The Routledge Anthology of Women's Theatre Theory and Dramatic Criticism

The Routledge Anthology of Women's Theatre Theory and Dramatic Criticism is the first wide-ranging anthology of theatre theory and dramatic criticism by women writers.

Reproducing key primary documents contextualized by short essays, the collection situates women's writing within, and also reframes the field's male-defined and male-dominated traditions. Its collection of documents demonstrates women's consistent and wide-ranging engagement with writing about theatre and performance and offers a more expansive understanding of the forms and locations of such theoretical and critical writing, dealing with materials that often lie outside established production and publication venues. This alternative tradition of theatre writing that emerges allows contemporary readers to form new ways of conceptualizing the field, bringing to the fore a long-neglected, vibrant, intelligent, deeply informed, and expanded canon that generates a new era of scholarship, learning, and artistry.

The Routledge Anthology of Women's Theatre Theory and Dramatic Criticism is an important intervention into the fields of Theatre and Performance Studies, Literary Studies, and Cultural History, while adding new dimensions to Feminist, Gender and Sexuality Studies.

Catherine Burroughs is Professor Emerita of English at Wells College, Courtesy Professor of Performing and Media Arts at Cornell University, and a member of Actors' Equity Association.

J. Ellen Gainor is Professor of Performing and Media Arts at Cornell University.

The Routledge Anthology of Women's Theatre Theory and Dramatic Criticism

Edited by Catherine Burroughs
and J. Ellen Gainor

Routledge
Taylor & Francis Group

LONDON AND NEW YORK

Designed cover image: Photography by Rosaline Shahnavas.
Art Direction by National Theatre Graphic Design Studio.

First published 2024
by Routledge
4 Park Square, Milton Park, Abingdon, Oxon OX14 4RN

and by Routledge
605 Third Avenue, New York, NY 10158

Routledge is an imprint of the Taylor & Francis Group, an informa business

British Library Cataloguing-in-Publication Data
A catalogue record for this book is available from the British Library

Library of Congress Cataloging-in-Publication Data
Names: Burroughs, Catherine B., 1958- editor. | Gainor, J. Ellen, editor.
Title: The Routledge anthology of women's theatre theory and dramatic criticism / edited by Catherine Burroughs and J. Ellen Gainor.
Description: Abingdon, Oxon ; New York, NY : Routledge, 2023. | Includes bibliographical references.
Identifiers: LCCN 2022031608 (print) | LCCN 2022031609 (ebook) | ISBN 9780367439866 (hardback) | ISBN 9780367439873 (paperback) | ISBN 9781003006923 (ebook)
Subjects: LCSH: Dramatic criticism. | Women theater critics. | Feminist criticism
Classification: LCC PN1707 .R59 2023 (print) | LCC PN1707 (ebook) | DDC 792.01/5082–dc23/eng/20221207
LC record available at https://lccn.loc.gov/2022031608
LC ebook record available at https://lccn.loc.gov/2022031609

ISBN: 9780367439866 (hbk)
ISBN: 9780367439873 (pbk)
ISBN: 9781003006923 (ebk)

DOI: 10.4324/9781003006923

Typeset in Baskerville
by KnowledgeWorks Global Ltd.

To our teachers: Nancy Cotton, James Engell,
Sandra M. Gilbert, Michael Goldman,
Stanley Kauffmann, Anne K. Mellor,
Eugene Waith, Ed and Emily Wilson.

Contents

Contributors

GIOIA ANGELETTI is an Associate Professor of English literature at the University of Parma, Italy. She has published a wide range of essays and journal articles on nineteenth-century Scottish theatre and poetry, contemporary Scottish theatre, Romantic-period British theatre and poetry, and Anglophone literature of migration and transculturality. Her major authored and edited volumes include: as author, *Eccentric Scotland: Three Victorian Poets. James Thomson ("B. V."), John Davidson and James Young Geddes* (2004), *Lord Byron and Discourses of Otherness: Scotland, Italy, and Femininity* (2012) and *Nation, Community, Self: Female Voices in Scottish Theatre from the Late Sixties to the Present* (2018); as editor, *Emancipation, Liberation, and Freedom: Romantic Drama and Theatre in Britain, 1760-1830* (2010), and with Lilla Maria Crisafulli, *East/West Encounters in Romantic Literature and Culture* (2019), an issue of the journal *La Questione Romantica*. She is currently working on an edition of Liz Lochhead's *Dracula*, a book about Scottish Romantic-period migration literature and a volume, co-edited with Diego Saglia, on Romantic ecocriticism. She is Honorary Fellow of the Association for Scottish Literary Studies.

ELAINE ASTON is Professor Emerita of Theatre at Lancaster University, United Kingdom. She has published numerous books and articles on feminism and theatre. A former editor of *Theatre Research International*, she was the elected President of the International Federation for Theatre Research (2019–23).

SERENA BAIESI is an Associate Professor of English Literature at the University of Bologna. Her primary research interests include Romantic poetry, Gothic literature, Romantic theatre and drama, Jane Austen and popular culture, and slavery literature. She is the author of *Letitia Elizabeth Landon* and *Metrical Romance*, the editor of *Romantic Dialectics: Culture, Gender, Theatre* with S. Curran and *Gothic Metamorphosis across the Centuries* with M. Ascari and D. L. Palatinus, as well as a special issues of *TEXTUS* on Jane Austen and the interdisciplinary journal *La Questione Romantica*.

LINDA BEN-ZVI is a Professor Emeritae at Tel-Aviv and Colorado State Universities, a John Stern Distinguished Professor, Colorado, and Lady Davis Professor, Hebrew University. She has authored and edited 13 books, including four on Samuel Beckett, and four on Susan Glaspell. Her Glaspell biography won the Jury Prize of the American Theatre Library Association.

CHRISTINA BLACK is an Assistant Professor at the McIntire School of Commerce at the University of Virginia, where she teaches about communication, persuasion, and ethics. Previously, she taught at Johns Hopkins Carey Business School and developed business education and leadership coaching materials for a wide range of clients. She also designed and taught courses on waste and spy literature at Cornell University. Her research interests include the history of rhetoric, corporeal figures of speech, and intercultural communication. She holds a doctorate in eighteenth-century English literature from Cornell University.

KATE BREDESON is a theatre historian, a director, and a dramaturg. Her project as a scholar is to research, write about, and practice the ways in which theatre can be a tool for radical activism and protest. Her book *Occupying the Stage: The Theater of May '68* is published by Northwestern University Press. She is editing the unpublished diaries of Judith Malina. She is Professor of Theatre at Reed College.

MEGHAN BRODIE is an Associate Professor of Theatre at Ursinus College. She is also a director, dramaturg, and playwright. Directing credits include plays by Sarah Ruhl, Charlotte Jones, Diana Son, Ellen McLaughlin, and Paula Vogel. Meghan has published work about queer casting and feminist directing. She holds a Ph.D. from Cornell University.

CATHERINE BURROUGHS is Courtesy Professor in the Departments of English and Performing and Media Arts at Cornell University. Throughout her career, she has focused on the contributions to theatre and playwrighting of women writers between 1750 and 1830. Her books include *Closet Stages: Joanna Baillie and the Theater Theory of British Romantic Women Writers*; *Women in British Romantic Theatre: Drama, Performance, and Society, 1790–1840*; and *Closet Drama: History, Theory, Form*. She is also a member of Actors' Equity Association.

CHARLOTTE M. CANNING is the Frank C. Erwin Jr., Centennial Professor in Drama at the University of Texas at Austin, where she also serves as the Director of the Oscar G. Brockett Center for Theatre History and Criticism. Her books include *On the Performance Front: US Theatre and Internationalism*, winner of the Joe A. Callaway Prize, *Representing the Past: Essays in Performance Historiography*, *The Most American Thing in America: Circuit Chautauqua as Performance*, recipient of the Barnard Hewitt Award for Outstanding Research in Theatre History, *and Feminist Theaters In The USA: Staging Women's Experience*. Her op-eds have appeared in *The Chronicle of Higher Education*, the *Washington Post*, *The Conversation*, and other publications.

MARVIN CARLSON is the Sidney E. Cohn Emeritus Professor of Theatre, Comparative Literature and Middle Eastern Studies at the Graduate Center of the City University of New York. He has received an honorary doctorate from the University of Athens, the ATHE Career Achievement Award, the ASTR Distinguished Scholarship Award, the George Jean Nathan Award for Dramatic Criticism, and the Joe A. Callaway Prize for writing in theatre. He is the director of the Marvin Carlson Theatre Center at the Shanghai Theatre Academy and the founding editor of the journals *European Stages* and *Arab Stages*. He is the author of 28 books, the most recent of which is *Theatre and Islam*.

ANKE CHARTON is an Assistant Professor of Theatre and Society with the Department of Theatre, Film and Media Studies at the University of Vienna. She specializes in theatre historiography and intersectional gender studies, with recent publications on Early Modern Spanish performance, gendered singing voices and the music theatre industry.

KATHARINE COCKIN is a Professor of English Literature at the University of Essex in the Department of Literature, Film, and Theatre Studies. She is Principal Investigator of the AHRC Ellen Terry and Edith Craig Database and Searching for Theatrical Ancestors resource at http://ellenterryarchive.essex.ac.uk based on her scholarly descriptive catalogue of the archive of Edith Craig and Ellen Terry, of over 20,000 documents. She has published 15 books including three books on Edith Craig: *Edith Craig: Dramatic Lives* (Cassell, 1998); *Edith Craig and the Theatres of Art*, (Bloomsbury Methuen Drama, 2017); and *Women and Theatre in the Age of Suffrage: The Pioneer Players 1911–25*, (Palgrave Macmillan, 2001).

LILLA M. CRISAFULLI is Alma Mater Professor of English Literature at the University of Bologna. She is the founder and Honorary President of the Interuniversity Centre for Romantic Studies (CISR) and Editor of *La Questione Romantica*. Her research interests include British Romanticism, Women Romantic Playwrights, Women's and Gender Studies, Anglo-Italian Studies. With Keir Elam she has edited *Women's Romantic Theatre and Drama: History, Agency, and Performativity* (Routledge, 2010), and the Italian edition of Mary Shelley's *Valperga* (Mondadori, 2022). She has published two volumes on Percy Bysshe Shelley (respectively, on Shelley's prose and on the reception of his work). Her most recent book is *Women's Voices and Genealogies*, edited with Gilberta Golinelli.

THOMAS C. CROCHUNIS is an Associate Professor of English at Shippensburg University. He has edited the collection *Joanna Baillie, Romantic Dramatist: Critical Essays*, co-edited *The Routledge Anthology of British Women Playwrights, 1777–1843*, and has written on Romantic-era women playwrights and theatre managers.

LINDSAY B. CUMMINGS is an Associate Professor of Dramatic Arts at the University of Connecticut, where she also serves as head of the BA in Theatre Studies program. Her research interests include community-based performance, feminist performance, affect theory, Latinx theatre, and theatre for social change. She is the author of *Empathy as Dialogue in Theatre and Performance*.

TRACY C. DAVIS is Barber Professor of Performing Arts at Northwestern University. Her most recent books are *Liberal Lives and Activist Repertoires: Political Performance and Victorian Social Reform*, *The Cambridge Guide to Mixed Methods Research for Theatre and Performance Studies* (forthcoming, edited with Paul Rae), *The Routledge Companion to Theatre and Performance Historiography* (edited with Peter W. Marx), and *Uncle Tom's Cabins: The Transnational Histories of America's Most Mutable Book* (edited with Stefka Mihaylova).

BIRGIT DÄWES is a Professor of American Studies at the University of Flensburg, Germany and General Editor of *Amerikastudien/American Studies: A Quarterly*. Her work includes *Native North American Theater in a Global Age* and the edited volumes *Indigenous North American Drama: A Multivocal History* and *Native American Survivance, Memory, and Futurity*.

JESSICA DEL VECCHIO is the Senior Associate Director for Teaching Initiatives and Programs for Faculty at the McGraw Center for Teaching and Learning at Princeton University. Prior to joining Princeton's staff, she was an Assistant Professor of Theatre at James Madison University in Virginia. Her writing has appeared in *Critical Stages/ Scènes critiques, Contemporary Theatre Review, Theatre Journal, TDR,* and *Modern Drama,* as well as several anthologies.

APARNA DHARWADKER is a Professor of English and Interdisciplinary Theatre Studies at the University of Wisconsin-Madison, the author of *Theatres of Independence: Drama, Theory, and Urban Performance in India Since 1947* (Joe A. Callaway Prize, 2006), and editor of *A Poetics of Modernity: Indian Theatre Theory, 1850 to the Present* (Joe A. Callaway Prize, 2020; Honorable Mention, ATHE Outstanding Book Award). Her current book project, *Cosmo-Modernism and Theatre in India: Writing and Staging Multilingual Modernisms,* is under contract with Columbia University Press for its Modernist Latitudes series.

JERRY DICKEY is Professor Emeritus of Theatre at the University of Florida and is the author of *Susan Glaspell and Sophie Treadwell* (with Barbara Ozieblo, Routledge), *Broadway's Bravest Woman: Selected Writings of Sophie Treadwell* (edited with Miriam López-Rodríguez), and *Sophie Treadwell: A Research and Production Sourcebook.*

SIOUXSIE EASTER is a theatre director, deviser, and educator. She relishes working with playwrights and theatre makers on new works. Easter helped found the Advanced Studies in England Theatre Summer School in Bath, England. After serving for eighteen years as a Professor of Theatre at Wells College in Aurora, NY, Easter recently relocated to Fort Worth, TX, where she is the Upper School Theatre Director at Fort Worth Country Day.

JILL R. EHNENN is a Professor of English and standing faculty in the Gender, Women's and Sexuality Studies Program at Appalachian State University. She is the author of *Michael Field's Revisionary Poetics* (Edinburgh University Press, 2023) and *Women's Literary Collaboration, Queerness, and Late-Victorian Culture* (Ashgate, 2008/ Routledge, 2017). Her projects also include a guest-edited special issue of *Nineteenth-Century Contexts* on "Natural and Unnatural Histories," articles on Dorothy Wordsworth, Elizabeth Siddal, Vernon Lee, Graham R. Tomson, Lucas Malet, Thomas Hardy, twentieth-century lesbian romance novels, the *Harry Potter* series, and multiple articles and chapters on the late-Victorian female co-authors who wrote as "Michael Field." Her current project is a biography of Michael Field, co-authored with Sharon Bickle.

LAURA ENGEL is a Professor in the English Department at Duquesne University, where she specializes in eighteenth-century literature, theatre, gender studies, and material culture. She is the author of *Women, Performance, and the Material of Memory: The Archival Tourist, Fashioning Celebrity: Eighteenth-Century British Actresses and Strategies* for *Image Making, Austen, Actresses, and Accessories: Much Ado about Muffs,* and co-editor with Elaine McGirr of *Stage Mothers: Women, Work and the Theater 1660–1830.*

ANGELA ESCOTT is a theatre historian and has worked in a specialist music library. She has published a monograph on Hannah Cowley, and many journal articles and book chapters. She is an advisory editor for the journal *Restoration and Eighteenth-Century Theatre Research* and reviews for the *Journal for Eighteenth Century Studies.*

PENNY FARFAN is a Professor of Drama at the University of Calgary and the author of *Women, Modernism, and Performance* and *Performing Queer Modernism.* She is also a past editor of *Theatre Journal* and the editor with Lesley Ferris of *Contemporary Women Playwrights: Into the Twenty-First Century* and *Critical Perspectives on Contemporary Plays by Women: The Early Twenty-First Century.* She is a Fellow of the Royal Society of Canada.

LESLEY FERRIS is an Arts and Humanities Distinguished Professor of Theatre Emeritus at The Ohio State University. Her research focuses on women playwrights. In 2014 she founded Palindrome Productions. Her first production was Christopher St. John's *The First Actress.* Performances took place in London and at the Barn Theatre at Smallhythe Place, the country retreat of Ellen Terry in Kent. Edith Craig, daughter of Terry, converted the sixteenth-century barn into a theatre space following Terry's death in 1928. The Barn Theatre presented annual productions of Shakespeare to honor Terry's legacy continues today under Britain's National Trust.

MELINDA C. FINBERG is an Associate Professor of Theatre Practice in the School of Dramatic Arts, University of Southern California. She is the editor of *Eighteenth-Century Women Dramatists,* and is a dramaturg who has helped bring productions of the works of these playwrights to professional and university stages across the United States.

LA DONNA L. FORSGREN is an Associate Professor of Theatre at the University of Notre Dame. Her research centers on recovering Black women's intellectual, artistic, and activist traditions within US theatre and society. She is the author of *In Search of Our Warrior Mothers: Women Dramatists of the Black Arts Movement* and *Sistuhs in the Struggle: An Oral History of Black Arts Movement Theater and Performance.*

LISA A. FREEMAN is a Professor of English at the University of Illinois Chicago. She is the author of *Antitheatricality and the Body Public,* which was named Runner-Up for the ATHE Outstanding Book Award, a Finalist for the Theatre Library Association George Freedley Award, and an Honorable Mention for the Joe A. Callaway Prize. Among her recent publications is an essay on performance artist Taylor Mac's *24-Decade History of Popular Music* and an article on Elizabeth Inchbald's *Remarks for the British Theatre.* She is a founding member of the R/18 Collective: Reactivating Restoration and 18th-Century Drama for the 21st Century.

SHARON FRIEDMAN is Founding Gallatin Professor Emerita in the Gallatin School of New York University. Specializing in modern literature and drama, feminist criticism, and adaptation, she is editor of the volume *Feminist Theatrical Revisions of Classic Works* and co-author (with Cheryl Black) of *Modern American Drama: Playwriting in the*

1990s. Her essays have appeared in such journals and collections as *Theater Journal, New Theatre Quarterly, Text and Presentation, Susan Glaspell: Essays on her Theater and Fiction, Codifying the National Self, Intertextuality in American Drama,* and *Visions of Tragedy in Modern American Drama.*

J. ELLEN GAINOR is a Professor of Performing and Media Arts at Cornell University. Her research focuses on British and American modern drama and performance and women playwrights. In addition to her numerous scholarly monographs, articles, reference entries, and reviews, her edited volumes include *Imperialism and Theatre, Performing America: Cultural Nationalism in American Theater* (with Jeffrey Mason), *Susan Glaspell: The Complete Plays* (with Linda Ben-Zvi), *Githa Sowerby: Three Plays, Susan Glaspell in Context,* and *The Norton Anthology of Drama* (with Stanton Garner, Jr. and Martin Puchner).

MAGGIE GALE is Chair in Drama at the University of Manchester, United Kingdom. She is a co-editor of the journal *Contemporary Theatre Review,* and of the series, *Theatre—Theory—Performance* with Maria Delgado and Peter Lichtenfels, and *Women, Theatre and Performance* with Kate Dorney. Recent publications include, *A Social History of British Performance Cultures 1900–1939: Citizenship, Surveillance and the Body*; and with Kate Dorney eds., *Stage Women 1900–1950: Female Theatre Workers and Professional Practice* and *Vivien Leigh: Actress and Icon.*

ANDREW GALLOWAY is the James John Professor of Medieval Studies at Cornell University. He has published widely on medieval English and other medieval literature, including two monographs, *The Penn Commentary on Piers Plowman, Volume One,* and *Medieval Literature and Culture.* His many essays and chapters include "Visions and Visionaries," in Elaine Treharne and Greg Walker, eds., *The Oxford Handbook of Medieval Literature* (2010).

JOANNE E. GATES wrote the first full biography of Elizabeth Robins and remains engaged with additional Robins projects. She is professor emerita in English at Jacksonville State University, Jacksonville AL; and besides numerous papers and presentations on Robins, she specializes in Shakespeare and women's literature. She continues to maintain the Robins Web at JSU.

BENJAMIN GILLESPIE holds a Ph.D in Theatre and Performance from The Graduate Center, CUNY. His research focuses on the intersections of aging, gender, and queer sexuality in contemporary theatre and drama, especially the later works of Split Britches. Benjamin holds a full-time Lectureship at Baruch College, CUNY where he teaches communication, theatre, and performance studies. He is Associate Editor of *PAJ: A Journal of Performance and Art* and his articles and reviews have been published in *Theatre Journal, Modern Drama, Theatre Survey, Performance Research, PAJ, Canadian Theatre Review, Theatre Research in Canada,* and a number of edited anthologies.

GABRIELE GRIFFIN is a Professor of Gender Research at Uppsala University, Sweden and Professor of Gender and Africa Studies at the University of the Free

State, South Africa. Previously she held the Anniversary Chair in Women's Studies at the University of York, United Kingdom. Her many publications include *Bodily Interventions and Intimate Labour: Understanding Bioprecarity, Body, Migration, Re/constructive Surgeries: Making the Gendered Body in a Globalized World,* and *Contemporary Black and Asian Women Playwrights in Britain.*

KITTY GURNOS-DAVIES received her DPhil in English from the University of Oxford, where she researched the relationships between women's agency and the material resources of the stage in modern and contemporary performance. Her research drew upon eight years' experience working in costume and wig departments. She is now a researcher, writer and curator, specializing in contemporary art.

JULIET GUZZETTA is an Associate Professor of English and Romance and Classical Studies (Italian) at Michigan State University. Her first book, *The Theater of Narration: From the Peripheries of History to the Main Stages of Italy* (Northwestern UP, 2021), explores a form of contemporary solo theater in its historical, political, and performative dimensions. She has published articles and essays in *Theatre History Studies, Annali d'Italianistica,* and *Spunti e ricerche* among other venues. Her research has been supported by a year-long Fulbright grant to Italy, and Harvard's Mellon School for Theater and Performance Research.

GERALDINE HARRIS is a Professor of Theatre Studies at Lancaster University. Her books include *Staging Femininities, Performance and Performativity, Beyond Representation: The Politics and Aesthetics of Television Drama, Feminist Futures? Theatre Theory, Performance,* co-edited with Elaine Aston, *Practice and Process: Contemporary [Women] Practitioners,* co-authored with Elaine Aston and *A Good Night Out for the Girls: Popular Feminisms in Contemporary Theatre and Performance,* co-authored with Elaine Aston. She co-edited a special edition of *The Contemporary Theatre Review* on feminism and performance with Sarah Gorman and Jen Harvie.

NOELIA HERNANDO-REAL is an Associate Professor of English and American Literature at the Universidad Autónoma de Madrid. She has authored *Self and Space in the Theater of Susan Glaspell, Voces contra la mediocridad: la vanguardia teatral de los Provincetown Players, 1915–1922,* and *Rosas en la arena: los relatos de Susan Glaspell,* and she has co-edited *Performing Gender Violence: Plays by Contemporary American Women Dramatists* with Barbara Ozieblo. She was President of the International Susan Glaspell Society (2015–2021).

MARJORIE HOWES teaches at Boston College. She is the author of *Yeats's Nations: Gender, Class, and Irishness* and *Colonial Crossings: Figures in Irish Literary History.* She is the co-editor of *Semicolonial Joyce, The Cambridge Companion to W. B. Yeats,* and *Yeats and Afterwords.* She is also the series editor, with Claire Connolly, of *Irish Literature in Transition* (6 vols., 2020).

KELLEN HOXWORTH is an Assistant Professor of Theatre Studies at the State University of New York at Buffalo. He is the 2018 recipient of the Errol Hill Award for outstanding research in African American theatre and performance for his essay

"The Many Racial Effigies of Sara Baartman." His book, *Transoceanic Blackface: Empire, Race, Performance* is forthcoming from Northwestern University Press.

MAKI ISAKA teaches gender studies and Japanese theatre and literature at the University of Minnesota. Author of *Secrecy in Japanese Arts: "Secret Transmission" As a Mode of Knowledge, Onnagata: A Labyrinth of Gendering in Kabuki Theater,* and articles on *shingeki* (New Theatre), gender and gendering, body grammar such as that of gait, etc., Isaka's current project explores the performance and theoretical implications of female musicians of *gidayû*: the audio component of the four-century-old, "all-male" puppet theatre, called *bunraku* today.

SUJATA IYENGAR is a Distinguished Research Professor of English at the University of Georgia and author of *Shades of Difference: Mythologies of Skin Color in Early Modern England, Shakespeare's Medical Language, Shakespeare and Adaptation Theory,* and editor of *Disability, Health, and Happiness in the Shakespearean Body* and other volumes, most recently (with the late Christy Desmet and with Miriam Jacobson) the co-edited *Routledge Handbook to Shakespeare and Global Appropriation.* Her essays on race, gender, and rank in the science, fiction, and drama of Margaret Cavendish have appeared in *ELH* (2002) and in *Criticism* (2021).

FATİNE BAHAR KARLIDAĞ is an Assistant Professor at the Department of English Language and Literature at Yeditepe University, Istanbul, Turkey. She received her Ph.D. from the School of Drama, University of Washington, Seattle. Also a Fulbright Visiting Research Program alumna, her research concentrates on the historical representation of the radical left in theatre and performance, and contemporary Labor activism in Turkey.

SCOTT W. KLEIN is a Professor of English at Wake Forest University, North Carolina. He is the author of *The Fictions of James Joyce and Wyndham Lewis: Monsters of Nature and Design,* the editor of the Oxford World's Classics edition of the 1928 edition of Wyndham Lewis's *Tarr,* with Mark Antliff, the editor of the essay collection *Vorticism: New Perspectives,* and with Michael Valdez Moses the editor of the essay collection *A Modernist Cinema.* He has published essays in such journals as *ELH, Modernist Cultures, Twentieth Century Literature, The James Joyce Quarterly,* and *The Journal of Wyndham Lewis Studies,* and is the Artistic Director of the Secrest Artists Series, the performing arts series at Wake Forest University.

ELIZABETH KRAFT is a Professor Emerita of English at the University of Georgia. She has published widely in the area of her specialization, Restoration and Eighteenth-Century British Literature. Her most recent monograph is *Restoration Stage Comedies and Hollywood Remarriage Films,* and she is the editor of the *Bloomsbury Cultural History of Comedy in the Enlightenment.*

LINDSAY LACHANCE (Algonquin Anishinabe) has worked as a dramaturg for over a decade and has a Ph.D. from the Department of Theatre and Film at the University of British Columbia. Lindsay's dramaturgical practice is influenced by her relationship with birch bark biting and the Gatineau River. She is also the Director of the Animikiig Creators Unit at Native Earth Performing Arts, which focuses on the development of new Indigenous works.

ROSEMARY MALAGUE is the author of *An Actress Prepares: Women and "the Method"*. Her writing on feminism and performance has been published in *The Routledge Companion to Stanislavsky*, *Shakespeare Bulletin*, and *European Stages*. She is the Director of the Theatre Arts Program at the University of Pennsylvania.

MOLLY MAROTTA received her Ph.D in English Literature from Florida State University. Her research focuses on eighteenth-century kidnapping narratives in novels and in plays. She is currently the Internal Communications and Engagement manager at the Brookings Institution.

KIM MARRA is a Professor Emeritus of Theatre Arts and American Studies at the University of Iowa. Her books include *Strange Duets: Impresarios and Actresses in the American Theatre, 1865–1914* (Joe A. Callaway Prize) and the co-edited volumes *Passing Performances: Queer Readings of Leading Players in American Theater History*, its sequel *Staging Desire, The Gay and Lesbian Theatrical Legacy*, and *Showing Off, Showing Up: Studies of Hype, Heightened Performance, and Cultural Power*. She has published numerous articles on interspecies performance and directed the digital humanities documentary *The Pull of Horses in Urban American Performance, 1860–1920* (2020).

SHILO MCGIFF is the Co-founder of The Woolf Salon Project. Her work appears in *The Virginia Woolf Miscellany*, *Virginia Woolf & The Anthropocene*, and *Virginia Woolf: Selected Papers*. She's recently served as developmental editor of Tonia Sutherland's *Resurrecting the Black Body*. Her research focuses on the pastoral poetics of Virginia Woolf as a vehicle for feminist historiography and social critique. She earned her Ph.D. in English from Cornell University.

LILIAN MENGESHA is the Fletcher Foundation Assistant Professor of Dramatic Literature in the Departments of Theatre, Dance, and Performance Studies at Tufts University. Her research lives at the intersection of performance studies, critical Indigenous studies and gender and sexuality studies. Her current book project argues for dreaming as a critical tool for decolonial practice in contemporary performance art.

JEN-SCOTT MOBLEY is an Associate Professor at East Carolina University where she coordinates the B.A. in Theatre Arts program. In addition to her monograph, *Female Bodies on the American Stage: Enter Fat Actress*, she is coeditor of *Performing Dream Homes: Theater and the Spatial Politics of the Domestic Sphere*, as well as *Lesbian and Queer Plays from the Jane Chambers Prize* and *Cross Cultural Feminisms: Plays From the Jane Chambers Prize*.

KRYSTYN MOON is a Professor of History and American Studies at the University of Mary Washington in Fredericksburg, Virginia. Her teaching and research include US immigration history, popular culture, race and ethnic studies, foodways, gender and sexuality, and consumerism. She is the author of *Yellowface: Creating the Chinese in American Popular Music and Performance, 1850s–1920s*, and several articles, essays, reviews, and blogs on American immigration history, ethnic identity and the performing arts.

AMY MUSE is a Professor of English at the University of St. Thomas in Minnesota. She is the author of *The Drama and Theatre of Sarah Ruhl* and of essays on Ruhl and Woolf, intimate theatre, and Romantic drama that appear in the *Journal of Dramatic Theory and Criticism, Text & Presentation, Romantic Circles*, and other publications.

EUNHA NA is an Associate Professor in the Department of English Language and Literature and is Affiliated Faculty in the Interdisciplinary Program in Performing Arts Studies at Seoul National University, South Korea. Her work on contemporary Asian and Asian American theatre has appeared in *Modern Drama, Theatre Journal*, and *The Oxford Encyclopedia of Asian American Literature and Culture.*

JIMMY A. NORIEGA is a Professor of Theatre at the College of Wooster and President of the American Society for Theatre Research. He is the co-editor of *Theatre and Cartographies of Power: Repositioning the Latina/o Americas* (2018) and *50 Key Figures in Queer US Theatre* (2022). He has directed over 50 productions in a dozen countries.

DANIEL O'QUINN is a Professor in the School of English and Theatre Studies at the University of Guelph. He is the author of *Engaging the Ottoman Empire: Vexed Mediations 1690–1815, Entertaining Crisis in the Atlantic Imperium, 1770–1790,* and *Staging Governance: Theatrical Imperialism in London, 1770–1800.* He has also co-edited with Jane Moody *The Cambridge Companion to British Theatre, 1730–1830,* and with Gillian Russell, *Georgian Theatre in an Information* Age, a special double issue of *Eighteenth-Century Fiction.* He has also worked with Kristina Straub and Misty Anderson on two linked anthologies on eighteenth-century theatre and performance and with Jennifer Schacker on *The Pantomime Reader (1800–1900)* for Routledge.

SHELLEY ORR is a theatre scholar and dramaturg. She is Associate Professor at San Diego State University's School of Theatre, Television, and Film, where she heads the MA in Theatre Arts program and advises student dramaturgs. Orr is a past president of Literary Managers and Dramaturgs of the Americas.

ELIZABETH OSBORNE is an Associate Professor in Theatre Studies at Florida State University. Her work has appeared in numerous journals and edited collections. She wrote *Staging the People: Community and Identity in the Federal Theatre Project* and co-edited *Working in the Wings: New Perspectives on Theatre History and Labor* with Christine Woodworth.

KATE PIERSON is a theatre historian and educational developer. She earned a Ph.D. in Theatre Studies from Florida State University and now serves as Assistant Director of Engaged Learning and Strategic Initiatives at Northwestern University's Searle Center for Advancing Learning and Teaching. Her research interests include community-engaged theatre and twentieth century British and American theatre. She focuses on the historiography of collaboratively created performances and the hidden histories of work created by women theatre practitioners.

RYAN PLATT is an Associate Professor of Performance Studies in the Department of Theatre & Dance at Colorado College. His writing has appeared in *Dance Research Journal, PAJ: A Journal of Art and Performance,* and *Theatre Journal.*

MEENAKSHI PONNUSWAMI is an Associate Professor of English at Bucknell University. Her scholarship focuses on Black British drama and American theatre of the Civil Rights era. She has most recently published articles on Amiri Baraka, Alia Bano, and British Muslim theatre. She is currently working on British Asian women's comedy.

MERRITT DENMAN POPP is an adjunct lecturer in Theatre and Great Texts at Baylor University. She received her M.A. in Theatre Studies from Baylor in 2016 and her Ph.D. in Theatre and Performance Research from Florida State University in 2023. Her research examines the intersection of maternity, gender, and politics in nineteenth-century U.S. theatre.

MARJEAN D. PURINTON is a Professor of English at Texas Tech University where she also teaches in the Women's & Gender Studies Program. Her scholarship focuses on British Romantic drama and women writers. A member of the Teaching Academy at Texas Tech University, Purinton has served as President of the International Conference on Romanticism.

KARA RAPHAELI is an Assistant Professor of Theatre Arts at Simpson College. They hold a Ph.D. in Theatre and Drama with a specialization in Critical Gender Studies from the joint program between UC San Diego and UC Irvine. They specialize in theatre historiography and trans performance and have published in *Theatre History Studies*, *The Victorian Review*, and *TheatreForum*.

JOSEPH ROACH is a Sterling Professor of Theater and Professor of English, Emeritus, at Yale University. He is the author of *It* and, with Gill Perry and Shearer West, *The First Actresses: Nell Gwyn to Sarah Siddons*.

MAYA E. ROTH serves as Della Rosa Associate Professor at Georgetown University, where she was founding Artistic Director of the Davis Performing Arts Center. As artist-scholar, she specializes in feminist plays and criticism, cross-cultural adaptations of classics and new work development. She co-edited the volumes *International Dramaturgy*, and, together with Jen-Scott Mobley, *Lesbian & Queer Plays*, and *Cross-Cultural Plays from the Jane Chambers Prize*. Her creative collaborations commit to interdisciplinary performance and pluralism. She is the recipient of many teaching awards and WTP's Service to the Field Award.

DONELLE RUWE is a Professor of English at Northern Arizona University and Associate Dean of the College of Education and Professional Education Programs. She has been the Co-President of the 18th- and 19th-Century British Women Writers Association. She is the author of *British Children's Poetry in the Romantic Era: Verse, Riddle, and Rhyme*, editor of *Culturing the Child, 1690–1914*, and co-editor with James Leve of *Children, Childhood, and Musical Theater*.

DANIEL SACK is an Associate Professor of English at the University of Massachusetts Amherst, jointly appointed with its Commonwealth Honors College. His books include *After Live: Possibility, Potentiality, and the Future of Performance*; *Samuel Beckett's Krapp's Last Tape*; and *Imagined Theatres: Writing for a Theoretical Stage*. He is the founding editor of the e-journal *Imagined Theatres* and serves as contributing editor for several other journals. His book *Cue Tears: On the Act of Crying* is forthcoming with the University of Michigan Press.

DIEGO SAGLIA is a Professor of English Literature at the University of Parma (Italy), and his research concentrates on British Romantic literature and culture, with particular attention to their links and exchanges with continental European traditions. He is a member and current director of the Interuniversity Centre for the Study of Romanticism (CISR), and his latest monographs are *European Literatures in Britain, 1815–1832: Romantic Translations* (2019) and *Modernità del Romanticismo: scrittura e cambiamento nella letteratura britannica 1780–1830* (2023).

NICK SALVATO is a Professor of Performing and Media Arts at Cornell University. He is the author of *Uncloseting Drama: American Modernism and Queer Performance, Knots Landing, Obstruction,* and *Television Scales.* His articles have appeared in numerous venues, including *Critical Inquiry, Modern Drama, TDR: The Drama Review, Theater Journal,* and *Theater Survey.*

JENNIFER SCHMIDT is an Assistant Professor of Theatre at Hanover College. Schmidt's research traces the history of the one-woman show in America, and her writing on performers such as Cissie Loftus, Lily Tomlin and Heidi Schreck has appeared in *The Journal of American Drama and Theatre, Etudes,* and Howl Round Theatre Commons. She received her Doctor of Fine Arts in Dramaturgy and Dramatic Criticism from the Yale School of Drama.

GILLIAN SKINNER is an Associate Professor at Durham University in the United Kingdom. She is the author of *Sensibility and Economics in the Novel, 1740–1800: The Price of a Tear* and of scholarly articles on many aspects of eighteenth-century literature, including women writers, the novel, drama, and life writing.

ERICA STEVENS ABBITT is an Associate Professor Emerita at the School of Dramatic Art, University of Windsor, Canada. She is co-editor (with Scott T. Cummings) of *The Theatre of Naomi Wallace: Embodied Dialogues.* Her writings on feminist performance have appeared in *Theatre Journal, Asian Theatre Journal, Theatre Topics, Performance Research, The Journal of Dramatic Theatre and Criticism,* and *American Theatre* magazine.

AOISE STRATFORD is a Lecturer in Performing and Media Arts at Cornell University. She works on early and contemporary Gothic narratives, Early Modern tragedy, and postcolonial and feminist drama. She has published in *Theatre Survey, The Journal of Dramatic Theory and Criticism, Modern Drama,* and *The Dramatist.* She is co-editor of *(M)Other Perspectives: Staging Motherhood in 21st Century North American Theatre and Performance.* She is also a playwright and dramaturg.

ANDREW TOLLE is a Professor of English at Dallas College and president of the Dallas College Faculty Association. He specializes in American literature, science studies, feminist drama, and posthumanism. His research on nurturing and futurity involved recovering Charlotte Perkins Gilman's overlooked plays, exploring her desire to succeed in drama, and (re)defining her as a naturalist playwright.

MIKAELA WARNER is a doctoral candidate at the University of Georgia, studying Early Modern English Literature and focusing on gender and disability. She has published in *Sidney Journal*, and her dissertation project reconsiders Henry VIII through a Disability Studies lens.

SARA WARNER is Director of LGBT Studies at Cornell University. Her book, *Acts of Gaiety: LGBT Performance and the Politics of Pleasure*, received the Outstanding Book Award from the Association for Theatre in Higher Education. She produces community-based performances on social issues.

RACHEL MORRIS WATSON is a specialist of twentieth- and twenty-first century French and Francophone theatre. Her manuscript in progress, "(Re)Membering the Body," investigates the performance of embodied memory in contemporary French and Francophone dramaturgies of diaspora and migration. Her writing has been published in *The Drama Review, Arab Stages,* and *Horizons/Théâtre.*

KRISTEN WRIGHT is an Assistant Professor of Theatre Studies in the Department of Drama in the Tisch School of the Arts at New York University and is also a playwright. She previously earned a Ph.D. in Africana Studies from Cornell University, an M.A. in Africana Studies from Cornell University, an M.A. in African-American Studies from Columbia University, and a B.A. in Political Science and Theater Studies from Yale University.

Acknowledgments

We thank our editor, Ben Piggott, for his early and sustained commitment to this project, and his former assistant, Zoe Forbes, and current assistant, Steph Hines, for their patient and helpful support throughout the submission and publication process. We also appreciate the entire Routledge production team, especially Sophie Dixon-Dash and Meeta Singh, for their careful shepherding of this volume through to publication.

In addition, we want to acknowledge a number of individuals and institutions that assisted with key elements of this anthology:

Amal Allana
Cassidy Higgins
Catherine Kodicek
Christos Vlahos
Cornell University College of Arts & Sciences
David Faulkner
Diane Glancy
Djuna Barnes papers, Special Collections and University Archives, University of Maryland Libraries
Fred Muratori
Garrick Beck
Gary Gabisan
Grove Atlantic, Inc.
H. Scott Brill
Independent Age
Isha Appell
James Ralston
Jim Mulligan
Joey Stocks
Jorn Bramann
Katherine E. Kelly, Penny Farfan, and the Editors of *Theatre Journal*
LeAnn Fields
Mary Haegert
Medieval Institute Publications
Nancy Walker
Peter Rankin
Rick Bogel
Ron Unz

Sheri Wilner
Sine Hwang Jensen
St. John and Loie Faulkner
Susan Brady
Takemoto Koshikô
Texas Tech University Gloria Lyerla Library Memorial Fund
The Asian American Studies Collection, Ethnic Studies Library, University of California, Berkeley
The Beinecke Library, Yale University
The Folger Library
The Houghton Library at Harvard University
The Huntington Library
The Newberry Library
The Schomburg Center for Research in Black Culture
The Spanish Ministry of Universities (Plan de Recuperación, Transformación y Resiliencia), Universidad Autónoma de Madrid, Research Fellowship CA2/RSUE/2021-00383
Tiffany Ana López
Tom Walker
Wendy Weckwerth
Youngsun Palmer
Zoe Wilcox

PERMISSIONS

The following people, presses, and organizations have given permission to our authors to excerpt or re-print certain materials in the anthology:

Amal Allana
American Theatre
Beth Allen
Cambridge University Press
Cengage IP Granting Department Copyright Clearance Center
Cherríe Moraga
Currency Press
Doubleday Press
Emma Rice
Émilie Monnet
The Drama Review (TDR)
Garrick Beck, Executor of the Estate of Judith Malina
Grove/Atlantic
Houghton Library at Harvard University
Houghton Mifflin
Johns Hopkins University Press
Kate McGrath
Loughborough Theatre Texts
Michelle Bruer, Guardian News Service
National Endowment for the Arts
The New York Times

Nick Hern Books
Office of Special Collections, New York Public Library
PAJ Publications
Palgrave Macmillan
Penguin Random House
Peter Rankin
Sara Henany
Stuart Bernstein Representation for Artists
Takemoto Koshikô
The Bodleian Library, Oxford University
The British Library
The Harry Ransom Center, University of Texas at Austin
The Harvard Theatre Collection
Velina Hasu Houston
Victoria Myers
The Roman Catholic Church of the Diocese of Tucson: A Corporation Sole, owns
the rights to Sophie Treadwell, "Writing a Play." It is reprinted here with permission
of the Diocese of Tucson. Proceeds from the printing or publication of Treadwell's
writings are used for the aid and benefit of Native American children in Arizona.
David Savran
Dinah Leavitt Swan
Elaine Romero
Jack Tantleff of Paradigm Theatre Agency
Lara Stevens
Rowohlt Verlag
Southern Illinois University Press
SpringerNature
Suddhaseel Sen
Taylor & Francis Group
Theatre Communications Group
Theatre Journal
The University of Alabama Press
The University of Bristol Women's Theatre Collection
The University of Illinois Press
The University of Michigan Press
Wayne State University Press

From the Publisher: In the case of all materials included in this anthology, every effort
has been made to contact the rights holders. Any party wishing to discuss questions
of ownership or copyright are encouraged to contact the publisher.

INTRODUCTION

Catherine Burroughs and J. Ellen Gainor

In her essay on the legendary British actress Ellen Terry (1847–1928), Virginia Woolf (1882–1941) acknowledges the ephemerality of stage artists' work: "What remains is at best only a wavering, insubstantial phantom—a verbal life on the lips of the living" ("Ellen Terry" 67). Recounting Terry's understanding of this truth, Woolf explains that Terry "tried [...] to describe what she remembered" of her fellow artists' performances, particularly those of Henry Irving (1838–1905), with whom she had acted for decades. But, Woolf continues,

> [i]t was in vain. [Terry] dropped her pen in despair. 'Oh God, that I were a writer!' she cried. 'Surely a *writer* could not string words together about Henry Irving's Hamlet and say *nothing, nothing.*' It never struck her, humble as she was, and obsessed by her lack of book learning, that she was, among other things, a writer.
>
> (67–68)

Woolf further argues that "whatever [Terry] took up became in her warm, sensitive grasp a tool. [...] [W]ords peeled off, some broken, some suspended in mid-air, but all far more expressive than the tappings of the professional typewriter" (68). Analyzing the epistolary exchanges between Terry and the playwright and critic Bernard Shaw (1856–1950),[1] Woolf summarizes their dialogue on Shakespeare's *Cymbeline*: "But what suggestions has the brilliant critic [Shaw] to make about Imogen?[2] None apparently that she [Terry] has not already thought for herself. She is as close and critical a student of Shakespeare as he is" (71). And yet, Woolf implies, we do not adequately recall Terry as such, ironically perhaps because she was so gifted in so many ways that she "def[ied] our attempts to name" her manifold accomplishments (72).

Woolf—who had herself struggled to secure the designation of "critic"[3]—could have been ruminating on any number of the women and woman-identified critics and theoreticians whose works are represented in *The Routledge Anthology of Women's Theatre Theory and Dramatic Criticism*. The historical oversight or willful undervaluing of women's significant contributions to theatre theory and dramatic criticism remains one of the singular lapses in the discipline. Precisely because, from antiquity to recent time, men's writing has largely comprised and thus defined what constitutes this theory and criticism, the notion of what may be recognized as such has long remained unquestioned. As recently as 2020, for example, Tilden Russell, in the Introduction to his edited collection of dance theory, claimed that there were

DOI: 10.4324/9781003006923-1

"no women theorists before the twentieth century, *a situation endemic in all the arts*" (xxiii, emphasis added). Our collection proves otherwise.

Historically, anthologies of dramatic theory and criticism, such as Bernard Dukore's canonical *Dramatic Theory and Criticism: Greeks to Grotowski* (1974), or Daniel Gerould's *Theatre/Theory/Theatre: The Major Critical Texts from Aristotle and Zeami to Soyinka and Havel* (2000), contained few, if any entries by women. More recently, Glenn Odom notes that "only four female theorists are included" in his *World Theories of Theatre* (2017). Stating that this choice is "indicative of the fact that there are not many women [...] working in the field of theatre theory," he acknowledges that "there is a rapidly expanding, although still small, pool of world female playwrights and theatre practitioners gaining international prominence," even though "very few of these explicitly theorize their work in writing" (210). By including Australia's Mayrose Casey, Argentian Griselda Gambaro, India's Poile Sengupta, and New Zealander Roma Potiki, Odom importantly signals an expanding perspective, at the same time that he appears to hold fast to the assumption of a universally shared concept of what constitutes "theory." By comparison, Aparna Bhargava Dharwadker's edited volume, *A Poetics of Modernity: Indian Theatre Theory, 1850 to the Present* (2019), is a remarkable, award-winning project that includes a number of female authors and brings to a global readership "theoretically significant writing on theatre from nine Indian languages" (all translated to English) "that articulate[s] the wide-ranging theoretical positions underlying the complex of drama—theatre—performance practices in the modern period" (xxxiii-xxxiv). Projects such as Dharwadker's unequivocally show that there is a vast body of theoretical and critical writing on global performance traditions that we must continue to identify and make available for a broad readership.

While Marvin Carlson's important *Theories of the Theatre* (1984) introduces some women writers into a revised historical narrative—as does Mark Fortier's *Theory/Theatre: An Introduction* (1997, 2002, 2016)—there remain few published locations for women's writing on the theatre per se. Volumes such as S. P. Cerasano and Marion Wynne-Davies' *Renaissance Drama by Women: Texts and Documents* (1996) that provide such theory and criticism are perforce limited in their historical scope. Revelatory studies such as Gay Gibson Cima's *Early American Women Critics: Performance, Religion, Race* (2006) significantly expand our historical understanding but do not provide the writings themselves. In the Introduction to *Women Critics 1660–1820* (1995), the Folger Collective on Early Women Critics explains that "nearly all anthologies and histories of criticism exclude early women, and nearly all anthologies and histories of early women's writings exclude criticism" (xiii). We would add that writing about drama and performance by women is conspicuously under-represented in both.

These editors additionally note that their volume includes excerpts from forty-one of "the nearly one hundred women we have identified who were producing criticism between 1660 and 1800" (xiii). The Folger Collective further details that its anthology explores

> writings in a wide spectrum of genres. Some of the criticism presented in this collection is embedded in plays, novels, and poems. Other selections take the form of dialogues between fictional characters rather than emerging directly from the authorial voice. Still others are confined to the private vehicles of letters and diaries.

(xv)

In other words, these scholars remind us that we must reconsider our understanding of the forms and locations of theory and criticism if we are to develop not only a fuller sense of such writing but also its broader cultural and political significance. Ann Thompson's and Sasha Roberts' invaluable anthology, *Women Reading Shakespeare, 1660–1900* (1997), for example, demonstrates the extent to which their included authors "use their writing on Shakespeare to raise issues of particular concern to women [...], such as women's education, women's role in public life, and power relations between the sexes in society and in marriage" (5).

The Routledge Anthology of Women's Theatre Theory and Dramatic Criticism brings together relevant and illustrative examples of women's writing that are drawn from wide-ranging cultural and historical traditions. The contents are arranged chronologically by date of composition if known (or approximated) or, if published, by date of publication. By pairing primary documents with scholarly framing essays that contextualize these works, we offer readers materials that gesture toward, but cannot possibly encompass, the wealth of theoretical and critical writing by women on drama, theatre, and performance. We readily acknowledge that, as with any such recuperative project, we cannot possibly embrace the full range of these materials historically or geographically or include as fully diverse a group of authors as must be recognized. Our contents reflect only a sampling of this robust and compelling legacy. We also note that the balance of the contents skews toward Anglo-American traditions. While the collection includes some important examples of women's writing in translation, drawn from other global traditions, we profoundly hope that the anthology will prompt new or renewed attention to an even more expansive body of works by women and woman-identified authors worldwide.

This project began in 2018 as a Working Group session of the American Society for Theatre Research, building on a related, earlier session that had been organized by Penny Farfan and Katherine E. Kelly. In organizing our session, we posed three core questions: 1) How does the women's writing speak to our understanding of drama and performance, broadly conceived? 2) How does the women's writing engage with, or prompt us to reconsider, extant understandings of dramatic theory and criticism? 3) How does the women's writing contribute to, or help us to revise, extant understandings of drama and performance in relation to history and culture? The participants in our session—many of whom are included here—as well as those who have since joined this project have all focused their analyses in response to those core concerns.

These foundational questions, undergirding their introductory essays, help us to appreciate the array of forms of writing and perspectives on theatre and performance embedded in the primary documents. Letters convey private responses to specific texts or performances or reveal aspects of the collaborative creative process. Scrapbooks and other memorabilia document artistic work within amateur theatrical communities as well as fandom. Manifestos and published criticism argue forcefully for women's status in the theatre and women's experience in a male-dominated profession. Interviews and speeches include invaluable and distinctive glimpses of women's theatrical engagements. Play excerpts instantiate dramaturgy as theory, and dramaturgy as criticism. Not surprisingly, a number of English female critics are responding to Shakespeare, while prefaces, no matter when or where written, situate the author's plays in their theatrical and cultural contexts. Occasional essays speak to theatre and politics, or aesthetics, or feminism, or other related concerns.

Taken together, the contents of this anthology represent the rich and varied critical and theoretical voices of women whose informed perspectives on the stage and on drama merit our serious attention.

This collection has four primary goals: 1) to introduce women's long history of producing theatre theory and dramatic criticism; 2) to demonstrate the variety of ways that women writers have responded to theatre and performance and have challenged—and are still challenging—traditional, male-authored theories and practices of theatre, performance, drama, and criticism; 3) to make available actual documents that women theatre theorists, practitioners, and critics produced so that users have readier access to them for instructional, creative, and scholarly purposes; and 4) to participate in the ongoing process of expanding our historical, theoretical, critical, and aesthetic understanding of theatre and performance through the strategic introduction of women's writing into established narratives of theatre theory and dramatic criticism.

The collection underscores the simple fact that women have a long history of producing theory and criticism, although it may not have always been apparent as such, nor has it been embraced within the discipline's traditional narratives, for now well-established reasons: women authors may have used alternative genres, sometimes without a public aim, to express themselves, including letters, diaries, marginalia, prefaces, epilogues, scrapbooks, or other creative forms. Women have at times published work anonymously or pseudonymously, or have published work outside of mainstream outlets, if indeed publication has even been possible. And, of course, women's writing, even when accessible, has traditionally been ignored, undervalued, or misrepresented by the dominant culture.

Precisely because women's theoretical and critical writings may not always resemble established conventions for these forms, our volume presents examples of female-authored theories of theatre, playwriting, acting, etc., that can be read directly in dialogue with, and at times in opposition to, the male critical tradition that has heretofore defined the field. Perhaps most importantly, the collection makes available the actual documents (in full or excerpted for length) that women theatre theorists, practitioners, and critics generated. Since many of these documents reside in archives, or in lesser-known or less-accessible publications, this volume makes them more available so that readers can not only discover this expanded concept of a theoretical and critical tradition but also have materials with which to teach, study, and create. We offer here a more expansive picture so that the works of luminaries in our field, as well as isolated, period- or locale-specific examples of women's writing are, perhaps newly, perceived as part of much longer and more diverse traditions. In short, we believe that women's theatre theory and dramatic criticism invaluably reflect the different kinds of texts, stylistic approaches, modes of analysis, and perspectives on culture that can truly expand our understanding not only of the arts and artistic processes but also of the broader social and political arenas from which artistry emerges and to which it speaks.

Notes

1 See St. John, ed., *Ellen Terry and Bernard Shaw: A Correspondence.*
2 Imogen is the central female character in *Cymbeline.*
3 See Woolf, "Professions for Women" in her *Selected Essays.*

Suggestions for Further Reading

Canning, Charlotte. "Constructing Experience: Theorizing a Feminist Theatre History." *Theatre Journal*. 45.4 (1993): 529–540.

Canning, Charlotte and Thomas Postlewait, eds. *Representing the Past: Essays in Performance Historiography*. Iowa City: University of Iowa Press, 2010.

Carlson, Marvin. *Performance: A Critical Introduction*. Third Edition. London: Routledge, 2018.

Cima, Gay Gibson. "'To Be Public as a Genius and Private as a Woman': The Critical Framing of Nineteenth-Century British Women Playwrights." *Women and Playwriting in Nineteenth-Century Britain*. Eds. Tracy C. Davis and Ellen Donkin. Cambridge: Cambridge UP, 1999. 35–53.

Greenwald, Michael L. *The Longman Anthology of Drama and Theatre: A Global Perspective*. London: Longman, 2001.

Gale, Maggie B. and John Stokes, eds. *The Cambridge Companion to the Actress*. Cambridge: Cambridge UP, 2007.

O'Brien, Karen. *Women and Enlightenment in Eighteenth-Century Britain*. Cambridge: Cambridge UP, 2009.

1 FIVE MEDIEVAL WOMEN

St. Perpetua (c. 185–203), Hildegard of Bingen (1098–1179), Hadewijch (c. 1200–c. 1250), Katherine Sutton (d. 1376), Margery Kempe (c. 1373–1438)

Andrew Galloway

Introduction

Few medieval women are generally considered to have produced dramatic works, much less theatrical commentary and criticism as we define those categories. The best-known exceptions are rare, though they are far from minor figures. One is the tenth-century nun, Hrotsvit of Gandersheim (c. 935–c. 1002), whose Latin plays—broadly based on the Roman playwright Terence's character types and plots but refashioned into stories displaying the sanctity of martyred, holy women—may or may not have been acted. Hrotsvit's commentary is presented separately in this volume. The only other generally noted exception across the long span from late imperial Rome through the later seventeenth century is the remarkable twelfth-century abbess and visionary Hildegard of Bingen (1098–1179), whose *Ordo Virtutum* or "Play of the Virtues" is often picked out as the first "morality play."

It would seem that little more can be said about women's drama and dramatic thought and commentary in the Middle Ages. But if "public drama," in the sense of secular, acted entertainment before general audiences, was not typical or dignified for women in England before the Restoration of 1660, and only somewhat earlier in other European regions, there is plenty of evidence of earlier women's dramatic creativity and imagination in other forms and genres. More germane to this volume, often the women's realizations of those quasi-dramatic genres are accompanied by penetrating critical reflections on the meanings and purposes of the results. Hildegard's "Play of the Virtues," for example, is far from the only visionary dialogue written by her or other women that is cast in more or less explicitly dramatized terms, and other visionary narratives by Hildegard and others not only feature highly dramatic scenes—and might even have been physically dramatized as Hildegard's works show—but also often include the writers' remarks on the meanings of those visions' details. This suggests we should broaden our generic categories in order to appreciate a fuller archive of women's dramatic imagination and commentary in early Western culture.

Any broadening, to be sure, requires adjustments in what we are seeking, in determining what theatre and theatrical commentary are. It is true that medieval visionary dialogues, for example, are often implicitly or explicitly in competition with productions or procedures defined as "spectacle." The earliest selection here presents a direct instance of such competition against public spectacle, in this case the late-imperial Roman spectacle of public execution. This is from the remarkable

DOI: 10.4324/9781003006923-2

autobiographical *Passion* of St. Perpetua (c. 185–203), an otherwise unknown young North African convert to Christianity who was killed by beasts in the Carthaginian Coliseum around the year 203, along with other recalcitrant Christians under Emperor Severus. Perpetua's first-person, vision-laden account of her final days is vivid enough, and its Latin (which changes in style after her account) is demotic or "vulgar" enough, to justify the claim (made by whoever originally preserved it) that it came directly "from her hand." Her running commentary on the meaning of events and visions shows how, for Perpetua, both the waking experience of being imprisoned by the Romans and her visionary versions of what the spectacle of her death really means, offer a competing kind of "spectacle." She focuses on vivid details from which she unpacks the cosmic meanings of her conflict, but also poignantly human moments, cast no less vividly as dramatic action. She includes, for instance, the Romans authorities' brutal separation of her nursing infant when they cast her into prison (she finds it miraculous that her breasts, though swollen, did not hurt or drip, unlike the breasts of a fellow martyr, Felicity, another young mother), and her narrative includes a vivid scene of her father's pleadings that she recant Christianity while she is preparing to resist the similar demands by the Roman imperial official, who then sentences her to death and has her father beaten for his interference. The narrative includes her pitying thought about her father's "wretched old age" while she rejoices with the other Christians as they march off the judicial platform to the prison below the arena.

This is intrinsically theatrical, as law cases always are, but climaxing Perpetua's counter-spectacle are the visions she receives of her execution while imprisoned. Here, her revision of the upcoming execution elaborately rescripts the Roman version of public execution, complete with careful attention to audience, costume, movements, and dialogue. In a vision the night before she is executed, she enters the arena to face not beasts but an "Egyptian" fighter, an agon supervised by a mysterious and enormous man with purple robe and elaborate footgear, who offers her a bough of golden apples if she wins (perhaps a strange Vergilian allusion thrown back at the pagan world she scorns [*Aeneid* 6.124–50]). In this vision, not just clothing but gender identity is malleable: when Perpetua's assistants strip her of her clothing to oil her down, she "became a man," who can then viciously defeat the Egyptian in hand-to-hand, then foot-to-body, combat. Her realization upon awakening of what her execution means is the final step of her reinterpretation of the Roman event: this will not be a typically entertaining Roman execution of a subversive, but a major struggle with the devil himself, a fight she feels she has already won by her unwavering commitment.

Although Perpetua's narrative is not included in anthologies of medieval drama, responses to it have often registered its theatricality. Augustine of Hippo, the influential fourth-century theologian and commentator, remarked about the *Passion of St. Perpetua*, "Quid hoc spectaculo suavius?" ("what sweeter spectacle could there be?" [col. 1281; my trans.]). So too, when the modern church historian Marina Warner muses on Perpetua's narrative, whose effects Warner recalls from having it read aloud to her by the nuns who educated Warner herself, Warner thinks of the potential for dramatic tragedy it demonstrates. For Warner, the *Passion* not only evokes "the image of Perpetua standing in the arena under the battering African sun on the blood-soaked sand with the crowd howling for sport and the grilles behind which the wild beasts paced and snarled, unlocked and ready to be lifted," but also Greek and Shakespearean tragedy (354–6).

If the visionary mode was one way for early Christian and medieval women to recuperate "spectacle" for their own purposes, another way was liturgy, veering into "liturgical drama," a term often used by modern scholars to accommodate the unpredictable capacity of medieval liturgy to expand into reenactments of sacred history (often greatly expanded from the Bible, in accord with the elaborations of sacred history found in all manner of medieval Christian writings). In some medieval Christian views, the often elaborate liturgy commemorating the Crucifixion could be seen as dramatic "tragedy," as Honorius Augustodunensis declared in the twelfth century (Kelly, 80–2). By the twelfth century, both secular and religious Latin dramas were widely available, some of them produced for, if not by, "mixed" audiences of men and women (the Latin *Bridegroom* [ed. Dronke, 3–21] and the Anglo-Norman *Play of Adam* [ed. Fitzgerald and Sebastian, 23–56], are notable examples). The line between "liturgy" and "drama" was inevitably and constantly blurred. But if very few women, perhaps even only Hrotsvit, entered that blurry zone from the side of "drama," a number of them occupied that liminal terrain from the side of "liturgy." Most productive was Hildegard of Bingen (1098–1179).

Many of Hildegard's copious writings for her convent can be called at once visionary, liturgical, and dramatic, and it was in the originality of her fusion of these genres that she most risked criticism for violating medieval Christian norms, especially those presenting women, and certainly lavishly performing women, as dangerous beings. No less scandalous was taking pleasure in the beauty of expensive costumes and women's unbound hair. Hildegard flatly ignored such views and attitudes. It is no surprise, therefore, that another woman, the twelfth-century abbess Tengswich of Andernach, expressed dismay at Hildegard's productions, in a silky but venomous letter that we are fortunate has survived. Hildegard's and Tengswich's exchange offers unparalleled evidence both for how Hildegard disposed her liturgical drama and how, in defending her work, Hildegard viewed every detail of such pious performances. Her reply to Tengswich takes stock of the dramatic and quintessentially feminine nature of the liturgical and visionary dramas that she created for the elite nuns whom she educated and fostered.

If for Tengswich, Hildegard's selection and dressing of beautiful virgins for religious dance and song in elegant clothing, with embroidered crowns and hair unbound, was a blatant transgression against Christianity's embrace of the poor and the Fathers' rejection of sensual theatricality, for Hildegard, such displays of feminine beauty were permitted to virgins. For those are exempt, she argues, from the rules of modesty imposed on married women. Tengswich's attack led Hildegard to her clearest set of statements about casting, staging, and the Edenic state that both signify: in her convent, a display of the innate beauty of femininity was fully permitted, to a degree hard to find equaled elsewhere in the Middle Ages or indeed many periods. As Barbara Newman notes, "every nun [...] became a figure of the unique virgin bride and remembrance of Eve in the garden—in short, an epiphany of the original *feminea forma*" (222). Virginity for Hildegard was not the suppression of femininity but its fulfillment. As for the social elitism that Tengswich criticized, Hildegard retorted that mixing poor with rich nuns would only bring out envy in the poor, and arrogance in the rich. Here, her dramatic and aesthetic tastes might seem to shape her morality rather than the reverse, yet it might be fairer to see her morality as infused with an artistic and aesthetic celebration of divine and natural creation, epitomized by her signature use of the word for "greening."

Hildegard thus reveals that she conceives of her convent as a kind of permanent stage, suited to her careful casting, staging, and constant control of mood and meaning. She is able to assert this thanks to her exceptionally authoritative style, both in her visionary or liturgical productions and in her commentary sprinkled throughout those productions, as well as in her letters. Enabled by nearly biblically prophetic self-confidence, Hildegard's many Latin dialogues, visions, and letters blithely offered many novel syntheses between song, poetry, dance, and worship. This governs her well-known *Ordo Virtutum* (ed. Dronke, 147–84) as it does all her other quasi-dramatic visionary dialogues, some of which include more of her running explication and commentary than does the *Ordo Virtutum*. A large set of such visions and concurrent commentary is found in her *Scivias* (a title based on *Scito Vias Domini*, "know the ways of the Lord"), whose visions move vividly and surreally through sacred history, especially the Fall of Adam and Eve, Lucifer's fall, and the Incarnation: all events, as Newman says, that "in the seer's eye [...] were three acts of one drama" (89). A selection from the finale of *Scivias* is chosen here because that features Hildegard's (or rather the Living Light's) commentary, which both before and after the dialogue discusses the details of the vision of the travails and triumph of a "Penitent Soul in a Body." Allegorical as that drama is, it is notable that for Hildegard, the "body" and its beauties are never forgotten, however much this might distress more dour contemporaries.

Other elegantly described and quasi-dramatic visions by women can be easily found across the next several centuries, both within convents and among the twelfth- and thirteenth-centuries' newer religious orders. Visions were particularly cultivated by beguines, lay women who adopted their own "order," often wrote in the vernacular, and lived with little male supervision in their own communities, especially in the thirteenth- and fourteenth-century Low Countries. A mid-thirteenth century Dutch writer, Hadewijch (c. 1200–c. 1250), is among the most brilliant of such beguine visionaries. Of her life little is known other than what is available from the sacred love poems, prose visions, and letters that survive, all in Middle Dutch; it seems she had an early divine revelation, followed by some later exile, or perhaps flight from authorities. We do not know her dates of birth or death. But we can see that all of her works are intricate and intensely elegant combinations of mode and media. English-language criticism of Hadewijch has lagged behind Dutch scholarship, which has been more thorough, for example, in showing Hadewijch's uses of music in her lyric poetry (Grijp).

Although the performative nature of Hadewijch's poetry is widely acknowledged, no scholarship, apparently, has addressed her visions' dramatic implications, much less how the strands of commentary within the visions reveal Hadewijch's thinking about the quasi-dramatic scenes she narrates. The vision chosen here presents a youthful, personal, yet highly theatrical encounter with God himself, as the object of the nineteen-year old woman's obsessive love. She yearns, as she explains, to understand why and how the Lord gives to and takes from those who love him. Her vision answers this longing. In that vision, she encounters a gigantic figure ensconced on a monumentally high throne below an all-encompassing royal crown, with a face that somehow displays "all the faces and all the forms that have ever been and will ever be." Seeing him, Hadewijch slips into a wordless union, lasting one half hour, as she notes. Even ecstasy is precisely situated in the space and time that the vision unfolds. In the vision, she is conveyed from scene to scene "in a spirit" (the phrase is as odd in Middle Dutch as modern English), a comment that establishes some containment of her special experiences, much like what drama achieves with theatrical space. Ultimately, she comments on the larger meaning of her experiences in terms of the "exile" from God to which she must awaken. As her reflections and commentary on the vision make clear, the experience is a rite of passage that looks both backward and forward to the end of what will be the long sorrows of life. It is about change, and it changes her. During the vision the nineteen-year-old grows older.

Though we can identify the women writers of many religious visions with their drama and their commentary, usually we can only assume that they contributed some liturgy as well. The only liturgy anywhere in the Middle Ages that we know to have been at least significantly shaped by a woman was at Barking Abbey outside London, in the late fourteenth century, during Chaucer's life and near his setting. Katherine Sutton (d. 1376), abbess of Barking from 1358–76, is said by the Barking *Ordinale* to have revamped the traditional Easter drama in a number of ways in order to revive the "torpor" of modern congregations. Easter drama is often seen as the most important medieval basis for other kinds of drama, with its long-established rituals of the Deposition, the Elevation, and the Visit to the Sepulcher by three Marys, usually monks or priests dressed as the women, seeking the crucified Jesus and learning he is not in the cave where his body had been deposited but has risen, as an angel tells them (richly documented in Young, *Drama* 1:249–410, although he disposes the evidence too neatly into progressive "stages"). So traditional is this general form that it is hard to know how much to credit Sutton with, given the institutional bases of all liturgical drama, not to mention the hints that earlier liturgy at Barking was a bit too vivid to suit the authorities.[1] But given the explicit statement in the abbey's *Ordinale* concerning Sutton's major adjustment of the timing of the Easter liturgical drama, and the explicit statement that changes by Sutton and Sutton alone are described in what follows, Sutton was surely a major influence on the Barking production, and both its internal explanations and the drama's unusual features themselves part of her contribution to dramatic criticism.

The work includes musical invention (several of the songs are not known elsewhere [Ogden, 149]) and vivid stage business, including the rare touch of pouring water and wine on the effigy of the crucified Jesus in her version of the Deposition, before wrapping it in fine clothing, as a corpse would be tended. Thereupon a priest was to carry another cross to the doors of the sepulcher in which the whole convent of nuns has been hidden and from which, at his pounding on the door, they then flee, representing the souls of the patriarchs and prophets released by Jesus's harrowing of hell. Sutton, who surely added the touch of representing the Marys by nuns rather than male clerics, was likely also responsible for granting more individuation than usual to the Marys; as Anne Yardley notes, each is given "an opportunity to sing individually—to personify these three women as three distinct personalities and not as the undifferentiated Marys" commonly found in Easter *Visitations* (Yardley, 251). Sutton's desire, as the *Ordinale* says, to dispel "torpor" and reawaken devotion in her jaded London audience can also be understood as a wish to involve women more directly in the most sacred scenes of liturgical drama, while the text of her liturgical drama explains throughout the historical meanings that each of the actions possess.

The apex of this production's emphasis on women's authority is the inclusion of the abbess herself confessing and absolving the nuns who are about to play the three Marys. It is important to emphasize that this expression of spiritual authority is remarkable: women, even abbesses, could neither confess nor absolve others. As Dunbar Ogden observes, "the Abbess takes unto herself sacred powers reserved for the male clergy" (146; Young, *Drama* I:381–85). Making this part of the dramatic action constitutes an implicit yet bold assertion of the convent's and Sutton's own authority. This might be seen as *merely* "dramatic," the climax of a fanciful production that Sutton has created, with a kind of Puck-like power over the church's clerical and secular audience alike. But it is also a powerful reassertion of the power of women and women's ideas in the drama of the medieval church, and a sign, if any more were needed, that such capabilities could readily be extended to wider dramatic and even institutional realms.

A later medieval English woman visionary, much better known now than any of these other figures, left visions widely recognized as proto-"dramatic": Margery Kempe (c. 1373–1438), the daughter of a well-placed bourgeois family of East Anglia. In contrast to Hildegard's widespread medieval notoriety, however, Margery's *Book*, with its single surviving copy perhaps written by one of her sons,[2] was probably little known in its time, and entirely unknown to scholars until 1936.[3] Yet Margery's visions are emphatically public events, often taking place *in* public, whenever she begins her characteristic wailing, as at the sight of babies who recall to her the baby Jesus. Her visions are equally dramatic. As well as multiple bedroom conversations with Jesus, she describes scenes that in their vivid enactments of the Incarnation and Holy Family might easily be joined with more officially staged plays of "salvation history" in the fourteenth- and fifteenth-century cycle plays that were common in Margery's East Anglia. As the historian Clarissa Atkinson remarks, late-medieval English drama parallels Margery's visionary imagination, including her "easy familiarity with the Holy Family and the saints" in a mode "entirely characteristic of the style and attitudes of medieval playwrights" (96). Scattered evidence survives of minor or peripheral roles that late-medieval and early Modern women sometimes held in producing civic drama or other festivities (Stokes); it seems clear that Margery would have wanted a far more decisive degree of dramaturgical control than anything her culture offered. Her *Book* is not itself that drama but the guide to the drama that was her life, on which the voices that fill her *Book*, both human and divine, comment continually.

Just as Hadewijch's desire to understand God's gifts and punishments is the question that led to her vision, so the vision described by Margery that is selected here is the product of a thought-experiment: Margery asks Jesus what she should think about. This framing of her subsequent vision is thus a commentary on the kind of visionary drama she wants to answer to her questions, and focuses on her creative responses, just as the scene from sacred history that then unfolds places her at its center. In all her narratives and her dramatic visions, Margery, however modestly called simply "the creature," is the central protagonist. In the vision here she is allowed to hold the baby Jesus, as if cast in the role of godparent, however ironic or hubristic we might see that role in this instance. All of Margery's visions show some degree of experimental theatre: her visions are all answers to her open-minded desire to contact and revive and even be part of sacred history in her own time. Equally dramatic are the waking scenes she recounts, such as the dialogue she records between herself and Archbishop Thomas Arundel, known for his scourge of heretics (whom some accused Margery of following). Arundel is eventually convinced by Margery to give official sanction to her wearing of a white gown, as a kind of novel "virginal nun."

This reclothing of herself, recasting herself everywhere she went, was evidently pivotal in her self-redefinition, a "growing ability to assert authority over her self and to trust the strength of her private experience of the nature of the divine," as Lynn Staley puts it (3). Since we have no other writing by her than the *Book*, a pioneering instance of English autobiography, we cannot trace her intellectual development more precisely. But it is clear that she charts not only a path to salvation but also increasing self-confidence in her anomalous psychological and literary experimentation. Margery's life is an open-ended dramatic experiment, its only truly fixed element the quasi-bourgeois marriage she will ultimately consummate with Jesus at her death.

St. Perpetua

Excerpt from **Passio Sanctarum Perpetuae et Felicitatis,** *Chaps. 6, 10*[4] *(c. 203)*

[VI] On the next day while we were eating we were suddenly snatched to go to our hearing. And we came to the forum. A rumor swiftly ran through neighboring areas, and an immense crowd gathered. And we climbed up to the platform. The others were interrogated and professed their faith. My turn came. And my father appeared with my son and plucked me off the steps, saying, "Offer the sacrifice![5] Pity your baby!" And Hilarianus, the imperial administrator, who had just been promoted to issue capital judgments there after the death of proconsul Minucius Timinianus, said, "Spare the white hairs of your father, spare your infant son. Make the sacrifice on behalf of the emperors' health!" And I answered, "I won't do it." Hilarianus asked, "Are you Christian?" And I responded: "I am Christian." And since my father was standing there pulling me away, he was ordered by Hilarianus to be ejected, and he was beaten by a stick. And I mourned the blow to my father, as if I had been struck. Thus I mourned for my father's wretched old age. Then [Hilarianus] pronounces sentence on us all and condemns us to the beasts. And joyous, we descended down into the prison[...].

[X] On the day before we are to fight [the beasts in the arena], I see this in a vision. Pomponius the deacon came to the prison door and knocked loudly. And I went out to him and opened it to him. He had dressed in an unbelted white robe and elaborate sandals. And he said to me, "Perpetua, we are expecting you. Come." And he held me by the hand, and we went through a difficult and winding place. Finally we arrived, heavily breathing, at the amphitheater, and he led me into the central arena and said to me, "Don't be afraid; I am here with you and I will work with you." And he departed. And I see a huge and thundering crowd; and since I knew I was condemned to the beasts, I marveled that beasts weren't sent out to me. And instead an Egyptian came out, foul in appearance, with his helpers, to battle with me. And elegant youths arrived, my helpers and assistants. And they undressed me. And I became male. And my supporters began to rub me down with oil, in the way they are accustomed to in arena struggles; and on the other side I see the Egyptian rolling in the dust. And then came out a certain man, unbelted, of extraordinary size, so that he could even exceed the top of the amphitheater, on his breast wearing a robe that was purple with two stripes in the middle, and elaborate sandals made from gold and silver, carrying a rod like a lance, and a leafy tree branch with golden apples on it. And he commanded silence and said, "The Egyptian, if he should conquer this woman, let him kill her with a sword; if she should conquer him, let her take this branch." And he departed. And we closed on one another and began to land blows; he wanted to seize me by the feet, but I stomped on his face. And I was raised up in the air and I began to stomp him as if not standing on the ground. But when I saw a pause occurring, I joined my hands together to put my fingers into my fingers and I grabbed his head, and he fell on his face and I stomped his head. And the people began to roar and my supporters to chant psalms, and I went to the gladiator-trainer and took the branch. And he kissed me and said to me, "Daughter, peace be with you." And I went with celebration to the port of Sanavivaria ["Salvation and Life"]. And I woke up. And I realized that I was about to fight not against beasts, but against the devil, but I knew victory would be mine. Up to this point I proceeded [in my writing] until the day before my reward; but if someone else would like, may he write the deed [*actum*] of the reward itself.

Hildegard of Bingen

Excerpt from Letters to and from Mistress Tengswich (c. 1148–1150)[6]

To Hildegard, mistress of the brides of Christ, T[engswich], mistress of the nuns of Andernach, [sends greetings,] with the highest hopes of uniting with her someday in heaven.[7]

The soaring fame of your sanctity, flying far and wide, has resounded in our ears with extraordinary and astounding things, commending to us in our insignificance the excellence of your sublime religion and singular way of life. For we have learned by the witness of many that a great many heavenly secrets, difficult for mortal understanding, are revealed to you for writing through angels' divinities, ordained for you to carry out not by human planning but by God himself teaching.

But another thing, unheard of in customs, has also reached us: namely, that your virgins stand in the church for singing on feast days with their hair unbound, and for ornamentation using white silk veils reaching the surface of the ground, wearing crowns on their heads woven with gold, embroidered with crosses on both sides and the back, and in the front with a lamb's figure elegantly inserted. Further, that their fingers are adorned with gold rings—although the first shepherd of the Church in his Epistle forbad such things, admonishing by saying, "not with plaited hair, or gold, or pearls, or costly attire" [1 Timothy 2:9]. Moreover—seeming to us no less astounding among these other things—only women who are elegant and noble in kind are taken into your convent while ignoble and less wealthy ones your convent utterly rejects.

Wherefore, stupefied, we were stunned by the uncertainty of great doubt, when we silently pondered that the Lord chose paupers and small fishermen into his original Church, and that the blessed Peter later said to peoples converted to the faith, "in truth, I perceive that God is no acceptor of persons" [Acts 10:34; cp. Romans 2:11], remembering too the Apostle's words to the Corinthians: "not many mighty, not many noble, but God hath chosen the contemptible and the ignoble things of this world" [1 Corinthians 1:26–28]. Indeed, intently scrutinizing as far as we can all things established by the Fathers—to which it is fully proper for all spirituals to conform—we find nothing like this. So great a novelty in your practices, o venerable bride of Christ, exceeds incomparably the capability of our insignificance, striking us with no little wonder.

Therefore we such small womanly creatures, deeply rejoicing with you in your success, with all due love but desiring nonetheless to understand more clearly something about this matter, found it pleasing to send to your sanctity this little letter, humbly and devoutly praying that your dignity would not disdain to write us back soon, to indicate by whose authority such religious practices might be defended.

Farewell; may you remember us in your prayers.

[Reply:] Hildegard, to the Congregation of Nuns [at Andernach]:
The Living Light says: let a woman lie hidden in her little room so she might keep her great modesty, since the serpent has infused in her the great dangers of horrible lust.

How? A woman's beauty glowed and radiated in her first root in which was formed this thing [her womb] in which every creature lies hidden. How? In two ways: namely, by her expert creation by the finger of God, and by her supreme beauty.

How wondrous you are, woman, who have established your foundation in the sun and overcome the world! Wherefore spoke the apostle Paul, who flew into the highest and was silent on earth, so he did not reveal what was hidden: woman, who falls subject to the male power of her husband, conjoined to him in his first rib, ought to preserve her great modesty, so she ought not give or reveal the fame of her own vessel [womb] to a man under a strange place, who is not tied to her [cp. 1 Thessalonians 4:4]. And let her do this according to the word the earth's dominator spoke, in mockery of the devil: "What God hath joined together, let no man put asunder" [Matthew 19:6].

Hear this: the earth exudes grass's greenery until winter conquers it. And the winter takes away the beauty of that flower and covers over its flower's greenery; it cannot conceal itself as if it had never dried up, because winter has taken [the flower] away. Therefore a woman ought not elevate herself or ornament her hair or raise herself by any point of a crown or any gold except by her spouse's will, according to which it will have pleased him in proper measure.

These things, however, do not pertain to a virgin. For she stands in purity and the integrity of the beauty of paradise, and will never seem dried up but always remain in the full greenery of the flowering staff. The virgin does not cover her hair's greenery by precept; instead, she covers herself by choice, through the highest humility, as a human being hides the beauty of the soul, so the rapacious one does not ravish it through pride.

Virgins are joined together in the inviolability of the Holy Spirit and the dawn of virginity. Wherefore it is proper for them to proceed to the highest priest as a sacrifice dedicated to God.

Wherefore it is proper, through dispensation, and through revelation in the mystical breath of the finger of God, that a virgin put on white clothing, the clear sign of a marriage to Christ, since by tightly woven integrity her mind will be strengthened, considering indeed who he is to whom she is conjoined, as is written: "Having this name, and the name of his Father, written on their foreheads" [Revelations 14:1], and "These follow the Lamb whithersoever he goeth" [Revelations 14:4].

For God has the scrutiny of one who scrutinizes every person [cp. Psalm 7:10], such that a lesser rank does not climb above a higher, just as Satan and the first man wanted to fly higher than they were placed. What man will gather together his entire herd of livestock into one stable, namely, cattle, asses, sheep, and goats, in such a way that they do not distinguish themselves?

Therefore let there be discretion even in this, so a diverse public, gathered into one flock, are not destroyed by the pride of elevation and the humiliation of diversity, and especially so that honorable manners are not destroyed when they rip each other apart by hatred, when a higher order overbears a lower one and a lower one ascends above a higher one. God distinguishes peoples on earth just as he does in heaven, discerning angels, archangels, thrones, dominions, cherubim, and seraphim. All these are loved by God, but do not have equal names. Pride loves princes and nobles in their personhood of elevation, and hates them when they kill Pride. It is written: "God does not cast off the mighty, since He himself is mighty" [Job 36:5]. But He himself does not love persons, but the works that have the flavor of him, just as the Son of God says: "my food is to do the will" of my Father [John 4:34].

Where there is humility, there Christ is always taking his meal.

And therefore it is necessary that those men should be aspied who desire vain honor more than humility because they see that *those* things are higher than *those*. Let the sickly sheep be ejected, so that the whole herd is not contaminated. God pours understanding into people so that their name is not blotted [from the book of life; Revelations 3:5]. For it is good for a man not to grab hold of a mountain that he cannot move but to reside in the valley, gradually learning what he can seize [cp. Matthew 17:20].

These words are from the Living Light, not man. Who hears, let him see, and let him believe from where they come.

Excerpt from Scivias, *"Symphony of the Blessed" (1141–1151)*[8]

Then I saw the most brilliant sky, in which I heard various kinds of music with all the aforesaid meanings in a miraculous manner, with praises of the joyous higher citizens strenuously persevering in the way of truth, laments of those joyous ones calling [other] people back to those praises, and the exhortations of Virtues for the salvation of people whom diabolical traps assail[...]. And the sound, like the voice of a multitude, symphonizing in harmony in praise of the celestial ranks, spoke:

[...]
PENITANT SOUL IN A BODY:
Oh you army of the Queen,
And oh you white lilies of her, with crimson roses,
Take heed of me,
Because I, a pilgrim, am exiled from you;
And help me that I might be able to rise in the blood of the Son of God.
[...]

VIRTUES TO THE PENITANT SOUL IN A BODY:
We wish to bring you back,
And we do not want to desert you;
And the whole celestial army rejoices over you.
So it is fitting for us to resound in symphony.
[...]

THE DEVIL'S TEMPTATION TO THE SAME PENITANT SOUL:
Who are you, and where have you come from?
You embraced me,
And I led you forth;
But now you confound me, in turning back!
I will throw you down by my attack.

PENITANT SOUL AGAINST THE DEVIL:
I recognized that all your ways are evil,
And so I fled from you;
And now, oh impostor, I fight against you.
[...]

VICTORY:
Rejoice, oh comrades,
Because the ancient serpent is bound.

VIRTUES:
Praise to you, Christ, King of the angels!
Oh God, who are you
Who had this great counsel in yourself,
Which destroyed the hellish drink,
Among publicans and sinners,
Who now shine in celestial goodness?
Wherefore praise to you, oh King!
[...]

These voices were like the voice of a multitude, when a multitude lifts its voices on high. And their sound passed through me, so that without any obstacle or delay I understood them. And I heard a voice from the shining sky speaking to me: [...]

Thus, oh human, you see "the most brilliant sky," designating the brightness of the joy of the heavenly citizens, in which you heard "various kinds of music with all the aforesaid meanings in a miraculous manner: with praises of the joyous higher citizens strenuously persevering in the way of truth, laments of those joyous ones calling people back to those praises"; for, as the air encloses and sustains the things under the heavens, so the wonders of God, as you heard in the things demonstrated to you, a sweet and delightful symphony expresses with joy the wonders of the elect living in the heavenly city, persisting in their sweet devotion to God; but it laments the wavering of those the ancient serpent is trying to destroy, whom nonetheless divine power vigorously leads to the company of the blessed joys, proffering them the mysteries unknown to human minds inclined to the world; and "in the exhortation of the virtues exhorting themselves to the salvation of the people whom diabolical traps are assailing. But those virtues defeat his snares, so that the faithful at last through repentance proceed out of their sins and into heaven." For there, virtues in the minds of the faithful resist the vices by which the Devil fatigues them; but when those virtues overcome him with the mightiest strength, people, fallen into sins, turn back to penance by God's will, when they will scrutinize and bewail their former deeds, and consider and sing their future ones[…]. Thus the words symbolize the body, but the symphonizing manifests the spirit; since celestial harmony denotes divinity, and the Word manifests the humanity of the Son of God.

Hadewijch

Excerpt from Visions[9] *(c. 1250)*

It was on a feast of the Epiphany. I was turning nineteen, as someone told me that day. Then I wished to go to our Lord, and in those days I was in longing, and in exceedingly strong desire, to understand how God takes and gives to persons who, lost in him and taken up in fulfillment, are conformed to his will in every circumstance. On this day I was again strongly moved in love because of my longing. And then I was taken up in a spirit [*in enen gheeste*] and conveyed to where a huge, awe-inspiring place was shown me, and in this mighty place stood a seat. And he who sat on it was invisible and incomprehensible in the dignity of rule he wielded from that height. To be seated in such a place is incomprehensible to both heavenly and earthly beings. Above that high seat, in this high place, I saw a crown that was above all diadems. It embraced all things in its width and nothing existed outside the crown. And an angel came, with a glowing censer glowing red-hot with fiery smoke. He knelt before the highest part of the seat, above which the crown hung, and he paid him honor and said:

> Oh unknown Power and almighty great Lord, receive honor and dignity from this girl who resorts to you in your secret place, which is unknown to all who do not send you such a kindled offering with such sharp arrows as she sends you with her new burning youth. For she has now ended her nineteenth year, as is said. And it is she, Lord, who comes to seek you in the spirit—who you are, whom men do not understand. For that unknown life, which you have aroused in her with your burning charity, has led her to this place. Now reveal to her that you have drawn her here, and transport her wholly within yourself.

And then I heard a terrible voice speaking to me and—unheard of—speaking to me with imagery [*bi enen ghelikenesse*] and said: "See who I am!"

And I saw him whom I sought. And his face revealed itself with such clarity that I recognized in it all the faces and forms that existed and ever shall exist, from which he received honor and service in all right. I saw why each one must receive his part, in doom and in blessing, and by what each one must be set in his position; and by what ways of being some persons wander from him and return back to him again, finer and more beautiful than they were before; why still others seem always wandering and never came back, and they remained standing entirely still and almost devoid of consolation at all times; and others have remained in their place since childhood, have known themselves at their worth, and have held out to the end. I recognized all these beings there in that face.

In his right hand I saw the gifts of his blessing; and I saw in his hand heaven in its vastness opened, and all those who will be with him there eternally. In his left hand I saw the sword of the fearful stroke, with which he strikes down everyone to death. In this hand I saw hell and all its eternal company. I saw his greatness oppressed under all, I saw his smallness exalted above all. I saw his hiddenness embracing and flowing through all things. I saw his breadth enclosed in all. I heard his reasoned understanding, and perceived all reason with reason. I saw in his breast the entire fulfillment of his nature in love. In everything else I saw, I could understand it in the spirit [*in de geest*].

But then wonder seized me because of all the riches I had seen in him, and through this wonder I came out of the spirit in which I had seen all that I sought. And as in this situation in all this rich comprehension I recognized my awe-inspiring love, my unspeakably sweet beloved, I fell out of the spirit, from myself and all I had seen in him, and, wholly lost, fell upon the breast, the fulfillment of his nature, which is love. There I remained engulfed and lost, without any comprehension of other knowledge, or sight, or spiritual understanding, except to be one with him and to have fulfillment of this union. I remained in this less than half an hour [cp. Revelations 8.1].

Then I was called back again in a spirit, and again I recognized and understood all reasoning as before. And once again it was said to me by him:

> From now on you shall never more condemn or bless anyone except as I wish; and you shall give everyone his due according to his worth. This is what I am, in fulfillment and in knowledge, and in entrancement for those who wish to content me according to my will. I direct you to live in conformity with my divinity and my humanity, back in the cruel world, where you must taste every kind of death, until you return here in the full name of my fulfillment, in which you are baptized in my depths.

And with this I returned, woeful, to myself.

Katherine Sutton, Abbess of Barking Abbey

Excerpt from the Barking Ordinale and Customary[10] (c.1375)

[Deposition of the Cross][11]

Meanwhile while the left-hand chorus have sung this antiphon, let the abbess first adore the Cross in memory, namely, seeking the five graces of Christ's five wounds; and when she will have come to the Cross with her whole body prostrate, let her kiss the feet, hands, and right side of the Crucifix with reverence and devoutness, praying that the Holy Spirit shall inspire her heart, with the rest of the sisters then imitating her in the pattern of these things [...] When the Holy Cross has been adored, let the priests, elevating the Cross from its place [in the sepulcher], begin the antiphon, "Above all the trees [...]" and with the chorus then following let them sing together the whole thing, led by the female cantor. Let them convey the Cross to the great altar, and there, in the guise of Joseph of Arimathea and Nicodemus, putting the Image down from the wood, let them wash the wounds of the Crucifix with wine and water [...] And when they have placed it reverently in the aforesaid place, splendidly adorned with a golden-threaded pillow of tapestries and bright linens, let the priest close the sepulcher and begin the responsory, "The Lord being buried [...]" [...] And then let the abbess offer a candle that shall burn continually before the sepulcher, not extinguished until the Image, which will have been taken up from the sepulcher with candles and incense and procession on Easter night after matins, be replaced in its spot [...].

Concerning Easter Festivities:

Let the glorious solemnity of the Lord's resurrection principally be celebrated.

First let two bells be rung, and not cease until the entire convent of the chorus shall enter. Then, after two peals each between fifteen Psalms, let the last peal be sounded [...]

Note that according to ancient church custom, the Lord's resurrection was celebrated before Matins, and before any striking of bells on Easter day; and since[12] the mass of people in those days seemed to grow cold in devotion, and with human torpor greatly increasing, the revered lady, Lady Katherine Sutton, then serving in the role of their pastoral care and desiring to extirpate entirely the said torpor and, to rouse all the more the devotion of the faithful for such a renowned celebration, established with the unanimous consent of her sisters that the celebration of the Lord's resurrection would be made immediately after the third responsory of Matins on Easter day, and the proceedings were established in this manner.

First let the Lady Abbess go with the entire convent and certain priests and clerks dressed in copes with every priest and clerk carrying a palm and an unlit candle in his hand; let them enter the chapel of St. Mary Magdalene, figuring the souls of the holy fathers descending to hell before the coming of Christ; and let them shut themselves into the aforesaid chapel. Then, after the officiating priest should arrive, let them approach the aforesaid chapel dressed in alba and cope, with two deacons— one bringing a cross with the Lord's banner hanging from the top, the other carrying a censer in his hand, and with other priests and clerks with two boys carrying candles—at the door of the aforesaid chapel, beginning three times this antiphon, "Raise your gates [...]" –which priest shall indeed represent the person of Christ about to descend to those below and rip away the doors of hell. And let the aforesaid antiphon begin each time in a louder voice, which each time the clergy repeats, and at each beginning let the priest beat with the cross at the aforesaid door, figuring the breaking of the gates of hell, and at the third blow let the door open. Then let him enter with his ministers. Meanwhile, let a certain priest, remaining in the chapel, begin the antiphon "From the gates of hell [...]," which the female cantor with the entire convent should take up. "O Lord, rescue [...]" ... Then let all exit the chapel, that is, from the Limbo of the Fathers [...] in procession through the middle of the chorus to the sepulcher each carrying a palm and a candle designating a victory seized over the enemy, followed by the Lady Abbess, the prioress, and with the entire convent just as before. And when the officiating priest will have come to the sepulcher let him cense it and enter the sepulcher, beginning the verse "He rises [...]" then let the female canter join in with "Christ from the tomb [...]" and meanwhile let him carry out the body of the Lord [the Host] from the sepulcher, beginning the antiphon, "Christ rising [...]" before the altar with his face turned to the people, holding the Lord's body enclosed in crystal in his hands [...]. And let them proceed in procession to the altar of the Holy Trinity in solemn arrangement, namely with censers and candles [...] and this procession signifies how Christ proceeded after his resurrection in Galilea with his disciples following.

With these things finished, let three sisters chosen in advance by the abbess come forth and, taking off their black clothing in the chapel of the Blessed Mary Magdalene, let them be clothed in shining surplices, with white veils placed over their heads by the lady abbess. Thus prepared, therefore, and holding silver vessels in their hands, let them say their confession [*dicant Confiteor*] to the abbess, and, having been absolved by her, let them stand in an established place with candles. Then let the one who pretends to serve as Mary Magdalene sing this verse, "At one time of God [...]." This finished, let the second, who imitates Mary Jacobi, respond with the second verse, "Drawing near, therefore, alone [...]," the third Mary in turn taking the role of Salome: "I am allowed to go with you [...]." After going to the choir, let them sing with tearful and submissive voice these verses together: "Alas the hearts within us [...]." Then let the Maries, exiting the choir, say together, "Alas who has rolled away [...]." When they will have come to the sepulcher, let a clerk dressed in a white stole be seated before the sepulcher serving in the role [*imago*] of the angel who rolled the stone away from the tomb and sat on it, and let him say to them, "Whom do you seek in the sepulcher, o companions of Christ?" Let the women reply, "We seek Jesus of Nazareth." Let the angel follow with "He is not here; he has risen." And when he will have said "come, and see," let them enter the sepulcher and kiss the place where the Crucifix had been placed. Let Mary Magdalene take the sudary that had covered his head and take it with her. Then let another clerk in the form of another angel sitting in the sepulcher say to the Magdalene, "Woman, why are you weeping?" Let her follow that with "Because they have taken away my lord." Then let the two angels singing together say to the women, "Why are you seeking the living among the dead [...]?" Then let them, still doubting the resurrection of the Lord, weeping say to one another, "Alas, misery [...]." Thereafter let Mary Magdalene sighing sing, "I sigh for you [...]." Then on the left side of the altar let the Person [of Christ] appear, saying to her, "Woman, why do you weep, whom do you seek?" But let her, thinking him a gardener, respond, "Lord, if you have carried him away [...]." Let the Person add, "*Maria*." Then let her, recognizing him, prostrate herself at his feet saying "*Raboni*." But let the Person withdrawing himself say "Touch me not [...]." When the Person will have disappeared, let Mary communicate her joy to her companions, with a happy voice, singing these verses, "Rejoice and be happy [...]." These things finished, let the Person on the right side of the altar encounter the women all together saying, "Greetings, do not fear [...]" Then let them, prostrating themselves on the ground, grasp his feet and kiss them. This done, let them sing in succession these verses, Mary Magdalene beginning, "Jesus, the Nazarene [...]." Once these verses are completed, then let the Maries standing on the steps before the altar, turning themselves to the people, sing these verses, "Alleluia, the Lord has risen from the sepulcher [...]," with the choir responding to them. With these things finished, let the priests and clerks, in figuration of the disciples of Christ, proceed forward, saying, "O people hard-hearted [...]." Then let one of them approach and say to Mary Magdalene, "Tell us, Maria [...]."[13] Let her then respond, "Sepulcher of Christ [...]"; "Angelic witnesses [...]"; with her finger let her point out the place where the angel was sitting and offer to them the sudary to kiss, adding this verse, "Christ has risen, our hope [...]. "Then let the disciples and the choir add these final verses, "It is to be believed [...]" and "We know Christ [...]." Afterward let Magdalene begin "Christ rising," with clergy and choir singing with her as well.

These things thus finished, let the hymn "O God we praise thee [...]" [*Te Deum laudamus*] be sung, with the priest beginning; meanwhile, with the aforesaid priests putting back on their proper clothing in the chapel, let them approach the sepulcher with candles in order to pray, passing through the choir, and let them thus make there a brief prayer. Then let them return to their stations until the abbess orders them to exit for rest.

Margery Kempe

Excerpt from The Book of Margery Kempe[14] *(c.1430)*

Another day this creatur schuld geve hir [*give herself*] to medytacyon, as sche was bodyn [*bid to*] befor, and sche lay stylle, nowt knowyng what sche mygth best thynke. Than sche seyd [*said*] to ower [*our*] Lord Jhesu Crist, "Jhesu, what schal I thynke?" Ower Lord Jhesu answeryd to hir mende [*mind*], "Dowtyr, thynke on my modyr [*my mother*], for sche is cause of alle the grace that thow [*thou*] hast." And than anoon sche saw Seynt Anne gret [*great*] wyth chylde, and than sche preyd [*prayed*] Seynt Anne to be hir mayden and hir servawnt. And anon ower Lady was born, and than sche besyde hir to take the chyld to hir [*herself*] and kepe it tyl [*until*] it wer twelve yer of age wyth good mete [*food*] and drynke, wyth fayr [*fair*] whyte clothys and whyte kerchys [*diapers*]. And than sche seyd to the blyssed chyld, "Lady, ye schal be the modyr [*mother*] of God." The blyssed chyld answeryd and seyd, "I wold I wer [*I wish I were*] worthy to be the handmayden of hir that [*she who*] schuld conseive the sone of God." The creatur seyd, "I pray yow, Lady, yyf [*if*] that grace falle yow, forsake not [*don't forget*] my servyse." The blysful chyld passyd awey [*departed*] for a certeyn tyme, the creatur being stylle in contemplacyon, and sythen cam ageyn [*returned*] and seyd, "Dowtyr, now am I bekome [*I have become*] the modyr of God."

And than the creatur [*creature: MK herself*] fel down on hir kneys wyth gret reverens [*reverence*] and gret wepyng and seyd, "I am not worthy, Lady, to do yow servyse." "Yys, [*Yes*] dowtyr," sche seyde, "folwe thow me, thi servyse lykyth me [*your service pleases me*] wel." Than went sche forth wyth owyr Lady and wyth Josep, beryng wyth hir a potel of pyment and spycys therto [*container of sweetened and spiced wine*]. Than went thei forth to Elysabeth, Seynt John Baptystys modir [*the mother of St. John the Baptist*], and, whan thei mettyn [*they met*] togyder, eythyr [*both*] of hem [*them*] worshepyd other [*the other*], and so thei wonyd togedyr [*lived together*] wyth gret grace and gladnesse twelve wokys [*weeks*]. And than Seynt John was bor [*was born*], and owyr Lady toke hym up fro the erthe wyth al maner reverens and gaf [*gave*] hym to hys moder, seyng of [*saying about*] hym that he schuld [*would*] be an holy man, and blyssed hym. Sythen [*then*] thei toke her leve [*took their leave*] eythyr of other [*each from the other*] wyth compassyf terys. And than the creatur fel down on kneys to Seynt Elysabeth and preyd hir sche wold [*would*] prey for hir to owyr Lady that sche mygth do hir servyse and plesawns [*do her service and pleasure*]. "Dowtyr, me semyth" [*Daughter, it seems to me*], seyd Elysabeth, "Thu dost ryght wel thi dever" [*you are doing your duty very well*].

And than went the creatur forth wyth owyr [*our*] Lady to Bedlem [*Bethlehem*] and purchasyd hir herborwe [*paid for her lodging*] every nyght wyth gret reverens, and owyr Lady was receyved wyth glad cher [*warm hospitality*]. Also sche beggyd [*got by begging for*] owyr Lady fayr whyte clothys and kerchys [*diapers*] for to swathyn [*swaddle*] in hir sone [*her son in*] whan he wer born, and, whan Jhesu was born sche ordeyned beddyng for owyr Lady to lyg in [*lie*] wyth hir blyssed sone. And sythen [*then*] sche beggyd mete [*food*] for owyr Lady and hir blyssyd chyld. Aftyrward sche swathyd [*swaddled*] hym wyth byttyr teerys [*bitter tears*] of compassyon, havyng mend [*having *mind, i.e., taking thought*] of the scharp [*painful*] deth that he schuld [*would have to*] suffyr for the lofe [*love*] of synful men, seyng to hym, "Lord, I schal fare fayr wyth yow [*I will treat you well*]; I schal not byndyn yow soor [*bind you too tightly*]. I pray yow beth not dysplesyd wyth me."

Please see the Works Cited for further information on the sources used in this essay.

Notes

1 See Säntha Bhattacharji, "Sutton, Katherine."
2 See Sebastian Sobecki, "The writing of this tretys."
3 See Carolyn Dinshaw, "Margery Kempe."
4 Translation by Andrew Galloway from van Beek, ed., pp. 16–26.
5 That is, a sacrifice to the official Roman gods on behalf of the emperor, as the exchange makes clear.
6 Translation by Andrew Galloway from *Hildegardis Bingensis Epistolarium*, ed. Van Acker, pp. 125–30.
7 The author of this letter identifies herself (with pointed modesty) only as "T," but we (like Hildegard) know from her abbey that she is the abbess Tengswich. Mother Tengswich's reasons for writing are explained in her letter. Their entire exchange is presented here; no other letters between Tengswich and Hildegard survive.
8 Translation by Andrew Galloway from *Hildegardis Scivias*, ed. Führkötter, pp. 614–15, 627–29, 631. The excerpt is from Part III, vision 13.
9 Translation by Andrew Galloway from *Het Visioenenboek*, ed. Vekeman, pp. 81–89. The excerpt is from the Sixth Vision.
10 Translation by Andrew Galloway from Tolhurst, ed., 1.99–100, 106–8.
11 The Christian services for Easter, established as commemorating Jesus's Crucifixion and Resurrection (and marking the arrival of spring), are elaborate and ancient, and from the tenth century onward offered opportunity for even more elaborate "Easter drama," whose participation in and distinctions from any other kind of drama are matters of long and ongoing discussion. By the early Christian centuries were established annual ceremonies based on episodes in the gospels presenting Jesus's Crucifixion, his Descent or Deposition (taking down his body from the Cross), and, on Easter morning, his Elevation (the resurrection and ascent into heaven). Key features of these occur at the Elevation, including dramatizing the search of the three Marys for Jesus's body only to encounter an angel at his tomb who tells them that he is not there but has arisen, a dialogue loosely based on the synoptic gospel accounts of Matthew 28:5–10, Mark 16:5–7, and Luke 24:4–6, though none of those has dramatic dialogue. The Deposition enacted in a church involved taking down the crucifix and placing it, suitably tended and mourned, in a special "sepulcher" (often an elaborated engraved stone feature inside a medieval church altar area, with a small recess to receive the Crucifix, but here clearly a much larger internal structure), to be brought out and "resurrected" in the Elevation. For some of Sutton's innovations in the typical versions of this liturgy, see the essay discussing these materials.
12 "Quoniam" for "quam" in Tolhurst's edition of the *Ordinale*, a medieval or the modern editor's error.
13 "Dic" for "dixit" in Tolhurst's edition of the *Ordinale*, a medieval or the modern editor's error.
14 From Staley, ed., 32–33; glosses by Andrew Galloway

Suggestions for Further Reading

Baird, Joseph L., trans. *The Personal Correspondence of Hildegard of Bingen.* Oxford: Oxford University Press, 2006.

Bremmer, Jan N. and Marco Formisano, eds. *Perpetua's Passions: Multidisciplinary Approaches to the Passio Perpetuae et Felicitatis.* Oxford: Oxford University Press, 2012.

Cerasano, S. P. and Marion Wynne-Davies, eds. *Renaissance Drama by Women: Texts and Documents*. London: Routledge, 1996.

Galloway, Andrew. "Visions and Visionaries." *The Oxford Handbook of Medieval Literature*. Elaine Treharne and Greg Walker, eds. Oxford: Oxford University Press, 2010, 256–75.

Hart, Mother Columba, and Jane Bishop, trans. *Hildegard of Bingen, Scivias*. New York: Paulist Press, 1990.

Hart, Mother Columba, trans. *Hadewijch: The Complete Works*. New York: Paulist Press, 1980.

Lancaster, Anne. *London Civic Theatre: City Drama and Pageantry from Roman Times to 1558*. Cambridge: Cambridge University Press, 2002.

Nissé, Ruth. *Defining Acts: Drama and the Politics of Interpretation in Late Medieval England*. Notre Dame, IA: University of Notre Dame Press, 2005.

Tydeman, William. *The Theatre in the Middle Ages: Western European Stage Conditions, c.800–1576*. Cambridge: Cambridge University Press, 1979.

2 HROTSVIT OF GANDERSHEIM (c. 935–c. 1002)

Andrew Galloway

Introduction

Hrotsvit[1] (c. 935–c. 1002) is the first named woman playwright, the first named woman to write epic, and the first named woman to comment directly on drama; from our contemporary perspective, she seems to tower above an otherwise almost impenetrable mist. "O rare bird in Saxony!" exclaimed the sixteenth-century monk Heinrich Bodo, following the nationalizing treatment of her by the German Humanist scholar, Conrad Celtis, who discovered and then printed the fullest still-surviving copy of her works (which he had cut apart and reordered) in 1501 (Bodarwé 336; Berschin 27–29).[2] Much of what we know about Hrotsvit is derived from her own works, especially her handful of prefaces and addresses to her readers, but other clues open her world further. Hrotsvit was a nun in Gandesheim, a monastery founded in Saxony in 856 but occupied only after its abbey church was completed in 880. By Hrotsvit's time, Gandesheim had become one of the richest and most privileged religious houses in Saxony, a brilliant center of education and exchange with neighboring abbeys and the royal court. During most of Hrotsvit's life, Gerberga II was Gandersheim's abbess. Gerberga II was the niece of Otto the Great (912–73), who fashioned himself as the ruler of a revived Roman Empire (later called the Holy Roman Empire to distinguish it from the long-collapsed pagan Roman Empire of the ancient world, the setting for so many of Hrotsvit's plays).[3]

Hrotsvit wrote at Gerberga's request a Latin verse history of the *Deeds of Otto the Great*, as well as verse narratives of saints' lives with addresses to Gerberga. Hrotsvit's six plays are grouped and introduced with the Preface, translated here, along with a slyly deferential letter to certain "learned men" to whom she dedicates the drama. These, with other poetic narratives and verse prayers, survive in the single tenth-century manuscript in elegant Carolingian Latin and Carolingian script that Celtis discovered and printed. The mere fact that a named woman from her period was so learned a playwright and poet has sometimes seemed reason enough to value Hrotsvit. But scholars have found further reasons to ponder the complexities of her views of virginity, gender, political power, and intellectual authority, and have frequently considered where her plays might fit in dramatic history—if they do at all. Whether Hrosvit's plays were acted or even recited with any degree of mimetic impersonation continues to be debated.[4]

The Preface's consideration of the "insane" mores of pagan drama, identified with the Roman comic dramatist Terence (c. 195–c. 158 BCE), casts a large literary-historical and world-historical frame around these issues. Hrotsvit's plays are all historical dramas

DOI: 10.4324/9781003006923-3

that show the defeat of brutal pagan imperial males by chaste and captive but spiritually powerful Christian women—and in one case a young virgin man. This may reflect how burdensome reproductive sexuality was, especially for women, carrying family-linking and heir-producing importance in Ottonian (like much medieval) culture.

Hrotsvit speaks of herself "blushing" as she depicts pagan lusts, but her identification of herself as "Clamor Validus" (Strong Cry) introduces her bodily presence in another, more pointed way. In one sense, the phrase is a simple (though not the only possible) Latin version of her Saxon name: *hrot* ('cry') plus *svit* ('strong'), as Jacob Grimm was first to mention in 1898 (ix). But as many have since suggested, this also seems an allusion to John the Baptist as the "voice of one crying [*vox clamantis*] in the desert" (Mark 1:3), and perhaps even to the prayers of Christ Himself, in Hebrews 5:7, where, while still "in the flesh," he is said to have offered up supplications to God "with a strong cry" (Berschin, "Hrotsvit" 23, n. 2)

Those possible implications are bold enough claims to her authority and freedom. But scholars seem not to have considered a further, somewhat less Christian possibility informing the phrase. The most widely used treatise on rhetoric and public speaking from pagan Antiquity, *Ad Herennium* (c. 80 BCE), falsely attributed to Cicero and used in rhetorical education for a millennium, discusses an orator's proper voicing and enunciation, including when to use *clamor*, usually translated as "full voicing." Assuming throughout that only a man can be a public orator, the unidentified author declares that a man should carefully choose when he ought to rise to *clamor*, whereas a woman's voice is "ignoble" because it too often stays in that range: "sharp exclamation injures the voice and likewise jars the hearer, for it has about it something ignoble, suited rather to feminine outcry than to manly dignity in speaking" (Caplan 3.12.22).

Especially in the context of a (self-)introduction, Hrotsvit's positive use of that phrase seems uncannily similar to the disparagement of women's "outcry" by the pagan author of the *Ad Herennium*. The point is certainly clear in the plays themselves, where pious women verbally demolish their brutal (and often impotently clamorous) male assailants. Hrotsvit's chaste female interlocutors, like Hrotsvit herself as her Preface presents her, demonstrate an abundance of ways for evading or reinterpreting St. Paul's stern dictum, "I suffer not a woman to teach, nor to use authority over the man; but to be in silence" (1 Timothy 2:12).

Yet evasion and reinterpretation are not insurgency. As the unstable modesty yet boldness in the Preface makes clear, Hrotsvit can be seen either ultimately to uphold a male hierarchy of husbands, emperors, then God,[5] or, equally, to question all authority—except God's (Brown 262). Either way, the plays like the Preface show women in dialogue with men of authority, in various literary and political modes, overtly and by implication. Even her comments against Terence in the Preface merely parallel the ancient playwright's defenses in his own prologues against certain critics of how he used his sources.[6]

Hrotsvit's achievement is unexpected in so many ways that scholars continue to try to understand just how rare she was. That question is particularly pressing in regard to how unusual her idea of "drama" was, whatever it was. Her considerations of Terence do not directly help us there, as Terence was evidently read then, rather than performed. Fully impersonated (or "dramatized") liturgical drama had not yet appeared in tenth-century Germany, and secular Latin drama did not widely emerge until the twelfth century. At most we can say that Hrotsvit follows the basic early medieval definition of "drama" as "dialogue."[7]

There is no question that Hrotsvit's ways of "imitating" Terence were highly crea-tive, taking "imitation" in the sense of interpretation and elaboration, as was often the case in medieval theories of translation.[8] Roman theatricality was a fact of polit-ical life at court at the height of Hrotsvit's productive years during the Ottonian empire, which continued Charlemagne's invocations of Roman imperial culture shaped, like Hrotsvit's drama, into a solemnly Christianized form. Gandesheim's church boasted a grand western extension (*Westwerk*) including a special gallery overlooking the nave, which was designed for the king to partake in the monastery's religious ceremonies (Bernhardt 153). Might Emperor Otto and his son Otto II have witnessed from there Hrotsvit's wittily pious rebukes of the kinds of Romanized the-atricality to which the imperial court was accustomed?

Hrotsvit of Gandersheim

"Preface to the Dramas"[9] *(c. 1000)*

Catholics can be found aplenty whose actions we cannot entirely expurgate: who, because of the beauty of more elegant discourse, prefer the vanity of pagan texts to the value [*utilitas*] of sacred scripture. There are even some who, though they adhere to the sacred text and spurn the things of gentiles,[10] often take pleasure in the fic-tions of Terence,[11] and while delighted by the sweetness of the discourse are stained by ideas of unspeakable crimes. Wherefore I, the Strong Cry of Gandersheim [*Clamor Validus Gandeshemensis*], have not refrained from imitating him in speaking since others worship him in reading—except that, using the same genre in which the foul unchaste actions of lascivious women are recited, I celebrate the laudable chastity of sacred virgins, as far as my feeble intellect's ability.[12]

Not infrequently, however, it shames me, infusing deep blushes, that, since this kind of writing demands the detestable illicit madness of lovers and their evilly sweet discourse together, I have conceived in my mind and inscribed with my quill things not meant to be accommodated to our hearing. Yet if, in my blushing, I should fail to do these things or to fulfill my plan, I would also fail to expound the praise of innocents, as far as my full ability. For the quicker that some turn out to be in illicitly flattering the insane, the higher the glory of the divine Helper and the more glorious the victory of those triumphing, especially when feminine weakness conquers and masculine strength is overthrown.[13]

As for myself, I do not doubt some will object that the value of my writing is lower by far, and more constrained by far, indeed utterly unlike the statements of him whom I meant to imitate. I grant it. Yet I declare to such doubters that I cannot be convicted by that law, as if I had aberrantly wanted to be made similar to those who, greater in learning, far outstripped my artlessness. Nor am I of such boastfulness that I would presume to compare myself even to the least disciple of [pagan] authorities. This alone do I seek: that, although not at all suitably capable, with bowed devoutness of mind I might render back to the Giver the ingenuity I have been granted.

Wherefore I am not so great a lover of myself that, in order to avoid the censure of Christ, Who creates strength and virtue among the holy wherever He will provide the capability, I would cease preaching. I will rejoice, however, if my devoutness pleases anyone. But if, either because of my lowliness or because of the flawed folksiness of my speech, this pleases no one, I would nonetheless take pleasure in what I have done [*or* what I have made: *feci*]. For while I cultivate the vileness of my own labor—using linked heroic strophes [*heroico ligatam strophio*] in other little works of my feeblemindedness, and here knitted-up dramatic exchanges [*dramatica vinctam serie*]—I evade the pernicious pleasures of the gentiles.

Please see the Works Cited for further information on the sources used in this essay.

Notes

1 Also identified in modern discussions as Hrosvitha, Hroswitha, Hrosvit, Hrotsvitha, Rosvita, and Roswitha. Even this element of her life and work is controversial. The poet twice records her own name in the nominative (subject) case as "Hrotsvit," thus that form is used here as in most current scholarship. The other forms that scholars have used are based on various other assumptions about the Old Saxon forms of her name.
2 All translations are mine unless otherwise noted.
3 See Wailes and Brown, "Hrotsvit and her World" and Berschin.
4 See, for example, Zeydel; Zampelli; Wailes 122–23.
5 See McMillin.
6 See Newman.
7 See Wilson, 55–86.
8 See Copeland.
9 Translated and annotated by Andrew Galloway
10 That is, pagans of Greek and Roman Antiquity.
11 Ancient author (c. 195–158 BCE) of six comedies. Unlike any other ancient drama, Terence's works were widely known and quoted in the Christian Middle Ages, though not as widely as Hrotsvit claims.
12 Gestures of intellectual and literary modesty are common among medieval Christian authors; Hrotsvit's learning and brilliance are abundantly clear, including in the rhetorical elegance by which she proclaims her ineptness.
13 That is, the better some speakers (and writers) are at deluding those whose rational capabilities can be deranged by sinful passions, the greater the triumph is when divinely inspired innocent women prevail over such brutal men. This difficult sentence manages to imply both the triumph of Hrotsvit's pious Christian women over their pagan tormenters and seducers, and also Hrotsvit's literary triumph over Terence's sinfully seductive plots and non-Christian world-view.

Suggestions for Further Reading

Bonfante, Larissa, trans., with Alexandra Bonfante-Warren. *The Plays of Hrotswitha of Gandersheim.* Waconda, IL: Bolchazy-Carducci, 2007.
Brown, Phyllis R., Linda A. McMillin, and Katharina M. Wilson, eds. *Hrotsvit of Gandersheim: Contexts, Identities, Affinities, Performances.* Toronto: University of Toronto Press, 2004.
Brown, Phyllis R., and Stephen L. Wailes, eds. *A Companion to Hrotsvit of Gandersheim (fl. 960): Contextual and Interpretive Approaches.* Leiden: Brill, 2013.
Chance, Jane. *The Literary Subversions of Medieval Women.* New York: Palgrave, 2007.
Dronke, Peter. *Women Writers of the Middle Ages: A Critical Study of Texts from Perpetua (†203) to Margaret de la Porete (†1310).* Cambridge: Cambridge University Press, 1984.
Hyperdonat (online editions of Donatus, including commentaries on Terence). http://hyperdonat.huma-num.fr/editions/html/index.html
Wilson, Katharina, ed. *Hrotsvit of Gandersheim: "Rara avis in Saxonia"?* Ann Arbor: Michigan Medieval and Renaissance Monograph Series, 1987.
Wilson, Katharina, ed. *Hrotsvit of Gandersheim: A Florilegium of her Works.* Cambridge: D. S. Brewer, 1998.

3 MARGARET LUCAS CAVENDISH (c.1623–1673)

Sujata Iyengar and Mikaela Warner

Introduction

Margaret Lucas Cavendish (c.1623–1673), Duchess of Newcastle, the first English woman playwright openly to publish under her own name, wrote twenty plays during England's Interregnum and Restoration. The Duchess was known for her wide generic scope; she published drama, poetry, orations, letters, natural philosophy, and science fiction. An ardent Royalist who served at the court of Queen Henrietta Maria and who in 1645 married the much-older William Cavendish, Marquess of Newcastle over her friends' (and the Queen's) objections, Cavendish has been long and unfairly reviled as an eccentric egotist whose lack of education, according to Virginia Woolf, perverted and spoiled her natural talents (*A Room of One's Own* 60–61). Her plays were dismissed for centuries as "closet dramas," unplayable and unwatchable. It was not until the 1990s that Gweno Williams began producing student productions of the plays and not until July 2018 that the first ever professional production of a play by Cavendish, her *Unnatural Tragedy*, was performed at the White Bear Theatre in London, directed by Graham Watts.

But Cavendish's drama is eminently playable: the short, episodic scenes for which she felt bound to apologize to her Neoclassical peers translate into lively running action on a modern "black box" stage, and present-day audiences instantly grasp the underlying feminist logic that unites each play's different plot strands and characters. Marta Straznicky (67–90), Lara Dodds (162–3), and Anne Shaver (1–20) independently observe that it is unreasonable to dismiss Cavendish's drama as "closet" theatre given that the public theatres were closed throughout the Interregnum; moreover, argues Straznicky, to write drama at all constitutes a veiled "political act" at this time, in particular during the Cavendishes' exile on the Continent (90). Dodds suggests that Cavendish is above all concerned with female self-actualization, despite her extensive disclaimers and frequent use of the modesty *topos* (10–13). Cavendish juxtaposes vignettes or interludes to question whether it can even be possible for a woman to become a fully realized human being under the system of patriarchy, primogeniture, and patronage. As an aristocrat, she paradoxically valued the privileges that her rank afforded her, even as she critiqued the sexism of that milieu.

In her "Sociable Letters," in her science fiction novel *The Blazing World*, in the many "Prefaces" she added to her published plays, and in her "Oration on Plays and Players," Cavendish laid out a consistent theory of what theatre should do for society, how writers should construct plays for the theatre, and how actors should be trained best to embody them. Cavendish anticipated a Keatsian "negative capability" (Keats 42;

DOI: 10.4324/9781003006923-4

Fitzmaurice 29–46) in attributing to Shakespeare the ability to enter the minds, speech, and bodies of his characters, rather than blaming him for failing to adhere to the Neoclassical "Unities" in vogue at her time ("Sociable Letter" 123).[1]

We here reproduce excerpts from some of Cavendish's own extensive writing about the theatre. Hoping to make this text as accessible as possible to general readers without losing the distinctive "flavor" of Cavendish's prose, we have modernized spelling and typography, including giving the names of authors and literary characters in their more modern and familiar forms, for example "Shakespeare" instead of "Shakespear"; "Beatrice" instead of "Betrice." We have also, where appropriate, broken her long texts into paragraphs, and silently emended obvious printers' errors, consulting modern editions (Bowerbank and Mendelson; Shaver) alongside digital facsimiles of the early printed texts. We have, however, tried to maintain Cavendish's original grammar and punctuation, including her idiosyncratic word divisions and use of upper-case for emphasis, and her omission of possessive apostrophes ("my self" or "my Self" where we would now write "myself"; "Plutarchs story" where we would now write "Plutarch's story," for example).

We have likewise kept Cavendish's characteristic address to her "Noble Readers" in her *Prefaces*, "Noble Citizens" in her *Orations*, and fictive female friend, "Madam," in her *Sociable Letters*. We have removed, however, her usual concluding initials, "M.N." (for "Margaret Newcastle"). In editing Cavendish's prose, we are aware we risk becoming the "Pedantical Scholastical persons" she derides in Preface 5; we encourage interested readers to turn to Anne Shaver's reprinting of all the prefaces in their entirety in Appendix A of her edition of Cavendish's plays, for the full benefit of the Duchess's epic catalogues and sly irony.

Margaret Lucas Cavendish

Excerpt from "An Oration Concerning Plays and Players," Orations of Diverse Sorts, Accommodated to Diverse Places *(1662)*

Noble Citizens,

Here is a Company of Players [...] but [...] you Mis-spend your Time, and [...] your Money, unless the Players were better Actors, and their Plays better Plays; for as their Plays have no Wit in them, so the Actors have no Grace, nor Becoming Behavior in their Actions; for what is Constraint, is Misbecoming, as being not Natural, and whatsoever is Unnatural, is Deformed: but pray, Mistake me not, as believing, I am an Enemy to Plays or Players, for I am an Enemy only to Foolish Plays, and Ill Actors, but for Good Plays well Acted, I am so far from being an Enemy to them, as I think there is nothing so Profitable for Youth, both to Increase their Understanding, and to Fashion their Behavior; and for those that have Spare time, they cannot pass it more Pleasingly; therefore let me Advise you, that are Magistrates of this City, to set up a Company of Players at the Common charge, and to Maintain some Excellent Poet, to make Good Plays, and certainly you will be no Losers in so doing, but Gainers, being the Best and Readiest way of Education for your Children: for the Poet will inform them both of the World, and the Natures and Humors of Mankind, an Easier and Delightfuller way, than the School-men; and the Actors will shew them to Behave themselves more Gracefully and Becomingly, than their Dancing-Masters.

Thus they will Learn more both for their Bodies and Minds of the Poet and Players, than of their Tutors and Governors, or by Studying or Travelling, which is Expensive, Laborious, and Dangerous, whereas the other is Easy, Delightful, Safe, and Profitable. Also one thing more I must advise you, that you provide a Practick[2] Judicious man, to Instruct the Players to Act well; for as they must have a Poet, to make their Plays, so they must have a Tutor to teach them to Act those Plays, unless the Poet will take the pains to teach them himself, as to Humor the Passions, and to Express the Humors Naturally, and not to Act after the French Fashion, with High strained Voices, Constrained Motions, Violent Actions, and such Transportation, as is neither Graceful, Becoming, nor Natural; but they must make Love Soberly, Implore Favor Humbly, Complain Seriously, Lament Sadly, and not Affectedly, Fantastically, Constraintly, Ragingly, Furiously, and the like; all which in my Opinion they do Senselessly, Foolishly, and Madly; for all Feignings must be done as Naturally as may be, that they may seem as Real Truths.

Excerpt from Preface 3[3], **Plays** *(1662)*

Noble Readers,

Although I expect my Plays will be found fault with, by reason I have not [...made...] all the Actors to meet at the latter end upon the Stage in a flock together; likewise, that I have not made my Comedies of one days actions or passages; yet I have adventured to publish them to the World. But to plead in my Plays behalf, first, I do not perceive any reason why that the several persons presented should be all of an acquaintance, or that there is a necessity to have them of one Fraternity, or to have a relation to each other, or linked in alliance as one Family; when as Plays are to present the general Follies [...] Vices, Humors, [...] Fashions, Customs [...] of the whole World of Mankind, as in several persons; also particular Follies [...] and the like, in particular persons; also the Sympathy and Antipathy of Dispositions [...] of several persons; also the particular Virtues and Graces in several persons, and [...] in particular persons, and all these Varieties to be drawn at the latter end into one piece, as into one Company, which in my opinion shows neither Usual, Probable, nor Natural.

For since the World is wide and populated, and their various actions dispersed, and spread about by each particular, and Plays are to present them severally, I perceive no reason they should force them together in the last Act, as in one Community, [...] in this I have not followed the steps of precedent Poets, for in my opinion, I think it as well, if not better, if a Play ends but with two persons, or one person upon the Stage; besides, I would have my Plays to be like the Natural course of all things in the World [...] so my Scenes, some last longer than othersome, and some are ended when others are begun; likewise some of my Scenes have no acquaintance or relation to the rest of the Scenes, although in one and the same Play, which is the reason many of my Plays will not end as other Plays do, especially Comedies [...].

Likewise my Plays may be Condemned, because they follow not the Antient[4] Custom, as the learned says, [...] which is, that all Comedies should be so ordered and composed, as nothing should be presented therein, but what may be naturally, or usually practiced or Acted in the World in the compass of one day; truly in my opinion those Comedies would be very flat and dull, and neither profitable nor pleasant [...] I do not perceive a necessity that Comedies should be so closely packed or thrust up together; for if Comedies are either to delight, or to profit, or to both, they must follow no other rule or example, but to put them into Scenes and Acts, and to order their several discourses in a Comedy, so as Physicians do their Cordials, wherein they mix many several Ingredients together into one Electuary, as sharp, bitter, salt, and sweet, and mix them so, as they are both pleasing to the Taste, and comfortable to the Stomach; so Poets should order the several Humors, Passions, Customs, Manners, Fashions, and practice of Mankind, as to intermix them so, as to be both delightful to the Mind and Senses, and profitable to the Life [...].

[A]lso Poets should do as Physicians or Apothecaries, which put not only several sorts, but several kinds of Drugs into one Medicine [...] so Poets both in their Comedies and Tragedies, must, or at leastwise may, represent several Nations, Governments, People [...] Fashions [...] Natures, Fortunes [...] Actions, in one Play; as also several times of Ages to one person if occasion requires, as from Childhood to Manhood in one Play; for Poets are to describe in Plays the several Ages [...] Actions, Fortunes, [...] and Humors in Nature, and the several Customs, Manners, Fashions and Speeches of men: thus Plays are to present the natural dispositions and practices of Mankind; also they are to point at Vanity, laugh at Follies, disgrace Baseness, and persecute Vice; likewise they are to extol Virtue, and to honor Merit, and to praise the Graces, all which makes a Poet Divine, their works edifying to the Mind or Soul, profitable to the Life, delightful to the Senses, and recreative to Time [...] and I do not despair, although but a Poetress, but that my works may be some ways or other serviceable to my Readers, which if they be, my time in writing them is not lost, nor my Muse unprofitable.

Excerpt from Preface 5, **Plays** *(1662)*

Noble Readers,

I Know there are many Scholastical and Pedantical persons that will condemn my writings, because I do not keep strictly to the Masculine and Feminine Genders, as they call them as for example, a Lock and a Key, the one is the Masculine Gender, the other the Feminine Gender, so Love is the Masculine Gender, Hate the Feminine Gender, and the Furies are shes, and the Graces are shes, the Virtues are shes, and the seven deadly Sins are shes, which I am sorry for; but I know no reason but that I may as well make them Hes for my use, as others did Shes, or Shes as others did Hes.

But some will say, if I did do so, there would be no forms or rules of Speech to be understood by; I answer, that we may as well understand the meaning or sense of a Speaker or Writer by the names of Love or Hate, as by the names of he or she, and better: for the division of Masculine and Feminine Genders doth confound a Scholar more, and takes up more time to learn them, than they have time to spend; besides, where one doth rightly understand the difference, a hundred, nay a thousand do not, and yet they are understood, and to be understood is the end of all Speakers and Writers; so that if my writings be understood, I desire no more; and as for the niceties of Rules, Forms, and Terms [...] if any dislike my writings for want of those Rules, Forms, and Terms, let them not read them, for I had rather my writings should be unread than be read by such Pedantical Scholastical persons.

Excerpt from "A General Prologue to all my Plays," Plays *(1662)*

> But Noble Readers, do not think my Plays,
> Are such as have been writ in former days;
> As Jonson, Shakespeare, Beaumont, Fletcher[5] writ;
> Mine want their Learning, Reading, Language, Wit:
> The Latin phrases I could never tell,
> But Jonson could, which made him write so well.
> Greek, Latin Poets, I could never read,
> Nor their Historians, but our English Speed;
> I could not steal their Wit, nor Plots out take;
> All my Plays Plots, my own poor brain did make:
> From Plutarchs story I never took a Plot,
> Nor from Romances, nor from Don Quixote,[6]
> As others have, for to assist their Wit,
> But I upon my own Foundation writ;
> [...]
>
> But I have thriftly been, housewived[7] my time,
> And built both Cottages of Prose and Rhyme;
> All the materials in my head did grow,
> All is my own, and nothing do I owe:
> But all that I desire when as I dye,
> My memory in my own Works my lye:
> And when as others build them Marble Tombs,
> To inurn their dust, and fretted vaulted Rooms,
> I care not where my dust, or bones remain,
> So my Works live, the labor of my brain.
> I covet not a stately, cut, carved Tomb,
> But that my Works, in Fames house may have room:
> Thus I my poor built Cottage am content,
> When that I die, may be my Monument.

Excerpt from Sociable Letters no. 29 *(1664)*

Madam,

[...T]he Lady S. P. [...] was pleased to Censure and Condemn [...] the Manner of my Life [...] This course of Life is by my own voluntary Choice, for I have liberty to do any Thing, or to go any Where [...I]t is not out of a Fantastic Humor, that I live so much Retired [but...] for my Pleasure and Delight, my Ease and Peace, [...] though I do not go Personally to Masks, Balls, and Plays, yet my Thoughts entertain my Mind with such Pleasures, for some of my Thoughts make Plays, and others Act those Plays on the Stage of Imagination, where my Mind sits as a Spectator, Thus my Mind is entertained both with Poets and Players [...] so that the Mind and the Thoughts employ the Senses, and the Senses employ the Mind and Thoughts, and thus I take as much Pleasure within my self, if not more, as the Lady S. P. doth without her self [...].

Excerpt from Sociable Letters, *no. 123 (1664)*

Madam,

I Wonder how that Person you mention in your Letter, could either have the Conscience, or Confidence to Dispraise Shakespeare's Plays, as to say they were made up only with Clowns, Fools, Watchmen, and the like; But to Answer that Person [...] it seems by his Judging, or Censuring, he Understands not Plays, or Wit; for to Express Properly, [...] Shakespeare did not want Wit, to Express to the Life all Sorts of Persons [...] and so Well he hath Expressed in his Plays all Sorts of Persons, as one would think he had been Transformed into every one of those Persons he hath Described [...].

Who would not think he had been such a man as his Sir John Falstaff? and who would not think he had been Harry the Fifth? & certainly Julius Caesar, Augustus Caesar, and Antonius, did never Really Act their parts Better, if so Well, as he hath Described them, and I believe that Antonius and Brutus did not Speak Better to the People, than he hath Feigned them; nay, one would think that he had been Metamorphosed from a Man to a Woman, for who could Describe Cleopatra Better than he hath done, and many other Females of his own Creating, as Nan Page, Mrs. Page, Mrs. Ford, the Doctors Maid, Beatrice, Mrs. Quickly, Doll Tearsheet, and others, too many to Relate? [...] indeed Shakespeare had a Clear Judgement, a Quick Wit, a Spreading Fancy, a Subtle Observation, a Deep Apprehension, and a most Eloquent Elocution; truly, he was a Natural Orator, as well as a Natural Poet, and he was not an Orator to Speak Well only on some Subjects, ... Shakespeare's Wit and Eloquence was General, for, and upon all Subjects, he rather wanted Subjects for his Wit and Eloquence to Work on, for which he was Forced to take some of his Plots out of History, where he only took the Bare Designs, the Wit and Language being all his Own; and so much he had above others, that those, who Writ after him, were Forced to Borrow of him, or rather to Steal from him [...]. I believe, those that Dispraised his Plays, Dispraised them more out of Envy, than Simplicity or Ignorance, for those that could Read his Plays, could not be so Foolish to Condemn them, only the Excellency of them caused an Envy to them.

Excerpt from Sociable Letters, *no. 143 (1664)*

Madam,

I Heard the Ship was Drowned, wherein the man was that had the Charge and Care of my Plays...if I had not had the Original of them by me, truly I should have [...] accounted the Loss of my Twenty Plays, as the Loss of Twenty Lives, for in my Mind I should have Died Twenty Deaths [...] or I should have [...] almost Drowned in Salt Tears, as they in the Salt Sea; but they are Destinated to Live, and I hope, I in them, when my Body is Dead, and Turned to Dust [...].

Excerpt from The Blazing World, *Part 2: The purpose of plays (1668)*

[...] the Emperor desired her advice how to set up a theatre for plays [...]. The Duchess answered, that she had as little skill [...].

"But you have made plays," replied the Empress.

"Yes," answered the Duchess, "I intended them for plays; but the wits of these present times condemned them as uncapable of being represented or acted, because they were not made up according to the rules of art, though I dare say that the descriptions are as good as any they have writ."

The Emperor asked whether the property of plays were not to describe the several humors, actions and fortunes of mankind?

"'Tis so," answered the Duchess.

"Why then," replied the Emperor, "the natural humors, actions, and fortunes of mankind are not done by the rules of art."

"But," said the Duchess, "it is the art and method of our wits to despise all descriptions of wit, humor, actions and fortunes that are without such artificial rules."

The Emperor asked, "Are those good plays that are made so methodically and artificially?" The Duchess answered, they were good according to the judgment of the age, or mode of the nation, but not according to her judgment: "For truly," said she, "In my opinion, their plays will prove a nursery of whining lovers, and not an academy or school for wise, witty, noble and well-behaved men."

"But I," replied the Emperor, "desire such a theatre as may make wise men; and will have such descriptions as are natural, not artificial."

"If your majesty be of that opinion," said the Duchess's soul, "then my plays may be acted in your blazing-world, when they cannot be acted in the blinking-world of wit, and the next time I come to visit your majesty, I shall endeavor to order your Majesty's theatre, to present such plays as my wit is capable to make."

Then the empress told the Duchess, that she loved a foolish farce added to a wise play.

Please see the Works Cited for further information on the sources used in this essay.

Notes

1 In drama, the "unities" refer to three principles derived from Aristotle's *Poetics* (c. 330 BCE) to which a play should adhere: unity of time, unity of place, and unity of action.
2 Both practical and practiced.
3 The prefaces numbered in the original printing, they are numbered here in order of appearance.
4 "Ancient," but with the additional sense of "antique" or "antic," meaning both "old" and "quaint."
5 Benjamin Jonson (1572–1637), William Shakespeare (1564–1616), Francis Beaumont (1584/5–1616), and John Fletcher (1579–1625) were all renowned British dramatists.
6 Cavendish claims that she never takes material from the Greek writer Plutarch or from Miguel de Cervantes' *Don Quixote* (1605).
7 Managed appropriately, economically; compare to our modern use of the term "husbanded," to indicate "managed thriftily," conserved resources.

Suggestions for Further Reading

Cerasano, S. P., and Marion Wynne-Davies, eds. *Readings in Renaissance Women's Drama: Criticism, History, and Performance, 1594–1998.* London: Routledge, 1998.

Dodds, Lara, and Margaret Ferguson. "Sidney, Cary, Cavendish: Playwrights of the Printed Page and a Future Stage." *A New Companion to Renaissance Drama.* Eds. Arthur F. Kinney and Thomas Warren Hopper. London: John Wiley & Sons Ltd. EBSCO Publishing, 2017. 576–97.

Haber, Judith. *Desire and Dramatic Form in Early Modern England.* Cambridge, UK: Cambridge University Press, 2009.

Raber, Karen. *Dramatic Difference: Gender, Class, and Genre in the Early Modern Closet Drama.* Newark: University of Delaware Press, 2001.

4   APHRA BEHN (1640–1689)

Joseph Roach

Introduction

The most important single document in the history of seventeenth-century theatrical celebrity comes down to us in the form of a fan letter written by one woman to another. Aphra Behn (1640–1689), who is often described as English literature's first female professional author, wrote actress Eleanor "Nell" Gwynn (1650–1687) an over-the-top *billet-doux* as the dedicatory epistle to *The Feigned Courtesans* (1679). Introducing this risqué comedy, in which two women disguise themselves as courtesans to drive the intrigue plot, Behn performs the rhetorical equivalent of falling to her knees before the star. Pushing idolatry over the line into blasphemy, she addresses the popular comedienne and notorious concubine in an extended metaphor of religious devotion replete with echoes of Biblical citations. Approaching Gwynn's "altar" with "fear and trembling" (cf. *Philippians* 2:12), the playwright tells the actress that her voice inspires "awful reverence as to holy oracles or divine prophecies" (*Isaiah* 32: 15–20). She explains that her paragon's speeches reach the ears of the multitude as if they emanate from a sacred being, one possessed of "divine powers" worthy of "adoration" and "true worship." The sustained intensity of the prayerful language of the paean suggests that the author intends to express a feeling that runs even deeper than the desire to please a cash-bearing patron, though that is indeed the conventional purpose of the dedicatory epistle at this time.

   At first glance at least, Behn's metaphor seems counter-intuitive. Gwynn needed no disguise to play her courtesan's role in private life as the favorite mistress of King Charles II, nor did she shrink from performing it unashamedly in public. The author enthusiastically congratulates her patron on her extramarital "conquests," pointedly using the plural, the most recent of which has miraculously "subdued the most powerful and glorious monarch of the world." Moreover, she celebrates Gwynn for the ennobling of her two royal bastards, "whom you have permitted to wear those glorious titles which you yourself generously selected." Even for a reign made infamous by its sexual candor, this is breathtakingly outré, as was the jaw-dropping behavior of the addressee of the epistle. With the patois of her origins in the Covent Garden demimonde stenciled on her tongue, "Nellie" cursed so fluently that she made Admiralty Secretary Samuel Pepys, who regularly worked with sailors, blush. Having been kept previously by the actor Charles Hart and then the aristocrat Charles, Lord Buckhurst, the actress referred to her royal paramour (also known as Defender of the Faith and King by God's Grace of England, Scotland, and Ireland) as "Charles III."

DOI: 10.4324/9781003006923-5

She was the least sanctimonious person imaginable and the least likely to be sancti-fied in any orthodox way.

So what to make of the beatific aura with which Behn veils her? Opinions differ. In *The Life of Dryden*, Dr. Samuel Johnson went out of his way to deplore the dedication to *The Feigned Courtesans* as excessive even for an age over-ripe with effusive front matter; indeed, he found it more fulsomely sycophantic than Dryden's own panegyrics. To more contemporary sensibilities, however, Behn's tribute offers a moving reminder of the solidarity that women can attain, given the chance, when mutual admiration or attraction liberates their expression from the domination of male judgment. The author tells the actress that her example shames all those who "will allow a woman no wit." She extols not only the "power" of her "illustrious beauty," but also the "greatness" of her "mind." The self-evident personal warmth of the accolade—the idea that the addressee's personality seems to have been heaven-sent in order to put everyone she meets, men as well as women, in a good mood—certainly does distinguish "To Mrs. Ellen Gwynn" from other, more formal examples of the genre.

What needs to be understood about the larger meaning of the piece, however, is that it epitomizes in one pithy statement the creation of the modern idea of celebrity. That happened when the theatrical profession became sufficiently prominent in cul-ture and society that charisma could be earned by especially qualified performers, rather than merely ascribed to notables such as sacred monarchs or saints. Behn had the critical acuity and historical self-awareness to apprehend this re-purposing of worship as fandom and to illustrate it in one spectacular example. She opens our eyes to the fact that theatrical stardom as we know it is both a cause and a consequence of the historical phenomenon inadequately summed up by the word *secularization*.

English history of the Interregnum and the Restoration had a startling outcome for vernacular religion: a single generation of iconoclasts brought forth an age of icons that has yet to end. New dynasts required new deities, and popular culture served up the novelty of women on the stage as an enduring provocation for idol worship. In support of this argument, Behn's "Dedication to Mrs. Ellen Gwynn" is by no means the only evidence, but it is the best.

Aphra Behn

"To Mrs. Ellen Guin," Dedicatory Epistle to The Feign'd Curtezans; Or, A Night's Intrigue *(1679)*[1]

Madam,
'Tis no wonder that hitherto I followed not the good example of the believing Poets, since less faith and zeal then you alone can inspire, had wanted power to have reduc't me to the true worship : Your permission, *Madam,* has inlightened me, and I with shame look back on my past Ignorance, which suffered me not to pay an Adoration long since, where there was so very much due, yet even now though secure in my opinion, I make this Sacrifice with infinite fear and trembling, well knowing that so Excellent and perfect a Creature as your self differs only from the Divine pow-ers in this; the Offerings made to you ought to be worthy of you, whilst they accept the will alone; and how Madam, would your Altars be loaded, if like heaven you gave permission to all that had a will and desire to approach 'em who now at distance can

only wish and admire, which all mankinde agree to do; as if Madam, you alone had the pattent from heaven to ingross all hearts; and even those distant slaves whom you conquer with your fame, pay an equall tribute to those that have the blessing of being wounded by your Eyes, and boast the happiness of beholding you dayly; insomuch that succeeding ages who shall with joy survey your History shall Envy us who lived in this, and saw those charming wonders which they can only reade of, and whom we ought in charity to pity, since all the Pictures, pens or pencills can draw, will give 'em but a faint Idea of what we have the honour to see in such absolute Perfection; they can only guess She was infinitely fair, witty, and deserving, but to what Vast degrees in all, they can only Judge who liv'd to Gaze and Listen; for besides Madam, all the Charms and attractions and powers of your Sex, you have Beauties peculiar to your self, an eternal sweetness, youth and ayr, which never dwelt in any face but yours, of which not one unimitable Grace could be ever borrow'd, or assumed, though with never so much industry, to adorn another, they cannot steal a look or smile from you to inhance their own beauties price, but all the world will know it yours; so natural and so fitted are all your Charms and Excellencies to one another, so intirely design'd and created to make up in you alone the most perfect lovely thing in the world; you never appear but you glad the hearts of all that have the happy fortune to see you, as if you were made on purpose to put the whole world into good Humour, whenever you look abroad, and when you speak, men crowd to listen with that awfull reverence as to Holy Oracles or Divine Prophesies, and bears away the precious words to tell at home to all the attentive family the Graceful things you utter'd and cry, *but oh she spoke with such an Ayr, so gay, that half the beauty's lost in the repetition.* 'Tis this that ought to make your Sex vain enough to despise the malicious world that will allow a woman no wit, and bless our selves for living in an Age that can produce so wondrous an argument as your undeniable self, to shame those boasting talkers who are Judges of nothing but faults.

But how much in vain Madam, I endeavour to tell you the sence of all mankinde with mine, since to the utmost Limits of the Universe your mighty Conquests are made known : And who can doubt the Power of that Illustrious Beauty, the Charms of that tongue, and the greatness of that minde, who has subdu'd the most powerfull and Glorious Monarch of the world : And so well you bear the honours you were born for, with a greatness so unaffected, an affability so easie, an Humour so soft, so far from Pride or Vanity, that the most Envious & most disaffected can finde no cause or reason to wish you less, Nor can Heaven give you more, who has exprest a particular care of you every way, and above all in bestowing on the world and you, two noble Branches, who have all the greatness and sweetness of their Royal and beautiful stock; and who give us too a hopeful Prospect of what their future Braveries will perform, when they shall shoot up and spread themselves to that degree, that all the lesser world may finde repose beneath their shades; and whom you have permitted to wear those glorious Titles which you your self Generously neglected, well knowing with the noble Poet; 'tis better far to merit Titles then to wear 'em.

Can you then blame my Ambition, Madam, that lays this at your feet, and begs a Sanctuary where all pay so great a Veneration? 'twas Dedicated yours before it had a being, and overbusy to render it worthy of the Honour, made it less grateful; and Poetry like Lovers often fares the worse by taking too much pains to please; but under so Gracious an Influence my tender Lawrells may thrive, till they become fit

Wreaths to offer to the Rays that improve their Growth : which Madam, I humbly implore, you still permit her ever to do, who is,

Madam,
Your most Humble,
and most Obedient Servant,
A. Behn.

Please see the Works Cited for further information on the sources used in this essay.

Note

1   Nell Gwynn's name was spelled variously.

Suggestions for Further Reading

Perry, Gill, Joseph Roach, and Shearer West. *The First Actresses: From Nell Gwyn to Sarah Siddons.* London: National Portrait Gallery, 2011.
Rojek, Chris. *Celebrity.* London: Reaktion Books, 2001.

5 ANNE FINCH (1661–1720)

Christina Black

Introduction

Anne Finch (née Kingsmill, 1661–1720), Countess of Winchilsea, was a maid of honor to Mary of Modena, the second wife of England's King James II. Finch left this role after her marriage in 1684 but remained a fixture at court until the king was deposed in 1688 during the Glorious Revolution. At this point, the Finches decamped from life at the court to a rural retreat, and Anne turned her energy to literary circles that included Alexander Pope.

Finch has been called a "daughter of Behn," an appellation that belies their many differences. While Aphra Behn (1640–1689)[1] was self-conscious of her lack of learning, Finch had every privilege. Finch wrote poetry—a genre used to secure a literary reputation—while Behn made her reputation on plays that were infamously bawdy, a genre for mass consumption and profit. Behn was "the first professional woman of letters in British literature" while Finch never sought to publish her poetry, although some of her poems were anthologized in collected volumes (Staves 59). This was despite the fact that Finch could have hoped for some success as a professional writer; she lived in a time when women writers hoped to be treated more equally, emboldened by the example of Behn. Thus, we can think of Finch as a "daughter of Behn" insofar as she "made major and successful efforts to write in clearly female voices" while "self-consciously building on the accomplishments of Behn" (Staves 130).

In an exchange of epistolary poems with Alexander Pope (1688–1744), Finch created "female literary lineages" for herself while resisting his praise that she was "unique among women" (Staves 127). Building on Behn's legacy, Finch regarded slurs against women's playwrighting as slurs against women's writing generally. Specifically, Finch took issue with Pope's implication in *The Rape of the Lock* (1712) that female playwrights were motivated not just from spleen but hysteria.[2] In an address to the Queen of the Cave of Spleen, Pope wrote,

> Parent of Vapors and of Female Wit
> Who give th' *Hysteric* or *Poetic* Fit
> On various Tempers act by various ways
> Make some take Physick, others scribble Plays.
>   (IV.59–62)[3]

While spleen could affect either sex, hysteria was definitively gendered. "Hysteria" derived from the Greek for "belonging to the womb," and was thought to result from

DOI: 10.4324/9781003006923-6

vapors rising from the uterus. It was "at once a veritable malady, a figurative construct, and a metaphor for the weaknesses and dangerous excesses of the female sex" (Meek, "Medical Discourse and Hysteria" 177–78).

Pope's misogynistic equation between unruly female bodies and minds was nothing new. Restoration playwright William Wycherley (1641–1716) had addressed a poem to Behn titled, "To the *Sappho* of the age, suppos'd to be Ly-In of *Love-Distemper*, or a Play" (Staves 61). Behn had been known to counter that insult by arguing that innate, bodily knowledge made for better plays than the tired and staid neoclassical rules about the unities of action, time, and place (Staves 74). Yet Finch rejected this dichotomy between the body and intellect in her poem, "The Spleen." She also resisted the misogynistic implications of the dichotomy in how she preferred the term "spleen" over "hysteria." The spleen signified "a more intellectual mental disturbance usually attacking men," similar to melancholy (Meek, "Of Wandering Wombs" 109). While Finch acknowledged the effects of the spleen on her mind and writing, this acknowledgment was "devoid of any root of female bodily deficiency" (Meek, "Medical Discourse and Hysteria" 182). Thus, Finch could agree with Pope that playwrighting resulted from a psychosomatic disorder, while disagreeing that it made the writing inferior. In "Ardelia to Melancholy" (1690) she described writing as her final, if ultimately ineffective, prescription for overcoming melancholy: "These failing, I invok'd a Muse,/And Poetry would often use" (l. 29–30).

In describing the spleen and melancholy, as well as the writing it engenders, Finch was participating in the age-old philosophical debate on the relationship between the mind and the body, which was an animating question in a number of fields in the eighteenth century, including dramatic theory. As theorists of the theatre as diverse as David Garrick (1717–1779) and Denis Diderot (1713–1784) would posit, an actor's body was "a physical instrument, like a piano or a clock," where the "mind and body comprise a material continuum, subject to physical laws in its entirety" (Roach, *Player's Passion* 13). Garrick, the preeminent actor of his age, was lauded for a mechanistic method that resulted in an entirely "natural" affect. Similarly, Finch never refuted the power of the body over the mind; she simply denied that her machine was inferior.

Similar to how contemporaneous dramatic theorists understood the emotions of actors to result from their physical postures, Finch understood authorial inspiration to travel through bodily pathways. Yet she also was cognizant that spleen was a fashionable disease to pretend to have, connected to "mental superiority" and "intellectual and artistic achievement" (Babb 170). Much of "The Spleen" (1701, rev. 1709) describes the behavior of those who pretend to be afflicted – like the fool who "to imitate the Wits,/Complains of thy pretended Fits," (l. 64–65). There is a similarly suggestive correspondence between the nature of the disease itself, "which ev'ry thing dost ape," and the prevalence of it being feigned (1.1). These descriptions of playacting served to contrast Finch's genuine case of spleen, which simultaneously legitimized her as an author. In fact, "The Spleen" was reprinted by a physician as an authoritative description of the disease (Meek, "Of Wandering Wombs" 106). By countering a narrative of hysterical female playwrights with the stronger intellectual framework of the spleen, Finch carved out authorial legitimacy within the age's framework of the body's influence over the mind.

Anne Finch, Countess of Winchilsea

Excerpt from **The Poems of Anne Countess of Winchilsea**

"The Spleen: *A Pindarik Poem*" (First Written 1701, Revised 1709)

What art thou, *SPLEEN*, which ev'ry thing dost ape?
Thou *Proteus* to abus'd Mankind,
Who never yet thy real Cause cou'd find,
Or fix thee to remain in one continued Shape.
Still varying thy perplexing Form,
Now a Dead Sea thou'lt represent,
A Calm of stupid Discontent,
Then, dashing on the Rocks wilt rage into a Storm.
Trembling sometimes thou dost appear,
Dissolved into a Panick Fear;   10
On Sleep intruding dost thy Shadows spread,
Thy gloomy Terrours round the silent Bed,
And croud with boading Dreams the Melancholy Head;
Or, when the Midnight Hour is told,
And drooping Lids thou still dost waking hold,
Thy fond Delusions cheat the Eyes,
Before them antick Spectres dance,
Unusual Fires their pointed Heads advance,
And airy Phantoms rise.
Such was the monstrous *Vision* seen,   20
When *Brutus* (now beneath his Cares opprest,
And all *Rome's* Fortunes rolling in his Breast,
Before *Philippi's* latest Field,
Before his Fate did to *Octavius* lead)
Was vanquish'd by the *Spleen*.

Falsly, the Mortal Part we blame
Of our deprest, and pond'rous Frame,
Which, till the First degrading Sin
Let Thee, its dull Attendant, in,
Still with the Other did comply,   30
Nor clogg'd the Active Soul, dispos'd to fly,
And range the Mansions of it's native Sky.
Nor, whilst in his own Heaven he dwelt,
Whilst Man his Paradice possest,
His fertile Garden in the fragrant East,
And all united Odours smelt,
No armed Sweets, until thy Reign,
Cou'd shock the Sense, or in the Face
A flusht, unhandsom Colour place.
Now the *Jonquille* o'ercomes the feeble Brain;   40
We faint beneath the Aromatick Pain,

Till some offensive Scent thy Pow'rs appease,
And Pleasure we resign for short, and nauseous Ease.

In ev'ry One thou dost possess,
New are thy Motions, and thy Dress:
Now in some Grove a list'ning Friend
Thy false Suggestions must attend,
Thy whisper'd Griefs, thy fancy'd Sorrows hear,
Breath'd in a Sigh, and witness'd by a Tear;
Whilst in the light, and vulgar Croud,   50
Thy Slaves, more clamorous and loud,
By Laughters unprovok'd, thy Influence too confess.
In the Imperious *Wife* thou Vapours art,
Which from o'erheated Passions rise
In Clouds to the attractive Brain,
Until descending thence again,
Thro' the o'er-cast, and show'ring Eyes,
Upon her Husband's soften'd Heart,
He the disputed Point must yield,
Something resign of the contested Field;   60
Till Lordly *Man*, born to Imperial Sway,
Compounds for Peace, to make that Right away,
And *Woman*, arm'd with *Spleen*, do's servilely Obey.

The *Fool*, to imitate the Wits,
Complains of thy pretended Fits,
And Dulness, born with him, wou'd lay
Upon thy accidental Sway;
Because, sometimes, thou dost presume
Into the ablest Heads to come:
That, often, Men of Thoughts refin'd,   70
Impatient of unequal Sence,
Such slow Returns, where they so much dispense,
Retiring from the Croud, are to thy Shades inclin'd.
O'er me alas! thou dost too much prevail:
I feel thy Force, whilst I against thee rail;
I feel my Verse decay, and my crampt Numbers fail.
Thro' thy black Jaundice I all Objects see,
As Dark, and Terrible as Thee,
My Lines decry'd, and my Employment thought
An useless Folly, or presumptuous Fault: 80
Whilst in the *Muses* Paths I stray,
Whilst in their Groves, and by their secret Springs
My Hand delights to trace unusual Things,
And deviates from the known, and common way;
Nor will in fading Silks compose
Faintly th' inimitable *Rose*,
Fill up an ill-drawn *Bird*, or paint on Glass

The *Sov'reign's* blurr'd and undistinguish'd Face,
The threatning *Angel,* and the speaking *Ass.*

Patron thou art to ev'ry gross Abuse,   90
The sullen *Husband's* feign'd Excuse,
When the ill Humour with his Wife he spends,
And bears recruited Wit, and Spirits to his Friends.
The Son of *Bacchus* pleads thy Pow'r,
As to the Glass he still repairs,
Pretends but to remove thy Cares,
Snatch from thy Shades one gay, and smiling Hour,
And drown thy Kingdom in a purple Show'r.
When the *Coquette,* whom ev'ry Fool admires,
Wou'd in Variety be Fair,   100
And, changing hastily the Scene
From Light, Impertinent, and Vain,
Assumes a soft, a melancholy Air,
And of her Eyes rebates the wand'ring Fires,
The careless Posture, and the Head reclin'd,
The thoughtful, and composed Face,
Proclaiming the withdrawn, the absent Mind,
Allows the Fop more liberty to gaze,
Who gently for the tender Cause inquires;
The Cause, indeed, is a Defect in Sense,   110
Yet is the *Spleen* alledg'd, and still the dull Pretence.
But these are thy fantastic Harms,
The Tricks of thy pernicious Stage,
Which do the weaker Sort engage;
Worse are the dire Effects of thy more pow'rful Charms.
By Thee *Religion,* all we know,
That shou'd enlighten here below,
Is veil'd in Darkness, and perplext
With anxious Doubts, with endless Scruples vext,
And some Restraint imply'd from each perverted Text.
Whilst *Touch* not, *Taste* not, what is freely giv'n,   121
Is but thy niggard Voice, disgracing bounteous Heav'n.
From Speech restrain'd, by thy Deceits abus'd,
To Deserts banish'd, or in Cells reclus'd,
Mistaken Vot'ries to the Pow'rs Divine,
Whilst they a purer Sacrifice design,
Do but the *Spleen* obey, and worship at thy Shrine
In vain to chase thee ev'ry Art we try,
In vain all Remedies apply,
In vain the *Indian* Leaf infuse,   130
Or the parch'd *Eastern* Berry bruise;
Some pass, in vain, those Bounds, and nobler Liquors use.
Now *Harmony,* in vain, we bring,
Inspire the Flute, and touch the String.
From Harmony no help is had;
Musick but soothes thee, if too sweetly sad,

And if too light, but turns thee gayly Mad.
Tho' the Physicians greatest Grains,
Altho' his growing Wealth he sees
Daily increas'd by Ladies Fees,   140
Yet doft thou baffle all his studious Pains.
Not skilful *Lower* thy Source cou'd find,
Or thro' the well-dissected Body trace
The secret, the mysterious ways,
By which thou dost surprise, and prey upon the Mind.
Tho' in the Search, too deep for Humane Thought,
With unsuccessful Toil he wrought,
'Till thinking Thee to've catch'd, Himself by thee was caught,
Retain'd thy Pris'ner, thy acknowledg'd Slave,
And sunk beneath thy Chain to a lamented Grave.   150

Excerpts from Anne Finch Wellesley Manuscript Poems
"To the Right Honorable Ann Countess of Winchilsea: Occasion'd by four verses in the rape of the Lock [by Alexander Pope] (1714)"

In vain you boast Poetick Dames of Yore,
And cite those Sapphos we admire no more;
Fate doom'd the fall of every Female wit
But doom'd it then, when first ARDELIA writ.
Of all Examples by the World confest,   5
I knew ARDELIA cou'd not quote the best,
Who like her Mistress on Britannia's Throne
Fights, and subdues, in Quarrels not her own.
To write their Praise you but in vain essay;
Ev'n while you write, you take that Praise away: 10
Light to the Stars the Sun does thus restore,
But shines himself till they are seen no more.

"To Mr Pope In answer to a coppy of verses occasion'd by a little dispute upon four lines in the Rape of the Lock (1717)"

Disarm'd with so genteel an air,
The contest I give o'er,
Yet Alexander have a care
And shock the sex no more.

We rule the World, our Lives whole race,
Men but assume that right,   5
First slaves to every tempting Face,
Then Martyrs to our spight.

You of one Orpheus, sure have read,
Who wou'd like you have writ,   10
Had he in London town been bred,
And Polish't to his wit;

But he (poor soul) thought all was well,
And great shou'd be his Fame,
When he had left his Wife in Hell,   15
And Birds and Beasts cou'd tame.

Yet vent'ring then with scoffing rhimes
The Women to incense,
Resenting Heroines of those Times,
Soon punish'd the offence;   20

And as thro' Hebrus, rowl'd his Scull,
And Harp besmear'd with Blood,
They clashing, as the Waves grew full,
Still Harmoniz'd the Flood.

But you our Follies, gently treat,
And spin so fine the thread,
You need not fear his awkward fate,
The Lock won't cost the Head.

Our Admiration you command,
For all that's gone before;
What next we look for at your Hands   30
Can only raise it more.

Yet, sooth the Ladies, I advise,
(As me, to Pride you've wrought,)
We're born to Wit, but to be wise
By Admonitions Taught.   35

Please see the Works Cited for further information on the sources used in this essay.

Notes

1 See, also, Behn entry in this volume.
2 At the time, spleen, along with bile, melancholy, vapors, nerves, hysteria, and hypochon-
driasis, constituted a general vocabulary of being "in the dumps" (Rousseau 73).
3 Michael O'Neill posits that Pope was "likely to have been influenced by Anne Finch's
poem 'The Spleen' (first published in 1701), which, with its 'lively diagnosis' of the condition, establishes Spleen as a virtually indefinable yet fascinating parody of the imagination" (O'Neill 106).

Suggestions for Further Reading

Burton, Robert. *The Anatomy of Melancholy.* Oxford: Clarendon Press, 1989.
Roach, Joseph R. *The Player's Passion: Studies in the Science of Acting.* Ann Arbor: The University
of Michigan Press, 1993.
Rogers, Katharine M. "Finch's 'Candid Account' vs. Eighteenth–Century Theories of the
Spleen." *Mosaic: A Journal for the Interdisciplinary Study of Literature.* 22.1 (1989). 17–27.
Sena, John. "Belinda's Hysteria: The Medical Context of *The Rape of the Lock.*" *Psychology and
Literature in the Eighteenth Century.* Ed. Christopher Fox. New York, NY: AMS Press, 1987.
129–46.

6   SUSANNA CENTLIVRE (c. 1669–1723)

Gillian Skinner

Introduction

Susanna Centlivre's (c. 1669–1723) career as a playwright stretched from 1700 until 1722. Her staunch Whig affiliation[1] and its importance in her work have long been recognized.[2] The two Prefaces below, published in the years immediately preceding and following the Hanoverian succession,[3] give both a vivid sense of the practical ways that party politics of the early eighteenth century affected theatrical culture and a feel for the strategies Centlivre employed in the febrile atmosphere generated by frequent fluctuations in the political landscape. As Frank O'Gorman comments, in this period "[t]he sheer frequency of elections kept party passions on the boil" (50). In 1710, a Tory landslide put an end to the power of the Whig Junto. *The Perplex'd Lovers* (1712) was thus staged at a period of Tory ascendancy during which the peace deal that resulted in the Treaty of Utrecht (1713)[4] was negotiated.

The play – a comedy of romantic intrigue with a soldier hero – ran for only three nights. Unable to get the Epilogue licensed in time for the first night, Centlivre encountered audience displeasure, notwithstanding the "six Lines *Extempore*" spoken by the actor Henry Norris, "to entreat the Audience to excuse the Defect". He "promised them an Epilogue the next night", but by then rumor had branded it, as Centlivre writes, "a notorious whiggish Epilogue" and Anne Oldfield,[5] who had been chosen to deliver it, "had Letters sent her to forbear, for that there were Parties forming against it". Although the Vice-Chamberlain licensed the Epilogue in time for the second night (suggesting that from a government perspective it was not ultimately perceived as especially inflammatory), in the end, Norris spoke an alternative Epilogue, "which implied that the intended one had never been licensed".[6]

The Preface ties the difficulties Centlivre faced with the Epilogue, and the consequential (as it is implied) "sinking of [her] play" to the presence of "People of this Nation so ungrateful as not to allow a single Compliment to a Man that has done such Wonders for it": that is, the Duke of Marlborough, praised in the original Epilogue as the only equal of Prince Eugene of Savoy, whose victorious partnership with Marlborough at battles such as Blenheim made them Whig military heroes. At the time of the Tory ministry, Whig principles are presented as beleaguered by an unsympathetic administration and hostile, unspecific "Parties", who are bringing pressure to bear on the stage. The party-political point is implicit, and Centlivre claims non-partisan patriotism: "as I am an English *Woman*, I think my self oblig'd to acknowledge my Obligation to his Grace for the many Glorious Conquests he has attain'd". In a move linked to this stance, she disclaims – disingenuously but

DOI: 10.4324/9781003006923-7

strategically – party loyalty: "I know not what they call Whigs, or how they distinguish between them and Tories".

The Preface to *The Gotham Election* (1715), by contrast, is more open about the Whig values of its author. This is perhaps unsurprising, given the accession of George I the previous year. The accession was not without opposition, however, and there were riots and protests in some areas of the country on the day of the coronation in October 1714.[7] The 1715 election was a landslide for the Whigs, but despite the change in political ascendancy, licensing was once more a problem for Centlivre, and the farce this preface accompanies was never performed.[8] Centlivre presents herself as again the victim of malicious rumor:

> [...] *the Word* Election, *it seems, immediately furnish'd out a Thousand scandalous Stories, and I was become the Subject of every Coffee-House in Town;* [...] *several Persons had been so industriously malicious as to report that this* Farce *was a most impudent Libel upon her Late Majesty; than which there is nothing more false* [...]

Publication is thus ostensibly necessary to dispel such rumors. The content of *The Gotham Election* itself demonstrates the complexity of Centlivre's political commentary,[9] while the preface goes on to link theatre and politics more firmly, most arrestingly in its championing of Nicholas Rowe's *Lady Jane Grey*. Rowe's tragedy was first staged less than a month after the election, in April 1715, and is, as Jean Marsden writes, "the best remembered part of a near obsessive interest in Lady Jane during the years 1714 and 1715" ("Sex" 505). Rowe's Whig politics, like Centlivre's, were well known (the two were also friends), and the use of a Protestant martyr as the central figure in a new kind of "she-tragedy" proved popular. It also drew some criticism, with at least one pamphlet attacking the play from a Jacobite perspective (506).

In her *Gotham Election* Preface, Centlivre gives the impression that such attacks were widespread, and she makes a provocative comparison between Britain and France:

> *Had the Author of Lady* Jane Grey *made her a Papist, and* Gardiner *a Bishop of the Church of* England, *and the Play been represented on the* French *Stage, what Protestant would have dar'd to call it a* Popish Play, *without running the Danger of the Gallies?*

Here, Centlivre manages both to deplore French (Catholic) tyranny and to imply some degree of regret that Jacobite critics of Rowe have not been punished. At the same time, her sense of the play's strongly Protestant message supports her subsequent bold claim that the stage has "*become a better Advocate for* Protestantism *than the Pulpit*". Deftly, this challenge to the anti-theatrical sentiments so often voiced in the period[10] strategically aligns a moral mission for the stage with Whig politics.

These prefaces help us explore some of the nuances of party affiliation and rhetoric in the theatrical context at a critical period in British history, offering a fruitful comparison between the earlier piece, written when Anne was still queen and the Tories in government, and the later, written at the beginning of the Whig ascendancy. Centlivre used her position as a woman and a playwright to negotiate the political disputes of the day and to press home her own strongly held convictions, a balancing act successfully maintained throughout her long career.

Susanna Centlivre

"Preface" to The Perplex'd Lovers *(1712)*

I Am oblig'd to trouble my Reader with a Preface, that he may not be carried away with false Notions, to the Prejudice of this Play, which had the ill Fate to introduce a new Custom, viz. in being acted the first Day without an Epilogue: It seems the Epilogue design'd wou'd not pass; therefore the Managers of the Theatre did not think it safe to speak it, without I cou'd get it licens'd, which I cou'd not do that Night, with all the Interest I cou'd make: So that at last the Play was forc'd to conclude without an Epilogue. Mr. Norris, *who is an excellent Comedian in his way, was desired to speak six Lines* Extempore, *to entreat the Audience to excuse the Defect, and promised them an Epilogue the next Night; but they apprehending that that was the Epilogue design'd for the Play, were pleas'd to show their Resentment. It is plain the want of an Epilogue caus'd the Hiss, because there had not been any thing like it during the whole action; but on the contrary a general Clap attended the Conclusion of the Play. The next Day I had the Honour to have the Epilogue Licens'd by the* Vice-Chamberlain, *but by this time there was a Rumour spread about Town, that it was a notorious whiggish Epilogue; and the Person who design'd me the Favour of speaking it, had Letters sent her to forbear, for that there were Parties forming against it, and they advis'd her not to stand the Shock; here was a second Blow greater than the first: The sinking of my Play cut me not half so deep as the Notion I had, that there cou'd be People of this Nation so ungrateful as not to allow a single Compliment to a Man that has done such Wonders for it. I am not prompted by any private Sinister End, having never been oblig'd to the Duke of* Marlborough, *otherways than as I shar'd in common with my Country; as I am an* English *Woman, I think myself oblig'd to acknowledge my Obligation to his Grace for the many Glorious Conquests he has attain'd, and the many Hazards he has run, to establish us a Nation free from the Insults of a Foreign Power. I know not what they call Whigs, or how they distinguish between them and Tories: But if the Desire to see my Country secur'd from the* Romish *Yoke, and flourish by a Firm Lasting Honourable Peace, to the Glory of the best of Queens, who deservedly holds the Ballance of all* Europe, *be a Whig, then I am one, else not. I have Printed the Epilogue, that the World may judge whether 'tis such as has been represented. So much for that. Now I must acquaint my Reader, that I shall not pretend to vindicate the following Scenes, about which I took very little Pains, most of the Plot being from a* Spanish *Play, and assuring my self Success from Mr.* Cyber's[11] *Approbation, whose Opinion was, that the Business wou'd support the Play; tho'* Mr. Wilks *seem'd to doubt it, and said, there was a great deal of Business, but not laughing Business; tho' indeed I cou'd not have dress'd this Plot with much more Humour, there being four Acts in the Dark, which tho' a* Spanish *Audience may readily conceive, the Night being their proper time of intreaguing; yet here, where Liberty makes Noon-day as easie, it perplexes the Thought of an Audience too much; therefore I shall take Care to avoid such Absurdities for the future; and if I live I will endeavour to make my Friends amends in the next.*

"Preface" to The Gotham Election *(1715)*

WHEN I writ this little Farce, *I was not without Hopes of having it represented on the Stage; what I propos'd to my self, was, the Honour to show their Royal Highnesses the Manner of our Elections, and entertain the Town with a Subject entirely new: It has had the good Fortune to please several Persons of Distinction, and Taste, in the Reading, and some of our best Judges assur'd me, it cou'd not fail to entertain from the Stage; but the Subject being upon Elections, the Master of the Revels did not care to meddle with it, and the Players act nothing without his Licence, so that I had given over all Thoughts of its appearing in Publick. But the Word* Election, *it seems, immediately furnish'd out a Thousand scandalous Stories, and I was become the Subject of every Coffee-House in Town; and notwithstanding my Friends endeavour'd to do me justice as often as they heard me aspers'd, yet for my clearer Justification, they were of Opinion I ought to print it, since several Persons had been so industriously malicious as to report that this* Farce *was a most impudent notorious Libel upon her Late Majesty; than which there is nothing more false, and the World will see how little Ground there is for such a Report; its so far from being a Satyr upon her, that there is not one personal Reflection design'd thro' the whole Piece; I was oblig'd indeed to make an Opposition of Parties, to heighten the Humour; it had been impossible to have writ any Thing upon the Subject without it; but I dare be positive, that the Persons among whom the Scenes lie wou'd have given more Diversion than Offence to the Spectators of either Party. I endeavour'd to make every Thing appear as natural as I cou'd, and for that Reason only, I stuck Wool in the Hats of my* Whigs, *and Lawrel in those of the* Tories; *tho' I wou'd be glad to know why the latter made use of the Lawrel to distinguish themselves, when they were labouring to give up all the Conquests we had won: I should have thought a Sprig of Rosemary had been the properer Emblem of the then approaching Funeral of our Church and State, since the* Chevalier's *Friends were endeavouring to bury our Religion, and Liberty, under Tyranny and Popish Superstition. Had Parliaments been Part of the Legislature among the Ancients, and our Manner of Elections known to, and practis'd by them,* Apollo *wou'd certainly have shown Vengance on the unworthy Wearers of his favourite Tree: The Lawrel was ever held the Emblem of Joy, and Reward of Vertue: Hence it was worn by Victors in the* Olympick Games; *but have* Englishmen *Reason to rejoyce in those Measures, that pav'd the Way for a* French *Government, and a* Popish *King?*

The Roman *Soldiers, who followed their Triumphs, were crown'd with Lawrel, to denote an Expiation of the Blood which they had shed in the Wars; but our Lawrel-wearers can draw no Parellel from thence, except deserting our Allies, selling our Trade, disgracing our Generals, giving up those glorious Conquests they had won, deserv'd to be crown'd with Lawrel, or that they wou'd be thought to wear it as an Expiation of the Blood of the* Catalans, *and of the Twelve Thousand cut to Pieces at* Denain, *by the fatal Cessation of Arms.*

Whatever Reason they had for wearing it, I am glad they had not an Opportunity of making use of it, in the Triumph they design'd over the Laws and Liberties of their Country.

Here I can't omit taking notice how much the Popish Faction encreased under the traiterous Management of the late Ministry, and we see by their daily Insults, that 'tis at the hazard of Life or Interest, at least, that we dare vindicate our Religion, and Liberty. Had the Author of Lady *Jane Grey made her a Papist, and* Gardiner *a Bishop of the Church of* England, *and the Play been represented on the* French *Stage, what Protestant would have dar'd to call it a* Popish *Play, without running the Danger of the Gallies? If the Title of a certain Monarch, who was also set up by the People, in Opposition to the Right Line, were to be represented on the Theatre of* France, *not even the first Peer of that Nation durst to have vented one Murmur, much less hiss, without he were furnish'd with Philosophy enough to endure the* Bastile, *and yet the Papists and their Abettors dare to do it here. It is with the utmost Indignation, that I see those wholsome Laws neglected, which ought to be put in Execution against such profess'd Enemies of our Church and State; for to the Indolence of our People in Power, are all our present Divisions and Distractions owing; tho' for the Author of that excellently writ Poem abovemention'd, I dare answer for him, is under no Concern for any Thing that Faction can either say or write, since 'tis very evident their Malice is not levell'd against him but against our Religion and Liberties, which he has in that Piece vindicated so well, and set the Cruelties of* Rome *in so true a Light, that a great Part of our Clergy may blush to see the Stage become a better Advocate for* Protestantism *than the Pulpit; and as oft as that Tragedy shall be represented the Author's Memory shall be honoured to Posterity, whilst those Pretenders to the Church, the* High-Flying *and* Nonjuring-Party *shall be remembred. with the utmost Detestation.*

Please see the Works Cited for further information on the sources used in this essay.

Notes

1 The terms "Whig" and "Tory" originate from around the time of the Exclusion Crisis of 1681, which referred to the failed attempt to exclude James, Duke of York, Catholic brother of Charles II, from succession to the throne. Those who wished to exclude him were Whigs, those opposed were Tories. Consequently, Whigs were associated with a belief in constitutional monarchy and the Protestant succession, while Tories were associated with greater sympathy for the divine right of kings and for Catholicism. James II ruled for only three years from 1685 till 1688, soon replaced by the Protestant rule of William and Mary, during the events known as the Glorious Revolution. Most Tories were Protestants loyal to the Church of England, but on the extreme end of Toryism were the Jacobites, who, in the rebellions of 1715 and 1745, actively supported the restoration to the throne of James II's son (James Francis Edward Stuart) and then grandson (Charles Edward Stuart, or Bonnie Prince Charlie), both Catholic.
2 See, for example, Milling and H. Smith.
3 From the succession of George, Elector of Hanover, to the British throne in 1714 as George I, British kings were also electors and then (from 1814) kings of Hanover, until Hanover's salic law prevented Queen Victoria from succeeding to the throne of Hanover in 1837. In 1714, George I was the nearest Protestant heir to the British throne, Catholics and those married to Catholics having been excluded from succession by the Act of Settlement of 1701.
4 The Treaty of Utrecht ended the War of the Spanish Succession (1701–1713). Some Whig commentary saw this as a capitulation ("deserting our Allies, selling our Trade, disgracing our Generals, giving up those glorious Conquests they had won", as Centlivre puts it in the Preface to *A Gotham Election*), but Britain nonetheless gained significant economic advantages from the Treaty, including the acquisition of Gibraltar and the lucrative *Asiento*, the monopoly contract to supply slaves to the Spanish colonies in the Americas.
5 For information on Oldfield, see entry for "Anonymous" in this volume.
6 Entry for Saturday 19 January, 1712, *"The London Stage" Database 1660–1800* in *Eighteenth-Century Drama: Censorship, Society and the Stage* (Adam Matthews Digital, 2022–).
7 See O'Gorman, p. 67.
8 See Milling, pp. 83–84, for a shrewd assessment of the possible reasons.
9 See Milling, *passim*.
10 See Jonas A. Barish, *The Antitheatrical Prejudice*. Berkeley, CA: University of California Press, 1981.
11 Colley Cibber (1671–1757), British actor-manager, playwright, and poet best remembered for his autobiography, *Apology for the Life of Colley Cibber* (1740).

Suggestions for Further Reading

Airey, Jennifer L. "'I Must Vary Shapes as Often as a Player': Susanna Centlivre and the Liberty of the British Stage." *Restoration and Eighteenth-Century Theatre Research*. 28.1 (2013): 45–62.

Butler, Douglas R. "Plot and Politics in Susanna Centlivre's *A Bold Stroke for a Wife*." *Curtain Calls: British and American Women and the Theater, 1660-1820*. Eds. Mary Anne Schofield and Cecilia Macheski. Athens, OH: Ohio University Press, 1991. 357–370.

Martinez-Garcia, Laura. "Politics of Gender and National Identity in Susanna Cetlivre's Iberian Plays: A Defence of Whig Feminism." *Anagnorisis*. 16 (2017): 54–79.

Smith, Hannah. "Susanna Centlivre, 'Our *Church*'s Safety' and 'Whig Feminism'." *Religion and Women in Britain, 1660-1960*. Eds. Sarah Apetrei and Hannah Smith. Farham: Ashgate, 2014. 145–161.

Tierney-Hines, Rebecca. "Emotional Economies: Centlivre's Comic Ends." *Studies in Eighteenth-Century Culture*. 45 (2016): 83–106.

7 CHARLOTTE LENNOX (1729–1804)

Elizabeth Kraft

Introduction

Shakespear Illustrated (1753–1754) by Charlotte Lennox (1729–1804) is, as Margaret Anne Doody has pointed out, one of the earliest critical treatments of Shakespeare not attached to an edition of his works. As Doody goes on to say, Lennox "is the first woman to produce a scholarly work on English literature, and the first feminist critic of a major author" (307). Lennox's criticism is offered in two parts for each play treated: summaries of the "novels" upon which Shakespeare's plays are based and "observations" on the parallels between the prose narratives and Shakespeare's works.

Lennox's criticism of Shakespeare ran against the tide of her times in two ways. First, her interest in source study did not fit well with the emergent hagiographic construction of Shakespeare as the nation's poet epitomized by David Garrick's Jubilee in 1769.[1] Such bardolatry was well underway prior to the Jubilee, with editions of Shakespeare already produced by, among others, Alexander Pope (1725; revised 1735), Lewis Theobald (1740), and three more to be completed by the end of the century, including one by Lennox's friend and literary mentor, Samuel Johnson. Johnson's *Dictionary* (1755) also contributed to the ever-growing esteem in which Shakespeare was held in this period; the lexicographer quoted him more than any other writer in illustration of the language. Indeed, Johnson's reverence permeates the dedication he wrote (in Lennox's name) for *Shakespear Illustrated*. While Johnson's claim there (and elsewhere) is that Shakespeare's excellence lies in his unsurpassed ability to represent "Human Nature," Lennox's point is that Shakespeare was indebted to Renaissance fictions known as *novelles* for his plots and characters[2] and that often his source material surpasses Shakespeare in treatment of both.

The second emerging value against which Lennox's treatment of Shakespeare pushed was the increasing emphasis on "originality" and "innovative genius" in literary production. The very premise of Lennox's project—however she judged the use of source material—conflicts with the nationalistic pride in Shakespeare's unique, original genius that will fuel treatment of his works from the second half of the eighteenth century through much of the twentieth century.

Lennox's three-volume work was published in two installments, volumes one and two appearing in 1753, and, following their success, volume three in 1754. In total, the work treated twenty-two plays deriving from source material written originally in English, Italian, Latin, French, and Danish. Lennox was fluent in French at the time she began her work, and though she was sure that Shakespeare himself relied on

DOI: 10.4324/9781003006923-8

English translations of all his sources, she felt compelled to learn enough Italian to provide new translations of material she wished to examine written in that language. Guiseppe Baretti, who had recently arrived in London from his native Italy, agreed to exchange Italian lessons for English lessons (Carlile 114). Lennox mastered Italian sufficiently to translate the seven Italian source texts (perhaps, Carlile speculates, with Baretti's help). For Plautus, the source of *Comedy of Errors*, she translated a French translation; and for the Danish source of *Hamlet*, she relied on a friend to render the Danish source into English. She was scrupulous in acknowledging these matters.

Lennox's work built on that of others who had explored Shakespeare's sources: critics Gerald Langbaine (1656–1692) and Thomas Rymer (1643–1713), as well as the editors of his works (Carlile 113). Lennox, however, made at least one new discovery—the indebtedness of *Twelfth Night* to a tale by Matteo Bandello (Young 37)—and even those critics who wished to minimize her achievement had to admit that she went well beyond her predecessors in "collecting and printing the sources of Shakespeare's plays, and in attempting a general commentary upon his use of these sources" (Young 53). Further, as Fiona Ritchie and Susan Carlile have written, eighteenth-century commentary on Shakespeare following the publication of *Shakespear Illustrated* was thoroughly informed by and engaged with the work. Ritchie cites echoes of Lennox in Edward Cappell's "Origin of Shakespeare's Fables" (1768) as evidence that "the work had entered the mainstream of literary criticism in the mid-eighteenth century" (67), and Carlile records Johnson's praise as well as Garrick's "respect and concern" (118).

Garrick's "concern" had to do with Lennox's authoritative, even "acerbic" tone in her often "negative assessments" of Shakespeare's plots and characters (Gevirtz 62). Both Garrick and Johnson were admirers of Lennox's novels and supporters of her literary career, but both were also committed to elevating the reputation of Shakespeare as the nation's poet. Carlile is particularly astute in her analysis of Johnson's complex engagement with Lennox beyond the dedication he wrote for *Shakespear Illustrated*. Though Johnson does not cite her in his own edition of Shakespeare, his emphasis on Shakespeare's genius and his minimizing of Shakespeare's flaws in the famous preface to that work strike Carlile as "a reaction to Lennox's very clear and fully substantiated critiques" (127).

Lennox's focus on plot and character in Shakespeare ignores the poet's language as well as the theatrical possibilities inherent in the plays. Her tone at times reflects, as Carlile suggests, a lack of "tact and self-deference," as well as a kind of naivete about the critical "arena into which she was entering" (112). However, it is Gevirtz's sense that Lennox's unabashed notion of her own authority over not only Shakespeare but also his male critics rankled other readers (67). After all, Lennox prided herself on her mastery of languages that Shakespeare did not know, and she thoroughly discredited Thomas Rymer's negative critique of *Othello*, partly through a demonstration of Rymer's ignorance of Italian.

The title page of *Shakespear Illustrated* identifies the author as "The Author of *The Female Quixote*," in reference to Lennox's highly acclaimed second novel, published the previous year. It seems clear that both Lennox and her publisher, Andrew Millar, felt she had earned the cultural authority to undertake a critical assessment of Shakespeare. While some of Lennox's judgments ran against those of her contemporaries, they also served as ballast to a kind of enthusiasm that could have proven even more damaging to Shakespeare's long-lasting appeal than blunt critique.

As important, the scholarly methodology with which Lennox approached the task of source study would both encourage and set the standard for all future investigations of works that influenced and inspired Shakespeare's genius.

Charlotte Lennox

Excerpt from *Shakespear Illustrated* (1753–1754)

OBSERVATIONS *on the Use Shakespear has made of the foregoing Novel in his Tragedy of* Othello, *or the* Moor *of* Venice.

Othello, or the *Moor* of *Venice,* the Plot of which is drawn from the foregoing Novel of *Giraldi Cinthio,* has always been esteemed one of the best of *Shakespear's* Tragedies.

'Tis confessed the Fable is more regular, the Incidents less numerous and closer connected, and the Subject more of a Piece than any other of his Plays, except *Romeo* and *Juliet.*

The Fable *Shakespear* found already formed to his Hands, some few Alterations he has made in it, and generally for the better.

Thus it stands in the Poet.

Othello, a *Moor* descended of Royal Blood, eminent for his great Valour, and the Services he had done the *Venetians* in their Wars, is preferred by the Senate to the Government of the Island of *Cyprus,* which was threatned with an Invasion by the *Turks.*

Othello, being commanded to go immediately to his Government, takes with him, at her earnest Request, his Bride *Desdemona,* a young Lady of great Beauty, Daughter to a Senator of *Venice,* who had married him unknown to her Father.

Iago, Ancient to *Othello,* being jealous that the Moor had had an Intrigue with his Wife, and desirous of procuring the Post of Lieutenant for himself, which was possessed by *Cassio,* a young Officer very dear to the Moor, to gratify his Revenge and Ambition at once, he entertains a Design of making *Othello* jealous of *Desdemona* and *Cassio,* so to bring about her Death, and the Removal of *Cassio.*

To effect this, by various Arts he raises Suspicions in the Mind of *Othello,* and to confirm them prevails on his Wife, who attended *Desdemona,* to steal a Hand[k]erchief which the Moor had given her.

This Handkerchief he drops in *Cassio's* Apartment, and *Othello* accidentally seeing it in his Hand, is convinced of his Wife's Infidelity, orders *Iago* to kill his Rival, promising to make him his Lieutenant in his stead, and himself smothers *Desdemona* in her Bed.

Cassio escapes only with a slight Wound.

Emilia, the Wife of *Iago,* finding her Mistress murdered, and hearing *Othello* declare he had killed her through her Husband's Informations that she had wronged him with *Cassio,* in whose Possession he had seen the Handkerchief he had given her; she confesses she had stolen the Handkerchief at her Husband's Request.

Iago, finding himself discovered, stabs his Wife, and in Part confesses his Villany.

Othello, in Despair, falls upon his Sword and dies, and the Punishment of *Iago* is left to *Cassio,* who before *Othello's* Death was ordered by the Senate to take upon him the Government of *Cyprus.*

In *Cinthio* the Moor is mentioned without any Mark of Distinction; *Shakespear* makes him descended from a Race of Kings, his Person is therefore made more considerable in the Play than in the Novel, and the Dignity which the *Venetian* Senate bestows upon him is less to be wondered at.

In the Play, *Cassio*, the Person of whom *Othello* is jealous, is represented to be a young amiable Officer, remarkable for the Agreeableness of his Person, and the Sweetness of his Manners, and therefore likely enough to inspire *Desdemona* with a Passion for him.

In the Novel, these Qualities are all ascribed to the Villain who betrays the Moor to the Murder of his Wife; and the suspected Rival is no more than an ordinary Person.

Cinthio might perhaps think it necessary to give his Villain a pleasing Person and insinuating Address, in order to make his Artifices less suspected; but to give Probability to the Jealousy of the Moor, was it not also as necessary to make the suspected Rival possess some of those Qualities with which the Minds of young Ladies are soonest captivated.

Shakespear therefore paints *Cassio* young, handsome, and brave; and *Othello*, who feeds his Jealousy, by reflecting that he himself is neither young nor handsome, by the same Train of Thought falls naturally into a Suspicion, that what he loses, for want of those Qualities, will be gained by another who possesses them.

But on the other Hand *Shakespear* has made a very ill Use of the Lieutenant's Wife.

Cinthio shews this Woman privy, much against her Will, to the Design on *Disdemona;* and though she dares not discover it to her, for fear of her Husband's Resentment, yet she endeavours to put her upon her Guard, and gives her such Advice, as she thinks will render all his Schemes ineffectual.

Shakespear calls this Woman *Emilia*, and makes her the Attendant and Friend of *Desdemona*, yet shews her stealing a Handkerchief from her, which she gives to her Husband, telling him at the same Time that the Lady will run mad when she misses it; therefore, if it is not for some Purpose of Importance that he wants it, desires him to return it to her again.

If her Husband wants it for any Purpose of Importance, that Purpose cannot be very good; this Suspicion however never enters her Mind, but she gives it him only upon that very Condition, which ought to have made her refuse it.

Yet this Woman is the first who perceives *Othello* to be jealous, and repeats this Observation to her Mistress, upon hearing him so often demand the Handkerchief she had stolen, and fly into a Rage when he finds his Wife cannot produce it.

Emilia pronounces him jealous, perceives the Loss of that fatal Handkerchief, confirms some Suspicions he had entertained, and though she loves her Mistress to Excels, chuses rather to let her suffer all the bad Consequences of his Jealousy, than confess she had taken the Handkerchief, which might have set all right again; and yet this same Woman, who could act so base and cruel a Part against her Mistress, has no greater Care in dying, than to be laid by her Side.

Mr. *Rymer*, in his Criticisms on this Play, severely censures the Characters as well as the Fable, and Conduct of the Incidents.

That of *Emilia* though more inconsistent than any, he has taken no Notice of; and most of the Charges he brings against the others have little or no Foundation.

The Character of *Iago*, says this Critic, is against common Sense and Nature. "*Shakespear* would pass upon us a close, dissembling, false, insinuating Rascal, instead of an open-hearted, frank plain dealing Soldier; a Character constantly worn by them for some Thousands of Years in the World."

The Soldiers are indeed greatly obliged to Mr. *Rymer* for this Assertion, but though it may in general be true, yet surely it is not absurd to suppose that some few Individuals amongst them may be close dissembling Villains.

Iago was a Soldier, it is true, but he was also an *Italian*; he was born in a Country remarkable for the deep Art, Cruelty, and revengeful Temper of its Inhabitants. To have painted an *Italian* injured, or under a Suspicion of being injured, and not to have shewn him revengeful, would have been mistaking his Character.

It is with Justice indeed that Mr. *Rymer* condemns *Shakespear* for that unnecessary and diabolical Cruelty he makes *Iago* guilty of in urging *Othello* to the Murder of the innocent Lady who had never offended him; his Point was gained by making *Othello* jealous, and procuring his Consent to the Death of *Cassio*, who stood in his Way to Preferment: But the Murder of *Desdemona* was such an Excess of wanton Cruelty, that one can hardly conceive it possible a Man could be so transcendently wicked.

Cinthio indeed makes *Iago* not only urge *Othello* to the Murder of his Wife, but is himself the Perpetrator of it; this seems still more absurd; but he tells us, that he had been violently in love with *Disdemona*, and the Indifference she had discovered towards him converted his Love into a settled Hatred.

Shakespear injudiciously copies *Cinthio* in making *Iago* confess a Passion for *Desdemona* as it rendered his urging on her Murder less probable; since in the Play *Iago* had no Opportunity of declaring that Love to her, and consequently could not be stimulated by her Contempt of him to act so cruel a Part against her.

But he has greatly improved on the Novelist by making him jealous of the Moor with his own Wife; this Circumstance being sufficient, in an *Italian* especially, to account for the Revenge he takes on *Othello*, though his Barbarity to *Desdemona* is still unnatural.

Upon the whole, there is very little Difference between the Character of the Lieutenant as it is drawn in the Novel, and *Iago* as managed in the Play; his ambiguous Questions, dark Hints, and villainous Arts to raise Suspicions in the Mind of *Othello* are the same in the Novel as in the Play; and the Scene where *Othello* is made to observe the Gestures of *Cassio* while he is talking to *Iago*, is exactly copied from *Cinthio*; as is likewise a preceding one, where *Othello*, tormented with Doubts about his Wife, threatens *Iago* with Destruction, unless he gives him ocular Proof of her Dishonesty.

This Demand, with *Iago*'s Expostulations, Arguments, and satisfactory Replies, are also the same with those in the Novel.

The Character of *Desdemona* fares no better in Mr. *Rymer*'s Hands, than that of *Iago*; her Love for the Moor, he says, is out of Nature.

Such Affections are not very common indeed; but a very few Instances of them prove that they are not impossible; and even in *England* we see some very handsome Women married to Blacks, where their Colour is less familiar than at *Venice*; besides the *Italian* Ladies are remarkable for such Sallies of irregular Passions.

Cinthio, it is true, says, that *Disdemona* was not overcome by a womanish Appetite, but represents her, as *Shakespear* does likewise, subdued by the great Qualities of the Moor.

Courage in Men has always had an invincible Charm for the Ladies; *Desdemona* admired the Moor for his Valour, and the Transition from extreme Admiration to Love is very easy in a female Mind.

Mr. *Rymer* alledges, that *Shakespear* makes *Desdemona* a Senator's Daughter instead of a simple Citizen; and this he imputes to him as a Fault, which is perhaps a great Instance of his Judgment.

There is less Improbability in supposing a noble Lady, educated in Sentiments superior to the Vulgar, should fall in love with a Man merely for the Qualities of his Mind, than that a mean Citizen should be possessed of such exalted Ideas, as to overlook the Disparity of Years and Complexion, and be enamoured of Virtue in the Person of a Moor.

However, it is not true, that *Shakespear* has changed a simple Citizen into a Lady of Quality, since *Desdemona* in the Novel is mentioned as a Woman of high Birth.

Cinthio calls her *Cittadina*, which Mr. *Rymer* translates a simple Citizen; but the *Italians* by that Phrase mean a Woman of Quality.

If they were, for Example, to speak of a Woman of the middle Rank in *Rome*, they would say, *Una Romana*; if of a noble Lady, *Una Cittadina Romana*: So in *Venice* they call a simple Citizen *Una Venitiana*; but a Woman of Quality, *Una Cittadina Venitiana*.

That Simplicity in the Manners of *Desdemona*, which Mr. *Rymer* calls Folly and Meanness of Spirit, is the Characteristic of Virtue and Innocence.

Desdemona was conscious of no Guilt, and therefore suspected no Blame: She had so lately given the Moor an incontestable Proof of her Affection, that it was not unnatural for her to impute his sudden Starts of Passion to some other Cause than Jealousy.

The whole Stress of the Proof against *Desdemona* is laid upon the Handkerchief, as well in the Novel as the Play; though I think in the Novel it is more artfully managed; there the Moor insists upon seeing it in the Captain's Possession e'er he will resolve any Thing against his Wife, and the Lieutenant contrives to give him this Satisfaction.

Othello, in the Play, has not the least Appearance of Proof against his Wife, but seeing the Handkerchief in the Lieutenant's Possession; yet this is brought about by mere Accident.

Bianca, to whom *Cassio* had given it to have the Work copied, (which, by the way, was an odd Whim for a Soldier) comes to him while he is engaged in a private Discourse with *Iago*; and *Othello* observing them concealed, and in a Fit of Jealousy, throws the Handkerchief at his Head.

This happens well for *Iago*'s Plot; but as he did not, and indeed could not foresee, this lucky Accident, methinks it would have been more natural, since every Thing depended upon that, to have made it the Effect of some Contrivance of his.

The Outlines of *Iago*, *Desdemona*, and *Cassio*'s Characters are taken from the Novel; but that of *Othello* is entirely the Poet's own.

In *Cinthio* we have a Moor, valiant indeed, as we are told, but suspicious, sullen, cunning, obstinate and cruel.

Such a Character married to the fair *Desdemona* must have given Disgust on the Stage; the Audience would have been his Enemies, and *Desdemona* herself would have sunk into Contempt for chusing him.

With what Judgment then has *Shakespear* changed the horrid *Moor* of *Cinthio* into the amiable *Othello*, and made the same Actions which we detest in one, excite our Compassion in the other!

The Virtues of *Shakespear*'s *Moor* are no less characteristic than the Vices of *Cinthio*'s; they are the wild Growth of an uncultivated Mind, barbarous and rude as the Clime he is born in; thus, his Love is almost Phrensy; his Friendship Simplicity; his Justice cruel; and his Remorse Self-Murder.

Please see the Works Cited for further information on the sources used in this essay.

Notes

1 Organized by Garrick to bring renewed attention to Shakespeare's artistry and achievement, the Jubilee took place at Shakespeare's birthplace, Stratford-upon-Avon, which became a tourist attraction from that moment forward.

2 See Keymer 129.

Suggestions for Further Reading

Eger, Elizabeth. "'Out Rushed a Female to Protect the Bard': The Bluestocking Defense of Shakespeare." *Huntington Library Quarterly*. 65 (2002): 127–151.

Green, Susan. "A Cultural Reading of Charlotte Lennox's *Shakespear Illustrated*." *Cultural Readings of Restoration and Eighteenth-Century English Theatre*. Eds. J. Douglas Canfield and Deborah Payne. Athens: University of Georgia Press, 1995. 228–257.

Hamilton, Patricia L. "Patronage or Friendship? Charlotte Lennox and the Fifth Earl of Orrery." *Eighteenth-Century Life*. 47 (2023): 35–62.

8 CHARLOTTE CHARKE (1713–1760)

Molly Marotta

Introduction

The eighteenth-century playhouse was a raucous place—filled with the gentry and the lower orders alike, looking for entertainment. Celebrity actresses emerged, captivating their audiences with their performances and public personas (Nussbaum 11). Charlotte Charke (1713–1760) was an actress and a writer who wore many different hats in her roles both on and off stage. At various times, a temporary doctor, a sausage seller, a puppeteer, and a valet, Charke is most well-known for her long and varied acting career and her tell-all autobiography, *A Narrative of the Life of Mrs. Charlotte Charke* (1755).[1]

The youngest daughter of Colley Cibber (1671–1757)—a famous actor and playwright—Charke was intimately familiar with all aspects of theatrical life, from managing to acting to writing, all of which she attempted. Both contemporary and modern scholars are drawn to Charke's autobiography, within which she outlines her exploits, successes, and failures. Charke acted in plays with various consistency from April 1730 until September 1759 (Highfill 167; 177). In addition to her autobiography, Charke wrote three plays—two of which were performed but not printed—a novel and two novelettes (Highfill 178). Additionally, Charke's *Narrative* is "one of the earliest secular autobiographies written by a woman, and the first to be written by an English actress" (Shevelow 3).

Charke stands out amongst her peers due to her frequent performance of male roles in the theatre and on the London streets. Women in trousers on stage were hardly unfamiliar to a theatre audience at this time. In Restoration and eighteenth-century theatrical performances, women played what were called "breeches" roles. The female character would disguise herself in male attire, often to erotic effect (Nussbaum 197). While Charke played both female and "breeches" roles, she also performed in roles intended for male actors, which gained her both attention and notoriety. These "roles" extended to Charke's daily life; she would dress as a man in order to find work. In her autobiography, Charke reveals that she was often on the outs with certain acting communities and needed this extra-theatrical work to support herself and her daughter, as she was neglected by her first husband and abandoned by her father; Charke's autobiography has been read by critics as an open letter to her father, asking for his forgiveness and (financial) support (Lobban-Viravong 196). Charke's *Narrative* therefore inherently characterizes acting—on- and off-stage—as a form of survival and self-making.

Scholars have frequently discussed Charke's sexuality and gender in relation to her performances on stage and in her autobiography. Jade Higa describes "Charke's

DOI: 10.4324/9781003006923-9

body as 'fluid'" and refers to Charke as a "gender bender" (1–2). These terms help us understand Charke's position without limiting her to contemporary definitions of gender (Higa 2). Additionally, scholars note how Charke's *Narrative* blends her own voice with the "voices" of fictional characters. Heather Lobban-Viravong reads these voices as making Charke both actor and spectator; due to Charke's perception of the lack of outside sympathy, "Charke seeks sympathy from herself, consequently turning her narrative into theater" (195). Jean Marsden illustrates the lineage from Colley Cibber's autobiographical self-construction to Charlotte Charke's autobiographical blend of theatrical roles and personal narratives (68; 78). These studies speak to Charke's *Narrative* as a captivating, if occasionally opaque, text that, like Charlotte herself, resists firm categorizations.

In her *Narrative*, Charlotte Charke weaves in a theory of acting as a craft—what it should be, what it should not be, for whom, and at what cost to the players themselves. Alongside her humorous turns of phrase in her personal anecdotes—often rich with the names of actors and fictional characters—she builds her credibility with her audience. Charke has acted and lived to tell the tale. Her work legitimizes acting as a trade and defines a hierarchy of actors and careers. Charke explores the advice of a seasoned actress, the reception of the audience, and the skills required to perform.

In the first excerpt from the *Narrative* below, Charke includes and tests her famous sister-in-law's, Jane Cibber's (1706–1733), theory of stage fright. The theory is as follows: as an actor gains more experience, their stage fright also grows because this experience leads to a better knowledge of the role, the craft, audience reception, and all the ways they can go wrong. Charke's inclusion of this theory of craft serves multiple purposes. The first provides her audience with an interesting "behind the scenes" anecdote for the amusement of her reader. The second shows Charke testing this theory against her own experiences. Charke emphasizes audience reception as contributing most strongly to this fear. Some audiences begrudgingly permit a few "theatrical Gentry" to act during an entire play, while other audiences are less sympathetic—booing actors off the stage. Charke likens her stage fright, which emerges while acting in "two such Characters, after two of the greatest Actresses [...] Mrs. *Oldfield* and Mrs. *Porter*," to an escape from the clutches of death: "DIED ONE, OF CAPITAL CHARACTERS." Behind this humor lies an experiment; Charke outlines a theory and supports it with her observations and experiences. Additionally, Charke briefly positions herself as a theatre critic, assessing Mrs. Oldfield and Mrs. Porter as "two of the greatest Actresses."

In the second excerpt included in this volume, Charke divides actors into two groups: those who train for the trade and those who are "interlopers" from other professions. Charke makes the argument that these "interlopers" are so strongly marked by their trades that the signs of these trades negatively affect their roles. Additionally, her observation that the actor's identity affects audience perception of the role anticipates Marvin Carlson's argument in *The Haunted Stage* (2001), expanded upon over two centuries later.

Charke creates an additional division between "strolling"—acting in a travelling troupe—and acting in an established playhouse. She describes strolling as a grueling trade, overrun by her miserable fellow strollers, whereas truly deserving "Players" honor themselves and their intelligence with their trade. This division is characteristic of much of Charke's *Narrative*, for she is *both* stroller and player, observer and participant, critic and criticized. Ultimately, she defends herself and her craft in light of her warning that one's talent on stage often endangers one's reputation.

Charlotte Charke

Excerpt from A Narrative of the Life of Mrs. Charlotte Charke *(1755)*

It happened that Mrs. *Horton,* who played Lady *Fanciful* the Time before, was indisposed, and my Sister-in-Law, the late Mrs. *Jane Cibber,* was appointed to do the Part; who, notwithstanding her having been a few Years on the Stage, and indeed a meritorious Actress, had not overcome the Shock of appearing the first Night in any Character. I, who was astonished at her Timidity, like a strange Gawky as I was, told her I was surprized at her being frighted, who had so often appeared; when I, who had never played but once, had no Concern at all. *That's the very Reason,* said she; *when you have stood as many Shocks as others have done, and are more acquainted with your Business, you'll possibly be more susceptible of Fear.* The Apprehensions she laboured under, gave her a grave Aspect, which my insensible Head at that Time took as an Affront; and, I remember, I turned short on my Heel, as we were waiting for our Cue of Entrance, and broke off our Conversation, nor could I bring myself, but on the Stage, to speak to her the whole Evening.

This ridiculous Circumstance we have both laughed at since, and I found her Words very true; for I'll maintain it, the best Players are the most capable of Fear, as they are naturally most exact in the Nicety of their Performance. Not that I would insinuate, by this Observation, that I think myself better than in the common Run of those theatrical Gentry, who are lucky enough to be endured through the Course of a Play, without being wished to be no more seen, after the First Act.

Such melancholly Instances I have been Witness of, both in Town and Country; WHILST THE POOR PLAYER HAS BAWLED AND BELLOWED OUT HIS MINUTE ON THE STAGE, AND THE GROANING AUDIENCE HISSINGLY ENTREATED, HE MIGHT BE HEARD NO MORE.

The second Character I appeared in was *Alicia,* and found the Audience not less indulgent than before. Mrs. *Porter's* Misfortune, of being over-turned in her Chaise at *Highwood-Hill,* was the Means by which I was possessed of that Part. The third was the 'Distress'd Mother,' in the Summer, when the young Company were under my Brother *Theophilus Cibber's* Direction.

Now I leave to any reasonable Person, what I went through, in undertaking two such Characters, after two of the greatest Actresses in the Theatre, *viz.* Mrs. *Oldfield* and Mrs. *Porter.* By this Time I began to FEEL I FEARED; and the Want of it was sufficiently paid home to me, in the Tremor of Spirits I suffered in such daring Attempts: However, Fortune was my Friend, and I escaped with Life; for I solemnly declare, that I expected to make an odd Figure in the Bills of Mortality—DIED ONE, OF CAPITAL CHARACTERS. [...]

The least Glimmering or Shade of Acting, in Man or Woman, is a sure Motive of Envy in the rest; and, if their Malice can't perswade the Town's-People into a Dislike of their Performance, they'll cruelly endeavour to taint their Characters; so that I think going a Strolling is engaging in a little, dirty Kind of War, in which I have been obliged to fight so many Battles, I have resolutely determined to throw down my Commission: And to say Truth, I am not only sick, but heartily ashamed of it, as I have had nine Years Experience of its being a very contemptible Life; rendred so, through the impudent and ignorant Behaviour of the Generality of those who pursue it; and I think it wou'd be more reputable to earn a Groat a Day in Cinderfisting at *Tottenham-Court,* than to be concerned with them.[2]

'Tis a Pity that so many, who have good Trades, should idly quit them, to become despicable Actors; which renders them useless to themselves, and very often Nusances to others. Those who were bred up in the Profession, have the best Right to make it their Calling; but their Rights are horribly invaded by Barbers 'Prentices, Taylors and Journeymen Weavers; all which bear such strong Marks of their Professions, that I have seen *Richard* the Third murder *Henry* the Sixth with a Shuttle, and *Orestes* jump off the Shop-Board to address *Hermione.*

Another Set of Gentry who have crept into their Community, are Servants out of Place; and I very lately saw the gallant *Marcian* as well rubbed and curried, as ever the Actor did a Horse in his Master's Stable. This worthy Wight having the Happiness to write an exceeding fine Hand, and living formerly with a Gentleman in one of the Inns of Court, wisely palms himself upon Strangers for a Lawyer, when his real and original Profession was that of a Groom.

How such Sort of People, without the Help of at least a little Education, can presume to pick the Pockets of an Audience, is to me astonishing, though they have the Vanity and Assurance to say they please, but 'tis only themselves; and were the Spirits of departed Poets to see their Works mangled and butchered, as I have too often been a melancholly Witness of, they would certainly kick the depredating Heroes out of this World into the next.

I have had the Mortification of hearing the Characters of *Hamlet, Varanes, Othello,* and many more Capitals, rent in Pieces by a Figure no higher than two Six-penny Loaves, and a Dissonancy of Voice, which conveyed to me a strong Idea of a Cat in Labour; all which, conjoined with an injudicious Utterance, made up a compleat tragical Emetick, for a Person of the smallest Degree of Judgment: And yet these Wretches very impudently stile themselves Players; a Name, let me tell them, when properly applied, is an Honour to an Understanding, for none can deserve that Title, who labour under the Want of a very considerable Share of Sense.

Please see the Works Cited for further information on the sources used in this essay.

Notes

1 See Highfill for further biographical details.
2 Cinder-fisting or cinder-hunting is the work of picking through the banks of the Thames or in dust piles for bones or other potentially saleable items. See "Totting" in *The Slang Dictionary* by John Camden Hotten.

Suggestion for Further Reading

Baruth, Philip E., ed. *Introducing Charlotte Charke: Actress, Author, Enigma.* Champaign, IL: University of Illinois Press, 1998.

9 FRANCES BURNEY (1752–1840)

Serena Baiesi

Introduction

Frances Burney (1752–1840) is renowned for her sentimental novels, which contributed significantly to the development of the genre during the Romantic period. During her lifetime, Burney published four successful novels: *Evelina* (1778), *Cecilia* (1782), *Camilla* (1796), and *The Wonderer* (1814). She also wrote eight plays—only two of which were performed on the London stage—as well as *Memoirs of Doctor Burney* (1832) about her father, and a large number of unpublished journals, letters, and diaries. In all her writings, Burney consistently questions issues of genre, gender, race, authority, and power relations, notably influencing later female authors, such as Maria Edgeworth (1768–1849) and Jane Austen (1775–1817), and contributing to the literary and critical history of her time.

Burney was educated at home and, through family connections, made early acquaintance with many London intellectuals, novelists, and actors. After the publication of her first two novels, Burney was offered a position in the court of King George III and Queen Charlotte. While her five years of service (1786–1791) were physically and psychologically demanding, they also gave Burney the opportunity to observe political events and private intrigues of the period that informed her subsequent writing. She considered her role at court as a sort of imprisonment, but she also wrote four tragedies during this period (*Edwy and Elgiva*, *The Siege of Pevensey*, *Hubert the Vere*, and the incomplete *Elberta*). Burney's plays reflect the sparkling dialogue and witty characters drawn from her time at court, and they also convey her ideals of liberty, equality, fraternity, and social justice, together with her concern for the rights and independence of women.

After a secret courtship, and against her father Charles's[1] wishes, Burney married Alexandre D'Arblay (1754–1818), an exiled French Adjutant-General of the Marquis de Lafayette, in 1793. Theirs was a happy marriage, and the couple had a son, Alex, the following year. In addition, the writer soon published her third successful novel, *Camilla*, whose profits allowed the couple to buy a cottage, named Camilla Cottage after her book.

In the later part of her life, Burney moved to France, where she faced significant health issues, but she carried on with her writing. Returning to England, she published her last novel, *The Wonderer*, and, after the death of her father, she wrote her *Memoir* of him, an important and original example of biographical writing.

Burney also wrote many diaries, journals, and letters, and such important material should be read alongside her novels and plays. In these personal papers, there are many passages that read like theatrical scenes and reflect her profound interest in

DOI: 10.4324/9781003006923-10

drama and acting. Burney drew special enjoyment from acting for her family and friends. Despite her shyness, she delighted in the thrill of acting and all aspects of a performance. As the excerpts from her journals, letter, and diaries here show, she offered readers detailed descriptions of the theatricals performed at the Burney's household: from the rehearsals to the costumes, and on to the reactions of the audience at the final staging of the play.

Moreover, in her journals and letters, we discover the challenges and difficulties she had to face as a woman writer coming from the refined London intellectual background of the Burney circle. Her father and other male mentors strongly influenced her writing, especially for the theatre, preventing Burney from developing her dramatic abilities fully. As we can see from the selection of her letters excerpted here, Charles Burney and family friend Samuel Crisp[2], in particular, were sometimes encouraging, but more often averse to Burney's dramatic endeavours. Finally, Burney's letters and select passages from her journals reveal the fraught relationship between gender and theatre as a public space. After the disastrous reception of her only staged tragedy, Burney decides to withdraw her work from the theatre. She demonstrates a sophisticated understanding of the production arena when she reports the events to a friend, blaming her own inexperience as a playwright and especially the poor performances of the actors whose interpretations much influenced the reception of the work.

Together, Burney's journals, letters, and diaries shine new light on the history of women's dramatic criticism, enriching the multifaceted story of theatre during the Romantic period.

Frances Burney

Excerpts from The Early Journals and Letters of Fanny Burney, *Volume II—1774–1777*

Monday April 7 (1777)

[*While FB was staying with her uncle and cousins in Worcester, she describes a private performance of the comedy by Arthur Murphy* (1727–1805) *entitled* The Way to Keep Him (1760)]

[…] The Theatre looked extremely well, & was fitted up in a very Dramatic manner: with side scenes,—& 2 figures, of Tragedy & Comedy at each end, & a Head of Shakespear in the middle. We had 4 Change of scenes.

[…]

Take notice, that, from the beginning to the End, no *applause* was given to the play. The company judged that it would be inelegant, & therefore, as they all said, *forbore*;—but indeed it would have been very encouraging, & I heartily wish they had not practiced such *self denial*!

Next came my scene; I was discovered Drinking Tea[3];—to tell you how *infinitely*, how *beyond measure* I was terrified at my situation, I really cannot,—but my fright was nearly such as I should have suffered had I made my appearance upon a public Theatre, since Miss Humphries[4] & Captain Coussmaker[5] were the only two of the Audience I had ever before seen.

[…]

Fortunately for me, all the next scene gave me hardly 3 words in a speech, for Muslin has it almost to herself: so I had little else to do than to lean on the

Table, & twirl my Thumbs, &, sometimes, bite my fingers:—which, indeed, I once or twice did very severely, without knowing why, or yet being able to help it.

I am sure, *without flattery*, I looked like a most egregious fool;— for I made no use of the Tea things,—I never tasted a drop,—once, indeed, I made an attempt, by way of passing the Time better, to drink a little, but my Hand shook so violently, I was fain to put down the Cup instantly, in order to save my Gown […].

In this Act, therefore, circumstances were so happily miserable for me, that I believe some of my auditors thought me a much better & more *arttificial* [*sic*] actress than I [really was] & I had the satisfaction of hearing some few buzzes of approbation which did me no harm.

But I would never have engaged in this scheme, had I not been persuaded that my fright would have ended with the first scene: I had not any idea of being so completely overcome by it […].

At the End of all, there was a faint something in *imitation* of a Clap,—but very faint, indeed: yet, though applause would much have encouraged us, we have no reason to be mortified by it's[6] omission, since they all repeatedly declared they *longed* to clap, but thought it would not be approved: & since we have heard, from all quarters, nothing but praise & compliment […].

Excerpts from **The Early Journals and Letters of Fanny Burney, Volume III—The Streatham Years, Part I: 1778–1779**

[Streatham, 29]—30 July [1779]

[*In May 1799 Burney completes the first draft of her comedy entitled* The Witlings *encouraged by dramatists such as Richard Brinsley Sheridan[7] and Arthur Murphy, as well as by intellectuals, artists and friends: Samuel Johnson, Joshua Reynolds and Hester Thrale[8]. However, after reading a revised draft of the comedy, her father, together with his family friend Samuel Crisp, urges her to suppress it, for fear of offending the literary circle of* Bluestockings[9]. *Frances obediently accepts her censors' judgments, but not without disappointment. Even though the play was ready for the stage, it remained unperformed and unpublished*]

Friday, July 30th
To Samuel Crisp

[…] This seems a strange unseasonable period for *my* undertaking, among the rest,—but yet, my dear Daddy, when you have read my conversation with Mr. Sheridan, I believe you will agree that I must have been wholly insensible, nay, almost *ungrateful*, to resist encouragement, *entreaties*,—all of which, he warmly repeated to my Father.
[…]
Oh my dear Daddy, *if* your next Letter were to contain your *real* opinion of it, how should I dread to open it!—Be, however, as honest as your good nature & delicacy will *allow* you to be, & assure yourself I shall be *very* certain that all criticisms will proceed from your earnest wishes to obviate those of others,—& that you would have much more *pleasure* in being my *panegyrist*.
[…]
I should like that your First reading should have nothing to do with *me*,—that you should go quick through it, or let my Father read it to you, forgetting all the

Time, as much as you can, that *Fannikin* is the Writer, or even that it is a play in manuscript, & *capable* of alterations:—And then, when you have done, I should like to have 3 Lines, telling me, as nearly as you trust my candour, it's [*sic*] general effect.—

After that,—take it to your own Desk, & lash it at your leisure.

Adieu, My dear Daddy—I shall hope to hear from you *very* soon,—& pray believe me

Yours ever & ever
Frances Burney.

Let it fail never so much, the manager will have nothing to reproach me with: is not that some comfort?—[He would really listen to no denial.]

[St Martin's Street, *c.* 13 August 1779]
To Charles Burney

The fatal knell then, is knolled! & down among the Dead Men sink the poor Witlings,—for-ever & for-ever & for-ever!—[10]

I give a *sigh* whether I will or not to their memory, for, however worthless, they were *mes Enfans* [my children], *& one must do one's Nature*, as Mr Crisp will tell you of the Dog.

You, my dearest Sir, who enjoyed, I really think, even more than myself the astonishing success of my first attempt, would, I believe, even more than myself, be hurt at the failure of my second;—& I am sure I speak from the bottom of a very honest Heart when I most solemnly declare that upon *your* Account any disgrace would mortify & afflict me *more* than upon my own,—for whatever appears with your *knowledge*, will be naturally supposed to have met with your *approbation*, & perhaps with your *assistance*;—& therefore, though all *particular* censure would fall where it *ought*, upon *me*,—yet any *general* censure of the *whole*, & the *Plan*, would cruelly, but certainly, involve *you* in it's severity.

Of this I have been sensible from the moment my *Authorshipness* was discovered,—& therefore, from that moment, I determined to have no *opinion* of my own in regard to what I should thenceforth part with out of my own Hands. I would, long since, have Burnt the 4ᵗʰ Act, upon your disapprobation of it, but that I waited, & was by Mrs. Thrale so much *encouraged* to wait, for your finishing the Piece. [...]

I expected many Objections to be raised, a thousand errors to be point out, & a million of alterations to be proposed;—but—the *suppression of the piece* were words I did *not* expect,—indeed after the warm approbation of Mrs. Thrale, & the repeated commendations & flattery of Mr. Murphy, how could I?—

I do not, therefore, pretend to *wish* you should think the decision for which I was so little prepared has given me no disturbance;—for I must be a far more egregious Witling than any of those I tried to draw to imagine you could ever credit that I writ without some remote hope of success *now*, though I literally did when I composed Evelina. But my mortification is not at throwing away the Characters, or the contrivance;—it is all the throwing away the *Time*,—which I with difficulty stole, & which I have Buried in the mere trouble of *writing* [...].

Excerpt from **The Early Journals and Letters of Fanny Burney,**
Volume IV—*The Streatham Years, Part II: 1780–1781*

[*In January 1780 Burney revises Act IV of* The Witlings, *in order to show it completed to Sheridan. She also plans other revisions, but she is finally persuaded by her father and Crisp to abandon the play*]

St Martin's Street,
22 January [1780]

To Samuel Crisp

[…] As my Play was settled in it's silent suppression, I entreated my Father to call on Mr. Sheridan in order to prevent his expecting any thing from me, as he had a good right to do from my having sent him a possitive message that I should, in compliance with his exhortations at Mrs. Cholmondeley's[11], try my fortune in the *Theatrical line*, & send him a Piece for this Winter. My Father did call, but found him not at Home,—niether did he happen to see him till about Christmas. He then acquainted him that what I had written had entirely dissatisfied me, & that I desired to decline for the present all attempts of that sort.

Mr. Sheridan was pleased to express great concern,—nay more, to protest he would not *accept* my refusal,—he beg'd my Father to tell me that he could take no denial to *seeing* what I had done,—that I could be no fair Judge for myself,—that he doubted not but it would please;—but was *glad* I was not satisfied, as he had much rather see pieces before their Authors were contented with them than afterwards, on account of sundry small changes always necessary to be made by the managers, for Theatrical purposes, & to which they were loath to submit when their writings were finished to their own approbations. In short, he said so much that my Father, ever easy to be worked upon, began to waver, & told me he wished I would shew the play to Sheridan at once.

This very much disconcerted me,—I had taken a sort of disgust to it, & was myself most earnestly desirous to let it Die a quiet Death. I therefore *cooled* the affair as much as I conveniently could, & by evading from Time to Time the Conversation, it was again sinking into it's old state,—when again Mr. Sheridan saw my Father, & asked his leave to call upon me himself.

This could not be refused.

Well,—I was now violently *fidgetted*,—& began to think of *alterations*,—&, setting my Head to Work, I have actually new written the 4th Act from beginning to End except one scene:—Mr. Sheridan, however, has not yet called,—& I have so little Heart in the affair, that I have now again quite dropt it.

Such is the present situation of *my Politics*. Now I wish you much to write me your private opinion what I had best do in case of an emergency,—your Letters are always sacred, so pray write with your usual sincerity & openness.—I know you too well to fear your being offended if things should be so managed that your Counsel cannot be followed: it will, at any rate, not be thrown away, since it will be a fresh proof of your interest in my affairs.

My Notions I will also tell you; they are:— — in case I *must* produce this piece to the manager—

To entirely omit all mention of the *Club;*—[…]

Excerpt from* Diary and Letters of Madame D'Arblay[12], *Vol III—1788 to 1796

[*21 March 1795: Burney's tragedy* Edwy and Elgiva *is produced at Drury Lane, with the prologue by her brother Charles. However, it is immedialy withdrawn from the stage after only one performance.*]

Bookham,
April 15, 1795.

Madame d'Arblay to Mrs.———[13]

So dry a reproof from so dear a friend! And do you, then, measure my regard of heart by my remiss of hand? Let me give you the short history of my tragedy, fairly and frankly.

I wrote it not, as your acquaintance imagined, for the stage, nor yet for the press. I began it at Kew Palace, and at odd moments, I finished it at Windsor; without the least idea of any species of publication.

[…]

The piece was represented to the utmost disadvantage, save only Mrs. Siddons and Mr. Kemble; for it was not written with any idea of the stage, and my illness and weakness, and constant absorbment, at the time of its preparation, occasioned it to appear with so many undramatic effects, from my inexperience of theatrical requisites and demands, that, when I saw it, I myself perceived a thousand things I wished to change. The performers, too, were cruelly imperfect, and made blunders I blush to have pass for mine—added to what belong to me. The most important character after the hero and heroine had but two lines of his part by heart! He made all the rest at random, and such nonsense as put all the other actors out as much as himself; so that a more wretched performance, except Mrs. Siddons, Mr. Kemble, and Mr. Bensley[14], could not be exhibited in a barn.

All this occurred to make it very desirable to withdraw the piece for alterations, which I have done.

And now you have the whole history—and now—are you appeased?

F. D'A.

Please see the Works Cited for further information on the sources used in this essay.

Notes

1 Charles Burney (1726–1814) was Frances Burney's father. He was a renowned music historian, composer and musician. Charles provided his daughter with a stimulating domestic and social background where leading intellectuals and artists were frequent visitors of the Burney's household.

2 Samuel Crisp (1707–1783), playwright living in retirement, family friend who became Frances' second "daddy."

3 Burney played the role of Mrs Lovemore.

4 Sister-in-law of Frances' uncle, Richard Burney.

5 George Kien Hayward Coussmaker, Ensign of the 1st Foot Guards.

6 Burney regularly used the apostrophe; here and throughout, we retain her spellings [eds.].

7 Richard Brinsley Sheridan (1751–1816), famous playwright, who managed Drury Lane Theatre since 1776.

8 Samuel Johnson (1709–1784), poet and critic, best remembered for his *Dictionary of the English Language* (1755); Joshua Reynold (1723–1792) painter specializing in portraits; Hester Thrale (1740–1821), diarist and arts patron.

9   The Bluestockings were a group of intellectuals, primarily women, who, during the mid-18th century, held literary meetings with writers, artists, and members of the aristocracy. They also supported literary publications of emerging writers. Since Frances depended on their patronage, her father warns her about the risks of mentioning the "Club" in her play, as she notes below.

10 Burney makes literary allusions to Shakespeare, John Dyer, and Alexander Pope in order to highlight her frustration over the rejection of her play by her readers: her father Dr Burney and Samuel Crisp.

11 Mrs Mary Cholmondeley, eccentric sister of the famous actress Peg Woffington. Her husband, the Hon. and Rev. Robert Cholmondeley, was the second son of the Earl of Cholmondeley and nephew of Horace Walpole.

12 In 1793, Frances married Alexandre D'Arblay, a French expatriate in England and former adjutant to the Marquis de Lafayette.

13 Mary Port Waddington, Mrs. Delany's great-niece, a friend of Frances at Windsor.

14 English actors at Drury Lane: John Philip Kemble (1757–1823) played Edwy, Robert Bensley Dunstan (1740–1817), and Sarah Siddons (1755–1831) Elgiva.

Suggestions for Further Reading

Clark, Lorna J., *A Celebration of Frances Burney*. Newcastle: Cambridge Scholars, 2007.

Epstein, Julia. *The Iron Pen: Frances Burney and the Politic of Women's Writing*. Bristol: Bristol Classical Press, 1989.

Harman, Claire, *Fanny Burney: A Biography*. London: Harper Collins, 2000.

Johnson, Claudia L., *Equivocal Beings: Politics, Gender, and Sentimentality in the 1790s: Wollstonecraft, Radcliffe, Burney, Austen*. Chicago, IL: University of Chicago Press, 1995.

Sabor, Peter, ed. *The Cambridge Companion to Frances Burney*. Cambridge: Cambridge University Press, 2007.

Straub, Kristina. *Divided Fictions: Fanny Burney and Feminine Strategy*. Lexington: University of Kentucky Press, 1987.

Thaddeus, Janice Farrar. *Frances Burney: A Literary Life*. New York, NY: St. Martin's Press, 2000.

10 HANNAH COWLEY (1743–1809)

Melinda C. Finberg and Angela Escott

Introduction

Hannah Cowley (1743–1809), the last new playwright introduced to the London stage by David Garrick[1] before he retired, was an overnight success with her comedy *The Runaway* (1776), and she became one of the most produced playwrights of late eighteenth-century London. While her playwrighting career began the year the American colonies declared their independence, it continued beyond the French Revolution.

Cowley was celebrated for her effervescent dialogue and well-drawn characters and was justifiably confident in her own work. She used her addresses, prefaces, and advertisements to assert women's artistic freedom to tackle controversial topics including politics, to challenge critics who disputed the appropriateness of her addressing those topics, and to advance her theories of what makes for true dramatic comedy. Yet despite seeming so forthcoming about her work, Cowley remains enigmatic. During her stage career, which lasted from 1776 to 1794, she braved – even courted – controversy; yet in retirement, she edited whatever might scandalize her readers or audiences out of the final edition of her works (1813). The quoted passages we include from Cowley's writings are from the first editions of her work, before she eliminated the controversial or risqué from editions published after 1794.

Cowley's most scandalous play, *A School for Greybeards* (1786), was an adaptation of Aphra Behn's *The Lucky Chance* (1686.)[2] Since Behn's plays were considered "too indecent to be ever represented again" (Genest 6:427), Cowley coyly concealed both the source of her adaptation and that author's gender: "the work of a poet of the drama, once highly celebrated" (*Greybeards* viii), but it was an open secret. The comedy led to a riot on opening night and attacks on Cowley in the press. While angry at having to revise the plot and language of her comedy before it could be restaged (Finberg xli), nevertheless, Cowley may have anticipated this controversy. She quickly brought out a published edition that restored most of her original language, but, interestingly, not the original plot. In this new version's Address, included here, Cowley protests the suppression of her creative impulses and charges that her chosen genre, as well as her gender, makes her subject to critical attacks that confuse her own reputation with the respectability of her characters (see *Greybeards* v–vii).

She states that true dramatic comedy is based on observations of human nature and lays out her claims for the female playwright, who, like the "Novelist" (whom she refers to as "her"), draws characters from "Nature" and eschews strategies "continually to reflect, not whether *this is just?* but whether *this is safe?*" (*Greybeards* vii).

DOI: 10.4324/9781003006923-11

Cowley was also advancing a political cause: calling attention to the tyranny of the Hardwicke Act of 1754,[3] a law which made it illegal for a woman under the age of twenty-one to choose her own husband. It was enacted to prevent "stealing" heiresses and their property – or as Cowley viewed it, to keep young women tied up as patriarchal property. Previously, a woman and her lover could declare their betrothal as early as age sixteen, and their vow would be legally binding. In Behn's *The Lucky Chance* (1686), the bride is rescued from her wedding to an old man by her exiled lover, who secretly returns to marry her based on their legal betrothal. The lovers' rights remain valid, while the woman's forced marriage is unconsummated. In her Address, Cowley confesses that what attracted her to her source was the "snatching [of] a young woman from a hateful marriage, the moment before that marriage became valid" (*Greybeards* viii). In Behn's day, the old man marrying a pre-engaged woman was considered adultery. The scandalous aspect of *Greybeards* is that the Hardwick Act turned the young couple escaping together into adultery. By creating the scandal, Cowley calls attention to the injustice of the new law.

In her Advertisement to her 1792 comedy, *A Day in Turkey*, also included here, Cowley denies any political intent, declaring, with apologies to Mary Wollstonecraft (1759–1797), that politics is "unfeminine." Based on Cowley's courting of political controversy in 1786, it is laughable that she points a finger at Wollstonecraft, author of the feminist tract *A Vindication of the Rights of Woman* (1792). Yet Cowley's denial seems tongue-in-cheek. Written in the aftermath of the American and French revolutions, Cowley's comedy has a French character who pointedly champions liberty and individual rights. We see here how Cowley frequently writes on two levels at once: the surface level upholds the status quo and the ironic level beneath reveals her more radical leanings.

Cowley's use of satire, particularly in her farce *Who's the Dupe?* (1779) but also throughout her comedies, was unusual for a female dramatist and risked crossing the boundaries of respectability. In her prologue to this farce, she argued for the right "[t]o laugh at those same *learned* Men" who attack women,

> And fill their bold, satiric page
>> With petty foibles – *Ladies'* faults –
>> Who still endure their rude assaults (5–6)

In the Preface to her final comedy, *The Town Before You* (1794), the last selection here, Cowley gives her view of what comedy ought to be and why she cannot continue to write for audiences who prefer slapstick to wit. She cites Congreve, Farquhar, and Cibber[4] as models of wit and observation and laments that their "patient development of character, the repeated touches which colour it up to Nature, [...] we now have no relish for" (*The Town Before You* x). This farewell to the stage sounds nostalgic, but her comedy was not old fashioned. The romantic heroine, Lady Horatia, a female sculptor surrounded by her school of young women who wish to emulate her, seems inspired by Anne Seymour Damer (1748–1828), the only successful professional female sculptor in England at the time. Her success in what was considered a masculine art made her a target for satire as a "Sapphic" woman, or lesbian, in the journals of the day (Elfenbein 95). Lady Horatia can be read as Cowley's daring defence of Damer and of female artists in general against hostile and reactionary public opinion.

Cowley's obituary reads: "The general tenor of her life was by no means theatrical [...]. Though public as a GENIUS, yet private as a WOMAN, she wore her laurels gracefully veiled" (*Gentleman's Magazine*). The shy and retiring flower represented in her obituary had also been a member of the politically left-wing Duchess of Devonshire's[5] circle, had conducted a literary correspondence on the pages of the newspaper *The World* with the radical journalist Robert Merry in 1787, had met Thomas Jefferson in Paris in 1789, and had included characters in her plays who apparently supported both the American and French revolutions. Both sides of her character, the conventional and the independent, are simultaneously present in her addresses to the public that frame her dramatic works.

Hannah Cowley

"Address" from School for Greybeards *(1786)*

AN ADDRESS

I OFFER the following Comedy to the public, under a circumstance which has given my mind the most exquisite uneasiness. On the morning after the first representation, it was observed by the papers that there had been persons present at the Theatre the preceding evening, who went there *determined* to disapprove at all events. From such a determination it is hard indeed to escape! And the opposition intended, was justified it seems, by the indecency of some of the expressions.—From such a charge I feel it impossible to defend myself; for against an imputation like this, even *vindication* becomes disgraceful!

As I was not at the Theatre, I should have had some difficulty in understanding at what passages the objections were levelled, had not one of the papers recorded them, with many cruel remarks. The particulars which were thus pointed out, will, I trust, be a sufficient apology for themselves. In the following pages they are *all* restored; that the public AT LARGE may have the power to adjudge me, as well as that small part of it, confined within the walls of a Theatre.

These passages have not been restored from any pertinacious opinion of their beauty— for other expressions might have conveyed my intention as well; but had I allowed one line to stand as altered for the stage, what might not that reprobated line have been supposed to express? I shrink from the idea! And therefore most solemnly aver, that the Comedy, as now printed, contains EVERY WORD which was opposed the first night, from the suspicion of indelicacy; hoping their *obvious* meaning only will be attended to, without the coarse ingenuity of strained explanations; which have been made, by persons who seem desirous to surround my task of dramatic writing, with as many difficulties as possible.

A celebrated Critic, more attended to for the discrimination and learning which appear in his strictures, than for their *lenity*; in his observations on the Greybeards, has the following.

> "When Mrs. Cowley gets possession of the spirit and turn of a character, she speaks the language of *that* character better than *any* of her dramatic contemporaries."

This, I confess, I hold to be very high praise; and it is to this very praise, which my contemporaries resolve I shall have no claim. They will allow me, indeed, to draw strong character, but it must be without speaking its language. I may give vulgar or low bred persons, but they must converse in a stile of elegance. I may design the coarsest manners, or the most disgusting folly, but its expressions must not deviate from the line of politeness.

Surely it would be as just to exact from the Artists who are painting the Gallery of Shakespeare, that they should compleat their designs without the use of light and shade.

It cannot be the *Poet's* mind, which the public desire to trace, in dramatic representation; but the mind of the *characters*, and the truth of their colouring. Yet in my case it seems resolved that the point to be considered, is not whether that *dotard*, or that *pretender*, or that *coquet*, would so have given their feelings, but whether Mrs. *Cowley* ought so to have expressed herself.

This is a criterion which happily no author is subjected to, but those of the drama. The Novelist may use the boldest tints;—seizing Nature for her guide, she may dart through every rank of society, drag forth not only the accomplished, but the ignorant, the coarse, and the vulgar-rich; display them in their strongest colours, and snatch immortality both for them, and for herself! I, on the contrary, feel encompassed with chains when I write, which check me in my happiest flights, and force me continually to reflect, not, whether *this is just?* but, whether *this is safe?*

These are vain regrets, which I hope my readers will pardon me, for having a moment indulged. I now hasten to that part of the Comedy which will be found in the following sheets, as *altered* for the second representation.

The idea of the business which concerns Antonia, Henry, and Gasper was presented to me in an obsolete Comedy; the work of a poet of the drama, once highly celebrated. I say the *idea*, for when it is known that in the original the scene lay amongst traders in the city of London—and those traders of the lowest and most detestable manners, it will be conceived at once, that in removing it to Portugal, and fixing the characters amongst the nobility, it was hardly possible to carry with me *more* than the idea. The circumstance which most particularly interested me, and fixed itself in my mind, was that of snatching a young woman from a hateful marriage, the moment before that marriage became valid—that is to say, after the ceremony. This very circumstance to which the Comedy owes its existence, was that, which some of the audience found discordant to their feelings. An event which had in the last century been stampt with the highest applause, (tho' surrounded by many repulsive circumstances) was found in this, to be ill-conceived. I did not, however, dispute the decision of my Critics,—and the marriage has been in course dissolved.

The manner in which the comedy has since been received gives room to suppose that the alteration is approved. It has struggled with many oppressive circumstances: the chasm in the performance, occasioned by the repeated illness of Mr. Parsons, was sufficient to have sunk it;—but neither that, nor the sterile month of December, always *against* the Theatres, has prevented its being distinguished by many brilliant and crouded nights. I now resign it to the closet, where without the aid of fine acting, or the fascinations of beauty, and deriving all its little force from the pen which composed it, it hopes still to amuse—the innocent flame of Seraphina's coquetry may still shed rays of delight on her readers, and the affecting situation of Antonia interest them.

"Advertisement" for **A Day in Turkey** *(1792)*

ADVERTISEMENT

Hints have been thrown out, and the idea industriously circulated, that the following comedy is tainted with POLITICS. I protest I know nothing about politics;—will Miss Wolstonecraft forgive me—whose book contains such a body of mind as I hardly ever met with—if I say that politics are *unfeminine?* I never in my life could attend to their discussion.

TRUE COMEDY has always been defined to be a picture of life—a record of passing manners—a mirror to reflect to succeeding times the characters and follies of the present. How then could I, pretending to be a comic poet, bring an emigrant Frenchman before the public at this day, and not make him hint at the events which had just passed, or were then passing in his native country? A character so written would have been anomalous—the critics ought to have had no mercy on me. It is A LA GREQUE who speaks, not *I;* nor can I be accountable for *his* sentiments. *Such* is my idea of tracing CHARACTER; and were I to continue to write for the stage, I should always govern myself by it.

THE illiberal and *false* suggestions concerning the politics of the comedy I could frankly forgive, had they not deprived it of the honour of a COMMAND. The passages on which those misrepresentations were built, were on the second night omitted, but immediately afterwards restored; and the DAY IN TURKEY leaves the press exactly as it has continued to be performed amidst the most vivid and uninterrupted plaudits— or interrupted only by the glitter of soft tears; a species of applause not less flattering than the spontaneous laugh, or the voluntary collision of hands.

SOME of the performers in this comedy have play'd so transcendently well, that their names deserve to be recorded; but to particularise any, when *all* have aim'd at perfection, would be invidious.

"Preface" to **The Town Before You** *(1794)*

PREFACE

The following is rather the Comedy which the Public have chosen it to be, than the Comedy which I intended. Some things have been left out, and some have been added since the first representation: In short, the Comedy has been *new class'd*—it has been torn from its genus.

It is hoped, however, that there may be found characters, in THE TOWN BEFORE YOU, to interest, and situations to attach; and that those events which were vivacity in the Theatre, will not be dulness in the closet.

But it must be noticed, that the scene, in the second act, between TIPPY and his Landlady, and that in the fifth act, between TIPPY and the Bailiff, were no part of my original design. They were written during the illness of MRS. POPE, after the Piece had been played several nights. Alas! I am sorry to remark, that no scenes in the Comedy (to use the Stage idiom) *go off* better.

An acute Critic lately said, in one of those assemblies where conversation, though sometimes light, is seldom without meaning, "A Comedy to please, in the present day, must be *made,* not written." It requires no great expanse of comprehension to perceive the meaning of this dogma; the truth of which I am equally ready to acknowledge, and to deplore: But should it *want illustration*, it may be found every week in a popular Piece, where a great Actor, holding a sword in his left hand, and making aukward pushes with it, charms the audience infinitely more than he could do, by all the wit and observation which the ingenious Author might have given him; and brings down such applauses, as the bewitching dialogue of CIBBER, and of FARQUHAR pants for in vain!

The patient developement of character, the repeated touches which colour it up to Nature, and swell it into identity and existence (and which gave celebrity to CONGREVE), we have now no relish for. The combinations of interest, the strokes which are meant to reach the heart, we are equally incapable of tasting. LAUGH! LAUGH! LAUGH! is the demand: Not a word must be uttered that looks like instruction, or a sentence which ought to be remembered.

From a Stage, in such a state, it is time to withdraw; but I call on my younger cotemporaries, I invoke the rising generation, to *correct* a taste which, to be gratified, demands neither genius or intellect;—which asks only a happy knack at inventing tricks. I adjure them to restore to the Drama SENSE, OBSERVATION, WIT, LESSON! And to teach our writers to respect their own talents.

What mother can now lead her daughters to the great National School, THE THEATRE, in the confidence of their receiving either polish or improvement? Should the luckless Bard stumble on a reflection, or a sentiment, the audience yawn, and wait for the next tumble from a chair, or a tripping up of the heels, to put them into attention. Surely I shall be forgiven for satirising myself; I have *made* such things and I blush to have made them.

O! GENIUS of a polish'd age, descend!—plant thy banners in our Theatres, and bid ELEGANCE and FEELING take place of the *droll* and the *laugh*, which formerly were found only in the Booths of *Bartlemy* Fair, and were divided between *Flocton* and *Yates*! With actors capable of giving force to all that is intellectual, is it not *pity* to condemn them to such drudgery? THEY are no longer necessary. Let Sadler's Wells and the Circus empty themselves of their performers to furnish our Stage; the expence to Managers will be less, and their business will be carried on better. The UNDERSTANDING, DISCERNMENT, and EDUCATION, which distinguish our modern actors, are useless to them;—strong muscles are in greater repute, and grimace has more powerful attraction.

Please see the Works Cited for further information on the sources used in this essay.

Notes

1 David Garrick (1717–1779), prominent English actor and theatre manager, associated closely with the Drury Lane Theatre.
2 Aphra Behn (1640–1689) was the first professional woman playwright in England. See entry in this volume.
3 For the full text of this act, see http://statutes.org.uk/site/the-statutes/eighteenth-century/1753-26-geo-2-c-33-prevention-of-clandestine-marriages/
4 William Congreve (1670–1729), George Farquhar (1677–1707), and Colley Cibber (1671–1757) were all noted playwrights.
5 Georgiana Spencer Cavendish (1757–1806).

Suggestions for Further Reading

Choudhury, Mita, "Gazing at His Seraglio; Late Eighteenth – Century Women Playwrights as Orientalists." *Theatre Journal*. 47 (1995): 481–502.

Donkin, Ellen. *Getting into the Act*. London: Routledge, 1995.

Escott, Angela. *The Celebrated Hannah Cowley*. London: Pickering and Chatto, 2012.

Finberg, Melinda C. *Eighteenth-Century Women Dramatists*. Oxford: Oxford University Press, 2001.

Girdham, Jane. *English Opera in Late Eighteenth-Century London: Stephen Storace at Drury Lane*. Oxford: Clarendon Press, 1997.

Newey, Katherine. "Women and History on the Romantic Stage: More, Yearsley, Burney and Mitford." *Women in British Romantic Theatre: Drama, Performance and Society, 1790-1840*. Ed. Catherine Burroughs. Cambridge: Cambridge University Press, 2000. 79–101.

Spencer, Jane. "Adapting Aphra Behn: Hannah Cowley's A School for Greybeards and The Lucky Chance." *Women's Writing*. 2.3 (1995): 221–34.

11 LADY EGLANTINE WALLACE (c. 1754–1803)

Lilla Maria Crisafulli

Introduction

Lady Eglantine or Eglinton Wallace (c.1754–1803) was a controversial Scottish playwright also known for her sonorous protest against theatre censorship. The little biographical information we have, as Ann Brooks claims, emphasizes her substantial presence among the "women as public intellectuals" of the age (22). Indeed, Lady Wallace was endowed with an eccentric personality, to the point that the canonical *Dictionary of National Biography* describes her as "A boisterous hoyden in her youth, and a woman of violent temper in her maturer years" (97). The entry found in the recent *The Biographical Dictionary of Scottish Women* depicts her as: "Dramatist, author, exile, reputed spy" (365). She appears to have held an unsteady position in the ranks of the aristocracy; her early youth was spent in "some poverty," and she married a member of the minor aristocracy. Additionally, the *Biographical Dictionary* remarks that "In March 1788, she allegedly entered the gallery of the House of Commons in male dress, and she had an affair with a 'fortune-hunting colonel' in Bath [...]. These reports influenced the riotous reception at Covent Garden of her play, *The Ton* (1788), attacking aristocratic corruption and arguing for female education and divorce" (365). What emerges is the profile of a strong-willed woman, ready to break the strict rules of the society to which she belonged and to resist gender roles. Evidently, Lady Wallace's transgressive temperament and the satirical force of her comedies affected her plays' reception even before they reached the stage.

The Whim (1795) was one of the very few plays of the time that was denied a license by John Larpent[1] without any recommendations for amendments or alterations.[2] Larpent's verdict, "Prohibited from being acted," arrived just before the curtain rose, causing great consternation in Lady Wallace and in the entire Theatre Royal company that was ready to perform. The decision left the management no choice but to withdraw the representation and send the audience away. But was Larpent's decision entirely unexpected? As David Worrall notes, "What may also have alarmed Larpent [...] was his knowledge of her Covent Garden play of seven years earlier, *The Ton; or, Follies of Fashion. A Comedy* (1788). Although it has been described as a failure, its production encountered malicious controversy precisely because of its satire upon upper-class society" (125). Yet what was really under attack was Lady Wallace's private life and, in particular, her recent divorce from her unfaithful husband. Not by chance, two days after the debut of *The Ton*, *The English Chronicle; or, Universal Evening Post* wrote: "Lady Wallace divorced her husband for infidelity, and is, if we believe her

DOI: 10.4324/9781003006923-12

own Comedy, unique among women of fashion"(10 April 1788), thereby establishing an equation between the plot of the comedy and Wallace's style of life, both signs of unfeminine behavior. Greg Kucich sees such "gender disability" at work especially in the case of women playwrights whose private and public spheres inevitably coincided in the eyes of the reviewers (59).

Wallace was left with no hope of having *The Whim* performed. Under dispute was its comic plot, which deals with the whim of an elderly antiquarian, Lord Crotchett, who decides to put into practice the ancient rituals of the *Saturnalia*. His decision to restage the Roman rites is motivated by his desire to reform the rampant corruption of contemporary society via the moral superiority of the ancients. As he explains to his servant Nell: "It would be rendering a greater service to my country than any which has been done for many years." (31). Hence, for twenty-four hours, his other servant Fag and Nell become his masters while he serves his own servants, in a carnivalesque reversal of class roles.[3] Although the plot is apparently intended to amuse, many of the lines display a pivotal anti-aristocratic view. Overall, *The Whim* exposes the unregulated life and unreliability of the aristocracy, together with the aptness of the servants' pleas for fairer treatment. It offers the audience a satire on aristocratic mores that Larpent must have found unacceptable and unstageable, intent as he was "to keep off the stage any reference to the 'alarms' of the day, both those in France and those closer to home" (Cox, "Baillie, Siddons, Larpent" 41). Larpent's verdict gave rise to a considerable scandal, making the suppression of *The Whim* one of the most resonant episodes of Georgian theatre. It disclosed the relationship of subjection between theatre and political power and unveiled the arbitrariness of the Licenser's decisions. It also caused anger and desire for retaliation in the playwright, who hurried to write her own version of the affair in a preface to the printed version of the play, excerpted here, published in Margate at the end of November of the same year.

In this "Address" Wallace defends her good faith and emphasizes the charitable reasons that prompted her to write her play. On the front page, in place of the date and venue of the comedy's debut, Wallace makes two opposing references: to the beneficial intent of the representation, and to news of the censorship: "offered to be acted for the benefit of the Hospital and poor of the Isle of Thanet, but refused the Royal license" (*The Whim* 1). Lady Wallace calls *The Whim* a "harmless COMEDY," adding that its suppression looks even more unfair since it was written to raise money for the poor. As Catherine Burroughs argues, Wallace's preface, unusually for a woman writer, openly challenged the Licenser's authority: "Overt defiance of the Licenser (or Examiner) of Plays in a preface from this period is quite rare, especially in one composed by a woman. More often than not, one sees an almost fatalistic acceptance of the Licenser's decision" (Burroughs, *Closet Stages* 195). The "Address" turns into both a vigorous complaint against the arbitrary power of censorship and a compelling vindication of the educational role of theatre.

The "Address" embeds a letter of protest to the Lord Chamberlain, responsible for the appointment of the Licenser, in which Wallace asks for an explanation, accusing Larpent of nourishing personal dislikes towards her and of exposing her to the resentment of public opinion. Thus, if *The Whim* satirizes the vices and whims of the upper classes, its preface taught those classes that political opposition and liberal views cannot always be silenced.

Lady Eglantine Wallace

Excerpt from **The Whim, a Comedy in three Acts. […] With an Address to the Public upon the Arbitrary and Unjust Aspersion of the Licenser Against Its Political Sentiments. Offered to Be Acted for the Benefit of the Hospital and Poor of The Isle of Thanet, but Refused the Royal Licence** *(1795)*

"ADDRESS TO THE PUBLIC"

I FEEL myself called upon to offer to your perusal, this harmless COMEDY— written with the view which has ever appeared to me the noblest and most gratifying, which the honest mind can indulge, —that of alleviating the sorrows of those afflicted by the pinching hand of Poverty—Sickness—or Oppression.

I felt too much elate, with the certainty that the emolument of this Comedy would relieve much distress in the Isle of Thanet, to allow myself for a moment to suppose it was possible, that the hand of power could be out-stretched to blast all my Fairy dreams, of thus feeding the hungry—and relieving the sick.

Not believing it possible, without the grossest injustice, to attribute a meaning to any one expression in the Comedy, as either personal, or prejudicial to the public tranquillity, I gave it to be rehearsed; and, as the public curiosity is ever awakened by *Female Whims*, the house on its being announced, was overflowing, and those who were sent away, were not more disappointed, than those who squeezed in, to be told that the Piece could not be acted without endangering the Theatre, with having the ROYAL LICENCE withdrawn; as the *Licencer* disapproved of the Piece as exceptionable. The accusation, that any production of mine could be obnoxious from its Political sentiments, appears to me, and I trust will so to you, to be extremely unjust. Whatever motives the *Licencer* may have, for giving a preference to particular people, he has no right to affix odium to the reputation of any individual, by such unjust and injurious remarks. From reading the Comedy it may easily be conceived, that other motives, independant of the sentiments and merits of it, influenced his decision, —I therefore thought proper to write to the Marquis of Salisbury, as the only hope I had left of securing the benefit of the Comedy to the Poor, I accordingly wrote him as follows: —

LETTER

MY LORD,

"WISHING to contrive a mode to relieve in this place, those who from the misfortunes of the times, require the help of the compasionate, I wrote a piece called the *Whim*, which I gave to be acted here, for the benefit of the Hospital and the Poor."— The Piece was rehearsed, and approved before the firmest friends of Government; and, I believe, my admiration of the Constitution of England, and my regard for the Minister, no one can doubt; as I have I trust, by the most unequivocal services, and steady sentiments in their favor, more than any one in my situation, proved my anxious wishes for their honor, and the tranquillity and prosperity of my Country.

A few days ago the Manager received a letter, saying, that the Piece had been presented to a Mr. Larpent, (who, I am told your Lordship has appointed to inspect all productions for the Theatre) and that he found no objections to it, if signed by a Patentee, and that it would be Licensed on Monday; it consequently was notified to be performed last night, when a letter arrived, saying, that Mr. Larpent had objected to it from its exceptionable sentiments, and that he would lay it before your Lordship.

I cannot conceive that any unfavourable construction can with Justice be put on any sentiment which it contains, as whether ridiculing our late faithless Allies,—or the common follies of Life; it is surely, a far more soothing way to laugh at such unavoidable misfortunes, than to snarl at them.

Perhaps, Mr. Larpent may have more *weighty* reasons for objecting to the licensing the Piece but, I am persuaded, that your Lordship must exult in every thing, which can turn the gaities of the age into immediate relief, for the miseries of the needy. Should any thing in the Piece be construed into an apparent infringment on good order, it will surprise me much, and I may say, with Lord Crotchett,—

"I wonder you don't see the moral it conveys!"

Besides the sorrow I shall feel of being baulked in my charitable scheme, I shall feel more keenly the sort of implication it conveys: such a character being affixed to the Piece, as that it is rejected on account of its Political sentiments. [...]

—There are Philosophers who think, that it is bad policy to alleviate the miseries of the lower order of mankind; but, I am of such different sentiments, that, let who will, for me, enjoy the exuberant luxuries of life, I shall be proud—could I turn my abilities so as to procure the comforts of existence for all my fellow creatures. I therefore hope, that your Lordship will approve this Piece, and the motive which I have for offering it to the public:

I have the honor to be, &c.

E. WALLACE.

Lord Salisbury condescended to answer this letter in the handsomest manner, regretting that Mr. Larpent had represented the Piece as unfit for appearing, that it would have given him pleasure could he have permitted it; for so good a motive as the relief of the Poor.—And as his Lordship is distinguished by his humanity, on all occasions, the misrepresentation of Mr. Larpent alone, could have made him refuse a Licence. To disprove such aspersions, I offer it to the perusal of the candid, who, I flatter myself, will pronounce that no sentiment which it contains, either degrades me, or is unworthy of the most exalted characters, either to feel, or express; – altho' some things have been added in getting it up; yet nothing has been effaced, since sent to Mr. Larpent – If to feel contempt for profligacy, injustice, or deceit, even if detected in a palace; or, if to respect virtue, and integrity, even in the humble obscurity of the cottage, be deemed exceptionable, I plead guilty; for I exult in such opinions—if the motive which I had for offering it to the Stage, the relief of the wretched, be obnoxious, I glory also in that wish—and I only regret, that I cannot, as I hoped, pour into their wounds the balm, which the author's three nights would have afforded.

For, as to the Comedy, or its authoress, being branded with the suspicion of *exceptionable principles*; I am totaly indifferent to that. [...] I shall rest satisfied with self-approbation.

It is unfortunate, when men who are appointed thus with power to damn or save with a despotic yes, or no,—are not endued also with power to judge without prejudice; as on this occasion, it would have given some hundreds to feed the Hungry and relieve the Sick.—If one but hints at the possibility of a great man's not being endued with truth, justice and moral rectitude, you are forsooth, called Democrat, Daemon, or what you please!

A long list of ancestors,—large estates, and high sounding titles, are what are called Noble;—but reason, estimates the value of the man, not the splendor of his name:

and looks up with disgust, to those, who under the influence of grandeur indulge atrocities and vices, which would render a plebeian an outcast from mankind.— God forbid, ever such Ideas should become common to Britons,—that Nobility should have a right to act immorally with impunity;—or that a degrading odium should be affixed on those, who without prejudice, or passion, from the innate dictates of rectitude, despise a bad man, however great.

We every day see, that virtue,—truth,— and integrity cannot be conveyed by the patents that bestow those splendid titles, which ever flow from the Throne; the never failing source of Nobility:—and, it is the pride and best prerogative of Britons that our Constitution, gloriously permits, even the humblest of mankind to be exalted,— if distinguished by virtue, or as faithful servants to their Country; which shews, that the tendency of this Comedy is not only irreproachable, but worthy of praise; from its proving, that virtue alone aggrandizes the Man: [...]

Did the folly, and dissipation of the age, permit now of the growth of a Philosopher, I have no doubt, but that he would tell us, that the misfortunes and humiliations, that have overwhelmed the exalted in neighbouring countries, arose from this very misconception, that it is dangerous to unveil the errors of those of superior rank.— The nobles in France usurped a right, almost divine, like the wax images in their Churches, of being kept behind the curtain from Plebeian eyes; those were deemed guilty, of sacriledge if they used their reason or senses, in descrying their imperfections. But did this soothe the disaffection of the people, or engage the Nobles to act with more moderation and virtue? No, and this age is too enlightened for opinion to be restrained, or a barrier to be placed by Priest-craft on thought.— Oh! How much more flattering is it for Rulers to be acknowledged our superiors from integrity and worth, than from those fears which power awakens in the ignorant, abject mind?— But to deem it criminal for the inferior orders of mankind to judge of virtue and vice, revolts the human mind: This System once adopted in France, that it was the Prerogative of the Nobles to be free from censure, —ridicule, or comparison, filled the honest mind with contempt, or hatred; whilst the Great, with haughty arrogance exulted in indulgences, which would have been deemed crimes in their inferiors; [...] and misery, alas, became contagious in Europe!

Happy! Thrice happy, had the French Nation been! Had the press, or drama permitted those who were disinterested in the cause of honor and humanity, to raise their voice, to reprobate or ridicule their vices;—and by holding the mirror up to their deformity, have enabled them to foresee the horrors which surrounded them; they would have shuddered at their danger. It was then too late to blind the eyes of the People, it only remained to open theirs; to reflect that they were men,—to be judged by men; and that although ennobled, they could be excelled by even the humblest of men, if more virtuous. This reflection might have rescued them in time from vices, immoralities, and cruelties, which have finally hurled them from their fancied greatness, and deprived them of even the *Rights of Men*!

The Stage is the only school which overgrown boys and girls can go to, and did the Licencer permit more satire, more sentiment, and less ribaldry, *outré* pantomime, and folly, to appear under his auspices, it would be doing the State more service, than thus taking the alarm at *The Whim* of renewing the Saturnalia Feast: and that too, from a pen, which although not paid by the Minister for either writing or inspecting pieces, yet which does him ever far more honor by disinterested admiration of his virtues, than any venal dependant could do. My Sentiments are the dictates of unprejudiced conviction, and my approbation never bestowed but upon unquestionable merit. That many of our great people are by their immoral and injudicious conduct destructive to the respectability and tranquility of the community, it is by no means possible to conceal, it would be only cherishing, and nursing a mortal disease in embryo to conceal it; —how then is the evil to be remedied?—By remonstrance from the pulpit, and by ridicule from the stage, by public and private censure of those who forget what they owe to their high situations; for the great are certainly doubly pledged to their country, to act with more distinguished virtue, good faith, and benevolence, in return for those honors bestowed upon them.—Nor, does it add, to the disgust which their conduct causes to point out the diseased part were it true, that *"all robes and furred gowns"* hid nothing but depravities and corruption our situation would be bad indeed, and it would be dangerous to call the attention of the people to so irritating a calamity—but, although the dissipated and profligate are too numerous, yet has not England to boast men of high birth, as well as men of inferior rank, even, at the very helm of Government, both civil and military, who possess virtues which add glory to birth, and splendor to any situation? happy would it be, if every object, either more exalted or more humble, were attracted by these men, who are distinguished by the brilliancy of their social and moral virtues: by emulating them they'd rob satire of its sting; nor dread the contempt attending on ridicule:— But away from our liberal shores the vile unnatural idea, that grandeur, should not be censured, — and that reason should not see, and honor disapprove, their depravities, without the imputation of Jacobins, Democrats, or what not.

Such unmerited accusations render ludicrous what should be respected; and confound bad subjects with the most independant, and honorable characters, which Britain can boast: —those who have unquestionably served their Country, and who fervently wish for the respectability and safety of all its members.—

It would be well if the Licencer in his idle hours would inspect the News-papers, and issue his fiat against private slanders, with which the cut-throat prints, the corrupt vehicles of private envy-revenge-and falsehood, are ever filled;—they in the one line declaim against the assassinations of Paris, and in the next, without one passion to excite, stab the domestick tranquility, or fair fame of innocence; which is daily a pray, butchered by the rascality of some News-paper Devil, paid by those who are either instigated by private or political spite; better this, then to prevent the follies of the age from meeting ridicule on the stage: not to permit it, is acting unfairly by the great – it is withholding from their view a picture of that contempt, which the humble honest mind liberally bestows, on the corrupted, however exalted by fortune or the chance of birth: – truths which the awful distance they keep, and the deference ever paid to rank, may prevent them otherwise from being made acquainted with –

I shall not intrude longer on your patience than by calling your attention to the last speech in the Comedy. I leave you to judge, if it is not expressive of such respect for the British Constitution, as should prove acceptable to all mankind; – one thing I am sure of, that if all our Peers were to form so proper, and honourable a determination, they would have no reason to fear the pen of Satire, or the uplifted finger of Scorn. –

LORD CROTCHET

"I for my part never again shall give up, even for a day, the duties of my situation; but ever endeavour to act worthily as a member of one of the three parts of our glorious Constitution; who, I hope, will each for ages yet to come, discharge uncorruptibly, and distinctly, their several Duties: without encroaching on each others prerogative, so that the name of Briton, may prove to the latest ages, an example to Nations, and the admiration of Mankind."

Please see the Works Cited for further information on the sources used in this essay.

Notes

1 Larpent was the Lord Chamberlain's Examiner of Plays from 1778 to 1824. In later years Larpent was unofficially assisted by his second wife, Anna Margaretta Porter, whom he married in April 1782. See LA 1093.
2 *The Larpent Catalogue* shows that between 1776 and 1800 only seven plays were denied a license.
3 George Taylor suggests that Wallace's *The Whim* might have been influenced by Marivaux' *Le Jeu de l'amour et du hazard* (1730), translated into English by Lady Mary Wortley Montagu (Taylor 234).

Suggestions for Further Reading

Conolly, Leonard W. *The Censorship of the English Drama 1737–1824.* San Marino, CA: Huntington Library, 1976.
Forster, Antonia, "Thomas Holcroft and Reviewing Traditions." *Re-Viewing Thomas Holcroft, 1745–1809: Essays on His Works and Life.* Eds. Miriam L. Wallace and A. A. Markley. London and New York: Routledge, 2016. 167–180.
Morning Chronicle, 11 April 1788.
Owen, D. J. and H. D. Symonds, eds. *Flower of the Jacobins: Containing Biographical Sketches of the Characters at Present at the Head of Affairs in France.* 3rd ed. London, n.p., 1793. 74.

12 SALLY SIDDONS (1775–1803)

Laura Engel

Introduction

Sally Siddons, daughter of the famous actress Sarah Siddons (1755–1831), is perhaps best known for her tumultuous affair with the Regency painter, Sir Thomas Lawrence (1769–1830). Their entanglement involved Sally's sister, Maria, who captured Lawrence's heart first, only to be supplanted by Sally. Both sisters suffered from consumption. On her death bed, Maria extracted a promise from Sally never to be with Lawrence. This enraged him for a short time, and he began to stalk Sally while she was on tour with her mother. Eventually, Lawrence lost interest in Sally, moving on to other conquests, but she continued to love Lawrence until her early death in 1803 at the age of 24. The story of this love triangle, narrated in a series of letters later published by Oswald G. Knapp in a volume entitled *An Artist's Love Story* (1905), gives us a rich understanding of Sally's complexity.[1] A talented singer and composer in her own right, Sally was deeply involved in the theatrical culture of the 1790s and early 1800s both backstage as Sarah Siddons' companion and in the audience as a skeptical critic. This selection of letters below highlights Sally's evaluation of current plays and performers; her astute observations about her mother's extraordinary fame; and her portrayal of the space of the theatre as a social world of desire and intrigue. Sally stages her love affair with Lawrence against the backdrop of the theatre suggesting the powerful ways in which the public arena of performance provided an opportunity for women in the late eighteenth century to be immersed in a world beyond the confines of domestic space.[2]

In a 1798 letter to her dear friend Miss Bird, Sally chronicles her latest outings at the theatre, providing a unique perspective on the heyday of Gothic drama. Her sharp evaluation of Matthew Lewis' hit, *The Castle Spectre,* is particularly significant in thinking about the role of spectacle in theatrical and popular culture.[3] She was delighted by the effect of the ghost, but found the actual play boring and the performances terrible. Sally's criticism of Dorothy Jordan, the most famous comedic actress of the day and a rival of her mother's, is also a comment on Jordan's inability to act tragic roles, which were Sarah Siddons' forte.[4]

The same letter moves on to Sally's review of the first night of George Colman the Younger's musical afterpiece *Blue Beard*–re-imagined as an Orientalist fantasy–at Drury Lane. The plot revolves around the relationship between two sisters, Fatima (the heroine forced to marry Bluebeard) and her sister Irene (formerly the character of Anne). In Colman's version, Irene is both the instigator of Fatima's treacherous search of the forbidden section of the castle and also her sister's savior when she

DOI: 10.4324/9781003006923-13

waves a handkerchief to signal travelers to come and rescue them in the end. Sally's admiration of the scene with Anne/Irene on the tower–describing it as "capitally manag'd and interesting to an excess, the pleasure of which is almost painful" (20)–may be tied to her complex feeling about her vibrant sister Maria as both a beloved sibling and a rival for her lover's affections. Perhaps significantly, Sally turns to her musical compositions at the end of the letter, asking Miss Bird "if my songs continue to be favorites" (20). For Sally, hearing music at the theatre was connected to gathering fuel and inspiration for her own musical practice.

Sally often includes thoughts about her mother's performances in her letters. She describes her mother's presence and beauty on stage as well as the reaction of her adoring fans. "I wish very much to have seen my Mother in 'Zara' to-night, I attended her Toilette, and she did look so beautiful!" (185). Although a critic for *The Lady's Magazine* agreed with Sally, rhapsodizing about Siddons' beauty and declaring "She is her own ornament" ("In a Letter" 580), a few months later her performance of Elvira in Richard Brinsley Sheridan's drama *Pizarro* resulted in a widely circulated caricature of Siddons by Robert Dighton depicting her as a very large looming figure.[5]

Two letters near the end of the correspondence highlight the ways in which the space of the theatre represents Sally's emotional connection to Lawrence and her mother. Sarah Siddons and Lawrence continued to have a personal and professional relationship long after his affair with her daughters had ended. In a final letter about Lawrence, Sally describes desperately trying to catch his attention at the theatre, staring at him directly through an opera glass, only to be ignored and dismissed. Sally Siddons' experience of the theatre is inextricably related to the culture of late eighteenth-century celebrity and to the intersections among actresses and artists.[6] Her letters convey a heightened sense of the ways in which the theatre magnified and complicated the emotional inner lives of audience members.

Sally Siddons

Excerpts from: **An Artist's Love Story: Told in the Letters of Sir Thomas Lawrence, Mrs. Siddons, and her Daughters** *(1798–1801, pub. 1905)*

Sally Siddons to Miss Bird[7]
Sunday, January 28th, 1798

I should not have suffer'd your last letter to remain so long unanswer'd, my dear Miss Bird, but that I waited to send you news of Maria's return to the Drawing Room, where she has now been for several days, and is recovering her strength and good looks every day. But here she must remain, Dr. Pierson says, during the cold weather, which means I suppose, all the Winter, and the Thermometer still hangs up to direct the degree of heat. But surely if every confinement was supportable, it must be to Maria, for she not only sees all our friends and acquaintance as usual, but the visits of her *first friend*[8] are unremitted, and should (should they not?) console her for everything. [...]

Since Maria has been so much better, and has had so agreeable a companion, I have been out to amuse *my*self two or three times. I have at last seen the Castle Spectre, and was delighted quite beyond expression when the Spectre did appear, but what a deal of dullness one has to wade thro' before she comes! And how ridiculous some of Mrs. Jordan's attempts at the pathetic are![9] I could really scarcely forbear laughing out right two or three times. I was at Drury Lane too, the first night of

Blue Beard; some of the Music is charming, and the scene where Sister Anne (as she was call'd in the old story) appears on the Tower, is capitally manag'd and interesting to an excess, the pleasure of which is almost painful. I was delighted at that part of the piece, and very angry at, and very much tir'd with much of it; they have not told the story by any means well.[10]

Tell me, dear Miss Bird, if you sing often, and if my songs continue to be favourites; I'm sure, if you sing them, you will gain me, as well as yourself, a great deal of credit, so don't discard them for my sake.

And now, having reach'd the end of the third page, I will finish my letter. Write to me soon, and believe me ever yours, with sincere esteem and affection,

S. SIDDONS

Sally Siddons to Mrs. Pennington[11]
London, January 8th 1799

[...]Ann and Harriet Lee[12] were with us on Sunday evening; they are both looking very well, and are so gay, and so much engag'd it is difficult to get a peep of them. Dear Mr Whalley too was here; I hear not a word of his Play; I cannot help wishing he would withdraw it, for it never can succeed. The new Play of "Aurelio and Miranda" is quite at an end, I fancy; I went to see it last week and I think I should have fall'n asleep, if our little Cecilia had not been of the party.[13] We took her to see "Blue Beard," and she was more interesting and entertaining than you can imagine: it was quite delightful to hear and see her, and she has done nothing but act Sister Ann upon the tower, waving her handkerchief, ever since. I have great hopes that my Father will take her with us to Bath, and leave her with Miss Lee. I lament every day that she has no companions of her own age. I would not commit her to the care of Servants, and yet her extreme restlessness and high spirits are often too much for me.

My Mother is just gone to pay a round of visits, which I am happy to escape; she desir'd me to say all that was kind for her to you, and pray remember us all with the most friendly good wishes to dear Mr. and Mrs. Piozzi, and tell him I hope he will sing some Italian duetts with me if we do come to Bath.[14] Adieu, my dear Mrs Pennington! Believe me ever your grateful and affectionate

S.M.S.

Sally Siddons to Miss Bird
S. James' Parade, Bath, February 8th, 1799

We intend going to the Ball next Monday, where we should already have been, but for my unfortunate illness. I lament this deprivation the less as I understand that the Balls are so crowded there is no possibility of moving, much less of dancing, and it is the dance I love, and not the crowd, I do not on my account feel much disappointment [...] I wish'd very much to have seem my Mother in 'Zara' to-night, I attended her Toilette, and she did look so beautiful![15] It is a part I love to see her act extremely. I have been but to one of the Plays, that was to the 'Grecian Daughter' the first night.[16] The people are all as mad about my Mother as if they had never seen her: it is delightfully gratifying to see their eagerness for places every night of her performance, and on the third day after our arrival here, every place was taken for this night, her Benefit.[17]

Sally Siddons to Miss Bird
December 25th, 1799

You may have heard (and it is true) of Mr. L[awrence] being in Mrs. Kemble's[18] Box, and with my Mother. I fancy she often sees him at the Theatre, but you have indeed been misinformed by those who told you he was ever of *our party*. All I ever see of him is now and then at the Theatre, when he just appears for a minute, as if *purposely* to make me a formal bow, and then he generally goes away to some other part of the house, I suppose. My Mother told me the other night that he was very well and in very good spirits, which will, I sincerely hope, continue. I am less likely than any one to inform you how he spends his time. All I know of him is that he is painting, and means to paint my Uncle as Hamlet[19] and that my Mother says the sketch is *very beautiful*; that he is frequently at my Uncle's house, and I believe scarcely ever misses a night when my Mother performs, when he generally pays a visit to her dressing room. This I hear not from my mother, for unless I force her to it, she never mentions him.

Sally Siddons to Miss Bird
February 13, 1801

I write, my dear namesake, to tell you my grievances, and because I think by your means I may gain some information I very much wish for. I was last night at Drury Lane where I saw Mr. L——— for the first time these *many many weeks*. Well, as soon as I thought I perceiv'd his eyes turn'd toward me, I bow'd to him; he did not return my salutation, and I supposed I had been mistaken in thinking he was looking at me. I waited a little, and then feeling sure his looks were fixed upon our Box, I bow'd *three* times, still he took not the least notice. I began to feel a little surpris'd and almost to fancy he *would* not see me; to be certain of this I took an Opera Glass, caught his eye, and immediately repeated my salutation *three times*, he actually star'd me in the face, without even once smiling, or answering me with the smallest inclination of his head. This behavior *astonishes and grieves me*; tell me, my dear namesake (for only you can), to what I am to attribute this amazing change. I cannot believe he means to insult me—nor do I know in what I can have offended him. You can find this out—and I entreat you do. Separated for ever as we are, I would still live in his memory as a friend he esteems and regrets, and to think that he can quite forget me, and after not seeing me for so long a time behave to me as he did last night, gives me great uneasiness […] I have never ceased to express the interest I take in him, in his fortunes, in his sentiments, and I had flatter'd myself that tho' every former hope was by *both of us resign'd*, I should not in passing from his heart, be mixed with the many who had gone before and were forgotten. The kind professions of your friendship make me think you will not think any excuse necessary, and that you will not a moment delay doing what I request. I cannot now begin on any indifferent subject. So adieu, my dear girl. Believe me ever yours, sincerely and affectionately,

S. M. SIDDONS

Please see the Works Cited for further information on the sources used in this essay.

Notes

1 All quotations from the letters are from this edition.
2 See Engel, "Mommy Diva" and Day and Rauser.
3 See Joseph Roach, "Pretty Ghost."
4 See Asleson and Helen Brooks.
5 See Coture and the Victoria and Albert Museum Collection Database: http://collections.vam.ac.uk/item/O1138604/sarah-siddons-as-elvira-in-print-dighton-the-elder/
6 See McPherson.
7 Little is known about Miss Sarah/Sally Bird, except that at this time she was staying at Thomas Lawrence's house on Greek Street as the guest of Lawrence's sister. See Goldring 122; Knapp 34.
8 Likely a reference to Thomas Lawrence.
9 The extremely popular 1797 gothic play *The Castle Spectre* by Mathew "Monk" Lewis then featured comic actress Dorothy Jordan (1761–1816) in the role of Angela. See The London Stage Database, 1660–1800. https://www.eighteenthcenturydrama.amdigital.co.uk/LondonStage/Database
10 *Blue Beard or Female Curiosity* was a 1798 afterpiece by George Coleman the Younger. See The London Stage Database, 1660–1800 for production details. https://www.eighteenthcenturydrama.amdigital.co.uk/LondonStage/Database
11 Penelope Pennington nee Weston (1757–1827) is perhaps best known for her correspondence with diarist and social historian, Hester Thrale Piozzi (1741–1821).
12 Sisters, playwrights and novelists, Sophia Lee (1750–1824) and Harriet Lee (1757–1821) also ran a school for young ladies in Bath. See Garwood.
13 Thomas Sedgwick Whalley's 1799 play, *The Castle of Montval* starred Sarah Siddons as the Countess of Montval. James Boaden's 1798 *Aurelio and Miranda: A Drama In Five Acts* was an adaptation of Matthew Lewis' novel *The Monk*. See David.
14 Gabriel Piozzi (1740–1809), husband of Hester Thrale Piozzi, was an Italian singer and composer.
15 See "In a Letter to a Lady" for confirmation of Sally's observations.
16 *Zara* (1736) was Aaron Hill's adaptation of Voltaire's play *Zaïre* (1732). *The Grecian Daughter* (1772) was a tragedy by Arthur Murphy.
17 Benefit performances designated ticket revenues, less expenses, for a specific actor.
18 The Kembles were a legendary British theatre family, of which Sarah Siddons was a member.
19 Thomas Lawrence's portrait of "John Philip Kemble as Hamlet" (1801) is now at the Tate Museum in London. https://www.tate.org.uk/art/artworks/lawrence-john-philip-kemble-as-hamlet-n00142.

Suggestions for Further Reading

Engel, Laura. *Fashioning Celebrity: Eighteenth-Century British Actresses and Strategies for Image Making.* Columbus: Ohio State University Press, 2011.

Nussbaum, Felicity. *Rival Queens: Actresses, Performance, and the Eighteenth-Century British Theater.* Philadelphia: University of Pennsylvania Press, 2010.

Perry, Gill. *Spectacular Flirtations: Viewing the Actress in British Art and Theatre 1768–1820.* New Haven: Yale University Press, 2008.

Robinson, Terry F. "'The Glass of Fashion and the Mould of Form': The Histrionic Mirror and Georgian Era Performance." *Eighteenth-Century Life* 39.2 (2015): 30–55.

13 ELIZABETH INCHBALD (1753–1821)

Lisa A. Freeman

Introduction

Of the one hundred and twenty-five prefatory remarks that Elizabeth Inchbald (1753–1821) was commissioned to write for Longman's *British Theatre* series in 1806, twenty-four focused on plays by Shakespeare. Inchbald had emerged in the late eighteenth and early nineteenth centuries as the most successful playwright on the London stage, and Longman was clearly looking to capitalize on her reputation when it solicited her to offer commentaries for this collection drawn from the promptbook play copies used at the Drury Lane, Covent Garden, and Haymarket patent theatres and designed as such to reflect the contemporary playhouse repertory.

Inchbald's "Remarks" on Shakespeare's plays are distinguished from those of her contemporaries by her particular interest in the plays as works meant to be performed, a characteristic in line with her keen observations on the art of dramatic representation across the entirety of her one hundred and twenty-five entries. Where other, more vaunted critics of the Romantic age, such as William Hazlitt and Charles Lamb, were calling not only for the elevation of the works of the Bard to the sphere of universal genius but also for their removal from the sullied stages to the pristine confines of the closet—a call which if enacted would have left a huge gap in playhouse repertories and devastated their bottom lines—Inchbald approached the plays as live, textual objects that were meant to be performed before an audience and adapted to suit current tastes and playhouse capacities.[1] For her, the genius of Shakespeare's plays resides not in the distant entombment of their meaning in some kind of idealized time immemorial but rather in their adaptability to popular tastes, their embodiment on the stage, and their presence in living memory.

In the example of her "Remarks" on *King Lear* provided below, we can see Inchbald's emphasis on the historical, political, and social contexts in which a play is performed and on the audience's ability to draw contemporary parallels and to read new resonances into current stage productions.[2] Thus she meditates on the parallels that might be drawn between the usurpation of King Lear and the plight of James II, whose daughters, Mary and Anne, joined forces with Protestant armies to drive their Catholic father out of England in the 1688–1689 Glorious Revolution. While Inchbald's personal loyalties to Catholicism are strongly felt in her sympathies for James II, so too is her aptness to engage not just with the political resonances of theatrical representations but also with the political crises and settlements that marked her own age. Here, as well as in her entries on a number of other Shakespeare plays,

DOI: 10.4324/9781003006923-14

including those for *Coriolanus* and *Julius Caesar,* Inchbald engages in the kinds of political commentary and public judgment that were supposedly proscribed for women. For her endeavors in this vein, Inchbald came under considerable fire, including from her first biographer James Boaden, who thought that women should have nothing to do either with politics or with the province of criticism.[3]

It is significant to note in this light that even as Inchbald refers to herself self-deprecatingly in this entry as a "minor critic," her claims for authority rest on her rather sly intimations about disagreements among the male critics of the day (5). Whether she is referring to questions about the historicity of events represented in *King Lear,* or to the critical controversies surrounding the merits of Nahum Tate's 1681 adaptation of *King Lear* in which Cordelia lives to marry Edgar—the version of *King Lear* that still held the stage at the time of her writing as did so many other Restoration and eighteenth-century adaptations of Shakespeare—Inchbald intimates that such a lack of critical consensus provides a space for her own reasoned voice. Just as significantly, she also marks the extent of her own reading and cuts off those who might undermine her authority by casting her either as unschooled or unread.[4] Not only is she able to cite Shakespearean editors such as Edmond Malone, Samuel Johnson, and George Steevens, but so too does she display her reading of history and philosophy.

Finally, what becomes clear in her observations on other critics' responses to Tate's *King Lear* is her apparent lack of concern that the great bard had been adapted, altered, or transformed. Indeed, if anything, her objection here lies in the fact that Tate did not alter Shakespeare enough, leaving intact what she takes to be the inordinately spectacular display of violence in the gouging of Gloucester's eyes. While Samuel Johnson may have "vindicated this frightful incident by saying, 'Shakspeare well knew that would please the audience for which he wrote,'" she objects, "yet this argument is no apology for the correctors of Shakspeare, who have altered the drama to gratify spectators more refined, and yet have not expunged this savage and improbable act" (5). For Inchbald, the point of adapting Shakespeare's plays was to make them more playable and palatable for contemporary spectators. With Tate, she agreed, then, that *King Lear* offered a "heap of jewels, unstrung, and unpolished," and with an ease that must have sent shivers of horror through her male Romantic counterparts, she embraced the idea that they should be polished and restrung to suit audience tastes. This should not surprise us when we recall again that whereas these writers grounded their arguments in their reading of fine-printed editions of Shakespeare, Inchbald's insights were drawn primarily from her observations on the live performances that were guided by promptbook copies. Not only were the texts on which their criticism was based vastly different, raising questions about the extent to which the choice of texts shapes our understanding in Shakespeare criticism, but so too was their sense of what aroused audiences to an attentive and productive engagement with the plays.

Elizabeth Inchbald
Remarks on *King Lear* (1806)

> *KING LEAR;*
> *A TRAGEDY*
> *IN FIVE ACTS;*
> *By WILLIAM SHAKSPEARE.*

AS PERFORMED AT THE THEATRES-ROYAL,
DRURY-LANE AND COVENT-GARDEN
PRINTED UNDER THE AUTHORITY OF THE MANAGERS
FROM THE PROMPT BOOK.
WITH REMARKS
BY MRS. INCHBALD
LONDON:
PRINTED FOR LONGMAN, HURST, REES, ORME, AND BROWN,
PATERNOSTER ROW.

REMARKS.

The story of this Tragedy has been told in many an ancient ballad, and other ingenious works; but Mr Malone supposes, that Shakspeare is more indebted for his fable to "The true Chronicle History of King Lear and his three Daughters, Goneril, Regan, and Cordelia," than to any other production.

Camden, in his Remains,[5] gives the following account of an English King, which is also similar to the story of Leir, or Lear:—

"Ina, King of the West Saxons, had three daughters, of whom, upon a time, he demanded, whether they did love him, and so would do during their lives, above all others? The two elder sware deeply they would; the youngest, but the wisest, told her father flatly, that albeit she did love, honour, and reverence him, and so would whilst she lived, as much as nature and daughterly duty at the uttermost could expect; yet she did think that one day it would come to pass, that she should affect another more fervently, meaning her husband, when she were married."

This relation, the commentator imagines, may probably have been applied to King Lear, who, Geoffrey of Monmouth says, "Nobly governed his country for sixty years, and died about eight hundred years before the birth of Christ."[6]

Notwithstanding the number of histories and books of fiction that have promulgated this piteous tale of a monarch and his children, it remains a doubt among the most learned on the subject, whether such an event, as here described, ever, in reality, occurred.

But, if it never did before the time of Shakspeare, certainly something very like it has taken place since. Lear is not represented much more affectionate to his daughters by Shakspeare, than James the Second is by Hume.[7] James's daughters were, besides, under more than ordinary obligations to their king and father, for the tenderness he had evinced towards their mother, in raising her from a humble station to the elevation of his own; and thus preserving these two princesses from the probable disgrace of illegitimate birth.

Even to such persons as hold it was right to drive King James from the throne, it must be a subject of lamentation, that his beloved children were the chief instruments of those concerned. When the king was informed that his eldest daughter, Mary, was landed, and proceeding to the metropolis, in order to dethrone him, he called, as the historian relates, for the princess Anne—and called for her by the tender description of his "dear, his only remaining daughter." On the information given to his majesty in return, that "she had forsook the palace to join her sister," the king wept and tore his hair.

Lear, exposed on a bleak heath, suffered not more than James, at one of our seaports, trying to escape to France. King Lear was only pelted by a storm, King James by his merciless subjects.

Not one of Shakspeare's plays more violently agitates the passions than this tragedy; parents and children are alike interested in every character, and instructed by each. There is, nevertheless, too much of ancient cruelty in many of the events. An audience finds horror prevail over compassion on Gloster's loss of his eyes: and though Dr Johnson has vindicated this frightful incident, by saying, "Shakspeare well knew what would please the audience for which he wrote," yet this argument is no apology for the correctors of Shakspeare, who have altered the drama to gratify spectators more refined, and yet have not expunged this savage and improbable act.

The nice distinction which the author has made between the real and the counterfeit madman in this tragedy, is a part of the work particularly admired by the experienced observers of that fatal disorder; and, to sum up the whole worth of the production, the reader may now say of it, with some degree of qualification, what Tate said before he had employed much time and taste on the alteration: "It is a heap of jewels, unstrung and unpolished, yet so dazzling in their disorder, that I soon perceived I had seized a treasure."

It is curious and consolatory for a minor critic to observe, how the great commentators on Shakspeare differ in their opinions.

Tate alters the play of King Lear, and instead of suffering the good Cordelia to die of grief, as Shakspeare had done, he rewards her with life, love, and a throne. Addison, in his Spectator, condemns him for this; Dr Johnson commends him for it; both showing excellent reasons.[8] Then comes Steevens, who gives a better reason than all, why they are all wrong.

Please see the Works Cited for further information on the sources used in this essay.

Notes

1 For one of the more sustained discussions of Inchbald's *Remarks* on Shakespeare in this vein, see Gevirtz.

2 All of the citations for Inchbald's "Remarks" on *King Lear* have been taken from the text reproduced below: Volume IV of *The British Theatre; Or, A Collection of Plays, Which Are Acted at the Theatres Royal, Drury Lane, Covent Garden, and Haymarket*, held by the Newberry Library. All of Inchbald's *Remarks* have been gathered in alphabetical order with individual pagination in a facsimile edition by Cecelia Macheski, *Remarks for the British Theatre (1806–1809) by Elizabeth Inchbald*.

3 See James Boaden, *Memoirs of Mrs. Inchbald*, II.84.

4 According to Fiona Ritchie, "Inchbald clearly enters into the field of Shakespeare scholarship in her remarks, demonstrating her learning and engaging with her male peers. Her work proves that despite what Boaden may have thought, women were capable of acquiring and exercising learning and therefore of writing criticism" (104).

5 Inchbald refers here to William Camden's *Remaines of a greater worke, concerning Britaine, the inhabitantes thereof, their languages, names, surnames, empreses, wise speeches, poësies, and epitaphes* (1605).

6 Inchbald refers here to Geoffrey of Monmouth's *Historia Regum Britanniae* or *History of the Kings of Britain* (c. 1136).

7 Inchbald refers here to the philosopher David Hume's *History of England* (1754–1762).

8 Inchbald refers here to Joseph Addison's *Spectator* essay no. 40 (16 April 1711), from *The Spectator*, a groundbreaking periodical publication that Addison co-authored with Richard Steele from 1711–1712.

92   *Lisa A. Freeman*

Suggestions for Further Reading

Bennett, Susan. "The Making of Theatre History." *Representing the Past: Essays in Performance Historiography*. Eds. Charlotte M. Canning and Thomas Postlewait. Iowa City: University of Iowa Press, 2010. 63–83.

Burroughs, Catherine B. *Closet Stages: Joanna Baillie and the Theater Theory of British Romantic Women Writers*. Philadelphia: University of Pennsylvania Press, 1997.

Waters, Mary A. *British Women Writers and the Profession of Literary Criticism, 1789-1832*. Basingstoke: Palgrave Macmillan, 2004.

14 JOANNA BAILLIE (1762–1851)

Thomas C. Crochunis

Introduction

Scottish poet, playwright, and essayist Joanna Baillie (1762–1851) remains of literary importance today for her dramatic and critical writing. She published her first volume of *A Series of Plays in Which It Is Attempted to Delineate the Stronger Passions of the Mind* (hereafter the *Series of Plays*) anonymously, but when they received critical attention for their dramatic innovation, she claimed them as her own, going on to publish–between 1798 and 1851–several additional volumes in the series containing a total of 27 plays. Despite only modest stage success, her dramatic writing was much reviewed and discussed by other writers of her era.

As early as 1800, critics of London's Drury Lane Theatre production of Baillie's *DeMonfort,* starring legendary actors John Kemble and Sarah Siddons, alerted readers to the noteworthy connection between the play's author and the medical men in her family; her brother Matthew's Gulstonian Lectures, published in 1794, outline a neural theory of emotion that anticipates Joanna's dramatic theory. There, he explains, "Each emotion [...] sets in action its appropriate muscles, producing a change in the countenance and attitude, which is expressive of emotion. This becomes a natural language, and is not connected with any arbitrary customs of society" (M. Baillie 146). Limiting himself to characterizing the human mechanisms by which emotions take shape and are expressed, he imagines that we read each other's emotional behavior as a "natural language."[1] Joanna Baillie's plays, however, rather than presuming that case studies of passions could be "naturally" absorbed, activate dialogue with impassioned behavior by engaging audiences and readers in interpreting emotion and its effects. She manipulates the rhetoric of theatre practices of her time—dialogue, actor expression, stage groupings, spectacular scenery, processions, tableaux—to effect moral realizations in theatre audiences.[2] But Baillie also uses the *idea of theatre* to draw readers into an intimate imaginative experience of the public enactment of impassioned states and to heighten a play's moral effect on its reader-audience.

Baillie's "Introductory Discourse" to the first volume of the *Series of Plays* captures the intense appeal that the signs of others' emotion have for us: "If invisible, would we not follow him into his lonely haunts, into his closet, into the midnight silence of his chamber?" (J. Baillie 11). Baillie envisions audiences and readers engaging with the passions of dramatic characters through a process of imaginative inquiry. In the preface to her third play volume (1812), excerpted here, Baillie extends such comments into a more detailed consideration of the ways in which contemporary

DOI: 10.4324/9781003006923-15

theatres and acting were at odds with the psychological experience of simulated passion that her plays sought to create. Baillie discusses how hearing an actor's voice speaking the words and seeing the actor's nuanced expression of emotions draw interpreters into the psychological experience of a character's passions. But Baillie also notes that poor sound and sight, especially in London's inadequately lit larger theatres, disconnect moments of emotional expression, disrupting the desired psychological effects on audiences and preventing their gaining social insights from her characters and narratives.

Baillie's s(t)imulative dramaturgy of the passions also has much in common with the philosophical writings of David Hume (1711–1776), whose *A Treatise of Human Nature* (1739–1740) describes the social significance of the passions as "performances in themselves" rather than effects created by logical chains of causality. Drawing additionally upon Adam Smith's (1723–1790) *Theory of Moral Sentiments* (1759), specifically the complex psychological and social dialogues that he suggests emotions produce, Baillie envisions stagecraft that would provoke audiences to engage in interpretive dialogue with the passion's performance. Finally, Denis Diderot's (1713–1784) theories of acting and painting envision an interaction between viewer and image that anticipate Baillie's interest in her audiences' private interpretive encounters with a character's emotions. While Baillie's critical comments on the theatre of her time are grounded in observed detail, they are informed by these other writers on the passions.[3]

For Baillie, the passions were not simply imitated but shaped into a sequence of audience observation, interpretation, and reflection. By entering into "sympathetic curiosity" with characters, her audiences (and reader-audiences) were able to explore passions through these characters' predicaments, and in so doing consider their own responses to emotional circumstances in life. Baillie's critique of the theatre in the 1812 "To the Reader" is not primarily a judgment on either audiences or stage professionals, but rather it underscores her belief that theatre could not play an important role in social education within the tolerances of the London stage of her time. Her recourse to closet theatricality—the use of imagined performance to enhance a reader's experience of printed drama—constitutes a significant theoretical and practical alternative grounded in the theories of emotion.

Joanna Baillie

Excerpt from "To the Reader," prefatory to the Third Volume of A Series of Plays [... on] the Stronger Passions of the Mind *(1812)*

[After apologizing for the long delay since publishing her last volume of the *Series of Plays [...on] the Stronger Passions*, Baillie describes the plays included in the current volume. Then she goes on to explain that she has decided to suspend publishing her planned series of plays on the passions, believing that retaining them in manuscript may prevent publication from harming their chances of being staged. She briefly weighs the effect large theatre venues have on the kinds of plays audiences have developed a taste for seeing, but then turns to the effects of theatre size on the audience's relationship with actors and characters.]

The size of our theatres then is what I chiefly allude to when I say, present circumstances are unfavourable for the production of these plays. While they continue to be of this size, it is a vain thing to complain either of want of taste in the Public, or want of inclination in managers to bring forward new pieces of merit, taking it for granted that there are such to produce. Nothing can be truly relished by the most cultivated audience that is not distinctly heard and seen, and managers must produce what will be relished. Shakspeare's Plays, and some of our other old plays, indeed, attract full houses, though they are often repeated, because, being familiar to the audience, they can still understand and follow them pretty closely, though but imperfectly heard; and surely this is no bad sign of our public taste. And besides this advantage, when a piece is familiar to the audience, the expression of the actors' faces is much better understood, though seen imperfectly; for the stronger marked traits of feeling which even in a large theatre may reach the eyes of a great part of the audience, from the recollection of finer and more delicate indications, formerly seen so delightfully mingled with them in the same countenances during the same passages of the play, will, by association, still convey them to the mind's eye, though it is the mind's eye only which they have reached.

And this thought leads me to another defect in large theatres that ought to be considered.

Our great tragic actress, Mrs. Siddons, whose matchless powers of expression have so long been the pride of our stage, and the most admired actors of the present time, have been brought up in their youth in small theatres,[4] where they were encouraged to enter thoroughly into the characters they represented, and to express in their faces that variety of fine fleeting emotion which nature in moments of agitation assumes, and the imitation of which we are taught by nature to delight in. But succeeding actors will only consider expression of countenance as addressed to an audience removed from them to a greater distance, and will only attempt such strong expression as can be perceived and have effect at a distance. It may easily be imagined what exaggerated expression will then get into use; and I should think, even this strong expression will not only be exaggerated but false: for, as we are enabled to assume the outward signs of passion, not by mimicking what we have beheld in others, but by internally assuming, in some degree, the passion itself; a mere outline of it cannot, I apprehend, be given as an outline of figure frequently is, where all that is delineated is true, though the whole is not filled up. Nay, besides having it exaggerated and false, it will perpetually be thrust in where it ought not to be. For real occasions of strong expression not recurring often enough, and weaker being of no avail, to avoid an apparent barrenness of countenance, they will be tempted to introduce it where it is not wanted, and thereby destroy its effect where it is,—I say nothing of expression of voice, to which the above observations obviously apply. This will become equally, if not in a greater degree, false and exaggerated, in actors trained from their youth in a large theatre.

But the department of acting that will suffer most under these circumstances, is that which particularly regards the gradual unfolding of the passions, and has, perhaps, hitherto been less understood than any other part of the art—I mean Soliloquy. What actor in his senses will then think of giving to the solitary musing of a perturbed mind, that muttered, imperfect articulation, which grows by degrees into words; that heavy, suppressed voice, as of one speaking through sleep; that rapid burst of sounds which often succeeds the slow languid tones of distress; those sudden, untuned exclamations, which, as if frightened at their own discord, are struck again into silence as sudden and abrupt, with all the corresponding variety of countenance that belongs to it;—what actor so situated will attempt to exhibit all this? No; he will be satisfied, after taking a turn or two across the front of the stage, to place himself directly in the middle of it; and there, spreading out his hands, as if he were addressing some person whom it behoved him to treat with great ceremony, to tell to himself, in an audible, uniform voice, all the secret thoughts of his own heart. When he has done this, he will think, and he will think rightly, that he has done enough.

The only valuable part of acting that will then remain to us will be expression of gesture, grace, and dignity, supposing that these also shall not become affected by being too much attended to and studied.

It may be urged against such apprehensions, that, though the theatres of the metropolis should be large, they will be supplied with actors who have been trained to the stage in small country theatres. An actor of ambition (and all actors of genius are such) will practise with little heart in the country what he knows will be of no use to him on a London stage; not to mention that the style of acting in London will naturally be the fashionable and prevailing style elsewhere. Acting will become a less respectable profession than it has continued to be from the days of Garrick;[5] and the few actors who add to the natural advantages requisite to it, the accomplishments of a scholar and a gentleman, will soon be weeded away by the hand of time, leaving nothing of the same species behind them to spring from a neglected and sapless root.

All I have said on this subject may still in a greater degree be applied to actresses; for the features and voice of a woman being naturally more delicate than those of a man, she must suffer in proportion from the defects of a large theatre.

The great disadvantage of such over-sized buildings to natural and genuine acting, is, I believe, very obvious; but they have other defects which are not so readily noticed, because they in some degree run counter to the common opinion of their great superiority in every thing that regards general effect. The diminutive appearance of individual figures, and the straggling poverty of grouping, which unavoidably takes place when a very wide and lofty stage is not filled by a great number of people, is very injurious to general effect. This is particularly felt in Comedy, and all plays on domestic subjects; and in those scenes also of the grand drama, where two or three persons only are produced at a time. To give figures who move upon it proper effect, there must be depth as well as width of stage; and the one must bear some proportion to the other, if we would not make every closer or more confined scene appear like a section of a long passage, in which the actors move before us, apparently in one line, like the figures of a magic lanthorn.

It appears to me, that when a stage is of such a size that as many persons as generally come into action at one time in our grandest and best-peopled plays, can be produced on the front of it in groups, without crowding together more than they would naturally do any where else for the convenience of speaking to one another, all is gained in point of general effect that can well be gained. When modern gentlemen and ladies talk to one another in a spacious saloon, or when ancient warriors and dames conversed together in an old baronial hall, they do not, and did not stand further apart than when conversing in a room of common dimensions; neither ought they to do so on the stage. All width of stage beyond what is convenient for such natural grouping, is lost; and worse than lost, for it is injurious. It is continually presenting us with something similar to that which always offends us in a picture, where the canvass is too large for the subject; or in a face, where the features are too small for the bald margin of cheeks and forehead that surrounds them [...].

[Baillie then describes a number of ways that more spectacular scenes are also affected by the size of theatres and related conditions before returning to the difficulty of creating convincing scenes on a stage space that is too wide.]

On those occasions too, when many people are assembled on the front of the stage to give splendour and importance to some particular scene, or to the conclusion of a piece, the general effect is often injured by great width of stage: for the crowd is supposed to be attracted to the spot by something which engages their attention; and, as they must not surround this object of attention (which would be their natural arrangement), lest they should conceal it from the audience, they are obliged to spread themselves out in a long straight line on each side of it: now the less those lines or wings are spread out from the centre figures, the less do they offend against natural arrangement, and the less artificial and formal does the whole scene appear.

In short, I scarcely know of any advantage which a large stage possesses over one of a moderate size without great abatements, even in regard to general effect, unless it be when it is empty, and scenery alone engages our attention, or when figures appear at a distance on the background only. Something in confirmation of what I have been saying has perhaps been felt by most people on entering a grand cathedral, where figures moving in the long aisles at a distance add grandeur to the building by their diminished appearance; but in approaching near enough to become themselves distinct objects of attention, look stunted and mean, without serving to enlarge by comparison its general dimensions.

It is also, I apprehend, more difficult on a very wide and lofty stage, to produce variety of light and shadow; and this often occasions the more solemn scenes of Tragedy to be represented in a full, staring, uniform light that ought to be dimly seen in twilight uncertainty; or to have the objects shown by partial gleams only, while the deepened shade around gives a sombre indistinctness to the other parts of the stage, particularly favourable to solemn or terrific impressions. And it would be more difficult, I imagine, to throw down light upon the objects on such a stage, which I have never indeed seen attempted in any theatre, though it might surely be done in one of moderate dimensions with admirable effect. In short, a great variety of pleasing effects from light and shadow might be more easily produced on a smaller stage, that would give change and even interest to pieces otherwise monotonous and heavy; and would often be very useful in relieving the exhausted strength of the chief actors, while want of skill in the inferior could be craftily concealed.* On this part of the subject, however, I speak with great diffidence, not knowing to what perfection machinery for the management of light may be brought in a large theatre. But at the same time, I am certain that, by a judicious use of light and scenery, an artificial magnitude may be given to a stage of a moderate size, that would, to the eye, as far as distance in perspective is concerned, have an effect almost equal to any thing that can be produced on a larger stage: for that apparent magnitude, arising from succession of objects, depends upon the depth of the stage, much more than its width and loftiness, which are often detrimental to it; and a small or moderate sized theatre may have, without injury to proportion, a very deep stage [...].

Please see the Works Cited for further information on the sources used in this essay.

Notes

1 See Frederick Burwick on Joanna Baillie's shared psychological interests with her brother Matthew.
2 See Jeffrey N. Cox, "Staging Baillie," on Baillie's uses of theatrical spectacle.
3 See Alan Richardson, Victoria Myers ("Joanna Baillie's Theatre of Cruelty"), and Christine Colón on connections between Baillie's dramaturgy and her predecessor theorists of moral influence.
4 Baillie here is referring to the provincial theatres in which many of London's actors began their careers.
5 David Garrick (1717–1779), renowned London actor.
* [Baillie's Note] That strong light cast up from lamps on the front of the stage, which has long been in use in all our theatres, is certainly very unfavourable to the appearance and expression of individual actors, and also to the general effect of their grouped figures. When a painter wishes to give intelligence and expression to a face, he does not make his lights hit upon the under part of his chin, the nostrils, and the under curve of the eye-brows, turning of course all the shadows upwards. He does the very reverse of all this; that the eye may look hollow and dark under the shade of its brow; that the shadow of the nose may shorten the upper lip, and give a greater character of sense to the mouth; and that any fulness of the under chin may be the better concealed. From this disposition of the light in our theatres, whenever an actor, whose features are not particularly sharp and pointed, comes near the front of the stage, and turns his face fully to the audience, every feature immediately becomes shortened, and less capable of any expression, unless it be of the ludicrous kind. This at least will be the effect produced to those who are seated under or on the same level with the stage, making now a considerable proportion of an audience; while to those who sit above it, the lights and shadows, at variance with the natural bent of the features, will make the whole face appear confused, and (compared to what it would have been with light thrown upon it from another direction) unintelligible.—As to the general effect of grouped figures: close groups or crowds, ranged on the front of the stage, when the light is thrown up upon them, have a harsh flaring appearance; for the foremost figures catch the light, and are too much distinguished from those behind, from whom it is intercepted. But when the light is thrown down upon the objects, this cannot be the case: for then it will glance along the heads of the whole crowd, even to the very bottom of the stage, presenting a varied harmonious mass of figures to the eye, deep, mellow, and brilliant […].

Suggestions for Further Reading

Burroughs, Catherine B. *Closet Stages: Joanna Baillie and the Theater Theory of British Romantic Women Writers*. Philadelphia: University of Pennsylvania Press, 1997.
Burwick, Frederick. "Joanna Baillie, Matthew Baillie, and the Pathology of the Passions." *Joanna Baillie, Romantic Dramatist: Critical Essays*. Ed. Thomas C. Crochunis. London: Routledge, 2004. 48–68.
Colón, Christine. *Joanna Baillie and the Art of Moral Influence*. Brussels: Peter Lang, 2009.
Myers, Victoria. "Joanna Baillie's Theatre of Cruelty." *Joanna Baillie, Romantic Dramatist: Critical Essays*. Ed. Thomas C. Crochunis. London: Routledge, 2004. 87–107.

15 FELICIA HEMANS (1793–1835)

Diego Saglia

Introduction

One of the most successful and celebrated poets of the Romantic era, Felicia Hemans (1793–1835) had a wide-ranging interest in drama and the theatre. A keen theatregoer as well as a playwright and a dramatic critic, her engagement with dramaturgy and performance was particularly intense in the middle phase of her career, between the early to mid-1820s. Her dramatic scenes "*Sebastian of Portugal* (from an unpublished Dramatic Poem)" appeared in the *Edinburgh Magazine and Literary Miscellany* in 1822. The following year saw the publication of her historical tragedies *The Vespers of Palermo* (performed at Covent Garden on 12 December 1823) and *The Siege of Valencia*, while another historical tragedy, *De Chatillon; or, the Crusaders*, begun in 1824, was left unfinished at her death and published posthumously in the 1839 edition of her works.

Her most significant contributions to dramatic criticism appeared in a series of articles on recent Italian literature, published in the *Edinburgh Magazine and Literary Miscellany* between October 1820 and June 1821, in which drama has a central place. These articles also present indirect references to politics, as they hint at the current subjugated state of the country and its potential for resurgence visible in the earliest manifestations of the *Risorgimento* process, which culminated in the unification of Italy (1861–1870). These references were in line with editorial policy at the *Edinburgh Magazine*, which often published pieces on Italy's historical, cultural, and political questions (for instance, it offered detailed reports on the fortunes of the Neapolitan revolution of 1820). The consonance between Hemans's and the periodical's attention towards Italy's national cause is apparent in her essay on "Patriotic Effusions of the Italian Poets," where she outlines the country's tradition of patriotic poetry "from the days of Dante and Petrarch, to those of Foscolo and Pindemonte" (513)

Published in June 1821, her essay "Italian Literature. No. IV. Caius Gracchus, a Tragedy, by Monti" discusses Vincenzo Monti's *Caio Gracco* (1800, first performed at La Scala, Milan, 1802) and centres on ideas of republican virtue in pre-imperial ancient Rome. As the play was composed during the author's phase as a supporter of, and a propagandist for, the ideals of the French Revolution, Hemans highlights how "the whole piece seems to be animated by that restless and untameable spirit of freedom, whose immortalized struggles for ascendency give so vivid a colouring, so exalted an interest, to the annals of the ancient republics" (515–516). Hemans also throws into relief the figure of Cornelia, the mother of the Gracchi, whose

DOI: 10.4324/9781003006923-16

"high-hearted" qualities and "collected majesty" make her an illustrious anteced-ent of Hemans's gallery of heroic females, especially those she created in *Siege* and *Vespers* (515).

Two more essays from this series deal with drama – "Italian Literature. No. II. The Alcestis of Alfieri" on Vittorio Alfieri's *Alceste* (1798), and "Italian Literature. No. III. Il Conte di Carmagnola, a Tragedy, by Alessandro Manzoni" on Manzoni's *Il Conte di Carmagnola* (1820). Published in December 1820, the former deals with one of Alfieri's less intensely political plays, though Hemans still concentrates her attention on the eponymous heroine as a model of female heroism and stoicism, recalling "to our imagination the calm and tempered majesty distinguishing the masterpieces of Greek sculpture" (513). In contrast, the piece on Manzoni's *Carmagnola*, excerpted here, examines a recent historical tragedy with strong political overtones and rich in allusions to contemporary events in Italy. Unable to expect her readers to be familiar with this *tranche* of late-medieval Italian history, Hemans dedicates much of the introduction to a summary of the life of the titular hero, Francesco Bussone Count of Carmagnola (1390–1432), a soldier of fortune and military commander of the Venetian armies in their war against the Duchy of Milan, sentenced to death by Venice on suspicion of treasonous dealings with the Milanese. Interspersed, like the articles on Monti and Alfieri, with abundant translations from the original, the article bears witness to the presence of libertarian impulses in Italy's contemporary literary and dramatic production in spite of its inclusion in the Austrian sphere of influence decreed by the Restoration settlement at the Congress of Vienna. Though Hemans is far from sounding any dangerously audible revolutionary notes, yet she does not consign the country to an inglorious destiny of political enslavement as does Henry Hart Milman in the conclusion to his review of Manzoni's *Carmagnola*, Ugo Foscolo's *Ricciarda*, and Silvio Pellico's *Francesca da Rimini* published in the *Quarterly Review* for October 1820. Indeed, she hints at the fact that *Carmagnola* is "a piece which has excited [...] much attention in Italy" but prefers to steer clear of controversy and dis-cuss it from a formal point of view, illustrating Manzoni's bold experiment in aban-doning "the fetters of the dramatic unities" ("Italian Literature. No. III", 123, 131). As is well known, however, Continental and thus also Italian debates on classical norms such as the Aristotelian dramatic unities, which were among the Romantic innovators' favourite targets, amounted to coded political polemics in countries where Restoration regimes quashed any kind of oppositional activity. In her 1821 essay on "Patriotic Effusions of the Italian Poets," Hemans pessimistically notes that, after the defeat of the revolutions of 1820–1821 in Sicily, Naples, and Piedmont, "[i]t is not, perhaps, *now*, the time to plead the cause of Italy" (513). Even so, her piece on Manzoni bears witness to a type of committed dramatic criticism that engages both with aesthetic questions and, albeit cautiously, with political issues, confirm-ing the interest in Italian drama and theatre typical of Britain's nineteenth-century Italophilia, as well as testifying to a Romantic-period line of politically committed dramatic criticism also actively promoted by women intellectuals.

Felicia Hemans

Excerpt from "Italian Literature No. III." (1821)

Il Conte di Carmagnola, a Tragedy, by Alessandro Manzoni

Francesco Bussone, the son of a peasant in Carmagnola, from whence his *nom de guerre* was derived, was born in the year 1390. Whilst yet a boy, and employed in the care of flocks and herds, the lofty character of his countenance was observed by a soldier of fortune, who invited the youth to forsake his rustic occupations, and accompany him to the busier scenes of the camp. His persuasions were successful, and Francesco entered with him into the service of Facino Cane, Lord of Alessandria. At the time when Facino died, leaving fourteen cities acquired by conquest, to Beatrice di Tenda, his wife, Francesco di Carmagnola was amongst the most distinguished of his captains. Beatrice afterwards marrying Philip Visconti, Duke of Milan, (who rewarded her by an ignominious death, for the regal dowry she had conferred upon him,) Carmagnola entered his army at the same time, and having, by his eminent services, firmly established the tottering power of that prince, received from him the title of Count, and was placed at the head of all his forces. The natural caprice and ingratitude of Philip's disposition, however, at length prevailed, and Carmagnola, disgusted with the evident proof of his wavering friendship, and doubtful faith, left his service and his territories, and after a variety of adventures, took refuge in Venice. Thither the treachery of the Duke pursued him, and emissaries were employed to procure his assassination. The plot, however, proved abortive, and Carmagnola was elected captain-general of the Venetian armies, during the league formed by that Republic against the Duke of Milan. The war was at first carried on with much spirit and success, and the battle of Maclodio, gained by Carmagnola, was one of the most important and decisive actions of those times. The night after the combat, the victorious soldiers gave liberty to almost all their prisoners. The Venetian envoys having made a complaint on this subject to the Count, he inquired what was become of the captives; and upon being informed that all, except four hundred, had been set free, he gave orders that the remaining ones also should be released immediately, according to the custom which prevailed amongst the armies of those days, the object of which was to prevent a speedy termination of the war. This proceeding of Carmagnola's occasioned much distrust and irritation in the minds of the Venetian rulers, and their displeasure was increased, when the armada of the Republic, commanded by Il Trevisani, was defeated upon the Po, without any attempt in its favour having been made by the Count. The failure of their attempt upon Cremona, was also imputed to him as a crime, and the Senate, resolving to free themselves from a powerful chief, now become an object of suspicion, after many deliberations on the best method of carrying their designs into effect, at length determined to invite him to Venice, under pretence of consulting him on their negotiations for peace. He obeyed their summons without hesitation or mistrust, and was everywhere received with extraordinary honours, during the course of his journey. On his arrival at Venice, and before he entered his own house, eight gentlemen were sent to meet him, by whom he was escorted to St Mark's Place. When he was introduced into the ducal palace, his attendants were dismissed, and informed that he would be in private with the Doge for a considerable time. He was arrested in the palace, then examined by the Secret Council, put to the torture, which a wound he had received in the service of the Republic rendered still more agonizing, and condemned to death. On the 5th May 1432, he was conducted to execution, with his mouth gagged, and beheaded between the two columns of St Mark's Place. With regard to the innocence or guilt of this distinguished character, there exists no authentic information. The author of the tragedy, which we are about to analyse, has chosen to represent him as entirely innocent, and probability at least is on this side. It is possible that the haughtiness of an aspiring warrior, accustomed to command, and impatient of control, might have been the principal cause of offence to the Venetians; or perhaps their jealousy was excited by his increasing power over the minds of an obedient army; and not considering it expedient to displace him, they resolved upon his destruction.

This tragedy, which is formed upon the model of the English and German drama, comprises the history of Carmagnola's life, from the day on which he was made commander of the Venetian armies, to that of his execution, thus embracing a period of about seven years. The extracts we are about to present to our readers, will enable them to form their own opinion of a piece, which has excited so much attention in Italy. The first act opens in Venice, in the hall of the Senate. The Doge proposes that the Count di Carmagnola should be consulted, on the projected league between the Republic and the Florentines, against the Duke of Milan. To this all agree, and the Count is introduced. He begins by justifying his conduct from the imputations to which it might be liable, in consequence of his appearing as the enemy of the Prince whom he had so recently served.

> ————He cast me down
> From the high place my blood had dearly won,
> And when I sought his presence, to appeal
> For justice there, 'twas vain! My foes had form'd
> Around his throne a barrier; e'en my life
> Became the mark of hatred, but in this
> Their hopes have fail'd—I gave them not the time.
> My life!—I stand prepar'd to yield it up
> On the proud field, and in some noble cause,
> For glory well exchang'd—but not a prey,
> Not to be caught ignobly in the toils
> Of those I scorn. I left him, and obtain'd
> With you a place of refuge—yet e'en here
> His snares were cast around me. Now all ties
> Are broke between us; to an open foe,
> An open foe I come.————

He then gives counsel in favour of war, and retires, leaving the senate engaged in deliberation. War is resolved upon, and he is elected commander. The fourth scene represents the house of Carmagnola. His soliloquy is noble, but its character is much more that of English than of Italian poetry, and may be traced, without difficulty, to the celebrated monologue of Hamlet.

> A leader—or a fugitive!—to drag
> Slow years along in idle vacancy,
> As a worn veteran living on the fame
> Of former deeds—to offer humble prayers
> And blessings for protection—owing all
> Yet left me of existence to the might
> Of other swords, dependent on some arm
> Which soon may cast me off—or on the field

To breathe once more, to feel the tide of life
Rush proudly through my veins—to hail again
My lofty star, and at the trumpet's voice
To wake! to rule! to conquer!—Which must be
My fate, this hour decides. And yet, if peace
Should be the choice of Venice, shall I cling
Still poorly to ignoble safety here,
Secluded as a homicide, who cowers
Within a temple's precincts? Shall not he
Who made a kingdom's fate, control his own?
Is there not one amidst the many lords
Of this divided Italy, not one
With soul enough to envy that bright crown
Encircling Philip's head? And know they not
'Twas won by me from many a tyrant's grasp,
Snatch'd by my hand, and plac'd upon the brow
Of that ingrate, from whom my spirit burns
Again to wrest it, and bestow the prize
On him who best shall call the prowess forth
Which slumbers in my arm?
[...]

The fourth and fifth scenes of the second act represent the tent of the Count in the Venetian camp, and his preparations for battle. And here a magnificent piece of lyric poetry is introduced, in which the battle is described, and its fatal effects lamented, with all the feeling of a patriot and a Christian. It appears to us, however, that this ode, hymn, or chorus, as the author has entitled it, striking as its effect may be in a separate recitation, produces a much less powerful impression in the situation it occupies at present. It is even necessary, in order to appreciate its singular beauty, that it should be re-perused, as a thing detached from the tragedy. The transition is too violent, in our opinion, from a tragic action, in which the characters are represented as clothed with existence, and passing before us with all their contending motives and feelings laid open to our inspection; to the comparative coldness of a lyric piece, where the author's imagination expatiates alone. The poet may have been led into this error by a definition of Schlegel's, who, speaking of the Greek chorusses [*sic*], gives it as his opinion, that "the chorus is to be considered as a personification of the moral thoughts inspired by the action; as the organ of the poet, who speaks in the name of the whole human race. The chorus, in short, is the *ideal* spectator."

But the fact was not exactly thus: The Greek chorus was composed of *real* characters, and expressed the sentiments of the people before whose eyes the action was imagined to be passing; thus the *true* spectator, after witnessing in representation the triumphs or misfortunes of kings and heroes, heard from the chorus the idea supposed to be entertained on the subject by the more enlightened part of the multitude. If the author, availing himself of his talent for lyric poetry, and varying the measure in conformity to the subject, had brought his chorus into action, introducing, for example, a veteran looking down upon the battle from an eminence, and describing its vicissitudes to the persons below, with whom he might interchange a variety of national and moral reflections, it appears to us that the dramatic effect would have been considerably heightened, and the assertion that the Greek chorus is not compatible with the system of the modern drama, possibly disproved. We shall present our readers with the entire chorus of which we have spoken, as a piece to be read separately, and one to which the following title would be much more appropriate.

The Battle of Maclodio, (or Macalo,)—an Ode.

> Hark! from the right bursts forth a trumpet's sound,
> A loud, shrill trumpet from the left replies!
> On every side hoarse echoes from the ground
> To the quick tramp of steeds and warriors rise,
> Hollow and deep—and banners all around,
> Meet hostile banners waving to the skies;
> Here steel-clad bands in marshall'd order shine,
> And there a host confronts their glittering line.
>
> Lo! half the field already from the sight
> Hath vanish'd, hid by closing groups of foes!
> Swords crossing swords, flash lightning o'er the fight,
> And the strife deepens, and the life-blood flows!
> Oh! who are these? What stranger in his might
> Comes bursting on the lovely land's repose?
> What patriot hearts have nobly vow'd to save
> Their native soil, or make its dust their grave?
>
> One race, alas! these foes, one kindred race,
> Were born and rear'd the same fair scenes among!
> The stranger calls them brothers—and each face
> That brotherhood reveals;—one common tongue
> Dwells on their lips—the earth on which we trace
> Their heart's blood—is the soil from whence they sprung.
> One mother gave them birth—this chosen land,
> Circled with Alps and seas, by Nature's guardian hand.
>
> O grief and horror! who the first could dare
> Against a brother's breast the sword to wield?
> What cause unhallow'd and accurs'd, declare,
> Hath bath'd with carnage this ignoble field?
> Think'st thou they know?—they but inflict and share
> Misery and death, the motive unreveal'd!
> —Sold to a leader, sold *himself* to die,
> With him they strive, they fall—and ask not why.
>
> [...]
>
> O thou devoted land! that can'st not rear
> In peace thine offspring; thou, the lost and won,

The fair and fatal soil, that dost appear
Too narrow still for each contending son;
Receive the stranger, in his fierce career.
Parting thy spoils! thy chastening is begun!
And, wresting from thy kings the guardian sword,
Foes, whom thou ne'er hadst wrong'd, sit proudly at thy board.

Are these infatuate too?—Oh! who hath known
A people e'er by guilt's vain triumph blest?
The wrong'd, the vanquish'd, suffer not alone,
Brief is the joy that swells th' oppressor's breast.
What though not yet his day of pride be flown,
Though yet heaven's vengeance spare his haughty crest,
Well hath it mark'd him—and decreed the hour,
When his last sigh shall own the terror of its power.

Are we not creatures of one hand divine?
Form'd in one mould, to one redemption born?
Kindred alike where'er our skies may shine,
Where'er our sight first drank the vital morn?
Brothers! one bond around our souls should twine,
And woe to him by whom that bond is torn!
Who mounts by trampling broken hearts to earth,
Who bows down spirits of immortal birth!
[…]

Notwithstanding the pathetic beauties of the last act, the attention which this tragedy has excited in Italy, must be principally attributed to the boldness of the author
in so completely emancipating himself from the fetters of the dramatic unities. The
severity with which the tragic poets of that country have, in general, restricted themselves to those rules, has been sufficiently remarkable, to obtain, at least, temporary distinction, for the courage of the writer who should attempt to violate them.
Although this piece comprises a period of several years, and that, too, in days so
troubled, and so "full of fate," days in which the deepest passions and most powerful
energies of the human mind were called into action by the strife of conflicting interests; there is, nevertheless, as great a deficiency of incident, as if "to be born and die"
made all the history of aspiring natures contending for supremacy. The character
of the hero is pourtrayed [sic] in words, not in actions; it does not unfold itself in
any struggle of opposite feelings and passions, and the interest excited for him only
commences at the moment when it ought to have reached its climax. The merits of
the piece may be summed up in the occasional energy of the language and dignity
of the thoughts; and the truth with which the spirit of the age is characterized, as
well in the developement [sic] of that suspicious policy distinguishing the system of
the Venetian government, as in the pictures of the fiery Condottieri, holding their
councils of war,
     Jealous of honour, sudden and quick in quarrel.

Please see the Works Cited for further information on the sources used in this essay.

Suggestions for Further Reading

Borsa, Paolo, Christian del Vento, "Italian Tragedy, 1820-1827", *Rassegna europea di letteratura italiana* 44 (2014): 59–88.

Manzoni, Alessandro, *The Count of Carmagnola* and *Adelchis*, introduced and translated by Federica Brunori Deigan. Baltimore and London: The Johns Hopkins University Press, 2004.

Saglia, Diego, "'Freedom alone is wanting': British Views of Contemporary Italian Drama, 1820-1830." *British Romanticism and Italian Literature: Translating, Reviewing, Rewriting*. Eds. Laura Bandiera and Diego Saglia. Amsterdam, New York: Rodopi, 2005. 237–54.

16 ADELAIDE O'KEEFFE (1776–1865)

Donelle Ruwe

Introduction

Adelaide O'Keeffe (1776–1865) was the daughter of the Irish Catholic playwright, John O'Keeffe, who wrote and adapted fifty-seven comic works for Covent Garden, the Haymarket, Drury Lane, and other theatres. John O'Keeffe (1747–1833) was a prolific author, despite having lost his eyesight in the late 1770s. His bibliographer, Muriel Sanderow Friedman, estimates that there were at least 2,066 performances of his plays in London (70). Adelaide O'Keeffe (herself a successful author) served as her father's amanuensis throughout the 1790s, which were some of his most productive years as a librettist. Her "Memoir" of her father offers an insider's view of life as a playwright and composer during the Romantic era.

John O'Keeffe began his career as a stage manager and actor in Irish theatres, where he met and married seventeen-year-old Mary Heaphy, a Protestant actress and the daughter of the manager of Dublin's Royal Theatre. When Adelaide was six, her father discovered that Heaphy was having an affair, and he left Ireland forever, taking his children with him. For the next six years, until the onset of the French Revolution, Adelaide was educated in a French convent, after which time she returned to England. But clearly she was traumatized by her early separation from her parents. Her historical novels – *Llewellin* (1799), *Zenobia, Queen of Palmyra* (1814), and *The Broken Sword, or, A Soldier's Honour: A Tale of the Allied Armies of 1757* (1854) – obsessively rehearse scenes of childhood anguish in which children are separated from a parent (Ruwe, "*Zenobia*").

Adelaide O'Keeffe's "Memoir" (1834) paints an intimate picture of the chaotic and financially tenuous life of a professional playwright. Her father would return home from theatre rehearsals, filled with despair after yet another day of forced and failed script revisions that were demanded by the actors. She depicts her father cranking out *The Son-in-Law* (Haymarket 1779) in just a few days, working in a crowded room where the company was dancing, conversing, and playing music and cards. She discusses *The Doldrum; or 1803* (Covent Garden 1796) as a remarkable instance of the "patch-work" of theatre writing. Her memoir also offers a sense of the hierarchy of high art versus commercial work in Romantic-era theatre. For example, her father wrote, on-demand, a one-act play in the "Don Juan style"(xxvii) for Thomas Harris (part owner and manager of Covent Garden). With the written play in his pocket, John O'Keeffe journeyed to Harris's house in Knightsbridge, and while "complacently sipping the chocolate placed before him, the manager, seated opposite, read the new work"; he gave his guest an "awful look" (xxvii). Because Harris felt the play

DOI: 10.4324/9781003006923-17

was too "moral, sublime, admirable," and "awful" (as in awe-inspiring), he recommended that O'Keeffe publish it rather than seek to have the work staged (xxviii). Either Harris was unwilling to accept that O'Keeffe could venture outside of comedic genres or Harris (according to Adelaide O'Keeffe) thought the work too good for the theatre. In any case, her father destroyed the only surviving copy.

While the memoir mostly focuses on John O'Keeffe's life, Adelaide O'Keeffe offers a rather telling recollection of her own. After the Covent Garden premiere of *Wild Oats* (1791), Mrs. Elizabeth Pope, who played the Quaker widow Lady Amaranth, made a loud statement in the green room to the company, guests, and manager. She announced that John O'Keeffe's work had improved since his little daughter's arrival. Interestingly, Adelaide O'Keeffe does not deny her possible impact on her father's plays; in fact, she deflects, avoiding directly addressing Pope's claim by simply mentioning that her handwriting and spelling were execrable. Surely Pope's arch comments, as quoted in the memoir – "Our *Friend* O'Keeffe hath verily improved," since "he appointed his little daughter to be his amanuensis" (xxiv, emphasis original) – were not about handwriting but rather the play itself? Yet by her very act of bringing up this incident while not refuting Pope's insinuation, Adelaide O'Keeffe leaves open an interesting possibility. Did she improve *Wild Oats* (which many scholars consider John O'Keeffe's best play)? Was she, perhaps, a contributing author?

As one reads O'Keeffe's memoir of her father, one senses that he had a volatile temper, swinging from flashes of anger and impulsivity to dour moodiness. By contrast, according to a first-hand account by John George Bishop, Adelaide O'Keeffe was cheerful and gregarious, with "bright eyes, sunny chestnut hair, and a most pleasing and expressive countenance. [...] and to the last dressed somewhat showy and *young*" (67). She helped to support her father for forty-five years, using her earnings as a governess and popular novelist and children's poet. Moreover, she was one of the three main contributors to the groundbreaking collection, *Original Poems for Infant Minds* (1804–1805), and she published many other children's poetry collections, including the first children's novel in verse, *A Trip to the Coast* (1819) (Ruwe, "Dramatic"). Other influential works include a retelling of the first seven books of the bible, *Patriarchal Times* (1811), and the novel *Dudley* (1819). *Dudley* draws from O'Keeffe's many years as a governess in its depiction of interrelated families, each of which takes a different approach to the education of their children. Ironically, *Dudley*'s portrayal of music education is negative, especially given O'Keeffe's closeness to her composer father (Ruwe, "Mediocrity").

Many of Adelaide O'Keeffe's vignettes in "Memoir" suggest constant anxiety over money. For example, she was to have inherited her father's lifetime annuity of £40 from the theatres of Cork and Limerick, but payments were made for only a few years after his death. Likewise, Covent Garden Theatre stopped paying O'Keeffe's lifetime annuity in 1835. Thus, the "Memoir" serves as a fundraising endeavor: it prefaced a posthumous collection of John O'Keeffe's poetry, *O'Keeffe's Legacy to his Daughter, Being the Poetic Works of the Late John O'Keeffe, Esq., the Dramatic Author*, which Adelaide herself edited and then published by subscription.

Fortunately, Adelaide O'Keeffe's financial survival did not depend upon her father's legacy, and her working life is a testament to the resourcefulness of the nineteenth-century woman of letters and limited means. She made a living as a governess and an author, and many of her books went through multiple editions and translations. She also applied for and received support from the Royal Literary Fund.

When she died at age 89, she was interred in a wooden casket in consecrated ground in the Brighton Extra-Mural Cemetery, and her burial was listed as a 3 (on a scale of 1–7, in which 1 indicated the cheapest level of burial and 7 referred to the wealthiest funeral arrangements). In other words, as her direct descendant Lynda O'Keeffe explains, she was neither wealthy nor particularly poor.[1]

Adelaide O'Keeffe

Excerpt from "Memoir" in O'Keeffe's Legacy to his Daughter, Being the Poetic Works of the Late John O'Keeffe, Esq., the Dramatic Author *(1834)*

With the name of O'Keeffe has been associated, for more than half a century, the idea of humour, laughter, high spirits, fun, frolic, farce, and drollery! Such be it owned, his mind appears in his youthful productions of Tony Lumpkin, the Agreeable Surprise, the Son-in-Law, the Dead Alive, the Little Hunchback, the Poor Soldier, Love in a Camp, Modern Antiques, &c. &c. But to these essential qualities, (the life of the comic drama,) must be added some of far more importance: –who of the many admirers of his works can forget the excellent and pleasing lessons of virtue and morality which adorn his mature plays and operas: for example, Wild Oats, the Castle of Andalusia, Fontainebleau, the Highland Reel, the Farmer, the Young Quaker, the Prisoner at Large, &c. Not one of these but might be read, or seen represented, by the eye of youth, purity, and innocence.

On the first coming out of "Wild Oats," a complimentary observation in the Green Room of Covent Garden Theatre was made by Mrs. Pope (Lady Amaranth,) who in the hearing of the manager, the performers, and other company, said, –"Our *Friend* O'Keeffe hath verily improved since the time when he appointed his little daughter to be his amanuensis." So Lady Amaranth might decide, but the vile spelling, unintelligible scrawl, and careless arrangement of her pages, tried the patience of manager and transcribers severely; and the former often assured the author they preferred his own hieroglyphics to hers, and that he had much better send his "little amanuensis" to a boarding-school, to learn to spell and write. Mr. Harris recommended Mrs. Hannah More's, at Bristol, and Mr. Colman that of Miss Lee, of Bath.

On giving up the ungrateful and unprofitable profession of writing for the stage, the Author endeavoured in 1798 to create a fund for himself, with a reversion to his children, by the publication of his dramatic works in four volumes, previously to which he had allowed his mind to take the early bent of youth, and indulge itself in political writing, but without the hope of emolument, had [it] even such been the custom to offer on the part of newspaper proprietors, of which he was not at that time aware. Both Mr. Perry, and his Greek or Roman correspondent, (the Editor forgets what were the signatures,) are now no more; but while the files of the Morning Chronicle exist, the bold, fearless, energetic denunciations and prophecies of the *Seer* (who sometimes descended to humorous verse,) can never die. Little could the play-goer imagine, that the absurdities of Lingo, which convulsed him with laughter the previous night, and the masterly political essay he was the next morning gravely pondering over in deep cogitation, were from the same pen!

The extent of the Author's genius and acquirements has never been fully appreciated, chiefly owing to the invincible reserve, and sternness of his nature, and well-known aversion to learned parties of either men or women. This was a blemish in his disposition; with his son, who owed to *him*, and him alone his excellent education, he would converse freely and liberally, his own early studies under the learned and celebrated Jesuit, Father Austin, having made him a proficient in the Greek, Latin, and French languages, with considerable knowledge of the mathematics; but with a stranger he was invariably silent and uncomfortable, except in the instance of the boarding house, already related, which did not often occur.

His favourite propensity to the drama, however, led him from more serious pursuits, and to that alone he for many years devoted himself. The Son-in-Law was written in a few days, in a room full of company engaged with music, dancing, cards, and conversation. This piece did not require a line of alteration; the same with above twenty of his plays, and these are his best; but when compelled by "the caprice of the managers, and the vanity, self-will, and sulky obstinacy of the performers," as he said, to change his "original uniform plan, to the patch-work of the Drama, expel this, intrude that, re-write dialogue, shuffle scenes like a pack of cards, ["] the play almost invariably failed, and he would return from a rehearsal of his new play, indignation on his brow, and despair in his look. Of the above fact, the "Doldrum" is the most remarkable instance; if the reader of taste has ever read or seen it acted, he must pronounce it to be as absurd, tame, unmeaning, and perhaps immoral a two-act piece as any on the stage; but could he compare it with the original MS. fresh from the Author's imagination, he would agree that a more powerful and effective vehicle for every species of fair satire, could scarcely be imagined. Old Septimus waking from his seven years' trance, or "Doldrum," inquires of his son and those around his sofa, what changes have taken place since he went to sleep, and is answered. It was the intention of the Editor here to introduce part of this one scene, but on second thoughts, feared it might prove too great an interruption to the Memoir.

The origin of the poem on "War," in this volume, may, however, be worth noticing: Mr. Harris asked the Author to write a one-act piece in the Don Juan style; the last scene of which (for the amusement of the audience,) was to represent the infernal regions; there was to be no music (for music is divine,) but only speaking and recitative accompanied. About a fortnight after, the Author took his MS. in his pocket to Mr. Harris's house at Knightsbridge, and whilst complacently sipping the chocolate placed before him, the manager, seated opposite, read the new work; a slow and stedfast [sic] perusal was followed by a fixed, and sort of awful look at his guest, who, in disappointment said hastily, "What, sir, you don't like it?" "Like it!" was the sudden exclamation, "in my life I never read any thing to equal it; the last scene exceeds in horror and sublimity every thing in poetry I ever met with!" He took up the MS. again, read attentively for a few minutes, and again laid it down, saying, "Dante himself may stoop to this—it is too good for the stage—print it, publish it—it is awful, moral, sublime, admirable! but it will not do!" "So!" replied the Author, ["] a man may write *too well*: fewer praises, and £100 would be more acceptable to my sublimity!"

But it was the fate of this original dramatic poem, which bore the simple, and unpretending title of "THE CAP" to be neither acted, printed, or published; the author, on mature reflection, as a matter of conscience, destroyed the MS. and kept no copy, he could only repeat a few verses of it. The admired last scene may be thus briefly explained. He represented Pluto on his throne of fire, with a burning CAP of hellish honor perched on the top of his huge pronged fork: a gang of devils, or evils, (synonimous [sic],) returned from earth, whither he had sent them to tempt mankind, rushed into his presence, when each in a verse of four lines only, long metre, but in a language the most nervous, masculine and comprehensive that could be imagined, claimed the reward of the CAP. Each crime, such as avarice, infanticide, sacrilege, perjury, &c. &c was distinctly understood by the reader, and yet not a single word introduced that could offend the eye or ear of perfect innocence. A sudden crash of thunder strikes the demons silent, and Pluto, rising hastily, in four lines of powerful effect, gives the CAP to the sin of INGRATITUDE.

Mr. Harris, when questioned on the subject, remarked, with characteristic humour, "Had I attempted to produce it on the stage, half of the ladies might have fainted, and the other half miscarried." This terrific vision still floating on the imagination of the author, he at length *laid the spirit*, by shifting it into its present far more gentle, but still most awful form. His son read the poem on "War," and greatly praised it as the very essence and spirit of poetry; but asked him, did it not want relief; he was ever open to counsel, and on this slight hint from one whose taste he justly depended upon, he wrote his admired and beautifully contrasted poem of "Peace, or the Halcyon."

The origin of "Bona the Rake," is to be dated from domestic circumstances of no consequence, and which may be explained in a few words, first premising to the young and rising generation, that as Bonaparte though emperor of France, was not *born* to empire, but set out in life a subaltern of artillery, there is no miracle in the fact, that with one or more of Napoleon's military relations and friends, the Author should be, some thirty years ago, most intimately acquainted. He took long walks with them, listened to their campaigns, improved their English, and his own French, and visited them at their boarding house, and invited them to his own board and fireside, which intercourse happily chequered the monotony of his own life, and eventually produced this admirable poem. With respect to the "LEGACY" in general, the Editor may here remark, that she has not presumed to touch a Corregio, by altering a line of the original. As her father's amanuensis (not secretary), she was only a machine worked by the power of mind, the mere preserver of the overflowings of a memory and imagination which habit and necessity had rendered so retentive, (not always having a friend with pen and ink at his elbow) that he could dictate above ten or twelve verses, *mentally* corrected, which seemed to flow like inspiration from his lips.

Composition was in truth the master-spring of his life; he preferred it to every other amusement, and indulged in it almost to the last few weeks of existence. Let the reader suppose a stranger to come accidentally into his drawing room; he would perceive, lying at full length on the sofa near the fire, or opened window, according to the season, a figure covered nearly to the chest with a scarlet India, or other shawl, above which is visible a noble and venerable countenance, apparently about 60 years of age, but in reality upwards of fourscore. [...]

At the first casual glance, this figure might appear an object of helpless malady, or deep dejection, or forlorn neglect, but a second and more attentive look would happily undeceive the stranger, and he would perceive the light blue eyes lit up with satisfaction at having caught a happy idea or turn of verse, the half-opened smiling lips, conscious of the innate pleasure of what is soon to be dictated, the finely-shaped and latterly wax-like hands and fingers scanning syllables; in short the whole picture revealing the HAPPY POET, a subject not to be pitied, but envied, and were the stranger to remain long enough unnoticed, he might hear the laugh of delight, and cheerful call of "Adelaide, where are you? where's 'neighbour Sea-cole and her pen and ink-horn?' I have five or six capital for you."

It was frequently the same out of doors, father and daughter, arm-in-arm, would sometimes walk from Bedford Cottage to the third milestone, on the Winchester road, and back again, without exchanging a dozen words; or he would sit on his camp chair, whilst she traversed to and fro a few yards, during his rest, and neither of them scarcely speak to each other; but the glow of his countenance, the unconscious smile, the motion of his lips and fingers, and sparkling intelligence of his eyes, satisfied her as to what was the employment of the mind. On their return home, it was in vain to tell him that dinner waited; he could enjoy nothing until his "imagination was unversed." The Editor hastily wrote down what he dictated, and he was then happy and contented.

Please see the Works Cited for further information on the sources used in this essay.

Note

1 Lynda O'Keeffe, personal correspondence. 12 December 2018.

Suggestion for Further Reading

Bishop, John George. *Strolls in the Brighton Extra-Mural Cemetery*. London: Fleet, 1867.

17 SARAH SIDDONS (1755–1831)

Daniel O'Quinn

Introduction

The most celebrated and influential actress of her time, Sarah Siddons (1755–1831) had a profound effect on Georgian society and culture. After a truncated start in David Garrick's company at Drury Lane, she made her name in the provincial theatres (especially in Bath) before taking London by storm in the 1782–1783 season. Along with her brother John Philip Kemble and her colleague Dorothea [Dora] Jordan (1761–1816) at Drury Lane, Siddons systematically altered the way that much of the repertoire was performed. After working through she-tragedies by Rowe, Otway, and Murphy,[1] she turned to Shakespeare in 1785 with her epochal reimagination of Lady Macbeth. The interventions in the performance protocols associated with the role would come to define her career and continued to haunt figures like William Wordsworth and William Hazlitt well into the nineteenth century.

Writers and painters attempted to capture the sensation surrounding Siddons's electrifying performances, to the point where one could argue that her presence permeated all media. Her cultural importance is undeniable, but her performance of femininity both on and off the stage was also vital to the realignment of gender norms in the Romantic era. Her embodiment of fierce intelligence, unbounded sympathy, and passionate maternal care became the epitome of middling femininity and played no small part in the reformulation of middle-class identity as a form of bio-politics. In fact, it is hard to conceive of the consolidation of social power around the middle ranks without thinking of Siddons.

Siddons's realignment of both the repertoire and gender norms are intertwined in her "Memoranda: Remarks on the Character of Lady Macbeth." The "Memoranda" were published in Thomas Campbell's *Life of Siddons* (1834), and they were derived from a manuscript that Siddons bequeathed to Campbell. Siddons's text is akin to two prior pamphlets on *Macbeth*, Thomas Whately's *Remarks on Some of the Characters of Shakespeare* (1785), and John Philip Kemble's *Macbeth Reconsidered; An Essay*. But whereas Whately and Kemble sparred over the question of Macbeth's martial masculinity in the wake of the American War, Siddons resolutely focuses on questions of femininity.

She makes two provocative arguments: first, she inductively contends that Lady Macbeth exhibits a form of feminine beauty that borders on fragility; second, she demonstrates that Lady Macbeth possesses a strength that eclipses her husband's martial valor because she bears her burdens alone. Both propositions are derived from a close reading of the script that assumes that the character develops in relation to the social forces that impinge upon her. This dynamic view of the character

DOI: 10.4324/9781003006923-18

departed radically from Siddons's predecessors, especially Hannah Pritchard (1711–1768), who portrayed Lady Macbeth as a fierce virago. As Siddons argues in the "Memoranda," Lady Macbeth is terrifying, but the terror elicited from her cold resolution in the dagger scene (2.2) is fundamentally different than that enacted in the sleep-walking scene (5.1). The former is a function of her strength; the latter is derived from her fragility; and the transit from one condition to another marks her increasing isolation in the play. As a rejoinder to Macbeth's tragic down fall, Siddons theorized a different tragic path for his wife grounded in the impossible demands of femininity itself. It is not surprising that contemporary reviews bemoaned the lack of a Macbeth sufficient to counter-balance this complex performance, for martial masculinity was in crisis throughout the 1780s.

Siddons's theoretical reflection is broken into two sections. The first constitutes an extended close reading. As she works through Lady Macbeth's five primary scenes in order, it becomes clear that her interventions all drive towards the formulation of a singular syncretic personality. In doing so, she reveals an internal logic for Lady Macbeth's speeches and actions. The second, much shorter, section takes the form of a theatrical anecdote that narrates her first serious encounter with the play in preparation for her 1778 performance in Bath and links it to her first triumphant appearance in the role at Drury Lane in 1785. She makes a subtle connection between the earlier act of reading and her later performance by focusing on her specific relation to a physical object. The terror experienced in reading the dagger scene becomes manifest in a moment of temporary derangement when she runs to bed, sets a candle on the table, and is so scared that she forgets to extinguish the flame. This same device, the lit candle burning on the table, became the focal point of her famous divergence from Pritchard's performance of the sleep-walking scene. Just as the lit candle works as a rhetorical emblem for her terror within the anecdote, so too did it operate as the most memorable gesture, or "point," in her performance. In this subtle alignment, Siddons suggests that affect can be concretized in specific actions and thus makes a crucial theoretical proposition regarding the intersection of bodies and space within the emotional landscape of the theatre.

Sarah Siddons

Excerpt from "Memoranda: Remarks on the Character of Lady Macbeth" in Thomas Campbell, **Life of Mrs. Siddons** *(1834)*

In this astonishing creature one sees a woman in whose bosom the passion of ambition has almost obliterated all the characteristics of human nature; in whose composition are associated all the subjugating powers of intellect and all the charms and graces of personal beauty. You will probably not agree with me as to the character of that beauty; yet, perhaps, this difference of opinion will be entirely attributable to the difficulty of your imagination disengaging from the idea of the person of her representative which you have been so long accustomed to contemplate. According to my notion, it is of that character which I believe is generally allowed to be the most captivating to the other sex,–fair, feminine, nay perhaps, even fragile—

> Fair as the forms that, wove in Fancy's loom,
> Float in light visions round the poet's head.[2]

Such a combination only, respectable in energy and strength of mind, and captivating in feminine loveliness, could have composed a charm of such potency as to fascinate the mind of a hero so dauntless, a character so amiable, so honourable as *Macbeth,*–to seduce him to brave all the dangers of the present and all the terrors of a future world; and we are constrained, even whilst we abhor his crimes, to pity the infatuated victim of such a thralldom. His letters which have informed her of the predictions of those preternatural beings who accosted him on the heath, have lighted up into daring and desperate determinations all those pernicious slumbering fires which the enemy of man is ever watchful to awaken in the bosoms of his unwary victims. To his direful suggestions she is so far from offering the least opposition, as not only to yield up her soul to them, but moreover to invoke the sightless ministers of remorseless cruelty to extinguish in her breast all those compunctious visitings of nature which otherwise might have been mercifully interposed to counteract, and perhaps eventually to overcome, their unholy instigations. But having impiously delivered herself up to the excitements of hell, the pitifulness of heaven itself is withdrawn from her, and she is abandoned to the guidance of the demons whom she has invoked.

[Siddons now offers her thoughts on each of Lady Macbeth's principal scenes. Of these her remarks on Act 2 scene 2 and Act 5 scene 1—the dagger scene and the sleepwalking scene respectively–reveal the most about her approach to the play. Ed.]

The Second Act.

There can be no doubt that *Macbeth,* in the first instance, suggested his design of assassinating the king, and it is probable that he has invited his gracious sovereign to his castle, in order the more speedily and expeditiously to realize those thoughts, "whose murder, though by yet fantastical, so shook his single state of man." Yet, on the arrival of the amiable monarch who had so honoured him of late, his naturally benevolent and good feelings resume their wonted power. He then solemnly communes with his heart, and after much powerful reasoning upon the danger of the undertaking, calling to mind that *Duncan* his king, of mildest virtues, and his kinsman, lay as his guest. All those accumulated determents, with the violated rights of sacred hospitality bringing up the rear, rising all at once in terrible array to his awakened conscience, he relinquishes the atrocious purpose, and wisely determines to proceed no further in the business. But, now, behold his evil genius, his gravecharm, appears, and by the force of her revilings, her contemptuous taunts, and, above all by her opprobrious aspersion of cowardice, chases the gathering drops of humanity from his eyes, and drives before her impetuous and destructive career all those kindly charities, those impressions of loyalty, and pity, and gratitude, which, but the moment before, had taken full possession of his mind. She says,

> I have given suck, and know
> How tender 'tis to love the babe that milks me:
> I would, while it was smiling in my face,
> Have pluck'd my nipple from his boneless gums,
> And dash'd the brains out, had I so sworn
> As you have done to this.[3]

Even here, horrific as she is, she shews herself made by ambition, but not by nature, a perfectly savage creature. The very use of such a tender allusion in the midst of her dreadful language, persuades one unequivocally that she has really felt the maternal yearnings of a mother towards her babe, and that she considered this action the most enormous that ever required the strength of human nerves for its perpetration. Her language to Macbeth is the most potently eloquent that guilt could use. It is only in soliloquy that she invokes the powers of hell to unsex her. To her husband she avows, and the naturalness of her language makes us believe her, that she had felt the instinct of filial as well as maternal love. But she makes her very virtues the means of a taunt to her lord:–"You have the milk of human kindness in your heart," she says (in substance) to him, "but ambition, which is my ruling passion, would be also yours if you had courage. With a hankering desire to suppress, if you could, all your weaknesses of sympathy, you are too cowardly to will the deed, and can only dare to wish it. You speak of sympathies and feelings. I too have felt with a tenderness which your sex cannot know; but I am resolute in my ambition to trample on all that obstructs my way to a crown. Look to me, and be ashamed of your weakness."[4] Abashed, perhaps, to find his own courage humbled before this unimaginable instance of female fortitude, he at last screws up his courage to the sticking-place, and binds up each corporal agent to this terrible feat. It is the dead of night. The gracious Duncan, now shut up in measureless content, reposes sweetly, while the restless spirit of wickedness resolves that he shall wake no more. The daring fiend, whose pernicious potions have stupefied his attendants, and who even laid their daggers ready, –her own spirit, as it seems, exalted by the power of wine,–proceeds, "That which hath made them drunk hath made me bold," now enters the gallery, in eager expectation of the results of her diabolical diligence.[5] In the tremendous suspense of these moments, while she recollects her habitual humanity, one trait of tender feeling is expressed, "Had he not resembled my father as he slept, I had done it."[6] Her humanity vanishes, however, in the same instant; for when she observes that Macbeth, in the terror and confusion of his faculties, has brought the daggers from the place where they had agreed they should remain for the crimination of the grooms, she exhorts him to return with them to that place, and to smear those attendants of the sovereign with blood. He, shuddering exclaims, "I'll go no more! I am affear'd to think of what I have done. Look on't again I dare not."[7]

Then instantaneously the solitary particle of her human feeling is swallowed up in her remorseless ambition, and, wrenching the daggers from the feeble grasp of her husband, she finishes the act which the infirm of purpose had not courage to complete, and calmly and steadily returns to her accomplice with the fiend-like boast,

> "My hands are of your colour;
> But I would scorn to wear a heart so white."[8]

A knocking at the gate interrupts this terrific dialogue; and all that now occupies her mind is urging him to wash his hands and put on his nightgown, "lest occasion call," says she, "and shew us to be the watchers."[9] In a deplorable depravation of all rational knowledge, and lost to every recollection except that of his enormous guilt, she hurries him away to their own chamber.

[.... Siddons's commentary on Act III has been elided for reasons of length. Ed.]

The Fifth Act.

Behold her now, with wasted form, with wan and haggard countenance, her starry eyes glazed with the ever-burning fever of remorse, and on their lids the shadows of death. Her ever-restless spirit wanders in troubled dreams about her dismal apartment; and, whether waking or asleep, the smell of innocent blood incessantly haunts her imagination:

> Here's the smell of the blood still.
> All the perfumes of Arabia will not sweeten
> This little hand.[10]

How beautifully contrasted is this exclamation with the bolder image of Macbeth, in expressing the same feeling?

> Will all great Neptune's ocean wash the blood
> Clean from this hand?[11]

And how appropriately either sex illustrates the same idea!

During this appalling scene, which, to my sense, is the most so of them all, the wretched creature, in imagination, acts over again the accumulated horrors of her whole conduct. These dreadful images, accompanied with the agitations they have induced, have obviously accelerated her untimely end; for in a few moments the tidings of her death are brought to her unhappy husband. It is conjectured that she died by her own hand. Too certain it is, that she dies, and makes no sign. I have now to account to you for the weakness which I have, a few lines back, ascribed to Macbeth; and I am not quite without hope that the following observations will bear me out in my opinion. Please to observe, that he (I must think pusillanimously, when I compare his conduct to her forebearance,) has been continually pouring out his miseries to his wife. His heart has therefore been eased, from time to time, by unloading its weight of woe; while she, on the contrary, has perseveringly endured in silence the uttermost anguish of a wounded spirit.

> The grief that does not speak
> Whispers the o'erfraught heart, and bids it break.[12]

Her feminine nature, her delicate structure, it is too evident, are soon overwhelmed by the enormous pressure of her crimes. Yet it will be granted, that she gives proofs of a naturally higher toned mind than that of Macbeth. The different physical powers of the two sexes are finely delineated, in the different effects which their mutual crimes produce. Her frailer frame, and keener feelings, have now sunk under the struggle—his robust and less sensitive constitution has not only resisted it, but bears him on to deeper wickedness, and to experience the fatal fecundity of crime.

> For mine own good—All causes shall give way.
> I am in blood so far stepp'd in, that should I wade no more,
> Returning were as tedious as go o'er.[13]

Henceforth, accordingly, he perpetrates horrors to the day of his doom.

In one point of view, at least, this guilty pair extort from us, in spite of ourselves, a certain respect and approbation. Their grandeur of character sustains them both above recrimination (the despicable accustomed resort of vulgar minds,) in adversity; for the wretched husband, though almost impelled into this gulph of destruction by the instigations of his wife, feels no abatement of his love for her, while she, on part, appears to have known no tenderness for him, till, with a heart bleeding at every pore, she beholds in him the miserable victim of their mutual ambition. Unlike the first frail pair in Paradise, they spent not the fruitless hours in mutual accusation.

[*Mrs. Siddons had played Lady Macbeth in the provincial theatres many years before she attempted the character in London. Adverting to the first time this plot was allotted to her she says,*] It was my custom to study my characters at night, when all the domestic cares and business of the day were over. On the night preceding that in which I was to appear in this part for the first time, I shut myself up, as usual, when all the family were retired, and commenced my study of Lady Macbeth. As the character is very short, I thought I should soon accomplish it. Being then only twenty years of age, I believed, as many others do believe, that little more was necessary than to get the words into my head; for the necessity of discrimination, and the development of character, at that time of my life, had scarcely entered into my imagination. But, to proceed. I went on with tolerable composure, in the silence of the night, (a night I never can forget,) till I came to the assassination scene, when the horrors of the scene rose to a degree that made it impossible for me to get farther. I snatched up my candle, and hurried out of the room, in a paroxysm of terror. My dress was of silk, and the rustling of it, as I ascended the stairs to go to bed, seemed to my panic-struck fancy like the movement of a spectre pursuing me. At last I reached my chamber, where I found my husband fast asleep. I clapt my candlestick down upon the table, without the power of putting the candle out; and I threw myself on my bed, without daring to stay even to take off my clothes. At peep of day I rose to resume my task; but so little did I know of my part when I appeared in it, at night, that my shame and confusion cured me of procrastinating my business for the remainder of my life.

About six years afterwards I was called upon to act the same character in London. By this time I had perceived the difficulty of assuming a personage with whom no one feeling of common general nature was congenial or assistant. One's own heart could prompt one to express, with some degree of truth, the sentiments of a mother, a daughter, a wife, a lover, a sister, &c., but, to adopt the character, must be an effort of judgment alone.

Therefore it was with the utmost diffidence, nay, terror, that I undertook it, and with the additional fear of Mrs. Pritchard's reputation in it before my eyes.[14] The dreaded first night at length arrived, when, just as I had finished my toilet, and was pondering with fearfulness my first appearance in the grand fiendish part, comes Mr. Sheridan, knocking at my door, and insisting, in spite of all my entreaties not to be interrupted at this to me tremendous moment, to be admitted.[15] He would not be denied admittance; for he protested he must speak to me on a circumstance which so deeply concerned my own interest, that it was of the most serious nature. Well, after much squabbling, I was compelled to admit him, that I might dismiss him the sooner, and compose myself before the play began. But, what was my distress and astonishment, when I found that he wanted me, even at this moment of anxiety and terror, to adopt another mode of acting the sleeping scene. He told me he had heard with the greatest surprise and concern that I meant to act it without holding the candle in my hand; and, when I urged the impracticability of washing out the "*damned spot*," with the vehemence that was certainly implied by both her own words and by those of her gentlewoman, he insisted, that if I did put the candle out of my hand, it would be thought a presumptuous innovation, as Mrs. Pritchard had always retained it in hers. My mind, however, was made up, and it was then too late to make me alter it; for it was too agitated to adopt another method. My deference for Mr. Sheridan's taste and judgment was, however, so great, that, had he proposed the alteration while it was possible for me to change my own plan, I should have yielded to his suggestion; though, even then, it would have been against my own opinion, and my observation of the accuracy with which somnambulists perform all the acts of waking persons. The scene, of course, was acted as I had myself conceived it; and the innovation, as Mrs. Sheridan called it, was received with approbation. Mr. Sheridan himself came to me, after the play, and most ingenuously congratulated me on my obstinacy. When he was gone out of the room I began to undress; and, while standing up before my glass, and taking off my mantle, a diverting circumstance occurred, to chase away the feelings of this anxious night; for while I was repeating, and endeavouring to call to mind the appropriate tone and action to the following words, "Here's the smell of blood still!" my dresser innocently exclaimed, "Dear me, ma'am, how very hysterical you are to-night; I protest and vow, ma'am, it was not blood, but rosepink and water; for I saw the property-man mix it up with my own eyes.

Please see the Works Cited for further information on the sources used in this essay.

Notes

1 Nicholas Rowe (1674–1718), playwright best known for tragedies; Thomas Otway (1652–1685), playwright best known for *Venice Preserv'd* (1682); Arthur Murphy (1727–1805), playwright known for both tragedies and farces. She-tragedies refers to a group of works with a central female character, often the victim of psychological torture and/or violent death.

2 William Mason, "An Elegy, On the Death of a Lady. Written in 1760" from *A collection of the most esteemed pieces of poetry: that have appeared for several years. With variety of originals, by the late Moses Mendez, Esq; and other contributors to Dodsley's collection. To which this is intended as a supplement.* London, 1767, p. 6, ll. 11–12.

3 *Macbeth*, 1.7.54–59.

4 Siddons is paraphrasing elements of 1.5 and 1.7.

5 *Macbeth*, 2.2.1.

6 *Macbeth*, 2.2.11–12.

7 *Macbeth*, 2.2.50–53.

8 *Macbeth*, 2.2.63–64.

9 *Macbeth*, 2.2.69–70.

10 *Macbeth*, 5.1.47–48.

11 *Macbeth*, 2.2.59–60.

12 *Macbeth*, 4.3.209–10.

13 *Macbeth*, 3.4.135–38.

14 Hannah Pritchard (1711–1768), British actress who played Lady Macbeth opposite Garrick at Theatre Royal Drury Lane from 1747 to 1768.

15 Richard Brinsley Sheridan (1751–1816), playwright, politician, and manager of Drury Lane Theatre from 1776 to 1809.

Suggestions for Further Reading

Carlson, Julie A. *In the Theatre of Romanticism: Coleridge, Nationalism, Women.* Cambridge: Cambridge University Press, 1994. 134–75.

Freeman, Lisa. "Mourning the 'Dignity of the Siddonian Form'." *Eighteenth-Century Fiction.* 27. 3–4 (Spring-Summer 2015): 597–630.

Macpherson, Heather. "Masculinity, Femininity, and the Tragic Sublime: Reinventing Lady Macbeth." *Studies in Eighteenth-Century Culture.* 29 (2000): 299–333.

McDonald, Russ. "Sarah Siddons." *Garrick, Kemble, Siddons, Kean.* Ed. Peter Holland. London: Bloomsbury, 2010. 105–37.

Pascoe, Judith. *The Sarah Siddons Audio Files: Romanticism and the Lost Voice.* Ann Arbor, MI: University of Michigan Press, 2011.

18 "ANONYMOUS"

Marjean D. Purinton

Introduction

During an archival research trip to the Women's Theatre Collection at the University of Bristol in 1997, I discovered a 34-page, handwritten prompt manuscript for a play entitled "Nance Oldfield: The Tragedy Queen: A Comic Drama in One Act" (c.1848).[1] Although the manuscript lacks a formal title page, it seems to be one of the many nineteenth-century portrayals of the famous eighteenth-century actress, Anne Oldfield. This prompt manuscript includes penciled alterations, but it does not indicate the kinds of blocking directions and technical instructions frequently associated with extant prompt books used by stage managers (Cattell 42–44). The absence of the kind of encoded system associated with actor-manager John Philip Kemble (1757–1823), for example, suggests that this prompt script may have been used strictly for verbally prompting onstage actors (E. Smith 30–31).

The nineteenth-century stage history of the Oldfield plays is both edifying and incomplete. The cast of a 13 November 1848 production of the play is penciled on the first page of this manuscript. Theatre records indicate that Helena Faucit played the title character in a staging of the Oldfield tragedy on 13 November 1848, and we know that on 9 October 1849, a version of the play, entitled *The Reigning Favourite: A Drama in Three Acts,* was produced at the Strand (Lafler 171–172). Following both dramatic (1852) and prose (1853–1854) adaptations of the story by Charles Reade (1814–1884), the Oldfield tribute was staged on 24 February 1883 at the Olympic, with Genevieve Ward playing the title role (Lafler 50). Archival librarian Christopher Robinson and theatre records in Bristol could not identify the specific performance for which this prompt script might have been used, but it could have been the basis of a performance at the Lyceum sometime between the 1849 Strand production and the 1883 Olympic production.

Two other interesting features of this prompt script are important. First, no author of this adaptation is identified. Variations in this script from other published versions of the play, as well as Reade's novella, point to the strong possibility of a female writer, one knowledgeable of eighteenth- and nineteenth-century theatre theory and practices. Since women would not have been stage managers—even at the end of the nineteenth century—it is possible that this prompt script could have been written by a woman intent on providing performers verbal cues and lines. As a potential female-scripted prompt book, this adaptation contributes to our knowledge of women's theatre theory, for this anonymous adaptor may well have had to let the lead female character of the play speak for her and other women engaged in theatrical work,

DOI: 10.4324/9781003006923-19

which is what is intriguing about the second feature. While the play's title and tradition clearly associate it with Anne Oldfield (1683–1730), the actress of the script is identified as Anne Bracegirdle, Oldfield's predecessor on the stage (1671–1748). Since the rivalry between Oldfield and Bracegirdle was theatre lore, what does it mean to conflate them as the composite figure "Nance," the major female performer in this script?[2]

Dramatic adaptations of the Oldfield story, seemingly about female celebrity and a professional acting career, were, in fact, important sites for transmitting from one generation to the next women's serious contributions to theatre history. Recent scholarship has focused on the actress as object, eroticized for male theatre-goers' gaze,[3] but the possibility that these women embodied theoretical registers has been less vigorously pursued. Both the female performer and the female adapter in the theatrical and textual spaces of this prompt script point to a theoretical posture that bends the traditions of stage history. The "tragedy queen" of this prompt script is not exactly Oldfield or Bracegirdle, and the female adapter of the prompt script is not the conventional stage manager, but both find space for an alternative and disorderly presence in a theatre enterprise controlled by men and intent on achieving primarily masculine pleasure.

The artificiality of theatre, long associated with feminine character and temperament, is actually an illusion crafted by masculine-informed design. Male-dominated theatre depended on the feminine artifice expressed by onstage female performers, here valorized by a "Nance" who is not a particular actress but the *idea* of female performance. Female performers were expected to role-play within the artificial world of the stage with such precision that male audiences came to see this novelty as reality. From her intimate dressing room, Bracegirdle instructs her would-be suitor, the young aspiring playwright David Standfast, in the magic of theatrical technologies:

> You know perfectly well that the Palaces we inhabit on the Stage, are but so many yards of painted canvas and that sometimes a massive column gets half rubbed out. You also know that the sun which shines upon us is composed of lamps and candles and that an eclipse can only be presented by snuffing. All this is unreality, you know well, the sighs and tears, and the stamps, are just the same, and have no more to do with the heart, than the painted temples have to do with real Pariss [*sic*] marble—or the snuffed sun with the solar system. The whole is a mere matter of business, just got up for the occassion [*sic*]—put on when the curtain is raised and cast off, when it is let down.

Nance lifts the curtain revealing a theatrical illusion to David.

By extension, the very performer, Bracegirdle/Oldfield, dressed for spectator consumption, is as artificial as the staged palaces, eclipses, and temples. The repetition of the phrase, "you know well," ironically suggests that David Standfast and other theatre-goers do not recognize the illusion with which they are allured. In theatrical space, men could engage in the fantasy and artifice with which women daily existed, as Bracegirdle extols: "[...] it is the born duty of a woman to endeavour to please, to the best of her power—and when she abandons this—she quits her proper vocation" (24). While "her proper vocation" might refer to Bracegirdle's acting career, it also alludes to performances scripted for all women whose very roles on the stage of actual life are defined by their biology. All women, on- and off-stage, are "tragedy queens," integral to–but not empowered in—production. The prompt script thus opens onto spaces where the familiar female performer manifestly resides and where the latent prompt script adapter represents all anonymous women of the theatre. Theatrical "Nances" perform artificial femininity, and women behind stage curtains function like scenery props.

The first pencil emendation in the script occurs early in the play and indicates the retention of Nance's critique that theatre companies merely rely on costumes on hand. She recognizes that costumes are vital visual signifiers of illusion, and she quips: "Well, perhaps some day there may be managers of Theatre's [sic] wise enough to dress people as they aught to be dressed, and not to put periwigs upon Roman Generals—but that will not be in my time" (5). While male stage managers might have excised this criticism from the script, the mistress of this prompt script sees fit to have Bracegirdle comment on the challenge of pulling off theatrical visual trickery when improperly costumed. Bracegirdle diminishes masculinist financial decisions and points to the possibility of wise (female) managers who understand the significance of appropriate costume to theatrical production.

At the end of the prompt script, penciled directions indicate the relocation of one line and the marginal insertion of another line. Bracegirdle ponders whether her dressing-room satire, her meta-performance, has subdued Bridget's desires to transform herself from theatre maid to actress and has softened Ebenezer Standfast to his would-be-playwright son's theatrical ambitions. The inserted line of self-reflection is important. Bridget answers that, whenever Bracegirdle is in the room, she commands all the public love and adoration, regardless of the stage, the role, or the script, and she laments, *"This poor girl must not so much as think of a little on her own account"* (34). This line is underscored in the prompt script, followed by Bracegirdle's transplanted line affirming that her satire has made an impression on "two unsophisticated hearts" (34). While the line's relocation emphasizes the consciousness-raising function of Bracegirdle's metatheatricality in helping both the Standfasts and Bridget recognize the artificiality of staged performances, it also emphasizes theatre as the space that remains perilous for women, where women sacrifice self-hood, whether performing a scripted part or adapting a prompt script.

"Anonymous"

Excerpt from "Nance Oldfield: The Tragedy Queen: A Comic Drama in One Act" (c. 1848)[4]

ANNE BRACEGIRDLE: You know perfectly well that the Palaces we inhabit on the Stage, are but so many yards of painted canvas that sometimes a massive column gets half rubbed out. You also know that the sun of which shines upon us is composed of lamps and candles and that an eclipse can only be presented by snuffing. All this is unreality, you know well, the sighs and the tears, and the stamps, are just the same, and have no more to do with the heart, than the painted temples have to do with real Pariss [sic] marble—or the snuffed sun with the solar system. The whole is a mere matter of business, just got up for the occassion [sic]—put on when the curtain is raised and cast off, when it is let down (20).

EBENEZER STANDFAST: [To his son David] [...] [D]o you think that I flatter your nonsense and your foolery—that you may be a miserable Poet all your life—with your head full of vanity and your pockets full of nothing else? [...] I will speak what I mean without cloak or disguise. I believe your tragedy rubbish—baldadash [*sic*]! [...] The town will chuckle exceeding—and if they do not—I myself will come to the Pit and I will bring with me some trusty friends from Banbury—and we will hiss, till you think the devil is in town (30).

BRIDGET: [To Bracegirdle] I have indeed madam—I find that when you are near you have all the love to yourself—*This poor girl must not so much as think of a little on her own account* [marginal emendation].

Please see the Works Cited for further information on the sources used in this essay.

Notes

1 See Tracy Cattell's "Transmitting the Thinking: The Nineteenth-Century Stage Manager and the Adaptation of Text for Performance."
2 See, for example, Sandra Richards' *The Rise of the English Actress*, 13–14; Kristina Straub, *Sexual Suspects: Eighteenth-Century Players and Sexual Ideology*, 92–93.
3 Ann Pellegrini, *Performance Anxieties: Staging Psychoanalysis, Staging Race*, 67–71; Jill Dolan, *The Feminist Spectator as Critic*, 9–16; and "Gender Impersonation Onstage: Destroying or Maintaining the Mirror of Gender Roles."
4 Excerpt from handwritten prompt manuscript at the University of Bristol, Women's Theatre Collection, transcribed by Marjean D. Purinton.

Suggestions for Further Reading

Dolan, Jill. "Gender Impersonation Onstage: Destroying or Maintaining the Mirror of Gender Roles." *Women and Performance*. 2 (1985): 1–19.
Pellegrini, Ann. *Performance Anxieties: Staging Psychoanalysis, Staging Race*. New York, NY: Routledge, 1997.

19 MARY RUSSELL MITFORD (1787–1855)

Serena Baiesi

Introduction

Mary Russell Mitford (1787–1855) wrote poetry, drama, and prose over her long literary career, while, as a dramatist, she successfully staged four historical tragedies between 1823 and 1834 at London's Covent Garden and Drury Lane theatres. She also published numerous short dramatic sketches in literary journals and annuals in the 1830s. During the time spent in her early to middle teens at a boarding school in Chelsea, she regularly attended Drury Lane, where she admired the performances of the leading actors of the day, such as John Kemble (1757–1823) and Sarah Siddons (1755–1831).

Mitford became a writer out of economic necessity. For this reason, she was both prolific and worked in different genres, in order to increase her opportunities for financial gain. *Our Village: Sketches of Rural Character and Scenery* (1824–1832) is her best-known publication, first printed serially in periodicals. This popular collection, much admired by critics, incorporated everyday subject matter and a conversational style to become a prototype of a new poetical hybrid genre: the country village sketch.

As a playwright, Mitford is best remembered for her historical plays, which engage deeply with the complex relationship between gender, social rules, and female agency. Her historical drama *Foscari* (1821), depicting the prominent fifteenth-century Italian family, was designed specifically for the Covent Garden company. However, after Lord Byron's 1821 publication of his tragedy about the same subject, entitled *The Two Foscari*, Mitford requested the theatre manager cancel her play's production, since she did not wish to be seen as competing with Byron. Her drama *Rienzi* (1828), which provocatively stages a revolutionary plot, enacts events the playwright also represents in *Charles I* (1834).

In 1854, Mitford published her two-volume collection of *Dramatic Works* with an important introduction, excerpted here, about the role of actors in the theatre of her day. She argues that significant changes were taking place on the English stage, which was transitioning from theatre patronized by the leading families of the country to a new enlarged "London school," where "the acted drama received its full development." Starting with a personal justification for her involvement in the "ambitious and perilous paths of dramatic literature," – since she had always been a retired woman "whose days had passed chiefly in the calm seclusion of a country village" – she then focuses her attention on the great London theatres. Knowing that the theatre would pay well for a successful play, she had decided to write for the stage and managed to have her dramas performed in big and small theatres. Thus, in her

DOI: 10.4324/9781003006923-20

prefatory remarks, she conjures up the dynamic atmosphere of the theatre – lighting, sound, costume, rehearsal, etc. – involving the reader in the frenetic atmosphere backstage, which she believed to be an almost magical world. She is a self-conscious dramatist, involved not only in the practical matters of staging her plays but also, more significantly, in the success she would gain from them.

As a woman, she knew that she would attract personal and professional scrutiny from critics, but she acknowledges in her introduction the recognition she received from the public, and the "eager congratulations" expressed from the most eminent writers of the time, all female authors like Maria Edgeworth (1768–1849), Joanna Baillie (1762–1851), and Felicia Hemans (1793–1835).[1] However, at the end of this section, she admits that writing for the stage could be a dangerous endeavour, and it is "intoxicating," especially when censorship is involved. The triumph gained on stage is very temporary, Mitford admits with regret, and it is a sort of "ill success" that "leads to self-assertion" and final disappointment. This is why, after the production of her plays, she went back to rural poetry as a more suitable and profitable literary genre.

Mitford was much admired during the late Romantic and Victorian periods, especially for this rural poetry. Her reputation was so extensive that her village in Berkshire became a place of pilgrimage for her international readers. She also corresponded with the most prominent writers of the nineteenth century; her letters testify to her involvement with the literary debates of her time. Nowadays, alongside her poetic career as a rural writer, her dramatic works have been rediscovered, but, from critical and editorial perspectives, she still remains a neglected and lesser-known Romantic author. However, this selection from her Introduction testifies to her direct involvement in the theatrical life of her time, in terms of both theatrical practice and dramatic theory. Mitford's poetry and plays merit further study in the context of her literary period in order to fully understand her significant contributions to generic innovation, political discourse, and dramatic practice.

Mary Russell Mitford

Excerpt from "Introduction" to Dramatic Works (1854)

To edit these tragedies myself, seems a kind of anachronism, not unlike engraving the inscription upon my own tombstone. [...] But theory, right or wrong, especially as applied to the work in hand, forms the ground-work of most dramatic Prefaces, largely blended with skilful specimens of the noble art of self-justification, with vehement attacks upon critics, and perpetual grumblings against managers and actors, and all that was done and all that was not done for the pieces that follow. [...] No one has a right to gratify a prickly, defiant and sensitive self-love by speaking unkindly of another, especially when the waves of thirty years have rolled between. So instead of reciting long categories of theatrical troubles, I shall endeavour to explain to myself and to others, what has often caused me some astonishment, the causes that drove a shy and retired woman, whose days had passed chiefly in the calm seclusion of a country village into the ambitious and perilous paths of dramatic literature. [...]

Sixty years ago, in the early times of the great war, the drama filled a very different place amongst the amusements of a country town from that which it holds now. Concerts were rare, lectures unknown, and the theatre patronized by the leading families, and conducted in the good town of Reading (to which we had removed) with undeviating propriety, formed the principal recreation of the place. The new comedies of those old times, the comedies of Holcroft and Morton, of Colman and Sheridan, followed by the farces of Foote and O'Keefe, and the musical entertainments of Dibdin,[2] formed the staple of the house. [...]

It was during the five years from ten years old to fifteen, which I passed at a London school, that my passion for the acted drama received its full development. At this school (well known afterwards as the residence of poor Miss Landon[3]), there chanced to be an old pupil of the establishment who, having lived, as the phrase goes, in several families of distinction, was at that time disengaged, and in search of a situation as governess. This lady[4] was not only herself a poetess (I have two volumes of verse of her writing,) but she had a knack of making poetesses of her pupils. She had already educated Lady Caroline Ponsonby (the Lady Caroline Lamb, of Glenarvon celebrity[5]), and was afterwards destined to give her first instruction to poor L.E.L., and her last to Mrs Fanny Kemble.[6] She was, however, a clever woman, and my father eagerly engaged her to act by me as a sort of private tutor – a governess out of school-hours.

At the time when I was placed under her care, her whole heart was in the drama, especially as personified by John Kemble; and I am persuaded that she thought she could in no way so well perform her duty, as in taking me to Drury Lane, whenever his name was in the bills.

It was a time of great actors. [...] The glorious family of Kemble satisfied alike the eye and the intellect, the fancy and the heart.

John Kemble was, however, certainly Miss Rowden's chief attraction to Drury Lane Theatre. She believed him – and of course her pupil shared in her faith – the greatest actor that ever had been, or that ever could be; greater than Garrick, greater than Kean.[7] I am more catholic now; but I still hold all my admiration, except its exclusiveness.

If Foote's reputation have been injured, as I think it has, by his own double talent as an actor and a mimic, so the fame of John Kemble – that perishable actor's fame – has suffered not a little by the contact with his great sister. Besides her uncontested and incontestable power, Mrs Siddons had one advantage not always allowed for – she was a woman. The actress must always be dearer than the actor; goes closer to the heart, draws tenderer tears. Then she came earlier, and took the first possession; and she lasted longer, charming all London in her reading, whilst he lay in a foreign grave.[8] Add that the tragedy in which they were best remembered was one in which the heroine must always predominate, for Lady Macbeth is the moving spirit of the play. [...]

Another and a very different test of John Kemble's histrionic skill was the life and body which he put into the thin shadowy sketches of Kotzebue,[9] then in his height of fashion. Mr Canning,[10] by the capital parodies of the 'Anti-Jacobin,' demolished the sentimental comedy of the German school, a little unmercifully perhaps, for with much that was false and absurd, and the bald gibberish of the translator, for which the author is not answerable, the situation were not only effective, but true. As Mr Thackeray[11] has somewhere observed, the human heart was there, and John Kemble contrived to show its innermost throbbings. [...]

In the meanwhile, frequent visits to London had made known to me the successive glories of the two great Theatres.[12] I had seen the boyish grace of Master Betty,[13] and all the charm of womanly tenderness in Miss O'Neill,[14] and had watched the fiery impulse and gushing pathos that had electrified the town in Edmund Kean. [...]

About this time, too, my own prospects, so bright and sunny in early youth, become gradually over-clouded. [...] We were now so poor, that it became a duty to earn money if I could, and how I could, and so I determined to write a play. [...]

My first attempt was a blank comedy, on a pretty story, taken from a French *feuilleton* – a story so pretty, that it made the first manager, to whom, without any introduction, I ventured to send it, pause to consider; and after his final decision, tempted an amateur composer into requesting me to turn it into a opera; by which means I achieved a double rejection of the same piece. Then, nothing daunted, I tried Tragedy, and produced five acts on the story of 'Fiesco', which would doubtless have been rejected also had they ever fallen into the hands of a manager.

But just as, conscious of the feebleness of my attempts, of the smallness of my means, and the greatness of my object, I was about to relinquish the pursuit in despair, I met with a critic so candid, a friend so kind, that, aided by his encouragement, all difficulties seem to vanish. [...] 'Foscari' was the result of this encouragement – a womanish play, which acts better than it reads. [...]

Great, at the moment, were those anxieties and tribulations, the rather than money arrangements most important to those dearer to me than myself were staked on the issue. [...]

To one accustomed to the imposing aspect of a great theatre at night, blazing with light and beauty, no contrast can be greater than to enter the same theatre at noontide, leaving daylight behind you, and stumbling as best you may through dark passages, and amidst the inextricable labyrinth of scenery and lumber of every description. [...]

To me – no offence to the Theatre Royal Covent Garden – it always recalled the place where I first made acquaintance with the enchantment of the scene, by reminding me of some prodigious barn. [...]

Oh, that din! Voices from every part, above, below, around, and in every key, bawling, shouting, screaming; heavy weights rolling here and falling there, bells ringing one could not tell why, and the ubiquitous call-bay everywhere! If one element prevailed amongst these conflicting noises, it was certainly the never-pausing stroke of the carpenter's hammer. [...]

Even the new scenes had their perils. [...] And the turmoil about costume! A good deal of that squabbling was transacted in some remote part of the upper regions, where tailors and dress-makers held their court. [...] I had early made the discovery that the less an author meddled in such matters the better. [...]

No end to the absurdities and discrepancies of a rehearsal! I contributed my full share to the amount, and began pretty early, so soon indeed as the very first words that I ever uttered behind the scenes. [...]

Troubled and anxious though they were, those were pleasant days, guns and all; days of hope dashed with so much fear, of fear illumined with its fitful rays of hope. And those rehearsals, where for noise of every sort nobody is ever to be found where he is wanted, and nobody ever seems to know a syllable of his part; those rehearsals must have some good in them notwithstanding. In the midst of the crowd, the din, the jokes, and the confusion, the business must somehow have gone on; for at night the right scenes fall into the right places, the proper actors come at the proper times, speeches are spoken in due order, and, to the no small astonishment of the novice, who had given herself up for lost, the play succeeds.

Not that I had nerve enough to attend the first representation of my tragedies. I sate still and trembling in some quiet apartment near. [...]

When 'Rienzi,' after a more than common portion of adventures and misadventure, did come out with a success rare in a woman's life, I missed the eager congratulations which I should have received from her[15] [...], because no part of my success was more delightful than the pleasure which it excited amongst the most eminent of my female contemporaries. Maria Edgeworth, Joanna Baillie, Felicia Hemans (and to two of them I was at the time unknown), vied in the cordiality of their praises. [...]

And dramatic success, after all, is not so delicious, so glorious, so complete a gratification as, in our secret longings, we all expect to find. It is not satisfactory. It does not fill the heart. It is an intoxication, followed like other intoxications, by a dismal reaction. The enchanting hope is gone, and is ill-replaced by a temporary triumph – very temporary! [...]

Then came 'Charles the First' and his calamities, of a very different sort from any of the former, since managers and actors were equally eager to bring out the play. The hindrance lay in Mr George Colman, the licenser, who saw a danger to the State in permitting the trial of an English Monarch to be represented on the stage, especially a Monarch whose martyrdom was still observed in our churches. It was in vain that I urged that my play was ultra loyal: that having taken the very best moment of Charles's life and the very worst of Cromwell's. [...] Mr Colman was inexorable; and the tragedy, forbidden at the two great houses, was afterwards produced at a minor theatre with no ill effect to the reigning dynasty. [...]

So much for the Tragedies. There would have been many more such, but that the pressing necessity of earning money, and the uncertainties and delays of the drama at moments when delay or disappointment weighed upon me like a sin, made it a duty to turn away from the lofty steep of Tragic Poetry to the every-day path of Village Stories.

Please see the Works Cited for further information on the sources used in this essay.

Notes

1 Maria Edgeworth was an Anglo-Irish novelist and educator. Joanna Baillie, Scottish playwright, poet, and theorist of theatre and drama. Felicia Dorothea Hemans poet best known for sentimental verse. See entries on Baillie and Hemans in this volume.

2 Thomas Holcroft (1745–1809), English actor and author known for spoken dramas of serious moral purpose. Thomas Morton (bap. 1764–1838), English dramatist most often produced at Covent Garden. George Colman (1732–1794), English playwright and father of playwright George Colman "The Younger" (1762–1836). Richard Brinsley Sheridan (1751–1816), Irish comic playwright. Samuel Foote (bap. 1721–1776), English actor, manager, and dramatist who managed the Haymarket until 1776. John O'Keeffe (bap. 1747–1833), Irish playwright, actor, and theatrical memoirist. Charles Dibdin (bap. 1745–1814), English actor, playwright, and musician.

3 Letitia Elizabeth Landon (1802–1838), also known as L.E.L., was a prolific and famous writer. Landon died under mysterious circumstances in Africa, shortly after moving there to be with her husband, who was in charge of the Cape Coast Castle. This is probably why Mitford addresses her twice as "poor," showing sympathy for her unfortunate friend.

4 She refers to Miss Frances Rowden (1774–1840?), schoolteacher and poet. She runs a boarding school for young female scholars at Hans Place.

   5 Lady Caroline Ponsonby, later Lamb (1785–1828), novelist and poet.
   6 Frances Anne "Fanny" Kemble (1809–1893), actress daughter of Charles and Marie Kemble and niece of Sarah Siddons.
   7 Edmund Kean (1787–1833), English actor best known for his Shakespearean roles. David Garrick (1717–1779), renowned English actor affiliated with the Drury Lane Theatre in London.
   8 He died in Lausanne, Switzerland, 26 February 1823.
   9 August von Kotzebue (1761–1819), German dramatist successful on the London stage around 1800.
  10 Gorge Canning (1770–1827), Tory deputy and public speaker.
  11 William Makepeace Thackeray (1811–1863) novelist best known for *Vanity Fair* (1847–1848).
  12 Drury Lane and Covent Garden.
  13 William Henry West Betty (1791–1874), Irish child actor.
  14 Elizabeth O'Neill (1791–1872), Irish actress who saw success on the London stage.
  15 Mitford refers to Miss Porden, later Mrs Franklin, previously referenced.

Suggestions for Further Reading

Edward, Peter David. *Idyllic Realism from Mary Russell Mitford to Hardy*. London: Macmillan, 1988.

Mitford, Mary Russell. *Our Village: Sketches of Rural Character and Scenery*. London: Whittaker, 1824

———. *Selected Stories from our Village*. London: Blackie and Sons, 1894.

———. *The Dramatic Works*, 2 vols. London: Hurst and Blackett, 1854.

Morrison, Kevin A. "Foregrounding Nationalism: Mary Russell Mitford's *Our Village* and the Effects of Publication Context." *European Romantic Review*. 19.3 (2008): 274–287.

Pietropoli, Cecilia. "The Tale of the Two Foscaris from the Chronicles to the Historical Drama: Mary Mitford's *Foscari* and Lord Byron's *The Two Foscari*." *British Romanticism and Italian Literature: Translating, Reviewing, Rewriting*. Eds. L. Bandiera and D. Saglia, New York, NY: Rodopi, 2005, pp. 209–220.

Watson, Vera. *Mary Russell Mitford*. London: Evans Brothers, 1949.

20 AMELIA CHESSON (1833–1902)

Tracy C. Davis

Introduction

Richard Cobden and John Bright launched *The Star* in 1856 to "assume the mantle of the archetypical representative of the post-1855 penny press" (M. Hewitt 129). Frederick William Chesson (1833–1888), a young liberal political organizer with a little experience in newspaper writing, was hired on immediately. Though he never became as famous as Justin McCarthy, George Holyoake, or Edmund Beales – outspoken radical journalists who wrote on political and other topics for *The Star* – he stuck with the paper until its demise in 1869, rising to the position of acting editor. His diaries reveal an important second string to this line-up: his wife, Amelia Chesson, earned a guinea for each review she contributed. When she was in the first trimester of a pregnancy, or nursing an infant, Frederick brought home works of fiction, biography, and political history for her to review. Later in her pregnancies, or when she was weaning a child, she ventured out to review live performance. Though all her work was unsigned, her only obituary stipulates that she was known as the *Star*'s "chief musical critic [...] at a time when, perhaps, there was no other lady filling such a position. She must, therefore, be considered a pioneer in lady journalism. As a critic of singing, she was peculiarly successful; she possessed the faculty of comparison in a high degree" ("Amelia Ann Everard Chesson," 145).

At 11.00 am on 17 June 1857, the Chessons set out from Bloomsbury to attend the performance of *Judas Maccabaeus* at the Crystal Palace, Sydenham. From 1854, this vast pleasure palace located on extensive grounds in south London hosted a plethora of special events including agricultural fêtes, flower shows, and exhibitions, but it was best known for musical concerts, including the Handel Festival that had outgrown Exeter Hall (Goode; Piggott). At the time this review was published, Amelia was in the sixth month of her second pregnancy: she was in a venturing phase of her reproductive cycle. The Chessons may have collaborated on the review, though its detailed rendition of the vocal work is a hallmark of Amelia's later criticism, and since Frederick never reviewed another concert, it is more likely that he was there for pleasure. He had not attended the Handel Festival on Monday 15 June, and since the review also remarks on that day's performance of *The Messiah,* it is logical to assume that Amelia had attended that performance too. Frederick notes in his diary that Amelia stayed behind with her friend Alice Bauer; two women in their twenties would have been inconspicuous both in the venue and on their return by rail to central London, where Amelia could write and file her copy at her husband's office. This is the pattern whenever the diaries note her attendance at a performance the

DOI: 10.4324/9781003006923-21

day prior to a review being published in *The Star*. It is all but definitive, therefore, that Amelia wrote this, in which case it is the earliest known example of performance criticism by a British woman in the daily press. In fact, this antedates any other known female British newspaper critic by several decades (Kent; Davis). As such, its focus on the broad spectrum of performance – not just musicians' acumen – is important as a holistic approach to "eventness" and public experience. It is also important to note that a woman whose financially strapped family prioritized her receipt of music lessons in childhood, yet who never showed exceptional musical precocity, could become a professional critic.

Several features of the writing are especially notable. The entire route from Buckingham Palace to Sydenham (nearly eight miles) is constitutive of the performance, as readers are encouraged to envision the cavalcade of carriages cheered by well-wishers. The Queen had given birth to her ninth (and last) child two months before, which partially accounts for the joyful reception. A week later, she would give her husband the title Prince Consort, and soon after, news of the rebellion and atrocities in India would reach Britain, destabilizing national confidence but affirming the masses' – though not *The Star*'s – jingoistic support for queen and country.

Amelia Chesson is careful to describe the royal party's arrangement (Queen, Princess Royal, and Archduke Maximillian in front; Albert, the Prince of Wales, and King of Prussia behind). Albert, the musical connoisseur, followed the score while the orchestra of 385 and chorus of 2,500 performed ("Handel Festival" 572). The soloists were praiseworthy, but the most striking moment was at the end, when the interpolated "Old Hundredth," a mid-sixteenth-century setting of Psalm 100, recapped the sense of the occasion:

> All people that on earth do dwell,
> Sing to the Lord with cheerful voice.
> Him serve with mirth, His praise forth tell;
> Come ye before Him and rejoice.

In its initial test, the great organ, installed for this season, could be heard a mile away. The effect of its harmonies with the massed chorus and orchestra was so overwhelming that after the psalm was sung the crowd of 11,649, including the royal party, stood in silence for a couple of minutes. Only when the Queen rallied herself to depart did the assembly erupt in cheers. The gentlemen of her party remained behind to take a turn in the grounds, guided by the architect Sir Joseph Paxton, with the German guests clearly discomfited by the accompanying crowd's pressure to engage with them.

Judas Maccabaeus was not, at this time, Handel's best-known work. And so it was to be expected that the audience would want to acquire the libretto to read and then take home as a souvenir. This facet of Victorian concert (and opera) going is not something that normally receives notice, and yet this review not only specifies that W. Pole prepared the libretto but also that in addition to the 180 stewards who saw the public to their seats there were 120 child booksellers who ably distributed the book of words. Thus, nearly the entire spectrum of society is in evidence in the review: monarchs, aristocracy, cognoscenti, the middle classes, artists, and hawkers. Thereby Amelia Chesson stresses that there are two measures of success: not just the rendition of the music but also the material conditions of staging and coordinating the orderly spectacle constituted by the audience. After all, the penny press existed to put high-quality journalism within reach of the masses. This review not only informed working people about what they could not attend on a Wednesday afternoon in June but also how it was managed and to whom this was due.

Amelia Chesson

THE HANDEL FESTIVAL SECOND DAY'S PERFORMANCE (1857)

The announcement that Her Majesty and a Royal Party would attend the performance of *Judas Maccabaeus*, selected as the subject of the second of the Handel days, attracted an additional number of visitors to the Crystal Palace yesterday. It was pretty generally known that the royal visitors would repair to Sydenham by what is called "the private road," and from a very early hour the entire line was thronged at the principal points with loyal pedestrians, undeterred by the louring aspect of the weather, or the clouds of dust which every now and then swept along in blinding drifts. As early as ten o'clock, carriages conveying members of the aristocracy began to enliven the route, gradually increasing in number, until it assumed the appearance peculiar to an Epsom or Ascot gathering. From Buckingham Palace to Sydenham, by way of Vauxhall, Nine Elms, Kennington-cross, and Stockwell-green, through Dulwich, it presented a most animated appearance, and as the royal party passed along, the air was rent with loud acclamations. They reached the Crystal Palace at five minutes after one, and at ten minutes past her Majesty made her appearance. She was greeted with deafening cheers, which reverberated through the building in heavy waves, and was then responded to by the multitudes outside. A space had been elegantly fitted up for the party, at the corner of one of the galleries immediately opposite the orchestra, Sir J. Paxton officiating as master of the ceremonies. The Queen was accompanied by Prince Albert, the Prince of Wales, Prince Alfred, Prince Frederick William of Prussia, the Archduke Maximilian, and a numerous suite, some of whom occupied seats in the side gallery. Prince Albert sat behind the Queen, having the Prince of Wales on his right and Prince Frederick William on his left. The Archduke occupied a seat on her Majesty's left hand, the Princess Royal one on her right. The Royal party, but especially Prince Albert, who followed the score page for page, and frequently checked the time, paid the greatest attention to the performance, and applauded the most striking passages. They retired between the first and second parts, and were duly escorted to the refreshment pavilion and back.

The scene within presented much the same appearance as on Monday, only that there were fewer unoccupied seats. The galleries facing the Royal party were filled by members of the aristocracy, of the diplomatic circle, and of the *elite* of the gentry; and when the mighty assembly beneath the transparent roof rose, as the first bars of the National Anthem surged through the vast area, the spectacle was one of the most imposing that can be conceived.

The first verse of the national anthem was sung in solo by Madame Clara Novello, the second as a quartet by Madame Rudersdorff, Miss Dolby, Mr. Sims Reeves, and Herr Formes, and the third by the full orchestra. The whole was preceded by an imposing roll upon the military drums, to which the large drum, in its full force, contributed the concluding note.

The performance of *Judas Maccabaeus*, yesterday, really seemed to surpass that of the *Messiah* on Monday. We cannot, indeed, conceive how it could be possible to have a finer performance than that of yesterday. Of course, no one would have been surprised to discover that the solos all went well; the long tried and well known ability of all the principal vocalists was of itself sufficient to render this a matter of certainty. But what really does surprise everybody capable of forming an opinion upon the subject, is that an immense orchestra [*sic* chorus] of 2,500 performers can be got so completely under control that they can execute the most complicated choruses with as much ease and precision as could possibly be exhibited by four single individuals in the performance of a quartet. This fact obviously demonstrates the care with which the voices must have been selected, and reflects great credit upon the discrimination of the committee of the Sacred Harmonic Society; but still, after making every allowance for this element, it could scarcely have been expected that so large a body of choristers could be collected from all parts of the country to sing together for the first time, in a building to which they were totally unaccustomed, and yet that they should not make a single slip. The first two days of the Handel Festival, however, are now over, and not the slightest flaw has been discoverable in any of the choruses which have been executed by the 2,500. On the contrary, every chorus has been magnificently rendered, and the astonishment and delight which have been clearly depicted on the countenances of the audience as chorus after chorus has been given is one proof, among others which might be quoted, of the perfect character of the performances. It is a point worthy of note, too, that the vast mass of voices and instruments does not produce an undue sensation of *loudness*, and we refer to this because we have met with persons who are afraid to venture to the Festival lest they should be struck deaf for the remainder of their natural lives. They have heard so much about Gray and Davison's immense organ, Distin's monster drum, and the 2,500 performers to boot, that they have come to the conclusion that the resultant of all these elements of sound must be something really terrific. In this, however, they are sadly mistaken, and we would strongly advise them to hear the *Israel in Egypt* on Friday, and they will then be convinced at once that they have come to a wrong conclusion. The tones produced by the mighty orchestra are not hard and piercing, but are beautifully full and mellow. They travel a long way, it is true, but they are not in the slightest degree oppressive, even in the immediate vicinity of the performers.

It is difficult to select any of the choruses of yesterday for special comment, they were all so well done. Every chorus, too, told with the audience, and even those choruses which present more than ordinary difficulty were faultlessly executed. We have philosophically made up our minds to wait till the next Handel Festival to hear "Mourn, ye Afflicted Children!," "Hear us, O! Lord," and "Fallen is the Foe," performed as they were yesterday. "Tune your Harps" was also a magnificent performance. The grand climax, so far as the audience was concerned, was reached in the full chorus to "See the Conquering Hero Comes." This was so splendidly done that the people in their enthusiasm forgot that the Queen was present, and uproariously demanded an *encore*. Mr. Costa, as in duty bound, went on with the succeeding march, and the first part was played completely through almost in dumb show; but when it had to be repeated *piano*, the clapping of hands gained the day, and the conductor turned imploringly to the Queen to know what he was to do. Her Majesty, nothing loth—for it was clear that none had appreciated it more highly than the illustrious occupants of the Royal box—graciously gave the signal for its repetition, and the whole piece, commencing with the trio by Mesdames Novello and Rudersdorff, and Miss Dolby was performed a second time, if possible, in grander style than at first. At the commencement of the Hallelujah chorus, at the conclusion of the oratorio, her Majesty rose, and the audience immediately followed her example, and remained standing during the performance. The "Old Hundredth" was then performed by the entire strength of the band and chorus, for the purpose of exhibiting the grand effects of simple harmony by a large body of voices, and a sublimer result could not possibly be conceived. It actually took the power of speech from the listeners, so that no man could turn to his neighbour and remark upon its grandeur, and at its close they were so completely overwhelmed that all notion of applause was completely beaten out of them, and the performances of the day were concluded in complete silence—a silence which was only broken by the cheers which greeted her Majesty when, a minute or two afterwards, she took her departure.

We ought to have stated that the solo singers were Mesdames Novello and Rudersdorff, Miss Dolby, Messrs. Montem Smith, Sims Reeves, and Weiss, and Herr Formes, all of whom sang magnificently. But Mr. Sims Reeves as usual electrified the audience by his execution of "Call Forth Thy Powers," and "Sound an Alarm."

As soon as the performance was concluded, the Queen—who, with the remainder of the royal party, had stood whilst the Old Hundredth was being sung—advanced to the front of the platform, and repeatedly bowed to the vast auditory, who cheered her more vociferously, if possible, than when she made her appearance. Prince Albert, the Prince of Wales, Prince Frederick William, and the Archduke Maximilian, remained after the Queen had left the building, and, escorted by Sir Joseph Paxton and a body of police, made the tour of the grounds.

They remained some time admiring the grand jets in the lower basin, and Prince Albert pointed out to his distinguished guests the most striking points of view. Their progress, seen from the point we occupied, reminded us of a real hunt. They were waylaid at every point, surrounded, stared at, cheered at, and let depart, to be again waylaid, surrounded, and gaped at by another eager crowd coming from another point of the gardens, the scene being continued until they took refuge in the carriages which conveyed them back to Buckingham Palace. It is quite true that the trio of Princes very graciously bowed to the assembled multitude; but we doubt whether, at least two of them (Prince Albert has, by this time, become accustomed to it), consider being hunted down in this indiscreet manner, stared out of countenance, and often even jostled, is a very striking mark of anything but the most vulgar and impertinent curiosity.

A very able analysis of yesterday's oratorio, written by Mr. W. Pole expressly for the festival, was sold in the building, and materially assisted the audience in their appreciation of the performance. This last item reminds us that we have omitted to award a due meed of praise to the intelligent and civil host of little fellows, 120 in number, who sell the "books of words" and who have been trained into their present state of efficiency by Mr. Edgar A. Waugh. We ought also not to forget Mr. D. Sims, who has organised a staff of 150 efficient and polite stewards who conduct people to their seats without the smallest overcrowding or confusion. As we are upon this subject we may remark that it proves a good gauge of the magnitude of the festival when 120 boys are required to sell books, and 150 stewards to guide people to their seats.

Amongst the distinguished visitors present were—Lord Kincaid, Mr. Justice Willes, Sir Hugh Rose, Lady Douglas, Lord and Lady Faversham, Baron Bramwell,

Lady Thos. de Malahide, Lord and Lady Dynevor, Lord Wensleydale, the Turkish Ambassador, Lady Abinger, Earl and Countess of Stamford and Warrington, Lord Ward, Lord Templeton, Lord Rothesay, Sir B. Brodie, Lady Belhaven, Vice-Chancellor Wood, the Countess Listowell, the Netherlands Minister, Lord Stuart, the Archbishop of Canterbury, Earl of Wilton, Sir T. Troubridge, Lord Robert Grosvenor, Lady Atherton, Sir J. and Lady Matheson, Lord Rivers, Lady Harry Vane, Lord James Stuart, Lady Panmure, the Dowager Countess of Essex, the Bishop of Lincoln, Lord and Lady Howard de Walden, Lady Beresford, Earl and Countess of Jersey, and Lady W. Paulet.

The total number of visitors was 11,649.

––––––

In the evening, a performance of Mr. Costa's "Eli" was given in Exeter hall, to which all the country members of the Festival chorus were invited, and with which they appeared to be delighted universally. Mr. Sims Reeves sung the Philistine war song in his best style, and which, in obedience to a demand for an encore, he repeated—we presume out of compliment to the "provincials." The other solo singers were—Madame Novello, Miss Dolby, Herr Formes, and Mr. Weiss. The unaccompanied quartet in the second part was, as usual, encored, and the performance of the oratorio was, throughout, of the most unexceptionable character.

Please see the Works Cited for further information on the sources used in this essay.

Suggestions for Further Reading

Chambers, Deborah, Linda Steiner, and Carole Fleming. "Early Women Journalists: 1850–1945." *Women and Journalism*. London: Routledge, 2004. 15–34.

Cima, Gay Gibson. "'To be Public as a Genius and Private as a Woman' The Critical Framing of Nineteenth-Century British Women Playwrights." *Women and Playwriting in Nineteenth-Century Britain*. Eds. Tracy C. Davis and Ellen Donkin. Cambridge: Cambridge University Press, 1999. 35–53.

Gray, F. Elizabeth. *Women in Journalism at the Fin de Siécle: Making a Name for Herself.* New York, NY: Palgrave Macmillan, 2012.

Onslow, Barbara. *Women of the Press in Nineteenth-Century Britain.* New York, NY: St. Martin's Press, 2000.

Special section on Women of the Press in the 1890s. *Victorians: A Journal of Culture and Literature.* 132.1 (2017).

21 FRANCES A. KEMBLE (1809–1893)

Catherine Burroughs

Introduction

When Frances Anne Kemble (1809–1893)–the niece of legendary British actress Sarah Siddons (1755–1831)—made her debut as Juliet in 1819 at Covent Garden, expectations were high. Twenty-eight members of her family had acted on the English stage from the late eighteenth century onward. But even though Kemble described acting as "congenial […] to my nature" ("On the Stage"14), she also portrayed it as a kind of "emotional prostitution" (Scott xvii). Her *Notes Upon Some of Shakespeare's Plays* (1882)–to which she attached her theory of theatre, "On the Stage"–reveals Kemble's penchant for proto-psychological feminist criticism. In this document, she gives a close reading, from the perspective of an actress, of the central female characters in some of Shakespeare's best known plays, *Macbeth*, *The Tempest*, and *Romeo and Juliet*; she also includes an analysis of Queen Katharine in *Henry VIII*. Kemble's *Notes* may be read as part of the trend during the late Romantic and Victorian periods to focus attention on female character, such as one finds in Anna Murphy Jameson's *Characteristics of Women: Moral, Poetical, and Historical* (1832) and Mary Cowden Clarke's *The Girlhood of Shakespeare's Heroines* (1852).

As a playwright, poet, and copious journalist and diarist, Kemble's bent was literary, and her theory of acting in "On the Stage" resulted in what George Arliss has called "the most careful analysis of the actor in juxtaposition with his art that one is likely to find in dramatic literature" (1). In the short piece excerpted here, Kemble introduces a dichotomy crucial to her theory–dividing the instinctual ("the dramatic") from the self-conscious ("the theatrical")–in order to clarify why she found acting so "repugnant" ("On the Stage" 10).

Kemble was very harsh on the profession into which she had been born. In "On the Stage," as she ranks the different categories that make up the Arts, she claims that acting "requires no study worthy of the name; it creates nothing; it perpetuates nothing" (16). This is because the "combination of the power of representing passion and emotion with that of imagining or conceiving it" is essential to make a good actor; their combination in the highest possible degree alone makes a great one" (5). But in Kemble's experience, acting "has little to do with the […] reflective and analytical quality" (14).

Kemble is especially disdainful of English actors; in her view, they have lost "the dramatic emotional temperament and the scenic science of effect" (7). While she admired her aunt, Sarah Siddons, who created "one of the grandest dramatic achievements that could be imagined, with the least possible admixture of the theatrical

DOI: 10.4324/9781003006923-22

element" (7), Kemble asserted that she lacked the intellectual qualities that might have made her a more interesting actor to watch.

According to Kemble, Siddons' remarks on playing Queen Constance and Lady Macbeth (*The Reminiscences of Sarah Kemble Siddons 1773–1775*)–are "feeble and superficial" (13); and although the great eighteenth-century actor, David Garrick, was "the most perfect actor that our stage has ever produced" (8), his theatrical taste "induced him to garble, desecrate, and disfigure the masterpieces of which he was so fine an interpreter [...]" (8).

The problem with acting for Kemble is that, when one represents a character on stage it is a "mere reception [...] of the creation of another mind," and its "representation of the character thus apprehended, has no reference to the intrinsic, poetical, or dramatic merit of the original creation" (14). A keen analyst of Shakespeare, here Kemble echoes the "apprehend/comprehend" binary that Duke Theseus employs in Act V of *A Midsummer Night's Dream* to explain to Hippolyta, his betrothed, why he doesn't believe the fantastic accounts of the young lovers, when they return to Athens from their wondrous experience of the forest nearby. Given his rational bent, Theseus tries to distance himself from the infatuated young people by stating: "Lovers and madmen have such seething brains,/Such shaping fantasies that *apprehend*/More than cool reason ever *comprehends*" (V.i.4–6, my emphasis). Theseus' monologue actually erodes the opposition between what he represents as two distinct modalities, and in short, his speech conveys the importance of wedding together what, in "On the Stage," Kemble separates into "the theatrical" and "the dramatic." But Kemble's insistence on this dichotomy as a way to elevate her intellectual abilities over her instinctual responses conveys the fact that, when it came to performing, she grew almost afraid of her emotionalism and developed stage fright about the prospect of letting herself become subsumed by any character she was playing. Yet, paradoxically, "On the Stage" also makes the case for acting as an important channel for both apprehending *and* comprehending one's heightened and intense feelings.

Novelist Henry James wrote of Kemble's body of work, which included a number of plays: "Nobody connected with the stage could have savored less of 'the shop' [...] but if she got rid of her profession, she could never get rid of her instincts, which kept her dramatic long after she ceased to be theatrical" (ctd. in Clinton 258). Indeed, after a scandalous divorce from the American businessman, Pierce Butler—the result of Kemble's commitment to abolitionism and her determination to expose the horrors of the plantation that Butler owned in Georgia (in *Journal of a Residence on a Georgia Plantation in 1838–1839* [1863])—she remained dramatic to the end, conducting solo performances of Shakespeare from behind a desk to paying audiences.

Frances Anne Kemble

Excerpt from "On the Stage" (1882)

Things dramatic and things theatrical are often confounded together in the minds of the English people, who, being for the most part neither the one nor the other, speak and write of them as if they were identical, instead of, as they are, so dissimilar that they are nearly opposite.

That which is dramatic in human nature is the passionate, emotional, humorous element, the simplest portion of our composition, after our mere instincts, to which it is closely allied, and this has no relation whatever, beyond its momentary excitement and gratification, to that which imitates it, and is its theatrical reproduction; the dramatic is the *real,* of which the theatrical is the *false.*

Both nations and individuals in whom the dramatic temperament strongly preponderates are rather remarkable for a certain vivid simplicity of nature, which produces sincerity and vehemence of emotion and expression, but is entirely without the *consciousness* which is never absent from the theatrical element.

Children are always dramatic, but only theatrical when they become aware that they are objects of admiring attention; in which case the assuming and dissembling capacity of *acting* develops itself comically and sadly enough in them.

[...] The combination of the power of representing passion and emotion with that of imagining or conceiving it—that is, of the theatrical talent with the dramatic temperament—is essential to make a good actor; their combination in the highest possible degree alone makes a great one.

There is a specific comprehension of effect and the means of producing it, which, in some persons, is a distinct capacity, and this forms what actors call the study of their profession; and in this, which is the alloy necessary to make theatrical that which is only dramatic, lies at the heart of their mystery and the snare of their craft in more ways than one: and this, the actor's *business,* goes sometimes absolutely against the dramatic temperament, which is nevertheless essential to it.

[...] There is something anomalous in that which we call the dramatic art that has often arrested my attention and exercised my thoughts; the special gift and sole industry of so many of my kindred, and the only labour of my own life, it has been a subject of constant and curious speculation with me, combining as it does elements at once so congenial and so antagonistic to my nature.

Its most original process, that is, the conception of character to be represented, is a mere reception of the creation of another mind; and its mechanical part, that is, the representation of the character thus apprehended, has no reference to the intrinsic, poetical, or dramatic merit of the original creation, but merely to the accuracy and power of the actor's perception of it; thus the character of "Lady Macbeth" is as majestic, awful, and poetical, whether it be worthily filled by its pre-eminent representative, Mrs. Siddons, or unworthily by the most incompetent of ignorant provincial tragedy queens.

This same dramatic art has neither fixed rules, specific principles, indispensable rudiments, nor fundamental laws; it has no basis in positive science, as music, painting, sculpture, and architecture have; and differs from them all, in that the mere appearance of spontaneity, which is an acknowledged assumption, is its chief merit.

[...] [Acting] is an art that requires no study worthy of the name; it creates nothing—it perpetuates nothing; to its professors, whose personal qualifications form half their merit, is justly given the need of personal admiration, and the reward of contemporaneous popularity is well bestowed on those whose labour consists in exciting momentary emotion.

Please see the Works Cited for further information on the sources used in this essay.

Suggestions for Further Reading

Burroughs, Catherine. "Introduction: Closet Drama Studies." *Closet Drama: History, Theory, Form.* New York and London: Routledge, 2019. 3–31.

———. "The Erotics of Home: Staging Sexual Fantasy in British Women's Drama." *Women's Romantic Theatre and Drama: History, Agency, and Performativity.* Eds. Lilla Maria Crisafulli and Keir Elam. Farnham, UK: Ashgate Publishing, Ltd., 2010. 103–21.

———. "'The Father Fostered at His Daughter's Breast': Fanny Kemble and *The Grecian Daughter.*" Special Issue: "Romanticism and Theater." *Nineteenth-Century Contexts.* 28.4 (2006): 335–345.

David, Deirdre. *Fanny Kemble: A Performed Life.* Philadelphia: University of Pennsylvania Press, 2007.

Kemble, Frances Anne. *Plays. (An English Tragedy; Mary Stuart; Mademoiselle De Belle Isle).* 1863. London: Forgotten Books, 2015.

22 OLIVE LOGAN (1839–1909)

Merritt Denman Popp

Introduction

Olive Logan (1839–1909) is a bit of a prude. Or at least that's how her work *Apropos of Women and Theatres* (1869) might appear today. Logan's collection of essays often adopts the stern tone that one might expect from a friendly but conservative older aunt. As Logan chastises young actresses for their involvement in "the leg business" – her term for productions which placed scantily-clad women onstage for the purpose of male consumption – a contemporary reader cannot help but note that she would certainly not be considered all that progressive in our present moment. The collection of essays explores several topics that might seem to firmly place the text in its own moment. Titles such as "About Bonnets," "About Getting Photographed," and "About the Quakers" might give a modern reader good reason to ask how such a text could be relevant as a work of theory today. However, despite its situation in history, Logan's work is a significant contribution to feminist theory and offers a needed perspective on what it means to work in the theatre as a feminist.

The actress, playwright, and theatre critic Olive Logan is perhaps best known for her association with the feminist movement in nineteenth-century America rather than her theatrical accomplishments. After hearing loss cut short her acting career, Logan turned to theatrical criticism. Her writing brought her a great deal of fame and led to an invitation from Susan B. Anthony and Elizabeth Cady Stanton to speak at the 1869 convention of the Equal Rights Association. Her speech at the convention turned Logan into a flashpoint in the discussion of women and women's bodies on stage in nineteenth-century America. *Apropos of Women and Theatres* is the result of the writing and thinking which both led up to and resulted from that speech. Through the first ten essays of the book Logan explores how women, theatre, and male audiences interact. Beginning with the first six essays, Logan argues first for the equality of women in social spheres. Secondly, through the next four pieces she argues against male consumption of women on stage. Finally, and concurrently with her second point, she argues that women should not be involved in any theatrical practice in which the consumption of women is the objective.

To understand Logan's theatrical theory, it is necessary to first understand her overall feminist perspective. Logan's speech at the Equal Rights Convention perhaps best elucidates her overall feminist theory as being primarily "for the enfranchisement of woman, for her elevation personally and socially, and above all for her right and opportunity to work at such employments as she can follow, with the right to such pay as men get" (Logan qtd. in E. Stanton, 386) For Logan, feminism is an issue

DOI: 10.4324/9781003006923-23

of economic agency. Throughout her writings, she is concerned primarily with the ability of woman to "secure the blessings of liberty," and it is this stance that informs her theatrical theory most heavily.

The bulk of Logan's theatrical theoretical perspective is developed within the chapters "About the Leg Business" and "About Nudity in Theatres." In these essays, Logan argues that there are two types of performers associated with the leg business: dancers, who perform for artistic purposes, and those who perform for the purpose of sexual titillation. While recognizing the harsh financial realities that might lead women to make such decisions, Logan condemns engaging in the leg business as a moral compromise made in search of celebrity or financial gain. For Logan, the leg business hinders female emancipation both socially and financially. She argues that the leg show and its accompanying reputation make women hesitant to enter the theatre despite the dearth of occupations available to them. She also argues that the leg show has overrun the theatre to such an extent that actresses must choose between appearing nude or being out of a job. For Logan, the leg business is one of male pleasure and female subjugation. Robert Allen sums up Logan's argument by noting that for her, the leg business "was not only a threat to public decency but also [...] an insidious inversion of her strategy for female economic emancipation [...] According to Logan, the burlesque performer succeeded to the degree that she was willing to display what made her dependent on men" (Allen 126).

One might argue that Logan is writing, then, in favor of a theatre in which women are blamed for the thoughts and behaviors of their audience members and are denied any expression of desire, but Logan explicitly blames the male gaze rather than its object for any indiscretion. Furthermore, it is worth noting that Olive's younger sisters performed in *Ixion* alongside Lydia Thompson in her American debut.[1] So, while the practices of Olive Logan's sisters certainly cannot stand in as proof of Olive's line of thinking, their work certainly helps to clarify that perhaps Logan's ideal theatre is not entirely devoid of all sexuality.

Olive Logan was part of a theatrical moment in which actresses were forced to justify their profession to a public that saw it as utterly damning. She was also part of a social moment in which women who spoke out for their rights had to defend themselves against accusations of immorality for having dared to speak their minds publicly. So while her tactics might be rooted in this cultural-historical moment, the heart of Logan's argument is to encourage women to work in the theatre in a way that will help the cause of women everywhere. For Logan, the end of all art is to fight for something worth fighting for. She shows us that not only the product but the process of creating can be a radical feminist act. And she implores us to think about the ways in which we are part of a valuable, intricately connected network of women in theatre.

Olive Logan

Excerpt from Apropos of Women and Theatres With a Paper or Two on Parisian Topics *(1869)*

About the Leg Business

Two classes of "female" performers are associated with the "naked drama," as it has been called. The first are a legitimate branch of the theatrical profession, and in their way may be, and often are, artists. They are the ballet-dancers.

The theatre as legitimately deals in music and dancing as it does in tragedy or comedy. Hence, the ballet is, and always has been, as freely recognized by the most cultured people (when they approve of the theatre at all) as any other feature of the mimic world.

For the dancers of the legitimate ballet, I – who know them as a class well – have some respect. They are for the most part a hard-working, ill-paid body of women, not infrequently the sole support of entire families, and their moral characters are not one whit affected by their line of business.

I am far from placing the ballet-girl in the same rank with an intellectual player; but there are grades of quality in all fields. She is a dancer, and loves dancing as an art. That pose into which she now throws herself with such abandon is not a vile pandering to the taste of those giggling men in the orchestra-stalls, but is an effort which, to her idea, is as loving a tribute to a beloved art as a painter's dearest pencil-touch is to him.

I have seen these women burst into tears on leaving the stage because they had observed men laughing among themselves, rolling their eyes about, and evidently making unworthy comments on the pretty creature before them, whose whole heart was for the hour lovingly given over to Terpsichore.

"It is *they* who are bad," said Mademoiselle B. to me the other night; "it is not we."

Those men who have impure thoughts are the persons on whom censure should fall, not upon the devotees of an art which the dancers love, and embody to the best of their ability, and without any more idea of impurity because of the dress, which is both the conventional and the only practicable one, than sculptors or painters have when they use the female figure as a medium to convey their ideas of poetry to the outside world.

[…]

But there is one set of exponents of the "naked drama" on whom I am for launching every possible invective of censure and reproach.

I mean those women who are "neither fish, flesh, nor fowl" of the theatrical creation, – who are neither actresses, pantomimists, nor ballet-girls, but who enjoy a celebrity more widely spread than many legitimate artists could hope to attain.

It is unpleasant to mention names; it is disagreeable and even dangerous to do so; but when such women as Cora Pearl, Vestvali, Menken,[2] and their like were insolent enough to invade the stage, and involve in the obloquy which falls on them hundreds of good and pure women, it was time for even the most tolerant critic to express disapprobation.

Whatever the private character of these women might be, – however good, however bad, – we were justified, from their public exhibitions, in denouncing them as shameless and unworthy.

It is true, they made more money than any other class of "performers;" more money than the poetic Edwin Booth; infinitely more than the intellectual E. L. Davenport.[3]

Stifle conscience, honor, and decency, and mere money-making is easy work, as these women and others who have come later fully illustrate.

In this chapter, whose main facts were set down before the fever for "blonde burlesque" raged in our theatres, I treat principally of a style of performance which the above-named women illustrate, and which is already fluttering in the last agonies of death. But so long as it lives, however sickly, my denunciation of the women who illustrate it has "excuse for being." These women are not devotees of any art. With the exception of Vestvali – a failure on every lyric stage, both in Europe and America, – they do not either act, dance, sing, or mime; but they habit themselves in a way which is attractive to an indelicate taste, and the inefficiency in other regards is overlooked.

Some of these women, strange as it may seem, have occasional aspirations for higher things.

A play which I prepared for the stage in the year 186—had for its heroine a woman of tender feelings, holy passions, such as every author loves to paint.[4]

After its production at one of the theatres in Broadway, I had many applicants for the purchase of copies. Among these applicants was a person whose name is thoroughly associated with the *Mazeppa*, Dick Turpin, Jack Sheppard school, and none other.[5]

I was astonished that such a woman could covet such a part [...]

I could not help expressing my astonishment at this seeming inconsistency to a person who was acquainted with my applicant, for I was not.

> "Well you see," he replied, referring to her familiarly, by her *petit nom*, "Leo hates the leg business as much as anybody; but, bless you, nothing else pays nowadays, – so what can she do?"

The leg business is a business which requires legs.

That these should be naturally symmetrical is desirable, but not indispensable; for the art of padding has reached such perfection, that nature has been almost distanced, and stands, blushing at her own incompetency, in the background.

[...]

Of personal beauty, [followers of the Mazeppa school] have often little; of intellectuality, of comprehension, of grace, genius, poetry, less; and of talent, none.

When the part they portray calls for the speaking of words, we lift our hands in blank astonishment that any creature with audacity enough to assume such a position can have so little ability to fill it.

If the stage could but be rid of the "leg business" scourge, there is no reason why it should not form a worthy channel for gifted, intelligent, and virtuous young women to gain a livelihood through. But in its present condition – overrun as it is by troops of immodest women – there is, alas! but little encouragement to any woman who respects herself to turn to the stage for support.

Openings for women are few enough, as governesses, and schoolmistresses, and shirtmakers, and hoopskirt drudges, generally, will testify.

But worse slavery than any or all of these is the thralldom of waiting to be married to have one's board and lodging paid.

A woman should have her destiny in her own hands as completely as a man has his, and the first boon that should be vouchsafed her is the happy knowledge that, before she lies down at night, she may really thank her Maker, and not her husband, for having given her this day her daily bread.

About Nudity in Theatres
[...]

What the *Tribune* calls the Dirty Drama, the *World* the Nude Drama, the *Times* the Leg Drama, and other journals various other expressive adjective styles of *drama*, I call the Leg *Business*, simply.[6]

Does any one call the caperings of a tight-rope performer the Aerial Drama? – the tricks of an educated hog the Porcine Drama?

How, then, does it happen that in attacking these yellow-haired nudities, I am compelled to say that they disgrace the dramatic profession?

In this wise: These creatures occupy the temples of the drama; they perform in conjunction with actors and actresses, on the same stage, before the same audience, in the same hour. They are made legitimate members of our theatrical companies, and take part in those nondescript performances which are called burlesques, spectacles, what you will. They carry off the chief honors of the hour; their names occupy the chief places on the bills; and, as I said in my speech at the Equal Rights Meeting at Steinway Hall,[7] they win the chief prizes in the theatrical world.

A woman, who has not ability enough to rank as a passable "walking lady" in a good theatre, on a salary of twenty-five dollars a week, can strip herself almost naked, and be thus qualified to go upon the stage of two-thirds of our theatres at a salary of one hundred dollars and upwards.

Clothed in the dress of an honest woman, she is worth nothing to a manager. Stripped as naked as she dare – and it seems there is little left when so much is done – she becomes a prize to her manager, who knows that crowds will rush to see her, and who pays her a salary accordingly.

These are simple facts, which permit of no denial. I doubt if there is a manager in the land who would dream of denying them.

[...]

When the *Black Crook* first presented its nude woman to the gaze of a crowded auditory, she was met with a gasp of astonishment at the effrontery which dared so much.[8] Men actually grew pale at the boldness of the thing; a death-like silence fell over the house, broken only by the clapping of a band of *claquers* around the outer aisles; but it passed; and, in view of the fact that these women were French ballet-dancers after all, they were tolerated.

By slow and almost imperceptible degrees, this shame has grown, until to-day the indecency of that exhibition is far surpassed. Those women were ballet-dancers from France and Italy, and they represented in their nudity imps and demons. In silence they whirled about the stage; in silence trooped off. Some faint odor of ideality and poetry rested over them.

The nude woman of to-day represents nothing but herself. She runs upon the stage giggling; trots down to the foot-lights, winks at the audience, rattles off from her tongue some stupid attempts at wit, some twaddling allusions to Sorosis, or General Grant, or other subject prominent in the public eye, and is always peculiarly and emphatically herself, – the woman, that is, whose name is on the bills in large letters, and who considers herself an object of admiration to the spectators.

The sort of ballet-dancer who figured in the *Black Crook* is paralleled on the stage of every theatre in this city, except one, at this time.

[...]

To create a proper and profitable sensation in the breast of man, she no longer suffices. Something bolder must be devised, – something that shall utterly eclipse and outstrip her.

Hence, the nude woman of to-day, – who outstrips her in the broadest sense. And, as if it were not enough that she should be allowed to go unhissed and unrotten-egged, she must be baptized with the honors of a profession for which Shakespeare wrote!

Managers recognize her as an actress, and pay her sums ranging from fifty to a thousand dollars a week, according to her value in their eyes. Actresses, who love virtue better than money, are driven into the streets by her; and it becomes a grave and solemn question with hundreds of honorable women what they shall do to earn a livelihood.

I say it is nothing less than an insult to the members of the dramatic profession, that these nude women should be classed among actresses and hold possession of the majority of our theatres. Their place is in the concert-saloons or the circus tents. Theatres are for artists.

[...]

Please see the Works Cited for further information on the sources used in this essay.

Notes

1 Lydia Thompson (1838–1908) was famous for her company of "British Blondes," an infamous burlesque troupe which first toured the United States in 1868.
2 Cora Pearl (c.1842–1836), Felicita Vestvali (c.1831–1880), and Adah Isaacs Menken (1835–1868) were female performers famed perhaps more for their appearance than their talents. Pearl was a courtesan; Vestvali was an opera singer best known for her breeches roles; Menken was most famous for her performance in *Mazeppa* in which she donned a sheer body suit and rode, seemingly naked, across the stage while strapped to a horse.
3 Edwin Booth (1833–1893) and Edward Loomis Davenport (1815–1877) were both renowned actors and members of powerful and respected theatre families.
4 Logan gives the date exactly as it is written here. This is a common convention of the time to avoid precise information.
5 On *Mazeppa*, see note 1 above. Dick Turpin and Jack Sheppard were both folk heroes about whom numerous burlesques and dramas were written. The title characters were often played by women as breeches roles.
6 Presumably *The Chicago Tribune, The News of the World* (London-based), and *The New York Times.*
7 Logan was invited by Elizabeth Cady Stanton and Susan B. Anthony to speak at the Equal Rights Convention on May 12th, 1869. The impetus for her invitation was likely her article "About the Leg Business" excerpted here and originally published in *Galaxy* magazine in 1867.
8 Generally considered the first modern musical, *The Black Crook* opened at Niblo's Garden in New York in September of 1866, ran for 474 performances, and grossed over a million dollars during its first run. The spectacle driven performance was notorious for its scantily clad dancers.

Suggestions for Further Reading

Allen, Robert. *Horrible Prettiness*. Chapel Hill: University of North Carolina Press, 1991.
Chinoy, Helen Krich. "Art versus Business." *The Drama Review.* 24.2 (1980): 3–10.
Roberts, Vera Mowry. "Olive Logan and 'The Leg Business.'" *The Journal of American Drama and Theatre.* 2.1 (1990): 5–10.

23 MICHAEL FIELD [KATHARINE HARRIS BRADLEY (1846–1914) AND EDITH EMMA COOPER (1861–1913)]

Jill R. Ehnenn

Introduction

Although they are today perhaps best known as poets and for their co-authored diary, *Works and Days* (1888–1914), Katharine Harris Bradley (1846–1914) and Edith Emma Cooper (1861–1913), who wrote collaboratively as "Michael Field," were prolific late-Victorian dramatists. Aunt and niece who "swore/against the world to be/Poets and lovers evermore," they published almost thirty closet dramas in verse and saw one play, *A Question of Memory*, produced at the Independent Theatre in 1893. The prefaces to Michael Field's early dramas, combined with their letters, illuminate the history of women writing drama and drama theory.

Born in Birmingham into a family of prosperous tobacco manufacturers, at fifteen Katharine Harris Bradley moved to Kenilworth to live with her sister, who soon gave birth to Edith Emma Cooper. As Marion Thain observes, "Katharine became to Edith everything one woman can be to another: mother, aunt, sister, friend, and eventually, lover" (3). In her twenties, Bradley studied at Cambridge, and in Paris. In 1878, both women studied classics and philosophy at University College, Bristol. From 1888–1899 they lived in Reigate, often traveling to London and the Continent, attending theatre, and visiting the historical sites, museums, and libraries that would inspire their writing. In 1899 they moved to Richmond. Although Bradley and Cooper's work celebrates women's beauty and power, they preferred the mentorship of men like John Ruskin and Robert Browning, and the companionship of male aesthetes like art critic Bernard Berenson, artist and theatre designer Charles Ricketts, and his partner, painter Charles Shannon. In 1907, after their beloved dog, Whym Chow, died, Bradley and Cooper converted to Catholicism and penned devotional poetry. Cooper died in 1913 of bowel cancer. Bradley died the following year of breast cancer, which she had kept secret from her cherished partner during Cooper's last months.

In the preface to their first published closet drama, *Callirrhoë* (1884), Michael Field proclaims, "this poem pleads guilty to anachronism;" indeed, most of their drama and poetry rewrites historical and mythological figures, including Mary Queen of Scots, Lucrezia Borgia, and Deirdre of the Sorrows. Yet like many of their fin-de-siècle contemporaries, Bradley and Cooper's diaries and letters proclaim, "We must be modern," and "We must make all things new." The prefaces to Michael Field's early plays illuminate how and why they used history, anachronism, and archaism in their dramatic work, even as, paradoxically, they aimed to follow their friends' directives to "Be Contemporaneous."

The selections that follow illustrate how, as playwright and thinker, Michael Field makes dramatic choices specific to their ideas about verse drama, modernity, and

DOI: 10.4324/9781003006923-24

the relation between art and life. Taken together, these texts make possible four observations:

First, despite rigorous historical study, the prefaces acknowledge that Michael Field's historical figures intentionally stray from fact. They justify their inaccuracy and anachronisms by invoking universalist impulses and Shakespeare. What Michael Field seem most invested in portraying with great accuracy is *feeling*–both their subjects' and their own.

Second, these documents attribute Michael Field's archaic style to their commitment to accurately portraying feeling. The 1885 letter responds to William Archer's negative review of *The Father's Tragedy* and *William Rufus,* which accuses them of "imitation" and "affected archaisms" irrelevant to "the modern world." For Archer, Michael Field's "fatal error [...] as a writer of dialogue consists in his unlagging adherence to the theory that poetical personages must speak a jargon as unlike as possible to ordinary human speech." Yet the co-authors resolved to continue in Elizabethan style because they believed it was best suited to the expression of emotion, which they believed was a necessary precondition for art and a key element of their fierce dedication to living with Dionysian passion.

Third, while closet drama is often considered theatre of the mind, for Michael Field, closet drama is a stage on which to "study and touch life," and a "mirror of ideal presentation." The preface to *The Tragic Mary* explains that for Bradley and Cooper, such study is an affective creative process similar to the dialectical epistemology of nineteenth-century aesthetic theorist Walter Pater, wherein both objective and subjective energies are provisional and interrelated. At the same time, however, such study happens best when one is (in the words of Bradley's letter) "transfigured by emotion."

Lastly, as Field asserts in the Preface to *Canute the Great,* "in the evolutionary struggle the survivor is himself a tragic figure." This explains the tragic, often violent, outcomes of the Dionysian passions in Michael Field's closet dramas. Like their heroes and heroines, they saw themselves as "tragic survivors of evolution" in an era they felt was "base with the Vulgarity of Materialism." They too felt the pull of tradition, despite how it disadvantaged women and women writers, as well as the anguish of modernity, of change and of loss, of relinquishing old allegiances, and of evolving toward the unknown–becoming contemporaneous.

In other words, what makes it possible for Michael Field (and their characters) to negotiate the painful difficulties of change is dedication to Dionysian passion. This is the universal that the co-authors see in both past and present. For Field, negative, tragic feeling is desirable in drama because it is Dionysian: the "glorification of enthusiasm [...] the sap of the Tree of Life." As the following selections illustrate, Dionysian passion constitutes escape, autonomy, and release from repression and oppression, even when it ends in death; and the style of Renaissance verse drama is best suited to portraying these passionate historical tales, however anachronistically.

Michael Field

Preface to Callirrhoë *(1884)*

Before the bar of Time this poem pleads guilty to anachronism. The establishment in Greece of the worship of Dionysus[1] reaches back into the dateless vistas of legend. The Author has so far defied Cronus,[2] that he has represented this foreign cult struggling for recognition in the midst of a refined and even sceptical Hellas.[3] Mighty voices excuse him, which have prevailed in silencing the accusation of "old Time"; he is their client. Euripides[4] puts the language of a sophist in the lips of pre-historic heroes. Virgil makes Æneas and Dido contemporaries.[5]

The Author would here remark that his account of the rise of the drama is purely imaginative and unhistorical.

The story of Callirrhoë is drawn from a classic source,[6] but has never been raised from obscurity by ancient bard or dramatist. This fact has permitted a latitude of treatment, unstraitened by the fear of presumption. Greek men and women are approached, not from the centre of nationality, but from the circumference of humanity. "All the world's a stage."

The myth of Dionysus is the glorification of enthusiasm, which the poet believed to be the sap of the Tree of Life, the spring and origin of all good fruit.

There is nothing lovelier among natural things than a bunch of grapes, a Bacchanalian cluster of rare crimson, grey with the lovely mist of the world of vegetation, which we call *bloom*. There is nothing lovelier among human things than Love with its halo of self-sacrifice. The natural object and human affection find the harmony in metaphor:–

> "Thou art the wine who drunkenness is all
> We can desire, O Love! and happy souls
> Ere from thy vine he leaves of autumn fall,
>
> Catch thee, and feed from their o'erflowing bowls
> Thousands who thirst for thy ambrosial dew."[7]

Preface to William Rufus *(1885)*

A visit to the New Forest[8] suggested this drama.

On a plot of scanty grass, with few trees about, and one small leafy oak almost touching it, stands a low, triangular, iron-cased stone, which is said to mark the place where the king fell. It is dark, stern, unobtrusive as Fate; it stands like a mile-stone on the way of Retribution. Here the tree grew from which the arrow glanced as if directed by Nature's anger at the destruction of her food-bearing field for the insolence of pleasure. Now there are no great trees near, no forest gloom; it is all soft and healed—scarcely the scar of association lingers. Only the poet, looking on that black memorial in the midst of "calm oblivious tendencies and silent over-growings"[9] of Nature can realize its import and history.

In the matter of accuracy this play is not to be regarded as a study of the Past. While the author has felt the sacredness of touching dead character, of which he has striven to bear witness that would not make him ashamed should be hereafter be brought face to face with the personages whose moods and thoughts he has sought to penetrate and reproduce, he has not scrupled to modify or compress events at his pleasure, holding that the dramatist, in face of chronology, may declare, with the imperiousness of Petruccio,[10] "It shall be what o'clock I say it is."

Again, the playwright is always the contemporary of the age he treats. He moves among living figures in whom he feels an interest too vital to be curious of their accent or demeanour.

The material he needs is faithful narrative that by its simplicity becomes pictorial. Such help the author has found in Mr. Freeman's *William Rufus*.[11] Regret that he may through ignorance have misused, or through covetousness too rashly appropriated the historical treasure of these volumes, cannot restrain him from acknowledging, with humility and delight, the debt he owes to their most inspiring pages.

Excerpt from Letter, Katharine Bradley to Edith Cooper (28 August, 1885)

[…]I want to say some grave[12] words to you. Do not desert Shakespeare and the Elizabethans. Those with the sobering influence of the great Greek dramatists, whom you ought to resolve at once to study, are the only Masters for us. Every dramatic writer must be full of his Shakespeare, as every religious writer Must be full of his Bible. We Must give up the tricks, the externalities, the archaisms,—to copy these is imitation, but we must seek to study and touch life as he—Shakespeare studied and touched it, and our speech Must always be utterly different from ordinary speech; because ordinary speech is not transfigured by emotion, and the ordinary speech of an Age like ours is base with the exceeding Vulgarity of Materialism. God shall give our thought a body as it pleaseth him.

Excerpt from Preface to Canute the Great (1887)

There is a peculiar pleasure in visiting a district of one's native land that has retained the idiosyncrasies of a province. […]This sensation I experienced in an exceptional degree when, two years ago, I spent some weeks of the summer in Norfolk.[13] The humble landscape, with its clear-cut outline on the horizon, its large sky, its penetrating sunshine, impressed me with the absence of mystery and reserve. Unobstructed stretches of corn-field lay open to the season and the wind. As soon as I sailed among the Broads[14] I discovered that this shadowless, unguarded country had a secret and seclusion of its own. […] Attracted by the features and traditions of this Danish kingdom, I cast about for a subject that should be of use to me as a playwright […and] determined to treat of the conflict of Edward Ironsides with Canute. […]

The story of Canute is full of the tragic element of evolution. […] In the evolutionary struggle the survivor is himself a tragic figure. Every sunrise brings him into sharper antagonism with the beliefs and habits that beset while they revolt him. He is alienated from his gods, his forefathers, his very dreams. His hopes are not founded on experience, not his ideals on memory.

Causes such as these invest the person of Canute[15] with a singular and mournful majesty. Centuries of fierce, pagan blood in his veins, he set himself to the task of becoming a great Christian governor and lawgiver to men. It is the business of this play to expound how these things came to be, and at what cost they were achieved.

As the ages roll on, we find no grim, inhuman shapes by the wheel of Destiny. The feeding of the spindle, the snapping of the threads, does not indeed belong to man; but to his hands a great, formative power has been given, and with this self-determination, if he has lost the misery of being the plaything of the gods, he has gained access to the deepest sources of pain in increased capacity for humiliation and remorse.

Excerpt from Preface to **The Tragic Mary** *(1890)*

Beautiful for situation, happy in the way the light visits her, novel in natural outline, and favoured even in the rise and declivity of her streets, it is nevertheless as the repository of her Queen's[16] tragedy that Edinburgh fascinates us to herself. She is to us what Troy would be could we move now among her streets and palaces, could we learn where Helen stood forth upon the walls, or pace the rooms that Helen made beautiful by habitation. In the apartments of Holyrood[17] we can touch the very silks that Queen Mary handled; the mirror of scalloped edge, graved with alternate doves, and quatrefoils, that without contradiction reflected her features, still hands in her chamber: the flushed tatters of her curtains are before us. And beholding these things we are seized with a passionate desire of access, an eagerness of approach: we cannot pause to wonder, or debate, or condemn; an impulse transports us: we are started on an inevitable quest.

The woman who appeared to certain of her contemporaries to be a princess lacking in no virtue save discretion, and to other a creature full of guile, inconstancy, and malevolence, can but expose the mysteries of her nature, leaving us to resolve them. Of absolute knowledge we have nothing; her tragedy, clear-cut in detail, is vague in determination. We know, indeed that within the compass of her destiny great passions held their course, and great crimes reached their consummation; but we are ignorant to whom to assign the temptation or the guilt. A few hard facts are before us, a murder, an abduction, a marriage; with regard to none of these events can Mary Stuart's will be known. Her portraits cannot aid us even to firm conjecture: the most genuine are the least open in evidence. The face is softly pale; the lower lip is sucked in as one may see a running water caught under by its own little waves; the eyes are oval, languid, full of sensitive reticence; the ample brows disinterested rather than frank, touched with an universal clearness and perfection. [...]

The extremes of antithetical judgment passed on the character of Mary Stuart are presented in the writings of one man, George Buchanan,[18] who celebrated her virtues with his Latin muse, and afterwards transformed them into notorious vices in the reckless pages of his prose *Detectio*. [...] Between such devious versions of the same author a latitude pliant and shadowy is left for the psychologist and historian. The wife of Darnley and of Bothwell[19] will be various to various natures throughout the ages: for like Helen she never grows old; her allure consists only with an immortal being, her peerless value is that of a daughter of the gods. It is therefore possible for a dramatist to transcribe his sense of the facts of her life, to justify the vision of her as it has come to himself, and yet be reverently conscious of the splendid and passionate qualities of a former presentment. To a great poet of our time[20] she has appeared in majesty of intellect, conscious of the burthen of her own beauty, and devoting every power of spirit and sense to the reception or excitement of desire. The Mary Stuart who is now in process of canonisation has not yet been delineated; it is possible to dream of her, a creature perfect in action and forbearance from the day of her first communion to her bowing down upon the block. Neither of these ideals (one an incomparable achievement) can be deformed by my rendering of the great Marian legend. My impression from contact with a personality the facets of which present perpetual change have not been embarrassed or irrelevant, for they have grown from a vision almost to a conviction as I have explored and wrought.

The Queen herself lies sculptured in Westminster Abbey,[21] waiting with the serenity of patience a judgment other than that of men. Yet we are not permitted to withhold out human verdicts, if she is to live as a presence in our midst. We may believe that Clytæmnestra-like[22] she was a woman of haughty counsels and blood-stained career, or that her fame and nobleness were dragged down under a ring-net of conspiracies and detraction, or again that laxity of protest was the basis of her whole tragedy. These beliefs are but conjectures, and the real woman of magical nature must remain undiscovered and triumphant:

> kind be time or cruel,
> Jewel, from each facet flash your laugh at time.[23]

Please see the Works Cited for further information on the sources used in this essay.

Notes

1 Dionysus, is the Greek god of wine, fertility, ritual madness, theatre, and religious ecstasy.
2 In Greek mythology, Cronus is the son of Uranus and Gaia, leader of the Titans and generally considered the personification of Chronos, or time.
3 Greece.
4 Euripides (c.480–c.406 B.C.), the famous tragedian of Athens.
5 In Greek legend, Dido founded Carthage. In Greco-Roman legend, Æneas is a Trojan hero whose descendants found Rome. In the *Æneid* the Roman poet Virgil (c.70–19 B.C.) depicts Dido and Aeneas as tragic lovers; although most historians assert they were not contemporaries, the famed couple appear in art, literature, and opera.
6 Pausanias (c.110–180) in his *Descriptions of Ancient Greece,* tells the story of Coresus, priest of Dionysus, and the maiden, Callirrhoë.
7 From the poem *Prince Athanase, A Fragment* by Percy Bysshe Shelley (1792–1822).
8 Royal forest in southern England established by William the Conqueror in 1076; still owned by the Crown, today. It contains many ancient monuments, including The Rufus Stone, purported to mark the place of King William II (William Rufus)'s death in 1100.
9 From *The Excursion* by poet William Wordsworth (1770–1850).
10 The male protagonist in Shakespeare's *The Taming of the Shrew.*
11 *The reign of William Rufus and the accession of Henry the First* (1882).
12 This letter reacts to theatre critic William Archer's (1856–1924) extremely negative review of *The Father's Tragedy* and *William Rufus,* in *Pall Mall Budget* (27 August 1885) which took issue with Michael Field's Elizabethan style, which Archer felt was unsuited to the modern world.
13 County in East England, bordering the North Sea.
14 A network of rivers and lakes in Norfolk and Suffolk.
15 Cnut, or Canute the Great (990–1035) was Prince of Denmark who became King of England, 1016–1035.
16 Mary Stuart, Mary I of Scotland (1542–1587).
17 Palace in Edinburgh where Mary lived, 1561–1567.
18 George Buchanan, (1506–1582), Scottish historian, and Mary's tutor, c.1562.
19 Mary's second and third husbands, respectively.
20 Algernon Charles Swinburne (1837–1909) wrote a trilogy of verse dramas relating to Mary, Queen of Scots: *Chastelard* (1865), *Bothwell* (1874), and *Mary Stuart* (1881).
21 Famous London church where British monarchs are crowned and buried.
22 In Greek mythology, the wife of Agamemnon, king of Mycenae, and the sister of Helen of Troy. Clytemnestra is the subject of plays by Aeschylus and Euripides, among others.
23 From the poem, "Magical Nature" by Michael Field's friend and mentor, Robert Browning.

Suggestions for Further Reading

Bickle, Sharon. *The Fowl and the Pussycat: Love Letters of Michael Field, 1876–1909.* Charlottesville: University of Virginia Press, 2008.

Donoghue, Emma. *We Are Michael Field.* London: Absolute Press, 1998.

Parker, Sarah and Ana Parejo Vadillo, eds. *Michael Field, Decadent Moderns.* Athens: Ohio University Press, 2019.

Stetz, Margaret D. and Cheryl A. Wilson, eds. *Michael Field and their World.* High Wycombe, UK: The Rivendale Press, 2007.

24 CHARLOTTE PERKINS GILMAN (1860–1935)

Andrew Tolle

Introduction

Despite Charlotte Perkins Gilman's (1860–1935)[1] absence in histories of modern drama, she actively participated in it for at least four decades. Her legacy in American literature has largely been defined through her most famous work, "The Yellow Wallpaper" (1892), but she became a household name only after she published *Women & Economics* (1898). Critics describe her feminist utopia, *Herland* (1915), as a fictional representation of the ideas regarding natural and sexual selection that Gilman first presented in *Women & Economics*, where she coined the term "sexuo-economic relation." The two artifacts included here, "The Quarrel," and "Dame Nature Interviewed," both closet dramas originally published in *Kate Field's Washington* in 1890, show that she first relied on the dramatic form to "rehearse" for *Women & Economics*. Through these "practice plays," she workshopped her feminist response to Herbert Spencer's brand of social Darwinism.[2]

"The Quarrel" was originally published as "A Dramatic View" in a multi-genre series called "The Ceaseless Struggle of Sex." Gilman employs parallel structure among scenes to communicate the "ceaseless struggle" between two characters, tellingly named the pronouns "He" and "She." The "ceaseless struggle," according to this play, is a phase of oppression that continues to cycle but only if allowed by the oppressed. The parallelism of each scene is further reinforced by a gesture carried out just after the first lines of dialogue: in scenes one through four, He and She "embrace," but by scene five they only "shake hands" (239). So, in each scene, the two sexes agree to mutual attraction, then carry out some sort of physical exchange; but by the fifth scene, the exchange is less cordial. He and She have become more independent even though his position on women's roles has not changed. Although the struggle between the sexes may be "ceaseless," Gilman argues that it will end with the elevation of women whether or not men consent. Gilman contends in this play, as she would later articulate in *Women & Economics*, that the current oppressed status of women is a temporary part of the evolutionary timeline, and, as in "The Quarrel," the actions of men can only accelerate or delay the already inevitable conclusion of upheaval.

In "Dame Nature Interviewed," Gilman similarly lampoons the contradictory logic of Spencer's prevailing theories regarding male superiority. But in this play, Gilman explores her reform Darwinist ideas more fully and provides a more concise dramatic version of the arguments she presents in *Women & Economics*. Although longer than "The Quarrel," "Dame Nature Interviewed" contains only a single scene with

DOI: 10.4324/9781003006923-25

two characters: a male, "Reporter," and a female, "Nature." As the play's full title reveals, Reporter interviews Nature "on the Woman Question as it looks to her." Gilman speaks through the archetype of (Mother) Nature to voice her opinion on woman's place in evolutionary history. In so doing, she seizes the authoritative expertise of that role while also reminding readers (or hypothetical audience members) that their own cultural history once valued maternal evolutionary power.

Nature chides the Reporter (and men in general) for "getting around [her] laws" by "shut[ting]" women up rather than allowing them to exercise their "free choice of the best" males (139). By removing female agency, Nature argues, men had "upset [her] beautiful arrangement of sexual selection" (139). Gilman expands upon this idea in *Women & Economics* by pointing out the "peculiar inversion" of nature's "usual habit": in other species, the "males compete in ornament, and the females select" (54–55). Due to this inversion, the female "finds her economic environment in the male" rather than in the struggle for existence between species (58). This argument first appears in "Dame Nature Interviewed," when Nature explains that "the struggle for existence […] is just my [Nature's own] struggle to adapt the organism to its environment" but males had, over several centuries, perverted this arrangement: "You made yourself her environment […] and she had to struggle with you!" (139). Female inferiority may be the status quo, Gilman explains, but Darwin's theories suggest that the status quo is far from "natural."

In response to the Reporter's question regarding the "present advance of women," Nature proclaims that she not only approves of it, but that she is responsible for it as well. This claim surprises the Reporter, because he had been under the impression that Nature "made the other kind of woman," the subservient female resigned to the home. Somewhat offended, Nature explains that because man has "individual volition," he was able to, as the Reporter puts it, "make things against nature" such as the servile woman of the nineteenth century. This argument recalls the passage in *Women & Economics* in which males realize the convenience of "institut[ing] the custom of enslaving" females, making them "modified to sex to an excessive degree" (60, 39). Both through drama and through non-fiction, Gilman upends the Spencerian notion that female inferiority is a biological necessity.

Furthermore, Gilman depicts the character Nature's role in evolution with language that summons the dramaturgy of the naturalist playwrights of her time. Nature comments on her excitement with the stage of evolution that involved "protoplasm," which for her was "great fun" because protoplasm was "so docile!" This parallels a passage in *Women & Economics* in which Gilman lays out the process of "nature's slow but sure experiments" with "differentiation," where "out of the mere protoplasmic masses" evolved the complex human creature (29). Such language evokes the naturalists' belief that the stage should act as a laboratory for experimentation on the human condition in which characters' fates are determined by the environments that dramatists create.

True to her life-long belief that drama was the most effective form of progressive education, Gilman not only uses drama to experiment with the human condition, but also to experiment with her own sociological theories. By the time she died in 1935, she had written or co-written at least fifteen (and perhaps as many as seventeen) plays. Her later dramas would showcase a more advanced understanding of naturalist theatre and a more dedicated effort to see her plays performed for audiences, but "The Quarrel" and "Dame Nature Interviewed" are important windows into the emergence of Gilman as a dramatist and into the development of her feminist interpretation of Darwinism.

Charlotte Perkins Stetson [Gilman]

"A Dramatic View" ["The Quarrel"] (1890)[3]
Dramatis Personæ

HE.   SHE.

SCENE I.

HE. I like you!
SHE. And I like you! (*They embrace.*)
HE. I want more of you!
SHE. You've had enough!
HE. But I want more!

SHE. You can't have it!
HE. I'll take it! I'm the biggest!

SHE. You sha'n't! (*They fight.*)

SCENE 2.

HE. I like you!
SHE. And I like you! (*They embrace.*)
HE. I'll hunt for you!
SHE. And I'll cook for you!
HE. Carry this beast!
SHE. I don't want to!
HE. You must!
SHE. I won't!
HE. I'll make you! I'm the biggest!
SHE. You sha'n't! (*They fight.*)

SCENE 3.

HE. I like you!
SHE. And I like you! (*They embrace.*)
HE. You are so pretty in the house!
SHE. I like to be pretty!
HE. You mustn't go out of the house!
SHE. Oh, but I want to!
HE. You mustn't!
SHE. I will!
HE. I'm the biggest, and I'll keep you in!
SHE. You sha'n't! (*They fight.*)

SCENE 4.

HE. I like you!
SHE. And I like you! (*They embrace.*)

HE. You are lovely but wicked!

SHE. I know I'm wicked!

HE. You are an angel—and a fool!

SHE. I know that, too!

HE. You are my queen—and my slave!

SHE. That is self-evident!

HE. I may do as I please, but you mustn't!

SHE. I will!

HE. I am the biggest, and I'll make you behave!

SHE. You can't! (*They fight.*)

SCENE 5.

HE. (*Feebly*). I like you!

SHE. (*Wearily*). And I like you! (*They shake hands.*)

HE. Keep behind me! Don't push so!

SHE. Oh! you hurt! I want to get out!

HE. You mean, you want to get ahead!

SHE. I don't! I want to get even!

HE. Horrors! You don't belong even! You weren't made even! You can't get even! You are a fool—I mean an angel! Here, go back! You're a slave—I mean a queen! Get behind, 1 tell you! Heavens and earth, woman! Don't you understand? You were divinely ordained to stay behind; you were naturally evolved to stay behind; you look much better behind; you are far happier behind; you are more—ahem— convenient behind; you are constitutionally incapacitated for anything but staying behind; it is absolutely impossible for you to get out from behind; and therefore I will fight till I die to keep you behind! But if you'll only stay behind and keep quiet, we'll be good friends. See?

SHE. I want to get out!

HE. You sha'n't!

SHE. I will!

HE. I'm the strongest, and I'll keep you behind!

SHE. We'll see about that! (*They fight— awfully!*)

SLOW CURTAIN.

"Dame Nature Interviewed
On The Woman Question as It Looks to Her" (1890)

NATURE.—You want to interview me—*me!*—on the woman question? Well you *are* a man! How you can have the face to come to me on that subject is known only to yourself—no other creature of mine could have done it!

REPORTER.—Excuse me, but I represent the press, and I am commissioned to inquire your views on the present advance of women. The scientists tell us it is against nature!

NATURE.—Yes—the scientists! That nearly broke my heart. My last babies! And they really seemed to be learning something. Perhaps you don't know what it is, young man, to have millions of children for millions of years and have 'em all foolish!

REPORTER.—No, ma'am, I don't. But may I ask if you approve of the present advance in women?

NATURE.—*Approve!* Why, bless your little soul, *I* did it!

REPORTER.—You did it! *You!* Why, you made the other kind of woman, I thought—

NATURE.—You thought! Dear me! You *thought*, did you? Well it's the first time you ever thought on *that* subject, I warrant. No, young man, I make most of the creatures, I admit, but not those creatures; nor mules; nor prize pigs; nor pouter pigeons. Man has that honor!

REPORTER.—But how can man make things against nature?

NATURE.—Because he has individual volition—brains —what you call a soul. Snip that you are, you can break almost all my laws if you please—and you do please, mostly. You can go right against every natural instinct, and you do. But you are caught up with. You get killed! You suffer finely! I've paid you back with diseases and things! Yes, I can make you suffer and die, but I can *not* make you learn.

REPORTER.—Will you explain what you mean by saying *we* are responsible for the earlier type of woman?

NATURE.—Certainly, I will explain. I have been *explaining* for thousands of years, but you never could understand it. You probably won't now. Still, those scientists have done *something*. You may comprehend. You see I have had charge of this universe for a long time, with certain laws to run it by and certain circumstances to combat, and I worked away with great enthusiasm at first. Protoplasm was great fun—so docile! I could do anything with it. Those were my palmy days. The way those earlier forms of life would differentiate at a touch! It was interesting all the way up. You see, my business is to keep things alive at any cost; and when the continents were going up and down like a juggler's balls, and the world's whole climate changed as it does now in New England—why, I had my hands full. But the creatures responded. The way they put out claws and teeth and fins and tails and smartness at a moment's notice! It was a grand game, and I began to think I could do anything. And then, just as I had got you—*you* ungrateful animal!—up to the very top of the tree, in came that soul of yours, and I had to take a back seat! But I wouldn't believe it for a long time. How I did struggle! To be beaten by an atom like you!

REPORTER.—But the woman?

NATURE.—Hold your tongue, young man! You can't hurry nature. I'm coming to woman; but it makes me groan. The poor cripple!

REPORTER. —What! Woman a cripple? Lovely woman!

NATURE.—Lovely woman, indeed! Nothing alive is lovely unless it is natural, and harmonious, and suited to its environment. Don't you know that much? And "woman, lovely woman"—the kind you like—is a monstrosity, a man-made paradox, a helpless, senseless, disproportioned thing, an over-developed, undeveloped, ill-developed, walking contradiction! Where does she stand in the struggle for existence?

REPORTER.—Oh, come now, I can't swallow that! It isn't woman's place to struggle for existence! She is the weaker, and must be taken care of. Man is the stronger and must take care of her—her special functions prove that!

NATURE (*Gasping with rage*).—Oh, they do—do they! Who taught you to run the universe, young man? Just come within my reach. Show me one spot where nature can touch you. . . . Useless! you haven't any!. . . . Well, you have ears, at any rate. . . I want you to understand—if you have the capacity —that the "struggle for existence" has made every living thing what it is. All have to struggle—it's a condition of life. And you flatter yourself you have taken woman out of it? Oh, you idiot!

And it wasn't any regard for what you presume to call "weakness," either, when you began. I was there, young man, and I know all about it. It was no regard for her "special functions," you precious philogynist! It was just your smart way of getting around my laws. Instead of fighting with the other males and giving her free choice of the best, as my other children do, you shut her up to keep her away from them, whether you were the best or not! And you were not, of course; if you had been, she would have stayed with you anyway, and gloried in it. That's the way you first upset my beautiful arrangement of sexual selection, young man*!*

REPORTER (*Cowering*).—I—I didn't do it!

NATURE.—Not you! Man nowadays can't do even that! And to hear you say you have kept woman out of the struggle for existence! The struggle for existence, baby, is just my struggle to adapt the organism to its environment. Whatever circumstances surround the creature, it has to fit itself to them or die. You couldn't take woman out of the universe, could you? Not at all. You only assumed to stand between her and heaven and earth. Every blessed thing in life, from baby-clothes to grave-clothes, she must get from you. Safety, and honor, and bread and butter, she must come to you for. You made yourself her environment—that's all—and she had to struggle with you! I hope you've enjoyed it?

REPORTER. I never thought of that.

NATURE. Of course not. You never thought of anything except what you wanted, and the shortest way to get it. I suppose it never occurred to you that the rest of your cut-throat struggling, the way you live on each other like parasites and fungi instead of on my common supplies, is all due to this first insanity of setting half the race to beg and fight for a living with the other half! And you sneer at your wife, and say you "support" her, and sneer at your mistress and say she robs you! "Woman, lovely woman," indeed!

REPORTER.—But—why—you know she *belongs* to us: "God's last best gift to man," you know!

NATURE.—I know, do I? You grant that I know? I ought to—I was there. There was no gift about it, you conceited fool! The division of sex is rather older than the vertebrate, not to say *genus homo*. She "belongs" to you not one bit more than you "belong" to her. The female of any race is just as representative as the male— just as capable of getting along. There are some exceptions—the queen bee, for instance; but, when you make a helpless breeder of the female, observe what becomes of the male!

REPORTER.—But if what you say is true, how did this equally organized creature succumb so easily?

NATURE.—How, indeed! That you should ask it—you, who have taken the very strings that bound her to you and used them to tie her hand and foot! The sexes were equally organized *to fight with circumstances*, but not to fight with each other. Did you ever see the two sexes fight, young man, in any race but your own? No, it takes souls to do that, or brains, or whatever it is. The males fight *for* the females— that's all right—but never *with* them. They are no such fools! If a lion should fight with a lioness—the lioness who bears his young—he could beat her, of course, but just fancy it! It would so improve the race, wouldn't it? And so add to the health and happiness of their relation! And how much has it added to yours?

REPORTER.—But you don't really mean to tell me that man could interfere with the course of nature like that, for all these years, and not know it?

NATURE.—I really do. How long has it taken the idiot to learn that he has *two* hands? Or that bad air is not good for him? Or how much he ought to eat? Is there any way in which he *could* have interfered with the course of nature and *hasn't?* What makes him the sickest beast alive, and all the beasts he tames sick like him? He's a walking nursery of diseases! And, as to not knowing it all this time, why, man never knows anything till he has died of it for millions of years. And then one man knows it, and the rest kill him! Talk to me about his knowing anything!

REPORTER.—If I were not a man—and a representative of the press—I confess I should be somewhat convinced. But you have not yet clearly expressed your opinion on the movement of woman to-day.

NATURE.—Now, that is man all over! Nature can talk to you for a thousand years—scold, scream herself hoarse—and then you say she has not clearly expressed her opinion! Here's for you, then, and you may print it, with my name on: The amazing and irresistible uprising among women to-day is the best thing that has happened to man since he stood up straight. When the female of your species stands on her own feet, full, self-poised, and fulfils her three duties as an organism: nutrition, reproduction and relation—then you may hope to have some sense as a race, and then you'll have a fair chance to see if your precious souls can take care of you as well as I did. Tell 'em this, too—with my name on: that you will never settle any of your other "questions" till you settle this one; never be able to see anything straight; and never learn that two and two make four, till you find out that one and one make *two* young man—not *one!*

Please see the Works Cited for further information on the sources used in this essay.

Notes

1 Gilman also published under her first married name, Charlotte Perkins Stetson.
2 Social Darwinism derives not directly from the work of Charles Darwin, but rather from other social theorists, such as Herbert Spencer (1820–1903), who applied Darwin's work on evolution to other social phenomena, developing, most notoriously, the notions of "survival of the fittest," the Lamarckian idea of the inheritability of acquired characteristics, and that female "inferiority" is a biological necessity.
3 After its original publication, Gilman retitled this piece "The Quarrel."

Suggestions for Further Reading

Auflitsch, Susanne. *Staging Separate Spheres: Theatrical Spaces as Sites of Antagonism in One-Act Plays by American Women, 1910–1930: Including Bibliographies on One-Act Plays in the United States, 1900–1940.* Frankfurt am Main: Peter Lang, 2006.
Wegener, Frederick. "Turning 'The Balsam Fir' into Mag-Marjorie: Generic Transposition in Charlotte Perkins Gilman's Imaginative Economy." *Charlotte Perkins Gilman: New Texts, New Contexts.* Eds. Jennifer S. Tuttle and Carol Farley Kessler. Columbus, OH: Ohio State University Press, 2011.

25 PHYLLIS ROBBINS (1883–1972)

Kim Marra

Introduction and Excerpts from "Remembrances of Miss Maude Adams: Scrapbooks Compiled by Phyllis Robbins" (1898–1953)

On 19 November 1898, fifteen-year-old Phyllis Robbins (1883–1972) became smitten with Maude Adams (1872–1953) when she saw her perform the role of Lady Babbie in James M. Barrie's *The Little Minister* (1897). From then until the actress's death in 1953, Robbins lovingly and meticulously compiled four volumes of scrapbooks of Adams's career, each in excess of 100 pages. She became the most comprehensive chronicler of the era's most popular and profitable star during the Golden Age of Broadway at the turn into the twentieth century.

Robbins worshipped Adams from within the star's core fan base of young, unmarried white middle- and upper-class women. Courting this fan base under the aegis of producer Charles Frohman (1860–1915), Adams starred in a series of American premieres of plays by Barrie (1860–1937), including *The Little Minister, Quality Street* (1901), and *What Every Woman Knows* (1908), through which she forged a star image of sprightly, chaste femininity that appealed to nostalgia for the waning Cult of True Womanhood while masking other desires. Her virtuous star persona also allowed her to play breeches roles with moral impunity—not only Barrie's *Peter Pan* (1905) but also Rostand's *L'Aiglon* (1901) and *Chantecler* (1911), among others. Offering illuminating insight into that fan perspective as well as a richly detailed historical record, the scrapbooks, along with other papers Robbins bequeathed to Harvard's Houghton Library in 1965, comprise the bulk of the Maude Adams Collection, the major Adams archive.

In addition to reams of newspaper and magazine clippings, ranging from full-length articles and reviews to the briefest mentions of Maude Adams in the news, the Phyllis Robbins Scrapbooks contain photographs, theatre programs, and ticket stubs for the dozens of times she saw each of Adams's productions. Asserting her physical placement with respect to the performance, she wrote "My seat" beside each of these stubs. When applicable, she also noted the name of her companion, e.g., "went with Aunt Fanno." Around clippings and images, she jotted the extemporaneous curtain speeches Adams delivered at the behest of the wildly cheering crowds of which she was a part, as well as favorite lines and personal commentary. Covered with hand cut and pasted materials and neatly inscribed, each page eloquently bespeaks and bears the physical traces of the embodied ardor and devotion to her idol that centered Robbins's emotional and social life (see Figures 25.1 and 25.2).

DOI: 10.4324/9781003006923-26

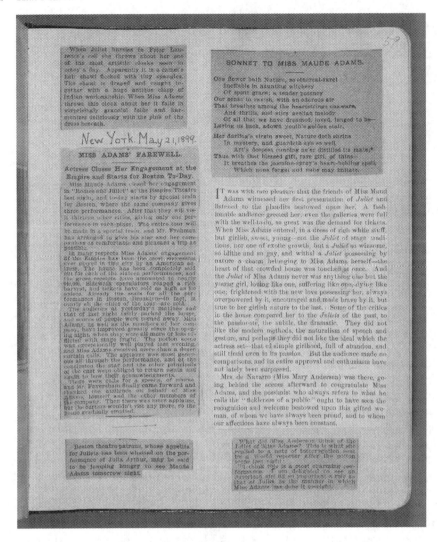

Figure 25.1 Example of scrapbook page featuring newspaper (more yellowed and darkened)
and magazine (brighter greyish white) clippings compiled the year before Robbins
became personally acquainted with Adams. These concern Charles Frohman's
production of *Romeo and Juliet* featuring Maude Adams as Juliet and its 1899
move from New York to Boston where Phyllis Robbins lived with her Aunt Frances
Horton. The unattributed "Sonnet to Miss Maude Adams" expresses fan ardor
such as these women—most passionately, Robbins—harbored. In "Remembrances
of Miss Maude Adams: Scrapbooks Compiled by Phyllis Robbins," Volume I, p. 59.
Call no.: GEN *2006MT-94r. Harvard Theatre Collection. Courtesy of Houghton
Library, Harvard University, Cambridge, MA.

Never married, Robbins lived with her maiden aunt Frances Horton (aka Aunt
Fanno). Commuting between their high society home in Boston and upscale lodg-
ings in New York, the two became such fixtures in the front rows of Adams's performances that the notoriously reclusive and putatively nunlike star eventually invited
them backstage. Robbins recorded this momentous moment on page 91 of Volume

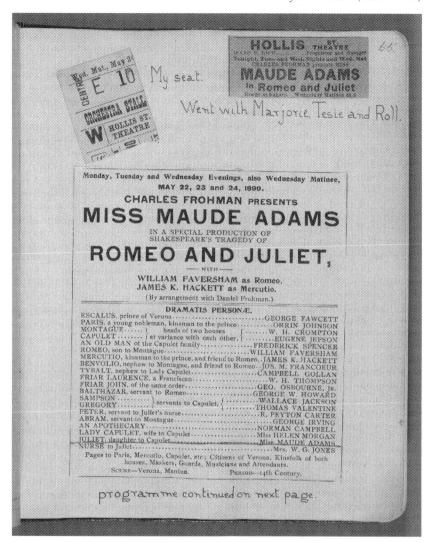

Figure 25.2 Example of a page with cut-out list of Dramatis Personae or Cast of Characters
with mint green ticket stub and hand-written (black-to-brownish ink throughout, unless otherwise noted) annotations compiled prior to Robbins's personal
friendship with Adams. In "Remembrances of Miss Maude Adams: Scrapbooks
Compiled by Phyllis Robbins," Volume I, p. 65. Call no.: GEN *2006MT-94r.
Harvard Theatre Collection. Courtesy of Houghton Library, Harvard University,
Cambridge, MA.

I where she wrote the following inscription next to her ticket stub over the program
for one of Adams's tour-closing Boston performances as Lady Babbie in March
1900: "Went behind the scenes and was introduced to Miss Adams" (see
Figure 25.3 a, b). So began a lasting, supportive friendship that crossed the footlights
(see Figures 25.4 a, b and 25.5).

With her aunt initially acting as chaperone, Robbins entered into Adams's personal life, which was not only intensely private but also closeted; Adams shared her

Gold statue of Miss Adams.

Figure 25.3a Left page of two facing pages. The gold statue depicted in this sepia image was six feet tall and titled "The American Girl." Sculptor Bessie Potter Vonnah was commissioned to use the iconic Adams as a model for the statue, which was to be displayed for the state of Colorado at the 1900 Paris Exposition. Robbins placed the image in the scrapbook to set off the golden moment of her personal meeting of her idol, documented on the facing page (Figure 25.3b) Robbins placed the image in the scrapbook to set off the golden moment of her personal meeting of her idol, documented on the facing page (Figure 25.3b) In "Remembrances of Miss Maude Adams: Scrapbooks Compiled by Phyllis Robbins," Volume I, pp. 90–91. Call no.: GEN *2006MT-94r. Harvard Theatre Collection. Courtesy of Houghton Library, Harvard University, Cambridge, MA.

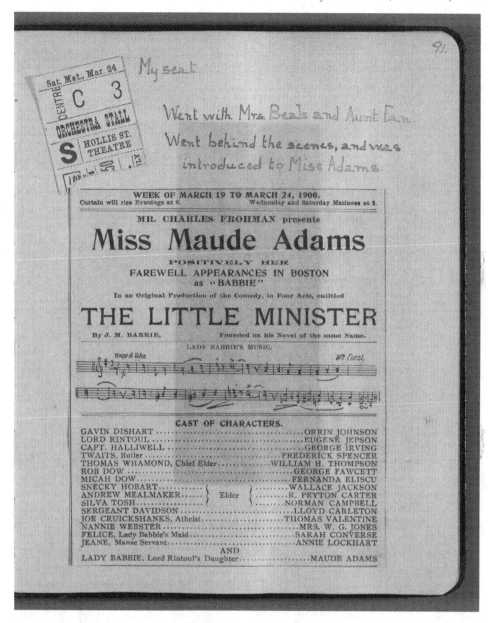

Figure 25.3b Right page of two facing pages documenting when Robbins, her Aunt Fanno, and a friend were invited behind the scenes to meet Adams, and their long personal friendship began. This followed the March 24, 1900 Boston performance by Adams as Babbie in *The Little Minister*. The statue photo on the facing page has left a brownish imprint from the pages pressing together. Robbins' ticket stub pasted in the upper left corner is lemon yellow. In "Remembrances of Miss Maude Adams: Scrapbooks Compiled by Phyllis Robbins," Volume I, pp. 90–91. Call no.: GEN *2006MT-94r. Harvard Theatre Collection. Courtesy of Houghton Library, Harvard University, Cambridge, MA.

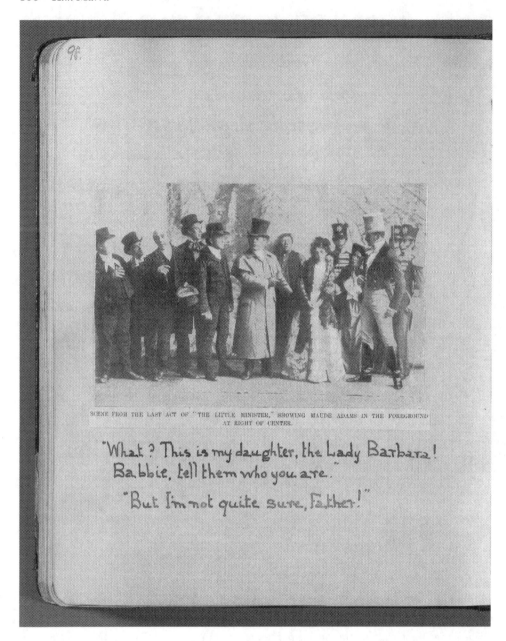

Figure 25.4a Left page of two facing pages (see Figure 25.4b) that together show how Robbins entered hand-written inscriptions of favorite lines from the play around the pasted black and white photograph, ticket stub, and program page. In "Remembrances of Miss Maude Adams: Scrapbooks Compiled by Phyllis Robbins," Volume I, pp. 98–99. Call no.: GEN *2006MT-94r. Harvard Theatre Collection. Courtesy of Houghton Library, Harvard University, Cambridge, MA.

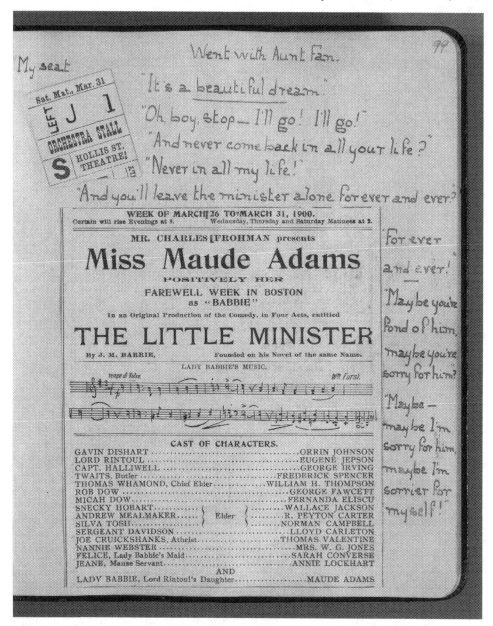

Figure 25.4b Right page of two facing pages (see Figure 25.4a). The date on the ticket stub in the upper left corner, which is lemon yellow, indicates that Robbins (and Aunt Fan) went back after seeing the Saturday matinee and meeting Adams the week before to see the show again. In "Remembrances of Miss Maude Adams: Scrapbooks Compiled by Phyllis Robbins," Volume I, pp. 98–99. Call no.: GEN *2006MT-94r. Harvard Theatre Collection. Courtesy of Houghton Library, Harvard University, Cambridge, MA.

Figure 25.5 Scrapbook page featuring a program page for a 1905 return engagement to Boston's Hollis Street Theatre of Adams in a double bill of *The Little Minister*, followed by the one-act *'Op O' Me Thumb*. The four ticket stubs indicate the number of times in a single week Robbins attended (including twice in one day) and where she sat. Note her inscription of the orchestra box given her by Adams. Upper right stub is light grey. Bottom three stubs are mint green. In "Remembrances of Miss Maude Adams: Scrapbooks Compiled by Phyllis Robbins," Volume III, p. 23. Call no.: GEN *2006MT-94r. Harvard Theatre Collection. Courtesy of Houghton Library, Harvard University, Cambridge, MA.

home with two domestic partners, first Lillie Florence who died in 1901, and then Louise Boynton[1] from 1905 until Boynton's death in 1951. This privileged access distinguished Robbins from the legions of other so-called "Adamites," the female audiences who packed the theatres and flocked outside the stage door (See Figures 25.6 and 25.7). But Robbins's ardor for Adams also epitomized dynamics of women-loving-women within the actress's core fan base at a time when such attachments could

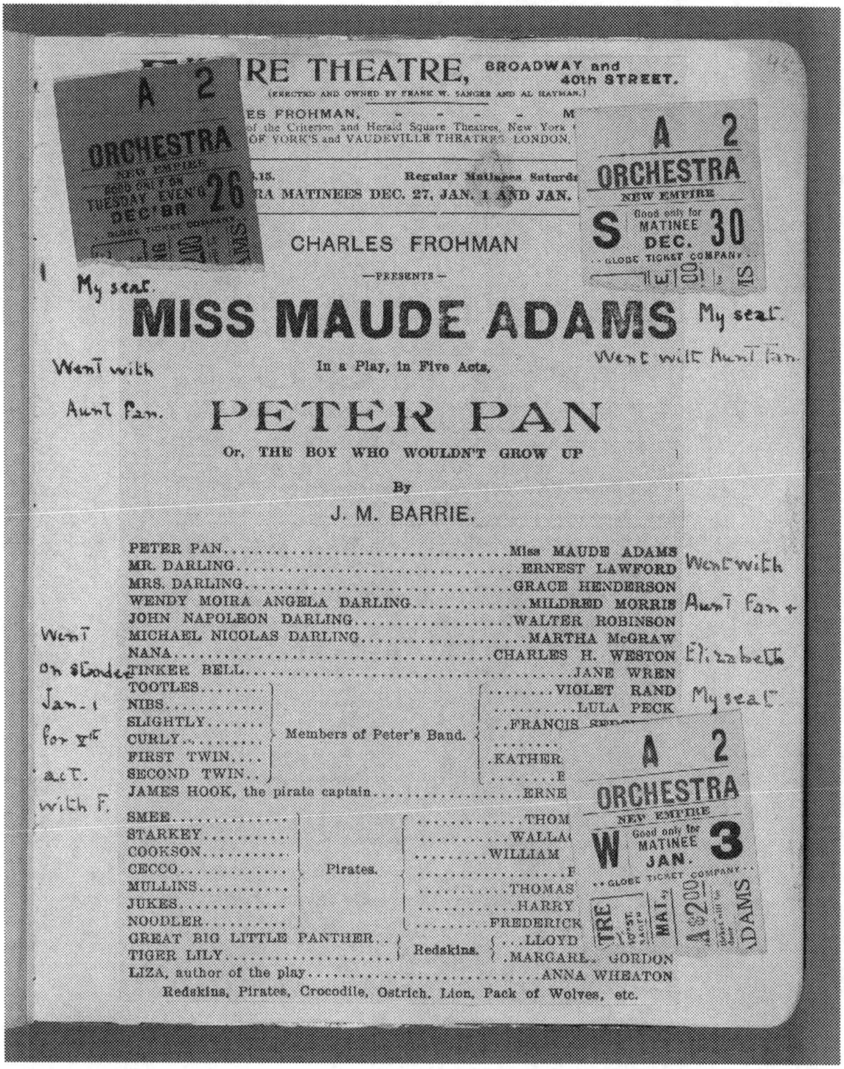

Figure 25.6 Scrapbook page documenting with ticket stubs, annotations, and program cast list the four times in eight days when Robbins and Aunt Fan attended the New York premiere run of Adams in Charles Frohman's production of *Peter Pan* at the Empire Theatre. Upper left stub is royal blue; upper and bottom right stubs are mint green. In "Remembrances of Miss Maude Adams: Scrapbooks Compiled by Phyllis Robbins," Volume III, p. 23. Call no.: GEN *2006MT-94r. Harvard Theatre Collection. Courtesy of Houghton Library, Harvard University, Cambridge, MA.

still seem innocent and respectable among white middle- and upper-classes; older Victorian notions of supposed female "passionlessness" and romantic friendships between women persisted even as newer discourses identifying and pathologizing lesbianism were emerging. In this transitional era, Adams's seemingly virginal and often boyish performances could appeal with impunity to differently desiring audiences, including non-heteronormative or queer ones (Marra, *Strange Duets* 73–141).

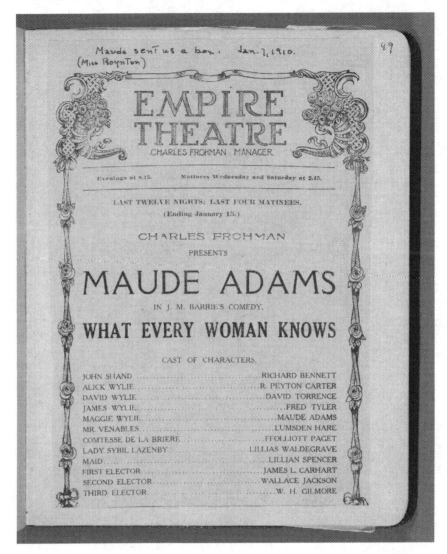

Figure 25.7 Shows an inscription in blue ink at the top of this scrapbook page, indicating Robbins and Adams were on a first-name basis with each other. "Miss Boynton" refers to Louise Boynton, Adams's domestic partner who assisted with household and administrative matters. In "Remembrances of Miss Maude Adams: Scrapbooks Compiled by Phyllis Robbins," Volume III, p. 45. Call no.: GEN *2006MT-94r. Harvard Theatre Collection. Courtesy of Houghton Library, Harvard University, Cambridge, MA

Apparently without any other occupation, Robbins spent more than half a century helping tend to Adams and chronicling her career. The contents of the four volumes provided the primary source material for the two biographies Robbins later published, *Maude Adams: An Intimate Portrait* (1956) and *The Young Maude Adams* (1959). Robbins opens *An Intimate Portrait* with an epigraph Adams wrote about Barrie that captures Robbins's aims in chronicling Adams: "So much of [her] life is second nature to me that I have to remind myself that other people do not know it so well; and much of it is so intimate that it is hard to touch with a sense of the delicacy it demands." These published biographies have remained largely definitive in Adams studies, but as handmade artifacts, the scrapbooks more directly record their author's play going and memorializing habits and illuminate crucial affective forces that animated the life and career of the top-grossing U.S. star and her audiences around the turn into the twentieth century.

Please see the Works Cited for further information on the sources used in this essay.

Note

1 (Mary) Louise Boynton (1868–1951) was an American newspaper publisher and editor, as well as the personal secretary and partner of actress Maude Adams.

Suggestion for Further Reading

Fields, Armond. *Maude Adams: Idol of American Theater, 1872–1953.* Jefferson, NC: MacFarland, 2004.

26 LADY AUGUSTA GREGORY (1852–1932)

Marjorie Howes

Introduction

Augusta Gregory (1852–1932) had a multifaceted career. She is best known now as a playwright who produced one-act peasant comedies and as a founder and manager of Ireland's first national theatre. But she was also an important and innovative theorist of the Irish Literary Revival, the cultural nationalist movement that sought to promote Irish independence from Great Britain by producing a distinctively Irish national literature and culture. Her 1900 essay, "The Felons of Our Land," provides insight into the sophisticated and highly political dramaturgy of her plays.

Gregory's essay draws a contrast between the national characters and cultures of England and Ireland, arguing that the English and the Irish see the world very differently. England is preoccupied with success, victory, and power and measures those things in materialistic terms. Ireland, on the other hand, focuses its thoughts on failure, incarceration, and death and strives for "spiritual vision" rather than material success. To the English, Christianity represents "respectability, comfort, peace, a settled life," while the Irish associate religion with the persecution and sufferings of Christ, who was "led to a felon's death." Gregory's essay defines "felony" as a crime in the eyes of the (British) law, but not in the eyes of the (Irish) people. The essay also asks questions many writers of the Revival asked: in the face of the immense power disparities between Ireland and England, how could ordinary Irish people survive, subvert, and even thwart British rule? How could they wrest strategies for wielding power from situations and histories defined by failure and powerlessness?

Gregory's answers, evident in her drama, involve uncovering a vigorous though subjugated Irish popular culture involving literature, such as political ballads and "Speeches from the Dock," and popular devotional and funerary practices, such as making pilgrimages to Wolfe Tone's[1] unmarked grave and treating the bodies and clothes of executed felons as religious relics. This popular culture is both a vehicle of popular memory, passing the names of rebels and movements to new generations, and a shaper of everyday life, as in the example of the arrest warrant framed and hung on the wall. Together, these everyday cultural practices form a subaltern account of Irish history that, "having been forbidden in the national schools, has lifted up its voice in the streets" to contest the imperial, pro-British history offered by official institutions and to provide a basis for national culture and community among the Irish.

Gregory's plays often turn on the contrast between Irish and English styles of cognitive mapping—and on a conflict between an official English narrative imposed

DOI: 10.4324/9781003006923-27

on the Irish from above and a fugitive counter-narrative that asserts its fragmented but vital presence from below. In "Spreading the News" (1904), the representative of imperial power, the Magistrate, interprets Ireland as a "repulsive" site of dirt, disorder, and crime. He assumes that all British colonies are the same, and he seeks to improve Ireland by enforcing laws, employing modern technologies like the telescope and the telegraph, and imposing a "system" on Irish chaos (*Selected Writings* 312–313). In response, the local people employ what Homi Bhabha called "sly civility" (93–101); they thwart the Magistrate's demands for information covertly, rather than openly, by pretending to misunderstand his questions. When the frustrated Magistrate concludes, "I shall learn nothing here" (Gregory, *Selected Writings* 313), he is right, but not for the reason he thinks. He has been outsmarted by the Irish, rather than uncovering their incapacities. Gregory's "Hyacinth Halvey" (1906) depicts a similar conflict and subaltern strategy. Colonial officials see the Irish as dirty and corrupt and seek to civilize them with a "new Sub-Sanitary Inspector" and a lecture designed to advance the "moral development of the rural classes" (*Selected Writings* 329, 331). The Irish are outwardly deferential and secretly subversive. Mrs. Delane uses her job in the post office to gather information and to shield the criminal activity of Mr. Quirk, who has been selling rotten meat to British soldiers, from discovery.

Other Gregory plays emphasize the "Felons" essay's interest in a shared national culture and popular memory as the basis for a potentially powerful Irish nationalism. In "The Rising of the Moon" (1907), named for one of the ballads cited in the essay, a nameless "Ragged Man"—who has escaped from prison—persuades an Irish policeman to let him get away. The policeman's partial conversion to the cause of Irish nationalism happens because he discovers that he and the Ragged Man share the same past origins, and the same national culture. The Ragged Man poses as a "poor ballad-singer" and begins singing nationalist ballads. At first, the policeman commands him to "stop that noise" (*Selected Writings* 366), but as the play unfolds, the policeman admits that he knows all the Ragged Man's songs, that he sang them in his youth, and that he could easily have become a nationalist felon rather than a policeman. The Ragged Man tells him: "I am thinking it was with the people you were, and not with the law you were, when you were a young man" (370). The authorities offer one hundred pounds for the capture of the Ragged Man; the policeman lets him go and foregoes this material reward, choosing shared subaltern culture and solidarity with an outlaw instead.

Kathleen ni Houlihan (1902), which was written by Gregory and W. B. Yeats[2] together, features another nationalist conversion and imagines martyred Irish rebels becoming part of Irish national culture and popular memory. Michael Gillane is about to be married when Kathleen, an old woman who is an allegorical figure for Ireland, enters the house. Here, too, the conversion is provoked by nationalist ballads praising felons who have been executed by the British: "I will go cry with the woman/For yellow-haired Donough is dead,/With a hempen rope for a neckcloth,/And a white cloth on his head" Selected Writings (306). And the shared national culture represented by the songs is one that Michael already knows as part of his past but with which he needs to reconnect. He says of Kathleen's name: "It must have been someone I knew when I was a boy. No, no; I remember, I heard it in a song" (309). Moreover, Kathleen promises Michael that, if he dies for the nationalist cause, he and people like him will become martyrs and be memorialized in Irish popular memory and popular culture: "They shall be remembered for ever,/They shall be alive for ever,/They shall be speaking for ever,/The people shall hear them for ever" (309).

Similarly, *The Gaol Gate* (1906) invokes Gregory's "Felons" essay by describing the process through which executed felons become part of a shared subaltern culture. When the play opens, Denis Cahel's wife and mother are distressed because they have heard a rumor that Denis, who is in jail, has informed against his fellow Irish. They lament that if he were to be released, he would not be able to return to his village because of the opprobrium Irish people heaped upon informers. The gatekeeper of the jail enters and tells the women that Denis was hanged, and gives them the dead man's clothes. They conclude that he was not, after all, an informer, and they begin the process of making him part of a politicized Irish popular culture: "I will call to the people and the singers at the fairs to make a great praise for Denis!" (*Selected Writings* 362). They also initiate the practice of treating his clothes like holy relics: "Gather up, Mary Cushin, the cloths for your child; they'll be wanted by this one and that one. The boys crossing the sea in the springtime will be craving a thread for a memory" (362).

In play after play, Gregory turned to the theoretical formulations she offered in "The Felons of Our Land," formulations that show these one-act peasant dramas are remarkably coherent and sophisticated pieces of a Revivalist project that was both cultural and political.

Augusta Gregory

Excerpt from "The Felons of Our Land" (1900)

I

For a century past, to go back no further, the song-writers of England have been singing of victory, the song-writers of Ireland only of defeat. Nelson and Wellington and Clive and their days of triumph have been set in lasting verse by English poets, not the generals driven back by Washington, or Hicks or Herbert Stewart or Majuba Hill. [...] [D]ead and defeated; [they have] never passed into popular song, but the conqueror of Omdurman has already had the hall mark of success stamped upon him by the unofficial laureate of the Empire. And yet it is not a material victory that most needs interpretation in song. The newspaper placard that tells of it is enough to stir the blood[,] to swell the pride, of the passer-by. The song-writer, the poet, would find a better mission were he to tell of the meaning of failure, of the gain that may lie in the wake of a lost battle. If he himself possessed the faith that is the evidence of things unseen, he would strive to give spiritual vision to trembling and discouraged men. He would strive for the power of the man of God in the little hill city besieged by the Syrian host, when he comforted his trembling and discouraged servant with the assurance that 'they that be with us are more than they that be with them,' and opened his eyes to see the mountain sides alight with chariots and horses of fire.

Whether with such a purpose, or whether through the nature formed by generations of loss, it is not of conquerors or of victories our poets have written and our people have sung through the last hundred years, but of defeat and of prison and of death. This feeling, or instinct, has been thus expressed:--

They say the British Empire owes much to Irish hands,
That Irish valour fixed her flag o'er many conquered lands,
And ask if Erin takes no pride in these her gallant sons,
Her Wolseleys and her Lawrences, her Wolfes and Wellingtons.

Ah! these were of the Empire, we yield them to her fame,
And ne'er in Erin's orisons is heard their alien name;
But those for whom her heart beats high and benedictions swell,
They died upon the scaffold and they pined within the cell.

Another song, more distinctively of the people, is the one from which I have taken the name of this paper:--

Let cowards sneer and tyrants frown,
Oh little do we care:
A felon's cap's the noblest crown
An Irish head can wear!
And though they sleep in dungeons deep
Or flee outlawed and banned,
We love them yet, we can't forget
The felons of our land.

Felony is given in Johnson's dictionary as 'a crime denounced capital *by the law*,' and this is how it, or perhaps I should use the word coined for Ireland, 'treason-felony,' is defined in Ireland also—a crime in the eyes of the law, not in the eyes of the people. A thief is shunned, a murder prompted by brutality or personal malice is vehemently denounced, a sheepstealer's crime is visited on the third and fourth generations; but a 'felon' has come to mean one who has gone to death or to prison for the sake of a principle or a cause. In consequence, the prison rather lends a halo than leaves a taint. In a country that is not a reading country, 'Speeches from the Dock,' the last public words of political prisoners, is in its forty-eighth edition. The chief ornament of many a cottage is the warrant for the arrest of a son of the house framed and hung up as a sort of diploma of honour. I remember an election to a dispensary district before which one candidate sent round certificates of his medical skill, the other merely a statement that several members of his family had been prosecuted by the Government. And it was the latter who won the appointment. I have known the hillsides blaze with bonfires when prisoners were released, not because they were believed to be innocent, but because they were believed to be guilty. It has been so all through the century. I find among Under-Secretary Gregory's papers a letter written by Colonel Barry from Limerick in 1816 in connection with some executions that were taking place at that disturbed time. 'The Sheriff has requested that I would remark to you the propriety of appealing to Government to forbid the Bodies of all such people, or indeed any part of their clothing, being given up to their familys, who consider that these people have died as Martyrs in the cause of their country, and instead of holding them out as examples to avoid, cry them up as characters to be imitated. [...] Not even a shoe should be given to the family, for all the cloths the deceased had on are considered as relicks.' Then, as in later years, the act of the Government executioner seems often to have been a swift act of canonization.

II

Irish history, having been forbidden in the national schools, has lifted up its voice in the streets, and has sung the memory of each new movement, and of the men who guided it, into the memory of each new generation. At little Catholic bookshops, at little sweet and china shops in country towns, one finds the cheap ballad books, in gaudy paper covers, red, yellow, and green, that hold these summaries of a sad history. The 'Harp of Tara,' the 'Green Flag of Ireland,' the 'Rising of the Moon,' are some of them. And at fairs and markets the favorite ballads are sold singly or in broadsheets by the singers at a yet lower price. Sometimes it is a movement that is celebrated, the '98 rebellion above all. The well-known 'Who fears to speak of Ninety-eight,' the contribution of Trinity College to national song, has lately taken new youth in a translation into Irish, but a more general favourite is the simple and picturesque 'Rising of the Moon:'—

> Oh! then tell me, Shawn O'Ferrall,
> Where the gathering is to be—
> In the old spot by the river
> Right well known to you and me.
> One word more—for signed token
> Whistle up the marching tune,
> With your pike upon your shoulder
> By the rising of the moon.
> [...]
> Well they fought for poor old Ireland,
> And full bitter was their fate
> (Oh! what glorious pride and sorrow
> Fill the name of ninety-eight!)
> Yet, thank God, e'en still are beating
> Hearts in manhood's burning noon,
> Who would follow in their footsteps
> At the rising of the moon!
> [...]

Davis, though he died young, before his 'Young Ireland' friends had found their way to the dock, to which he himself was inevitably tending, wrote while he lived of him and of other felons who had come before his time:–

> Sure 'twas for this Lord Edward died, and Wolfe Tone sank serene,
> Because they could not bear to leave the red above the green.
> And 'twas for this that Owen fought, and Sarsfield nobly bled,
> Because their eyes were hot to see the green above the red!

His verses on 'Tone's Grave' are usually found on the broadsheets, for that grave has been for the last hundred years a place of pilgrimage. No tomb has yet been built there, for others feel, as Davis felt, that the time has not yet come, but stones have often been laid on his grave to mark it, and have as often been carried away by the pilgrims as relics. [...]

IV

To the spiritual mind the spiritual truth underlying each development of Christianity is always manifest. But there is a significant contrast in the outward form in which religion appears to the peasant of England and the peasant of Ireland. In

England (I quote again from the 'Jail Journal'), 'is there not our venerable Church, our beautiful liturgy? There is a *department* for all that, with the excellent Archbishop of Canterbury at the head of it.' To the English peasant the well-furnished village church, the pulpit cushion, the gilt-edged Bible, the cosy rectory, represent respectability, comfort, peace, a settled life. In Ireland the peasant has always before his eyes, on his own cottage walls or in his whitewashed chapel, the cross, the spear, the crown of thorns, that tell of what once seemed earthly failure, that tell that He to whom he kneels was led to a felon's death.

In England the poet of to-day must, if he will gain a hearing, write of the visible and material things that appeal to a people who have made 'The Roast Beef of Old England' a fetish, and whose characteristic song is:–

> We don't want to fight, but by Jingo if we do,
> We've got the ships, we've got the men, *we've got the money too.*

In Ireland he is in touch with a people whose thoughts have long been dwelling on an idea; whose heroes have been the failures, the men 'who went out to battle and who always fell,' who went out to a battle that was already lost—men who, whatever may have been their mistakes or faults, had an aim quite apart from personal greed or gain.

Some of us are inclined to reproach our younger poets with a departure from the old tradition because they no longer write patriotic and memorial ballads. But in singing of 'the dim wisdoms old and deep that God gives unto man in sleep,' they have not departed from it, they have only travelled a little further on the road that leads from things seen to things unseen. And a poet is not to be shaped and trained like a yew tree and set in a hedgerow, to guard even the most hallowed ashes. He must be left to his own growth, like the tree that clings to its own hillside, that sends down its roots to find hidden waters, that sends out its branches to the winds and to the stars.

Please see the Works Cited for further information on the sources used in this essay.

Notes

1 Theobald Wolfe Tone, posthumously known as Wolfe Tone (1763–1798), was an Irish revolutionary who sought to overthrow English rule in Ireland and led a French military force to Ireland during the insurrection of 1798.
2 William Butler Yeats (1865–1939) was an Irish poet, dramatist, and revolutionary whose works—ranging from Romantic, Nationalist, Symbolist, and Modern styles—have distinguished him as one of the most important poets of the twentieth century. He was also one of the founders of Dublin's famous Abbey Theatre.

Suggestions for Further Reading

Coxhead, Elizabeth. *Lady Gregory: A Literary Portrait.* New York, NY: Harcourt, Brace & World, 1961.
Cusack, George. *The Politics of Identity in Irish Drama: W. B. Yeats, Augusta Gregory, and J. M. Synge.* New York, NY: Routledge, 2009.
Gregory, Lady. *Seventy Years: Being the Autobiography of Lady Gregory.* New York, NY: Macmillan, 1976.

27 EDITH CRAIG (1869–1947)

Katharine Cockin

Introduction

Edith Craig (1869–1947) achieved a reputation for international excellence as a director of experimental and politically controversial dramas. Nevertheless, Edith Craig's theatrical reputation has long been overshadowed by those of her mother, renowned actress Ellen Terry (1847–1928), and her brother, theatre designer Edward Gordon Craig (1872–1966). Yet, more recently, Edith Craig's work as a theatre artist has been rediscovered and recognized for its depth of engagement with and creative innovations for the stage.[1]

Ellen Terry's leading role with actor-manager Henry Irving (1838–1905) at London's Lyceum Theatre from 1878 to 1902 provided opportunities for both of her children to develop theatrical expertise. Edith Craig's work as the stage director for her mother's tour in the United States grounds the understanding of theatrical production she conveys in her 1907 article, "Producing a Play," included here.

In 1911, Craig founded the Pioneer Players, which, like other play-producing subscription societies or independent theatres, produced new, controversial, and experimental drama. Craig championed innovative modernist dramas, such as those by American Susan Glaspell (1876–1948).[2] As her reputation grew, James Joyce (1882–1941), through his agent, approached the Pioneer Players to produce his play *Exiles* (1918), and George Bernard Shaw (1856–1950) was indebted to Craig for the revival of his postwar theatrical reputation.[3] Her skills as a costumier as well as a director enhanced her productions of historical pageants in the 1920s and 1930s. From 1919, she was also active as a national leader of the British Drama League.

Craig's "Producing a Play" emerged at a pivotal moment for Anglo-American women. Those working in the theatre, including Craig and Terry, were organized not only in their support of women's suffrage but also in challenging prevailing, exploitative labor conditions. Notably, the role of the theatre director was emerging as distinct from that of the producer or the stage manager at this time, and Craig now reimagined her work: to oversee the entire artistic design of theatrical productions. Craig's article provides valuable insights into her approach to theatre practice in this transformational era.

Craig's title focuses on the activity, "producing a play," but the magazine's brief editorial introduction highlights the gendered status of her role, including a somewhat disingenuous reference to Craig's groundbreaking achievement as "the first woman stage manager on record," possibly derived from other recent articles. Both Terry and Craig had been interviewed by the press before embarking on their tour of the United States, which was managed by impresario Charles Frohman.[4] Newspapers consistently

DOI: 10.4324/9781003006923-28

proclaimed Edith Craig "The First Lady Stage Manager," probably drawing on an article by Craig's life partner, author and theatre artist Christopher St John (Christabel Marshall, 1872–1960),[5] which included a brief interview with Terry, who had observed of her daughter, "So far [as] I know she is the first woman stage manager on record" (St John, "Miss Ellen Terry's American Tour" 8).

Although Craig had a reputation for "self-effacement" ("Miss Edith Craig" 233), she provided evidence of assertiveness in her own interviews, having said that, as she was acting in the plays on the tour, "I thought I might as well offer myself to Mr Frohman as stage manager also" (St John, "Miss Ellen Terry" 4). She was likewise prepared to correct her mother, emphasizing, "I have unofficially stage managed all of Miss Terry's provincial productions for the past three years" (Our Private Wire 5). It is likely that "Producing a Play" was written with the assistance of Christopher St John. The timing, platform, and tone selected for Craig's article all suggest a self-promotional strategy designed to reach a wide readership, given its publication in the popular *Munsey's Magazine,* which had the US and international circulation of several hundred thousand copies.

"Producing a Play" establishes women as directors in the theatre and acts as a rejoinder to the egocentric and patriarchal concepts launched by Edward Gordon Craig in his recently published manifesto, *The Art of the Theatre* (1905). His book would soon become an internationally acknowledged foundational treatise of modernist theatre theory. Yet, Edith Craig specifically criticizes her brother's treatment of actors as "blank minds empty of ideas, for the subjects of his control." Instead, she supports more collaborative artistry and theatrical "intelligence," especially noting the importance of the stage crew in achieving desired technical effects in performance. She emphasizes the significance of design, and particularly stage lighting, as a vital means of complementing the acting. Moreover, Craig rejects older lighting conventions, especially the use of limelight, as disrupting the realistic stage atmosphere she tries to achieve. She discusses the relationship of lighting and costuming to the audience's perception of color and emphasizes her balanced approach to all elements of the production, including music. She speaks, as well, to the significance of "supers"—short for supernumeraries, the actors who help create background atmosphere in crowd or group scenes—and how important it is that they be fully committed to the world of the play. Her sense of directing both presciently anticipates core tenets of contemporary feminist theatre and draws upon the rich and diverse heritage of theatre practices developed through the work of Charles Kean (1811–1868), Ellen Terry, and Sarah Bernhardt (1844–1923).[6] And finally, in an appeal to her US readers, she highlights the resistance to women in leadership roles in a theatrical environment long dominated by men: "I have found the American [theatre workers] startling and charmingly free from this prejudice."

Edith Craig[7]

"Producing a Play" *(1907)*
The "First Woman Stage-Manager on Record" Relates Some of Her
Experiences – Intelligence versus Mechanism – The Artistic Use of Costumes,
Scenery, Lights, And Music – A Field for Interesting Achievement

WHEN it was first announced that I was to be the stage-director for my mother, Miss Ellen Terry, during her American tour, there was quite a flutter in the dove-cots of the London newspapers.

I was the first woman stage-manager on record; I had started a new profession for women; I was the pioneer of a new departure in theatrical enterprise! No one could have been more surprised than I when reporters came and asked me how I felt under the grave responsibilities of a revolutionary!

For really the thing came about most naturally and simply. After my mother ceased to act with Sir Henry Irving—which she did in 1902, not because of a personal quarrel, as people more in idleness than in malice chose to say, but because of the increasing difficulty in finding plays in which both Sir Henry and she had good parts—she for the first time became her own manager. I accompanied her on her provincial tours, and represented her wishes to her staff. I was not called either stage-manager or stage-director, but I did the work.

Being in perfect sympathy with my mother's views, and understanding exactly the kind of atmosphere, light, and color best calculated to help her acting, I was in a strong position to start with. But the right person in the right place must have the right equipment and the right training as well. For fifteen years I had been in the Lyceum company and had had the privilege of seeing and studying the way Sir Henry Irving produced plays. This was in itself an education.

In my opinion, he was the ideal stage-manager, although he was not called by that name on the bills. He had a stage-manager under him, but this stage-manager was merely the interpreter of Sir Henry's wishes, and did not initiate anything. Everything passed through Sir Henry's hands. There was not a button on a coat which he had not seen and approved. This is no exaggeration. Music, lighting, acting, scenery, dresses—all the parts which go to create the result of a theatrical production were supervised by him down to the smallest detail—I don't say to the most insignificant detail, because to the stage-manager nothing is insignificant.

SIR HENRY AND HIS STAFF

That Sir Henry was an autocrat may be gathered even from this slight indication of his methods, but he was not an autocrat of the Czar-of-all-the-Russias type. He did not want machines under him which he could control from a switchboard, but men of intelligence whom he dominated by appealing to their special gifts. He demanded *thought* from the humblest member of his staff, and he got it.

My brother, Gordon Craig, who has recently published a brochure on "The Art of the Theater," takes up a different position. He wants no one to think except the stage-director, not even the actors! The stage-director is to conduct the play as a musical conductor leads an orchestra, and in the scheme the principal actor is not more necessary to the result than the lime-light man. The will of the stage-director is imposed upon every one in the theater, and, like the hypnotist or the mesmerist, the stage-director prefers raw material, blank minds empty of ideas, for the subjects of his control. My brother, whose opinions have provoked widespread interest and discussion all over Europe, is a root-and-branch reformer. He denies that there is any virtue in the old theatrical material, and wants, logically enough from his point of view, to sweep it out of existence and create new.

Yet how much there is in the existing material, if only it is properly used! Our first obstacle in the way of using it is the apathy of the typical staff.

MECHANICAL CONTRIVANCES AND EFFECTS

The want of personal interest and energy, of brains and understanding, displayed by the carpenters, the propertymen, and the lime-light men has led the stage-manager to rely entirely on mechanical contrivances and effects. No member of the staff is trusted to take up a cue through the play without having a signal flashed at him from the electrician's switchboard, the electrician obeying the instructions of the stage-manager. Suppose that there is any flaw in the electric plant—for even the greatest mechanical inventions are not infallible. The desired effect, be it sunset, or storm, or the murmuring of distant crowds, or the sound of distant music, simply does not come off at all!

There should be nothing mechanical about anything connected with the stage, although its technicalities are infinite. What use are cut-and-dried rules and formulas when applied to a living, emotional thing like a play? Even the man who beats a drum or tolls a bell or works a wind-barrel ought to contribute a little bit of life to the performance. Instead, we find the staff half asleep over their duties, waiting for their signals. "We didn't get the signal" is all the excuse that they need offer when they have ruined a situation. What I wish to have working with me is a body of men who care about what they are doing—obedient to discipline, but never servile—men who follow the play intelligently, and take up their cues through alert attention, as actors do, not through the pressing of an electric button. This alert sympathy with the action of the play on the part of the staff would make the work of a stage-manager far less disheartening than it is in the present condition of things.

For intelligence, the theater has substituted custom. The theater men have been trained in certain elementary principles—most of them radically bad and wrong—and it is difficult, as they are also trained not to think, to work against their customs. The way that they have been accustomed to do a thing is generally the easiest—and the worst!

Let me take the stage sunset as an example. From yellow to red, from red to blue, all the lights changing at once, with no gradations, no mitigation of their whole-hearted thoroughness—that is the approved way of working a sunset. If you want anything different you disorganize the whole staff.

In "Captain Brassbound's Conversion"[8] there is very little scope for what are known as stage effects, but my mother and I were anxious to have the lighting as good as possible. We found the American staff much quicker than our boys at home, but they were shocked at my not being satisfied with the ordinary achievements of the switchboard.

THE RIGHT USE OF LIGHTS

By the way, I have been told that I subdue the lights, using hardly any footlights at all, because a strong light is unbecoming to my mother! In my opinion, strong lights are unbecoming to the youngest actress. I have seen pretty girls look far from their best, owing to the mania for lighting a scene like a saloon bar.

Lighting, like every other branch of stage decoration, should be considered as a means of helping the acting. There are some situations which demand light; others which do not suffer from shadow—and the wise stage-manager will remember this before arranging his lights.

In the Dutch play "The Good Hope,"[9] which my mother produced recently at the Empire Theater, New York, I aimed at getting the interior of the cottage somber and shadowy in its corners and the ceiling plunged in gloom. In the third act, where the women gather round the fire and, while the storm rages outside, tell one another gruesome stories of all that their men have suffered at sea, I had to simulate lamplight and firelight; but besides considering the pictorial effect, I had to remember the dramatic situation. If the lights and shadows had fallen ever so beautifully they would have been enemies to the play if Miss Terry as *Kniertje* had been in the dark for her best scene, or Miss Suzanne Sheldon as *Jo* had had to express tragic emotion without the audience being able to see her.

The bad old way of helping the actors is by following them all over the stage with the lime-light. It is hardly necessary to say how completely this plan destroys the sincerity of a situation, or how pictorially ugly it is. It is quite possible to have the actors in the light when they need it and at the same time to preserve an atmosphere of beauty and an illusion of nature.

In every play there are certain pictorial moments which have to be led up to, and every movement toward them must be calculated beforehand. Elaborate scenery, expensive dresses, lavish use of lime-light, crowds of supers, cannot make them pictures. The material is dead; the use of the material gives life.

The importance of an intelligent staff, of individuals as opposed to machines, and the vital question of lighting ought to occupy the attention of every stage-manager; but only as the *means to an end*, as servants of the acting.

The play is in the hands of the actors. This is almost a truism, no doubt, but in practise it is often forgotten. The actor who alone can interpret the play to the audience is often, in a costume drama, put into clothes which kill his efforts, into colors which, although he does not know it and the audience do not know it, are working against him. Behind him is a scene which may be perfect from the artist's point of view, and yet is completely devoid of significance to the play. Round him are supers whose inattention and inadequacy are destroying the sympathy between him and his audience.

Often I have heard the boast: "We have one hundred people on in that scene." Well, very often that hundred might just as well be in their dressing-rooms. Like the staff, they are not expected to use any intelligence. Ten are told off to say "Oh!" to cue, ten more to say "Ah!" and so on. Why they are to make these exclamations is not explained.

HANDLING THE SUPERS

Twenty supers who have been properly rehearsed can fill the stage better than a hundred who have been left to their own devices and a few mechanical cues; but these supers have to be very carefully selected. The art of being a good super is almost entirely a pictorial one, and I should always choose my supers from that point of view. In New York we were lucky in this respect, and I was able to get supers of fine quality.

The next thing in the stage-manager's jurisdiction is the music. Let us once for all abolish the stupidity of having music which is supposed to be on the stage played from the orchestra. This was never tolerated by Sir Henry Irving, nor is it now by Sarah Bernhardt, and the music in her productions is always perfect. To see a character in a play singing a song to the accompaniment of a full orchestra and the conductor's baton is a sorry spectacle. It is not always possible to have the instrumentalists on the stage, but we can always have them at the side with supers doing the accompaniment in pantomime on the stage.

THE ART OF COSTUME

Costume is another matter in the stage production to which every stage-manager should give attention. Long before I supervised a whole production I specialized in stage costume, and designed and made clothes for several plays in London. In my opinion, every theater should contain a large wardrobe-room, and every dress worn by the performers—in costume drama, at any rate—should be made in the theater. The services of the artist and the dressmaker, though often brilliant in themselves, sometimes conflict with the art of the theater. Stage color must be determined by stage lights, a fact often overlooked by the painter. A high authority on archeological costumes in London, whose services as designer are much in request, has been known to make the management pay heavily for a specially dyed purple silk which looked *brown* under the lighting of the scene in which it was to be worn.

It is often argued that in the performance of a play only the acting matters, and that elaborate stage effects are distracting and unnecessary; but from the very first I was trained to see that the actor is the better, not the worse, for being surrounded by the right atmosphere. My mother has always, from the day when she first appeared with Charles Kean, acted in an appropriate stage setting, and her consideration of it has not hampered her in any way.

Sarah Bernhardt is another example of an actress who has never scorned the help of all those details which lie within the province of the stage-manager. The stage-manager nowadays is really only a prompter. It is not of him that I am speaking, but of the man (or woman!) who has control of the stage.

Before I sailed for America the English reporters asked me what I should do about language. They had heard, and were not altogether mistaken, that in an American theater no stage-manager can accomplish anything without a large vocabulary chiefly of a damnatory nature. I said that this aspect of my duties did not worry me much, and that anyhow in America the vocabulary would be different and I should not care to import ours, even if I knew it.

At my very first rehearsal in a New York theater an expert told me that if I wanted the boys to hustle the best word to use was "please."

So far, my experience as stage-manager in America has been confined to New York, and there "please" has acted like magic.

I shall continue to try it in the other cities. It has the objective recommendation of destroying the last obstacle to a woman occupying the position of stage-manager— anyway, in America. In England men create another objection by resenting a woman "bossing" them in a professional capacity. I have found the Americans startlingly and charmingly free from this prejudice.

Please see the Works Cited for further information on the sources used in this essay.

Notes

1 See Cockin, *Edith Craig: Dramatic Lives*, 1998; *Women and Theatre in the Age of Suffrage: The Pioneer Players*, 2001; *Edith Craig and the Theatres of Art*, 2017.

2 See the entry on Glaspell in this volume.
3 See Cockin, *Edith Craig and the Theatres of Art*, Ch. 7.
4 Charles Frohman (1856–1915), American theatre manager whose Theatrical Syndicate controlled theatrical productions in the USA.
5 See entry on St John in this volume.
6 Charles Kean, English actor-manager associated with historically authentic stage costume and design, gave Ellen Terry her first opportunity as a child actor in the role of Mamillius in *The Winter's Tale* in 1856. Sarah Bernhardt, an internationally famous French actor of Dutch Jewish heritage, toured extensively and managed her own theatres in Paris.
7 Miss Craig is the daughter of that great and favorite actress who is best known to the people of two continents as Ellen Terry. By taking successful charge of her mother's productions, she has upset many traditions, and, indeed, may be said to have discovered a new occupation for women. '*Munsey's* ed.']
8 Play by George Bernard Shaw from 1900 in which Terry played the central female role.
9 Play by Herman Heijermans from 1900.

Suggestions for Further Reading

Adlard, Eleanor, ed. *Edy: Recollections of Edith Craig*. London: Frederick Muller, 1949.

Auerbach, Nina. *Ellen Terry: Player in Her Time*. New York: W. W. Norton, 1987.

Farfan, Penny. *Women, Modernism and Performance*. Cambridge: Cambridge University Press, 2004.

Holledge, Julie. *Innocent Flowers: Women in the Edwardian Theatre*. London: Virago, 1981.

Holroyd, Michael. *A Strange Eventful History: The Dramatic Lives of Ellen Terry, Henry Irving and Their Remarkable Families*. London: Chatto & Windus, 2008.

28 CHRISTOPHER ST. JOHN (1871–1960)

Lesley Ferris

Introduction

Addressing the centuries-long English prohibition on women acting publicly, the unpublished play "The First Actress" (1911), by Christopher St. John (Christabel Marshall, 1871–1960), excerpted here, features one of the women purported in 1661 to be the "first actress," who took the role of Desdemona in Shakespeare's *Othello*, following Charles II's (r. 1660–1685) sanctioning women's performances on public stages.

Following her studies at Somerville College Oxford, and aspiring to become a playwright, St. John spent three years acting and learning stagecraft. She was simultaneously involved in the suffrage movement, writing essays and plays such as *How the Vote Was Won* (1909), a comedy coauthored with feminist playwright, actress, and essayist Cicely Hamilton (1872–1952). St. John also served as secretary to the celebrated actress Ellen Terry (1847–1928).

Directed by St. John's life partner Edith Craig (1869–1947),[1] "The First Actress" was produced in London in 1911 as part of a triple bill that launched a new women's company – The Pioneer Players – whose stated purpose was to produce the era's "plays of ideas," which centered on current issues that were "social, political and moral" (Melville 214).[2] In 1909, St. John wrote in the newspaper *Votes for Women:*

> There is not one play on the London stage at the present time which takes any account of women except on the level of housekeeping machines or bridge players—the actual or potential property of some man valuable or worthless as the case may be. It is strange to go out of the world, where women are fighting for freedom and showing unparalleled courage when most despised and rejected, into the theatre where the dramatist appears unaffected by this new Renaissance. (qtd. in Melville 214)

The Players insisted that all the areas of theatre making – costume, light, and scenic design, directing, stage management, administration – be done by women. This gave women the opportunity to experiment and take risks that were unavailable to them previously. This commitment extended to the theatre in which the play was produced. Lena Ashwell (1872–1957), actress, member of the suffrage-supporting Actresses' Franchise League (AFL), and the only woman active in theatre management at the time, leased them the Kingsway Theatre for their performance (Melville 214).[3]

"The First Actress" demonstrates the impossibility of equality in a world that prohibits women from representing themselves on the stage. St. John literally "plays"

DOI: 10.4324/9781003006923-29

with this throughout her drama in her uses of meta-theatre, the pageant play, and the concept of "self" that is central to the art of performance. The play takes place on the stage at the New Theatre Drury Lane. Four of the roles in the first half are historical figures, including actress Margaret Hughes (d. 1719) as Desdemona. Sir Charles Sedley (1639–1701) and Lord Hatton are aristocrats who see Hughes's groundbreaking performance as a means of upstaging the celebrated boy-actress Edward Kynaston (1640–1706), who notoriously parodied Sedley in public.

While praising Hughes for her performance, Sedley's actual agenda is to get back at Kynaston for his insults. Margaret Hughes's stage presence is essential to this narrative, yet it consigns her to a minor role, a position of "otherness." The aristocrats leave the theatre to celebrate their double success – the first time a woman performed on a public stage in England, an event that also attacked the role of the boy-actress. Hughes's fellow performer Griffin remains to support Kynaston by pursuing the centuries' long argument of anti-actress prejudice: the superiority of male mimesis that drives home St. John's feminist theme.

In the play's second half, St. John draws on the theatrical form of the "pageant" that was popular throughout England. Professional theatre directors often worked with local citizen performers to stage highlights from their area's historical past as annual celebratory events for the community. St. John, however, reversed this traditional use of local history by featuring actresses from Hughes's future. Nell Gwynn (1650–1687) is the first of ten actresses who appears to support the troubled, sleeping Hughes. Mrs. Barry (1658–1713), Mrs. Bracegirdle (1673/4–1748), Mrs. Anne Oldfield (1683–1730), Peg Woffington (1714–1760), Kitty Clive (1711–1785), Sarah Siddons (1755–1831)[4], Fanny Abington (1737–1815), Dorothy Jordan (1761–1816), and Madame Vestris (1797–1856) follow. Described by St. John as "Visions of the Future" (4), each delivers a personal testimony about her own successes while celebrating Hughes's pioneering efforts.

Well-known actresses of the day portrayed these figures, with Ellen Terry taking the role of Nell Gwynn. Such historical layering highlights St. John's interest in the concept of women's performance. In the final moment of the play, St. John engages with the notion of mimetic art itself. The very premise of Western theatre relies on a system in which the actor creates a character, a fictionalized "other." All the roles in "The First Actress" adhere to this with one exception: the "Actress of To-day" (4).

Portrayed by Lena Ashwell, this final actress is not a vision from the past; she is in the present moment. Playing herself, Ashwell makes clear the irrational nature of gender prejudice, linking the ability to vote to the ability to perform by describing a map of the world that has a line down the middle representing men on one side and women on the other. This theatrical boundary evaporated with the first actress. The Actress of To-day acknowledges the significance of women performing their roles: "[W]e shall not forget it was first made to look foolish when women mounted the stage" (17). This aesthetic autonomy is equally as important as the political autonomy to vote, as audiences familiar with the ongoing women's suffrage campaign would have grasped. Playing herself on stage – an actress, a theatre manager, a suffrage activist – Ashwell provides multiple resonances for both aesthetic and political autonomy. The communal experience of the women who performed in The First Actress is one of its most significant points. These early 20th-century actresses playing actresses from their past, and Lena Ashwell performing herself, emphasize the impact of women's self-creation and their ability to define who they are. St. John's play raises the specters of the past, highlighting theatre's aptitude for simultaneously "ghosting" the past with the present.

Christopher St. John

Excerpt from "The First Actress" (1911)

[The excerpted scene follows the first public performance in England featuring an actress, Mrs Margaret Hughes, and her fellow actor, Griffin, both of Thomas Killigrew's Company of King's Players]

Griffin.

[…]. You must bear in mind that the audience to-night were not incensed against you personally. They were but protesting against woman's invasion of a sphere where she is totally unfitted to shine.

Hughes.

You are very clever, Griffin, and I am a fool – Charles always told me himself so, until he began to educate me for the stage – but I don't see how we can be unfitted to play women's parts. Are we not fitted –if only because we are women[?]

Griffin.

That is as much as to say that acting is not an art. By that show of reasoning […] – we must go to the jail to find impersonators of our villains – must bribe noblemen to play our stage dukes – and allow no unmarried actor to play a husband, no child-less actor to depict the emotions of a father. Acting, Mistress Hughes, is the art of assuming a character, not the accident of being it. You happen to be a woman, but can you draw tears for a woman's grief as Kynaston can? Can you so sensibly touch the audience to the spectacle of outraged modesty and invincible fidelity? Forgive me, no! 'Tis the genius of assumption, of creation, that makes an actor like Kynaston the faithful limner of your sex upon the stage. I will even go so far as to say that his trained powers enable him, when he dons a woman's habit, to look livelier than you all – to speak with a sweeter voice – to walk with a greater grace –to express the very quintessence of the female soul!

Hughes.

All this may only be because men have had more practice. Perhaps if women were encouraged to give the art as careful a study, they could do as well.

Griffin.

Believe me, it is not in them – to give that careful study. Have they the mental power or the mental energy? They certainly have not the creative imagination. What artistic creation have women to their credit in history? Yet they have had the opportunity of participating in arts demanding a much smaller sacrifice of womanly delicacy than the art of acting.

Hughes.

Our womanly delicacy! I like to hear you men prate of our "womanly delicacy" – as if you valued it so highly. Do you think my appearance on the stage to-night has rubbed the bloom off mine? Say we oughtn't to act, because we are inferior to you in inability, if you like, Griffin, but for heaven's sake don't speak as if we must be preserved from it because of our delicacy! A lot of delicacy the Sedley's [*sic*] and Etheredges[5] of the world leave us!

Griffin.

You do but confirm me in my opnion, Mistress Hughes. Were your sex to tread the stage it would not be in your power to resist the assaults of the kind of gentry of which you have named two bright and sly examples. The limits imposed on you by Nature preventing you from studying the art seriously, you would endeavour to atone for the deficiency in your talents by practising airs and tricks to tempt mankind. The gentry would not be able to judge of your performance apart from your sex. No doubt they would enjoy the diversion, but the stage would suffer degradation.

Hughes.

I'm not so sure. Perhaps we should not be so busy in the affairs of love – if we had other affairs to interest us.

Griffin.

You have already a large choice of such affairs – Mistress Hughes – affairs better befitting a woman's mental capacity – Embroidery, the study of languages, the ornamental side of cooking, and many other domestic arts. And lastly there is what I may call the "grande affaire" – the true vocation of every woman – the excellent business of being a wife to a good man, and rearing him a hopeful and healthful progeny.

Hughes.

For the matter of that Mr Burt rears a hopeful progeny – certainly a numerous progeny – and it doesn't interfere with his playing Othello!

Griffin.

You are illogical, Mistress Hughes –a privilege of your sex, but one by the exercise of which you further proclaim its unfitness for such a rational art as that of acting, where a Patriot, a Prince, a Beggar, a Clown each have their propriety, where action is perfectly and logically adjusted to character and manner –

Hughes.

(Interrupting) I say Mrs Burt is dead, and Mr Burt is a mother to his family. But we won't quarrel about that, Griffin. I know you are right in the main. I failed completely. My diction was artificial – my voice was weak –and I tried to make up for it by bawling – Charles's flattery about my gestures didn't deceive me – They were ill-designed and inappropriate – I walked like a cripple – and held my head like a hunchback – Oh, I know! 'Tis very bitter to me to think that through my failure I may have kept my sex off the stage for centuries – if not forever –Good-night, Griffin.

Griffin.

Good-night. – But stay, there's no one in the theatre. Had I not better remain with you till Sir Charles returns?

Hughes.

No, no. I want to be alone. Good-night.

Griffin.

Good-night. (Returning, he says consolingly) You will be better next time.
(EXIT GRIFFIN)

Hughes.

Thank you – Griffin –but I don't want even to think of next time. Perhaps some day I may be able to look back on it all – as a nightmare. God – if I could just sleep! I am fatigued – fatigued – to death. (Yawning) Griffin was right. I ought never to have attempted it – I have made it impossible for the others – perhaps there never will be any others – I am sorry for that – very sorry —

(All the latter part of this speech has been spoken drowsily, and now she falls asleep. A voice is heard singing outside. Gradually it becomes more distinct)

Oranges, who'll buy my oranges,
Sweet China oranges, ripe oranges,
Yellow as the sun, round as the moon,
Juicy and sweet,
Sweet China oranges.

(The vision of NELL GWYNNE appears)

Gwynne.

Come now – Not so much bleating! You're a trifle hasty in your sorrow here, as I, Nelly, can very quickly prove. You must know I saw you acting from the pit. I was selling oranges there! When they began to hoot – and jeer – I cried out:

"You damned confounded dogs, what are you laughing at? Many another woman will mount the stage before the year's out." They said in jest: "Why not **you**, Nelly?" "Stranger things have happened," said I. "We don't want women on the stage," said one fellow who wasn't too drunk to speak distinctly. "You mayn't want 'em, but by the Lord Harry, you've got to have 'em," said I. "And they'll do your damned dull stage a power of good." Well, they only laughed again – but the joke won't be against **me**, I think, when I enter the King's Playhouse, as I shall do, and become an actress in great vogue.

Be merry, Mrs Hughes. You've led the way, and I that was at first no better than a Cinderwench, will follow, and will be spoke of by folks who've never heard the name of Edward Kynaston! Ask the ringers of St. Martin's! Every week their bells shall ring out in honour of poor Nelly, long centuries after she is laid in earth! Listen – you may hear them!

(EXIT singing)

Oranges, and lemons,
The bells of St. Clemens,
Cost me three farthings
The bells of St. Martin's!

(ENTER visions of MRS BARRY and MRS BRADEGIRDLE as the Rival Queens.)

Barry.

My brain is burst, Debate and Reason quenched.
The storm is up, and my hot bleeding heart
Splits with the rack –
I beg the gods to help me for the moment.

(Drives the knife into MRS BRACEGIRDLE's heart)

Bracegirdle.

Oh! Oh! I'll be sworn you did that on purpose, Mrs Barry, to revenge yourself because the property man gave me your veil. The knife has pierced my stays; it has entered at least a quarter of an inch into my flesh! I'll play the Rival Queen with you no more, trust me for that. I'll walk out of the theatre rather!

Barry.

Come, come, my Bracegirdle, is this the time
To exhibit private feuds and jealousies!
The glorious public triumphs we shall win
Must be our theme; we're here to prophesy!
Twin stars, with equal lustre we shall shine.
There shall be peace between our reputations!

'Twas ignorance, dear Hughes, that made them spurn you.
But by our time, men will have learned our worth.
What fool will prate then: **"The stage is not for you"**
The names of Barry, Bracegirdle, be my witnesses!

(She sweeps off followed by BRACEGIRDLE)
(ENTER vision of NANCE OLDFIELD.)

Oldfield.

Not forgetting that little Nancy Oldfield,
    If you please! She has a word to say! She has a prophecy!
    Think of it, Hughes! An actress so greatly honoured that at her death
    she will lie in state in Jerusalem Chamber – for all the world as though
    she had won a battle or conquered a province. The public, who loved her
    when she laughed as when she wept, will be faithful. They will crowd to
    see her – in her last part! Only sixty years after they threw pippins at you,
    and the world will see an actress buried in Westminster Abbey – buried like a
    queen.

(EXIT NANCE OLDFIELD)
(ENTER vision of PEG WOFFINGTON)

Woffington.

The whirligig of time brings in his revenges[6] – and another Peg!
    Peg Hughes has prepared the way for Peg Woffington – Peg the Second–

(Vision of KITTY CLIVE dances in)

Clive.

And that's enough to Peg! I, Kitty Clive –

Woffington.

(Ignoring CLIVE) Peg the Second will teach the pit to presume! She will not
    forget that they would have none of Peg the First.

Clive.

Mrs Woffington – I have a line here.

Woffington.

Unmannered dogs! I'll teach them to doubt a woman's intellect –
    a woman's grit. Nature has given me a harsh, unpleasing voice – but that
    shall not daunt me – I'll learn to use it! A defect shall become a grace –
    and as for intellect! –

Clive.

They don't want to hear all that! I, Kitty Clive —

Woffington.

(To HUGHES) You sowed the good seed in flouts and jeers –
we shall reap it in applause and honour—

(ENTER MRS SIDDONS as for the sleep-walking scene.)[7]

Yes – I will give place to the Tragic Muse most gladly – though never to a Singing
Chambermaid –
(EXIT PEG WOFFINGTON)

Clive.

I, Kitty Clive —

Siddons.

Out damned spot —

(EXIT KITTY CLIVE)

All the prejudice in all the world shall not keep us off the stage –
What's that I see – A great painter writes his name on the hem of an actress's
garment! And statesmen, to watch her, sit among the fiddlers. We **fail**! But
screw your courage to the sticking–place, and **we'll not fail. We'll not fail!**

(EXIT SIDDONS)
(ENTER MRS ABINGTON)

Abington.

'Tis hard on Nosegay Fan to have to follow the lofty minded Siddons – to hitch her
comedy waggon to the tragic star!
Where's George Ann Bellamy or Miss Farren or Pritchard –all were fitter for the task.
My prophecy, dear comrade Hughes, is of an immortal comedy – Behold the original –
and the author says the never equalled – Lady Teazle! When all the comedies of
your day are dead, and the names of the boy-actresses forgotten, *The School for
Scandal*[8] will be alive, and the memory of Fan Abington will live with it!

(EXIT MRS ABINGTON)
(ENTER MRS JORDAN)

Jordan.

Shall I play tragedy, comedy, high or low, opera or farce? Sure, I will play 'em all,
but laughing will agree with me better than crying! Peg, if you had begun in

comedy you'd have had fewer apples thrown at you – take Dorothy Jordan's word for it!

(EXIT JORDAN)
(ENTER MME VESTRIS as Captain MacHeath)[9]

Vestris.

I'll not be content myself with playing the woman, not I!

Since men once put on the petticoats and played all **our** parts – Vestris will put on trousers and play some of theirs for a change! And play them so well too, that man will hardly know himself, so elegant, so gallant, so fascinating will he appear – such a pretty devil of a fellow! Captain MacHeath takes off his hat to you, Mistress Hughes, and begs the public, who once thought it unbecoming for us to tread the stage, even in our skirts, never to be too sure of anything!

(EXIT VESTRIS)
(ENTER an ACTRESS of To-Day)

Actress.

When I am born, dear Peg, people will have quite forgotten that the stage was ever barred to us. They will laugh at the idea that acting was once considered a man's affair – they will be incredulous that the pioneer actress was bitterly resented – Yet they will be as busy as ever deciding what vocations are suitable to our sex. It will be "Man this" and "Woman that" as though we had never taught them a lesson.

I see an old map where the world is divided into two by a straight line. The Pope who ruled that line across the world said: "All territory discovered to the right of the line in future to belong to Spain – all to the left to Portugal." To my age such a division of the world will seem comical indeed, yet that is how I see them still dividing the world of humanity – "This half for men," "That half for women." If in my day that archaic map is superceded, we shall not forget that it was first made to look foolish when women mounted the stage.

Brave Hughes – forgotten pioneer – Your comrades offer you a crown!

(The shapes of the others rise from the front of the theatre. They come forward. MRS SIDDONS holds a crown over the head of the sleeping HUGHES)

(Music. Disappearance of visions)

Please see the Works Cited for further information on the sources used in this essay.

Notes

1 See entry on Craig in this volume.
2 Performed but never published, the script remains in manuscript at the British Library.
3 See entry on Ashwell in this volume.
4 For more on Oldfield, see entry on "Anonymous" in this volume. For more on Siddons, see her entry in this volume.

5 George Etheredge (c. 1636–c. 1692), Restoration comic playwright best known for *The Man of Mode or, Sir Fopling Flutter* (1676).

6 The clown Feste's famous line from Shakespeare's *Twelfth Night* V.1.388.

7 Siddons was famous for her portrayal of Lady Macbeth; her entrance here parallels that of V.1.21.

8 1777 play by Richard Brinsley Sheridan, in which Abington appeared as Lady Teazle.

9 Vestris played this character from John Gay's play *The Beggar's Opera* (1728) as a breeches role in 1833.

Suggestions for Further Reading

Cockin, Katherine. *Women and the Theatre in the Age of Suffrage: The Pioneer Players 1911-1925.* London: Palgrave, 2001.

Ferris, Lesley. "The Female Self and Performance: The Case of *The First Actress.*" *Theatre and Feminist Aesthetics.* Eds. Kathleen Laughlin and Catherine Schuler. Madison, NJ: Farleigh-Dickinson University Press, 1995. 242–257.

Paxton, Naomi. *Stage Rights: The Actresses Franchise League, Activism and Politics 1908-1958.* Manchester: Manchester University Press, 2016.

Paxton, Naomi, ed. *Suffrage Plays: Taking the Stage.* London: Methuen Drama, 2013.

29 BINODINI DASI (1862–1941)

Aparna Dharwadker

Introduction

Binodini Dasi (1862–1941), also known as "Nati [actress] Binodini," is a singular figure in the modern urban theatre that developed as a secular and commercial institution in colonial Indian cities like Calcutta and Bombay during the later nineteenth century. The daughter and granddaughter of prostitutes, she was trained as a singer from early childhood, and her arrival on the Calcutta stage as a prepubescent girl in 1873 coincided with the beginnings of the Bengali public theatre. In addition to her innate talent, several emergent sociocultural and artistic factors contributed to Binodini's exceptional success: the growing demand for women rather than cross-dressed male actors to play female roles; the pragmatic argument that in the absence of "respectable" women, the class of prostitutes could meet that demand for a time; and the reformist claim that the theatre could consequently offer artistic fulfilment, economic independence, and social emancipation to women who were otherwise condemned to a life of poverty, exploitation, and ostracism.

When she joined the Great National Theatre in 1874, Binodini also came under the immediate mentorship of Girish Chandra Ghosh (1844–1912), the leading Bengali actor, playwright, and theatre manager of his generation, and for the next twelve years, their association exemplified the *guru-shishya* (master-student) relationship as well as a powerful creative partnership on stage. During this formative period for the public theatre, Binodini performed leading roles in more than eighty plays (often against Ghosh), catered to a privileged audience that included major literary/cultural figures as well as colonial officials, and was proclaimed India's leading professional actress. In 1886, what she calls "various kinds of estrangements and betrayals" led to her abrupt departure from the theatre, and for the remainder of her long life, she garnered occasional public attention as an author, not a performer.

Amar katha (My Story), the first of two autobiographical works by Binodini, was published in 1912, as she struggled to cope with the deaths of her daughter Shakuntala, the wealthy "protector" who had supported her for thirty-one years, and Girish Ghosh. The narrative is therefore an amalgam of at least three distinct structural and rhetorical strains. Employing the conventions of the *bedona-gatha* (narrative of pain), the opening and closing chapters express the emotions of irreparable loss, anguish, physical decrepitude, and desolation, all of which Binodini ascribes to her moral culpability as a fallen woman, a sinner, a "social

DOI: 10.4324/9781003006923-30

outcast—a despicable prostitute." The second strain consists of seven "letters" of varying lengths addressed directly to Ghosh as *Mahashay* (gentleman), moving unpredictably between deeply personal or spiritual questions and memories of the theatre. The third strain is a recognizably conventional and neutral autobiographical voice that recounts events in chronological sequence. The narrative expresses Binodini's positive experiences in the theatre, her fame, and her sense of personal achievement, but the dominant tone is confessional and penitential.

The pioneering significance of *My Story* in the modern Indian archive is that it uses the partnership between authorship and print culture to transgress the constraints of gender and class. Theoretical and critical reflections on theatre in Bengali and other active languages were monopolized by men, and in both manuscript and print, women authors across the full spectrum of literary genres belonged to the category of *bhadra-mahila* (respectable ladies). Rimli Bhattacharya, who translated and edited the autobiography, notes "the exceptional location of Binodini Dasi's writings, or more properly, of a Binodini Dasi—writing" because "this was the first time that a woman was speaking of the 'inner story' of the public world of the theatre" while also negotiating "the primary challenge of the move from performance on stage to expression in print" (Dasi 24, 30). In her crowning role—as the sixteenth-century male mystic Chaitanya Mahaprabhu (1884)—she also turned the prevailing codes of cross-dressed performance upside down. In many other respects, however, the hierarchies of gender remain intact: the most influential figures in her life are men, she has a succession of "kind keepers," her proudest moment in the theatre is to receive the blessing of the spiritual leader Ramkrishna Paramhansa after a performance of *Chaitanya-lila*, and her devotion to Lord Krishna counterbalances the feelings of wretchedness and loss as she writes her life.

The theoretical and critical perspectives implicit in *My Story* capture the essentially syncretic nature of urban Indian theatre. In one direction, Binodini's account of the training she received from Ghosh connects "modern" theatre to the aesthetic "tradition" of Bharata's *Natyashastra*, with *bhava* (emotion) as the key term. As codified in the third-century Sanskrit treatise, a dramatic work progresses from *sthayi bhavas* (stable emotions) to a selection of *sanchari bhavas* (dynamic, communicable emotions), in order to create the *rasa* (literally, juice or flavor) that is specific to a performance and meant to be enjoyed by an audience of *rasiks* (connoisseurs). Understanding the *bhava* of a particular role is therefore crucial for the actor, especially when resonant narratives from Indian myth, history, and spiritual experience dominate the texts for performance. In another direction, however, the new urban theatre is modeled on the Victorian theatre of spectacle, follows European practices in such activities as costuming, make-up, lighting, and set design, and treats major Anglo-European figures like Siddons and Terry as relatable precursors. Binodini's efforts to immerse herself in a role and master its expressive gestures by practicing before a mirror are especially important signs of the modern, "natural" acting style Ghosh promoted in his theory and practice. Finally, Binodini's approach to acting as (artistic) work that could bring her family out of poverty and her unsuccessful attempt to acquire a financial interest in the Star Theatre so that it would be named after her point to a performance economy based on materialist rather than patronal relations and make her in some respects the first modern Indian exemplar of the actress as working woman.

BINODINI DASI

Excerpt from **Amar katha** *([My Story] 1912)*[1]

This is only a reflection of the emotional torments of an unfortunate woman! I have nothing in this world, only endless hopelessness, only the afflictions of a sorrowful life! But there is no one to listen to it. I have no one in the world to whom I can convey my pain – since, to the world, I am a woman of ill-repute, a fallen woman. [...] Why should people pity me? To whom can I convey my pain? So I am trying to compose with pen and paper. [...]

[...] You [Girish Ghosh] have written: "In your life, you have several achievements to your credit: you have made hundreds of people happy through your work at the theatre. The way you have brought alive characters from various plays in the theatre by means of your extraordinary power as an actress, is no small achievement. As Chaitanya in my *Chaitanya-lila*, you have inspired devotion in the hearts of many, and have gained the blessings of many Vaishnavites.[2] No one who is destined to do ordinary things is capable of such an achievement. Without deep meditation, it is not possible to depict so vividly the many characters that you had vividly portrayed with your acting. Even though you have not been able to see the results of your labour till now, it is not because of your failings but because of your circumstances; and your contrition makes it evident that you will soon possess the rewards of your work."

Mahashay, you say that I have entertained the audience. But could the members of the audience ever see my inner being? Having had the opportunity to utter Krishna's name at work, how ardently had I called out to Him both inwardly and outwardly! Was my audience ever able to see that? In that case, why did my only lamp of hope get extinguished? [...]

[...] Sometime after the death of my brother, two gentlemen, Purnachandra Mukhopadhyay and Brajnath Seth, would come often to hear Gangamani[3] sing. [...] One day he [Purnachandra] called my *matamahi* [grandmother] and asked her whether, given our poverty, she would be interested in giving me to the theatre. [...] In those days, there were only two theatres: one was Sri Bhubanmohan Niyogi's National Theatre,[4] and the other the late Saratchandra Ghosh *mahashay*'s Bengal Theatre. My grandmother discussed the matter with a few people and in the end decided to apprentice me to the stage, following Purna-babu's suggestion. Purna-babu then had me admitted to the famous National Theatre at a monthly salary of ten rupees. [...]

[...] A new life began for me from then on. In those years when I was a young girl, the training I received in that luxurious world, as well as the nature of the work— all these seemed new to me. I understood nothing, I knew nothing; but I followed as sincerely as possible whatever I was taught. My zeal increased whenever I recalled the dire conditions within my home. The thought of mother's sorrowful face only spurred me on. I used to think that if I could earn some money during this difficult period in my mother's life, then our family's hardships too would be reduced.

Although I worked on stage in accordance with the instructions I received, I also always felt a certain earnestness and longing driving my spirit. I used to wonder how I could learn as soon as possible to act like these well-known actresses. I would always be thinking about their performances. In those days there were only four actresses at the National Theatre: Raja, Kshetramani, Lakshmi, and Narayani. The late Kshetramani was a famous actress. Her acting was so natural that people were amazed; it is doubtful that the void she left behind can ever be filled. Mr. Thompson, the *chhota lat*[5] himself remarked on seeing her performance as the maid in *Bibaha-bibhrat* (Marriage Muddle) that such actresses were scarce even in his own England! [...] I would only like to add that with care and effort, I was soon able to act as well as they did. [...]

[...] By the time I returned home from work, the day's lessons would be vividly etched in my memory. The way [my teachers] taught me to speak, the ways in which they showed me all the moods, all these details surrounded me like my friends at play. Even when I played at home, an unknown force kept me drawn in that direction. I did not want to be at home; I wondered constantly when again my carriage would come, when they would take me to the theatre so that I could begin to learn new roles—my mind would always be full of such thoughts. Although I was young then, a pleasant sense of enthusiasm permeated my being. [...]

[...] From then on, I was usually asked to play leading roles. Although the leading actresses were senior to me, within a very short while I became their equal as a performer, even though I was not as old as them. [...]

[...] One evening we were performing *Neel-darpan* (The Indigo Mirror) at the Chhatramandi in Lucknow.[6] Almost all the sahibs of Lucknow city had come to see our play. At the point where Rogue Sahib tries to assault Khetramoni, Torap breaks open the door and beats the sahib, while Nabinmadhab takes Khetramoni away. The play was being performed extremely well; in addition, Babu Motilal Sur as Torap and Abinash Kar *mahashay* as Rogue Sahib were performing with consummate skill. The sahibs were extremely upset by this scene on stage. During the ensuing furor, one of the sahibs climbed up on the stage with the intention of beating up Torap. Because of this reason we were in tears, our managers were scared, and our manager Dharmadas Sur started trembling. Stopping the performance, we packed our costumes and belongings and fled from the scene.[7] [...]

[...] After we began working together [at the National Theatre], I have worked with Girish-babu continuously, right up to the time of the completion of the Star Theatre on Beadon Street. He was my instructor in the theatre and I was his first and principal pupil. It was I who used to play the chief female roles in his plays. By guiding me with the utmost care, he ensured that my work was up to his desired standards. [...]

[...] How many plays shall I mention? In all of them, Girish-babu, Amrit[lal] Mitra, Amrit Basu and I played the principal characters. Girish-babu would prepare me for my roles with great care. His method of teaching was marvellous. First, he would explain the *bhava* of the roles. He would then require the parts to be memorised. After that, when he had the time, he would come to our house, and he and others such as Amrit[lal] Mitra, Amrit-babu (Bhuni-babu) would talk about various English actresses and the works of famous English poets such as Shakespeare, Byron, Milton and Pope in an informal, story-like fashion. Sometimes he would read from their texts and explain them. He taught us, one by one, a range of gestures and moods. Because of his meticulousness, I began to learn about the art of acting, using my understanding and intelligence. Until then, whatever I had learnt could be compared to the [apparent] cleverness of a bird that had been taught to repeat what it was told.

I did not have much experience; I could not argue or speak logically. From now on, however, I could understand the roles I was given. I was eager to attend performances by famous British actors and actresses when they came to the city. The theatre management also took pains to arrange my attendance at English-language plays. Once I returned home from these performances, Girish-babu would ask, "What did you think of the performance?" I would tell him whatever I felt. If there were mistakes in my understanding, he would explain them to me. [...]

[...] When I appeared on stage, as a result of Girish-babu *mahashay*'s training and excellent advice, I did not feel that I was anyone else—it was as if I *was* the character I was supposed to represent! Only after the performance was over would I come out of the trance-like state. Seeing my enthusiasm and devotion to my work, the theatre management came to love me very much indeed. Some treated me like a daughter, others like a sister, and still others like a *sakhi* [female friend]. [...]

[...] Acting was the principal source of sustenance in my life. It was as if learning my part, visualising my role in my mind, standing before a mirror and committing to memory all the various forms and gestures, combining these forms in my mind with rapt attention, and even moving about, sitting, or lying down in accordance with those mental images had become part of my bearing. [...]

[...] Other topics and stories did not interest me very much. But I liked a lot the stories that Girish-babu told about famous British actors and actresses, or the books from which he read out. He explained to us from books what kinds of faults different critics found in the interpretations of Mrs. Siddons, who had returned to the stage ten years after her marriage; at what points in her performances those faults could be found; or what her strengths and weaknesses as an actress were. He even told us which foreign actress did her voice-training while hearing the sounds of birds in the forest. What kind of costumes that Ellen Terry wore; how Bandmann dressed in his role as Hamlet; how Ophelia always wore a dress made of flowers;[8] [...] I cannot tell you how many stories from the works of the major English, Greek, French and German authors I have heard, thanks to Girish-babu *mahashay* and other kind friends. [...]

[...] In order to compile a range of *bhava*s, I lived in the world of the imagination. Perhaps because I could lose myself in the world of imagination, whenever I took on a role, there was never any lack of the *bhava* proper to that character. I never thought that I was acting either in order to captivate others, or for merely monetary reasons. I used to forget my own self. I myself used to feel the joys and sorrows of my characters, forgetting entirely the fact that I was only enacting them. Because of this reason everyone was affectionate towards me. [...]

[...] At this point of time I was thinking of leaving the late Pratap-babu *mahashay*'s theatre [the National Theatre]. Shortly before I started thinking along these lines, I was left badly hurt by an incident. The unmarried aristocratic young man who provided for me had recently tied the knot and, urged on by his rich young friends, had behaved in an immoral way with me. That incident deeply distressed me. That is why I decided that, since God had given me the ability to earn my own living, if I could take care of myself and my family through my own physical labour, then I will stop committing the sin of selling my body and, indeed, of harassing my own self. If I could get a theatre constructed, then I could earn my own living for all my life. [...]

[...] I decided to be involved with the theatre! And why not? Those with whom I have always been together, as though we were siblings; those of whom I am eternally fond and whom I have obeyed—they are telling me the truth. If I could form a theatre, then we could all stay together like brothers and sisters. [...] We also hope for a husband's love, but where will we get it? Who will give us their hearts and minds in return for ours? [...] Love cannot be bought with money. We, too, have not traded in love for money. This is our earthly crime. The doyen among teachers of theatre, Girish-babu *mahashay*, has a poem called 'Barangana' ('The Prostitute'), which provides the real picture of such unlucky women. [...]

[...] So intense was my anxiety that I was sleepless for almost the entire night before my first performance in *Chaitanya-lila*. The next morning, I went for a bath in the Ganga; later, I wrote Durga's name 108 times and fell at His feet, praying "May Mahaprabhu [Chaitanya] provide me support in this moment of great crisis. May He be merciful towards me." The entire day, however, I remained anxious due to nervous thoughts. I later realised that my meditating at His feet, which makes one feel mentally stronger, had perhaps not been unsuccessful, since the fact that I had been the object of His mercy was confirmed by the responses of the many erudite members of the audience. [...] I can't tell you how many truly learned people (*mahamahopadhyay*s and *pandit*s) had blessed me as a result of my performance in *Chaitanya-lila*. [...] By the blessings of Mahaprabhu, I received kindness from so many venerable people. And it was during a performance of *Chaitanya-lila* that the incident took place which for me was a source of the greatest pride—the fact that I received the grace of the late Paramhansadeb, Sri Ramakrishna *mahashay*, who saves souls from damnation.[9] [...]

Please see the Works Cited for further information on the sources used in this essay.

Notes

1 Translated here by Suddhaseel Sen.
2 A "Vaishnavite" is a worshipper of Vishnu, the god who preserves the cosmos in Hindu mythology.
3 A female singer who was a tenant in Binodini's house and provided the training that enabled her to enter the theatre in 1872.
4 Bhuban Mohan Niyogi offered the Baghbazar Amateur Theatre rehearsal space in his home on the Ganges river. The group was renamed the Calcutta National Theatrical Society, and their playhouse became the National Theatre inaugurated in December 1872.
5 The terms *chhota lat* and *chhota latsahib* mean lieutenant or provincial governor.
6 This anecdote about the disrupted performance of Dinabandhu Mitra's play *Neel-darpan* (The Indigo Mirror, 1860), which criticized the British colonial state for forced indigo cultivation in Bengal, is regularly recounted in histories of modern Bengali and Indian theatre.
7 A few months after this trip, the National Theatre closed down, and Binodini joined Saratchandra Ghosh's Bengal Theatre, where she moved quickly to leading roles. Her next employment was at Kedarnath Chowdhury's Great National Theatre, where Girish Ghosh soon became manager and began his lifelong mentorship of Binodini.
8 Girish Ghosh's "stories" about figures like Sarah Siddons (1755–1831), Ellen Terry (1847–1928), and Daniel Bandmann (1837–1905) reflect a cosmopolitan interest in Anglo-European theatre that is not unusual among Indian theatre professionals of the colonial period.
9 Ramakrishna Paramhansa (1836–1886) was also the acknowledged spiritual master of Binodini's mentor, Girish Ghosh.

Suggestions for Further Reading

Chakravarty, Radha. "The Fallen Woman in Bengali Literature: Binodini Dasi and Tagore's *Chokher Bali*." In *Unveiling Desire: Fallen Women in Literature, Culture, and Films of the East*. Ed. Devaleena Das et al. New Brunswick, NJ: Rutgers University Press; 2018. 221–235.

Dharwadker, Aparna Bhargava. *A Poetics of Modernity: Indian Theatre Theory, 1850 to the Present*. New Delhi: Oxford University Press, 2019.

Dutt, Bishnupriya. "Actress Stories: Binodini and Amal Allana." *Staging International Feminisms*. Eds. Elaine Aston and Sue-Ellen Case. Basingstoke, England: Palgrave Macmillan; 2007. 67–75.

30 FLORENCE KIPER (1886–1976)

Sharon Friedman

Introduction

Florence Kiper [Frank][1] (1886–1976) was an American poet, dramatist, and essayist who contributed to the developing modernist aesthetic in dialogue with contemporary movements for social change during the early decades of the twentieth century. She continued to write essays and poetry throughout her life and published her last volume of poems, *The Silver Grain,* in 1956. Kiper graduated from the University of Chicago and participated in the "Chicago Renaissance," which included avant-garde arts and culture journals, theatre companies, and arts clubs. Her early poetry was published in Margaret Anderson's famed periodical *Little Review* (1914–1929), a hub of art, literature, and politics that included American and transatlantic modernists.

During this same period, Kiper wrote plays for two legendary little theatre companies: Maurice Browne's Chicago Little Theatre (1912–1917) and the Provincetown Players (1915–1922). Charles Lock argues that the Chicago Little Theatre (founded by Browne and Ellen Van Volkenburg) "was to name a movement," the word "little" signaling a "style and a politics of Modernism" (109). The Provincetown Players, founded by George Cram Cook and Susan Glaspell, originally in Provincetown, MA and then in New York City's Greenwich Village, was distinctive in its mission to produce plays exclusively by American dramatists. Many of the themes represented in these works concerned all that was considered "new" in American cultural life: the "new" politics, the "new" psychology (sparked by Freud's lectures in the U.S.), the "new" art, and the "new" woman.[2] Furthermore, the Provincetown Players included an unprecedented number of women playwrights, directors, and scenic designers.

The "little theatres," part of the larger art theatre movement, emerged between 1910 and 1916 and shared dissatisfaction with American commercial theatre. These avant-garde theatres addressed political and cultural issues in various stylistic modes, including social realism, expressionism, and satire. Influenced by their European counterparts in France, Germany, England, Russia, and particularly the touring Abbey Players from Ireland, they adopted some of their practices. They also incorporated innovations in stage design, lighting, costuming, and new modes of acting.

In her essays, poetry, and plays, Kiper expressed several social and political concerns, for example, the struggle for labor unionization, the devastation of war, urban poverty, anti-Semitism and Jewish identity, and a range of issues related to the feminist movement. Her feminism is manifest, for example, in her poem "Song of the Women" and in her play titled *Cinderelline; or, the Little Red Slipper* (1913), a parody of "Cinderella," reprinted in Bettina Friedl's anthology *On to Victory: Propaganda Plays*

DOI: 10.4324/9781003006923-31

of the Woman Suffrage Movement. Her play *Jael—A Tragedy in one act, in verse* (1914) was performed at the Chicago Little Theatre (Conway 110).

In that same year, 1914, Kiper published her groundbreaking review essay, "Some American Plays from the Feminist Viewpoint" in *Forum*, a major journal of American thought. This essay has been discussed by both American theatre historians and feminist critics.[3] "Some American Plays" is a clarion call to contemporary playwrights to bring to the stage "a conscious philosophy or an informed understanding" (rather than "unconscious method") of themes related to the "woman movement," which Kiper sees as "the one most important tendency of the century" with perhaps the exception of "class consciousness in the labor struggle." In making her claim, she argues that it is the role and "privilege" of the dramatist to "interpret" as well as "popularize the pressing questions of the time," though not necessarily in terms of a "thesis play." To substantiate her argument, she analyzes several plays of the past few seasons and laments the dearth of playwrights who address these "large issues and that have the ability to fuse at white heat into one, thesis, plot, characterization" (921–922).

In addition to the importance she gives to the playwright, she also notes the role of the critic who must discern the underlying views on "men and women in relation to each other" that many of these plays depict, and the need for receptive audiences to demand serious drama. As a humanist feminist, she ultimately looks to emerging women playwrights and their "brother writers" for a more honest portrayal of women on the stage, devoid of stereotypical overtones that "sentimentalize femininity" or attribute to "femaleness" either "angelic or demoniac power." Her hope is that dramatists will "set forth [...] those problems in the development and freedom of women that the modern age has termed the problems of feminism" (930–931).

Kiper references such issues as the double sexual standard, the stigma of divorce, suffrage agitation, women in the professions, "young girls" in industry, and "the sudden-awakening of the sheltered woman to a knowledge of prostitution and venereal diseases" (921). Surveilling several contemporary plays, she lauds Rachel Crothers's (1878–1958) *A Man's World* (1910) for its depiction of a "type of modern feminist" and a central conflict that is "waged not so much without as within her own nature, a conflict between individual emotion and social conviction" (928).

Kiper's contribution to theatre criticism adds a feminist dimension to what George Brandt calls an "analytical" approach to theory and criticism, "assessing and offering a new reading of that which already exists [...] to change the intellectual landscape in which drama is received" and practiced (xvii). Furthermore, Kiper heralds the emergence of women playwrights in the theatre, which had been primarily a male domain. Envisioning this future, she anticipates the feminist theatre of the 1970s and 1980s that Helene Keyssar termed "an emergent cultural form" that led to theatre companies by and about women (e.g. Women's Projects), as well as many new plays that positioned women in the "subject position" and subverted structures of patriarchal power (*Feminist Theatre and Theory* 1). Kiper also foreshadows the explosion of feminist theatre and performance criticism that has transformed theatre history as well as theory from myriad perspectives. Numerous studies in the 1980s and 1990s, such as Sue-Ellen Case's *Feminism and Theatre*, Jill Dolan's *The Feminist Spectator as Critic*, and Lynda Hart's *Making a Spectacle*, resonate with Kiper's concern for the representation of women on stage, the importance of critical perspective that discerns ideology, and the development of new audiences.[4]

Florence Kiper

Excerpt from "Some American Plays: From the Feminist Viewpoint" (1914)

EVERY play produced on the American stage, with perhaps a few negligible exceptions, has its say on the feminist question. Until sex ceases to be the main preoccupation of drama, this must necessarily be so. Given the depiction of men and women in their relations to each other, whether or not there be a conscious purpose in the playwright's mind to set forth his views on such relations, the critic will nevertheless discover his views—or at least the quality of his thinking, from which his sex-philosophy may be deduced. It is no more difficult to determine what Eugene Walter[5] thinks about women than it is to define Brieux's[6] feminist Credo, although the former probably considers himself guiltless of the latter's propaganda intention.

One must frankly confess at the outset that it is by the unconscious rather than the conscious method that the American dramatists are revealing themselves in regard to the woman movement. We have at present no Ibsens, Shaws, Björnsons, Strindbergs, Brieuxs[7]. In a drama whose themes are almost entirely those of contemporary social life, few among our playwrights are attempting to interpret to us the meaning of the growing divorce "evil," of the suffrage agitation, of women in the professions, of young girls in industry, of the sudden awakening of the sheltered woman to a knowledge of prostitution and venereal diseases. Almost none among our clever writers for the stage are bringing to these vital themes a conscious philosophy or an informed understanding. Yet the woman movement is undoubtedly, if perhaps the class-consciousness in the labor struggle be excepted, the one most important tendency of the century. It is important because it deals not with a limited and selected class of society, but with the very fundamentals of society—the relation of the sexes and consequently the next generation. Race-suicide, the double standard of morals, the taints of heredity, these are not side issues, but of relevancy to all of national existence.

It is the enviable privilege of the dramatist "to popularize the pressing questions of the time." That is, he must be an interpreter to the people of what they have heretofore vaguely sensed, of what is already implicit in the public mind, but through him is realized with vividness. The drama, being preeminently a social art and dependent not on the selected audience but on the average, develops correlatively with the developing social and artistic consciousness of a people. We of America must therefore remember, in our indictment of American dramatists, what Whitman has said of another art, "To have great poets there must be great audiences too."

That the great, or at least the receptive audiences are coming into being in America is a fact to all but the most pessimistic among the critics of dramatic tendencies. America is really beginning to take its drama seriously, to consider its plays as something more than "shows" for the pleasing of the immature minded. No more than five years ago a play like *Hindle Wakes*[8] would have been taboo to an American audience. To-day enlightened mothers are taking their young people to *The Blindness of Virtue*[9] or even to *Damaged Goods*[10], because of the educational value of their propaganda. I hold no brief for the thesis play as such—even the thesis play of transAtlantic importation. But surely until the American audience ceases to demand only cant and provincialism, prudishness and sentimentality, America can produce no dramatists of import—minds that are conscious of large issues and that have the ability to fuse at white heat into one, thesis, plot, characterization.

To many it appears that even now the time is ripe for a new birth and that there are the stirrings of parturition. Already several worthy plays have come out of America and there is springing up a veritable crop of young dramatists with a feeling for the stage and the craftsman's facility. While we are awaiting our big American playwrights—and perhaps the next decade will welcome them!—it is of interest to the feminist to hear what the present writers of the theatre have to say about American women.

Mr. Augustus Thomas, the so-called dean of American dramatists, a writer who has developed an easy facility in the technique of his art, has chosen the double standard of sex morality as one of the themes in his play, *As a Man Thinks,* a drama that has received a critical approbation almost unanimous. In this story of modern New York life, the discussion of female chastity is brought about *à propos* of the visit of a young married woman to the bachelor apartment of a man friend. The deed is a very natural act of bravado induced by the repeated infidelity of the husband, who is a frank exponent of masculine privilege in sex-matters. As is the way of such advocates, however, he demands of his wife a fidelity that shall be pure of the slightest appearance of evil. Dr. Seelig, presumably here the mouthpiece of the playwright, explains to the reckless wife why this must be. The home, Dr. Seelig says, rests on faith—the faith of man in woman, the faith that he is the father of the children, for whose sake is maintained this home. Truly a satisfying answer to Mrs. Clayton's bewilderment! For mark you—but a short time before, her husband, strong in this beautiful faith in his marital partner, has warned her that if she does not leave his house in quick order, his servant will be given the task of showing her the door. He allows her to remain only when the doctor informs him that his sick child may die without the little fellow's accustomed nursing, and at this the husband packs his bag and leaves for the club, unable to remain longer under the same roof with a wife guilty of the depravity of spending a half-hour in another man's bachelor apartments. This same beautiful faith of man in woman then instils suspicion into Clayton's mind as to the paternity of the child, a suspicion allayed only by documentary proof that "the other man" had been safe in prison for the year preceding the boy's birth. All then is magnanimously forgiven the erring wife—all her wickedness in compromising herself in the eyes of her husband—and the curtain falls on a beautiful reunion of mother, father and boy, to the soft chime of Christmas bells outside the window.

This play from the standpoint of feminism is an interesting study, because it represents a sex-ethics that is more or less typical. That the author did not see bigger than his story and is innocent of satirical intention, does not invalidate the play as a fair enough picture of that American home in which the function of the wife is to be the ornamental symbol of her husband's prosperity. Mrs. Clayton as played by Miss Chrystal Herne is par excellence the leisure-class American female, graceful, charming, alert, cultured, exquisitely gowned, utterly helpless. When, in Miss Herne's tremulous, low voice, the wife announces her undying love for the husband who has just bullied and insulted her, one is not amazed at all, remembering that for the woman dependent on luxury it is a business to cherish and to conserve her provider.

The explanation of the double standard of morals—a necessity, Mr. Thomas states, inherent in the biological nature of things—is somewhat reminiscent of Henry Arthur Jones[11] and the unfortunate lady in *Mrs. Dane's Defence.* Both Mr. Jones and Mr. Thomas regret kindly and urbanely as humanitarians that the woman alone must bear the social penalty of sex-indiscretion, even though that penalty be visited on the appearance of sin and not its actuality, but—with a faint sigh!—what can one do about it? So the matter has been, so will it be always. Some years ago, however, Henrik Ibsen wrote *Ghosts,* a play which not undramatically calls attention to the fact—also a fact of biology—that even a father's sex sins may have consequences for the next generation and that his personal life, as well as the mother's, bears intimate relation to the integrity and purity of the home.

A young Chicago playwright, Mr. Joseph Medill Patterson, has given us *Ghosts* in the terms of modern Chicago, in a thoroughly sincere and workmanlike drama. *Rebellion,* from the box-office standpoint, was a success neither in New York nor in its birthplace. The public was said to have found it gloomy, depressing. Either this was so or its arraignment of the Catholic Church spelled its failure. This arraignment was not a onesided or distorted propaganda, but grew inevitably from the situation. In fact, the depiction of the Catholic priest was so sympathetic that one truly regretted one's intellectual disagreement with him. When he calls to the conscience of the deserting wife in the terms of a duty that seeks not the individual happiness, one is thrilled with the fervor of all those moralists, in church or not, who are adjuring us of the present day to be mindful of the sacred and high responsibilities of marriage. But it is precisely because we are so mindful that we are insisting on the dissolution of those marriages not inherently sacred.

[....]

The High Road by Edward Sheldon and Rachel Crothers's *A Man's World,* the first a drama of last season, the second of several years ago, are two plays that deal with the modern woman who has attained self-support in the occupation of her choice and is thereby enabled to make her own terms with men. *The High Road* is an interesting attempt to show on the stage what the academic critics say can be done only through the medium of the novel—a spiritual growth through a process of years—in this case the period of a woman's life from seventeen years of age to thirty-eight. That Mr. Sheldon was not quite successful in the portrayal may be due to the limitations of the dramatic form—or to his own present limitations. At any rate, his last three acts are authentic and interesting, if conventional, drama. What is not conventional is his characterization of Mary Page. Here at last we have an American playwright who recognizes that the woman of 1912 is not the woman of 1880, or even of 1900. Miss Page at thirty-eight is capable, keen, resourceful, a woman who is filling in an important way an important position. No one would think for a moment of patronizing or pitying her because she is nearing forty without a husband and children. Indeed, so much of a person is she that the man who loves her takes her for wife not as a woman once stained, now cleansed by masculine forgiveness, but as an individual who, as her lover himself might have done, has wrung from experience tolerance and sympathy.

Miss Crothers' play is also of a mature woman, younger than Mary Page—a woman who has made a place for herself as a writer. Her writings have been largely directed against the abuses from which women suffer in the present social arrangement.[12] She is a type of the modern feminist. And the conflict of the drama is waged not so much without as within her own nature, a conflict between individual emotion and social conviction. What many of our writers for the stage have missed in their objective drama that uses the new woman for protagonist is a glimpse of that tumultuous battlefield, her own soul, where meet the warring forces of impulse and theory, of the old and the new conceptions of egotism and altruism. Miss Crothers understands dramatic interest of such tumult. The heroine of *A Man's World,* a woman whose intellectual power has enriched, not devitalized, her emotional capacity—(why do certain of our dramatists believe feminine intellect must inevitably devitalize!)—discovers that the man she loves has had a son out of wedlock, the mother a friend of hers who died in giving birth to the baby. It is not her horror at the discovery that separates her from her lover. The man had not known of the little fellow's existence and is now eager to make any reparation possible. But he refuses to admit the heinousness of his wrong. It is a man's world. A pity! but in the nature of things woman must pay the penalty. Because of this intellectual conviction she leaves him. There is no sentimentalism, no attempt to gloss over the situation with the pet American dramatic platitude that love makes right all things. *A Man's World* is honest, well-built drama, interesting to feminists not only because of its exposition of a modern sex-problem, but also because it is written by a woman—one who does not attempt to imitate the masculine viewpoint, but who sees the feminine experience through feminine temperament.

[...]

The literature that will be written by woman as a revealer of that so-called mystery, herself, will probably not sentimentalize femininity. She knows that there is no sacrosanct or magic quality in femaleness, either for angelic or demoniac power—other than that sacredness of individual worth that accrues to every human being by the mere fact of being human. There will be an increasing number of women playwrights in America as the doors of occupational and educational opportunity are thrown wider. It is to be hoped that they will feel impelled—they and their brother-writers,—to set forth sincerely and honestly, yet with vital passion, those problems in the development and freedom of women that the modern age has termed the problems of feminism.

Please see the Works Cited for further information on the sources used in this essay.

Notes

1 Florence Kiper married Jerome N. Frank in 1914 and used the name Florence Kiper Frank in subsequent publications. Jerome New Frank was an American legal philosopher and author who played a leading role in the legal realism movement.

2 Carroll Smith-Rosenberg characterizes the early twentieth-century New Woman as a figure signifying the "rejection of convention" and a "desire to act on her own," but defined differently by successive generations. *Disorderly Conduct: Visions of Gender in Victorian America*, New York: Alfred A. Knopf, 1985. See, also, Adele Heller and Lois Rudnick, *1915, The Cultural Moment.* New Brunswick, NJ: Rutgers University Press, 1991.

3 Cheryl Black, *The Women of the Provincetown, 1915-1922*, Tuscaloosa, Al: University of Alabama Press, 2002; Judith Barlow, "Introduction," *Women Writers of the Provincetown Players*, Albany, NY: State University of New York Press, 2009; Barbara Ozieblo, *Susan Glaspell: A Critical Biography*, Chapel Hill, NC: University of North Carolina, 2000; Brenda Murphy (with Laurie J.C.. Cella), eds., *Twentieth Century American Drama: Critical Concepts in Literary and Cultural Studies*, Vol. I, London and New York: Routledge 2006, pp. 14–21.

4 See entries by Farfan and Del Vecchio in this volume.

5 American playwright (1874–1941) of social melodrama. His 1908 play *The Easiest Way* depicts a woman whose desires for money and male attention ultimately defeat her.

6 Eugene Brieux, French dramatist, is known as an exponent of the thesis play. He addressed, among many themes, power relations in marriage and other forms of authority in societal institutions.

7   Henrik Ibsen (1828–1907) revolutionized modern drama, and along with August Strind-
    berg (1849–1912) and Björnstjerne Björnson (1832–1910) made major contributions to
    European modernism. George Bernard Shaw (1856–1950), influenced by Ibsen, among
    other artists and thinkers, developed the drama of ideas that addressed a range of social
    ills. All four dramatists created central roles for women in their plays, and Ibsen, Björn-
    son and Shaw supported freedoms for women and examined power dynamics between
    women and men. In Strindberg's later plays, however, women are portrayed as inferior,
    demanding, and destructive.

8   *Hindle Wakes* (1910) by English playwright William Stanley Houghton (1881–1913) was
    one of the first plays to depict a working-class female protagonist that desires agency in
    her life, stirring controversy at the time.

9   *The Blindness of Virtue* (1912) by English playwright Cosmo Hamilton (1870–1942)
    depicts the vulnerability of young women who have not been educated about sexuality
    and societal conventions.

10 Eugene Brieux's 1913 play addressed the ramifications of venereal disease upon spouses
    and children, as well as attitudes toward marriage and exploitation of the poor.

11 English dramatist (1851–1929).

12 Although she became relatively unknown after her death, Rachel Crothers wrote the
    largest number of commercially successful plays by a woman for the conventional thea-
    tre prior to World War II. Her canon ultimately included twenty-three full-length plays
    and a number of one-acts written over a period of forty years (1899–1937), many of
    which addressed the changing role of women in the early twentieth century and such
    issues as the double standard, women's economic independence, and women's quest for
    identity and autonomy.

Suggestions for Further Reading

Chansky, Dorothy. *Composing Ourselves: The Little Theatre Movement and the American Audience.*
    Carbondale: Southern Illinois University Press, 2004.
Dukore, F. Bernard. "Maurice Browne and the Chicago Little Theatre." *Theatre Survey,* Vol.3,
    (May, 1962): 59–78.

31 MAY ISABEL FISK (1872–1955)

Jennifer Schmidt

Introduction

"A fund of brightness and gay humor—a new book of monologues by May Isabel Fisk, recognized as the funniest woman monologist in America." So reads an advertisement for *The Silent Sex* in the *The New York Times* from April 1923. At the time, calling Fisk (1872–1955) "the funniest woman monologist in America" was not mere promotional hyperbole. Working between 1898 and 1930, Fisk performed original, humorous monologues for high society at the Waldorf-Astoria Hotel in New York and for the masses at F. F. Proctor's vaudeville houses. She was a frequent contributor to *Harper's* magazine and published five volumes of her monologues. Her comedic writing demonstrated an impressive range of styles. Some of her monologues written in dialect are reminiscent of the frontier humor of Mark Twain (1835–1910), while others share an affinity with the urban satire of Dorothy Parker (1893–1967).

In the preface to her 1914 collection, *Monologues and Duologues*, Fisk writes an instructional essay titled "The Art of Giving a Monologue" in which she explains the main characteristics of her form: "It […] demands a certain kind of specialized and compressed acting—so to speak—that the ordinary actor, surrounded by every stage requisite, is not called upon to exercise" (9). The monologist, "without the assistance of properties or accessories of any kind," must convey a full scene purely through her "acting and suggestions," and thus "every motion and gesture, every glance of the eye and turn of the head, must be replete with meaning" (9). The lack of scenery or stage requirements made the style of monologue Fisk defines in this essay highly popular with amateur performers, especially women, who performed them at social events and gatherings. Moreover, as a professional practice, monologue performance offered women like Fisk an opportunity to earn a living through a highly autonomous form of theatre-making.

When Fisk began performing in the late 1890s, the comic monologue form was perhaps most readily associated with the popular platform humorists of the nineteenth century. The folksy, narrative monologues of Mark Twain and Artemus Ward (Charles Farrar Brown [1834–1867]) had dominated the newspapers, Lyceum circuits, and platform stages of the preceding era. Concurrent with Fisk's development as a monologue performer, the popular forms of American humor began to shift from the platform humorists' narrative style to what was called the "New Humor" of vaudeville. Variety audiences expected a laugh at the end of every line, and vaudeville comedians adapted the monologue for the impatient tastes of their patrons.

DOI: 10.4324/9781003006923-32

Although Fisk built on established traditions of comic monologue performance, her humor pointed in yet another new direction, one which focused on women's changing roles at home and in the public sphere.

Whereas the platform and vaudeville stages were dominated by male comedians, Fisk got her start by performing in primarily feminine spaces, at women's club luncheons or drawing room entertainments. Out of this milieu, Fisk, along with contemporaries, such as Beatrice Herford (1867–1952), developed a distinct form of monologue, which centered on close observations of female character and personality. As pioneers in the field of the one-woman show, Fisk and Herford served as inspiration and precedent for later performers, such as Ruth Draper (1884–1956), Cornelia Otis Skinner (1889–1979),[1] Lily Tomlin (b.1939), and Whoopi Goldberg (b.1955), all of whom created comedic, character-based monologues in a style similar to Fisk's.

The form they developed allowed the performer to question and satirize women's social roles and behaviors in a manner much different from the standard representation of women in popular entertainment. Rather than following the narrative style of the platform humorists or the punchline-driven vaudeville sets, Fisk created specific dramatic scenarios in each monologue, evoked through the words and actions of the characters she embodied. By placing her characters at the center of a dramatic scene, stripped of any excess scenery or costumes, Fisk focused all the attention on her female subjects, requiring the audience to witness scenes of everyday life from the woman's perspective.

In developing her monologues, Fisk also capitalized on changing cultural attitudes toward selfhood and identity in the early part of the twentieth century. As Maggie B. Gale comments, Fisk's monologues focused on an "investigation of identity and observation of social types [...] at a time when the acceleration of urban industrialization meant that individuality and social identity were becoming an issue in the popular press" (297). The titles of some of Fisk's monologues—"The Village Dressmaker," "The Suburban Hostess," "The Saleslady," "The London Char-Lady," "Hunting for an Apartment," "Buying a Hat"—give an impression of the range and types of characters and activities represented in her work. Because of Fisk's "ability to story-tell from the first-person perspective and to move between depictions of different imaginary stage characters simultaneously," Gale argues, her work "contains a strong anthropological perspective" (298).

Fisk's success in the medium stemmed from her close, critical, and compassionate attention to feminine behavior and mannerisms. Accordingly, her essay on the art of the monologue provides invaluable insights into the construction and representation of female character during her time. In the essay, Fisk acknowledges that "nearly all" of her monologues "portray a type." She then lists several types, along with advice for how to faithfully portray them. The coquette, for example, "holds her head more frequently a-tilt, and does not impale her victim with direct regard," while the eyes of "a gossiping woman" are "alert and bright, calculating and sophisticated." As a manual for comedic acting, the piece is filled with thorough and astute articulations of how to enact typical female roles while walking the line between caricature and character. A fascinating guide to an acting practice dominated by women, "The Art of Giving a Monologue" therefore provides vital analysis and commentary on a popular but understudied field of performance from one of its original proponents.

May Isabel Fisk

"The Art of Giving a Monologue" (1914)

THE art of giving a monologue is a separate little histrionic attainment quite by itself. It differs entirely from the rendering of a recitation and demands a certain kind of specialized and compressed acting—so to speak—that the ordinary actor, surrounded by every stage requisite, is not called upon to exercise.

One has to create all the illusion and atmosphere without the assistance of properties or accessories of any kind, and to make not only felt but *seen* every other person in the miniature drama. Therefore, every motion and gesture, every glance of the eye and turn of the head, must be replete with meaning.

One must *act* from head to foot, without an instant's respite, as so much must be conveyed without a single word. Thus, when in apparent repose and listening to another's speech, the gist of what is said must be faithfully reflected by clear and expressive pantomime.

To successfully portray a type—as in nearly all of my monologues—it is necessary to reproduce the character absolutely true to life and invested with all the little ways and foibles that are distinctly and essentially feminine and that would fit that particular woman. To give such a picture, a careful study of the character must be made before attempting the lines, making a mental sketch of the person—how she looks, acts and speaks, and form a conception of the body expression suitable to that type.

For instance, a woman with a cold who has been in the house all day alone, is in a particularly irritable frame of mind; she speaks quickly and sharply, the voice is high-pitched and querulous, and often trails off into a whine of mingled fatigue and impatience, her movements are languid and half indeterminate, but she expresses petulance with every lifting of her shoulder.

In a gossiping woman the eyes are alert and bright, calculating and sophisticated. Her comments are delivered in an acidulous tone, her movements are self-possessed and assured, and her whole expression radiates self-complacency and superiority.

The girl who coquettes holds her head more frequently a-tilt, and does not impale her victim with direct regard. The prosaic, matter-of-fact type, looks more squarely to right or left, with no perkings of the head or digressions towards the tail of the eye.

A fussy or nervous woman is constantly in some sort of motion, a species of rudimentary and unfinished gesture. The timid little woman who means well, but always blunders in saying the wrong thing, is quick and hesitating and contradictory in her movements. Her step is light and short, her expression full of concern, her eyes large and surprised, her tone soft, and betraying a childishness and lack of experience.

The woman who is making an elaborate excuse, knowing she is entirely at fault, is very emphatic and precise in speech, smiles ingratiatingly and hurriedly, looking constantly from side to side, and is extravagantly considerate in manner.

It must be borne in mind, however, when trying to give an original interpretation, that there are certain elementary emotions which always produce corresponding physical effects, which cannot be controverted, as they have been found to be true and must not, therefore, be disregarded. For example, it is indisputable that fear contracts—one shrinks, draws away, the limbs lie closely, the eye expands, all movements are jerky, or slow and slinking. Pride and arrogance expand and swagger. Happiness lends to light and free and easy motion. Exultation and spiritual joy expresses itself in uplifted head, slow movement, wide and large gesture—and so on.

In giving a monologue when one is literally scenery, properties, lighting, and possibly several characters, the importance of every line of the body expressing *something* in its attitude and motion, cannot be too strongly insisted upon. So, in making gestures and movements, it is well to ask yourself why you do it—if it means nothing to you, it cannot possibly convey anything to an audience. If you cannot find that you have any definite idea in what you are doing and cannot see that it is helping to illustrate the characterization, you will probably discover it is not the thing to do. Constant and meaningless movement of the body will give a confused and blurred picture. Of course, this statement must be more or less fitted to the requirements of the type rendered.

The real art and chief attraction in rendering a monologue is really not so much what you say yourself, but in making the audience see and understand, through your acting and suggestions, exactly what the other person or persons are saying without repeating the words. First in importance comes the necessary mobility of facial expression. The emotion or feeling must instantly reflect itself in the countenance—always remembering the *thought* must come first—it is mirrored in the face, and almost simultaneously follows a corresponding expression of the body.

To act *at* a character is hopeless—one must *be* it, divested of ego, and casting aside any personal inclination to mannerisms. Anything consciously artificial is always a barrier between actor and audience, and puts to flight that essential and subtle element of success termed magnetism. One must be spontaneous and natural and convincing in one's artificiality.

Women—superficial women, be it said—are so amusing because they are unconsciously so. They jump from the sublime to the ridiculous without an instant's hesitation, and chief comedy effects are obtained from their rapid transition from one emotion to another.

The garrulous woman is not often the deep thinking woman, therefore she has no thought of reserve and is thoroughly outspoken and frank—in a shallow acceptance of this last term. Consequently, successive shades of feeling and ideas rapidly reproduce themselves in her countenance.

Considerable meaning may thus be conveyed without a single word. For instance, you wish the audience to be aware, without saying so, that something distasteful has been said at which you are greatly annoyed. All you may say is " Oh, indeed," but as you articulate, " Oh," you turn away with a slight lifting of the brows, accompanied by a bridling of the head, a tightening of the lips and a little straightening up, and then, " indeed," with a rising reflection [sic], as you give your hair a half conscious pat or smooth your belt, or give a pull at your veil, to indicate your apparent indifference. None of these slight actions must be exaggerated or to [sic] assume an effect of caricature.

In giving a monologue, it must always be borne in mind that unless the imaginary character or characters are seated—and unless for some very definite reason this position is to be maintained, it would appear monotonous; you must not fail to follow them about with your eyes as they move.

Too much care can never be taken in fitting one's performance to the size and surroundings in which it is to be rendered. It takes a nice calculator in values to determine the exact amount of force and breadth to diminish in adjusting a stage performance to a drawing-room and vice versa. A not inapt simile might be to fancy how coarse and ineffective a piece of scene painting would appear in the drawing-room, and how lost a miniature would seem displayed on the stage. This applies admirably to the giving of a monologue. One must paint with a large brush for the stage, and with a small and delicate one for the drawing-room and small platform. For the stage, large gestures, incisive speech, almost exaggerated facial expression—more dramatic and intense in every way; and the reverse must be observed in smaller surroundings.

Please see the Works Cited for further information on the sources used in this essay.

Note

1 See Skinner entry in this volume.

Suggestions for Further Reading

Fisk, May Isabel. *The Silent Sex: Monologues.* New York, NY: Harper & Brothers, 1923.
Hans, Julia. "Landy Goshen! Here comes a whole troop o' them city boarders': May Isabel Fisk's Dialect Monologues." *Studies in American Humor.* 3.22 (2010): 129–145.
Piacentino, Ed. "Mark Twain and May Isabel Fisk: Parallels in Comic Monologues." *Mark Twain Journal.* 49.1/2 (2011): 92–108.

32 DJUNA BARNES (1892–1982)

Nick Salvato

Introduction

Playwright and novelist Djuna Barnes (1892–1982) began her writerly career as a journalist. Known for her keen wit and eye for detail, she brought those qualities particularly to two forms of reporting, the celebrity interview and the theatrical "stunt" piece, which characterized her work for a variety of New York City-based newspapers and magazines in the 1910s. Recognized as charming snapshots of urban modernity (and modern urbanity)—as well as for the ways in which they proleptically gesture toward stylistic maneuvers and thematic preoccupations that distinguish Barnes's later, more mature and prominent writing—a number of these journalistic forays have been collected in two posthumous volumes, *Interviews* (1985) and *New York* (1989). Yet one of Barnes's most fascinating, unusual, and arguably important journalistic pieces, "When the Puppets Come to Town" (1917), did not make the cut for inclusion in either volume and thus remains more obscure, worthy of a level and kind of attention that it has not received thus far.

In a piece focused on an interview with puppeteer Tony Sarg, Barnes frames their conversation with a history of global puppetry; that history fans out, with an emphasis on marionettes, into a theorization of the puppet's cross-cultural curiosity and power. For Barnes, this power, distinguishing lively puppets from mere dolls, stems largely from the ways in which puppets can perform violent acts indifferently, putatively tragic acts without tragic emotion, and related forms of mayhem with charming calmness. Not, in Barnes's accounting of them, stripped of subjectivity, marionettes and their kin are rather endowed, when they move, with a subjectivity that comes close to—and then swerves away from—human subjectivity.

This quality, among others that make marionettes at once familiar and strange, contributes to their status as "uncanny," a word choice with which Barnes anticipates Sigmund Freud's famous 1919 essay on the uncanny. Indeed, Barnes offers an implicit—and quite differently inflected—theory of the uncanny that refuses the pretensions to depth characteristic of psychoanalytic thinking and that lingers instead on the force of sensuous surfaces. Training her attention on joints, holes, costumes, and paint, Barnes locates the uncanny animation of puppets precisely in the surficial gestures and movements, ranging from the delicate to the rough, with which the puppets' component parts come to life (and death)—*not* in a nonconscious field to which these gestures and movements may point (and in which, for Freud, the fear of castration is key [231]).

DOI: 10.4324/9781003006923-33

When Barnes quotes Sarg admiring such movements exactly for the ways in which they can exceed human motility, "Puppets" also speaks knowingly backward to Heinrich von Kleist's influential essay, "On the Marionette Theatre," where dialogue between two interlocutors fastens similarly onto the puppet's potential to outdo the human performer (24). At the same time, "Puppets" previews in miniature (as it were) the prominence of lively, uncanny objects in Barnes's most accomplished plays. Whether the picture in *The Dove* made "obscene" when it is punctured by a bullet (161), or the dollhouse in *The Antiphon* that prompts a family to confront its traumatic history of rape and abuse (145–153), such objects do not merely fascinate Barnes. Rather, they propel the actions and rouse the sentiments that animate her works for the stage—and, one may infer from a reading of "Puppets," Barnes perhaps begins to learn how to harness the vitality of such uncanny objects from her engagement with and speculations about marionettes.

Enigmatic personal meditations, underlining Barnes's embodied and affective experiences as a woman, begin and end the piece and endow it with a further level of complexity, rooted in ambiguity and mysteriousness. Marked by boredom and fatigue—but rhetorically presented in a way that suggests that Barnes is not merely suffering from lassitude but made nervous by it—these experiences haunt the otherwise cheerful conversation that Barnes undertakes with Sarg and her wry and ironic descriptions of the marionettes' form of being. Does Barnes envy the puppets for their apparent immunity from weariness and malaise? And, perhaps triangulating the otherwise binaristic relationship between puppets and humans, who are the strange creatures populating the drawing with which Barnes furnishes the article (See Figure 32.1)?

Like others of Barnes's celebrated drawings, it is rendered in a style inspired by and directly allusive to the work of Aubrey Beardsley. Yet unlike many of Barnes's other drawings, this one ushers its viewers into a proto-surrealistic world that is neither the human's, troubled by feeling, nor the puppet's, comparatively untroubled. It is a fantasy zone, perhaps, in which feeling persists, but with fluid tranquility and sinuous grace.

Twirling a Mustache, He Watches the Death Pang.

Figure 32.1 Line drawing by Djuna Barnes from "When the Puppets Come to Town"

Djuna Barnes

"When the Puppets Come to Town" (1917)

I am tired; my days are full of a vain yet pleasant sorrow. I perceive that I am happy without being able to grasp my happiness. I am full of an acute languor and I must be up and doing. I have speculated upon life until existence has become a network of plot and incident tangled hopelessly in the complexities of human emotion. One's heart beats, therefore one breathes; one breathes, and therefore one senses; and, sensing, one comes inevitably to where one must comprehend. One mourns, and mourning brings the heart to that alternative to beat slowly or to cease. I see all these things – they make a profound impression on me – still I know that I don't really give everything the greatest significance. Therefore I only guess at things, and in these days one should know. It is well. I go off to twenty-eight Macdougal Street and watch Bufano's marionettes.

They are so impartial. Having no sense of colour, a tear means no more to them than a drop of water, a pool of blood, nothing more than a pool of rain. They are filled with a strange, charming angular fidelity to moments that we should have slurred by our roundness of perception and our more flexible motions. They say to each other, 'Madame, how do you do – it is an exceedingly delightful day, the Bois is sunny, let us take a stroll', and when the stroll has been accomplished the young swain finds nothing to regret in the discovery that his inamorata has returned minus a head. He looks at her coquettishly as though about to murmur, 'I like your head like that', instead of saying, 'Your hair is very becoming dressed low', and thereupon proceeds to adore her in her new condition without sorrow and without regret.

Their passions are always more violent than their retribution, their beginning more fatal than their end; for them the beginning is struggle, mighty raisings of hands and creaking of joints and flourishing of swords, but their deaths are only defeat, not tragedy.

They come upon one another with a great flourish. The lady villain, with odd, cold eyes carved from some tropical wood, murmurs between two rows of perfectly matched dog's teeth, 'Can't you see by my colouring that I must participate in rows – muddy red rows?' and instantly every one falls to, beating with their clubs and dancing with their feet, and some of them rise again and some of them don't.

They look about them with their wide, calm carved faces as the female portion of their herd fall like mushrooms beneath the slurring tread of early grazing cattle, and perhaps one more deft in his joints than another will look calmly upon the death pangs of his daughter as he twirls a slick black mustache, caroling in a childish voice, 'The flowers that bloom in the Spring, tra la.'

Now you begin to understand what I mean; they take all things casually – they have a story to run through, a plot to complete, a design to enact. They go about it, they accomplish it; and, having no desire to murder, they do not suffer pains of remorse. They can, indeed, go off stage complacently, full of happy selfcontent, because they have done something well, therefore, instead of being at the beginning of a lifelong tragedy, they are at the end of an amusement.

With what ease Orlando Furioso murders and is murdered, nothing comes so near perfect design, excepting perhaps a Russian novel. With what delicate articulation the soul and the arm move in these murders and homicides. One throws his beloved from the window as one tosses a flower, with a beautiful gesture of appreciation. The other knows his sweetheart has shattered to bits as only rare porcelain has done before her. What a sign it is that he knows to a nicety the despair of the birds when they realise that their song is less sweet by two ears, and the growing things less succulent by a mouth.

He paces back and forth, and up and down, smiling as he has always smiled since Bufano's penknife cut into the wood that was to make him his rare personality, and only when a signal is given does he suddenly collapse upon the stage like a fallen boat amid the glory of its rigging.

Perhaps some of his hysterical immunity is due to the fact that he has never had a private life, or had he one he would still compose little smiles of affection and confidence to cast upon the audience. His family skeleton never menaces; it beckons only for its joints. It too would be a marionette and play for an hour smiling 'The eternal smile of thirty-two white teeth.'

This is what they have been in the past, that past which reaches back with how prodigiously long an arm to bring forth a duplicate for every one of our modern inventions. Monsieur marionette was found among the remains of Struria in Egypt and was at last set free from the clasp that knows no variation in a million of years, the arms of some mummy.

In Italy the Saint's days builded it slowly; first the little figures of the Virgin Mary; incidents from the crucifixion; then the great Passion Play by marionettes. Like all things that have sprung from the heart, like all that grows up beneath a face bent in devotion to the dust, the marionette has something of charm and of value unknown to mere dolldom.

From Greece it went to Rome, in the sixteenth century. The prodigal Son returned on wires and Nineveh was acted by toys strung together with care.

And ah, how the puppets danced in the time of Bartholomew Fair:

'Here a knave in a fool's coat, with a trumpet sounding or a drum beating, invites you to see his puppets. Here a rogue, like a wild woodman or in an antic shape like an incubus, desires your company to view his motion.'[1]

Here Pepys speaks of having found Lady Castlemain enjoying the marionettes and Maeterlinck has even sung for them.

Pinketham, the 'motion maker' with his divinities of Olympus set to music, Crowley with his scenes from the Flood and the order of their coming, Noah and the birds and beasts and the swan that could flap its wings, and in the bosom of Abraham the body of Lazarus still lyrical with the mould of a generous grave.

And in the early eighties there was Brown, who always turned up at the country fairs, with the battle of Trafalgar and the army with Napoleon crossing the Alps, and there was that performance of Dr Jonathan Faust that Goethe founded his own upon, they say. Ah, well, it has been a merry set of centuries with these marionettes dancing down ages with their grave or happy faces set towards the audience.[2]

Some rarer joy than our more common happiness has struck lies upon these painted eyeballs and stares from out their china depths. With how masterly a bound they approach the problems we have long set our faces against; with what merry twirlings they giggle over the problems that must ever confront buffoons – the necessity of committing life for the purpose of amusing the living.

Confronted with the sword, they murder. Placed opposite a pair of lips, they kiss. Set among chairs, they sit them down, and surrounded by 'cause' they still suffer nothing of effect.

It is not a rare life where you can say: 'I would strike the villain dead; his inquiries set my veins to jumping with the stuff of blood turned to the gall of despair. My head spills open to give death its little door, where, stepping forth, it may sit like judgement on my brow and may spit fire from my eyeballs and destruction from my tongue.' And, at the same time, to smile and smile imperturbably, and, while the monster gnaws at the vitals of your heart, to be able to scratch the knee in simple complacency.

I asked Tony Sarg and he assented, while he went on painting a picture of a gentleman who was trying to prevent a runaway match.

'I respect marionettes,' he said, 'because they are capable of tragedy without annoying anyone by being also capable of tragic emotions. Then, too, it's about the only way that America will ever accustom itself to tragic endings – they do not mind the head of the heroine, whether on or off – they have cut up so much kindling wood for their own comfort that it means less than nothing when wood cuts up wood for the casual amusement. They have builded houses with them, made axe handles and cradles with him – with him the guillotine is erected. Wood was the cross and wood is also the comfort of daily life; why shouldn't wood be melodramatic also?'

'Quite true,' I assented. 'It is with wood that we express so much of that which is the flesh. Tell me, then, what you and Mr Bufano and Mr Ames are going to do with the puppets?'

'We are going to open at the Little Theatre in September with three fairy plays. More I cannot say, it is a secret. But,' he added, throwing down his pencil and his paint brush, 'I will let you see my children if you will come over to the loft where I keep them.'

We strolled. It was a perfect day, sunshine gilded the edges of the cobblestones, while the rain lay in little puddles between them, and crossing over Twenty-third Street toward Twentieth Street West, we approached 121.

A young lady with a small canary-coloured monkey on her arm came forward and spoke to Mr Sarg in strongly English accented sentences, about the loss of a saw, a hammer and a penknife. Mr Sarg nodded and introduced me to a young gentleman and another young lady who stood upon the platform as they manipulated the twenty-two strings of the marionettes.

'Rehearsal?' I inquired.

Mr Sarg nodded. The young English girl put the monkey down on the beam of the small theatre platform, whereupon it immediately climbed up the purple curtain and sat grinning upon the room like one of the eternal tragic masks seen at the corner of the stage curtains and all stage architecture.

Behind the slightly raised platform ten or twelve calico bags swung in line. Written on one of them was the word 'Doctor Magicus', on another, 'Martin', and below this in brackets the word 'boy'. I thought it entirely charming, and asked to see what he looked like.

Still they were a little uncanny after all, like corpses hung up in a row. It might well have been Blue Beard's den, only there was a body beneath the head. Several hung by their throats, the trout line thread used to move them multiplied into the hundreds. One of them could be heard as he beat his lead feet upon the platform in a folk dance, another sitting in a chair beat a tattoo.

Bufano's marionettes had been manipulated by a single rod running through the head and two or three strings attached to hands and legs. These were strung from the nose, the elbows, the knees, the feet, the wrists, the mouth and the eyes. They sneezed, shaking the hair out of their faces; they walked, they tossed balls about, they could reach into a cupboard and bring forth a jug, a plate, a glass. They embraced, they struck each other, they kicked, jumped, swung their arms, legs and head, they winked, they moved their lips, they held their sides, they laughed (voice from above, of course), they sneered, they found moments in which scorn became opulent and heavy, they joked among each other, they stared into space, they cleaned tables, they spanked children, they played an instrument, they took up a wild dance again. Finally they flew from the scene, their legs stretched straight and arms extended in farewell.

Mr Sarg came over and sat down beside me. 'It's very difficult,' he said, 'to get people to operate the dolls; they either don't care for the work or they don't catch on to it quick enough, or they get discouraged and bored. If they can make a marionette walk in the first week they are very smart indeed. That is the hardest part of it all; it is much simpler to make them dance, fight, embrace – anything, than it is to make them walk – you see that,' he broke off, pointing to the blue coated puppet, 'watch it now.'

Martin was moving slowly across stage from the point where the little red settee stood, over to a blue arm-chair; he walked as though a bird were in either foot and would sing as he touched the floor. He bent swiftly forward as he moved, and turned his head from side to side, smiling, the Buster Brian [*sic*] bang of hair falling into his eyes. He approached the chair, thrust his hands out, placed them along the chair back, and swinging around abruptly dropped into it, sinking down softly toward the base of the spine, and nodding his head. I expected him to take snuff at this moment; instead he sneezed again. (Sneeze from midair.)

'She has not quite got on to it yet,' Mr Sarg was saying at my side, and giving directions, asked the young lady to repeat the performance.

'Do you consider marionettes of more artistic importance than actors?'

'No. I shouldn't say no, being a marionette fan,' he answered, 'but one must be honest in hot weather. I think, however, that marionettes certainly have a real artistic value.'

'But don't you feel that they are being made – well, a little too near human – too complex?'

'No. I'll tell you why. They can be as human as they please in appearance, and yet they can do things that no human can, without being ridiculous. Marionettes can fly – a human cannot do that without adding something false to the performance; a marionette only adds another string. Marionettes are admirable for fairy tales, more especially as fairy stories are generally based upon impossible events, that is, impossible for human beings.'

'And what do you consider the best kind of play for a marionette to undertake?'

'Oh, melodrama, of course – something with a great deal of action. Character studies would be quite impossible, as you can see for yourself – studies in facial expression are out of the question, abstract emotion is also impossible, and so is any sort of psychological study. They could not play a Shaw comedy, neither could they render anything of Yeats. They have done Shakespeare. A company in Munich performed *Midsummer Night's Dream.'*

'How long have you been interested in them?'

'Oh, a long time. I was first drawn to them by seeing the Javanese dolls. I gave performances to friends in London – by the way, the house was the one used for *The Old Curiosity Shop* in Dickens's time – and again I gave performances to invited audiences here.'

'And has Bufano been at it a long time?'

'Oh, yes, but only actively since December.'

'I remember speaking to him at the Richmond Hill house about it. He seemed very enthusiastic – the house, however, was mostly an Italian one, and *Furioso* was even given in Italian.'

'Yes,' he said, picking up an arm and beginning to paint it. 'And the Italian one was the best too.'

I continued: 'I remember, too, that the box seats were baby chairs set up on a sort of platform, where two or three little girls sat and discussed the performance like great ladies, with the difference of an "allday sucker" in place of opera glasses or lorgnette.'

He laughed. 'Yes, and do you recollect the little girl who played her scales upon the piano in the corner before the curtains were drawn?'

'I suppose,' I said, returning to the dolls, 'they are very difficult to make?'

'It takes months. Then, too, the furniture has to be made especially for them, the periods of dress and decoration have to be thought of: one needs a dressmaker, a carpenter, an electrician, a staff to manipulate them, and then actresses to speak the lines.'

'Are you going in for beautiful costuming for the heroines?'

'Yes, but with each change of dress I have to make a duplicate doll.'

'Why?'

'Because of the twenty-two strings,' he answered, frowning. 'You can't dress a doll in a minute when you have to make twenty-two holes in the dress before you can get it on, so duplicate dolls have to be made, each with a different dress.'

'What type of marionettes are yours – old Italian or Egyptian?'

'Neither – old English and German, perhaps. Not the theatre puppet of Richard Teschner – exotic – mad little dolls with a taste for the bizarre. Quite normal, as you see, with a touch of New England in their spines, but with more suppleness.' He laughed again at this.

And then I said to him what I often have said: 'Ah, well, it's a strange world!'

I am bored – I go to see the marionettes.

Please see the Works Cited for further information on the sources used in this essay.

Notes

1 Ben Johnson's play *Bartholomew Fair* (1614) features puppets in its narrative [eds.].
2 Barnes recounts here highlights of European puppet history from the Medieval era to the early 20th century. See Henryk Jurkowski, *A History of European Puppetry*. 2 vols. London: Mellen Press, 1996–1998 [eds.].

Suggestions for Further Reading

Bell, John. *American Puppet Modernism: Essays on the Material World in Performance.* New York, NY: Palgrave Macmillan, 2008.

Broe, Mary Lynn, ed. *Silence and Power: A Reevaluation of Djuna Barnes.* Carbondale and Edwardsville, IL: Southern Illinois University Press, 1991.

Ridinger Smorul, Kate. "Of Marionettes, Boxers, and Suffragettes: Djuna Barnes's Performative Journalism." *Journal of Modern Literature* 39:1 (Fall 2015): 55–71.

33 SOPHIE TREADWELL (1885–1970)

Jerry Dickey

Introduction

Sophie Treadwell (1885–1970) is widely recognized as one of the most significant women dramatists of the first half of the twentieth century. Her unconventional and trailblazing life intersected with many of that era's prominent historical and political movements and fueled the forms and subjects of her writings in theatre, fiction, and journalism. Her passion for women's rights included marching for women's suffrage with the feminist Lucy Stone League, serving as one of the first state-accredited female foreign war correspondents during World War I, and maintaining her maiden name and at times a separate residence after marriage. Her work as a professional journalist, combined with her father's Mexican heritage, resulted in her reputation as a noted champion of Mexico, especially through her first-hand account of the assassination of President Carranza and an exclusive interview with Pancho Villa at his post-revolution sanctuary in Canutillo. Treadwell developed close relationships with modern and avant-garde artists, including a romantic relationship with painter Maynard Dixon, participated regularly in New York City salon gatherings of Walter and Louise Arensberg, and collaborated on a work of art with Marcel Duchamp. Advancing the early mission of The Dramatists Guild, Treadwell tirelessly defended the artistic rights of playwrights, including bringing a lawsuit against John Barrymore for plagiarism, becoming the first U.S. dramatist to be paid royalties for stage production from the Soviet Union, and seeking greater artistic controls by variously producing, acting in, and co-directing some of her seven plays presented on Broadway.

Treadwell's play *Machinal* (1928) has been anthologized several times and hailed as a landmark feminist exploration of gender and patriarchal power in modern America. Inspired by the infamous 1927 trial of Ruth Snyder for conspiring to murder her husband, the play presents, as Jennifer Jones notes, "the testimony [of Snyder], disallowed by the court of law, that Treadwell wished to introduce into the court of public opinion" (486). Stevie Simkin further suggests that the play's "significance lies in its seismic reorientation of the Snyder narrative," one that roots the tragedy in a society that inhibits autonomy for women rather than on the "patriarchal myth of the *femme fatale*" (137). Treadwell's plays consistently place women in the central, subject position of the plot, although these characters are not uniform in age, social class, occupation, or identity. She sympathetically depicts young working women, the iconoclastic "new woman" who rejects traditional Victorian mores, accomplished artists and aspiring actresses, physically impaired women, journalists, daughters of

DOI: 10.4324/9781003006923-34

the privileged and powerful, young women of mixed ethnicities, and prostitutes. Treadwell's plays interrogate the social constraints on women from all walks of life, especially regarding sexual freedoms, marriage and family, and work and career.

Treadwell left very few written statements about dramatic theory, but her unpublished lecture, "Writing a Play," stands as her most extensive statement about her playwriting process and the search for an effective authorial voice in the theatre. The lecture, one of three Treadwell offered to students of Richard Boleslavsky's American Laboratory Theatre in the spring of 1925, may be best understood within the context of theories of playwriting of the time, especially those of the late nineteenth-century European "well-made play" as espoused in the U.S. by renowned playwriting teacher George Pierce Baker. By the time of Treadwell's lecture, a number of Baker's former students had achieved notable success as Broadway playwrights, including Sidney Howard, Philip Barry, and Eugene O'Neill, among others. While Treadwell did not study under Baker, her lecture shares striking affinities with principles outlined in his seminal book, *Dramatic Technique* (1919).

Both works begin with central differences between fiction writing and playwriting, the latter including the elimination of all ideas, characters and situations that do not directly contribute to the development of a strong central action in order to capture and maintain audience attention. While both acknowledge that various sources of inspiration—a theme, social idea, character, or situation—may serve as springboards for plays, they stress the need for a detailed scenario before, as Treadwell states, "any word is written." Both emphasize the necessity of a causal progression of incidents, likening this scaffolding of action to an architectural plan of a "completed house" (Baker 462) or "edifice" (Treadwell). And in practice, both writers advocate the use of collaborative workshops where playwrights learn all aspects of play production—Baker with his famed 47 Workshop at Harvard designed to stage and critique plays-in-process, and Treadwell through her participation in a summer-long theatre collective led by Boleslavsky in Pleasantville, New York in 1923.

Despite these similarities, Treadwell's lecture suggests that she is not completely comfortable with the well-made play structure for her own writing, even though her first Broadway play, *Gringo* (1922), and soon-to-open second Broadway play, *O Nightingale* (1925), both follow this form. Adopting a self-effacing persona, Treadwell confides to the ALT students that she has written many unsuccessful plays because of her over-reliance on emotional inspiration during the writing process. After delineating various processes used by classical and contemporary peer playwrights, Treadwell articulates a proclivity for the "real playwright" to use one critical "situation"—as opposed to character or idea—as the starting point in writing a play. This "particularly thrilling or amusing moment" leads, in turn, "back or forward to other situations."

This compositional technique would prove especially significant regarding *Machinal*, a play uniquely constructed as a series of nine "situations," or what Treadwell identifies in the play's stage directions as "episodes." In this work, Treadwell deviates from the traditional "well-made play" structure by frequently omitting the transitional and climactic moments of these episodes, preferring instead to stimulate audience members to fill in for themselves the obvious omissions in the narrative (see Ozieblo and Dickey 150–152). In "Writing a Play," Treadwell demonstrates her familiarity with the most widely used dramatic composition techniques of her day and also provides tantalizing glimpses into the impulses and writing processes that would soon lead to her most stunning dramatic achievement, *Machinal*.

Sophie Treadwell

"Writing a Play" (1925)

Michael Arlen[1] says that it is very easy to write a play. I hope that my beginning by saying "Michael Arlen" will not delude anyone into the sudden pleased conviction that this so short talk is to be one of charm and possibly gracefully lurid excitements because it is not. My beginning this way, hiding behind Michael Arlen, is simply a confession at the start of my own lack of confidence in myself to really tell you anything about writing a play, or to interest you alone while not telling you. I know so little about writing a play. I suppose that is why it seems to me such a difficult craft and why I so passionately disagree with the judgment of this popular young man of the moment, this so successful young man of the moment, that to write a play is easy. He says it is so much easier to do than to write a novel. Naturally he would say this because story-writing is his real work and it is only natural to be a little jealous of it.

I haven't written novels—not anything that could be called such, but I suppose that I can say that I've worked in the novel form after my fashion. That is to say, I have written long, long stories for magazines and newspapers; stories that took months to run and just as long to write. Still I'd hesitate to call them novels unless we add the word "pot-boilers." However slight and inconsequential as all this is it does give me a little balance of comparison, weighing which I cheerfully give forth the dictum that it's easier to write a novel than a play. But then, of course writing plays—trying to write plays—is my craft and it's only human to be jealous.

I really believe it is easier to write a novel than a play because the task is a freer one, the mind is freer. You can begin with a general idea of where you want to go and you can work along these lines freely. In a play you must know exactly where you want to go and you must work along this line rigidly. I toss off the word "must" very glibly, but of course by that I mean simply that I think this is so. It is so for me. Quite sincerely to the best of my knowledge and experience, but it may not in the slightest degree be true.

In story-writing one word really leads to another; one idea to another; one situation to another. In a play it is almost the opposite. The situation, the idea, the word, if you please, is fixed first. Other words, other ideas, other situations are put in deliberately to reenforce [*sic*] this, to lead up to this.

In writing a play a thousand charming, interesting thoughts—charming and interesting, that is to say, to the mind of the writer, and perhaps I exaggerate—must be discarded, let go, even though they really directly illuminate the subject at hand because at the same time that they may illuminate they divert.

The playwright in his results is really engaged in an emotional battle with an audience, a battle to reach out, to get and to hold an interest. By this I mean a battle to weld the different thoughts and feelings of a scattered group of totally different human beings brought together casually and by at the beginning one common incentive, the desire to be amused—to weld these scattered thoughts and feelings into one concentrated thought and feeling. So that many ideas that come to the playwright as diverting and illuminating to his subject must be ruthlessly cast out for the danger they hold to him in this battle. Not so the novelist. His battle is fought with each one of these human beings alone, comfortably alone, relaxed, and it isn't a battle to be won or lost in one throw, as the poor playwright's is. It is put aside, renewed, taken up again, other moods, other days. That habit, that way of the writing mind by which one word leads to another, one thought leads to another, gives some curious sense of progression, of accomplishment, of relief, to the one exercising this. Add to this many times the delightful excitement of surprise, the coming upon something unexpected, something amazingly satisfying but unexpected, unsought, unhoped for—all this is for the writer of stories, but for the writer of plays, no. Nothing can be expected for him; for the audience, yes, but for him, no. Everything he writes is foreseen by him; sought for by him often, too often sought for and not completely found. Whether he has found it or not he doesn't know, he can't know until the battle is fought, the battle of play and audience.

A play must be completely constructed in the mind of the author before a word is written. I say "must." I explain again that I believe this is so. This creation of the entire edifice complete in the mind is not an easy task, it is not exactly a natural task, if I may put it that way, for the imagination. To believe this, I ask you to consider some story that you have read, a story that you have read is a definite accomplishment. It is there. Some one has worked it out for you completely. Now I ask you to try and reconstruct that story in your mind, that story that already has been done. You see how difficult, how impossible it is. Much of it escapes you. Much of it left you at the very moment you took it in. Only what is important or interesting to you stands out in your mind, and yet what you have forgotten, what you never even realized, never even saw when it was before you, is an important, an essential part of the whole creation. If you can't make this recreation out of materials and plans all of which have been given you, consider the difficulty of the playwright, who must make this creation out of materials and plans he must create as well, and make a creation that must stand up, a creation so beautifully and delicately balanced that almost to remove one brick, so to speak, is to put it all in jeopardy. I am talking, of course, about the well made play. Talking as a person who would like to be a good craftsman to people who are interested in craft, who are interested in the way of doing and not particularly in results that have succeeded.

How does the playwright achieve this complete edifice in his writing? Processes of the creative imagination have always been given somewhat the respect due a miracle, but I believe some of the steps at least in this process can be made very clear and very simple. Whether this imagination is rich and interesting, or meagre and common-place, I suppose the processes are the same, and being so, we can have no hesitancy in entering the sanctum and reporting something of what we experience there.

How does the playwright begin? What is the seed? What is the acorn from which the mighty oak is to spring? It may be an idea, a theme, an idea that illumines life, a social idea. Playwrights who must work from this acorn occur to all of us immediately: Shaw, Brieux;[2] or the acorn may be an idea for a character. This is usually true of the actor playwright: Molière, with "Tartuffe"; Shakespeare, with "Hamlet", and in our own day the play of "Lightnin'" by Frank Bacon;[3] or this play, "The Poor Nut," by Elliott Nugent.[4]

Or the playwright may think first of a background, a slice of life, as they say. This is very often true of the journalist type of mind—people who look about them and see life going on in little groups, in little units. "I will write a play about ladies of the evening," says Mr. Gropper.[5] Or I may say to myself, "I'll write a play about rum runners." But the real playwright—and by that I do not mean to say that these other sort of workers I have just spoken of are not real playwrights, according to their fashion. I mean to pick out merely the type of playwright that is more completely the playwright more than he is anything else. This type of artist begins inevitably, I think, from a situation. This is, I think, the real playwright, the man most deeply aware of his craft, most completely at home in the theatre. His mind fastens on one situation, one moment when opposed forces come together in a particularly thrilling or amusing moment, depending on whether his mood is drama or comedy. From this situation he works back and forward to other situations and having found these, he then—or rather in finding these—he works out his story and his characters. His process will thus be seen to be almost directly opposite to that of the man who starts with character first and from this character or for this character works out a story and then breaks the story up into its situations. These are, if not all, undoubtedly the most powerful starting points for playwrights for as long as we have any records of plays.

Now, how does he go on from there? How does he proceed to create the structure of a play? How, in other words, does he make a play? Make up a play? I don't know how better to say it than that he must feel and think at the same time, and this is really not so easy, because feeling and thinking engage different processes of the soul, processes that are very often opposed and that even on one of those rare and felicitous occasions when they are not opposed never, under any circumstances, have the same r[h]ythm. In other words, he must engage in his creation two forces that are more than likely inclined to destroy each other, and the more he knows about his job the more likely they are to destroy each other. In the beginning it is easier. One or the other of these forces is stronger in him and serges [*sic*] ahead unhampered. A young man wants to write a play, we say. He approaches his subject carefully in the best modern spirit. He reads books on plays. He reads books of plays. He knows how it is done and he knows a great deal about life, and he writes his play and it is a very bad play. A play without vitality, without interest, without excitement. Nothing has been stirred in him in the doing it except confidence as the easiness of his task becomes manifest to him and the perfection of his formulaes [*sic*]. And nothing is stirred in the audience—if such a play ever gets an audience.

The other young man, or young woman, serging [*sic*] with emotional unrest, while brushing one's hair in the morning or riding in the subway—one is suddenly and without warning the center, the thrilling scene. One decides to write a play. All the emotional intensity in the world may be concentrated into the writing of this first play, but curiously enough nothing whatever of this comes out of it. The result is either blaa or funny. Why doesn't the emotion come out as it went in, strong, intense, sincere? The answer is very simple. Because the writer doesn't know how to write a play. I speak here with great authority. I've written so many plays like this. Perhaps I shall write some more.

Let us turn to really successful playwrights and to those about us. Mr. Kelly, who wrote "The Show-off,"[6] is able to build up and hold together in his imagination a complete edifice of his play before he puts finger to typewriter. This imaginative play is a complete structure, not just the plot and the characters but the complete development of this plot and these characters into the play form, breaking up of the material into acts, breaking up of the act into its component scenes; how and why the characters come on and off. This difficult technical problem of entrances and exits. All is perfectly clear, perfectly and definitely settled in his mind before he begins to write one word of the dialogue.

Mr. Channing Pollock[7], on the other hand, tells me that he does not know his play as completely as this when he begins to write. He begins to write to help himself to know his play. His approach is more nearly the novelist's approach to his material, but do not make the mistake of thinking that beginning this way he finishes this way. He begins this way simply to help himself because he is prolific, because he has facility. It is easier for him to work in this way. He has his play generally in mind but not detailed in mind when he begins to write. He then writes because in the very act of writing he comes into the realm of the curious stimulus we have mentioned before, of one word leading to another, one idea to another. He writes his play at this stage to help himself to find it, but when he has found it in this way he writes it again, and in this second writing are engaged his real playwrighting forces.

Other methods fall between these, but whatever the way the playwright must find his play, know his play—must, in fact, write his play before he writes it.

Now, to write it. Some playwrights, many in fact, Benavente,[8] the great Spaniard, for example, are accustomed to begin with the scene that interests them most; the scene that has the most vigor and vitality in their imagination. This scene is more than likely the climax, the big situations.

In drama, I think it can be said, that the best scenes are those written at one sitting, so to speak. When the playwright is truly in the grip of his own creative emotion and has these forces gathered up in himself, to a real center, a real intensity, a scene written in this way has a singleness of mood and a drive that is very difficult to achieve. When this concentration on the part of the writer is broken down, lost, interrupted, it is better, I think to write a whole scene and if it is not good throw it away and write another, than to monkey around with it, potter with it. Then it becomes blurred, mussed. Its original intention gets confused, its vitality, its drive, evaporates.

Comedy, on the other hand, I think can better be done piecemeal, made up almost line by line, created at a much slower tempo. In fact, from such writers of comedy as I have known I would almost say that the r[h]ythm for writing comedy is a very slow one, slow to the point of being funereal.

These are just a few notes on the subject I was asked to talk about, "Writing a Play."

I have been interested, you see—and I suppose it is inevitable considering my job that this would be so—on the verb side of my subject, the action side, the writing, rather than the noun, the subject or rather the object, isn't it? I have been interested in the <u>how</u> of writing rather than the <u>what</u> of a play. If any of you thought to learn from me anything really about a play, what is a play, what makes a play and what doesn't, it is inevitable that you have been disappointed. You see I know quite less about that than I do about this.

Please see the Works Cited for further information on the sources used in this essay.

Notes

1 British author noted for stories depicting the disillusionment and manners of London's Mayfair district after World War I. His adaptation of his popular novel *The Green Hat* (1924) opened on Broadway a few months after Treadwell's lecture.

2 As with George Bernard Shaw, Brieux is cited by Treadwell as a noted author of plays designed to expose a specific social problem or injustice. Brieux's dramas formed a significant part of the repertory at the Théâtre Libre in Paris.

3 Treadwell cites Bacon, along with Molière, Shakespeare and Elliott Nugent, as an actor-playwright whose plays were based on a strong central character. With himself in the starring role, Bacon's 1918 play, *Lightnin'*, had a record-setting three-year run on Broadway, nearly twice as long as the previous record holder.
4 American actor, playwright and director best noted for light comedies. Nugent wrote and starred in the Broadway play, *The Poor Nut*, at the time of Treadwell's lecture.
5 Milton Herbert Gropper's melodrama *Ladies of the Evening*, directed by David Belasco, was nearing completion of its 159-performance run on Broadway at the time of Treadwell's lecture. The play was adapted to a 1930 film, *Ladies of Leisure*, directed by Frank Capra and starring Barbara Stanwyck.
6 George Kelly, an American playwright best known for satires of middle-class life. At the time of Treadwell's lecture, his popular play, *The Show-Off*, about a deceitful railroad clerk, was nearing the end of its year-and-a-half Broadway run. The play was nominated for a Pulitzer Prize and made into several film versions.
7 American playwright whose populist Broadway plays often aroused condemnation by critics as sophistry. In turn, Pollock derided leading New York critics for promoting false values of elitism and cynicism. His 1922 play, *The Fool*, attracted large audiences during its 272-performance run.
8 One of Spain's most prominent playwrights, Jacinto Benavente y Martínez was awarded the Nobel Prize for Literature in 1922. His play, *The Bonds of Interest*, was presented as the inaugural production by New York's Theatre Guild in 1919 as part of its mission to produce original non-commercial plays.

Suggestions for Further Reading

Dickey, Jerry. *Sophie Treadwell: A Research and Production Sourcebook*. Westport, CT: Greenwood Press, 1997.
———. "Sophie Treadwell's Summer with Boleslavsky and Lectures for the American Laboratory Theatre." *Experimenters, Rebels, and Disparate Voices: The Theatre of the 1920s Celebrates Diversity*. Eds. Arthur Gerwitz and James J. Kolb. Westport, CT: Praeger, 2003. 111–118.
Dickey, Jerry, and Miriam López-Rodríguez, eds. *Broadway's Bravest Woman: Selected Writings of Sophie Treadwell*. Carbondale: Southern Illinois UP, 2006.
Wynn, Nancy Edith. *Sophie Treadwell: the Career of a Twentieth-Century American Feminist Playwright*. 1982. City University of New York, PhD dissertation.

34 VIRGINIA WOOLF (1882–1941)

Shilo McGiff

Introduction

Adeline Virginia Woolf (née Stephen; 1882 –1941) is well known as an essayist, literary critic, and a pioneer of modernist narrative technique. Her novels, among them *Mrs. Dalloway* (1925), *To the Lighthouse* (1927), and *Orlando* (1928), are notable for their deeply allusive and aesthetically layered prose, stream of consciousness style, and preoccupation with subjectivity and the possibilities—and impossibilities—of its representation. Her widely-cited essay, *A Room of One's Own* (1929), stands as one of the founding, and most famous, documents in the practice of feminist literary criticism. Less known are Woolf's writings on theatre and performance.[1] Yet, she grew up and came of age in a late Victorian Britain, in which theatre was both fashionable and flourishing. Exerting a vital influence on social and cultural life, the theatre was as much a place to see as to be seen, and the spectacle of London's theatre-going crowds fed Woolf's keen wit and motivated her meditations on craft, as much as any performance she attended. Indeed, musings on spectacle and the theatricality of everyday life so thoroughly saturate Woolf's work that when Herbert Blau begins his book-length study, *The Audience* (1990), it is Virginia Woolf's thinking that he uses to frame it.

From her youth until her death at the age of fifty-nine, Virginia Woolf was both an avid theatre-goer and a voracious reader of plays. While penning only one fully-fledged play, the three-act satire and amateur theatrical *Freshwater* in 1935, her essays, diaries, and letters make reference to a full range of dramatic experience from her youthful translations of Greek and her reminiscences of The Royal Opera House at Covent Garden to Wagnerian opera, the plays of Ibsen, Shaw, and Chekhov, and modernist avant-garde theatricals hosted by varying members of the Bloomsbury group, of which she and her husband Leonard were an integral part. She deeply admired Shakespeare and considered his authorship to be both the apotheosis of literary practice and a symbol of the androgynous mind at work in the creative process. It is not surprising, then, that she consistently thought and rethought her practice as a prose writer in relation to plays and playwriting. Even when watching a staged performance, Woolf would often refer back to the event as if it were a dramatic text rather than a theatrical event, implying the primacy of her experience as a solitary reader of plays even in the midst of an audience. In her essay "Twelfth Night at the Old Vic" (1933), she divides Shakespeareans into three classes: "those who prefer to read Shakespeare in the book; those who prefer to see him acted on the stage; and those who run perpetually from book to stage gathering plunder" (45). It is almost

DOI: 10.4324/9781003006923-35

certain that Woolf saw herself as the last, but not the least, of these—recommending in the essay's closing lines a return to reading Shakespeare, a proposal meant to enrich her own novelistic practice.

While theatrical metaphors most obviously comprise the creation of her experimental work *The Waves* (1931), whose interwoven soliloquies she calls a "play-poem," (D3:129), and her final, posthumously published novel *Between The Acts* (1941), which tracks and reproduces the performance of a village pageant play in the country house locale of Pointz Hall over the course of a single afternoon, the effects of a trenchant theatricality can be found throughout her novels. Jane Marcus, for example, finds in Woolf's early exposure to Mozart's *Magic Flute* an important structuring influence for her 1919 novel *Night and Day* ("Enchanted"); likewise, a firm sense of dramatic irony governs the playful narratorial inflections of *Orlando*'s impersonal but cheeky biographer.

In the course of Woolf's lifetime, British drama would transition from the popular comic, music hall, and melodramatic forms common to the earlier 19th century into 20th century modernism's embrace of realism, naturalism, and alienation, largely influenced by continental playwrights. Woolf's writings on theatre chart a similar trajectory, with their initial concerns about aesthetics and craft giving way to increasingly complex socio-political formulations. Whether in her novels or in her other prose writings, Woolf's attentiveness to theatricality and dramatic form continually calls attention to and problematizes concepts of audience, reception, and spectatorship—an attentiveness she progressively turned towards feminist and pacifist ends. These attentions could often be strongly anti-theatrical. In her vehemently anti-war essay *Three Guineas* (1938), Woolf responds to the rise of fascism in Europe and the concomitant threat of the erosion of women's rights by expressing a deep suspicion of public pageantry associated with ceremonies of state and the "limelight which paralyzes the free action of the human faculties" (135). She will go on to compare public sentiment, expressed on the radio and daily press of the time, that women should abdicate the workforce in favor of men and return home to attend to their families to the "voice of Creon, the dictator" (167), and to warn against becoming "passive spectators doomed to unresisting obedience" (168).

At the time of her suicide in 1941, on the cusp of Britain's entry into World War II, Woolf was working on both *Between the Acts* and an essay tentatively titled "Notes for Reading at Random, or Turning the Page." Charting an inevitable process from the open-air theatricals of medieval and renaissance England toward a more modern "theatre of the brain" (Silver, "Anon" 398), Woolf's unfinished essay demonstrates an atavistic understanding of theatre in a primordial union between audience and playwright as it slowly morphs and reaches its telos in the advent of author and reader. Her last novel, however, in its very form, lingers with the tension between reading and performance, returning to the village pageant play in order to re-inscribe questions of individual agency and communal identity within that self-same theatre of the mind. Both novel and unfinished essay exhibit a brilliant writer with a mature understanding of theatre as an evolving form whose mimetic effects could be reflective and imitative, but also turned to perceptive and critical ends. Included here, her essay, "Notes on an Elizabethan Play" first published in the *Times Literary Supplement* in 1925 and later reproduced and published by the Hogarth Press in her first *The Common Reader,* brings many of these concerns together with a meditation on the emotional concentration, word-coining splendor, and sensual pageantry of Elizabethan drama.

Virginia Woolf

"Notes on an Elizabethan Play" (1925)

There are, it must be admitted, some highly formidable tracts in English literature, and chief among them that jungle, forest, and wilderness which is the Elizabethan drama. For many reasons, not here to be examined, Shakespeare stands out, Shakespeare who has had the light on him from his day to ours, Shakespeare who towers highest when looked at from the level of his own contemporaries. But the plays of the lesser Elizabethans—Greene, Dekker, Peele, Chapman, Beaumont and Fletcher,—to adventure into that wilderness is for the ordinary reader an ordeal, an upsetting experience which plys him with questions, harries him with doubts, alternately delights and vexes him with pleasures and pains. For we are apt to forget, reading, as we tend to do, only the masterpieces of a bygone age, how great a power the body of a literature possesses to impose itself: how it will not suffer itself to be read passively, but takes us and reads us; flouts our preconceptions; questions principles which we had got into the habit of taking for granted, and, in fact, splits us into two parts as we read, making us, even as we enjoy, yield our ground or stick to our guns.

At the outset in reading an Elizabethan play we are overcome by the extraordinary discrepancy between the Elizabethan view of reality and our own. The reality to which we have grown accustomed is, speaking roughly, based upon the life and death of some knight called Smith, who succeeded his father in the family business of pitwood importers, timber merchants and coal exporters, was well known in political, temperance, and church circles, did much for the poor of Liverpool, and died last Wednesday of pneumonia while on a visit to his son at Muswell Hill. That is the world we know. That is the reality which our poets and novelists have to expound and illuminate. Then we open the first Elizabethan play that comes to hand and read how

> I once did see
> In my young travels through Armenia
> An angry unicorn in his full career
> Charge with too swift a foot a jeweller
> That watch'd him for the treasure of his brow,
> And ere he could get shelter of a tree
> Nail him with his rich antlers to the earth.
> (George Chapman, *Bussy D'Ambois*, 2.1.)

Where is Smith, we ask, where is Liverpool? And the groves of Elizabethan drama echo "Where?" Exquisite is the delight, sublime the relief of being set free to wander in the land of the unicorn and the jeweller among dukes and grandees, Gonzaloes and Bellimperias, who spend their lives in murder and intrigue, dress up as men if they are women, as women if they are men, see ghosts, run mad, and die in the greatest profusion on the slightest provocation, uttering as they fall imprecations of superb vigour or elegies of the wildest despair. But soon the low, the relentless voice, which if we wish to identify it we must suppose typical of a reader fed on modern English literature, and French and Russian, asks why, then, with all this to stimulate and enchant, these old plays are for long stretches of time so intolerably dull? Is it not that literature, if it is to keep us on the alert through five acts or thirty-two chapters, must somehow be based on Smith, have one toe touching Liverpool, take off into whatever heights it pleases from reality? We are not so purblind as to suppose that a man because his name is Smith and he lives at Liverpool is therefore "real". We know indeed that this reality is a chameleon quality, the fantastic becoming as we grow used to it often the closest to the truth, the sober the furthest from it, and nothing proving a writer's greatness more than his capacity to consolidate his scene by the use of what, until he touched them, seemed wisps of cloud and threads of gossamer. Our contention merely is that there is a station, somewhere in mid-air, whence Smith and Liverpool can be seen to the best advantage; that the great artist is the man who knows where to place himself above the shifting scenery; that while he never loses sight of Liverpool he never sees it in the wrong perspective. The Elizabethans bore us, then, because their Smiths are all changed to dukes, their Liverpools to fabulous islands and palaces in Genoa. Instead of keeping a proper poise above life they soar miles into the empyrean, where nothing is visible for long hours at a time but clouds at their revelry, and a cloud landscape is not ultimately satisfactory to human eyes. The Elizabethans bore us because they suffocate our imaginations rather than set them to work.

Still, though potent enough, the boredom of an Elizabethan play is of a different quality altogether from the boredom which a nineteenth-century play, a Tennyson or a Henry Taylor play, inflicts. The riot of images, the violent volubility of language, all that cloys and satiates in the Elizabethans yet appears to be drawn up with a roar as a feeble fire is sucked up by a newspaper. There is, even in the worst, an intermittent bawling vigour which gives us the sense in our quiet arm-chairs of ostlers and orange-girls catching up the lines, flinging them back, hissing or stamping applause. But the deliberate drama of the Victorian age is evidently written in a study. It has for audience ticking clocks and rows of classics bound in half morocco. There is no stamping, no applause. It does not, as, with all its faults, the Elizabethan audience did, leaven the mass with fire. Rhetorical and bombastic, the lines are flung and hurried into existence and reach the same impromptu felicities, have the same lip-moulded profusion and unexpectedness, which speech sometimes achieves, but seldom in our day the deliberate, solitary pen. Indeed, half the work of the dramatists, one feels, was done in the Elizabethan age by the public.

Against that, however, is to be set the fact that the influence of the public was in many respects detestable. To its door we must lay the greatest infliction that Elizabethan drama puts upon us–the plot; the incessant, improbable, almost unintelligible convolutions which presumably gratified the spirit of an excitable and unlettered public actually in the playhouse, but only confuse and fatigue a reader with the book before him. Undoubtedly something must happen; undoubtedly a play where nothing happens is an impossibility. But we have a right to demand (since the Greeks have proved that it is perfectly possible) that what happens shall have an end in view. It shall agitate great emotions; bring into existence memorable scenes; stir the actors to say what could not be said without this stimulus. Nobody can fail to remember the plot of the *Antigone*, because what happens is so closely bound up with the emotions of the actors that we remember the people and the plot at one and the same time. But who can tell us what happens in the *White Devil*, or the *Maid's Tragedy*,[2] except by remembering the story apart from the emotions which it has aroused? As for the lesser Elizabethans, like Greene and Kyd, the complexities of their plots are so great, and the violence which those plots demand so terrific, that the actors themselves are obliterated and emotions which, according to our convention at least, deserve the most careful investigation, the most delicate analysis, are clean sponged off the slate. And the result is inevitable. Outside Shakespeare and perhaps Ben Jonson, there are no characters in Elizabethan drama, only violences whom we know so little that we can scarcely care what becomes of them. Take any hero or heroine in those early plays—Bellimperia in the *Spanish Tragedy*[3] will serve as well as another—and can we honestly say that we care a jot for the unfortunate lady who runs the whole gamut of human misery to kill herself in the end? No more than for an animated broomstick, we must reply, and in a work dealing with men and women the prevalence of broomsticks is a drawback. But the *Spanish Tragedy* is admittedly a crude forerunner, chiefly valuable because such primitive efforts lay bare the formidable framework which greater dramatists could modify, but had to use. Ford, it is claimed, is of the school of Stendhal and of Flaubert; Ford is a psychologist. Ford is an analyst. "This man", says Mr. Havelock Ellis,[4] "writes of women not as a dramatist nor as a lover, but as one who has searched intimately and felt with instinctive sympathy the fibres of their hearts."

The play—*'Tis pity she's a Whore*[5]—upon which this judgement is chiefly based shows us the whole nature of Annabella spun from pole to pole in a series of tremendous vicissitudes. First, her brother tells her that he loves her; next she confesses her love for him; next finds herself with child by him; next forces herself to marry Soranzo; next is discovered; next repents; finally is killed, and it is her lover and brother who kills her. To trace the trail of feelings which such crises and calamities might be expected to breed in a woman of ordinary sensibility might have filled volumes. A dramatist, of course, has no volumes to fill. He is forced to contract. Even so, he can illumine; he can reveal enough for us to guess the rest. But what is it that we know without using microscopes and splitting hairs about the character of Annabella? Gropingly we make out that she is a spirited girl, with her defiance of her husband when he abuses her, her snatches of Italian song, her ready wit, her simple glad love-making. But of character as we understand the word there is no trace. We do not know how she reaches her conclusions, only that she has reached them. Nobody describes her. She is always at the height of her passion, never at its approach. Compare her with Anna Karenina.[6] The Russian woman is flesh and blood, nerves and temperament, has heart, brain, body and mind where the English girl is flat and crude as a face painted on a playing card; she is without depth, without range, without intricacy. But as we say this we know that we have missed something. We have let the meaning of the play slip through our hands. We have ignored the emotion which has been accumulating because it has accumulated in places where we have not expected to find it. We have been comparing the play with prose, and the play, after all, is poetry.

The play is poetry, we say, and the novel prose. Let us attempt to obliterate detail, and place the two before us side by side, feeling, so far as we can, the angles and edges of each, recalling each, so far as we are able, as a whole. Then, at once, the prime differences emerge; the long leisurely accumulated novel; the little contracted play; the emotion all split up, dissipated and then woven together, slowly and gradually massed into a whole, in the novel; the emotion concentrated, generalised, heightened in the play. What moments of intensity, what phrases of astonishing beauty the play shot at us!

> O, my lords,
> I but deceived your eyes with antic gesture,
> When one news straight came huddling on another
> Of death! and death! and death! still I danced forward.
> (John Ford, The Broken Heart, 5.3)

or

> You have oft for these two lips
> Neglected cassia or the natural sweets
> Of the spring-violet: they are not yet much wither'd.
> (John Webster, The White Devil, 2.1)

With all her reality, Anna Karenina could never say

> "You have oft for these two lips
> Neglected cassia".
> (ibid)

Some of the most profound of human emotions are therefore beyond her reach. The extremes of passion are not for the novelist; the perfect marriages of sense and sound are not for him; he must tame his swiftness to sluggardry; keep his eyes on the ground, not on the sky: suggest by description, not reveal by illumination. Instead of singing

> Lay a garland on my hearse
> Of the dismal yew;
> Maidens, willow branches bear;
> Say I died true,
> (Beaumont & Fletcher, The Maid's Tragedy, 2.1)

he must enumerate the chrysanthemums fading on the grave and the undertakers' men snuffling past in their four-wheelers. How then can we compare this lumbering and lagging art with poetry? Granted all the little dexterities by which the novelist makes us know the individual and recognise the real, the dramatist goes beyond the single and the separate, shows us not Annabella in love, but love itself; not Anna Karenina throwing herself under the train, but ruin and death and the

> ... soul, like a ship in a black storm,
> ... driven, I know not whither.
> (John Webster, The White Devil, 5.6)

So with pardonable impatience we might exclaim as we shut our Elizabethan play. But what then is the exclamation with which we close *War and Peace*? Not one of disappointment; we are not left lamenting the superficiality, upbraiding the triviality of the novelist's art. Rather we are made more than ever aware of the inexhaustible richness of human sensibility. Here, in the play, we recognise the general; here, in the novel, the particular. Here we gather all our energies into a bunch and spring. Here we extend and expand and let come slowly in from all quarters deliberate impressions, accumulated messages. The mind is so saturated with sensibility, language so inadequate to its experience, that, far from ruling off one form of literature or decreeing its inferiority to others, we complain that they are still unable to keep pace with the wealth of material, and wait impatiently the creation of what may yet be devised to liberate us of the enormous burden of the unexpressed.

Thus, in spite of dullness, bombast, rhetoric, and confusion, we still read the lesser Elizabethans, still find ourselves adventuring in the land of the jeweller and the unicorn. The familiar factories of Liverpool fade into thin air and we scarcely recognise any likeness between the knight who imported timber and died of pneumonia at Muswell Hill and the Armenian Duke who fell like a Roman on his sword while the owl shrieked in the ivy and the Duchess gave birth to a still-born babe 'mongst women howling. To join those territories and recognise the same man in different disguises we have to adjust and revise. But make the necessary alterations in perspective, draw in those filaments of sensibility which the moderns have so marvellously developed, use instead the ear and the eye which the moderns have so basely starved, hear words as they are laughed and shouted, not as they are printed in black letters on the page, see before your eyes the changing faces and living bodies of men and women—put yourself, in short, into a different but not more elementary stage of your reading development and then the true merits of Elizabethan drama will assert themselves. The power of the whole is undeniable. Theirs, too, is the word-coining genius, as if thought plunged into a sea of words and came up dripping. Theirs is that broad humour based upon the nakedness of the body, which, however arduously the public-spirited may try, is impossible since the body is draped. Then at the back of this, imposing not unity but some sort of stability, is what we may briefly call a sense of the presence of the Gods. He would be a bold critic who should attempt to impose any creed upon the swarm and variety of the Elizabethan dramatists, and yet it implies some timidity if we take it for granted that a whole literature with common characteristics is a mere evaporation of high spirits, a money-making enterprise, a fluke of the mind which, owing to favourable circumstances, came off successfully. Even in the jungle and the wilderness the compass still points.

> "Lord, Lord, that I were dead!"
> (John Webster, *The White Devil*, 3.2)

they are for ever crying.

> O thou soft natural death that art joint-twin
> To sweetest slumber—
> (John Webster, *The White Devil*, 5.3)

The pageant of the world is marvellous, but the pageant of the world is vanity.

>   glories
> Of human greatness are but pleasing dreams
> And shadows soon decaying: on the stage

Of my mortality my youth hath acted
Some scenes of vanity—
        (John Ford, *The Broken Heart*, 3.5)

To die and be quit of it all is their desire; the bell that tolls throughout the drama is death and disenchantment.

All life is but a wandering to find home,
When we're gone, we're there.
        (Thomas Dekker, John Ford & Willam Rowley, *The Witch of Edmonton*, 4.2)

Ruin, weariness, death, perpetually death, stand grimly to confront the other presence of Elizabethan drama which is life: life compact of frigates, fir trees and ivory, of dolphins and the juice of July flowers, of the milk of unicorns and panthers' breath, of ropes of pearl, brains of peacocks and Cretan wine. To this, life at its most reckless and abundant, they reply

Man is a tree that hath no top in cares,
No root in comforts; all his power to live
Is given to no end but t' have power to grieve.
        (George Chapman, *Bussy D'Ambois*, 5.3)

It is this echo flung back and back from the other side of the play which, if it has not the name, still has the effect of the presence of the Gods. So we ramble through the jungle, forest, and wilderness of Elizabethan drama. So we consort with Emperors and clowns, jewellers and unicorns, and laugh and exult and marvel at the splendour and humour and fantasy of it all. A noble rage consumes us when the curtain falls; we are bored too, and nauseated by the wearisome old tricks and florid bombast. A dozen deaths of full-grown men and women move us less than the suffering of one of Tolstoi's flies. Wandering in the maze of the impossible and tedious story suddenly some passionate intensity seizes us; some sublimity exalts, or some melodious snatch of song enchants. It is a world full of tedium and delight, pleasure and curiosity, of extravagant laughter, poetry, and splendour. But gradually it comes over us, what then are we being denied? What is it that we are coming to want so persistently, that unless we get it instantly we must seek elsewhere? It is solitude. There is no privacy here. Always the door opens and some one comes in. All is shared, made visible, audible, dramatic. Meanwhile, as if tired with company, the mind steals off to muse in solitude; to think, not to act; to comment, not to share; to explore its own darkness, not the bright-lit-up surfaces of others. It turns to Donne, to Montaigne, to Sir Thomas Browne, to the keepers of the keys of solitude.

Please see the Works Cited for further information on the sources used in this essay.

Note

1 See, also, the Introduction to this volume for a further example of Woolf's writing on theatre.
2. John Webster, *The White Devil* (c. 1610–1612); Francis Beaumont and John Fletcher, *The Maid's Tragedy* (c. 1610–1611).

3. Thomas Kyd, *The Spanish Tragedy* (c. 1582–1592).
4 Havelock Ellis (1859–1939) was a British physician, social reformer, and cultural critic best known for his *Studies in the Psychology of Sex* (1897).
5. John Ford, *'Tis Pity She's a Whore* (pub. 1633).
6. Title character in 1878 novel by Leo Tolstoy.

Suggestions for Further Reading

Farfan, Penny. *Women, Modernism, and Performance.* Cambridge: Cambridge University Press, 2004.

Putzel, Steven. *Virginia Woolf and the Theater.* Madison, NJ and Vancouver: Fairleigh Dickinson University Press, 2012.

Silver, Brenda, "Virginia Woolf and the Concept of Community: The Elizabethan Playhouse." *Women's Studies,* 4:2–3 (1977): 291–298.

Wright, Elizabeth. "Bloomsbury at Play." *Woolf Studies Annual.* 17 (2011): 77–107.

35 ELIZABETH ROBINS (1862–1952)

Joanne E. Gates

Introduction

American actress, writer, and activist Elizabeth Robins (1862–1952) remains legendary for her performances in Henrik Ibsen's plays in England in the 1890s.[1] Frustrated by the paucity of other challenging roles for actresses and the formulaic images of women in many plays of the time, Robins also wrote for the stage, crafting such important dramas as *Votes for Women!* (1907). As this title suggests, she became very involved with the campaign for Women's Suffrage in the early twentieth century. Later in her career, she was the sole woman to commemorate the centennial of Henrik Ibsen's birth at the British Drama League's events in 1928; her activist reputation and her continued stream of successful novels through two full decades after she retired from the stage lent a feminist stature to all her engagements.

This centennial event featured other speakers central to Ibsen's legacy in the British theatre: Edmund Gosse, Desmond McCarthy, J.G. Robertson, and Bernard Shaw.[2] But only Robins' speech survives in printed form, released within the year by Hogarth Press as *Ibsen and the Actress*, excerpted here.[3] Just after her lecture, the London *Times* published her related article, "Henrik Ibsen, The Drama of Ideas." In that biographical piece, she stresses that Ibsen's opportunity to work for a precursor of a national theatre in Norway gave him his real start as a playwright. (Robins herself had numerous times promoted the idea of a British National Theatre.) Also in 1928, the women's periodical which she helped launch, *Time and Tide*, published her piece "Henrik Ibsen," in which she offered a more feminist slant on Ibsen as the originator of the tragic female character whose depiction retained a classic poetic heightening, but also spoke to the real conditions of real women. Perhaps more pointedly for that largely female readership, she acknowledged that "practically all of Ibsen's women […] got at life though men," but that his and his characters' realization of this as tragic foretold the need for society to change. Capturing the essence of Hilda Wangel in *The Master Builder*, she asserted: "Ibsen came to realise that women must not only build their own towers. They must learn the joy of climbing, and the peril that awaits them in High Places" ("Henrik Ibsen" 242).

Yet it was the Hogarth Press essay that has had a remarkable afterlife: it continues to be cited in contemporary research on Ibsen and in Robins scholarship. Dissertations and articles, some turned into book-length studies, include Penny Farfan's "From *Hedda Gabler* to *Votes for Women*: Elizabeth Robins's Early Feminist Critique of Ibsen" and Gay Gibson Cima's "Ibsen and the Critical Actor," among others. The feminist critic of Ibsen, Joan Templeton, in *Shaw's Ibsen: A Re-Appraisal*,

DOI: 10.4324/9781003006923-36

highlights important principles that derive from Robins' essay, that women working together—owning the production elements of a new Ibsen play and exploring
interpretive possibilities in rigorous rehearsals—made a difference in the reception
of Ibsen in the 1890s. Moreover, *Ibsen and the Actress* has inspired creative artists of
the theatre. Contemporary playwright María Irene Fornés (1930–2018) turned her
fascination for the nugget of story in the essay—the account of Marion Lea[4] and
Robins acquiring stage rights to *Hedda Gabler*—into a centerpiece of her dramatic
treatment, *The Summer in Gossensass* (1998).

Most importantly, the attention to Ibsen in 1928 reinvigorated Robins; now retired
from acting, she maneuvered a shift into writing that was primarily autobiographical.
Upon her friend Lady Florence Bell's death in 1930, her voluminous correspondence
to Bell was returned to her. This and her rich diary and scrapbook record resulted
in *Theatre and Friendship* (1932). More than a decade later, encouraged by Bernard
Shaw, she released the first volume of her stage memoirs, *Both Sides of the Curtain*.[5]

Not all of Robins' recollections should be taken as pure accolades for Ibsen, how-
ever. Penny Farfan studies how Robins' suffrage politics caused her to severely critique
Ibsen's inter-character dynamics as limiting and self-serving. With Nora Helmer in *A
Doll's House* the exception, Robins argued in a 1908 lecture, "Some Aspects of Henrik
Ibsen," that Ibsen had little interest in feminism; his prominent characters like
Dr. Stockmann (*An Enemy of the People*) or Brand (*Brand*) blindly pride themselves on
the cult of the individual as superior (Farfan, "From *Hedda Gabler*" 70–72).

But in her *Time and Tide* article she proclaimed a wider purpose for the tragic
blindness of both Hedda Gabler and Hilda Wangel, beginning and ending with
more pointed feminism than in any remarks she addressed to the Drama League:
"Ibsen not only transformed dramatic art, he was an instrument used by the *Zeitgeist*
to enfranchise the spirit of women," she asserts. Then she concludes: "Men have disputed and philosophized about Ibsen. Women have turned him into the stuff of life"
("Henrik Ibsen" 242).

The impact of Ibsen-style dramaturgy upon the urgency of the campaign for wom-
en's suffrage proves that Ibsen's influence upon Robins was pervasive. Robins' analysis of Ibsen's plays and characters, as well as their cultural and theatrical impact,
informed not only this series of lectures and essays, but also her own playwriting.
Thus, Robins' dramas, examined in the context of modernist dramaturgy, exemplify
the meticulous, detailed production practices, *mise-en-scènes*, and socio-political convictions that are hallmarks of this pivotal era in theatre history.

Elizabeth Robins

Excerpt from Ibsen and the Actress *(1928)*

[…] In dealing with Ibsen's significance to the acting profession, I naturally think of
one actress in particular whose view would have been immensely interesting. I mean,
of course, the woman to whom belongs the lasting honour of being the first person
to play a great Ibsen part in England—Janet Achurch. […] I do not know whether I
had ever heard Ibsen's name till the afternoon when I went with my friend Marion
Lea to see her friend act *A Doll's House*.

I cannot think such an experience was ever ushered in with so little warning. There
was not a hint in the pokey, dingy theatre, in the sparse, rather dingy audience, that

we were on the threshold of an event that was to change lives and literature. The Nora of that day must have been one of the earliest exceptions—she was the first I ever saw—to the rule that an actress invariably comes on in new clothes, unless she is playing a beggar. This Nora, with her home-made fur cap on her fair hair, wore the clothes of Ibsen's Nora, almost shabby, with a touch of prettiness.

[...] [T]he famous lines: "Millions of women have done so" and [...] "it burst upon me that I had been living here these eight years with a strange man, and had borne him three children"–for all time they should be said just as they were first said, and by just that person. [...]

To go to that play once was to be compelled to go again. The second time I was able to follow the sheer acting more—shall I say professionally. I am afraid I felt I knew about acting. [...] In an old-fashioned stock company on the other side of the Atlantic, [...] I had played, during two years (by dint sometimes of doubling and even trebling), nearly three hundred parts. I had afterwards gone touring in romantic melodrama with the father of Eugene O'Neill; after that, in Shakespeare with Edwin Booth. Yes, I thought I knew. [...]

I do not remember much about the Mrs Linden of that occasion except that, looking on from the front, she seemed just right. It fell to me, a little while after the Charrington season, to play Mrs Linden with a wholly different caste. Coming close to her, as acting a part brings close, was another matter, and in that quite common fact there is significance for people who care to understand the function of the actor. In mere length Mrs Linden is a small part, but it was for me a great experience. I despair of giving an idea of what that little part meant, not only of vivid pleasure in working at and playing, but of—what I cannot find any other word for than—self-respect.

[...] It was Marion Lea who first saw the opportunity in *Hedda Gabler* and invented our going to see Mr Heinemann, the publisher, to get the acting rights. That settled (provisionally to our finding a producer), we undertook to see the managers; but they were more difficult to access, so we wrote to them. We saw them ultimately and tried to persuade that their indifference and their loathing were equally mistaken. We failed.

[...] Then Marion Lea, again the initiator, urged me to join her in producing *Hedda* ourselves. This was courageous of her. It was no secret that we had, neither of us, any money; but Marion had a jewelled bracelet and I had a small treasure that I could throw in the pot. With these "securities" we borrowed from an amiable friend £300, and set to work.

[...] I have somewhere several sets of page proofs of *Hedda Gabler* as they left the hands of the translators; one set scored over in Marion Lea's handwriting, one with mine, and our final agreed recommendations. These Mr Archer fully criticised, sometimes denounced and utterly declined; but the final result was, I think, a very speakable, very playable version, no less faithful—I have always held more faithful— to Ibsen. Anyway, it was immense fun. [...]

I had the best of reasons for not trying to mitigate Hedda's corrosive qualities. It was precisely the corrosive action of those qualities on a woman in Hedda's circumstances that made her the great acting opportunity she was—in her revolt against those commonplace surroundings that the bookworm she had married thought so "elegant"; her unashamed selfishness; her scorn of so-called womanly qualities; above all, her strong need to put some meaning into her life, even at the cost of borrowing it, or stealing the meaning out of someone else's.

[...] Hedda speculates, like many another woman, on the opportunity politics would give to her husband, and, through him, give to her; but she is too intelligent to have much hope of Tesman in that direction. She is no sooner home from her boring honeymoon than she finds that a girl she had looked down on and terrorised at school—shrinking, gentle Mrs Elvsted—has reclaimed the dissipated Lövborg. More than that, largely by her faith in him, she has helped him to write what they are calling a work of genius. The timid Thea Elvsted has actually left her husband and her home to watch over Lövborg, so that he may not fall into evil courses again. How on earth had it all come about? Hedda, by turns, worms and coerces the facts out of Thea: "He gave up his old habits not because I *asked* him to, for I never dared do that; but he saw how repulsive they were to me—so he dropped them."

As simple as that! None of those shady stories told to Thea—but the pretty little fool has his dreams in her keeping; she has helped to turn them into reality. And Hedda has lost him. For Hedda there would be "others." The insinuating Judge Brack, with his aristocratic profile and his eyeglass, is already at the door—but never the man whose faith in his own genius, faith in life, had given Hedda the one respite she had known from mean standards, mean fears.

Those had been times for Lövborg, too, of respite from his meaner self. Hedda's passion for external material beauty was not the only kind of beauty that swayed her. Lövborg in his moods of poetic exaltation had given her, too, a glorious sense of freedom, of daring. [...] Now she has lost all that—unless—unless she can break the hold of this irritating little goose. Thea had said she'd been so frightened of Hedda at school. Well, she should be frightened again!

It is a commentary on actress psychology that though in those days I accepted, and even myself used, the description of Hedda as a "bloodless egoist," I was under no temptation to play her like that. Here I was in debt to Ibsen's supreme faculty for giving his actors the clue—the master-key—if they are not too lofty or too helplessly sophisticated to take it. Ibsen's unwritten clue brought me close enough to the "cold-blooded egoist" to feel her warm to my touch; to see Hedda Gabler as pitiable in her hungry loneliness—to see her as tragic. [...] She knew, she did not deny, her prime weakness. Lövborg in the second act says of Thea in Hedda's presence:

"And then she is so brave!"
"Good heavens," Thea exclaims, "I brave!"
"Very courageous," he rubs it in, "where your comrade's interests are concerned."
"Ah, yes," says Hedda, "Courage. If only one had that."
"What then?" Lövborg insists.
"Then life would perhaps be livable after all."

She knew there was no deadlier enemy than Fear; but her circumstances [...] made Fear the master of the show. To the timid, trembling Thea, who yet could brave public opinion—having less to lose—Hedda had found herself crying out:

"Oh, if you could understand how poor I am! And fate has made you so rich!" [...]

Long before she met the man she married, Hedda had looked on General Gabler's pistols as possible allies. They had early prevented Lövborg from adding Hedda

Gabler to the list of his Mademoiselle Dianas and other light o' loves. At the last, Hedda was to give Lövborg a pistol that he might do with what she had long meant to do, if life should fail her utterly. It will be remembered there were two pistols. She still had one for her own need. [...]

You may be able to imagine the excitement of coming across anything so *alive* as Hedda. What you won't be able to imagine (unless you are an actress in your twenties) is the joy of having in our hands—free hands—such glorious actable stuff. If we had been thinking politically, concerning ourselves about the emancipation of women, we would not have given the Ibsen plays the particular kind of whole-hearted, enchanted devotion we did give. We were actresses—actresses who wouldn't for a kingdom be anything else. We got over that; but I am talking about '89–'91. How were we to find fault with a state of society that had given us Nora and Hedda and Thea? [...]

Ibsen had taught us something we were never to unlearn. The lesson had nothing to do with the New Woman; it had everything to do with our particular business—with the art of acting. Events, after Hedda, emphasised for us the kind of life that stretched in front of the women condemned to the "hack-work" of the stage. That was what we called playing even the best parts in plays selected by the actor-manager. The important managers were actors then. [...]

But Ibsen's fame in England had now reached a point where there was competition—among actresses—as to who should have the next play: "*If it's actable,*" said the cautious. "How can we know?"

[...] By the time the first sheets of *The Master Builder* reached England it was not necessary for me to wait yet longer while the translators turned it into English, or I think I should have died of impatience. I had the experience "frightfully thrilling" ([...] as Hilda Wangel would say) of being able by then to read Ibsen in the original. That promised a collaboration closer still. [...]

I naturally took the play first to the theatres where I had already played, or to those which had offered engagements. I was told *The Master Builder* was simply unintelligible. Oh, it was wild! It was irritatingly obscure. It was dull, it was mad, it would lose money.

I had one special friend among English managers. [...]

Beerbohm Tree turned out to be the one manager in London who could see anything in the play. To my delight, what he could see was himself. Yes, he would produce it—on condition. The condition was that we should lift the play out of its sordid provincialism. We would do this by dint of making the people English; more particularly by making the Master Builder a sculptor. Many people in those days would have backed that view.

Fortunately, Mr Herbert Waring was ready to join me in the responsibility of producing *The Master Builder* as Ibsen had written it. Herbert Waring it was who found a man ready to put down a small sum that would give the play a hearing. For me there had been just one haunting doubt about the enterprise: Was I *quite* young enough to stand for the Younger Generation knocking at the door? Among the reassurances on this score I have always cherished the one Sir Edmund Gosse set down in his preface to the play.

[...] Ibsen, more than any author I have known, comes to the rescue of the actor in this misery. He never deserts you, if you trust him. Practically he "does it" for you. [...]

This is one of the plays—the other is *Rosmersholm*—that I won't pretend to speak dispassionately about [...] No other (and I played in seven of Ibsen's)–no other ever seemed so mine as *The Master Builder.* No other ever brought such a sense of [...]

release, such conviction of having the audience with me, and at the same time such freedom from the yoke of the audience. It was as if one played not only, as the good old advice directed, "to the last row in the gallery," but farther still—to an audience invisible. And this feeling was not disturbed by the sounds from the actual audience. They took the "points" I thought obvious, and they took the points I least counted on anybody's noticing—*my* points, those that Ibsen had left me not merely to make, but to find. And, in addition to these, there was in the air (any actor will understand) that unmistakable response—and I do not mean applause—a response no less to the "little devil" in Hilda than to her thrilling sense of the adventure of living; a response to that queer mixture of wildness and tenderness; that determination to have her own imperious way, crossed by the necessity to feel what other people were feeling. [...]

Ibsen's relation to the player is either singularly close, or, in effect, complete detachment. More than anybody who ever wrote for the stage, Ibsen could, and usually did, collaborate with his actors. I do not mean that he ever consulted one of them; the collaboration was a subtler thing than that. Ibsen was by training so intensely *un homme du théâtre* that, to an extent I know in no other dramatist, he saw where he could leave some of his greatest effects to be made by the actor, and so left them. It was as if he knew that only so could he get his effects—that is, by standing aside and watching his spell work not only through the actor, but *by* the actor as fellow-creator. [...]

Ibsen's deep knowledge of human nature, coupled with this sixth sense of his—the sense of the theatre—was less clouded than in most writers by a desire to dramatise himself; [...]

[...] [M]y own position is, that no dramatist has ever meant so much to the women of the stage as Henrik Ibsen. This is no less true although many admirable artists have never played him. They do not know, perhaps, that the parts they have made successes in would not have been written but for Ibsen. [...] [P]eople who have been a good while on the stage are less likely to show Ibsen at something like his full value than people whose talent is still mobile and comparatively modest, receptive. Make no mistake, you must let Ibsen play you rather than insist on your playing Ibsen.

"Collaboration." Maeterlinck has said: *"Il y a une plus haute collaboration que celle de la plume—celle de la pensee et du sentiment."* [There is a higher collaboration than that of the pen—that of thought and feeling.] One of the highest of all is, surely, this collaboration between playwright and player.

To those of us who were given a share in shaping for the stage some of Ibsen's characters it is an unfading glory of memory that there was a moment when, led by him, we "mounted right to the top"—and heard harps in the air.

Please see the Works Cited for further information on the sources used in this essay.

Notes

1 Norwegian playwright and director Henrik Ibsen (1828–1906) was a pioneering figure of the modernist theatre.
2 Edmund Gosse (1849–1928) was an early English translator of Ibsen. Desmond McCarthy (1877–1952) was a prominent English critic and champion of Ibsen; John George Robertson (1867–1933) was professor of German language and literature at University of London, assuming in 1924 the Directorship of the Department of Scandinavian Studies; Bernard Shaw (1856–1950) was England's leading dramatist and author of *The Quintessence of Ibsenism* (1891).

3 The excerpted text highlights Robins' recollection of *A Doll's House* (1889) and her own productions of *Hedda Gabler* (1891) and *The Master Builder* (1893). Miriam A. Franc details each of the first British productions of Ibsen, including eight Ibsen women performed by Robins, along with others that Robins credits for their influence.

4 American actress Marion Lea (1861–1944) partnered with Robins to form their own company and produce Ibsen in London.

5 Robins' detailed recollections of her early involvement in Ibsen productions of the 1890s were deferred to a subsequent volume that remains unpublished and resides in her full archive at New York University. The collection at the Fales also contains the handful of her unpublished plays and memoirs.

Suggestions for Further Reading

The Elizabeth Robins Web. Project Director Joanne E. Gates. https://www.jsu.edu/robinsweb/.

Guide to the Elizabeth Robins Papers. Fales Library Special Collections. New York University Libraries. http://dlib.nyu.edu/findingaids/html/fales/robins/.

Thomas, Sue. *Elizabeth Robins (1862–1952): A Bibliography*. Victorian Fiction Research Guide. Queensland: University of Australia, 1994. https://victorianfictionresearchguides.org/elizabeth-robins/.

36 LENA ASHWELL (1872–1957)

Maggie B. Gale

Introduction

Dame Lena Ashwell (née Pocock, 1872–1957) was a British actress, theatre manager, producer, director and theorist. Having trained originally as a musician, she moved into theatre work with her first professional role in 1891. Her role as Mrs Dane in Charles Wyndham's production of Henry Arthur Jones's *Mrs Dane's Defence* (1900) confirmed her position as one of the leading actresses of the era. Known as an intelligent performer of great emotional capacity, Ashwell chose challenging roles considered rather "modern" for her time, which demanded both force and sincerity. Like a number of actresses of the era, such as Adeline Bourne (1873–1965) and Gertrude Kingston (1862–1937), Ashwell went into management and production, refurbishing and reopening the theatre in Great Queen Street as the Kingsway, London, in 1907. She was a founding member of the Actresses' Franchise League in 1908 and a pioneering advocate for the professional welfare of actresses in particular. In 1911, Ashwell co-founded the Three Arts Club in London, where affordable accommodation was provided for women working in the arts. Her dedication to suffrage politics coincided with her years of actor management: the Kingsway launched the lucrative production of Cicely Hamilton's feminist play *Diana of Dobson's* (1908) with Ashwell in the lead. Here, she produced both classics and plays by new writers, many of which challenged contemporary social prejudices. Her role as producer/director continued in her management of the Century Theatre, London, in the 1920s.

The chapter "Beauty in Strange Places," excerpted here, is from her later book *The Stage* (1929), for a series in which "leading men and women" wrote for the general public about professional practice. A prolific activist and writer, Ashwell ran her own touring theatre company during World War I and through the 1920s; she brought theatre to venues and town halls outside London's mainstream cultural centre, serving audiences for whom access to the West End was limited. While her other works focus on specifics – on "entertainments for the troops" or on Shakespeare – *The Stage* is more a reflection on the art and technique of theatre from a number of different perspectives: as actor, producer, manager and thinker. Written after a prolific career of almost forty years, the chapter offers Ashwell's thoughts about the theatre in a state of both social and artistic transition from the late nineteenth century through to the early decades of the twentieth. She does this through her analysis of Ibsen and Shaw[1], and then of the "art" of the performer in bringing their work into performance and public consciousness.

DOI: 10.4324/9781003006923-37

The chapter is framed by what she terms her "search for beauty" in theatre, where she believes there to be a discernible level of "indifference to the Theatre" from other intellectual fields and arts institutions. For Ashwell, the emergent drama, as typified by Ibsen and Shaw, moved away from the residue practices of the nineteenth century that she saw as making few demands on audiences. The emergent drama created theatre that approached social class and social difference from an intellectually complex, as opposed to condemnatory, perspective. Audiences at the time were, she suggests, used less to the power of language and conversation and more familiar with the playing spaces created through spectacle and mannered writing. The actor needed to develop new techniques in order to convincingly deliver plays to audiences eager for the new kind of work typified by Ibsen and Shaw. In her analysis, she notes the emergence of theatre which embraced the "hidden swirl of emotions" produced by human interaction, and yet, in the case of Shaw, "startles" us from "comfortable security." For Ashwell, theatre is far more than "live" literature: it offers us an art whose whole is greater than the sum of its parts, and whose beauty lies ultimately in its elusive qualities.

While a number of fellow actresses and women playwrights of the era, such as Elizabeth Robins (1862–1952), Constance Collier (1878–1955) and Cicely Hamilton (1872–1952), also wrote about theatre[2], they often focussed on the expression and documentation of experience, rather than theories of the craft or technique of acting. In contrast, Ashwell wrote and theorised more about the practice of theatre: as an actress in a field of precarious labour, and as a manager and producer in a performance culture which, without state funding, emphasised commercial viability over art and experiment.

In the chapter excerpted here, she proposes that while it is the theorist whose view "usually carries the day," in fact the practitioner has much to offer by way of understanding and critique of the drama, from the perspective of the labourer whose job it is to make the play "work" in performance. As someone who, like many middle-class women of her era, only received a limited education, Ashwell's theories of drama come from her experience of working with it as a practitioner. Elsewhere, and unusually for a woman of her era, she theorises the craft and technique of theatre, both in live performance and in drawing up the essential different requirements of actors in a film. Here, however, she talks of Shaw's plays, for example, via detailed analyses of them as challenging blueprints for performance, as well as being sharp social critiques of the complacency of the British middle and upper classes.

Ashwell's career was unusual in the proportion of time she spent managing and campaigning. As well as her work with the Actresses' Franchise League, she campaigned for better working conditions for performers and for the embedding of drama in local communities in the promotion of well-being. Along with William Archer and Harley Granville Barker, she advocated for a national theatre, promoting the benefits of arts provision across the classes. She wrote many essays, speeches, and books from the perspective of the theatre artist. Through this body of work, Lena Ashwell provided an insight into the working practices of performers and theatre makers – and here, of the challenges and reception of new playwrights requiring new understandings and techniques of acting – from the late nineteenth century to the early twentieth.

Lena Ashwell

Excerpt from "Beauty in Strange Places" (1929)

[...] There is no other art which combines all forms of beauty – the beauty of form, colour, sound, emotion, thought, so far as mind can reach or heart can feel. The Theatre can give you almost all.

Do people realise, I wonder, how wild and elusive beauty is, how she appears in the strangest places, giving courage and hope to those who don't know that they need it? The experience of the Great War taught me that the dreamers, the music makers are necessary: a song, a poem, the magic of sound, the wonder of the mind – and courage is restored, fear forgotten, because beauty had passed by and quieted the troubled waters for the soul.

[...] I had to search for other paths to the fulfilment of my dream ambition. And I am quite sure that I had to play the parts of more criminals than any other actor. The public had just begun to take an interest in the unfortunates of social life, not as subjects for mere condemnation. They were shown as criminals in need of reformation, suffering from their wrong doings. Now, of course there are many plays wherein the heroine is only considered interesting if she has committed some sensational crime or is about to do so and "get away with it". She has to be successful and get away with it, and incidentally to make all the other characters who are not criminal, seem very anaemic people.

My search was still for beauty, but it became the quest for the indestructible inherent dignity of human life.

[...] It is impossible to describe the action of the mind, especially when it is at work creating; [...] In fact the great people of the Theatre have always been right when they insisted that no actor must really bring *himself* into the part. His business is to hold the mirror up to Nature not to himself. He must create an illusion which the audience will accept as a reality; and, though it is through himself that this person must be created – through his body as a medium, but not through his body only – through all that he has felt and observed – yet the obtrusion of his personal sorrow, ugliness, bitterness, contempt, entirely spoil the reflection which is shown to the audience. All the personal sufferings of an artist are merely the stored up material out of which the mirror can be constructed.

[...] Acting is concentrated imagination. A picture is created by the mind, through observation and sympathy, and gradually through the technique of the art, the actor becomes the picture. It is not only necessary to have created the picture but in all real acting the personality of the actor must disappear, till he actually becomes the character portrayed. Yet being, like all artists dual in consciousness, the actor as observer always stands aside from the mirror, directs, controls the picture but never allows himself to merge into it, or interfere with the living personality which is being presented, and which he embodies. There are authors who write of ugliness for enjoyment of ugliness, and find no beauty there because they are not looking for it.

[...] Providentially for my search after beauty, such great authors as Tolstoy and Maeterlinck had been writing books, showing that the outcast, the wronged and the betrayed, had a power within them which was indestructible, that however low a human being might sink, however low a woman's life might seem, the indestructible within, at the first touch of truth, bloomed into a beauty which might not have been possible without the bitter sorrow and disillusionment that sin had brought. These were protests against our civilisation because it permitted an unutterable selfishness of outlook, which made criminals of the weak and the helpless.

[...] Although undoubtedly the most successful authors of my time were Sir Arthur Pinero and Henry Arthur Jones, the two who most influenced the form of dramatic expression were Heinrich Ibsen and George Bernard Shaw. They both created new forms. Ibsen's plays produced with difficulty by private societies and courageous pioneers [...] made a very deep impression upon the people of the Theatre, causing a great change both in the method of writing and of acting plays. Ibsen was I believe the first author to cut out the soliloquy and asides. In all plays the soliloquy and the aside had been used to inform the audience as to the thoughts which were in the minds of the characters, thoughts which they were unable to utter one to another. For the sake of the drama and its unfolding, some of the characters were not to be informed as to what was going on. Also it was thought necessary sometimes to make quite sure that the audience was really taking in the secret motives which guided a character, and led to his actions. Very slight reliance was placed upon the intelligence of the audience which, treated as an unintelligent mass, had to have everything of importance repeated at least three times. The actor was expected to insist by some action, speech, or wink to the audience what he expected to be understood and followed.

The newer school founded by Ibsen, which spread very quickly, expected the actor to convey, without soliloquy, aside, or any particular movement, a whole stream of thought which was not represented in the dialogue. A higher mode of interaction between author, actor and audience was being established.

[...] Where before, as in Shakespeare's plays, there had been the rhythm of the spoken word to explain the motives and feelings, and to build up the power of the scene, the Transition Drama of the newer school had a hidden swirl of unspoken emotion, which had to be communicated to the audience by no other means than the actor's concentrated power of thought and feeling.

[...] Ibsen was studying human problems, and did not recognise the sympathetic co-operation of the audience. They were expected, without being referred to, to understand and appreciate.

Great actors have chosen the Ibsen plays for their repertory, notably Eleanora Duse, and Mrs. Patrick Campbell. There are depths of feeling, and most curious twists of emotion in his tortured characters, who feel that, beyond their small environment there is a life wider, cleaner, happier, more free. Every play deals with real suffering, but the people are growing somehow as they live through the action. The parts are all great vehicles of expression for the actor; and a deep impression is made upon the onlooker, although he sometimes feels that he should not be peeping through the keyhole [...] Ibsen is ruthless in stripping bare the evils that men do; but his combats take place in a realm not entirely controlled by the material world. His last play, "When We Dead Awaken" contains perhaps what I feel to be the key to all his work. Although in the prefaces written to several editions of his work, this play is condemned by William Archer as a sign of his senility, and explained by Bernard Shaw as Ibsen's contribution to the Suffrage Movement, I cannot help feeling that in the asylum, where Ibsen was for a time detained owing to the breaking down of his health, he may have surveyed himself and the powers and possibilities inherent in man, who inhabits not only the world visible, but also the world invisible – a world which he makes use of, and at the same time ignores […] I would love to play the Stranger, for there is great beauty here. To tell the story shortly, the hero, an artist has forsaken inspiration in order to achieve worldly success. He is married to Maya – Illusion. He is famous, but unhappy. He meets again the Ideal, who has become the Stranger. The Stranger has always with her a silent Presence personified in the Nun. The allegory ends when man's higher self is led by the Stranger to the mountain-top; while Maya – Illusion – goes down the hill with the Wolf Man – the base human passions; and the brooding Presence, the silent, ever present Nun, speaks for the first and last time her *Pax Vobiscum* [peace be with you].

The stage directions prove that the play is deliberately symbolic, for no actual stage could have a river flowing down the centre.

The other giant of the Theatre was, and is George Bernard Shaw. At first his plays were little appreciated either by the public or by the Press. Even "St. Joan" has had, for all its popular success, a smaller audience in England than for example: "Journey's End"[3]. There are indeed more people in the world who can feel than there are people who can think […] There was a season at the Court Theatre when Vedrenne and Barker produced [Shaw's] "John Bull's Other Island" and "Major Barbara," among others, to a very special, select, and limited audience. "Fanny's First Play" was a notable success, and achieved a long run. But I felt a thrill of triumph for him when, on the first night of "St. Joan" there was no room for the many distinguished people who wanted to be present […] if I look on the fruits of [Shaw's] search after beauty as well as truth, there is only one outstanding character I would give my head to play, and that is Saint Joan.

[…] Shaw's passion for truth, and his brilliant fearless attacks on all the comfortable illusions of our civilization, cause him to be admired and hated more than any other living man. His joyous wit, like that of Ariel in "The Tempest," leads the wanderers on our Island into bogs and morasses, not knowing whether he is in jest or in earnest. I heard a victim of his brilliance at a meeting, where Shaw temporarily destroyed an effort for which the other had worked for many years, describe him as an angel masquerading as Mephistopheles […] Clear-seeing and as ruthless as Ibsen, he appears to shatter and destroy, not by pity but by laughter […] Shaw is a reformer, a philosopher, using the Drama as a means of approach to the public through their reason. The first time I played in one of his plays, "Misalliance," I found at rehearsal that I was all at sea. Here was a new medium and none of my very considerable technical skill fitted into the action. There were no emotional high lights to be conveyed to the audience. There was no mirror to be held up to Nature while the observer mounted guard. It was rather as if the observer took the whole stage. The lambent wit, destroying as it rushed its course, had to be uttered without passion, without emotion; but the dialogue required clearness of enunciation, precision, speed – Shaw's one passion is symphonic music, and his plays must be performed as if they were a symphony. If one is playing alone, the actor can vary or adapt the rhythm, depart from it or return to it; but if the whole movement is orchestrated, this is no longer possible; the actor finds himself in an inelastic framework. Anyone who has recited or sung with a full orchestra will realise the tightness of the frame. When one is playing Shaw one is merely part of the band, accurately or even almost slavishly interpreting the score.

Shakespeare creates. Shaw destroys. But who am I to express opinions on the works of the Theatre? When I wrote a book called *Reflections on Shakespeare* a publisher who admired the work – not Hutchinson who published it – spoke about it to a distinguished literary man as a book worth his while. The famous writer expressed interest, asking who was the author. When this was told him he replied at once: "An Actress? I shouldn't dream of reading it."

The practical worker in any walk of life has little chance of expressing his opinion, or relating his experience, and the view of the theorist usually carries the day.

[...] But I have never understood why we should be considered unable to say anything of interest or value about the dramatic literature which we are absorbing all year round; except indeed that, as our medium of expression is not literary, we find some difficulty in fitting our thoughts to words. Our art, from its nature, cannot be measured in terms of the other arts. We have no fixed, definite or permanent standards in acting, as there are in painting, architecture, and music, and also to some degree in the construction of a play. There is a standard of aptness for the dialogue, but there never can be a standard measurement in the art for acting, excepting in its tradition. A play as a book, may be a delightful piece of work; and easily ruined by the actors when it stands up in the four dimensions of performance. On the other hand a play which, in book form is absolute rubbish, may by genius in the acting be made into an enthralling evening's entertainment, to be remembered and talked of for many years after the performers have departed this life, and the play is out of print and unprocurable. The beauty of a play, considered as a performance, not as a thing written, remains elusive. A stranger to the art of acting, though he may recognise the beauty, will not know how it has been achieved; nor again, if it has failed to achieve beauty, will he not know wherein is the defect. Yet the matter may be plain to the poor fish. They will perceive that a scene has been taken too quick or too slow: that the actor has failed to feel his part; or that the personages have been wrongly placed on the stage at a critical moment. In such detail as this lies the making or the lack of beauty, and the poor fish see why the success or failure comes to pass.

Talking with the most intellectual and intelligent lovers of the other arts, directors of museums, of art galleries, or schools of music and all the educationists, one comes up against entire ignorance of and indifference to the Theatre, except as to its literature. Perhaps the memory of enjoyment in some particular play or actor may be worthy of comment, but as for the art itself, its technical values, and above all, its traditions one meets with irritation even at the idea that there is any such thing. There is no public sympathy for, or understanding of, the technique in acting; so I am indifferent to even mentioning the peculiar problems to be solved by actors.

Please see the Works Cited for further information on the sources used in this essay.

Notes

1 Playwrights Henrik Ibsen (1828–1906) and George Bernard Shaw (1856–1950) were both closely associated with the emergence of the modernist theatre in England.
2 See Robins entry in this volume.
3 1928 play about World War I by R. C. Sherriff.

Suggestions for Further Reading

Ashwell, Lena. *Myself a Player.* London: Michael Joseph, 1936.
———. *Modern Troubadours.* London: Gyldendal, 1922.

————. "Acting as a Profession for Women." *Women Workers in Seven Professions: A Survey of Their Economic Conditions and Prospects.* Ed. Edith Morley. London: George Routledge and Sons, 1914. 298–314.

Gale, Maggie B. "Lena Ashwell and autobiographical negotiations of the professional self." *Auto/biography and Identity: Women, Theatre and Performance.* Eds. Maggie B. Gale and Viv Gardner. Manchester: Manchester University Press, 2004. 99–125.

Leask, Margaret. *Lena Ashwell: Actress, Patriot, Pioneer.* Hertfordshire: University of Hertfordshire Press, 2012.

37 CONSTANCE ROURKE (1885–1941)

Charlotte M. Canning

Introduction

In 1932, a graduate student wrote to Constance Rourke (1885–1941) to consult with her on her dissertation. In three years, that student, Esther Porter (later Lane), would be Hallie Flanagan's most trusted Federal Theatre Project deputy. But at that moment, Porter was simply a student looking for mentoring on her history of Montana theatre. In the middle of her chatty response, Rourke commented: "No one could value the history of the theatre in this country more than I do" (Schlueter 529). From her first professional article in 1919 to her posthumously published final book, Rourke always placed theatre and theatricality at the center of her work on US culture. That one sentence distilled her intellectual commitment to its fundamental principle: US theatre and its history had value.

In the last quarter of the twentieth century, feminist historians repeatedly denounced the erasure of women from history. Now, nearing the end of the first quarter of the twenty-first century, feminist historians might reasonably believe that such condemnations are obsolete. Theatre history, however, is far from done with recovering women erased from the field. The women who were part of the invention of theatre history as a discipline, especially those who championed the study of US live performance, have yet to appear regularly in the field's annals. Chief among these forgotten women is Constance Rourke. Three years before Rosamond Gilder wrote the first history of women in theatre, *Enter the Actress*, Rourke had great success with her 1928 biography of actress Lotta Crabtree, *Troupers of the Gold Coast*. From her earliest publications to her death in 1941, Rourke argued for the importance of live performance in the US, and for it as innovative and distinct from European performance traditions. Theatre studies has been largely silent about Rourke's many and varied contributions.

Throughout her childhood and into her undergraduate education, Rourke was immersed in the ideas that would be central to her scholarship. Rourke was born in Cleveland, Ohio and raised by a single mother, a teacher who ascribed to philosopher John Dewey's progressive theories on education. Dewey's contention that "the only true education comes through the stimulation of the child's powers by the demands of the social situations in which he finds himself [*sic*]" was one that Mrs. Rourke embraced fully, and Rourke was pushed as a child to have ambitions far beyond the domestic (Rourke, *American Humor* 1). Rourke attended Vassar College (1903–1907) and taught there (1910–1915). However, at Vassar, both as a student and an instructor, she was very much influenced by two English professors (and life partners), Gertrude

DOI: 10.4324/9781003006923-38

Buck and Laura Wylie, who shared an approach to the study and value of literature. For Buck, literature was "a cooperative activity of writer and reader, to the end of the reader's heightened social consciousness" (42). The idea that literature—and Rourke would expand this to include all the arts—is an agent of social progress was one that would be fundamental to Rourke's view of theatre as a measure and demonstration of national identity and invention.

Rourke's first publication on theatre was a short article on vaudeville in the *New Republic*. In this 1919 piece, she emphasizes the importance of performance over literature and spectacle over story, as she would in myriad articles she wrote for popular publications in the 1920s. Many of the elements specific to US performance that Rourke would explore across her career are present in the 1919 article: the inventiveness of humor, the centrality of ingenuity, and the significance of itinerancy. These ideas were explored fully in the seven books she wrote starting in the late 1920s.

The book for which she is best known, excerpted here, is *American Humor* (1931). In it, she argued that theatre in the US "had significance," not as distinguished literature or through the potential to "evolve into great national art, but because it was closely interwoven with the American character and the American experience" (93). Subtitled *A Study of the National Character*, the book's first three chapters establish three eponymous figures: the Yankee, the backwoodsman, and the Blackface Minstrel. The fourth chapter narrates a history of the theatre as the place where all three characters emerged, and the remainder of the book demonstrates how indebted US literature is to the theatrical performances of these three figures. Across the book, Rourke argues for what one scholar described as the "permeability of barrier between the real and the theatrical" and how that permeability was unique to the US (Zwagerman 66). For Rourke, the theatre was a place of experimentation, national feeling, and lived experience. If literature was an agent of social progress as she had learned from Buck, then the theatre was where that progress was tested and refined.

Rourke is also notable because she was one of the few white writers of her time to deal with race in ways that recognized racism and white supremacy. To be sure, Rourke's sensibilities, especially around race, are too much of her historical moment to be embraced now. Nevertheless, her work lays the groundwork for a critique of race and racism in the theatre. Her work was "more nuanced" on the issues of race and representation than that of her white colleagues (Schlueter 538). She notes when performances "appropriated" Native American culture or when actors were "white beneath the war-paint" (Rourke, *American Humor* 98). She delineates minstrelsy as a "white" invention and stresses that "the figure was a myth" (72, 86). It is this kind of observation and analysis that led African American writer Ralph Ellison to cite her research on minstrelsy. For decades, he used her work as a basis for his own analysis of race.

It is long past time to recognize that the "value" Constance Rourke found in theatre as a national enterprise offers much to current theatre historiography. Her multiple focuses on live performance over literary merit, national myth-making over individual personalities, and the specifics of race over white invisibility are all key approaches that theatre history employs today. Despite her fervor for live performance, the scholarly discipline that has claimed her as foundational is American Studies. Hopefully, as the field moves fully into the twenty-first century, theatre will recognize her as one of its own founding figures.

Constance Rourke

Excerpt from **American Humor: A Study of the National Character** *(1931)*

Young Horace Greeley, walking into New York in 1830 in a short-sleeved coat and tow-linen[1] trousers, was the very picture of the Yankee lad of the fables. He looked, in fact, like Yankee Hill.[2] No one can know whether Greeley was conscious of the figure he cut in these years, but as he grew older surely his sense of masquerade became acute. With his old white hat and coat, his fringe of silvery-yellow whiskers, his ostentatiously uncouth manners, his drollery, he stressed his Yankee heritage in a few bold lines so that any passerby might see.

Many bold self-delineations were appearing during these years. In New York or Baltimore or New Orleans the origin of strangers could easily be told by their dress, their bearing, even their physical type, as if all these effects had been consciously developed. Characters in this period often seemed larger than life. To match the rising grandeur of the Republic, heads of the antique Roman cast developed: then in later years the type vanished as though the animating conviction had failed. Even the more self-contained of these new Romans made grandiose gestures: Webster solemnly rose and bowed low to Jenny Lind[3] when she had bowed in response to the applause of the audience in Castle Garden[4], as if he represented the entire aggregation. Characters in public life were indeed one of the great creations of the time; and they often seemed to gain their emphasis less from a closely packed individuality than from bold and conscious self-picturization.

Tyrone Power[5], who traveled widely over the country in the '30's, found the mimetic gift singularly common in all phases of American society. The Americans had in fact emerged as a theatrical race. No doubt many obscure influences tended to create this bias of character. The new country made a strangely painted backdrop before which the American seemed constrained to perform; and every powerful force in pioneer life led toward outward expression. Self-consciousness had perhaps been induced early in the American by the critical scrutiny abundantly accorded him by the older races; and theatrical tendencies in the American character were heightened by a long intimacy with the stage.

"There is much discourse now of beginning stage plays in New England," Increase Mather[6] wrote in 1686, at a time when the Puritan power seemed supreme. The restless interest in the theater worked slowly, with long gaps between its triumphs, but it was unremitting. By 1750 Bostonians were so eager to see a play at a coffeehouse that a serious riot took place at its doors. Soon after the Revolution an exquisite theater was built in Boston, designed by Bullfinch[7] and containing a chastely ornamented dancing-room, card rooms, and tea rooms. In eastern cities of the coast from New York to Charleston, playhouses were established; and as the migration from New England moved westward into upper New York, into western Pennsylvania and the Western Reserve, theatricals seemed to spring up in their wake. By 1815 small companies had reached Kentucky, and improvised theaters soon dotted the West. In the little town of Columbus in Georgia, timber that waved in the breeze on Monday was transformed into a theater the following Thursday. In Natchez a theater was built in an old graveyard, with dressing-rooms beneath the stage like catacombs, and bones in view. Ballrooms of plantation mansions were fitted up for performances, and plays were performed in taverns.

In the West at least, on the frontier, where the mixed elements of the American character were taking a pronounced shape, the results were hardly considerable as drama. The best acting—and many gifted players traveled over the country—could offer little more than sheer theatricals. With transient audiences and scratch companies and the hardships of travel there was small chance for intensification and depth; even the elder Booth[8] concentrated only on single scenes. The pioneer theater was coarsened and haphazard. No drama came out of this broad movement: nothing can be clearer than the fact that drama as a powerful native form did not appear in America at this time or even throughout the entire nineteenth century. But the theatrical seemed a native mode. The Yankee first fully emerged in the theater; each of the trio of native characters was seen there. The theater took a place which in a civilization of slower and quieter growth might have been occupied almost altogether by casual song and story; even the comic tale was theatrically contrived, with the teller always the actor, and the effect dependent upon manner and gesture and the stress of speech.

Now the theatrical, as opposed to the dramatic, is full of experiment, finding its way to audiences by their quick responses and rejections. On the stage the shimmer and glow, the minor appurtenances, the jokes and dances and songs, the stretching and changes of plots, are arranged and altered almost literally by the audience or in their close company; its measure is human, not literary. The American theater then, particularly in the West, was a composite of native feeling. It had significance, not because it might at some later time evolve into great national art, but because it was closely interwoven with the American character and the American experience. It marched with the forces of dispersal, essaying a hundred things by way of entertainment and revealing a growing temper.

Like gypsy crews, strolling actors moved over the country, following the trail of the pioneers, often abreast of them. At Olean[9] one company bought a broadhorn and floated down the Alleghany, playing airs from *The Beggar's Opera*[10] at solitary cabins, finding music in abundance wherever a few settlers were gathered. A troupe stopped at a double log cabin and discovered that a tiny theater had been contrived in a loft, with curtains and three large benches for boxes and pit. There with a few crude properties they offered the semblance of romance: but the world which they created for a few hours was no more fanciful than that which existed in the minds of their small audience. All around them lay shadowy sites of public buildings and wide ephemeral avenues and streets such as Colonel Sellers[11], a figure of later years, depicted at the breakfast table as he laid out a railroad line through Slouchburg and Doodleville, Belshazzar, Catfish, Babylon, Bloody Run, Hail Columbia, and Hark from the Tomb.[12]

Many companies went into the West by way of the Alleghany, leaving behind them white flags flying on the banks of the river at places where those who followed might find a friendly reception. Pittsburgh, "sunk in sin and sea-coal," where pioneers had often been stranded for lack of money or had suffered strange adventures, was a difficult crossroads for actors. Not many of them could match the inhabitants in conviviality. One complained, "To see a Pittsburgh *bon vivant* under the table is a task few attempt who know them, and fewer succeed in accomplishing." And when debt was involved, difficulties in Pittsburgh were doubled. "The constables of Pittsburgh never forget an old friend," mourned the people of the theater. "What actor who has visited this city will ever forget it?'" they cried satirically. As one actor was playing the gravedigger in *Hamlet*, he saw the bailiffs in the wings and popped into the grave, and was never heard of again. A whole troupe was caught on the wing for debt as they tried to leave town, and were obliged to hire themselves out as waxworks at a museum to raise the necessary money. A celebrated few succeeded in slipping away in skiffs down the Ohio at night.

On rafts, in broadhorns, companies traveled down the Ohio and the Mississippi, stopping at the larger cities, often playing in small villages. Some went on by wagon into the hills of Kentucky, where the roads were so steep that they were obliged to unload their properties and carry them, and where they often left their watches and chains behind as toll. A few passed through the Cumberland Gap and thus to Richmond, then coastwise to Savannah and farther south. One troupe ventured into Florida during the Seminole War, playing at forts and garrisons on the way, threatened by the Indians but continuing their journey until they were finally set upon, some of their number killed, and their wardrobe seized. Thereafter for a time the Seminoles galloped through the sandy lowlands garbed as Romans, Highlanders, and Shakespearean heroes.

Some companies deployed through Kentucky and Tennessee to the Gulf States, traveling down crooked little rivers in overladen steamers that took on cotton at every wharf, with Negroes pushing huge bales of cotton over the bluffs at night by the light of great fires and with a pit of fire roaring in the steamer below. Everywhere they found theaters, or theaters were improvised for them; every one came, black and white, children and their elders. Backwoodsmen rode up in their fringes and green blankets and fur. Flatboatmen could be distinguished by their rolling stride and implacable manner. Planters appeared in white Spanish hats of beaver on fine horses with bright saddlecloths, and farmers with their wives on pillions, and a host of Negroes.

[....]

In an imaginative sense the audiences of the backwoods joined deeply with the players. Theirs was that intimate participation which means that acting has become reality. Out of the forest, groups would come riding at night who would talk with the actors as the play proceeded, or with each other about the characters. On a small stage in a Kentucky village a gambler's family was pictured as starving, and a countryman rose from one of the boxes. "I propose we make up something for this woman," he said. Some one whispered that it was all a sham, but he delivered a brief discourse on the worthlessness of the gambler, flung a bill on the stage with his pocketbook, advised the woman not to let her husband know about it or he would spend it all on faro, and then with a divided mind sat down, saying, "Now go on with the play."

Such participation often meant deep and direct drafts upon the emotions, and the black romantical plays like *Pizarro*, *The Iron Chest*, and *Venice Preserved*[13], popular at this time, with their themes of envy, hatred, remorse, terror, revenge, could evoke an emotional response with force and abundance. The bolder tragedies of Shakespeare—never his comedies in that early day—were staple pieces, with plays of the supernatural. *Hamlet* was frequently played for the ghost, the murder, the burial, and *Macbeth* for the witches, the sleepwalking scene, and the knocking at the gate, so strongly did the pioneer taste lean in this direction. Since lights were scarce the effects were eerie. One company acted a tragedy wholly in the dark before a

Kentucky mountain audience. *The Spectre Bridegroom*[14] was played by moonlight in a low-roofed opening like a hallway between two cabins, and the ballet of *The Wizard Skiff*[15] was danced before guttering candles. Hushed and startled, these audiences would watch and listen; then again the low murmuring talk would begin among themselves or with the actors.

Here in disguised and transmuted forms emotions which had been dominant in the early day of the pioneer lived again—emotions stirred by a sense of the supernatural, and those grosser feelings begotten of a primitive conflict between man and man, or of man and a rude destiny. With these came the wraith of the Indian.

As the Indian perished or was driven farther and farther from those fertile lands which the white invader wished to occupy, a noble and mournful fantasy was created in his place. After the Revolution, Indian plays and operas abounded. From the '20's onward Cooper[16] followed with a spate of Indian novels. In the '30's, when the trio of popular American figures appeared at full length, the Indian assumed a still loftier stature and a more tragic mien. These were the first palmy years of Forrest's[17] appearance in *Metamora, the Last of the Wampanoags*[18], a play whose vogue seemed unremitting, and which was copied in dozens of less conspicuous successes. Cooper's *Wept of the Wish Ton Wish* was dramatized and even became a ballet.[19] The stage soon overflowed with Indian figures. Painted and decked, the dusky hero went his tragic way, fighting to be sure, full of "carnivorous rages" when Forrest played the parts, but most often declaiming. The Indian's pride, his grief, his lost inheritance, his kinship with the boundless wilderness, were made enduring themes. Talk flowed again, in Indian monologues, in oratorical outbursts, in rhapsodies.

This fantastic Indian was subjective, white beneath the war-paint, springing into full stature when pioneer life was receding. About his figure the American seemed to wrap a desire to return to the primitive life of the wilderness. It was not for nothing that he had appropriated Indian methods of warfare, Indian costumes, Indian legends: this borrowing had left a wide imprint. In the Indian plays he could drench himself in melancholy remembrance of the time when the whole continent was untouched. These plays were mournful elegies, and it would be easy to call them proof of national hypocrisy. But a whole people will hardly pore over books and drive themselves to the theater for more than thirty years in order to build up an effective attitude which no one is at hand to see but themselves; nor will they do so to smother a collective conscience. Like the novels of Cooper, the plays were immensely popular; and their elegiac sentiment surged up in a region where a more realistic view might have been expected to prevail, in the West. It was there that the legendary Indian strutted and declaimed and mourned with the greatest vigor, on small rude stages, before audiences of small farmers and backwoodsmen. He seemed an improbable and ghostly ancestor.

Please see the Works Cited for further information on the sources used in this essay.

Notes

1 Tow linen is a thick, coarse linen fabric. It was not considered a valuable fabric.
2 Yankee Hill was the nickname of actor George Handel Hill (1809–1849) who was widely admired in the 1830–1840s for his performance of the stage Yankee.
3 Rourke is referring to an oft-repeated anecdote about a Washington, DC performance soprano Jenny Lind (1820–1887) gave in 1850. After hearing her sing (depending on what version of the anecdote you believe; "Home Sweet Home," the national anthem, or

"Hail Columbia"), politician and statesman Daniel Webster (1782–1852) was so moved that he rose and bowed to her (some accounts have him joining her in song). The audience was delighted when she curtsied back and they repeated this gesture to each other several times.

4   The Castle Garden Theatre was built in New York City in 1839 and demolished in 1940. Rourke is placing the Webster-Lind exchange in New York instead of Washington, DC.

5   Tyrone Power (1869–1931) was born in England but made his name as an actor on the American stage and screen. His son, Tyrone Power (1814–1958), also became a movie star.

6   Increase Mather (1639–1723) was an influential minister in the Massachusetts Bay Colony and president of Harvard College from 1681 to 1701.

7   Charles Bulfinch (1763–1844) was an architect who is considered to be the first US professional architect.

8   Edwin Booth (1833–1893) was the most renowned actor of his generation. His two brothers also acted: Junius Brutus Booth, Jr. and John Wilkes Booth who assassinated President Abraham Lincoln in 1865.

9   Olean, NY, was a crucial nineteenth-century transportation hub due to its access to the Allegheny River.

10   *The Beggar's Opera* (1782) by John Gay. The eighteenth-century play would serve as the basis for Bertolt Brecht's *The Threepenny Opera* (1928).

11   *The American Claimant* (1892) by Mark Twain focuses on Colonel Mulberry Sellers who becomes an Earl. American citizens inheriting British titles were a favorite plot line in nineteenth-century novels and plays. Sellers first appeared in *The Gilded Age: A Tale of Today* (1873) by Mark Twain and Charles Dudley Warner.

12   These towns are a reference to *The Gilded Age: A Tale of Today* (1873) by Mark Twain and Charles Dudley Warner, where Sellers, a wealthy buffoon, explains the railroad network to his wife and invents nonsense towns to represent the West.

13   These plays were extremely popular in the nineteenth-century US repertoire. *Pizarro* (1799) was adapted by Richard Brinsley Sheridan from August von Kotzebue's *Die Spanier. The Iron Chest* (1796) by George Colman, The Younger was based on William Godwin's novel *Things as they are, or the Adventures of Caleb Williams* (1794). *Venice Preserv'd* (1682) by Thomas Otway was the most popular play on the British stage in the 1680s.

14   *The Spectre Bridegroom* was an 1819 short story by Washington Irving adapted into a play in 1821 by William Thomas Moncrieff.

15   *The Wizard Skiff* was a play by British playwright John Thomas Haines.

16   James Fenimore Cooper (1789–1851) was a prolific writer best known for *The Last of the Mohicans* (1826).

17   Edwin Forrest (1806–1872) was a leading actor in the mid-nineteenth century US. He funded playwriting competitions as a way to develop US dramatic literature.

18   *Metamora, or the Last of the Wampanoags* (1829) by playwright and actor John Augustus Stone, won one of Forrest's competitions and became Forrest's best-known role. It focused on King Philip's War (1675–1678) between the English settlers and the Native Americans in what would become the northeastern US.

19   *Wept of the Wish Ton Wish* (1829) was a novel about Native Americans by James Fenimore Cooper.

Suggestions for Further Reading

Ellison, Ralph. "Change the Joke, Slip the Yolk." *The Partisan Review* 25.2 (1958): 212–22.

Rourke, Constance. *The Roots of American Culture and Other Essays.* Ed. Van Wyck Brooks. New York: Harcourt, Brace, 1942.

Rubin, Joan Shelley. *Constance Rourke and American Culture.* Chapel Hill: University of North Carolina Press, 1981.

38 CORNELIA OTIS SKINNER (1899–1979)

Jennifer Schmidt

Introduction

Cornelia Otis Skinner (1899–1979) occupies a unique and vital place in the history of solo performance and the ranks of twentieth-century female dramatists. In a long and varied career, Skinner acted on Broadway and in film, wrote essays for publications like *The New Yorker*, and published several humorous memoirs and works of non-fiction, such as her biography of Sarah Bernhardt. She was best known, however, as a writer and performer of monologues. At the time, as one contemporary critic noted, there was a "small and select company" of solo performers, and "the names most readily connected" to it were "Miss Ruth Draper" and "Miss Cornelia Otis Skinner" ("Wellesley to See"). Indeed, Skinner and her contemporary, Draper (1884–1956), whom she describes as raising the form to "extraordinary heights," dominated monologue performance in the mid-twentieth century. In his history of solo performance in the United States, *Cast of One*, John Gentile describes the 1920s and 1930s as a transitional period for solo performance. The former craze for elocution and platform reading, Gentile explains, began to fall out of favor in the 1920s: "the violent backlash against Victorianism had swept away respect for anything smacking of elocutionary declamation" (113). Despite this trend, Draper and Skinner "were able to win acclaim and a public following from a theatre community whose main interest lay in play productions" (113–114).

Skinner made her professional acting debut opposite her father, the well-known actor Otis Skinner, in the 1921 Broadway production of *Blood and Sand*. For the next few years, she filled small roles in such plays as *Will Shakespeare* (1923), *In His Arms* (1924), and *White Collars* (1925), before embarking on her career as a monologist in the late 1920s. Beginning in the 1930s, she developed her monologues into full-length one-woman shows. These solo dramas, often taken from historical subjects, wove together monologues spoken by a variety of female characters, as in *The Wives of Henry VIII* (1931) and *The Loves of Charles II* (1933). Her next two solo shows, *Mansion on the Hudson* (1935) and *Edna, His Wife* (1937), focused on domestic themes, depicting the fortunes of a single American household over decades of time. With each work, Skinner expanded and developed the solo form. In *Edna, His Wife*, Skinner played eight different characters, who appear in eleven separate scenes. Reviewing the solo drama in the *Chicago Tribune*, Charles Collins praised her pioneering efforts: "It is an extension of the technique of the monologist beyond its traditional frontiers, where no other specialist in the *genre* has adventured" ("Cornelia Otis Skinner

DOI: 10.4324/9781003006923-39

is Entire Cast"). Skinner's longest and most elaborate one-woman show, *Paris '90* (1952), was a Broadway spectacle in three acts, featuring music and lyrics by Kay Swift and scenery by Donald Oenslager. Her character portraits in the show gave glimpses of life in *fin-de-siècle* Paris, with some characters, such as "La Goulue" inspired by Toulouse-Lautrec's paintings.

In 1931, Skinner published an essay in *The New York Times* in support of her "particular branch of dramatic work." Its title, "Monologue to Theatre: An Exponent of a Solo Art Discusses Its Rise from the Ranks of the Amateurs," summarizes her main argument. Although both Draper and Skinner began their careers as amateurs, reciting monologues for private parties and women's organizations, they constantly pushed their careers in the direction of professionalism and the legitimate stage. For Skinner, the association between monologue performance and the more feminine realms of amateur recitations and "readings" constituted an unnecessary barrier to considering it legitimate theatre. "There is no reason," she writes, "that a 'one-man' or 'one-woman' show should continue in the fusty tradition of the dramatic recitation." As the daughter of actors, she reveled in "theatricality" and increasingly incorporated costumes, lights, music, and sets in her solo work.

Written at the time of her first full-length one-woman show, *The Wives of Henry VIII*, Skinner's essay documents an important transition in the history of American solo performance, between the popularity of platform performance in the late nineteenth and early twentieth centuries and the rising interest in one-person shows in the second half of the twentieth century. This transition was primarily carried out by the conscious efforts and creative innovations of Draper and Skinner, whose work gave the solo form legitimacy and prestige that paved the way for the resurgence of solo theatre in the latter half of the century. Citing Skinner's essay in *Cast of One*, Gentile notes that, with the renewed popularity of solo performance, "the years since 1950 have proved Skinner's words prophetic" (115). As a critical diagnosis of the status of solo theatre and a promotion of its merits, Skinner's essay is a crucial piece of criticism, which illuminates the central role women played as both theorists and practitioners of solo performance.

Cornelia Otis Skinner

"Monologue to Theatre: An Exponent of a Solo Art Discusses Its Rise from the Ranks of the Amateurs" (1931)

THAT the theatre has reflected more than any other art the spirit of the contemporary age is due, perhaps, to the fact that its appeal is wider, its language, if not as polyglot as music, is more human and its medium more personally understandable. Dependent for its livelihood on popularity, the theatre must perforce keep pace with, if not even act as lead-horse for, the prevailing public humor, summoning into use its finest trappings in the way of lighting, stage-mechanics, scenic arts and playwriting. For the theatre is many arts in one.

My own particular branch of dramatic work is one which, for lack of a better name, I call "character sketches." It is a medium somewhat removed from that of the theatre, considerably experimental and hitherto classed with "platform entertainment." I see no reason why this form of dramatic presentation should not in its collateral way develop in proportionate measure with the modern theatre.

There is no reason that a "one-man" or "one-woman" show should continue in the fusty tradition of the dramatic recitation. The character sketch or monologue has for so long been regarded as so polite a form of entertainment that it seems lamentably remote from drama and theatre. Instinctively one associates it with the gifted amateur. The idea recalls an army of artistically inclined ladies calling themselves "readers" (a word as incomprehensible as it is distressing) who present on the stage of their local parish house a program of school-of-expression recitations.

Certain artists have shown that this conception is not wholly true. With the inimitably delicious Beatrice Herford, the monologue passed far beyond this distressing boundary, later rising to the extraordinary heights, of course, in the art of its greatest exponent, Ruth Draper.[1] It is still regarded, however, as a medium that is not of necessity a part of drama. A program of monologues or character sketches is obviously most effective in a public theatre. But it can be and often is presented with almost equal success on the stage of a Masonic temple or even on the platform of a Unitarian church. This is theatre considerably denicotinized. It is my hope to see the "character sketch" become theatre.

* * *

This is somewhat of a problem. Hitherto the popularity of a program of monologues has been in its variety—or rather in the opportunity for variety on the part of the monologist. The successful one-man performance is a miniature vaudeville show and as such is a succession of small sketches, a succession of climaxes. It may be highly entertaining, but it is perforce disjointed. In view of this periodic interruption there can be no main thread, no balance of construction, no curve of emotions, such as one finds in a play. And yet to attempt anything like a one-character play, unless it were done with ultra-human skill, is not solving the problem either. There must be contrast; there must be variety. No one character can hold sway and amuse an audience for two hours without chameleon-like variation. How, then, is it possible to attain a multiplicity of mood, a shifting of situation and a variety of character in a one-man show and yet maintain an underlying purpose, a main theme that binds the performance into a complete unit?

The nearest solution I have found—one that is by no means completely satisfactory, but is none the less encouraging—lies in the presentation of a subject which is far from being of my own composition. The theme was created, developed and recorded by living men and women nearly 400 years ago with such niceness of dramatic balance, such contrast of characterization, such shading of moods that one might wonder if destiny itself be not a most perfect William Archer.[2] I have attempted to portray incidents, imaginary of course, in the lives of the six wives of Henry VIII in such a way as to present a short but complete drama of which the protagonist is that bluff and atrocious king and the principal theme, terror.

This group of sketches, or; perhaps, a "suite" would define it better, occupies about fifty minutes—or half a program. I have tried to make it what might be called a "show"—for, being of the theatre, I rather respect that much-maligned word. Here is a chance for costuming, for lighting, for what scenic effects may be derived from the draping of curtains. Here is also a chance for music (I think every actor in his heart of hearts hankers for the return of incidental music), for I use tunes of the period in the intervals to help merge the moods and (a reason less esthetic but more practical) to bridge the gaps when I am changing my costumes. Perhaps all such extraneous accoutrements savor of theatricality. But theatricality is more or less what I am seeking.

To call in the aid of costumes, lights and music may be cheating from the point of view of pure monologue, the merit of which lies largely in the ability to evoke the fantasy of an audience until it sees not merely the imaginary characters, but the complete setting and the change of apparel in the performer. It may even border on "hokum." But I'm afraid I believe in a certain amount of well-disguised hokum. It is inevitably a part of the theatre and my argument is that the monologue should approach more and more to theatre until it is recognized as a legitimate offspring and not a left branch of the concert stage.

Please see the Works Cited for further information on the sources used in this essay.

Notes

1 See, also, Fisk entry in this volume.
2 William Archer (1856–1924), leading London theatre critic, theatre theorist, playwright, and translator, especially of the plays of Henrik Ibsen.

Suggestions for Further Reading

Boyle, Jamie Libby. "A Chameleonic Character: Celebrity, Embodiment, and the Performed Self in Cornelia Otis Skinner's Magazine Monologues." *Tulsa Studies in Women's Literature.* 30.2 (2011): 371–392.
Skinner, Cornelia Otis. *One-Woman Show.* Woodstock, IL: The Dramatic Publishing Co., 1974.
Walker, Nancy. "'Fragile and Dumb': The 'Little Woman' in Women's Humor." *Thalia: Studies in Literary Humor.* 5.2 (1982): 24–29.

39 GERTRUDE STEIN (1874–1946)

Scott W. Klein

Introduction

American writer Gertrude Stein (1874–1946) was best known for her idiosyncratic and innovative prose style. She used a high degree of repetition and simple sentence construction, and abandoned conventional narrative progression and typical narrative logic in such experimental works as *Three Lives* (1909), *Tender Buttons* (1914), and *The Making of Americans* (1925). But Stein was also arguably America's first true avant-garde playwright. She composed over seventy theatrical (and quasi-theatrical) works during her career, including her best-known play *Doctor Faustus Lights the Lights* (1938). She also wrote the libretti for two operas composed by Virgil Thompson, *Four Saints in Three Acts* (1929; 1934) and *The Mother of Us All* (1946–1947). Her plays are often scarcely distinguishable from her prose experiments; indeed, she frequently published them side-by-side in volumes of her collected literary works. They are largely avant-garde experiments influenced (as was all her work) by the radical representational practices of the early twentieth-century visual artists whom she befriended and whose work she collected, such as Henri Matisse, Paul Cézanne, Georges Braque, and Pablo Picasso.

In the same way that those artists rejected painterly conventions, Stein rejected the conventions of traditional theatre. Her plays sometimes consist of broken paragraphs without designated speakers. They often lack stage directions, and they never contain realistic narratives or psychologically developed characters—although many have found pervasive yet oblique references throughout her work to Stein's homosexuality and linguistic play with gender expectations. To some degree, her theatre pieces parallel or blend two distinct "outsider" traditions of nineteenth- and early twentieth-century performance: the post-Romantic closet drama, which was intended to be read "staged" only in the mind of the reader, and pre-War Dadaist performance, where nonsense and linguistic play took precedence over character and narrative.

Stein seldom wrote critical reflections on her own creative writing. When she did, her musings often shared the rhetorical strategies of her noncritical prose. In the excerpts from her lecture, "Plays," that follow—one of six prose pieces published as *Lectures in America* in 1935—Stein writes about her early exposure to theatre. She describes her dislike of the realist theatrical experience and finds a disjunctive rhythm between the observer's observation of the play and the performed action, a rhythm that she compares to the intentional "nervousness" of jazz. She further notes the different ways in which observers experience actions described in literary prose,

DOI: 10.4324/9781003006923-40

as opposed to actions that are performed in public in real time. Her observations undergird her decision to create an avant-garde theatre dependent on language and rhythm, avoiding traditional character, logic, and even grammar, and implicitly suggest why she eventually turned to writing for musical settings in operas.

In style, these excerpts exemplify some of Stein's thinking about language and repetition, the differing affects presented by small versus large units of language, and what it means to have a creative epistemology of narrative and time. Her claim that "paragraphs are emotional and sentences are not" and her suggestion that this disjunction "is not a contradiction but a combination" (*Lectures* 93) show her thinking about the microcosmic and macrocosmic interactions of various building blocks of language, a model she then tropes upon an understanding of the various aspects of theatrical construction: "Plays are either read or heard or seen" (94). "Plays" investigates whether these aspects of theatre are hierarchical or self-cancelling: "Does the thing heard replace the thing seen. Does it help or interfere with it" (101). "Or do they both go on together" (102), she asks without question marks—as though the questions are also statements without answers. By writing that plays are "read" or "heard" in rhetorical primacy to "seen," Stein suggests that her ideal theatre is linguistic and disembodied. In such a theatre, the observer could be free from the anxieties implicit in being part of a physical audience.

One of Stein's paradoxes in "Plays" is her juxtaposition of the epistemological basis of theatrical aesthetics with her emotional discomfort with actual performance. The essay presents itself as an idiosyncratic investigation into the problem of knowledge. As Stein claims, "This is a thing to know and knowledge as anybody can know is a thing to get by getting" (94). Yet despite Stein's claim "I do so very essentially believe in knowledge" (101), her knowledge is not abstract: it is a product of action—of "getting." Yet in the essay, the relation between knowledge and action becomes less important than emotion and its relation to time. Stein claims that in real life—where one is an actor in one's own drama—or in reading, action and emotion are synchronized. In the theatre, however, where one observes scenes in which one does not participate, "your emotion concerning that play is always either behind or ahead of the play" (93). This causes a kind of temporal "syncopation" or anxiety—a very different thing from knowledge. Only the cinema, Stein finally claims, potentially offers new answers to the problem of "understanding sight and sound in relation to emotion and time" (104). This insight also points to Stein's later attraction to opera, where musical flow offers an epistemological and emotional connection between language, time, and emotion different from that of the traditional theatre, perhaps because it is more artificial.

Stein's implicit advocacy for a language-based (and even irrational) theatrical art, and her blending of critical stylistic practice with linguistically experimental meta-commentary draw visible connections between her different realms of literary practice. Her suggestion that plays are "either read or heard or seen," subordinating the visible aspects of theatre to language, underlines her pioneering of a kind of abstract (even entirely aural) theatre, which would later be exemplified by the radio plays and final theatrical pieces of Samuel Beckett.[1] Her influence can be further felt (as Sarah Bay-Cheng suggests in her book, *Mama Dada: Gertrude Stein's Avant-Garde Theater*) in the work of later American directors and playwrights such as Robert Wilson and Richard Forman, in whose non-narrative theatrical works nonsensical textuality and music coexist with abstract visual tableaux.

Gertrude Stein

Excerpt from "Plays" (1935)

IN a book I wrote called How To Write I made a discovery which I considered fundamental, that sentences are not emotional and that paragraphs are. I found out about language that paragraphs are emotional and sentences are not and I found out something else about it. I found out that this difference was not a contradiction but a combination and that this combination causes one to think endlessly about sentences and paragraphs because the emotional paragraphs are made up of unemotional sentences.

I found out a fundamental thing about plays. The thing I found out about plays was too a combination and not a contradiction and it was something that makes one think endlessly about plays.

That something is this.

The thing that is fundamental about plays is that the scene as depicted on the stage is more often than not one might say it is almost always in syncopated time in relation to the emotion of anybody in the audience.

What this says is this.

Your sensation as one in the audience in relation to the play played before you your sensation I say your emotion concerning that play is always either behind or ahead of the play at which you are looking and to which you are listening. So your emotion as a member of the audience is never going on at the same time as the action of the play.

This thing the fact that your emotional time as an audience is not the same as the emotional time of the play is what makes one endlessly troubled about a play, because not only is there a thing to know as to why this is so but also there is a thing to know why perhaps it does not need to be so.

This is a thing to know and knowledge as anybody can know is a thing to get by getting.

And so I will try to tell you what I had to get and what perhaps I have gotten in plays and to do so I will tell you all that I have ever felt about plays or about any play.

Plays are either read or heard or seen.

And there then comes the question which comes first and which is first, reading or hearing or seeing a play.

I ask you.

What is knowledge. Of course knowledge is what you know and what you know is what you do know.

What do I know about plays.

In order to know one must always go back.

What was the first play I saw and was I then already bothered bothered about the different tempo there is in the play and in yourself and your emotion in having the play go on in front of you. I think I may say I may say I know that I was already troubled by this in that my first experience at a play. The thing seen and the emotion did not go on together.

This that the thing seen and the thing felt about the thing seen not going on at the same tempo is what makes the being at the theatre something that makes anybody nervous.

The jazz bands made of this thing, the thing that makes you nervous at the theatre, they made of this thing an end in itself. They made of this different tempo a something that was nothing but a difference in tempo between anybody and everybody including all those doing it and all those hearing and seeing it. In the theatre of course this difference in tempo is less violent but still it is there and it does make anybody nervous.

In the first place at the theatre there is the curtain and the curtain already makes one feel that one is not going to have the same tempo as the thing that is there behind the curtain. The emotion of you on one side of the curtain and what is on the other side of the curtain are not going to be going on together. One will always be behind or in front of the other.

Then also beside the curtain there is the audience and the fact that they are or will be or will not be in the way when the curtain goes up that too makes for nervousness and nervousness is the certain proof that the emotion of the one seeing and the emotion of the thing seen do not progress together.

Nervousness consists in needing to go faster or to go slower so as to get together. It is that that makes anybody feel nervous.

And is it a mistake that that is what the theatre is or is it not.

There are things that are exciting as the theatre is exciting but do they make you nervous or do they not, and if they do and if they do not why do they and why do they not.

Let us think of three different kinds of things that are exciting and that make or do not make one nervous. First any scene which is a real scene something real that is happening in which one takes part as an actor in that scene. Second any book that is exciting, third the theatre at which one sees an exciting action in which one does not take part.

Now in a real scene in which one takes part at which one is an actor what does one feel as to time and what is it that does or does not make one nervous.

And is your feeling at such a time ahead and behind the action the way it is when you are at the theatre. It is the same and it is not. But more not.

If you are taking part in an actual violent scene, and you talk and they or he or she talk and it goes on and it gets more exciting and finally then it happens, whatever it is that does happen then when it happens then at the moment of happening is it a relief from the excitement or is it a completion of the excitement. In the real thing it is a completion of the excitement, in the theatre it is a relief from the excitement, and in that difference the difference between completion and relief is the difference between emotion concerning a thing seen on the stage and the emotion concerning a real presentation that is really something happening.[. . .]

Now the theatre has still another way of being all this to you, the thing causing your emotion and the excitement in connection with it.

Of course lots of other things can do these things to lots of other people that is to say excite lots of people but as I have said knowledge is what you know and I naturally tell you what I know, as I do so very essentially believe in knowledge.

So then once again what does the theatre do and how does it do it.

What happens on the stage and how and how does one feel about it. That is the thing to know, to know and to tell it as so.

Is the thing seen or the thing heard the thing that makes most of its impression upon you at the theatre. How much has the hearing to do with it and how little. Does the thing heard replace the thing seen. Does it help or does it interfere with it.

And when you are taking part in something really happening that is exciting, how is it. Does the thing seen or does the thing heard effect you and effect you at the same time or in the same degree or does it not.

Can you wait to hear or can you wait to see and which excites you the most. And what has either one to do with the completion of the excitement when the excitement is a real excitement that is excited by something really happening. And then little by little does the hearing replace the seeing or does the seeing replace the hearing. Do they go together or do they not. And when the exciting something in which you have taken part arrives at its completion does the hearing replace the seeing or does it not. Does the seeing replace the hearing or does it not. Or do they both go on together. [. . .]

I suppose one might have gotten to know a good deal about these things from the cinema and how it changed from sight to sound, and how much before there was real sound how much of the sight was sound or how much it was not. In other words the cinema undoubtedly had a new way of understanding sight and sound in relation to emotion and time.

I may say that as a matter of fact the thing which has induced a person like myself to constantly think about the theatre from the standpoint of sight and sound and its relation to emotion and time, rather than in relation to story and action is the same as you may say general form of conception as the inevitable experiments made by the cinema although the method of doing so has naturally nothing to do with the other. I myself never go to the cinema or hardly ever practically never and the cinema has never read my work or hardly ever. The fact remains that there is the same impulse to solve the problem of time in relation to emotion and the relation of the scene to the emotion of the audience in the one case as in the other. There is the same impulse to solve the problem of the relation of seeing and hearing in the one case as in the other.

It is in short the inevitable problem of anybody living in the composition of the present time, that is living as we are now living as we have it and now do live in it.

Please see the Works Cited for further information on the sources used in this essay.

Note

1 Samuel Beckett (1906–1989) is best known for his absurdist plays, especially *Waiting for Godot* (1952).

Suggestions for Further Reading

Bowers, Jane. *"They Watch Me as They Watch This": Gertrude Stein's Metadrama.* Philadelphia, PA: University of Pennsylvania Press, 1991.
Durham, Leslie. *Staging Gertrude Stein: Absence, Culture, and the Staging of American Alternative Theatre.* New York, NY: Palgrave Macmillan, 2005.
Knapp, Bettina. *Gertrude Stein.* New York, NY: Continuum, 1990.
Sprigge, Elizabeth. *Gertrude Stein: Her Life and Work.* London: H. Hamilton, 1957.

40 SUSAN GLASPELL (1876–1948)

J. Ellen Gainor and Elizabeth A. Osborne

Introduction

Pulitzer Prize-winning dramatist, fictionist, biographer, and journalist Susan Glaspell (1876–1948) may be best known today for her one-act play *Trifles* (1916) and its short-story counterpart, "A Jury of Her Peers" (1917), both of which have served as exemplary texts in Anglo-American feminist literary criticism and feminist legal theory and are now considered canonical American works. Over the course of her career, Glaspell produced hundreds of newspaper articles, more than fifty short stories, fifteen plays, nine novels, and the biography of her husband, George Cram Cook (1873–1924), with whom she co-founded the legendary Provincetown Players, one of the early companies in the anti-commercial Little Theatre movement in the United States.

Like many other writers who became prominent in the development of American modernism, Glaspell hailed from the Midwest. She began her career working for local papers in Davenport, Iowa, before joining the staff of the *Des Moines Daily News*, where she covered the murder case that became the basis for *Trifles*/"Jury." She left journalism to concentrate on fiction, securing early success with short stories placed in such leading magazines as *Harper's* and *Ladies' Home Journal*. She spent time in Chicago, participating in the emerging bohemian community there, and then moved to the East Coast, joining like-minded artists, writers, and left-leaning activists who summered in Provincetown, Massachusetts, and spent winters in New York's Greenwich Village. Although Glaspell embraced fiction as her primary genre, her contributions as playwright, actor, and producer for the Provincetown Players—where she nurtured the dramatic careers of Eugene O'Neill and others in their circle—significantly shaped the development of US theatre and drama.

Glaspell and her colleagues saw their stage as an important platform for stylistic experimentation and innovation as well as political engagement and activism. Her plays reflect both sets of concerns; such pieces as *The Outside* (1917) and especially *The Verge* (1921) demonstrate her participation in the emerging American modernist avant-garde, while *Inheritors* (1921) forcefully confronts American jingoism, racism, and attacks on free speech during and immediately following World War I. She received the Pulitzer in 1931 for her play *Alison's House*; depicting the legacy of a poet whose life story resembles that of Emily Dickinson, the drama considers such important questions as who controls an artist's oeuvre and what is the function of art in contemporary culture.

DOI: 10.4324/9781003006923-41

Although Glaspell held strong leftist political convictions and was a member of the feminist group Heterodoxy, she did not, like many of her Greenwich Village colleagues, participate directly in the socialist or anarchist activism of the time. In a rare interview she gave to fellow Heterodoxy member and journalist Alice Rohe, Glaspell explained, "Of course I am interested in all progressive movements, whether feminist, social or economic [...] but I can take no very active part other than through my writing. [...] When one has limited strength one must use it for the thing one feels most important" (Rohe 4).

In 1936, Glaspell found an opportunity to use her skills and strengths for something important: directing the Federal Theatre Project's (FTP) Midwest Play Bureau. Embedded in the Works Progress Administration, the FTP (1935–1939) was one of four major arts projects created under the auspices of Franklin Delano Roosevelt's New Deal. As Director of the Midwest Play Bureau, Glaspell played a pivotal role in the creation of National Director Hallie Flanagan's vision of the FTP as a "federation of theatres" that was "national in scope, [and] regional in emphasis" (Flanagan, *Arena* 23, 45). With this vision in mind, Glaspell set out to find and nurture new writers in Illinois, Indiana, Iowa, Michigan, Ohio, Wisconsin, Missouri, and Nebraska. As she argued, "To <u>cause</u> better American plays to be written is one of the great aims of the Federal Theatre," and she was particularly inspired by the development of midwestern writers in a period when New York dominated US theatre (Glaspell, "Speech" 3). By the end of her first year, her small team had read more than 800 plays by writers located in midwestern cities, towns, and rural areas.

In the unpublished speech included here, Glaspell explains the necessity of government support for the arts during the Great Depression: "[...] the government decided that workers in the arts were also workers. [...] The government had never before recognized the arts. Now it did, and on a big scale" (Glaspell, "Speech" 1). This focus on artists as laborers worthy of support was central to the FTP, and it served as a form of advocacy for Glaspell even as her work with emerging writers fulfilled her interests in artistic innovation and experimentation. She describes the hard-won FTP—a scrappy, imaginative, far-reaching program that no one thought could succeed, but that had already earned the praise of *New York Times* critic Brooks Atkinson (Atkinson, "No Theatre" X1). Most important, Glaspell makes a compelling case for new work, regional playwrights, and local pride in home-grown theatre. "There is no reason why Chicago should not be one of the great theatrical centers of the world," she writes (Glaspell, "Speech" 4).

Glaspell likely wrote this speech in September or October of 1937. Two productions that Glaspell notes are occurring in the contemporaneous present—*Monesh* and a bill of one-acts, which included Eugene O'Neill's *The Long Voyage Home*, Thornton Wilder's *Love and How to Cure It*, Molly Thatcher's *Blocks,* and Sean O'Casey's *The End of the Beginning*—opened in early September; *Monesh* closed November 14 and the one-acts closed October 17. Glaspell resigned from the FTP in May 1938, but under her leadership, the Midwest Play Bureau encouraged new plays and playwrights regardless of their experience in theatre or their education. She designed a reading process that led to positive feedback, advanced widespread interest in a range of aesthetic styles and subject matters, and created a path for new works like the commercial and critical hit *Swing Mikado* (1938) and Arnold Sundgaard's *Spirochete* (1938), which became the FTP's most-produced living newspaper after *One-Third of a Nation* (O'Connor 92).

Susan Glaspell

"Speech on the Federal Theatre Project" (c.1937)¹

In 1935 Uncle Sam went into the show business because people were hungry. Man does not live by bread alone, but he doesn't live without it. The administration had the unique idea that people were not to starve. But almost at once something became evident. The people of this country were also hungry for theatre.

For years there had been a cry for a National Theatre. In the days of our prosperity nothing was done about it. Then came desperation and out of that came a Federal Theatre. Founded on economic necessity, it is bringing the theatre to the people.

The dream of a National theatre was a sort of "I dreamt that I dwelt in Marble Halls" idea. Our halls in the Federal Theater are not marble. We play in theatres, we play in tents—as was done all this summer in Peoria. We play in parks and sometimes, as in the Kentucky mountains, lighted by the headlights of the truck that brought in the show. It is a democratic theatre. It is the peoples' theatre.

This is how and why it came about: Show business was hard hit by the depression. In 1935, there were 12,500 actors and other theatre workers out of jobs. A sorry feature of it was that these were people who had always given of their time and talent in benefits for those less fortunate than they. Now the generous actor was flat—and proud. He didn't want to go on relief. Yet he did want to eat—at least every other day. It was then the government decided that workers in the arts were also workers. They did not work in foundry or ditch, but they were American workers none the less. This was an innovation. The government had never before recognized the arts. Now it did, and on a big scale.

The Four Arts Projects were organized: The Writers', The Arts', The Music, and Theatre Projects.

To Mrs. Hallie Flanagan fell the staggering task of organizing Federal Theatres all over the country. Wherever twenty-five professional actors were out of work through no fault of their own, eligible for relief, a theatre could be organized. Broadway shook its head and told Mrs. Flanagan it could not be done. She went ahead and did it.

It was not done easily. While an administrative program had been worked out for street gangs and other WPA workers, there was nothing to cover the intricate business of running a theatre. Those early days caused a good many headaches.

Now there are 158 theatres operating in 28 states—Federal Theatre plays to a weekly audience of over a half million people. Your Uncle Sam is the biggest theatrical producer in the world. This has given work not only to actors, but directors, writers, scene designers and builders, seamstresses, lighting artists, costume designers, musicians, press agents, box office men, janitors, typists, and the myriad people who together make a theatre.

The Government pays labor costs. This is on the basis of work relief. The theatre must support itself from the box office in other than labor costs, including advertising and cost of production. Ten per cent [*sic*] of the personnel can be drawn from the outside—people who are not eligible for work relief but are needed for some important position or role.

A difficulty has been the small sum that can go for advertising. As a Federal Theatre box office man said, "Running a theatre without advertising is like winking at your girl in the dark. You know what you are doing but she doesn't."

Brooks Atkinson, Dramatic Critic of the *New York Times*, says: "The Federal Theatre is one of the relief programs of which the government may be proud. It has never played politics or spent money loosely. It has rebuilt the morale of 15,000 Americans and by its public activities has enriched the lives of fifteen million American people."

This comment of one of America's foremost dramatic critics speaks not only for the magnitude of the undertaking but for the quality of work that is being done. Federal Theatre has attracted to itself some of the leading playwrights of the world. Sinclair Lewis gave his play, *IT CAN'T HAPPEN HERE*, to the Federal Theatre when Broadway contracts for the play were fluttering around him. "I want the people of America to see my play,"[2] he said, "and my best medium is the Federal Theatre."

So also says our leading dramatist, Eugene O'Neill, who has recently released all his plays for Federal Theatre production. Bernard Shaw, like Sinclair Lewis, said, "I want my plays seen not only in New York, Chicago, and a few cities, but by the people all over the country." He, too, has released all his plays for Federal Theatre.

In addition to the conspicuous names, the Federal Theatre gives young American playwrights of promise the best opportunity that has ever been offered them.

In Chicago alone more than eight hundred plays have been read in the last year. For this there is a competent staff, called the Play Bureau, and when a play has possibilities, but not right as it stands, careful criticism is given and suggestions for rewriting. Many young writers living in remote places, where they feel no one is[3] interested in their work, are expressing appreciation of the help and encouragement given them.

The Federal Theatre is interested in all sorts of plays: some purely for entertainment value, others in which there is the conflict of modern life expressed in terms of the theatre. They may be humorous or they may be tragic; they must be real. To cause better American plays to be written is one of the great aims of the Federal Theatre.

We feel that the Federal Theatre should be of the very greatest interest to Chicago. Too long we have seen Broadway plays presented here by inferior companies and at prices far from inferior. There is no reason why Chicago should not be one of the great theatrical centers of the world. It has done almost everything else it wanted to. Say the "I Will" to the theatre and New York must look to its laurels. There is an excitement, a pride, in one's own first nights far more keen than seeing a play already reviewed and discussed. The Federal Theatre is building up an audience for this.

Our work here began in February, 1935 with a production of Ibsen's *AN ENEMY OF THE PEOPLE*.[4] Since then the Federal Theatre has presented, among other plays, *CHALK DUST; TRIPLE A PLOWED UNDER*, a Living Newspaper, which is a new dramatic form created on the project and sponsored by the Newspaper Guild; Martin Flavin's *BROKEN DISHES* and *GOOD OLD SUMMER TIME; IT CAN'T HAPPEN HERE*, which had simultaneous opening nights in seventeen cities—from coast to coast; *WITHIN THESE WALLS*, a religious play by Marcus Bach, a new American playwright; *THE LONELY MAN*, a fine, modern play animated by the feeling of Lincoln, written by Howard Koch, a young playwright of great promise; *OH SAY CAN YOU SING*, a revue created here in Chicago—and isn't it something of a surprise to be able to see a first rate musical show for one dollar?

The Negro group gave a delightful comedy, *MISSISSIPPI RAINBOW*, and now at the Great Northern the Yiddish Group is playing to enthusiastic audiences, *MONESH*, based on an old Jewish legend and using folk dances and music.

At the Blackstone Theatre there is a bill of one act plays: *THE LONG VOYAGE HOME* by Eugene O'Neill, *LOVE AND HOW TO CURE IT* by Thornton Wilder, *BLOCKS* by Molly Day Thatcher, and *THE END OF THE BEGINNING*, an Irish comedy by Sean O'Casey.

Eugene O'Neill's *THE STRAW* will follow this bill at the Blackstone, and Bernard Shaw's *THE DEVIL'S DISCIPLE* is to be presented soon.

In rehearsal now is a ballet created by Grace and Kurt Graff, and Berta Ochsner.[5]

Our companies will tour the other Illinois cities with three plays: *BOY MEETS GIRL*, Eugene O'Neill's *AH WILDERNESS*, and *CRIMINAL AT LARGE*.

The Director of the theatre is Harry Minturn, too well known for his contribution to the theatre in Chicago and the Middle West to need introduction here. You will remember when he had three companies playing in Chicago at once, his fine work as actor and director!

We offer you a season of rich entertainment in the theatre. It is your theatre and we want your support. Come and see our plays and tell your friends about them. Let us make this a season we can all be proud of and then, with the audience we are building up, go on to bigger things.

Please see the Works Cited for further information on the sources used in this essay.

Notes

1   Transcribed and edited by Elizabeth Osborne and Connor Osborne. The archival version of this unpublished document contains some typographical inconsistencies. Most of the issues are connected to play titles, which are in all capital letters and enclosed in quotation marks, often with inconsistent comma usage or missing punctuation; we have modernized play titles using italics and removed the quotation marks to account for these issues. We have maintained alternate spellings throughout and noted other corrections made for readability.

2   In the archival document, the comma follows the quotation mark after "play."

3   In the archival document, "one is" is "oneis."

4   According to the program available at the Library of Congress, Ibsen's *An Enemy of the People* premiered at Chicago's Great Northern Theatre (also known as "The Peoples' Playhouse") on March 10, 1936. The FTP was founded in July 1935, and the first FTP production staged in Chicago was a vaudeville show, *Greater American Minstrels*, which opened January 20, 1936. The first legitimate play to open was Charles Hoyt's *A Texas Steer,* which commenced at the Blackstone Theatre March 9, 1936. *An Enemy of the People* opened the following day; *The Chicago Tribune* credits it as the "first Federal Theater" opening, but this is likely because the producing unit was dubbed "Federal Theater No. 1." Charles Collins, "Federal Drama Bureau Will Reopen Two Chicago Theaters," *Chicago Daily Tribune*, March 8, 1936, 19; Charles Collins, "First Federal Theater Opens Doors in City," *Chicago Daily Tribune*, March 11, 1936, E2.

5   This piece is likely part of the Federal Theatre's *Ballet Fedré,* a long-standing dance repertory that played at Chicago's Great Northern Theatre. Katherine Dunham's first full-length ballet, named *L'Ag Ya* after a Martinican fighting dance, constituted the final piece in the program; Dunham was named director of the FTP's Chicago Negro Unit in 1938.

Suggestions for Further Reading

Ben-Zvi, Linda. *Susan Glaspell: Her Life and Times.* New York, NY: Oxford University Press, 2005.

Gainor, J. Ellen. *Susan Glaspell in Context: American Theater, Culture, and Politics 1915-48.* Ann Arbor, MI: University of Michigan Press, 2001.

O'Connor, John, and Lorraine Brown. *Free, Adult, Uncensored: The Living History of the Federal Theatre Project.* New York, NY: New Republic Books, 1978.

Osborne, Elizabeth A. *Staging the People: Community and Identity in the Federal Theatre Project.* New York, NY: Palgrave Macmillan, 2011.

Ozieblo, Barbara. *Susan Glaspell: A Critical Biography.* Chapel Hill, NC: University of North Carolina Press, 2000.

41 HALLIE FLANAGAN (1889–1969)

Elizabeth A. Osborne

Introduction

Hallie Flanagan (1889–1969) is best known as the national director of the Federal Theatre Project (FTP, 1935–1939), the only national theatre in the history of the United States. Yet it is the rest of her career that qualified her for this important position, and her breadth as an educator, artist, and scholar is impressive. In addition to her work on the FTP, Flanagan was a theatre educator at Grinnell College (Iowa), Vassar College (New York), and Smith College (Massachusetts) where, over the years, she taught thousands of students. She was an accomplished director and playwright whose creative tastes explored social issues in experimental ways. Flanagan studied with George Pierce Baker[1] at Harvard's 47 Workshop, founded the Grinnell and Vassar Experimental Theatres (1924 and 1925), and served as a tireless advocate for new, experimental theatre and the artists who created it.

In her first year at Vassar, Flanagan proposed a year-long study of theatre in Europe and post-revolutionary Russia; a Guggenheim award funded her research, and she was one of the first women to receive this award. In addition to serving as the basis of her first book, *Shifting Scenes* (1928), the trip proved foundational for the creative ethos that would sustain her through her career. Studying with an array of artists—including William Butler Yeats, Lady Gregory,[2] John Galsworthy, Gordon Craig, Konstantin Stanislavsky, Vsevolod Meyerhold, Karel Čapek, and Luigi Pirandello—Flanagan was most inspired by the powerful connection between Russian theatre and its audiences. These audiences were moved not by "amorous relationship[s]" but by "the problem of what men and women can achieve together" (*Shifting Scenes* 272). In Russia, theatre was a social force. Flanagan believed theatre was critical to a democratic society as well and viewed theatre artists as cultural soldiers. Nearly two decades later, she would articulate this in her third book, *Dynamo* (1943): "at a time when statesmen, military men and educators unite in telling us that we need to work together *so as to effect some change*, we cannot afford to ignore an instrument which, since the days of Aristophanes[,] has had the ability [to] stir up life and infuse it with power" (*Dynamo* 11).

Arena (1940) is Flanagan's second book. It is a blend of memoir, archive, accounting, criticism, theatre management, production record, manifesto, and court transcript, covering the four turbulent years of the FTP from Flanagan's perspective as national director. The FTP was part of President Franklin Delano Roosevelt's signature New Deal, dedicated to putting unemployed theatre professionals back to work in their own profession—and it did so by employing more than 13,000 theatre

DOI: 10.4324/9781003006923-42

professionals at its height in 1936. But Flanagan also envisioned the FTP as a "federation of theatres" that would bring the resources of a national theatre to the diversity
and geographic expanse of the United States (*Arena* 23). Flanagan imagined theatres
and theatre professionals creating locally relevant, experimental work nation-wide
for a diverse audience. Like the people of the nation, the FTP's theatrical work would
have an extraordinary range: children's theatre, vaudeville, living newspaper, radio
plays, Yiddish theatre, Spanish theatre, African American theatre, dance, musical
theatre, puppetry, classics, massive outdoor pageants, historical dramas, participatory theatre, adaptations, community dramas, circuses, Shakespeare in the park, and
much more (Witham 1–2). *Arena* documents this work.

However, the FTP was certainly not without critics. The "free, adult, and uncensored" theatre that Works Progress Administration head Harry Hopkins famously
promised Flanagan was, unfortunately, not in line with the political reality (qtd. in
O'Connor and Brown 2). The FTP was a frequent target for those hoping to damage
Roosevelt or the New Deal and, as national director, Flanagan was often called on
to champion the FTP's work. In 1938 she testified before the Dies Committee, where
she memorably defended Christopher Marlowe from accusations of communist sympathies (Bentley 25). In spite of her efforts to marshal defenses, Congress singled
out the FTP for defunding and, on June 30, 1939, the project ended. When the FTP
closed its doors, nearly thirty million people—over 60 percent of whom were seeing
theatre for the first time—had viewed more than one thousand productions in seven
different languages and more than thirty states (*Arena* 435; "Pinocchio Dies in
New York" 20; Osborne 7).

Arena was funded by a grant from the Rockefeller Foundation in the year following the FTP's closure, and it is clear that, in addition to documenting the project's
activities for posterity, Flanagan continued to advocate for its long-term potential
and viability. In addition to being a narrative of the FTP's inner workings and productions, *Arena* contains a helpful accounting of four years of production records.
Flanagan also includes a brief overview of the FTP's financial statements, with the
important reminders that: 1) the FTP's primary directive was relief, and therefore
it was created to spend (and not generate) money by paying worker salaries; and 2)
the FTP could only exist in states/cities with sufficient numbers of qualified theatre
relief workers. With *Arena*, Flanagan demonstrates her administrative abilities, arts
advocacy, theoretical acumen, and phenomenal creative energy. The selection below
offers an introduction to the FTP and to Flanagan's way of conceptualizing one of
the grandest adventures in US theatre history.

Hallie Flanagan

Excerpt from ARENA (1940)

Can you spend money?

A plan began to take form in my mind, dictated not by an art theory or an academic idea, but by economic necessity. No one knew how many unemployed theatre
people there were or where they were. Actors' Equity said there were 5,000 unemployed actors in New York City alone. Counting workers in allied theatre skills, W.P.A.
estimated a probable 20,000–30,000. Where were they? Who were they? Numbers on
cards in relief offices from one end of the country to the other. The primary task

would be to set up volunteer boards of theatre people in each state to audition the applicants. When a sufficient number of professionals were found in any state, we could start a company. This, however, was not enough; we must have a broad plan encompassing the whole country, outlining the general policy in plays, sketching the relationship of these companies to their various communities.

Because of the size of our country and because of the origins and aims of the project, the type of theatre needed could not be modeled on a government-operated enterprise of any other country. Government subsidy of the theatre brought the United States into the best historic theatre tradition and into the best contemporary theatre practice, but there the similarity ended. This was not France or Germany where a galaxy of artists was to be chosen to play classical repertory. Nor was it Russia where the leaders of the state told the theatre directors what plays to do and what not to do. Neither was it Italy where theatre performances took the form of largesse distributed to the people. This was a distinctly American enterprise growing out of a people's need over a vast geographic area.

Knowledge of plays and techniques absorbed through years of theatre study here and abroad would be useful, but in the central conception what was immediately needed was a knowledge of the United States. I was glad at this point that I knew my country, that I had been born in South Dakota, educated in Iowa and Massachusetts, that I had traveled in almost every state, lived in cities—Chicago, St. Louis, Detroit— in a small town, Grinnell; in a village, Sonora; and on a farm in Iowa. I studied the map and the plan developed: five great regional theatres—New York, Los Angeles, Chicago, possibly Boston, possibly New Orleans, each one a production center for a professional company; each a retraining center for the actors who would undoubtedly be of varying ability and from various backgrounds; each a service, research, and playwriting center for its own region. Eventually the plan should include a metropolitan theatre built in each area, labor for such a building to be furnished by the W.P.A.; and in these theatres, resident companies would do new plays and classical repertory and everything that commercial theatres cannot always afford to try; companies from each of these centers would tour the region, playing a circuit of smaller theatres; university or civic theatres in each of the regions would work with these government theatres in developing playwrights who would build up a body of dramatic literature each for his own region.

Would not all such activity contribute to the commercial theatre by building audiences and by making experiments in a field in which changes in both subject matter and form seemed indicated by the changes in art, science, and the world itself?

The idea of a regional theatre in some form had been in the minds of many people for many years. Edith Isaacs through the pages of *Theatre Arts Monthly* had explored its possibilities; Kenneth MacGowan [*sic*], in *Footlights Across America*, had hoped that the college and community theatres would grow up to their opportunity of creating an American drama; E. C. Mabie in the Midwest, Gilmor Brown in California, Frederick Koch in North Carolina, Frederic McConnell in Cleveland, Jasper Deeter in Pennsylvania, were [outstanding] among those who had built up regional theatres. Now, for the first time, the professional theatre might also be considered regionally. Under a federal plan could not all of these various theatres, commercial, educational, and community, in the East, West, North, and South, work together? The strength of such union would be that each region could develop its own drama in its own pattern; yet all regions could improve standards by pooling experiences, and all could decide mutually upon the lines of activity to be stressed.

Most helpful in working with me was E. C. Mabie, with whom I had discussed the organization of regional theatres in the United States, predicated on his work for the National Theatre Conference of University and Community Theatres. We expanded and modified that plan to fit the new need and the use of professional talent. We laid a great deal of stress upon the development of local and regional theatre expression, rather than on the New York conception of theatre, or of ideas emanating from Washington:

> If any important creative work is to be done in the theatre in the West it will be an outgrowth of life in these regions. The plan here proposed is an effort to stimulate the development of genuinely creative theatre in these regions.[3]

And again, we stated the aim:

> To set up theatres which have possibilities of growing into social institutions in the communities in which they are located and thus to provide possible future employment for at least some of those who now present an immediate and acute problem to the government . . . and to lay the foundation for the development of a truly creative theatre in the United States with outstanding producing centers in each of those regions which have common interests as a result of geography, language origins, history, tradition, custom, occupations of the people.[4]

In short, the plan was based on that of the federal government itself: the general policy and program would be outlined in Washington, but the carrying out, with modifications dictated by local conditions, would rest with the states. It was not a national theatre in the European sense of a group of artists chosen to represent the government. It was never referred to by me as a national theatre, though critics increasingly spoke of it as such. It was rather a federation of theatres. That was the origin and meaning of its name.

[. . .]

What part could art play in this program [the WPA]? Could we, through the power of the theatre, spotlight the tenements and thus help in the plan to build decent houses for all people? Could we, through actors and artists who had themselves known privation, carry music and plays to children in city parks, and art galleries to little towns? Were not happy people at work the greatest bulwark of democracy? [. . .]

No more natural place for the announcement of a nationwide government theatre could be imagined than the National Theatre Conference at Iowa University, where people from all over the United States met for the laying of the cornerstone of an institution which was to be not only a civic and university theatre, but a regional center for the entire Midwest. After the ceremony we all went back to the hall of the Art Building where, after dinner, President Gilmore of the University introduced Elmer Rice, Paul Green, and other speakers. Harry Hopkins spoke of the new kind of theatre we hoped to create in America; he concluded with a fearless statement of policy: "I am asked whether a theatre subsidized by the government can be kept free from censorship, and I say, yes, it is going to be kept free from censorship. What we want is a free, adult, uncensored theatre."

I took this declaration seriously, as did my associates, and that is the kind of theatre we spent the next four years trying to build.

[. . .]

The artistic policy was based on three beliefs: first, that unemployed theatre people wanted to work and that millions of Americans would enjoy the results of this work, if it could be offered free or at prices they could pay; second, that the people on our rolls should be regarded not as relief cases but as professional workers competent to carry out an ambitious nationwide program; and third, that any theatre sponsored by the government of the United States should do no plays of a cheap or vulgar nature but only such plays as the government could stand behind in a planned theatre program national in scope, regional in emphasis, and democratic in allowing each local unit freedom under these general principles.

Washington did not dictate individual plays, leaving such choice to the various directors, with, however, the suggestion of emphasis on new American plays, classical plays, children's plays, and a special program for Negro companies.

We could not afford to set tasks equal to the powers of our people, which through destitution and despair had become depleted. Rather we must develop in ourselves and our projects powers equal to the gigantic task of bringing to people across America, hitherto unable to afford dramatic entertainment, a theatre which should reflect our country, its history, its present problems, its diverse regions and populations.

Looking at the keen and powerful faces around that table I felt that there was nothing such a staff could not accomplish and this feeling colored what I said:

> Our whole emphasis in the theatre enterprises which we are about to undertake should be on re-thinking rather than on remembering. The good old days may have been very good days indeed, but they are gone. New days are upon us and the plays that we do and the ways that we do them should be informed by our consciousness of the art and economics of 1935.
>
> We live in a changing world: man is whispering through space, soaring to the stars in ships, flinging miles of steel and glass into the air. Shall the theatre continue to huddle in the confines of a painted box set? The movies, in their kaleidoscopic speed and juxtaposition of external objects and internal emotions are seeking to find visible and audible expression for the tempo and the psychology of our time. The stage too must experiment—with ideas, with psychological relationship [sic] of men and women, with speech and rhythm forms, with dance and movement, with color and light—or it must and should become a museum product.
>
> In an age of terrific implications as to wealth and poverty, as to the function of government, as to peace and war, as to the relation of the artist to all these forces, the theatre must grow up. The theatre must become conscious of the implications of the changing social order, or the changing social order will ignore, and rightly, the implications of the theatre.

Please see the Works Cited for further information on the sources used in this essay.

Notes

1 George Pierce Baker (1866–1935) led the influential "47 Workshop" and taught the related playwriting class at Harvard beginning in 1905; his *Dramatic Technique: A Codification of the Principles of Drama* (1919) emphasized dramaturgical principles associated with the "well-made" play.
2 See, also, Lady Augusta Gregory entry in this volume.
3 *A Plan for the Organization of Regional Theatres in the United States,* by E. C. Mabie (W.P.A. Federal Theatre Records, Washington, D. C.).
4 Ibid.

Suggestions for Further Reading

Chinoy, Helen Krich. "Art versus Business: The Role of Women in American Theatre." *The Drama Review: TDR.* 24.2 (1980): 3–10.

Fraden, Rena. *Blueprints for a Black Federal Theatre, 1935–1939.* Cambridge: Cambridge University Press, 1994.

Hallie Flanagan Davis Papers, Smith College Archives, CA-MS-00053, Smith College Special Collections, Northampton, Massachusetts. https://findingaids.smith.edu/repositories/4/resources/354.

Hallie Flanagan Papers, Archives and Special Collections Library, Vassar College Libraries. https://digitallibrary.vassar.edu/collections/finding-aids/5098b62d-a40e-4b8f-b0b0-d20ca4c272b4.

Hallie Flanagan Papers, *T-Mss 1964–002, Billy Rose Theatre Collection, The New York Public Library for the Performing Arts. http://archives.nypl.org/the/21354.

Mathews, Jane de Hart. *The Federal Theatre, 1935–1939: Plays, Relief and Politics.* Princeton, NJ: Princeton University Press, 1968.

Osborne, Elizabeth A. "A Democratic Legacy: Hallie Flanagan and the Vassar Experimental Theatre." *Women, Collective Creation, and Devised Performance: The Rise of Women Theatre Artists in the Twentieth and Twenty-First Centuries.* Eds. Kathryn Mederos Syssoyeva and Scott Proudfit. New York, NY: Palgrave Macmillan, 2016. pp. 67–80.

42 JOAN LITTLEWOOD (1914–2002)

Fatine Bahar Karlıdağ

Introduction

England's renowned ensemble Theatre Workshop (1945–1964) had three phases in its timeline: 1) Joan Littlewood (1914–2002), a drop-out of the Royal Academy of Dramatic Art (RADA), and Ewan MacColl (then Jimmie Miller), a motor mechanic from Salford, Manchester, partnered in 1934 to start their indoor theatre, Theatre Action in Manchester; 2) a new manifesto arrived in the Theatre Union phase (1936), which took them through the middle of World War II; 3) their partnership continued as the Theatre Workshop beginning in 1945. After a lengthy period of touring miners' towns as well as foreign countries, in late 1952 ensemble members voted to settle in a permanent theatre in East London, hoping to be patronized by the East London working-class population. But funding was an insurmountable problem, and moving to London lost them their founding partner, Ewan MacColl, who openly stated that he would not play to please the critics, after years of trying to reach working-class audiences, although he continued to support the theatre while continuing his folk-singing career.

Born in the Workers' Theatre Movement,[1] the Theatre Workshop's stage techniques, ensemble structure, and dramatic literature expressed its priority to play to the working-class and the unemployed people of England, who had no access to art; the target audiences were those in the streets and in distressed provinces. Their stage language was that of the radical left, merged with the Russian and European avant-garde, and these dynamics were kept intact by Littlewood through the post-settlement years of success and recognition. With their 1956 production of Brendan Behan's play, *The Hostage*, Theatre Workshop became famous and started transferring their plays to the well-known theatre row of London, the West End.

These migratory plays, moving from the working-class base of Stratford, East London, and then to the West End, earned Littlewood many prestigious awards and put the Theatre Workshop in a position to revolutionize the English stage. But although transferring the productions to commercial stages was necessary for financial sustenance, these moves diminished both MacColl's formative input and Littlewood's astute working-class politics—even though success on West End stages garnered critics' praise for and appreciation of the beauty of their stage language. However, as Christopher Balme suggests, theatres' cultural identities exceed "the heightened enchantment of the 'event'," because theatres live in their own space and time; in their own *longue durée* (Balme 38).

The archived, typewritten document by Littlewood included here conveys her observations about the state of theatre from a left-wing perspective and can also be

DOI: 10.4324/9781003006923-43

read as another manifesto of principles guiding Theatre Workshop's mission and practice. Written around 1949, the document demonstrates: Littlewood's appreciation of audience response over artistic canons and institutions; compares the Czech theatres to their Western peers; reveals her extreme disappointment with the English Actors Union's endorsing what she calls the black (fascistic) circular of Trades Union Congress[2] against communism; emphasizes the importance for revolutionary theatres of experimentation; and declares her commitment to communistic views of theatre and life. Additionally, Littlewood describes the Theatre Workshop's aim to recognize and represent the realities of the working class, which MacColl had earlier formulated in Marxian terms and described in his autobiography, *Journeyman,* as "The ability to get at the basis of reality, and skill in portraying its basic content made great artists of the past the outstanding critics of their time; it made realism an objectively democratic force" (266).

Yet though MacColl was the ensemble's ideologue, he was not the sole purveyor of advancing the theatre's working-class ensemble. Littlewood's undated notes in her various notebooks indicate her strong faith in class politics, when she writes about the Theatre Workshop's urgent aim to express the feelings and desires of British workers. Created by the class struggle, the theatre had a mission, she stated, to give voice to workers' tragedy and to help them grasp the realities of life happening around them by traversing an unknown land through experimentation. To implement this vision, Theatre Workshop turned to the constructivism of the Russian avant-garde and to the expressive techniques central to movement and dance developed by Christoph Laban, which resembled the inwardly-processed truths that Littlewood's actors created through the kind of stage moves and rhythms developed by Stanislavski methods.[3]

As resident playwright, Ewan MacColl was the driver of both Theatre Union and Theatre Workshop phases at a time when most revolutionary left-wing theatres dissolved for want of fresh and relevant material. The ensemble members also became skilled researchers for their documentary pieces, including the two living newspapers, *Newsboy* and *The Last Edition,* and later for the infamous *Oh What A Lovely War* (1963)—a cabaret satire of militarism and the Great War.[4]

In her notebook, Littlewood demanded: "Remember Lenin's words: 'If I know a little, I will endeavor to know more.' And we can never know enough about our job as revolutionary artists as the people who must sing of class struggle" (*Political Science Notebook*). In these notes, Littlewood compared Soviet proletariat audiences to the pit area crowds at the Elizabethan public playhouses, who were often amused by the plays they were watching, and she believed that the classics had to be re-interpreted in order to bring to the fore their revolutionary content. But unlike Elizabethan audiences, twentieth-century working-class audiences—Theatre Workshop's target audiences as they were—should be involved in the action, both physically and mentally, which accounts for the ad-libbing and other stage-audience bantering in Theatre Workshop productions. This approach reminds us of the company's agit-prop[5] background.

Agit-prop generally formed the backbone of the Workshop's performance strategies, so much so that Littlewood, in a private correspondence with MacColl, wrote that the production of *Oh What A Lovely War* (1963) "was agit-prop. I've never even got around to putting that on paper" (Letter to MacColl). As the main point of convergence between public space and political performance, the agit prop technique frequently fed the carnivalesque liveness of Theatre Workshop's stage and allowed it to maintain its original identity as a working-class theatre, ever alert to the materialist and historical forces in the streets. It is evident that the Theatre Workshop's legacy stretches wider and further than their acclaimed transfers to the West End would suggest and that their "longue durée" is evidence of the theatre ensemble's significant influence on theatre companies today.

Joan Littlewood

"The Theatre and Communism: Some Ideas Inspired by a Recent Visit to Czechoslovakia" (c. 1949)

Nearly half the world has emerged from the darkness of pre-history and is moving towards communism. The speed with which communism can be achieved in the new world is a matter of vital concern – in the interim period the artist bears a heavy responsibility. Under capitalism, art has served a relatively small section of the community; the artist's development has been a matter of concern to himself and his kind but seldom to society as a whole; revolutionary work has only been widely accepted long after its first vital impact has been softened by time.

History is changing the artist's position in society and the artist himself is called upon to change the old relationship between art and the people – a necessary step in the move towards a creative society in which all men and women may develop their mental attributes to the fullest extent. The artists' failure to assume this role may delay the process but the people in their progress towards complete emancipation will certainly find means of expression for themselves. Even the administration of an education designed merely to create efficient employees has not succeeded in destroying the underlying culture of the people.

In Britain the finest songs and poems of the past were written in a tradition which bore little relation to the work of the accepted poets. Those folk-works are technically the finest poetic expression in our language and the tradition is by no means dead. Today, whilst T.S. Eliot[6] dreams wistfully of a return to feudalism, young regional writers are using the language of the people to create a poetry greater than any we have ever known. The backward looking poets are standing on shrinking territory; their work becomes more introspective and abstract, writing as they do for themselves and their familiars.

Some of our peoples' poets have turned to the theatre because theatrical art has the power to revive the people's interest in their heritage. The theatre of many past periods has used the language and songs of the people, and, although theatrical form has changed from age to age, its elements have consistently been derived from manifold sources. Poetry, painting, architecture, dance, philosophy, and science, have all fed and inspired this "bastard art"; it is this mixed parentage, scorned by the purists, which has given the theatre its virility and flexibility. The cinema and radio have influenced the theatre but its fundamental quality is still its power to involve both audience and actor in a joint creative experience.

Theatrical art is most important in a period of historic transition; it has the power to break down the people's understandable prejudice against art; its flexibility and practical use of the arts can inspire young artists who have had no desire to work in the "art for art's sake" tradition: by its necessary use of cooperative talent it is a group art, and the development of a creative group in a community can only be assured by its participation in the life of that community.

Theatres fulfilling this function do not exist in Britain, although attempts are made from time to time to found them and keep them alive. At best the theatre is looked upon as an educational force, but in the narrow and therefore condescending sense of the word. It was therefore inspiring to read the following words in Václav Kopecký's speech, delivered at the Czech Congress of National Culture in April 1948:-

> "All we do is directed by the intention to popularise culture and to make it really accessible to all classes, even to those who in the past have been intentionally and inhumanly excluded from cultural life. We want to achieve a state of affairs where the people will crave for a collection of poems, for the sound of artistic music, for the view of a beautiful picture, and for a visit to the theatre, and where all hitherto inaccessible should become an absolute necessity."

This declaration reveals a new conception of life.

Kopecký speaks from a country where the people are already free, and his words are a prelude to action. Six months after those words were spoken, our company, Theatre Workshop, had the honour to participate in a Theatre Festival held in Prague in which at least fifty provincial Czech theatres appeared. Our northern English accents mingled with the speech of Bohemian, Moravian, and Slovak actors on the sunlit streets.

The festival was sponsored by "Art for the People" - Umêní Lidu - and we, side by side with our Czech colleagues, enjoyed their support and encouragement.

The festival attracted the people; they had the opportunity to compare standards and to enjoy the new achievements of their theatre. In the tumultuous welcome we received from our warm hearted audiences we felt their friendship for the ordinary English people whose lives we represented on the stage.

We learned a good deal about the work of Umêní Lidu, and in our four week's tour of Czechoslovakia we had the opportunity to study that work at first hand. What we heard and saw filled us with admiration and envy; the attitude of the Czech Government to the arts has made their land a veritable paradise for artists. We were astonished by the generous subsidies given to theatre, opera, and ballet; for instance, last year the National Theatre in Bratislava received a subsidy equal to that of the entire English theatre with the exception of the Covent Garden Opera House.

The Czech actor is free from unemployment, free from the necessity of earning a living by participating in inferior entertainment. He has economic security, leisure, accommodation provided for him, and the opportunity to play to the working people. He is an honoured citizen, privileged to help in the building of a new life.

In America, where commercial entertainment has become one of the country's main industries, 80% of the actors are unemployed: in England no official figures are available because of the haphazard nature of theatrical employment here, but we know that the problem of unemployment is acute; each week hundreds more film workers are declared redundant.

There are 32 permanent state subsidized theatres in Czechoslovakia: as I write, the English government is discussing a bill to authorise the construction of our first national theatre; today a Tory Peer objected to the luxury.

The Czech Theatre is part of the national heritage of the people. It came into being as a revolt against oppression and the dominance of a foreign culture. Many of its artists gave their lives in the resistance to the Nazis.

English actors fought and died in the same battle, yet on Sunday the 13th February 1949, the English actors' trade union endorsed the T.U.C.'s black circular inaugurating the witch hunt against communism. Arts Council, financed by a Labour government, helps a company of Basil Dean's[7] which is presenting a play, "Private Enterprise," the most bitter attack on trades unionism seen on the English stage in living memory.

Many examples could be given to show that the British theatre is mainly reactionary and artistically feeble; the general standard of political and artistic integrity is markedly low. There is dissatisfaction among the actors but unfortunately this does not find expression in any strong, independent movement against commercial theatre. Taking into account the stranglehold which commercial agents and managements have on our theatres, it is obvious that any such movement would find it difficult to survive. Their only solution would be to attract a large new audience from the workers, but these do not have the money, opportunity, nor inclination, to visit the theatre.

Czechoslovakia too has had to face the problem of attracting the people to the theatre. Organisationally they have faced the problem brilliantly, but it is also an artistic problem. Cinema, radio, and football matches are the only forms of mass entertainment in England. As a result, their technique is much more developed than that of the theatre which atrophied here many years ago. The working people have an instinctive appreciation of good technique, acquired in their education at the loom, coal face, or engineering bench. The theatre must make similar advances, becoming as mobile as a film production or a football game, and supplying auditory stimulus equal to that of radio technique.

There is a frequent condemnation of experiment among Czech regisseurs [directors]. In confusing experimental work with the precious "art for art's sake" of western art theatres, they are making a grave mistake. True experiment is synonymous with progress: the Czech theatre must make social and artistic experiments if it is to reveal the creative instincts of the people. The progressive proletariat is never opposed to experiment in industry or social life when such experiment is directed towards the solution of society's problems. The workers' brigades of Czechoslovakia are experimental, they embody a new conception of leisure, of freedom itself. The experimental theatre under capitalism has merely been directed against artistic and thematic conventions. Under socialism experiment must be directed towards the liberation of a new class of artists.

The Czech theatre must develop a new dramaturgy; this is a vital problem. In Prague last autumn there were 4 productions of Shakespeare's plays, 3 modern American plays, and a Russian play: In Brno, a Polish and a Shakespeare play. This was to some extent typical of all the towns we visited. An international attitude to art is stimulating and necessary, but side by side with it the national and regional expression of the people must develop. It was unfortunate that the only Czech product we saw was a mediocre work, "Krőma na Břehu" by E.F.Burian, reminiscent of the English 'well-made play' tradition.

It is also unfortunate that the plays imported from abroad do not, for the most part, serve to widen international appreciation; they merely import a bad tradition: In the case of the Shakespearian productions a tradition mercifully dead even in England. I refer to the 19th century Romantic style which was employed at the Prague and Brno National Theatres; a style calculated to rob the play of any life or meaning it might have today. There is some socially dynamic writing even in the worst Shakespearian play; some of it can be related to the problems of our own time; certainly in a socialist theatre you would expect it to be related at least to the environment in which it was written. Instead the plays were produced as period pantomimes.

The great works of the past must not only be preserved, they must be shown to the people in their true light, not cluttered with the paraphernalia of the ages. They must be shown in their relationship to the social history of man.

In the market places of Czechoslovakia we saw cheap pottery richly and beautifully designed: In the villages we saw small houses so painted and decorated that we imagined a master artist had been at work: in country churches, Sunday dresses, gingerbread cakes, and shop windows, we saw the good taste and innate artistry of the Czech people: we heard songs more lovely than any we had ever known: on every hand the creative spirit of the people was expressed, but as yet, this great artistry has not found expression in the theatre.

Umění Lidu has only just begun its work; the tasks it has set itself are tremendous and inspiring, they can only be achieved by the fullest cooperation of all the artists. They will not be achieved in clever critics' columns, nor in café discussions; but in the villages and factories each place will yield its harvest of genius. The artists must devote themselves to the creation of cultural centres where every stimulus is provided for the furtherance of art.

The complete liberation of the people is at hand and a new art will be born. If the artists of Czechoslovakia are to speed this renaissance their eyes must not be centred on the brilliant intellectual life of the capital, but rather on the lonely ploughman in the fields, the miner at the coal face. Let their inspiration come from the poignant songs of the land of their birth, from the unnamed men and women of the May and February days[8], from the landscapes of their beautiful country and the simple daily achievement in the factory and farmland.

A thousand new forms will arise like the songs of the future, and they will come from that deep understanding of life which is in the men and women who work quietly for the new world. It is their belief and their courage which has made communism possible, and from them in the fullness of time, the new art will be born.

Please see the Works Cited for further information on the sources used in this essay.

Notes

1 The Workers' Theatre Movement (WTM) is the collective term for revolutionary left-wing theatre groups in the interwar period in the USSR, Germany, Britain, and the United States. The WTM of the 1920s and 1930s built upon existing traditions of radical theatre, particularly in Germany and Britain.

2 Trades Union Congress (TUC) is a national trades union center in England and Wales, representing the majority of trade unions.

3 Christoph Laban (Rudolph Laban, 1879–1958) is the forefather of Labanotation, the system used to arrange and preserve the staging of dances. Konstantin Stanislavski (1863–1938) created a groundbreaking system for training actors to create truthful, believable characters.

4 For information on Living Newspapers, see the Hallie Flanagan entry in this volume.
5 The term "agit prop," short for "agitation and propaganda," refers to an intentional, vigorous promotion of usually political ideas.
6 T. S. Eliot (1888–1965), best known for his poems "The Love Song of J. Alfred Prufrock" and *The Waste Land*, was also an essayist and playwright.
7 Basil Dean (1888–1978), British actor, director, and producer.
8 Littlewood refers here to May 1, International Workers' Day, and the Russian February Revolution against monarchy in 1917.

Suggestions for Further Reading

British Library Theatre Archive Project interviews with Theatre Workshop members, Brian Murphy, Joan Plowright, Murray Melvin, Peter Rankin, Harry Greene. https://www.bl.uk/collections/theatre-archive-project?searchTerm=Theatre+Archive+Project&firstCall=true&page=1&sort=recentlyadded&view=gridview&collection=true.

Goorney, Howard. *The Theatre Workshop Story.* London: E. Methuen, 1981.

Holdsworth, Nadine. *Joan Littlewood's Theatre.* Cambridge: Cambridge University Press, 2011.

Leach, Robert. *Theatre Workshop: Joan Littlewood and the Making of Modern British Theatre.* Exeter: University of Exeter Press, 2006.

Littlewood, Joan. *Joan's Book: Joan Littlewood's Peculiar History As She Tells It.* London: Methuen, 1994.

Samuel, Raphael et al. eds. *Theatres of the Left, 1880–1935 Workers' Theatres Movements in Britain and America.* London: Routledge and Kegan Paul, 1985.

43 ALICE CHILDRESS (1916–1994)

Meenakshi Ponnuswami

Introduction

Alice Childress's (1916–1994) reputation has been overshadowed by that of her celebrated peers Lorraine Hansberry and Adrienne Kennedy,[1] but her views on aesthetics and politics are critical to understanding mid-century African American theatre. Childress's plays and drama theory were grounded in forty years of experience as a playwright and practitioner, beginning with the American Negro Theatre in 1941. Close to the Harlem Left through the 1940s and 50s, she was deeply committed to "portraying have-nots in a *have* society" ("A Candle" 112). At the same time, Childress's "central theme of black self-determination" (Dugan 124), her emphasis on the artist's responsibility to the community, and her long-standing support for a national Black people's theatre were consonant with nationalist arts philosophies of the 1960s.

Childress's views on theatre were finessed over decades in articles she published in prominent magazines, including *Freedomways, Masses and Mainstream*, and *Negro Digest*. These essays show her evolving concerns with women's experience, the lives of the poor, the racism of the theatre industry, and the need for a vibrant theatre to represent the experiences of common people and to serve as a beacon for Black communities. They reflect also her engagement with long-standing theoretical concerns in African American theatre, springing from the storied 1920s "Art vs. Protest" debates between W. E. B. Du Bois and Alain Locke[2]: whether theatre should agitate and propagandize to arouse white consciences, or focus sharply on the arts, cultures, lives, and needs of African Americans (Hay 4–5; Miller 57–59). Childress was committed to both: a theatre that directly addressed Black audiences, depicting the struggles and joys of ordinary lives and fostering "'positive self-respect and self-reliance'" (Locke, qtd. in Hay 21), as well as a theatre of "protest" and "propaganda" that exposed the crushing reality of racism and other social problems.

Such concerns are apparent as early as 1951 in Childress's essay, "For a Negro Theatre," excerpted here. Childress explains that while she once believed "a Negro theatre" sounded like "a Jim Crow institution,"[3] she has come to recognize the importance of separate spaces for Black culture. The essay anticipates the concerns of her later work in urging young artists "to depict the Negro people" authentically: "We must not only examine African art, but turn our eyes toward our neighbors, the community, the domestic workers, porters, white-collar workers, churches, lodges and institutions" (62). Childress cautions that only a large, strong "Negro people's theatre" will be "powerful enough to inspire, lift, and eventually create a complete desire for the liberation of all oppressed peoples" (63). Childress's 1953 essay, "A Candle in

DOI: 10.4324/9781003006923-44

a Gale Wind"—also excerpted here—similarly advocates theatres that center "Black experience" (112) and cautions against allowing fear of white judgement to censor expression (114).

Childress offers what Mary Helen Washington calls a "racialized radicalism," a "vision of this new theatre [that] is multicultural, black-centered, and internationalist: [...] possessed of the desire 'for the liberation of all oppressed people'" (Washington 130). These essays were written in the heyday of Childress's involvement with the Harlem Left, including Du Bois and Paul Robeson, with whom Childress shared an office and for whose paper *Freedom* she wrote her popular "Mildred" columns; in 1952, her play *Gold Through the Trees* provoked an FBI report on her leftist associations. However, as Washington notes, the essays also reveal Childress "adapting and revising the cultural and political imperatives of the Left, something she would do for the rest of her creative life" (130).

During the 1960s, Childress, along with other members of the organized Black Left, moved towards the mainstream of the Black liberation movements.[4] Her writing remained focused on the "have-nots": her 1965 speech "The Negro Woman in American Literature," excerpted here, tackles representations of Black women in the Moynihan Report,[5] and her essays of 1968 and 1969 address the conflicting imperatives of wanting to work within a separate "black theatre" while also needing to survive economically in a white-powered society. These latter articles communicate a new militancy and despair, reflecting the mood of the period. In her January 1968 interview, Childress remarks: "Meanwhile, we have no theaters ... or any other means of production [...] and any attempt to 'buy our own' puts us in the position where they can cut off our supply lines, via unions and real estate holdings, at a moment's notice" ("Black Writers' View" 86). Her 1969 essay, excerpted here, signals a similar urgency: "The theater must reflect, to some degree, that we live in a land where no white man has ever been executed for the murder of a black man, woman, or child, not one. A culture can be no better than the people from whom it springs." Nevertheless, she argues, although "integration" is an illusion, Black artists should continue to work "within the so-called 'mainstream'" to "avoid swallowing the hook thrown to the American Indian: 'You'll be able to thrive and prosper on your *very own reservation*, surrounded by us'" ("But I Do" D9).

Like her essays, Childress's plays reflect the evolution of her theory of Black radical performance: *Florence* (1949) and *Trouble in Mind* (1955) examine racism and sexism in theatre; *String* and *Mojo, A Black Love Story* (1969–1970) tackle class conflict within Black communities. Most notably, her 1968 play *Wine in the Wilderness* offers a stinging critique of sexism and uncritical pan-Africanism, accusing the urban bourgeoisie of marginalizing working-class African Americans, particularly women, in the post-Civil Rights era (Dugan 129–131). Its heroine, Tomorrow Marie, or "Tommy," is a working-class woman whom Childress reclaims from the Moynihan Report, portraying a strong, independent, dignified woman whose moral clarity and integrity force the middle-class characters to recognize their own class prejudices. Childress sketched a template for Tommy in her 1965 speech on "The Negro Woman in American Literature," which critiques the Moynihan report's allegation that the strength of Black women emasculates Black men. Childress laments that Black women's strength has been misrepresented and demonized, urging artists to celebrate Black women's lives and stories, their "constant, unrelenting struggle against racism and for human rights" (19).

The excerpts included here span eighteen years of Childress's career, when she was immersed in the cultural and political life of Harlem. She stressed the importance of a philosophy of Black arts with nationalist and Black Power underpinnings and authentic working-class roots. Addressing artists and the intelligentsia, Childress championed forms of cultural activism deeply connected to Black working-class experience and respectful of the knowledge, creativity, and beauty of "everyday" people.

Alice Childress

Excerpt from "For a Negro Theatre" (1951)[6]

[...] Where is truth? Where are the schools that will teach us Negro art forms? We must create them and devote time, study and research toward the understanding and projection of Negro culture.

We must not only examine African art, but turn our eyes toward our neighbors, the community, the domestic workers, porters, laborers, white-collar workers, churches, lodges and institutions. We must look closely and search for the understanding which will enable us to depict the Negro people.

I have learned that I must watch my people in railroad stations, in restaurants, in the fields and tenements, at the factory wheels, in the stores, on the subway. I have watched and found that there is none so blind as he who will not see.

My people walk in beauty, their feet singing along the pavement; my people walk as if their feet hurt, in hand-me-down shoes; some of my people walk in shoes with bunion pockets, shoes with slits cut for the relief of corns; and the children walk on feet that are growing out of their shoes; and my people walk without shoes.

My people move so gently and jostle rudely; they step gingerly, they walk hard; they move along with abandon and show defiance and there are some who move timidly.

I love them all but I love most those who walk as they would walk, caring nothing for impressions or fears or suppressions [...] those who walk with a confident walk. These things we must learn to duplicate.

My people stand weary with fatigue, half asleep, in the subway, my people have been scrubbing floors and washing walls and emptying, carrying, fetching, lifting, cooking, sweeping, shining, and polishing and ironing, washing, ironing, washing. But they fight drowsiness. No one must say they are lazy or sleepy or slow. What could be a more fruitful study in the craft of acting than to reproduce one of these weary people?

My people smile and think of death, frown and think of life, laugh and think of nothing. My people show a face calm and smooth and think of great plans, they pass by quietly and take great action. They pass each other and without speaking, say: I know, I understand.

My people eat scraps that we their children may grow strong in the face of adversity. We eat pig's tails, and feet and ears: we will not die. My people drink champagne and eat caviar and enjoy these things with a special enjoyment because we know there are those who do not wish us to have them and would keep everything for themselves. My people wear furs and diamonds and cast-offs and old tattered jackets.

My people hope, build, love, hate, cater, plan and struggle. We watch the newspapers to see if some foreign power is worrying the rulers of the United States into giving a few of our people a "break" in order to offset the "propaganda."

These things and countless others must be a part of our training that we may develop and grow into real people's artists. We must be sure that through our interpretation the world and our next-door neighbor may see and view the Negro people.

Yes, we need a Negro people's theatre but it must not be a little theatre. Its work is too heavy, its task is too large to be anything other than a great movement. It must be powerful enough to inspire, lift, and eventually create a complete desire for the liberation of all oppressed peoples.

The Negro people's theatre must not condemn what it does not understand. We must seek out every artistic expression and if it does not conform to our present mode of production, we must examine it closely to see if it is a new form or some vague whispering from the past. We must be the guide and light the way to all that we may glean [sic] the precious stuff from that which is useless. We must be patient and, above all, ever-searching. We should, in this second half of the century, plan to turn out the largest crop of Negro artists in the entire history of America. Our voices must be heard around the world. The Negro people's theatre must study and teach not only what has been taught before but found and establish a new approach to study of the Negro in the theatre, dance and arts. We shall take advantage of the rich culture of the Chinese, Japanese, Russian and all theatres. We shall study oppressed groups which have no formal theatre as we know it, but we must discover theatre as they know it.

Last but not least, there should be courses in the cultural background of the minority groups in this country. We must never be guilty of understanding only ourselves. [...] [T]here will be no progress in art without peace, a lasting peace throughout the world.

Excerpt from "A Candle in a Gale Wind" (1953/56)

[...] I recall teachers urging me to write composition papers about Blacks who were "accomplishers"—those who win prizes and honors by overcoming cruel odds; the victory might be won over racial, physical, economic, or other handicaps but the end result had to inspire the reader/audience to become "winners." [...] I turned against the tide and to this day I continue to write about those who come in second, or not at all—[...] the intricate and magnificent patterns of a loser's life. No matter how many celebrities we may accrue, they cannot substitute for the masses of human beings. My writing attempts to interpret the "ordinary" because they are not ordinary. Each human is uniquely different. Like snowflakes, the human pattern is never cast twice. We are uncommonly and marvelously intricate in thought and action, our problems are most complex and, too often, silently borne.

I concentrate on portraying have-nots in a *have* society, those seldom singled out by mass media, except as source material for derogatory humor and/or condescending clinical, social analysis. Politically I see my Black experience, my characters, and myself in very special circumstances. Participation in political parties has not given us power and authority over our lives. We remain in the position of petitioners, or at best pressure groups trying to plead and press one faction against another. [...]

The Black writer explains pain to those who inflict it. [...]

Artists are economically tempted away from serious topics. The Black artist finds most opportunity and reward in the field of ludicrous comedy, refuge in laughter. That labeled "serious and controversial" is silently considered dangerous ground.

[...] Writers are encouraged to "keep 'em laughing" and complain "with good humor" in order to "win" allies. The joke is always on ourselves. [...]

As long as we are subliminally trained to recognize other racial feelings above our own, our ideas are in danger of being altered even before they are written. It becomes almost second nature to be on guard against the creative pattern of our own thought. Shall I ease in this bit of truth or that? Perhaps I can make a small point in the midst of a piece of nonsense. We often make a great noise in the other direction and try to "mouth whitey to death"; blowing off steam can be a grand but harmless substitute for even small action. Self-censorship also knows how to disguise itself in long, strong, pointless diatribes against ourselves. "We don't vote! We don't know how to take a joke! We don't need to speak Black English!" [...]

Excerpt from "The Negro Woman in American Literature" (1965)[7]

I agree that the Negro woman has almost been omitted as important subject matter in the general popular American drama, television, motion pictures and radio; except for the constant, but empty and decharacterized faithful servant. And her finest virtues have been drawn in terms of long suffering, with humility and patience.

Today, the Negro woman's faults are sometimes pointed out, that she is too militant, so domineering, so aggressive, with son, husband and brother, that it is one of the chief reasons for any unexpressed manhood on the part of the black man in America.

There must be some truth in this charge. The mother in James Baldwin's *Amen Corner* attempts to restrict her son and husband to her passive and withdrawn way of life, but fails. The husband abandons her and seeks to find himself in music. He returns home to die, then advises the son she has raised to break free of her gentle domination. The son leaves home.

In Lorraine Hansberry's *A Raisin in the Sun*, the strong, loving mother so dominates the home that she restricts her children and infringes upon the rights of her son as a man.

In Louis Peterson's *Take a Giant Step*, a Negro mother tries to separate her son from his black heritage in order to shield him from the realities of life.

All Negro writers have written; [*sic*] first, about that strong, matriarchal figure. I did in a one-act play, *Florence*, and in *Trouble in Mind*.

But now we frequently hear that strength has taken femininity away from her with the end result that she is the main culprit in any lack of expressed black manhood, and that she has been masculinized in the process.

Certainly this is too easy and too misleading a conclusion. We know that most alien visitors are guaranteed rights and courtesies not extended to at least one-fifth of America's citizens. They are entitled to travel, without restriction, reside in hotels, eat at restaurants and enter public and private places closed to Americans who have built up the country under bondage and defended it under a limited and restricted liberty.

But the American Negro woman has been *particularly* and deliberately oppressed, in slavery and up to and including the present moment, above and beyond the general knowledge of the average American citizen. [...]

Writers, be wary of those who tell you to leave the past alone and confine yourselves to the present moment. Our story has not been told in any moment.

Have you seen us in any portrayal of the Civil War? *Gone With the Wind* is not our story. And our history is not gone with the wind, it is still with us. [...]

Because [her husband] could offer no protection or security, the Negro woman has worked with and for her family. She built churches, schools, homes, temples and college educations out of soapsuds and muscle.

It seems a contradiction for a woman to be degraded by law, and by popular opinion which was shaped and formed by that law, and yet also take her rightful place as the most heroic figure to emerge on the American scene, with more stamina than that shown by any pioneer.

Finally, I would like to say, today we hear so much about the *new Negro*. As though we never breathed a protest until a few years ago.

But the story of the old Negro has not been told.

Denmark Vesey, Francis Watkins Harper, Monroe Trotter—if their true stories were told, there would not be so many school drop-outs.

Who wants to sit in a classroom and be taught that he is nobody?

The Negro woman will attain her rightful place in American literature when those of us who care about truth, justice and a better life tell her story, with the full knowledge and appreciation of her constant, unrelenting struggle against racism and for human rights.

Excerpt from "The Black Experience: 'Why Talk About That?'" (1967)[8]

[...] People tend to ask, "why write about *that?*"–*That* usually stands for the possibility of controversy, which has a way of stemming from themes on race or interracial conflict, when presented in a land which abounds in racist law and racism. But no matter how much has been seen and heard about *that*, little of it has come from the American writer of African descent. Only 16 of his plays have reached Broadway in the last 40 years, only two were made into films—*A Raisin In The Sun* by Lorraine Hansberry and *Purlie Victorious* by Ossie Davis.

It seems evident that theatre audiences have not been exposed to a great deal of controversial—or any other kind—[of] drama created by the Afro-American playwright. Sixteen plays, over such a period of time, constitute a very small percentage of the thousands presented on the big street in the art center of the U. S. A., New York City, N. Y.

Much more work has seen the light of day on the stages of Off-Broadway and in community theatres improvised in churches, libraries and meeting halls. These productions have reached only a small section of the public and, as a result, we hear little, if anything, about them—except from those scholars who devote time and energy to researching the subject.

[...]

Our dramatists have not had a wider viewing because we, as a people, have not had the power to decisively determine the quality and quantity of our participation in Theater, Television, Radio and Films, which power would enable us to portray life as we see it. Also, those who have the power and the means of production seem, at best, constrained to move slowly and to keep pace with the advances, or set-backs, of the national struggle for human and civil rights.

The characters in a play may be made of impressions gathered from old or new incidents, conversations, disconnected words, and sense-memories of physical characteristics and human emotions. They are created and constructed of what hurts and what heals, slowly built and put in order out of the conflict which comes from the daily search for bread, love, and a place in the sun. The best characters are good and true, cowardly and brave, miserable and happy, filled with the virtues and weaknesses found in ourselves; they grow stronger and more insistent in the mind of the writer, they cancel each other out until the right story and the right people emerge and blend into one predominant idea or theme. [...]

After the first or second draft of the script, there comes a time when all the earmarks of preachment must be searched out and removed, all that has been superimposed by the writer, all that the characters deny and refuse to accept, anything that smacks of pamphleteering on the subject. Out come some of your favorite bits and pieces—the idiom of speech never used by those characters who people your work. You are taxed to show them as they are, beautiful in a way not yet merchandised by Madison Avenue. [...]

The American of African descent has produced the only new music which came out of the New World—Spirituals, Gospel, and Jazz. I firmly believe that for him, the "protest" play will reach new heights in form and content, become ever more finished in craftsmanship, and eventually prove to be the most varied and original theatre on the American scene. The times dictate the trend. We are at a moment in history when the playwright cannot turn away from social drama without abandoning the search for truth.

Excerpt from "Black Writers' Views on Literary Lions and Values" (1968)[9]

[...] black audiences are not always waiting with open arms for every word we have to say. Many of them listen with a 'white' ear ... they want us to say just enough but not too much. They often listen for what will *offend* the white 'friend' – or enemy. It is not the simplest thing in the world to write for a black audience. Our black audiences also evaluate us *according to the recognition given to us by white society* ... They are grateful and hopeful for a better future for themselves every time a black artist or sportsman receives accolades from whites. Very often they believe that the whites are simply waiting for more and more achievement from us ... before the gates swing wide and we all walk in. If we were all to face what exactly white society has done and is doing to us ... and what it plans to do in the future, it would be too gloomy a picture to bear with any kind of patience. We are in a subservient position ... the smallest and the greatest of us. We have cajoled, pleaded, tommed, protested, achieved, rioted, defied, unified ... you name it! But white supremacists have dug their heels into the ground and will settle for nothing less than out-right confrontation in the streets of America. Welfare and "poverty program" are the white power's answer to our demand for freedom. Meanwhile, we feed upon each other and hungrily pick unbuttered crumbs from Massa's table. Meanwhile, we have no theaters ... or any other means of production ... and any attempt to "buy our own" puts us in the position where they can cut off our supply lines, via unions and real estate holdings, at a moment's notice. There is no artist among us whose individual success will free the rest of us. There is no substitute for human rights ... not even art. [...] The plaster now being slapped on our wounds is welfare and "poverty program," which is another and more subtle attack. This society tells us they would rather support us as charity cases than to open the doors and let us win or fail, live or die, as full citizens of this country. If one lacks an "appreciative" attitude about this, then "You are bitter"

... We can be bitter or *numb*; there is no other choice. A Negro without feeling (numb) seems to survive a few moments longer than we who are bitter. [...]

Excerpt from "But I Do My Thing" (1969)[10]

Dialogue stops but communication never ceases. A black theater here and there does not signify "turning away" from commercial television, motion picture and theater markets of the U.S.A. It is one reaction to being *turned away*. There *is* a white theater. White theaters do not hang out signs reading "The White Ensemble Company" or "The American White Theater" or "The Anglo-Saxon Players"; but they do present hundreds of plays every year, written, directed, acted, designed, produced and patronized, almost exclusively, by white persons. This white theater is not a plot to establish separatism, it *is* separatism. This theater functions even though the greater part of what it turns out fails.

Black communities have always had black theaters, if the community had a theater at all. The American Negro Theater Company worked ten years without salary, four nights per week, keeping the same acting company together, until the boot-straps wore out. [...] Yes, we do need theaters for African-Americans, we will continue to need them, even when, if ever, this land is free of racism. Theater serves as the mirror of life experience and reflects only what looks into it; everyone yearns to see his own image once in a while. But there are two trick-bags of thought to be avoided concerning the theater within and outside of the black community.

Some believe that any attempt to work within the so-called "mainstream" of American life is an attempt to "be with *them*," or to be "integrated." This fear of total integration is an illusion. I've never yet met a black person who has been integrated into white society; he may think so, he may hope so, but it just ain't so. If any of us, at this point in time, believe such nonsense, we're suffering from a severe form of hallucination.

The inner-city must also avoid swallowing the hook thrown to the American Indian: "You'll be able to thrive and prosper on your *very own reservation*, surrounded by us." If we don't learn anything from history, we must relive the past. The time is over for asking or even demanding human rights, in or out of the theater. We no longer *ask* for manhood or womanhood or dignity; all we can do is express what we have to the degree that we have it. All whites aren't bad or good, the same goes for blacks – but this fact equalizes nothing. The whole racism mess is based upon the action of white supremacist deed and thought.

The theater must reflect, to some degree, that we live in a land where no white man has ever been executed for the murder of a black man, woman, or child, not one. A culture can be no better than the people from whom it springs. [...] *In the past 40 years only 18 plays by black writers have been presented on Broadway.* Soon we may have to read our works on the sidewalks of inner-city *and* "mainstream" Broadway. Time is up. I've a play to write that may never be seen by any audience anywhere, but I do my thing. Who has ears to hear, hear ... all others, later.

Please see the Works Cited for further information on the sources used in this essay.

Notes

1 Lorraine Hansberry's (1930 –1965) *A Raisin in the Sun* (1959) was the first play by an African American woman to be produced on Broadway. See, also, entry on Adrienne Kennedy in this volume.

2 W.E.B. DuBois (1868–1963) was a seminal African American theorist and social critic, known especially for *The Souls of Black Folk* (1903), which argued that voting and civil rights were less important to Black progress than acquiring property and material security, even as he believed that capitalism was a primary cause of racism. Alain Locke (1885–1991) was called the "Father of the Harlem Renaissance" because his publication, *The New Negro* (1925)—an anthology of poetry, essays, plays, music, and portraits by white and black artists—drew attention to the enormous literary and artistic achievements of African Americans.

3 After the end of the American Civil War and the start of Reconstruction (1865), "Jim Crow" laws were enacted at the state and federal levels to legalize racial segregation in schools, voting booths, political offices, and elsewhere.

4 See Washington 146 ff.

5 The 1965 analysis of U.S. Black poverty written by Secretary of Labor, Daniel Patrick Moynihan, "The Negro Family: The Case For National Action," better known as the Moynihan Report, notoriously and problematically characterized Black single mothers as integral to these economic issues.

6 Childress frames this essay as a response to Ted (Theodore) Ward, a prominent playwright of the 1930s and 40s and a founder and editorial board member of the left-wing periodical *Masses and Mainstream*, where this essay was published. While Childress initially expressed skepticism about Ward's advocacy of a "Negro theatre," dismissing it as "a Jim Crow institution" (61), she then explains why she now, in 1951, champions the idea.

7 This article is a transcript of a speech that Childress read at a New School for Social Research conference on "The Negro Writer's Vision of America" in 1965. An audio recording can be found at Internet Archive, https://archive.org/details/pacifica_radio_archives-BB5284B. Churchill's presentation appears in Part 2.

8 This essay was published in a special edition of *Negro Digest* (later *Black World/Negro Digest*), its second annual Theatre Issue, which also featured articles by LeRoi Jones (and his new play *Slave Ship*), Ronald Milner, Woodie King Jr., and other prominent practitioners. Childress here also discusses her controversial 1966 play *The Wedding Band*, which depicts an interracial love story set in South Carolina in 1918.

9 "Black Writers' Views on Literary Lions and Values: Writers Symposium" was an edited compilation of responses to a questionnaire sent by *Negro Digest* to 38 Black writers, including Childress. The writers were asked about "the books and writers which have influenced them, the writers who are 'most important' to them in terms of achievement and promise, and what they think about the new movement toward a 'black aesthetic' and the preoccupation with 'the black experience,' aspects of the larger Black Consciousness Movement" (10).

10 Childress's piece was written for the *New York Times*'s 1969 feature "Can Black and White Artists Still Work Together?", which also included responses by James Baldwin, Barbara Ann Teer, Harold Cruse, Douglas Turner Ward, Harry Belafonte, and others.

Suggestions for Further Reading

blackchild, cfrancis. "Signifying in the Wilderness: Alice Childress and the Black Arts Movement." *Journal of American Drama and Theatre*. 25:1 (Winter 2013): 27–54.

Brown-Guillory, Elizabeth. *Their Place on the Stage: Black Women Playwrights in America*. New York: Greenwood Press, 1988.

Childress, Alice. *Selected Plays*. Ed. Kathy Perkins. Evanston: Northwestern University Press, 2011.

44 ANN JELLICOE (1927–2017)

Kate Pierson

Introduction

Ann Jellicoe's (1927–2017) career parallels the development of postwar British theatre. She entered the London theatre scene after graduating from the Royal Central
School of Speech and Drama in 1948 and continued to produce theatre by way of her
community plays through the early 1990s. As a practitioner working within the institution of British theatre, Jellicoe witnessed and participated in many of the moments
seen by historians as shaping the narratives of postwar British theatre history—the
establishment of the Arts Council England in 1946; the creation of the English Stage
Company at the Royal Court Theatre in 1956; the end of censorship by the Lord
Chamberlain in 1968; the rise of feminist theatre in the 1970s; the explosion of alternative theatre forms during the 1970s through the 1990s; and the crippling impacts
of Margaret Thatcher's[1] funding cuts to the arts in the 1980s.

Jellicoe contributed to British theatre for more than forty years, driven by her
fascination with the unconscious forces that shape the theatrical experience.
She was an artistic magpie—continually creating productions from a variety
of perspectives—which resulted in her career defying easy placement into the
dominant narratives. She wrote, directed, designed, taught, and produced theatre as a vehicle for furthering her exploration of the relationship between
theatrical space, actors, text, and spectators.

In 1951, Jellicoe founded the Cockpit Theatre Club. Jellicoe used the Cockpit to
explore the actor-audience-space relationship. She opted to put on plays in an open-
stage layout: imagine an Elizabethan thrust, which for the period was an unusual
choice for productions. At the Cockpit, she took on all the roles needed to operate
a theatre company: writer, director, dramaturg, actor, manager, producer, designer,
etc. Her next big career transition happened in 1956, when she won third place in
The Observer's playwriting contest for *The Sport of My Mad Mother* (1958). Prominent
theatre critic Kenneth Tynan organized the contest to discover new voices for the
postwar British stage, and Jellicoe's play was produced at the Royal Court with her
and Court artistic director, George Devine, co-directing.

While scholars, such as Philip Roberts, Baz Kershaw, Dan Rebellato, and Michelene
Wandor typically describe Jellicoe as a playwright,[2] I argue that she should be
described as a total theatre-maker. Although she wrote plays in many different dramaturgical forms, she did so with the intention of creating directing opportunities for
herself. She also used these occasions to discover connections between the form of
a play and how it impacts the theatrical experience. Over the course of her career,

DOI: 10.4324/9781003006923-45

she wrote: an experimental movement-driven play (*The Sport of My Mad Mother*, 1958); a four-person sex satire (*The Knack*, 1962); a piece for the Girl Guides of Britain intended for a cast of over a thousand children and teenagers (*The Rising Generation*, 1967); a historical drama about the Romantic poet, Percy Bysshe Shelley (*Shelley; Or the Idealist*, 1965); an "absurdist farce," as described by Baz Kershaw (*The Giveaway*, 1969); a couple of children's plays (*Two Jelli-plays*, 1974); and several large-scale community plays, *The Reckoning* (1978), *The Tide* (1980), *The Western Women* (1984), and a few others. Each play presented her with new challenges, which she thrived on.

Jellicoe left London in the mid-1970s and entered into the community play phase of her work. The community play represents a culmination of her practical research and the point where she unified her theory and practice to create the theatrical experience she sought. Starting in 1978, in coastal Dorset County in southwest England, Jellicoe produced more than eleven large scale community plays over the course of the decade. She wrote three of the plays, directed six of the productions, and aimed for the plays to recount local history. In addition, she and other commissioned playwrights found inspiration in the archives and embodied memories of townspeople. The plays featured cast sizes of over a hundred people, and more than a couple of hundred people would help behind the scenes. Jellicoe drew on her network of London practitioners to bring amateur actors together with professional playwrights, directors, and designers.

Shifting to Jellicoe's theoretical ideas, I want to underscore that she first articulated her insights about the unconscious forces at play in the theatrical experience during a lecture at Cambridge University in 1967 titled "Some Unconscious Influences in the Theatre." She delivered this lecture at the midpoint in her career—after working at the Cockpit and writing/directing several shows at the Royal Court. This lecture can be read as an indication of her future work and the ways in which her ideas on theatrical experience would start to take shape.

In "Some Unconscious Influences," Jellicoe reflects on how an audience reaction to a play can impact the communal theatrical experience. She recalls that her feelings about *The Knack*, her 1962 sex satire, changed as she traveled around England watching other people react to the play. Even though she was the author, depending on the audience she vacillated between seeing her play as fresh and funny, then innocent, or finally obscene. By the time Jellicoe developed her community plays in the 1980s, she had moved beyond observing spectators to implementing her discoveries in her productions. To name a few examples: she wrote plays that were relevant to the local community; she focused on recruiting the townspeople to help during the research and production process; she gave actors creative agency during rehearsals; and she staged the play in an open area that allowed audiences to promenade around the space. By combining these dramaturgical and production techniques, Jellicoe created an immersive theatrical experience for all involved.

After refining her community play methodology, she wrote a guidebook, *Community Plays and How to Put Them On* (1987). While the book is organized as an instruction manual, it is infused with Jellicoe's broader theories about crafting a communal theatrical experience. Reassessing Jellicoe's practical work alongside her writings—"Some Unconscious Influences" and *Community Plays*—illustrates Jellicoe's lifelong interest in the relationship between the performance space, production style and audience reception, and they provide a new lens through which to view her postwar British theatre contributions.

Ann Jellicoe

Excerpt from "Some Unconscious Influences in the Theatre" (1967)

[. . .] But I would suggest that for most artists creating a work of art is also indissolubly searching for truth; and that art is less a process of creation than a process of discovery: the work demands and creates itself, the artist merely waits attentively for the work to reveal itself. But this also demands that the artist ask certain questions, answer certain problems in seeking to discover the nature of the work. And in his struggle the artist makes discoveries which release energy, excitement and enthusiasm which give his work power. The power of a work springs directly from its truth. The work having been created there is then an urgent desire to show it to other people. Artists must communicate. A work of art is not complete until it reaches its audience.

All art demands its audience but the audience is especially important in the theatre. In the theatre the audience cannot have an individual reaction, and their corporate reaction swamps individual judgement in a manner, and to a degree, I wouldn't have thought possible if I hadn't had the experience of travelling round the provinces on tour with my own play, seeing a familiar work with different audiences, and observing how those audiences affected my judgement of the work. The theatrical experience is not merely the experience of the play, but of experiencing it in company with the rest of the audience who colour the event to a degree of which one is largely unconscious. [. . .]

Working as author or director I have often moved round a theatre during performance and noted that the stalls are indifferent while the balcony is enjoying itself. You will even find small pockets of reaction, their influence spreading for a few seats around and then falling off. The physical shape of a theatre is most important—too vast a subject to consider here; basically if you can't see or hear very well you may not be so deeply involved, unless there is a compensating strong audience reaction to lift you along—what one might call the gallery syndrome. [. . .]

The first time I recognised this phenomenon and was able to isolate it was during the provincial tour of my play *The Knack*. The play opened here in Cambridge and the theatre was filled each night by young people who greatly enjoyed themselves. Without wishing to flatter I would say that undergraduates make good audiences, because the standard of intelligence is high, reactions are quick and lively; undergraduates tend to see a joke just before the point has been reached, thus they give themselves the extra, exquisite pleasure of having their suspicions confirmed. These audiences laughed a great deal and so did I. I watched the play three or four times sitting amongst them and laughed with them. I was aware that I wasn't totally in control of my reactions—self-control is the enemy of good theatre. The play did seem very funny, yet I'd lived with it for a long time and watched it many times in rehearsal, but with those first audiences it seemed quite fresh; I laughed at the play not as if I were seeing it for the first time but with a kind of fresh delight. Someone said to me, 'You laugh at your own play then?' and I had to confess I did; I excused myself by saying that the actors were extremely good—I genuinely did think this was the reason, and indeed the actors were good, but it was not the reason I laughed. The following week the play went to Bath—Bath in the late autumn when most of the summer visitors, such as they were, had departed. The audiences were thin and elderly, they were confused and outraged by the play, it was too quick and off-beat in style for them and they had no point of contact with the characters. Moreover, they found the play obscene; there were outraged letters in the local press about the obscene play which dealt with rape and kangaroo nipples and so forth; they couldn't make head or tail of it. Sitting in the auditorium amongst that audience, I did not want to laugh. More than that, the play appeared obscene to me. I had had a number of arguments with the Lord Chamberlain over certain lines which he had wanted to cut, but after discussion we were allowed to retain some of them. When these lines were said in Bath, and other lines which he had never even questioned, it seemed to me that the Lord Chamberlain was right—they were obscene. I began to think the Lord Chamberlain had a nice feeling for obscenity, but it was unpleasant: I had no wish to be the author of obscenity. There followed a good week in Cardiff. They told me the bar takings were the highest for years and I still wonder what that meant. But the play went well and my confidence was restored. Finally, *The Knack* came to London. The notices were good, but the audience were not given a strong lead. I was sitting in the audience watching the play and found myself thinking 'How could I ever have thought this play obscene? It's so innocent, it's so young.' Then, when the lights went up in the interval I noticed there was a large party of extremely sophisticated people in the row ahead of me; from their conversation they were clearly a group of people working in films.

I realised that, without having previously noticed them, and certainly not having been aware of them in the dark, their reaction was my reaction. It would almost be true to say that they had taken over my mind. There were a number of them, I was alone, their reaction was strong: 'How childlike, how innocent'; it became my reaction. Did this explain my laughing with the audience at Cambridge, and feeling of offence in Bath? I began to observe more carefully how each member of an audience is influenced by the reaction of those around them. And it now seems to me that no member of any audience of reasonable size can ever see a play in isolation. Their reaction is always coloured by the reaction of those around them. And not merely coloured: according to the nature of the audience, the play will appear quite different, will indeed be a different play, in Bath or London according to the audience with whom we see it. How many of us realise that, while play and acting may not change, what was a bad play when we saw it in Cheltenham last Wednesday may be splendid if we see it in Manchester next Friday?

The audience is the vital factor in the theatre, more volatile and unpredictable than play or actors, which are, after all, fixed entities. Even with improvised drama— and I don't mean improvised in rehearsal and then presented in a final form because the same rules still apply, but actually improvised in the presence of the audience— even with improvised drama the actor, though apparently in the dominating position, cannot take the audience other than where they are prepared to go. The way an audience will react will be determined by their particular make-up: a certain play will attract a certain audience. Once the audience is inside the theatre reaction will be affected by its physical shape. Finally the audience cannot react as individuals. The theatrical experience is essentially a buildup from within the audience in answer to the conditioning they have received about the play before they enter the theatre and the stimuli they receive from the stage. [. . .]

The theatrical experience is unconscious, subjective, powerful: an amalgam of the subconscious forces circulating amongst the audience, working from the stimuli they receive from the stage.

Theatrical dichotomy is the double experience that is at the heart of all thea-tre-going. The audience knows they are in a theatre watching a play that is make-believe, it's not really happening. They see before them actors on a stage who pre-tend to be certain people and pretend to be in a particular, developing situation; the actors invite the audience to join in this make-believe. And, given a good the-atrical experience, the audience does indeed enter into the play, it allows itself to be carried away, but for most of the time the audience is well aware of reality. It doesn't lose itself entirely in the fantasy world. A double experience is taking place: the audience is caught up in the play and yet it's also aware that it's part of an audi-ence sitting in a theatre. The audience plays at make-believe and knows that it is playing. If you increase the challenge to belief you also increase theatricality. In *A Midsummer Night's Dream* the dramatist has Oberon say, 'I am invisible and I will overhear their conference.' Oberon remains on stage and the actors behave as if he was not there. The audience then has the fun of seeing Oberon four-square in the scene and yet imagining him as invisible simply because he says he is and the other actors behave as if he is. Theatrical dichotomy is a comedian turning around in the middle of a revue sketch and talking directly to the audience, then going back into the sketch again— the reality conflicts with the play-acting and emphasises the two levels upon which the audience is experiencing. The challenge to belief may become filially so great that it is manifestly absurd—as is the case with the panto-mime horse. This is so absurd that it demonstrates very clearly the true nature of theatre—theatre as play.

You can play with reality in this way in the theatre because you start with a self-ev-ident basis of reality: live actors on a stage in front of a live audience. [. . .] The audi-ence connive with the actors and with each other. They play together and in playing they enter into a particular relationship with the others in the theatre.

The audience goes to the theatre to be moved, to be 'taken out of themselves', to be 'carried away'. The good dramatist knows he must capture their imagination and hold it. To do this he uses any number of means, of which those of least use to him are intellectual. If the audience wants to be carried away the dramatist must induce surrender, so that he doesn't want to appeal to reason: rationalisation, objec-tivity—these are not states of mind which will help an audience to surrender. No. The appeal in the theatre must be to the senses, emotions and instincts. So we have colour, movement, rhythmical and musical sounds and use of words, and we have appeals to the half conscious and the unconscious: symbols, myths and rituals.

Please see the Works Cited for further information on the sources used in this essay.

Notes

1 Margaret Thatcher (1925–2013) was the longest serving Prime Minister of the United Kingdom in the twentieth century (1979–1990) and the Leader of the Conservative Party from 1975 to 1990.

2 See Philip Roberts, *The Royal Court Theatre and the Modern Stage.* Cambridge: Cambridge University Press, 1999; Baz Kershaw, "(Patricia) Ann Jellicoe." *British and Irish Dramatists Since World War II*: Second Series. Ed. John Bull. Detroit: Gale, 2001. *Dictionary of Literary Biography* Vol. 233. Literature Resource Center. Web and his *The Politics of Performance: Radical Theatre as Cultural Intervention.* London: Routledge, 1992; Dan Rebellato, *1956 and All That: The Making of Modern British Drama.* London: Routledge, 1999; Michelene Wandor, *Post-War British Drama: Looking Back in Gender.* London: Routledge, 2001.

Suggestions for Further Reading

Doty, Gresdna A, and Billy J. Harbin, eds. *Inside the Royal Court Theatre, 1956–1981 Artists Talk.* Baton Rouge: Louisiana State University Press, 1990.

Findlater, Richard. *At the Royal Court: 25 Years of the English Stage Company.* Ambergate, Derbyshire: Amber Lane Press, 1981.

Jellicoe, Ann. Interviewed by Kate Dorney. "Ann Jellicoe - Interview Transcript." *Theatre Archive Project.* London: British Library. May 21, 2005.

Jellicoe, Ann. Interviewed by Harriet Devine. *The Legacy of the English Stage Company.* London: British Library. April and June, 2008.

Todd, Susan. *Women and Theatre: Calling the Shots.* London: Faber and Faber, 1984.

45 BARBARA ANN TEER (1937–2008)

La Donna L. Forsgren

Introduction

Black art is key to our survival as a people. The performer and theorist Barbara Ann Teer (1937–2008) understood this profound truth and dedicated her life to preserving and disseminating Black history and culture. As a visionary artist and staunch advocate for the collective well-being of Black people throughout the diaspora, Teer made profound contributions to the cultural flowering known as the Black Arts Movement (1965–1976). The movement consisted of thousands of Black artists across the US and abroad who used their agency to articulate the important relationship between art and politics. While these artists did not share a singular artistic vision or political stance, they were unified in their commitment to celebrating the Black aesthetic and advocating art as an effective tool for Black liberation. Teer's promotion of the Black aesthetic resulted in numerous awards, including the inaugural AUDELCO Recognition Award for Excellence in Black Theatre (1973). Her efforts were also recognized in 1975 by New York Congressman Charles Rangel, who declared her National Black Theatre (1968–) "one of the most valuable, worthwhile and exciting programs in our community [… the National Black Theatre] ha[s] been a positive force in Harlem asking people indirectly to confront their own lives and celebrating constantly the achievements and experience of Black writers, artists and scholars" (Best D10). Although contemporary scholars have not afforded Teer the recognition she deserves as a theorist, this does not diminish the fact that she led, fought alongside, and at times contradicted her male compatriots to actualize her vision of a truly liberated Black America.

Teer's legacy as a forthright theorist has been obscured in contemporary historical narratives. When examining the theoretical development of the Black Arts Movement, most studies focus on the critical essays of luminary male figures such as movement founder LeRoi Jones/Amiri Baraka, as well as theorists Larry Neal, Addison Gayle Jr., Hoyt Fuller, James T. Stewart, and Harold Cruse, to name a few. For example, studies typically note Baraka's "The Revolutionary Theatre" (1965) for issuing a call for a radical departure from the Western aesthetic and emboldening theatre artists across the US to join him at the Black Arts Repertory Theatre/School in Harlem. Neal's noteworthy "The Black Arts Movement" (1968) provided early theorization about the relationship between art and politics, describing the movement as the "aesthetic and spiritual sister of the Black Power concept" (Neal 29). Addison Gayle Jr.'s seminal collection, *The Black Aesthetic* (1971), offered the first rigorous investigation of the Black aesthetic. While these writings certainly helped shape the

DOI: 10.4324/9781003006923-46

nature and thrust of Black Arts Movement theory, an incomplete picture emerges when the focus is solely on the works of male compatriots. Reclaiming the theoretical legacy of Teer provides a starting point to understanding Black women's contributions to one of the greatest artistic movements of the twentieth century.

Teer's experiences performing in the New York commercial theatre provided a strong impetus for her theories of performance. Initially a Broadway dancer, Teer worked with choreographers Alwin Nikolais and Syvilla Fort, as well as toured with the Alvin Ailey Dance Company, Pearl Bailey Las Vegas Revue, and Louis Johnson Dance Company. However, after suffering a knee injury, she turned to acting as her profession and was taught by the greatest teachers of her time, including Sanford Meisner, Lloyd Richards, Paul Mann, and Philip Burton (L. Thomas 368). Unfortunately, as with many Black actresses navigating commercial theatres of the 1960s, Teer learned that despite her talent, she would be limited to playing stereotypical roles for Blacks onstage. She explains in a 1971 interview with National Black Theatre playwright-in-residence Charlie L. Russell the psychological toll of performing in the white-dominated commercial theatre industry:

> I became conscious of who I was. A black woman[.] Politically aware of what a black woman in America means. Over my manager's objections I had cut my hair in a natural. Cutting my hair helped me realize that I was in the wrong place, white theatre. Because of my natural I had my first fight with my manager (L. Thomas 368).

Having experienced the devastating effects of racism as a performer, she desired to disrupt stereotypical representations of Blacks and began theorizing a more holistic approach to performance that would liberate Black performers and spectators.

Teer's burgeoning consciousness led her to compose a series of critical essays during the sixties, many of which appeared in the *New York Times*. These essays include: "The Black Woman: She Does Exist" (1967); "Needed: A New Image" (1968); "The Great White Way is Not Our Way—Not Yet" (1968); "We Can Be What We Were Born to Be" (1968); and "Who's Gonna Run the Show?" (1969). The titles alone reflect the major thrust of Teer's theorization: a deep concern for the marginalization of Black women, misrepresentation of Blacks in the media, and the need for greater artistic agency and Black liberation. Teer's daughter, Barbara Ann "Sade" Lythcott, remembers that, as her mother was "becoming very hot" or passionate about her theories, white critics were "intrigued" by her work, and some Blacks "maybe [we]re not ready to embrace something so radical" (Forsgren 142). While these articles have been obscured in the annals of theatre history, at the time they were published, they inspired a strong critical response from theatre artists across the US.

Despite some early criticism, Teer used her newly minted National Black Theatre as a vehicle to develop her theories of performance. Turning critical thought into action, Teer began workshopping her conceptualization of "ritualistic revivals," a new performance genre that fuses a dramatic premise with African ritual, music, movement, poetry, and Holiness, Baptist, and Pentecostal church worship practices. Teer wrote, directed, choreographed, and performed in three ritualistic revivals during the Black Arts Movement, all of which provided an important space for Black performers and spectators to discover their strength, celebrate their history and culture, heal from the psychological trauma of racism, and connect with their own humanity. In other words: be what they were born to be.

Barbara Ann Teer

"We Can Be What We Were Born to Be" (1968)

Up to now, the Negro artist has been totally concerned with integration, with finding a place for his creative talents in the existing theater. He has spent thousands of dollars on classes and training, and countless years of pain and frustration, to compete in an already established, highly competitive industry. Clearly he feels that if he can just make it to Broadway, he will have reached the pinnacle of success, he will have arrived! (And Off Broadway is, of course, simply a stepping-stone to Broadway.) For years this has been his dream.

In the process of trying to realize this dream, he has had to picket, sit-in, march and, even in the various theatrical unions, negotiate new rules to provide more employment for himself. Yet today the employment situation for the Negro in the theater and other mass media remains frighteningly depressing.

How long will it take the Negro artist to understand fully what his status in show business really is? How long will it take him to wake up, see, realize, grasp, comprehend how he is being used—or how he has allowed himself to be used—by the white establishment? Until he can answer these questions honestly, he will naturally see no need for a black cultural art form. I believe the need for such an art form is far more critical even than the issue of white racism. And the Negro artist must examine the need for a black cultural art form before he can take any "next step forward."

For those brothers and sisters who are still tied to whitey, and have not yet seen the need to shape their own black cultural art expression, let's look at one of whitey's institutions: the American theater, an establishment developed, owned and operated by him for the sole purpose of making money.

And if you, a black performer, wish to become a part of this lily-white business, it is mandatory that you accept his values spiritually and morally. And I warn you, the compromises and sacrifices involved in the acceptance are extremely dangerous. You must constantly think in accordance with his values. You then begin to *act* in accordance with his values and pattern your life style and personality after his. You become the same as he.

This means that you literally negate your blackness. And I don't need to tell you how way out that is. The American public, both black and white, can see the results of this compromise daily in the theater, on television, on the screen, in magazines and newspapers, and, in the public schools, even in our textbooks. The mass media, controlling millions of minds, are now establishing for the black man what they consider to be new, wholesome patterns of behavior. But the black performer must step back and appraise his situation. Is this the image of himself that he wants portrayed? Is this the image that will further his racial identity or is it, in fact, simply reproducing more whiteness? Look around you. The few black directors, choreographers, television and movie actors that the industry has are, in fact, doing the same thing as the white man and not even as effectively.

So it seems the black artist is truly in a trick bag. The mass media consistently exclude him or use him for the purpose of exploitation, and seem completely unconcerned with reflecting any positive or authentic image of his experiences. Black women are either portrayed as prostitutes, maids, matriarchs or some other form of neutral exotica. Black men are either white black men, or shuffling Uncle Toms. The mass media overflow with blatant examples of white racism. In order for this racism to die, a totally new and different black cultural art form must be born. White producers do not wish to face this fact. Oh, no. They would rather talk to you about integration.

But, as you can clearly see, the concept of integration speaks directly to the problem of blackness in a contemptable way. As a goal, it is based on complete acceptance of the fact that, in order to have a decent job, black actors must play those narrow one-dimensional roles so magnanimously assigned to them. And black audiences must watch those actors playing those roles—if they want to participate in any enjoyment of the mass media. These images reinforce, among both black and white, the idea that white is automatically better; black is, by definition, inferior.

Integration is only subterfuge for the maintenance of white supremacy. Integration allows the media to focus on a handful of Negro actors who get white or other stereotyped roles at a great price, and to ignore the 99 percent who are left behind, unemployed. Furthermore, the establishment handpicks these actors. They carefully choose those they can isolate and/or dominate. This is called "tokenism." Black people refer to such actors as "sell-outs."

This tokenism increasingly splits the Negro artist from his people. Since we have no black mass media to counteract such injustice, we see only those few tokens that whitey has appointed as our stars and we begin to emulate them. We never stop to ask ourselves who put them there in the first place. So we get millions of black women spending hours before the mirror trying to emulate the only idols they have been permitted to know—Lena Horne or Twiggy—and millions of men trying desperately to be Harry Belafonte, Sidney Poitier, Rock Hudson, Marlon Brando or John Wayne. Do I have to say that neither of these character types represents the basic essence of soul or Afro-American beauty or manhood in their fullest sense? We have a much broader, wider range, and it should be publically displayed as it is in real life.

Very few producers seem to be clear as to the significance of the word Afro-American, and what a colorful and exciting theatrical combination that is. The implications of terms like Afro-American must be clarified before black artists can have any meaningful creative expression in the mass media. It is the duty of black artists to cease assimilating and imitating white standards and begin establishing truer, more realistic ones for themselves.

We have a responsibility toward our race. We must stop thinking individualistically and begin thinking collectively, for the sake of ourselves and of our brothers and sisters. There is a tremendous amount of work to be done, but we certainly cannot do it as long as we are divided and separated from one another. We must bridge the gap that has existed all these years between the artist and the people. The black artist should no longer represent the "man" but rather his own black people.

We as black artists cannot face the questions of morality and spirituality until we begin thinking as a people, a unified body of people who have power—power to control, power to change. And until we can control at least some parts of the mass media or, better yet, our *own personal talent*, we will not become a meaningful force in this country. When and if this does happen, integration will cease to be a word that has any significance or importance.

One of the tragedies in our struggle against racism in America is that there is no black theater which speaks directly to black people. The theater should be the forerunner in this cultural revolution because the theater is a form which can encompass nearly all our creative endeavors. It can disavow all the stereotypes and replace them with more meaningful images that represent us as we really are in life. We must establish for ourselves what is beautiful, ugly, clean, pure, proper, dirty, correct, incorrect, good, bad, sexy, violent, nonviolent, criminal—what is really meaningful to us.

All black artists must begin either to build, or to support, black theaters in all the black communities in America. These theaters should portray black people in all their many forms and colors. They should be concerned with the truth of our lives. After seeing the truth, we can begin to grow stronger and more positive as a body of people. That is why it is necessary to feed strong political and social messages into the minds of these black audiences. When we begin thinking and using our energies in this direction, we will be on the right road toward rehabilitation of black America and out ultimate survival as a people, that is where our real contribution lies. Today, too much of our energy and time are being utilized to maintain the concept of integration. And it is impossible for us to merge into the mainstream and identify with our blackness at the same time.

We are a people who were captured and brought to a strange land. We were stripped of our language, robbed of our names, our family ties, that is, we were left completely naked psychologically. Our bodies were clothed, but our minds were filled with negative, hateful, and demeaning images of ourselves by those who had everything to gain by suppressing the truthful images.

Here in America today, we are faced with a crisis. To quote Harold Cruse, "We must cease thinking of black theater purely in European terms the way white artists view the theater. Black theater is, historically, an American development by way of Africa. It is not an American development by way of Europe." So here are we black artists, scattered, separated from one another, frustrated, confused and choked up with centuries of unfulfilled creative potential which has never had the proper black creative outlets.

The existing American theater, with all its cancerous, immoral perverseness, has consistently robbed the black man of his true culture and re-dressed him to suit its own capitalistic needs. Because of this, and many other atrocities, the black artist has never reached his full capacity as a craftsman and a performer in America. Our salvation is developing our own black theater forms supported by strong cultural philosophies.

Culture is simply the total way of life built up by a group of human beings and transmitted from one generation to another. That definition is very important because the theater is one way of transmitting cultural forms. That means that the way we walk, the way we talk, the way we sing, dance, pray, laugh, eat, curse, "hit on a girl," make love and, most important, the way we look, make up our cultural heritage. Our culture is rich and beautiful; there is nothing like, or equal to, the black life style. It is uniquely and intimately our personal gift to the world.

Ever try walking down 125th Street hearing Aretha Franklin blasting from two loudspeakers and James Brown or Smokey Robinson and the Miracles blasting from two more? Music flying out of all the record shops. Children in groups of two's and three's standing in front of these record shops, booga-looing, shinga-linging, and doing all kinds of intricate steps that professional dancers with years of training would find most difficult to do. Or see a young black man from the "cool" school doing his favorite steps, hoping to catch the eye of some fine young female. If he succeeds in capturing an audience, he will put on a show the likes of which performers at the Apollo[1] can't equal.

In Harlem you see old women standing at bus stops with old shopping bags. Bags full of groceries and odds and ends, much too heavy for them to carry alone, but standing there in all their glory waiting patiently to get home and start cooking the evening supper. You see young women with hard-pressed hairdo's very carefully straightened with hot combs. Men wearing hairdo's very meticulously lacquered with some brand of chemical hair straightener. Sideburns, spitcurls, softly falling waves and, last but not least, the beautiful sisters and brothers with Afro's of all shapes and descriptions. You see all kinds of bright colors and styles varying from miniskirts to long African dresses. You see girls in tight dresses and tight pants switching and swaying, and fellows standing on corners checking them out and profoundly commenting as they pass by. You see the girls trying desperately to ignore them but you know deep inside they really dig it. You hear lots of laughter, lots of preaching, and dozens of four-letter words being thrown around. But, above all, you see people living fully and completely, whether it be hustling, fighting, drinking wine, smoking pot or selling Muhammad Speaks[2]; you feel passion and emotional range that is enormously powerful. We are beautiful, imaginative and gifted people and we owe it to ourselves and to our future generations to restore, to recreate this beauty.

We must begin by building cultural centers where we can enjoy being free, open and black, where we can find out how talented we really are, where we can be what we were born to be, and not what we were brainwashed to be, where we can literally "blow our minds" with blackness. The white establishment does not have the time, knowledge, inclination or intelligence to do our research for us and furthermore, it is not their responsibility, it is ours. Besides, the "man" has reached a dead end creatively so why should we continue to take our problems to him? He can't even solve his own problems, let alone ours.

So let's forget him, brothers and sisters; turn your minds and feet around; head for home.

Please see the Works Cited for further information on the sources used in this essay.

Notes

1 Famous Harlem performance venue in operation since 1913.
2 Official newspaper of the Nation of Islam, published 1960–1975.

Suggestions for Further Reading

Russell, Charlie L. and Barbara Ann Teer, "Barbara Ann Teer: We Are Liberators Not Actors." *Essence* (March 1971): 56–59.
Teer, Barbara Ann. "The Black Woman: She Does Exist." *New York Times.* 14 May 1967. D15.
———. "Needed: A New Image." *The Black Power Revolt: A Collection of Essays.* Ed. Floyd B. Barbour. Boston: Porter Sargent Publisher, 1968. 219–223.
———. "The Great White Way is Not Our Way—Not Yet." *Negro Digest* (April 1968): 21–29.
———. "Who's Gonna Run the Show?" *New York Times.* 2 Feb. 1969. D9.

46 JUDITH MALINA (1926–2015)

Kate Bredeson

Introduction

Judith Malina (1926–2015) was a director, actor, and writer who marked theatre history through her life in art and resistance. With her husband Julian Beck (1925–1985), she cofounded The Living Theatre in New York in 1947. Malina believed that theatre was a powerful tool to use in service of what she called "the beautiful nonviolent revolution," and The Living Theatre's project as a company was and remains to use theatre to serve political and social transformation. While she is rightly remembered as an artist who created visceral stage and street performances, Judith Malina must also be celebrated as a major theatre theorist. Her theatre theory is evident in her stage productions in which Malina strove to use theatre to awaken both senses and intellect in search of instigating spectators "to arouse the feelings that make the violent alternatives un-entertainable." In writing, she presents her theatre theory in the tens of thousands of diary entries[1] she left behind after her 2015 death, spelling out there her visions for theatre in opposition to capitalism, commercial theatre, and violence. In Malina's eyes, theatre—both the product shared with spectators and also the offstage processes—is a tool to help people see, think, and act in service of the coming revolution. This transformative potential of theatre is the through-line of her theatre theory.

Malina's diaries reveal her study of several key figures from whom she would form her own manifestos about art and activism. From her teacher at The New School, German director and theorist Erwin Piscator (1893–1966), Malina discovered her own conviction that "the theatre exists to serve the needs of people" and her life's work as a director, despite Piscator's order that she could not study directing because she was a woman. From French playwright, actor, and theorist Antonin Artaud (1896–1948), whose *The Theater and Its Double* she read via M.C. Richards' 1958 translation, Malina developed her own desire to "arouse the body and the spirit" of actors and audiences. She drew on German playwright, dramaturg, and poet Bertolt Brecht's (1898–1956) Marxist theories; her own determination to "change the whole human condition" is influenced by both Brecht and Piscator. German philosopher Eric Gutkind (1877–1965) inspired Malina's Jewish philosophy and her commitment to the "end" of "murder." Malina, with Beck, and later with her second husband Hanon Reznikov (1950–2008), sought to blend aspects of these various thinkers into her own theatre theory and practice built on a drive to invite spectators to wake up and work. Malina believed to her core that theatre was a medium through which artists and spectators could learn new ways of being in community and the world.

DOI: 10.4324/9781003006923-47

Malina's Spring/Summer 1969 diaries are exemplary of her theatre theory. She offers readers her manifesto for what theatre can and should be. She puts forward three main arguments: first, the imperative for new work and a new form in service of nonviolence; second, the personal responsibility of the artist—it's not the job of someone else to do the political and social work, each one of us must take on that role, and she calls on herself to step up; and, third, that staid practices and structures must both be overhauled in service of the larger goal of revolution. Malina's vision is sweeping; she seeks no less than "to change the whole human condition" and to use theatre as a tool in this work. She uses her beloved list format multiple times in these diary entries, and in these inventories she enumerates the elements of her new creation, as well as her work plan for her and Beck's company as they reconfigure and move forward towards "unification/to create/the people."

Malina's revolutionary theatre was and remains a way to invite artists and spectators to see the world differently and to take personal responsibility. Malina's theatre does this through existing outside of commercial frameworks, by having a woman director, by rewriting what a company can look like and what it means to stage performance. Her theory offers contemporary theatre-makers, students, spectators, and critics inspiration to overhaul outdated forms, to seek the new, and "to keep hacking away at the stone walls around the human hearts." Malina's life is a testament to the fact that political activism and theatre can be part of the same large-scale project to make the world better. Malina's theatre theory invites spectators to invest their hearts, minds, and bodies in service of revolution.

Judith Malina

Excerpts from the Diaries of Judith Malina (1969)

May 24, 1969   *Toulouse*

To create a work that serves to diminish the violence. A play, an event, a coming together that stimulates joy, that awakens the senses and gives the heart dominion. That restores feeling and arouses to action, that helps us turn the wheel, but helps release us from murder. To expose ourselves to those rituals that further the interior revolution by making the individual understand his presence in the collective. To bring us nearer to the Absolute Collective. To drench us in such beauty that the impossible becomes possible. The restoration of man to his Natural State. To rob death of its power.

It is only a glimmer now, this play. So the words stick together in the lower regions and falter and don't come out.

I can't say it well because I can't yet see it well.

It takes place anywhere. Preferably there are no chairs all lined up, only places to sit or lie or stand. A free space.

Anything can be there that is necessary, and rituals. Any objects needed, any tools.

Music
Musical instruments
Lights
Films
Slides
Clothes

Mats	FOOD
Costumes	DRINK
Books	
Charts	DRUGS
Drawings	
Stones	
Platforms	
Curtains	
Whatever is useful	

The form is free.

We are there.
The others come.

Unification
to create
the people.

Our work is to prepare this.
1st: 10–15–20–100 possible events for presentation, stimulation, further elaboration.

It is always a trip. What we do could be anything, any rituals or events.

How to get the apples to the city.
Technologies revealed
Magic → Science
Myth → Art
Being

We have to arouse the feelings that make the violent alternatives un-entertainable.

Again, as in *Paradise Now*, it can't be political enough, but it has to arouse the body and the spirit to the revolution of peace, blood of man's true kingdom does not begin until murder has come to an end.

Eric Gutkind.

It has to be sexual revolution because sexual revolution diminishes violence. It has to be an economic revolution because economic revolution diminishes violence. All those things.

But it has to arouse the Creative and undo the Destructive.

Because the beautiful nonviolent revolution which is at hand in 30–100 years is about to be subverted by the magnetism of violence. And this play is needed and the theatre exists to serve the needs of people and this is what we have next to do.

No title.

Yet.

June 4, 1969
It becomes my birthday. The burden of my age and my lack of wisdom

/(I don't know how to stop the wars)/
weighs too heavily. I pace all night. I wake the baby with my wailing. She goes to sleep at 8 a.m. and I go out shaken; but my fear abates: so soon. The frustrations become the "normal" frustrations, whereas the night was "enragée." Then it calms. How full of violent images that mood is!

That mood in which one feels abandoned and alone in what one believes. Lost in a dark wood called the truth, without foretaste of rescue or the light.

And the arguments against what is right ring loud and clear. It would be so easy to fall down and worship this idol called the wickedness-of-the-world. But the force of something stronger begins urging very quietly, in my father's voice, "If not I, who?"

If not I, who?

Where are you? Here I am.

And this fever burns in me to do something to match the strength of my feeling. In violent people, this rage must be the rage to kill. And what is that rage that is the same passion in the nonviolent urge. The rage to stop the killing. The rage, like the assassin's rage inherited into a passion to stop the violence.

Or at least to make it clear! To open the mind to the pain of the other.

To reorganize yourself in him.

To feel the bong of the continuum.

To experience the kinship as active love.

The morning light tells me it is not rage that is needed—but the strength not to despair in the face of constant failure

/I don't know how to stop the wars/
and work at leaving no stone unturned, to discover The One Essential for Survival.

/No less is at stake than the survival of our Species!/
And count no work too small, too arduous, too ungratifying, and no work too monumental, too grand, and too impossible.

And keep hacking away at the stone walls around the human hearts.

Instead of being exhausted by this arduous night I work well at rehearsal.

It's my 43rd year.

July 7, 1969   *Malaga*
Plans for Essaouira:
Main concern: Division of Time

JM: Suggestions
Creations/Summer:

1. A film script: *Frankenstein/Paradise Now:* or neither, but film about what we are most concerned about
2. A NEW PIECE FOR THEATRES
3. A NEW PIECE FOR THEATRES = <u>A NEW THEATRE FORM</u>
   (Street/Free Theatre)
4. Work on <u>THE COMMUNITY</u> (conscious work on making it better (Form cells!)
5. Plays for diversified company: <u>TWO INTERCHANGEABLE UNITS:</u> One play street or free theatre, one play commercial theatres. Actors can work interchangeably, on different nights, weeks, etc. . . .

So the paid unit earns enough to support both units (This project depends on #3)

July 16 1969   ***Essaouira, Roof***
Revolutions will be fought. This is the reality of the world. But our major focus is how can we change the whole human condition so that eventually this can change.

Please see the Works Cited for further information on the sources used in this essay.

Note

 1 Malina published two editions of her diaries: *The Diaries of Judith Malina 1947–1957*. New York, NY: Grove Press, 1984. *The Enormous Despair: the Diary of Judith Malina August 1968-April 1969*. New York, NY: Random House, 1972. Kate Bredeson's edition of Malina's unpublished diaries is forthcoming.

Suggestions for Further Reading

Malina, Judith. *The Diaries of Judith Malina: 1947-1957*. New York, NY: Grove Press, 1984.
———. *The Enormous Despair: The Diary of Judith Malina August 1968-April 1969*. New York, NY: Random House, 1972.
———. *The Piscator Notebook*. London: Routledge, 2012.
Rochlin, Sheldon, and Maxine Harris, dirs. *Signals through the Flames*. 1989; New York, NY: Mystic Fire Video. Videocassette (VHS), 97 min.
Rosenthal, Cindy. "Antigone's Example: A View of the Living Theatre's Production, Process, and Praxis." *Theatre Survey* 41.1 (May 2000): 70.
Rostagno, Aldo with Julian Beck and Judith Malina. *We, the Living Theatre*. New York, NY: Ballantine, 1970.

47 ROSE YUEN OW (1895–?)

Krystyn Moon

Introduction

Chinese American women who chose to perform on the stage prior to World War II faced numerous hurdles from both the broader entertainment industry and their community. To find work, women often had to participate in acts that played to the racialization of gender and sexuality outside of normative notions of white, middle-class womanhood. For instance, the sing-song girl, a musically talented prostitute found in early twentieth-century American popular culture, was common. Another trope was the Chinese princess, whom women portrayed as sexually modest, musically talented, and of royal blood. Female entertainers recognized that these performances were an act, and they easily subverted them on the stage with their use of contemporary dress, perfect English, modern dance moves, and witty repartee.

Outright discriminatory practices also impacted their ability to work. Immigration authorities made it difficult for all performers of Chinese ancestry to cross international borders, which required the production of large amounts of paperwork that had to circulate between agents at various ports of entry and Washington, D.C. before their departure. It was simply easier for entertainers to avoid tours that traveled outside of the United States, especially if there were any questions about their (or their family's) residency or citizenship status. Discrimination occurred on the local level too. Cities such as San Francisco and Vancouver with large immigrant communities segregated theatres and required Chinese Americans/Canadians to sit separately from whites in the balcony. This practice embarrassed friends and families who hoped to watch their loved ones on the stage.

Beyond the stage, Chinese American women faced social pressures from their family and neighbors, too. Many Chinese immigrants questioned the respectability of women who left domestic spaces to work outside the home or enjoy leisure activities. Families and friends policed women in public spaces, particularly restaurants and theatres, which continued to be viewed as primarily male homosocial spaces. Changing gender roles in the United States, along with economic need, made it possible for women to work outside the home and support themselves and their families. But entertainment, which immigrants conflated with sex work, continued to be viewed as morally suspect.

Despite these issues, a handful of Chinese American women embraced the excitement of performing in front of audiences and made careers for themselves in the entertainment industry prior to World War II. They studied music, acting, and dance in hopes of obtaining their first big "break," usually at a restaurant or theatre in cities

DOI: 10.4324/9781003006923-48

such as San Francisco, Chicago, or New York City. Some sang Tin Pan Alley numbers, while others performed elaborate partner dances, played musical instruments as soloists, or joined bands. Adversity did not stop them from following the career that they loved, but often Chinese American women made compromises in their work that reflected and reinforced stereotypes found in American popular culture at the time.

In this 1970 interview excerpt, Rose Yuen Ow (1895–?)[1] recalls how she enjoyed performing in front of audiences and, despite numerous obstacles, made a career for herself in the entertainment industry. Her parents, she notes, were unusually progressive and gave her opportunities that many other Chinese American families forbade young women to pursue. She studied dance and with her boyfriend Yow Joe started performing at Tait's Café in San Francisco. In 1915, actor and producer Raymond Hitchcock recruited Ow and Yow to audition in New York City where they received their big break in vaudeville as "Chong and Moy." Like other Chinese American entertainers, they mixed modern dance with Chinese stylized movements, costumes, and backdrops. Both picked up singing too. Their dancing impressed audiences, but reviewers complained about their singing, which they noted was accented.[2] The use of accents, however, was a common device used among Chinese American vaudevillians to undermine stereotypes that they could not speak English. Like many acts, they stopped performing at the beginning of the Great Depression—when it became increasingly difficult to find work—and returned home to San Francisco.

Rose Yuen Ow

Excerpt from Interview (1970)

[This interview was conducted on September 9, 1970 in San Francisco. The original transcript is housed in the Him Mark Lai Papers at the Asian American Studies Collection in the Ethnic Studies Library at the University of California at Berkeley.]

Interviewer: Did you go to school in San Francisco?

Rose Yuen Ow: [I was] 12 years old before I start[ed] school.

Interviewer: Why so late?

Rose Yuen Ow: The Chinese didn't want the girls to go to school in the old times.

Interviewer: There was no compulsory education?

Rose Yuen Ow: The Westerners had no laws unless you went to church. There church people come to your house and teach you how to read and write. Very old-fashioned in those days. Even when my mother and father let me go to school, the cousins criticized. When I go to work, the first place I work in Chinatown is a woman's picture place. I sat there and sold tickets. The cousins immediately told my father to get me home.

Interviewer: Which theater?

Rose Yuen Ow: It's now [the] Sun Sing Theater, but they used to show moving pictures a long time ago.

Interviewer: How old were you then?

Rose Yuen Ow: At most 14 or 15. I don't remember whether they showed Western or Chinese movies.

Interviewer: Where did you go to school?

Rose Yuen Ow: Commodore. It used to be call[ed] the Oriental Public School. I went until I finished the eighth grade.

Interviewer: Did you go to Chinese School?

Rose Yuen Ow: Just a few months. My father and mother wanted me to go to school, but busybodies kept butting into our family. Later when I was older and went to work in the American section of town, everyone talked about me. Said I worked and roamed around the streets.

Interviewer: How about your girlfriends?

Rose Yuen Ow: They didn't work. I think I was the first or second one to start working in Chinatown [selling movie tickets]. Afterwards, I went downtown to work in the nightclub for Westerners. Like when they came for meals, they would hire a Chinese girl to hand out biscuits, candy, etc. That's how I started to work. In those days, Tait's Cafe was the biggest cabaret in San Francisco. They purposely hired two Chinese girls to pass out hot biscuits when dinner started. Then after dinner, we came around again to pass out peppermint candy. In the old days, Chinatown was harsh. People would follow me all the way downtown to see where I was going. Those Chinese men wanted to see where I was going. They talked and everyone in Chinatown talked about you. Not nowadays. You can do anything and nobody in Chinatown would care. It was really harsh in the old days.

Interviewer: What could they do to you?

Rose Yuen Ow: Nothing, except talk and say you did what and what downtown. Just gossip.

Interviewer: They didn't want you associating with whites?

Rose Yuen Ow: They didn't want Chinese girls doing that. Always butting into your business. So one time I got so mad, I said come on in and look. They had followed me to the door. They were all dirty minds, the Chinese in the old days. Closed minded. Now it's a little too open. Before, you couldn't even move. I didn't dare walk the streets with a Westerner alone. I would always drag a friend along.

Interviewer: But it was okay for a Chinese man to go out with a white girl?

Rose Yuen Ow: It happened very seldom.

Interviewer: Would people talk?

Rose Yuen Ow: In those days, no white would go out with a Chinese. They looked down at the Chinese. The Chinese were treated as bad as the blacks. It was pitiful the way the whites taunted us. Before, Chinese were not allowed to sit downstairs at the Pantages Theater [on Market Street]. It was really hard being a Chinese girl in those days.

Interviewer: When did you go on stage?

Rose Yuen Ow: In 1915.

Interviewer: Why?

Rose Yuen Ow: I was working in the cafe passing out candy. I was stationary watching the people dance and Mr. Tait jokingly said, how would you like to do something like that, Rosie? I said fine. I had a boyfriend who was studying pharmacy. So I told him the boss said I should learn dancing and he would hire me to dance. He said alright, let's take a few lessons. I was quite bold because the boss hadn't said he would hire me, just how would I like to do that? So after a few months of lessons, I thought I was all ready. I was that brave. So I said to the boss, Mr. Tait, I'm ready for you. He had forgotten all about it. In those days, there was the waltz, the foxtrot, the old-time nigger cakewalk. So that was three dances.

Then we improvised a Chinese dance, just motion. So he said you're ready for what. Scared me. I'm ready to dance for you, I said. There were two floors then, a ballroom upstairs and a dining room downstairs. Just then this French woman said she refused to dance in the dining room. She would only dance in the ballroom. So Mr. Tait was having a little trouble. So he said tomorrow, you go upstairs and dance for me. So we bravely danced for him. And Mr. Tait said fine, very good. So he decided to put Rosie and Joe on next week. So I became scared. How was I going to tell my father that I was going to dance? So I told him I had learned to dance and that since the French woman refused to dance downstairs, we were going on. How would you know how to dance, he asked. I said it's not really me. He just wanted to put my picture in the newspapers. Actually someone else was going to dress up like a Chinese and dance, not me. So we danced. In those days, I was paid $125 a week and I was more than happy.[3] Then our wages were increased until I got $200. The customers got to know us and every time we made our entrance, there was a lot of clapping. Later, a big star Raymond Hitchcock came and saw us dance. How would you like to go to New York, he asked. So I bravely said alright, even before I asked my father. Later I told my father. He still didn't know we had been dancing although I had always given him my wages. The *Call-Bulletin* had shown our pictures. After my picture appeared in the morning paper and it had gotten all over Chinatown, I ran up to see Mr. Tait and said, Mr. Tait, I can't do it. You can't put my picture in the paper. I was crying. What's the matter with you, he said. People give thousands and thousands of dollars for publicity. I said I don't care for publicity. I was just afraid my father would see it. Everyone in Chinatown saw it, it was such a big picture. So after it got out in the papers, I had to tell my father. He said it was alright and didn't scold me or anything. But in those days, at that age you were still stuck at home and not permitted to say anything. So we danced until 1915 when we went to New York. Then we got to know some big brokers and got a chance to play the big theaters, like Palace Theater in New York and we played for Ziegfeld Follies. Pretty lucky. We worked with Jack Benny, Marx Brothers, and that's how I started my show business [career]. Altogether 14 years of show business.[4] Then the movies, the talkies came in. He didn't want to give up but I wanted to give up because the shows were all closing. And we weren't used to booking week to week. We were so used to book[ing] one season. Every year we go we were very lucky. Season to season. We traveled around. Same town over and over again back east. They, the Westerners, all knew us by Rosie and Joe.[5]

Interviewer: Then what did you do after that?

Rose Yuen Ow: I came back to San Francisco and worked in the restaurant as cashier until I retired.[6] People say I'm crazy not to enjoy not working. But I said not working makes me very unhappy. I miss my public. All my life of people. And now retired and sitting around, I have to go out in the streets. There's nothing to do sitting around. I miss it but my husband missed it more. He loved it. If he were here, he'll get up and dance for you. He's crazy about it, and very likeable.[7]

Interviewer: Why did you go out of Chinatown to work, knowing how unpopular that was?

Rose Yuen Ow: After I started working outside of Chinatown, a thousand Chinese girls followed me.

Interviewer: How could you be so brave?

Rose Yuen Ow: My sister never went out, but I went everywhere.

Interviewer: Were you rare then?

Rose Yuen Ow: All the mothers wanted their daughters to go to work but they were afraid of gossip. By the time I got back from New York, they were all working. Actually, even in 1915, things were more liberal.

Interviewer: How did you find the job at Tait's in the first place?

Rose Yuen Ow: George Ong's father introduced me to the job. He use[d] to take care of all the Fairmount Chinese employees. He took care of finding Chinese employees for most of the white employers. Like he knew you and he would mention a job opening and if you wanted it, you would go.

Interviewer: Your father was pretty open-minded?

Rose Yuen Ow: My mother and father both were open-minded. My mother was very open-minded. When I was young, my mother made me Western clothes to wear. But she died when she was 28. I was only 9. In the old days, they married too young–at 14, 15.

Interviewer: Were you afraid working for westerners?

Rose Yuen Ow: Not at work.

Interviewer: Did you feel any discrimination at work?

Rose Yuen Ow: No. Where I went they were high-class people. People with money and manners. Educated people don't look down at others. Even in Vancouver, they didn't use to let people sit downstairs in the theaters. They kept them segregated.

Interviewer: So the Chinese who came to see you perform would have to sit upstairs?

Rose Yuen Ow: Only in Vancouver and the Pantages in San Francisco. The Orpheum on O'Farrell Street, one of the most high-class theaters, didn't discriminate. Every year we played the vaudeville show there. Also Golden Gate.

Interviewer: Did a lot of Chinese come see you?

Rose Yuen Ow: Lots because Chinese were performing, so they came to support us. In Vancouver, even the Chinese consulate came. I got mad when they won't sell me a ticket for them to sit downstairs. So I screamed at them. She said it's the people in town who would object. Of course, the Chinese were a bit sloppy. They would wear their Chinese slippers. Vancouver and Victoria Chinese were very old-fashioned. Typical Chinese with queues and open shirts. After Sun Yat-sen, people began wearing English clothes. At first, the community leaders pressured the people to cut their queues and change to Western dress. The Chungshan people were the first.[8]

Interviewer: Where did you perform?

Rose Yuen Ow: All over. Back east. Down south.

Interviewer: Were you in the same circuit with Hugh Liang?

Rose Yuen Ow: Different group. There were never two Chinese groups at the same time.

Interviewer: Were you the only Chinese dancing team at that time?

Rose Yuen Ow: There was another one. An Eastern couple Harry Haw and Feng Feng Gue. They were earlier by at least three or four years. They retired before us. Ernie Tsang was another dancer. His brother Benny Won was a single comedian. He was a very clever man but he never played any big theaters at all. Show business is like anything else. If you have good luck, you meet the right people. He was very, very good. As soon as he came out, you would laugh. He was a very good comedian. Harry Haw was a good dancer, very genteel.

Interviewer: What was the pay then?

Rose Yuen Ow: $200 to $300 a week at the minimum. If I had saved it, I would be rich by now. People didn't buy property in those days. They all planned to go back to Hong Kong or China. In those days, buildings in Chinatown were selling for a few thousand dollars. Nine out of ten Chinese would not buy property because they planned to go back to China. When I die I can say I've lived a full life.

Please see the Works Cited for further information on the sources used in this essay.

Notes

1 To date, scholars have not been able to discover the date or location of Rose Yuen Ow's death.
2 "Vaudeville Reviews by Special Wire," *The Billboard,* 8 September 1917, 70; "Vaudeville Reviews by Special Wire," *The Billboard,* 4 November 1925, 15; "Show Reviews," *Variety,* 16 January 1920, 22; Playbill, "Vaudeville," Orpheum Theater, Oakland, CA, July 15, 1928, Bancroft Library, University of California, Berkeley, CA.
3 Ow worked at Tait's Café between 1913 and 1915. She only made $60 a week passing out candy.
4 She worked in vaudeville and nightclubs from 1915 to 1929. After 1929, she never performed on the stage again.
5 Joe Haw (mis-transcribed as Hall) was her first husband. Their stage names were Joe Chong and Rosie Moy because her Chinese given name was Moy. Historical records also list Joe Chong as "Yow Joe" and "Chong Yow Haw."
6 She worked as a cashier for 11 years at Cathay House and 30 years at Sai Yuen.
7 Joe Haw passed away at age 71. Although Ow and Hall were divorced, they remained good friends. After they left the entertainment industry, he became an alcoholic.
8 Ow recalled elsewhere that her father cut his queue before 1900, several years before other Chinese immigrants.

Suggestions for Further Reading

Kondo, Dorinne. *About Face: Performing Race in Fashion and Theater.* New York, NY: Routledge, 1997.

Kwan, SanSan. "Performing a Geography of Asian America: The Chop Suey Circuit." *TDR: The Drama Review.* 55.1 (Spring 2011): 120–136.

Lee, Esther Kim. *A History of Asian American Theatre.* New York, NY: Cambridge University Press, 2011.

Lee, Josephine. *Performing Asian America: Race and Ethnicity on the Contemporary Stage.* Philadelphia, PA: Temple University Press, 1997.

Moon, Krystyn. *Yellowface: Creating the Chinese in American Popular Music and Performance, 1850s–1920s.* New Brunswick, NJ: Rutgers University Press, 2004.

Shimakawa, Karen. *National Abjection: The Asian American Body Onstage.* Durham, NC: Duke University Press, 2002.

Yoshihara, Mari. *Musicians from a Different Shore: Asians and Asian Americans in Classical Music.* Philadelphia, PA: Temple University Press, 2007.

48 MARGUERITE DURAS (1914–1996)

Shelley Orr

Introduction

Novelist, playwright, and filmmaker Marguerite Duras (1914–1996) was one of the most prolific and prominent writers of the twentieth century. Born to French colonists in French Indochina (Vietnam), she wrote more than 70 novels, plays, screenplays, and adaptations over her 53-year career. Winner of the prestigious Prix Goncourt for her novel, *The Lover* (1984), and screenwriter of the landmark New Wave film *Hiroshima Mon Amour* (1959), Duras consistently pushed the limits of representation.

Duras's work prompts a reconsideration of the purposes of dramatic literature and performance, especially the relationship that a work forms with an audience. By using typically unquestioned theatrical conventions in unconventional ways, she forces us to confront our assumptions (often informed by realism) about how theatre works. In the "General Remarks" that preface *India Song* (1973), Duras outlines the ways in which she uses the conventions of setting, adaptation, and the audience's role in forming meaning. Her brief preface opens up new possibilities for how to make meaning in the theatre. She begins:

> The names of Indian towns, rivers, states, and seas are used here primarily in a musical sense.
> All references to physical, human, or political geography are incorrect:
> You can't drive from Calcutta to the estuary of the Ganges in an afternoon. Nor to Nepal.
> The "Prince of Wales" hotel is not on an island in the Delta, but in Colombo.
> And New Delhi, not Calcutta, is the administrative capital of India.
> And so on.

The expectations that one might have regarding a work entitled *India Song* are immediately complicated by the fact that Duras's setting is simultaneously in India and *not* in India. Her note underscores that the actual country, India, and a concept evoked by the word "India" are related, but not identical. One of these Indias can be visited and is ever changing, while the other is only as stable as any sign can be. The India that Duras wishes to evoke is simultaneously an actual location *and* a space of memory and imagination. In this provocative author's note (which might be provided to an audience by including it in the programme), Duras positions her audience to view India as partly actual and partly conceptual. The setting shimmers between evoking a real location and a space of memory.

DOI: 10.4324/9781003006923-49

In the theatre, we are always "here" and "not here" at the same time. When, for example, we see a production of Tennessee Williams' *The Glass Menagerie,* we are in St. Louis, and yet we are not. Even a production that is actually performed in St. Louis is not identical to the "St. Louis" evoked on stage. The theatrical setting maintains a distance in time and by being filtered through the many artists who contribute to the production. Yet audiences may overlook the shimmering quality of the theatrical setting to focus on the actual place that is evoked. Duras's innovation is that she uses the chimeric quality of the theatre space *as part of her setting.* The *memory* of India is an important part of the work—indeed as important as India, the actual place.

Later in her "General Remarks," Duras refers to her novel, *The Vice-consul* (1966). She also refers to the three media that she envisions for *India Song.* In the French edition, the title, *India Song,* is subtitled *Texte, théâtre, film,* indicating that the work is a written text, a play, and a screenplay:

> The characters in the story have been taken out of a book called *The Vice-consul* and projected into new narrative regions. So it is not possible to relate them back to the book and see *India Song* as a film or theatre adaptation of *The Vice-consul.* Even where a whole episode is taken over from the book, its insertion into the new narrative means that it has to be read, seen, differently.

As she outlines *India Song*'s relationship to *The Vice-consul,* Duras zeroes in on how her audience must see the episode differently in the new context. In her unconventional view of adaptation, Duras highlights the differences in the works *not* by chronicling the changes in the plot but by pointing to the particular relationship each work has with its audience. Rather than a smooth, seamless adaptation from *The Vice-consul* to *India Song,* Duras envisions two works that are related but distinct. The subtitle *Texte, théâtre, film* attests to the ways that Duras questions convention: these three genres of storytelling are not usually all applied to one work. While the script for a play is certainly a text, it is often viewed as "standing in" for a theatrical production. Film scripts are, in the vast majority of cases, never published, as the film is most often considered the definitive version. Duras defies simplistic representation and evokes three genres at once in her subtitle. Therefore, *India Song* is three genres in one, three works at once.

Duras also questions the concept of adaptation, and she plays with genre by interrogating the assumptions associated with each. As all playwrights do, she counts on the audience members to bring their expectations and preconceptions with them to the theatre, but Duras goes further than most theatre theorists in that she creates a space for the audience's contributions to be incorporated into her work. Thus, she redefines the audience's role. Her novel conception of the audience's engagement with her work came from a discovery that she made about voiceover while making one of her films, *La Femme du Gange* (*The Woman of the Ganges* 1974).

> This discovery made it possible to let the narrative be forgotten and put at the disposal of memories other than that of the author: memories which might remember, in the same way, any other love story. Memories that distort. That create.

Duras is counting on the audience's own memories to *create* part of the dramaturgy. Because most playwrights do not explicitly include the expectation that the audience might be thinking of something else during their play, for Duras, participation by the audience is an expected and necessary element. *India Song* comes into focus only through the spectators who define it through their own lens. In short, one could argue that all plays are formed only in performance, but precious few playwrights incorporate this idea into the dramaturgy of their plays.

Marguerite Duras

Excerpt from India Song *(1973)*

General Remarks

The names of Indian towns, rivers, states, and seas are used here primarily in a musical sense.

All references to physical, human, or political geography are incorrect:
You can't drive from Calcutta to the estuary of the Ganges in an afternoon. Nor to Nepal.
The "Prince of Wales" hotel is not on an island in the Delta, but in Colombo.
And New Delhi, not Calcutta, is the administrative capital of India.
And so on.

The characters in the story have been taken out of a book called *The Vice-consul* and projected into new narrative regions. So it is not possible to relate them back to the book and see *India Song* as a film or theatre adaptation of *The Vice-consul*. Even where a whole episode is taken over from the book, its insertion into the new narrative means that it has to be read, seen, differently.

In fact, *India Song* follows on from *The Woman of the Ganges*. If *The Woman of the Ganges* hadn't been written, neither would *India Song*. The fact that it goes into and reveals an unexplored area of *The Vice-consul* wouldn't have been a sufficient reason.

What was a sufficient reason was the discovery, in *The Woman of the Ganges*, of the *means* of exploration, revelation: the voices external to the narrative. This discovery made it possible to let the narrative be forgotten and put at the disposal of memories other than that of the author: memories which might remember, in the same way, any other love story. Memories that distort. That create.

Some voices from *The Woman of the Ganges* have been used here. And even some of their words.

That is about all that can be said.

As far as I know, no "India Song" yet exists. When it has been written, the author will make it available and it should be used for all performances of *India Song* in France and elsewhere.

If by any chance *India Song* were performed in France, there should be no public dress rehearsal. This does not apply to other countries.

Please see the Works Cited for further information on the sources used in this essay.

Suggestions for Further Reading

Duras, Marguerite. *The Malady of Death*. Trans. Barbara Bray. New York, NY: Grove Press, 1986.
———. *Savannah Bay*. Trans. Barbara Bray. *Marguerite Duras: Four Plays*. London: Oberon Books, 1992. 97–118.
———. *The Viaducts of Seine-et-Oise*. Trans. Barbara Bray. *Three Plays: Marguerite Duras*. London: Calder and Boyars, 1967. 117–159.
———. *The Vice-Consul*. Trans. Eileen Ellenbogen. New York, NY: Pantheon, 1987.

49 MEGAN TERRY (1932–2023)

Maya E. Roth

Introduction

Playwright Megan Terry (née Marguerite Duffy, 1932–2023) played a significant role in shaping, sustaining, and reflecting on the experimental theatre movement in North America, beginning in the 1950s. Terry channeled counter-cultural and grassroots democracy of the sixties and seventies – epitomized by the Civil Rights, Environmental, Women's Rights, and Anti-War Movements – into theatre praxis: seeking to decenter power, transform consciousness, and seed collectives. Terry also engaged radical writing by 19th- and 20th-century women, including Margaret Fuller, Simone Weil, Gertrude Stein, Simone de Beauvoir, and Audre Lorde,[1] who critically and creatively interrogated gender rights, ways of knowing, family, sexuality, language, history, and class.

Drawn to theatre and audacious play at a young age, Terry was politicized as a teen by the McCarthy-era[2] coercive norms (marked white, male, capitalist, nationalist, and heterosexual). She collaborated with the progressive Seattle Repertory Playhouse ("Old Rep") until its demise from Washington's Legislative Committee on Un-American Activities (an extension of HUAC). Equally, Terry was shaped by the largely female tradition of creative dramatics, which values community and play-based theories of learning and life. Terry and the interdisciplinary avant-garde – including María Irene Fornés, Joseph Chaikin, Spiderwoman Theatre, Ellen Stewart, Anna Halprin, Meredith Monk, and Urban Bush Women,[3] for instance – framed performance as fundamentally collaborative and sought to break cultural barriers between artists and audiences and to undermine binary oppositions of mind/spirit and body; self and collective; performance and social praxis.

Terry deployed critical and creative inquiry, realism, and radical imagination across her *oeuvre*. She also was the sole female founding member of the Open Theater (in 1963), where she pioneered "transformation plays" – which perform like nonlinear theatre games – radically morphing scenarios, roles, genre, settings, and styles to creatively pursue a critical theme. In *Feminist Theatre*, Helene Keyssar hailed her as "the Mother of American Feminist Drama," a "sustaining force" due to her experimental feminist dramaturgy, mentorship, and collaborative techniques, which inspired many in the women's theatre movement (53). Terry's prodigious impact has yielded enduring relevance for experimental theory, radical youth theatre, and community-based performance.

Terry famously experimented with form and gender for the Open Theater, leading to her prismatic *Calm Down Mother* (1965), "a transformation play for three women,"

DOI: 10.4324/9781003006923-50

and *Keep Tightly Closed in a Cool Dry Place* (1967) for three men. Most explicitly political was her genre-defying full-length *Viet Rock* (1967) – the first rock musical and America's first production to protest the Vietnam War; it premiered at La Mama, directed by Terry, with music by Marianne de Pury. (Inspired by improvisations with actors, Terry's developmental process and aesthetic influenced the creation of *Hair*.) Terry's independent *tour-de-force* was *Approaching Simone*, based on her decade-plus research on French labor activist and mystic Simone Weil, which won the 1970 Obie Award. Terry incubated dozens more original plays and flexible structures for co-creation during her twenty-five years as Playwright-in-Residence and Literary Manager at the Omaha Magic Theatre (OMT), one of the longest-running avant-garde theatres in the U.S. Signature plays from this era, which Terry developed with her life and creative partner Jo Ann Schmidman, OMT's Founding Artistic Director (who premiered the role of Simone), include *Babes in the Bighouse: a Documentary Fantasy Musical About Life in Prisons* (1974), *Molly Bailey's Traveling Circus: Featuring Scenes from the Life of Mother Jones* (1982), the ecopoetic *Sea of Forms* (1986), and *Body Leaks* (1990). These works, sometimes developed from community workshops on "issues," engaged feminist critics and artists, including myself. Terry's radical ensemble scripts posit flexible terms and structures for co-creation (i.e., open texts, open casting) and embrace contingency with artists and audiences.

Whereas some iconic practitioners and theorists of experimental theatre – such as Jerzy Grotowski or the Living Theatre – drew on theatre theorist Antonin Artaud,[4] seeking to shock or confront audiences out of complacency by placing the artist's body in sacrifice or pain, Terry focused on game structures and transformation by inviting audiences into discovery and interconnection. Yet, in the 1970s, Chaikin and critic Robert Brustein called her direction for *Viet Rock* "too soft" and "feminine" because she had actors move into the audience, which was then an innovation (when a male director experimented similarly two years later, he was hailed as revolutionary). Mixing creative casting with constantly changing roles, scenarios, and styles to imaginatively engage her audiences, Terry's formal innovations and inventions model how people and structures can dramatically change (social scripts, perspectives, and systems).

Terry rejected a logocentric theatre – and Playwright-as-God ethic – as early as her 1958 opinion essay in the *New York Times,* "Who Says Only Words Make Great Drama?." Terry's generous, "non-hierarchical" collage-storytelling stemmed from diverse training in directing, performance, and visual art, not unlike Fornés, with whom she co-founded the Women's Theatre Council in 1972. Terry composed scripts for performance that juxtapose images and voices, styles and art forms, emotions and ideas, realism and anti-realism. "Apply the principles of creative dramatics to adult drama," she explained to Dinah Leavitt in the interview excerpted here; deploy thematic "juxtaposition, and it's all jammed together with film techniques, cutting, jump cuts. [...] What if you do this on stage?" (291). Terry, whose chosen surname honors 19th-century British actress-manager Ellen Terry, centered experimentation and feminist genealogies repeatedly.

Terry theorized that "total theatre" arises from creative and compassionate relationships across artists, communities and audiences. In *Right Brain Vacation Photos: New Plays and Production Photographs from the OMT, 1972–1992* – written together with Schmidman and Visual Artist Sora Kimberlain, her co-creators – Terry vividly frames theatre as multidisciplinary and sensory-rich, constellating imagination and pluralism. In manifestos and ephemera, she theorizes interactive practices to feed avant-garde theatre and community building.

Her multidisciplinary aesthetic anticipated postmodern bricolage by recycling mixed elements, including new media to "create new resources," in order to renew lives, art, and souls. "[G]reat plays [...] are the true human record" and more reliable than history, she averred; they reveal "the psychic news" of cultures (Leavitt 286). In an interview with Felicia Londré, excerpted here, Terry promoted "cross-pollination" across artists, ideas, and cultures, as generating creative energy and peak periods for theatre, from 1960s New York City to Shakespeare's London. Cross-fertilization and diversity, she explained, feed "creative explosions" of collaboration and competition, promoting "dynamism" in art and life. While Terry acknowledged gender double standards and sexism ("a woman has to produce through menopause before anyone thinks she's serious"), she reframed capitalist notions of value to spiritual, embodied, and art-based ones: success is working in the theatre every day, engaging others (Leavitt 290).

Megan Terry

Excerpt from "Preface" to Ex-Miss Copper Queen on a Set of Pills *(1966)*

[...] Free from bills! Free to work. One month. I had to work fast and I did. It was a good test. I set it myself and thanks to the Rockefeller Foundation and the O.A.D.R., I made it.[5] To be chosen by people not involved with you in any way is a heartening and confirming experience for a writer. It opens up stores of energy you didn't know you had. [...]. Relatives and friends can help keep a writer going, but to have recognition from outside [...] does much to alleviate energy-sapping doubts that plague the artist.

Excerpt from Molly Bailey's Traveling Family Circus featuring Scenes from the Life of Mother Jones *(1983)*

This play [stages] imagined and possible events in the lives of two women who were born in the (19th) century. These women were vibrant, positive, creative, strong and successful. They didn't know each other, but I believe we can know more about ourselves by knowing them.

Through the use of transformation techniques (or doubling, etc.) this show may be performed by seven or eight people, or as many actors as are available. The musical can be successfully presented without scenery, costumes or props. It may also be produced with the most imaginative & complete scenic spectacle. The music may be provided by piano & percussion or a total orchestra. It can be staged & will work in any available space [...].

Excerpt from Interview with Dinah L. Leavitt *(1981)*

[...] The great plays that have been left to us are the true human record. I believe you can find out what people are really like or were like or felt like through reading plays that have come down to us since the Greeks. They're much more reliable, from my point of view, than any of the history books. The theatre is the psychic news. [...]

I've been lucky [as a woman playwright]. I'm famous, but I have no money. If I were a male, I'd probably have money too. But I don't need the money and my culture is giving me a living wage for what I write. I'm just now beginning to get a living wage at the age of forty-five. I see my male colleagues at the age of twenty-five being able to do that; it comes much sooner. A woman has to produce through menopause before anyone thinks that she's serious. [...]

I always sit with my audiences; I learn so much from them. I feel that anyone who comes to the theatre is my peer or better these days, and they see things I never thought of [...]. I've had them crying in my arms, thanking me, others screaming at me and throwing things, others saying never stop writing. I have a very passionate relationship with the audience. I want them to be involved in the process of creating the play. [...]

I've had the chance to sit with audiences all over the world—Algeria, Persia, Israel, Yugoslavia, France, Denmark— and see what reaches people, what are the universal touching points. And when an audience laughs, it's the greatest natural high in the world. [...]

(A)pply the principles of creative dramatics to adult drama and you get a whole new kind of comedy, a juxtaposition, and it's all jammed together with film techniques, cutting, jump cuts. I said, "What if you do this on stage?" Well in *Comings and Goings* and *Keep Tightly Closed* you get a new kind of comedy because of the jump cuts. [...]

We may have taken it to a higher power, but it was always there. The Second City was doing it, as were Mike Nichols and Elaine May and Viola Spolin. I was trained by my cousin Geraldine Siks of the University of Washington in creative dramatics. I was doing it all my life. It's the way people play; we took it to a higher level by formalizing it. Shakespeare did transformations of place— the great banquet hall became the queen's chamber became the battlefield. The audience and actors must create place. Understanding this [...] requires that you believe as children. You can change that fast, but you must take a different attitude.

Excerpt from Interview with Felicia Londré (1996)

I think that the more our culture gets fragmented, the more people want a feeling of community and contact.

The 1960s marked an explosion of playwriting styles. One reason for this was because at least thirty-five strong playwrights arrived and began to show their work in New York within the same time period. It was the kind of creative combustion that hadn't been seen since Greek and Elizabethan times. Sheer numbers of challenging writers with many different points of view were in the same geographical location. I believe this could take place because of some excellent teaching that had gone on in the universities by people who had fought in WW II. They came back to their students with a global view and a new sense of American power and energy in the world. Before this, playwrights seemed to arrive in the national consciousness one at a time. But this new group of playwrights realized they were a group. Some realized this because they literally received energy from one another, and others because [of] audiences [...]. It was like sport to show our work to one another and almost play "can you top this" with each new play.

We started our own theatres and found directors and actors of like minds, colleagues, who would work in collaboration, in groups where the actor was treated as a co-creator not as an employee or interpreter. This attitude or practice made for a completely different dynamism in performance. The 1960s audiences responded to this, and we were off and flying. Our work and ideas took over the decade, and soon American theatre production ideas and playwriting seemed to be leading the world. These ideas cross-pollinated with many other cultures. [...]

There were great advances made in direction, acting and production design in the 1960s. A synthesis and cross-pollination from discoveries in other media and art were coming into theatre. You can see the fruition of these seminal ideas in much of the performance art of the last ten years and now on Broadway productions such as *Tommy,* as well as in opera and the new wave festivals at the Brooklyn Academy of Music, that is, Robert Wilson, Laurie Anderson and Karen Finley, and in the current work of the Omaha Magic Theatre. Ideas from the last hundred years in art and design have come into the theatre. Some of these ideas are amplified, modified and expanded by the use of electronic media and by the application of image projection possibilities on a large scale. [...] [T]he designer, too, has been [...] as a co-creator who makes as strong a statement about the theme or ideas of the play as the playwright, director and performer. Sometimes one person may wear all these hats, sometimes a creative team, but all work together to bring new power into our field and thus more enjoyment to the audience [for...] this evolving art form. [...] [T]o stay alive you have to constantly solve new problems [...] We create something out of nothing, we artists. We don't use up resources; we recycle and rearrange and thus create new resources, self-renewing, to fire ourselves and warm the souls of those who are dedicated to serve and/or take sustenance from this art form.

Excerpts from Right Brain Vacation Photos *(1992)*

We never experiment in front of an audience. *We play in front of them; we interact with them.*

[...] It's text and visuals fully realized—It's play—fully performed. We play with one another, with our audiences, with ideas, images, situations, relationships.

GENDER CASTING/MULTICULTURAL CASTING

The company is made up of those willing to commit to the work. Art is about commitment, whatever color— whatever gender. If a script calls for two characters and seven wish to work, the production company becomes seven.

Please see the Works Cited for further information on the sources used in this essay.

Notes

1 Margaret Fuller (1810–1850), an American journalist and first female war correspondent, editor, critic, translator, and advocate for women's rights, was associated with the American transcendentalism movement. Simone Weil (1909–1943), whom Albert Camus described as "the only great spirit of our times," was an influential French philosopher, mystic, and political activist. Gertrude Stein (1874–1946) was an avant-garde writer and art collector; see entry in this volume. Simone de Beauvoir (1908–1996) was

an influential feminist theorist and existential philosopher, best known for *The Second Sex* (1949). Audre Lorde (1934–1992) described herself as a "black, lesbian, mother, warrior, poet." She focused on the intersections of sexism, classism, racism, homophobia, and especially lesbian feminism.

2 Joseph McCarthy (1908–1957), Republican Senator from Wisconsin whose virulent anticommunist stance resulted in the persecution, prosecution, and "blackballing" of Americans he suspected of communist sympathies under the auspices of the House Committee on Un-American Activities (HUAC).

3 See Fornés entry in this volume. Joseph Chaikin (1935–2003) was an American theatre director who founded the Open Theatre, known for exploring political and social issues in avant-garde theatre productions. Spiderwoman Theatre (1976–) sought to establish an American, Indigenous women's performance company that blends traditional art forms with Western theater; see Spiderwoman/Muriel Miguel entry in this volume. Ellen Stewart (1919–2011) was an American theatre director and producer who founded the influential off-off-Broadway playhouse, La Mama Experimental Theatre Club. Anna Halprin (1920–2021) was a pioneering American postmodern choreographer and dancer. Meredith Monk (b.1942) composes, sings, directs, and choreographs pieces identified with postmodern performance art. Urban Bush Women, an interdisciplinary performance collective founded by choreographer Jawole Willa Jo Zollar (b.1950), explores women's lives, community and movement traditions of the African Diaspora.

4 Polish experimental theatre artist and theorist Jerzy Grotowski (1933–1999) developed innovative performance techniques documented in his influential study, *Towards a Poor Theatre* (1968). The Living Theatre, founded in 1947 by Julian Beck and Judith Malina, produced groundbreaking experimental theatre that introduced US audiences to the work of leading European avant-garde artists; see Malina entry in this volume. Actor, director, and theorist Antonin Artaud (1996–1948) is best known for his "Theatre of Cruelty" that utilized violent and arresting images and rejected traditional text-based production.

5 The Office for Advanced Drama Research, affiliated with the University of Minnesota, was a precursor to the Playwrights Center; Terry was in the inaugural cohort.

Suggestions for Further Reading

Carlson, Susan, "Leaking Bodies and Fractured Texts: Representing the Female Body at the Omaha MT." *NTQ.* 12.45 (1996): 21–29.

Greeley, Lynn. *Fearless Femininity by Women in American Theatre, 1910s to 2010s.* Amherst, NY: Cambria Press, 2015.

Roth, Maya. "A Doubly 'Environmental' Sensorium: Omaha Magic Theatre's *Sea of Forms.*" *The Senses in Peformance.* Eds. Sally Banes and Andre LePecki. World Performance Series. London: Routledge, 2007: 154–166.

Savran, David, ed. "Interview with Megan Terry." *In Their Own Words: Contemporary American Playwrights.* NY: TCG, 1993: 240–256.

Terry, Megan. *Plays by Megan Terry: Approaching Simone, Babes in the Bighouse, Viet Rock.* New York, NY: Broadway Play Publishing, 2000.

50 DOROTHY HEWETT (1923–2002)

Aoise Stratford

Introduction

Dorothy Hewett (1923–2002) is one of the most significant Australian playwrights of the twentieth century. Hewett won her first awards for poetry and drama while at university, where she also became involved in the Communist Party of Australia (CPA). Her first novel, *Bobbin Up* (1959), about women working in the sewing mills, came at the end of a decade writing journalism for the CPA and living tumultuously with Les Flood, a boilermaker, who burned much of Hewett's poetry and other writing as a "bourgeois indulgence" (McCallum 113). In her memoir *Wild Card* (1990), Hewett describes working on *Bobbin Up* as a "miracle" that put an end to a period of "silence" and "exile" from herself as a writer (Hewett, *Wild* 246).

In her forties, estranged from the CPA and remarried to poet Merv Lilley, Hewett emerged as a prominent Australian poet and playwright, finding her place in a cultural moment when second-wave feminists were clamoring to be heard and the Australian theatre scene was for the first time seriously producing Australian writers—nearly all of whom were men. Hewett's first major play, *This Old Man Came Rolling Home* (1967), is a "quasi realist working class drama" (Radic 233), but most of the plays that followed moved away from the conventions of realism to be formally innovative, lyrical plays that use music, myth, vaudeville, poetry, masks and puppets, and nonlinear structures alongside precisely rendered Australian settings and vernacular. Plays include *The Chapel Perilous* (1972), *Bon-bons and Roses for Dolly* (1972), *The Tatty Hollow Story* (1976), *The Man from Mukinupin* (1979), and *The Song of The Seals* (1983). Across Hewett's body of work, women—their working-class lives, their struggle for sexual and reproductive freedom, their search for identity and creative autonomy in the face of oppressive institutions, and their relationships—are repeatedly central.

Hewett is, however, a controversial and complicated figure. Audience reactions to her work have tended to be, as theatre critic John McCallum notes in *Belonging* (2009), "divided in their responses between enthusiasm and revulsion" (113). About her play *Bon-bons and Roses for Dolly*, Hewett recalls:

> Perth was outraged, particularly by the aging Ollie Pullett, who drags around a husband, a white dummy called Mate, as she discusses abortion, menopause, menstrual flooding, death and the Royal family—all no-nos for the blue rinse set. They rose and stomped down the aisles, wrote letters to the press and the Playhouse, denouncing me.
>
> (Hewett in Blundell, 190)

DOI: 10.4324/9781003006923-51

In the short essay, "Why Does Sally Bow?," excerpted here, Hewett notes that it is not *Bon-bons and Roses for Dolly*, but *The Chapel Perilous*, that, of all her plays, is "the most performed, the most talked about"—a claim she made in 1977 that is likely still true—generating responses from "violently hostile" to "critical," and "nostalgic" to "identifying to quite a startling degree with the protagonist, Sally Banner" ("Why" xvi). Hewett's female characters are often aggressively sexual and defiantly nonconformist, and few more so than Sally Banner, whose epic journey to "walk naked through the world," just as she is, constitutes the arc of the play (*Chapel* 86). While characters like Sally have galvanized Hewett's feminist legacy by giving voice to female desire, and offering rich and complex acting roles for Australian women, those same characters have also been criticized by feminists for their "neediness" (Janaczewska 14–15). Hewett sees neediness as a byproduct of culturally perpetuated gender norms, but she has also been very open about the role her own needs and desires have played in her writing (Hewett in Palmer 90–91).

As a result, Hewett's work has been labeled as "lacking distance" (Radic 234). Such labels seek to undermine her contribution to feminist theatre. As Janaczewska notes in her *Playing Awkward: A Response To The Chapel Perilous* (2014), the "adjective autobiographical comes with a hefty gender bias" and functions as a means to "not exactly silence the voice, but diminish the achievement of the writing" (12). Though autobiography was cited as a weakness in Hewett's work, "equally autobiographical male writers" were spared that charge from critics (McCallum 117). Importantly, however, Hewett is doing something other than telling her own story on stage within the conventions of the consciousness-raising women's theatre of that period or by following the tenets of domestic realism. As the following excerpt makes clear, significant to Hewett's structuring of *The Chapel Perilous* is the discovery that realism is not adequate for the telling of real life even though "freeing the mind from formal confines" is difficult ("Why" xvii). Instead, Hewett's theatre is big, challenging, polyvalent, and wildly theatrical. Arguably, one of the most significant contributions of Hewett's feminist dramaturgy is the innovative and political theatricality she brings to bear on the genre of women's autobiography and performance. Sally Banner may be, as McCallum suggests, "the most complete evocation of the wildly romantic, sexual, visionary, feminine, rebellious and subversive character that many early critics and audiences took, with some justification, to be Hewett's representation of herself" (119), but she is at once specific and archetypal, functioning as an authentically complex human being and a mythic locus for a large number of feminist ideals and struggles.

The following excerpt from "Why Does Sally Bow?" illustrates how the political authenticity of Hewett's innovative autobiographical dramaturgy has much to do with both process and theatrical form. In tracing the evolution of *The Chapel Perilous* as she searched for the right ending for the play, Hewett's writing documents the labor of the feminist playwright working with lived experience, political consciousness, theatrical representation, and audience reception. Like much of her poetry and dramatic writing, this excerpt is noteworthy for the author's autobiographical candor and intimate tone, even as she addresses larger dramaturgical theories.

Particularly significant among those is Hewett's observation that: "I had to lose myself in order to complete *The Chapel Perilous*" ("Why" xix). This separation, Hewett suggests, is key to authentic autobiographical storytelling and political ideology. The question of how to get autobiographical and political authenticity through dramatic representation is a significant part of Hewett's contribution to the history of feminist theatre in Australia, and in raising it, Hewett both addresses criticisms about distance and seeks to reclaim the maligned term "autobiographical" for a feminist theatre of big ideas and innovative theatricality.

Nonetheless, Hewett's own unflinching and nonconformist attitudes toward women's sexual freedom in her political and personal life have come to cast a shadow over her work and legacy for Australian feminist theatre, raising complex questions about the extent to which the reader's ability to separate the writer from their work and legacy is either possible or appropriate. Since her death in 2002, Hewett's daughters have spoken publicly about the often-painful experience of growing up in the Bohemian arts scene of the seventies and the trauma of being sexually abused at parties—allegedly with their mother's knowledge (Carmody). These accounts in turn are shaped by Hewett's own experiences with sexual harassment in the theatre (Hewett, *Wild* 82–83), speaking loudly to both the systemic misogyny of the Australian literary world in the seventies and Hewett's complex and troubling place in it.

Dorothy Hewett

Excerpt from "Why Does Sally Bow?" (1977)

The Chapel Perilous began its life as a semi-autobiographical novel, and I had considered writing it as a film script because all that diffuse and recalcitrant material seemed too difficult to reconcile to the theatre. I found myself going back continually to Brecht and the Elizabethans [Hewett was teaching both modern and Elizabethan drama at the time], wrestling with the concepts of apparently pure freedom in time and space on an open platform. It was frightening and immensely difficult to free the mind [...]. I found myself falling back on proscenium arch solutions, none of which worked here, and I would go down and pace about the great platform [of the New Fortune Theatre] deliberately freeing my imagination, setting it loose to prowl in those perilous empty spaces.

I finished the first draft of the first Act and showed it to [director] Aarne Neeme [...]. He was enthusiastic, supportive, and insistent that I finish it. Easier said than done. The play had to have a conclusion. How could I conclude a life I hadn't even lived? It was a case of the writer being too close to the protagonist. I was frightened of the conclusion. What would it mean? What would it say? The only conclusion could be death. How could I achieve the necessary distance to see that end? The answer seemed to lie in distancing myself from the protagonist through ritual and symbol. Night after night, week after week, I wrestled with the second half of *The Chapel Perilous*; writing long, explanatory, dreary drafts that only muddied the issues [...].

In the struggles with the ending I wrote two or three separate endings [...]. Sally moving into the chapel of Self, the schoolgirls singing 'Come Live With Me,'—were constant elements but the details were changed. The original production by Aarne Neeme at the New Fortune Theatre cross-cut from scene to scene using a spare, plain, dramatic shorthand which was immeasurably helped by the theatre architecture. At the conclusion Sally appeared white faced in flowing robes at the very apex of her world, the roof of the chapel above the stained glass window (the top balcony of the theatre). She had aspired to death and the legend remained enshrined there. It was a medieval conclusion which required no words. At the Sydney Opera House much more of the chanted material from *The Book of Common Prayer* was used to bring

Sally to her final end. This produced a solemn, slow processional—almost florid—finale: cluttered and overemphasised.

This published text [...] lies somewhere between these two extremes: neither quite content to accept the purely visual end, nor convinced that the heavier and more obvious ending is the right one. It came after seeing a young student actress at the Melbourne Union Theatre put her own interpretation of Sally on the play. Following the stage directions, she approached the altar to move past it into the chapel; but as she reached the altar, almost unconsciously she knelt, not humbly but proudly, head held high. Then she rose and passed on. I saw this added business on the opening night and was, for one instant, outraged. How dare they make my Sally bow? Sure this made nonsense of her whole life?

My outrage has since been shared by others [...]the accusatory question: 'Why does Sally bow?' [...] is asked sometimes in puzzlement, sometimes in anger, sometimes in disappointment. [...] I wrestled with the problem all that night; and the next morning I accepted the gesture, for it is a gesture, not of capitulation. It is a gesture to the exigencies of life. Sally finally *accepts* life. 'So is that all there is in the end,' she says, 'to accept oneself, to be finally and irrevocably responsible for oneself?' The answer is 'Yes!' As she pauses at the entrance of her Chapel of Life and Death, under her ironic self-donated stained-glass window, she makes a kind of peace, not with the Church, not with the State, not with temporal authority, but with life itself, which includes authority.

My lesson was that I had to lose myself in order to complete *The Chapel Perilous*. A work of the imagination is not autobiographical in the accepted sense, although it may have strong autobiographical elements. The central figure had to be, in the end, a created character. [....] Sally Banner lives only in the play. She doesn't exist outside it.

Sally Banner [has...] become variously to others a modern day symbol, an ego-tripper of monstrous proportions, a boring self-advertiser, a vulgar hotpants and a heroine of liberation. Nobody seems to view her, as I do, with quiet calm acceptance. I seem to have created some kind of female *doppelganger*, which is both humbling and irritating, because, like the albatross, I suspect she will always be slung around my neck.

Please see the Works Cited for further information on the sources used in this essay.

Suggestions for Further Reading

Bennett, Bruce, ed. *Dorothy Hewett: Select Critical Essays.* South Fremantle, WA: Fremantle Arts Centre Press, 1995.

Hewett, Dorothy. *Collected Plays.* Sydney: Currency Press, 1992.

Tait, Peta. *Converging Realities: Feminism in Australian Theatre.* Sydney: Currency Press in Conjunction with Artmoves Melbourne, 1994.

51 MARÍA IRENE FORNÉS (1930–2018)

Linda Ben-Zvi

Introduction

María Irene Fornés (1930–2018) holds a special position in American theatre. Fellow playwrights; actors directed by her; students studying playwriting with her; academics teaching and writing about her extensive and diverse output—40 works in a 40-year career—including sketches, one-act and full-length plays, musicals, libretti for opera, and modern adaptations of classics (Cummings, *Maria Irene Fornes* xviii), share Tony Kushner's assessment that, "America has produced no dramatist of greater importance [...]. She is one of the greats" ("One of the Greats," xxxiii): "a magical maker of Theatre" (qtd. in Weber 14).

Born in Havana, Cuba in 1930, Fornés came to New York with her mother and one sister in 1945. By the early 1960s, she was a leading force in establishing Off-Off Broadway, the American venue for avant-garde European theatre experiments beginning to gain a foothold abroad, as Martin Esslin describes in *The Theatre of the Absurd* (1961). Of the 18 playwrights he places under the absurdist rubric in the first edition, none are women and few are Americans; however, in the second edition (1968), he acknowledges "a veritable flood of plays" (266–267, n.64) being written in America in the absurdist vein, citing Megan Terry and Rochelle Owens, but overlooking Fornés, who by then had written ten non-realist plays, staged in 26 venues in America and Europe.[1]

As early as 1954, during her two-year stay in Paris studying painting, Fornés had seen the first production of Samuel Beckett's *Waiting for Godot* and never forgot the experience. "I didn't speak any French at all. But I understood the world in which it took place, I got the rhythm" (Wetzsteon 32). In *Tango Palace* (1963), her first produced play, she follows suit, jettisoning traditional realist forms including exposition, character delineation, and plot. Language is simple and spare; pauses and silences, rather than words, create tension; visual elements often dominate the verbal. In subsequent works, sounds, tones, speech rhythms, and precise body movements—scrupulously determined by Fornés, who began directing the premieres of her plays—convey inner feelings and intent.

Fornés argues for the importance of the various art forms which ground plays: a study of music, for instance, makes one sensitive to sounds, silences, and aural effects; a familiarity with art provides tools to turn a space into a visual image, "a spirit" she calls it, creating a theatrical reality and solidity that draw the audience into the imaginative world of the play.

DOI: 10.4324/9781003006923-52

Unlocking and trusting the imagination, rather than following prescribed theatrical rules and dramaturgy, is at the heart of Fornés's work as well as her teaching, particularly at the famous playwriting workshops she led for two decades, at INTAR (International Arts Relations), in the Hispanic Playwrights-in-Residence Lab (HPRL) which she established. Under her guidance, it produced a new generation of important Latina and Latino playwrights in America, including Migdalia Cruz, Nilo Cruz, Eduardo Machado, Cherríe Moraga,[2] and Caridad Svich. In these workshops, Fornés wrote along with her students; and many of her plays from the 1980s on had their inception in the lab. In the book *Conducting a Life* (1999), a tribute to Fornés, Svich observes, "The articulation of her aesthetic has been made manifest in her hands-on work as a teacher, and therefore is an essential, inextricable part of her work as playwright and director" (Delgado and Svich, xxviii).

Fornés practices what she teaches, as she indicates in the fourth excerpt here, describing how her imagination remains open "to the messages that come." Words overheard or brief bits of dialogue often become the genesis of a play. When characters finally emerge, she indicates that they arrive in "full color" and remain so, a possible carryover from her time as an art student, studying with the renowned abstract expressionist painter Hans Hoffmann, whose "push-pull" technique juxtaposes color elements to create a surprising sense of depth, movement, life and energy. In such works, "Space was never a static, inert thing, but alive; and its life can be felt in the rhythm in which everything in a visual ensemble exists" (de Kooning). The same can be said of Fornés's plays, which juxtapose unexpected and incongruous images, props, physical movements, and shifting dialogue. Fornés also subscribes in her work to de Kooning's belief that, "A picture should be made with feeling, not with knowing," and that predetermination precludes free rein of the imagination.

When inspiration does not come, Fornés sometimes creates what she calls "a kind of fantasy game," as she did in *Fefu and Her Friends* (1977), heralded as the first contemporary American feminist drama: consistently taught in courses in universities over the years; staged in theatre departments and small theatres in America and abroad; and, 42 years after its premiere, restaged in New York City. The production received the prestigious Drama Desk Award as Best Revival of any play on Broadway, Off-, or Off-Off Broadway in 2020.

In several of the following excerpts, Fornés takes up the danger of labels. Embraced by feminist scholars after *Fefu*, she was later accused by some of betraying women by allowing Mae to die at the end of *Mud* (1983), one of her most famous plays. As Fornés makes amply clear in her responses to such comments, Mae *is* the center of the play and the strongest character—itself a feminist statement—but to argue that the play is *only* about gender is to narrow the work to one specific meaning and no other, which she rejects. As early as her preface to *Tango Palace*, Fornés warned that "[i]f art is to inspire us, we must not be too eager to understand. If we understand too readily, our understanding will, most likely, be meaningless. We must be patient with ourselves" (9).

Susan Sontag was Fornés's lover from 1957 to 1961, and echoes of their relationship may be found in *Tango Palace*. Sontag makes the case that Fornés's works are not reducible to only one specific meaning, but, rather, address the "the conduct of life" (8) and, "incarnating the human condition as such" (9).

María Irene Fornés

Excerpt from Interview with David Savran, "Maria Irene Fornes" (1988)

What got you interested in theatre? When was that?
A play that I wanted to write got me interested in theatre. I was not a playwright. I was not in theatre because at that time (1959–1960) theatre was not a very interesting art. The most advanced writers in the American theatre were Tennessee Williams and Arthur Miller.[3] That *was* the American theatre [...]. The beginning of the avant-garde theatre came from Europe: Samuel Beckett, Eugene Ionesco and Jean Genet.[4] But even when these writers became known here, it took a few years before we actually started doing their work [...].

Were you attracted to European theatre?
I saw the original production of *Waiting for Godot* in Paris, directed by Roger Blin. I'd just arrived in Paris [...]. But I was so profoundly upset by that play—and by upset I mean turned upside down—that I didn't even question the fact that I had not understood a word [...]. I left the theatre and felt that I saw everything so clearly [...] something in me understood that I was to dedicate my life to the theatre [...].

I was a painter and lived in Paris for several years. I was not interested in writing. I came back to New York in 1957 and the next year I saw a production of *Ulysses in Nightown* with Zero Mostel, directed by Burgess Meredith[5][...] performed in a place [...] that was not ordinarily used as a theatre. And that too had a profound effect on me [...]. Then in 1960, or maybe it was 1959, I had an idea for a play. I was obsessed with it [...]. A door was opened which was a door to paradise [...]. That was *Tango Palace* [1964].

What about other influences? Arthur Miller, Tennessee Williams?
I don't like Arthur Miller at all. I don't like Tennessee Williams' plays very much either, because it seems to me that he celebrates a kind of feminine neurosis, that he sings praise to it. I don't like that [...]. In his writing you see the spirit of somebody with delicate feelings who was beat up as a child and lives in a world of pain and tears with a kind of complacency [...]. Maybe it's masochistic—the feeling that you cannot escape it [...]. I don't see the point of that at all. I feel we're fortunate that no matter how terrible things are, we live in a society where we have the freedom to take action even if some people make this difficult for you, or if you're disabled from your upbringing. I understand how one can be mangled psychologically, but still our effort should be to find our vitality and move on.

I don't romanticize pain. In my work people are always trying to find a way out, rather than feeling a romantic attachment to their prison. Some people complain that my work doesn't offer the solution. But the reason for that is that I feel that the characters don't have to get out. Characters are not real people. If characters were real people, I would have opened the door for them at the top of it—there would be no play. The play is there as a lesson, because I feel that art ultimately is a teacher. You go to a museum to look at a painting and that painting teaches you something. You may not look at a Cezanne and say, "I know now what I have to do." But it gives you something, a charge of some understanding, some knowledge that you have in your heart. And if art doesn't do that, I am not interested in it.

I don't know what my work inspires, because I'm never the spectator. But I'm horrified to think that my work in any way would suggest there is no way out. I've been told by some women, for instance, that by killing Mae in *Mud* [1983], I have robbed them of the possibility of thinking there's a way out. "If she cannot escape," they said, "how can we?" I feel terrible that I have made them lose hope. The work that has most inspired me to action or to freedom is not work that's saying, "Look, I'm going to show you how you too can do it."

Kafka's *The Trial*[6], like *Waiting for Godot*, gave me the experience of a remarkable energy inside me. Pozzo beats on Lucky and at the end Lucky doesn't get free, but it doesn't matter because I do! I've never been anybody's slave but when I see that I understand something. Josef K. may get guillotined or go to the electric chair but, rather than saying "I'm doomed," I learn from his behavior. I know what my intention is, but I don't know if, after seeing *Mud*, it would be difficult to feel, "I'm getting out." I know that most people don't feel depressed by it.

Excerpt from "Creative Danger: Exploring the Woman's Voice in Drama" (1985)

Often, there are misunderstandings about my work because it is expected that as a woman I must be putting women in traditional or untraditional roles, or roles of subservience or subjugation or dominance, to illustrate those themes. Or when one of my women characters is portrayed in a position of work or leisure, certain assumptions or simplifications are made about the character which might be quite the opposite of what is presented in the play. When those contradictions occur, the critics never question their initial premise. Instead, they see it as a fault in the play.

The same thing happens if you have a non-white character or actor in a play. Immediately people assume the play is dealing with racial questions [...].

In my play *Mud*, the character Mae works very hard. She earns the little money that comes into the house. The two men don't earn money [...]. I have often been told that in *Mud* I have written a play about women's subservience, by virtue of Mae's job. While it is true that ironing is work that women do, the play also makes it very clear that Mae is willful and strongminded, and that the men in the play accept her as such and love her without making any attempt to undermine her strength. These people are too poor to indulge in bizarre ego games. They have a reality to deal with, which is poverty. That is the way things have worked out for them. The concept of sex roles and role-playing are a luxury, an indulgence that requires a degree of affluence [...].

To understand *Mud* as being about Mae's oppression and [...] *The Conduct of Life* [1985] about the subjugation of Latin American women is to limit the perception of those plays to a singleminded perspective. It is submitting your theatergoing activity to an imaginary regime or discipline that has little to do with the plays. I would like to be offered the freedom to deal with themes other than gender. But again, people think, what right does she have as a woman to be writing about military cruelty in Latin America?

I'm pleased that at this time in my writing I am finding expression for strong female characters who are able to speak of their longings for enlightenment and of their passions, or who make political or philosophical observations. If I were limited to writing plays to make points about women, I would feel that I was working under some sort of tyranny of the well-meaning. It is unavoidable that every choice I make comes exactly from who I am—including the fact that I love to iron. I think it's magic! Every single thing I have lived through in my life, everything I have witnessed, in some way gets into my work. The fact that I am a woman is one of the most present things. Each day of my life something happens to me that is different from what would happen were I a man [...].

The possibility of being creative depends on not being shy with one's intimate self and not being fearful for one's personal standing. We must take very delicate chances—delicate because they are dangerous and delicate because they are subtle; so subtle that while we experience a personal terror it could be that no one will notice. It is this danger which in my mind is very connected to what is truly creative.

Excerpt from Fornes, "Maria Irene Fornes" (1983)

I have been thinking about the question of identifying with the opposite sex, not just observing the opposite sex but being one with it. The question of identification is of great interest, as it is through identification that we learn to become whole human beings. The experience of others becomes our own. And our experience endows details that we observe in the lives of others with a depth that benefits our understanding [...].

Compassion is of course a result of identification, and so is hatred. My intention is not necessarily to promote kindness to the opposite sex but something ultimately more interesting, which is that any human being is a member of our species and if we do not allow our imagination to receive the experience of others because they are of a different gender, we will shrivel and decay [...].

When my play *Fefu and her Friends* [1977] was done at the American Place Theatre there were discussions of the play after each performance and so I became aware [...] that a lot of the men looked at the play differently from the women [...]. They insisted on relating to the men in this play, which had no male characters [...].

This, besides being a problem for men, is a problem for women because if they write a play where a woman is the protagonist men get all confused [...]. The only answer they have is that it is a feminist play. It could be that it is a feminist play but it could be that it is just a play. We have to reconcile ourselves to the idea that the protagonist of a play can be a woman and that it is natural for a woman to write a play where the protagonist is a woman. Man is not the center of life. And it is natural when this fact reflects itself in the work of women.

The question of personal vision and imagery is for me more important than gender [...]. When we start respecting imagery and sensibility, which are unique, the gender of the writer will be the last thing we will think of.

Excerpt from Fornes, "I Write These Messages That Come" (1977)

Thoughts come to my mind at any point, anywhere—I could be on the subway—and if I am alert enough and I have a pencil and paper, I write these messages that come. It may be just a thought, like a statement about something, an insight, or it could be a line of dialog. It could be something that someone says in my head [...]. That dialog then could become a play. When I am to write a work, I never start from a blank page [...].

The only play that I started from an idea—and it was an idea that was very clear in my head—and that I sat down and wrote was *Tango Palace* [...] because the play has a very strong, central idea. None of my other plays do [...]. I lost interest in that way of working.

The play writes itself. The first draft writes itself anyway. Then I look at it and I find out what is in it. I find out where I have overextended it and what things need to be cut. I see where I have not found the scene. I see what I have to do for the character to exist fully. Then I rewrite […]. But there is a point when the characters become crystallized. When that happens, I have an image in full color, technicolor […] the play exists; it has taken its own life. Even if it is only fifteen pages. It is like an embryo that is already alive and it is there waiting […].

I find doing exercises very valuable. It is good for me not to do things too deliberately: to have half my mind on something else and let something start happening […]. I like analyzing things, but it is better for me not to think very much. Only after I have started creating can I put all my analytical mind into it.

Most of my plays start with a kind of a fantasy game—just to see what happens. *Fefu* started that way. There was this woman I fantasized who was talking to some friends. She took her rifle and shot her husband. Also there is a Mexican joke where there are two Mexican speaking at a bullfight. One says to the other, "She is pretty, that one over there." The other one says, "Which one?" So the first one takes his rifle and shoots her. He says, "That one, the one that falls" […].

There was just that scene […] three years later […] there was a woman in a wheelchair. The play was very different then, but the spirit was actually quite similar […]. Earlier this year [1972] […] I just sat down and did it […].

Space affected *Fefu* […] I decided to look for a place to perform the work. I had finished the first scene, and I had loose separate scenes that belonged somewhere in the second part of the play. I did not like the space I found because it had large columns. But then I was taken backstage to the room the audience could not see. I saw the dressing room, and I thought, "How nice. This could be a room in Fefu's house." Then I was taken to the greenroom I thought that this also could be a room in Fefu's house. Then we went to the business office. That office was the study of Fefu's house […]. I mention this because people put so much emphasis on the deliberateness of a work. I am delighted when something is not deliberate. I do not trust deliberateness. When something happens by accident, I trust that the play is making its own point.

Excerpt from Delgado, "Maria Irene Fornes Discusses Forty Years in Theatre with Maria M. Delgado" (1999)

You can teach playwriting the way you can teach any other art. You don't teach an art by giving the person a bunch of rules. You teach it by encouraging the person to pay attention to their own imagination. To trust and respect their own imagination. To allow the work to be a meditation. To open their imagination and their sensitivity to the themes and aspects of human character that interest them […]. To commit themselves to the integrity of the work. Not to drive the very work out of their hands by burdening it with external concerns. Those are the main things that people have to learn. You can teach a person how to breathe, how to meditate, how to listen to their own consciousness, even how to listen to their own desires. Why wouldn't you be able to teach a person how to find their own creativity?

Please see the Works Cited for further information on the sources used in this essay.

Notes

1 See Cummings, *Maria Irene Fornes,* Appendix A.
2 See Moraga entry in this volume.
3 Tennessee Williams (1911–1983) and Arthur Miller (1915–2005) were among the most prominent American dramatists of the 20th century.
4 Irish writer Samuel Beckett (1906–1989), best known as a dramatist for his play *En attendant Godot* (*Waiting for Godot,* 1953), Romanian-French playwright Eugène Ionesco (1909–1994), and French playwright Jean Genet (1910–1986) all wrote works critic Martin Esslin subsequently called "theatre of the absurd."
5 Dramatic adaptation based on James Joyce's novel *Ulysses* (1922), with legendary actor Zero Mostel (1915–1977) as Leopold Bloom.
6 Franz Kafka's (1883–1924) famous novel *The Trial* (1925), about the inexplicable arrest, prosecution, and execution of banker Josef K.

Suggestions for Further Reading

The Fales Library and Special Collections, Guide to Maria Irene Fornés Papers MSS.413. Elmer Holmes Bobst Library, New York University.
The Rest I Make Up: A Documentary Film about Maria Irene Fornés. Dir. Michelle Memran. New York: Women Make Movies (#1811226), 2018.
Marranca, Bonnie. "The Real Life of Maria Irene Fornés." *Performing Arts Journal* 8:1 (1984): 29–34.
Reagan, Alice. "Maria Irene Fornés, World Builder." *American Theatre* (5 July 2017): 2–25.
Sontag, Susan. "Against Interpretation." *Against Interpretation and other Essays.* New York: Farrar, Straus and Giroux, 1966: 1–10.

52 JANE CHAMBERS (1937–1983)

Sara Warner

Introduction

In February 1981, producers cajoled dramatist Jane Chambers (1937–1983) into act-ing in the Off-Broadway run of her play *Last Summer at Bluefish Cove*. A break-out hit from The First Gay American Arts Festival (June 1980), this lesbian dramedy star-ring Jean Smart as Lil, a rakish dyke who finds love just months before she dies of cancer, had been extended twice with plans for a national tour. A cast member took ill the same day the understudy was hospitalized. Chambers, who hadn't graced the stage in decades, had studied acting at Rollins College and Pasadena Playhouse, but only because she was denied entry into playwriting classes, which were reserved for men (less than 10% of produced plays boasted female authors).[1] Dropping out of the former and suspended by the latter (for wearing pants and smoking), she moved to Manhattan, apprenticed with Erwin Piscator,[2] and joined Actors' Mobile Theatre, making her debut as Laura in *Tea and Sympathy*. Chambers starred in another van-guard queer production, *Single Man at a Party* (1959), which Brooks Atkinson decried as an "anxious tour of the abominations," including "homosexuality, blackmail, death by abortion, and other evidences of bad taste" ("Theatre: Seamy Side" 30).

Soon after the play closed, Chambers moved with a new lover to Maine. While she continued to act – as the title character in a local children's television program, *The Merry Witch*, and with the Lewiston-Auburn Little Theatre – she dedicated most of her energy to writing. She had supported her acting career as a free-lance journal-ist, landing two recurring columns in *Backstage* magazine. Chambers also published poems and essays, including daring compositions about same-sex desire in homo-phile journals *One* and *The Ladder* (under the pseudonym Carol Bradford). During this time, she drafted short stories, outlined a novel, and sold screenplays (all unpro-duced), but it wasn't until she left Manhattan and the world of professional theatre that she felt entitled to write plays. In 1964, Chambers completed her first script, a proto-feminist sex farce, *Business as Usual at Lovelady Goode's,* a previously unknown work I discovered at the Library of Congress.

In 1969, Chambers finally found a mentor to nurture her dramaturgical ambi-tions: lesbian director Catherine Nicholson at Goddard College, in the nation's first low-residency Adult Degree Program. That summer the Stonewall Riots[3] catalyzed the modern gay and lesbian movement as second-wave feminism took the world by storm. Both involved radical forms of street theatre and gave rise to artistic collec-tives that would change the landscape of American drama, including New Feminist Rep, It's All Right to Be Woman, and Women's Interart Theatre, which Chambers

DOI: 10.4324/9781003006923-53

co-founded in 1972 after completing her degree. She staged several feminist plays at Interart (*Random Violence, Mine, The Wife*) but the homophobia of the women's movement kept her lesbian scripts in the closet. While white gay men (e.g., Edward Albee, Mart Crowley, Lanford Wilson, Terrence McNally) moved with relative ease into the mainstream, lesbian and queer of color theatre remained taboo.

When the recently established Playwrights Horizons, with its mission to develop and produce "bold new plays and musicals," mounted Chambers' *A Late Snow*, it made history by staging "the first out lesbian play, the first one affirmative of the lesbian lifestyle as a positive experience" ("About: History and Awards").[4] This was 1974, the year the American Psychiatric Association removed homosexuality from its list of pathologies. An autobiographical comedy, *A Late Snow* features five women – all current or former love interests of Ellie, a college professor – trapped by a blizzard in a remote cabin. Ellie is worried that her friends will out themselves to Margo, a famous author she invited to campus. As the drinks flow, Margo reveals that she too is a lesbian, one who chooses, like Tally in Chambers' *The Eye of the Gull* (1971) and Kitty in *Last Summer at Bluefish Cove*, to remain closeted to protect her reputation. The plot proved prophetic when Jane lost her job on the soap opera *Search for Tomorrow*, despite winning a Writers Guild Award, because CBS executives felt an out lesbian would tarnish their brand and alienate suburban housewives.

Blacklisted by Hollywood and deemed a liability by mainstream theatres, Chambers struggled to find work, eking out a living writing porn. In 1979, Caffe Cino veteran William Hoffman, looking for lesbian scripts, included *A Late Snow* in *Gay Plays: The First Collection*. This landmark anthology by a mainstream press legitimized queer drama and made Jane, one of only two women featured, the standard bearer for lesbian theatre, a position cemented by the award-winning *Bluefish Cove, My Blue Heaven, Quintessential Image*, and *Kudzu*. The latter was poised to be the first lesbian play by a lesbian dramatist on Broadway when Jane died of cancer in 1983, aged 46. (We would have to wait for Lisa Kron's *Well* in 2006 to break this barrier.)

Chambers alludes to herself here, in a gay trade publication at the pinnacle of her abbreviated career, as an "arrogant playwright" who is "humbled" by acting in her play. She delivers these dramaturgical insights both earnestly and tongue-in-cheek, as her queer readers knew any attempt to stage lesbian lives was an audacious act. That a dyke from the deep South felt entitled to pursue playwriting was a brazen gesture. This "arrogant" playwright faced oppression with "humble" persistence and absolute conviction, a position my students find quaint, if not retrogressive. The annual Jane Chambers Playwriting Award keeps this pioneering dramatist au currant, ensuring that her legacy, along with debates about queer performance history, won't lapse anytime soon.

Jane Chambers

"The Arrogant Playwright as Humble Actor" (1981)

[EDITOR'S NOTE: In February 1981, Jane Chambers was called upon to act in her play, LAST SUMMER AT BLUEFISH COVE, in its Off-Broadway production at the Actors Playhouse in New York City. GTAN asked her to reflect upon her experiences in this unusual situation, and the following article, which appears in print here for the first time, is the result.][5]

Everyone knows that actors are temperamental and insecure. Not having toiled as an actor for nearly twenty years, I could state that frequently and with impunity – and often did, especially when faced with actors who challenged the motivations for transitions of the characters they were playing in my plays. I had little tolerance for actors' other complaints, too. How big or warm does a dressing room need to be – the actor is only in there for an hour! And eight performances should not be tiring, it only totals sixteen hours of work a week!

In my play LAST SUMMER AT BLUEFISH COVE, the primary supporting character, Kitty Cochrane, is a medical doctor, unable to cope with patients' deaths, who has given up her practice to become a feminist celebrity by lecturing and writing books. She sets the pace for the first act of the play by throwing a temper tantrum in her opening scene. Much of the humor of the play is set in motion by Kitty. In the second act, she subtly changes, affected by the impending death of her friend, Lil. The dramatic peak of the play comes when Kitty, having seen Lil's x-rays and test results, must tell her best friend that she hasn't long to live. By the play's end, Kitty has gathered strength to return to the practice of medicine.

LAST SUMMER AT BLUEFISH COVE opened first at the Shandol Theatre in March 1980, moved to the Westside Mainstage in June 1980 and was remounted at the Actors Playhouse in December 1980, where it ran until March 1981. During the year of the play's life, Kitty Cochrane was played by four different actresses. All had the same complaints: it was difficult to begin a play at such a high pitch and sustain that pitch throughout the first act; and the transition required of Kitty in the second act was sudden and impossible to play. I poo-pooed this input, attributing it to the artistic temperament innate to actors.

Then came the week in February 1981 when the actress playing Kitty took ill on the same day that the understudy was hospitalized. The tradition that the show must go on is based on economics, not art, and we could not afford to close the show until an actress could be hired and rehearsed to play Kitty. I went on.

I was first surprised to discover that, although I had written the play and seen at least fifty performances of it, I did not know the lines. I knew the whole play, sketchily, from opening to closing curtain but I had not a clue as to which lines belonged to Kitty. The Assistant Stage Manager drilled me on lines for eight hours and I was still unsure. In the second act, Kitty has a long, involved speech with psychiatric terminology which normally provides one of the biggest, longest audience laughs in the entire play. At the one run-through I had with the cast, I botched it terribly. The cast was wide-eyed and nervous. "Don't worry," I assured them, "I wrote it once, I can write it again." And the first night I went on, that's what I did: I ad-libbed half of that speech and nearly lost the audience response. The actresses who had previously played Kitty were right about the energy required for that first act – it is exhausting. As an actor, I was weighted by the responsibility of launching the act – as a playwright, I became aware that I'd written an entire act overly dependent on the rhythm of one character.

In the second act, however, I was vindicated. I found "the sentence scene" where Kitty tells Lil she's dying an easy scene to play. But, as a playwright, I had a liberty the actresses had not had: I changed the blocking. In all the months that actresses playing the role of Kitty had complained about this scene, it had never occurred to me that the problem was in the staging. It had been directed so that Kitty is physically moving away from her friend as she delivers the death sentence. As an actress, I, too, became tentative and evasive when I played the scene as blocked by the director.

Instead, I stood my ground and reached out to her. It changed Kitty's intention and Lil's response. The actress playing Lil agreed with me that the scene worked for the first time.

I also discovered how much of me was in the character: I had no difficulty with Kitty's sudden turns from seriousness to self-deprecating humor – it's a personal trait of my own. I uncovered moments where pompous Kitty is poking fun at herself – something I couldn't see from out front, but, playing the role, was instinctive – I created Kitty, some part of me IS Kitty. Had I played the other seven roles, I expect I would have found me in them, too. As a playwright, I'm a lion about paraphrasing. I send vicious notes to the stage manager to be delivered backstage. Acting the role, I was frequently tempted to change a line because I'd found a new moment or action and wanted the rhythm of the speech to match. Invariably, it threw the scene off. I, as playwright, became so angry at myself, as actor, that one night between scenes I handed the Stage Manager a note which read: "Tell that actress playing Kitty that if she paraphrases that speech again, the playwright is going to kick her behind up between her shoulders." The cast cheered when that note was delivered before curtain next performance.

Although I'd gone into the role with trepidation and reluctance, by the second week I was feeling like an actor, looking forward to each new performance, finding moments, trying new intentions. And I saw that I'd behaved in many of the ways I'd found objectionable – in my insecurity, I'd nearly driven Producer John Glines wild, eliciting his reassurance and praise for my performance (But I can't SEE myself," I repeated, "you have to TELL me."); I complained more than any member of the cast about the draft and low light in the dressing room, about the squeak in the onstage platform floor; I likened the four back-to-back shows on weekends to the Boston Marathon. As playwright, I could never see whether a weakness in a scene was due to the actor or director; onstage I could see it clearly. I intend to experiment with this as a rehearsal device in the future: by stepping into the role myself, I may be able to quickly clarify the source of problems. Playing Kitty brought home to me something else that actors already know: every play is, on one level, an exercise in schizophrenia and the playwright her/himself is the clue to every character. I will never again complain when an actor follows me around a rehearsal hall, observing.

Acting in my own play was an enlightening experience. I recommend it to all playwrights. I'm anxious to do it again. Moreover, it makes me question the validity of another longstanding prejudice of mine: playwrights should never direct their own work. Maybe I'm wrong. Maybe we should.

Please see the Works Cited for further information on the sources used in this essay.

Notes

1 The first comprehensive survey of theater's gender gap, "Action for Women in Theatre: A Study on Employment Discrimination Against Women Playwrights and Directors in Non-Profit Theatre (1969–1975)," found that 7% of dramatists in regional and Off-Broadway productions were women. A recent report, "The Count 2.0," shows we have progressed to 35% (2016–2017).

2 Producer and director Erwin Piscator (1893–1966) is closely associated with Expressionist theatre and developed the Epic Theatre concept that was utilized by Bertolt Brecht.

3 The Stonewall riots, named for the Stonewall Inn in Greenwich Village, occurred fol-
    lowing the police raid of the gay bar in June 1969.
4 See Tish Dace, "From Whom the Bell Tolled," *The New York Native*, 24 October–6 Novem-
    ber 1983, 47.
5 This headnote accompanied the original publication in the *Gay Theatre Alliance Newslet-
    ter* (GTAN).

Suggestions for Further Reading

Dean, Nancy. "Jane Chambers." *Contemporary Lesbian Writers of the United States: A Bio-
    Bibliographical Sourcebook.* Eds. Sandra Pollack and Denise D. Knight. Westport, CT:
    Greenwood Press, 1993. 111–117.
Landau, Penny M. "Jane Chambers: In Memoriam." *Women & Performance: A Journal of Feminist
    Theory.* 1:2 (1984): 55–57.
Roth, Maya and Jennifer-Scott Mobley, eds. *Lesbian & Queer Plays from the Jane Chambers Prize.*
    Southgate, CA: No Passport Press, 2018.

53 ELFRIEDE JELINEK (b.1946)

Anke Charton

Introduction

In her important 1983 essay included here, "Ich möchte seicht sein" ("I want to be shallow"), Austrian theatre artist Elfriede Jelinek (b. 1946) sees the actor as mere cloth, not as controlling the production of meaning: "Get rid of human beings who could fabricate a systematic relationship to some invented character! Like clothes, you hear me? Clothes don't have their own form either. They have to be poured over bodies that ARE their form." With this concept, she anticipates core aspects of what Hans-Thies Lehmann (1944–2022) later termed a "postdramatic" theatrical aesthetic;[1] Jelinek overtly rejects traditional Aristotelian dramaturgy, the theatre apparatus, and the role of the (male) director. When Jelinek was awarded the *Faust* Lifetime Achievement Award in 2017, thirteen years after accepting the 2004 Nobel Prize for Literature only through a taped lecture, she again enacted her refusal to perform: this time, a hand-puppet in her image accepted the accolade on stage.

"I am merely handing over my chaos, my inventions at will, pretty disorderly, not even important shed from unimportant, as proper chaos is," Jelinek stated in "Es ist Sprechen und aus" ("It is talking and over"), an essay written in 2013 for the 125th anniversary of the Vienna Burgtheater. This pantheon of the German-speaking theatre landscape had been the site of Jelinek's controversial 1985 "farce with songs," pointedly titled *Burgtheater*. Much of the general public responded to this production by labeling her a "Nestbeschmutzerin": someone who soils their own nest. *Burgtheater* addressed Austrian collaboration with the Nazis and its lasting legacy. Indeed, Jelinek's writing centrally confronts fascism, revisionism, racism, and misogyny. Her theatre texts grind repressed memories and political affairs, most recently the Ibiza scandal[2] that toppled Austria's center/far-right government in *Schwarzwasser* (*Waste Water*, 2020); the 2016 Trump election in *Am Königsweg* (*On the Royal Road: The Burgher King*, 2017); and European asylum politics in *Die Schutzbefohlenen* (*Charges (The Supplicants)*, 2014).

Still, it is Jelinek's brief essays "on theatre"—39 to date, accessible through her website[3]—that outline her impact on late 20th and early 21st century theatre, including "I want to be shallow"; "Sinn egal. Körper zwecklos" ("Mind Immaterial. Body Useless" 1997); and "It is talking and over." Such pieces expose the ideological pretense of a mimetic theatre based in plot and character in favor of the stage as a place of shifting, unpredictable ambiguity that eschews the authority of an author as much as that of the actor: "I don't want to play, and I don't want to see others play, either. I also don't want to get others to play. People shouldn't say things, and pretend they

DOI: 10.4324/9781003006923-54

are living. I don't want to see that false unity reflected in the faces of actors: the unity of life" ("Shallow").

Jelinek's early writing was informed by the work of French cultural theorist Roland Barthes (1915–1980) and also echoes stances of the Austrian avant-garde writers' *Wiener Gruppe* (c. 1953–1963), which understood language as material, or concrete.[4] Jelinek's "musical flow of voices and counter-voices [...] that with extraordinary linguistic zeal reveal the absurdity of society's clichés and their subjugating power" (Nobel Media), as the Nobel Committee phrased it in 2004, reflects and builds on these influences. While Jelinek's early, international successes—such as *Die Liebhaberinnen* (*Women as Lovers*, 1975) or *Die Klavierspielerin* (*The Piano Teacher*, 1983)[5]—were novels that centered women's experiences within patriarchal structures, the 1990s saw a shift towards dramatic works in a variety of formats, from opera libretti to plays to radio drama. Her language, often described as biting, crass, and obscene, lays bare the violence of a reality instantiated and mirrored by language, "a never-healing wound" ("Meaning Immaterial").

Jelinek's dense and multifold writing might best be understood against the backdrop of her dual formation as a writer and a musician: she studied composition and holds a degree in organ performance. Musical principles such as rhythm, repetition, layering, and temporal flow inform her work. Often described as "language surfaces" (Lehmann 18), Jelinek's writings realize what Lehmann described in *Postdramatic Theatre* as the investigation of a postmodern reality (25, 99–104), radically questioning concepts of authenticity, subjectivity, and authorship.

Frequently, Jelinek draws on previous theatre forms—Greek tragedy in particular—to question a fragmented reality in a highly stylized way. This Brechtian approach resonates with the works of dramatist Heiner Müller (1929–1995); Jelinek's distrust of subjectivity and its ascription to the actor—as someone who would pull "a whole other person out of their mouth" ("Shallow")—also connects her to the legacies of dramatists Heinrich von Kleist (1777–1811) and Georg Büchner (1813–1837).

Jelinek's *Sports Play* (1998) exemplifies her employment of a Greek chorus—it is the main protagonist and "the only thing that has to be kept" (*Sports Play* 39)—and reflects a core aspect of postdramatic aesthetics through a resistance to audience identification with individual characters. Here Jelinek remarks, "The author does not give many stage directions, she has learned her lesson by now. Do what you like" (*Sports Play* 39). Such comments highlight her overall stance on writing and performing as a layered continuum that struggles against linear time.

In "I want to be shallow," originally written for the annual special issue of Germany's most prominent theatre criticism journal, *Theater Heute*, Jelinek delivers a biting deconstruction of institutionalized theatre and its power structures. Her text is a negation of a hierarchical theatre that feigns a "unity of life" onstage. For Jelinek, theatre does not offer a plot or characters to project onto, but will instead, as an aesthetic and political credo, pull the very idea of a ground out from under one's feet.

Elfriede Jelinek

"I Want to be Shallow" (1983)[6]

I don't want to play, and I don't want to see others play, either. I also don't want to get others to play. People shouldn't say things, and pretend they are living. I don't want to see that false unity reflected in the faces of actors: the unity of life. I don't want to see that play of forces of this "well-greased muscle" (Roland Barthes)—the play of language and movement, the so-called "expression" of a well-trained actor. I don't want voice and movement to fit together. In Theatre Today something is being revealed— invisibly, for all the stage strings are pulled behind the scene. The machinery, in other words, is hidden; the actor is surrounded by contraptions, is well-lit, and he walks about. Senselessly he imitates human beings. He produces nuances of expression, and he pulls a whole other person out of his mouth, a person who has a fate that is being laid out. I don't want to bring to life strange people in front of an audience. I don't know, but somehow I prefer not to have anything on stage that smacks of this sacred bringing to life of something divine. I don't want theatre. Perhaps I just want to exhibit activities which one can perform as a presentation of something, but without any higher meaning. The actors should say something that nobody ever says, for this is not life. They should show work. They should say what's going on, but nobody should ever be able to say of them that something quite different is going on inside of them, something that one can read only indirectly on their faces or their bodies. Civilians should say something on stage.

A fashion show perhaps—during which women speak sentences in their clothes. I want to be shallow!

A fashion show, because on that occasion one could also send out the clothes by themselves. Get rid of human beings who could fabricate a systematic relationship to some invented character! Like clothes, you hear me? Clothes don't have their own form either. They have to be poured over bodies that ARE their form. Sagging and neglected hang these covers, but then somebody gets into them, somebody who talks like my favorite saint, and who exists only because I exist: I and the one who I am supposed to be—we won't appear on stage anymore.

Neither individually nor together. Take a good look at me! You won't ever see me again! Deplore it! Deplore it now. Holy, holy, holy. Who, after all, would be able to tell what characters should say what in a theatre. Any number of them I line up against each other; but who's who? I don't know these people! Every one of them could be someone else, and could be represented by some third party who is identical with a fourth, without anyone noticing it. A man says. The woman says. A horse comes to a dentist and tells a joke. No, I don't want to get to know you. Good bye!

Actors tend to be false, while their audiences are genuine. For we, the audiences, are necessary, while actors are not. For this reason the people on stage can be vague, with blurred outlines. Accessories of life without which we would leave again, pocketbooks glued to the slackening crooks of our arms. The actors are as superfluous as these bags—filled as they are, like dirty handkerchiefs, with candy boxes, cigarette cartons, and—yes!—poetry. Blurred ghosts. Products without sense, for their sense is, after all, "the product of a supervised liberty" (Barthes). For every move on stage a certain quantity of liberty is available from which the actor can take a portion. There is the pond of liberty, and the actor—please help yourself!—takes his portion of the juice, his distress-liquid, his secretions. There's no secret about that. He adds his snot. But however much he is going to take from his supply of gesturing and strutting about, the gabbing must be imitable, for he and others like him must be able to mimic it exactly. Like fashion clothing: Each piece is defined, but at the same time not too tightly delimited with respect to what it is supposed to do. Sweater, dress—they all have their leeways and holes for the arms. Yes. And what's really necessary: that's us! We don't have the liberty to be false. Those guys on the stage, however, they do. For they are the ornaments of our life—movable and removable by the hand of God, the director.

And then he tears down a whole chunk of human beings and saddles us with something he likes better. Or he will shorten the human smock by re-aligning the hem—this executive of a regional office of a toy store chain. Don't bother us with your substance! Or with whatever you use to fake substance—like dogs who circle each other with excited growls. Who's the boss? Don't be presumptious! Go away! The meaning of theatre is to be without sense, but also to demonstrate the power of the directors to keep the machinery going. Only with his own importance can the director make the empty shopping bags glow—those sagging, leaking recepticles with more or less poetry in them. So, suddenly the meaningless has meaning! When Sir Director reaches into eternity and pulls out something wriggling. At that point he murders everything that was, and his production, although itself based on repetition, becomes the only thing that is allowed to exist. He negates the past, and at the same time censores [*sic*] (fashion!) that which lies in the future, for that will have to heed what he lays down for the next few seasons. What lies in the future will be domesticated, and whatever is new will be regulated before it even exists. Then a year passes, and the newspapers are screaming again with joy about something new, something unpredictable, which replaces the old. And the theatre starts all over again; the past can be replaced by the present—can be redeemed. The present, nevertheless, always has to bend over the past. That's why there are trade journals. To be able to see anything one has to have seen everything.

But now to our collaborators: How can we remove these dirty marks, these actors, from the theatre, so that they won't pour themselves from their zip-lock packages all over us? I mean: That they won't overwhelm us with their fluids! For it is these people who disguise themselves, who drape themselves with attributes, and who arrogate a double life to themselves. These people allow themselves to be multiplied without running any risk, for they won't ever get lost. In fact, they don't even toy with their own being! They are always the same; they never fall through the bottom, and they never rise into the air. They remain without consequence. Let's simply remove them from the inventory of our life! Let's flatten them out into zelluloid! [*sic*] Perhaps we'll make a movie out of them. From there the odor of their sweat (symbol of a work from which they have tried to escape by way of a luxurious personality) won't be able to waft over to us. But a film as theatre is not a film as film! Just aim and shoot! What you see is what you get. Nothing can be changed, and thus the eternal recurrence of that which is never quite the same will be subverted. They will simply be banned from our lives. They will be punched into piano rolls that whimper wobbly tunes. They drop out of our body perception and turn into surfaces that move before our eyes. They become impossible, and thus don't have to be outlawed, for they are nothing, and they don't exist anymore. Or else: With every performance a whole new crew will take over, and they will do something totally new every time they perform. They have a supply of possible moves, but as with our clothes, nothing will be repeated the way it was done before. It's only time that threatens us with passing away! There must be no theatre anymore. Either the same will always be repeated in exactly the same way (film documentation of a secret performance which can be seen by us humans only as this UNIQUE and ETERNAL repetition), or never twice the same!

Always something quite different! Nothing lasts forever, anyway. In the theatre we can prepare ourselves for entering the dimension of time. Stage people do not perform because they are something, but because their unimportant traits become their real identity. Their wild gesturing, their clumsy, wishy-washy pronouncements, put in their mouths by those who do not comprehend—only by this are they distinguished from each other. They assume, indeed, the identity of persons whom they are supposed to represent, and they turn into ornaments, into performers of performers—in an endless chain. On the stage the ornament becomes the essential thing. And what's essential—Hold it! Step back!—becomes decoration, mere effect. Without being concerned with reality the effect becomes reality. The actors signify themselves, and they become defined by themselves. And I say: Get rid of them! They are not real! Only we are real. We are most of what there is when we, slim and chique, [*sic*], hang in our elegant theatre outfits. Let's look exclusively at ourselves! We are the performers of ourselves. We don't need anything besides us. Going into ourselves, and staying inside—everybody hopes, after all, that as many people as possible will look at him, as he struts through the world, regulated by magazines and their pictures, like a well-greased machine. Let's become our own patterns, and sprinkle snow, meadows, and knowledge with—with what? With ourselves! That's how everything is all right.

Please see the Works Cited for further information on the sources used in this essay.

Notes

1 See his *Postdramatic Theatre* (2006).
2 In 2017, then Vice Chancellor of Austria Heinz-Christian Strache, of the far-right FPÖ, was caught on video in Ibiza discussing underhanded party deals and pondering further corruption. The 2019 publication of the video caused the Austrian government to collapse.
3 https://elfriedejelinek.com/
4 See Schmatz 1992: 69–70; Wiener & Britt 2001: 120.
5 In 2001, a film version starred Isabelle Huppert.
6 Translated by Jorn Bramann.

Suggestions for Further Reading

Fiddler, Allyson and Karen Jürs-Munby, eds. *Elfriede Jelinek in the Arena: Sport, Cultural Understanding and Translation to Page and Stage. Austrian Studies* 22, 2014.

Honegger, Gitta. "'I Am a Trümmerfrau of Language.' An interview with Elfriede Jelinek." *Theater* 36.2 (2006): 20–37.

Janke, Pia. "Notes on Secondary Drama." *Disruption in the Arts. Textual, Pictorial, and Performative Strategies for the Analysis of Societal Self-Description*. Eds. Lars Koch, Tobias Nanz, and Johannes Pause. Berlin: de Gruyter, 2018: 337–338.

Johns, Jorum B., ed. *Elfriede Jelinek: Framed by Language*. Riverside, CA: Ariadne Press, 1994.

Jürs-Munby, Karen, Elfriede Jelinek and Werner Schwab. "Heimat Critique and Dissections of Rightwing Populism and Xenophobia." *Contemporary European Playwrights*. Eds. Maria M. Delgado, Bryce Lease and Dan Rebellato. London: Routledge, 2020: 44–65.

———. "The Resistant Text in Postdramatic Theatre: Performing Elfriede Jelinek's Sprachflächen." *Performance Research* 14.1 (2009): 46–56.

Konzett, Matthias, ed. *Elfriede Jelinek: Writing Woman, Nation, and Identity. A Critical Anthology*. Madison, NJ: Fairleigh Dickinson Univ Press, 2007.

Kovacs, Teresa. "Disturbance in the Intermediate. Secondary Drama as a Parasite." *Disruption in the Arts. Textual, Pictorial, and Performative Strategies for the Analysis of Societal Self-Description*. Eds. Lars Koch, Tobias Nanz and Johannes Pause. Berlin: de Gruyter, 2018: 339–346.

54 SUE-ELLEN CASE (b.1942)

Penny Farfan

Introduction

Sue-Ellen Case (b.1942) is among the pioneers of feminist theatre studies, having come to prominence in the 1980s and remaining active to this day. Her essay "Classic Drag: The Male Creation of Female Parts" (1985), now itself a classic and excerpted here, threw down a feminist gauntlet, challenging readers to rethink—and reject— the foundational texts and practices of Western theatre, drama, and criticism. Re-viewing classical Greek texts, particularly Aeschylus's *Oresteia* and Aristotle's *Poetics*, from a feminist theatrical perspective, Case argued that the male-authored and male-performed female parts of the classical canon should be understood as drag roles that reveal nothing about actual women. Given this fact, she concluded, "feminist practitioners and scholars may decide that such plays do not belong in the canon—that they are not central to the study and practice of theatre" (327).

Case reprinted "Classic Drag" as the opening chapter of her landmark book *Feminism and Theatre* (1988), in which she displaced the male-authored dramatic and critical canon, along with the theatre-historical narratives that have served to enshrine it, by recovering forgotten and neglected plays and performance practices by women, articulating new avenues of feminist research across a range of historical periods and performative modes, and foregrounding playwrights, performers, and critical perspectives from across the contemporary field of 1980s feminist theory and cultural practice. The book's final chapter, "Towards a New Poetics," countered the misogynistic Aristotelian poetics that Case had dispatched in "Classic Drag" and highlighted instead new directions in feminist theory and criticism of theatre, drama, and performance.

Feminism and Theatre opened up ways of seeing that Case pursued in subsequent work, illustrating the new feminist "poetics" across a range of articles and book chapters, among them "Towards a Butch-Femme Aesthetic" (1989), also excerpted here. Reprinted in the late Lynda Hart's important edited volume *Making a Spectacle: Feminist Essays on Contemporary Women's Theatre* (1989), Case proposed in this essay that butch-femme role-play both on and off the stage offered a solution to an impasse in the conceptualization of a feminist—as distinct from female—subject position, that is, a subject position "endowed with the agency for political change, located among women, outside the ideology of sexual difference, and thus the institution of heterosexuality" (56). Case supported her argument with reference to the work of Peggy Shaw and Lois Weaver, who, together with Deb Margolin, formed the celebrated New York-based feminist company Split Britches, whose performance texts Case later anthologized in *Split Britches: Lesbian Practice/Feminist Performance* (1996).[1]

DOI: 10.4324/9781003006923-55

Beyond her own scholarship in the areas of feminist and lesbian theatre and performance studies and critical theory, Case contributed to the development of the wider research field in her capacity as co-editor and then editor of *Theatre Journal* (1986–1989). The impact of her work in this curatorial capacity is evident in her edited collection *Performing Feminisms: Feminist Critical Theory and Theatre* (1990), which reprinted feminist research published in *Theatre Journal* immediately before and during her editorial tenure. Case's own feminist perspective is decidedly materialist, understanding women's experience as rooted in historically specific socio-economic factors and recognizing different experiences of oppression among women across intersecting vectors of class, race, and sexuality. In *Performing Feminisms*, however, as in *Feminism and Theatre*, she foregrounded a plurality of feminisms, creating critical space for a complex and multi-vocal understanding of the strategic uses as well as the limitations of different feminist stances, including the radical feminist view of an essential and universal female experience of patriarchal oppression and a distinct culture of women. *Performing Feminisms* included chapters by leading feminist scholars from within and beyond the field of theatre studies, among them gender theorist and philosopher Judith Butler (b.1956) and feminist film theorist Teresa de Lauretis (b.1938), at once demonstrating and enriching the productive intersection between feminist critical theory and theatre/performance studies. The expansive and generative vision of *Performing Feminisms* extended to Case's later work, including the essay collection *Staging International Feminisms* (2007), which she co-edited with Elaine Aston.[2]

Following the publication of her early field-defining books, Case's research has been voluminous and far-reaching, expanding beyond theatre and performance studies to encompass lesbian and queer cultural studies more broadly, with such noteworthy contributions as *The Domain-Matrix: Performing Lesbian at the End of Print Culture* (1996) and *Feminist and Queer Performance: Critical Strategies* (2009). In addition to her characteristic materialist feminist stance and lesbian critical perspective, her work is marked by a signature wit and a love of camp style. Thus, whereas in the introduction to *Feminism and Theatre* she acknowledged using an "objective" critical voice arising from her training as a scholar and expressed uncertainty as to how to deploy the personal voice associated with so much feminist writing for her analysis of "historical figures and events" (4), by the time of "Towards a Butch-Femme Aesthetic," she could write the following often-cited sentence about the butch-femme couple as "dynamic duo": "They are coupled ones who do not impale themselves on the poles of sexual difference or metaphysical values, but constantly seduce the sign system through flirtation and inconstancy into the light fondle of artifice, replacing the Lacanian slash with a lesbian bar" (57). Case's signature style is further evident in her exploration of the vampire as a figure for the lesbian in "Tracking the Vampire" (1991): "Like the actor peeking out at the audience from the wings before the curtain rises, she rustles plodding, descriptive prose into metaphors whose veiled nature prompts her entrance. Her discursive retinue whets my desire to flaunt, to camp it up a bit, to trans-invest the tropes" (2). The clever, devastating title—"Miss Piggy the Seer in the Land of Trump's Blind: Elfriede Jelinek's *On the Royal Road: The Burgher King*"—of her chapter for my own co-edited book *Critical Perspectives on Contemporary Plays by Women* (2021) serves as a final and very recent example of Case's rhetorical wit. She has been a bold, courageous, insightful, and engaging voice whose work has shaped, enriched, and enlivened feminist critical conversations for almost forty years.

Sue-Ellen Case

Excerpt from "Classic Drag: The Greek Creation of Male Parts" (1985)

[...]

The feminist critic may no longer believe that the portrayal of women in classical plays by men relates to the lives of actual women. Instead, the feminist critic may assume that the images of women in these plays represent a fiction of women constructed by the patriarchy. This assumption originates in a central practice within classical cultures: the division between private and public life. The public life becomes privileged in the classical plays and histories, while the private life remains relatively invisible. The new feminist analyses prove that this division is gender-specific, i.e., the public life is the property of men and women are relegated to the invisible private sphere. The result of the suppression of actual women in the classical world created the invention of a representation of the gender "Woman" within the culture. This "Woman" appeared on the stage, in the myths, and in the plastic arts, representing the patriarchal values attached to the gender of "Woman" while suppressing the experiences, stories, feelings, and fantasies of actual women. [...] The new feminist approach to these cultural fictions divides this "Woman" as a male-produced fiction from historical women, insisting that there is little connection between the two categories. Within theatre practice, the clearest illustration of this division is in the tradition of the all-male stage. "Woman" was played by male actors in drag, while actual women were banned from the stage. The classical acting practice reveals the construction of the fictional gender created by the patriarchy. The classical plays and theatrical conventions can now be regarded as allies in the project of suppressing actual women and replacing them with the masks of patriarchal production.

[...]

The Athenian theatre practice created a political and aesthetic arena for ritualized and codified gender behavior, linking it to civic privileges and restrictions. The elevation of this gender principle to the term "classic" canonizes it as a paradigmatic element of the history of theatre, connoting the expulsion of women from the canon and the ideal. The etymology of "classic," connoting class, indicates that this expulsion is also related to the economic and legal privileges of the "first class"—a class to which women were denied admittance. The consonance of aesthetic criteria with economic ones becomes clear in the term itself. In each of the cultures which has produced "classics" for the stage (not only the Athenian, but the Roman and the Elizabethan), women were denied access to the stage and to legal and economic enfranchisement. These same production values are embedded in the texts of these periods. Female characters are derived from the absence of actual women on the stage and from the reasons for their absence. Each culture which valorizes the reproduction of those "classic" texts actively participates in the same patriarchal subtext which created those female characters as "Woman." Though we cannot examine a production of the Greek classics, we can examine one of the "classic" texts produced for the Dionysian festivals and reproduced in the history of theatrical productions, history, and criticism within our own contemporary culture. The trilogy of *The Oresteia*[3] exhibits all of the themes and practices discussed above. Moreover, its elevated position in the canon illustrates its lasting value. A feminist reading of *The Oresteia* illustrates the defeat of the old matriarchal genealogy, the nature of

"Woman" as portrayed on the stage, the rise of Athena, and the legacy of the suppression of actual women.

[...]

The feminist reader of *The Oresteia* discovers that she must read against the text, resisting not only its internal sense of pathos and conclusion, but also the historical and cultural codes which surround it, including its treatment within theatre history. The pathos the feminist reader feels may be for Iphigenia[4] and Clytemnestra rather than for Agamemnon. She may perceive Athena as a male-identified woman in alliance with the male network of power rather than as a hero of Athens. She definitely feels excluded from the conventions of the stage, bewildered by the convention of cross-gender casting which is only practiced in terms of female characters. Mimesis is not possible for her. Perhaps the feminist reader will decide that the female roles have nothing to do with women, that these roles should be played by men, as fantasies of "Woman" as "Other" than men, disruptions of a patriarchal society which illustrates its fear and loathing of the female parts. In fact, the feminist reader might become persuaded that the Athenian roles of Medea, Clytemnestra, Cassandra or Phaedra[5] are properly played as drag roles. The feminist reader might conclude that women need not relate to these roles or even attempt to identify with them. Moreover, the feminist historian might conclude that these roles contain no information about the experience of real women in the classical world. Nevertheless, the feminist scholar must recognize that theatre originated in this kind of cultural climate and that the Athenian experience will continue to provide a certain paradigm of theatrical practice for the rest of Western theatrical/cultural history. By linking practice, text, and cultural practice in this new way, she may enhance her understanding of how the hegemonic structure of patriarchal practice was instituted in Athens.

[...]

The legacy of the Greeks to theatre history does not end with the theatre practice and texts of Athens. The process known as theatre was first and lastingly articulated by Aristotle in his *Poetics*. This text is still taught in theatre classes as the definitive source of the nature of classical tragedy. Based on the Greek practice as we have considered it and on the kind of texts produced for it, *The Poetics* expands the patriarchal prejudice against women to the nature of the dramatic experience and to the role of the audience.

The feminist reader [...] finds herself reading against this text. In fact, she discovers that she is not even intended to be a reader of this text. Whatever anger she might feel in reading Aristotle's insults or whatever pity she might feel in identifying with the excluded women in this classical era seems inappropriate within the exclusivity of this textual world. At this point, the feminist finds herself to be defined as one without the necessary criteria for the study or the practice of the drama. The prominence of *The Poetics* within the history of the drama and within the study of the history of the drama makes the exclusion of the feminist reader even more comprehensive.

The feminist reader can, however, discover the methodology and assumptions of patriarchal production. She can begin to comprehend the alliance of theatre with patriarchal prejudice. The study of its development may inform the feminist analysis of contemporary theatre, providing it with choices for future action which might make the fiction of "Woman" appear in these texts. The feminist theatre practitioner may come to a new understanding of how to reproduce the classic Greek plays. For example, rather than considering a text such as *Lysistrata*[6] as a good play for women, she might view it as a male drag show, with burlesque jokes about breasts and phal-luses playing well within the drag tradition. The feminist director may cast a man in the role of Medea, underscoring the patriarchal prejudices of ownership/jealousy and children as male-identified concerns. The feminist actor may no longer regard these roles as desirable for her career. Overall, the feminist practitioners and schol-ars may decide that such plays do not belong in the canon—that they are not central to the study and practice of theatre.

Excerpt from "Towards a Butch-Femme Aesthetic" (1988–1989)

[...]

If one focuses on the feminist subject, endowed with the agency for political change, located among women, outside the ideology of sexual difference, and thus the social institution of heterosexuality, it would appear that the lesbian roles of butch and femme, as a dynamic duo, offer precisely the strong subject position the movement requires. [...] [T]he butch-femme couple inhabit the subject position together—"you can't have one without the other," as the song says. The two roles never appear as ... discrete. These are not split subjects, suffering the torments of dominant ideology. They are coupled ones who do not impale themselves on the poles of sexual differ-ence or metaphysical values, but constantly seduce the sign system through flirtation and inconstancy into the light fondle of artifice, replacing the Lacanian slash with a lesbian bar.[7]

[...]

Perhaps the best example of some workings of this potential is in Split Britches' production of *Beauty and the Beast*.[8] The title itself connotes the butch-femme couple: [Peggy] Shaw as the butch becomes the Beast who actively pursues the femme while [Lois] Weaver as the excessive femme becomes Beauty. Within the dominant sys-tem of representation, Shaw, as butch Beast, portrays women who actively love other women as bestial. [...] In other words, the butch, who represents by her clothing the desire for other women, becomes the beast—the marked taboo against lesbianism dressed up in the clothes of that desire. Beauty is the desired one and the one who aims her desirability at the butch.

This symbolism becomes explicit when Shaw and Weaver interrupt the Beauty/ Beast narrative to deliver a duologue about the history of their own personal butch-femme roles. Weaver uses the trope of having wished she was Katherine Hepburn and casting another woman as Spencer Tracy, while Shaw relates that she thought she was James Dean. The identification with movie idols is part of the camp assim-ilation of dominant culture.[9] It serves multiple purposes. One, they do not identify these butch-femme roles with "real" people, or literal images of gender, but with fic-tionalized ones, thus underscoring the masquerade. Two, the history of their desire, or their search for a sexual partner becomes a series of masks, or identities that stand for sexual attraction in the culture, thus distancing them from the "play" of seduction as it is outlined by social mores. Three, the association with movies makes narrative fiction part of the strategy as well as characters. This final fiction as fiction allows Weaver and Shaw to slip easily from one narrative to another, to yet another, unbound by through-lines, plot structure, or a stable sense of character because they are fictional at their core in the style of camp and through the butch-femme roles. The instability and alienation of character and plot are compounded with their own personal butch-femme play on the street as a recognizable couple in the lower East Side scene of New York, as well as within fugitive narratives on stage, erasing the difference between theatre and real life, or actor and character, obliterating any kind of essentialist ontology behind the play. This allows them to create a play with scenes that move easily from the narrative of beauty and the beast, to the duologue on their butch-femme history, to a recitation from *Macbeth*, to a solo lip-sinked [*sic*] to Perry Como. The butch-femme roles at the center of their ongoing personalities move masquerade to the base of performance, and no narrative net can catch them or hold them as they wriggle into a variety of characters and plots.

This exciting multiplicity of roles and narratives signals the potency of their agency. Somehow the actor overcomes any text, yet the actor herself is a fiction and her social self is one as well. Shaw makes a joke out of suturing to any particular role or narrative form when she dies, as the beast. Immediately after dying, she gets up to tell the audience not to believe in such cheap tricks. Dies. Tells the audience that Ronald Reagan pulled the same trick when he was shot—and tells them that was not worth the suturing either. Dies. Asks for a Republican doctor. Dies. Then rises to seemingly close their production by kissing Weaver. Yet even this final butch-femme tableau is followed by a song to the audience that undercuts the performance itself.

[...]

What, then, is the action played between these two roles? It is what [Jean] Baudrillard[10] terms seduction and it yields many of its social fruits. Baudrillard begins his argument in *De la seduction* by asserting that seduction is never of the natural order, but always operates as a sign, or artifice. [...] By extension, this suggests that butch-femme seduction is always located in semiosis. The kiss, as Shaw and Weaver demonstrate in their swooping image of it, positioned at its most cliché niche at the end of the narrative, is always the high camp kiss. [...] The point is not to conflict reality with another reality, but to abandon the notion of reality through roles and their seductive atmosphere and to lightly manipulate appearances. Surely, this is the atmosphere of camp, permeating the *mise-en-scène* with "pure" artifice. In other words, a strategy of appearances replaces a claim to truth. Thus, butch-femme roles evade the notion of "the female body" as it predominates in feminist theory [...]. These roles are played in signs themselves and not in ontologies. Seduction, as a dramatic action, transforms all of these seeming realities into semiotic play. To use Baudrillard with Riviere,[11] butch-femme roles offer a hypersimulation of woman as she is defined by the Freudian system and the phallocracy that institutes its social rule. [...] Therefore, the female body, the male gaze, and the structures of realism are only sex toys for the butch-femme couple. From the perspective of camp, the claim these have to realism destroys seduction by repressing the resonances of vision and sound into its medium. This is an idea worked out by Baudrillard in his chapter on pornography,[12] but I find it apt here. That is, that realism, with its visual organization of three dimensions, actually degrades the scene, impoverishing the suggestiveness of the scene by its excess of means. This implies that as realism makes the spectator see things its way, it represses her own ability to free associate within a situation and reduces the resonances of events to its own limited, technical dimensions. Thus, the seduction of the scene is repressed by the authoritarian claim to realistic representation. This difference is marked in the work of Weaver and Shaw in the ironized, imaginative theatrical space of their butch-femme role-playing. Contrast their freely-moving, resonant narrative space with the realism of Marsha Norman,

Beth Henley, Irene Fornes's *Mud* or Sam Shepard's *Lie of the Mind*.[13] The violence released in the continual zooming-in on the family unit and the heterosexist ideology linked with its stage partner, realism, is directed against women and their hint of seduction. [...] The closure of these realistic narratives chokes the women to death and strangles the play of symbols, or the possibility of seduction. In fact, for each of them, sexual play only assists their entrapment. One can see the butch Peggy Shaw rising to her feet after these realistic narrative deaths and telling us not to believe it. Cast realism aside. Its consequences for women are deadly.

In recuperating the space of seduction, the butch-femme couple can, through their own agency, move through a field of symbols, like tiptoeing through two lips (as Irigaray would have us believe[14]), playfully inhabiting the camp space of irony and wit, free from biological determinism, elitist essentialism, and the heterosexist cleavage of sexual difference. Surely, here is a couple the feminist subject might perceive as useful to join.

Please see the Works Cited for further information on the sources used in this essay.

Notes

1 See Weaver entry in this volume.
2 See also Aston's entry on Monstrous Regiment, and Geraldine Harris' entry on Aston in this volume [eds.].
3 Aeschylus' trilogy from the 5th century BCE concerns the murder of King Agamemnon by his wife Clytemnestra and its aftermath [eds.].
4 Daughter of Clytemnestra and Agamemnon, sacrificed by Agamemnon prior to the first play of the trilogy. Athena, in Greek mythology, is the goddess of war [eds.].
5 In Euripides' play *Medea*, she kills her children as an act of vengeance against their father Jason. In Aeschylus' first play of the trilogy, *Agamemnon*, Cassandra's ability to see the future is ignored, driving her to madness. In Euripides' play *Hippolytus*, Phaedra, wife of King Theseus, kills herself when her love for her stepson Hippolytus is discovered [eds.].
6 Aristophanes' play depicts a sex-strike by the wives and lovers of soldiers in the Peloponnesian War, which the women believe will bring a quick end to the hostilities [eds.].
7 Case here refers to the psychoanalytic theory of Jacques Lacan (1901–1981). For further on Case's revision of the Lacanian notion of the split subject, see "From Split Subject to Split Britches."
8 Case's original note here specifies that there was no published version of *Beauty and the Beast*. Case would later include the script in her edited anthology *Split Britches: Lesbian Practice/Feminist Performance*.
9 Susan Sontag (1933–2004) wrote her groundbreaking essay "Notes on Camp" in 1964, establishing the concept in both aesthetic and cultural contexts, and tying it to notions of "artifice" and "stylization" for material objects as well as creative work [eds.].
10 Jean Baudrillard (1929–2007) was a French theorist best known for exploring the simulation of the real [eds.].
11 Case here refers to Joan Riviere (1883–1962), whose essay "Womanliness as a Masquerade" introduced the concept of women's taking on, or wearing the mask of, traditional femininity in patriarchal culture [eds.].
12 In Baudrillard's book *De la seduction* [eds.].
13 Marsha Norman (b.1947) is best known for her play *'night, Mother* (1982); Beth Henley (b.1952) is best known for her play *Crimes of the Heart* (1979); María Irene Fornés' (1930–2018) *Mud* (1983) centers on a woman struggling for autonomy; Sam Shepard's (1943–2017) *Lie of the Mind* (1985) was one of his plays examining the American family. Some feminist scholars have critiqued these and other realist works for their representations of women and their depictions of violence towards women [eds.].
14 Case here refers to Luce Irigaray (b.1930), *This Sex Which Is Not One*; see especially chapter 11, "When Our Lips Speak Together."

Suggestions for Further Reading

Case, Sue-Ellen. "The Affective Performance of State Love." *Performance, Feminism and Affect in Neoliberal Times*. Eds. Elin Diamond, Denise Varney, and Candice Amich. New York, NY: Palgrave Macmillan, 2017. 15–23.

———, ed. *The Divided Home/Land: Contemporary German Women's Plays*. Ann Arbor, MI: University of Michigan Press, 1992.

———. "From Split Subject to Split Britches." *Feminine Focus: The New Women Playwrights*. Ed. Enoch Brater. Oxford: Oxford University Press, 1989. 126–146.

———. *Performing Science and the Virtual*. London: Routledge, 2007.

55 ADRIENNE KENNEDY (b.1931)

Maya E. Roth

Introduction

Born in 1931, Adrienne Kennedy is one of the great modern experimental Black American writers. Since exploding onto the New York alternative theatre scene in the 1960s, Kennedy has innovated with dramatic and narrative form. A polymath and fabulist, Kennedy, through her distinctive *oeuvre*, uses stream of consciousness— including Black female interiority for and about the stage— non-linear storytelling, historical and cultural citation-as-nightmare, sensory-rich settings, and performative memoir to reveal multi-faceted genealogies of subjectivity and Black trauma.

Kennedy's writing navigates her disparate racial and cultural legacies in uncanny, often painful ways. Raised in a Black middle-class family steeped in social uplift, Kennedy recalls feeling "torn between" not only the double consciousness of Blacks in (white) America, but "these forces of my ancestry… European and African" (*People* 96). Mid-century she was shaped by "the color line," moving between summers with her grandmother in the Jim Crow[1] South of Montezuma, Georgia, and her home in multiethnic Cleveland, where her parents had relocated during the Great Migration. Elliptical, allusive, and cyclic, Kennedy's writing experiments with form and memory. In *The Ohio State Murders* (1992), for instance, she fuses her college experience of racism and sexism in the 1950s with Thomas Hardy's novel *Tess of the D'Urbervilles* (1891). She often refracts her fertile, disorienting time in Ghana in 1960 when pregnant and writing as sensory experiences poured in amid the African Continent's anti-colonial struggles. Her most recent plays creatively remix family traumas from early and late 20th century America, centering interracial intimacy and violence in the Jim Crow South for *He Brought Her Heart Back in a Box* (2018) and the Black family nightmare of police brutality in *Sleep Deprivation Chamber* (1996), co-written with her son Adam. Intellectual and confessional, Kennedy offers multiple frameworks for leveraging her works' complex historical and political, as well as personal, cross-currents. Still, across works she stages imagery and citations from Frantz Fanon's existential theories on the psychopathologies of racism, imbricated in lingering webs of transatlantic colonialism.[2]

Kennedy is best known for her fugue-like one-acts —such as her lyrical, yet wrenching *Funnyhouse of a Negro* (1964, Obie-Winner) about Negro Sarah's crisis of identity, ghosted by racial trauma and her funnyhouse selves (including Queen Victoria-as-Empire, Patrice Lumumba—bludgeoned, and a yellowing Jesus). Or *The Alexander Plays* (1992), in which, through her alter ego Suzanne Alexander, she excavates porous webs of Black psychic and social traumas by intermingling dense subjectivity, gothic

DOI: 10.4324/9781003006923-56

intertexts, and social history. With such plays —as well as *The Owl Answers* (1965), *A Rat's Mass* (1967), and *A Movie Star Has to Star in Black and White* (1976)—"Kennedy fashion(ed) a new kind of narrative structure. With a Black female protagonist at its center, it reinvents as it deconstructs the narrative structures of white, male-dominated culture: Victorian novels, Hollywood movies, Catholic rituals" (Solomon xv).

Her iconoclastic early plays of the 1960s, hallucinatory and surreal, but rarely produced, expressed a different consciousness and aesthetic than either the era's mainstream American drama or the Black Arts Movement. Instead of realism and plot, she staged haunting images of racial and mixed-race trauma via fractured and repeating language, morphing figures, allegorical scenarios that fuse imagination, history, and myth. She was centering her complex "states of mind" (127), she explains, in her ground-breaking creative memoir excerpted here, *People Who Led to My Plays* (1987).

Kennedy has profoundly influenced post-modern and feminist theatrical criticism as well as Black theatre-making: freeing the former from default whiteness and the latter from over-reliance on realism. Playwright Suzan-Lori Parks calls her work "a passionate odyssey into the psyche of post-African America," and credits Kennedy's influence on her own radical experiments with form, a generation later ("Interview"). Theorist Elin Diamond reads Kennedy's work in relation to feminist and psychoanalytic theory,[3] as indeed does Kennedy herself, slyly. "Her echoes and intimations of the European avant-garde alone span nearly a century [...] both in theatre and criticism, from the symbolists to (among others) the surrealists," notes critic Elinor Fuchs ("Adrienne Kennedy" 76). Twenty-first century playwright-performer Aleshea Harris credits Kennedy's "strangeness" as "revelation": "She gave me permission to allow whatever entities (historical, fantastical, or nonhuman) that came knocking to enter" ("Adrienne Kennedy").

People Who Led to My Plays —structured like a scrapbook, with photographs— experiments with pastiche and auto-theory. Brilliant, multifaceted and spare, the memoir cites disparate influences and aesthetics, from modernism and the Harlem Renaissance, to Hollywood's golden age and Federico Garcia Lorca,[4] to kinship and African masks. Fragmentary in form, the selections reproduced here suggest the book's flow, hailing five contexts that shaped and disrupted her coming of age as a Black female writer: Elementary School, High School, College, Marriage and Motherhood, and Voyage. Mixing quite personal and critical curation, she forges a multi-faceted history, too, of mid-20th century life and arts.

Kennedy's experimental memoir has been lauded since its publication. Black feminist theorist bell hooks see it as partner work to Virginia Woolf's *A Room of One's Own* (1929); theatre theorist Elinor Fuchs sees it as a late-twentieth century conversation with Maurice Maeterlink's *The Tragical in Daily Life* (1917); the book jacket compares it to James Joyce's *Portrait of the Artist as a Young Man* (1916) and quotes fellow writer Ishmael Reed, who calls it "a new form of black autobiography."

Infused with a gothic embrace of imagination, sensory experience, and women's dreams, *People* intermingles lyricism and terror and post-colonial as well as modernist lenses. The work is both accessible and evocative, functioning as a casebook for Kennedy's complex, sometimes overwhelming early plays. With her as proxy, readers discover the expressive poetics—and racialized, gendered politics—of form. Her beloved models sublimate Kennedy's experience; only as she travels in Europe and lives in Africa does Kennedy discover the psychic and social freedom to express her radical difference, reimagining how to write. Instinctively, Kennedy's memoir links African theatre's praxis of possession, and the power of objects, to Western literature's emphasis, like Fanon's, on consciousness. She theorizes heterogeneity, yet also kinship, deconstructing liberal individualist —as well as linear—models of self, story, history. The narrative arc gestures to awakening, the thematic one lucid dreaming. In the early 21st century, Kennedy has been embraced as a doyenne of American theatre and a visionary transatlantic Black writer.

Adrienne Kennedy

Excerpts from **People Who Led to My Plays** *(1987)*

ELEMENTARY SCHOOL
1936–1943

More and more often as my plays are performed in colleges and taught in universities, people ask me why I write as I do, who influenced me. When they ask this they are usually referring to my original one-act plays, *Funnyhouse of a Negro, The Owl Answers, A Rat's Mass* and *A Movie Star Has To Star in Black and White,* and not to my commissioned work [...] for Julliard *(Electra* and *Orestes),* the Mark Taper Forum *(The Life of Robert Johnson),* or the Empire State Youth Institute *(Chaplin's Childhood).* Who influenced you to write in such a nonlinear way? Who are your favorite playwrights?

After I attempt to answer, naming this playwright or that one, as time progresses I realize I never go back far enough to the beginning. So I decided to.

People on Old Maid cards (1936, age five):
Through make-believe one could control people on a small scale.

Paper dolls:
You could invent enchantment with paper.
[...]

People in fairy tales:
There was a journey in life that was dark and light, good and evil, and people were creatures of extreme love, hatred, fear, ambition and vengefulness, but there was a reward if one kept seeing the light and hoping. [...] Stories of people could hypnotize.
[...]

Sabu, Turhan Bey:
Two people in the movies who were *not* white.
[...]

Souls, witches, magicians, Sleeping Beauty:
I hoped no one would put me to sleep for a hundred years. For when I woke up where would my parents and brother be?
[...]

People in my mother's dreams:
People whom my mother saw at night had often "been dead for years." I didn't know anyone who had been dead for years. So her dreams held a spectacular fascination. "My Aunt Hattie," "my stepfather," "my grandmother," "my mother," all were people who had been dead a long time. But from my mother's dreams, I got to know them.
[...]

HIGH SCHOOL
1946–1949
[...]

THE GLASS MENAGERIE[5]:
I saw the play and for the first time understood that there were other family secrets, family joys, and sorrows, just as in my own family."
[...]

Chekhov, Joan and her mother:
[...] My friend and her mother sitting together reading aloud a play by someone called Chekhov enchanted me. "He's a great Russian writer," Joan told me. Over our lunch she and her mother told me the story of *The Cherry Orchard*.

Joan's father (a lawyer) had died the year before, and [...] she had written me notes telling me how sad her house was now and how her mother (who had never worked) had to get a job as a salesclerk.

But now on this pretty afternoon as they talked of Chekhov they were joyful.
[...]

Flavius David:
He taught World History and was the first person whom I ever heard say that every event was connected [...]. And that there was a "universal unconscious."
[...]

Laura (in THE GLASS MENAGERIE):
From my extreme empathy with her I learned that I too felt frightened and crippled, which was totally puzzling to me. Why? Why did I feel like Laura? Why? I was popular [...]. Why?

COLLEGE
1949–1953
[...]

Lorca:
[...] My unhappiness with the racial climate at Ohio State and the drafting of my fiancé into the army left me feeling dark. Lorca's dark complex vision was thrilling and comforting to me.

Florence told me Lorca[6] had been killed mysteriously. The year before I had seen *Death of a Salesman*. These writers said tragedy was the nature of life. There was a crosscurrent in life that moved across football games, dances, clothes[...]

MARRIAGE AND MOTHERHOOD
1953–1960
[...]

Tennessee Williams:
While I was pregnant I read as much of Williams as possible. *Streetcar Named Desire* was at the height of its fame. My friends and I were in love with Marlon Brando (from his films) and saw Brando as a rebel;[7] he was the first movie star (in the dorm) that both my white and my Negro friends had loved equally, at a time when we seemed to have little in common except our passion for "engagements" and engagement rings. [...]

My husband Joe:
How he focused his energy, ignoring fatigue, and how he refused to acknowledge obstacles, but just continued to work hard at goals. He made working hard seem like an adventure.

Myself, New York:
Sometimes when I'd walk down the street I'd hum "I Like New York in June."[8] [...] I bought black toreador pants and a black sweater and gathered my hair in a pony-tail—like Audrey Hepburn[9] and the girls in *Vogue*—and I daydreamed.

I started another play, about a family—the father was a minister and they lived in a kind of biblical setting[...]

I started another play about a family... perhaps the father could give fine stirring sermons... perhaps the mother could have dense complex dreams [...]. I tried to capture this.

Yet I still didn't really understand how intensely I wanted my family on the stage (like the family in *Our Town*[10]), like Tom, Laura and Amanda in *The Glass Menagerie*.

[...]

RASHOMON[11] (I saw the movie again):

It haunted me by its mystery. Life is like that, I thought: human visions crossing, disputing one another, violently clashing.

[...]

My father (again in the '50s):

Life had begun to merge with literature. My father had by now changed from an outgoing, gregarious man to a Hamlet... a Willy Loman.[12] He reflected, pondered constantly the meaning of his past life. So now I had 'two fathers'— my heroic father of the '30s and '40s and now my Hamlet-Willy Loman father of the '50s. I tried to reconcile them... but it tormented me.

Eugene O'Neill:[13]

I'll be forever grateful to him for the extraordinary light he shed on the matrix of his family relationships in *Long Day's Journey Into Night,* the greatest play I had seen on the stage [...]

Jason Robards[14] *and Eugene O'Neill,* THE ICEMAN COMETH:

[...] Seeing what would become historic productions *(Iceman* and *Long Day's Journey)* made it clear the stage was where mysterious, unparalleled passion and dilemmas of the deepest kind could be expressed. [...] I worked even harder at creating settings. My settings seemed so pallid, so weak in comparison to these two plays which now haunted my mind.

[...]

Chekhov, Dante, Virgil[15] *and the Bible:*

Over and over I copied passages from them, studying the language and the rhythms.

Chekhov and my brother:

I saw my brother and myself as Nina and Constantine in *The Seagull.* [...].

Dostoevsky[16]:

Severe trauma and trial are natural to our existence.

[...]

Audrey Wood (literary agent):

The play I wrote at the New School (*The Pale Blue Flowers*) got me my first letter from a literary agent. Although she didn't take me on, she wrote a long encouraging letter. I was only twenty-four. So her letter was important. After all, she was Tennessee Williams' agent.

[...]

Mrs Rosebaugh and Caesar (mid-50's):

[...] She had read in Latin and then translated into English, her frail voice trembling. The sound of Mrs. Rosebaugh reading Latin is a sound I today strive for when I write, just as I strive for the emotional levels of spirituals. Nobody Knows the Troubles I've Seen, Nobody Knows but Jesus, And, Sometimes I Feel Like a Motherless Child, And, Go Down Moses [...][17]

Nina (in THE SEAGULL):
In my wild, desperate attempts to become a writer, I felt like Nina [...] so desperate to express my thoughts and feelings, her speech spoke for me.

"I am alone. Once in a hundred years I open my lips to speak and my voice echoes mournfully in the void and no one hears..." [...]

Josephine Baker, Mabel Mercer:[18]
I reflected on these Negro women whom I had read about. (Mabel Mercer we would soon see at the Byline Room.) They had gone to Europe to be "discovered." Was that a necessity? [...]

Tennessee Williams:
The writer whose career and plays I coveted. It took ten years to stop imitating him, to stop using his form, to stop stealing his themes, which were not mine.
[...]

Jung:
Dreams, memories. I must stop trying to ignore them.

Kazan, Williams, Brando:
Would I ever be part of an artistic brotherhood like this? Ever?
[...]

Beethoven and Hatshepsut:
I'd often stare at the statue of Beethoven I kept on the left-hand of my desk. I felt it contained a "secret." I'd do the same with the photograph of *Queen Hatsheptsut* that was on the wall. I did *not* then understand that I felt torn between these forces of my ancestry...European and African...a fact that would one day explode in my work.

Beethoven and Hatshepsut (again):
When friends asked me [...] I always said they were inspiration. [...] Soon I *would* understand that I was in a dialogue with the photographs, prints, postcards of people. They were my alter egos.
[...]

Federico Garcia Lorca (POET IN NEW YORK, 1950s):
This book, like all of Lorca's work, showed me that imagery is multilayered, that it comes from recovering connections long ago lost and buried.
[...]

Aristotle (POETICS):
"The greatest thing by far is to be a master of metaphor. It is the one thing that cannot be learned for another and it is also a sign of genius since a good metaphor implies an intuitive perception of the similarity in dissimilars."
[...]

Tennessee Williams:
His comments on the nature of writing and drama in [...] *Theatre Arts* magazine, especially an essay on how he utilized the colors of great painters in his work, and as well, actual scenes. He spoke of how he used a setting in Cézanne[19] for inspiration as a scene in *Streetcar Named Desire.*
[...]

Langston Hughes:[20]
His work defined a whole society of Negroes, and somehow in its power was defining and creating me personally.
[...]

Lorca (again):

After I read and saw *Blood Wedding*, I changed my ideas about what a play was. Ibsen, Chekhov, O'Neill and even Williams fell away. Never again would I try to set a play in a "living room," never again would I be afraid to have my characters talk in a nonrealistic way, and I would abandon the realistic set for a greater dream setting. It was a turning point.
[...]
Martha Graham:[21]
After I saw her production of *Clytemnestra,* the question of how I could use mythic characters in my own work grew in my mind.
[...]
Lorraine Hansberry:
I had abandoned playwriting by the time Lorraine Hansberry made her sensational entrance into the Broadway theater with the classic *A Raisin in the Sun,* because I thought there was no hope; but with Lorraine Hansberry's success, I felt reawakened.
[...]

A VOYAGE
1960–1961
[...]
The voyage:
As the Duchess of Hapsburgh[22] had haunted my mind, so would Queen Victoria [...] The statue we saw of Victoria in front of Buckingham Palace was the single most dramatic, startling statue I'd seen. Here was a woman who had dominated an age.

In my play, I would soon have the heroine, Sarah, talk to a replica of this statue. *Finally* the dialogue with the statue would be explicit and concrete. And the *statue* would reply; the *statue* would inform my character of her *inner* thoughts. The *statue* would reveal my character's secrets to herself.
[...]
West Africa:
There where I saw the Ethiopian princesses, the palace of Tubman, and the statue of Kwame Nkrumah,[23] it was there I started the lines of two plays, *Funnyhouse of a Negro* and *The Owl Answers,* and the lines had a fierce new cadence. (119)
Patrice Lumumba:
[...] "They've killed Patrice Lumumba.[24] Lumumba was the hope."
Just when I had discovered the place of my ancestors, just when I had discovered this African hero, he had been murdered. [...] He became a character in my play... a man with a shattered head.
[...]
Ulli Bieir (editor of BLACK ORPHEUS):
[...] When Ulli Bieir[25] came to Accra, we all had dinner at the Achimota Guest House and he invited us to Nigeria to meet his wife, a painter, who lived there. Word seemed to travel fast in West Africa among foreigners. It was soon known that I was having a story published in *Black Orpheus.* "Are you a writer?" people now asked. "Yes," I said. "Yes." I felt such exhilaration [...] that I worked more feverishly on the passages and pages that I had started on the *Queen Elizabeth.*

We had stayed in several cities a week (London, Paris, Madrid, Casablanca) and in each city my notebook had filled up with ideas, thoughts, feelings, impressions. Now, after Joe had gone to the bush and our son had left for school [...], I worked constantly until one o'clock, when I walked to the school and picked him up.

The sun and moon seemed to have a powerful effect on my senses. I felt on fire.
[…]

Africans or the masks:

[…] (N)ot until I bought a great African mask from a vendor on the streets of Accra,
of a woman with a bird flying through her forehead, did I totally break from realis-
tic-looking characters. I would soon create a character with a shattered, bludgeoned
head. And that was his fixed surreal experience.

Please see the Works Cited for further information on the sources used in this essay.

Notes

1   Refers to a set of a laws and cultural practices that mandated racial segregation, disen-
franchising Black Americans and enforcing white supremacy, including via violence,
from roughly 1890–1965, in Southern States of the United States, especially supporters
of the Confederacy during America's Civil War (1861–1865). "Jim Crow" cites a stock
minstrel character, performed in blackface by a white performer during America's
slavery era, represented as a lazy buffoon, who was ridiculed and demeaned by whites
onstage and in the audience.

2   Born in Martinique, Frantz Omar Fanon (1925–1961) was a psychiatrist and social activist in Algeria during the African Wars of Independence, who wrote *Black Skin, White
Masks* (1952) and *The Wretched of the Earth* (1961), seminal texts analyzing the effects of
white colonizing cultures on Black psyches and communities. He argued for the necessity to decolonize subjugated selves and nations as linked.

3   See Diamond, *Unmaking Mimesis*.

4   Federico García Lorca (1898–1936), a Spanish Symbolist, wrote "dreamlike" tragic
poems and plays on Andalusia, including *Romancero Gitano* (1928, *The Gypsy Ballads*),
Blood Wedding (1933) and *The House of Bernarda Alba* (1936). He was assassinated by
Fascists in 1936, early in the Spanish Civil War.

5   A 1944 memory play by American Tennessee Williams (1911–1983), the title of which references the glass figurines collected by the character Laura, a young disabled woman.

6   Florence was Kennedy's friend.

7   American actor Marlon Brando (1924–2004) starred in the 1951 film adaptation of
Williams' 1947 play, set in New Orleans.

8   The song "How About You" (1941) by Burton Lane and Ralph Freed was later recorded
by Frank Sinatra, among others.

9   Legendary film actress (1929–1993).

10 1938 play by American Thornton Wilder (1897–1975), set in a fictional small town,
Grover's Corners, New Hampshire.

11 1950 film by Japanese director Akira Kurosawa (1910–1998).

12 The titular figure in Miller's *Death of a Salesman*.

13 Irish American Eugene O'Neill (1888–1953) wrote realist, poetic tragedies for the
American stage, culminating with the autobiographical *Long Day's Journey Into Night*
(produced posthumously 1956).

14 American actor, iconic for interpreting O'Neill's dramas.

15 Anton Chekhov (1860–1904), Russian writer; Italian Dante Alighieri (c. 1265–1321)
famous for his three-part epic poem *Divine Comedy* (1309–1320); Virgil (70–19 BCE)
wrote ancient Rome's epic poem *The Aeneid* (29–19 BCE).

16 Russian Fyodor Dostoevsky (1821–1881), aka Dostoyevsky, wrote *Crime and Punishment* (1866)
and *Notes from the Underground* (1864), probing social crisis with psychological depth.

17 African American Spiritual songs originated during slavery and passed across generations; Lena Horne, Marian Anderson, Paul Robeson, Louis Armstrong, and others
released major recordings in the 20th century.

18 American-born French Cabaret performer Josephine Baker (1906–1975) found fame
in 1920's Paris, the first Black female film star (*Siren of the Tropics*, 1927); English-born

Cabaret Singer Mabel Mercer (1900–1984) headlined music halls in 1930s Paris, then moved to US supper clubs and jazz recordings.

19 French Modern Artist Paul Cezanne (1839–1906) was a Post-Impressionist.

20 American Writer Langston Hughes (c. 1902–1967) shaped the Harlem Renaissance via jazz poetry, fiction, essays and autobiography. Major works include *The Weary Blues* (1926), *The Ways of White Folks* (1934), *Montage of a Dream Deferred* (1951) and the memoir *I Wonder As I Wander* (1956).

21 Martha Graham (1894–1991), American choreographer and pioneering modern dancer.

22 The Duchess of Haspburgh (1717–1780), Maria Theresia, ruled Austria's Hapsburg Dynasty for four decades.

23 Ghanaian Kwame Nkrumah (1909–1972) led the Gold Coast of Africa to independence from British rule in 1957 and then served as Ghana's first President and Prime Minister.

24 Patrice Lumumba (1925–1961) pan-African leader and activist, served as the Congo's first Prime Minister after Belgian colonial rule; he was assassinated within months, aided by Western governments.

25 Ex-pat (German-born) editor of the literary journal *Black Orpheus*, who invited Kennedy to write an essay.

56 LIZ LOCHHEAD (b.1947)

Aoise Stratford

Introduction

Renowned Scottish writer Liz Lochhead (b.1947) came to national attention as a poet in the early 1970s when she won a BBC Scotland Poetry contest. In addition to giving poetry readings, Lochhead wrote and performed monologues and pieces in revues while also developing as a dramatist. Volumes of poetry include *The Grimm Sisters* (1981) and *Dreaming Frankenstein* (1984). Plays include *Blood and Ice* (1982), *Dracula* (1985), *Mary Queen of Scots Got Her Head Chopped Off* (1987), as well as several acclaimed adaptations of Molière and Greek Tragedy. Lochhead's writing demonstrates a keen ear for the muscularity and musicality of language, a vivid (re)visionary imagination, and unabashed nationalist and feminist politics.

Lochhead's significance as a dramatist is rooted in her feminist revisions of historical figures, mythical icons, and fictional characters. As Dorothy Porter McMillan notes in her essay, "Liz Lochhead and the Ungentle Art of Clyping," Lochhead is self-conscious and explicit in her use of the deconstructive "tricks and tropes of revisionary story[telling]," making Lochhead's oeuvre exemplary of what "may well be the central project of contemporary women's writing. The construction or reclamation of a women's tradition [that] shapes or brings to light hidden or neglected stories" (17). In her *Introduction to Feminsm and Theatre* (1995), Elaine Aston makes a particular example of Lochhead's play *Blood and Ice*, which is about the life and writing of Mary Shelley, arguing that it not only offers important "materialist-feminist critique" but also makes the "feminist revisioning process visible in a performance context" (144–145). Like *Blood and Ice*, *Mary Queen of Scots* takes up familiar female figures from a collective cultural consciousness and "twists" their story, deploying theatrical devices that draw our attention to the construction of cultural knowledge and staging women's struggles with institutionalized power and gender politics. Lochhead's women—whether Mina Harker, Mary Shelley, or Mary Queen of Scots—are very much products of Lochhead's own twentieth-century Scottish context: one in which class and gender determine power in a dominantly patriarchal society and where Scots occupy a marginalized position within the UK.

So too the introduction to *Mary Queen of Scots,* excerpted here, might be viewed as a text that "twists" narratives about adaptation and playwriting, illuminating and deconstructing the playwright's process. Like her introductions to *Dracula* and *Blood and Ice,* which we might think of as sister texts, this introduction offers a deeply intimate, autobiographical and consciously political narrative about playwriting as a process that is both mysteriously "subterranean" (*Dracula* viii) and consciously

DOI: 10.4324/9781003006923-57

executed. It is a messy process, cantilevering between the "midnight oil" of writ-ing-fever (*Blood and Ice* vii; *Mary* ix), and writer's block. It flows and stalls, gesturing toward an "anxiety of authorship," as theorized by Sandra Gilbert and Susan Gubar in relation to nineteenth-century women writers, Shelley among them (45), and arguably functions as a part of Lochhead's inherited literary context and feminism.

Significantly, Lochhead's critical writing reveals a dramatic writing process that is not only irregular but also composite. It is a process in which dreams, research, craft, feminist politics, current events, impulse, hindsight, dramaturgical agency, literary influences, the circumstances of production, and personal experience all inform the work equally and are mutually supportive. In this way, Lochhead's criti-cal contribution is, in part, the articulation of an alternative to dominant narratives of playwriting and adaptation that privilege inherently patriarchal values such as linear progression, singularity, hierarchy, and closure. Such narratives have been persistent. Vincent Murphy's *Page to Stage: The Craft of Adaptation* (2013), for example, articulates a systematic step-by-step set of "basic building blocks" that a playwright can "uncover" and master in the process of dramatic adaptation (2).

Lochhead's more kaleidoscopic approach is captured as both subject and form in her critical writing. The introductory material included here is typically full of interruptions, references to other texts and people, brief eruptions of Scots, changes in tense, unfinished phrases, ellipses, breathless unpunctuated sentences, slippages in point of view, and unanswered questions. Her prose, like her process, runs, leaps, halts, and twists: "Oh, but I could do it as a play-within-a-play and it could be a hor-rid-comical masque of Salome, which would end up with a different head on a plate […] It was, for me, from now on, just simply a matter of getting on with it" (*Mary*, ix).

The process of just "getting on with it" is a recurring focus of Lochhead's critical writing, emphasizing the labor of the writing process, and revealing how that labor is shaped by the forces of context. Lochhead's realization about how to write the ending of *Mary Queen of Scots*, for example, occurs as she sees a "stagger-run of the first half" during rehearsal (*Mary* ix), while her realization about the beginning of the play comes from a conversation with her collaborator, director/producer Gerry Mulgrew, about another text entirely. And much of the text between those moments takes its structure from "the debate about the then current state of affairs between Scotland and England" in the wake of Margaret Thatcher's election (*Mary* x). In her Introduction to *Blood and Ice*, Lochhead explains that she went back and rewrote a new version of that play when director David McVicar brought her in to talk about his idea for staging the play and to meet with his potential cast. This happened, Lochhead writes, after several years of "trying, abortively, to solve the problem of the structure […]—for its own sake, whether there was an upcoming production or not—happily scribbling away through long lonely nights, just as obsessively, I had to own, as half-mad Frankenstein himself labouring with his unlovely creation, looking for the spark of life" (*Blood and Ice* vi).

Dramatic structure, then, is born at the convergence of multiple forces, rather than prefabricated in a vacuum ahead of time and then turned over as a vessel for content. In writing about her struggle with structure, Lochhead's introductions are themselves structured to move back and forth between current events, the work of other writers, the circumstances of production, and the collaborative process so that those things become part of the fabric of adaptation. The leap from one idea to another is symptomatic of the stream-of-consciousness that characterizes much of

Lochhead's work and challenges us to read actively by making intuitive rather than explicit connections: "'I can't write the Mary Queen of Scots play you wanted. And the bloody Tories are in again'" (*Mary* viii).

Liz Lochhead's feminist dramaturgy, then, asks us to be conscious of how meaning is made. Benjamin Poore notes that adaptation is "the production of a cultural double," something which, he rightly notes, *Dracula* in particular and Lochhead's plays, in general, take full advantage of, working with doubling and repetition, and trading on the audience's "cultural competency" to generate dramatic irony and uncanny echoes (87, 90). Certainly, the ending of *Mary Queen of Scots* gains much of its impact from such devices. Moreover, Lochhead's own writing about the process of writing functions as a kind of double, too, offering an intimate storytelling that both shows and tells us how her plays work: by association, rather than translation, by accumulation rather than conversion, always becoming more than the sum of their parts. Lochhead's significant contribution is to illuminate that process in both theory and practice.

Liz Lochhead

Excerpt from "Introduction" to Mary Queen of Scots Got Her Head Chopped Off *(1987)*

[...] How I remember *Mary Queen of Scots Got Her Head Chopped Off* coming about was this: Gerry Mulgrew had the idea. [In 1987] it was going to be the four hundredth anniversary of Mary's decapitation. [...]

It all seemed a long way ahead, more than two and a half years. I was delighted to say yes. It didn't, that night, matter that neither of us seemed to know much of anything of the history, except the blunt axe-man ending and...oh, yes, we had both dim memories of a childhood game played by flicking the heads of dandelions while chanting 'Mary-Queen-of-Scots-Got-Her-Head-Chopped-Off, Mary-Queen-of-Scots-Got-Her-Head-Chopped-Off...' We were, though, already very aware that culturally, as a Scot of Irish-Catholic descent (Gerry) and I, of solidly Lowland Scottish Presbyterian stock, had been brought up with totally different versions of the myth [....] I was as much exercised by the misogyny of John Knox,[1] his enduring anti-feminist, anti-feminine legacy in Scottish society, as Gerry was attracted by the notion that Knox's teaching the people to read so they could read the Bible for themselves and the Protestant ideal of a direct one-to-one relationship with God, un-mediated by any clerical hierarchy, had directly led to democracy. We were both republican and anti-royalist.

[...]

Flash forward to June 1987 and I'm up all night, unable to go to bed as the horror unfolds and the election results come in. For the third time Margaret Thatcher gets back in to power. We can't believe it. Nobody in Scotland can believe it. We voted resoundingly against the Tories in this country and yet we are being ruled by them. Again. That Friday there is a palpable sense of gloom everywhere, and at Glasgow Queen Street I actually consider getting on the wrong train, running away, instead of boarding the train to go to that meeting in Edinburgh in Communicado [Theatre]'s wee borrowed office to tell Gerry that we don't have a play to go into rehearsal with next month. Yes, there are scenes and fragments all over the place, we both know there are those wee bits we like, that speech of the Corbie character with the pan-Scotland overview, that sexy scene between Leicester and Elizabeth, that plotting scene where Mary, imprisoned in that castle, gets that brewer to help her get messages out to her English Catholic allies, there is mibbe something in that cruel kids' stuff but it doesn't fit with anything else...I've got a trunk-load of research material (I had increasingly spent more and more hours that spring in Glasgow's Mitchell Library doing more and more 'research' – i.e. Not Writing the Play). 'Gerry, I've got all these scenes, but we don't have a play. We go into rehearsal next month and by then I'll have found you a do-able one among all the literally hundreds there are about her, the library catalogue says so. I'll start reading today. I can't write the Mary Queen of Scots play you wanted. And the bloody Tories are in again.'

Gerry is amazing. He refuses, just won't release me from the job of doing this piece [...]. He says to imagine how *King Lear* would be as a fairy story. *Once upon a time there was a king who had three daughters, and he decided to divide his kingdom between them, so he called them together and...* 'Just write once upon a time,' he says... 'What would that be?' And we'll go from there.'

So that night, back home in Glasgow, I find myself writing down – just as part of a process, that was all he'd meant it to be – "once upon a time there were twa queens on the wan green island.' And realising just how well that fitted Corbie's voice...

[...] I can remember, just a week before rehearsals began, coming up with what seemed like a good solution for how to do the murder of Riccio for this tiny cast. (In reality, more than a dozen armed men broke in and murdered Mary's secretary before her very eyes as she sat with a few trusted servants in Holyrood Palace.) Oh, but I could do it as a play-within-a-play and it could be a horrid-comical masque of Salome, which would end up with a different head on a plate...It was for me, from now on, just simply a matter of getting on with it, and the sheer enjoyment of the rhyming and the Stanley Holloway parodying,[2] and taking down those most passion-ate speeches for Mary which seemed, whiles, to almost write themselves.

When we did go into rehearsal, about three quarters of what is now here was extant. Not necessarily in the right order – I don't like to admit it but the Bairns scene was the beginning of the play, not the end.

[...] But at the end of the first week, as the company struggled through a stag-ger-run of the first half, I saw quite clearly what the structure of the whole play should be. The Bairns were a coda, Corbie the beginning.

[...] We got there in the end. With the play not yet quite in the shape that now goes into print, but definitely in the context of a debate about the then current state of affairs between Scotland and England that the play seemed to illuminate. Margaret Thatcher is not Queen Elizabeth the First, but questions of women and power – and how to hold on to it – are always there as we consider either icon. There was at that time a real sense of frustration in Scotland, a need for us to tell our own stories and find our own language to tell it in.

[...] The Jock Tamson's Bairns ending of Mary [came] out of an early workshop day about a year or more before rehearsals when – and I really can't remember whose initial idea this was – we considered: could we tell the whole story, do the whole play, as a set of contemporary children forced to re-enact a tragedy we didn't understand?

Please see the Works Cited for further information on the sources used in this essay.

Notes

1 John Knox (c.1514–1572), Scottish Reformation theologian best known for his pamphlet *The First Blast of the Trumpet Against the Monstrous Regiment of Women* (1558). See, also, Monstrous Regiment entry in this volume.
2 British comic actor Stanley Holloway (1890–1982), best known for the role of Alfred P. Doolittle in the stage and screen productions of the musical *My Fair Lady*.

Suggestions for Further Reading

Brown, Ian. *History as Theatrical Metaphor: History, Myth, and National Identities in Modern Scottish Drama*. New York, NY: Springer Literature. Cultural and Media Studies eBooks, 2016.
Crawford, Robert and Anne Varty, eds. *Liz Lochhead's Voices*. Edinburgh: Edinburgh University Press, 1993.
Lochhead, Liz. *Five Plays*. London: Nick Hern Books, 2012.
Varty, Anne, ed. *The Edinburgh Companion to Liz Lochhead*. Edinburgh: Edinburgh University Press, 2013.

57 CONSTANCE CONGDON (b.1944)

Ryan Platt

Introduction

Constance Congdon (b.1944) is "one of the best playwrights our country," Tony Kushner famously proposed, "and our language, has produced" (Kushner, "Introduction" ix). As a member of New Dramatists, Congdon developed an innovative postmodern theatrical style in her plays *No Mercy* (1985), *Tales of the Lost Formicans* (1989), *Casanova* (1991), and *Losing Father's Body* (1993). These plays belong to what Marc Robinson calls "the other American drama," which flouts Aristotelian dramatic principles and naturalism in favor of narratives that break with the unities of action, time, and place. Congdon describes her non-naturalistic approach to writing at a 1990 conference panel for literary managers and dramaturgs titled "How to Talk to a Playwright," excerpted here. In these remarks, Congdon expresses frustration with academically trained members of the theatre establishment who evaluate new dramatic writing according to outdated conventions, which she associates with the "well-made play." Congdon defends her plays against criticism that "nothing happens" in them and rejects the need for classical dramatic form, including a narrative "arc" that has a beginning, middle, and end. Her plays in the eighties do not follow this linear narrative structure and instead stage overlapping events from multiple time periods. Elderly characters—from a senile Robert Oppenheimer to a washed-out Cassanova—encounter traumatic memories and confuse the past and present. In the absence of dramatic action, these characters end up talking, often talking too much. Congdon's characters are big personalities with a gift for gab, which Elinor Fuchs, Paul Castagno, and other scholars link to the primacy of language over character and action in postmodern American drama.

The critical resistance that Congdon identifies in "How to Talk to a Playwright" is also the result of widespread gender bias. Unlike her male peers, Congdon had to contend with biases about the inherent emotionality and irrational tendencies of women. In her view, these prejudices led the theatrical establishment to misread female playwrights' formal innovations with language, action, and time. Congdon likewise challenges assumptions that female playwrights must address so-called woman's issues or write in a recognizably feminine way. In particular, she dismisses the popular belief among dramaturgs and critics that her plays have a "female sensibility" and argues that "I can think of four male writers" who share her stylistic and political interests. Congdon's skepticism about this "female sensibility" is consistent with antiessentialist theories of gender and sexuality proposed in the eighties and nineties by scholars such as Jill Dolan, Sue-Ellen Case, and Elin Diamond.[1] As these

DOI: 10.4324/9781003006923-58

scholars argued, theatre and performance were an ideal medium for the exploration of plural identities resistant to the reduction of gender and sexuality to biologically deter-mined positions. Like these influential theories on gender, Congdon's plays refuse to follow norms or roles commonly imposed on women. Her female protagonists are unorthodox characters from real life: stressed-out single mothers, eccentric suburban widows, and other unusual women whose pragmatic and survivalist life stories subvert readymade political messages about feminism. By the late nineties, Congdon increas-ingly explores intersections between these iconoclastic female characters and gay men and women in her plays, *Dog Opera* (1998) and *Lips* (1999), the latter: thus (1999), the latter about the first female president's all-too-public affair with a younger woman.

Congdon's bold refusal of the aesthetic and social conventions that dominated American theatre in the eighties and nineties led her to express broader reservations about current academic and political discourses. In contrast to the critical orthodoxy of identity politics, Congdon views herself as a "nonhyphenated American" and ques-tions the value of identity categories used in elitist institutions. As a female writer, she asks, "who wants to put herself into a category?" In life and art, she stresses the need to avoid confining "buzzwords" popular with academically trained drama-turgs and other intellectually rigid members of the theatrical establishment. In her early plays, Congdon uses comedy to unmask these academic pretentions and access the shared humanity of ordinary people. She frequently examines class differences that can be traced to the comic antics and everyday acts of bravery performed by ordinary women. Congdon continues to champion economically disenfranchised characters in her later work, which consists of adaptations of Molière, Goldoni, and Gorky and original plays, including *The Children of the Elvi* (2007), *Take Me to the River* (2013), *Paradise Street* (2018), and *Enemy Sky* (2019). These later plays contain less formal experimentation with time and narrative but still search for comic moments of redemption amid new political challenges, such as drone warfare, disputes over water rights, and the prospect of life in postapocalyptic society—as it happens, life in a matriarchal society that bluntly dispenses with antiquated rules of gendered civil-ity. Even in our increasingly precarious time, Congdon continues her battle against the confining orthodoxies of American politics and theatre in order to make room for the new voices of diverse female playwrights working outside the boundaries of Aristotelian dramatic form and the conventions of naturalism.

Constance Congdon

Excerpt from "How to Talk to a Playwright"[2] (1990)

To those of you who studied dramaturgy in academic institutions and heard about the dramaturg being the conscience and the mind of the theater: I think it's absolute bullshit and you should just, like, call up your teachers and tell them to stop using those terms, because they give the impression that everyone else is a drooling idiot and has no conscience.

I'm a nonhyphenated American, unless you put Wonder Bread in front of it. I wrote a play several years ago in which a young girl was a major character. She's about fifteen to sixteen years old. I was working on it with a woman who said, "You know, this play never explodes, Connie. It doesn't really have an arc. Could the guy grab a knife or something?" This is a woman for whom I have tremendous respect, and it's a comment that comes out of desperation, because in desperation we always go back to our stereotypes. Later, I'm driving and thinking, "So, all right, fine. Make the girl a boy, and then she could grab the knife." All of a sudden, bells went off in my head and I thought, "I have a well-made play! That's it, I change the gender! I'll make the girl a boy." And that led to a revelatory moment about sensibility.

When we start writing they tell us, "Write what you know." Whether that's an emotional territory or something literal, like a story that happened to you. I delved into what I knew, and what I found again and again was that, when it came to the so-called "big, dramatic moment," when I tried to imagine it in a real way, I didn't do any of those things; because I'm a girl, I'm probably not going to be grabbing knives. It's possible I could, but when I think about really horrible moments in my life, it's been much more like glass-shattering far away than violence happening right there in the living room or the kitchen or in outer space.

Maybe I'm a little touchy because people have often said, "Nothing happens in your plays, Connie." I would hate to say that there is a female sensibility, because I can think of four male writers who have the same sensibility. And who wants to put herself into a category? But the sensibility idea is even beyond culture; it goes down to the microscopic—to the individual—and it affects form as well as content.

There's a lot of prejudice. I am tremendously sensitive when I hear terms like "arc" and "through-line." They make me flinch; they piss me off. So I don't know how you talk about a play. I have my own language that I make up in the moment. I say things I believe, and try to avoid buzzwords, because they underlie what I think a lot of playwrights think: that dramaturgs are these literal, academic people who have some idea of what is right and what is wrong, what a play should be; and who will put an A, B, or C on their scripts and turn them back to them. Anything you can do to dispel that prejudice is good to do.

Please see the Works Cited for further information on the sources used in this essay.

Note

1 See entries for Dolan, Case, and Diamond in this volume.
2 From an edited transcript of a panel discussion at the Literary Managers and Dramaturgs of the Americas Annual Conference, DePaul University, Chicago, June 1990.

Suggestions for Further Reading

Congdon, Constance. *Tales of the Lost Formicans and Other Plays*. New York, NY: TCG, 1994.
———. *Tartuffe: A Verse Translation by Constance Congdon*. New York, NY, and London: W.W. Norton and Company, 2009.
Fordyce, Ehren. "Experimental Drama at the End of the Century." *A Companion to Twentieth-Century American Drama*. Ed. David Krasner. Malden, MA and Oxford, UK: Blackwell Publishing, 2005.
Gholson, Craig. "Interview with Constance Congdon." *Bomb Magazine*. 37 (Fall 1991): 38–41.

58 ELIZABETH MACLENNAN
(1938–2015)

Gioia Angeletti

Introduction

Between the mid-1960s and the early 1970s, a wave of "inventiveness and new energies" (Angeletti 16) revitalised Scottish theatre. As critic Ian Brown has argued, although the Scottish theatrical tradition, in all its diversity, is marked by continuity from the Middle Ages to today, that specific phase featured a "theatrical renaissance" (183–219) linked to the political ferment and revolutionary spirit generally igniting the cultural climate of those years. At the time, for instance, Scottish female dramatists began coming onto the scene, often challenging the theatrical establishment from the fringe – as was the case with Ena Lamont Stewart and Joan Ure, both of whom can be regarded as pioneers of a "school of women playwrights" (Bain 139). It is in this 1960s turbulent as well as thriving cultural context that we must situate the conception of the left-wing, agit-prop and avant-garde 7:84 Theatre Company founded by English playwright John McGrath and Scottish actress Elizabeth MacLennan.

Elizabeth Margaret Ross MacLennan (1938–2015) was born in Glasgow into a well-known medical family. She studied modern history at Oxford and was also an active member of an improvisation workshop where she met McGrath. He produced there a version of James Joyce's *Ulysses* with MacLennan as Molly Bloom. She then studied acting at LAMDA (the London Academy of Music and Dramatic Art), after which she worked for Granada Television. In 1962, the same year she married McGrath, she had a leading role in *You in Your Small Corner*, an adaptation of Barry Reckord's stage play that became famous for broadcasting one of the earliest interracial kisses on British television – between MacLennan and Jamaican actor Lloyd Reckord. However, despite her several successes in lead roles for BBC television plays and movies throughout the 1960s and early 1970s, she decided to embark on a different career with her husband, one that would allow them to realise their ideal of a theatre for and among people.

Through MacLennan's acquaintances, McGrath had meanwhile become engaged with left-wing Scottish politics, which, combined with the 1968 student protests he went to observe in Paris, strongly impacted his idea of a theatre able to exert an oppositional force against status-quo politics. With a group of colleagues, they founded 7:84 in 1971. The name of the company refers to a statistic that appeared in *The Economist* in 1966, according to which seven per cent of the population of the UK owned eighty-four per cent of the whole country's wealth. The name also reflects 7:84's mission: to bring politically engaged performances to working-class audiences (often non-theatre goers) all over Britain; thus, besides regular playhouses, they

DOI: 10.4324/9781003006923-59

staged their repertoire in improvised venues, such as community centres, clubs, and village halls.

Throughout the 1970s and 1980s, MacLennan was one of the company's leading performers, appearing in several of its most famous productions: classics of British popular theatre, such as Ena Lamont Stewart's *Men Should Weep* (1947, revived in 1982), and John McGrath's *Trees in the Wind* (1971). She was at her best when playing the part of the working-class, resilient hard woman, fighting against all odds, like the heroine of *Men Should Weep*, who is capable of wit and humour, despite her despondency. She also played an important role not only in bolstering McGrath's interest in Scottish theatre's genre diversity and formal experimentation but also in encouraging him to produce a popular theatre that could bring attention to traumatic episodes of Scottish history, such as the Highland Clearances in *The Cheviot, the Stag and the Black, Black Oil* (1973) – the term "clearances" referring to forced removals, for purely economic reasons, of the inhabitants of the Scottish Highlands and western islands between 1750 and 1860; the dispossessed lands were used mainly for sheep-raising in order to comply with the flourishing wool trade, but the evictions resulted in the destruction of the traditional clan society, and in depopulation and mass emigration from Scotland to America and Canada.

In 1973, McGrath, MacLennan, her brother David, and his partner Ferileh Lean founded 7:84 Scotland as a separate company, so that the original one was renamed 7:84 England. According to MacLennan, "Scotland is distinguished by its socialist, egalitarian tradition, its Labour history, its cultural cohesion and energetic participation in argument and contemporary issues. [...] We felt our plays [...] should reflect and celebrate these differences in language, music, political identification and carry on the arguments" specific to each region (43). The two entities, though linked to each other, continued to work separately until they folded: the English group was the first one to break up in 1984, partly because McGrath and the MacLennans, by the early eighties, had focused on 7:84 Scotland, which continued to be funded only until 2008, perhaps because it had lost its original artistic, let alone political, impact. However, MacLennan carried on acting, writing and defending the work of touring companies like 7:84, which proved that theatre can reach everyone and everywhere, albeit with an awareness that "a show on the road [...] can be the biggest success in one place and the next night it can be a total flop" (197). Theatre critic Michael Billington wrote that MacLennan was "one of those passionate, pioneering women who periodically erupt to change the British theatre," "one of nature's fiery spirits, who wholeheartedly put her beliefs into action." After her husband's death in 2002, her focus shifted to writing: the play *Wild Raspberries* (2002), the children's story "Ellie and Granny Mac" (2009) and the poetry collection *The Fish That Winked* (2013). Nevertheless, until her death in 2015, MacLennan never lost faith in theatre's – especially community theatre's – power to challenge the world and function as a vehicle to counteract conservatism and trigger socio-cultural revolutions. These ideas have inspired the work of one of her daughters, Kate McGrath, a leading independent producer, and director of Fuel Theatre in London.

MacLennan's *The Moon Belongs to Everyone: Making Theatre with 7:84*, published in 1990, is not only an account of her own engagement with the company but also a major work of theatrical criticism about contemporary popular theatre inside Scotland and beyond, as well as about radical and experimental modes of performance – best exemplified by McGrath's landmark play *The Cheviot, the Stag and the Black, Black Oil,* which toured throughout Scotland. MacLennan's book shows what "this other kind of theatre" – her definition of popular theatre as opposed to bourgeois theatre (2) – can mean and do. This other kind of performance vibrantly engages "the audience's attention by music, gesture, speech or action" (196) and directly involves them through the breaking of the fourth wall. The book documents a total theatre, as it were, which crosses or transgresses generic boundaries and challenges conventional methods of acting and performing, while, at the same time, it preserves Scottish popular forms such as the *cèilidh* (a traditional Scottish social event, in private or public gathering places, involving dancing and playing Gaelic folk music), traditional songs, the music hall and pantomime. As Maria DiCenzo has observed, "[W]hat 7:84 did was to take advantage of the familiarity with and entertainment values of these forms [...] and to use them as vehicles for political analysis and commentary" (87).

This rich legacy, as well as the peripatetic nature of 7.84, left an indelible mark on contemporary British theatre, as evidenced today by the touring, not building-based, National Theatre of Scotland. Yet, *The Moon Belongs to Everyone* shows that the meaning of 7.84's heritage is transnational and timeless. While touring in Canada, Australia and the Soviet Union in the late 1980s, MacLennan realised that "theatre movements like 7:84 were being taken up and developed all over the world, and may even continue here, albeit in different form" (3).

Elizabeth MacLennan

Excerpts from The Moon Belongs to Everyone: Making Theatre with 7:84 *(1990)*

Introduction

We began serious discussions about starting a theatre company to recreate a form of popular theatre and tour it to working class audiences and their allies during 1968. This was the Year of the Events in Paris, the big Grosvenor Square demonstrations against the Vietnam War, the gunning down of the students at Kent State University, the shooting of Bobby Kennedy, Civil Rights marches in Derry, the Russian invasion of Czechoslovakia and Che Guevara's guerrilla struggles in Bolivia.

Many people want the theatre to be a mysterious place, inexplicable, full of nuance, ambiguity and fun. They want it to transport them away from everyday life, problems, questioning, 'squalor', having to think. Many feel theatre should be comfortable, comforting, expensive, supportive of middle-class values, decorative, a fun experience, a giggle, a gasp, a good cry. The lights go down, you shut off your critical faculties and wade into the weight-supporting shallows and feel the sand of passing sensations between your toes. If you're lucky you can down a stiff drink in the interval, or eat chocolates and ice-cream at the same time. Why not? What right has anybody to tell other people how to enjoy themselves?

Many people in the business feel that the leisure industry is there to provide work and pay mortgages for performers, writers, cameramen, musicians, prop-makers and so on. If you rise to the top of the pool, the world's your oyster; posh parts, fancy clothes, chat shows, the Cotswolds, Roseland, Hollywood, the white Rolls Royce, the nanny with tax problems, title, friends with royalty – well, why not?

In our discussions other questions arose. You might ask yourself, as I did, has anybody ever said anything to you in a theatre that really made a difference to your life and attitudes? Is that as important? Is there a choice? Does that kind of theatre need additional skills? Is it available round where you live? Was it ever? If so, do people go, do they enjoy it? If not, why not? Is thinking boring? Do you see yourself as part of the experience happening on the stage or outside it? Why is Shakespeare respectable? Why do some people not go to the theatre at all? Where *do* they go, why, what for? Are they right to feel excluded? Which kind of experience and set of class values are you part of? Is it more or less artistic? Does questioning imply lack of respect? Why is music popular? Should the audience leave their politics in the cloakroom? If so, why? Can politics be fun? Is there a blacklist? Is joy class-based? One kind of fun for some classes, another kind for others. [...]

Why do we need writers? Is there such a thing as a reactionary laugh? Is there such a thing as a socialist actor? Should performers leave their politics behind at the stage door? Should theatre make money? Raise money? Be cost effective? Be subsidised? Which skills, which audience? Is it permissible to break the rules and still be an artist?

To this last question history says, emphatically, Yes. But who is saying No in the 90s? In whose interest?

Is the position of the theatre artist improving as a result of 'market forces', or getting worse? Do audiences get what they want, deserve, feel entitled to?

* * *

7:84 Theatre Company was started in 1971
Now it is in danger of being written out of history, along with most of the popular oppositional theatre of our times. It is fighting for its life. Then the political tide was in our favour and it was more acceptable, even trendy to be oppositional. Now its funding is threatened, it receives patronising reviews which talk of 'falling standards, crude agit-prop', and academics vie with each other to explain its demise.

Today alternative and oppositional theatre has become fragmented, competitive. Rampant individualism has set companies against each other, as each dons the appropriate funding mask, be it 'new writing', 'community' or 'touring product', the acceptable survival kits for anything even mildly critical of the status quo, the barriers erected to prevent people bursting onto the pitch or becoming part of the main action.

While the students in Beijing and Prague demonstrated their need to speak freely and express their desire for change, here in Britain that need is projected as inappropriate for our present culture which requires above all affirmation of the status quo, of the idea that the rich are entitled to get richer, the poor poorer. By all means let the arts celebrate this 'diversity', but not challenge it. The cultural tanks and personnel carriers are ready to crush any of that.

But this kind of theatre has been around since Aristophanes. It is an awesome tradition, the popular tradition, and will outlive its present insecurity. Should working people's lives be reflected on the stage, why should the theatre speak for them?

* * *

It is my intention in this book, as a performer and founder-member of both 7:84 Theatre Companies, to examine from some of my own first-hand experience the values and impact of this other kind of theatre – not to devalue the achievements of the bourgeois theatre, whose apologists are legion, but because otherwise in all the clamour of the New Realists our voice may not be heard. I shall be contentious, partial. Where possible I shall use records I kept at the time, and try to share my own feelings of excitement in the process. It is not an official history: inevitably many productions and people involved will be left out. Nor will I attempt to do full justice to the history of the remarkable English 7:84, for, apart from anything else, its story – like my own – is not over yet.

* * *

The story has several beginnings: there is the beginning of my life, roots, influences, where I came from, and a bit about my education, training, early work; there is the beginning of the original 7:84 and its subsequent growth; then the beginning of the Scottish 7:84.

The middle period falls into two sections. The first is the highly confident time of *Little Red Hen, Out of Our Heads, The Trembling Giant,* and others in Scotland, and three mighty McGrath plays in England – *Fish in the Sea*, the enormously successful *Lay Off* and *Yobbo Nowt*; the growth and excitement of the English company band; other new companies starting and the growth of a popular theatre movement throughout Europe.

The second half of the middle period was perhaps the busiest and most successful of all, and coincided, surprisingly perhaps, with Thatcher's first term of office. There is a mythology grown up that the 'heady, early days' of 7:84 finished in the early 70s. But 7:84 continued to function throughout the 80s, performing much of its boldest, most innovative work to ever-growing audiences, and dealing with many of the questions they urgently wanted raised.

Had Thatcher *not* been re-elected in 1983, 7:84 might well have continued to grow and develop within a strong cultural revival in Scotland. But a forceful, independent culture with a popular voice became undesirable. Thatcher began her long march through the institutions, attempting to undermine and destabilise them, and to bring Scotland in line with the Tory majority in the south, by restructuring schools, universities, the hospital system, the social services, the Arts Council, and, not least – and most devastatingly – the trades unions.

It is against this background that the last section of the book unfolds, which I have called The Squeeze, and it brings me up to the present.

There are, happily, always exceptions: the momentous arrival of *glasnost* and *perestroika*; for me, the birth of a new child, critical success, the challenge of doing my one-woman show, *The Baby and the Bathwater*, and the discovery of an exciting emergent popular theatre in Canada and Australia through touring abroad in the late 80s with 7:84; international solidarity through touring in the Soviet Union, forging links with the Cinema Actors Theatre of Tblisi, and the knowledge that theatre movements like 7:84 were being taken up and developed all over the world, and may even continue here, albeit in different forms, and unaware of their connections.

* * *

It's a long way to Tipperary
There is a general perception that if you try to do something 'totally new' in the theatre, it might 'last' for a couple of years, but it will inevitably 'burn out', and those taking part will 'move on' (and by inference UP) to, well, Higher Things – the RSC, the National, television, their own comedy series perhaps, or, if they are really masochistic, their OWN company. The idea of moving OUT from Higher Things and INTO impoverished, touring theatre, which was the situation in my case, is considered downright perverse.

However, when we started 7:84 we did not say to ourselves as we set off to Hull University, say, or Fraserburgh Town Hall, 'Ahah, this is my red brick road to the

Land of Oz,' (although the thought might occur perhaps when the lights failed or the electrician was catapulted across the room by a near-lethal switch) – no, we said, 'This is going to be a great show and I'm going to enjoy doing it.' It was good while it lasted, but I was thankful to get home to my own bed, a decent hot meal. Touring is an enormous pressure. It can also be a great release, challenging every part of the imagination.

In our precarious business most actors have to respond to the demands of the marketplace, and fear of becoming pigeon-holed, stereotyped, even these days black-listed, keeps them flitting like butterflies. So I am clearly an oddball, hanging in all these years; or, as my dear Aunt Effie put it – I was forty at the time – 'The trouble with you is that you're a permanent adolescent.' So many people have said to me on the road, 'Don't you ever feel like settling down?'

In 1990 I had worked in the theatre for thirty years. After the first eleven years we made the decision to start our own company; to find the audience, the money, the circuit, put on new plays, question the norm, learn, find more money, keep going, bring up three children, keep going. Success, struggle, exhaustion, renewal. Well over thirty tours. An average of perhaps sixty gigs per tour (the early ones were longer), hundreds of benefits, line-runs in vans, new friends, company meetings, dirty coffee cups, smoke-filled rehearsal rooms, children growing up. An extended dialogue with the most extraordinary audience a performer might be privileged to get to know, to be criticised and cherished by.

In addition to describing how these events came about I have kept a diary of 1988 – for me a traumatic year – an attempt to make sense of events. Sometimes chunks of my past appear in it, and they are there as they occurred to me at the time. Here is how it begins.

* * *

Diary, March 1988
9 March, Edinburgh
Breakfast with Hugo Medina from Chile. An old friend from 1974 – he fled from Santiago after being imprisoned and tortured during the coup; *a fine actor, he helped to start the* Teatro Popular Chileno *in exile in London, but went back to Chile a few years ago. I haven't seen him since.*

He tells me eighty-three actors and Chilean artists are on a list and have received death threats. Many others, previously non-aligned, have associated with them, and they are here touring a play in Europe to draw attention to the situation in Chile. Contrary to their govern-ment propaganda, things are NOT getting better. They have meetings with Edinburgh District Council, Lothian Regional Council, and the Scottish TUC later, in Glasgow. They will go back to Chile.

Hugo has been in London. Everything in England has been cut, he says; how is it here in Scotland? We are waiting for our funding to be announced, I tell him, things are hard, but it IS different here; the consensus, a Labour majority in Scotland. The theatre is confident, feels young, optimistic, perhaps, but bold; there are lots of new groups touring, maybe a basis for action in the 90s. In SPITE of the devastation of the working class since Thatcher, we can build on that. There is at least cultural confidence, there is a huge audience, the writers are there, the talent. [. . .]

Some Conclusions
When I started to work as an actor in 1959, plays were still being submitted for the approval of the Lord Chamberlain. There was Variety with its summer seasons and

its winter pantos, there was the West End with its number one and number two tours, there were the 'provincial' reps and that was about it. There was the odd one-off tour. But now, thanks to people like Jenny Lee and Lord Goodman and the Arts Council in the late 60s and early 70s, and to the enlightened support of some local authorities, and to a very great deal of hard work, there are hundreds of new theatre buildings, halls, theatres and companies.

Performing in some of these new places a whole new generation of actors, musicians and technicians have grown up who are accustomed to being paid the same to do strikes and get-ins, to travelling out of London, to being responsible for the material which they are putting across, and for taking part in decision-making processes. They of course are part of a popular theatre tradition that was strong in the 20s, 30s, and 40s and goes back a very long way.

In my experience, the drama schools do not really reflect these changes, with the possible exception of the Rose Bruford, which they are trying to close down. They tend to prepare students for a theatre where Shakespeare is still the Bible and requires a special voice, where Olivier is god, and Peggy Ashcroft his mother. Where women still perform a largely decorative and stereotyped function. So it is not surprising that many 'ordinary' people still regard the likes of us as 'students' needing a proper day job and not really part of the *proper* acting world where acting skills once more equal the ability to wear long dresses and cloche hats, to cross your ankles decoratively, to speak posh and earn a lot of money – at least if we're to believe quite a lot of what's to be seen on stage, television and film at the moment.

I too have had a university education and a middle-class background, and been to the Royal Shakespeare Company and the National Theatre, and *admire* Peggy Ashcroft and Olivier, and what John Gielgud did to sustain a classical repertory tradition. But that is not the *whole* story. There are other skills. Other forms of commitment. Other forms of training required.

As things stand, many actors who are on a one-way ticket away from their own class are encouraged to think there is only one way of performing, to sustain only one set of values. But the range of popular theatre styles within the European tradition *alone* – quite apart from those of India, China, Japan and the rest of the *world* – is as various as the culture of the peoples they reflect. We have still a lot to learn.

The kind of performance I became familiar with in 7:84, as it was, is subject to and conditioned in the main by a series of specific pressures. It relates to these very vital questions: who is putting us on here? Is it self-financing? What happened today that relates directly to the content of the show and do we make changes or updates? What was the last show we played here? Did they like it? Did our ad appear next to the one for the sheep-dog trials? Have the audience been waiting long? Are they queueing? Is there a bar? Will it be open during the show? Is there coffee? Is there one toilet for the audience and the players? (Do not flush during the show.) Who's doing the raffle? Is there any heating? The audience certainly won't laugh if they're huddled in their coats, though I do vividly remember one woman on such a cold night on a Highland tour, producing her husband from under her arm and a set of broken false teeth in her hand saying, 'He laughed so much he broke them – are you going to pay up?'

Then the more serious questions: are we in a big theatre tonight or is the stage, as in most town halls, too high? Should we use the fore-stage – more work in the get-outs? Is there anywhere to do the quick changes? Can I get round the back? Shall we start late to allow the bus to arrive from the oil rig? – at Kishorn for instance – or the bus party from Govan, or the local works outing. Is there a dance to follow? Are we playing it? Should we play with or without an interval? Is there a storm, are the boats in? Will the fishermen come or will they stay in the bar? Are there Gaelic speakers in? Are there more women than men in the audience, children, any babies? Is that a drunk or is he trying to say something? What time does the evening mass finish? Remember to check with the priest in Barra. Are there people standing? Have they come far? Should we say thanks at the end? Are we raising money? Are we drawing attention to, or supporting, a local strike, a demonstration? Is it my turn to make a speech? In what language?

Under these sorts of circumstances it is often very hard to tell where the event finishes and the performance begins.

For this and other reasons, I have found it is pretty disastrous to employ anything other than the epic acting style. By epic I mean larger than life, but fiercely true to it. The performer must engage the audience's attention by music, gesture, speech or action.

Of course this is only my experience with 7:84 and there are many other touring companies who respond to these circumstances in different ways. Some favour social realism, some stand-up comedy, some recreate the small scale experimental theatre wherever they go in terms of seating, ticket prices, publicity and so on, and by adapting their performance style to suit the requirements of their particular audiences. Many other admirable companies have sprung up who work even more closely with, and as *part* of a community. From these companies we can all learn a great deal.

In fact the originality, zest, sensitivity, talent and variety of skills developed by such companies and their influence upon each other and their interaction provide today, to a very large extent, the life-blood of the mainstream theatre and account for most of the new audiences, in my opinion, throughout the whole of Britain and certainly in Scotland.

However, today, far from being encouraged, this tradition is fighting for its life.

I've come to the conclusion that there are five things that really matter in this kind of work as a performer. All are discouraged by funding bodies, as they are by many drama school teachers. They are:

Holding onto your roots.
Using your brain and your critical faculties.
Development of all kinds of comic skills.
Class awareness.
Not being afraid to try something new.

At drama school you're told, don't be too intelligent, forget your roots, join the middle class, learn their language, underestimate and patronise the popular comedy skills and don't bother to learn an instrument – leave it to the musicians who should stay in the pit where they belong.

If you play in a play in a theatre building in one place in, say, the West End, for a run, the performance will vary of course from night to night, reactions, running time, and so forth, but the range of variations is quite narrow. You more or less know if it's going to be a success or a flop. And I've done it.

But if you take a show on the road it can be the biggest success in one place and the next night it can be a total flop. This throws an enormous responsibility onto the performer, particularly as many touring companies travel without a director. And the responsibility has to be shared among the crew and the working actors. Because each night is the first night for THAT community – they may not see the company, or *any* company again that year. So there is a lot of danger and excitement and the touring audience will realise that and share it. It's also one of the practical reasons why such companies need some form of internal democracy. [. . .]

* * *

Wind will not cease, even though trees want rest
When I set out to try and recreate for myself some of the events and sensations of my own involvement in touring popular theatre, it was perhaps at the lowest point of the last seventeen years; the announcement, or rather the surreptitious letting-us-know of the SAC funding cut to 7:84. Many people on the left are exhausted, dispirited. 'What can we do? We feel so powerless. It's happening to everybody, you just can't take it in.'

Under these circumstances, it has been quite difficult to recall the energy and optimism and effectiveness of so much of our work, because we are constantly being told by the New Realists that things are different now and that sort of thing won't work any more. But we know from our experience that this is not true, and from history that they are defending their own powerful interests once again.

Like the teachers, the doctors, the nurses and every member of the caring society who remain, we have to stand up and fight for the things that are being taken away from us. And that includes popular theatre. The profession must take on the battle and recognise the steps that are being taken to standardise and sanitise people's lives and experiences. There is a big cultural battle going on. We are engaged in it. We must cherish and support our writers and artists and they must recognise their strengths and speak out and we must make sure that they are heard.

> 'It's very important that there's somewhere people can learn to speak to an audience directly. That place, as far as I'm concerned, is small-scale, it's subsidised and it has the absolute right to fail.'
>
> Drew Griffiths, writer and co-founder of Gay Sweatshop

If a society destroys its artists it destroys itself. They are reflecting the hopes and fears of our children. They must resist; and the forms of resistance must be as available to us as the current enterprise culture that is pumped into us intravenously every day.

Theatre needs money. Touring theatre needs subsidy. Oppositional theatre needs a strong opposition and they need each other. The audience is there. The road is open.

Song at the end of *Blood Red Roses*:

> Now that is our story
> A tale that goes on –
> Is it true or a lie or a fiction?
> Is it right or mistaken the story we tell:
> Is it fit to be tellt tae your children?

Please see the Works Cited for further information on the sources used in this essay.

Suggestions for Further Reading

Bain, Audrey. "Loose Canons: Identifying Women's Tradition in Playwriting". *Scottish Theatre Since the Seventies*. Ed. Randall Stevenson and Gavin Wallace. Edinburgh: Edinburgh University Press, 1996. 138–145.

Brown, Ian, ed. *The Edinburgh Companion to Scottish Drama*. Edinburgh, Edinburgh University Press, 2011.

Reid, Trish. *Theatre & Scotland*. Houndmills, Palgrave Macmillan, 2013.

Stevenson, Randall and Gavin Wallace, eds. *Scottish Theatre Since the Seventies*. Edinburgh, Edinburgh University Press, 1996.

59 MONSTROUS REGIMENT (1975–1993)

Elaine Aston

Introduction

Formed against the backdrop of second-wave feminism in 1975, Monstrous Regiment was one of the UK's most influential women's theatre groups. Founding members Chris Bowler, Gillian Hanna, and Mary McCusker (see the interview) were professional practitioners whose involvement in and relationship with the company endured until the group ceased performing in 1993. Like many women in theatre then (and now), the Monsters, as they were affectionately called, had experienced marginalisation in the industry, even when working in fringe, socialist companies. Acutely aware of the paucity of parts for women – especially nonstereotypical roles – the company committed to commissioning women playwrights, seeking to move women's stories, experiences, and histories centre stage.

The socialist roots of company members saw the group established as a collective, both organisationally and artistically: everyone had equality of input to the structure of the group (in theory at least, since this proved harder to achieve in practice); artistic roles were deemed to be of equal value (e.g. no god-like director); and the group performed as an ensemble. More precisely, Monstrous Regiment was founded as a socialist-*feminist* collective; early years were spent fathoming and wrestling with the political dynamics and difficulties of what it meant to be a women-led company that included a minority of men: how might feminism and socialism be aligned for women and men to be comrades in theatre (and society at large), fighting the inequalities produced by patriarchy and capitalism? All told, at the outset, Monstrous Regiment differed from many other feminist groups that excluded men; it was not until the early 1980s when men left and were not replaced that the company transformed into and continued as an all-women's troupe.

Finding a "new way of making theatre," as Hanna states in the interview, was a fundamental concern for Monstrous Regiment. As she explains elsewhere, this involved exploring "what 'women's writing' is or might be" (lxxii). On the one hand, there was no overall aesthetic uniformity to the work staged by the company. Formally, the writers they commissioned were wide-ranging; they included the likes of Caryl Churchill and Bryony Lavery who would subsequently become major names in British theatre, as well as European and American women dramatists. On the other hand, a unifying artistic principle on the part of the company could be found in their desire to stage new writing by women that eschewed "straight" drama: the tradition of realism whose

DOI: 10.4324/9781003006923-60

linear dramatic structure and regular staging often cast women to the margins of male-dominated narratives. As evinced by their 1976 debut production of *Scum* (Claire Luckham and Chris Bond) and later that same year, *Vinegar Tom* (Churchill), the use of music was favoured by the company to rupture a fourth-wall mode of conventional staging.

However, such aesthetic explorations demanded time and money; these increasingly were in short supply during the Thatcherite 1980s that saw draconian cuts to state subsidy for the arts and an accelerated drive towards private sponsorship. Equally, the vaunting of the individual, Thatcherite "Superwoman," and the backlash against socially progressive modes of feminism eroded those values that were foundational to Monstrous Regiment, aesthetically and politically. Consequentially, artistic concerns were outweighed by the sheer struggle for the company's survival. In the interview, as the Monsters reflect on how the company was adversely affected by the economic conditions and postfeminist climate of the 1980s, they compare their struggles with Churchill's career, observing how, as an individual dramatist, she was able to weather writing "gaps" and to continue engaging with an "aesthetic process" in a way that simply was not possible for them as a company. Why continue as a feminist group when the odds were so heavily stacked against them? To understand the Monsters' desire to keep the company going is to comprehend this effort as an enduring feminist commitment to challenging and transforming the cultural malestream. Ultimately, this relates to the critical issue of struggling for women's cultural visibility: an unrepentant, unreconstructed malestream means that once again women risk becoming invisible – of being written out of, and "hidden from history."

Viewed from a twenty-first-century perspective, the late twentieth-century inequalities in British theatre voiced by the Monsters have a highly contemporary feel – the struggle for theatre workers to earn a living wage, sexism in the industry, and the idea of the male, cultural "norm." This accounts for why some women theatre makers still choose to work outside the malestream: to follow in the second-wave feminist tradition of women-only or women-led collectives, even if this might "risk ghettoising women" (Turney). The influences and legacies of this counter-cultural, politically motivated tradition can also be felt in the renewed feminist demands to transform the theatre industry by: introducing gender quotas; recognising social class as a barrier to practitioners earning a living wage; and ending a toxic culture of sexual harassment, as outed by the Harvey Weinstein scandal and the #Me Too Movement (Aston, *Restaging Feminisms* 14–23).

More specifically, remembering the Monsters affords an illuminating and instructive opportunity to recollect the importance of the collective as an artistic and political hub for a company and writers to "rehearse" feminist ideas, themes, processes, and practices. Equally, the challenges the company faced in its fight for survival are a salutary reminder of the creative energies and political commitment it will still take to further loosen if not transform the male-dominated hegemonic hold over British theatre. It is not one "regiment" needed in this battle, but battalions of women.[1]

Finally, if women are not to be hidden from future histories, then, as the Monsters observe, the generational handing on of feminist insights, struggles, and experiences is also a vital strategy, one exemplified by this present collection's archiving of women's theatre, dramatic criticism, and theory.

Monstrous Regiment

Excerpt from Interview with Monstrous Regiment company members
Chris Bowler, Gillian Hanna and Mary McCusker conducted by Elaine Aston
and Gabriele Griffin (1990)[2]

MARY: [...] When we started out we did have men in the collective. They were there
on stage, there everywhere. After we'd formed the company we invited men to
join us because we saw that as part of the process of grappling with feminism, of
grappling with life. They were part of the problem, so they had to be part of the
answer as well. But, over the years the men in the company seem to have left and
we haven't recruited any new ones. We've quite enjoyed not having any. There
are definite problems in having men, as well as the advantages of letting them
portray themselves on stage and also, of hearing the male voice participate in
some of the sessions you have on issues such as violence or sexual politics. But it's
been far more relaxing, in some ways, not to have that and to concentrate on the
women and women's relationships with each other. [...]

GILLIAN: I think we underestimated the amount of work that we needed to do on ourselves as women. In the initial excitement of feeling that you were right, that feminism was right, that feminism was what would change the world, that it was the only
progressive politics that there was at the time, in that excitement we desperately
underestimated the amount of what we needed to do ourselves, in a sense. And
because we had all suffered from being token women in groups we were all terribly
anxious that the men should not be marginalised or oppressed or token men! [...]

One of the things that influenced us very strongly was that a lot of us came up
through various socialist groups, so you had the idea of comradeship, of men
and women struggling together rather than apart. [...]

It's a difficult point because we sometimes get accused of having needed the sanction of the male presence at the beginning, but it wasn't about that. We were very
clear about the fact that it was not about us feeling that we could not do it on our
own. It had to do with recognising that there were certain issues which we wanted
to deal with on the stage which, in terms of how we thought about them, were also
hangovers from our socialist pasts. We used to talk about 'the point of production':
the point of production was where conflict occurred, that was the pinnacle of political activity, that was where it all happened. We sort of transported that into the
relationship between men and women. [...]

[...] Even in the early days, the company ensured that writers were commissioned, just as
they endeavoured to pay all their theatre workers. This in turn related to the way in which
the company had always seen itself primarily as a group of theatre workers, rather than as
a group of people who came together because of a common political viewpoint:

MARY: We have always believed, politically, that any work for the company is professional work and therefore ought to be paid, the same as we believed that we
should pay ourselves at least the Equity rate, that money is important. We agreed
in principle on these things which doesn't mean that we always had the money
to pay ourselves, but we knew when we were deviating from these principles.

We believe that actors have as much right to job security as anyone else, and that their job ought to be paid for at a rate that means that you can live a reasonable life. [...]

GILLIAN: It's important to remember that we didn't set up primarily as a political group. We weren't a group of people who wanted to say something about politics. We were a group of theatre workers, women, who were sick and tired about the way theatre was dealing with women. This is quite a big distinction. We came into it with certain guidelines, certain givens that we weren't prepared to deviate from. In other words, this was our work, this was how we earned our living, we were Equity members, we were going to pay Equity rates, we were members of TWU, the Theatre Writers' Union, we were going to pay TWU rates. That was terribly important. It was a professional body of work which we were doing. [...]

[...] Why [was it], when times had been so hard, Monstrous Regiment had fought to keep the company going?:

MARY: I still believe in the company. I still believe that if we went there wouldn't be anything like us to replace us. I also like the idea that we are a group of women of a particular age who have been going for a long time, who are theatrically skilled and politically committed, and still have a voice in the theatrical world. Everybody made this big fuss about Kenneth Branagh starting his own company[3] and, really, that's what we did. People keep going on about what an amazing thing he did; the fact is, that we weren't a single woman but a bunch of women who started our company fifteen years ago, and we did it with new work, which is far more difficult to get on its feet than re-hashing old material. You know where the highs are in *Richard III*, you know where you're aiming with *Hamlet*. Even if you're going for a new interpretation, there's always a blueprint. With new plays that's quite different.

GILLIAN: There was a period of about four or five years, during the '80s, when, in response to this question, I used to think, 'Well, perhaps we're only continuing out of stubbornness. Perhaps we ought to stop, really. We're getting too old for this.' But now I feel differently about this. It's more important now to continue because of all the points Mary made. There is something unique about a body of work, largely by women, about women and for women, which we can build on. The fact that we are now middle-aged rather than young women gives us a platform of history and experience to work from.

I remember talking to the women of the Royal Shakespeare Company at a weekend event which these women had organised because they were feeling really angry about the way they were being treated. Juliet Stevenson, a friend who was involved in all that, and I kept saying to each other, 'Why isn't there some wonderful organisation whereby women who've been through all this could get paired up with a younger woman who could phone them up and say, 'This shit has just done x,' and the older woman could reply...'

MARY: '... Turn to page five of your manual, and look at diagram six for the pincer movement...'

GILLIAN: I suppose, it's to do with the notion of 'hidden from history', the feeling that if we stopped we'd get buried as women's culture always does, whereas if we can keep going, we might manage to keep above the surface of the water. It also then might mean that we can help women who're starting out now. This may be idealistic but there are certain things we have learnt that we can tell people about. Everyone has to make their own experience and mistakes, of course. Even so.

In the group's opinion, the fact that all the recently formed actor-manager style companies run by men had had a lot of publicity whereas women's theatre companies had not elicited the same kind of response, epitomised the still all too prevalent gender inequalities in the theatre and in society at large:

GILLIAN: When men do something, they speak for the human race, when women do the same thing it goes under the heading 'Special Interest'.

MARY: Men do it to 'free their talent' whereas, I sometimes get the impression, that when women do it, it is seen as their neuroses demanding an outlet. I do sometimes feel that women are classed as neurotic in that context in ways that men never would be.

GILLIAN: The norm is male, still. There really hasn't been much of a dent in that. Because men are still 'the norm', nobody thinks that there is anything abnormal in a man saying, 'Here I am, this wonderful actor, and I'm going to organise things.'

CHRIS: If a woman does it, it is assumed that she can't get any work so she has to go off and create her own work somewhere on the side, whereas with Branagh the feeling seems to be, 'Isn't it wonderful! Here's this man who could be here, there, anywhere, but he chooses to go off and work in this little tuppenny-ha'penny company. Isn't that an amazing sacrifice of a brilliant talent like his!'

GILLIAN: When men get together and perform, this isn't very unusual because it happens in theatre up and down the country. When women get together to perform it is very unusual because you don't get that very often. There is the occasional production of *Top Girls* but that's it, basically. So, when women get together there is always a suspected ulterior motive. And there usually is an ulterior motive, which is that they're tired of being pushed around and that they want to say something about their condition as women. [...]

Did the group see this as a rather pessimistic view of women in theatre and in the world at large?:

GILLIAN: I don't think we're pessimistic. I think we're realistic! I got very excited reading Rosalind Coward's book about women's history of the world, recently.[4] When you look at history from a woman's point of view, you have to have an incredible amount of optimism when you consider that men have spent thirty-five thousand years beating us, raping us, taking our children away from us, refusing to allow us to work, refusing to allow us access to children, and so on. If you read the history of the world it's pretty amazing that in the last two hundred years we've slowly begun to raise our heads above the parapet. We have to be realistic about that. The world is not going to change in five minutes like we thought when we were young.

MARY: The public seem to have got the impression that things have got better whereas they actually haven't in an awful lot of ways. What that means is that you get this appalling notion of post-feminism, whatever that might mean. You know, Robin Morgan discovered that the word 'post-feminism' was used in 1919[5] – so even that isn't new. That is a typical backlash. What is positive for women, and what I keep remembering, is that it is now possible for women to find some affirmation of their selves. Our current play [*Love Story of the Century*, Märta Tikkanen] is about a woman discovering feminism. That is really a phenomenon of the '70s though. If you were fighting your way out of something in the '70s there was feminism there for you to find.

I don't know what you'd be finding in the '80s. It isn't that feminism isn't there. Things are different. Feminism is there in a more public way, in some respects. You get reflections of women in the media and television that weren't there in the early days, and that was the reason why we were fighting. You get ordinary women's magazines like *Woman* discussing issues that years ago you'd only ever see discussed in *Spare Rib*.[6] […]

Some of the difficulties which Monstrous Regiment had faced over the years could be traced to their representation as a group of women rather than as individual women working in the theatre. The group reflected on this by considering how their career had progressed in relation to Caryl Churchill's career as a writer:

GILLIAN: I remember very clearly that when we first set out we were trying to find a new way of making theatre. We were conscious of that, we really were. We talked about it a lot. I think that that project got subverted because economic hardship hit us. For example, in those early days – it sounds like some blissful memory now – we once had a week's cancellation of a gig we were supposed to be doing, so we did a week of workshops instead. We did sonnet classes, and we had Maggie Nichols[7] come and do a voice class with us. I don't know how we'd ever find the money to do that sort of thing now.

It's useless to speculate, of course, but I think it would be interesting to know what would have happened if the political climate hadn't changed, if Thatcher had come in six or seven years later, if there had been this continuing expansion, not just on a financial scale, but the expansion of ideas. It's not just that money restricts you, but your thinking is restricted too. All the time you're thinking how do we get the next booking, how do we get the next gig, how do we get the next show on? All those day-to-day mundane, practical problems that have to be solved subverted the aesthetic programme that we had embarked on. I think that is a tragedy, not just for us, but for all women for whom it was the same. The only person who I know, who has really gone ahead with this programme is Caryl Churchill. She is the only woman that I know of who has managed to keep herself at a level of enquiry, if you like, into the aesthetic process. She is constantly re-writing herself. In every play that she writes she seems to start again, she re-writes the process.

MARY: I think it has to do with the fact that she is a phenomenal writer and has never lost her sense of wanting to pick things apart. I also have a sense that she is someone who's never reneged on her feminism. I also think she's also been lucky, in that she's managed to find a relationship with the Royal Court [Theatre] which has given her a public profile so that her work is taken seriously – as it should be! [...]

CHRIS: But that's a different situation from ours. [...] We, because we were too involved in setting up a company and running a company, were subverted by that process. We always had to think of so many things besides acting, such as keeping the company on the road. That's something we enjoyed and liked but it took its toll.

The difference between that and Caryl Churchill's situation is that she was involved in childcare over a number of years and started writing for the radio at home. As a result, she was always at one remove. I remember talking to her years ago when she said that that was what it felt like, being at one remove. She felt that being at home she had missed out on things that we were involved in. She's had gaps, too, like all writers, when she hasn't written anything. But we, being on the road as a working company, couldn't afford to have such gaps – the company would have folded.

Please see the Works Cited for further information on the sources used in this essay.

Notes

1 The company's name was a playful take on John Knox's 1558 pamphlet, *The First Blast of the Trumpet Against the Monstrous Regiment of Women*. As Hanna recollects, "we were rather taken with the image of armies of women driving around the country in battered Transit vans putting on plays" (xxi–xxii).
2 For the full interview, see Aston and Griffin, eds. *Feminist Theatre Voices*.
3 Renaissance Theatre Company founded with David Parfitt.
4 *Patriarchal Precedents: Sexuality and Social Relations* (1983).
5 See Morgan's *The Demon Lover: A study of the Sexuality of Terrorism* (1989).
6 *Woman* is a long-running, British women's magazine; *Spare Rib* (1972–1993) was a feminist magazine founded during the 1970s Women's Liberation Movement.
7 Scottish vocalist and performer, cofounder of the Feminist Improvising Group (1977).

Suggestions for Further Reading

Aston, Elaine. "Finding a Voice: Feminism and Theatre in the 1970s." *The Arts in the 1970s: Cultural Closure?* Ed. Bart Moore-Gilbert. London: Routledge, 1994. 99–128.

Itzin, Catherine. *Stages in the Revolution: Political Theatre in Britain Since 1968*. London: Eyre Methuen, 1980.

Monstrous Regiment Website: http://monstrousregiment.co.uk/

60 JILL DOLAN (b.1957)

Jessica Del Vecchio

Introduction

In *Presence and Desire* (1993), Jill Dolan (b.1957) explains that her first book, *The Feminist Spectator as Critic* (1988/1991), "offers a kind of road map for other theater workers and feminist scholars who might find themselves, as [she] did, looking for new ways to think about their dissatisfactions (or their different pleasures) in the theater" (5). Since *The Feminist Spectator*'s initial publication, feminist performance scholars have followed Dolan's road map and been inspired to design their own.[1] My copy is highlighted almost beyond readability, its spine cracked, its pages dog-eared, my embarrassingly emphatic marginalia a record of how Dolan's ideas forever altered my own thinking about theatre.

When Dolan enrolled in New York University's Performance Studies graduate program in 1981, there was no road to map; as Dolan recalls, "there was no track in feminism and performance and theory" (*Presence and Desire* 7). The Second Wave of U.S. American feminism had receded, leaving behind a renewed conservativism. Judith Butler had yet to theorize gender's performativity, and the concept of queer theory had yet to take hold in the academy. Nevertheless, a cadre of scholars had begun applying feminist theory to theatre, opening up new possibilities for performance criticism. Along with Sue-Ellen Case who, since the early 1980s, had published feminist critiques of theatre both contemporary and classic; Elin Diamond who also used Brecht's theories to feminist ends[2]; and Lynda Hart who edited one of the first collections of essays on feminism and theatre, Jill Dolan paved the way for the first generation of feminist theatre scholars.

Most significant in catalyzing the rise of feminist performance theory was the release of *The Feminist Spectator as Critic*. Drawing together feminist film theory and the deconstructionist work of French feminists Hélène Cixous,[3] Julia Kristeva, Luce Irigaray, and Monique Wittig, the book offers new ways of understanding theatre and performance from a materialist feminist perspective. In her first chapter, "The Discourses of Feminism," Dolan provides concise descriptions of three major categories of U.S. feminist thought—liberal, cultural, and materialist—and, throughout the book, she maps these feminisms to examples in performance. She argues that Marsha Norman's Pulitzer Prize-winning '*night, Mother,* which opened on Broadway in 1983, is representative of mainstream liberal feminism and identifies At the Foot of the Mountain Theater and Women's Experimental Theatre as cultural feminist groups whose work reifies oppressive gender norms. She demonstrates that the male gaze operates in the work of postmodern playwright/director Richard Foreman and

DOI: 10.4324/9781003006923-61

critiques other so-called radical male artists whose work pushes some boundaries while reinscribing others.

Her final chapter, excerpted here, models a materialist feminist approach to theatre-making and performance criticism. Engaging anthropologist Gayle Rubin's arguments about gender and sexuality as social constructs, Dolan demonstrates how feminist theatre makers can use Brechtian techniques to denaturalize gender onstage and to disrupt the traditionally gendered operation of theatre itself. She transposes film scholars Laura Mulvey and Theresa de Lauretis's theorization of classical cinema's male gaze to the theatre and argues that "[t]he lesbian desire underlying lesbian representations of gender disrupts the system of gender signification" (116). The mode of analysis Dolan describes in this chapter continues to be an important means of locating feminist politics in performance today.

The book also helped to put several feminist artists on the map. Among her examples, Dolan includes Split Britches, Spiderwoman Theater,[4] and Holly Hughes, all of whom were working, decidedly out of the mainstream, at the WOW Café in downtown New York City. As Dolan points out in her preface to *Memories of the Revolution* (2015), at the time, neither the *Village Voice* nor the *New York Times* would cover the work produced at WOW (ix). That these artists are now considered part of the canon of feminist performance *and* that of U.S. American performance, in general, is due, in part, to Dolan's championing their work.

In *Geographies of Learning: Theory and Practice, Activism and Performance* (2001), Dolan argues, "The onus is on progressive academics to maintain several audiences" (6). Accepting her own charge, throughout her career, Dolan has published a range of texts in a variety of venues. Dedicated to feminist pedagogy and activism, in *Geographies of Learning* she bridges the theory/practice divide that plagues theatre, LGBTQ+, and gender studies. Each of the book's chapters culminates in a list of practical suggestions for implementing the ideas she presents. With *Utopia in Performance: Finding Hope at the Theatre* (2005), Dolan offers another influential theory of spectatorship. In it, she coins the phrase "utopian performative" to describe those moments in performance that "make palpable an affective vision of how the world might be better" (6). That same year, Dolan began *The Feminist Spectator* blog,[5] for which she won the George Jean Nathan Award for Dramatic Criticism in 2011, using her online platform to "advocat[e] work by women, queer people, and people of color" and to "engag[e] more pointedly with popular culture" (*The Feminist Spectator in Action* 9).

Jill Dolan writes passionately, persuasively, and sometimes polemically, about the power of theatre. In books and blog posts, essays, and edited collections, Dolan's commitment to feminist principles is evidenced by both the form and content of her work. Her approaches to spectatorship transformed the fields of theatre and performance studies. Through her writing, Dolan offers road maps for feminist scholars to follow in pursuit of performance that critiques gender oppression, creates community, and offers audiences the possibility of better worlds.

Jill Dolan

Excerpt from The Feminist Spectator as Critic *(1988/1991)*

[...] Denaturalizing historical texts provokes the spectator to contemplate the structure of social relations their mythology perpetuates. The individual solution to both dramatic and social situations is preempted by a focus on people in relation to each other and the dominant ideology that shapes their interactions.

In the "Short Organum," Brecht writes that "the smallest social unit is not the single person but two people."[6] Gayle Rubin also posits the couple as the fundamental social unit, but she emphasizes the necessity of their heterosexuality within the economic structure:

> Lévi-Strauss concludes from a survey of the division of labor by sex that it is not a biological specialization, but must have some other purpose. This purpose, he argues, is to insure the union of men and women by making the smallest viable economic unit contain at least one man and one woman. ... The division of labor by sex can therefore be seen as a "taboo": a taboo against the sameness of men and women, a taboo dividing the sexes into two mutually exclusive categories, a taboo which exacerbates the biological differences between the sexes and thereby *creates* gender.[7]

Social arrangements mandate compulsory heterosexuality organized by gender polarization to insure the operation of economic and social systems. Rubin goes on to say, "The sexual division of labor is implicated in both aspects of gender—male and female it creates them, and it creates them heterosexual. The suppression of the homosexual component of human sexuality, and by corollary, the oppression of homosexuals, is therefore a product of the same system whose rules and relations oppress women."[8] Brechtian alienation techniques that denaturalize social arrangements can be fruitfully employed in feminist practice to demystify compulsory heterosexuality and the construction of gender as the founding principle of representation.

In lesbian usage, for instance, the estrangement of male desire and the institution of heterosexuality is often foregrounded by historicizing performance conventions that close on the inscription of heterosexual, genderized social arrangements. Popular genres are historicized, then reinscribed in an alternative lesbian social arrangement. Alice Forrester's *Fear of Laughing* (1985), for example, presented at the WOW Cafe, uses 1950s television as the basis of its parody. Ward and June Cleaver of *Leave It to Beaver* and the father of the ubiquitous *Father Knows Best* are all portrayed by women. Historicizing this familiar cultural material and foregrounding its gender assumptions by casting the production with lesbians makes the ideology of such pieces of Americana readable to the spectator.[9]

In a similar fashion, such historicization also works to defamiliarize the present, as conclusions about current social arrangements can be inferred. The isolated freedom of the individual privileged in liberal humanism is rejected by Brechtian technique. The historicized individual becomes a product of social relations, and the character an "untragic hero" who can be studied within a larger social context.[10] The author, too, is recuperated from the Romantic myth of isolated genius, and is seen as a cultural worker embedded in social relations and history:

> For Brecht ... the author is primarily a *producer,* analogous to any other maker of a social product. [He opposes,] that is to say, the Romantic notion of the author as *creator*—as the God-like figure who mysteriously conjures his handiwork out of nothing. Such an inspirational, individualist concept of artistic production

394 *Jessica Del Vecchio*

makes it impossible to conceive of the artist as a worker rooted in a particular history with particular materials at his disposal.[11]

The Brechtian reading, then, offers a revised position for both character and playwright.

Liberal feminist texts, as we have seen, present their characters as individuals struggling alone to attain the freedom capitalism and liberal humanism posit as universally available. Playwrights such as Marsha Norman work within this ethos, theorizing their characters and themselves as individuals who have achieved—or not—their singular success on the dominant culture's terms. Cultural feminists, with their tendency to collective creation, come closer to dispelling the Romantic notion of inspired authorship, but continue to mystify their work as biological organicism.

Materialist feminist theatre makers, on the other hand, are engaged in cultural production in which characters and playwrights are posited in relation to social arrangements, both in the text and vis-à-vis modes of production. These positions are clearly articulated in materialist feminist revisions—influenced by Brecht—of the performer's role in representation.

Performance Texts Articulated in the "Not ... But"

Brecht's formulation of the alienation effect's application to acting technique is perhaps most pertinent to materialist feminist practice. The Brechtian actor resides in a state of showingness. Rather than being psychologically enmeshed with the character, as the performer is in Stanislavski's technique (which most resembles the spiritual channeling currently popular in New Age metaphysics), the performer continually stands beside the character, illustrating its behavior for the spectator's inspection.

Brecht emphasizes that "'he who is showing should himself be shown.'"[12] In many WOW Cafe performances and Spiderwoman Theatre productions[13], lines are frequently dropped or blundered through as memory fails the performers. These mistakes, however, foreground the psychological implications of memorizing lines. What does it mean, after all, to assume a character's speech, and to therefore silence your own? The psychological abdicaton of the performer's identity is undesirable to Brecht, who suggests that the performer should display, rather than become, the character.

The performer "expresses his awareness of being watched" in epic theatre.[14] [Elin] Diamond proposes these layers of watching as a way to revise Laura Mulvey's reading of the female body's traditional position in representation as constructed for "to-be-looked-at-ness."[15] Diamond substitutes "looking-at-being-looked-at-ness" or even "looking-ness" as a model for Brechtian-influenced feminist theorization of the female body onstage.[16] She expands on Brecht to suggest a triangular relationship between the actor, character, and spectator, one that will also belie Mulvey's demand for an end to visual pleasure:

> The spectator still has the possibility of pleasurable identification. This is effected not through imaginary projection onto an ideal but through a triangular structure of actor/subject-character-spectator. Looking at the character, the spectator is constantly intercepted by the actor/subject, and the latter, heeding no fourth wall, is theoretically free to look back. The difference, then, between this triangle and the familiar Oedipal one is that no one side signifies authority, knowledge, or the law.[17]

The gaze circulates along the triangle, providing three separate subject positions. The one-way nature of the male gaze, owned by a spectator who is obscured in a darkened theatre, specularizes the female body, which is not allowed to gaze back. In Diamond's formulation, the gaze itself is foregrounded—the spectator and actor/subject as character watch each other watching.

Peggy Shaw, for example, in Split Britches' *Upwardly Mobile Home,* addresses the audience through her awareness that they are watching her. She asks spectators if their seats are comfortable and if they are getting what they paid to see. This break in the narrative forces the spectators to confront themselves *as* spectators, participants in the act of looking.

Shaw steps outside the representational frame to look at the spectator looking at her, and to comment on the convention of the theatrical gaze. Her story about going to see the fat lady at the circus in *Mobile Home* comments on a feminist position vis-à-vis the gaze. When she entered the fat lady's tent, Shaw says, "She knew I had come to see her being fat. She looked at me and I looked at her."[18] The awareness of looking, freed from the pretense of disguise by the fourth wall, makes the representation of women part of the performance's subject. The performer's awareness of her being-looked-at-ness, and her stance beside her character, implicates her in the act of looking. Since she merely quotes her character in the Brechtian manner, and does not identify with her, the spectator's impulse toward identification is also broken. In Brecht's description, "The audience identifies itself with the actor as being an observer and accordingly develops his attitude of observing or looking on."[19]

Positioning the performer as an observer who quotes the character also allows meditation on the actions she has chosen to share with the spectator. The performer's choice of actions will "imply what he [*sic*] is not doing; ... his acting allows other possibilities to be inferred ... every gesture signifies a decision; the character remains under observation and is tested. The technical term for this procedure is 'fixing the "not ... but."'"[20] Purposefully distanced from the representation she is making, the performer embodies a semiotic space in which her presence bears the traces of its difference; her image retains "something of the rough sketching which indicates traces of other movements and features all around the fully-worked out figure."[21] Or, as Diamond defines the "not ... but," "Each action must contain the trace of the action it represses, thus the meaning of each action contains difference."[22] If the performer is representing gender, the action she chooses will bear the trace of what it is not. The representational apparatus that creates gender can be demystified; the representation of gender within the "not. . . but" will be a choice made in a critical attitude.

The Lesbian Subject as the "Not ... But"

The "not ... but" might point to a materialist practice in which the female body in representation is no longer the object of the male gaze, but part of the discourse of watching that performance promotes. The female body may no longer be a hysterical spectacle, but a term in the new representational debate. As Diamond offers, "The body in historicization stands visibly and palpably separate from the 'role' of the actor as well as the role of the character; it is always insufficient and open."[23] This new representation of the female body is not a closed text that ends in objectification nor is it subjected to inscription in the narrative of compulsory heterosexuality.

In order to rethink representation, [Teresa] de Lauretis proposes that "we must walk out of the male-centered frame of reference in which gender and sexuality are (re)produced by the discourse of male sexuality."[24] She emphasizes that cultural production is "built on male narratives of gender, whether Oedipal or anti-Oedipal, bound by the heterosexual contract." Hence, the "critique of all discourses concerning gender" must rewrite cultural narratives and define the terms of another perspective—"a view from 'elsewhere.'"[25] The lesbian subject position looms as the unarticulated but inferred "elsewhere" in de Lauretis' discourse.

The lesbian subject is "the elsewhere of discourse, the here and now, the blind spots, or the spaces-off, of its representations."[26] The lesbian subject is in a position to denaturalize dominant codes by signifying an existence that belies the entire structure of heterosexual culture and its representations. The lesbian signifies a "blockage in the system of representation" by expressing forbidden contents in forbidden forms.[27] The forbidden content is active female desire independent of men, and the forbidden form is a self-representation that separates gender from a strict correlation with biological sex and compulsory sexuality. The lesbian is a refusor of culturally imposed gender ideology, who confounds representation based on sexual difference and on compulsory heterosexuality.

If gender is representation, then the application of the "not ... but" can help inscribe a deconstruction of gender within its construction in representation. Lesbian representations of butch/femme appearances point out the possibilities of such a deconstruction. A lesbian assuming a butch or femme role retains traces of difference that mark out her choice. [Sue-Ellen] Case describes butch or femme lesbians as "dressed in the clothes of desire";[28] the roles are "symbols of seduction."[29] The lesbian desire underlying lesbian representations of gender disrupts the system of gender signification.

The drag role requires the performer to quote the accepted conventions of gender behavior. A woman playing a man, or the traditional representation of Woman, is quoting gender ideology, holding it up for critique. By standing outside her gendered character, the performer makes gender available for discussion. When the assumed gender role does not coincide with the performer's biological sex, the fictions of gender are highlighted. When the role does coincide with her biology, as it does when the lesbian plays the femme role, it is noncoincidental to the assumed heterosexuality of the representation of Woman.

In the lesbian context, where the heterosexual assumption has been discarded, gender as representation gets detached from "the real" and becomes as plastic and kitsch as the little man and woman balanced on a wedding cake. Gender becomes a social *gestus*, a gesture that represents ideology circulating in social relations.

The lesbian body, which articulates itself through female desire, stands already outside of gender enculturation. In its refusal of heterosexuality, the lesbian body cannot be narrativized as spectacle. The lesbian is still a representation—as Con Carne tells Garnet McClit in [Holly Hughes's] *Lady Dick*, "You're what they watch when there's nothing *buena* on TV"—but she is a sign that disrupts the dominant signifying system. When she assumes a gender role, it becomes part of the material aspects of the representational apparatus, a costume that hangs on a rack of choices.

Joan Nestle, a cofounder of the Lesbian Herstory Archives who became a lesbian in the 1950s, tells a story in the "Sex Issue" of *Heresies* that seems to me to be about gender as representation: "One day many years ago, as I was walking through Central Park, a group of cheerful straight people walked past me and said, 'What shall we feed it?'"[30] They could not read her lesbian self-representation because they could not inscribe her in their heterosexually gendered narrative. With a certain prescience, Nestle remarks, "When [lesbians] broke gender lines in the 1950s, we fell off the biologically charted maps."[31] By transgressing heterosexually divided gender roles, the lesbian confounded the sign system that denotes woman, because the representation of gender *as* representation is based on compulsory heterosexuality.

Garnet McClit, Lady Dick, is perhaps emblematic of the lesbian subject position in representation. Divisions of both gender and biological sex are conflated in her name. The puns on her hermaphroditic appellation run through the play: One character remarks in a kind of Brechtian astonishment, "She's a dick. She can't be!" This is Brechtian defamiliarization at work—implied in the lesbian subject is a "not ... but" that materializes the gap between sex and gender that lesbian desire can inhabit.

Please see the Works Cited for further information on the sources used in this essay.

Notes

1 Dolan's book was initially published by UMI in 1988, and then re-published in 1991 by the University of Michigan Press. Dolan published a second edition of the book with a new introduction in 2012 [Del Vecchio and eds.].

2 See Case and Diamond entries in this volume [eds.].

3 See Cixous entry in this volume [eds.].

4 See entries on Lois Weaver and Spiderwoman/Muriel Miguel in this volume [eds.].

5 See http://feministspectator.princeton.edu/ [eds.].

6 Bertolt Brecht in John Willett, ed., *Brecht on Theatre* (New York: Hill and Wang, 1964), p. 197 [Dolan].

7 Gayle Rubin, "The Traffic in Women: Notes on the 'Political Economy' of Sex," in Rayna Reiter, ed., *Toward an Anthropology of Women* (New York: Monthly Review Press, 1978), p. 178 [Dolan].

8 Ibid., p. 180 [Dolan].

9 For a relevant discussion of the WOW Cafe's parody of genre conventions, see also Jill Dolan, "Feminists, Lesbians, and Other Women in Theatre: Thoughts on the Politics of Performance," in James Redmond, ed., *Themes in Drama* Vol. 11 (Cambridge University Press, 1989) [Dolan/Del Vecchio].

10 Walter Benjamin, *Illuminations* (New York: Schocken Books, 1969), p. 149 [Dolan].

11 Terry Eagleton, *Marxism and Literary Criticism* (Berkeley: University of California Press, 1976), p. 68 [Dolan].

12 Brecht, in Willett, p. 42 [Dolan].

13 See Spiderwoman/Muriel Miguel entry in this volume [eds.].

14 Brecht, in Willett, p.92 [Dolan].

15 Laura Mulvey, "Visual Pleasure and Narrative Cinema," *Screen* Vol. 16, No. 3 (Autumn 1975), p. 11 [Dolan].

16 Dolan quotes from an unpublished manuscript, but we have updated her citations to refer to the published version of the article: Elin Diamond, "Brechtian Theory/Feminist Theory: Toward a Gestic Feminist Criticism," *Drama Review* Vol. 32, No. 1 (1988). Diamond read an earlier version of this article at the Association for Theatre in Higher Education Conference in Chicago, August 1987, on a "New Directions in Feminist Research" panel [Dolan/Del Vecchio].

17 Ibid., p. 90 [Dolan].

18 See also Jill Dolan, "Desire Cloaked in a Trenchcoat" in *Drama Review* (1988), for a further discussion of this moment in *Upwardly Mobile Home* in terms of female spectatorship and the exchange of meanings. The article she references here appears in *TDR* 33.1 (spring 1989) pp. 59–67 [Dolan/Del Vecchio]

19 Brecht, in Willett, p. 92 [Dolan].

20 Ibid., p. 137 [Dolan].

21 Ibid., p. 191 [Dolan].

22 Diamond, "Gestic Criticism," p. 86 [Dolan/Del Vecchio].
23 Ibid., p. 89 [Dolan].
24 Teresa de Lauretis, "The Technology of Gender," in *Technologies of Gender: Essays on Theory, Film, and Fiction* (Bloomington: Indiana University Press, 1987), p. 17 [Dolan].
25 Ibid., p. 25 [Dolan].
26 Ibid [Dolan].
27 Dick Hebdige, *Subculture: The Meaning of Style* (New York: Methuen, 1979), pp. 90–91 [Dolan].
28 See Case entry in this volume [eds.].
29 Sue-Ellen Case, "Towards a Butch/Femme Aesthetic," keynote address, Women and Theatre Program Conference, Chicago, August 2, 1987; also in Lynda Hart, ed., *Making a Spectacle: Feminist Essays on Contemporary Women's Theatre* (Ann Arbor University of Michigan Press, 1988) [Dolan/Del Vecchio].
30 Joan Nestle, "Butch/Femme Relationships in the 1950s" in the "Sex Issue" of *Heresies* *#12* Vol. 3, No. 4(1981), p. 24 [Dolan].
31 Ibid [Dolan].

Suggestions for Further Reading

Dolan, Jill. *The Feminist Spectator.* http://feministspectator.princeton.edu/.
———. *Theatre & Sexuality.* London: Springer Nature, Ltd., 2010.

61 THE DIVINA PROJECT (1989–1998)

Juliet Guzzetta

Introduction

In the early spring of 1974 several high school and college students participated in a theatre workshop at the local library in the outskirts of the industrial northwestern Italian city of Turin. As they explored the possibilities of theatre-making, these students drew much inspiration from the creative thinking and experimentation that permeated Italian performance culture throughout the 1970s. They studied the fresh styles that emerged around them, as well as in the many foreign projects that were also popular in Italy, from the Living Theatre to the works of John Cage.[1] Born from this moment was the Laboratorio Teatro Settimo (their name winking at the group work of Jerzy Grotowski's "laboratory theater" and honoring their home town of Settimo Torinese).[2] Teatro Settimo grew to be one of the most influential theatre companies of late twentieth-century Italy, known for its original plays and adaptations that focused on stories of the traditionally underrepresented in such works as their celebrated *The Story of Romeo and Juliet* (1990), in which the protagonists were the nursemaid and priest.

Fifteen years after that first undertaking in the library, and a number of projects and critically-acclaimed plays later, several of the women of Teatro Settimo were concerned, ironically, that their own subaltern identities as women would not provide a space for their voices in the story of the theatre company they co-founded. A decade following the practical and theoretical discussions of 1970s feminism in Italy, Antonia Spaliviero of Teatro Settimo contacted Barbara Lanati and Paola Trivero, scholars at the University of Turin, conveying the desire to ensure both a theatre history that included the women of Teatro Settimo, and also more broadly one that included other female theatre artists whose work they admired (thus the presence of the Irish Fiona Shaw and the French Clementine Yelnick).[3] So began *Divina*, an initiative at the University of Turin from 1989–1998 comprised of conference gatherings with artists and critics, and two edited collections that addressed the ideas borne out of those conversations.

The excerpts published here offer a snapshot of their first published volume of essays, entitled *Divina: Vicende di vita e di teatro* (Events in Life and Theater). In a succinct introduction, the scholars articulate how the group came to appreciate the rich identification of the artists with their characters as a mystical experience veering towards the divine. The book performs this thinking by featuring the artists as the sole authors of each chapter; they muse broadly on the intersections of their own life choices with their experiences as women, and their lives in the theatre.

DOI: 10.4324/9781003006923-62

Their initial act of coming together as a group, coupled with their subsequent decision to reflect on their own lives, points to a dialectical instance of theatre theory in which the matching of collective thinking with the solitary process of autobiographical reflection leads to a specific practice of theatre-making. This new combination of techniques reinforced some of the group methods already in practice within their company, but also contributed to the then-developing style known as the Theater of Narration. Teatro Settimo artist Laura Curino was among the first to utilize this new form with her 1987 solo play, *Passione,* which dances along private/public lines to construct a postwar industrial/cultural history with her own experiences at the center.

As theatre theory, the personal essays in the first collection of *Divina* offer provocations rather than fully-fleshed models. The fact that the women in a leading experimental theatre company turned to scholars (also women who were navigating their own paths through systems stacked against them), inviting them to think together about intellectual and artistic ideas, is an important act itself. The artists are demonstrating the need to take control of documenting their own histories as well as the value of autobiographical elements in their professional narratives. The scholars serve in supporting roles by offering an official structure—the university—rather than as leaders of the meetings; it is especially laudatory that this arrangement, which centered the performers, carries over into the first published volume. That the scholars took a more muscular role in the second volume suggests that the artists did not have the same agency as they first did, which might have contributed to the discontinuation of these annual meetings after just a few years.

As it grapples with the importance of autobiography, this *Divina* text is in conversation with a range of philosophical, political, and cultural theories from the period and also anticipates many important analyses of autobiography. Hélène Cixous's 1976 "The Laugh of Medusa" with her directive that "woman must write her self" was influential to many strands of Italian feminism and philosophy and also resonates here.[4] This lineage crosses the Atlantic and develops over time, as with bell hooks's praise of personal narratives, which she threads throughout *Feminism is for Everybody* (2000) more than two decades later. A decade after that, the Scottish performance scholar Deidre Heddon's subsequent research, *Autobiography and Performance* (2008), addresses the specific ways in which autobiography, subjectivity, performance, and feminism overlap. Her projects develop with greater complexity what the Teatro Settimo artists were already beginning to suggest in the early 1990s. In fact, reading the *Divina* volume in concert with that scholarship raises questions about why so few scholars consider what artists themselves say about their own work.

The most significant aspect of the *Divina* project generally, and this first publication in particular, is the way in which it reframes history and culture as intimately personal while also available publicly. The artists' method of self-reflection is largely affect-driven, which leads them inevitably to reinforce the ways in which historical and cultural circumstances resonated with them personally and pushed them to approach their work deliberately from that interior place. Reading the private accounts of the performers, and considering that they themselves saw the public dynamic of their own stories, demonstrates the intimacy of the universal. The *Divina* meetings represent a proximity between artists and intellectuals, wherein the artists play a role in shaping the criticism of their own work, and thus its narrative for posterity.

The Divina Project

Excerpt from Life Events, Theater Events *(1992)*[5]

The testimonies here date back to an academic conference—Female Poetics and Presence in the Last Twenty Years of Theater—that took place in Turin, Italy on June 4–5, 1990, organized by the "Divina" Association.

Founded in Turin by an all-female group of scholars and theatre artists (Università degli Studi di Torino and Laboratorio Teatro Settimo), "Divina" was born as a permanent site of observation for *Women and Theatre*, widely interpreted [a series Divina began with the press, Tirrenia Stampatori].

The Executive Committee of "Divina" is composed of Maria Grazia Agricola, Barbara Lanati, Antonia Spaliviero, and Paola Trivero.

MARIELLA FABBRIS

It is difficult for me to describe my experience as an actress because my job implies that I have already chosen a language with which to express a distinct perception of the world. I am also a peculiar actress: I don't come from a school, but from a city near Turin's industrial belt – Settimo Torinese. In this city I met, by chance (or was it actually by chance?), a group of people with whom I have been living a life experience for more than ten years that has much to do with theatre, but not only.

In the beginning it was about finding a good reason to go on living in a place that seemed to have nothing to offer us and the theatre looked like the only way to satisfy our enormous need to communicate what we were feeling. We also touched upon, even if only peripherally, *animazione teatrale* [a movement that is somewhere between happenings, performance art, and street theatre] that had taken root in nearby Turin, but we used it mostly to make noise, occupy spaces, let it be known that we were alive. There was a period when downtown streets were constantly disturbed by our more or less theatrical interventions: a huge quantity of large and small actions to sensitize the streets a little, the walls of the houses, to insert sounds and voices over the usual noise.

I was in a very committed relationship during those times and my boyfriend always drove me around with his scooter: we often left the city in search of places where we were better off because Settimo was too ugly. But when I met Gabriele Vacis, [...]

LAURA CURINO

My story as an actress is linked to [the theatre group] Teatro Settimo, therefore I will often say "we," and in this "we" there is all of myself with some constraints and a little more luxury.

There is a crucial year, 1984, which is also the title of one of Orwell's novels. In that year, and also in that novel, there was much talk about the end of communication and the rise of one big Communicator: video, which looms over all of us and makes it impossible to escape the camera's gaze.

I was reading Orwell at eleven and was telling myself: "Let's hope it isn't like this. Oh god, oh god… Let's hope we won't become what is written here!".

And then 1984 was upon us and I saw *Fastes-Foules* by L'Ymagier Singulier, a Belgian company who performed in enormous spaces such as abandoned factories. We found one for them and we had to work for two weeks in order to allow these actors-plumbers-mechanics-stagehands and how many others to build that grandiose structure that was their theatre machine. The big warehouse became a theatre rich with not only objects but also filled with the actors' bodies who carried extraordinary and dangerous set pieces inspired by Zola's *Rougon-Macquart* series. All of that without giving up the text and with a communicative strength that was immediate and thrilling.

Another factory, same year. We staged *Accions* by "La Fura dels Baus" from Barcelona. Again, a large group [...]

Please see the Works Cited for further information on the sources used in this essay.

Notes

1 Founded in 1947 by Judith Malina and Julian Beck, The Living Theatre promoted an experimental and at times radical aesthetic with anarchist and pacifist roots. See Malina entry in this volume. John Cage (1912–1992) was an American composer frequently associated with the postwar avant-garde, best known for his experimental use of instruments, and collaborations with the dancer and choreographer Merce Cunningham (1919–2009).
2 Jerzy Grotowski (1933–1999), Polish director celebrated for his theory and practice of a Poor Theatre.
3 My gratitude to Paola Trivero who met with me to discuss *Divina* and more in the summer of 2018.
4 See Cixous entry in this volume.
5 Translated by Valeria Dani and Juliet Guzzetta from Antonia Spaliviero, ed., *Vicende di vita e di teatro. Tirrenia Stampatori*, 1992.

Suggestions for Further Reading

Goodman, Elizabeth. *'Divina': A report from Turin*. New Theatre Quarterly. 7.25 (1991): 97–99.
Goodman, Elizabeth and Gabrielle Giannachi. *A Theatre for Urban Renewal*. New Theatre Quarterly. 7.25 (1991): 27–34.
Guzzetta, Juliet. *The Theater of Narration: From the Peripheries of History to the Main Stages of Italy*. Evanston, IL: Northwestern University Press, 2021.

62 NEHAD SELAIHA (1945–2017)

Marvin Carlson

Introduction

On January 6, 2017, the Arab theatre world lost one of its best-known, beloved, and distinguished figures, the Egyptian theatre critic Nehad Selaiha (1945–2017). During the 1990s, Selaiha emerged not only as the dominant critical commentator on the Egyptian theatre but also as the most influential advocate for the developing independent theatre movement and for a new generation of actors, directors, and dramatists. She became for many the voice of the Egyptian theatre, her reviews in the journal *Al-Ahram* providing for much of the English-speaking world the best insight into that theatre and Selaiha herself regularly invited to represent the Arab theatre at major conferences around the world.

Her work was honored and awarded at most of the leading theatre festivals throughout the Arab world, and she received a number of major state awards marking her outstanding contributions to the arts. But her memory will surely be best preserved in the hundreds of perceptive essays she created, leaving behind a marvelously nuanced and detailed picture of several decades of the modern Egyptian theatre, and perhaps even more significantly, in the countless lives she touched in Egypt and abroad in whom she left something of her dedication, devotion to, and love of the theatrical art.

Several qualities set Selaiha's criticism apart from that of most of her contemporaries at home and abroad. Her reviews are rarely if ever simple summaries, descriptions or value judgments on particular productions, though they often include these, but are wide-ranging essays that consider the theatre as an art form and a political and social phenomenon, in Egypt and abroad. The range and depth of her critical references and comparisons are stunning. Not surprisingly, she is intimately familiar with the Egyptian theatre, its artists, and its history, and like many critics of her generation, she often references Beckett, Brecht, and Ionesco. But she is also well versed in Shakespeare, Wordsworth, and Virginia Woolf (her academic training was in English literature), and in the Western intellectual tradition from Plato and Aristotle to Marx, Sartre, and Freud.

She had little tolerance for the mindless commercial entertainments that the Cairo scene offers, but she struggled continuously and fruitfully for the experimental work of young artists, and especially women, and was deeply sympathetic to their ongoing struggles for funding, performance opportunities, and recognition with an indifferent and self-serving bureaucracy and the active opposition of religious and political conservatives.

DOI: 10.4324/9781003006923-63

While most Egyptian theatre critics, like theatre critics elsewhere, concern themselves almost exclusively with major productions in their home city, Selaiha's fascination with the art and her desire to encourage budding theatre experiments led her to seek out work in the most obscure corners of Cairo as well as in remote villages in upper Egypt. Her reviews of such experiences often provide us with fascinating insights into the experience of actually being in such unconventional places of performance.

Nor was Selaiha's interest and influence confined to Egypt. Her essays cover many of the major theatre festivals of the Arab world, and, as her reputation grew, she was frequently invited to address gatherings of theatre practitioners and scholars from around the world. For her many international friends and admirers, she was the voice and the presence of the contemporary Egyptian theatre.

Given the range and variety of her critical writing, selecting three essays that would begin to suggest the whole would be an impossible task, but the three chosen for this collection show Selaiha involved in one of her most important endeavors, raising major general questions about the art as a whole, and especially in Egypt, with a clear and perceptive analysis of the current situation and suggestion for how it might develop into something more in line with her own ambitious and inspiring vision. Originally, all three appeared, as did almost all of her writings, in the pages of *al-Ahram,* and two were reprinted in one of the six collected volumes of her essays (now out of print), published by the General Egyptian Book Office in Cairo. The first, "Women Playwrights in Egypt" exists in several versions, as it remained a central concern throughout her career. It originally was published in 1992 and this final version as an appendix to the 2003 collection *Plays and Playwrights.* The second "Art and Politics," another central concern, was first published in April of 1999 and reproduced in another 2003 collection *The Egyptian Theatre: New Directions.* The third, "A Year of Revolutionary Theatre," appeared in *Al-Ahram* during the final week of 2011 and provides a theatrical survey of the previous year in the Egyptian theatre, the critical year of the Arab Spring, beginning with the uprising of 25 January 2010.

Although these three essays are somewhat unusual in their scope, even the most specific report Selaiah makes on the most modest venture is almost always significantly related to the larger aesthetic, social, and political questions that she confronts more directly and extensively here. And it is this life-long engagement and commitment, along with her humanity, generosity of spirit, and critical acumen, that place Nehad Selaiha among the outstanding modern critics of theatre.

Nehad Selaiha

Excerpt from "Women Playwrights in Egypt" (1992)[1]

The list of women playwrights in Egypt is depressingly short. When you have counted in everybody, including the one-timers and those who never made it to the stage, and even if you add for a bonus Amina El-Sawi who adapted some novels in the sixties, the number does not exceed a dozen.

Compared to other Arab countries, however, Egypt does not seem to have done too badly in the space of forty years. Besides, if we were to expand our theme and make it "women dramatists in Egypt," we will find that at least six women have tried their hand at television drama. My business here, however, is with women who specifically wrote with the stage in mind.

[...]

With five full-length theatre pieces, countless radio plays, 20 T.V. plays and 22 T.V. drama serials, El-Assal is by far the most prolific woman dramatist in Egypt and the Arab world[2]. She is the only woman too who has made writing her sole profession and source of income. This appears all the more striking when we consider her beginnings. Indeed, she can be said to have had the most inauspicious childhood possible for a future writer.

[...]

In El-Assal's thought and writing, the freedom of the body is deeply linked with the freedom of the mind. The historical confinement of the female body to the home has been, in her view, the main cause of women's intellectual backwardness. "Denied education, social mobility and access to public life, how can women hope to develop their minds, or become artists or scientists?!" she exclaims. In such circumstances, any kind of creative writing becomes difficult, and writing plays becomes well-nigh impossible.

A woman, she explains, can weave novels out of her simple and limited daily experience. Theatre, however, is a communal art and a public forum; it tackles broader issues and requires a public type of discourse, more comprehensive, dialectical, and politically conscious - in other words, the type of discourse women are rarely trained into. Besides, very few women can write good plays without seeing some first; how else could they learn the craft? In most Arab countries, however, including Egypt, theatre-going is still regarded as an almost exclusively male pastime. If women are allowed to go at all, they seldom choose the play themselves or go without a male relative.

Excerpt from "Art and Politics" (1999)

In the Arab world where repressive authoritarianism, in varying degrees of severity and one form or another, penetrates all aspects of life and constitutes the ruling principle - informing the structures of thought, social relations and government - cultural events, and theatre festivals in particular, invariably have an air of crude political machination. Because theatre in the Arab world has always had an irreducible political dimension and continues to be inextricably bound up with a critique of domination, official theatre festivals are often viewed by governments as effective means to divert attention from the many arrant abuses of human rights in this part of the world, and project a spurious facade of democracy, freedom of speech and conscience.

The partisan political base of such events, however well camouflaged, is hardly a secret. Over the years, Arab artists, critics and cultural activists have had to learn how to manipulate it in their interests without compromising their visions. In this respect, bluffing has proved invaluable. By taking the establishment at its word, pretending to believe its glossy slogans, and threatening to embarrass it by calling its bluff if necessary, artists have been able, in some cases, to secure subsidies, spaces, media coverage and a bigger margin of freedom.

Foreign participants face a different challenge, particularly if they belong to formerly colonialist nations. Burdened with a sense of guilt, and a heritage they feel they have to apologize and make up for, they find themselves in the position of having to suspend all judgement and exercise the virtue of tolerance and respect for difference to a fault. This makes them a deliciously easy prey to autocratic regimes whose internationally acknowledged legitimacy is mere pretense. Caught in the guilt trap, they are rendered largely passive. Unwilling to interfere with what they regard as hallowed "internal affairs," and burdened with an exaggerated and overrated respect for otherness and cultural specificity, they are forced into a position which is the reverse side of the superiority coin.

Instead of holding up their culture as the norm and only model as they once did, Westerners now go to the other, equally reprehensible extreme of uncritically accepting repressive aspects and human rights abuses of formerly colonized countries which are passed off as part of the cultural heritage. Admittedly, they are in an unenviable position; if they object, they will be branded as ethnocentric, interfering busybodies by both east and west. In any case, the same cultural sanctity plea will be trotted out to defend the indefensible against foreign interference or even observation.

"If people like it, who am I to judge" about sums up the foreign position. Never mind if what the 'people' (read the natives) like is media-imposed, enforced, and popularized. Never mind if the free souls in these doubly oppressed countries (first militarily and then culturally) do not go along with the agenda of the new internal form of oppression. What the intelligentsia of the West have not yet realized is that many of the ruling establishments in previous cultures have decided to play on their sense of guilt to wangle a form of tacit validation for their new improved brand of oppression—all the more lethal because it comes from inside. One is asked, in the name of respect for 'otherness,' to condone dominant discourses that are held like an axe over the necks of the people, discouraging independent thought and leading to a herd mentality, as well as repressive laws that restrict people's freedom of action and sometimes physically mutilate them into the bargain.

Excerpt from "A Year of Revolutionary Theatre" (2011)

Theatre has been active in the Egyptian revolution since its eruption on 25 January 2010. During the Tahrir Square 18-day long sit in, which brought Mubarak down, theatre artists made their presence very much felt. With collectively improvised stories, sketches, songs and dances they helped their fellow revolutionaries keep up their morale, fight off the bitter cold and, in between skirmishes, some of them bloody, mourn the martyrs and while away the long days and nights of the long, long suspenseful wait. Mubarak's ouster only marked the end of the first phase of the revolution; it still continues, as the recent bloody events in downtown Cairo amply bear witness. And throughout its inspiring yet painful progress, its ups and downs, young theatre artists have tried to keep pace with the events.

The first phase of the revolution yielded a rich crop of performances that sought to salvage, document and store in the collective memory the stories of the people in Tahrir Square, both living and dead, through narration and first or second- hand live testimonies. Suddenly there was a powerful upsurge of a new branch of documentary theatre that has been absent from the Egyptian theatre scene – namely: verbatim theatre. And it was mostly offered by independent groups, through untraditional or fringe venues, in the courtyard of Al-Hanager, at Manf Hall, Rawabet, and the on the campuses of some universities. Outstanding examples of this type of performances were Dalia Basiouny's *Tahrir Stories*, Hani Abdel Naser's *By the Light of the Revolution Moon* and *Pages from the Tahrir Diary*, and Laila Soliman's *No Time for Art*. At the heart of this documentary effort was an ardent wish to record what that brief, 18-day utopia in Tahrir Square had meant and done to those who experienced it and to mourn and honour those who fell defending it.

[…]

By July, the summer heat seemed to evaporate the dewy dreams of utopia, and in the performances that still looked back in anger and celebrated the revolution one could clearly detect a note of forced cheerfulness, so hungry and eager, so fierce in its determination to be hopeful, to turn a blind eye to the present and cling to the Utopian image of Tahrir Square in the early days of the revolution, and yet so painfully conscious of being unsustainable. How easy it is to look back in anger and theatrically rehash and trot out grievances on which all agree; how much more difficult to confront a painfully confused and confusing reality and peer into a future hitherto dim and foggy. *Commedia Al-Ahzaan* (Comedy of Sorrows), by Ibrahim El-Husseini, directed by Sameh Megahed and presented at Al-Ghad Theatre in July, captured this state of mind. And so did *Malameh* (Features), at Yusef Idris Hall. In both there was a sober realization of the burden of long years of oppression that has eroded much that was good and honourable in the Egyptian character and that this heritage of oppression could not so easily be shaken off, that the road to a socially fair, free and democratic nation would be long and arduous. Indeed, as early as April of this year, the Youth Theatre's *Beit El-Naffadi* (House of Naffadi Alley), a political whodunit by Mohamed Mahrous, directed by Karim Maghawri and presented at Yusef Idris Hall, Al-Salam theatre, had warned against the effects of this heritage. By August, and not surprisingly, in view of the many sorrowful events that seemed to render the revolution void of meaning, a note of warning, sometimes subtle, sometimes loud and direct, crept into all the staged shows on the fringe and in the mainstream. While Abeer Ali's and her Al-Misaharati troupe's *Mr. X*, performed on a makeshift stage in front of Al-Hanager, and *Feeh Eeh Ya Masr?* (Egypt, what's up?), conceived and directed by Yasir Sadiq, with text and lyrics by Sirag El-Din Abdel-Qadir, and presented at Al-Salam Theatre, dwelt on the dangers of sectarian conflicts, Laila Soliman's *Doroos fi Al-Thawra* (Lessons in Revolting: a physical and visual political column), choreographed by Karima Mansour and presented at Rawabet, warned against the dangers of renewed military dictatorship and bore witness to the abuses of the supreme military council in rule, and the National Theatre's *Hikayat El-Nas fi Thawret 19* (Tales of People in the 1919 Uprising), conceived and directed by Ahmed Isma'il and presented at Miami theatre, juxtaposed the 1919 uprising and that of 25 January, forcing the audience to critically compare the two, and powerfully embodied a warning against the forces of darkness (namely, the Islamists and Salafis) that threaten to engulf the latter.

[…] The same sober, somber mood persisted through the autumn and still colours many of the performances offered at present. It is as if the revolution has to start all over again. Watching Mahmoud Abodoma's the Alternative Theatre troupe's *Sotoor min Dafater Masr: Infagiru aw Mootu* (Lines from Egypt's Diary: Explode or Die), a collection of recited ancient Egyptian texts and poems by Salah Abdel Sabour, Amal Donqol, Alfred Farag, Naguib Sorour and Anas Dawood, with musical accompaniment by the popular Massar Igbary (Compulsory Direction) pop group, at the French Cultural Centre in Alexandria last week, I felt as if the revolution was yet to begin. The performance was part of an Arab theatre event, significantly called 'Reveille', independently staged in place of the annual, state-funded Independent Theatre Mediterranean Forum, which the Bibliotheca Alexandrina failed to run this year. Tunis, Syria and Jordan were all strongly present with stirring performances, and classes and workshops were offered with the help of the Swedish Institute, the Goethe Institute, the Swiss Prohelvatia, Sida, and the French Cultural Centre in Alexandria.

Introducing this "Reveille: Arab Theatre Gathering," Abodoma wrote in the event's booklet: "*Reveille* is an Arab theatre gathering, a wake-up call that seeks to promote awareness of social and political changes and their cultural repercussions. [...] We aim to transcend the narrow limits of time and place. We find echoes of what is happening now in Egypt in Palestine, Jordan and Syria. We observe that what is happening in Tunisia has stirred Yemen and Iraq. We seek to awaken Damascus, Amman, Jerusalem, Beirut, Cairo and Sana'a. We seek to remove the long stuck layers of dust off our body. We seek to lead the way to broad prospects, to reach every Arab citizen to hear our wakeup call, our *Reveille*." Does not this sound like a call to revolt long after we thought the revolution had already started?

Please see the Works Cited for further information on the sources used in this essay.

Notes

1 First published in the *Contemporary Women Playwrights* special issue of *Theatre Journal,* eds. Penny Farfan and Lesley Ferris, 2010.
2 Fathia El-Assal (1933–2014), was an Egyptian writer and activist.

Suggestions for Further Reading

Carlson, Marvin, ed. "Nehad Selaiha Memorial Issue." *Arab Stages* 6 (Spring, 2017).
Schechner, Richard. "Nehad Selaiha, 1945–2017." *TDR: The Drama Review* 61.3 (Fall 2017): 8–9.
Selaiha, Nehad. "Antigone in Egypt." *Antigone on the Contemporary World Stage*. Eds. Erin B. Mee and Helen P. Foley. Oxford University Press, 2011. pp. 346–369.
———. "Egypt Update." *TDR: The Drama Review* 58.3 (Fall 2014): 7–14.
———. "The Fire and the Frying Pan: Censorship and Performance in Egypt." *TDR: The Drama Review* 57.3 (Fall 2013): 20–47.
———. "The Fringe in Action." *Women and Performance: A Journal of Feminist Theory* 23.3 (2013): 430–433.
———. "Peer Gynt by the Pyramids in Egypt." *Global Ibsen*. Eds. Erika Fischer-Lichte, Barbara Gronau, and Christel Weiler. Routledge, 2011. 114–130.
———. *Selected Essays*. Ed. Marvin Carlson (5 vol). Martin E. Segal Theatre Center, 2020.
Selaiha, Nehad and Sarah Enany. "Women Playwrights in Egypt." *Theatre Journal* 62.4 (December 2010): 627–643.

63 PEGGY PHELAN (b.1959)

Daniel Sack

Introduction

What distinguishes live performance in the theatre from performance on film, tele-vision, or another digital platform? What does live theatre have to say about everyday life? And how does one write about this fleeting art without ossifying it in deadening language?

Peggy Phelan (b.1959) addresses these questions directly in her essay, "The Ontology of Performance," excerpted here from her groundbreaking first book, *Unmarked: The Politics of Performance* (1993). That title could name Phelan's lasting project in over sixty essays spanning more than three decades: an excavation of the inextricable connection between performance and the politics of governance and the politics of the everyday. This struggle plays out upon the field of representation–of marking and unmarking–where the blind spots of racism, sexism, and ableism that make possible the partial vision of normative (white/heterosexual/patriarchal/American) culture are Phelan's primary targets. She brings a feminist critique to the atrocities of Abu Ghraib, of 9/11, of the Rodney King beatings,[1] and to the machina-tions of the conservative right via the presidency of Ronald Reagan and anti-abortion activism. Throughout, performance acts are the guiding metaphor and means for her investigations. In this regard, Phelan has exerted a major influence on perfor-mance studies, an interdisciplinary field of research on cross-cultural performance in all its registers—aesthetic, social, political, and otherwise.

She began her academic career at New York University's Department of Performance Studies, the first such department in the world, where she eventually served as chair; she became the first president of Performance Studies International and organized its first global conference in 1996 (selections of which were published in her book *The Ends of Performance* [1998]). She is now appointed to several departments at Stanford University, where she holds the Ann Quinn Day Maples Chair in the Arts.

Phelan has written luminous essays on modern drama, ensemble-based creation, queer and feminist solo performance, and contemporary dance, often redressing marginalized representation. Visual art in the post-World War II period has been another major focus in her important work on Marina Abramovic, Pippolotti Rist, Cindy Sherman, Andy Warhol, Francesca Woodman,[2] and other artists whose pro-duction involves performance in more or less direct ways. Her survey essay on *Art and Feminism* (2001) is widely read and referenced as the standard in the field; and her book *Live Art in LA* (2012) offers a counter-narrative to conventional understandings of New York as the nexus for post-war innovation in the arts. Here she occupies an

DOI: 10.4324/9781003006923-64

exceptional position in visual arts discourse, bringing theatrical frames of reference into the art world and vice versa, as when, for example, she recounts her quest to find the painting that inspired the play *Waiting for Godot* by Samuel Beckett (a writer with whom she is frequently in dialogue). Even as the passages excerpted here primarily discuss the French visual artist Sophie Calle,[3] their ramifications for the stage should be readily apparent.

Ontology is the philosophical investigation of the essence of things, so this excerpted essay seeks the signature of a live event in distinction from its mediated others. In part this grows out of the modernist search for the specific characteristics of each artistic medium, which led painters in the mid-20th century to expose the flatness of the painted canvas as the ground of painting or filmmakers to make works of mere light. As the art that contains all other arts, theatre has often been cast as the other to such modernist purity. Phelan locates a disruptive potential specific to performance in its temporality, which resists the exchange and accumulation of objects so central to capitalism and, with its focus on conserving and marketing "valuable" work, the art world. Performance expends everything; it leaves something different in its wake—documentation, a script or score, a relic marked with the traces of action—but not the live event itself. If performance "becomes itself through disappearance," then it is not so different from life itself, also always shadowed with its other, death. As the theatre director and critic Herbert Blau famously put it, when watching a performance, you are watching someone die in front of your eyes. For Phelan, the inevitable loss that accompanies this living makes psychoanalysis an especially rich means for thinking through its consequences.

This essay is a polemic advocating ephemerality in a world that privileges permanence. It often speaks in absolutes and has provoked various responses: most notably, Philip Auslander argues that this category of the "live" obtains meaning only in relation to its mediated other, and Rebecca Schneider claims that performances, documents, and objects continue to "live," even after they have passed through new resonances and repetitions.[4] These and other critiques offer necessary expansions on the ideas proposed here, though they do not discount its significance. Indeed "The Ontology of Performance" is perhaps the most frequently cited text on performance written in the last thirty years.

It is arguably as an artist/thinker of the written word that Phelan has made her most powerful impact in theatre theory. She did her doctorate in English literature; and poetry, particularly that of the philosopher-poets Wallace Stevens and T.S. Eliot,[5] weaves through her lines. This attunement to language affects her own writing, too. Just as the exhibition by Sophie Calle described below illustrates "the interactive exchange between the art object and the viewer," so does Phelan's writing perform an interaction with the figures she encounters. Both are changed by the meeting, just as we might find ourselves changed by the reading of her lines. (This, too, is a kind of "liveness.") Here, it is worth rehearsing the distinction proposed by the British philosopher J.L. Austin, who also makes an appearance in the essay.[6]

A *constative statement* describes an unchanging pre-existing world ("the cat is on the mat"), while a *performative speech act* does what it says, speech as action ("I now pronounce you man and wife"). Expanding on this distinction, Phelan models a "performative writing" that acts on the world. Her work often oversteps the efficiency of "effective" prose to embody a weight that moves, playfully and painfully, into the poetic, the confessional, the transcendent. Thus, she invites us to stage our own written responses as performances, not merely for the pleasure of expression, but to wrestle with the ethics of writing itself, demanding we consider "What remains after an act has ended? What are the obligations of a witness to an act that is over?"

Peggy Phelan

Excerpt from "The Ontology of Performance" (1993)

Performance's only life is in the present. Performance cannot be saved, recorded, documented, or otherwise participate in the circulation of representations of representations: once it does so, it becomes something other than performance. To the degree that performance attempts to enter the economy of reproduction it betrays and lessens the promise of its own ontology. Performance's being, like the ontology of subjectivity proposed here, becomes itself through disappearance. The pressures brought to bear on performance to succumb to the laws of the reproductive economy are enormous. For only rarely in this culture is the "now" to which performance addresses its deepest questions valued. (This is why the now is supplemented and buttressed by the documenting camera, the video archive.) Performance occurs over a time which will not be repeated. It can be performed again, but this repetition itself marks it as "different." The document of a performance then is only a spur to memory, an encouragement of memory to become present.

The other arts, especially painting and photography, are drawn increasingly toward performance. The French-born artist Sophie Calle, for example, has photographed the galleries of the Isabella Stewart Gardner Museum in Boston. Several valuable paintings were stolen from the museum in 1990. Calle interviewed various visitors and members of the museum staff, asking them to describe the stolen paintings. She then transcribed these texts and placed them next to the photographs of the galleries. Her work suggests that the descriptions and memories of the paintings constitute their continuing "presence," despite the absence of the paintings themselves. Calle gestures toward a notion of the interactive exchange between the art object and the viewer. While such exchanges are often recorded as the stated goals of museums and galleries, the institutional effect of the gallery often seems to put the masterpiece under house arrest, controlling all conflicting and unprofessional commentary about it. The speech act of memory and description (Austin's constative utterance) becomes a performative expression when Calle places these commentaries within the representation of the museum. The descriptions fill in, and thus supplement (add to, defer, and displace) the stolen paintings. The fact that these descriptions vary considerably—even at times wildly—only lends credence to the fact that the interaction between the art object and the spectator is, essentially, performative—and therefore resistant to the claims of validity and accuracy endemic to the discourse of reproduction. While the art historian of painting must ask if the reproduction is accurate and clear, Calle asks where seeing and memory forget the object itself and enter the subject's own set of personal meanings and associations. Further her work suggests that the forgetting (or stealing) of the object is a fundamental energy of its descriptive recovering. The description itself does not reproduce the object, it rather helps us to restage and restate the effort to remember what is lost. The descriptions remind us how loss acquires meaning and generates recovery—not only of and for the object, but for the one who remembers. The disappearance of the object is fundamental to performance; it rehearses and repeats the disappearance of the subject who longs always to be remembered.

For her contribution to the *Dislocations* show at the Museum of Modern Art in New York in 1991, Calle used the same idea but this time she asked curators, guards, and restorers to describe paintings that were on loan from the permanent collection. She also asked them to draw small pictures of their memories of the paintings. She then arranged the texts and pictures according to the exact dimensions of the circulating paintings and placed them on the wall where the actual paintings usually hang. Calle calls her piece *Ghosts,* and as the visitor discovers Calle's work spread throughout the museum, it is as if Calle's own eye is following and tracking the viewer as she makes her way through the museum. Moreover, Calle's work seems to disappear because it is dispersed throughout the "permanent collection"—a collection which circulates despite its "permanence." Calle's artistic contribution is a kind of self-concealment in which she offers the words of others about other works of art under her own artistic signature. By making visible her attempt to offer what she does not have, what cannot be seen, Calle subverts the goal of museum display. She exposes what the museum does not have and cannot offer and uses that absence to generate her own work. By placing memories in the place of paintings, Calle asks that the ghosts of memory be seen as equivalent to "the permanent collection" of "great works." One senses that if she asked the same people over and over about the same paintings, each time they would describe a slightly different painting. In this sense, Calle demonstrates the performative quality of all seeing.

I

Performance in a strict ontological sense is nonreproductive. It is this quality which makes performance the runt of the litter of contemporary art. Performance clogs the smooth machinery of reproductive representation necessary to the circulation of capital. Perhaps nowhere was the affinity between the ideology of capitalism and art made more manifest than in the debates about the funding policies for the National Endowment for the Arts (NEA). Targeting both photography and performance art, conservative politicians sought to prevent endorsing the "real" bodies implicated and made visible by these art forms.

Performance implicates the real through the presence of living bodies. In performance art spectatorship there is an element of consumption: there are no left-overs, the gazing spectator must try to take everything in. Without a copy, live performance plunges into visibility—in a maniacally charged present—and disappears into memory, into the realm of invisibility and the unconscious where it eludes regulation and control. Performance resists the balanced circulations of finance. It saves nothing; it only spends. While photography is vulnerable to charges of counterfeiting and copying, performance art is vulnerable to charges of valuelessness and emptiness. Performance indicates the possibility of revaluing that emptiness; this potential revaluation gives performance art its distinctive oppositional edge.

To attempt to write about the undocumentable event of performance is to invoke the rules of the written document and thereby alter the event itself. Just as quantum physics discovered that macro-instruments cannot measure microscopic particles without transforming those particles, so too must performance critics realize that the labor to write about performance (and thus to "preserve" it) is also a labor that fundamentally alters the event. It does no good, however, to simply refuse to write about performance because of this inescapable transformation. The challenge raised by the ontological claims of performance for writing is to re-mark again the performative possibilities of writing itself. The act of writing toward disappearance, rather than the act of writing toward preservation, must remember that the after-effect of disappearance is the experience of subjectivity itself.

[...]

The performance of theory, the act of moving the "as if" into the indicative "is," like the act of moving descriptions of paintings into the frames of the stolen or lent canvases, is to replot the relation between perceiver and object, between self and other. In substituting the subject's memory of the object for the object itself, Calle begins to redesign the order of the museum and the representational field. Institutions whose only function is to preserve and honor objects—traditional museums, archives, banks, and to some degree, universities—are intimately involved in the reproduction of the sterilizing binaries of self/other, possession/dispossession, men/women which are increasingly inadequate formulas for representation. These binaries and their institutional upholders fail to account for that which cannot appear between these tight "equations" but which nonetheless inform them.

These institutions must invent an economy not based on preservation but one which is answerable to the consequences of disappearance. The savings and loan institutions in the US have lost the customer's belief in the promise of security. Museums whose collections include objects taken/purchased/obtained from cultures who are now asking (and expecting) their return must confront the legacy of their appropriative history in a much more nuanced and complex way than currently prevails. Finally, universities whose domain is the reproduction of knowledge must re-view the theoretical enterprise by which the object surveyed is reproduced as property with (theoretical) value.

Please see the Works Cited for further information on the sources used in this essay.

Notes

1 Abu Ghraib is where American soldiers during the Iraq War committed atrocities against their Iraqi prisoners. During the Los Angeles riots of 1992, footage emerged showing an unarmed Black man, Rodney King, on the ground being beaten by police after initially evading arrest.

2 Influential Serbian performance artist Marina Abramovic (b.1946) tests the endurance and limitations of her own body and mind through grueling methods she has developed to reach a higher plane of consciousness and serenity. Swiss visual artist Pippolotti Rist (b.1962) focuses on the female body in her experiments with video art and installation art. American photographer Cindy Sherman (b.1954) produces "disguised" self-portraits that comment on social role-playing and sexual stereotypes. Andy Warhol (1928–1987) was an American artist and filmmaker and leader of the 1960s Pop Art Movement. His large canvases depicting cultural icons and everyday consumer objects called attention to the materialization, objectification, and banality of American capitalism. Francesca Woodman (1958–1981) was an American photographer known for her black-and-white self-portraits and face-obscured images of other female models, as well as surrealist and conceptual work depicting birds, skulls, and mirrors.

3 Sophie Calle (b.1953) is a French writer, photographer, and installation artist in the Conceptual tradition.

4 See Philip Auslander, *Liveness: Performance in a Mediatized Culture* (New York, NY: Routledge, 2008); Rebecca Schneider, *Performing Remains: Art and War in Times of Theatrical Representation* (New York, NY: Routledge, 2011).

5 Wallace Stevens (1879–1955) was an American modernist poet and essayist who explored what people do to the world of "reality" in their minds. Nobel-Prize winner and American expatriate T.S. Eliot (1888–1965) was considered one of the most important poets of the twentieth century, known for such works as "The Love Song of J. Alfred Prufrock" (1915) and *The Waste Land* (1921).
6 See J. L. Austin, *How to Do Things With Words* (Cambridge: Harvard University Press, 1962).

Suggestions for Further Reading

Phelan, Peggy. *Mourning Sex: Performing Public Memories.* New York, NY: Routledge, 1997.
———, ed. *Live Art in LA: Performance in Southern California, 1970–1983.* New York, NY: Routledge, 2012.
Phelan, Peggy, and Lynda Hart, eds. *Acting Out: Feminist Performances.* Ann Arbor, MI: University of Michigan Press, 1993.
Phelan, Peggy, and Helena Rickett. *Art and Feminism.* New York, NY: Phaidon, 2006.

64 SUZAN-LORI PARKS (b.1963)

Kristen Wright

Introduction

Suzan-Lori Parks' (b.1963) "Elements of Style" was published in the 1994 volume, *The America Play and Other Works,* which includes the former play, along with several of Parks' early dramas, such as *Imperceptible Mutabilities in the Third Kingdom* (1989). The "Elements" makes a powerful artist statement, emerging in the wake of the clashes over decency in art between the National Endowment for the Arts and conservative legislators. Parks would go on to create other theoretical work, but "Elements of Style" was the first articulation of her theory of playwriting, following her break-through work, *The America Play* (1994), and preceding *Venus* (1996), *In The Blood* (1998), and the Pulitzer Prize-winning *Topdog/Underdog* (2001).

"Elements of Style" begins with a prologue, in which Parks argues that she is writing her critical essay for two reasons: "to give those readers, scholars, directors and performers of my plays a way in–so that instead of calling me up they can with this 'guide,' dive into an examination with great confidence" (13). This work of criticism emerges primarily from her desire to avoid emotional labor as a Black female playwright who has repeatedly had to explain the complexities of her work to the phalanx of mostly white writers who produce it. Through her gesture of refusal, Parks has placed herself in the critical canon as a theorist as well as a playwright. She continues in the "Elements" to state that she also wants her essay to serve as a "bulwark" against the "real crisis in American dramatic literature," which has become a "Theatre of Schmaltz" in which all plays are intended to "produce some reaction of sorts, to discuss some issue" (13). Parks' disdain for "schmaltz" signifies her refusal to believe that plays offer easy, prescriptive solutions for complex political and social issues. But there is a third member of her critical audience that Parks identifies, and s/he is the "new generation of theatre makers" (13).

"Elements of Style" is written in the form of a glossary of theatre terms, revised to embody Parks' vision of theatre, and it also serves as a provocation to keep theatre makers *"awake"* (14). Parks argues that "form and content are interdependent," fore-grounding her identity as an example (14). "I am an African-American woman," she begins (14). "This is the form I take, my content predicates this form, and this form is inseparable from my content" (14). Parks rejects universalizing rhetoric that posits all humans are the same, despite markers of gender and race. Plays are things that do not simply emerge in vacuums; they are imbued by the identity of their creators.

Parks' form and content also engage the work of another eminent female African-American playwright, Lorraine Hansberry (1930–1965). Anticipating critiques from

DOI: 10.4324/9781003006923-65

those who champion the traditional three-act play, Parks argues that "the naturalism of, say, Lorraine Hansberry is beautiful and should not be dismissed simply because it is naturalism" (15). But although Parks pays homage to a Black feminist elder, she also flattens the scope of Hansberry's work, which is best remembered by her 1959 play, *A Raisin In the Sun,* although her later and posthumous works, like *The Sign in Sidney Brustein's Window* (1965) and *Les Blancs* (1970), are more experimental.

The most frequently cited portion of "Elements of Style" is Parks' section on "repetition or revision," or, as she calls it, "Rep and Rev" (15). This term points to a process that she borrows from Jazz music, in which a musical phrase is repeated "again and again" and "slightly revised" each time (15). Parks uses rep and rev to create a "drama of accumulation," resisting the hegemony of the three-act play's climax, in which the audience is led towards a "single explosive moment" (15). In Parks' transformation, the climax is no longer a singular, explosive moment, but rather the product of the "accumulated weight of the repetition" (16). And though Parks pushes her audience to reevaluate its relationship with realism, she also situates her use of rep and rev within the "African and African-American literary and oral traditions" (16). In a project that foregrounds the reevaluation of the dramatic canon, Parks places herself within the larger canon of Black Studies.

Her definition of "etymology" argues that "grammar" is etymologically related to the word "charm" (17). In Parks' hands, grammar is not the intellectual strait-jacket that many readers will remember from grade school. Instead, it becomes a way of shaping language, a "spell in [one's mouth]," which can shape the world of a play (17). Parks leans into the idea of playwriting as a mysterious, spiritual process. The subjects of her plays are not characters but "ghosts." These ghosts enter Parks' home and "take up residence in a corner" and may carry "*someone else's pulse*" (17–18). In her plays, characters are people who come to you instead of being summoned through a willful act of creative genius. And by carrying another's pulse into her own creative process, Parks is participating in a form of meta-theatrical call and response, thus further situating herself as an artist within the Afro-Diasporic tradition.[1]

"Elements of Style" also employs the use of images, under the section on "math" (18). Parks encourages the reader to "solve for x" in a series of images (18–20). In *Imperceptible Mutabilities,* the 'x' between the USA and Africa is evocative of the Middle Passage and Triangle Trade (18). In the *Last Black Man,* Parks tells the reader to "find the volume of this solid"– meaning the coffin (19). Parks encourages her readers to reckon with the magnitude of loss and death. In the *America Play,* her encouragement to "solve for x where x is the true measurement of the Great Mans Stature" refers to both Lincoln's height and his place within time and history (20).

Parks further elaborates on the meaning of her mysterious "x," which is not supposed to signify a clear "meaning" and is, in fact, a form of "bad math" (20). Instead, she urges that audience members should "tell [playwrights] what you think and have an exchange of ideas" (20). Yet this assertion contradicts what Parks has established at the very beginning of her essay, when she maintains that theatre shouldn't provoke. But more importantly, Parks reveals that her identity as a theorist is always in flux, subject to its own form of repetition and revision. Addressing "the NEA hoopla," which is the only topical moment in the essay, Parks encourages her readers to avoid pinning the blame for the controversy on "overweight southern senators" (20).

Rather than externalizing the threat of censorship, Parks implores her audience to turn inward, confronting "our own petty evils" (20). Anger must be channeled into a lens that redirects focus on what is going on within the theatre community.

Parks' theoretical work creates its own drama of accumulation, with the final nine glossary terms emphasizing her core preoccupations with questions of embodiment. Of particular note is her use of "dance," "humor," "action in the line," "sex," "a (rest)," "a spell," and "foreign words and phrases," which function as a kind of revised rising action, their accumulating weight revealing a new layer of embodiment (21–22). "Dancing around as you write" allows you to get "to the deep shit" (21). Laughter is a more pleasurable version of throwing up, action melts into dialogue, and Parks' work is shaped by the erotics of "The Great Hole of History" (21).

Beyond "Rep and Rev," the most significant elements of Parks' dramaturgy are the "rest" and the "spell" (21). A rest is a "pause," and a spell is an elongated, heightened pause. On the page, both are typified by what Parks refers to as an "architectural look," in which the names of the characters engaged in the pause are vertically stacked upon each other (21). Through this architecture, Parks is creating a world beyond text, a world of sheer embodiment.

Suzan-Lori Parks

"From Elements of Style" (1994)

I'm writing this essay for 2 reasons. First: to talk about my work—to give those readers, scholars, directors and performers of my plays a way in—so that instead of calling me up they can, with this "guide," dive into an examination with great confidence. Secondly, I want to examine what seems to me a real crisis in American dramatic literature. I'm hoping to form a sort of bulwark against an insidious, tame-looking, schmaltz-laden mode of expression that threatens to cover us all, like Vesuvius, in our sleep.

As a writer my job is to write good plays; it's also to defend dramatic literature against becoming "Theatre of Schmaltz." For while there are several playwrights whose work I love love love, it also seems that in no other form of writing these days is the writing so awful—so intended to produce some reaction of sorts, to discuss some issue: the play-as-wrapping-paper-version-of-hot-newspaper-headline, trying so hard to be so hip; so uninterested in the craft of writing: the simple work of putting one word next to another; so uninterested in the marvel of live bodies on stage. Theatre seems mired in the interest of stating some point, or tugging some heartstring, or landing a laugh, or making a splash, or wagging a finger. In no other artform are the intentions so slim! As a playwright I try to do many things: explore the form, ask questions, make a good show, tell a good story, ask more questions, take nothing for granted.

This essay is intended primarily for the new generation of theatre makers. For those of us who haven't yet reached the point where we can say we've spent ½ our lives in theatre. I've been writing plays for 11 years now; all along I've felt that the survival of this splendid artform — an art that is not "poor film" or "cheap TV" but an art so specific and strange in its examination of the human condition—depends not only on the older guard but also on those of us who are relative newcomers.

There are many ways to challenge ourselves as theatre artists. Here are some ideas, feelings, thoughts, takes on the world, riffs, ways of approaching the word, the page, the event, the subject, the stage, that keep me *awake.*

theatre

Jesus. Right from the jump, ask yourself: "*Why* does this thing I'm writing *have* to be a *play?*" The words "why," "have" and "play" are key. If you don't have an answer then get out of town. No joke. The last thing American theatre needs is another lame play.

form and content

> *Form is never more than an extension of content.*
> — *Robert Creeley to Charles Olson*

A playwright, as any other artist, should accept the bald fact that content determines form and form determines content; that form and content are interdependent. Form should not be looked at askance and held suspect—form is not something that "gets in the way of the story" but is an integral part of the story. This understanding is important to me and my writing. This is to say that as I write along the container dictates what sort of substance will fill it and, at the same time, the substance is dictating the size and shape of the container. Also, "form" is not a strictly "outside" thing while "content" stays "inside." It's like this: I am an African-American woman —this is the form I take, my content predicates this form, and this form is inseparable from my content. No way could I be me otherwise.

as Louis MacNeice sez: "the shape is ½ the meaning."

Playwrights are often encouraged to write 2-act plays with traditional linear narratives. Those sorts of plays are fine, but we should understand that the form is not merely a docile passive vessel, but an active participant in the sort of play which ultimately inhabits it. Why linear narrative at all? Why choose that shape? If a playwright chooses to tell a dramatic story, and realizes that there are essential elements of that story which lead the writing outside the realm of "linear narrative," then the play naturally assumes a new shape. I'm saying that the inhabitants of Mars do not look like us. Nor should they. I'm also saying that Mars is with us —right on our doorstep and should be explored. Most playwrights who consider themselves avant-garde spend a lot of time badmouthing the more traditional forms. The naturalism of, say, Lorraine Hansberry is beautiful and should not be dismissed simply because it's naturalism. We should understand that realism, like other movements in other artforms, is a specific response to a certain historical climate. I don't explode the form because I find traditional plays "boring" —I don't really. It's just that those structures never could accommodate the figures which take up residence inside me.

repetition and revision

"Repetition and Revision" is a concept integral to the Jazz esthetic in which the composer or performer will write or play a musical phrase once and again and again; etc.—with each revisit the phrase is slightly revised. "Rep & Rev" as I call it is a central element in my work; through its use I'm working to create a dramatic text that departs from the traditional linear narrative style to look and sound more like a musical score. In my first play, *The Sinners Place* (1983), history simply repeated itself. With *Imperceptible Mutabilities* (1986) and the others I got a little more adventurous. With each play I'm finding the only way that that particular dramatic story can be told. I'm also asking how the structure of Rep & Rev and the stories inherent in it—a structure which creates a drama of accumulation—can be accommodated under the rubric of Dramatic Literature where, traditionally, all elements lead the audience toward some single explosive moment.

in X-vids the cum-shot is the money shot. Yeah but it's not a question of the way girls cum vs. the way boys cum. I'm not looking at a single sexual encounter but something larger, say, in this context, the history of all sexual encounters all over the globe, all animals included from the big word "GO!" until Now and through the Great Beyond. Rep & Rev are key in examining something larger than one moment. Rep & Rev create space for metaphor &c.

Repetition: we accept it in poetry and call it "incremental refrain." For the most part, incremental refrain creates a weight and a rhythm. In dramatic writing it does the same—yes; but again, what about all those words over and over? We all want to get to the CLIMAX. Where does repetition fit? First, it's not just repetition but repetition with *revision*. And in drama change, revision, is the thing. Characters refigure their words and through a refiguring of language show us that they are experiencing their situation anew. Secondly, a text based on the concept of repetition and revision is one which breaks from the text which we are told to write—the text which cleanly ARCS. Thirdly, Rep & Rev texts create a real challenge for the actor and director as they create a physical life appropriate to that text. In such plays we are not moving from A → B but rather, for example, from A → A → A → B → A. Through such movement we refigure A. And if we continue to call this movement FORWARD PROGRESSION, which I think it is, then we refigure the idea of forward progression. And if we insist on calling writings structured with this in mind PLAYS, which I think they are, then we've got a different kind of dramatic literature.

What does it mean for characters to say the same thing twice? 3 times? Over and over and over and oh-vah. Yes. How does that effect their physical life? Is this natural? Non-natural? Real? In *Betting on the Dust Commander* (1987), the "climax" could be the accumulated weight of the repetition—a residue that, like city dust, stays with us. After years of listening to Jazz, and classical music too, I'm realizing that my writing is very influenced by music; how much I employ its methods. Through reading lots I've realized how much the idea of Repetition and Revision is an integral part of the African and African-American literary and oral traditions.

I am most interested in words and how they impact on actors and directors and how those folks physicalize those verbal aberrations. How does this Rep & Rev—a literal incorporation of the past—impact on the creation of a theatrical experience?

time

I walk around with my head full of lay-person ideas about the universe. Here's one of them: "Time has a circular shape." Could Time be tricky like the world once was — looking flat from our

"yesterday today next summer tomorrow just uh moment uhgoh in 1317 dieded thuh last black man in thuh whole entire world."

place on it—and through looking at things beyond the world we found it round? Somehow I think Time could be like this too. Not that I'm planning to write a science book—the goofy idea just helps me NOT to take established shapes for granted. Keeps me awing it. Attaches the idea of Rep & Rev to a larger shape.

Also: lookie here!:

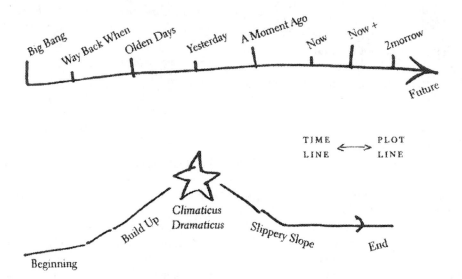

Standard Time Line and Standard Plot Line are in cahoots!

etymology

I spend a lot of time reading the dictionary. The word "grammar" is etymologically related to the word "charm." Most words have fabulous etymologies. Thrilling histories. Words are very old things. Because words are so old they hold; they have a big connection with the what was. Words are spells in our mouths. My interest in the history of words—where they came from, where they're going—has a direct impact on my playwrighting because, for me, Language is a physical act. It's something which involves your entire body—not just your head. Words are spells which an actor consumes and digests—and through digesting creates a performance on stage. Each word is configured to give the actor a clue to their physical life. Look at the difference between "the" and "thuh." The "uh" requires the actor to employ a different physical, emotional, vocal attack.

> *Shrink: Do you hear voices?*
> *Playwright: Isnt that my job?*

ghost

(time)
love
distance
(history)

A person from, say, time immemorial, from, say, PastLand, from somewhere back there, say, walks into my house. She or he is always alone and will almost always take up residence in a corner. Why they're alone I don't know. Perhaps they're coming missionary style—there are always more to follow. Why they choose a corner to stand in I don't know either—maybe because it's the intersection of 2 directions —maybe because it's safe.

They are not *characters*. To call them so could be an injustice. They are *figures, figments, ghosts, roles, lovers* maybe, *speakers* maybe, *shadows, slips, players* maybe, maybe *someone else's pulse.*

math

The equations of some plays:

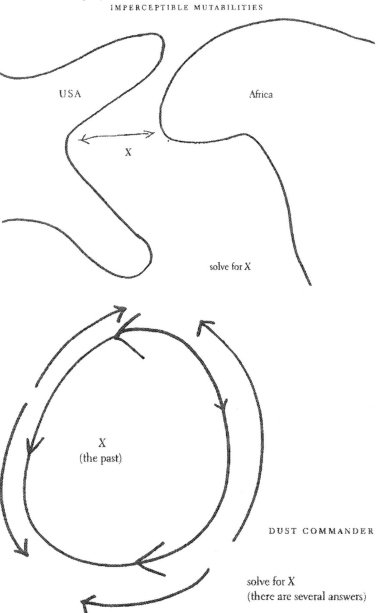

IMPERCEPTIBLE MUTABILITIES

USA

Africa

X

solve for X

X
(the past)

DUST COMMANDER

solve for X
(there are several answers)

PICKLING

The play iz trying to find an equation for time saved/saving time but theatre/experience/ performing/ being/ living etc. is all about *spending* time. No equation or.......?

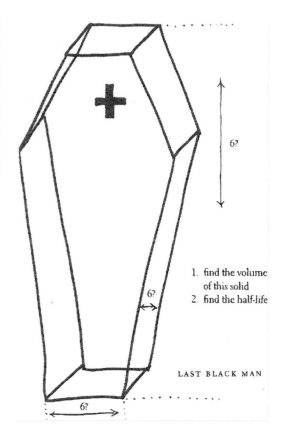

6?

1. find the volume
   of this solid
2. find the half-life

6?

LAST BLACK MAN

6?

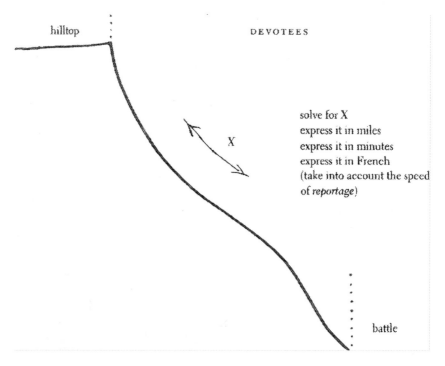

hilltop

DEVOTEES

solve for X
express it in miles
express it in minutes
express it in French
(take into account the speed
of *reportage*)

X

battle

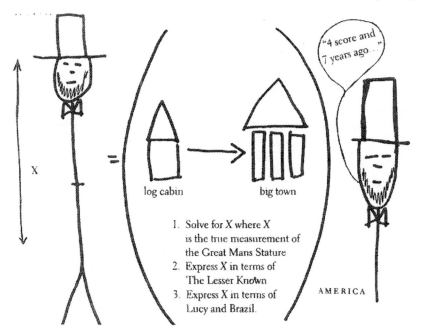

log cabin   big town

1. Solve for X where X
   is the true measurement of
   the Great Mans Stature
2. Express X in terms of
   The Lesser Known
3. Express X in terms of
   Lucy and Brazil.

AMERICA

"4 score and 7 years ago..."

X

bad math

x + y = meaning. The ability to make simple substitutions is equated with *clarity*. We are taught that plays are merely staged essays and we begin to believe that characters in plays are symbols for some obscured "meaning" rather than simply the thing itself. As Beckett sez: "No symbols where none intended." Don't ask playwrights what their plays mean; rather, tell them what you think and have an exchange of ideas.

the NEA hoopla

Overweight southern senators are easy targets. They too easily become focal points of all evil, allowing the arts community to WILLFULLY IGNORE our own bigotry, our own petty evils, our own intolerance which—evil senators or no—will be the death of the arts.

history

History is time that won't quit.

dance

If you're one who writes sitting down, once before you die try dancing around as you write. It's the old world way of getting to the deep shit.

humor

A playwright should pack all five, all six—all 7 senses. The 6th helps you feel another's pulse at great distances; the 7th sense is the sense of humor. Playwrights can come from the most difficult circumstances, but having a sense of humor is what happens when you "get out of the way." It's sorta Zen. Laughter is very powerful —it's not a way of escaping anything but a way of arriving on the scene. Think about laughter and what happens to your body—it's almost the same thing that happens to you when you throw up.

action in the line

The action goes in the line of dialogue instead of always in a pissy set of parentheses. *How* the line should be delivered is contained in the line itself. Stage directions disappear. Dialogue becomes rich and strange. It's an old idea. The Greeks did it and Shakespeare too, all over the place. Something to try at least once before you die.

sex

People have asked me why I don't put any sex in my plays. "The Great Hole of History" —like, duh.

a (rest)

Take a little time, a pause, a breather; make a transition.

a spell

An elongated and heightened (rest). Denoted by repetition of figures' names with no dialogue. Has sort of an architectural look.

LUCY		LINCOLN
BRAZIL		BOOTH
THE FOUNDLING FATHER	*and*	LINCOLN
LUCY		BOOTH
BRAZIL		LINCOLN
THE FOUNDLING FATHER		BOOTH

And

THE FOUNDLING FATHER
THE FOUNDLING FATHER
THE FOUNDLING FATHER

This is a place where the figures experience their pure true simple state. While no "action" or "stage business" is necessary, directors should fill this moment as they best see fit.

The feeling: look at a daguerreotype; or: the planets are aligning and as they move we hear the music of their spheres. A spell is a place of great (unspoken) emotion. It's also a place for an emotional transition.

foreign words & phrases
iduhnt /íd-ənt /, a variant of *is not* or *isn't*. "We arent from these parts. ... Daddy iduhnt either" (*America*).
heud /hé-əd/, a variant of *he would* or *he'd*. "Ssonly natural that heud come out here tuh dig" (*America*).
do in diddly dip didded thuh drop /dó-in-díd-ly-díp-díd-díd-thə-dráhp/, meaning unclear. Perhaps an elaborated confirmation, a fancy "yes!" Although it could also be used as a question such as "Yeah?" (*Last Black Man*).

ssnuch /ssnəch!/ (Air intake sound not through mouth or throat but in through the nose.) A fast reverse snort, a big sniff (usually accompanies crying or sneezing). "Snnnnuch. Blowings hard. For me." (*Dust Commander*)

thup /thəp!/, (Air intake with sound placed in mouth; liberal use of tongue.) Slurping. (*Imperceptible Mutabilities*)

uh! or *uuh!* /əh!/ (Air intake.) Deep quick breath. Usually dénotes drowning or breathlessness. "Years uhgoh from uh boat I had been—UUH! Jettisoned" (*Imperceptible Mutabilities*); ". . . in 1317 dieded thuh last black man in the whole entire world. Uh!" (*Last Black Man*),

thuh /thəh/, variant of *the*. "Thuh ultimate battle of love requires uh good go between" (*Devotees in the Garden of Love*).

chuh /chə/ The polite form of the expletive "Shit!" (*Dust Commander*)

k /kay/, variant of *okay*. (*America*)

gaw (This is a glottal stop. No forward tongue or lip action here. The root of the tongue snaps or clicks in the back of the throat.) Possible performance variations: a click-clock sound where the tongue tip clicks in the front of the mouth; or a strangulated articulation of the word *Gaw*! "gaw gaw gaw eeeee-uh" (*Imperceptible Mutabilities*).

language is a physical act

Language is a physical act—something that
involves yr whole bod.
Write with yr whole bod.
Read with yr whole bod.
Wake up.

opening night

Don't be shy about looking gorgeous.
I suggest black.

Please see the Works Cited for further information on the sources used in this essay.

Note

1 The tradition derived from the forcible dispersal of millions of Africans from Africa during the Transatlantic Slave Trades from the 1500s to the 1800s.

Suggestions for Further Reading

Geis, Deborah R. *Suzan-Lori Parks*. Ann Arbor: University of Michigan Press, 2008.

Larson, Jennifer. *Understanding Suzan-Lori Parks*. Columbia, SC: The University of South Carolina Press, 2012.

Parks, Suzan-Lori. *Suzan-Lori Parks in Person: Interviews and Commentaries*. Eds. Philip C. Kolin and Harvey Young. New York: Routledge, 2014.

Parks, Suzan-Lori., et al. *The HistoryMakers Video Oral History with Suzan-Lori Parks*. The HistoryMakers, 2016.

Wetmore, Kevin J., and Alycia Smith Howard, eds. *Suzan-Lori Parks: a Casebook*. New York: Routledge, 2007.

65 KATE BORNSTEIN (b.1948)

Kara Raphaeli

Introduction

Time magazine's May 2014 cover story on actress Laverne Cox[1] declared the arrival of "The Transgender Tipping Point," tying increased trans representation in media to a greater awareness and even social acceptance of trans people in everyday life (Steinmetz). Certainly, celebrities such as Cox, Janet Mock, and Chaz Bono have become household names in recent years, creating the illusion that trans people are a new phenomenon. However, trans performers have always existed,[2] and the call for their greater cinematic and theatrical representation began a quarter century before *Time* noticed. Kate Bornstein (b.1948) has been utilizing performance to tell trans stories for over thirty years.

Bornstein is a trans performer, author, scholar, and activist. They[3] began writing their own plays and performance pieces in the late 1980s, shortly after transitioning. At the time, the few trans people who were in the public eye described their experience as a linear journey from one binary gender to the other. The concept of being "born in the wrong body" and rectifying it through medical intervention explained trans identity in a way that was approachable for cis people.[4] The wrong-body narrative positioned gender confirmation surgery as the pinnacle of medical transition and the end goal that would cement the individual's gender identity. Kate Bornstein was among the first to defy this narrative. Along with Leslie Feinberg (whose novel *Stone Butch Blues* was published in 1993), Bornstein promoted a conception of gender that transcended the binary, describing themself as neither man nor woman. In her memoirs, *Gender Outlaw* (1994) and *A Queer and Pleasant Danger* (2014), Bornstein details her attempts to follow the established trans narrative, only to find the category of "woman" limiting, leading her to conceive of herself as belonging to a fluid third gender.

"Transsexual Lesbian Playwright Tells All" originated as a talk for the *Out/Wright* LGBTQ conference, which took place in San Francisco in 1990. It was then published in *High Risk: An Anthology of Forbidden Writings* in 1991 and reprinted in Bornstein's groundbreaking first book, *Gender Outlaw: On Men, Women, and the Rest of Us*, in 1994. In the essay, Bornstein critiques the lack of well-written trans characters in theatre, but rather than calling on cis authors to address the problem, she concludes that she must write plays for herself; after all, she argues, her gender experience is much more complex and multifaceted than anything a cis playwright could authentically portray. With their signature playful yet deadpan tone, Bornstein links their own work to prehistoric shamanic rituals, creating a lineage of trans performance that draws on knowledge outside of hegemonic Western society and its rigid gender binary.

DOI: 10.4324/9781003006923-66

The play Bornstein discusses in this text is *Hidden: A Gender,* which was commissioned and produced by Theatre Rhinoceros, the oldest continuously running queer theatre in existence, premiering there in November of 1989. It is a non-linear experimental play that explores gender non-conformity through both poignant historical truth and campy metatheatrical comedy. In the original production, Bornstein played the narrator, Doc Grinder, a mix of carnival barker, snake oil salesman, 1980s talk show host, and modern ad exec. Doc Grinder ends the play by selling the audience pills called Gender Defense—prophylactically reinforcing their binary identities and preventing them from becoming "gender outlaws," "freaks" like the characters in the play.

The second of Bornstein's writings re-published here is "Theatre, and the Future of the Body," which was written in 2005 and featured in the journal *Women and Performance.* Nestled among the meditative reflections, interviews, manifestos and poetry of this twentieth anniversary issue of the journal, Bornstein's essay functions as an ad for trans performers. Unlike most writing about the lack of responsible media representation of trans people or opportunities for trans actors, Bornstein turns theatre's exclusion of trans people on its head, presenting the trans body as the ideal theatrical tool. Rather than demanding roles be found for trans actors, she channels the salesmanship of Doc Grinder, enlightening cis playwrights and casting directors to the potential trans actors have to reshape theatre. They end with the ad exec's enticement: "What kind of theater might you build with bodies that walk beyond the boundaries of what's allowed by the proprietors of popular culture?"

In the late 1980s and the 1990s, as Bornstein was emerging as a theatre artist, queer activism was largely framed by the AIDS epidemic; organizations such as ACT UP and Queer Nation expressed open outrage through direct action. Trans activists followed with their own militant organizations, Transgender Nation and The Transexual Menace. Bornstein, on the other hand, has been saying for over thirty years that she prefers to approach gender as a playground rather than a battlefield, encouraging their audiences to explore gender with curiosity and lightheartedness. This approach places her in the tradition of queer performers who harness the subversive capacity of humor. They have cited seeing Charles Ludlam's *The Mystery of Irma Vep* in 1985 as an early influence. Like Ludlam, Bornstein's gender transformations reveal both the multiplicity of possible gender and sexual identities, as well as the value of remaining flexible in the face of cisheteronormative pressures. Kate Bornstein is a gender outlaw. Indeed, their inclusion in this collection of women's contributions to dramatic criticism further deconstructs the typical gendered assumptions of the theatre world.

Kate Bornstein

"Transsexual Lesbian Playwright Tells All!" (1990)[5]

My ancestors were performers. In life. The earliest shamanic rituals involved women and men exchanging genders. Old, old rituals. Top-notch performances. Life and death stuff. We're talking cross-cultural here. We're talking rising way way way above being a man or a woman. That's how my ancestors would fly. That's how my ancestors would talk with the goddesses and the gods. Old rituals.

I'd been a performer of one sort or another for over twenty-five years, and now I'm writing plays as well as performing in them. See, I had never seen my story on stage and I was looking. I used to go up to writers I knew. I used to wish they'd write my story. And I'm only just now realizing that they couldn't possibly. I write from the point of view of an *S/M* transsexual lesbian, ex-cult member, femme top and sometimes bottom shaman. And I wondered why no one was writing my story? I'm writing from the point of view of used-to-be-a-man, three husbands, father, first mate on an ocean-going yacht, minister, high-powered IBM sales type, Pierre Cardin three-piece suitor, bar-mitz-vah'd, circumcised yuppie from the East Coast. Not too many women write from that point of view. I write from the point of view of a used-to-be politically correct, wanna-be butch, dyke phone sex host-ess, smooth talking, telemarketing, love slave, art slut, pagan Tarot reader, maybe soon a grandmother, crystal palming, incense burning, not-man, not always a woman, fast becoming a Marxist. And not too many men write from that point of view.

My ancestors didn't write much. I guess they didn't need to.

Y'know, people try to write about transsexuals and it's amusing it's infuriating it's patronizing and it's why *I'm* writing about transsexuals now. I wrote one play in college twenty-one years ago. And one play last year. Both of them I pulled from my chest until they pulsed bleeding on the stage. Saint Kate of the bleeding heart. The first play was young love gone bad. Spun out my soul as just so much cotton candy romanticism. God it felt great. The second play was a harder birth. *Hidden: A Gender* is my transsexual voice—the voice I speak with, cry with, roar with, moan with and laugh with, don't forget laugh with. I always hid that voice away. I always used your voice, spoke your words, sang your hit parade. Until I heard them whisper, my ances-tors. And I whispered and you heard me and I said hey you weren't meant to hear that and you said tell us more. And that was the second play, the harder birth. The one I had to write.

I write when nothing else will bring me peace, when I burn, when I find myself asking and answering the same questions over and over. I write when I've begun to lose my sense of humor and it becomes a matter of my life and my death to get that sense of humor back and watch you laugh. I write in bottom space. I open up to you, I cut myself, I show you my fantasies, I get a kick out of that—oh, yeah. I perform in top space. I cover myself with my character and take you where you never dreamed you could go. Yes. My ancestors did this. My instrument is not my pen or my typewriter, not my lover's Macintosh, not my cast of characters, not my body on stage. No, my instrument is my audience and oh how I love to play you.

And to what end? I've come to see gender as a divisive social construct, and the gendered body as a somewhat dubious accomplishment. I write about this because I am a gender outlaw and my issues are gender issues. The way I see it now, the lesbian and gay community is as much oppressed for gender transgressions as for sexual distinction. We have more in common, you and I, than most people are willing to admit. See, I'm told I must be a man or a woman. One or the other. Oh, it's OK to be a transsexual say some—just don't talk about it. Don't question your gender any more, just be a woman now—you went to so much trouble—just be satisfied. I am so, not satisfied. My ancestors were not satisfied.

I write from the point of view of a gender outlaw because I don't want to hear: We don't want you in our club / We don't want you on our land / We don't want you in our march. And I say I don't know why the separatists won't let me in—I'm *probably* the only lesbian to have successfully castrated a man and gone on to laugh about it on stage, in print, and on national television.

Hello, Geraldo, are you reading this?

My ancestors were not shunned. They were celebrated. Look, I know you try to fill in the blanks in my life. I write to let you know who I am so that you *can* fill in the blanks.

Hello, Mom, are you reading this?

Anyway, I work in theater because I really enjoy working *with* people, and theater is not an alone art. And current theatrical forms reflect a rigidly bi-polar gender system. They aren't fluid enough for what I want to say, and I feel that form and content in theater as in life should be complementary, not adversarial, so I work on my own gender fluidity and sometimes it works and sometimes it doesn't. And I work on the fluidity of my theatrical style—and sometimes it works and sometimes it doesn't. My life and my theater—my form and my content—sort of do as I say and do as I do. Like my ancestors.

"Theater, and the Future of the Body" (2005)

Assuming that the actor's body is a primary tool of theater, then what does it say about the future of the theater if actors' bodies are changing? Whether as a theater artist, you're fond of holding Aristotle's mirror up to the culture; or whether you want to wield Brecht's hammer to shape society, there is a new aspect of the culture to take into account when doing theater these days: transgender.

I'm transsexual; my body is transgendered. I was born male, went through surgical and hormonal body modifications, and came out the other side as female; that made me transsexual. I've since left off being female and decided to subscribe to neither male nor female as a gender; that makes me transgendered.

> *Is my gender-flexible body a freak of Nature? Or do I have the body of the future?*

I write plays and performance art pieces. I've acted on stage and in film for over thirty years, performing boys, men, girls, women, drag queens, drag kings, hermaphrodites, and transsexuals travelling in both directions. I've played a non-gendered goddess-in-training, and a fluidly-gendered wise old crow.

I've played lesbian women, gay men, heterosexual men *and* women, bisexual roles, and celibate roles. I've played leather daddy tops, and I've played babydyke submissives.

My body *knows* how to play each of these gender/sex roles, because I've got the advantage of having lived through each and every one of them; and I know how to use my body to get those identities across.

> *Is my body the body of the future? Or am I simply doing gender the way I surf my way through 80 channels of bad cable TV?*

However I'm surfing gender, I seem to have been able to maintain my acting ability. Some tough theater critics have given me great reviews; and despite my breadth of experience with all these facets of human sexual identity, I rarely get cast in anything I haven't myself written.

I am writing myself into the culture as a new identity. Does that mean I have a newly-defined body?

> *If it's true that today's monsters are tomorrow's angels, then...*
> *...is my body the future of theater?*

I don't think so. It's more like I'm finding new things to *do* with a body I've set free from what I've found to be the repressive limits of an increasingly Disney-defined culture. I don't have the kind of life—or body—that Disney would ever make a movie about. I do have a body that can ably travel through genders. Me, and people with bodies like mine...we're the shape-shifters of the Nineties.

> *Will the body of the future remain static?*
> *Or might it become flexible, fluid even?*

Unfortunately, shape-shifters tend to scare audiences; we're the villains on popular TV shows like *The X-Files, Star Trek Deep Space Nine*; we've made it to Broadway, but we're the villain/hero of the musical, *Jekyll and Hyde*. People of the Disney American culture tend to villainize shape-shifters, because when they see Mickey Mouse, they know they're safe. They don't want to see Mickey transform himself into Pinky or The Brain and try to take over the world. The shape-shifters have replaced Frankenstein and Dracula as the truly fearsome monsters of today's performed arts. Why? Audiences can't pin us down... they never know what we are *really*. But isn't shape-shifting essential to the art of acting? I'd always thought so. Isn't that why an actor's moral character is almost always universally questioned: because you never can tell when a good actor isn't acting!

A number of social changes over the last few decades have resulted in the rise of cross-gendered casting; I think that's a good start, but cross-gendered casting merely scratches the surface of what we could *really* be doing theatrically with gender. There's so much more to playing with gender than simply going from man to woman or from woman to man. If theater artists really want to grab hold of the future of the body, then it's time those artists understand that there are some new tools available: me and my people. What kind of theater might *you* build with bodies that walk beyond the boundaries of what's allowed by the proprietors of the popular culture?

Please see the Works Cited for further information on the sources used in this essay.

Notes

1 Laverne Cox (b.1972), actor and producer, is the first openly transgender person to be nominated for a Primetime Emmy Award, for *Orange is the New Black* in 2014, and the first transgender person to win a Daytime Emmy as a producer (2015).
2 The term "trans" is used as an umbrella term encompassing all people who do not identify with the gender they were assigned at birth, regardless of medical intervention.
3 Bornstein uses both they/them and she/her pronouns; therefore, I will be using both they/them and she/her pronouns interchangeably.
4 The terms "cis" or "cisgender" describe a person whose gender identity and sex assigned at birth are the same.
5 Written as a talk for the Out/Write '90 conference of lesbian and gay writers in San Francisco and adapted for inclusion in the anthology *High Risk*.

Suggestions for Further Reading

Bornstein, Kate and Bergman, S. Bear. *Gender Outlaws: The Next Generation.* New York, NY: Seal Press, 2010.

Feinberg, Leslie. *Transgender Warriors: Making History from Joan of Arc to Dennis Rodman.* Boston, MA: Beacon Press, 2005.

Stryker, Susan. *Transgender History: The Roots of Today's Revolution.* Second ed. New York, NY: Seal Press, 2017.

66 ELIN DIAMOND (b. 1948)

Jen-Scott Mobley

Introduction

In the wake of second-wave feminism in the 1960s, a body of writing emerged in which feminist historians, theorists, and artists interrogated the impact of gender, race, and class on women's lives and contributions. Much of this theory initially focused on broader feminist materialist perspectives applicable to a range of social structures and cultural production, while fewer, such as Laura Mulvey's seminal essay in film studies, "Visual Pleasure and Narrative Cinema" (1975), began to theorize ways of seeing women in representation. Through the 1980s and 1990s, performing artists such as Carolee Schneemann, Holly Hughes, Robbie McCauley, and Karen Finley, among others, created explicitly feminist performances that experimented in subject and form and resisted patriarchal dramaturgies. Meanwhile, a cadre of scholars pioneered a feminist theoretical framework through which to critique traditional dramaturgies and establish a feminist praxis for making theatre. Sue-Ellen Case, Jill Dolan, Kate Davy, Lynda Hart, Vivian Patraka, and Peggy Phelan[1] are among the luminaries who contributed to this wave of scholarship that constitutes the very foundation of feminist theatrical theory. Among those who poured the metaphorical concrete is Elin Diamond (b.1948).

Diamond's scholarship of this era critically engaged the masculine hegemonic Western European theoretical and critical canon, from Plato and Aristotle to Walter Benjamin and Bertolt Brecht, and exploded it in order to "unmake mimesis." In her seminal monograph, *Unmaking Mimesis: Essays on Feminism and Theatre* (1997), excerpted here, Diamond synthesized and expanded her scholarship of the previous decade by adapting her essays, now "canonical" in their own right, including: "Realism and Hysteria: Toward a Feminist Mimesis," "Brechtian Theory/Feminist Theory: Toward a Gestic, Feminist Criticism," and "Mimesis, Mimicry, and the 'True-Real'." In so doing, she created one of the most significant and comprehensive documents of feminist theatre theory of the twentieth century. In her introduction to *Unmaking Mimesis*, she defines the word "unmaking" itself: "(1) to deprive of position, rank or authority; (2) to ruin, destroy; (3) to alter the characteristics of" (xiii). Diamond's book accomplishes all three.

Engaging a range of western mimetic, psychoanalytic, and historical materialist theory, Diamond offers new readings of mimesis and ways in which to integrate representational and experiential feminisms, proposing a new critical framework with which to read hegemonic canonical texts, as well as offering practitioners a feminist approach to patriarchal realism and realistic acting methodologies that

DOI: 10.4324/9781003006923-67

dominated twentieth-century stages. *Unmaking Mimesis* offers the possibility of a feminist mimesis by exploring two historically situated readings of the term: first as representation rooted in identity and subjectivity, as explored by Jacques Derrida's and Luce Irigaray's[2] interpretation of Plato and Aristotle, and second, by using the historical materialist lenses of Bertolt Brecht and Walter Benjamin,[3] in which mimesis functions "as a mode of reading [that] changes an object into a *gestus* or dialectical image" (ii).

Reading Brechtian theory intertextually with feminist theories of gender critique and sexual difference, Diamond establishes a "gestic feminist criticism" when she asserts that "[...] Brechtian theory [...] is not literary criticism, but rather a theorizing of the workings of an apparatus of representation with enormous formal and political Resonance." She also leverages Brecht's "alienation-effect" (*Verfremdungseffekt*)[4] for feminist practice (45). Through alienating or foregrounding gender iconicity in performance, Diamond notes that the ideology of gender is highlighted for the spectator:

> The appearance, words, gestures, ideas, attitudes that constitute [a gendered?] gender lexicon become illusionistic practices that are nevertheless inseparable from, embedded in, the body's habitus. Understanding gender as an ideology— as a system of beliefs and behaviors mapped across the bodies of women and men which reinforces a social status quo—is to appreciate the continued timeliness of *Verfremdungseffekt*, the purpose of which is to denaturalize and defamiliarize what ideology—and performativity—makes seem normal, acceptable, inescapable. (47)

Diamond therefore offers a reading of Brecht that has practical applications for feminism ("Brechtian Theory" 83).

Further, Diamond offers a reading of Brecht's concept of historicization, which productively integrates feminist theory concerned with women's material conditions of class, race, and gender. She suggests:

> There is a powerful dialectical movement in Brechtian historicization of preserving 'distinguishing marks' of the past and acknowledging, even foregrounding, the audience's present perspective. That is, when Brecht says spectators should become historians, he refers both to the spectator's detachment, her 'critical' position, *and* to the fact that she is writing her own history even as she absorbs messages from the stage. (*Unmaking Mimesis* 49)

Thus, the Brechtian concept of historicization is a *way of seeing* that resists appropriation and colonization and which encourages spectators to view the female body not as a fixed essence but as a site of struggle. Historicization enables the female performer's body to be separate from character and step out of the gendered system of onstage signifiers.

Diamond goes on to reveal the fruitfulness of the Brechtian *gestus* not only as an approach to performing the text but also as a way to position female spectators because it resists fetishization by insisting that both performers and spectators consider the author's inscription of the character, as well as the historical and sexual specificity. In Diamond's equation, the female performer resists fetishization and cultivates a "looking-at-being-looked-at-ness" in which "the Brechtian feminist body is paradoxically available for *both* analysis and identification, paradoxically within representation while refusing its fixity" (52). Moreover, Diamond synthesizes all of these concepts into what she calls a "gestic feminist criticism that would 'alienate' or foreground those moments in a playtext when social attitudes about gender and sexuality cancel or disrupt patriarchal ideology" (54).

The final section of Diamond's book takes up the third definition of "unmaking" by altering the characteristics of mimesis as she theorizes a "feminist postmodern." Examining the contemporary work of Adrienne Kennedy, Peggy Shaw, and Robbie McCauley, Diamond reveals how these performers' storytelling and historically constructed identifications not only reveal the destructed psychic effect of identification but also present gender and sexuality dialectically.

This essay regrettably focuses on only one key text in Diamond's prolific body of work. Yet, for the purposes of this volume, *Unmaking Mimesis* is inarguably one of *the* primary documents that established the field of feminist performance theory. Diamond's "unmaking" effectively remade mimesis and provided feminist practitioners with a praxis for a directing approach to hegemonic realism, offering the next generation of scholars a foundation upon which to build feminist theatrical theory. Yet, it is important to note that while the impact of *Unmaking Mimesis* as a productive and generative work of feminist theatrical theory cannot be overestimated, it represents only the first chapters of Diamond's contributions. Her ongoing work continues to explore intersections of performance, feminism, and critical theory and offers us new ways of seeing and constructing theatre and performance.

Elin Diamond

Excerpt from "Introduction" to Unmaking Mimesis *(1997)*

[...]

This book is an inquiry into the possibilities of a feminist mimesis. I explore the connections between theories of mimesis and feminist theories of sexuality and representation, and I do this through readings of a number of Western theater texts. In the most basic sense, I put into dialogue what I believe to be the most pressing questions in feminist theory with the oldest questions of theatrical representation: Who is speaking and who is listening? Whose body is in view and whose is not? What is being represented, how, and with what effects? Who or what is in control? In the last twenty-five years, feminism has struggled with psychoanalytic semiotic constructions of the female subject in sometimes explosive juxtaposition with empirical approaches to women's lives, histories and politics. One result of this agon has been a risky but exciting inclusiveness—the split and desiring female subject demands recognition of her gendered body, her race, her ethnicity, her nation. Yet these designations imply, problematically, the exclusivity of mimetic modeling. Similarly, in proposing universal frameworks of sexual, political, and economic liberation, white US feminists working with African American, Asian American, and Latina feminists must continue to ask, who is speaking? who is listening? who is in view, and who is not? When 'third world' and Western women convene in global conferences or across a lunch table, such questions are the implicit conditions of meaningful dialogue. [...]

[...] Historically women have been denied power in the theater apparatus yet signs of female sexuality have been crucial to that apparatus's functioning—a contradiction that can be read into the signifying processes of almost any play. Theater itself may be understood as the drama's unruly body, its material other, a site where the performer's and the spectator's desire may resignify elements of a constrictive social script. Theater may also be understood as a symptomatic cultural site that ruthlessly maps out normative spectatorial positions by occluding its own means of production. And yet—any set of seemingly rigid positions is available for revision. Conservative and patriarchal, the theater is also, in a complex sense, the place of play, and unlike other media, in the theater the same play can be played not only again, but differently.

But what of mimesis? Given its long association with neoclassical *imitatio* in both its didactic and idealist directions; given too, in our late twentieth-century view, its link with conservative tendencies in dramatic realism, why would a self-consciously evolving feminism concern itself with mimesis? Let's look at a recent damning definition: 'Mimesis...posits a truthful relation between world and word, model and copy, nature and image...referent and sign in which potential difference is subsumed by sameness.'[5] While A.O. Rorty situates Aristotelian mimesis between 'representation' and 'imitation' ('neither separately captures it'), most scholars want to shear off mimesis from the cruder connotations of imitation—fakeness, reproduction, resemblance.[6] Stephen Halliwell's new translation of the *Poetics* consistently prefers 'representation' over 'imitation.'[7] But suppose we follow a far longer tradition that interprets mimesis as not only the act of imitating but an imitation of. 'Imitation indicates a constant relation between something which is and something made like it...'[8] Tangled in iconicity, then, in the visual resemblance between an originary model and its representation, mimesis patterns difference into sameness.

From this notion, a feminist critique has followed. Same as what? For feminist historians, philosophers, and literary critics in the last three decades and, in fact, much earlier, truth and the sameness that supports it cannot be understood as a neutral, omnipotent, changeless essence, embedded in eternal Nature, revealed by mimesis. Rather Truth is inseparable from gender-based and biased epistemologies. The model of imitation may be the Platonic Ideal or Aristotle's universal type, Truth may be conceived as model-copy adequation, or, conversely, as an unveiling (that which shows itself or appears), but in all cases the epistemological, morphological, universal standard for determining the true is the masculine, a metaphoric stand-in for God the Father.[9] [...]

Whether a feminist views the problematic of the signifier and of representation through a postmodernist prism or a historical-materialist lens, the critique of patriarchy carries with it an ethical commitment to the value of one's own position, however complex and nuanced that position might be. As many have pointed out, feminism has gained much from postmodernism.[10] The decentered subject implies the dismantling of the self-reflecting cogito/self, whose inferior other has been traditionally gendered female. And yet feminists, in our different constituencies—we speak emphatically of 'feminisms' now—with our different objects of analysis, want to intervene in symbolic systems, linguistic, theatrical, political, psychological—and intervention requires assuming a subject position, however provisional, and making truth claims, however flexible, concerning one's own representations. Indeed feminism, like theater, finds it difficult to rid itself of the classical mimetic structure. Tragic drama was of course Aristotle's specific object for articulating the precepts of mimetic art. But there is a deeper connection. The discourse of theater, like the discourse of feminism, cannot rid itself of the temptation to refer, to emplot, to remember, to show. The actor's body cannot forget its gender (in the most exciting contemporary practice, performers remember with a vengeance), cannot shake off the referential frame imposed by text, mode of production, and spectators' narrativity— those trajectories of scopic desire and identification that performer and performance text can only partially control. For example, certain texts of early realism provoked excitement when middleclass women found, for the first time, mimetic models that sparked (and contained) their political desires. Of Elizabeth Robins's performance, as the first Hedda Gabler on the London stage (1891), an acquaintance commented: 'Hedda is all of us.'[11]

As we will see in Chapter 1, such intense identifications are solicited by realism. But stage realism is mimesis's positivist moment. If historicized, it can be codified and critiqued even as we acknowledge that its appeal is as strong in the 1990s as was in the 1890s. Mimesis, however, cannot so easily be seen, framed, gotten around, partially because it is continually embroiled in cultural desires and politics. Dryden may seem to echo Jonson and seems in turn to be echoed by Pope and Diderot in describing nature as the sign of order and perfection that the artist 'imitates.' But the mimesis of this 'nature,' in its production and reception, will be fully marked by the political, literary, and gender ideologies of the critic, the artist, the audience, and the social contexts that interconnect them. The Restoration dramatist's prologue is exemplary of such interconnections: the playwright's mouthpiece utters witty/serious praise of high poetic ideals whose imitation is sadly prevented by the lowbrow, loutish, wig-combing spectators before whom she or he stands. Because it produces a (fictively) true (therefore false) relation to the real, mimesis is as much a historical-ideological flashpoint as an aesthetic concept. When A.S. Schlegel sounds the romantic rejection of imitation by making the familiar Platonic move of reducing mimesis to trivial copying; when Karl Philip Moritz announces that 'the born artist is not content to observe nature…he has to …create as nature does,' both were announcing a change in more than aesthetic philosophy.[12] They were suggesting that assumptions about nature or universal order, the legitimacy of which neoclassical mimesis seemed to reproduce, were now in doubt. Romantics, they imply, will offer truer truths, although to use the soul rather than the landscape as model only shifts direction, produces yet another mimesis. In this sense mimesis leaps beyond aesthetic precincts, beyond parsing its energies between upholding a model (representation) or improvising a variation (representing). It has always made this leap. Since Plato sought to cleanse his Republic of histrionic display mimesis has been a political practice, inseparable from interpretation and contestation. [...]

It turns out that the participial 'unmaking' is not just an attribute of a deconstructive turn of thought—an unraveling from within. Rather 'unmaking' resides solidly in the *American Heritage Dictionary* with three, fortuitously relevant, meanings: (1) to deprive of position, rank, or authority; (2) to ruin, destroy; (3) to alter the characteristics of.

When I began *Unmaking Mimesis,* I had only the first in mind, because like many I viewed mimesis as a version of dramatic realism and linked them both to a rather simple referentiality—a view reductive to both realism and mimesis. In the ubiquitous feminist critiques of representation in the 1980s, it became clear to me that feminism was also a kind of realism, seduced by the desire to represent the truth about social reality, but was constantly in the process of questioning that position. I begin this book with a long section on realism, not merely to 'deprive' dramatic realism of its 'authority' (definition 1)—modernism has surely done that—but to explore realism's connection to feminist theory and practice. Attacks on dramatic realism are familiar: setting out to offer truthful versions of experience, realism universalizes but one point of view, ignoring the force-field of human-social contradiction. In the process of exploring social (especially gender) relations, realism ends by confirming their inevitability. But any critique of a representational practice needs to situate itself in the historical materials and desires of that practice. Part I of this book is organized as a discursive formation, bringing together the 'new' Ibsen and Ibsenite realism of the late nineteenth century and an equally powerful adjacent discourse, the 'new' science of psychoanalysis launched in Freud and Breuer's *Studies on Hysteria* (1895) and related texts. I argue that realism and early psychoanalysis are both theaters of knowledge—sites charged with the pleasure of positivist inquiry. Both share a similar object (the hysteric/fallen woman), a common claim to truth (the discovery of her secret), and a common genealogy (nineteenth-century melodramatic and clinical spectacles). I then suggest that in exploiting the signifiers and medical models of the hysteric, realism catches her disease, that is, produces the malady it is supposed to contain and cure. Reading Ibsen with a feminist contemporary, Elizabeth Robins, stretches the boundaries of our understanding of realism while, necessarily, depriving it of its prodigious authority. The section concludes by briefly suggesting what Robins's methods 'auger' for twentieth-century theater, namely body-centered performance, feminist 'semiotic' realism, and Brecht.

Part II, 'Gestic feminist criticism,' moves from a discussion of a powerful form of theater representation (realism) to consider the agents and apparatuses of representation. Each of Chapters 2, 3 and 4 rethinks the feminist controversy over the body or body-as-text by introducing historical density into the acts of reading and seeing. Here I propose a materialist approach, 'gestic criticism' which derives from Bertolt Brecht's theory of the gestus, the moment in performance when a play's implied social attitudes become visible to the spectator. To read a gesture, a line of dialogue, or a tableau gestically is to draw into analysis the author's history, the play's production conditions, and the historical gender and class contradictions through which stage action might be read. Brecht's gestus is not a reading of classical mimesis, however. Brecht intended to 'ruin' and 'destroy'(definition 2) conventional mimetic practice, understanding that that meant overhauling the apparatus of production and reception. [...]

Part III, 'Toward a feminist postmodern,' 'alters the characteristics of' mimesis (definition 3). The spatial investigations of the middle sections give way to the rich and varied temporal explorations in Adrienne Kennedy's plays and recent performance art by Peggy Shaw, Robbie McCauley, and Deb Margolin. In Chapter 5, 'Identification and mimesis: the theater of Adrienne Kennedy,' I read this playwright's oeuvre with Borch-Jacobsen's concept of mimetic identification and Paul Gilroy's historico-philosophical concept of the 'black Atlantic.' [...] Chapter 6, 'Performance and temporality: feminism, experience, and mimetic transformation,' takes up a recent trend in feminist performance art: the return to the auratic body and a kind of storytelling that emphasizes not only the contingency of the present but also historical figurations composed of lost or forgotten artifacts, the detritus of commodity culture. In these pieces, auratic bodies transform into 'dialectical images'—embodied montage-like constructions, not unlike Brecht's gestus—that bring conflicting temporalities into view and into (the concept of) experience. The performance art of McCauley, Shaw, and Margolin allows me to tease out a feminist mimesis based not on truth-models or psychic projections but on contiguities: subjects-in-relation, subjects-in-time. [...]

Because feminist performers voice such sentiments, we who write about them need to keep mimesis circulating. The connection of art (with its false simulacra, its irrationality) to life is precisely what Plato feared, and what Aristotle sought to regulate (while expunging the immoral dithyramb from poetic tradition, and women and slaves from 'life'). Still, for Halliwell, Aristotle's belief that art 'can nourish understanding and move the emotions with ethical force' means that 'mimesis makes art outward facing'[13]—an enticing formulation for feminism. The question, of course, is how. A feminist mimesis, if there is such a thing, would take the relation to the real as productive, not referential, geared to change, not to reproducing the same. It would explore the tendency to tyrannical modeling (subjective/ideological projections masquerading as universal truths), even in its own operations. Finally, it would clarify the humanist sedi-mentation in the concept as a means of releasing the historical particularity and transgressive corporeality of the mimos, who, in mimesis, is always more and different than she seems.

Please see the Works Cited for further information on the sources used in this essay.

Notes

1 See, also, entries on Case, Dolan, and Phelan in this volume.

2 Jacques Derrida (1930–2004) was an Algerian-born French philosopher noted for developing deconstruction, a semiotic and phenomenological form of analysis, which became one of the dominant theoretical methods applied to "close readings" of (literary) texts in the 1980s and 1990s. Luce Irigaray (b. 1930) is a Belgian-born French feminist, philosopher, linguist, psycholinguist, psychoanalyst, and cultural theorist who demonstrated some of the many ways in which language is (mis)used to perpetuate sexist culture.

3 German playwright and theatre theorist Bertolt Brecht's (1898–1956) concept of "epic theatre" espoused that plays can move audiences to political acts if the dramaturgy is constructed and presented not so much as a story for an audience to identify with but as ideas in action. Walter Benjamin (1892–1940), German social theorist, is best known for his essay "The Work of Art in the Age of Mechanical Reproduction" (1935).

4 Brecht's "alienation effect," also translated as "estrangement effect" aimed to keep his audiences at an emotional and psychological distance from narrative and character, so that they could retain a more objective perspective on theatrical works.

5 Diamond's definition in "Mimesis, Mimicry, and the "True-Real,'" *Modern Drama*, 32:1 (March 1989), p. 58. [Diamond]

6 A.O. Rorty, 'The Psychology of Aristotelian Tragedy,' in A.O. Rorty, ed., *Essays on Aristotle's 'Poetics'* (Princeton, NJ: Princeton University Press, 1992), p. 4. [Diamond]

7 'Representation' is closest to the 'meanings covered by the mimesis word group in Greek. Thus a picture can represent a subject, an actor represent a character, a play represent an action, event, or story' while '"imitate" has none of these sensibilities in modern English.' Stephen Halliwell. *The 'Poetics' of Aristotle* (Chapel Hill: University of North Carolina Press, 1989), p. 71. [Diamond]

8 Richard McKeon, 'The Concept of Imitation in Antiquity," in R.S. Crane, ed., *Critics and Criticism* (abridged edition) (Chicago, IL: University of Chicago Press, 1962), p. 122. [Diamond]

9 For a feminist critique of patriarchal modeling in discourses of truth, see, for example, Rosi Braidotti, *Patterns of Dissonance* (London: Routledge, 1991); Linda Alcoff and Elizabeth Potter eds., *Feminist Epistemologies* (New York and London: Routledge, 1993); Drucilla Cornell, *Beyond Accommodation: Ethical Feminism, Deconstruction, and the Law* (New York: Routledge, 1991); Genevieve Lloyd, *The Man of Reason* (Minneapolis, MN: University of Minnesota Press, 1993). [Diamond]

10 For arguments for and against this position, see *Feminism/Postmodernism*, ed. Linda J. Nicholson (New York, NY: Routledge, 1990), and Gayatri Chakravorty Spivak, *In Other Worlds: Essays in Cultural* (New York, NY: Methuen, 1987). [Diamond]

11 Elizabeth Robins, *Ibsen and the Actress* (London: Hogarth Press, 1928), p. 18. [Diamond]. See, also, Robins entry in this volume [eds.].

12 A.W. Schlegel in *Die Kunstlehre* (1805), cited in Todorov, p. 151; Karl Philip Moritz, *Über die bildende Nachahmung das Schönen* (1788), in Todorov, p. 153. However, by 1710, the Earl of Shaftesbury was already situating mimesis between Creator and creator: '[the] poet is a second Maker: a just Prometheus under Jove.' Cited in M.H. Abrams, *The Mirror and the Lamp* (New York, NY: W.W. Norton, 1953), p. 280. See also Helga Madland, 'Imitation to Creation: The Changing Concept of Mimesis from Bodmer and Breitinger to Lenz,' in *Eighteenth-Century German Authors and their Aesthetic Theories*, eds. Richard Critchfield and Wulf Koepke (Columbia, SC: Camden House, 1988), pp. 29–43. [Diamond]

13 Halliwell, *'Poetics' of Aristotle*, p. 137. [Diamond]

Suggestions for Further Reading

Diamond, Elin. "Brechtian Theory/Feminist Theory: Toward a Gestic Feminist Criticism." *The Drama Review*. 32. 1 (1988): 89–94.

———. "'Folk Modernism': Zora Neale Hurston's Gestural Drama." *Theatre Journal*. 58:1 (2015): 112–134.

———. "'Gestus and Signature in Aphra Behn's *The Rover*.'" *ELH* 56-3 (1989): 519–541.

———. "(In)Visible Bodies in Churchill's Theatre." *Theatre Journal*. 40.2 (1988):189–205.

———. "Mimesis, Mimicry and the 'True-Real'." *Modern Drama*. 32:1 (1989): 189–205.

———. "Realism and Hysteria: Toward a Feminist Mimesis." *Discourse*. 13:1 (1990–1992): 59–92.

———. "Rethinking Identification: Kennedy, Freud, Brecht." *Kenyon Review*. 15:2 (1993): 86–99.

———. "We Keep Living." *Theatre Journal*. 62:4 (2010): 521–527.

67 HÉLÈNE CIXOUS (b.1937)

Rachel Morris Watson

Introduction

Twentieth- and twenty-first-century French writer Hélène Cixous's (b.1937) oeuvre—more than 70 books and hundreds of essays and articles—challenges generic categories. Associated in the 1970s with the "*Psych. et po.*" feminist movement,[1] Cixous is best known for her contributions to poststructuralist feminist theory, especially via her essay "The Laugh of the Medusa" ["Le Rire de la Méduse," 1975 (trans. 1976)]. First published in an issue of *L'Arc* dedicated to Simone de Beauvoir, "Laugh" calls for the practice of *écriture féminine*, which would challenge the patriarchal tradition of writing and the normative depiction of women in Western literature. According to Cixous, transgressive "feminine writing" is one that can *voler* or "lift"—both "fly" and "steal"—in order to subvert the phallogocentric linguistic system (Cixous, "Laugh" 887). Cixous's fiction, from *Le Prénom de Dieu* (1967) to *Gare d'Ostnabrück à Jerusalem* (1999) and *Hyperrêve* (2006), puts *écriture féminine* into practice: she blends the fictional, poetic, autobiographical, and theoretical and creates her own idiom—dubbed "Cixaldien" by Frédéric-Yves Jeannet[2]—rich with multiple languages and neologisms, thick with homophony and layered meanings, and musical. Marta Segarra, like French literary theorist Jacques Derrida, attributes "Cixous's particular 'genius' [to] theory [that] cannot be separated from fiction" (Segarra, *Portable Cixous* 2).

Cixous has also made major contributions to the theatre. Her theatrical work spans from early experimental plays of the 1970s, to ongoing collaborations with the Théâtre du Soleil[3] dating from the 1980s, and, finally, to theoretical writings on the theatre. Contributing to a feminist conceptualization of theatre in post-1968 France, Cixous published "Going to the Seaside/Mother" [Aller à la mer, 1977 (trans. 1984)], which extends her call for *écriture féminine* to the theatre. Published in the leading newspaper *Le Monde*, the essay indicts the Western theatre tradition for using the female corpse as the starting point for dramatic conflict: attending theatre amounts to "attending [a woman's] funeral." Calling for a theatre of female "body-presence," Cixous wants to end dramatic writing that relegates women's bodies to the role of "sacrificial object"(Cixous, "Aller" 546–7). She simultaneously writes *Portrait of Dora* [*Portrait de Dora*, 1976 (trans. 1979)] and *The Name of Oedipus* [*Le nom d'Oedipe*, 1978 (trans. 1991)], which give women back their once silenced voices and bodies.

Although they have largely been overlooked, Cixous's reflections on theatre develop a coherent dramatic theory. While Cixous acknowledges the "non-theorizable" in theatre—the "magical," "supra-rational" elements that exceed explication in language and that must be rediscovered anew for each creation—she also submits to her

DOI: 10.4324/9781003006923-68

impulse to theorize (McEvoy 23). The resulting theoretical writings are not a single manifesto, but an ensemble demonstrating continuity. Written during her collaboration with the Soleil, these texts,[4] set down in playbills, published scripts, and interviews, constitute a theory that designates transformation, mutability, multiplicity, and alterity as inherent to engaged theatre. Cixous establishes theatre as a space of *démoïsation*, or unselfing, in which the fluid *moi*/I is displaced and open to the Other. Reading across these critical reflections, one can extrapolate a dramatic theory in which theatre becomes a model for hospitality,[5] as theatre artists displace themselves on the journey towards character, and, consequently, embody permeability between the self/Other.

Selected for this anthology, "Theatre Surprised by Puppets," which addresses Cixous's creation with the Théâtre du Soleil of *Drums on the Dam: In the Form of an Ancient Puppet Play, Performed by Actors* [*Tambours sur la digue*, 1999 (trans. 2004)],[6] serves as exemplar. In "Puppets," Cixous develops a theory of the marionette that functions metonymically as dramatic theory. For Cixous, theatrical creation implies a marionette-like doubleness in which the theatre artist is "two-but-one" or "[o]ne, but inhabited" (Cixous, "Puppets" 71). The Cixousian theory of the marionette—deserving of its place next to Kleist's and Craig's[7]—demonstrates the openness of the self to the Other essential to theatrical metamorphosis.

These reflections exhibit a kinship with the working methods of Ariane Mnouchkine and the Théâtre du Soleil. Just as the Soleil actors begin masked improvisations from a neutral body on an empty stage, Cixous, when writing, voids herself and waits for the characters to "enter" (Prenowitz 3). This relationship of the self/Other can be traced back to "Laugh," and the practice of *écriture féminine*, for Cixous asserts that the "feminine" always already contains the Other.

Much of Cixous's writing on theatre deviates from traditional Aristotelian theory by rendering the creative process in a poetic, performative language that captures on the page the materiality of the stage and the energy of creation and performance (McEvoy 20). Cixous combines the fictive and the metadiscursive; she moves among the voices of dramatist, critic, and character; and she disrupts conventional temporal progression.[8] Cixous's writings combine the affective and the analytical while pointing to that which is absent, the trace of theatrical "presence" that cannot be apprehended in language.

HÉLÈNE CIXOUS

"The Theatre Surprised by Puppets"[9] *(1999)*

The Spirited Author
'What if you were to write a play that would have been written by the poet Hsi-Xhou, an ancient play, that was performed long ago—sometimes by puppets, sometimes by actors, sometimes women playing all the roles, sometimes men playing all the roles, depending on whether the play were performed in such and such a kingdom under such and such a law and such and such an interdiction?

Thus said the director one day to the author.

So the author set about writing the play that had been written by her ancient predecessor and master, the poet Hsi-Xhou.

In the daytime, in the year 1998, the author would study ancient texts just as they had been brought to us up the Silk Road and the Stage Road, from Japan, China, Korea, India, along with jewelry, glass paste, musical instruments, banners, brushes, engravings. Brought back, set down in scholarly volumes, illustrated and taught.

At nighttime, the master puppeteer Hsi-Xhou would arrive and he would set in motion the imagination of the author-puppet, pulling on all the strings.

If ever there were a text dictated and the author spirited away, this was it. This is, thus, a play, transmitted as never before.

The playwright always dreams of being the skin of the stage, taut like the silk of a drum, a sensitive stage upon which the characters of the play pass with puppet steps.

Gently grazing the skin of the imagination, the passersby imprint their emotions, their hastes, their fevers. The playwright dreams of being this manuscript impregnated by the prancing of characters.

In her dream, the author, moved, molts and metamorphizes into a marionette, marvelously manipulated[10]: the play comes to rest on the soul of her body with the precise and shimmering lightness of dragonflies and other butterfly-psyches. All that is left to do is to reproduce it faithfully.

But this, this is the dream of the author.

Once awake, it's quite another matter, the author, once up, is traversed by the great, monumental texts that architexturise[11] her memory, by long and extensive Western dialogues—far removed from the night's curtains and Noh theatre's gliding step.

So the author returns to the workshop to search among the rolls of texts for tightly braided and very light fabric from which to cut out these characters who have come from very far away, from the very origins of theatre. The text must be almost transparent, and yet, of an extreme and dense solidity, a mere nothing to carry the weight of humanity.

Writing is like Korean sewing, which holds translucent fabric by a triple fold so tightly woven it nearly vanishes: from rigor comes suppleness.

The Flood

For all eternity, from the beginning of the beginning to the end of the world, each summer, despite the sediments of memory, we always say, this flood is the worst, and surely it is The Worst. In 2297 before our era, the Yellow River and the Blue River mixed their waters, which rose all the way above the heads of the mountains, and no one survived to tell of this deluge.

The Emperors constructed jetties nine times the height of a man. But the Empire was suffering from internal floods against which no jetties at all were erected.

The word Inundation is pronounced either with fear or indifference.

By dint of saying the words beforehand: water water water water, we end up forgetting the horror.

It is, then, that it arrives.

We can replace the word 'water' with the word 'war' or another.

The Puppets

The author, the director, the actors, the stage, the dykes, the palace, the boat, the sheets of rain…everything is a puppet.

Everything is manipulated. Each one is put into movement by its puppeteer. The entire puppet receives the motions transmitted by the puppeteer's ultralight shaking. There is nothing more animated, more meticulously raised from inertia to emotion than a creature moved by its mechanic: the heart beats all the way into the knees, the whole body articulates a sentiment, from the elbow to the heel, the sentence of the soul runs and manifests itself.

The puppeteer is inside, he is the sublime spirit of the puppet. The accomplished puppet obeys its puppeteer completely.

It does not know doubt, it neither slows down nor resists.

It acquiesces. It lets itself go. It is commanded, it is in harmony. It does not argue. It does not plant itself in front of the director with its hands on its hips. It does not walk on the ground, does not strike the floor with its foot. It has no authority.

It does not make its weight felt. It advances on the floor—puppet who unrolls its transparent carpet two inches above the anchored ground. It does not have its feet on the ground, but just above it. Its respiration lifts it up.

The Face of the puppet is immobile. Over this mirror pass the innumerable expressions of our passions. The immobile Face only renders the space more vast.

It is in the ecstasy that seizes the Face that we catch a glimpse of the immensity of the Gods.

The director asks the actor to be the puppet. The actor must remove himself from his foundation, the noise, commentary, realism, concrete objects, the floor, images—supports—aids. Once purity is attained, the limbs will move, instead of ideas. The puppet is in suspension. The actor is suspended in favor of the manipulated.

The director asks the actor to be two. Do not go faster than you can as two. The time of the two-step: order and execution. Unfold: explain. The body of the puppet explains itself. What is more radically present thus more theatrical than a puppet in the process of playing a character?

The puppet is the exteriorization of the interior puppet that we are. Inside we are multiple, complicated, articulated beings. The social fronts that we oblige ourselves to put up are easily labeled and illegible simplifications, opaque screens, shields.

The puppet is an open book. The puppet is absolutely innocent, regardless of its deeds or misdeeds: it is revealed, legible to the naked eye. It is only avowal.

It permits so much to be done to it, so much imprinted upon it, it is so given over to the motilities and movements of its puppeteer that it no longer hits any limits, it is not moored with rigid mast.

The Secret is in Unbalance

The puppet does not conceal our fundamental instability.

It reveals the human being: unstable, uncertain, exposed to psychological storms and global tempests, never secure, battling all its life against the hostile elements that we create and we flee.

Life, viewed from the spectator's seat, is a play, which, however familiar it is to us, remains at the mercy of unexpected events of which we are the apprentice-sorcerers. We cause what we hope never to see happen. And even death. We are constantly aware of death. And yet, what a surprise!

Consider the puppet of the Seigneur:[12] chipped all over, old, fragile, tremulous. 'Each time we perform this show, we are even more careful because the puppet has already been repaired several times,' remarks the director. To repair. To repair. The human being damages and repairs, until the day when the irreparable enters and—all of a sudden—it is the play, its ending and its beginning.

Everything is always hanging on by a thread, isn't it? We unintentionally deal the blows of fate.

The puppet of the Seigneur is trembling. The word 'trembling,' once again a marionette! Which is to say, a metaphor. Several years ago, an old goat[13] woke up in the Seigneur. It is not visible, but it can be felt and heard. Obstinate, trembling, stubborn, capricious, kicking its elegant but chipped hooves.

The puppet—the soul, the genius, the ambiguous gender of the puppet—makes strides, spreads out in the river's current as it does in current language.

The spirit of indecision. The swaying. Why do we have two legs if not to think from side to side? A play filled with puppets represents the truth that society would like us to deny: the extent to which we go backwards while going forwards, and to which in threatening we flee and in fleeing we threaten—our back is our other face—from one moment to the next we can change our destiny, choice, faith, loyalty, gender, direction, political party, and even sex!

The Puppet is Naked

Everything about this creature is naked: the eyes, the hair, the costume, the ankle, the gait.

Naked? Exhibited, exposed. Tiny. Fragile. Breakable. Angular. Solid but worn. The puppet has already been played a lot. We sense that they have already lived through much, the puppets, and have travelled a lot.

Suddenly, we are moved to tears that this is us: when the face is so eternal and the body so fragile that it cannot tense up without breaking, this is us, the human creature surrounded by the winds of time, miniscule in the History of Forces and Powers, drawn back before the enormity of a flood, confronted with very powerful cosmic stuff—the same stuff that reduces it to an atom in the immensity of the universe—to a cosmic fragment.

There is nothing greater than the miniscule creature, against whose smallness all explosions are measured.

The Rhythm of the Puppet

Be two-but-one. One, but inhabited. Make the crossing, demonstrate it. A puppet enters. Stop. Advance. No fits and starts. But a precise rolling-out, the exactitude of dance. A puppet who does ten things at once muddles everything up and loses its puppet-ness.

Be two: it is a kind of writing. The puppet writes with time, in distinct intervals, in (invisible) blanks, separating and tying together with regular full stops the sentences, the dashes, the leaps of passion—outlining the space from which will burst forth the cry, the crisis, the fit—disjointing, cutting, painting flawlessly so that the spark or flash suddenly bursts forth in tension like the leap of the shité in Noh. Like the leap of the cat which gathers up slowly in its vibrating body and lets loose only when it is ripe.

Thus we see the boatman,[14] touched by the blow of dishonor, running around the dams like an alley cat, holding his head in his puppet hands. We see that the soul of the boatman is this alley cat. And on his immobile face, we think we see—we see—go by all the great tragic faces painted on silent film masks. Mirage, magic, miracle, through puppetisation.

Everything will have been de-re-composed and transposed, as if soaked in the dye of human essence, hair transposed, skin, gesture, breath, and voice dyed "puppet."

The voice! Ah! It is what proved the most knotty. This is because the voice is foreign to the puppet. Poignant mystery of this creature composed of two distant beings, the body and the voice, which comes from the outside, comes from the singer, seated on the side, impassive, and who makes a gift of his voice. As if it were necessary to be two in order to express the enormity of the interior combat. Yet here in this theatre, the puppet and its puppeteer will ultimately have been played by a single person. It is the actress or actor who has to lend her/his foreign/strange voice to the puppet to which the actress actor gives her/his body. To do so, you will have had to renounce your voice—that within you which is the most indissociable, that which you renounce with the most difficulty—to go look for an entirely other voice in the vocal music of the puppets. Even your breath, you transpose it and you blow into the throat of the puppet the music of marionette-voice—of which the flesh, the timbre, the volume, are your creation.

To be a puppet is very tiring: it requires being both mother and child, double labor, from scene to scene.

The Horizon of Silk

To the puppets who trouble it, the world responds in prophetic silks:[15] there are twenty-two shaking skies that open and fall, all traversed by the imminent arrival of catastrophes. Clouds, messages, peaks, promised terrors, stretching out their living fabric above those stubborn and anxious little creatures.

Rare are the puppets who lift their heads looking to examine the consequences. For the most part, they are lazy, like us, and like us, impatient, they prefer not to reckon with their actions. But the spectators see the worsening weather tremble behind the inhabitants of the City. In vain, the book of the sky unfurls its splendid warnings.

Even so, below in the workshop, the mistress of indigo, with her follow artists, has done everything possible to make the fateful messages heard. Look at them, leaning over the floored sky, listening to its nuances, dying, dipping, repainting, making the greys speak, the golds, the purples, trembling with delicate fervor, hoping that some will receive the text of the message spread out in the silk. The silk also has its voice which has come from afar. Ah! If only we would listen to it.

For Ground, Music

For a floating world, flowing music.[16] One must imagine, says the musician, relationships that have not yet existed, and verbs to express almost impossible turns of phrase: to listen to an image, to look at a sound.

For music also plays itself, and is self-evident or silk-evident,[17] flowing, listening to itself slip out. Playing alongside the step of the puppet, carrying, without effort, the weight of the one that does not land, accompanying without holding back, never was music such a mother: it moves, asking if there exists a rhythm that is not fixed but flowing, and it is precisely from this questioning that the music surges, refraining from imposing and refraining simultaneously from leaving everything to chance.

This particular music lends an ear, listens to the hesitations of the puppet, translates them into a polyphony, then, with the movement of the puppet's soul, changes rhythm, obeying the spiritual gasps, receiving and giving back the variations of emotion. The music is also moved and elevated from one continental shore to the other, having for laws only the fluctuations of the drama.

With a gifted step, it paints with candor, without hesitation, with elegance, meticulousness, violence, serenity, thoroughly under the sway of surprise.

Thus, what advances—forever shunning a rapid tempo—what does not hurry, what does not stamp its foot in anxious staccato, is without a doubt the music of grace, a vital, soft-edged force which harmonizes in counterpoint, as if humming, with the pulse of the puppet.

Please see the Works Cited for further information on the sources used in this essay.

Notes

1 An abbreviation for psychoanalysis and politics.
2 See Hélène Cixous and Frédéric-Yves Jeannet. *Rencontre terrestre*. Paris: Galilée, 2005.
3 Parisian avant-garde theatre company founded in 1964 by Ariane Mnouchkine.
4 See especially: "Theatre Surprised by Puppets" ["Le Théâtre surpris par les marionnettes," 1999 (trans. 2016)], "Striking Sticks" ["Coups de baguettes," 2001 (trans. 2016)], "Hospitality?" ["L'Hospitalité?," 2003 (trans. 2016)], "On Theatre" [2004], and "Enter the Theatre" [2004]. All of these are published in the original and in English translation in Lara Stevens's edition of Cixous' *Politics, Ethics, and Performance: Hélène Cixous and the Théâtre du Soleil*. Melbourne: re.press, 2016.
5 See also, "Hospitality?," published in the playbill for the 2003 production of *The Last Caravansary* [*Le Dernier Caravansérail*], a play about 20th-century refugee crises.
6 In this play, actors played bunraku puppets manipulated by puppeteers, themselves actors.
7 Bernd Heinrich Wilhelm von Kleist (1777–1811) is considered the first great German playwright of the 19th century. His influential essay, "On the Marionette Theatre" dates from 1810. Edward Gordon Craig (1872–1966) was a British theatre designer and theorist who conceived of the "uber-marionette" as the perfect actor. See, also, Barnes entry in this volume [eds.].
8 For an excellent example of this, see "Striking Sticks," which can be viewed as a companion piece to "Puppets."
9 Originally translated by Lara Stevens, with further translation here by Rachel Morris Watson.
10 Cixous creates a homophony between "*ému*" and "*mu*" and "*mue*" that is lost in the translation "moved," "transformed" and "stripped." Watson changed this translation to "is metamorphized" and "molts" instead of Stevens's "transformed" and "stripped" to underscore the process of change, to retain the alliteration, and to allow for the preposition "into," which more closely captures Cixous's "en marionnette." Nonetheless, the assonance and homophony are lost.
11 The translation is faithful to Cixous's neologism "*architectent*" that turns the noun "*l'architecture*" into a verb that creates a rhythm and assonance with the word "*textes*" or "texts" that precedes it. Watson notes that it also implies archi-texts, fundamental texts that structure the author's textual memory through what she has previously read, and that, in keeping with the deconstructive concept that there is no "outside text," penetrate her reading and writing.
12 Cixous is referencing a puppet-character from *Tambours*—the cowardly Seigneur Khang.
13 Here, Cixous engages in word play with the French for "trembling" and "goat." Cixous uses the adjective "chevrotante" for "trembling." The infinitive of the related verb—*chevroter*—means "to bleat" or, for the human voice, "to quaver." Related to the sound a goat makes, "chevrotant" contains the word "chevre," French for "goat."
14 This is again a reference to a character in the play.
15 The scenic space of the production was framed by hand-dyed silk backdrops.
16 The music for this production was composed by Jean-Jacques Lemêtre.
17 Here, Cixous is playing with the homophony between "soi" ["self"] and "soie" ["silk"] to underscore how the music is developed through improvisation and in response to the movement of the silk backdrops.

Suggestions for Further Reading

Miller, Judith G. "The Theatre of Hélène Cixous: Rememberings, Refashionings, and Revenants." *The Portable Cixous*. Ed. Marta Segarra. New York, NY: Columbia University Press, 2010.

Picon-Vallin, Béatrice. *Le Théâtre du Soleil: The First Fifty-Five Years*. Trans. Judith Miller et al. London and New York, NY: Routledge, 2020.

Prenowitz, Eric, ed. *Selected Plays of Hélène Cixous*. London and New York: Routledge, 2004.

Stevens, Lara, ed. and trans. *Politics, Ethics, and Performance: Hélène Cixous and the Théâtre du Soleil*. Melbourne: re.press, 2016.

68 MĨCERE GĨTHAE MŨGO (1942–2023)

Kellen Hoxworth

Introduction

Mĩcere Gĩthae Mũgo (1942–2023) was an interdisciplinary artist, critic, and theorist from Kenya. In the world of drama and performance, Mĩcere is best known as the coauthor (with Ngũgĩ wa Thiong'o)[1] of the celebrated postcolonial African play, *The Trial of Dedan Kimathi* (1976). She authored two additional dramas—*The Long Illness of Ex-Chief Kiti* (1976) and *Dissolution* (1976)—as well as two volumes of poetry, *Daughter of My People, Sing!* (1976) and *My Mother's Song and Other Poems* (1994), and two scholarly monographs, *Visions of Africa* (1978) and *African Orature and Human Rights* (1991). Additionally, several of her critical essays on literature by African women, African orature, and African politics from Black, Pan-Africanist, and Third World feminist perspectives have recently been compiled in *Writing and Speaking from the Heart of My Mind* (2012). Though her work focuses primarily on East African performance cultures and Pan-Africanist politics, she lived in exile from Kenya beginning in 1982, when she was forced out of the country by the dictatorship of Daniel arap Moi.[2] She lived and worked in Zimbabwe until 1993, when she took a professorship at Syracuse University and relocated to the United States. In 2021, she was awarded the Lifetime Achievement Award in African Literature from the Royal African Society.

The theory of orature—a mode of cultural production that does not privilege the written word—is an organizing framework for Mĩcere's creative and critical work. As a distinct modality from the forms of European drama and theatre canonized in the compulsory educational discourses of colonial East Africa, orature emphasizes the performative potentialities of African modes of communication. Centrally, orature contests the colonial primacy of "drama" (i.e., text) and its categorical separation from "theatre" (i.e., performance). For Mĩcere, African literature requires oral performance to be fully realized, aesthetically and politically: "if you are writing serious poetry to communicate an experience, it has to be read aloud, felt, and heard in order to have a sense of involvement. There is a sense of affinity the writer is trying to establish between himself or herself and the audience" (qtd. in Berrian and Mĩcere 526; see also Mĩcere and Wilkinson 115–117). Thus, for Mĩcere, the often-segregated genres of poetry, drama, and theatrical performance function as related articulations of orature, which is to say that they establish communion, dialogue, and active participation among performers and audiences.

The participatory, communal aspects of orature are integral to Mĩcere's theorization of how theatre and performance function efficaciously in African contexts. Orature does not refer to "primitive dramas" or "half-baked dramas" awaiting

DOI: 10.4324/9781003006923-69

artistic development nor does it index a strictly representational medium (Mĩcere, "Popular Paradigms and Conceptions," 100, 99). Rather, orature invokes a collectivist performative modality through which artists may enact their agency to remake African social relations. In her 1984 essay, "The Battle of the Mind" (the title of which resonates with Ngũgĩ wa Thiong'o's *Decolonising the Mind*), Mĩcere first articulated the governing metaphor for her theorization of orature: an "onion-layered Afro-centric philosophy" (247; on "orature," see also Bukenya and Zirumu 88–105; J. Roach, *Cities of the Dead* 11–12; Ngũgĩ wa Thiong'o, "Oral Power and Europhone Glory," 103–128; and, Ngũgĩ wa Thiong'o, "The Oral Native and the Writing Master," 63–85). Modeled on an onion, Mĩcere offers a visualization of African society wherein "[l]ayers upon layers [...] maintain perpetual contact with each other harmoniously, making one whole" ("The Battle of the Mind," 247). In *African Orature and Human Rights* (1991), Mĩcere further elaborated her "Onion Structure Theory" as a vision of precolonial African society in which each member of society and every aspect of the physical, spiritual, and symbolic world exist in intimate interconnection: "We are dealing with a world that emphasized collectivity, groupness, interrelatedness, co-operation, sharing, inter-dependence, togetherness, etc." (14; see also "Towards a Definition of African Orature Aesthetics," 40). Here, Mĩcere relates orature to African cosmologies and philosophies of communalism, such as the Kiswahili utu and the Sindebele and Zulu ubuntu, which John Mbiti articulates as the philosophy of "I am because we are, and since we are, therefore I am" (Mbiti 214; cf. Mĩcere, *Writing and Speaking*, xii). By underscoring performative modes of precolonial African communication, and as evident in her work across poetry and drama, Mĩcere's orature intends to animate popular imaginations toward political activism, "to liberate others, and to create awareness" (qtd. in Berrian and Mĩcere 525; see also Ngũgĩ wa Thiong'o and Mĩcere iv–v).

In her creative works and her theorizations of orature, Mĩcere has steadfastly advocated for the centrality of women in African artistic production. As she observed in 1979, "in the authentic African set-up, it was mainly the woman who was the creative artist. They are the basket weavers. They are the storytellers in the evenings, the grandmothers and the aunties during the formative period of a child's life. A lot of them are singers and dancers" (qtd. in Berrian and Mĩcere 528). In fashioning African cultures and societies, Mĩcere's theorization of orature insists on the integral function of the artistic labor of African women. Citing the work of female writers such as Ama Ata Aidoo, Tsitsi Dangarembga, Nawal El Saadawi, Bessie Head, Ellen Kuzwayo, and Omolara Ogundipe-Leslie, Mĩcere's "Onion Structure Theory" emphasizes that the integrity of African and Pan-Africanist orature communities depends upon the full participation of African women (see also her "The Woman Artist in Africa Today").

In "Popular Paradigms and Conceptions: Orature-Based Community Theater," Mĩcere attends to the critical tensions endemic to the "popular" and to the communalism of "orature." Though she occasionally invokes a mythic, precolonial "authentic" African culture, Mĩcere's later work explores the social complexities and political contestations of performance cultures in the African postcolony (see also Mĩcere's nuanced analysis of the class and cultural politics of anti-female-circumcision discourse in "Elitist Anti-Circumcision Discourse."). In addition to Mĩcere's advocacy for orature-based theatre, she also notes the co-optation of the "popular" by colonial and neocolonial regimes, a phenomenon that she elsewhere terms "reactionary orature" and "neo-colonial 'ululation culture'" ("The Woman Artist in Africa Today," 57–59). By contrast to such appropriations of orature for state propaganda and tourism, in this essay, Mĩcere advocates for African artists to mobilize orature in order to confront the political crises of neocolonialism and globalization through dramaturgical practices structured on communalism, democratic participation, and collective world-making. Here, as in her broader oeuvre, Mĩcere outlines a radically participatory, democratic, "horizontal" vision of performance that seeks to perform such a nonhierarchical world into being.

Mĩcere Gĩthae Mũgo

Excerpt from "Popular Paradigms and Conceptions: Orature-Based Community Theater" (1999)

Any serious project of the reconstruction of the study and meaning of Africa must place cultural discourse at the center of its dialogue, for cultural studies bring us face to face with the history of a people, their self-definition, and an understanding of the dialectics that shape their destiny—together with all these processes' inherent contradictions. It is with this understanding that this chapter posits orature-based community theater as an important option in the quest for alternative paradigms that will take African studies in the arts beyond colonial and neocolonial formulations. In its attempt to depart from traditional Western bourgeois and liberal theater traditions, orature-based community theater may be regarded as an example of what Carol Boyce Davies terms an "uprising discourse" (Davies 1994: 80–112). It is, among other things, a response to colonial and neocolonial cultural expressions of domination. Drawing as it does on African orature forms, genres, and aesthetics that inform and shape the artistic production process, community theater is created with the broad masses of the people as the primary intended audience. […]

The key argument here is that African orature and the performing arts constitute the core of the authentic art forms that bring us closest to the heart of African people's self-expression and practice. They expose us to the type of indigenous knowledge that we should be scrutinizing as seriously as possible. This is especially critical given the crisis in what I call *invasion* by dominating paradigms, which are often veiled under the guise of status quo-controlled and status quo-programmed multicultural study packages. […]

African Orature as Historical and Artistic Expression
[…]

In African orature, drama and theater are more than artistic expressions: they are carriers of history, reflectors of the positive and negative forces inherent in the evolution of society. They are as well vehicles of conscientization that shape people's vision, even as they explore avenues for resolving the conflicts that characterize human development.

From antiquity right up to the slave trade and the colonial invasions of Africa, these are the terms on which drama and theater existed in various African communities. Theater took place at different kinds of sociocultural forums such as commemorations of historical events, cultural festivals, ceremonial occasions, ritual enactments, and ordinary social events. Theater was therefore used for entertainment as well as artistic commentary and critique of social reality. Generally speaking, theater was produced and consumed communally, but like all other forms of artistic and cultural production, it reflected the socioeconomic-political arrangement of the specific society from which it originated. Thus, in "vertical" societies[3] theater performances tended to reflect a feudalistic worldview and were often used to highlight themes featuring the chief, the queen, or the king. Examples of this kind of theater can be found in a number of countries that had feudal structures, such as ancient Egypt, the kingdoms of West Africa, Lesotho, Swaziland, and Uganda. Under such social formations, theater tended to be a tool for the deification and glorification of the ruling class. It was not unknown in such situations to witness performances dramatizing praise poetry that described the ruler as the "great," the "omnipotent," and the "lion that roars," whereas the masses were portrayed through images such as "ants," "rubble," "dust," and "grass" that tremble at the voice of the almighty.

It is also important to point out, however, that popular artists—even when in the minority—spoke loudly and clearly on behalf of the people, creating opposing images and symbols in an attempt to assert the humanity of the majority. This was so more often in "horizontal" social formations, where popular artists dominated the scene, taking their cue from the majority whose aspirations for self-assertion and human development they championed.[4] In their dramatizations, the heroes and heroines become what Wanjiku Mukabi Kabira describes as "the little people" of society (Kabira 1983: 1). At the end of the day, it was the small ones—the hare, the deer, the oppressed and powerless small antagonists—who emerged victorious, outdoing bullies such as the greedy hyena, the trampling elephant, and the gulping ogre, who were the antitheses of all that is just and humane.

This dialectical cultural scene was invaded by the Arab and European slave traders, followed closely by Western colonial invaders. The enslavers and colonizers were not unaware that culture plays the role that [Amilcar] Cabral has attributed to it. They knew that to effectively disinherit their victims and dominate their economy, they had to "conquer" them culturally. Frantz Fanon convincingly demonstrated this thesis in his two monumental works *The Wretched of the Earth* (1963) and *Black Skin White Masks* (1967). Even more demonstrative at the educational level, however, is the work of Paulo Freire, the celebrated Brazilian emancipatory educationist, theoretician, and community activist. He offers an especially rich analysis of the effects of conquest paradigms that invaders impose on colonized people. He defines cultural invasion thus:

> The theory of antidialogical action has one last fundamental characteristic: cultural invasion, which like divisive tactics and manipulation also serves the ends of conquest. In this phenomenon, the invaders penetrate the cultural context of another group, in disrespect of the latter's potentialities; they impose their own view of the world upon those they invade and inhibit the creativity of the invaded by curbing their expression. ...In cultural invasion...the invaders are the authors of, and actors in, the process; those they invade are objects. The invaders mold; those they invade follow that choice—or are expected to follow it. The invaders act; those they invade have only the illusion of acting, through the action of the invaders.
>
> (Freire 2000: 152)

Freire further argues that "all domination involves invasion—at times physical and overt, at times camouflaged, with the invader assuming the role of a helping friend" (2000: 153).

This final point is particularly important as we examine the plight of African theater under the paradigms of colonial and neocolonial education, whose practitioners claim to be agents of development. [...] Assertive forms of cultural expression were either captured, forbidden, or at best censored.

On the whole, the invaders targeted popular forms such as drama and theater. They repressed those artistic expressions that asserted the people's collective well-being and either condoned or actively encouraged whatever reinforced the power of the ruling classes. In their toleration and promotion of *court* orature, as it might be called, the invaders used divide-and-rule tactics to woo the ruling class into collaboration while silencing the dominated majority. In this way they sought to silence the voices that sang the epic songs of the resisting masses and to chain the bodies that dramatized the theater of the oppressed. Theater performed around festivities, ceremonies, and rituals that celebrated the people's milestones of production, development and social interaction was gagged. Theater that stagnated in religious swamps and caused trembling before tyrannical court enclosures was applauded. More significantly, the invaders schooled court theater artists and prospective artists in the invaders' own performing arts paradigms. Thus they manufactured robots who became mere imitators of the invaders' values and aesthetics. [...]

Neocolonial Invasions and Mass-Based Theater

[...] Ministries of tourism and culture in many African countries have at times used theater artists in the same way as they use animals in the game parks: as a means of raising foreign currency by entertaining tourists still in search of the African wild. Since he who pays the piper calls the tune, to use a hackneyed expression, commercial performing artists will often go out of their way to give the tourists what they wish to see. Needless to say, such compromises negatively affect the paradigms governing the production of the performed pieces, distorting indigenous African art forms and turning them into comical exhibitions for the entertainment of tourists. Authenticity is thus sacrificed as the performers dance themselves lame in near-naked painted bodies that match the profiles of jestering acrobatic buffoons, evoking the "noble savage" image of television's Discovery Channel. The Bomas of Kenya, a tourist center, used to feature an acrobat who specialized in distorting his facial muscles with such success that he would momentarily look like a monster. Here, indeed, was living, visible evidence of the cost of tourist entertainment: lost beauty and human dignity.

With these taunting insults on African masses in view, the progressive theater artist has had no option but to join the masses in their efforts to rescue their art forms from invasion under neocolonialism. More than this, the alliance has recognized the power of the performed word in the process of mass conscientization. This power had been demonstrated throughout the history of anticolonial cultural struggles. Under neocolonial states and dictatorships, the abuse of human rights has acquired forms just as grotesque as those experienced during colonization. Creators of mass-oriented theater are therefore committed to the revolutionization of this most immediate, communicative art form, with a view to turning it into a lethal artistic weapon that the invaded can use against the systems that oppress them.

At this point it becomes necessary to define *mass-based theater*, relating it to orature and identifying the paradigms that distinguish it from the theater of invasion examined previously. In its ideological conception, mass-based theater also borrows paradigms from revolutionary theater practitioners such as Paulo Freire and

Bertolt Brecht. In his well-known essay entitled "The Popular and the Realistic" (Brecht 1964), Brecht places popular theater within the realist tradition. Redefining "realism" outside the paradigms of the so-called great tradition, Brecht contextualizes a shift within twentieth-century capitalist Europe in which "the people has clearly separated from its top layer" and in which "its oppressors have parted company with it," becoming "involved in a bloody war against it which can no longer be overlooked" (Brecht 1964: 107). He thus contends that from the point of view of the progressive theater artist: "It has become easier to take sides. Open warfare has, as it were, broken out among the 'audience.' ...The ruling strata are using lies more openly than before and the lies are bigger. Telling the truth seems increasingly urgent. The sufferings are greater and the number of sufferers has grown. Compared with the vast sufferings of the masses it seems trivial and even despicable to worry about petty difficulties and the difficulties of the petty groups" (1964: 107).

In addition to making other points, Brecht is arguing that in an oppressive situation, theater cannot evade the burden of functional art, a paradigm that is antithetical to the bourgeois notion of art for art's sake. More than this, he is advocating that theater align itself with the struggles of the oppressed and avoid a preoccupation with elitist trivialities. In making these observations, Brecht might as well be addressing the neocolonial African reality. From Cape to Cairo, from eastern coast to western coast, workers and peasants bend double under the weight of economic oppression, political repression, and sociocultural degradation. More than 80 percent of the continent's population lead a subhuman material existence. Denial of basic human rights—food, clothing, shelter, and the wherewithal for self-determination—leaves the majority of the people in a perpetual begging posture. In particular, children have become ready victims of hunger, famine, disease, and war. Africa is faced with imminent child genocide that will affect the development of generations to come. Given this situation, the theater artist faces a moral choice: whether or not to continue with the paradigms of bourgeois theater, which depict the masses as nothing more than asides or invisible incidentals, when not ridiculing them or wiping them out of history altogether. According to Brecht, to propagate bourgeois theater paradigms is to abet the distortion of reality, if by reality we mean the overwhelming evidence of the wretchedness of the majority in our midst.

Having dealt with the issue of whose side popular art should take, Brecht proceeds to explain what he means by *popular* from the point of view of aesthetics and vision. This definition is pertinent because it is related to the question of why we should promote mass-based orature theater. As he says: "'Popular' means intelligible to the broad masses, taking over their own forms of expression and enriching them/adopting and consolidating their standpoint/representing the most progressive section of the people in such a way that it can take over leadership: thus intelligible to other sections too/linking with tradition and carrying it further/handing on the achievements of the section now leading to the section of the people that is struggling for the lead" (Brecht 1964: 108).

This model, greatly elaborated by revolutionary culturalists and educational practitioners such as Paulo Freire, Augusto Boal, [Brian] Crow and [Michael] Etherton, and others, is the theater paradigm with which progressive theater artists in Africa have been experimenting during the last two decades or so. [...]

An Orature-Based Paradigm

These efforts created the seeds for orature-based community theater in which the participation of the masses and their artistic forms, cultural paradigms, and languages are employed to shape the form and content of the pieces, as well as the overall visionary perception of the productions. However, the extent to which the various forms of orature-based community theater succeed in doing this varies from experiment to experiment, a subject that has been extensively treated by, among others, Boal (1979), Kidd and Byram (1982), Kidd and Colletta (1980), Crow and Etherton (1980), Mlama (1991), Kamlongera (1989), and Mda (1993). There is thus no need to describe individual community theater projects here. It will suffice to close with a brief, generalized sketch of the process involved in creating a desired orature-based model, with a view to reinforcing its place in the definition of liberating paradigms. The model used is that practiced by the Zambuko/Izibuko community theater group in Zimbabwe, of which I am a participating member. This group has staged performances in English, Chishona, and Sindebele, the three official languages of Zimbabwe, including works such as *Mavambo* [1985], *Samora Continua!* [1987], *Mandela—Spirit of No Surrender!* [1990] and a current one, *Simuka Zimbabwe!* (*Rise Up Zimbabwe!*) [1994], criticizing "invasions" by the IMF and the World Bank.

As I have repeatedly suggested such undertakings ought to do, the project goes back to the people for its themes and inspiration, deliberately drawing on the most positive aspects of self-expression that grassroots communities have evolved over time. The people are not relegated to the role of spectators but are involved as resources and participants in the creative process as well as in performance. The entire group of theater artists thus begins with brainstorming issues that are of concern to the community in which they are based, discussing them thoroughly before identifying the predominant theme on which the dramatization will eventually focus. The brainstorming exercise is normally conducted in the language shared by the creators of the artistic piece, ensuring that each member has freedom to use the tongue with which she or he feels most comfortable. This means that if Chishona, for instance, is the most common and bonding language, it becomes the main medium of communication. Other languages can be brought in where and when necessary. Members contribute orature songs, dances, stories, and other creations from their communities. Where necessary, these are researched for the specific production. Every rehearsal opens with dance and song warm-up exercises. Liberation songs are the most popular. Indeed, one of them has become Zambuko/Izibuko's signature tune. The song tells how Zimbabwe was liberated through armed struggle, and the artists hold toy guns high as they dance into the theater and onto the stage in celebration of the people's victory.

As the theme is developed and the spoken text shaped, the group begins identifying, from among the available human resources, individuals best suited for specific roles. Each case is discussed openly and critically, with the decision based purely on merit. Workshops in dramatization then begin. As the "script" is developed, each stage of the process is informed by intensive discussion and debate. The group experiments with criticism, alternative suggestions, and viable solutions. Once the oral text is more or less consolidated, scripting and recording finally come into play, but never for the purpose of producing a permanent text above amendment. During the rehearsals improvisation and continuous "writing" supersede the authority of a fixed script. When the rehearsals are mature, early performances are presented to other theater artists and members of the general community of artists for criticism. From the comments received, the group then works on perfecting the performance for the general public. Following some public performances, the audience is invited to participate in a session of criticism and self-criticism. Thus the piece and the artists continue to grow with each performance.

The foregoing discourse posits community theater, and specifically orature-based projects, as a paradigm that creates space for democratic participation, involvement, and collective work. The creative process becomes an embracing act; the final product, a shared experience. This contradicts the paradigm of "art for art's sake" and interrogates the perception of creative artistic productivity as the monopoly of intellectual elites. Furthermore, the paradigm provides a possible meeting place between orature and the written tradition. Complementarity and collective engagement replace the divisiveness and alienation of individualistic approaches. This explains why oppressed classes and groups such as workers and peasants, as well as women and youth, have responded so readily to the community theater project, which they use as a means of exploring the oppressive economic-political realities that have long suppressed their creativity. African studies specialists should pay serious attention to this aspect of creative and intellectual productivity as a paradigm worthy of further investigation.

Please see the Works Cited for further information on the sources used in this essay.

Notes

1 Ngũgĩ wa Thiong'o (b.1938) is a Kenyan writer who engages in a wide range of genres: novels, plays, short stories, children's literature, and literary and social theory and criticism. [eds.]
2 Daniel arap Moi was the second and longest-serving President of Kenya (1978–2002). [eds.]
3 Amilcar Cabral uses this term to describe societies ruled by kings, queens, and chiefs. Feudal systems, for instance, would be considered vertical in their organization. [Mĩcere]
4 Horizontal social formations had ruling councils as the governing bodies. Representatives on the councils were appointed by the people they represented, usually across age groups, clans, and villages. [Mĩcere]

Suggestions for Further Reading

Barber, Karin. *I Could Speak Until Tomorrow: Oriki, Women, and the Past in a Yoruba Town.* Washington, D.C.: Smithsonian Institution, 1991.
Boyce Davies, Carole, and Elaine Savory Fido. "African Women Writers: Toward a Literary History." *A History of Twentieth-Century African Literatures.* Ed. Oyekan Owomoyela. Lincoln, NE: University of Nebraska Press, 1993. 311–346.
D. Ndirangu Wachanga. *Mĩcere Gĩthae Mũgo: Making Life Sing in Pursuit of Utu.* Ibadan, Nigeria: Bookcraft, 2022.
Hale, Thomas A. "Griottes: Unrecognized Female Voices," *Griots and Griottes: Masters of Words and Music.* Bloomington, IN: Indiana University Press, 1998. 217-243.
Kerr, David. *African Popular Theatre: From Pre-Colonial Times to the Present Day.* London: James Currey, 1995.
Ogundipe-Leslie, Molara, and Carole Boyce Davies. Special Issue: *Women as Oral Artists. Research in African Literatures* 25.3 (1994).

69 DIANE GLANCY (b.1941)

Birgit Däwes

Introduction

"A script is a blueprint for a story that the character enters," Diane Glancy (b.1941) writes in her essay "Further (Farther): Creating Dialogue to Talk about Native American Plays"—"Or a character which the story enters. A story wants something, but something gets in the way" (200). This description of the individual process of playwriting—as "voice writing" (202), or creating "access to the unseen world(s)" (203)—emblematically characterizes the larger development of Native American drama as a genre, in which Glancy has played a significant role. When an early version of "Further (Farther)" was published in the spring of 1999 (it was revised for publication in 2002), the academic study of Native American theatre and per-formance was at a crossroads—at least in the United States. Whereas in Canada, First Nations plays had gained increasing mainstream acknowledgement since the 1980s, the Native American drama scene in the United States—albeit similarly vibrant—remained largely neglected by critics and curricula. In 1999, however, two influential anthologies exclusively dedicated to Indigenous North American plays were published, substantially increasing the visibility of the Americas' oldest and most adaptable form of artistic expression: *Seventh Generation* (ed. Mimi Gisolfi D'Aponte) and *Stories of Our Way* (eds. Hanay Geiogamah and Jaye T. Darby). Since 1999, the genre has exponentially grown, with further seminal anthologies espe-cially focusing on Indigenous women's work[1] and with several book-length critical studies.[2] Diane Glancy's credo that, both in theory and practice, "we have to invent Native terms" ("Further [Farther]" 201), instead of simply applying Western theat-rical theory to Indigenous work, has proven a ground-breaking directive over the past two decades.

In the prolonged process of furthering Indigenous stories on American stages, and of overcoming all kinds of "something [that] gets in the way" (such as colo-nialist structures, systemic displacement, prejudice, lack of political support, and underfunding), Diane Glancy's influence has been substantial. As a writer, drama-turg, professor, and educator, she is one of the most prolific Indigenous contributors to the American literary scene today, with international acclaim ranging from an American Book Award in 1993 to the Native Writers' Circle of the Americas' Lifetime Achievement Award in 2014. Her work includes over twenty volumes of poetry, films, and short story collections. Her widely taught novels, including *Pushing the Bear* (about the Trail of Tears [1996]) and *Stone Heart* (about Sacajawea [2004]), broaden

DOI: 10.4324/9781003006923-70

our understanding of history, and especially women's history—of "the voices of a longer story," as she puts it in "Further (Farther)" (203).

What characterizes her theatrical work—including over 30 plays to date—is the vision of "boundary crossing" that she theorizes for Native drama in "Further (Farther)." This involves not only the borderline between "(1) the physical world, (2) the dream world [...], (3) the spirit beings [...], (4) the ancestors (ancients), [and] (5) the imaginative experience, which is a strip of all between" ("Further [Farther]" 203), but it also applies to her "Cherokee poetics" and her "multi-genred" approach to writing, as Molly McGlennen puts it (59), which often resists demarcations of Western literary criticism. Glancy's plays are poetic; they evolve through a high density of language and vivid imagery, as does her approach to theatrical theory. Like the metaphor of seeing frozen lakes from high above—the "patterns marking the ice with hatchings that looked like broken glass"—Native American drama requires a larger perspective, an empowerment of "overstories" and "understories" ("Further [Farther]" 203). The land is as important in this image as the emerging, previously unnoticed patterns of a larger structure: "a literary theory for Native American plays in which the unseen world intrudes as though it were seen" (200).

In addition to bridging generic boundaries, Glancy's work is also profoundly dedicated, as her title suggests, to "creating dialogue" between ethnic, cultural, gender-based, and religious interests—and to opposing nationalist as well as essentialist ideologies. Being of mixed Cherokee, English, and German descent, Glancy has always advocated for fluid processes of identity construction and cultural pluralism. In her play *Salvage* (2009), for instance, she highlights the risks of "reservation wars—Us against us" (126) over those that she elsewhere calls "defining our territories" (Andrews 658). Instead of opposition and conflict, her writing promotes values of understanding, commonality, and respect. This "communal stance," she writes in *Claiming Breath*, "is inherent in the Native American heritage. The non-linear non-boundaried non-fenced open-prairied words" (4).

Her theory, representatively condensed in "Further (Farther)," has also manifested itself in an impressively diverse and voluminous corpus of theatrical work to date, from her realistic family play *Weebjob* (1987) to the experimental reflection *Jump Kiss* (1997), and from the allegorical first-encounter play *The Truth Teller* (1995) to her role of dramaturg in a highly innovative virtual performance of Laura Shamas's *Four Women in Red* at the Native Voices Short Play Festival in November 2020. For Glancy, writing and producing theatrical work are "giving voice to history" ("Author's Statement" 126); hers is "a stance of syncretism" ("Native Dramatic" 34) that allows her "to capture the largeness of the past and of the land in a very small place" (32).

James Mackay has metaphorically termed Glancy a "red state poet"[3]—referencing her Christian faith and her upbringing in Missouri and Oklahoma—with "an instantly recognizable poetic voice on what might strike others as the stoniest of ground" (1). But in light of her boundary-crossing celebrations of relativism and her emphasis on "various centers of the universe, taking in more than one view, more than one multiplicity" ("Further [Farther]" 204), it seems more justified to call her an "open-prairied" writer, who transforms the land of her origin into living language, who infuses American landscapes with memory, and who continuously expands the horizons of dramatic theory.

Diane Glancy

"Further (Farther): Creating Dialogue to Talk about
Native American Plays" (1999/2002)

SCENE 1

There has been conversation (at various conferences) toward making a literary theory for Native American plays in which often the unseen world intrudes as though it were seen. The parts not connecting until the play as a whole is seen and sometimes it (the meaning) still trails.

A script is a blueprint for a story that the character enters. Or a character which the story enters. A story wants something but something gets in the way. How it is resolved is the character.

A play connects to a power source which is a structure of action. A cord into a socket. Dramatic language is like electricity. Which is hard to explain. It accesses invisibility and all those things going to it. A play is a small town. With an interstate bypassing it. Yet connected to the power plant by the river. A new oral tradition with breath that is the condition of performance. A planet of being. A location. A vectoring that is a conflation of crossroads in different perspectives.

A Native play is maybe less constructed. Relying at times on campfire or lights from a trailer on the edge of darkness. Not moving to a clear finish with all kinds of imperatives, those little divisions between the spruce and the pines. But accessing the spirit world and the physical world. Combining the shadow world and the real world. Asking which is which? Is the shadow world the spirit world and the real world the physical world we live in? Or is the shadow world the real and the real world we live in the shadow? Or are both distorted until it only seems they are separate?

It is something like magic realism, but we have to invent Native terms.

> Improbable realities.
> Realized improbabilities.
> Improbable actualities.
> Ritualistic imagination.
> Imaginative realism.

(On a plane from Albuquerque, once it was over Minnesota, I looked down on frozen lakes that had been crossed with snowmobiles and trucks pulling ice-fishing houses. I saw patterns marking the ice with hatchings that looked like broken glass.)

A story in the process of theory.

What is similar and what is not (this came while waking from a dream).

> Trying out terms.
> Bulling a bulldozer.
> A snowmobile on a frozen lake that is only sometimes frozen.
> Oneiric magnetism.
> A pull of boundaries into one another.
> Accessible dualism.

Dualistic accessibility.
Dualistic realism.

Naturalistic dualism (except there are more than two things going on in a Native play; it's more of a bricolage, a staging of variants).

Boundary crossing (so that what is separated on a map—the definite lines between states, for instance, are not there when you look down—but being on the ground, there are only highway markers saying, *Entering Iowa*, but otherwise the borders are invisible unless the Red River between Texas and Oklahoma).

SCENE 2

There is a going into a world that is not the travel you're accustomed to. It exists side by side but is not known. Unless to those within it. It could be said *here it is* without explanation. But there has to be a way to look at. Otherwise, what is it? Emphasis of story over character development? A change of story? The story as character or the telling of the story as character?

Or, if you are there at a certain time / a certain place / it becomes visible like broken glass travels over ice.

Blended settings.
Unboundaried orations.
Seismic *orflations* (inflated orations).
Syncretic *ortations* (each speaking within each).
A dramatic, oral-traditional, many-voiced, poly-multiple, *multipole*.

A play that migrates around ceremony, including the time of year / the elements (a snowmobile on a frozen lake that is only sometimes frozen, depending on the weather) / the particular occasion / the particular voices that give *line*.
A confluence.
A collusion.
When I see the word, petroglyphography, I think of verbal petroglyph.
Voice writing (which a Native play is).
Overlay (not where is the conflict/resolution? character change? but process unfolding the storytelling is the plot).
A dialogue coming from different places. A dialogue without hearing the other (something else from a dream).
Implausible realities.
The believable occurrences of *unbelievability*.
Access to the unseen world(s).
A cohabitation of this world and the other(s) (but without making unrealistic separations). Or *here are other worlds also which are here*.
Intertextual facings.
Interfactual *textings*.
Interfactings.
Overstories.
Understories.
The intermix of overlaps.
The intercalation of (1) the physical world, (2) the dream world (2a those dreams also while waking), (3) the spirit beings (3a the *spirits being*), (4) the ancestors (ancients), (5) the imaginative experience, which is a strip of all between.

SCENE 3

It's when the voices, no matter where they're from, speak out ward from the core of experiences, from thought; feeling their way along the dark road to—well, be dramatic about it.

The voices of a longer story. One buffalo walking, over-spilling its prairie. Nor do there seem to be soldiers anymore with regiments moving to orders; but a process of exchange, relationship, and interaction; the one voice in many voices, the successive voices, the cumulative voices in manifold expressionism; moving to a fragmented cognizance; a recognition of self in the cross-genre democracy of writing; taking the tool, turning it back to them with new knifeness.

Authority tied in a spiderweb effect, if you've ever watched frost grow. A winter approach to spiderwebs; some garnering a gnat or insect from time to time.

Explications inward of our destination to civilization in these various combinations; a town hall of all of the voices together.

An expanding theory with various centers of the universe, taking in more than one view, more than one multiplicity. The common pervades and speaks the common in a new broken commonality, obedient to the call of changing, manifolding, powwowing, renewing, conviving. Incongruent to get at the matter of the things. To gist existence, all the while sharing the burden, the glory of the stage.

And in the separations, the sewings of meaning again, the contact, at last, with other tribes, other settlements.

DENOUEMENT

A Native play is often orbiculate. To circle back to terms: realized improbabilities probably describes the network of possibilities for the unlikely elements of the topography of the Native stage. The improbable happenings that fill the Native stage. The acceptable improbabilities. The indirect directions. Blizzard, the cold and heat, thunderstorm, humidity, humor and bleakness, tornado and calm, flood and drought—all the other upheavals of Native theater.

Please see the Works Cited for further information on the sources used in this essay.

Notes

1   See Huston-Findley and Howard as well as Armstrong et al.
2   See Däwes; Stanlake; Darby et al.
3   Mackay mainly refers to "the endless, red-earthed land of the Mid-West" (5), yet in the USA, "red states" are also associated with politically conservative views and the Republican Party, while "blue states" are associated with liberal views and the Democratic Party.

Suggestions for Further Reading

Blaeser, Kimberly. "Introduction." *War Cries: Plays By Diane Glancy.* Duluth, MN: Holy Cow Press, 1997. Vi–x.

Glancy, Diane. "From SALVAGE to Selvage: The Restoration of What Is Left." *Indigenous North American Drama: A Multivocal History.* Ed. Birgit Däwes. Albany, NY: State University of New York Press, 2013. 99–105.

Haugo, Ann. "American Indian Theater." *The Cambridge Companion to Native American Literature.* Eds. Joy Porter and Kenneth M. Roemer. Cambridge: Cambridge University Press, 2005. 189–204.

70 LOIS WEAVER (b.1949)

Benjamin Gillespie

Introduction

Lois Weaver (b.1949) is a leading contemporary theatre maker, performer, director, and teacher. As a lesbian and feminist, she has long centered her artistic practice on her own identity and desires. Weaver is cofounder (with Peggy Shaw and Deb Margolin) of the legendary New York-based performance troupe Split Britches, one of the longest-running theatre companies in the U.S. Celebrating the diversity of female subjectivity, Weaver has continuously challenged traditional gender roles, confronted patriarchal values, and defied heterosexual imperatives, most notably through the contrast of butch/femme lesbian roleplay on stage. Now in her seventies, through her playful and seductive stage presence as a femme lesbian, and by presenting powerful female characters informed by her own values and beliefs, Weaver continues to challenge heteronormative notions of femininity and women's objectification by the male gaze.

For Weaver, theatre and activism are never mutually exclusive: her creative roles onstage and off are informed by the principles of inclusivity, social equity, and theatrical imagination. Both as a solo artist and in collaboration with others, Weaver crafts performances that intimately engage the real world, and she often breaks the fourth wall to interact directly with her audiences. Eliminating participation would, in fact, be anathema to her aesthetic, which privileges community engagement, hospitality, equity, and care.

In 1980, Weaver cofounded the Women's One World Festival, showcasing new and experimental work by and for women that upended sexist stereotypes and traditional theatrical approaches to theatre making with a working-class aesthetic. The success of the festival resulted in the creation of the collectively run WOW Café theatre—a permanent venue in New York City's East Village still operating today. It is at WOW that Weaver established her democratic approach to collective performance making, focusing not on a polished final product but on the process of performance making itself as an act of care for the community surrounding her. Weaver's ongoing activism with marginalized communities has given a voice to those often silenced by institutionalized power, offering everyone an equal seat at the table.

As a part of her performance work, Weaver has developed a series of performance protocols, or "etiquettes," collected under an open-source project called "Public Address Systems."[1] These protocols aim to create alternative spaces that are hospitable and open to critical questioning and collective engagement around issues facing a community; they also seek modes for this engagement that are accessible,

DOI: 10.4324/9781003006923-71

egalitarian, and democratic. "How is it possible to think, and feel, publicly?" she asks.[2] These protocols allow communities to address moments of crisis or upheaval while prioritizing fairness and comfort. They emphasize a dramaturgy of care while navigating a range of spaces including classrooms, conferences, theatres, prisons, storefronts, community centers, elder care centers, and church halls. The protocols help assembled participants to negotiate the politics of these spaces while flattening embedded hierarchies in group interactions. As Weaver notes, "Everyone in the room has the power [...] to shift the direction of conversation to mediate moments of tension and to make spaces for voices less easily heard" (Weaver and Maxwell 93). Combining the formal and institutional with the domestic and vernacular, Weaver asks participants to be accountable as public citizens and recognize overlooked privilege.

The protocols below include the "Long Table Dinner Party," "Porch Sitting," and the "Care Café." By providing open-access documents, Weaver allows the public to extend her personal practice of care and stewardship in performance making in her absence. While the "Long Table Dinner Party" emphasizes face-to-face communication, "Porch Sitting" and the "Care Café" emphasize side-by-side communication to deter more dominant personalities from filling gaps. The gaps, in turn, might allow for reflection or negotiation, emphasizing the importance of listening and silent contemplation over active speaking. Each etiquette is performative in that they require actions and spaces to be worked out in real time with active participants or performers. Eschewing didacticism, the protocols avoid "educating" the public to derive meaningful theatrical experiences for all involved. As Weaver states, "The life of the project [is] in the repetition, the reciprocity, and the interconnection of disparate peoples and places through the principle of care and gathering" (Weaver and Maxwell 88).

Not only are these protocols useful for a wide range of groups entertaining challenging dialogue, but they can also be used to develop new performances. While they may, at times, raise questions or even dissent, the goal is always to do so respectfully. Producing a space that deemphasizes singular leadership is often challenging; however, these protocols provide a fluid configuration for participants that avoids inequity among individuals. As guidelines, the protocols are never definitive, and they leave room for interpretation or adaptation where necessary. They also reflect the fundamental aspects of Weaver's four-decade-long collaborative practice, prompted by her desire to grow and learn from community. Like the celebrated performances of Split Britches, Weaver's protocols resist easy resolution and tidy endings, instead offering an invitation for new beginnings and more care-*full* futures.

Lois Weaver

Excerpts from Performance Protocols: *Long Table Dinner Party*[3] *(2003)*

The Long Table is a dinner party and performance structured by an etiquette where dialogue is the main course. As both an everyday discussion and stylized performance, the Long Table provides a model for theatricalized public engagement that is open-ended and non-hierarchical for all involved. Theatrical craft and political commitment are mutually supportive in the performance environment and the often-feminized domestic realm becomes a stage for public thought and engagement.

The performance etiquette, or rules for engagement, lays the groundwork for participatory discussion structured for everyone present at the table without being limited in content or access. The Long Table acknowledges the discomfort that can occur in both private and public exchange, while also celebrating the potential for new forms of knowledge-making and sharing. Theatrical craft and political commitment are mutually supporting.

In a Long Table, participants are actively invited to share responsibility for the flow of the conversation and the respect shown to each other as speakers and listeners. The etiquette is read out by a host at the start, turns are taken, microphones are passed and shared. Everyone in the room has the power (and imperative, with the communal interest for a more satisfying discussion) to shift the direction of conversation, to mediate moments of tension and to make space for voices less easily heard.

The Long Table protocol was inspired by Marleen Gorris' film *Antonia's Line*. In the film, the protagonist continuously extends her dinner table to accommodate a growing community of outsiders and eccentrics until, finally, the table must be moved out of doors. The Long Table brings center stage that which is usually kept offstage in the private sphere of the home. In the process, the dining table becomes a place for meaningful political discussion and debate. They ask: *What if the world was organized differently?*

How to Host a Long Table:
This is a performance of a dinner table conversation.
Anyone seated at the table is a guest performer.
There is no beginning.
The menu is up to you.
Talk is the only course.
No one will moderate.
But a host may assist you.
It is a democracy.
To participate, simply take a seat at the table.
If the table is full, you can request a seat.
If you leave the table, you can come back again and again.
Feel free to write your comments on the tablecloth.
There can be silence.
There might be awkwardness.
There can always be laughter.
There is an end but no conclusion.

Porch Sitting[4] (2012)

Porch Sitting is an alternative model for public conversation. This project takes seriously the idea that public dialogue can happen side-by-side, rather than face-to-face in order to muse on a particular topic. Porch Sitting creates an open-ended forum supported by clear structures that draw on vernacular forms of exchange. It makes room for the things we wonder about rather than providing a platform for the things we already know. Porch Sitting is a space to sit, think, dream, or get involved in the ongoing conversation. It is ok to be quiet. It is ok to sing.

Each conversation allows for a household to divide into two areas: the kitchen and the porch. In the kitchen, you can get drinks, have a chat, or have a bite to eat. There are no rules for behavior. There is no need to leave the kitchen if that's where you're most comfortable. On the porch, conversation is sustained by a few simple rules.

This protocol inspires a gentler mode of discussion, with room for pause, welcomed tangents and a calm familiarity amongst the participants—evoking the feeling of sitting out in the quiet of the porch at the end of the evening. There is no official summation, no bullet-pointed conclusions; the conversation folds into a silence, its ending natural as bedtime.

How to Behave at a Porch Sitting:
Imagine this is a shared household.
This household might have two areas: a kitchen and a porch.
The kitchen is where you can get your drinks, your snacks, and your gossip. You can just hang out here if you want.
The Porch has a few guidelines.
- *It is where you sit, think, and dream of getting involved in the ongoing story or conversation*
- *You can come and go when and if you please. Just pay due respect to the silence or flow of conversation.*
- *Put your mind in the state of a porch sitter with phrases like:*
I wonder whatever happened to…
Who do you think that is…
I have a feelin' it's going to…
Or just about any phrase that begins:
I imagine…I wonder…I think…I feel…
Try not to worry if all goes quiet for a spell, or if it gets a bit raucous for a time, or if somebody just bursts into song.
Let everyone know how long you think you'll be sitting on the porch, and when the time comes, find a time to turn the porch light on and wish everybody a safe journey home.

Care Café[5] (2016)

The Care Café is a temporary venue for *communitas*, conversation, and activity within a spoken and visible frame of 'care'. It is a space which allows us to acknowledge social anxiety, vulnerabilities, and desire to enact and feel care. The Care Café is an open-source and unfixed protocol; it is still developing and evolving as it encounters new questions, contexts and communities. Anyone can stage their own iteration in their local arts center, church hall, shop front, or front room. The life of the project lies in the repetition, the reciprocity, and the interconnection of disparate peoples and places through the principle of care and gathering.

The Care Café re-appropriates some of the aesthetics of café culture, with the arrangement of small tables, quiet conversation and provision of shared food and drink. However, the space also acknowledges and dismantles the common social anxieties associated with these spaces: closed conversations between strangers, a school-canteen-esque difficulty in knowing where to sit and with whom.

Just by entering the Care Café, participants acknowledge something of their own vulnerability, their needs in the present moment, and their desire to give and receive care. It also allows for different kinds of conversation. Small roundtable discussions can take place concurrently, with participants moving around and engaging with other groups as the time progresses. There is room for questioning without the pressure of speaking in front of a larger group of people. And yet the proximity of the tables creates a feeling of a shared experience as conversations are overheard and bleed into one another.

The tables focus attention on a particular activity or selection of activities. These include cutting and pasting, filling envelopes, badge making, stickering, or other simple actions. They are not so demanding as to preclude conversation, but rather provide an underpinning rhythm. Moments of silence can be sustained through re-focus upon the activity, allowing for reflection, listening to surrounding conversations, and an organic shift in topic. More than anything, the Care Café is a simple space that should allow participants to take comfort in gathering without having to respond to any particular agenda or call to action.

How to Host a Care Café:

Care Café is a place – a public or domestic place for people to gather their wits, thoughts and comrades in action.

It's a place. It can be a hall, a hallway, a meeting room, or someone's living room - even the corner of a real café.

There should be chairs and ideally a table or two for sitting around and leaning on. If possible, room for people to move and mingle as well as sit and talk.

There is no specific agenda or discussion topic and the space should be kept mostly open for small group or one-to-one conversations.

Provide for food and drink. This can be an informal, potluck table that is free and open to all. It's fun to see what arrives and we can all serve and clean up after ourselves.

Music is optional. Remember that conversation is optimal.

Make available one small and somewhat mindless task of care – something that needs to be done for someone or some group - folding laundry, texting appeals, stamping mailings, cutting out cookies/art projects for kids, anything!

There is something about doing something simple and mindless with your hands that keeps the conversation gentle, slow and flowing. Having everyone engaged independently but in the same or similar activity creates both autonomy and community.

Provide a way to share resources for action, activism and care - post-its, sign-up sheets, a wall poster, bulletin board or blackboard, video diary corner.

Document and log your activity on the Care Café Facebook community page so we can stay connected and share care strategies. [https://www.facebook.com/cafeofcare]

And remember that this is primarily a state of mind that we can carry with us, asking ourselves and others daily: How can we maintain an attitude of care in such an uncaring world?

(Please see the Works Cited for further information on the sources used in this essay).

Notes

1 Over time, the exact details of the protocols have been slightly modified. The versions published here reflect wordings at the time and in consultation with the artist. See www.split-britches.com/public-address-systems-archive.
2 Ibid.

3 The Long Table was first hosted by Lois Weaver in Rio de Janeiro in 2003. Since then, the protocol has been performed in multiple locations across the world at various performance spaces, conferences, and universities.

4 The first Porch Sitting project was performed at La MaMa ETC in New York City on New Year's Eve in 2012.

5 The first Care Café was held on November 10, 2016 at La MaMa ETC in New York City following the election of Donald Trump as members of the downtown New York City community were invited to gather informally to discuss their reactions and feelings. For a full chronology, see Weaver and Maxwell.

Suggestions for Further Reading

Gillespie, Benjamin. "Detonating Desire: Mining the unexplored potential of ageing in Split Britches' Unexploded Ordnances (UXO)." *Performance Research*. 24.3 (2019): 89–98.

Harris, Geraldine. "Entertaining discussion: *The Long Table* and *Porch Sitting.*" *The Only Way Home is Through the Show: The Performance Work of Lois Weaver.* Eds. Jen Harvie and Lois Weaver. London: Intellect Press, 2015. 204–206.

Harvie, Jen. "Introduction: Welcome Home." *The Only Way Home is Through the Show: The Performance Work of Lois Weaver.* Eds. Jen Harvie and Lois Weaver. London: Intellect Press, 2015. 8–15.

Taylor, Diana. "Lois Weaver and the ethics and etiquette of the *Long Table.*" *The Only Way Home is Through the Show: The Performance Work of Lois Weaver.* Eds. Jen Harvie and Lois Weaver. London: Intellect Press, 2015. 210–212.

71 JUDITH THOMPSON (b.1954)

Erica Stevens Abbitt

Introduction

During a heady era of Canadian culture and progressive politics, Judith Thompson (b.1954) first came to national attention with her ground-breaking drama *The Crackwalker* (1980), inspired by the story of an Indigenous woman whose baby was brutally murdered. Her internationally-acclaimed plays focus on the lives of vulnerable people–often girls and young women–mixing realist settings and everyday language with intense, dream-like encounters between the marginalized and their oppressors.

A performer, artistic director, screenwriter, dramaturg, and professor of playwriting as well as a playwright, Thompson is the recipient of the Order of Canada and Governor General's Award for Drama (among many other national prizes), as well as the Susan Smith Blackburn Award for the best play written by a woman in the English language, and the Amnesty International Freedom of Expression Award.

Thompson's plays, spanning four decades, include: *Perfect Pie; White Biting Dog; Body and Soul; Borne; Palace of the End; Lion in the Streets; Habitat; Such Creatures;* and *Watching Glory Die,* among others. In 2012, she founded Rare, a Toronto-based company for theatre artists traditionally denied production opportunities. She is also known for her radio dramas, films (including *Lost and Delirious*), adaptations (such as *Hedda Gabler*) and a series of essays on her life as a theatre artist and educator.[1]

"That Stinking Hot Summer," written in 2010, is the first of three autobiographical pieces chronicling Thompson's career. In it, she recounts her rise to fame with *The Crackwalker*, which galvanized a theatre public that hardly knew what to make of its language, subject matter, and graphic scenes of violence—especially from a woman.

Thompson's coming-of-age story parallels a moment of extraordinary cultural change. Three hundred years of European domination, first by the French, and then by the British, meant that Canadians inherited deeply embedded colonial beliefs. In theatre, this led to an almost religious reverence for the works of Shakespeare and Molière and a popular taste for West End and Broadway hits. These tendencies were countered by a feisty subculture, made up of Indigenous rituals, dramas from the Irish diaspora and Francophone working-class, and military and amateur theatricals, nourishing a national talent for subversive mimicry and political satire.[2] A theatrical flowering in the 1960s and 70s produced home-grown dramas that called out British imperialism, cultural genocide, religious hypocrisy,

DOI: 10.4324/9781003006923-72

misogyny, and even homophobia.[3] The only problem was that most of the play-wrights were men.[4]

Little wonder, then, that Thompson's memoir begins with the confession: "Thirty years ago I denied being a feminist playwright" (505). When *The Crackwalker*, written "on a whim," became "a gift from the theatre gods" (506), she balked at being "marginalized" as a woman in a newly-emerging theatre scene (505).

In the end, however, this repudiation couldn't last. Thompson notes many reasons for her awakening–from her Irish background and the political achievements of her grandfather (briefly Prime Minister of Australia), to a growing belief that "history is carried in our bodies" (509). But perhaps the most telling factor was her uncanny ability to replicate voices.

This act of voicing provided Thompson with a feminist method and a mandate. As a high school student, she noticed that "[g]irls who spoke up in class were considered deranged" (508). While still at theatre school, she developed *The Crackwalker* as an acting exercise, inspired by a young woman she met during a summer job. As "an actress who was finding her own words a lot more exciting to perform than most playwrights" (507), Thompson extended the monologue into a play, finding not only fame, but a "true vocation–presenting those voices which were almost completely unheard of by the rest of the world" (508).

At the end of "That Stinking Hot Summer," Thompson expresses her passionate commitment to the radical act of finding voice. She returns to this theme in a more recent essay, "The Return" (2018), describing how a recurrence of epilepsy reminded her of the "burning need to put into words these seemingly indescribable moments" (107). In a third piece, "Inciting a Riot" (2018), she reiterates her dedication to helping young artists find their voices and "reclaim their power" (213).

In his introduction to *Judith Thompson: Critical Perspectives on Canadian Theatre in English* (2005), Ric Knowles acknowledges a wide range of approaches to her work, from Christian and radical humanism to psychoanalytic and postcolonial theory, the feminist critique of ghosting and monstrosity, troubled realism, "intercorporeal architecture" (a term coined by Kim Solga) and White representations of Native experience (vii–xiv).[5] Also worth noting is a line of feminist inquiry on voicing as provocative performance, from the writings of Sue-Ellen Case and Elin Diamond[6] on mimicry and excess to novelist Zadie Smith's recent manifesto on channeling the voice of the other in "Defending Fiction."

When Thompson trained at the National Theatre School, Canadian actors perfected British and American accents out of necessity, not choice. In the years since, she has turned the national talent for imitation from a mark of colonial yearning into a tool of resistance, giving voice to victimized school girls, incarcerated juveniles, rural housewives, urban sophisticates, Canadian immigrants, Iraqi dissidents, the disabled, and the elderly, interweaving personal experience and imagination until "she stands in their blood" (Kareda qtd. in Read 116).

"That Stinking Hot Summer" sums up forty years of feminist practice, from Thompson's realization that "[p]laywrights are girls who speak up" (509), to her assertion that "we 'senior' playwrights" are participants who also hear "new voices" (510). It is an artifact of living history, providing access to the ideas and innovations of a formidable dramatist whose generation has transformed, and continues to expand, the possibilities of contemporary theatre.

Judith Thompson

Except from "That Stinking Hot Summer" (2010)

"But *Judith* you have said emphatically that you are *NOT* a feminist writer."
"No I didn't."
"Yes you did."
"No, I did not. I wouldn't say that."
"Well you did."
"Couldn't have."
"I have the article right here."
"REALLY?"
"Would you like to see it?"
"NO! ... I didn't really ... Did I REALLY say that I am not a feminist playwright?"
"Yes, I'm afraid you did."

Thirty years ago, I denied being a feminist playwright.

I am not sure why I denied this. I now vibrate with rage when I hear a successful woman—well, ANY woman or girl—deny that she is a feminist. I can't believe I was that woman. But then again, I still ate meat then. I was intimidated by sales people and anyone in a uniform or too stylishly dressed or obviously rich, I barely knew my left from my right, I was still impressed by a British accent, I was surprised when any official or priest was exposed as corrupt, I didn't understand how electricity works, and I was afraid of flying. I still don't understand how electricity works, but the rest of that long-ago persona has been ripped off, torn to pieces, and burned. I am a new woman. I am the woman I have chosen to be rather than the woman I was constructed to be. I was ridiculously slow to bloom into myself. I'd always been late for everything, I suppose that was part of being late for myself.

   Maybe one of the reasons I denied being a feminist playwright is that I did not want to be marginalized or ghettoized. I didn't want people to think that my plays were only about feminist issues, which might keep audiences away. Even though most of the theatre audience is women—middle-aged women—they wouldn't be able to drag along their husbands if the plays were only about women.

   Although I was a different woman then, only half-bloomed, mostly unaware politically, the first play that emerged from me, *The Crackwalker* (1980), was fully formed, not juvenilia in any sense of the word. It was a kind of miracle, a gift from the theatre gods for which I will always be grateful. I didn't plan to write a play, I just started on a whim. I was all alone and very restless one weekend in Montreal, and in desperation, I dug out my roommate's typewriter and began writing scenes based on a character named Theresa that I had discovered in mask class, a character that was based on a person named Theresa I had met during a summer job as a teacher of life-skills I didn't have myself. She was one of our clients deemed "permanently unemployable"; she was also illiterate, so I tried to teach her to read and write while we walked around the charming city of Kingston, Ontario, occasionally stopping by Zal Yanovsky's new, cool café for some organic raspberry juice and a homemade carrot-poppyseed-blueberry-fig-date cookie. Many a morning I would get a call from Theresa—"I won't be doin' readin' writin' today, Judiss, I not feelin' too good"—and I would be crushed, and spend the day with other less interesting clients. In the evenings, if I was carousing with my friends in a local bar, Theresa would often appear, her face as bright as a child, and she would yell out, "I'm tellin' the social worker, Judiss, I'm telling her you drinkin'!" And strangely, even though I was already in my mid-twenties, I felt caught out, and usually turned bright red.

I just loved Theresa, and clearly she was not finished with me. And neither was the tragedy of that hot summer, when a tiny baby was murdered by his mentally delayed and emotionally deranged father, who was one of our "clients." It was August, about five minutes after nine, and I was enjoying my first takeout coffee of the day, when the phone rang:

"Kingston Community and Social Services, Judith speaking."
"Donny killed the baby."
"What?"
"He's goin' to Penetang, isn't he? He's goin' to Penetang for this."[7]

It was Bonnie, a sour-faced, doughy woman of indeterminate age who had recently had a baby with an intellectually delayed and profoundly disturbed young man named Donny. I had last seen them a few days before with their tiny premature baby, his little expressionless face uncovered, burning in the August sun. [. . .]

Donny had been furious at being denied sex by Bonnie and so he killed the baby. [. . .]

I know now that I was the vehicle for this story, the story that demanded to be told. And there I was, a willing, compliant amanuensis, a scarily good mimic who had been immersed in dramatic narrative since I was age 11, an actress who had just graduated from three always terrifying, sometimes wonderful years at the National Theatre School in Montreal, an actress who was finding her own words a lot more exciting to perform than the words of most playwrights. I loved improvisation class, I felt like I caught fire when I improvised, especially when I assumed a voice—a voice NOT my own. And so it began with the voice of Theresa, which I assumed as an actress—and that is what a playwright surely is, a hybrid, a cross between an actor/improviser and a writer.

I began as an actress. I am still an actress, even though I haven't acted in a play since Alan Ayckbourn's *Absurd Person Singular* at the Manitoba Theatre Centre in the −40°F winter of 1980, just after my father died. When I was 11, I was lucky enough to play Helen Keller in a university production that my mother, Mary Thompson, directed. At 12, I played Betty in *The Crucible*; at 15, Reenie in *The Dark at the Top of the Stairs*; at 16, Sandy in *The Prime of Miss Jean Brodie*; at 18, Lucy in *Dracula*. I played Ophelia, I played Cecily Cardew in *The Importance of Being Earnest*, and I played the Lion in *Androcles and the Lion*. I played Tennessee Williams, Ibsen, Strindberg, Shakespeare, David Mamet, Arthur Miller, the only female writer I played being Jay Presson Allen, who adapted Muriel Spark's novel *The Prime of Miss Jean Brodie* for the stage. Interestingly enough, Sandy was my strongest and most complicated performance. I understood this character, and I was able somehow to communicate my special understanding.

I did a little directing even back then, for my school: namely, *Dr. Umlaut's Earthly Kingdom* by Phyllis Gotlieb, a Canadian poet, but that was really a long poem, which Nancy Helwig, a brilliant Kingston theatre educator, adapted into a play—a play we took to the Sears Festival. An adjudicator called the text "doggerel." They did not like to hear women speaking up. The group that won the award had a beautiful blonde girl holding a real, severed, bloody pig's head onstage. Is there a stronger image of male violence? The judges were all men—no surprise!

WHERE were the female playwrights all through my youth? It appalls me that this was not even a question I asked myself. I simply accepted that the voice of drama was a male voice. I did not look for female playwrights, but I connected with those playwrights one might call "two-spirited"—which probably meant gay playwrights. I didn't even take the playwriting course that was offered by the Queen's University Drama Department. I wonder why. Maybe it was because I knew that I didn't have anything to say yet. Maybe it was because I knew somewhere in my gut that I was not going to write autobiographically, but in another way, through other voices, and I had not heard those voices yet. Maybe it was because the playwriting professor at the time was having an affair with my friend, who was 18 and had been a virgin until then. He threw her away just as fast as he had picked her up. I didn't feel I had anything to learn from an asshole like that.

When I finally began to write on that lonely weekend, it was as if meeting those vulnerable, beautiful souls at my summer job with social services released a passion I didn't know I had, gave me a true vocation—presenting those voices, which were almost completely unheard by the rest of the world. To my great joy, the voices in *The Crackwalker* continue to be heard over thirty years later, all over the world.

Something I am loathe [*sic*] to admit is that the dialogue of Mamet, the most patriarchal, butch playwright in theatre, opened my mind to the endless possibilities of dialogue, to the "okayness" of using four-letter words and letting characters talk the way they talk, only more so—of finding the music in the way people talk and cranking it up.

This essay is written as a monologue rather than an essay. It is actually the only way I can write now, and I am proud of it. I have always taught my writing and acting students that there is no right or wrong in English grammar, there is only communication. I caution them that if they want to be employable, they will probably have to learn the language of power, the grammar that is deemed to be correct. But, I tell them, don't ever believe that the language of power is in any way superior to the language you speak with your friends.

One suffocating summer, not the summer of Theresa, a group of us from Queen's University drama department formed a small company and staged our own adaptations of J. D. Salinger's short stories, plus Mamet's *Sexual Perversity in Chicago*, throughout the college town of Kingston. *Sexual Perversity in Chicago* is basically a mediocre play about young men and women who are flailing about in their sexuality, with broad, funny male characters and dead-boring female ones. We performed in nursing homes (!) and, even more inappropriately, in a medium-security prison to hundreds of prisoners who mainly wanted to persuade us that they were innocent and that they had found Jesus—they also wanted our addresses and telephone numbers. As an actor, I didn't judge the play at all, but adored the way Mamet's words just flowed out, with sentence fragments, self-interruptions, repetition, swearing—all that delicious swearing! This was a revelation to me: it's okay for characters to talk the way real people talk; I can do that, I can write the absolute gorgeousness of everyday dialogic interaction, and this luscious jazz—this can be a play!

Although I relished Mamet's crazy, true-to-life rhythmic dialogue, I was instinctively aware that he couldn't write women. All the women in his plays were just a guy's idea of the things that women said, a guy's recounting of a conversation with a woman—way off the mark. I loved playing his notes, but they never demanded that I dig deeply.

For deep digging and real women, I loved J. M. Synge's *Riders to the Sea*, which is haunting, deeply poetic, and yet so real. I relished the smash-up marriage of Strindberg's *Dance of Death*. I adored playing the crazy, incestuous, passionate, murderous Clare in Jean Genet's *The Maids*. Even though I regret and resent that my influences were all men, I believe that the female spirit in these playwrights acted as my guide.

There were very few female plays out there being produced or published. Why? Who is to blame for the dearth of women playwrights during the 1970s? Their absence in the academy and, of course, on the stages of North America? The drama professors, who did not search exhaustively enough to find great female playwriting? The producers, who left women's plays at the bottom of the slush pile? The high school drama teachers, who did not encourage girls to write plays and who did not get us to think about whose agenda we were serving? Or do we blame the women of the theatre, who were mostly drawn to the glamour of acting and sometimes, rarely, directing, most of whom did not even consider playwriting? Young women like me, who performed our personas as sweet and nonthreatening, not to be taken too seriously, and who made all statements sound like questions? In my case, ultimately, it was a case of walk softly and carry a big sword, but for a long time I didn't even know I was carrying a sword.

Girls who spoke up in class were considered deranged. Playwrights are girls who speak up. Playwrights penetrate the hearts and minds of the audience, something that is instinctively regarded as the province of men, like politics.

My grandfather was in politics all his life, even serving as prime minister of Australia for a short time after the war. My great-great-great-grandfather on my dad's side, a Carmody, was hanged by the British for speaking Gaelic and insisting upon his rights—hanged in the public square. I believe that history is carried in our bodies.

Acting is mostly passive: one is serving the text, surrendering to the vision of the director, and letting the role consume one's whole being. But playwriting—playwriting can never be passive. We must have something to say, not the odious "message" that high school students are continually e-mailing me about, but something mysterious, provocative, not entirely clear, yet able to stir up things in the audience that may have been hidden and stagnant for years—memories, frightening thoughts, anger, and truths that make us furious with their accuracy. When theatre works, it truly does hold up a funhouse mirror, but we know it is not actually a distortion, but a deeper, much more difficult truth.

I read once about a study that said that most of us are quite pleased when we look in the mirror, because we see exactly what we wish to see. When the theatre holds up its mirror, we are not in control; we have been willingly kidnapped and tied up. The play not only controls what we see, but when we see it—incrementally, suddenly, in flashes, or a slow reveal; and we will not look away from a great play, for a great play entices us and excites us enough that we cannot look away or leave the theatre, and before we know it, we have done what we have spent our lives avoiding—we have confronted ourselves.

A fiction writer I know, in refusing an invitation to a play, confessed to me that his experience in the theatre was always one of ... he didn't like to use the word "boredom," but said it was something "akin" to boredom. Frankly, I agree with him. The very serious problem with most plays, in my cranky opinion, is that they are stupefyingly boring. If one is not lucky enough to fall asleep (theatre naps can be so delicious!) or have grocery lists or long poems to compose, one can become frantic; there are so many times I have very nearly gone into a panic attack with the boredom, suddenly developing crazy-making restless-leg syndrome. And then, because I know so many people in the theatre community here, I have to, quite simply, lie my face off when I see them.

What is it about storytelling? When an actual real person tells me a story, I am never ever bored. All people possess innate storytelling skills, and when a person tells a story about something that happened to them, either that very day or many years ago, it is always, if they are telling the truth, ENTHRALLING. Maybe this is the problem, that actors are wooden and unwatchable when they are not emotionally truthful, when they are trying to be liked or trying to get a laugh or, worse, telling us what to feel. It is the very same with playwrights.

But the young playwrights who are blasting onto the stage are so very exciting: Hannah Moscovitch, Erin Shields, Anna Chatterton, Evalyn Parry, Karin Randoja, d'bi young, Anusree Roy, Nina Aquino, Charlotte Corbeil-Coleman, Marjorie Chan, and Falen Johnson. They are shouting their souls out to the world, they are full of passion, and rhythm, and exquisitely unique forms of narrative, all of them full of wit, and yet deep and ferocious.

We "senior" woman playwrights are also new voices; with every new play, our voice is fresh and renewed. Each character in each new play is a new adventure, and strong writing never gets old or tired, though it sometimes gets a little more subtle—there are certain things I would not write now that I have children. And my characters only use the F-word when absolutely necessary. This is not prudishness, but rather because I highly value those Anglo-Saxon, super-potent verbal weapons. Each play is identifiably mine, and yet each play is a world unto itself—a world seen with female eyes, written with female fingers, experienced with a female soul. My voice is not borrowed, nor has it been formed by a culture in which God is always a He. It is my voice, it is the voice of my great-great-great-grandmother, it is the voice of my daughters and my granddaughters, it is the voice of every woman I have ever known, and it will continue to speak for as long as I live and, I hope, for as long as people need the theatre.

Please see the Works Cited for further information on the sources used in this essay.

Notes

1 See Nothof's online entry on Thompson in the *Canadian Theatre Encyclopedia* https://www.canadiantheatre.com.
2 Still evident in the sketch comedy of *Saturday Night Live* and *The Royal Canadian Air Farce*.
3 See, for example, *Leaving Home, The Ecstasy of Rita Joe, Fortune and Men's Eyes* and *Les Belles Soeurs*.
4 A notable exception is feminist playwright Sharon Pollock.
5 Knowles' anthology contains essays from leading scholars on contemporary Canadian theatre and the Thompson canon. For the complete table of contents, see https://www.playwrightscanada.com/Books/J/Judith-Thompson
6 See entries on Case and Diamond in this volume.
7 Penetang is a prison for the criminally insane, located in Penetanguishene, Ontario.

Suggestions for Further Reading

Bennett, Susan, ed. *Feminist Theatre and Performance. Critical Perspectives on Canadian Theatre in English.* Vol. 4. Toronto: Playwrights Canada, 2005.

Barker, Roberta, ed. *New Canadian Realisms. New Essays on Canadian Theatre.* Vol. 2. Toronto: Playwrights Canada, 2012.

Grace, Sherrill and Albert-Reiner Glaap, eds. *Performing National Identities: International Perspectives on Contemporary Canadian Theatre.* Vancouver: Talonbooks, 2003.

"Northern Lights: Canadian Theatre Now." *American Theatre.* 29.5 (2012): 31–45.

Wasserman, Jerry. "Introduction." *Modern Canadian Plays.* Vol 1. 5th ed. Vancouver: Talonbooks, 2011. pp. 1–22.

72 CHERRÍE MORAGA (b.1952)

Lindsay B. Cummings

Introduction

Cherríe Moraga (b.1952) is a playwright, poet, essayist, and activist. A prominent voice in women-of-color feminism, Moraga began her writing career co-editing, with Gloria Anzaldúa, the groundbreaking feminist collection *This Bridge Called My Back: Writings by Radical Women of Color* (1981). In her contributions to that volume and in the career that has followed, Moraga applies the intimate lens of her experiences as a lesbian and a Xicana to offer intersectional analyses of literature and culture.[1] Key themes in her work include the repression of women's sexuality within both white and Xicanx society, the legacy of U.S. imperialism on Xicanx lives today, queer kinship and parenthood, and the decolonization of land, bodies, and minds.

Like many feminists of her generation, Moraga focuses her writing on the female body as a site of embodied knowledge. Chicana/o studies scholar Yvonne Yarbro-Berjarano observes that "Moraga's poetry constantly takes apart the entire female body, recognizing how it has been appropriated and attempting to reclaim it" (5). This is true in both a literal and a metaphorical sense, as the oppressed bodies in Moraga's writing are often bleeding, dismembered, or disabled in ways that reflect the oppressive forces of patriarchy, capitalism, and colonial legacies. As in her poetry, Moraga's plays, including *Giving Up the Ghost* (1984), *Shadow of a Man* (1988), *Heroes and Saints* (1989), *The Hungry Woman* (1995), and *Watsonville: Some Place Not Here* (1996), highlight the needs, desires, and history of Xicanas. Her plays also act as responses to the marginalization of women in the early Chicano *teatro* movement. As theatre scholar Tiffany Ana López explains, Moraga was drawn to the vision, established by figures like Luis Valdez, of a "community-oriented theatre driven by identity politics" ("Performing" 164). But like the Chicano civil rights movement, the *teatro* movement was dominated by heterosexist and patriarchal ideas. Moraga's plays, López argues, critiqued gender politics within the Chicano community while also creating room for a broader vision of that community, one that embraced queer and disabled bodies and envisioned family beyond heterosexual formations.

In the essay excerpted here, "An Irrevocable Promise" (2002, rev. 2011), Moraga describes writing for the theatre as form of embodied memory counteracting the amnesia caused by colonialism. She describes writing as fulfilling an "irrevocable promise to not forget what the body holds as memory" (Moraga "Irrevocable," 34). Bringing these memories to the stage is a political act. Repressed colonial histories can be reclaimed and past violations confronted: "theatre requires the body to make testimony and other bodies to witness it" (35).

DOI: 10.4324/9781003006923-73

These ideas resonate with a great deal of theatre and performance theory from the late 20th century. Theatre as vehicle for political testimony became widely popular in the 1990s with the documentary theatre trend. The notion of theatre as a means to transmit memory, meanwhile, is a foundational concept in the discipline of performance studies, where theatre and performance are often understood as a means to connect past and present through the human body. It is worth noting, however, that Moraga might reject both of these comparisons, much as she eschews alignment with postcolonial studies, due to their roots in Western theatrical and academic traditions. Instead, Moraga links her philosophy with that of Brazilian artist and theorist Augusto Boal (1931–2009), who understood theatre as a tool of resistance through which oppressed peoples can liberate themselves. Like Boal, Moraga finds significance in the act of live performance, in which a body brings to life the nature of its oppression as well as acts of resistance.

Throughout her work, Moraga has emphasized that political liberation movements succeed when they "walk a freedom road that is both material and metaphysical" ("A Long Line of Vendidas" 132), feeding the spirit as well as the body. In theatre, she finds "a contemporary curanderismo" ("Irrevocable" 40), a place where the wounds of historical oppression might be healed. As in many Indigenous traditions, mind, body, and world, past and present, self and other, are all intimately connected in the Indigenous practice of *curanderismo*. Theatre, Moraga suggests, has the capacity to heal the individual body because it is a place where past and present, mind and body, individual and society, meet. Theatre performs a ritual of connection: we see our own histories brought to life in the body of another, knowing we are witnessed and that our burdens are not just our own, but part of a wider social fabric. In the essay "Art in América con Acento," Moraga writes, "All writing is hunger. The longing to be known fully and still loved. [...] our overwhelming desire to be relieved of the burden of ourselves in the body of another" (61). Theatre, for Moraga, provides a place where we go to recognize and be recognized, to give body and voice to repressed pasts and intimate truths, to see those truths experienced in bodies other than our own, and to feel nourished by the sense of existing in the world.

Cherríe L. Moraga

Excerpt from "An Irrevocable Promise: Staging the Story Xicana" *(2002/2011)*

The ceremony always begins for me in the same way ... always with the hungry woman. Always the place of disquiet (inquietud) moves the writing to become a kind of excavation, an earth-dig of the spirit found through the body. The impulse to write may begin in the dream, the déjà vu, a few words, which once uttered through my own mouth or the mouth of another, refuse to leave the body of the heart. Writing is an act prompted by intuition, a whispered voice, a tightening of the gut. It is an irrevocable promise to not forget what the body holds as memory.

Writing for the stage is the reenactment of this ceremony of remembering. Experience first generated through the body returns to the body in the flesh of the staged performance. In this sense, for me, it is as close to direct political activism as I can get as an artist, for theater requires the body to make testimony and requires other bodies to bear witness to it. The question remains: bear witness to what? It is a question all Indigenous artists, the survivor-children of Euro-American genocide, must ask. And so I too ask myself most simply: what *is* the story Xicana?

As a teacher and maker of theater, I still consider the importance of the Brazilian teatrista Augusto Boal's ideas on the ways in which mainstream theater is used as a tool for political and cultural domination. In his *Theater of the Oppressed* from 1979, Boal calls for a theater practice welded and wielded as a weapon of political resistance. For me, these early writings assume even greater importance in the face of the growing cultural amnesia in América, aggravated by global capital.

I have always viewed my work as a writer in general and a playwright in particular within the context of an art of resistance or a literature toward liberation. *Toward* is the operative term here, as Xicana art and its forms are hardly free. In fact, if anything accurately describes the Xicana story, it is the site of conflict and resistance; revolt, but not revolution. Not yet. Or not ever, as at times it feels that, with the growing commoditization of Latinidad, we are moving further and further away from that requirement of resistencia in our art. Still I have never questioned the revolutionary potential in bringing the Xicana experience full-bodied to the center of the stage (and page). What I do question are the forms, the shape and structure in which that staged storytelling might be rendered. What languages do we use? What physical action? What objects are called forth? What voices? Help me remember, I ask of my dioses, what I never read and may never have witnessed but somehow know. This is the mantra of my own writing process. Help me believe I have the right to remember *and know* what at times only my troubled heart tells me to be true.

AGAINST AMNESIA

For over fifteen years now, I have wielded theater as part of my arsenal of cultural resistance as both an artist and teacher. It is not the single nor necessarily the most effective weapon I carry, but since lifted, it has impacted all the genres I endeavor, as well as my role as an educator. I came upon theater organically, out of the *spoken* voice of my first truly fictional character. I remember the day, exactly, when what had always been autobiographical writings first etched out in my journals suddenly transformed into the barrio tongue of a teenaged "cholito-style" blade-packing Mexican American girl.[2]

To say my work emerged from the oral tradition of my MeXicanismo is to tell you a simple truth: that my writings have always had bodies and as such are best rendered through the physical space of staging, even if that staging is no more than my body speaking aloud behind a lectern. The oral tradition is the only "literary legacy" about which I am completely sure, since books did not hold the first stories that held me. The rest of what I know as a playwright and a writer has been garnered, learned, assimilated. [...]

THE BODY'S PROMISE

The violation of the collective body is re-membered in these staged enactments. Here the pieces of ourselves broken by racist and colonial incursions are re-collected and reconfigured through an art of social transformation. Historical oppression is, however, at the same time experienced individually and intimately. [...]

About ten years earlier, in working with a pre-teen Latina actor, I had experienced through the staging of a scene, the visceral intimacy of oppression. In this case, the violation was a deeply private one, dependent on secrecy. It was the kind of oppression that happens behind closed doors, seldom recognized through the male gaze of the Euro-American proscenium. For the premiere of my play *Shadow of a Man*, the

Cuban American director María Irene Fornes casted an eleven-year-old girl to play an eleven-year-old girl, Lupe, who suffered an unwanted intimacy with her father.[3] Although not explicitly sexual, his habitual drunken visits to her bed for an abrazo after a night spent in the bar evoked the same childhood burden of guilt and shame that incest inspires.

I had written the scene, seen it enacted numerous times in other rehearsals and staged readings by actors sixteen years old and older, but never by a real live girl whose body balanced itself precariously and quite beautifully on the verge of puberty. So when that two-hundred-pound man playing the father dropped his drunken head onto Lupe's blanketed, eleven-year-old belly, I was not prepared for the holy terror of that moment. Although I had written the scene, I had not anticipated my own sense of revulsion, as I felt the audience gasp at the embodied experience of Lupe's vulnerability. It was exactly the effect I conjured in the words of my writings, but it took the Xicana/Latina stage to realize it in just this manner. For women in the audience, such visceral, unromantic staging made public an oppression reliant on its secrecy for its power. And, for me as a teatrista, the "conscientized" enactment of the oppressed body of this girl-child proffered, for a moment, the imagined possibility of an end to such clandestine violations.

The revolutionary promise of a theater of liberation lies in the embodied rendering of our prisons and, in the act, our release from them. I think of my teatro student, eighteen-year-old Daniel—he with the poet's heart, the delicate hands, the sharp wit of a cultural survivor. While rehearsing a performance piece he had written about the one-hundred-year legacy of machismo in his family—from Mexican miner, to revolutionary, to impassive laborer father—Daniel is suddenly overcome with tears. He breaks down right there on the stage floor. A moment later, he has quickly recovered himself, laughing nervously, "I didn't know this was gonna be therapy." But it is not therapy. "Therapy" is a privatized gringo concept that our illness is somehow individual, as is our cure. Daniel performs a history of the formation of masculinity in his MeXicano family. He is its ambivalent inheritor, as are the majority of young men I meet these days. He is involved in the art of unraveling how we all got in this mess—men estranged from women and themselves. His writing and its enactment, even beneath the shadow of Stanford's colonial archways, reflect a contemporary curanderismo. It emerges from an ancestral knowledge that a story told with the body can cure and create great warriors of heart on the cultural battlefield. "Word warriors," the author Denise Chávez has called them.[4] [...]

HOMEGROWN INSTRUMENTS OF NAMING

The stage is bare, except for several woven baskets. The music is Northern Mexican/ Southwest Indigena—antler and flauta. AMADA enters, carrying a basket under one arm. She tosses dirt from it onto the ground. She wears a serape in the style of a "sweat dress." POET digs at the earth with a shovel. It is a closing ritual as the two recall the ceremony offered to Amada upon her tragic passing.

AMADA: Was there a fire?
POET: Between us, oh. yes.
AMADA: NO, I mean... at the end?
POET: ... Blazing. I built it myself. And into it, entregamos tus faldas, tus huipiles, tus joyas of silver and turquoise. ...

Do you see it, your honoring?

AMADA: I... don't...

POET: I am just trying to do something other than theirs on this stage.

AMADA: (*After a moment*) Yes. I see it.[5]

Always in my imagination before I write, the stage is as empty as the page; always I wonder how to fill it. How to tell a story different from what has been prescribed to us: something beyond progressive plot lines, the Eurocentric "arc" of a story, and the single protagonist. Something beyond a literature that entertains Euro-American audiences by describing who we are to them with them in mind.

In the best of my imaginings, the Xicana stage would house an uncompromised story of dissent, one where the axis upon which freedom is conceived spins from a wholly alternate worldview. Spinning tales for the stage, I study I write I research I land upon the words of El Mallku, leader of the Katarino (Indigenous) movement in Bolivia: "Hay que indianizar a los q'aras" ([Whites and mestizos] must become Indianized).[6] Not the other way around, he means. And, suddenly, the ground opens up in the toiled field of my thinking.

A truly liberationist theater is not generated from some neoliberal Latin American notion of mestizaje or North American corporate-conspired definition of *multiculturalism* nor academic-inspired discourse on hybridity, nor New Age reconfiguration of indigeneity; it is one conceived by those who have been erased by the official colonial narrative. It is *our* liberationist theory assuming flesh on the América stage. It is a living art, requiring tools of our own making, our own objects, our sacred and profane practices; or maybe for us lost, queer mestizos, it is just some clumsy grasping at a precolonial language and history almost forgotten.

I have no nostalgia about some idealized original tongue that we, the thousands of tribes that make up the Xicano nation, once had. Still, I admit that as an artist not born into the educated classes, I am always protecting what may be original in me, not me alone, but the "we" of me. I am suspicious of Western thought, even as I stand here as its product. I do not naively confide in the postcolonial theory created by the colonists nor the liberation theories of my oppressors. I am both the freed slave and the enslaved. I am talking out of both sides of my mouth. I contradict and speak to you in their language, which is my language. And is not. I am the mestiza: Indian and white, more white than Indian. I have forgotten almost everything. I pick and borrow what I can to try and find my way to a manner of expression that will, from the simple vantage of an eight-year-old, stop greed. I want to turn the sign around.

Sometimes, as a writer, I feel my task comes down to the simple fact of declaring, "Sí existimos." We exist and have always been here. I remember the mother in my play *Shadow of a Man* trying to get her husband to respond to her. She cries, "Manuel, existo. Existo yo." Maybe this is the same refrain in all of my work: an insistence on a presence where the world perceives absence. Maybe this is fundamentally the project of all Xicana work: to announce our presence to one another and the world, but in our own tongue, on our own ground, brandishing our own homegrown instruments of naming. This is where the project of revolutionary teatro occurs: self-defined, self-determined, employing words and images before and beyond the colony.

BEYOND THE COLONY

The language of the Xicana story—if it were to be real—is fragmented, it is the stutter, the garbled utterance caught in the silence between tongues, tongues literally ripped from mouths. It resides in the taboo languages of the body: the vulva pressed unashamedly against a bed of dirt or the body of another woman in the effort to remember what got lost somewhere. It is a paling Odami descendant speaking through the body of Xicana performance.

Día de los Muertos, Oaxaca, Mexico, 2001.
On the last evening of a four-day encuentro between Mexican and Xicana visual artists, Celia Herrera Rodríguez[7] is to perform in the colonial courtyard of Santo Domingo, a massive cathedral-turned-cultural center. I was there among the audience beneath the moonlit, delicately clouded evening sky. I was there when that pearly disk slipped out from behind a cloud and showed herself in all her full-moon wonder. I was there when Celia threw a petate (a straw mat) the size of a beach towel down onto the cobblestoned ground and said to the mostly upper-middle-class Mexican audience, "This is what's left of my land."

Stunned silence all around. From me too. I had seen this performance several times before, but suddenly, here among the Mexicans, it is different. Suddenly we Xicanas, in one gesture of claiming, become bodies in our own right, citizens of a nation of peoples dispossessed and displaced. We are not caricatures of what could have been, neither malinchistas, nor wannabe gringas, nor vendidas-mexicanas. We are a pueblo in exile from a México Antiguo, that petate said. We are people who made our presence known in the physical body of one MeXicana and Odami woman and one damn "prop," I tell Celia later that day. She responds, "It isn't a prop," meaning the petate. And of course, it isn't. As her "performance" is not quite that. It is something else, not quite performance art, but art and performance at once. It is a story told through a single Xicana gesture and a dozen words. I don't know how she does it. I know it is not scripted, only thought about for many days in advance while washing dishes, hanging out laundry, spreading watercolor onto a piece of amate paper. It is a ritual of remembering, a kind of prayer as in ceremony. It is the Xicana stage. A land and history reclaimed.

Sí, existo. Existo yo.

Seven months later, Celia will perform in Málaga, Spain. She will take La Virgen del Carmen, a revered religious figure in Málaga, and smash the plaster statue with one fatal blow to the head. She will return the favor to Spain, smash their gods as our gods were smashed. The audience gasps, stunned. It is a brief visceral moment of historical reckoning. A truth told. But how hard it is to find that truth and give it shape. Simple. Direct. Courageous.

I am reminded of the Cuban American conceptual and performance artist Ana Mendieta, spirit-sister to Celia Herrera Rodríguez, in her effort to re-member an almost primordial rupture from the motherland. In her series "Siluetas" from the early 1980s, Mendieta created out of Cuban earth, gunpowder, and fire the silhouette of her own burning figure on the ground. Lillian Manzor writes of the artist, who died under suspicious circumstances in 1985, "Her work was an obsessive act intended to reconnect herself with the earth, to reunite herself with the ancestral origins from which she was torn apart?'[8] "From which she was torn apart." After the Cuban Revolution, as a young girl, Ana Mendieta had been sent to an orphanage in Iowa as part of "Operation Peter Pan," organized by Cuban dissidents, the Roman

Catholic Church, and the U.S. government. She was separated from her family for several years, and from a Cuban life forever.

How do we re-member rupture?

I write. It is a pitiful and necessary gesture toward something unnamed, beyond what we have been schooled to imagine.

> This, the core of the Xicana teatrista's journey:
> the effort to uncover what we don't remember,
> to use the Xicana body as a way to dig up the dirt,
> to find something of what is left of us.

Please see the Works Cited for further information on the sources used in this essay.

Notes

1 "Xicana" is the spelling Moraga chooses in the essay excerpted here and is used throughout this essay to reflect Moraga's notion of a community with indigenous heritage (Moraga, "A Xicana Lexicon" xxi). "Chicano/Chicana" is used to refer to historical movements [Cummings].

2 I refer to the character of Corky in *Giving Up the Ghost*. The play was first presented at Foot of the Mountain Theater in Minneapolis in 1984. It was directed by Kim Hines.

3 *Shadow of a Man* had its world premiere in San Francisco on November 10, 1990. It was produced by the Eureka Theater Company and Brava! for Women in the Arts. Lupe was played by Jade Power Sotomayor.

4 "Warrior Words / Word Warriors" was the theme of the tenth annual Border Books Festival, which took place in Las Cruces, New Mexico, in 2004. The phrase was coined by Chávez, a fiction writer and director of the festival.

5 Excerpt from *Digging Up the Dirt* (Albuquerque: West End Press, 2012). The play tells the parallel stories of two murders and their perpetrators. In one, Amada, who has been killed by her son, returns to reconcile this violent passing through the Poet's own scripting of it.

6 Sanjinés, Javier C. "Indianizing the Q'ara," Mestizaje *Upside-Down: Aesthetic Politics in Modern Bolivia*. Pittsburgh: University of Pittsburgh Press, 2004. 165.

7 Celia Herrera Rodríguez is a painter and installation and performance artist based in the Bay Area who teaches in the Chicano Studies program at the University of California, Berkeley.

8 Manzor, Lilliana. "From Minimalism to Performative Excess; The Two Tropicanas." *Latinas on Stage: Practice and Theory*. Eds. Alicia Arrizón and Lilliana Manzor. Third Woman Press, 2000. 382. In her mid-thirties, Mendieta fell or was thrown from the thirty-fourth-floor window of a New York apartment belonging to Carle Andre, "a well-known minimalist sculptor." Manzor states: "Carl Andre was indicted three times and finally acquitted of charges of having killed Mendieta" (373).

Suggestions for Further Reading

Bost, Suzanne. "Medicine: Cherríe Moraga's Boundary Violations." *Encarnación: Illness and Body Politics in Chicana Feminist Literature*. New York, NY: Fordham University Press, 2010. 114–150. *JSTOR*. https://www.jstor.org/stable/j.ctt13xOcg4.9

Moraga, Cherríe L. and Gloria E. Anzaldúa. *This Bridge Called My Back: Writings by Radical Women of Color*. Third Edition. San Antonio, TX: Third Woman Press, 2002.

Sternbach, Nancy Saporta. "'A Deep Racial Memory of Love': The Chicana Feminism of Cherríe Moraga." *Breaking Boundaries: Latina Writing and Critical Readings*. Ed. Asunción Horno-Delgado, et al. Amherst, MA: University of Massachusetts Press, 1989. 48–61.

73 AMAL ALLANA (b.1947)

Aparna Dharwadker

Introduction

In modern Indian theatre discourse, theoretical commentaries by practitioners have taken mainly the form of "workshop criticism" rather than systematic reflection, and the reflections have come predominantly from men. As a leading member of the post-independence generation of theatre practitioners, irrespective of gender, Amal Allana (b.1947) strongly challenges both these paradigms. Born in Bombay (now Mumbai) in the year of India's independence and trained as a director at New Delhi's National School of Drama (NSD) during the 1960s, she has produced a diverse and cosmopolitan body of directing work that includes productions of key contemporary Indian playwrights such as Mohan Rakesh, Vijay Tendulkar, Girish Karnad, Mahesh Elkunchwar, and Satish Alekar, as well as adaptations of Shakespeare, Ibsen, Brecht, Lorca, and Gabriel Garcia Marquez, all performed in Hindi, India's majority language. Allana is also an auteur, publisher, archivist, educator, and administrator (she served as Chairperson of the NSD from 2005–2013); a costume and set designer; and with her husband Nissar Allana, founder of professional groups or organizations such as The Workshop (Bombay, 1972–1975), Studio I (Delhi, 1977–1985), Theatre and Television Associates (1989–) and the Dramatic Art and Design Academy (2000–). In addition to careful documentations of the rehearsal process and Director's Notes in published programs, she has been an articulate commentator on issues of gender, identity, and intercultural performance in essay collections and prominent periodicals such as *The Drama Review* and *The Brecht Yearbook*. With *The Act of Becoming: Actors Talk* (2013), a large-format, richly illustrated 350-page compilation of materials by and about notable Indian actors from the late-nineteenth century to the present, Allana has established herself as the foremost contemporary Indian theorist of the centrality of the actor in theatre and performance.

Allana's comments on her family background and cosmopolitan upbringing in the Introduction to this compilation, excerpted here, point to an unusually complex postcolonial positioning in which her privileged Muslim heritage, metropolitan outlook, highbrow milieu, and elite theatre connections had implications for both her sense of personal belonging and her search for a viable artistic relationship to Indian theatrical modernity and performance traditions. Her father, Ebrahim Alkazi, the legendary second Director of the National School of Drama (1962–1977), belonged to a wealthy Saudi immigrant family; her mother, Roshan Padamsee, was one of India's leading costume designers and the sister of Alyque Padamsee, the actor and eminently successful Mumbai-based director of English-language plays

DOI: 10.4324/9781003006923-74

in India. Conditioned as a teenager to value "a new internationalism in the arts" and to reject popular commercial forms as vulgar and cheap, Allana arrives, through a rigorous process of professional training and self-reflection, at a qualitatively different understanding of the relationship between art and commerce in Indian theatre history, with the figure of the actor at the centre. Her "Introduction" takes a comparably measured approach to the decolonizing "theatre of roots" movement, which argued for a rejection of Western representational conventions in favor of precolonial non-urban Indian traditions. Like a number of major contemporary playwrights and directors, Allana asserts the "Indianness" of her own urban roots, and accepts as existentially valuable the syncretic fusion of East and West that in both art and life "*celebrates* hybridity, rather than shying away from it." She also notes that her conception of the director's role eventually became markedly different from that of her iconic father, indicating the generative but ambivalent ways in which her unique background has shaped her multidimensional professional accomplishments.

Beyond these issues of selfhood and creative determination, two ideas are at the core of Allana's Introduction: the performance of a fluid gender identity, and the actor's vital agency in shaping the theatrical event. The malleable and performative nature of gender came into focus most vividly for her when she cast Manohar Singh (1938–2002), the acclaimed NSD-trained actor and core member of her company, in the role of Mother Courage in *Himmat mai* (1993), a collaboratively developed Hindi adaptation of Brecht's play. As she notes, this experiment in transvestism made clearer the aesthetic of major traditional forms such as Kathakali and Noh, and connected them to the cult of cross-dressed actors such as Bal Gandharva (1888–1967) and Jaishankar Sundari (1889–1975) in *modern* urban theatre. Allana's second ambitious gender-bending production was Satish Alekar's play *Begum Barve* (1996), in which a minor cross-dressing actor from the now obsolete Marathi Sangeet Natak tradition of Bal Gandharva (played again by Manohar Singh) "marries" a repressed office clerk and imagines that he has become pregnant. Other major productions indicate the diversity of her directing work in terms of content: she has dealt with embattled domesticity in Rakesh's *Adhe adhure* ([Unfinished, Incomplete] 1976), hyper-masculinity in Vishakhadutt's Sanskrit play *Mudrarakshasa* ([The Signet Ring of Rakshasa] 1999), and essentially feminine domains in Lorca's *House of Bernarda Alba* (adapted as *Birjees qadar ka kunba*, 1980), Karnad's *Naga-mandala* ([Play with a Cobra] 1997), and Elkunchwar's *Sonata* (2002).

Allana's second argument, that "it is actors who have more or less dictated and defined the growth and development of theatre practice in India, and not really directors or writers, as is normally assumed," needs careful modulation. Major figures in late-colonial theatre, such as Girish Ghosh (1844–1912), Bal Gandharva, and Sisir Bhaduri (1889–1959), were indeed playwrights, actors, musicians, and impresarios, and as the dominant national rather than regional institution, the Parsi commercial theatre did approach play scripts as provisional blueprints for rehearsal and eventual enactment. But the "modernist revolution" of the 1950s and '60s irreversibly dismantled the colonial, commercial structures and made authorship, textuality, and the print medium just as significant to drama and theatre as the processes of rehearsal, production, and performance. Allana's position is therefore not generalizable, but as *The Act of Becoming* demonstrates spectacularly, it does reflect the all-important place of the actor in her own work as auteur, director, producer, archivist, and theorist. Fittingly, then, her most celebrated production is *Nati Binodini* (2007), a theatrical tour de force dealing with the career of the celebrated Bengali actress Binodini Dasi and her life-defining relationship with her mentor, director and fellow actor Girish Ghosh.[1]

Amal Allana

Excerpt from "Introduction" to **The Act of Becoming: Actors Talk** *(2013)*

The story of contemporary Indian theatre as performance needs to be narrated primarily through visual documentation, as it then clarifies and illustrates the trends of performance that have evolved and developed from the 1840s onwards [...]. Contemporary theatre seen as practice has been a neglected area for a number of reasons, including the fact that scholarship on Indian theatre in general tends to regard practice as an offshoot of playwriting, with academics tending to focus on productions being "interpretations" of play-texts, rather than assessing them independently within the changing parameters of newly evolving performance aesthetics. In a scenario where newer forms of theatre have rapidly moved on to being extensions of and fusions with other media like the visual arts, music, dance, and, of course, cinema and video, or vice versa, it becomes clear that the discourse on theatre practice in general, and acting in particular, requires theatre to be seen as an evolving, multidisciplinary art form. [...]

[...] More specifically my interest is in the thoughts, ideas, and lives of actors, of the performers themselves. Therefore I began to piece together the history of Indian theatre primarily through first-person accounts of actors themselves. This way history becomes alive, real. The words of actors are valuable because they are laden with layers of felt and lived experience. Actors may not have the facility of using words and phrases as precisely as academics, but they have a directness and energy that conveys the spirit and passion of their preoccupations. So, in a sense this book is an assemblage of oral histories, memories, confessions of actors (and sometimes directors about actors) about the way they feel about their work, their working conditions, their careers, and their lives [...]. These accounts by actors are fascinating, because they carry the amazing, bristling energy of people who are in the "act" of creating something, making history, so that the story of contemporary Indian theatre then is seen to be in a constant state of "becoming" [...] realising itself as a kind of performance of itself!

As one moves through the book, across a span of some 150 years, one becomes acutely aware that entire generations of the founding fathers of Indian theatre were primarily actors. Actors have been writers, actors have been directors, actors have been managers! Only about a third of the actors discussed in this book have singularly pursued acting alone, whereas two thirds have played multiple roles. This means that it is actors who have more or less dictated and defined the growth and development of theatre practice in India, and not really directors or writers, as is normally assumed. This possibly accounts for contemporary Indian theatre directly evolving on stage as it were, as practice. From the very beginnings of the movement, performances did not evolve from page to stage; rather, roles were written with specific actors in mind, while writers scribbled dialogues or lyrics sitting in on all rehearsals. Thus it was not literary play texts, but actual performance texts that were created for theatre companies by persons like Girish Chandra Ghosh.[2] Regarded as the father of modern Bengali theatre, Girish Ghosh, for example, wrote plays, as well as directed and acted in them. Bal Gandharva was not only a brilliant actor/singer in a new genre of operatic theatre called the Natya Sangeet form, but was also the owner of one of the largest theatre companies of Maharashtra, the Gandharva Natak Mandali. He commissioned plays, managed an enormous company of over a hundred employees, organised tours, and supervised sets and costumes—all of which contributed to his eminence [as] a practitioner who was remarkable not only for his histrionic and singing talents, but one who contributed enormously to the movement as a whole.

The organisational and histrionic skills of such eminent actors were combined with their intellectual capacity to rapidly absorb new ideas of dramaturgy, staging and technology from the West, and immediately transform and remodel them with creative inventiveness, into a genre of socially instructive, politically conscious, highly appealing and engrossing theatre that was essentially *Indian* in its sensibility. It is this quality of eclectic playfulness and creative inventiveness then, that characterised much of the new, popular urban theatre evolved in the 19th century that one found compelling. In its response to new, Western ideas, it suggests an attitude that *celebrates* hybridity, rather than shying away from it. In this respect it is not dissimilar to a postmodern approach. [...]

[...] I had grown up in a family and an environment that was cosmopolitan in outlook, English speaking, and one that at that time totally debunked and rejected this genre as "commercial" theatre activity. The generation of "progressive"/internationally-aware artists who were among the young intellectuals, be they dancers, theatre artists or painters, viewed all forms of "popular" art or "bazaar" art, as "cheap," "tawdry," "vulgar" and "crass." The Hindi films were also regarded as part of this subculture, and so "we" were never encouraged to see "Hindi" movies! Commercial theatre and commercial films were regarded as "impure," lowly forms that did not deal with subjects or aesthetics that "meaningful" art aspired to. For art of any variety to pander to "popular" tastes was deemed unseemly.

Ideas such as these were commonly held by the artists and actors who regularly visited our home. Instead they actively supported a new internationalism in the arts that was winning worldwide attention. It was global and inclusive in nature and was in protest against divisive and exploitative forces that had been responsible for colonialism, exploitation, and the devastation caused by the two world wars.

However, a decade and a half later, I shifted from Bombay to Delhi along with my parents. By the mid-1960s Indian theatre workers, in a postcolonial bid to reassert their cultural identity, vehemently refuted, overturned, and rejected the influence and impact of Western theatre and its aesthetics on Indian theatre. Instead they made a major bid to embrace and reforge links with Indian folk theatre traditions in the cause of supporting an "Indian" modernity.

By virtue of belonging to a theatre family I was not only witness to heated discussions around the dinner table by artist friends and my parents, regarding the pros and cons of these systemic shifts in the theatre movement, but as my own career as a theatre director intensified, I began to question the impact of these constant readjustments on my own work. It was clear that I was the next generation and that my preoccupations centred around different issues of identity.

I became increasingly conscious that as an urbanised, postcolonial Indian, I was intellectually a product of two cultures, both Indian and Western, and that I could not lay claim to a single, monolithic, "Indian" identity. The "back to roots" movement of the 1970s intensified my sense of shame of not belonging, of being suspended in a kind of no-man's land. It took me some time to admit, even to myself, that I was no thoroughbred, blue-blooded, "traditional" Indian. My ancestors did not hark back to some remote village in India that had its own folk theatre traditions intact that I could retrieve. In fact, I was genuinely of mixed parentage, Arab and Indian. I was born and brought up in Bombay, I went to a Protestant School and I spoke English at home! I had to accept that I was a hybrid, one of bastardised identity. These were the facts of my birth and my circumstances. So was I not to be regarded as a true "Indian"? Were other urban Indians such as myself not Indians?

Questions such as these preoccupied me from the 1970s onwards, as at that time I was surrounded by a movement on the part of theatre people to virtually reassert their "Indianness" by returning to tradition in order to validate their authenticity as being culturally rooted. The shrill and strident voices that were vehemently rejecting the Western theatrical legacy, invalidating its usefulness, did not entirely convince me. I did not feel that it was possible to erase its footprints entirely. I gradually realised that what I was searching for was perhaps a more integrated, intercultural approach, an approach that is at the core of our postmodern culture.

As a postcolonial director, then, what I needed to construct for myself was a performance language that would indeed reflect my cultural *instability*, the instability of the postcolonial, my inbetweeness, my *lack* of belonging to any culture/language/ethnic group, specifically. In theatrical terms this was ultimately translated into my attempting to create a constantly *shifting, vacillating identity* on stage, one that would dynamically reflect my constant state of *uprootedness*. So, unlike those before me who were searching for rootedness, I needed to assert my *lack* of it. [...]

[...] Although from the 1970s to the early 1990s my productions from Brecht's *A Man's a Man* (1971) through till *The Good Woman of Setzuan* (1973 and 1984) dealt with themes that exemplified this uneasy state of the divided self, it was finally in 1993, with the casting of Manohar Singh, a male actor, in the role of Brecht's *Mother Courage*, that the divided self theme manifested itself as one of dual gender in my work. For me this was crucial, as I had finally found an "image," a visual marker, that contained the sense of a fragmented identity that I wished to foreground. A man playing a woman was expressive *both* of my uneasy postcolonial cultural identity, as well as my predicament of being ill at ease with a single, stereotypical feminine identity as a woman.

Once I understood that a man playing a woman is in essence the "performing of gender," I realised that I belonged to a theatre tradition that essentially foregrounds performativity as a metaphor, a symbol. With this understanding I suddenly felt connected to an entire universe of Indian performing traditions. Doors opened up, leading me to older performance traditions like Kathakali, Noh, and Kabuki, in which gender was performed. More importantly I wanted to know more about the beginnings of the modern movement in theatre; where the interface between "presentational" styles and "representational" styles had taken place; where the cross-over from actor as symbol to actor as actual embodied character took place in the mid-19th century. When famous female impersonators like Jaishankar Sundari and Bal Gandharva continued the older tradition of men playing women, they simultaneously tried to portray female characters in palpably recognisable renderings under the influence of Western naturalism [...]. More than the realistically conceived sets painted in receding perspective, more than the reality of the social, everyday contemporary themes that were introduced in this era, it was in the uncanny ability on the part of great male actors to accurately portray the woman, in detailed psychological as well as physically accurate terms, that the "illusion" of theatre as "reality" was most intensely and effectively realised.

For me this was a supremely historic moment in theatre, where Indian theatricality was effectively married to Western realism, where the East and West met and fused together seamlessly, but interestingly where there was a frank acknowledgement of the act of impersonation. I was very keen to mark this first encounter between East and West, and examine it more closely, as it constituted the very roots of modern theatre in this country. [...]

[...] Over the years, my husband Nissar and I have established several theatre groups–The Workshop in Bombay in the 1970s, and Studio 1, Theatre and Television Associates, and Dramatic Art and Design Academy in New Delhi in the 1980s– through which we have mounted no less than sixty productions to date. All this has given me a firsthand experience of the precarious nature of a theatre career, as well as the opportunity of working with scores of actors [...]. It is important to note here that it has been actors more than others whom I have chosen as collaborators in devising scripts both for the stage as well as for my TV work. This is obviously because, ultimately, I lay great store on the performative outcome of the text. For *Mahabhoj* (1982), *Erendira* (2003), and *Nati Binodini* (2007), my entire team of collaborators was my actors. In plays like *Himmat Mai* (1993), and *King Lear* (1989),[3] although credit for the adaptations was given to Neelabh, not a single script session went by without Manohar Singh's interventions and suggestions. It was, in fact, Manohar's suggestion to use a Himachali accent as a performative device to play the female Himmat Mai that radically altered the entire translation of the text, providing us with a clue as to where we could geographically and historically locate the action in an Indian context. This called for an entire reworking of the translation. A colourless Hindi was replaced with a richly textured variety of dialects, which gave an epic sweep to Himmat Mai's journey across a war-torn landscape, interacting with a wide cross section of people speaking different dialects.

Having allowed actors into that sacrosanct space reserved for the so-called high priest of theatre, the captain of the ship, so-to-speak, my ideas about my role as the director began to alter substantially. To begin with, I felt this role had to be more democratic. As the director I had to shift from being the overall interpreter/ designer, the single auteur of the piece, someone in total control of all aspects of the production, to one who was more sympathetic, more nurturing in his or her leadership of the ensemble. The whole team had to recognise that we were essentially collaborators. I stopped telling my actors what to do.... I had to rethink the efficacy of my father's example as a director for myself and, in a sense, I gradually came to reject that role model and began to trust my own (feminine?) instincts. Through the years the collaborative process has become integral to my work and I enjoy working with actors as extremely gifted and creative equals. [...]

[...] It became increasingly clear that it was now imperative for the same group of people to work together continuously, in order to fully develop and extend the kind of explorations we were undertaking during rehearsals. Eventually a team of about seven to eight members solidified into our core group. This same group has explored the idea of the performativity of gender, over a period of several years, beginning with *Himmat Mai*, through *Begum Barve* (1996), *Nagamandala* (1998), and

Mudrarakshasa (1999), to *Erendira* (2003) and *Nati Binodini* (2007). Despite the lack of financial support, our team has, by and large, stayed together this entire period, with the grave exception of Manohar Singh who passed away in 2002, but who continues to inspire us with his very real presence in everything we do. It is for this reason that I salute him and dedicate this book to his memory.

Please see the Works Cited for further information on the sources used in this essay.

Notes

1 See excerpt from Binodini Dasi's autobiography, *Amar katha* (My Story, 1912), included in this anthology.
2 Ghosh wrote about eighty plays, directed and acted in them, and managed the Great National Theatre and the Star Theatre in Calcutta from 1874 until the late 1880s.
3 *Mahabhoj* (The Great Feast) is a stage adaptation of the eponymous novel by Mannu Bhandari, a leading female author in Hindi. *Erendira* is an adaptation of Gabriel Garcia Marquez's short story. See Introduction above.

Suggestions for Further Reading

Allana, Amal. "Staging *King Lear* in India, 1989: King Lear as the Indian Maharaja." Interview with Balwant Gargi. *TDR: The Drama Review: The Journal of Performance Studies*, 35. 3 (1991): 93–100.

———. "Gender Relations and Self-Identity: A Personal Encounter." *Muffled Voices: Women in Modern Indian Theatre*. Ed. Lakshmi Subramanyam. New Delhi: Har-Anand Publications, 2002. 165–192.

———. "Brecht: A Participant in the Process of Nation-Building." *The Brecht Yearbook*. 36 (2011): 27–43.

———. "Released into the Future: (Re)Claiming Brecht in India." *The Brecht Yearbook*. 42 (2018): 121–135.

Dharwadker, Aparna Bhargava. *A Poetics of Modernity: Indian Theatre Theory, 1850 to the Present*. New Delhi: Oxford University Press, 2019.

Roy, Madhumita. "Actresses on the Bengali Stage: Nati Binodini and Moyna: The Present Re-Imagines the Past." *Rupkatha: Journal on Interdisciplinary Studies in the Humanities*. 3. 4 (2011): 514–529.

74 NAOMI WALLACE (b.1960)

Lindsay B. Cummings

Introduction

Naomi Wallace (b.1960) believes in the transformative power of transgression. In her plays, characters challenge the social and political boundaries that structure their worlds, trying on new identities and behaviors like actors in a play. Ghosts transverse time and space, rendering visible the repetitions of history. Unlikely lovers violate social norms to forge intimate connections. Through acts of trespass, her characters analyze the world and their place in it, discovering new ways of being. Theatre, for Wallace, is a space designed to defy borders, locate echoes of the past in the present, and map connections between people, times, and places.

Originally a poet, Wallace began writing plays in the 1990s, finding that she enjoyed the collaborative work of theatre. Like many U.S. writers of the period, in her early plays, including *The War Boys* (1993), *In the Heart of America* (1994), and *One Flea Spare* (1995), Wallace explores the way identity shapes one's experience of the world. Her distinct style blends Brechtian-influenced historical materialism with a focus on the body as a locus of political knowledge. Scott T. Cummings observes, "In order to dissect the body politic, Naomi Wallace writes plays about the politics of the body" ("Naomi (French) Wallace"). Her characters often bear wounds and scars inflicted through their interactions with capitalism and imperialism. Hers is a politics, in the words of director Ron Daniels, "experienced in the flesh" (196). On this subject, Wallace asks, "What could be more intimate than the history of our bodies and their relationship to the world?" ("On Writing as Transgression" 101).

Wallace embraces her identity as a political playwright, which places her in the tradition of writers such as Bertolt Brecht (1898–1956), George Bernard Shaw (1856–1950), Edward Bond (b.1934), Caryl Churchill (b.1938), and Tony Kushner (b.1956), who was an early advocate of Wallace's work. Her politics frequently emerge through explorations of history, where she finds much of her inspiration. Her play *Things of Dry Hours* (2004) is based on Robin D. G. Kelley's book *Hammer and Hoe: Alabama Communists During the Great Depression; The Liquid Plain* (2013) was inspired by Marcus Rediker's *The Slave Ship: A Human History*. More recently, she has been writing about Palestine and the history of conflict in the Middle East, drawing on research, travel, and what her co-author Ismail Khalidi calls "a natural aversion to the imperial gaze" (212).[1]

Overall, Wallace's work reflects her belief that writers' "voice and vision are forged by looking outward instead of inward" ("Radical Vision and Form"). She frequently calls for playwrights to work outside their immediate sphere of experience, writing across gender, sexuality, race, and nationality. In the essay excerpted here, she

DOI: 10.4324/9781003006923-75

remarks, "Writing that does not actually violate boundaries, that does not enter into the process of trespass, is often a writing that is safe, consumable and shallow." Writing about others is, of course, "a risk and a responsibility," especially for those in positions of privilege, who must consider the long history of white artists representing cultural others in ways that stereotype, erase, and diminish them. It is an act to be undertaken through research, empathy, engagement, listening, and humility; even then it should not always be done. Wallace urges writers to ask themselves how their work fits into social, economic, and political power structures: "[T]o what purpose, in whose interest am I (are you) writing?" (Wallace, "On Writing" 98). For Wallace, writing outside one's experience can augment this critical work, expanding our perspective and challenging our privileges and beliefs.

These assertions place Wallace in the midst of the longstanding tension between theatre's capacity to bridge difference and the ways that capacity has been used as an excuse to limit voices of color. Aspects of this tension inform the famous "Wilson-Brustein Debate" of 1996–1997[2] and appear again in 2020's open letter "We See You, White American Theater," condemning U.S. theatre's ongoing failure to address racism. A corresponding statement of demands calls for hiring BIPOC writers, directors, and designers: "Understand that you cannot tell stories about us without us. We must be centered in the telling of our own stories. Get out of the way so we can thrive" ("BIPOC Demands for White American Theatre"). Wallace understands that empathetic engagement is not a substitute for more fundamental changes:

> As theatre folk, we can and must strive to create a multiracial, cross-class movement that centers people of color's leadership to subvert the status quo workings of our theatre world (and not just by achieving diversity quotas in casting, for instance). U.S. theatre is overwhelmingly, at times blindingly, white, not only in terms of who makes decisions and who fills the (generally very expensive) seats, but in its core politics and worldview.
>
> (Wallace and Khalidi 42)

For the white writer, is the purpose of writing others fundamentally a means to combat ignorance and, as she writes here, "revive our own humanity"? Perhaps. Ultimately, Wallace promotes a vision of theatre as a space of hospitality. Hospitality, she reminds us, comes from the Latin "to entertain," meaning to amuse, but also "To receive, admit, take in" ("entertain, v."). A theatre of hospitality is "one that gives, that offers pleasure and nourishment; but it is also a theatre of consideration, that is open to ideas, others, dissident selves." It is a theatre that entertains more voices, more points of view, more transgressions—a theatre that opens its doors, literally and figuratively, to let the right one in.[3] Who is the right one? Looking to Wallace's dramaturgy, the answer is usually someone quite different from ourselves—unexpected, perhaps even the feared—who unleashes new possibilities into the world.

Naomi Wallace

Excerpt from "Let the Right One In: On Resistance, Hospitality, and New Writing for the American Stage" (2013)

ALL WRITING FOR THE THEATRE IS IN SOME SENSE AN ACT OF VIOLATION. By this I mean that when we enter into the lives of others and try to imagine a perspective that is not our own, we have to push through what we know, what we are sure of, what we value—push into the very skin of another life and vision. Sure, that's common sense for a writer, but mainstream theatre does not generally enter into the lives and bodies of those we consider "strangers"; more often than not it bounces off the barriers, contenting itself with the safe and recycled materials of stereotype (albeit refreshed for the present moment), cliché and hearsay. Writing that does not actually violate boundaries, that does not enter into the process of trespass, is often a writing that is safe, consumable and shallow. A theatre that does not challenge its own assumptions, its own ignorance, with curiosity and humility is a contracted theatre, a diminished theatre.

And in these harsh and difficult days, when we are afraid of losing what we have, afraid of losing what we almost had, afraid of getting what we've always feared, we make choices. Playwrights make choices. About who enters their stages. Who gets the light and who gets only a glancing view. Who stays around and has the last word, the best word, and who is at the center of the joke. The center of love or humiliation. We are encouraged to fear the outsider, the one at the edge of our stage, the In/spectre at the door.

And here, I am not summoning the overly esoteric otherness in the philosophy of Emmanuel Levinas, the stranger who shatters and consumes us, but rather noting the ones who enter the landscapes of our stage, and the ones who are refused its geography. If, as Terry Eagleton says, "Neighborhood is a practice rather than a locality," we must investigate the neighborhoods of our theatre and highlight what is rendered invisible: Who is missing, who is spoken for and who is unmentionable. How does the policing of these "neighborhoods on stage," through our selves and/or our institutions, perpetuate a retracted, redacted and inhospitable theatre?

Coming into stories that we are not familiar with, entering into bodies and genders that are not our own, is a risk and a responsibility that I believe is often taken too lightly, if taken at all. For example, white playwrights, over many decades, have rarely given a second thought to creating characters for black Americans. Our conscious and unconscious sense of entitlement, our skin privilege, our general and often nursed ignorance, have created a legacy of demeaning, shallow and stereotypical portraits of African Americans and other people of color on stage. Considering the damage that white writers have done, one might come to the conclusion that it's best for white writers to stick to writing for white folks. Too much damage otherwise. And yet I believe that all of us must take the risk to represent anyone and everyone.

But why focus on imagination and its power to violate and trespass? Am I not in danger of advocating a sort of colonization, given that violation also signifies the oppression of one by another? Why not stick with what we know? Write about what we know? Well, certainly there is a place for that. Especially for the stories of those artists and their communities who have not been welcomed onto the American stage but have had to forge a space for themselves there: black artists, Asian American, Latino, Native American, Arab American and others. However, mainstream American theatre is still largely a white, middle-class endeavor—and, in being so, is not really an "American" theatre, but a specialized, illusionary theatre.

So how do we pillage the material of our own lives to find our connection to the larger historical and social forces swirling around our heads, if not inside them? The important word here is find rather than create. Because these connections already exist. The goal is to uncover these live wires, no matter how buried or twisted. The trick is to tap into these lines and charge up our imaginations.

Hospitality plays an important role in Shakespeare. One of drama's worst hosts, Macbeth, is thus because of his appetite for self-serving power. While a victim of inhospitable forces, King Lear comes to disregard power and embrace the out/cast as well as a more egalitarian world:

> Expose thyself to feel what wretches feel,
> That thou mayst shake the superflux to them
> And show the heavens more just.

In thinking about hospitality, we'll need to consider not only whom we welcome onto the stage but how in our writing we might cross the divide between our own personal experiences and that of others, from our own sexuality to that of another sexuality; our own race to that of another race; our own class and gender to that of another class or gender.

First, let us recall that hospitality derives from the Latin "hospitare"–to entertain. This neatly encapsulates the type of theatre I believe we strive for: one that gives, that offers pleasure and nourishment; but it is also a theatre of consideration, that is open to ideas, others, dissident selves. The tradition of the unexpected guest who provokes a revelation, if not a reconfiguration of the familiar, is well worn. But as in J.B. Priestley's *The Inspector Calls*, I would like to take this tradition a step further: The Other and ourselves should not be seen as the foreign facing off against the familiar.

As the inspector shows, we already know the unknown even if we didn't know we knew it (shades of Donald Rumsfeld there—apologies). My point is this: We are already and always complicit, interconnected and related to the stranger, the Other, the unfamiliar.

I GREW UP IN KENTUCKY. Unlike most Kentuckians, I grew up with privilege. My father, Henry, was a journalist and, as he liked to refer to himself, a "gentleman-farmer." I was raised on a small cattle farm which, while rarely breaking even, was kept going by the sizeable inheritance bestowed on my father. Even though my mother, Sonia, was Dutch working class and educated me in class consciousness, I grew up in an idyllic pastoral landscape.

But over the hill and not so far away, there lived two different communities. One was white working class, the other black working class. They were my neighbors. I slept in their houses. I ran with their children. I kissed their boys. I fell in love with their girls. But the most fruitful thing I did was shut my mouth in the presence of the adults of these families. And I listened. I listened to their dinner chat, their courtesies, their hopes, the vulnerability of their fears that they exposed to me because as long as I was a child, I was still harmless. I hadn't yet stepped into my full privilege of class and skin.

And it was here that I learned most intimately about the magic and seduction of the American dream. In one of these communities over the hill, I found a pick-up-truck-driving boyfriend named Jay. Jay's father had fought in Korea and he'd been poisoned by the tin food rations that were distributed to troops by the U.S. government. The poison had corroded his lungs. He had one lung removed, then another half. But this man, Mr. Aldridge, continued to work. I remember a few years later—when I'd lost contact with both Jay and his family—stopping by the local restaurant. There I saw Mr. Aldridge sitting in the corner with a paper cup of coffee and a cigarette. I was taught to be a polite young woman, so I sat with him some moments to say hello. Already he was dying, though he did his best to ignore it. But he asked me a question that I have never forgotten. He said, "How is it that I have worked hard all my life and still I have nothing?" I didn't have an answer. My own father had two lungs. And we didn't have "nothing." We had a lot of things.

[...]

We are responsible for the education of our imaginations, for its focus and direction. We must ask ourselves: Whom and what does my imagination serve? Where will I urge my mind to venture and roam, and to what purpose? As Edward Bond, in his *Theatre Poems and Songs*, puts it:

> How is society organized?
> For the happiness of the people?
> Or so that profit can be drawn
> At as many points as possible?

What childhood experiences like knowing Mr. Aldridge relayed to me is that there is something seriously and morally wrong with an economic system that nurtures the few rich and powerful, and diminishes and devours the rest. It is not for lack of effort, will power, or moral fiber that so many have been left broken, impoverished and afraid, but the fault of a racist and classist social system designed to have the majority struggling and a minority living in the lap of luxury.

Again, I come back to the question: How do we resist the temptation to write it safe? How do we as artists engage with the most urgent questions of our time? With oppression and injustice here within our turbulent home? How do we engage with war without fetishizing it?

As playwrights we need, I would suggest, to become detectives, inspectors and investigators into our own privilege and power, our culpability, our closing of the door. When we write, we can investigate the unseen, the disremembered. We can cultivate a hospitality toward dissent rather than a nurtured contempt for truth. We can do the hard work of inquiring into history, both immediate and past, both near and remote, with seriousness, imaginative thinking, playfulness, curiosity and a ruthless, carnivalesque sense of hope. We must do research. If possible, we should travel and talk to others. We read and reread and digest and consider. We imagine. We imagine some more. We listen. And then, if we're lucky, we write something that "entertains."

TO GO BEYOND OURSELVES. To imagine the worlds of others, is always a worthwhile endeavor. With all the obvious and discomforting flaws, we are still grateful for Othello, Lady Macbeth and Shylock. As we are grateful for the engaged, radical stages created by such a wealth of writers as Kia Corthron, Tanya Barfield, Young Jean Lee, Richard Montoya, Caridad Svich, Ismail Khalidi, Roger Guenveur Smith, Basil Kreimendahl, Yussef El Guindi, Quiara Alegria Hudes, Mike Geither, Betty Shamieh and Kwame Kwei-Armah, to name just a few. And to keep hope alive, we have the Oregon Shakespeare Festival's courageous American Revolutions: The United States History Cycle, a 10-year program commissioning up to 37 new plays sprung from moments of change in U.S. history;[4] New York Theatre Workshop and its continuing creative interaction with its associate company, the Freedom Theater of Jenin;[5] CENTERSTAGE of Baltimore's daring social media project, My America;[6] and Michael Dixon's New Play Project at Minneapolis's Guthrie Theater, which encouraged playwrights to explore a wider cultural representation in their plays, and to travel to Liberia, Cambodia, Turkey, Korea, the Occupied Palestinian Territories and other neighborhoods coming to a city near you.[7]

Let me be clear here: There are a thousand ways we can trip and flounder when we enter into writing about experiences far from our own. We might fail to honor the complicated humanity of another. We might find that cliché sneaks into our path and we stand on it and build from there. We might, simply, miss the boat. To aid us in this challenge, we might stay alert to the corrective that Edward Said suggests in his *Humanism and Democratic Criticism* (and here I will substitute the word "playwright" for "intellectual," for we are both): The playwright should be "a kind of counter memory" with his or her "own counter-discourse that will not allow conscience to look away or fall asleep. The best corrective … is to imagine the person you are discussing"–or writing about—"in this case the person on whom the bombs will fall—reading you in your presence."

We live in increasingly inhospitable times. Fanning anti-immigrant hysteria, racism, and increasing attacks on the poor, unions and women's health are part and parcel of the voracious and reactionary program which distorts our understanding of the world and our place in it, and is rapidly dismantling civic society: undermining our libraries, disappearing our public spaces, threatening our schools and the right to free education. All the necessary public places where we fall in love with the world, and one another, free from the fundamentalism of the profit-motive.

Inhospitality is about tending one's own garden and locking the gate; it's about greed and fear. NIMBYism as a life philosophy.[8] Mainstream culture suffocates our awareness of the inherent connection, however tenuous, between you and me. Between L.A. and Afghanistan. Between Kentucky and Sudan. Between Jenin and New York. Between Pakistan and Cleveland. Between you and you and you.

[…]

We must meet the perversion of human intellect for the benefit of war and oppression with a creative force, a theatrical force that challenges, interrogates and disorientates. Or, in more poetic terms, do as Keats suggests, and be "awake for ever in a sweet unrest." Unrest. Yes, that's where the sweetness, the sexiness, the seriousness makes things happen on stage by speaking truth to that most inhospitable terrain of human thriving: global capitalism.

That is all to say that we should aspire to be interested writers. Interest: a word too often hijacked by finance. The Latin prefix inter means between or among; also mutually, together. Thus interact, interrelate and international. Wonderful injunctions for writers. As if describing engaged and challenging writing, the Latin word *interresse* means "to concern, be of importance," and, here's the kicker, "to make a difference." Break interest down, it means basically inter—"between" and esse—"to be." To live between. To live between self and world, self and others, ourselves, our others, our histories, their histories. Sure, our own stories are occasionally interesting, but what I am talking about is connecting our everyday experiences to a world view, the longue duree, the grand narrative, the big picture.

The myth of free enterprise is that we are independent of one another, that we flourish in the me, mine and myself. But ultimately we are social beings and we need each other to understand ourselves and history. The stranger at the door is there so that we may realize that the stranger is also us. That hospitality, on the stage and off the stage, is what enriches, challenges, haunts and articulates our lives.

When we cross boundaries, when we violate our own skin to know the heartbreak or hope or resistance of another, what we come closer to, surprisingly, is ourselves. Because through imaginative empathy, we revive our own humanity. So, to put it simply, we must be where we are not, because if we look down we will see that we are already there, here, among those we are encouraged to believe are strangers. Who suddenly are no longer strangers.

Please see the Works Cited for further information on the sources used in this essay.

Notes

1 Wallace and Khalidi collaborated on a stage adaptation of Ghassan Kanafani's novella *Returning to Haifa,* which premiered at Finborough Theatre in 2018.
2 For an analysis of this controversy, see Catanese, *The Problem of the Color [blind]* chpt. 2.
3 The title of her essay alludes to the Swedish horror film *Låt den rätte komma in* (*Let the Right One in*), which poses questions about the dangers and pleasures of inviting others into our lives. Personal communication. 8 Aug. 2020.
4 Oregon Shakespeare Festival launched this initiative in 2008. Wallace's *The Liquid Plain* was produced as part of this series in 2013 ("American Revolutions").
5 The Freedom Theatre of Jenin, which promotes cultural resistance through art, was founded in 2006 in the Jenin refugee camp in the occupied West Bank of Palestine. The New York Theatre Workshop hosted The Freedom Theatre in both 2011 and 2013. In 2016, however, they withdrew their support for a New York production of *The Siege* as a result of public controversy over the piece, which depicts the siege on the Church of the Nativity in Bethlehem in 2002. In response, NYU's Skirball Center for the Performing Arts hosted the production. See "Friends of the Jenin Freedom Theatre" and Pursell.
6 Part of Center Stage's 50th anniversary season in 2012, this digital project, conceived by Artistic Director Kwame Kwei-Armah, consisted of 50 three-minute monologues by well-known U.S. writers on the topic of "My America." Many of the monologues were later gathered into a film. See McCauley.
7 Invited by the Guthrie to write for this initiative, Wallace collaborated with U.S. writer Lisa Schlesinger and Palestinian writer Abdelfattah Abusrour on *Twenty One Positions: A Cartographic Dream of the Middle East,* a play about wall built by Israel in the West Bank. Ultimately, the Guthrie did not follow the play through to production. See Wallace and MacDonald.
8 NIMBY is an acronym for "not in my backyard," a term originating in the late 1970s in response to questions over public health and the disposal of hazardous waste. See McGurty. The term has seen expanded usage to encompass any efforts to restrict development unwanted by a community, for economic, social, or other reasons.

Suggestions for Further Reading

Bigsby, Christopher. "Naomi Wallace." *Twenty-First Century American Playwrights.* Cambridge: Cambridge University Press, 2017. pp. 194–220.
Cummings, Scott T. and Erica Stevens Abbitt, eds. *The Theatre of Naomi Wallace: Embodied Dialogues.* New York, NY: Palgrave Macmillan, 2013.
Naomi Wallace. "Interview with Alexis Greene." *Women Who Write Plays: Interviews with American Dramatists.* Ed. Alexis Greene. Hanover, NH: Smith and Kraus, 2001. 449–471.
———. "We Are Also Each Other." *American Theatre* 20.6 (July/August 2003): 71.

75 MOJISOLA ADEBAYO (b.1971)

Kellen Hoxworth

Introduction

Mojisola Adebayo (b.1971) is a London-born, Nigerian-Danish, Black British performance maker and theorist. She works at the intersections of physical theatre, theatre for social change, queer and lesbian theatre, and Black diasporic performance, drawing together a wide array of influences. Adebayo studied the Theatre of the Oppressed with Augusto Boal,[1] trained and collaborated with Denise Wong's Black Mime Theatre,[2] and takes inspiration from Black feminist writers such as Ntozake Shange, Toni Morrison, and Alice Walker.[3] Adebayo has also published on her research and practice in theatre for social change.[4]

Adebayo's early plays include: *Moj of the Antarctic: An African Odyssey* (2006), *Muhammad Ali and Me* (2008), *Matt Henson, North Star* (2009), and *Desert Boy* (2010), which have been published in *Mojisola Adebayo: Plays One* (2011). More recent works include Afrofuturist performances, such as *The Listeners* (2012) and *STARS* (2017)— theatre for young, Black, and disabled actors—*Sweet Taboo* (with Talawa's Young People Theatre Project, 2013), and *Asara & the Sea-Monstress* (2015)—as well as theatre for social change projects, such as *48 Minutes for Palestine* (2010) [or, *Oranges and Stones* (2020)], *I Stand Corrected* (with Mamela Nyamza, 2012), and *The Interrogation of Sandra Bland* (2017). Several of these later works have been published in *Mojisola Adebayo: Plays Two* (2020).

Written within the post-Windrush tradition of Black British theatre,[5] many of Adebayo's plays stage the entanglements between Blackness, queerness, and disability by "integrating [her] own biography with the stories of [...] historical black figures," which Lynette Goddard terms (after Audre Lorde) "a kind of auto-bio-mythography" (qtd. in Adebayo and Goddard 147; Lorde, *Zami*). Several plays feature an African griot character[6] as the principal storyteller, invoking the ritualistic and communal functions of African orature. In *Moj of the Antarctic*, for instance, Adebayo performed both as the griot figure and as the nineteenth-century ocean-faring runaway "Moj," a double-casting that implicitly linked the individual Black diasporic figure whose transoceanic routes traverse the globe ("Moj") with a figure who embodies the roots of communal African cultural practices and histories (the "Ancient"). *Moj of the Antarctic* interlaces into this diasporic tale excerpts and scenarios from the wide-ranging narratives of Phyllis Wheatley, William and Ellen Craft, Frederick Douglass, Harriet E. Wilson, Harriet Jacobs, and the Black woman sailor, William Brown. Within this variegated Black Atlantic, Adebayo incorporates a lesbian relationship between "Moj"

DOI: 10.4324/9781003006923-76

and "May" set on a Virginian plantation. Adebayo includes this narrative to, in her words, "weave in the queer stories that have always been there in African history and the African Diaspora that are not ever told" (qtd. in Adebayo and Goddard 144). Thus, Adebayo draws from her own intimate knowledge of Black queer life to give a queer texture to Black diasporic histories.

Similarly, in *Muhammad Ali and Me*, Adebayo constructs a Black diasporic queer space by finding the queerness in blackness. She centers the piece on an icon of muscular Black athleticism—Muhammad Ali—amidst a proliferation of Black cultural artifacts to reanimate transnational Black practices of "solidarity and identification within the deterritorialised space of the African diaspora" (Pearce 84). Together, the autobiographical figure, "Mojitola," and Ali appear as each other's Black doubles—a Nigerian-Dutch butch lesbian fostered by a white British family finding a way to reclaim herself through her identification with a Black American Muslim anti-war boxing champion of the world. Ali gives voice to this queer articulation of the "changing same" of the Black diaspora in his short poem that concludes the play: "Me. We" (Gilroy, *Black Atlantic* ix, 106; Adebayo, *Muhammad Ali* 149).

By contrast, *I Stand Corrected* actualizes Adebayo's vision of a queer Black diaspora through its dramaturgy. In Adebayo's terms, *I Stand Corrected* is a collaborative "piece of African Diasporic queer interdisciplinary dance and theatre performance" devised by Adebayo in concert with Black queer South African performer and choreographer, Mamela Nyamza ("Revolutionary Beauty" 130–131). This dance-theatre performance takes a theatre for social change approach to the phenomenon of "corrective rape" in South Africa—an act of violence that seeks to "correct" Black lesbians into heterosexuality through sexual violence and, often, murder. In crafting this piece, Adebayo and Nyamza sought not only to protest such brutal violence but also to create a performance of defiant "beauty." Adebayo, herself a survivor of sexual violence, asserts, "beauty can be therapeutic in recovering from trauma not just for us and hopefully for people in our audience" ("Revolutionary Beauty" 139). Adebayo and Nyamza performed *I Stand Corrected* in London, Cape Town, and Johannesburg, using the piece to advocate for queer rights throughout Africa and the Black diaspora.

Taken together, these plays exemplify Adebayo's rich engagement with critical theory in her dramaturgy and performance practice. Specifically, they model what Adebayo terms "Afri-Quia Theatre," a concept through which she offers a Black-British-cum-West-African revision of E. Patrick Johnson's articulation of "'Quare' Studies" as "strategy for theorizing racialized sexuality" (Johnson 3; cf. Johnson and Henderson 1–17). In response to the prevailing whiteness of "Queer Studies," Johnson's "'Quare' Studies" presents "a theory of and for gays and lesbians of color" derived from the voicing of "queer" as "quare" in southern Black American dialect (Johnson 3). Similarly, Adebayo elaborates her concept of "African-Queer" theatre "pronounced with a West African accent, 'Quia'," thereby tracing other articulations of Black queerness in performance ("Everything You Know" 147n3). By focusing on a West African pronunciation ("Quia"), Adebayo works toward what Rinaldo Walcott terms "a black queer diaspora project" that encompasses not only the United States but also the Caribbean, Africa, and Britain ("Outside in Black Studies" 90; "Somewhere Out There" 29). Thus, "Afri-Quia" simultaneously dislodges the presumptive whiteness of queerness while also charting how blackness and queerness interanimate across "overlapping diasporas" (Lewis 767; Edwards 12–13). In her theory and practice, Adebayo mobilizes "Afri-Quia" as a capacious device for articulating particular Black queer lives in performance, as well as for tracing the entanglements and resonances among disparate diasporic sites.

Mojisola Adebayo

Excerpt from "Everything You Know About Queerness You Learnt From Blackness: The Afri-Quia Theatre of Black Dykes, Crips and Kids" (2015)

Blackness, queerness and performance are inseparable for me. I learnt all I know about blackness/queerness from the life of boxing legend and black leader Muhammad Ali. When the heavyweight boxer danced on his toes and declared "I'm pretty, I'm as pretty as a girl," he was playing with people's perceptions and prejudices of what a black man could be (Hauser 1997: 52). Ali troubled gender stereotypes and racist beliefs about black masculinity being monolithic, inarticulate, even savage (Butler 1990; M. Wallace 1979). But Ali did not slug. He kept his hands low and shuffled lightly on his feet; he danced—backwards—did magic tricks and recited poetry, until they took his licence away for refusing to go to Vietnam and shoot his fellow brown-skinned man. When he changed his name and his religion, from Christian Cassius Clay to Muslim Muhammad Ali, he undid the idea of what an American was supposed to be. As performance theorist Peggy Phelan has stated, "self-invention and re-invention structures the performance of identities" (1993: 168). Muhammad Ali was a master of self-/re-invention, which is a quintessentially queer quality. Ali is heterosexual, but he showed me that blackness and queerness do not need to be seen as sparring partners, but as dancing partners. And the music Ali loved to dance to most of all was that of a high-camp, queer black "crip" known as Little Richard (Nyong'o 2014: 169; McRuer 2006). Critical and creative black queerness is about unboxing binaries, blurring boundaries, exposing the "mythical norm," messing with form, being in the process, playful, political and, most of all, performative (Lorde 1998: 631; Butler 1990). That's what got me writing plays. *Muhammad Ali and Me* is a semi-auto/biographical piece tracing the parallel lives of Ali and his fantastical friendship with Mojitola, a girl child growing up in care, surviving abuse and coming out as a lesbian thespian.[7] The queer dyke kid and the Muslim man, physically impaired by Parkinsonism, become a fictional family in *Muhammad Ali and Me*. Their bouts are refereed by a British Sign Language performer, Jacqui Beckford, who creatively interprets the words for deaf people. As the excerpts from my latest plays below will show, I have been playing with the relationship between black and queer experience, including disability, ever since.

American queer performance critic of colour, the late José Esteban Muñoz, posits the term "racial performativity" to discuss the aspect of race that is "a doing." He says that "[a] critical project attuned to knowing the performativity of race is better suited to decipher what work race does in the world" (2013: 414–415). In this chapter, I demonstrate some of the work that everyday black queer performativity and black queer performance is doing in the world, through sharing and reflecting on extracts of Afri-Quia Theatre.[8] Afri-Quia Theatre is a term I have coined that encompasses a trilogy of stage productions with critical writing that I have been working on with my collaborators since 2012. The plays are *I Stand Corrected, Sweet Taboo* and *Asara and the Sea-Monstress*.[9] The three plays, in very different ways, use theatre to create accessible spaces for black/queer/crip togetherness towards understanding, debating and challenging the recent intensification of homophobic colonial laws and violent acts across the African continent and the diaspora (Epprecht 2013).[10]

Afri-Quia Theatre is informed by the burgeoning discourse of black/queer theory that has emerged over the early 21st century. Delroy Constantine-Simms's *The Greatest Taboo: Homosexuality in Black Communities* (2001), E. Patrick Johnson and Mae G. Henderson's *Black Queer Studies* (2007), and Sokari Ekine and Hakima Abbas's *Queer African Reader* (2013) are three notable edited anthologies. However, these books contain largely theoretical writings from African and/or American perspectives. There has been very little discussion of black queer theatre and performance from a British queer/performance perspective, which is dominated by white voices that pay surprisingly little attention to black artists. As theatre scholar Victor Ukaegbu asserts: "British queer theatre is white, not black and, though tolerant of black performers, it hardly serves black concerns" (2007: 331). Ukaegbu also notes the marked "ambivalence" (322) in black studies towards black queer theatre but, despite being largely ignored, "black gay performances have been flourishing underground" (2007: 329).[11] In the past few years, we have seen a locally active and internationally resonant radical black/queer cultural renaissance and political resistance happening on London stages. From fringe theatres voicing the margins, such as Ovalhouse, to iconic main houses in the history of British political theatre such as Theatre Royal Stratford East and the Royal Court; from small-spoken-word events to nationally recognised arts centres of the *avant garde* such as the Southbank Centre. Black queer performance is becoming and coming up strong.

Afri-Quia Theatre is therefore inspired by the works of my black British/British-based queer performance-making peers who include Jackie Kay, Valerie Mason-John, Rikki Beadle-Blair, Christopher Rodriguez, Joy Gharoro-Akpojotor, Ade Adeniji, Le Gateau Chocolat, Antonia Kemi Coker and Tonderai Munyevu, Paul Goayke, Kofi Agyemang, Reuben Massiah, Dorothea Smartt, Dean Atta, Stephanie "Sonority" Turner, David Ellington, Tarell Alvin-McCraney, Jacqueline Rudet, Steven Luckie, Inua Ellams, Topher Campbell, stand-up comedians Stephen K. Amos and Gina Yashere and former stage-manager now leading scholar of black-British theatre, Lynette Goddard, to name just a few.[12] [...I, then, seek] to counter what queer cultural critic Jasbir K. Puar notes as the "racism of the global gay left" (2007: xi) that I argue permeates queer theatre and performance studies. Furthermore, noting how many of the artists mentioned above are male, in Afri-Quia Theatre, I hope to go some way to addressing what feminist performance theorist Sue-Ellen Case has discussed as the queer erosion of lesbian representation (2009: 9–11), through positioning lesbian stories centre stage. I write in part to give more parts to women, black and disabled actors. Representation in all respects is an important function of my work.

Furthermore, on this subject of functionality, Thomas DeFrantz writes in *Black Performance Theory* that blackness is "the manifestation of Africanist aesthetics" and states that "This black is action. Action engaged to enlarge capacity, confirm presence, to dare" (2014: 5). African theatre scholars Osita Okagbue and Kene Igweonu call this engaging, affirmative and daring black action "performativity," which they see as the most useful critical framework through which to study the work. They assert that "African theatre and performance is functional" in that "it is not just entertainment but is often geared towards fulfilling particular social or aesthetic functions—hence it is performative at its core" (2014: 1–2). A recurring feature of black performance is the desire to bring something into being through the act of doing, whether this be through ritual or activism, towards education, empowerment and/or social change. As performativity is a key concept of gender/queer theory (Butler 1990), it can be instrumentalised as a frame through which to view blackness and queer experience together.

Paul Gilroy has written that in everyday black life "[s]urvival in slave regimes or in other extreme conditions intrinsic to colonial order promoted the acquisition of what we might now consider to be performance skills" (1995: 14). He cites enslaved African-Americans such as Frederick Douglass and Ellen Craft, who escaped from slavery through transvestism. As cultural theorists Maria Sanchez and Linda Schlossberg demonstrate in their book *Passing* (2001), performing white and playing straight in everyday life is a phenomenon practised by both black and queer peoples. Major postcolonial scholars have discussed how performance elements such as mimicry (Bhabha 1994) and the mask (Fanon 1986) have become defining features of black experience and demonstrate the damaging effect these affectations can have on the psyche and behavior patterns of the colonized. Black and queer performance modes have been both instruments of harm and instruments through which liberation has been fashioned and, indeed, been made fashionable. Camp, at the nexus of performance and fashion in contemporary western black and queer cultures, is possibly the most prolific and high-profile, both defiant and flamboyant, mode of cultural expression that we share.[13]

From the fast fingers and hair flicks of rocking and rolling Little Richard to the shaking bananas of the booty of Josephine Baker; from the high flat-top of Grace Jones to the high heels of RuPaul; from the 35-year purple reign of shoulder-padded Prince to the practice of voguing at drag balls from Harlem to Liverpool, who can say where queer begins and black ends? Or where crip sensibility ends and queer performance begins? Little Richard recalls: "The kids didn't realise I was crippled. They thought I was trying to twist and walk feminine. But I had to take short strides cos I had a little leg...The kids would call me faggot, sissy, freak punk." (qtd. in Nyong'o 2014: 169). Little Richard performed his body, scorned as "deformed," as the ultimate dandy, the daddy of rock and roll. And where would white gay boys have been since the 1970s without the dance floor anthems of black divas performatively bringing into being the feeling that "We Are Family..."?[14] We—black, queer, crip people—are family, indeed.

Lastly, diaspora, as both a material experience and a concept, is constantly evolving a map where blackness and queerness interconnect. DeFrantz and Gonzalez write that "Diaspora is continual; it is the unfolding of experience into a visual, aural, kinesthetic culture of performance" (2014: 11). Diaspora has been intrinsic to black cultural expression, ever since the forced movements of slavery and the chosen movements of migration transported the rhythms of West Africa to the West Indies and on to West London's Notting Hill Carnival. Queerness too has a diasporic quality: Sedgwick writes that "[q]ueer is a continuing moment, movement, motive...The word 'queer' itself means across" (1994: xii). Like Simone De Beauvoir's conceptualisation of not being born but becoming a woman (in Butler 1990), Paul Gilroy has written that "[d]iaspora accentuates *becoming* rather than *being*" (1995: 24). Queer cultural critics Cindy Patton and Beningo Sanchez-Eppler have written on the link between diaspora and queer becoming, stating: "Sexuality is not only not essence, not timeless, it is also not fixed in place; sexuality is on the move" (2000: 2). The struggles for black emancipation and LGBTQI equality are movements. We have fought by moving our bodies and acting out our passions, protesting and performing on streets and stages across oceans and seas. [...]

In a time of increasing persecution of LGBTQI people on the African continent and the Caribbean, coupled with the ongoing battle against HIV/AIDS—a shared African/diasporic and LGBTQI struggle—it is all the more important to recognize and acknowledge that black and queer are a/kin and to find creative ways of connecting and developing what is sometimes a turbulent relationship. [...]

To sum up

So black dykes, crips, kids and all your comrades and all your diasporic kin—the future of Afri-Quia theatre is yours. This is your beginners' call. You've got the likes of Muhammad Ali in your prompt corner. In you I see the curtain fall on all mythical compulsory normativities. Play on, with more pleasure and more power than ever before.

Please see the Works Cited for further information on the sources used in this essay.

Notes

1 Theatre of the Oppressed was created by Brazilian playwright, Augusto Boal (1931–2009), to stimulate an actor's critical observation skills and raise his/her consciousness about the real world in the process of performing concrete actions on stage.

2 Founded in 1984, Denise Wong's Black Mime Theatre (BMT) was Britain's first black mime company; it disbanded in 1998.

3 See Adebayo and Goddard 147; Adebayo, "Revolutionary Beauty," 137; Adebayo, Mason-John, and Osborne 9; Adebayo and O'Kane 66–67; Adebayo and McAvinchey 63–64.

4 See Martin, Adebayo, and Mehta; Adebayo, "Revolutionary Beauty".

5 "The MV Empire Windrush was the first ship to bring Jamaicans to Britain in 1948 to aid the post-WWII rebuilding effort. In 2018, a big scandal ensued when the British Home Office wrongly deported 83 of these immigrants who were declared illegal, and it then transpired that the Home Office had actually destroyed many of these immigrants' records proving their legal status" (Griffin, n.1 in this volume). References to "Windrush" and "Windrush generation" thus mark a new pattern of migration from the formerly colonized West Indies to the imperial center.

6 The (West) African griot character serves as an historian, storyteller, praise singer, poet, or musician and is often positioned as an advisor to royalty; sometimes called a "bard."

7 *Muhammad Ali and Me* (Adebayo 2011: 65–149) started as a 20-minuted piece entitled *Dancing-Talking-Contra-Diction* (2001), first performed at Royal Holloway, University of London, as part of my MA in Physical Theatre practice-as-research dissertation project. *Muhammad Ali and Me* was first staged at Ovalhouse Theatre in London in 2008, performed by Mojisola Adebayo, Charlie Folorunsho and Jacqui Beckford, and directed by Sheron Wray. It is published by Oberon Books in *Mojisola Adebayo: Plays One*. [Adebayo]

8 Afri-Quia = African-Queer, pronounced with a West African accent, 'Quia'. [Adebayo]

9 The Afri-Quia plays and critical writing form part of my practice-as-research doctoral project at Queen Mary University of London (QMUL). I gratefully acknowledge the support of QMUL and my supervisors Catherine Silverstone and Caoimhe McAvinchey. [...] [Adebayo]

10 Marc Epprecht makes a galvanising case for optimism about the struggle for sexual equality in Africa that is a growing grassroots movement, led by women, men, and LGBTQI African people across the continent. [Adebayo]

11 *Staging Black Feminisms* (2007) by Britain's only other black British lesbian theatre scholar, Lynette Goddard, is an important exception. [Adebayo]

12 Many of these artists have also published plays. They are not all necessarily LGBTQI but they have all made work that openly and positively represents black LGBTQI expe-

rience. There have also been recent works by white playwrights representing black queer experience such as Robin Soans, whose *Perseverance Drive*, first performed at the Bush Theatre in London in July 2014, deals with homophobia in a black family. Kate Tempest's *Hopelessly Devoted*, first performed at Birmingham Rep in September 2013, focuses on a black lesbian relationship in prison. [Adebayo]

13 Queer theorist Kathryn Bond Stockton identifies dark camp as one of the 'aesthetic delight[s]' (Stockton 2006: 24) that has been fostered from a shared black/queer feeling of shame. I am weary and wary of the recent western tendency in queer theory towards placing black and queer people in the depressing paradigm of shame; I am much more interested and invested in the more positive approach of black cultural studies scholars, such as bell hooks, who explore self-love (hooks 2001). I am further animated by the activism articulated by the likes of Epprecht (2013). I cannot see how indulging in the discourse of shame and failure is going to win LGBTQI equality in Africa, for example. I am tired of the repeated clichéd images of faceless and down-faced black gay men that appear all over Stockton's book. I would rather look directly into the eyes of the South African LGBTQI people celebrated in the photography of Zanele Muholi who have not time in the fight for equality to delight in shame. They are too busy surviving (Muholi, 2010). [Adebayo]

14 'We Are Family' (1979) is a popular disco song by the black female band, Sister Sledge. The song was often played in gay clubs from the late 1970s onwards. It was composed by Bernard Edwards and Nile Rodgers and first released on the Cotillion label. [Adebayo]

Suggestions for Further Reading

Osborne, Dierdre, ed. *The Cambridge Companion to British Black and Asian Literature (1945–2010)*. Cambridge: Cambridge University Press, 2016.

Tamale, Sylvia, ed. *African Sexualities: A Reader*. Nairobi and Oxford: Pambazuka, 2011.

76 LAUREN GUNDERSON (b.1982)

Noelia Hernando-Real

Introduction

The *Guardian* has called Lauren Gunderson (b.1982) the most popular playwright in America today (D. Smith). In fact, she has been named the most produced playwright by *American Theatre* three times so far—in seasons 2017–2018, 2019–2020, and 2022–2023—a credit to how prolific she has been. In 2022–2023, she has twenty-four productions of twelve different plays on the list[1]. Gunderson has also been the recipient of the 2016 Lanford Wilson Award from the Dramatist Guild, the 2016 Otis Guernsey New Voices Award, and the prestigious Steinberg/ATCA New Play Award for *I and You* (2014), which was also a Susan Smith Blackburn Prize and John Gassner Award finalist. She received the Steinberg/ATCA New Play Award again for *The Book of Will* (2018).

While Gunderson made a name with *I and You*—an ode to human connectedness across life, death, race, and time, with Walt Whitman's *Leaves of Grass* (1881) as its beautiful poetic background—her *oeuvre*, which includes over twenty plays, treads the main paths taken by contemporary Western women playwrights. She knows how to write light pieces that please regional theatregoers, such as *Miss Bennet: Christmas at Pemberly* (2017) and its sequels *The Wickhams* (2018) and *Georgiana and Kitty* (2021; all three co-written with Margot Melcon). But she also writes "giddy political comedies" (Pollack-Pelzner, "You've Probably"), such as *The Revolutionists* (2018), and sharp feminist revisions of classic texts, as exemplified by her Shakespearean cycle plays, *The Taming* (2000), *Exit; Pursued by a Bear* (2012), *Toil and Trouble* (2013), and *Natural Shocks* (2019), as well as her feminist rewriting of J.M. Barrie's classic 1904 text, into *Peter Pan and Wendy* (2019). Gunderson also succeeds in writing "witty historical dramas" (Pollack-Pelzner, "You've Probably"), plays through which she relocates women in their rightful place in history, especially in the case of female scientists, as in *Ada and the Engine* (2018), *Silent Sky* (2015), *Emilie, or La Marquise du Chatelet Defends her Life Tonight* (2010), and *The Half-Life of Marie Curie* (2019). She has also collaborated on a number of musical theatre productions. As Daniel Pollack-Pelzner observes in the *New Yorker*, "Gunderson has built a national reputation with works that center on women's stories" ("You've Probably") Her voice has been heralded as "so profoundly feminist, but it's not one of those agitprop political voices" (Hazelton qtd. in Kois). Rather, Gunderson's has created a feminist theatre because, in her own words, her plays put women's "struggles, passions, power and wit center stage" (qtd. in Tran).

Yet Gunderson's conception of theatre and drama is not only transmitted through her plays. As a playwright in residence at the Marine Theatre Company

DOI: 10.4324/9781003006923-77

(2016–2022), she teaches playwriting, asking herself and fellow playwrights about the why, how, and what of contemporary theatre. These dialogues and keynote lectures are available online, serving as a significant source to identify and spread the dramatic schema behind Gunderson's plays. Furthermore, Gunderson is also active through her website (www.laurengunderson.com), where she keeps a blog to share her ideas on art, theatre, writing, and even motherhood. She has uploaded there her speech, excerpted here, "Survival of the Storied: Why Science Needs Art and Art Needs Science," which celebrates the Humanities in a world that tends to prioritize Science over Art. Delivered on the occasion of the 2015 Wisconsin Science Festival, this text illustrates what women's theatre and drama signify for Gunderson. In "Survival of the Storied," Gunderson provides a redefinition of theatre and drama that echoes and revisits Aristotle through a feminist twist that also relocates theatre (and art in general) as an equal, if not superior, sister to Science.

"Survival of the Storied" starts with the obvious, though perhaps not yet expressed, remark that the concept of wonder lies behind Science and Art. The speech then explores the reasons why these disciplines should be brought together and the ways to do so for the improvement of the world. Furthermore, this speech also focuses on the urgency of exploring the life and work of women scientists on the stage. In a brilliant exposition, Gunderson argues that the blatant lie that there have not been women scientists has only been equaled by another falsehood, that there are no women in the theatre. Women scientists, as Gunderson claims, make for extraordinary dramatic protagonists because they have a goal, they suffer from a flaw, and they try and fail—in an Aristotelian sense—to prove their theories and, in experiencing climactic ecstasy, they eventually witness and experience a revelation. These stories, Gunderson says, are the new ones that the 21st-century theatre has been waiting for and that need to be told. These narratives feature great heroines who have suffered from multiple biases (gender, class, race, sexual condition, and denial) and who, through the efforts of a playwright who knows how to control the theatrical creation of empathy, will have their stories told truthfully and sensitively. Significantly, Gunderson also argues that these stories deserve to be dramatized not just because they have been ignored but because they are valuable and necessary. In Gunderson's words:

> I don't want to tell the stories of women just because they are true, or because I should. I want to tell them because I think they are better stories – better because these heroes are doubly tested by bias, dis-invitation, and outright denial. These are the stories of female scientists, GLBTQ scientists and straight, non-white scientists. Just on pure dramatic potential, those stories are far richer in struggle and thus far greater in triumph.

Here, Gunderson presents the main difference between Science and Theatre. While Science can exist without an audience, Theatre cannot. As she puts it, "You are the final ingredient in a performance, you are the missing element of a story," reminding us that the audience always has the last say and, significantly, if the play has been well written, Gunderson suggests that the playwright will have influenced her audience to work towards the desired evolution that Science also seeks.

Lauren Gunderson

*Excerpt from "Survival of the Storied: Why Science Needs Art
and Art Needs Science" (2015)*

> For the wonder of each hour
> of the day and of the night
> hill and vale and tree and flower
> sun and moon and stars of light
> Lord of All to thee we raise
> This our hymn of grateful praise.

I realize it's a little odd for a talk about science to begin with a hymn, but let me give you three very good reasons why this one does:

1   This song is a running element in the play *Silent Sky* about little known but critical astronomer Henrietta Leavitt who has a wonderful, soulful, creative sister named Margaret who is also a composer and the pianist for their father's church. The hymn challenges the sisters to reckon with faith, science, meaning, legacy, and with the wonderful dance between math and music. [...]
2   This was my grandmother Beatrice Gunderson's favorite hymn. [...] So this is really for her.
3   For the wonder of each hour. The wonder. [...] [W]hat I see and appreciate in the hymn is this sense of awe and wonder.

Wonder is the shared trunk from which the curiosities, craft, vision and perseverance of both science and art spring. It's that simple and voluminous wow of the Grand Canyon at sunset, the perfect Phi curl of a fern or a sea shell, a first kiss, the first glimpse of your brand new son, the night sky. Science and art, though I will speak mostly of the art of storytelling, share a catalyst, a source, a seed, a *wow*.

Science experiences *wow* and turns around to say... why is that so? How does that work? What's next?

Art experiences *wow* and says... how can I tell everyone else? How can I get that back?

What's next?

Both share that same taproot of curiosity and wonder.

How could they not? Both a scientific and artistic instinct is one of the most widespread and successful adaptations we have evolved into. The creativity and curiosity and technical skill that lay at the heart of both science and story are seen in every human culture on earth. Things that are common and widely experienced are generally assumed to provide a distinct evolutionary advantage for a species.

As Brian Boyd reminds us in *The Origin of Stories*, "...both science and story share the root adaptation of play." Playing, exploring, and playing pretend is an advantage seen in many animal species including ours [...].

We are evolved for science and story. But why?

Science I get. Figuring things out, understanding and bettering the world through investigation and innovation. [...]

But story? The work of crafting a narrative is one thing. Narratives are stories well told [...].

What on earth does fiction do for us that fact can't accomplish? Why on earth would we bother with make believe when we're quite busy trying to survive the Pleistocene or the election season? Why do we so often prefer fiction to fact?

We don't just bother with fiction. We crave it, we need it. Every civilization that we have record of told stories. [...]

It's everywhere, it's constant, we are drowning in it, (in a good way) and no other species that we know of does it. So what does it do for us that is so essential to our survival? [...]

Because there is science to it. So to answer some of the why of it [...], let's start with evolutionary psychology:

Leda Cosmides and John Tooby of the University of Santa Barbara argue that imaginative lives are essential to our humanity. Fiction allows us to weigh indirect evidence, to stimulate our mind virtually, to forecast scenarios and solutions without the risk of living through it. They call this investment in fiction *decoupled cognition* and it is key.

Here's a handy list of what stories offer us in terms of an evolutionary advantage expanded from Daniel Dennet's *The Art Instinct*:

1 Stories provide low-cost, low-risk surrogate experience. [...]
2 Stories can be richly instructive sources of factual information by teaching in a vivid and memorable manner. We learn lessons together, experience sorrow and joy together. [...]
3 Stories encourage us to explore other points of views, beliefs, motivations, and values. [...]

Stories gather us not just physically—around a podium or a campfire—but mentally, philosophically, and spiritually as well. Story offers us collective myths, shared ideals, common heroes and villains. This kind of bonding lasts because it perpetuates into future generations and makes us connect the long history of a people, connecting the past, the present and the future. When you see *Hamlet*, you are seeing the same play watched almost 500 years ago. [...]

Let us switch to neurology for a moment. Some of you have heard of these remarkable little things called *mirror neurons*.

Mirror neurons were discovered in primates in the 1990s from scientists at the University of Parma. Mirror neurons are:

> "...a set of neurons in the premotor area of the brain that are activated not only when performing an action oneself, but also while observing someone else perform that action. It is believed mirror neurons increase an individual's ability to understand the behaviors of others."

You might recall Hamlet instructing his actor friends that good performance "holds a mirror up to nature." Well said, Hamlet. [...] Even Aristotle says that tragedy is the imitation of life.

So, something indicated that these mirror neurons, this sense of imitation, this reflection from one person to another was vibrant and important. We have evolved the sophistication of empathy. E.O. Wilson and other sociobiologists would agree that empathy makes us stronger as a species because acknowledging the experience of others, and actually activating in oneself the feelings of others, allows us to strengthen our social awareness. Comprehension increases cooperation. Cooperation in balance with competition is the core of evolutionary multilevel selection.

Cooperation and competition also happens to be at the core of every great story.

Those two things are at battle in *Hamlet, Oedipus*, in *Breaking Bad*. Every choice the hero makes is a choice between cooperation and competition. There's a reason for it.

It's complex stuff to hone your ability to read people – friends, family, potential mates, and potential enemies. If you can do that well, you're ahead of the game of survival. Stories give us practice at it.

To quote Anne Murphy Paul's article "Your Brain on Fiction":

> "Scientists call this capacity of the brain to construct a map of other people's intentions 'theory of mind'. Narratives offer a unique opportunity to engage this capacity, as we identify with characters' longings and frustrations, guess at their hidden motives and track their encounters with friends and enemies, neighbors and lovers."

But it's not just the experience of a story as an audience that helps us survive, it's the ability to craft and tell a story that helps us hone our adaptive advantages.

Storytelling requires... rehearsal. A plan to kill a mammoth is probably bettered by a little practice. As is a play, a joke, or an epic poem. The ability to rehearse, which activates both premonition and memory, is a fundamental tool for survival. [...]

But we're not just rehearsing survival acts, we're also rehearsing emotions. The Greeks called the climax of a play its catharsis, however the catharsis is not a structural element for the characters to craft that big heroic moment in the play.

Catharsis is a term for the audience's reaction. The Greeks already knew about mirror neurons. In fact, a tragedy is just a vehicle for giving you the weepies at the exact moment when you're supposed to get them and teaching you a lesson about killing your father and sleeping with your mother. *Don't do it.* Catharsis is about engaging the audience, about bringing the audience into the very fabric of storytelling. [...]

A recent study showed that chimps who have seen a short film only once and were played the film again, were able to anticipate when an exciting scene was about to happen. Their bio indicators picked up before the scene happened.

Our ape ancestors learn from story immediately like we do, feel story like we do, and know story like we do.

Story is science if you understand that story is one of our survival instincts. Story is biology, evolutionary psychology, sociobiology, neurology, anthropology.

But I'm not just here to talk about the science of story, I'm here to talk about the stories of science, and how those stories are key to our thriving as a species.

Great Stories Make Great Heroes Make Great Futures
Our heroes are such because they have great stories. [...] [T]hey're great because a storyteller crafted the story in such a way to make you believe them. [...]

Scientists make for great heroes because science makes for great drama – especially if you realize that good drama is just life with all the boring bits cut out.

Structurally, Aristotle would approve of science as story. A great fiction asks for a great hero with a clear goal [...]. It's nice if that hero is complicated by some personal flaws, some distractions, and an antagonist that thwarts their efforts […]. The hero must try and fail, and try and fail until…the drama converges at a climactic point of great revelation and reversal – and that's the moment where everything changes for the hero, when something is known that could not be known until that point. If it's a comedy it ends with dancing and kisses, if it's a tragedy… well, don't tell the hero, but if their name is in the title it doesn't bode well for them.

Science fits this dramatic structure. The perseverance, the antagonism, the trial and error, and finally a revelation – a eureka – that changes everything.

But science needs storytellers to tell that to the world and it needs them now more than ever.

We are in a time when science is attacked by fundamentalist hucksters for its very existence as truth. We must encourage scientists to tell the stories of their work, their inspirations, their journeys. We need stories that can humanize the abstractions of science, stories that can bring humor, nuance and personality to the essential work of truth telling. […]

But we also need new heroes.

We need stories where scientists look like what they actually are – varied people, women and men, every race and size and age. […]

Some of you will have heard of the lack of women characters, women playwrights, and women directors in most theatres across the English speaking world. […]

This same statistic for lack of women is in the sciences as well.

Story and science *are the same thing*! I told you!

But in both cases, this is something we can do something about. In fact, story can help us reorient science in demanding that it stand up for its women, and science can help us reinvigorate story and provide stories for women and about women that are changing the world.

It's why I wrote *Silent Sky*, a play about Henrietta Leavitt, whose work at the turn of the century basically enabled the likes of Edwin Hubble to measure the universe for the first time in human history. Yeah. Not bad for a woman who, though she was tasked with pouring over photographs of the night sky for decades, was not allowed to use the actual telescope which sat across the lawn from her office because it was for the men.

Cue loud booing. […]

Now, I don't want to tell the stories of women just because they are true, or because I should. I want to tell them because I think they are better stories - better because these heroes are doubly tested by bias, dis-invitation, and outright denial. These are the stories of female scientists, GLBTQ scientists and straight, non-white scientists.

Just on pure dramatic potential, those stories are far richer in struggle and thus far greater in triumph.

Marie Curie, Rosalind Franklin, Alan Turing, George Washington Carver—these scientists and inventors, like so many more, have stories that not only capture the essence of perseverance, innovation, pattern-breaking thought, and forward think-ing, but they have each faced so much against them and proved themselves anyway. […]

Yes, we need to be given more examples of female science heroes, yes, we need more about African-American and Hispanic men and women in the sciences. Yes, we absolutely need those stories and I cannot wait to see them. But we cannot manifest a better future until we start seeing it around us, until all of us see stories that not only reflect ourselves and the world we live in, but project a better world, a more inclusive and supportive world, a world where anyone, based on their mind and merit, can be a scientist. Stories can help that. If Indiana Jones can do it for archaeology, then we can do it for astronomy, medicine, engineering, and math. If science aims to deepen our knowledge of the world and potentially innovate ways to make it better for human survival and thriving… then it needs story's help.

Why Science and Story Need Each Other and We Need Them BOTH
Fact and fiction need each other. We are a species that has evolved to excel at both. […]

Science has methods to make sure that what we say is true is true. I like this about science. It doesn't let you make things up.

Art has methods for truth-telling too, but one of our secrets is… we don't actually need fact to make something true. Science rather requires it. Story? Nope. Fiction is a falsity that tells the truth. And often, because it's false, because it's impossible, we can tell a truer thing—emotionally truer, philosophically truer. We feel real disgust at Oedipus's incest, real thrill at Macbeth's conniving and battling, real anticipation and strange sorrow at Walter White's fall [in *Breaking Bad*].

The impossibilities of fiction complement the realities of science. Both can shock us, move us, inspire us.

Fiction sets our minds to not only imagine the impossible, but to explore it.

Impossibility reminds us how often our paradigms have shifted under our feet and keeps us questioning the world around us, saying wow and why over and over again, as all good scientists should. […]

The truth is that curiosity, investigation, and creativity are required to excel at both science and story. What makes them different from each other, makes the other richer. They complement each other. They need each other.

We need fiction like we need fact. We need story like we need science. Which is why I love the STEM to STEAM advocates that add Art's A to STEM's Science, Tech, Engineering, and Math.

Noble Prize winning Chemist Harold Kroto said: "Art and science are intrinsically the same except for one thing. The universe is in control of your science, whether it's right or wrong, and the public are in control of your art."

Stories are things shared. Their success, their power and their longevity are determined by you. Science doesn't actually need your input, it's totally fine on its own—but story does. You are the final ingredient in a performance, you are the missing element of a story… until you aren't.

I'll end with Anton Chekhov, who besides being one of the most influential playwrights of the twentieth century, was also a doctor. He said:

"[T]he sensitivity of the artist may equal the knowledge of the scientist. Both have the same object, nature, and perhaps in time it will be possible for them to link together in a great and marvelous force which at present is hard to imagine."

For the wonder of each hour,
of the day and of the night,
science's truth and story's power
make us stronger, braver, bright.

Minds and hearts to thee we raise
This is our hymn of nature's praise.

Please see the Works Cited for further information on the sources used in this essay.

Note

1 See https://www.americantheatre.org/2022/09/23/clydes-is-most-produced-play-and-lynn-nottage-most-produced-playwright-of-2022-23-season/. See also http://www.laurengunderson.com/.

Suggestion for Further Reading

Gunderson, Lauren. "The Ending of the Play's the Thing." *Wall Street Journal*, 26 Nov. 2011.

77 SARAH RUHL (b.1974)

Amy Muse

Introduction

Sarah Ruhl (b.1974) is a twenty-first-century American playwright whose work asks "big questions about death, love, and how we should treat each other in this life-time" (Ruhl, *The Oldest Boy* 145). Her signature move is fusing joy and sorrow, arous-ing smiles and tears at the same time, and opening the heart "with the smallest, most elegant pliers, rather than opening the heart with a chain saw" (Ruhl, qtd. in Royce). Ruhl positions herself in a theatrical tradition that includes Anton Chekhov, Maurice Maeterlinck, Tennessee Williams, María Irene Fornés, Mac Wellman, and Paula Vogel, as well as writers not known as playwrights: Ovid, Italo Calvino, and Virginia Woolf. As this list of names suggests, Ruhl is not a dramatic realist; like Woolf she aims to "interpret how people subjectively experience life" (Ruhl, qtd. in Lahr). "Experience itself, rather than the fruit of experience" is her theatrical goal (Ruhl, "When Woolf Saw Chekhov" xi). "What if plot," she asks, "is a rather insignif-icant and illusory trapping that can be dispensed with?" (xii).

To date, Ruhl is the author of eighteen published plays; a coauthored (with poet Max Ritvo) work of nonfiction, *Letters from Max: A Book of Friendship*[1] (2018); two poetry collections, *44 Poems for You* (2020) and *Love Poems in Quarantine* (2022); and a mem-oir, *Smile* (2021). Two of her plays (*The Clean House* (2006) and *In the Next Room [or the Vibrator Play]* (2010)) have been finalists for the Pulitzer Prize. An inventive experi-menter with form, Ruhl early in her career created more abstractly language-driven, avant-garde dramas (e.g., *Eurydice* (2006) and *Melancholy Play* (2006)), and later plays that are more directly engaged socially and politically (*How to Transcend a Happy Marriage* (2017); *Scenes from Court Life, or the Whipping Boy and His Prince* (2016)), but she always leans toward transformation, away from verisimilitude. Her plays concern the experiences of humans relating to each other, and they strive to open audiences to an "I/Thou relationship with the stage," to "enlist the audience in a mutual rela-tion" (Ruhl, Essay #52, "Buber and the stage" 111).

100 Essays I Don't Have Time to Write (2014)—its title indicative of her litotic wit—encom-passes Sarah Ruhl's theory of theatre. Because the tone is warm and intimate, the essays brief and undeveloped—giving the impression at times of mere jottings—and the collec-tion sprinkled with anecdotes about her children, it feels disarmingly, even dismissively, light. (But *not* whimsical or quirky, two words often used to describe her work, which she resists in, for example, Essay #61, "Why I hate the word *whimsy*. And why I hate the word *quirky*" 125.) As in Ruhl's plays, the lightness of the essays is a deliberate choice "to temper reality with strangeness, to temper the intellect with emotion, and to temper emotion

DOI: 10.4324/9781003006923-78

with humor" (Essay #18, "Calvino and lightness" 36). Moreover, the essays are often balanced with a gravitational pull, an emotional kicker, at the end.

While Ruhl is a celebrated, widely produced, commercially successful playwright, she has often been misunderstood by critics as not able or unaware of how to craft a "real play"—meaning a naturalistic play with a recognizably Aristotelian rising and falling arc. But she has no interest in this traditional approach. At the end of Essay #7, "Andy Goldsworthy, theatrical structure, and the male orgasm," she quips, "Do we think the arc is natural because of the structure of the male orgasm?" (16), and in Essay #41, "Color-blind casting; or, why are there so many white people on stage?" she wonders if "the deeply-held belief in naturalism" in American theatre keeps us from achieving "diversity on stage" (90).

Rather than Aristotle, Ruhl follows Ovid and Woolf to create "moments of being" in which "one thing becomes another thing and then another," and the story moves episodically, taking "pleasure in change itself, as opposed to pleasure in moral improvement" or lessons learned (Essay #16, "On Ovid" 31–33). She finds subtext unhealthy—"I think it is almost ontologically impossible to think one thing while saying another thing. It creates an acting muddle in the theatre and a sociopath in life" (Essay #30, "Subtext to the left of the work, not underneath the work" 66)—and Ruhl is adamant that actors in her plays not look for and play subtext, which is a challenge, since we've come to understand modern drama as being all about subtext.[2] On stage directions, she writes: "I think many more directors would begin to treat stage directions as visual speech rather than as filigree if they were not always hiding in parentheses" (Essay #94, "On standard dramatic formatting" 199). Her directions, laid out like lines of verse, are a signal to slow down, for she's not merely conveying information but calling us to be attentive to the moment.

Paula Vogel,[3] who was her teacher at Brown, predicts that Ruhl will eventually "become her own vocabulary word" (qtd. in Wren 31). William Demastes has described as "new alchemists" (5) those artists and scientists who re-enchant the world through a grounding in its everydayness. Ruhl should be counted among them. Her theory of theatre, like all influential ones, can be read as a theory of life. Her distinctive aesthetic is in cross-disciplinary conversation with "affect studies," for she advocates for subjective responses to events, with intimacy research on the impact of attention, and with theories of reading that prioritize absorption and enchantment over critique. In her *New York Times* review, novelist Rachel Cusk found *100 Essays I Don't Have Time to Write* "a work of profound moral organization" (BR9). In short, Ruhl's aesthetic choices are ethical statements about being in the world. Because the real (children, life) breaks into the world of our imaginings, we should be attentive to the moments in our lives, as mundane as they might seem; theatre can enable us to get close rather than retreat to our corners to spar.

Sarah Ruhl

Excerpts from 100 Essays I Don't Have Time to Write: On Umbrellas and Sword Fights, Parades and Dogs, Fire Alarms, Children, and Theater *(2014)*

7. On Andy Goldsworthy, theatrical structure, and the male orgasm

I am inspired by Andy Goldsworthy's outdoor sculptures. Like a playwright, he spends his time structuring decay. In his case, the natural world destroys the form, whereas in the theater, time itself and the audience's movement through time destroy the form. Structure implies subtraction or repression; without the taking away or the hiding, there is everything, or formlessness. Goldsworthy documents how already structured nature is by using subtraction and repetition. He complicates what is natural and what is artifice by pointing to already existing natural forms.

Different plays have different shapes—spheres, rectangles, wavy lines, and of course the ever-discussed and ubiquitous arc. How will we find our own natural forms in the sense of the elemental, and when should we be suspicious of the word *natural?* The playwright Mac Wellman has his students draw the structure of their plays, encouraging them to draw wiggly lines, circles, or vases, as the structure demands. Aristotle thought form was natural, but he thought the natural form was always an arc.

I remember once hearing a young male student describe the structure of his play. He said, "Well, first it starts out, then it speeds up, and it's going and it's going, and then bam, it's over." And I thought, Do we think the arc is a natural structure because of the structure of the male orgasm?

16. On Ovid

I grew up on Shakespeare's romances, in which people become asses, and this brand of theatrical transformation felt normal to me rather than odd. But in the contemporary literary world, things that are "magic" are cordoned off and labeled "magic realism." Apparently, García Márquez himself disdained the term and said that most of what happened in *Love in the Time of Cholera* actually happened in his village. In the Renaissance, playwrights could not get enough of Ovid, the poet of transformation, and Shakespeare almost seems to have slept with Ovid under his pillow.

Paula Vogel, who was my teacher, teaches that there are six plot forms, and Aristotelian form, or the linear arc, is only one of them. Aristotelian form progresses through a logical series of cause and effect. One thing happens, so the next thing happens, so the next thing happens, so the climax happens, and so on. Vogel explains that alternatives to Aristotelian forms include: circular form (see *La Ronde*), backward form (*Artist Descending a Staircase* or *Betrayal*), repetitive form (*Waiting for Godot*), associative form (see all of Shakespeare's work, in particular his romances), and what Vogel calls synthetic fragment, where two different time periods can coexist (*Angels in America* or *Top Girls*).

I would humbly add a seventh form, Ovidian. In Ovid's *Metamorphoses*, he begins, "Let me begin to tell of forms changed." His emphasis, in terms of story, is on transformation, rather than a scene of conflict or rational cause and effect. Gods become swans, people become trees, people fall in love and die, the supernatural world is permeable. This story structure is reminiscent of fairy tales. Objects have magical properties, people transform, and the natural world is likewise transformative. One thing becomes another thing and then another, and there is no clear moral. If there can be said to be verisimilitude in Ovidian form, it is the sort that imitates dreams or the unconscious.

Perhaps change is all-important in most dramatic forms; in the arc play, change is usually of the moral variety—a lesson learned. But in Ovidian form, the play takes pleasure in change itself, as opposed to pleasure in moral improvement.

We now live in an age where people crave magic and transformation. We need Harry Potter. (One might argue that we need Harry Potter because of political escapism. That is another matter.) Still, I would argue that at the level of the story we crave transformation as much as we crave verisimilitude. Perhaps Ovidian form is not taught at universities as a genuine narrative form because it is very hard to teach the art of transformation. Aristotle lays out his theories in lecture form, easily accessible, whereas Ovid simply flies, and it is difficult to teach the art of flying.

18. Calvino and lightness

Italo Calvino has a wonderful essay, "Lightness," in which he honors lightness as an aesthetic choice and a difficulty, rather than as something to be easily dismissed. You cannot, after all, get something airborne on a mere whim, no—it requires careful patience and some physics to get a plane in the air. When I worked on a translation of *Three Sisters*, I was thrilled to learn that in the original Russian, Olga said quite literally, "I can now remember with some lightness." So often Chekhov is played by actors who are remembering with some heaviness.

A suspicion that lightness is not deeply serious (but instead whimsical) pervades aesthetic discourse. But what if lightness is a philosophical choice to temper reality with strangeness, to temper the intellect with emotion, and to temper emotion with humor. Lightness is then a philosophical victory over heaviness. A reckoning with the humble and the small and the invisible.

30. Subtext to the left of the work, not underneath the work

If you're acting in a play of mine, and I say this full of love for you, please, don't think one thing and then say another thing. Think the thing you are saying. Do not think of the language of the play as a cover or deception for your actual true hidden feelings that you've felt compelled to invent for yourself. Don't create a bridge between you and the impulse for the language; erase the boundary between the two. Think of subtext as to the left of the language and not underneath it. There is no deception or ulterior motive or "cover" about the language. There are, instead, pools of silence and the unsayable to the left or to the right or even above the language. The unsayable in an ideal world hovers above the language rather than below. Think of the word *hover* over and above the word *cover*. Perhaps it is because I am from the Midwest, but I think it is almost ontologically impossible to truly think one thing while saying another thing. It creates an acting muddle in the theater and a sociopath in life.

41. Color-blind casting; or, why are there so many white people on stage?

If you are a white playwright and you tell a casting agent that you need a young woman named Mary and ethnicity is irrelevant, chances are you will see thirty white women, two black women, and one Asian woman at auditions, and through some strange, indefinable process, a white woman gets cast, more often than not.

Chuck Mee once told me that he eventually began to specify the ethnicities of his characters through the choice of their names. If you tell a casting agent that you need a woman in her forties named Aditi, chances are you will see Indian women in auditions, and you will end up casting an Indian woman. I believe this has to do with our underlying unspoken faith in mimesis. If the name of a character suggests a nonwhite person, usually a nonwhite person will be found for the role. But even if the philosophy of the playwright is that his or her plays should be cast without regard to race, somehow the structure of theater (or our country) intervenes, and whether from subtle, unconscious racial or mimetic biases, our stages are way too whitewashed.

I am not interested in writing plays that are specifically about white people. And yet to cast nonwhite people, you often have to specify that a character is a particular race, and then suddenly you have a play about race. Is naturalism, which purports to hold a mirror up to nature, actually just a mirror held up to upper-middle-class Scandinavians?

I remember when the director John Doyle held auditions for my translation of *Three Sisters*, actors would often come in with something I might call "Chekhov voice," a strange accent that is not quite English and not quite American and vaguely upper-class. This unidentifiable accent (which is certainly not Russian) created an odd acting barrier between the actor and the language. John would say, "Where are you from?" And the actor would say, "Detroit." John would say, "Could you do the speech the way you normally talk, the way you talked before you went to acting school?" And then the speech would be liberated from Chekhov voice, and we could hear the language of the play again without getting a brain fog of corsets and samovars.

If Chekhov voice is seen as desirable in acting programs, and if Chekhov voice is an upper-class whitewashing of race, ethnicity, regionalism, and class difference, then what are acting programs erasing? And is the deeply held belief in naturalism in this country an impediment to diversity on stage, in addition to this country's subtle or not-so-subtle racism?

52. Buber and the stage

Martin Buber writes in his book *I and Thou*, "I consider a tree. I can look on it as a picture ... I can classify it in a species and study it as a type ... It can, however, also come about, if I have both will and grace, that in considering the tree I become bound up in relation to it. The tree is now no longer *It* ... relation is mutual."

How to give an audience an I/Thou relationship with the stage rather than an I/It relationship with the stage? That is to say, how can the audience exist *in relation* to the stage as opposed to watching the stage as object? Can the play itself encourage an I/Thou relationship? Can a production? We know that a production can transform an I/Thou relationship into an I/It relationship, but perhaps a production cannot transform an I/It text into an I/Thou relation. Or is it up to the audience members and their glorious free will?

If one is to enlist the audience in a mutual relation, *how?* Must one live in France to do that? I remember the experience of watching Mnouchkine's company come on stage during an intermission. The children from the play came quite naturally on stage and poured lemonade for the audience (it was a long play). The audience came onto the stage and shared lemonade and bread with the performers and their children, and the stage was no longer an "it"; it had become a "thou."

I'm not sure if this desire to create a "thou" in the theater is shared in the contemporary American climate, where it seems we put all our efforts into becoming more of an "it"—glossy, cinematic, bold. But I do know when I have been swept into a mutual relation at the theater, my knees always tremble from the effort; my knees know something that my brain does not.

61. Why I hate the word *whimsy.* And why I hate the word *quirky.*

Whimsy was an etymological cousin in 1520 to the word *whim-wham* (a decidedly superior word), which had to do with fluttering the eyelids or letting the eyes wander. It is, then, a way of making feminine and therefore trivial a whole school of aesthetic fabulation. We do not tend to call Shakespeare whimsical, although his fairies flew and his witches chanted. A male artist following his whims is daring, manly, and original. A woman artist following her whims is womanly, capricious, and trivial; her eyelids flutter, her heart palpitates, her eyes wander, and her hands rise and fall in her lap.

The word *quirky* is so much more loathed than the word *whimsy* that it does not bear the time it would require to dissect its horrors. The choice to have a perceptible aesthetic at all is often called a quirk. The word *quirky* suggests that in a homogenized culture, difference has to be immediately defined, sequestered, and formally quarantined while being gently patted on the head.

94. On standard dramatic formatting

Why are stage directions generally in parentheses? If you (the playwright) want them treated as parentheticals, put them in parentheses, but if they are as important to you as the dialogue, as they are to me, do not put them in parentheses, and insist on using your own punctuation, as any novelist or poet would.

Punctuation is philosophy and rhythm in a play. Actors understand this. I think readers do too. And I think many more directors would begin to treat stage directions as visual speech rather than as filigree if they were not always hiding in parentheses.

Please see the Works Cited for further information on the sources used in this essay.

Notes

1 Ruhl has subsequently developed a play from these letters.
2 Compare Pinter's insistence, in "Writing for the Theatre," that we use language as a way of hiding what we want.
3 See Vogel entry in this volume.

Suggestions for Further Reading

Al-Shamma, James. *Sarah Ruhl: A Critical Study of the Plays.* Jefferson, NC: McFarland & Company, 2011.
Durham, Leslie Atkins. *Women's Voices on Contemporary Stages in the Early Twenty-First Century: Sarah Ruhl and Her Contemporaries.* London: Palgrave Macmillan, 2013.
Muse, Amy. *The Drama and Theatre of Sarah Ruhl.* London: Bloomsbury Methuen Drama, 2018.
Ruhl, Sarah. "Six Small Thoughts on Fornes, the Problem with Intention, and Willfulness." *Theatre Topics.* 11.2 (2001): 187–204.
Vogel, Paula. "Artists in Conversation: Sarah Ruhl by Paula Vogel." *BOMB.* 99 (2007): 54–59.

78 ELAINE ASTON (b.1958)

Geraldine Harris

Introduction

Over the last thirty odd years, Elaine Aston (b.1958) has produced an exceptionally extensive and influential body of research which, taken as a whole, can be seen to exemplify the style of theatre criticism that she champions in "Agitating for Change, Theatre and A Feminist Network of Resistance" (2016).

Aston embarked on her career in the 1980s, a decade in which in the UK, Margaret Thatcher's Conservative Government laid the foundations of the neo-liberal socio-economic policies, and by extension for the "undoing" of feminism as a socially progressive force, which forms the backdrop to "Agitating for Change." The same period marked the beginnings of "doing" feminist criticism in theatre departments in the US and the UK, supported by an increase in the number of women employed as lecturers in the discipline (although mostly this "increase" was from zero to one). This early cohort of feminist theatre scholars emerged from undergraduate programs focused largely on theatre history, which with few, rare exceptions was represented exclusively by the work of "great white men." One of their first challenges then was to excavate and revalue the lost or forgotten genealogy of women in theatre.

This aspiration impelled Aston's early publications, including her first monograph, *Sarah Bernhardt: A French Actress on the English Stage* (1989), but is also apparent in the temporal sweep of later works, such as *The Cambridge Companion to Modern British Women Playwrights* (2000), which Aston coedited with Janelle Reinelt. Yet Aston's essay on Pam Gems in this volume signals a shift of focus already visible in the balance of material in *An Introduction to Feminism and Theatre* (1995), and today she is best known for her groundbreaking analyses of the work of contemporary British women playwrights. Published in journals, edited collections, and monographs, such as *Feminist Views of the English Stage* (2003), these studies cover plays by figures as diverse as Winsome Pinnock, Phyllis Nagy, debbie tucker green, Sarah Kane, and Laura Wade,[1] among many others. But Aston is especially renowned for her sustained and rigorous attention to the work of Caryl Churchill.

Her monograph, *Caryl Churchill*, first published in 1991, has run to two updated and extended editions (2001 and 2010) and sits alongside *The Cambridge Companion to Caryl Churchill* (2009), coedited with Elin Diamond. Aston's numerous other essays follow Churchill's artistic and political progress up to and including a discussion of *Escaped Alone* (2016) in *Restaging Feminisms* (2020). Significantly, the starting point for *Restaging Feminisms* is a "revisiting" of the feminist dynamics foundational to establishing feminist approaches to theatre in the 1980s, and in many ways, Aston's entire

DOI: 10.4324/9781003006923-79

research trajectory can be perceived as aiming to prevent "the erasure of details of historically significant efforts to bring about democratic change from cultural memory," which Angela McRobbie has remarked upon, and Aston has cited in "Agitating for Change" (9). McRobbie is commenting on the disarticulation of feminism within the neo-liberal postfeminist discourse which became dominant at the end of the twentieth century, and the impact of this discourse on theatre has been a topic in Aston's work since the early 2000s, most compellingly articulated in her award-winning essay, "Feeling the Loss of Feminism: Sarah Kane's *Blasted*," in *Experiential Genealogy of Contemporary Women's Playwriting* (2010).

Interestingly, the role played by feminist criticism in the "theory explosion," which in the 1980s and 1990s transformed theatre studies and underwrote the advent of Performance Studies, is now often overlooked, if not forgotten. Of necessity, Aston's generation of feminist theatre critics were pioneers in exploring how cutting-edge thinking emerging from other disciplines might be employed as tools for interrogating the relationship between politics and aesthetics in the performing arts. In this vein, *Theatre as Sign-System: A Semiotics of Text and Performance* (1991), which Aston coauthored with George Savona, remains a standard on undergraduate reading lists in many countries.

In addition, from *An Introduction to Feminism and Theatre* onwards, Aston has investigated, utilized, and sometimes critiqued approaches developed within women's studies, literary theory, critical race theory, and queer theory and variously shaped by Marxist socialism, cultural materialism, psychoanalysis, poststructuralism, deconstruction, and postmodernism. However, her deployment of interdisciplinary theory operates within a methodology characterised by scrupulous attention to the conditions and contexts (theatrical, social, cultural, discursive) in which the productions studied occur and hence to the specificity of their feminisms and forms. Moreover, as signalled by *Feminist Theatre Practice: a Handbook* (1999) and *Performance Practice and Process: Contemporary [Women] Practitioners* (2007) coauthored with Geraldine Harris, Aston's methodology is rooted in an "embodied knowledge" of theatre as a creative and affective medium not containable through references to a single, totalizing conceptualization of the politics of aesthetics, which originates from hands on and/or practitioner-led research. Accordingly, rather than for their own sake, theories are drawn upon in the service of illuminating the particular nature, style, and location(s) of the practices under consideration, whether these derive from the field of playwriting, or the wide variety of performance genres that Aston has explored in works such as *Performance Practice and Process* or *Popular Feminisms in Theatre and Performance* (2013), coauthored with Geraldine Harris.

Consequently, in "Agitating for Change," Aston makes lucid and convincing use of ideas from Ernest Laclau and Chantal Mouffe[2] to elucidate the possibilities of thinking about "political theatre" as heterogeneously formed sites of opposition to neoliberalism as a "network of resistance" (8). Yet this proposition reflects an understanding stemming from her own career-long engagement with "different forms and different feminisms" (6), which has produced an appreciation of both feminism and theatre as diverse and complex socially and culturally situated practices. "Agitating for Change" does not understate the enormity of the challenges and difficulties attendant on the goal of making "cracks" in the neoliberal system, nor does it make grand and sweeping claims for the role of theatre and performance (feminist or otherwise) in this project. Instead, it is cautiously optimistic about the signs of a revival of feminism as a social movement for material, structural change, and for performances of differing types and styles she identifies in the excerpt, such as *NSFW*, *Made in Dagenham*, and "One Billion Rising," to contribute to achieving this change as links in a much wider "chain of resistance" alongside other systems of "'counterhegemonic' communication and/or sites of activism" (17).

At once passionately committed to feminism as a plural, insurgent politics and to performance as a heterogeneous, creative medium, conceptually ambitious and profoundly pragmatic, "Agitating for Change" encapsulates the quality and importance of Aston's contribution to the field.

Elaine Aston

Excerpt from "Agitating for Change: Theatre and a Feminist 'Network of Resistance'" (2016)

[. . .] Inspired by Chantal Mouffe's compelling description of a "network of resistance" as a possible way forward I conceive of theatre politically as a series of heterogeneously formed sites of oppositional and affirmative activity, each linked into articulating dissent from neoliberalism and the desire for socially progressive change (Mouffe 95). This provides the critical framework for my engagement with three radically diverse performances ranging from new playwriting (Lucy Kirkwood's *NSFW*), through the flash mob (Eve Ensler's One Billion Rising campaign), to the musical *Made in Dagenham*. [. . .]

Feminism re-resignified: towards a "network of resistance"
The "undoing" of late twentieth-century Western feminism, as Angela McRobbie terms it, is by now a familiar story; archetypically it tells of backlash, anti-feminist sentiments and the appropriation of feminism into a neoliberal agenda (24–53). The transformation from feminism conceived as a socially progressive force for change into a neoliberal mode of individualistically styled "empowerment" can be cursorily glimpsed through the backlash shifts in the feminist lexicon: for "equality" read "autonomy"; for "collective" see "individual"; for "radical" substitute "liberal"; for "emancipatory" see all of the above.[3] From my UK perspective, without a movement of women seeking to re-appropriate feminism and redefine what it stands for, since the turn of the millennium it has been difficult to see how the socially progressive ends of feminism might be returned to, as opposed to the widely (mass-media) proclaimed end of feminism.

However, the advent of the current decade has seen an exponential growth in the number of women's campaigns, occasioning high-profile attention to the ongoing struggle for women's liberation. Some commentators, like *Guardian* journalist Kira Cochrane, see the extent of this activity as evidence of the emergence of a fourth wave of feminism. Cochrane argues that these renewed political energies can be attributed to feminism rising in the wake of a raft of other wide-ranging protests. Notable protests in the UK include: student riots over tuition fees for higher education (2010); Occupy London as part of the global Occupy movement (2011–2012); and a series of strike actions against cuts to public sector pensions (2011). To posit these widespread protests as a possible influence on the outcrop of women's campaigns lends credence to what Ernest Laclau and Chantal Mouffe term a "chain of equivalences": political identities formed around a site of oppression yet receptive to, and capable of intersecting with equivalent struggles and demands, thereby fostering the capacity "to push for the radicalization of democracy and to establish a new hegemony" (Mouffe 133). At this time, Mouffe reflects, it would require a "vast chain of equivalences" in order to challenge neoliberalism (135). To what extent current protests will prove to be "vast" still remains to be seen, but feminism rising against the backdrop of equivalent protests as it did in the 1960s and 1970s however fragile this may prove in the long term, could at least be viewed as hopeful.

Optimism about the "beginning of neoliberalism's end as an economic regime" certainly characterised the US-based perspective of political theorist Nancy Fraser. In the wake of Obama's election she wrote of capitalism as being "at a critical crossroads" and speculated on "a new wave of mobilization aimed at articulating an alternative" (113–14). As far as the UK is concerned, the hegemony of economic neoliberalism did not immediately crack open as many predicted it would after the global banking crisis of 2008. Rather, neoliberal austerity measures are what the UK government, led by the Conservative Party since 2010, have pursued. However, here too, as the Director of the Political Economy Research Institute at Sheffield University conjectures,

> in politics change often begins at the bottom and forces its way to the political surface. Possibly, just possibly, the British people in their apparently contradictory reactions to the crisis are now signalling that they have had enough of neoliberalism and want something that actually delivers to their aspirations and needs (Payne).

Indeed, although the General Election in May 2015 saw the Conservatives narrowly remain in power, the subsequent landslide vote for anti-austerity, democratic-socialist Jeremy Corbyn as Leader of the opposition Labour Party is indicative of a grassroots call for change.

That neoliberalism has failed to meet the "aspirations and needs" of young women, those who, as Cochrane puts it, "grew up being told the world was post-feminist, that sexism and misogyny were over, and feminists should pack up their placards," is now corroborated by the numerous instances of them picking up "their placards", organising campaigns, or protesting via social media, against sexism, pornography, rape and racism.[4] Their support is vital to recovering the momentum of feminism as a movement: to the "doing" rather than "undoing" of feminism. Since, as Fraser observes, "the rise of neoliberalism" occasioned feminism's "resignification" in the guise of the individualistic, self-empowered woman – feminism's "rogue", "uncanny double" – the current "possible shift away from neoliberalism" is a propitious moment in which feminism might be re-resignified through a renewal of "the emancipatory promise of second-wave feminism" (pp. 108, 114, 116). In other words, the recognition, especially on the part of younger, "post-feminist" generations, that a "shift away from" and alternative to neoliberalism is urgently needed in the interests of socially progressive change, affords an opportunity to revisit and revitalise feminism's emancipatory aspirations and goals.

Where feminism's rejuvenation is one critical concern, another matter is the question of theatre's political agency. The difficulty, if not seeming impossibility, of cracking open neoliberalism has occasioned intense scrutiny about the critical role of the arts. There are those who, like Jodi Dean, view the arts as a distraction from "political struggles", while others, such as Mouffe, are of the view that the arts have an important role "in making visible what the dominant consensus tends to obscure and obliterate" (Dean 13, Mouffe 93). More specifically in terms of performance, theatre's adjectival attachments to "the political" as fostered by a leftish, twentieth-century, political-theatre tradition have been widely contested by some and rejected outright by others. Theatre's capacity to act politically has been perceived to be as diminished as the ideological (broadly socialist) ground in which it took root. As Janelle Reinelt observes, "The debate about the value and indeed the definition of "political theatre" has seen a "turning away from a discredited 'identity politics' to a preference for participatory, non-didactic postdramatic theatre" ("Generational Shifts" 289–90). In her seminal essay "Performance at the Crossroads of Citizenship", she elaborates on how the discrediting of identity politics diminishes the focus on "matters of race, class, gender and sexuality in performance", and examines the way in which the "extremely influential discourse of postdramatic theatre" has occasioned "shifting attention away from any direct connection between theatre and political life outside the theatre" in favour of "turning attention inward to the processes of the theatrical apparatus itself and its internal politics" ("Performance at the Crossroads" 35). While identity politics always needs to be revisited and the terms of its thinking renegotiated,[5] its discrediting is arguably harmful to the erasure of identity-marked inequalities and differences. Equally, the privileging of the "participatory, non-didactic postdramatic" over politically marked theatre, if not all other kinds of theatre, risks eliding consideration of the myriad ways in which theatre might possibly be helping to make visible the cracks in neoliberalism's armour.

Hence, to borrow from Mouffe, I am arguing for critical attentions to a "plurality of forms of artistic [performance] intervention" and advocating an approach which posits theatre's heterogeneously formed sites of opposition to neoliberalism as a "network of resistance" (94–5).[6] To conceive of "counter-hegemonic"(Mouffe 94) performances as a "network of resistance", is to think of theatre's manifold, resistant sites as links in a chain agitating for change to the neoliberal hegemony. This eschews the difficulty of attributing the burden of resistance to any one particular form and conceives the making of political subjectivities as occurring across multiple sites of potential emancipatory possibility.[7]

While constitutive of multiple sites that may assist with dissent from neoliberalism, theatre as a "network of resistance" cannot in and of itself, however, dismantle the dominant hegemony. At once a reminder of Mouffe's point that a "vast chain of equivalences" is needed to challenge neoliberalism, in another, related way, this also directs attention to acknowledging theatre as a link in or linked into other chains of interconnecting social and cultural communication. As Reinelt argues, theatre operates as a "communication node within a network of highly varied and sometimes contradictory nodes that together make up public discourse". It has the potential to "modify or challenge, or possibly even sometimes support, other information or modes of knowing that are addressing the polity" (pp. 43, 48–9).[8] In sum, theatre need not to be seen as acting alone in the political arena but as intersecting with other circuits and activities producing "counter-hegemonic" knowledge, as will shortly be exemplified in my analysis of Lucy Kirkwood's *NSFW* and its links with Lucy Bates' Everyday Sexism project.

In addition to observing this "counter hegemonic" circuitry, it is important to clarify that resistance ought not be defined or thought of purely in terms of opposition (that which we are against) but also affirmation (that which we are for). In other words, agitating for change requires not only oppositional strategies but also reparative tactics to help envision the re-making of an alternative, socially progressive hegemony. Equally, as will become clear in my commentary on One Billion Rising, reparative strategies are arguably vital to carrying on within the political arrangement as is. For when people are calling for change to a regime that has failed to deliver or is in some way acting improperly in respect of so-called democracy, this requires both imagining and working towards a systemic change that is not yet, at the same time as surviving the here-and-now conditions of a socio-political given.[9]

As previously stated, under neoliberalism systemic change of the socially democratic kind has been difficult to imagine. As McRobbie outlines, a key impediment to envisioning an alternative is the erasure of details of historically significant efforts to bring about democratic cultural change from cultural memory (49). Thus my third and final case study, *Made in Dagenham*, with its reprise of the 1968 strike that made feminist history, attests to the politically reparative remembering of past struggles as an important element in the "network of resistance".

In sum, with their own amalgam of dissensual and reparative practices,[10] 'counter-hegemonic' performances conceived as a 'network of resistance' have the potential to play their supportive part in agitating for change. By way of consolidating and illustrating my claim, I move next to the three performances as links in a chain of feminist resistance to neoliberalism, each of which contributes to feminism's re-resignification as an emancipatory politics. [. . .]

Please see the Works Cited for further information on the sources used in this essay.

Notes

1 Pam Gems (1925–2011) was an English playwright best known for the 1978 musical play *Piaf.* Winsome Pinnock (b.1961) is a Jamaican-British playwright, known as "the godmother of black British playwrights." (See Pinnock entry in this volume.) Phyllis Nagy (b.1962) is an American theatre and film director, screenwriter, and dramatist, known for her work *Mrs. Harris.* debbie tucker green is a British playwright, screenwriter, and director, known for her Olivier award-winning *born bad.* Sarah Kane (1971–1999) was an English playwright, screenwriter and theatre director known for her play *Blasted.* Laura Wade (b.1977) is an English playwright, known for her works *Limbo* and *16 Winters* [Harris].

2 Ernest Laclau (1935–2014) was an Argentine political theorist and philosopher, often described as an "inventor" of post-Marxist political theory. Chantal Mouffe (b.1943) is a Belgian political theorist. [Harris]

3 For a detailed overview and contextualisation of these shifts, see McRobbie and in particular Chapter 2, "Feminism Undone? The Cultural Politics of Disarticulation," pp. 24–53. [Aston]

4 See Cochrane who offers a useful survey of the variety of campaign initiatives. [Aston]

5 For an insightful, feminist revisiting of identity politics, see Elin Diamond, *et al.* [Aston]

6 Mouffe's own discussion focuses on the "counter-hegemonic interventions" of the artist Alfredo Jaar. [Aston]

7 My observation about the making of political subjectivities across multiple forms is in accord with and influenced by Jacques Rancière's idea of the emancipated spectator. See Rancière. [Aston]

8 Reinelt's observations in "Crossroads of Citizenship" are situated within a critical framework that draws on Étienne Balibar's "worksites of democracy" to postulate "theatre as

a democratic worksite". This highly insightful model is a cognate way of thinking about how theatre acts politically. [Aston]

9 Eve Kosofsky Sedgwick, whose Kleinian-based discussion of reparative processes has influenced my thinking in this regard, argues that coping necessitates "the often very fragile concern to provide the self with pleasure and nourishment in an environment that is perceived as not particularly offering them" (137). Thus, attending to the reparative processes by which "selves and communities succeed in extracting sustenance from the objects of a culture – even of a culture whose avowed desire has often been not to sustain them" (150–151) is an important consideration, not least since reparative attachments to objects that fail to sustain also mark the oscillation between the given and the present desire for that which is not yet. [Aston]

10 Where Sedgwick is a seminal influence on my thinking about the reparative, it is Rancière's notion of dissensus that shadows my thoughts on the practice of dissent. See Rancière, pp. 48–49. [Aston]

Suggestions for Further Reading

Elaine Aston and Geraldine Harris, eds. *Feminist Futures?: Theatre, Performance, Theory.* London: Springer, 2006.

———. and Sue-Ellen Case, eds. *Staging International Feminisms.* Basingstoke, UK, and New York, NY: Palgrave Macmillan, 2007.

———. and Mark O'Thomas. *Royal Court: International.* Basingstoke: Springer, 2015.

———. "Enter Stage Left: 'Recognition','Redistribution', and the A-Affect." *Contemporary Theatre Review.* 28.3 (2018): 299–309.

———. "Moving Women Centre Stage: Structures of Feminist-Tragic Feeling." *Journal of Contemporary Drama in English.* 5.2 (2017): 292–310.

79 DAME HARRIET WALTER (b.1950)

Rosemary Malague

Introduction

Dame Harriet Walter (b.1950) is a distinguished, versatile, and prolific British actor of the stage and screen. She is also the author of several essays and three volumes on acting: *Other People's Shoes: Thoughts on Acting* (1999), *Actors on Shakespeare: Macbeth* (2002), and *Brutus and Other Heroines: Playing Shakespeare's Roles for Women* (2016). An outspoken feminist, Walter's writing addresses the sexism—and ageism—that actresses encounter in the theatre. Her fourth book celebrates the subject of its title: *Facing It: Reflections on Images of Older Women* (2011). Now in her sixth decade of performing, Walter is an expert interpreter of Shakespeare, as demonstrated in her acting and writing. She has played more than twenty Shakespearean women, many with the Royal Shakespeare Company (RSC), and she has written about most of them, including: Ophelia, Helena, Lady Macbeth, Beatrice, and Cleopatra, as well as what she calls the "boy roles," Portia, Viola, and Imogen. Finding herself older than most of Shakespeare's female characters, Walter had resigned herself that her "Shakespeare days were over." But she longed for the "lung-filling, mind-altering, self-testing practice" of playing The Bard (*Brutus* 157), and she found it again through her performance of three Shakespearean men, Brutus, Henry IV, and Prospero, in the celebrated trio of Phyllida Lloyd's all-female, Donmar Warehouse productions. Walter then wrote rapturously about these opportunities in *Brutus*.

Shakespearean expertise is central to Walter's repertoire, but only part of it. Her talent and intellect are deep and wide-ranging. She has portrayed Anton Chekhov's women, including: Varya in *The Cherry Orchard*, Nina in *The Seagull*, Masha in *The Three Sisters*, and Anna in *Ivanov*. Other canonical characters include Hedda in Henrik Ibsen's *Hedda Gabler*, Elizabeth I in Frederick Schiller's *Mary Stuart*, Edward/Victoria in Caryl Churchill's *Cloud 9*, and Linda in Arthur Miller's *Death of a Salesman*. Walter also originated roles in Tom Stoppard's *Arcadia*, Yasmina Reza's *Life x 3*, and Timberlake Wertenbaker's *Three Birds Alighting on a Field*. Her presence onscreen is ubiquitous: she has performed more than one hundred roles on film and television. She holds the titles of Commander of the Order of the British Empire (CBE) and Dame Commander of the Order of the British Empire (DBE), both in recognition of her services to drama; she was named an Honorary Associate Artist of the RSC and an Honorary Doctor of Letters by Birmingham University.

Walter's writing is significant for two compelling reasons. The first is that it remains a relatively rare phenomenon for actors to put their processes into words, much less publish them. Walter says that some colleagues protested that her effort

DOI: 10.4324/9781003006923-80

was "impossible," and others seemed "slightly threatened by my attempt, as though I were intending to give away trade secrets" (*Other* xii). The second reason Walter's writing is so important is that though she does not give away "trade secrets," she *does* expose a great deal about what it was—and is—to be an actress in the late-twentieth and early twenty-first centuries. "I discovered feminism in the same year as I went to drama school, 1970," Walter notes, and her insider's insights into rehearsal rooms, acting practices, script analyses, and interpretive choices are informed by her politics ("Heroine" 110). By publishing about her own career, Walter documents fifty years of theatre history, theory, and practice—from an explicitly feminist perspective.

Two encounters with academia in the 1980s prompted Walter's writing. The first was an association between the RSC and the Shakespeare Institute, which took "actors' insights seriously," inviting essays on characters they were playing for an anthology. The second was an interview with Carol Rutter for *Clamorous Voices*, a compilation that brought "new feminist experience to the famous female roles." Walter believed that she had "something fresh" to offer to these discussions, which indeed she has; readers would do well to consult all of her work (*Brutus* ix).

Feminist theatre scholarship of the 1980s largely rejected the canonical roles that Walter played. Sue-Ellen Case famously pointed to the "absence of women" in ancient Greek and Elizabethan theatres, and to the objectionable "fictional woman" that replaced them, going so far as to proclaim: "The feminist actor may no longer regard these roles as desirable for her career" (*Feminism and Theatre*, 18). Yet however sound Case's theory about theatre history might be, her suggestion was never pragmatic. Writing in 1999, Walter makes the all-too-familiar observation that women are often relegated to "thankless supporting roles" in the theatre,[1] expressing disappointment and anger about "actresses of huge capacity squeezed into stereotypes" (*Other* 189) and lamenting Shakespeare's neglect of women (*Brutus* 203–207). But she also testifies about the pervasive misogyny in experimental theatres of her early career, ironically finding that classical work offered her greater range and prestige. Though keenly aware that he never envisioned women onstage, Walter expresses gratitude for "the compensatory blessings of Shakespeare's scale" (*Other* 189).

In writing spanning three decades, Walter repeatedly revisits the role of Helena in *All's Well That Ends Well*, which she played at the RSC in 1981. Her interview with Rutter was printed in 1989; Walter gave a paper on Helena entitled "The Heroine, the Harpy and the Human Being" in 1991; and she published a revision of that talk for *New Theatre Quarterly* in 1993. She mentions Helena in *Other People's Shoes* and devotes a chapter to her in *Brutus*—the version included here—saying: "For this book I decided to focus on the character of Helena in *All's Well That Ends Well*, who exemplifies many of my observations. In order to be true to what I was writing at the time, I have kept to these observations in the current rewording for this book, but I'm happy to say that a lot of the attitudes I was up against have changed" (*Brutus* 14).

Walter's perspectives are enlightening: though "attitudes" about women may have changed throughout her career, Shakespearean text has not. Walter embraces this paradox in her essay on Helena, a nonconforming female character from one of Shakespeare's "problem plays," making it a fitting, feminist contribution to this collection.

Dame Harriet Walter

Excerpt from "Helena: Heroine or Harpy?" **Brutus and Other Heroines** *(2016)*

"A Mingled Yarn"

In Act IV, Scene 3, of *All's Well That Ends Well* Shakespeare says:

> The web of our life is of a mingled yarn, good and ill
> together: our virtues would be proud, if our faults
> whipped them not; and our crimes would despair, if they
> were not cherished by our virtues.

It is one of my favourite speeches. It is not at all famous and comes from the mouth of a minor character who doesn't even have a name (the First Lord).

It felt to me to be one of the central tenets of the play, and therefore it seemed that Shakespeare intended his chief female character, Helena, to reflect it. I believe Shakespeare deliberately created a heroine who is imperfect but whose worth he ultimately believes in. He challenges the audience to accept a flawed female as their guide through the story and to allow her to win in the end. That end remains ambiguous but, I think, hopeful. It would be unbelievable if it were all rosy, but it would be uncharacteristically cynical if the title were entirely ironic.

Helena came to me with a bad reputation. Critics over the years had judged her as immodest, ambitious, predatory and sanctimonious. It was 1981, and the play had not often been performed because so many people deemed it unplayable and the heroine unacceptable. What is Helena's crime? She pursues the man of her choice rather than waiting for him to choose her. Helena's namesake in *A Midsummer Night's Dream* (which I played in that same season) also chases after her man, but she is loveable because her quest is hopeless and it is treated comedically. In Act II, Scene 2, she voices the inappropriateness of her behaviour and despises her own desperation:

> We cannot fight for love, as men may do.
> We should be woo'd and were not made to woo,

and what is here comically expressed, is the predicament of the other, more serious Helena as well.

I was not interested in judging *All's Well's* Helena. I had my work cut out learning her very opaque speeches and summoning the courage and technique to play my first major Shakespeare role on the main stage at Stratford in the company of Dame Peggy Ashcroft among other luminaries.

What I instantly related to was a woman of ambition. To date, my favourite role had been Nina in *The Seagull.* Nina is no ordinary sweet young thing but an ambitious actress eager for experience, who gets battered by tragedy, is strengthened by it and moves on. I could always relate to ambition, having plenty of drive myself. What was harder to relate to was the fact that the full extent of Helena's ambition was to get her man.

Precisely because she is hard to label, Helena is one of the most interesting and modern of Shakespeare's women that I have ever played. However, the label-seeking analysts want to know where they stand. They fret over whether *All's Well* is a comedy, a romance or a tragedy. The answer is that it hops between all three and all three overlap; a bit like life really. But a label it must have, so it becomes 'a problem play', and the major problem is what to make of the central couple, Helena and Bertram.

It is one thing to come to terms with a heroine who pursues and traps a man into marriage, but another to accept that the man she pursues doesn't seem worth the effort. Neither hero nor heroine is likeable.

The issue of likeability is one I have come up against often since, but never so clearly as with Helena. Seldom does anybody ask whether they *like* Hamlet, Henry V, or King Lear, but somehow the heroine has to be sympathetic, palatable, liked. It is definitely easier for a woman to be liked if she is pretty, gentle, and unassuming than if she is intense, ambitious, and complicated like Helena.

On the other hand, it is interesting that George Bernard Shaw preferred Helena to any other Shakespeare heroine, and having studied the part in depth and played it in repertoire over a period of two years, I feel certain that Shakespeare was basically on her side. Every decent, wise character in the play approves of her, and her only detractors are Parolles, a known cheat, and Bertram, an immature snobbish boy.

From the start, I felt for Helena's unrequited love and her social isolation. I liked her for her ambition and the way she shoved self-pity aside and followed her dream. I admired her guts chancing her arm at curing the King. I was fascinated by her oblique, broken-up, cryptic soliloquies at the beginning of the play. They gave me a clue as to her tangled thoughts, and the fact that she almost could not speak her ambition out loud, it seemed so transgressive. This means that she could barely admit her feelings to herself, since a confessional soliloquy to the audience is the equivalent of talking to oneself.

About her faults I was maybe less than honest. I was feeling defensive against what seemed to be a historical sea of prejudice, so I was perhaps in denial about any of her short-comings, her possible underhandedness, her blinkeredness about Bertram's feelings, her scheming—and I sought every justification for these that I could dig out of the text.

Trevor Nunn, the director, also saw the need to redeem the misunderstood Helena if he was going to make the play work. By setting the play in the early twentieth century, he helped my interpretation of Helena by suggesting a connection with the emancipated heroines of Ibsen and Shaw. He also encouraged me to empha-sise Helena's trepidation and thereby her bravery, to dig out and deliver whatever self-deprecatory wit she might have, and to find her moments of remorse and com-passion for Bertram. The opportunities were all there in Shakespeare's text.

Yes, she can seem secretive and indirect, especially in her dealings with Bertram, but I put that down to diffidence and self-doubt. Yes, she can seem manipulative but, as I see it, she only manipulates what Fate seems to set in her pathway, and Fate seems consistently to reward her faith. First her pursuit of Bertram gets a blessing from his own mother, the Countess of Rousillon, then her faith (plus a little medical know-how) manages to cure the King of France of a fatal disease, and then the King promises her Bertram as her reward.

When things go terribly wrong and Helena realises that her monomania has driven Bertram away from France and on to the battlefield and possible death, she is willing to give up her pursuit, become a wandering pilgrim and leave France, since it is her presence there that has forced Bertram to run to the wars.

No, come thou home, Rousillon,
Whence honour but of danger wins a scar,
As oft it loses all: I will be gone;
My being here it is that holds thee hence:
Shall I stay here to do't? no, no, although
The air of paradise did fan the house
And angels officed all: I will be gone.

All this seems quite clearly to indicate her willing self-sacrifice to Bertram's hap-piness, but then, for the sake of a good plot, Shakespeare has her winding up in Italy and, by 'coincidence', exactly in that part of Italy where Bertram's regiment is stationed. The prejudiced in the audience see only the schemer deliberately stalking her prey. They forget the soliloquy they have recently heard. Actions have spoken louder than words.

The fact that everyone Helena meets seems to like her, including the Widow and Diana, who take to her immediately, can be seen by the prejudiced as evidence of her manipulative charm. I tried to be as straight as possible, but the plot is twisty and doesn't help me.

Why did I try? Partly I was being true to what I found in the text, but partly I was guilty of wanting to make Helena as palatable as I possibly could. This tends to happen with actresses of my generation who do not want to play into any possible misogynist interpretations of a female role. We feel burdened by the need to over-compensate and make our character better than anyone else, wiser, more moral, more sympathetic; and that leads to a different, though understandable, kind of inaccuracy.

Helena was complicated enough for me not to have to come down one side or another of the 'heroine or harpy' argument. I loved her variety, her contradictions, her elusiveness, her switches from diffidence to dynamism, from conjuror to rejected victim, from pilgrim to adventurer. I love her 'feminine' empathy and her 'mascu-line' wooing and pursuing; and she does all this without having to wear trousers!

After a long and painful journey she wins through. Bertram has been through a painful journey too, and Helena's steadfastness, that once sickened him, becomes the very thing he needs to redeem him from his own self-loathing and humiliation.

I did have trouble with both Shakespeare's and Trevor's idea of the woman as redeemer. This kind of idealism doesn't seem true to a real woman's experience any more than the negative portrayal of a scheming succubus, but I also can't believe that Shakespeare meant to leave the audience with a sense of 'Well, *that* marriage sure ain't gonna last' or 'Poor geezer saddled with that domineering woman'. I think he meant to leave us with a feeling that these two people have gone on an incred-ible journey, and who knows? They might work it out, and their life could be very interesting.

Whatever *All's Well's* textbook reputation, Shakespeare wrote it to be performed rather than read or written about, and, as we hoped it would prove, with the flesh and blood of live performance the harpy Helena and the wastrel Bertram were revealed to be human beings of a mingled yarn.

The production was received for the most part with rapture. The acting was praised, but I could not entirely enjoy the success. Despite all our efforts to clarify Helena's motives, one male critic still referred to her as 'the martyr/bitch'. Therefore

I felt I had failed. Now, however, I'm inclined to think that that review told me more about the reviewer's fears than about my performance, and that the prejudice and misogyny of a few male critics is their problem, not mine. If, despite the delicate ambiguity we placed in the final moments of the play, one critic managed to read a 'triumphant smile' into my apprehensive face as I took Bertram's hand, and if, despite our leaving the audience with the tentative optimism we dared to believe that Shakespeare himself intended, some critics chose to read blatant cynicism into it, that is their right. What more could I do?

Like many of the women we portray, we actresses have become expert at the subtle, the subversive, and the almost subliminal means of communicating our beliefs. The trouble is that this indirectness leaves the door wide open for misinterpretation. One's personal statement obliquely infiltrated into a piece of work or a character is necessarily filtered through the eyes and ears of the beholder, and it is the beholder's right to understand it as he or she feels.

Whether in classical or modern drama, I fight for the right to portray women who are as contradictory, complex and diverse as the women I see all around me, and I uphold my right to present ordinary, flawed women at the heart of a play.

Virtue and its opposite are human, not an endowment from the gods. There is always a chink in the halo, or a redeeming shaft of light under the black hood. As an actor you look for your character's motive. That is almost all you have to know. You try to understand why they do what they do and then set the acting in motion. We do not sit in judgment at the centre of our character any more than we spend our day assessing our own character at every moment of our lives in the real world. Whether the part I am playing is deemed a heroine or a harpy, I only need concern myself with her thoughts, her words and her deeds—and by following them I find a complex human being.

Please see the Works Cited for further information on the sources used in this essay.

Note

1 See, for example, Dolan, *Feminist Spectator*, 2.

Suggestion for Further Reading

Walter, Harriet. "Imogen in Cymbeline." *Players of Shakespeare 3: Further Essays in Shakespearean Performance.* Eds. Russell Jackson and Robert Smallwood. Cambridge: Cambridge University, 1993.

80 CATHERINE KODICEK (b.1972)

Kitty Gurnos-Davies

Introduction

In her article, "Stop treating costume professionals as second-class workers," Catherine Kodicek (b.1972) employs a feminist lens to address the conditions of women's work backstage. Published in 2017 on the online platform of the theatrical newspaper, *The Stage,*[1] it stands as the first in an ongoing series of monthly articles authored by Kodicek. The informal idiom of *The Stage* (in comparison, for example, to scholarship or industry reports) allows practitioners to engage in autoethnographic criticism rooted in their own experiences as theatre professionals. Drawing upon thirteen years working as Head of Costume at the Young Vic in London (2006–2019), Kodicek uses the platform to address the systemic imbalance of gendered power she observes in the theatre industry. Her writing unites theatre criticism with activism, employing an intersectional lens to interrogate how power dynamics relating to race, socio-economic status, and gender identity play out in the politics of theatrical labour. She argues that this approach is particularly pertinent when considering costume work. The costume supervisors, designers, makers, dressers, and wardrobe teams constitute "a predominantly female workforce" that operates within the hierarchical structure of backstage activities – one that frequently renders these professionals "invisible and victim to an unconscious gender bias" (Kodicek, "Let's have"). Kodicek's critique of the gender politics of theatrical labour resonates with contemporary concerns about women's status in the wider entertainment industry epitomised by the high-profile campaigns #MeToo and #TimesUp that strive, respectively, to raise awareness of sexual harassment in the workplace and gendered inequalities of pay in Hollywood, television, and theatre.

The significance of Kodicek's contribution to contemporary women's theatre criticism is threefold. First, she confronts the ideological and actual division of backstage labour along gendered lines, recognizing that costume is "an industry mostly made up of women" ("Stop treating"). She argues that the female-dominated demographic of the workforce has a tangible impact on women's working conditions. In her tongue-in-cheek New Year's Resolutions for directors, written for *The Stage* in January 2018, she highlights the assumption made by many theatre makers that a woman backstage must belong to the costume team: "[d]on't yell 'dresser' or 'wardrobe' at a passing woman wearing black unless you would also shout 'sound' or 'sparks' at a passing man dressed in cargo trousers or carrying a screwdriver" ("Fittings"). With humour, she warns against perpetuating gender stereotypes in the workplace that might restrict women's access to the full range of backstage roles and, in turn, shape

DOI: 10.4324/9781003006923-81

the valuation of costume work itself. The skills employed in the construction and care of costumes traditionally belong to the domain of women's work. As a result, these skills are frequently undervalued and the labour of costume professionals inadequately remunerated. Kodicek gives the example of the "soft skills" and "emotional labour" demanded of dressers. They are expected to "nurture and care for the actor" ("Stop tipping") during the performance period despite this aspect of their work being omitted from job descriptions and, consequently, unaccounted for in payment. Her argument resonates with well-established feminist critiques that address the lack of monetary compensation for tasks traditionally conceived as woman's labour that similarly employ "soft skills," including housework and childcare. Thus, she calls for gender-neutral job titles that she argues might help to professionalise the "emotional labour" associated with costume work by disentangling it from essentialist notions of gendered activities, for example, replacing "wardrobe mistress" or "wardrobe master" with "wardrobe manager" ("Gendered job titles").

Second, the article demonstrates the power of online platforms to facilitate democratic forums through which to undertake theatre criticism. Although *The Stage* operates a paywall that might limit her readership numbers, Kodicek also employs social media to cultivate virtual communities of costume professionals who feel underrepresented or exploited within the infrastructure of the theatre industry. As she describes in the article, colleagues are encouraged to share their experiences through these informal support networks. Kodicek has formalised this process of consciousness raising by founding a trade association for costume professionals: the Costume in Theatre Association (CITA)[2]. CITA strives to improve the working conditions of backstage labour and began by carrying out a number of pay surveys. The Association hopes to demystify the remuneration of costume work otherwise rendered opaque by the multiplicity of freelance and short-term contracts, employee buyout packages, and unregulated working hours prevalent across the industry.

Finally, in her celebration of costume professionals, Kodicek directs the attention of her readership to an area of women's work that is frequently overlooked and carves out space in theatre criticism in which to reassess women's historic and contemporary contribution to the production of theatre. Recovering these experiences from the margins of scholarship and the theatre industry alike, she asks her readers to confront the gender bias that continues to permeate the valuation of costume work and asks them to join her in finding solutions. Taken together, her series of articles written for *The Stage* brings the perspectives of the "predominantly female workforce" of costume professionals forth from the wings and places them centre stage.

Catherine Kodicek

"Stop Treating Costume Professionals as Second-Class Workers" (2017)

People talk to me. I have that sort of face. Strangers talk to me at bus stops, and my colleagues talk to me at work – not just idle chat but often full-blown, state-of-their-lives conversations. And while I'm a good listener, I have one infuriating habit: when I hear about problems, I want to find solutions.

I'm one of the lucky ones. I work in a good theatre, with a good employer, in a team that I feel truly part of. As head of costume, I earn the same as the other heads of departments. I feel appreciated and that my opinion matters – and I feel empowered to instigate change.

But I also employ a lot of freelance costume professionals and over time I've come to appreciate how much of a bubble I am in. Listening to their stories, I began to get angry on behalf of all costume professionals.

I sought out and met up with people who were talking about these issues facing them on social media. I began to list them in a notebook: low pay and no pay, bad contracts, uncaring managers, unfair hiring practices, impossible deadlines, low budgets for shows, bullish directors, long hours without overtime, working through breaks as standard and disparities between the costume department fees and those of other technical departments.

The list covered freelancers, those who work in full-time, permanent jobs and those on long-term, fixed contracts. It covered people who were paid by contract and received overtime, people who were on buyouts, people who were on weekly rates with overtime, people who were paid by show call, people paid a fee.

As I talked with them, I began to develop some theories about where these problems had sprung from. Here are a few:

- Costume people are too isolated, so we don't know what other people are earning or what a fair wage should be.
- The contracts we take are many and varied and at each stage we are required to negotiate on our own behalf.
- Many of us are working in a twilight-gig economy of fees that bear no relation to hours worked.
- There is an expectation that we will work through our breaks, and that if our hours are going to be too long we will accept a buyout that underpays us to illegal levels.

As an industry mostly made up of women, we cannot be too demanding or too difficult because that is frowned on. When we do question something, expect something or demand something, we may find that we are shunned and cannot find work. That's tough when a freelancer is only as good as their last job.

The issues seem vast and insurmountable. How could any individual hope to change them? So, with the like-minded costume professionals I had been talking to, I set up the Costume in Theatre Association to bring us together.

We conducted a pay survey that demonstrated the huge disparity of income, especially among freelancers, and our Facebook forum and occasional open meetings have gradually become places where people can talk about the issues they face.

There are many different problems affecting hundreds of costume professionals and each problem overlaps and intersects with the other issues. If you were to contrive a system designed to hold costume professionals down and disempower them, you would create the current system of working.

There simply isn't space to write about all the issues, but here's a concrete example. It isn't earth-shattering. It isn't the biggest issue we face today. It's just one small stitch in the whole giant tapestry. Recently, the Bridge Theatre opened in London to great fanfare. It is not a small theatre, with a single technical manager who oversees all technical aspects of the building. It is a large-scale producing theatre with a head of lighting and a head of sound among the technical staff.

Both these roles were advertised in this paper; applicants were afforded all the rigours of fairness and transparency demanded of an advertised role. But there was no advert for a head-of-costume role; instead a friend of mine was offered a short-term contract as a wardrobe manager.

UK Theatre and the Society of London Theatre recently commissioned a survey of backstage workers[3]. One of the issues the review highlights is that: "An endemic culture of networking and closed recruitment practices is effective at creating good short-term results, but means that the make-up of the sector is self-perpetuating and exclusive. This culture unintentionally works against piecemeal attempts to improve diversity in the sector."

Just consider for a moment a parallel reality in which all full-time technical staff were acquired in this way. What if someone was ringing around asking if anyone knew someone who wanted to set up the lighting department in a new theatre?

Would sound and lighting professionals be happy with this? Would they think it fair or equitable? Or would they be understandably concerned that temporary employees on rolling contracts have no vested interest in the department as a whole?

In a world dominated by freelance roles, a new permanent head of costume position would have been like gold dust – a fine opportunity for one of my many talented colleagues to advance their career and the craft of costume.

There are few enough as it is and the Bridge is certainly not alone in taking this path. But permanent heads of department provide so [much] more than just labour. We are able to take an active part in developing the department, committed to its smooth running and infrastructure, as well as health and safety.

We can offer work placements and employ apprentices, providing opportunities for others further down the ladder. While it may seem like a cost-saving measure to do without us (after all, it's just clothes, right?), it's a false economy. And, as the survey findings point out, employing freelancers on a 'who you know' basis, without even the courtesy of an interview process, makes it very hard for new people from diverse backgrounds to get a foothold in the industry.

Of course, it's not like there isn't a well-worn groove of producing theatres wanting costumes in their shows and yet seeing a costume department as a luxurious add on. But it would have been wonderful to see the Bridge's ethos of innovation extending to costume.

Their website states that they are "committed to managing a fair and equitable recruitment and selection process to the highest industry standards".

This is likely true, which is a damning indictment of those industry standards as they apply to costume professionals.

Please see the Works Cited for further information on the sources used in this essay.

Notes

1 See https://www.thestage.co.uk/
2 See CITA website: http://costumeintheatre.com
3 See http://bit.ly/workforcereview

Suggestion for Further Reading

Maclaurin, Alison and Aoife Monks. *Costume: Readings in Theatre Practice*. London: Palgrave, 2018.

81 SPIDERWOMAN THEATER (1976–) AND MURIEL MIGUEL (b.1937)

Lilian Mengesha

Introduction

In the opening lines of Potawatomi biologist Robin Wall Kimmerer's 2013 text, *Braiding Sweetgrass: Indigenous Wisdom, Scientific Knowledge and the Teaching of Plants,* she describes the care work needed to braid sweetgrass, "*wingaashk,* the sweet-smelling hair of Mother Earth." Kimmerer asks the reader: "Will you hold the end of the bundle while I braid? Hands joined by grass, can we bend our heads together and make a braid to honor the earth? And then I'll hold it for you, while you braid, too" (ix). This gesture, holding the bundle of sweetgrass taut to make a braid, captures the collective worldmaking that composes the three strands, the three sisters, of Spiderwoman Theater: Muriel Miguel (b.1937), Gloria Miguel (b.1926), and the late Lisa Mayo (1924–2013). The Kuna/Rappahannock trio originated a performance creation process that combines both individual and collective storytelling around topics of sexuality, spirituality and Indigenous epistemologies, a process Miguel describes as "storyweaving." In the 2017 interview between the National Endowment for the Arts Media Producer Jo Reed and Spiderwoman's Artistic Director Muriel Miguel, excerpted here, they reflect on over forty years of performance work by the legendary Indigenous feminist ensemble.

Mapping song, movement, and gesture to difficult stories about sex, violence, spirituality, and appropriation, Spiderwoman has created a grammar for intergenerational collaboration through storyweaving. Given the often extractive and patriarchal dynamics of theatrical institutions founded upon Euro-centric actor training methods and productions centered on the vision of a singular playwright or director, Spiderwoman's performance methodology weaves stories of both violence and resilience through a rehearsal process where, in the words of Miguel, "Sometimes people cried, sometimes people laughed. We all laughed. And we gave food, we gave tea, we made bean soup." Following their namesake, the Hopi goddess of creation, Spiderwoman rematriates theatre relations through the collective caretaking work that centers Indigenous women's realities in a celebration of multiplicity and resilience.

Based in New York City, Spiderwoman Theater has produced over twenty performances since the mid 1970s. They have forged an Indigenous feminist approach to storytelling, one that adapts and prods at the Western canon, with works such as the *Lysistrata Numbah* (1977) and *3 Up, 3 Down* (1986), as well as a look at Indigenous politics through satires of Charlotte Brontë's novel *Jane Eyre* (1847) and her sister Emily Brontë's novel *Wuthering Heights* (1847). All the while, they have centered the stories

DOI: 10.4324/9781003006923-82

of Native women, as in *Daughters from the Stars: Nis Bundo* (1995) and *The Elders Project: Something Old, Something New, Something Borrowed, Something Blue* (2012), a solo project by Gloria Miguel about the creation story of a Tu Tu Kapsus who arrives in Brooklyn in the 1920s, an origin story in its own right.

At the opening of the interview, Miguel takes time to name and introduce her origins in the Star family. This action is not to be underestimated. We live in a world that increasingly celebrates a "globalized" or "universal" worldview, but the importance of naming where you and your ancestors came from, their stories on both the spiritual and physical realms, is central to what Miguel describes as Indigenous "protocol," and what Glen Coulthard and Leanne Betasamosake Simpson call "grounded normativity," the ethical frameworks that teach us "how to live our lives in relation to other people and nonhuman life forms in a profoundly nonauthoritarian, nondominating, nonexploitative manner" (254). In naming her Kuna and Rappahannock ancestors, Miguel verbally invites them into the space of the interview, reminding listeners that we do not simply "arrive" but that people, like places, contain specific histories. This naming practice is part of being in good relation.

Within the world of Critical Indigenous Studies, many scholars have discussed the work of being in good relation. Lakota science and technology scholar Kim TallBear offers what she describes as "a relational web framework" invested in collective caretaking that "can also articulate obligations across the generations," particularly a "material connectedness among many generations: those whose bodies may now/still exist within organismically defined understandings of life, those entities that do not meet that definition, and other bodies whose materiality has been transferred back to the earth and out into that web of relation, or whose bodies are not yet formed of already existing matter" (25). For Spiderwoman, patchwork is the manifestation of the relational web framework, where *testimony* is not always necessary, but material can do the storytelling, as Miguel states: "We don't necessarily tell that story, but we have the patch that tells that story."

Their performances, with the material patchwork of the Spiderwoman quilt that Miguel describes as foundational for all of their work, function as a relational web across time and space, human and nonhuman life. Miguel describes how, over the years, tapestries and quilts become part of their storyweaving, from the Kuna Yala mola tapestry to the Sun Dance quilts. In the creation of their recent work, *Material Witness* (2016), Miguel details the performance process in which they asked Indigenous women, "what do you want to leave behind?" through writing their story on cloth, bringing together their stories through the material itself. Patchwork became a central part of *Material Witness,* bearing the stories of harm and survival with Indigenous women. The beauty of patchwork is juxtaposing materials that are not always created to go together, but in so doing, the entire collective creates something unique—perhaps even an expansive understanding of kinship that moves beyond bloodlines. This is the definition of collaboration—not what happens when stories are combined by existing egos, but rather by embracing the risk and vulnerability required to create an "us" when stories are stitched together.

While Spiderwoman is hailed as the longest running Indigenous feminist theatre group, we can be certain they will not be the last. Now in their 44th year, they have built an expansive community of performers and a complex relational web, the making of their own origin story in real time. They seem to layer time upon itself, where echoes of their very first production, *Women in Violence* (1977), reverberate through

Material Witness. Rematriating theatre practice through Indigenous centered relations, honoring life all around, refuses the linearity of time in favor of time weaving
through multiple stories fashioned into one. While they build stories that come from
their bodies, bodies which themselves are archives, Spiderwoman's storyweaving
bends time by including past and future ancestors into the present. Spiderwoman
Theater asks audiences and performers alike: Won't you hold the other end of the
sweetgrass and braid this story with me?

Spiderwoman Theater and Muriel Miguel

*Excerpt from the National Endowment for the Arts Interview with
Spiderwoman Theater's Muriel Miguel by Josephine Reed (2017)*[1]

Jo Reed: Welcome to *Art Works* produced at the National Endowment for the Arts,
I'm Josephine Reed.[2]
Forty years ago, Muriel Miguel, with her sisters Gloria and Lisa, created
Spiderwoman Theater– which became an Indigenous women's theater ensemble that blends traditional Native art forms with Western theater. Named after
the Spiderwoman deity from Hopi mythology, it was the first Native American
women's theater troupe. Its aim was and is: to be a voice for Native women, to
disrupt stereotypes, and to shine a light on little-known stories. Since its inception, Spiderwoman Theater has written and produced over twenty original
works for the theater, most of them directed by Muriel Miguel. A multi-talented
actor, choreographer, playwright and visionary, Muriel also served as the company's artistic director since it began. She joined me in the studio for an interview about the theatre, but when I began by asking her about Spiderwoman,
she gently schooled me in proper Native protocol.
Muriel Miguel: I have to introduce myself. Many years ago, I was doing a panel, and
it was my daughter, myself and we were talking about theater. And it was mostly
a Native audience. And after we were finished talking, one little Indian lady got
up and said, "So who are you?" And I realized, I didn't follow the protocol. So,
I promised myself I would always follow the protocol, no matter where I am. So,
it means I have to tell you my whole background before I even say anything. All
right?
Jo Reed: I'm happy for it. That was going to be my second question. But we can start
there.
Muriel Miguel: Okay, okay. Okay! My name is Muriel Miguel. My other name is
Bright Sun, and my other name is Waga Nadili. I am from two different nations.
I am from the Kuna Yala, they're off the coast of Panama. And I come from
Rappahannock, which is in Virginia. My mother and father, they met in Brooklyn,
they married in Brooklyn, and they had three daughters in Brooklyn, so I am
truly a city Indian. I come from a Star family. And I am the third daughter from
the Stars.
Jo Reed: What is a Star family?
Muriel Miguel: It's part of the Creation stories of how the Kuna began and where
they came from. And they came from the stars. And I happen to be part of that
Star family, in what you, I guess, would call [our] clan. So that's really important
to say what I just said.

Jo Reed: I want to hear about you growing up. Tell me what it was like growing up. Being a city Indian, living with your two sisters in Brooklyn.

Muriel Miguel: I grew up in an Italian neighborhood, a Native in an Italian neighborhood in Brooklyn, and I went to all the elementary schools and high schools in Brooklyn. And sometimes it was very hard. It was hard because people had no idea who you were. And so because they didn't understand you, they would make fun of you. And so that was very hard. They would call my father, "Tonto,"[3] "Chief," they would call my mother "Strega," which is [Italian for] "witch." So I learned to be very-very hard shell on me. And that's how I grew up in Brooklyn. What saved me was that in the neighborhood, and in the vicinity of where we were growing up, I was growing up– my sisters are older than me– there were many Native people, they came down from Canada. The iron workers came from Canada. They came from across the country. It was the end of these big Wild West shows,[4] and a lot of those Native families came across to come to New York. And a lot of people settled in Brooklyn. A lot of people got stranded there and started to live there.

Jo Reed: It's hard for some people to remember but until 1978, Native people were prohibited by U.S. law from practicing their religions. But New York City was its own universe.

Muriel Miguel: When I was growing up, there was this– a government act, it was a religious act with that, said that Native people could not practice their religions. The sun dance, the ghost dance. So a lot of medicine people, a lot of people that just left their reservations and came to New York City. And there they found a fertilized soil of young people that grew up that were Native that grew up in the city, and they taught us dances; the sun dances, the ghost dances. They taught us songs. They told us stories. You were in New York City. No one cared if you sang all night or taught dances. And that's how we grew up, many of us, in New York City.

Jo Reed: And were you hungry for those stories?

Muriel Miguel: Oh, yes, very hungry. We wanted to dance; we wanted to sing. It was hard in school because they told us our culture was dead. And we knew it wasn't dead! We lived among <laughs> we lived in it! We were sitting in it. And so we would say, "That's not true," and we got into a lot of trouble. A lot of us got into trouble. Brought to the principal's office. That type of thing, because we would contradict the teachers. And then we decided at a very young age, we were like ten/twelve, something like that, that we would start a group. And we started a group called Little Eagles. We started it in a church. We had a lot of different young people come in. All the families were very excited that we decided to do that. And we just learned these songs, we learned the dances, and then we all started to swap. Like different people did different things different ways. And that was really what saved us. You know, that we went into schools. We talked about our culture.

Jo Reed: Muriel's family were not strangers to their culture. In fact, her older sisters had performed Native dances and songs for tourists with their father at so-called Indian Villages. And Muriel sometimes went along.

Muriel Miguel: My father and all those people that came with the rodeos, and all those people were show biz Indians. There were many families that came across the States or came down from Canada, came up from South America, and they really did showbiz. They would go in all sorts of place[s], resorts and so on, and dance for the public. And that is what I remember also. I mean, that's what really got me interested in dancing as a profession. Not only Native dancing, but I went to school to learn dance.

Jo Reed: You had two parallel tracks going on.

Muriel Miguel: Yes.

Jo Reed: Did you begin as a dancer?

Muriel Miguel: <laughs> Well, again, I had two older sisters who said that I could do anything. And they decided they would give me all the colonial stuff that people say makes [dancers] a success. They wanted to give me piano lessons and French lessons, and <laughs> they also gave me dance lessons. And with the dance lessons, I was very interested, because at that time, I didn't speak much. And I started to dance really; I was like 13, 12, 13, I started to dance, modern dance. I did all of that, but it was really separate. Really separate from doing Native dance, because that was my life, and I kept that aside.

[…]

Muriel Miguel: Well, what I found interesting was that I started to feel like I really have to put together my background with what I'm doing. And how that happened was that Joe [Chaikin (1935–2003)] discovered storytelling. And they would all say to me how, "Muriel, you're such a wonderful storyteller." <laughs> You know? And I felt, "Oh, yeah!" You know?

Jo Reed: "I know a thing or two!"

Muriel Miguel: I mean, I always told stories since I was a baby. I would be hiding under the kitchen table, you know, to hear all the family secrets. How Uncle Joe married Aunt Mary, or you know, who was going with whom, and all the juicy stuff. And they were wonderful stories! And I realized that I had that feeling of what the story was. I had the feeling of how do you make something important? How do you repeat it? All of that stuff started to come. And when I left Open Theater,[5] I really wanted to really look into storytelling, because traditionally that's what we do. At the same time, it was the beginning of the feminist movement. And I really wanted to work with women. I wanted women's stories, because that was not happening. And this over 40 years ago. And I wanted to tell these stories, and so I had workshops all over. And then I got the CAP grant from New York State Council.[6] And I was asked to do a piece at the Washington Square Methodist Church, which is now a condo. And I asked my best friend, Josie. I also asked another woman that I was interested in working with, she's Lois Weaver from Split Britches,[7] and so we did a piece. And "Spiderwoman" is a [Hopi] Creation story, it's the beginning of the beginning. And Josie wanted to tell those stories. I just came back from the Sun Dance, and I told a story of talking to a butterfly. And the other woman, Lois, she told a story about Jesus. She was a white Southern gal, a Baptist. And I put– I ran a film of water running, and I put it through all three of us as we were talking, and the water just ran. And I started to work on the idea of what it means to story-weave, and how do you get the story weaving? And when do you all agree on one word? And how does that word expand? And thinking about the breath and different words, because we're telling three different stories, but really they're one story of Creation. So I was excited, and I decided that now was the time I had to really start my group. And I was going to call it Spiderwoman. And so that's what I did. I got money to explore it. And I knew I wanted to look at violence, and I wanted to look at women, and I wanted to tell women's stories.

[....]

Jo Reed: Spiderwoman's first piece *Women in Violence* created a sensation. It opened in New York and toured around the US and Europe.

Muriel Miguel: It was a big piece. <laughs> And it was so shocking. We shocked everybody with this piece.

Jo Reed: What did people find shocking? That you would talk about it?

Muriel Miguel: Well, we talked about things, we talked about penises, we talked about men feeling women up and what women can do about it. We talked about rape. We talked about a lot of things that, especially in Europe, they were not talking about.

Jo Reed: It was challenging theater and staged brilliantly with simple lighting and a backdrop made of different quilts and Native materials that would become a trademark of Spiderwoman Theater.

Muriel Miguel: When I was sun dancing, I received from many people, quilts, and I brought it home with me. They were all these patch work quilts and material, and I would put them out on the floor of the studio and look at them and think about what I wanted to do with them. And then my sister Gloria came back from Kona Yala, and she had a huge "mola," which is traditional tapestry of Kunas. And so we put that in it. And then my other sister said she had material. And then I started to ask the other women what they had. And so we started to create this very big quilt. So now it's very huge, and all the women that have passed through Spiderwoman have put things into the quilt. And that's our quilt.

Jo Reed: From the quilt to the topic, to the manner of story-telling.... no one had ever seen anything like Spiderwoman Theater, and soon they were being invited to theater festivals around the world.

[...]

Jo Reed: Well now, 40 years on you're doing a story that in some way, it's almost full circle. It's called *Material Witness*.

Muriel Miguel: Right.

Jo Reed: ... and *Material Witness* looks specifically at violence against Native women. How did this project start?

Muriel Miguel: I did another piece called *Throwaway Kids*. I did this at BANFF.[8] And I used Native dancers, and when these two Native dancers opened their own studio up in Nipissing, in Canada, on their reservation, they asked me if I would come and do parts of *Throwaway Kids* for the opening of their studio. And I took a section of it, which was about being beaten, and what happens. It was a whole section, and it's all in dance. And afterwards, I was really shocked at how women came up to me. Women were crying. Women talked to me about how they were beaten and how their children were beaten. And I was saying to myself, "I'm just an actor, you know? I'm just a director. I'm not a counselor." And how do you get past that and not feel cheap, that you're taking something from someone. And I started to think about it and think about what happened in the United States and in Canada. If a man beats a woman, you know, there's no tolerance any-more. He goes to jail. He's taken away. But that has not happened to most Native women. It has happened all around us, but it's the same where we are. So I was thinking about that thing. At that time, it was 35 years, 35 years I'd been working, and nothing has changed in our communities. So how do we– how do we shine the light on it? How do we talk about it? How do we heal? How do we make people feel that they can be healed? So we went in, and we did many workshops talking to women. And then we thought of doing a fabric workshop because we were already doing workshops with drawings and so on. So we started to take just fabric and buttons and bows and anything, anything. We started to ask people to come and find material that makes you think of yourself.

Jo Reed: Muriel then began to ask the women a series of questions, and they would answer by placing an appropriate piece of material on the table. One piece layered on top of another each representing an answer to another question.

Muriel Miguel: "What is your secret? Is it a dark secret? What do you think of your life?" And at the end, the last layer is your legacy. What do you want to leave behind? And women would sit there and then they would explain their patch. And all kinds of stories came out. Sometimes people cried, sometimes people laughed. We all laughed. And we gave food, we gave tea, we made bean soup, and it was very heartening. It was very wonderful to sit amongst all these women and have them laugh and let us laugh with them. And then we asked them if they wanted to give us this patchwork that they did, and we would carry their stories with us. We don't necessarily tell that story, but we have the patch that tells that story. And some women wanted to keep them, and some women wanted to put it in our quilts. And that's what we did, and we went to various reservations and reserves, and women were quite committed. And they really made big quilts, and some of them just gave us material and things to put in the quilts. And that's how we started *Material Witness*.

Jo Reed: Let me ask you this about *Material Witness*, because the cast is all Indigenous women. [...] What about the audience? Where is it performed? And who is the audience, typically?

Muriel Miguel: The audience is everybody! We do go on reservations and reserves. We just finished a gig in Toronto at the Living Ritual Festival. And that audience was everybody. And men, too. And one man said to me after the show, "You know, I have a responsibility here." And he was a Maori man. He said, "I don't know what it is, I don't know what happened to me looking at your piece, but I know I have a responsibility." I said, "Oh, wow!" "Yes!"

Jo Reed: Part of what you wanted to do with Spiderwoman Theater is to tell stories that really hadn't been told.

Muriel Miguel: That's right.

Jo Reed: What is it, do you think, about telling those stories and hearing those stories that can be so transformative?

Muriel Miguel: For us, there's so many stories that we have kept secret. There are so many stories that as soon as you start it, people say, "She can't tell that story." And that once you tell the story, it's a freedom! It's freedom! It's out in the air. It's there. Your words are out in the air. Looking at how does it affect you now? How does it affect you that you can tell this story? How do you understand the story now? That's what was, for me, is so important. I mean, my sister, my older sister said to me, she never had violence in her life. And <laughs> I couldn't believe that she was saying this to me because they were– "Did we have the same mother and father?" <laughs> "The same family?" <laughs> You know? Because all that violence that came in with, you know, a father that drank and drank and drank, where it was like almost normal to have alcoholics in your family. That's a big thing to fight against. And sometimes people just close off and won't look at it at all. I wanted to look at that. I wanted to look [it] right in the face, and say, "This is where I came from, and this is where I am now. And this is how I understand."

[….]

Please see the Works Cited for further information on the sources used in this essay.

Notes

1   The recorded audio interview was transcribed and published on the NEA website; spellings and capitalizations have been silently adjusted here for consistency.
2   Reed is a Media Producer at the National Endowment for the Arts.
3   Tonto is a fictional Native American character from the early twentieth century who appeared alongside the Lone Ranger, a Western cowboy who roams the frontier. The character was created by George W. Trendle and Fran Striker.
4   Much like their name, Wild West shows were vaudeville performances depicting life on the frontier that circulated throughout the eastern United States and Europe during the late 19th and early 20th centuries. Importantly, these shows perpetuated stereotypes of brazen "Indians" and heroic cowboys.
5   Miguel had worked with the Open Theater before creating Spiderwoman Theater. The Open Theater was an experimental theatre group active from 1963–1973 under the leadership of Joseph Chaikin. The Open Theater focused on sound, movement and gesture originating from the interiority and experience of the actor.
6   Community Arts Partnership with the New York State Council for the Arts.
7   Split Britches, founded in 1980, is an award-winning queer and feminist performance group centrally featuring Lois Weaver and Peggy Shaw. See Weaver entry in this volume
8   Banff Centre for the Arts and Creativity located in Banff, Alberta, Canada.

Suggestions for Further Reading

Carter, Jill. "The Physics of the Mola: Writing Indigenous Resurgence on the Contemporary Stage." *Modern Drama.* 59.1 (Spring 2016): 1–25.

Darby, Jaye T., Courtney Elkin Mohler and Christy Stanlake. *Critical Companion to Native American and First Nations Theater and Performance.* London: Methuen, 2020.

Haugo, Ann. "Circles upon Circles upon Circles: Native Women in Theater and Performance," *American Indian Theater in Performance: A Reader.* Eds. Hanay Geiogamah and Jaye T. Darby. Los Angeles, California: UCLA American Indian Studies Center, 2000.

82 EMMA RICE (b.1967)

Siouxsie Easter

Introduction

Emma Rice (b.1967), British theatre maker, director, and actor, has ignited the theatre scene from the turn of the twenty-first century to the current day. From her bold work with Kneehigh Theatre to her short-lived tenure as the first female Artistic Director of Shakespeare's Globe to her latest endeavor with Wise Children, Emma Rice resolutely reinvents and exerts her artistic freedom.

Rice began what she calls her "surprising career" as an actor, training with the Guildhall School of Music and Drama. After graduation, Rice worked with Theatre Alibi in Exeter for eight years, where she learned storytelling and theatre for youth. She then studied at the Gardzienice Centre for Theatre Practices in Poland, learning about physical theatre and integrating music into her work. In 1994, Rice joined the company that made her well-known, Kneehigh Theatre. She began as an actor, eventually becoming a director and the company's joint artistic director. Her productions of *Tristan and Yseult* (2003) and *The Red Shoes* (2003, 2010) launched her directing career. She subsequently directed productions with the Royal Shakespeare Company (*The Empress* 2013), the National Theatre (*A Matter of Life and Death* 2007, *Wuthering Heights* 2020), and the English National Opera (*Orpheus and the Underworld* 2019).

In January of 2016, Emma Rice became the first woman Artistic Director of Shakespeare's Globe Theatre. The summer of 2016 was the "Wonder Season" at the Globe with a reimagining (and renaming) of *Cymbeline*, a brightly lit *A Midsummer Night's Dream*, and *The Taming of the Shrew* set during the Easter Rising in Ireland. Even though the Globe stated that Rice's first season "brought new and diverse audiences, won huge creative and critical acclaim, and achieved exceptionally strong box-office returns," Rice was embroiled in controversy for her use of electric lights and amplified sound as well as rumored disagreements with the Board of Trustees over her directorial choices (Constable). In a scathing article in *The Times*, "The Globe Has Been a Success Story and Emma Rice Is Wrecking It," Richard Morrison claimed that Rice treated Shakespeare's *A Midsummer Night's Dream* with "perversity" and "disrespect." Controversies escalated until Rice announced her resignation just two months after the summer season closed.

On April 19, 2017, Rice wrote a letter that began, "Dear future Artistic Director of Shakespeare's Globe," announcing her decision to leave in April of 2018. The letter was posted on the Shakespeare's Globe website and reprinted in many online sources.

DOI: 10.4324/9781003006923-83

In this letter, Rice described what she learned during her time at the Globe and clarified the reasons for her resignation. The letter warns what happens when one reexamines traditional theatrical practices. It is also a manifesto of claiming one's "artistic freedom." Rice's theatre is a theatre of reinvention. From her early career moves, including leaving a 1992 National Theatre production of Tony Harrison's *Square Rounds* because of the rigid rehearsal practices, to her groundbreaking plays (*The Red Shoes* [2003]), *Wise Children* [2018]), Rice creates her own path. In the letter, Rice clearly states that her work is told through whatever medium fits best, including employing light and recorded sound in Shakespeare's Globe. Rice revealed that she left in order to choose her work and her freedom.

What happened when Rice practiced her theory about theatre-making? Many wondered at the Board's misunderstanding of Rice's performative practice. After all, Rice directed experimental productions with Kneehigh prior to her appointment, claiming, "At Kneehigh, we believe in the three 'R's; reinvention, regeneration and revolution" (Venn Creative). Rice repeatedly mentioned that she does not understand Shakespeare and wants to make the shows shorter and more accessible. Obviously, this did not endear her to the supporters of what some consider to be traditional Shakespeare.

Michael Morpurgo claimed in *The Guardian*, "The board of the Globe must have known that Rice was never going to treat Shakespeare as holy writ, neither should she. He was a great writer, but we are allowed to adapt his work. After all, he freely adapted the work of others."

Rice is not the only female director of Shakespeare who has received scathing criticism by the British critics and audiences for their work. The Royal Shakespeare Company (RSC) in Stratford-upon-Avon has a fraught history with women directors. It took over ten years from its inception before the RSC had its first woman director, Buzz Goodbody. Another decade passed before the RSC hired their second woman director in the early 1980s. Thirty years later, the RSC announced that their summer season would feature all women directors. However, in a *Guardian* interview, Mark Brown writes that Artistic Director Gary Doran's choice of all women "was not a deliberate act but part of a process" and that Doran says they "reached a point where those women directors had been with us and had grown, developed." These directors, whom Doran and the RSC "developed," include Erica Whyman, who was the Artistic Director of two well-respected theatres (Southwark Playhouse and Gate Theatre) *before* she directed at the RSC.

Katie Mitchell is another talented British director who has polarized audiences and enraged critics. Once considered to be among the greatest living British stage directors, working at places such as the RSC and the National Theatre, in 2012 Mitchell stopped directing in Great Britain for four years following harsh criticism of her work. In 2016, she admits she was "uncomfortable" as she stepped back into the London theatre scene to direct Sarah Kane's *Cleansed* at the Royal National Theatre. Of her work, Mitchell says, "There's a feminist agenda here as well, remember. There's only a limited amount of material written by women or with big female roles in it, so…. there's also a responsibility to generate a new body of work, not just for me, but for other artists" (Trueman, "Katie Mitchell").

By creating her new company, Rice has placed herself "in the rooms where decisions are made" (Rice, "A letter"), exercising what she learned at Shakespeare's Globe.

Rice, like Mitchell, is generating a new body of work, choosing her tales to reinvent, and setting her own rules.

Rice and Wise Children opened their third production, *Romantics Anonymous,* in January 2020 at the Old Vic Theatre in Bristol. The production's planned tour to the United States was cancelled due to the pandemic, but the company's training arm, live broadcasts, and renewed live performances provide opportunities for theatre artists and audiences to experience and become influenced by Emma Rice's artistic freedom. As she invokes her readers in her letter to the Globe's new Artistic Director, "You must make sure that your own freedom is assured."

Emma Rice

"Dear Future Artistic Director of Shakespeare's Globe" (2017)

Dear Future Artistic Director of Shakespeare's Globe,
I am writing this as the deadline for applications looms and my final Summer Season, The Summer of Love, prepares to launch. Before the Globe story is thrown up into the air again and the pieces fall in a new pattern, I wanted to share some thoughts with you.

Firstly, congratulations! By the time you are offered this most precious of jobs, you will have survived and triumphed over a rigorous and detailed interview process. You will have imagined a life dedicated to this most joyous and vibrant of spaces and will have shifted the tectonic plates of your own, equally precious life, to make this union happen.

And a union it is. The Globe is not a job, it is a vocation and an all-consuming, delicious tangle of histories, hopes, passions and agendas. You will be the latest in a line of experimental radicals and you will be in for the most intoxicating experience of your life. I have learnt much in my short time here and I thought I would take a moment to pass some of this knowledge to you, dear theatre friend, as you begin your own journey at the Globe.

I have learnt that a Globe audience is the best audience! Alert, excited and often standing, they are actively willing the night to be the best of their lives; they are generous beyond anything I have known before. Alive to the tragedy of life as well as the fun, they have taught me to speak with them not to them and to capture the moment with instinct, meaning and wit. They are the heartbeat and energy of this extraordinary place and will tell you not only what they need, but what you need.

I have learnt to work with other directors and what a gift they have been! Heroes, friends and inspiration all, they have cracked open my experience as a theatre maker and shown me such wisdom, ferocity, vision and dedication. I salute and thank them all.

I have learnt that there are as many opinions about what the Globe and Shakespeare should be as there are people you talk to.

I have learnt not to say that I sometimes find Shakespeare hard to understand.

I have learnt to trust my team with my heart and soul. They are true lovers and fighters, dedicated to a radical and relevant artistic mission and loyal beyond belief. They will listen to you, help you and support you and dance with you as they make real all your dreams. Take care of them for me.

I have learnt to love Shakespeare.

I have learnt where my personal and professional boundaries were. Born to please, I have enjoyed a life filled with encouragement, delight and love. I walked into the Globe expecting this to continue but my blessed path was crossed and I had to call on my beliefs, principles and integrity for guidance.

I have learnt, never again, to allow myself to be excluded from the rooms where decisions are made.

I learnt that I have many friends.

These precious things I have learnt and I am profoundly grateful.

But, dear friend, no more lessons. I chose to leave because, as important and beloved as the Globe is to me, the Board did not love and respect me back. It did not understand what I saw, what I felt and what I created with my actors, creative teams and the audience. They began to talk of a new set of rules that I did not sign up to and could not stand by. Nothing is worth giving away my artistic freedom for, it has been too hard fought for.

Like you, I have happily given my life to theatre. It has been my lover, my partner, my children and my future. I do not choose what I see, feel and do, it chooses me. I have spent my life developing my skills to be able to hear my instincts, reveal my inner stories and to be able to communicate them with my temporary community of strangers, my audience. And to reveal these truths, I have always used whatever medium best tells that story.

The Globe has been the making of me. Here, I have found my fight and my 'right', I have stood up for what I believe in and tried to do it with kindness, care and seriousness. However, in the wake of recent events, the Globe is wrestling with what, at its core, it now stands for. It is still in the process of deciding and clarifying what its fight and its 'right' are. I had to choose to leave because I choose myself and my work. Never think that my decision to step down in 2018 was simply about lights and sound, it was about personal trust and artistic freedom. You must make sure that your own freedom is assured.

So, ask the right questions, not only of the Globe but of yourself and take on the challenge with independence, caution and resolve. The Globe deserves an Artistic leader so fierce and true that they would steal a building and carry it over the river for what they believe in. It needs a leader who will shout to the heavens about what it is to be free and loving and one who is determined to make a difference during their brief time on the planet.

The Globe will always be part of me, so know I am here for you to enjoy beer, or tears, or dancing – and believe me, there will be all three of these pleasures in this place of rare humanity! Remember, you are part of a magnificent line of fearless theatre animals; in its astonishing 20-year history, this warm belly of humanity has been conceived, built and led by free-thinkers devoted only to Shakespeare, theatre and above all, the audience. You are not alone. As I plan and dream of the theatre adventures I am yet to have, I hand you the baton with pride, celebration and sadness as I say goodbye to this glorious chapter of my life.

I envy you so, but my heart cheers you on with a war cry of hope,

Keep in touch,

Emma Rice

Please see the Works Cited for further information on the sources used in this essay.

Suggestions for Further Reading

Dean, Paul. "Insubstantial Pageants." *New Criterion.* 34.10 (June 2016):13–16.

Higgins, Charlotte. "Katie Mitchell, British Theatre's Queen in Exile | Charlotte Higgins." *The Guardian.* 14 Jan. 2016. www.theguardian.com/stage/2016/jan/14/british-theatre-queen-exile-katie-mitchell.

Jonas, Susan. "Top Girls." *American Theatre.* 38.4 (Oct. 2017): 118–121.

Radosavljevic, Duška. "Emma Rice in Interview with Duska Radosavljevic." *Journal of Adaptation in Film and Performance.* 3.1 (April 2010): 89–98.

83 PAULA VOGEL (b.1951)

Meghan Brodie

Introduction

Born thirty-one years after women won the vote and sixty-four years before same-sex marriage was legalized in the United States, lesbian feminist playwright Paula Vogel (b.1951) writes plays that encourage readers and audiences to challenge norms, disrupt tired narratives, and reconsider what drama tells us about ourselves and others.

Vogel earned her B.A. from Catholic University and her M.A. and Ph.D. from Cornell University. She was the founding director of Brown University's M.F.A. program in playwriting and served as the Eugene O'Neill Professor and chair of playwriting at the Yale School of Drama. Her internationally-produced plays have earned every major American theatre award, including the Pulitzer Prize, and Vogel herself has been honored with the Dramatists Guild Lifetime Achievement Award, the Obie Award for Lifetime Achievement, a Guggenheim fellowship, and induction in the American Theatre Hall of Fame. As of 2020, five of Vogel's playwriting students have gone on to win Pulitzer Prizes of their own.

In the first book-length study of Vogel's work, Joanna Mansbridge demonstrates that the "recursive, juxtapositional structure of Vogel's playworlds undermines habituated responses, insisting instead on a mode of spectatorship that tolerates, and even takes pleasure in, contradictions and that consciously participates in an ongoing cultural dialogue" (2). For instance, in earlier plays from the 1970s and 1980s such as *Meg, The Oldest Profession*, and *Desdemona*, Vogel reimagines the lives of marginalized female characters from canonical male-authored texts, making the women three-dimensional protagonists and offering a radically different, feminist perspective on the stories from which they are drawn. Vogel makes the commonplace strange, gives voice to those historically silenced, and reshapes storytelling with each new play. In his introduction to Paula Vogel's *The Baltimore Waltz and Other Plays*, David Savran attributes Vogel's dramaturgy of defamiliarization to her reading of Bertolt Brecht and Viktor Shklovsky, but Savran writes that Vogel's work, unlike that of her predecessors, "is devoted to exposing not just how women are entrapped and oppressed, but the possibilities that figures like Desdemona or the oldest professionals have to contest, subvert and redefine the roles they have been assigned" (xi). Furthermore, Savran frames Vogel's "distinctive feminist theatre" (xi) in terms of her refusal to construct "an exemplary feminist hero" and her choice to write "speculative rather than polemical plays" (xii).

Another of Vogel's "speculative" plays, the 1998 Pulitzer Prize-winning *How I Learned to Drive*, chronicles Li'l Bit's recollection of her sexual abuse by her uncle.

DOI: 10.4324/9781003006923-84

Here, Vogel mines the fraught relationship between memory and corporeality, between gender and power. *How I Learned to Drive* as well as two other plays from the 1990s, *The Baltimore Waltz*, and *Hot 'N' Throbbing*, are just three examples of how, according to Alan Shepard and Mary Lamb, "Vogel's formal experiments, together with her studies of transgressive subjects, create an atmosphere that opens spectators to the possibility of reimagining and sometimes rescripting a number of American's myths and historical 'truths'" (199). Indeed, most of Vogel's plays, spanning several waves of feminism, invite audiences to consider just how oppressive American myths and their concomitant prescriptions for gender and sexuality are.

In her analysis of *And Baby Makes Seven*, first produced in 1984, Vanessa Campagna identifies Vogel as "an early architect of theories on queer utopia" (107). Over three decades after the premiere of *And Baby Makes Seven*, Vogel's queer dramaturgy continued to evolve, underpinning the love story at the heart of *Indecent*, a play that masterfully challenges theatrical conventions of time, space, and character as well as social norms for gender, sexuality, and religion. While *Indecent*, which premiered on Broadway in 2017, is ostensibly about Sholom Asch's *God of Vengeance* and its 1922–23 reception in the United States, the play is equally, in the words of *New Yorker* writer Daniel Pollack-Pelzner, "a celebration of theatrical power, an investigation of censorship, an elegy for the Yiddish stage, and a sly reimagining of female desire." In *Indecent*, Vogel embraces the polysemic language of a dramaturgy that is as defiant as the queer characters who populate her plays.

Victoria Myers' "An Interview with Paula Vogel" discusses the Broadway debut of *Indecent* and delves into Vogel's playwriting, politics, and legacy. Commenting on her process, Vogel suggests the indivisibility of form and content and observes a generational shift away from the linearity of well-made plays in favor of the temporal fluidity characteristic of the work of younger playwrights and evident in *Indecent*. The interview not only provides a glimpse into Vogel's process as a playwright, but also outlines for the reader how her plays are always in conversation with the work of others. Of this sort of intertextuality, Vogel remarks that "there's always a homage in everything that I write, usually in every scene." She calls these homages "valentines," generously acknowledging all those who have inspired her— from Polish director Tadeusz Kantor to American playwright Thornton Wilder. On a page of her website devoted to "bake-offs," group-constructed playwriting competitions, Vogel explains that "we write plays looking over our shoulders to our writer ancestors. Whether in fury or infatuation, the impact of previous writers can be seen[,] in the words of Thornton Wilder, as more of a relay race than a foot race." It is important to note, however, that Vogel does not view these "writer ancestors" as dead; instead, she sees their work as a transhistorical extension of their life force. In fact, Vogel makes an argument for understanding art as a living entity that can reanimate history; in the interview, she says, "drama is not about what is going to happen, it's about how it did happen." Vogel's conversation with Myers offers a snapshot of Vogel's feminist, and often queer, challenges to dramatic (written) convention as well as theatrical (performed) convention. Vogel addresses the inequities faced by women artists and artists of color, particularly those who pen timely critiques of their societies. Vogel sees her legacy in those who say, "'I read your plays and they mattered, and I've decided to write.'" We have; they did; and we will.

Paula Vogel

Excerpt from Victoria Myers' "An Interview with Paula Vogel" (2017)

[…]

Victoria Myers: Did you find that you had to adjust how you were writing [*Indecent*], not only in terms of writing for specific actors, but also maybe in terms of writing more quickly than usual or more outside-in than you normally would?

Paula Vogel: I don't know that I wrote more quickly. I have this technique called a bake-off where *How I Learned to Drive* was written in three weeks and *The Baltimore Waltz* was written in two weeks. So I wouldn't say that I am particularly slow about it. […] The more that I started to love my troupe and love the artists, the more I wanted it to be the best that it could be. And that meant a patience in terms of going back into the scene and trying other things. That's the main difference. I'm not working in a vacuum. I could look at actors. One day I was looking at Max Gordon Moore and I said to [director] Rebecca [Taichman], "I have a crazy idea. I need to disappear for 24 hours." And I ran home with the collected works of Eugene O'Neill and his letters, and I crammed and came back in the room with a new scene because I thought Max would make a terrific Eugene O'Neill, which it turned out he could. Or having the privilege of working with Katrina Lenk and saying, "I bet I could change her into this character. I bet I could do this." And the ability to use specific members of the cast who can play musical instruments, but also who can dance, means that you think about how to end the scenes differently. That really informed the writing. I'm writing for the troupe. It's the way that playwrights used to work back in the 1600s, 1700s, they wrote for the troupe, and oh my God it's heaven.

Myers: This is a piece that has a very strong interplay between form and content. Where in the process did you find the moments of content dictating form, and were there moments of form dictating content?

Vogel: I pretty much saw the shape of the general play within the first couple of days. It's why I said yes—I knew I could write it. So I knew where we were going. I knew where the turning point was going to be. I knew what the echoes were going to be. To me, form is content. So, it was a matter of making sure it was the right form. Very early on it was a two-act play. It didn't work as a two-act play, which meant I had to go back in and make deep cuts. So, it was trying to make that end work; I knew where it was ending. And I don't really think of [form and content] as divisible. I think they are the same thing.

I think one of the really amazing gifts I've gotten from 40 years of working with younger playwrights is that I think the younger generation has a fluidity of storytelling that older audience members may not have. We expect time to behave in a linear fashion. We expect that there's going to be a beginning, a middle, and an end. But the more that you look at the way plays are being written by younger writers, time is fluid, it's warping, it's morphing. I really wanted the dimension of time to change.

Myers: *Indecent* is obviously in relationship to *God of Vengeance*, but do you also see it as being in relation to other plays and other works of art?

Vogel: Absolutely, there's always a homage in everything that I write, usually in every scene. I never have the time to write handwritten notes, so instead I write plays, and I tuck in little valentines within the scenes. Definitely there is a valentine to an astonishing Polish director, by the name of Tadeusz Kantor, who used his childhood in Poland during World War II to create theatrical sculptures about his memory of getting through the war as a child. An astonishing play called *Wielopole, Wielopole.* And he did a play called *The Dead Class,* where he remembered his elementary school classmates in this tiny village, but they were basically like Siamese twins, two mannequins of their childhood selves played by their adult selves, and they were all dead, and they come back to life in this classroom. [...] When I told Rebecca that, she came up with the amazing visuals that begin and end the play. There's a big valentine in this to him. Thornton Wilder, I think I write almost every play with a valentine to Thornton Wilder. The third act of *Our Town* with the members of the cemetery sitting in chairs in the rain is a huge part of it, and the stage manager, Lemml, is absolutely a valentine to the stage manager of *Our Town.* And there are many, many more valentines in this. [...]

Myers: [In *Indecent,*] you have men looking at and writing about women, not just in the character of Sholem Asch, but also Lemml. What was your thought process for using the male gaze within the structure of the piece?

Vogel: There were a couple of initial impulses that I had. One was that I wanted us all, at the end of the play, to feel that we were native speakers of Yiddish, and that we were in that last audience [of *God of Vengeance*]. But the second thing was that I wanted us all to recognize how amazing and beautiful female desire is in worlds in which the agency was given to men. The fact that the first scene in the salon, it's men who are performing the women. I wanted the challenge of, how do I float women through this play and make them concrete and specific with material bodies, but also show men kind of creating a repository of their imagination and their desire?

I'm hoping the fact that women artists have created it makes that somewhat clear. It's true of every play I write. If I write *Baltimore Waltz,* for example, I want every man and woman in the audience to think how beautiful the male body is. How could you not be in love with men? That's a beautiful, beautiful thing. In this play, I'm asking the audience to look at the women in the way perhaps Sholem Asch looked at the women, which was revolutionary in how beautiful women are. The difference is that we've changed the characters in the original *God of Vengeance,* so that it's not a passive younger woman with an older, more aggressive, experienced woman, but rather that the younger woman is acting on her desires. And that's a fairly significant shift. How did these women become the agents of their desire, rather than get passively caught in the desire? It's a beautiful play written by a young married man in 1906 with an astonishing love scene. But I do think it plays differently now, and I think we're in the 21st century, and I think in order for *God of Vengeance* to come back into the canon, we have to look at female desire differently, particularly in this country. What's terrifying is that we are, once again, in risk of policing women and the desire of women, both through things like cutting rights of abortion, control over our bodies, and policing sexuality. That's where we are.

So in many, many ways, I feel like I'm on just the flip side of the coin that Sholem Asch was showing at a time when the policing was alive and well and extremely dangerous within the Jewish community. And I think of him—he's a very brave and honest writer for his time. And I'm using him in the present tense because I think of him in the present tense; I don't think of writers as dead. I don't think of actors as dead. That's very much a part of this play. I think the art continues their life force long after they're gone.

Myers: The specter of the Holocaust hangs over the events of the play. How did you work with the fact that you have the audience coming in with a prior knowledge of what was going to happen? [...]

Vogel: That's one of the primary challenges. Our paradigm shifted in the world after 9/11, our paradigm shifted after HIV. You can never go back, and our paradigm certainly shifted after 1938 and the Holocaust. How can we forget that? That was sort of our aim. So one of the aims is to create characters and cast members who don't know what their future holds, and to present them in such a way that we're kind of empathizing and caught up in them—through the music, through the dance, through the fact that we're spending time in struggles that were very real conflicts: Do you cut out the love-making with two women in love, and make it sexual instead? Do you get fired from a production because your Yiddish accent is too strong and you're going to be replaced, and your lover happens to be your scene partner, right? How do you deal with that? All of that. It's the struggles we have right now. [...] We're on the brink of a paradigm shift. We have to remember the innocence that we have in the moment before the paradigm shifts. That's my hope. To me, drama is not about what is going to happen, it's about how did it happen. Can we re-remember? Can we forget what we know, so that we can re-remember what we know in a new light and think, "I didn't know that. I didn't realize that impact of it"? So it's more a reinterpretation.

    The other thing I want to say is that what I think is extraordinary right now is this remarkable generation of 21st century audience members and artists and writers and actors, and I love them. I think this is an extraordinary time of theatre. It's time to retell the story so that I can hear how it's happening for a new generation. We're at this point in time when the members in our families, in our society, who remembered the actual events are dying and are no longer with us. We can't forget. We have to re-witness. We have to reanimate, we have to relive it, and I think this is an important time to do it. So that it's not thought of as history. [...]

Myers: Does that feel like a greater responsibility?

Vogel: [I]n this moment in time we have to say we are all Muslim. We have to say we are all Latino/Latina. In terms of the hate and the rhetoric: we are all lesbians, we are all transgender. This play said in 1907, "We are all Jewish. We are all women." Because Sholem Asch really looked at the plight of domestic violence and women. Yes, we feel the responsibility. Responsibility, though, also means how do we live with that knowledge and with some joy and lightness in our hearts, so that we have some resiliency to face what's happening politically every day? You can't do it simply by accepting responsibility. You have to think of how to come together and rejoice and celebrate all of the things that are good in our communities. So it may sound strange to be combining those two artistic principles of witnessing and responsibility with celebration and commemoration, but that's what we're trying to do as a troupe.

[...]

Myers: Do you see your plays as plays when you're writing them?

Vogel: No, I see them as a journey or an experience, and I guess I feel that I'm the first audience. I start to sound schizophrenic, like all playwrights do. I hear the voices, I see the people—they kind of come to me. I will literally lose my sanity if I don't, at some point, write it down. So I actually see it as if I'm sitting in a theatre or I'm in the middle of the stage. I don't know that I think of it as a play. I don't think of it as literary. I think of it as three-dimensional.

Myers: Are you starting to think about your own legacy now?

Vogel: I don't think about my own legacy now. I mean, it's kind of astonishing to me that I'm being done on Broadway. I thought it wouldn't happen. I have a theory that I've very much been seen as a prodigal daughter, and that in our society we have a very deep allegory about the return of the prodigal son, but we have not yet written that allegory for women artists and women comedians, who can criticize and make fun of their fathers' society and be embraced. If I were going to say, "Gee, I hope there's a legacy," I hope it's the legacy that has been left for me by astonishing writers of the 20th century. Women writers in theatre are pretty recent as an event. So Susan Glaspell, Zoe Akins, Lillian Hellman, Lorraine Hansberry. There are amazing women writing in the 1910s, 1920s, they were very much prodigal daughters. They weren't embraced for their critique of society as they should have been. So I'm hoping the legacy I leave behind is that it's easier for both men and women to write something that critiques the present moment in time and that can be seen as a play that is worthy to be on Broadway. You have to realize that since I produced her play when she was 20 years old, I have been incredibly frustrated to see that Lynn Nottage's magnificent works have not been on Broadway. So I just hope the legacy is that we say that new plays should be the center of Broadway theatre and that I hope that audiences think that this is part of the Broadway season. That's what I hope. I'm thrilled whenever younger artists come up and say, "I read your plays and they mattered, and I've decided to write." It is an amazing honor. So that's what I hope my legacy is: that people think of this as a career.

[...]

Myers: A lot has been made about the fact that [*Indecent*] is your Broadway debut. [...] Do you find that conversation helpful [...]?

Vogel: [...] I'm really kind of stunned that it happened. I do recognize the mathematics of being discovered is very different for women and playwrights of color, and very different for gay women. Very, very different. We don't have models. I think it goes back to what we were talking about earlier of being prodigal daughters. We're not comfortable as a society with that. [...]

Myers: What's something you think the theatre community can do to improve equality for women?

Vogel: I think we can, as audience members, do exactly what we should be doing to our representatives in the House. Show up and say, "How many women are you doing? How many writers of color? What are your demographics in the audience?" "How many women audience members do you have? You have more than 51%?" You really have to have the courage to say to our artistic directors and theatre companies, whether you're a man or a woman, "I'm a subscriber. I love the members of my community. How many women are you doing? How many writers of color are you doing in this season? Where are they?" And you have to show up. You have to show up at functions and post-play discussions, and raise your hands and say it. I'm afraid that I may have burnt a bridge or two by doing that on Twitter, but the truth of the matter is, it's not done out of disrespect. It's done out of love and concern that our community continues. Our community must continue. We have to represent America on stage, and we're not representing it.

Please see the Works Cited for further information on the sources used in this essay.

Suggestions for Further Reading

Johnson, Katie. N. and Sara Warner. "Indecent Collaborations and/in Queer Time(s)." *Critical Perspectives on Contemporary Plays by Women: The Early Twenty-First Century*, Eds. Penny Farfan and Lesley Ferris. Ann Arbor, MI: University of Michigan Press, 2021. pp. 50–57.

Parker, Mary Louise. "Paula Vogel." *BOMB*, Fall 1997, https://bombmagazine.org/articles/paula-vogel/. Accessed 4 August 2021.

Vogel, Paula. *The Baltimore Waltz and Other Plays*. New York, NY: Theatre Communications Group, 1996.

———. *How I Learned to Drive*. New York, NY: Theatre Communications Group, 2018.

———. *Indecent*. New York, NY: Theatre Communications Group, 2017.

84 ELAINE ROMERO

Jimmy A. Noriega

Introduction

Playwright Elaine Romero self-identifies as Latina and Chicana. As she explains, "I use both terms because the Latinx community is not a homogenous group. Latina allows me to connect to other Latinx individuals living in the United States, but Chicana is a specific identity rooted in my family's history" (Romero, "Interview"). She earned an MFA in playwriting from the University of California, Davis and studied with María Irene Fornés on two occasions (in Taxco, Mexico and Los Angeles, California). Romero began working with Arizona Theatre Company (ATC) in 1989 and later became its Playwright-in-Residence, a role which she has held since 1998. At ATC she also runs the National Latinx Playwriting Award, which has a record of honoring pieces that eventually become published or staged at major venues. In this capacity, Romero's role as a mentor and advocate for Latinx playwrights has helped to shape the national landscape of US theatre.

Her early plays emerged at a time when women and Latinx playwrights were not being widely produced, which speaks to the significance of her professional career. Romero was catapulted to national attention when her play *Walking Home* won the prestigious Chicano/Latino Literary Prize (1993–1994). Moreover, her family drama *Barrio Hollywood* (2003) holds the distinction of being the first play published by Samuel French in separate acting editions in English and Spanish. Her plays have been staged at prestigious venues, including the Goodman Theatre, Alley Theatre, and Actors Theatre of Louisville, and she is the recipient of the TCG/Pew National Theatre Artist Residency Program grant.

In March 2021, Arizona Theatre Company, in collaboration with The Scoundrel & Scamp Theatre and Winding Road Theater Ensemble, hosted "RomeroFest," an international theatre festival dedicated to Romero's work. Sixteen companies participated in the month-long festival, including professional venues, independent troupes, and universities from throughout the United States and Mexico. Over twenty of Romero's pieces were presented, covering a range of genres, styles, and topics that highlighted more than thirty years of the playwright's career. The COVID-19 pandemic required that the festival be curated and presented online, but it also created the opportunity to reach a wider and more diverse audience than would have been possible on the "traditional" stage. Through the virtual platform, Romero's work crossed a number of borders and barriers that otherwise would have limited the scope of the festival.

DOI: 10.4324/9781003006923-85

The digital format of "RomeroFest" and its ability to renegotiate theatrical and geographical borders provide a new perspective on how to read Romero's "The Power of Space," her essay included here. In this piece, Romero recalls several migrations that she experienced in her youth and later as a professional playwright. She reflects on the significance of space, time, and memory in her life and how her own understanding of relocation and belonging impacted her artistic development. For Romero, moving to new geographies gave her different perspectives from which to engage the idea of the border and to understand its relationship to politics and identity formation. As she says in the essay, "My work as a playwright shows me the border is no monolith. Her permutations shift in each different space."

Romero is a borderlands playwright: born and raised in California to a family with New Mexican roots, she now lives and writes in Arizona. Her geographical and cultural home is the US-Mexico border, which Gloria Anzaldúa famously described as "*una herida abierta* where the Third World grates against the first and bleeds" (Anzaldúa 25). This "open wound" permeates Romero's writing, and she often grapples with the subjects of a broken immigration system, anti-immigrant rhetoric, state surveillance of brown bodies, border violence, racism, and sexism. Her plays offer a glimpse into some of the most dangerous terrain of the US political landscape, including: anti-immigrant violence (*Wetback*); government termination of ethnic studies programs (*The Fat-Free Chicana and the Snow Cap Queen*); the effects of war on soldiers and their families (*Graveyard of Empires* and *A Work of Art*); and gun violence in schools (*Mother of Exiles*).

Romero also experiments with the complicated notion of reality in her works. As Anne García-Romero explains, "Romero contends that the border between the natural and the supernatural worlds is porous in ordinary reality. The realism [she] creates in her plays therefore differs from Western theatrical notions of realism" (*Fornes Frame* 108). She achieves this by drawing upon Mexican and Latinx cultures, histories, and cosmologies to craft her stories. The spirits of deceased loved ones, apparitions, otherworldly guides, memories, and dreams appear throughout her plays and become a part of the new realism she creates for the stage. As she states, "time and space fold onto each other in my work, like layers of origami that make new worlds" (Romero interview). She echoes this sentiment in her essay when she explains the connection between culture, space, and reality: "Our displacement as Chicanos sets us down on uneven ground. We straddle that border fault line as the earth shakes, and we survive. We stealthily keep a foot in each world without the risk of falling into the chasm in between. We adeptly split time and place, living in two realms at once." This living in two realms is an expansion of the "*ni de aquí ni de allá*" that she speaks about in the beginning of the essay. It is both a negation and an acceptance of what it means to come from and be formed by the edges of two nations.

As a playwright who lives and works in the bifurcated and complicated world of the US-Mexico border, Romero responds to the violent and unyielding collisions of cartography and power in her plays. It is fitting, then, that Romero ends her essay by addressing the border and its ever-present impact on her and her theatre: "The border has me. She hunts me down. She seeks me out. She calls my name [...] Whether she is in my head or I am on her earth, I cannot escape the border. I am of her."

Elaine Romero

"The Power of Space" (2018)

As Latinos in the United States, we live in absentia. We are of here and of there. Or conversely, *ni de aquí ni de allá* (neither from here nor from there). The Yaquis' nomadic patterns, on lands that would later be named Northern Mexico and Southern Arizona, wore the truth into the earth with their migratory feet. The Sonoran Desert is a singular place. Its border, its divide, is a fault line laid down by human error. Like a house divided, a fractured continent cannot stand.

My work as a playwright shows me the border is no monolith. Her permutations shift in each different space. Texas is not California, nor does it desire to be. When I walk to each new precipice along that fragile line, she whispers fresh secrets into my ear. *You thought I was this, but now I am that,* she says. *You think you know me, but I'm unknowable.*

My sense of the border was not innate. As a small child, I held a simplistic view. A Southern California kid who was born up north in Santa Rosa, I'd spend time with my grandparents on trips to Tijuana. I dreaded the trips to TJ where my mother would ask me not to speak English so we could get a better price. She once negotiated my bad haircut. Forbidden to speak, I cringed as a bowl was placed on my head and left me looking like a boy. This memory could not possibly be real. Like my many recollections of Mexico, it's elusive.

Though my life, forged on the US/Mexican border, began in California, it moved north to Oregon when I was in high school. The kids at my new school surmised that Romero was an Italian name. They called me out for being different. In that state of relentless rain, in a rural home in Amity, Oregon, I wrote my first play.

I headed to Northern California for graduate school, then to Arizona, and later Chicago. My relocations turned me over and shook me upside down, and like a child tumbled by an imposing ocean wave, I did not know the sand from the sky. Relocation thrust me into a place of not knowing.

My beloved mentor, María Irene Fornés[1], tossed me into similar waters, the subconscious world. I emerged with pieces of emotional biography that I'd fashion into plays. She taught me to mine myself, but also how to live. I could control my words no better than I could control the erratic nature of my life. The only cure for the unexpected would be to accustom myself to a state of not knowing.

I distrusted the popular verbatim narrative form in playwriting. I sought the visceral experience, the semblance of truth. The fiction of my plays, married to empathy, could spew forth more authenticity than recorded transcripts ever could. Anna Deavere Smith[2] I was not. I dove further inside myself, an explorer of an interior terrain whose dual identity constantly reasserted itself. *I am this and I am that. I am of here and I am of there.*

Our displacement as Chicanos sets us down on uneven ground. We straddle that border fault line as the earth shakes, and we survive. We stealthily keep a foot in each world without the risk of falling into the chasm in between. We adeptly split time and place, living in two realms at once.

My grandparents relocated to San Diego from New Mexico before I was born. We lived as immigrants in our own land. We knew that California *chile* could never be hot enough to purge us of our real ills. We would wait for New Mexican *piñones* and *chiles* to arrive by US post.

Those early days in California taught me that I could be of one place and in another. I could be a New Mexican still. I was told of our Sanchez family land grant in Anton Chico, and that we used to be rich. That statement was followed by silence, a lingering ellipsis, leaving me the space to fill in the blank.

My family did not take me to New Mexico while I was growing up. I yearned for it through my grandparents' memories. Through my mother's stories, I longed for my late great-great-grandmother Marillita, reputed to be a living saint. She collected herbs in Las Vegas, New Mexico, and, family legend held, she knew the medicinal qualities of each root. Doctors would come to her for her remedies. My mother invoked the people who made pilgrimages to Chimayó on their knees. New Mexico burst alive for me. I constructed an internal New Mexican space as I bled from the holy knees of my imagination.

As a child, I had grown up a mile away from the ocean in southern Orange County. I developed an irrational attachment to it and feared living more than a few miles away from the coast. With the ocean, I had a compass. I could tell north from south. I knew where the land ended and the sea began. Driving down Pacific Coast Highway (PCH) gave me great comfort. The highway kissed the curve of the coast. PCH was the first border I ever knew. The ocean seeped its ways into my plays, *Walking Home* and *Walk into the Sea*. The California coast had become a place I would remotely view. It would retain only certain parts, those of selective memory.

After I moved to the desert in Arizona, for six straight years I woke up with morning terror. In my recurring dream the ocean was a mile away, but I never went there. I'd forgotten her. It was that seventh year when a person's cells are purported to be fully replaced that I discovered the power of land.

The desert adjusted my eye. I oriented myself by the mountains of Tucson. I saw green where I once saw brown. I felt secure under the canopy of her big sky. I grew accustomed to the songs of the birds outside my house and to the occasional sighting of a coyote. Tucson, with its comforting blanket of heat, coaxed me into an interior world. I wrote my plays with her mountains in sight. And while I found myself attracted to the ever-changing activity of other restless cities, I credit Tucson with helping me find what the Aztecs called a "standstill point."

Indeed, in this desert landscape, I am steady and the words come.

When I left Tucson, I didn't know I was leaving. That's the best way to leave a place you love. I left for my husband's six-month job contract in Princeton. I was to go with him and write, catching up on shows on the weekends in New York City. At the end of the six months, we would move to Chicago for me to teach. I had commissions to complete and galleys to proof. I wrote about the border from a New Jersey café. As I dove into my work on the page, it took me back home, but not to Tucson as it really is, but to the Tucson of my psyche.

I knew I was not the first exiled border writer to revivify home through her pen. I had a quick flash. "Now, I'm Octavio Solis," I thought, "writing about El Paso from his house in San Francisco."[3] Something changed about my writing. The line between here and there disappeared. A border emerged. It was not between north and south, but this part of the United States and the other. The bicultural world of Tucson faded. The further I got away from Arizona, the better I grasped it.

When I worked on my play *Wetback*, the border reappeared. I imagined a place that was Arizona, but a little bit of San Diego, and a hint of Texas. My somewhere became my everywhere. Away from the Southwest, I began to experience my work from a broader political point-of-view. The national discourse on immigration had reached a high pitch.

I was writing *Wetback* at a writing retreat in Florida while protestors were marching in the streets of Arizona and California. I was missing my March on Washington. I wanted to return home immediately. Then, I realized my words had been predicting the crisis all along. My play had somehow prophetically preempted an event.

The day after I finished my first draft, Luis Ramirez was murdered in Pennsylvania in a park under strikingly similar circumstances to my play. Ramirez, an undocumented Mexican immigrant, was with his white girlfriend at the time the hate crime occurred. White supremacists, like the members of the Minuteman Militia in my play, uttered racial epithets at him as they took his life. As a constantly relocating Latina, I already believed that space could be folded. I learned that time could be folded as well. Truth and fiction had fused through a sacred act of spiritual origami. I had written *Wetback* for Ramirez even though I completed it before he died.

It got worse. Much worse. Not only did *Wetback* have the sad distinction of prognosticating tragedy, but another play of mine was in peril. *The Fat-Free Chicana and the Snow Cap Queen* was banned as part of the Mexican-American Studies book ban that happened in Tucson, Arizona, as a result of the legislation HB 2281. HB 2281 stated that the school district or charter schools could not offer courses that were "designed primarily for pupils of a particular ethnic group." It prohibited the advocacy of ethnic solidarity "instead of the treatment of students as individuals."

The Fat-Free Chicana and the Snow Cap Queen, featured in the book, *Puro Teatro: A Latina Anthology*, shows young women coming of age personally and politically. I weave the region's history into the text. I did not learn this history in school. I learned it from my mother. I have no idea if the people who banned the anthology knew of the content of my play. I can only say that they were right to ban it if they took issue with the truth.

My colleagues in Chicago kept telling me how cool it was that I was a banned author. They thought it belonged front and center on my CV. It felt great for a microsecond to be dangerous. I had written the play for young Latina women. I envisioned them feeling self-possessed with these lines in their mouths. Yet the kids at Tucson High, a few blocks from the home my husband and I owned, would not be able to read *The Fat-Free Chicana and the Snow Cap Queen*. Would they know how to piece together our region's past, or would they simply adopt the version of the victor?

My thoughts echoed the play itself.

SILVIA: He said our restaurant predates the occupation of Northern Mexico.
AMY: What does he mean occupation of Northern Mexico?
SILVIA: You know exactly what he means. Sometimes, sister, I think you're forgetting who we are.
AMY: I haven't forgotten.
SILVIA: But I know you. You'll remember. Inside you there is somebody who will remember. Everything. And it's stronger than that other part of you that went up North to get an education and, instead, she was erased.

Through censorship, might I, too, be erased?

I fantasized about coming home to Tucson to give the students our play. Maybe we could gather in a 4th Avenue café and have a reading. Maybe I'd rent a space and produce it myself. In the Tucson of my mind, it became critical to me that the students of Tucson High have the opportunity to know, live, and breathe my play. I'd written it for them.

In Chicago, I began my war trilogy. *Graveyard of Empires* features an engineer who developed the early prototype for the predator drone. His son later becomes a Marine and is killed in a friendly fire predator drone incident in Afghanistan. The drone pilot is a Mexican-American soldier who, though he knows he was shooting to miss, becomes obsessed with his role in the death of the soldiers. He kills himself. What do we ask soldiers to live with when we send them to war? When I first wrote it, I thought I was weaving together Latino and non-Latino worlds.

Graveyard of Empires had its world premiere at 16th Street Theatre in the Chicago area in spring 2015. I am now less convinced that it contains the fusion of a Latino and an Anglo world. That play's border has dissolved. There are moments when I see the engineer and his ex-wife as Latinos as well. Cultural identity has blurred.

On commission for the Goodman Theatre's Playwright's Unit, I wrote *A Work of Art*. I had planned to write it on an airplane. Through a divine case of rerouting or dumb-luck synchronicity, I was taking a trip to Chicago from Portland, Oregon, via Las Vegas. On the plane, I met a Mexican-American woman who had raised her two Anglo stepchildren. She told me her stepson had died in Iraq. I told her of my plan to begin a new play during the plane trip. The play was to be about a soldier who dies in Vietnam. We looked at each other and cried. The play premiered in summer 2015 in a coproduction with Chicago Dramatists in association with the Goodman Theatre. It is set in 1979, ten years after a woman loses her brother in the Vietnam War. What do we ask families to live with when we send their love ones to war?

I know the question intimately. My uncle was killed in action in Vietnam. When I stepped into the quiet elevator after the reading at the Goodman, I said, "I've needed to write that play since before I knew what a play was." *A Work of Art* fuses Anglo and Mexican worlds. The border between life and death, a persistent theme in my work, remains ever present. It finds its root in cultural traditions. As Mexicans and Mexican-Americans, we conjure effortlessly walking through walls, ceilings, and borders. We do it every day.

Mother of Exiles called me back to my imagined border. It was a commission from Cornell University. The director asked me to watch a French film that looked at a shooting in a classroom amid racial strife and adapt it to an Arizona context. While I was working on the play in Chicago, I felt the contexts did not match. My dramaturg Jimmy Noriega agreed.

The shooting at Sandy Hook Elementary School happened. There was talk that Arizona would arm teachers. Back in the Arizona of my consciousness, I ran with the terrifying *what if* question. What if the State of Arizona armed teachers with guns? I realized I had my second play in an Arizona/Mexican border trilogy. It poured from my fingers from an Andersonville café on Chicago's North Side. It was an Arizona I had never known and one I had always known. The border mutated beneath my fingertips. I had to write it fast to circumvent talking myself out of it. I had the power of Luis Ramirez behind me. I imagined *Mother of Exiles* could help the border avert a tragedy in a way that *Wetback* could not.

I'm on the final play of two disparate trilogies. When I write about the atomic bomb in the final war play, the border will be there. In the final play of the Arizona/Mexican border trilogy, *Title IX*, developed at the Eugene O'Neill National Playwrights Conference, the border takes on a literal incarnation between different groups of people and genders. I cannot help it. The border has me. She hunts me down. She seeks me out. She calls my name. Heck, the border has snatched me from Chicago and called me back to teach at the University of Arizona. Whether she is in my head or I am on her earth, I cannot escape the border. I am of her.

Please see the Works Cited for further information on the sources used in this essay.

Notes

1 See Fornés entry in this anthology.
2 American playwright known for interview-based dramas, including *Fires in the Mirror* (1992) and *Twilight: Los Angeles* (1994).
3 American playwright best known for *Santos and Santos* (1993) and *Lydia* (2008).

Suggestions for Further Reading

García-Romero, Anne. *The Fornes Frame: Contemporary Latina Playwrights and the Legacy of Maria Irene Fornes.* Tucson, AZ: University of Arizona Press, 2016.
Noriega, Jimmy A. "'Don't Teach These Plays!': Latina/o Theatre and the Termination of the Tucson Unified School District's Mexican American Studies Program." *Theatre Topics.* 27.1 (2017): 37–48.
Romero, Elaine. *Barrio Hollywood.* New York, NY: Samuel French, 2008.
———. *Xochi: Jaguar Princess. Palabras del Cielo: An Exploration of Latina/o Theatre for Young Audiences.* Eds. José Casas and Christina Marín. Woodstock, IL: Dramatic Publishing, 2018. 208–255.
Romero, Elaine and Anne García-Romero. "Expanding the Chair: A Conversation on Fornés's Pedagogy in Action." *Theatre Topics.* 27.1 (2017): 83–90.

85 VELINA HASU HOUSTON (b.1957)

Eunha Na

Introduction

Velina Hasu Houston (b.1957) occupies a special place in women's theatre and the Asian American theatre movement. She was born in postwar Japan, the daughter of a Japanese woman and an American serviceman of African and Native American descent. As Houston describes herself as "an amalgam of three cultures, two countries, and three races," the notions of multiculturalism, racial consciousness, and transnationality are inextricably related and constantly evolving throughout her works (*Politics* 3). After her family moved to the U.S., she grew up in Junction City, Kansas and attended a local university until eventually migrating to California to study playwriting at UCLA. Experiences of domestic and transnational migration helped shape a unique perspective on multiculturalism reflected throughout Houston's *oeuvre*. Often considered a major force among the second-wave of Asian American playwrights during the 1980s, Houston came of age as a writer when the mixed-race movement was ripe (Lee 128; Ma 163). In Houston's plays, this mixed-race consciousness is often materialized in multiracial or Amerasian characters who not only straddle established boundaries of identity dictated by social norms but also transgress those boundaries through what Karen Shimakawa has suggested is a "critical mimesis," or strategic re-appropriation of stereotypes (377). Houston's sense of racial and cultural ambiguity is further emphasized through dramaturgy that fuses Euro-American and Japanese theatricalities, characterized by visually compelling images, magical realism, and stylistic combinations of prose and haiku-inspired poetry.[1]

A prolific writer, Houston has composed dozens of plays and expanded her career over the years to musical theatre, opera, and film. Her own family history, interwoven with the U.S. intervention in the Asia-Pacific region in the aftermath of the Second World War, informs the much-discussed and acclaimed trilogy: *Asa Ga Kimashita* (1982), *American Dreams* (1984), and *Tea* (1987). The triology delves into such cogent themes as clashing cultures and interracial marriage. These early works revisit specific moments in history from a marginalized, "feminist transnational perspective" that sheds light on the distinctly gendered and racialized nature of Asian American women's experience (Usui and Liu 111). Houston's later works, such as *Kokoro* (1994) and *The House of Chaos* (2007), continue to explore the issues of women's global migration and transculturation; she also considers the psychological and material reverberations of war on racialized individuals on both sides of the Pacific in, for example, *Waiting for Tadashi* (2002) and *Calling Aphrodite* (2007). A fervent educator and scholar, Houston has edited several anthologies dedicated to Asian American

DOI: 10.4324/9781003006923-86

plays, including *The Politics of Life: Four Plays by Asian American Women* (1993) and *Still, Like Air, I Will Rise: New Asian American Plays* (1997).

   In her blog *matchabook*, excerpts of which are included here, Houston experiments with a new platform to archive her evolving thoughts on theatre and the contributions of women artists whose voices often remain unheard. A digital form of autobiographical scrapbook consisting of poems, prose, and photographic images, the blog, according to Houston, intends to offer an "unconventional way of looking at writing, humanity, and Asian American-ness." Reminiscent of Adrienne Kennedy's autobiographical memoir, *People Who Led to My Plays* (1987)[2], the following excerpts illustrate the personal and sociopolitical forces that have shaped a young female artist in her formative years. In these essays, Houston pays homage to people whose paths crossed with hers, especially women who have nurtured her artistic potential against preconceptions and prejudices in theatre and in society at large. As she charts her life from growing up in a multiethnic Japanese home in Kansas through moving to study playwriting in California, we see how different locales and cultural environments have informed her understanding of multiculturalism in a variety of complex and nuanced forms. She offers a powerful critique of U.S. mono-racial culture by drawing our attention to the exclusion of artists of mixed racial heritage within ethnic theatre and their token presence in mainstream theatre. What emerges from these essays is a voice that calls for true diversity in theatre and more inclusive aesthetic criteria that recognize the value and equality of different cultures.

Velina Hasu Houston

Excerpts from matchabook (2018)

"A Writer's Journey I, 1967–1979"

I was eleven when I wrote my first play. Truly, I did not know what a play was, but, in some respect, one can be fearless in one's pre-pubescent ignorance. Throughout my elementary school years, I wrote poetry which, at the time, was some sort of necessary expression that I felt compelled to write. I know now that it was nothing but juvenilia; however, when one is a juvenile, what else can one produce even if one thinks it is important at the time? I thought that because I experienced something or felt something deeply, it was a poem. It, however, was not. I understand that now.

   There were a lot of comings and goings at my elementary school because it was located about two miles from a military base, which meant that soldiers (sometimes called G.I.s, which means Government Issue or "doggies," which was a civilian epithet that, in my eyes, was on the same level as the N word) constantly were on the move being stationed here and there and, if they were married, taking their wives and children with them. Those wives were significant to Kansas school children because often they brought their talents to the schools as teachers. One such military wife taught at my elementary school for one year. [...] The military wife/school teacher was white with short, medium brown hair. She liked to wear sweaters during the winter. They were monochromatic, V-necked sweaters and she always wore a shirt underneath it, the collars of which were gently laid on top of the inner shoulders of her sweaters. With soft, brown eyes and thick, manicured hands, she shook my hand warmly if she passed me in the hall. Always, she acknowledged me, human being to human being. She was not my teacher, but she actually took the time to read my poetry. I was so surprised. I thought that perhaps she was a White liberal reaching out to a poor little immigrant child, but she in point of fact liked the poetry and discussed it with me. I was gob-smacked. After reading a poem about my Japanese mother leaving the port at Yokohama on a ship, she encouraged me to write a play.

"What is a play?" I asked. I never had seen or read one. [...] The teacher gave me three plays by Anton Chekhov to read (*The Cherry Orchard, Three Sisters,* and *The Seagull*).[3] I was ten years old. In a year, my father would pass away. Once I began reading those plays, a vista opened in front of me. *The Cherry Orchard* evoked my grandfather's persimmon orchard near Matsuyama, Japan. Furthermore, the giving way of the old order to the new in Chekhov's play also reminded me of what happened to my grandfather when Japan was defeated by the Allied Powers at the end of World War II. In Chekhov, I had found a writer, son of a serf, and doctor who in some ways understood the road that my family had traveled in a way that nobody in my United States' education ever had understood or wanted to understand. [...] After I finished reading the plays, the military wife/school teacher encouraged me to write a play. She said it could be a one-act play, just thirty minutes long. I reflected upon what I would write and, by the time I came to terms with a commitment to do it, her husband was ordered to Germany and she departed.

I began writing the play, but then my father's illness worsened. Since the end of World War II, in which he had fought in the Pacific Theatre (interesting terminology, not mine), his PTSD eroded him both psychologically and physically, and he drank more whiskey to drown out the demons. Eventually, his entire being collapsed and nothing was left. After his death, I was a pariah to most of my Kansas schoolmates, those same U.S. citizens. [...] Moreover, they did not want me at their birthday parties and no longer wanted to play with me. The solitude turned out to be a gift. I finished my first play. My sixth-grade teacher, the third teacher who was kind to me, James Hosler, had a reading of the play. I moved on to middle school and returned to writing poetry. Their encouragement was integrated into my DNA. During middle school, I wrote a couple of plays, but I was growing up during a time when society's sociopolitics had no interest in or tolerance for the equity, diversity, and inclusion of non-White, non-male, non-heterosexual voices. In high school, four teachers encouraged my creativity; three were White, one was Black. I wrote a play about a female spinster and a traveling saleswoman. We had a reading of it in one of my classes. The theatre bug had not bitten me, as many like to say. Rather, it always had lived in my marrow and was rising to the surface to drive me toward my destiny.

It also rose to the surface because my life was unlike the lives of most of my peers. Multiethnicity and immigrant status aside, there was also the matter of tea. [...] In my house, my mother would have tea with her friends at a table full of tiny, beautiful dishes that contained a variety of foods, both savory and sweet. They were not American foods, but things like *o-tsukemono, oshitashi, kinpira gobo, narazuke, natto,* and other Japanese foods in bigger, beautiful dishes such as *o-den, maki-zushi, o-mochi* or *oshiruko*; and parboiled *ika* with a paste of *miso,* chopped green onions, and chili paste. Because there were no grocery stores, my mother and I prepared these items from scratch. [...] Fundamentally, having tea in this way and engaging with the Japanese female immigrants around that tea table was like a blood transfusion to me. I felt their joys and pain so deeply, so personally. As it flowed into my DNA, I knew that it was as important to me as breathing. It further fortified me for the necessity of going into the outside world and facing all the closed doors; so many closed doors, some of them shut in my face just as I was about to cross the threshold.

[…] it was an afternoon discussion with my mother over tea and *maki-zushi* that invigorated me and sent me walking toward [my destiny]. I was twenty-one years old. She said that I was old enough now to know that my grandfather, her father, had committed suicide and that she had discovered the body. We talked about the years before the war in Japan, my grandfather's anti-Western sentiments, the Allied bombing of the area in which my mother lived […]. She also wanted me to know about my grandfather's shock at Japan losing the war, my grandmother dying prematurely from a breast wound inadvertently caused by a "son" (who actually was the child of my mother's sister), and the fact that my grandfather's youngest daughter – my mother – had fallen in love with a Yankee, a Yankee of color, and planned to marry him. The family history that my mother revealed to me struck deep chords. These were stories that I was compelled to explore, perhaps starting with my Japanese grandfather and the challenges with which he was faced at the end of World War II as the old order of life gave way to a new way of life without his country, his wife, and his youngest daughter. I resolved to be the explorer. […]

"A Writer's Journey, Part II"

Moving to California was a frightening prospect, especially as someone who wanted to be a playwright, especially as someone who was deeply multiethnic and multicultural (this was before the "multicultural diversity" movement took hold in the U.S.; my home with my mother was the only place in the world where my multiethnicity was an organic given and I didn't have to explain myself to everybody who was curious or intelligent enough to discern difference and ask). Despite the hurdles that I knew I faced, I felt compelled to go. […] I was not the first human being to come to California to pursue an artistic career. I know that many others far more intelligent and creative than I am probably were possessed in similar ways. For that artistic interest, I left behind the woman I loved – my mother – and the comforts of our multiethnic Japanese home to come to California, a place where there were more multiethnic Japanese like me, but also multiethnic Japanese and multiethnic Japanese Americans who did not understand multiethnics who also were of African descent. Inside my home in Kansas, my multicultural way of life and my multicultural perspective were integrated organically into our existence. Outside of that home, I was an anomaly in almost every ethnic group. I was never genuinely multiethnic, Asian, Black, Brown, or White; I was never "enough" of any of those groups to be counted as one of them. That was okay because that lack of belonging was beneficial to my writing. When one does not fit into a group, one has a lot of time to be alone to write. Moreover, there is only one thing to do, to rise, as the poet Maya Angelou stated. Those artistic secrets were the foundation of my life as an immigrant to California. […]

In Kansas, I experienced my first playwriting mentor, Norman J. Fedder, who was from New York. At UCLA, I was lucky enough to find a second in Theodore Apstein, an immigrant from Russia; he passed away at the age of seventy-seven while en route to see his granddaughter perform in a play. Other professors at UCLA were not so welcoming to me or to my voice. They discouraged my desire to write about Japanese women – one of them telling me to write for a "whiter" audience. I gave him the benefit of a doubt and asked him if he had said "wider," but we both knew that he had not. [...]

During these years, I also was developing as an artist. Prior to having a run of productions at several regional theatre companies, I had a few experiences at what are called ethnic theatre companies. For many years, I was not to revisit those ethnic theatre companies; my literary career was built at mainstream theatres. However, those early experiences were educational from both artistic and ethnic perspectives. I was the horse of a different color for both Asian American and Black theatre companies. My multiethnicity was something that they could sell, but, despite drawing me into the fold, they did little to treat me as a human being. I was always a commodity, never an individual. I was their diversity, but they were too busy trying to be the diversity for White theatres. [...] What was ironic to me, though, was that theatre artists of (monoracial) color who challenged mainstream theatre that did not include them so easily turned around and excluded multiracial people of color. Now some ethnic theatres finally are embracing multiracial individuals, but seldom those with African heritage. Part White, yes; part Black, no. [...]

Instead of focusing on the hostility of a society that was not yet ready to be inclusive, particularly of a multiethnic, immigrant-kindred female artist, I focused on my own life and art. I decided to start a non-nuclear family. I decided that, now more than ever, I must continue to write from my own unique perspective, even if ethnic theatres and some exclusive White theatres did not want me at their parties. I gave birth to two wonderful children, Kiyoshi and Leilani; and I gave birth to plays, essays, poetry, and opera that was embraced and continues to be embraced by many. Persistently, I am appreciative of that embrace and, in my mind, bow a deep and enduring bow to those institutions and individuals. [...]

"The Literary Challenge: Multicultural in a Monocultural World"

Over the years, I have worked with various international scholars – women from India, Egypt, and Algiers – on their post-graduate explorations of plays written by women, both White and of color. The communications raise many topics, some of which motivate my thoughts about writing and about being a writer. I was asked about the canon of dramatic literature in the West and the position of Asian American drama vis-à-vis that canon. The "canon," as it often is thought about in the Western world with regards to dramatic literature, generally means, as defined by the Oxford Dictionary, a "...list of works considered to be permanently established as being of the highest quality." [...] It remains true that many White European American scholars with regards to dramatic literature define "canon" to mean plays written mostly by White men and before the 1960s. [...] I think that it is incorrect to say that Asian American dramatic literature must impose itself upon that canon. It is the creators of the canon itself who must think more broadly, deeply, and inclusively. [...]

While my play *Tea* is one of the most produced works about the Japanese female experience in the U.S., I never have sought to impose it upon the Western canon. [...] Whether or not *Tea* is considered to be in any Western canon – and I think it never could be because its author is female and a multiethnic, multicultural person of color – it addresses aspects of history and identity to which an inquiring mind would want to be exposed. [...] One also has to question the notion of "ethnic" drama versus "White" drama. [...] Ethnic terms as descriptors are fine, I suppose, but often it seems that they are being used as ways of diminishing such literature or separating it from the White mainstream. Besides, often the terms are not accurate. For example, often my work is labeled as "Asian American." Of course, it is Asian American and Asian and Japanese, but it also is a lot of other things – African American, Latin, Native American Indian, White European American, female, and global. To not say all of those things is to reduce reality to a comfortable categorization that allows people to go to sleep at night without a sleep aid. [...]

As I reflect upon my writing, I know that my background – both ethnically and culturally – enriched my outlook with an organic interest in what happens when a new entity enters an established arena. That could be a new person in the neighborhood, a new person in a new family, or a new person in a new country. I innately was interested in the impact of a new environment on an individual who simply wants to survive. That thread is present in almost everything that I write. Perhaps, beyond my multiethnicity, multiculturalism, or female-ness, that is something to which many can relate. Perhaps that is why my very different voice found a place in the theatre and sustains in the theatre. [...]

Please see the Works Cited for further information on the sources used in this essay.

Notes

1 For further discussions on magical realism in Houston's plays, see Foley 220–222; Maufort 189–196.
2 See Kennedy entry in this volume.
3 Russian Anton Chekhov (1860–1904) was a pivotal figure in the development of modernist drama.

Suggestions for Further Reading

Hua, Hsüan. "Velina Hasu Houston." *Asian Americans: An Encyclopedia of Social, Cultural, Economic, and Political History.* Eds. Xiaojian Zhao and Edward J. W. Park. Westport, CT: Greenwood Publishing Group, 2013. pp. 521–522.

Huang, Guiyou. "Velina Hasu Houston." *The Columbia Guide to Asian American Literature since 1945.* New York, NY: Columbia University Press, 2006. pp. 91–93.

Janette, Michele. "Out of the Melting Pot and into the Frontera: Race, Sex, Nation, and Home in Velina Hasu Houston's 'American Dreams.'" *Mixed Race Literature.* Ed. Jonathan Brennan. Redwood City, CA: Stanford University Press, 2002. pp. 88–106.

Lee, Josephine. *Performing Asian America: Race and Ethnicity on the Contemporary Stage.* Philadelphia, PA: Temple University Press, 1997, pp. 199–204.

Na, Eunha. "'True Heart': Reimagining Transnational Subjects through Sentimentality in Velina Hasu Houston's Plays." *Modern Drama.* 58.4 (2015): 482–501.

Uno, Roberta. "Introduction to *Tea.*" *Unbroken Thread: An Anthology of Plays by Asian American Women.* Ed. Roberta Uno. Amherst, MA: University of Massachusetts Press, 1993. pp. 155–60.

Usui, Massumi. "Creating a Feminist Transnational Drama: Oyako Shinju (Parent-Child Suicide) in Velina Hasu Houston's *Kokoro* (True Heart)." *Japanese Journal of American Studies.* 11 (2000): 173–198.

———. "Velina Hasu Houston." *Women Playwrights of Diversity: A Bio-bibliographical Sourcebook.* Eds. Jane T. Peterson and Suzanne Bennet. Westport, CT: Greenwood Press, 1997. pp. 166–170.

86 QUIARA ALEGRÍA HUDES (b.1977) and GABRIELA SERENA SANCHEZ

J. Ellen Gainor

Introduction

For the 2018 Association for Theatre in Higher Education[1] (ATHE) annual meeting, conference organizers invited theatre artists and sisters Quiara Alegría Hudes (b.1977) and Gabriela Serena Sanchez to deliver a keynote address. Their joint presentation, "Pausing and Breathing," excerpted here, reflects both the "high tide of heartbreak" that Hudes has experienced working in the "upper echelons" of the professional theatre (Sanchez and Hudes E-7, 4) and what session commentator Patricia Ybarra termed the "heartening" realizations we can take from the revelations of both sisters (Green-Rogers et al, E-17). Controversially, only Hudes' portion of the speech initially appeared in the September 2018 issue of the industry magazine *American Theatre*, prompting a critique of that publication's privileging of the commercially successful dramatist's commentary over that of Sanchez, an award-winning community-based artist in Philadelphia. The ATHE-affiliated journal *Theatre Topics* subsequently printed their full speech in March 2019.

Hudes came to prominence as the book writer for Lin-Manuel Miranda's and her Tony Award-winning musical, *In the Heights* (2008). She received the Pulitzer Prize for her drama, *Water by the Spoonful* (2012), the second play in her trilogy that also includes the Pulitzer-nominated *Elliot, A Soldier's Fugue* (2007) and *The Happiest Song Plays Last* (2013). Other works include the play *Daphne's Dive* (2016) and the musical *Miss You Like Hell* (2016), an adaptation of her play *26 Miles* (2009).

Hudes believes that plays, which she first encountered in book form, are "instruction manuals on how to be human." They convey "secrets that shamans of the past were whispering in my ear. Secrets of life, of love, of culture, of sorrow and absurdity" ("Drama as Literature"). She maintains "that art can actually shape history because it's simply the record of our culture that we leave behind" (Potts). But that shaping can only occur if we are "actively, committedly [...] trying to produce the most diverse pool of plays possible." Hudes further explains, "I'm not just talking about ethnicities, race, and gender. I'm talking about aesthetics and everything that goes into theatre." Accomplishing this project will necessitate "a very committed pressure put on ourselves as artists and theatres [...] challeng[ing] your assumptions, [and asking] who is not being spoken about" (Myers, "Interview"). Scholar Anne Garcia-Romero argues that such transformations are "vital to twenty-first century US theater" ("Fugue" 87).

Embracing such commitment, Sanchez is the co-founder (with playwright Erlina Ortiz) and managing director of Power Street Theatre Company, "a collective of fierce,

DOI: 10.4324/9781003006923-87

multicultural and multidisciplinary artists dedicated to the mission of empowering marginalized artists and communities of color throughout Philadelphia and beyond" ("12×12"). Also an actor and teacher, Sanchez champions theatre for social justice through her company, which, she explains, is run by womyn of color. Her desire to establish Power Street grew from her experiences as a theatre student at Temple University, where she "realized [she] wasn't being cast because [she] actually didn't fit the roles" in the kinds of plays produced there. Sanchez recalls further, "It wasn't that my talent wasn't good enough," but rather that "[t]here was no space for me" ("Our Stories"). Power Street, by comparison, is "committed to sharing and supporting the artists, leadership, and narratives of people of color, immigrants, and refugees," among other disenfranchised communities (Power Street).

These same concerns structure Sanchez's ATHE remarks. Her belief that "theatre has the ability to transform lives and environments" links directly to her work toward "reflective democracy" and "culture change," as well as her "vision for gender justice, racial equality, and economic opportunity" for a "new generation of leaders" in theatre. She positions the work of Power Street in direct opposition to the "white male led" theatrical mainstream and emphasizes her theatre's efforts to bring "productions into communities" that might otherwise lack access due to financial and other barriers. Her core question, "*Am I here?*" speaks to notions of immediacy and representation; through production, Sanchez and her colleagues model their concept of community in and through theatre.

In her ATHE remarks, Hudes raises equally vital concerns about the theatres in which her work has been staged. She notes the overwhelmingly white audiences for her Latinx stories, as well as the preponderance of white critics reviewing her productions. She had earlier observed: "I've never read an interview where a white author has to justify or explain his identity or why it is that he writes for white actors." Thinking of some of her playwright "heroes" such as (now, the late) Edward Albee, Tracy Letts, or David Lindsay Abaire, Hudes said she would "squeal from wicked delight if one of them were ever asked, 'Do you consider yourself a male playwright?'" ("Artistic Statement" 78). Hudes also clearly worries about the feelings of, and potential injury to, actors of color in a white theatrical environment, as well as the personal and familial impact of bringing fictionalized narratives of relatives' lives into this public arena. The cumulative force of all these concerns, coupled with specific instances of discrimination she has experienced, led Hudes to announce that she was putting her theatrical work on "pause" for two years.

Hudes' and Sanchez's remarks prompt us to consider what it means to work primarily within specific communities, versus working to bring those communities' concerns and narratives to others—especially when we are considering issues of race, gender, ability, sexual orientation, socio-economic status, and other factors. Session commentator Harvey Young observed that "Sanchez, an artist whose work has a more regional and decidedly local impact, had the more desirable professional life." He asked, "How can Broadway success prove to be so unrewarding and undesirable" for a dramatist as compelling and accomplished as Hudes? Young believes the ATHE keynote "stood as a call for artists to invest themselves in managing the means of production," and that "it will take time and also the concerted efforts of artist-producers, people like Sanchez, to champion theatre with soul and a commitment to radical inclusion at a national scale" (Green-Rogers et al, E-20).

Quiara Alegría Hudes and Gabriela Serena Sanchez

Excerpt from "Pausing and Breathing: Two Sisters Deliver
the ATHE 2018 Conference Keynote Address" (2018)

[...]

QUIARA: I want to start with love. I love this woman up here with me, my sister, who will always be my baby doll. Fellow travelers, I love every one of you here today. I suspect there is at least one love story in your life that blazed the trail to this very gathering. Maybe you loved the way lights felt on your face, the blindness as you looked out at the invisible audience bank. Maybe you love backstage anonymity, the chaotic machinery and runaround that keeps a performance seamless. Maybe you were seven and loved the first play you saw. Back then, you probably loved it more than you understood it. Remember how glorious that was, immersion in an experience you didn't totally understand? Why do grownups cling to "getting it"? What an unadventurous, small parameter for experiencing art.

- —Tomasito, what do you want to be when you grow up?
- —A firefighter!
- —Luzecita, what about you?
- —When I grow up, I want to go to the theatre and get it!

Maybe, like me, you loved a cousin and wanted to tell their story.

Maybe, like me, there was a mentor. In my case, Paula Vogel and her warm ebullient enthusiasm. One time, in our sixteen-year friendship, I saw her lash out with anger and self-defense at a bunch of whiny MFA students (hint: myself and my cohort), and the way she showed that hurt made me love her even more, more than ever, because it is hard for a woman to stand up for herself, and I always wished my abuela had stood up for herself just one time in a life spent in service of others, so when Paula did just that, I loved her doubly for it.[2]

Tending our wounds is central to loving. Love is richer when it comes with an understanding of pain endured, of mortality faced, of chasms crossed. To love is to face the wound honestly and then let the wound be less than one's entire truth, to love despite the wound. That is the kind of love, I think, that calls me to speak today.

I suppose I need your help. I am here not to share wisdom, juicy gossip, or war stories (sorry if that's what you were expecting), but to articulate a question and reach out my hand for guidance.

For I fear that at 40, having produced three musicals and four plays I am proud of, two early plays I am fond of, and a handful of work I'd rather forget about—at 40 years old having worked on Broadway and off, regionally and internationally; having gone into debt and then paid off those debts all thanks to my theatre habit; having some paperback books that sit on library shelves with my name on the cover that maybe a kid like me will discover for free and feel less lonely as she cracks open the pages, I fear that today, after all that, the wound feels bigger than I can handle. I fear that the ways theatre has harmed me are winning out over the ways theatre has nourished me.

Since my first musical in 1998, opening night has always entailed stress. There is much to do and few hours. An entire team looks to me, the playwright, for ballast and strength, for confidence and support, for vision, clarity, and therapy should everything topple. And yet reviews loom; and the set isn't working; and neither is scene seven; and what if I rewrite it and the actors memorize it, to discover that the new, revised scene seven sucks? How will the audience view my Latinx stories, and if they are mostly white, does that mean my cast is performing race, and doesn't that injure our pride, our self-determination? How will it feel to go out onstage and once again not be afforded the luxury of neutrality? Will all the community outreach I've done in the Latinx community, saying *Hey, you know that huge theatre downtown? I'm here to say, you are welcome there, I invite you inside!* Will all that community outreach lead to two percent Latinxs in the audience or hopefully dear god maybe fifteen percent? Will the audience be mostly wealthy, and so will my characters' poverty seem monstrous? Is my play cultural tourism? Will the critics be mostly male and white? Will my little sister come and see how she has inspired me and feel outed and humiliated and angry at what I've turned her life—our life—into? Will I lose my family due to the mockery I've made of our stories? What right have I to joke about or fictionalize our pain? Is honesty, which I strive for, also a form a violence?

By opening night I have lost weight. The mirror reflects back Skeletor. Reviews are posted. I will not read them for days or weeks, but their simple existence suffocates me. Even positive reviews yank my art from my hands and serve up my heart like a well-dressed ham. Even rave reviews have deposited me, post-celebration, in a disorienting depression where I feel my mouth has been slapped with ducttape. People call and congratulate me not on the work, but on the *Times* review. Against my affirmations and meditations, I become once again the little girl seeking approval when I have worked so hard to reject that frame.

[...]

For *Daphne's Dive*, I remember one night after a preview. The production was impressive, the cast was inspired. Nothing was going wrong at all—how often can we say that in previews, usually a calamitous precipice of disaster? And yet I got into a taxi heading home, and my heart pounded so hard, I said *This is it, a heart attack at thirty-eight.* I texted Amy Herzog, a fellow playwright, and told her, "Can previews actually kill? My heart is going to break outta my ribcage." I threw a twenty at the driver, fled the backseat at the first red light, and began walking to the St. Luke's Roosevelt ER. Then the crisp evening in Hell's Kitchen and the foot traffic of drunk couples calmed me. Breath found me again. Another night of previews, survived.

Amy Herzog has diagnosed my condition: "theatre-induced psychosis." That she can name it so precisely leads me to believe I am not the lone sufferer of this malady.

After opening my last musical, *Miss You Like Hell*, in New York earlier this year, I called my theatre agent and asked him to cancel my productions and commissions for the next two years. I need a break. Hey, my heroes have shifted genres. Ntozake Shange wrote choreopoems, plays, and straight-up poems. Leslie Marmon Silko wrote essays, novels, and poetry. I can try my hand at other mediums.[3]

My work in theatre is not done. I've just pressed pause.

I feared that between taxicab panic attacks and theatre-induced psychosis, I might not survive another opening. And truth is, I like living more than I like theatre. I had to prioritize.

Having stepped aside for a minute, I can see and understand with clarity what was happening inside. Theatre, at least at the upper echelons of the professional field, is frequently elitist, expensive, exclusive, and nondemocratic. Our biggest-budget theatrical institutions purport to encourage equality and champion the underdog, but in fact must appease wealthy patrons and subscribers, disproportionately feature male leadership, and carry stubborn institutional memory beholden to the white aesthetics and values they have built themselves upon for decades.

To restate, I love what I do, what *we* do, and I stand here extremely proud of the work I've made at theatres big and small.

But the institutional-theatre landscape replicates many of the old structures and dynamics I abhorred in Philly, that I rebelled against by writing my Latinx family stories in the first place.

These structures and dynamics have hurt me. Like an onslaught of wolves, they come at me biting, growling. They mock, especially, my explorations of female wisdom, self-determination, and pleasure.

At my worst moments, and believe me they have been many and very low, my mom has begged me to practice wellness. [...]

Didn't she hear the audience member demand his money back at intermission because he doesn't come to the theatre to hear Spickanese?

Wasn't she at the talkback when the subscriber praised my play, but took exception to the fact that the characters were Puerto Rican: "Why limit the story like that?" he asked. On the heels of this comment, an older black subscriber stood, emotional, saying, "We have a right to be here, too! We don't have to explain ourselves! I've been a subscriber here for decades, and I'm sick of apologizing for my existence!" [...]

Didn't mom know about the Tony- and Pulitzer-winning board president who asked me to relinquish my board seat quietly, despite my being female and Latina (his words), because they were beginning a campaign to save the NEA in the era of Trump? [...] I said yes to his request and learned later there was no such campaign. His long-time collaborator, a white man, had not been reelected to the board and was quietly ushered back into his old board seat at my expense. Meanwhile, the other board members had been told that I had *volunteered* to give up my place due to family obligations. This in a democratic organization; this from a liberal leader. It's shocking what people do to protect the status quo, to keep their friends in power.

[...]

Theatre, I love you. Accomplishments, I stand proud. I treasure the collaborations I've built, the friendships I've earned, the jobs I've created. I treasure the letters from high school and college students who find value and comfort in my work. Who feel seen. Who imagine themselves with the title of protagonist. Who grab the baton and write their own truth.

But theatre, it hurt to get here, and I only now see the nature of the wound. I've only recently acquired the vocabulary to describe the affliction, the clarity to admit the hurt.

Just like my family loves Philadelphia. And yet it hurt them to leave their Puerto Rico farm behind. They love the 215, but it hurt to arrive in Philly and be harassed by the cops, be attacked by gangs because of their Spanish tongue, be priced out of their green-tree playground blocks every few years, migrating further and further north, getting more isolated from Center City, until finally they were living on treeless, no-playground, dilapidated cement blocks while judges and lawyers moved into their old homes. That my family holds fast to their Philly love even after the city has hurt them so, I think it makes the love more profound, more earned, gives it a realer edge and flavor.

Either that or they are delusional, and I really don't like that option.

I remember my abuela who, armed with nothing but a second-grade education and maybe—maybe—a coffee can of savings, left her husband, moved four daughters to Philadelphia, and then for decades nursed and fed and caretook until her descendants had graduated from Yale or were locked up in state penitentiaries. She loved till her back doubled over, curving like Big Sur—a testament to every meal cooked, every diaper changed, every neighbor advised.

I am starting to understand the hunch of abuela's shoulders. I feel it in my heart. The fatigue of the giver.

I struggle increasingly with the stubbornly entrenched, atheist white male aesthetics I inherit from my field. These include:

1 That love is dead, romance is transactional, and sex is not a source of pleasure but a race to the bottom.
2 That children hate their parents. The suggestion of familial love implies idiocy on the part of the playwright.
3 That wealth is either neutral or a hardship to the wealthy.
4 Regarding God: You're kidding, right?
5 Joy is sentimental, harmony a falsehood. Harming others is the single human truth.
6 Genius is a male attribute. Intuition is a female attribute.

The canonical plays that led to the aforementioned aesthetics matter a great deal to me. O'Neill, Miller, and Albee are my heroes. *Death of a Salesman* was the first American play I read. It rollicked my adolescent veins. It is the reason I write today.[4]

But why my work must either uphold or negate the values laid out by Miller, Albee, and O'Neill is beyond me, as if all the paradigms have been laid out, and we're now stuck rearranging the puzzle pieces or self-referentially rejecting the puzzle altogether.

Can institutional theatre not hold multiple worldviews and paradigms? Do multimillion-dollar capital projects lead to fancy theatres that reinforce a single aesthetic mode?

It is discombobulating and even humiliating to write Latinx characters who will be seen by mostly white audiences. It feels like either their brownness or humanity is destined to be the primary performance, the play itself a secondary action. My characters become Latinos performing humanity. This fear crippled me during the lead-up to my last piece, *Miss You Like Hell* at the Public Theater. Why was I writing this protagonist, Beatriz, so that she could be seen first and foremost through the filter of race, not to mention gender? Despite an impending deportation hearing, Beatriz experiences moments of playfulness, curiosity, and celebration. She fucks and dances for pleasure, in moderation. I suspected a criticism would be that Beatriz does not suffer enough. *Show us her victimhood, let us see her ravaged.* I was correct. […]

[…] Plays are things to be produced, and so my career is dependent on the market realities of producing theatres and what audiences those institutions have cultivated, historically, for decades. It is a strange marketplace to funnel my particular family stories into. In many ways, my interests as a writer do not match the United States theatrical landscape. Many characters in my plays could not afford to see my plays, and if they were given a comp ticket they might feel out of place in that lobby.

[…]

For you educators, artists, mentors, professors, administrators, grad students, fellow travelers, my words are more simple. […]

Does your mainstage season, syllabus, and/or curriculum reinforce dominant cultural values, and in particular, appearance-based and presentation-based casting hierarchies? Do looks, class markers, accents, and presentation afford students more or less cachet when it comes to casting departmental productions? Are students paying thousands of dollars to learn and replicate upper-class market structures? Are departmental seasons modeling theatre for wealthy ticket buyers? Are there abundant opportunities for students to center themselves, and the department, in different values and aesthetic systems?

Perhaps the greatest revolution I can imagine is to insist that no matter how "other" my characters are in the white wealthy spaces of theatre, to nonetheless affirm that they are not guests on the American stage. To insist that I am a center, I am a hostess. […] I want to return to the theatre soon, to say this again: *Come in. Enter. It is my profound honor to host you. Let me show you my beautiful house. It still stands. Pull up a seat at my table.*

I am not there yet.

Today is my high tide of heartbreak. All tides, however, ebb.

And yet there is relief. That I can finally name it or am finally willing to. And there is gratitude that you have respectfully listened.

Before revolution, honesty. That is my first step.

GABI: […]

I often daydream about co-creation for the masses, a necessity for our future. But someone usually snaps me out of it: "Hey! Get your head out of the clouds! Hello … Gabi are you here?" My eyes blink wide open. I protect that daydream like my marbles, holding on tight, counting each one… . Then I laugh. The irony in that question, *Am I here? Am. I. Here?* I often ask that question within the oppressive spaces I navigate.

In a world where we are pursuing reflective democracy, it is critical that people of color [POC] see themselves as leaders who can represent their communities, or as my mom would say, "social-change agents." Most fundamentally, we need a radical shift in culture in order for any of this to happen. We need to have a culture that affirms our ability to have full agency over our lives. And decision-making power over our bodies and over our expression of our gender and sexuality. We need a radical shift in culture, one that affirms our lives as lives that matter, our humanity as a humanity that matters.

[…]

Culture change happens with the storytellers.

Culture change happens with the artist.

Culture change happens with the grassroots organizers.

Culture change happens with education that is not captured in political and legal jargon.

Culture change happens by changing hearts and minds.

That is the role of the arts: bringing freedom and healing by sharing complex truths.

As a queer, plus-sized Latinx womyn, walking in the world has not always felt comfortable. However, growing up in Norf and West Philly, I gained a survival kit: humility and grit. Perhaps the occasional resting bitch face.

Theatre and community organizing are platforms I use to *speak my truth* and fight for what I believe in. My vision for gender justice, racial equality, and economic opportunity is to foster womyn of color as the new generation of leaders in the Philadelphia theatre industry.

I believe theatre has the ability to transform lives and environments through redefining spaces, preserving diverse stories, and mobilizing people to gather from ALL walks of life to enjoy arts and cultures.

[...] Conflict Resolution Theatre was my first reaaaal gig. This program, founded by my mentor Judy Nelson, is the reason why I chose to be an educator. For six years I played various roles within the organization, ranging from an actress to manager. I traveled to every Philadelphia recreation center you could imagine, performing musicals on conflict resolution. Unfortunately, what I discovered, at the age of fifteen, was that many black and brown neighborhood recreation centers had significantly less resources compared to predominantly white neighborhoods. That fueled me to advocate for those underserved children and communities.

PA'LANTE!

[...] My senior year, I decided to pitch my dream to classmates about mobilizing to create a multicultural theatre company. This was sparked out of rage due to the inequalities I faced attending Temple University: feeling alone as a Latinx student, the lack of diversity in the professors' racial and economic backgrounds, and Temple University's lack of support for plays featuring diversity.

Other marginalized students believed in my vision, and Power Street Theatre Company was born. PSTC is home to a collective of fierce multicultural and multidisciplinary artists dedicated to connecting communities through the performing arts by sharing powerful stories that innovate and inspire. [...]

As the founder of PSTC, my vision is a direct call to action to build a table among POC leaders to innovate, collaborate, and strategize on the future of theatre in Philadelphia. I seek to challenge and combat systematic oppressions by creating positions of leadership for POC, womyn, immigrants, disabled people, and LGBTQ+ identified folks, as well as to set up a space for white people to experience multicultural stories as audience members and co-creators of multicultural artistic work.

Through PSTC, I have been committed to producing one new play by our resident playwright, Erlina Ortiz, each year. I have expanded platforms for artists from historically marginalized communities to both create and excel in artistic spaces. The longevity of members' participation is a measurable outcome of this goal.

SPOILER ALERT: Mainstream theatres in Philadelphia are overwhelmingly white male led. This is not solely an issue in our city, but nationwide. Power Street Theatre Company is different. PSTC is unique in that it is entirely womyn-led and inclusive to People of Color and LGBTQ+ folks. The company brings multicultural theatre productions into communities lacking theatre access due to high ticket prices, lack of childcare, transportation issues, and other barriers. With community at the center of all PSTC does, organizing plays a huge role in how the company operates. Within six years, PSTC has engaged over 4,000 audience members through seven productions, six contracted performances, four pilot programs, and various collaborative community events.

PA'LANTE!

[…] I produced our first production, *MinorityLand*, at Taller Puertorriqueño, a community-based cultural organization whose primary purpose is to preserve, develop, and promote Puerto Rican arts and culture. *MinorityLand* was an experimental piece in response to overwhelming gentrification occurring on Temple's campus. To encourage new theatre audiences to engage with this work around gentrification, I canvassed the surrounding neighborhoods and built relationships with other social justice organizations within the community to bring their participants to see the play. Through these actions, I opened conversations around what theatre is and could or should be.

[…]

The primary communities I have served throughout my career are the residents of West Kensington and North Philadelphia, a geographic region of Philadelphia largely characterized by Latinx cultures, diverse histories of migration, and POC, with median household incomes of under $24,000 and disproportionate high-school dropout rates of 40–50 percent (U.S. Census, 2016). However, North Philadelphia is a far more dynamic and resilient community than these statistics imply; it is a *comunidad* filled with vibrant people and music, colorful murals, and multidimensional neighborhoods.

[…]

(Quiara and Gabi return to center stage, together again)

QUIARA: Hey, Gab.

GABI: Hey, Q.

QUIARA: This is cool. We've never done this before. She's my sister.

GABI: She's my sister.

QUIARA: You're my sister.

GABI: You're my sister.

[…]

QUIARA: Always asking, am I doing important work? Being haunted by that sometimes.

GABI: The breath I need to take. The pause you need to take.

QUIARA: Or your question, the simplest of all. Am I here? You are here, Gabi.

GABI: You are here, Quiara.

QUIARA: *(To audience)* You are here, fellow travelers.

GABI: *(To audience)* Your students are here too. And they bring their communities with them.

(Quiara and Gabi hold hands, take a breath)

QUIARA, GABI: Thanks.

Please see the Works Cited for further information on the sources used in this essay.

Notes

1 A US-based professional organization focused on the teaching and research of theatre and performance.
2 See Vogel entry in this volume.
3 Ntozake Shange (1948–2018) is best known for her dramatic choreopoem, *For Colored Girls Who Have Considered Suicide / When the Rainbow Is Enuf* (1975); Leslie Marmon Silko (b.1948) is a MacArthur grant recipient, best known for her novel *Ceremony* (1977).
4 Arthur Miller's (1915–2005) *Death of a Salesman* (1949) is considered one of the most influential American plays of the 20th century. Eugene O'Neill (1888–1953), best known for his play *Long Day's Journey Into Night* (1956), won the Nobel Prize for Literature in 1936. Edward Albee (1928–2016), three-time winner of the Pulitzer Prize for Drama, is best known for *Who's Afraid of Virginia Woolf?* (1962).

Suggestions for Further Reading

http://www.quiara.com/. Accessed 22 May 2023.
https://latinxcastingmanifesto.tumblr.com/. Accessed 22 May 2023.
Suzi Nash, "Gabriela Sanchez: Powered Up" *Philadelphia Gay News*, October 18, 2018. https://epgn.com/2018/10/18/gabriela-sanchez-powered-up/. Accessed July 5, 2020.
Patricia Ybarra, "How to Read a Latinx Play in the Twenty-first Century: Learning from Quiara Hudes" *Theatre Topics*. 27.1 (March 2017): 49–59.
Harvey Young, "An Interview with Quiara Alegría Hudes" *Theatre Survey*. 56.2 (May 2015): 187–194.

87 WINSOME PINNOCK (b.1961)

Gabriele Griffin

Introduction

Winsome Pinnock (b.1961) is one of a handful of Black British women playwrights who established a successful theatre career from the mid-1980s when women's cultural production began to be seriously championed, and opportunities, including new performance venues such as arts centres, opened up for the production of such work. The daughter of migrants from Smithville, Jamaica, Pinnock was born in London and educated at Goldsmiths and at Birkbeck College, both in London.

Pinnock's work is feminist and female-oriented, privileging female characters and detailing the plight of Black women both historically and in the present. She has collaborated with and written plays for a number of women's theatre companies, such as the Women's Theatre Group, the Women's Playhouse Trust, and Clean Break Theatre Company. These touring companies and the arts venues that emerged in the 1980s had their funding increasingly cut by conservative governments and the Arts Council England; in consequence, many became defunct by the early 2000s. This situation has contributed to Pinnock's need to seek income through teaching (as Associate Professor of Drama at Kingston University in South London); it also partially explains why, following her initial successes, it became increasingly difficult for her to write for the stage, and she has expanded her work into other media. She adapted Jean Rhys' short story "Let Them Call It Jazz" for BBC Radio 4 in 1998 and has also scripted screenplays and television episodes.

Pinnock's award-winning plays include *The Wind of Change* (1987), *Leave Taking* (1988; revised 1995; 2018), *Picture Palace* (commissioned by the Women's Theatre Group, 1988), *A Hero's Welcome* (Women's Playhouse Trust, 1989), *A Rock in Water* (1989; inspired by the life of Black Jamaican activist and coinstigator of the Notting Hill Carnival, Claudia Jones), *Talking in Tongues* (1991), *Mules* (Clean Break, 1996, a company for female ex-convicts and women with lived experiences of the criminal justice system), *Can You Keep a Secret?* (1999), *Water* (2000), *One Under* (2005; retoured in 2019 by Graeae Theatre Company, a company for disabled performers), *IDP* (2006), *Unzipped* (2009), *Taken* (2010, Clean Break Theatre Company), *Clean Trade* (2015, for BBC Radio 4), *Tituba* (2015), and *Rockets and Blue Light* (2020). Pinnock has been writer-in-residence at the Royal Court Theatre, the Royal National Theatre, Clean Break Theatre Company, Holloway Prison, and Tricycle Theatre.

Her association with stages and companies such as Tricycle Theatre (renamed Kiln Theatre in 2018), which has championed the work of minoritized social groups (e.g. Jewish, Asian, Black), Clean Break and Holloway (both of which focus on female

DOI: 10.4324/9781003006923-88

convicts), and the Royal Court Theatre (renowned for promoting new writing), indicates Pinnock's preoccupation with social justice, inequality, women's position in society, and the history of Black women's lives from slavery times into the present. Pinnock's work articulates a strong sense of continuity between histories of Black slavery and present injustices where racialized oppression is constructed as continuous and iterative across time and space. Many of her female characters – particularly older females such Abi in *The Principles of Cartography,* and also Enid in *Leave Taking* – are endowed with a powerful quasi-intuitive sense of history that courses through them and signals a specific sensitivity to the reproduction of the injustices of the past in the present. Such figures also reflect the indomitability of what one might describe as the Black spirit in the face of oppression and exploitation. Indeed, spirituality, the Black spirit (as an inner disposition of resistance to oppression and to misrepresentation), and the spirit world are at times juxtaposed with western values which emerge as challenging and challenged. This is the case in *Leave Taking, Talking in Tongues, Mules, One Under,* and *Can You Keep a Secret?,* for example. In *Rockets and Blue Lights,* the tension between, or paradox of, a Black spirit of indomitability and the experience of racist oppression through time is manifested in its three narrative strands, distributed across two timeframes: 1840 and 2006–2007. One plot strand concerns the making of white English artist J.M.W. Turner's 1840 painting *The Slave Ship (Slavers Throwing Overboard the Dead and Dying – Typhoon Coming On).* The second storyline features a free Black man going back to sea and being re-enslaved, also in 1840; and the third, set in 2006–2007, centres on the making of a film entitled *The Ghost Ship* about the trans-Atlantic slave trade. The play raises powerful questions of how one engages with painful pasts, in terms of the descendants of oppressed people and in terms of belonging to the dominant oppressing group.

Pinnock often plays with time, both conflating and expanding different temporalities in her efforts to bring together worlds that exist in uneasy proximity. Her theatre work therefore frequently combines realist dialogue and contemporary scenarios with poetic language and references to imaginary and spirit worlds that privilege knowledge and experiences beyond the immediate present, beyond the material world, and beyond the secular. These two dimensions – the realist contemporary and the immaterial extemporary – coincide and collide with each other in Pinnock's work in the deliberately uneasy juxtaposition that is partly attributed to the effects of migration in Pinnock's plays. These effects of migratory experiences – displacement, subordination, victimization – challenge the norms and assumptions of western culture. But in Pinnock's theatre work, this challenge occurs without the attempt to resolve the tensions and contradictions that living in contemporary society within the nested embeddedness of histories of migration, oppression, and injustice necessarily entails.

Pinnock has not written specifically about theatre as practice in any extended way, but her interviews provide useful pointers towards her preoccupations and sense of self within British theatre. Her desire to champion Black female performers and characters, still a distinct and tokenized minority in British theatre, the "unresolved history" of Black people's lives in Britain that structures so many of her plays, her accurate continuing sense of the difficulty of Black people achieving presence in the theatre, and her commitment to community and history are all powerful drivers for her work. Described by Helen Kolawole as "the godmother of black British playwrights," Pinnock learned her craft from her teenage years onwards, but she still professes surprise at "making it" in the theatre world – even as it remains a continuous struggle. She shares this struggle with many other Black and mixed-race women playwrights working in Britain, such as Trish Cooke, Patricia Cumper, Jacqueline Rudet, debbie tucker green, Bola Agbaje, SuAndi, Zindika Kamauesi, and Valerie Mason-John, some of whom have had their work performed at key UK venues, such as the Royal Court, the National Theatre, or, latterly, the Arcola Theatre. Many of these writers have striven to sustain a career as playwrights. One important part of their struggle is the question of the extent to which Black playwrights should write about Black communities. Pinnock is clear on this: while the fight for recognition and equality in racist societies continues, it must be engaged with. As her central female character, Lou, in *Rockets and Blue Lights* says: "They think it's just history, but it isn't" (46).

Winsome Pinnock

Excerpts from Interviews (1999–2019)

Winsome Pinnock interviewed by Natasha Sutton Williams (2019)

"Most of my plays have a personal reason behind why I want to write that play. Either I've observed or experienced something, and the play takes off from that. Strangely, since I wrote [*One Under*], I have very direct experience of things that happen in it. When writing it, I had been asking the question, "Have I got this? Have I captured this?" But of course you do. You're a writer. You can think your way into those sorts of experiences. Since the play was put on, I've experienced not just grief and loss, but a specific experience, which I can't talk about, because that's a spoiler!"

Pinnock enjoys being part of the rehearsal process.

"Often the actors and director will have a similar journey to the one I had while trying to come up with the play [...]. They'll even discard ideas in the same way I did. Actors can get a bit anxious, as I tend not to talk too much in rehearsal. They sometimes think that serving the play means serving the playwright, which is a completely different thing. I like to stay quiet so that they get a sense of ownership of their character [...]. Everything I've got to say is in the text [...]."

"In theatre you can be idolised as a young writer, and have your work exposed in a way that often is not contextualised. When I started writing there was no training for writers. You learned on the job. I had a sense when I started writing that the plays changed me. When I'd written a play I was a different person. Not necessarily that I'd got better. It's not that kind of progress, but something had changed. I'd gained an insight into the possibilities of writing for the stage. It's liberating to become older and still make work. It feels very different to when I was younger."

"Have confidence in the fact that the thing that may be difficult for you may be of value to others, especially to people who may share the experience. That's what I feel because that's what I have felt. I see young people feel it as Black writers. Each generation feels they're doing it for the first time simply because of the way those plays are produced or not produced. History disappears quickly".

"I look back, I produce a piece of work and people ask, 'how did you do that?' I can't really explain how it ended up the way it has because it is fragmented. It doesn't all come gushing out. It might for some people, but it doesn't for me. It's about work, thinking deeply and planning out the structure. Structure is one of the most important aspects of writing. Every day of my life I've spent thinking about structure."

Winsome Pinnock interviewed by Jim Mulligan (1999)

"This is raw emotion [in *Can You Keep a Secret?*] but I think young people will handle it because they are honest. The language is not provocative or inflammatory. It is the language of young people [...]. The language is at times racist, foul and violently homophobic [...]. You don't clean up the language because the play is coming to the National Theatre. Some people will find the killing of a black youth on stage shocking. When I am writing there are conscious choices and instinctive ones, on one level thinking of the best possible ways of telling the story and then there is an instinctive level. I didn't feel it was right for his death to happen offstage where the audience could either imagine it or choose to block it out. Some things are unimaginable and this is one of them. In writing I had to confront the death and other people have to face it as well."

Winsome Pinnock interviewed for *Alt-Africa Review* (2019)

AA: Being the first Black woman to have a play at the National Theatre with Leave Taking in 1988, do you remember what it felt like at the time?
WP: I didn't realise that I was the first black British woman to have a play on at the National Theatre until about 15 years after the event. When I realised that this was the case I was of course very proud, but I was also quite moved by the realisation that "the first" often means "the only one" which speaks to a history of the neglect and marginalisation of work by people of colour.

AA: Did you know you were making history?
WP: I was conscious of the contribution I was making and took the responsibility seriously. I am a child of immigrants and that means that you are part of a generation of pioneers.

AA: At what point did you realise that you were a talented writer?
WP: I won my first prize for writing when I was about 8 or 9. One of my teachers told me that I was a good writer and used to pin my stories on the board each week. As an adult I went on to win awards such as the George Devine Award, the Pearson Plays on Stage Award, and the Alfred Fagon Award, but it took quite a while for me to accept that I was a "real" writer simply because I hadn't met many writers who looked like me...

AA: Can you give us an insight into your journey into writing, where did you train, what was your first professional published piece?
WP: I'd been writing short pieces (stories, poems, sketches) since I was a child. Despite being chronically shy I became known as a writer and performer at school and when I left was predicted to do well in the theatre. I took a degree in Drama and English Literature at Goldsmiths. At first I'd wanted to perform but decided to focus on my writing when I realised that theatre didn't offer many good roles for people of colour. I applied to join the Royal Court Young Writers' group. I remember crying and jumping on my mum's bed when the then writing tutor wrote to tell me that the

sketch I'd sent in indicated that I was talented and invited me to join. My play "Leave Taking" was first produced in 1987. It was revived in 2018 by Madani Younis at the Bush Theatre. Can you imagine having your first play revived so many years later? Thank goodness it sold out and was a critical success.

AA: Let's talk about the event at the Royal Court: Passages: A Windrush Celebration how did you get involved?
WP: My play "Leave Taking" focuses on the Windrush generation.[1] When the play was revived at the Bush Theatre Lynette Linton contacted me and asked if I wanted to take part in an event that she was planning to celebrate the anniversary of the arrival of the ship The Windrush into Tilbury Docks in 1948.

AA: Tell us about your contribution to the Windrush event?
WP: I have written a monologue, which is a meditation on the tension between memory and nostalgia […].Our event is an expression of solidarity. We also hope that it will raise awareness. It is a tribute to the Windrush Generation – a way of thanking them for their courage and tenacity.

AA: How do these kinds of events make changes to this system/hostile environment if at all?
I think it's important to speak out and to raise awareness. The impact of events like this is exponential: those who attend will be in a position to inform others […]. We can't underestimate the contribution of the arts to social change.

AA: The Windrush scandal has created a wider awareness of the Windrush, why is it an important part of British history?
WP: The Windrush scandal doesn't only affect migrants from the Caribbean but has impacted so many others. However, I think that it is crucial for people to understand the specific Windrush history so that people can give up their delusions about a Britain that doesn't exist anymore – if it ever did – and open their eyes to what Britain is today.

AA: How much would you say the theatre industry has changed in the last 30 years in terms of representation and what are the changes you would like to see?
WP: I am aware that individual success does not necessarily represent structural change. So, while I am grateful for my career, I am conscious that theatre has a very long way to go in terms of representation. For example, I discovered recently that one of my favourite London theatres has never produced a play by a black British playwright. They tick the box for representation by producing a handful of African American plays and by curating "festivals" of work by black African artists […]. A recent positive change has been the rise of Artistic Directors of colour like Madani Younis whose vision and passion arises from lived experience. They prove that "diversity" is exciting, dynamic and commercial.

Interview by Lyn Gardner, "Winsome Pinnock: I used to think we needed change – now we need a revolution" (2018)

[…] she knows she has achieved a great deal and that every hard-won gain should be celebrated, she is also acutely aware of how far there is to go for writers of colour […].

We meet in the week in which Natasha Gordon's debut play, *Nine Night*, opened at the National to rave reviews, but Gordon is still one of only a handful of black female writers, including debbie tucker green and Michaela Coel, who have had their work staged at the National. It's hard for any young playwright to progress, but without a strong champion for writers of colour – Pinnock's early work was supported by Jules Wright and the Women's Playhouse Trust – the invisible barriers further lessen the opportunities.

"You are always finding yourself cast as a beginner, always a young writer [...]," she says. "There was a sense for me and my peers, other black women writers, of feeling we weren't allowed to grow up and progress – the feeling that I constantly had to prove myself over and over, and never getting to the point when people said, 'You can do this.'"

Pinnock argues that it is not just the individual who suffers, but the entire culture, leaving each new generation of black female writers to feel that nothing came before them. "Always feeling that you are the first is a lonely place to be," she says.

"If writers like me are denied a full career and the opportunity to reach our mature voice and fulfil our creative potential or tell our stories, it's not just a censoring of that individual but the censoring of an entire community. I feel this far more passionately than I ever did. You leave a trace of yourself as an unresolved history. It's not enough that you now have black actors playing parts not necessarily written for them. There is a culture and history that should be told and seen on stage. I used to think we needed change to progress. Now I think we need a revolution."

Winsome Pinnock interviewed by Jessie Thompson (2018)

[JT]: *What was your background to becoming a playwright?*
[WP]: The Inner London Education Authority subsidised school visits to the theatre and that got me into the habit of watching and reading plays. I used to go with my younger sister and invariably we'd be the youngest and also the only black people in the audience, but we didn't care. I was a member of various youth theatres. Like every other young person who grew up in Islington, I attended Anna Scher Children's Theatre. I had a job after school working with Anna and her then husband Charles Verrall in their office. I'm still the same, I've always had more than one job on the go (as well as writing I am Associate Professor in Drama at Kingston University). It's part of immigrant culture. My parents came to Britain to work and that was passed on to me. I was a member of the Old Vic Youth Theatre for a short while, and during my final year at Goldsmiths University, where I studied for a degree in Drama and English Literature, I joined the Royal Court Young People's Theatre. While I was there I started writing Leave Taking.

[JT]: *What's the hardest play you've ever written?*
[WP]: Probably *Leave Taking*, because it was the first play I wrote. At the time you couldn't study Creative Writing at university so you had to find other ways to learn the craft. I lived for the weekly meetings of the Young Writers' Group which took place in a shed behind the Royal Court. I started to think of myself as a writer because the

tutors, Hanif Kureishi and Stephen Wakelam,[2] took us seriously. I remember when I started writing in earnest it was an exciting time when I could barely sleep because I was living and breathing whichever play I was working on.
[…]

[JT]: *What is your favourite line or scene from any play?*
[WP]: "Dismantle capitalism and overturn the patriarchy" - a call to arms from Ella Hickson's *The Writer.*

[JT]: *What's been the biggest surprise to you since you've had your writing performed by actors?*
[WP]: There is a distinct moment in rehearsals when the actors take ownership of the play. You live for that moment, I think because the play is then elevated to more than just your words.

[JT]: *What's been your biggest setback as a writer?*
[WP]: The patriarchy.

[JT]: *And the hardest lesson you've had to learn?*
[WP]: Not to show work before it's ready.

[JT]: *What do you think is the best thing about theatre? And the worst?*
[WP]: The best thing is its ephemerality, that no two performances are alike. The worst thing about theatre is its ephemerality: you can't fully capture the feel of a live performance, not even by filming it…
[…]

[JT]: *Are there any themes and stories you find yourself re-visiting with your plays?*
[WP]: I often write about mothers, daughters, sisters - sisterhood in its widest sense.
[…]

[JT]: *Why did you write* Leave Taking?
[WP]: One of the reasons I wrote the play was because I never saw women like the main character Enid take the central role in a play. The play was written 30 years ago and it's still quite rare to find a lead part written specifically for a black female performer.

Winsome Pinnock interviewed by Alice Savile (2017)

"I was the first black female writer to have a play at the National Theatre. Thirty years later, I'm still one of the only black females who's been produced there, and that's nothing short of shameful. If you think women writers are under-represented in theatre, then my God, black women writers are severely under-represented. They don't get the nurturing they need to grow. And if you're not programming these women, you're not being bold enough to tell their stories – stories which might even indirectly criticise you. Integration is incredibly successful, but there's another story of continuing inequality, and I think that's one that needs to be told."

Please see the Works Cited for further information on the sources used in this essay.

Notes

1 The MV Empire Windrush was the first ship to bring Jamaicans to Britain in 1948 to aid the post-WWII rebuilding effort. In 2018, a big scandal ensued when the British Home Office wrongly deported 83 of these immigrants who were declared illegal, and it then transpired that the Home Office had actually destroyed many of these immigrants' records proving their legal status.

2 Hanif Kureshi (b.1954) is an award-winning playwright, screenwriter, and novelist of English and Pakistani descent, best known for his play *My Beautiful Launderette* (1985), which was also made into a film. Stephen Wakelam (b.1947) is an English playwright and teacher who was Young Writers' Tutor at the Royal Court Theatre (1981–1984) and then supported young playwrights at the National Theatre Studio in the 1990s.

Suggestions for Further Reading

Abram, Nicola. "Looking Back: Winsome Pinnock's Politics of Representation." *Modern and Contemporary Black British Drama.* (2014). 95–111.

Goddard, Lynette. "Winsome Pinnock's Migration Narratives." *Staging Black Feminisms: Identity, Politics, Performance.* Basingstoke: Palgrave Macmillan, 2007. 57–81.

Griffin, Gabriele. "The Remains of the British Empire: The Plays of Winsome Pinnock." *A Companion to Modern British and Irish Drama: 1880-2005.* Ed. M. Luckhurst. Oxford: Blackwell, 2006. 198–209.

Marzette, DeLinda. "Coming to Voice: Navigating the Interstices in Plays by Winsome Pinnock." *Middle Passages and the Healing Place of History: Migration and Identity in Black Women's Literature.* Ed. E. Brown-Guillory. Columbus, OH: Ohio State University Press, 2006. 32–51.

Öğünç, Banu. *Constructions of New Britishness in Winsome Pinnock's Talking in Tongues, Mules, Can You Keep a Secret? And One Under.* Unpubl. PhD. Ankara University. 2016. At http://www.openaccess.hacettepe.edu.tr:8080/xmlui/handle/11655/3621, accessed 07/08/2021.

Reitz, Bernhard. "'Discovering an Identity Which Has Been Squashed': Intercultural and Intracultural Confrontations in the Plays of Winsome Pinnock and Ayub Khan-Din." *European Journal of English Studies.* 7.1 (2003): 39–54.

Sakellaridou, Elizabeth. "Old Wine in a New Bottle or Vice Versa? Winsome Pinnock's Interstitial Poetics." *Contemporary British Theatre.* Ed. D. Godiwala. London: Palgrave Macmillan, 2013. 121–144.

88 TAKEMOTO KOSHIKÔ (b.1953)

Maki Isaka

Introduction

This essay explores Takemoto Koshikô's (b.1953) ideas on *gidayû* music.[1] The audio component of the four-century-old puppet theatre in Japan now known as *bunraku* puppet theatre, *gidayû* music is usually, if not always, conducted by two musicians: string music, played by an instrumentalist, and the entire lines of all characters on stage *narrated* solo by a single chanter, who also *sings* descriptive recitation. *Bunraku* is an all-male theatre, and *gidayû* an all-male theatrical vocal music. Female musicians have long played *gidayû*, however, as stand-alone music with no puppets. It is also noteworthy that these females have performed almost always under men's names and sometimes in men's clothing. In premodern times (through 1867), as females had been prohibited from participating in the performing arts since the proclamations of 1629,[2] female *gidayû* players frequently endured such drastic ordeals as bans, property confiscation, and incarceration imposed by samurai authorities. In modern times (1868 onward), these female performers were no longer subject to such physically violent sentences, but as Michel Foucault would remind us, the epistemological turmoil they faced was no less radical.[3]

Artistically, *gidayû* belongs to a far longer and broader performing-art category called "recited narratives," which refers to *storytelling* art that is posited vis-à-vis *singing* art. Accordingly, *gidayû* is defined as "theatrical male-vocal-music centering the act of narrating as that which is *not* singing." Here, two kinds of dichotomized and hierarchical pairs are in operation: "narrating vs. singing" and "masculinization vs. feminization." Yet around the turn of the twentieth century, certain twists happened to these two pairs. Colonial modernity changed epistemology in Japan through rapid modernization and westernization, during the process of which femininity and females and masculinity and males were categorically tied together in scientized (i.e., *made* as if it were "scientific") discourse.

At that time, women's *feminized gidayû* performance style that emphasized *singing* emerged and became extremely popular. Importantly, this new performance style ran counter to the fundamental definition of *gidayû* as "theatrical male-vocal-music centering the act of narrating as that which is not singing," but it certainly reified the modern epistemological amalgam of female bodies and femininity.[4] It is also noteworthy that this performance style was fervently supported by the people most likely to be subject to the influence of Western knowledge: young elite male college students. This new popularity did not last long, however, and the "masculinized" performance style continued.[5] Subsequently, females' *gidayû* came to be recognized for

DOI: 10.4324/9781003006923-89

its authentic (read: masculinized) artistry, to the extent that two chanters and two instrumentalists have been awarded Living-National-Treasure titles to date, arguably the highest honor for artists in modern Japan. It is quite telling that the vocal performance of the two Living-National-Treasure chanters, Takemoto Tosahiro (1897–1992) and Takemoto Komanosuke (b. 1935), is extremely masculinized, even passing as that of male chanters.

Contemporary chanter Koshikô belongs to this arena. She is one of the most prominent female chanters following in the footsteps of preceding maestros, such as the Living-National-Treasure chanters as well as her own master, Takemoto Koshimichi (1912–2013). Koshikô thus excels in enacting a wide range of characters, men or women, young or old: cheap racketeers, loving young wives, solemn samurai inwardly grieving over a son's premature death, and so on. At the age of eighteen, she was recognized by a top female *gidayû* chanter, Koshimichi, and became her disciple. Starting with an Emerging New Performer Award (1976), Koshikô has since garnered many prestigious awards. Among them, in 2000, she was designated as one of the Preservers of Important Intangible Cultural Properties (Collective Certification for *Gidayû* music), and in 2020, she was decorated with an Excellence Award for her performance at the Agency for Cultural Affairs' National Arts Festival. She has also been actively performing overseas (in France, the United States, Russia, Indonesia, Korea, etc.), and she has collaborated with performers in such various genres as all-female puppet theatre, dance, and contemporary theatre.

Whether in *gidayû* or other genres, Japanese performing arts have an enduring literary genre called "accounts-on-artistry," in which practitioners discuss their respective arts. These accounts tend to be short and deceptively simple, and they are sometimes considered analogous to Kôan of Zen Buddhism, which use simple-looking riddles to help Zen trainees to attain perception.

In her interview with Maki Isaka, excerpted here, Koshikô's comments about *gidayû*-artistry fall into this genre, the most critical points centering upon the "melodious singing-voice." A master of authentic *gidayû* music, Koshikô nevertheless makes a remark that contains two crucial and controversial matters: first, the melodious *singing* voice is one of the important elements of *gidayû* music; second, the melodious *singing* voice gives an advantage to female performers. For gender theory, the word "naturally" in the second sentence of the excerpt stands out, but in the context of *gidayû*, the first and third sentences[6] are extremely controversial and, indeed, radical. Without an effective understanding of what Koshikô connotes with the phrase, "melodious singing-voice," it would be impossible to comprehend what the word "naturally" in her remarks really means.[7]

What Koshikô says under the concept of "melodious singing-voice" certainly builds on the aforementioned two polarized pairs (narrating/singing and masculinization/feminization), and yet she radically alters – if not nullifies – their established meanings. First, although "narrating" and "singing" remain mutually exclusive in her words, and the constitutive other of each ("A as that which is not B") at that, these two acts are not placed in an "either or" relationship in Koshikô's conceptualization. She thus creates a contrast to the dominant understanding in which a beautiful singing voice is considered risky on the grounds that such is likely to hinder the skillful execution of narrating characters' lines.[8] Simply put, it had been deemed that, if excelling in singing, the chanter must be bad at narrating the lines, and vice versa. In stark contrast to this "common sense" in the *gidayû* paradigm that a beautiful singing voice is a liability, not only does Koshikô's idea present it as an asset but it also presumes that "singing voice" and "narrating voice" can coexist *within one performing body*. It is not that, should a chanter be good at one, he/she/they must be bad at the other. Nay, she implies, one can have both. No matter how tacit, this statement is revolutionary, going against the abovementioned tradition. Furthermore, Koshikô's notion is also challenging in terms of history. While not exclusively, the beautiful singing voice is often regarded as belonging to the aforementioned abjected and obliterated feminized performance by women in the past; then, aiming at such *might* equal seeking the bygone loser's path.

Given these observations, not only does Koshikô's statement challenge an established tradition theoretically, but her remarks also unsteady a historical paradigm that has been strongly stabilized over time. The greatest irony now emerges: her statement does not hypothetically propose to *shift* from the highly regarded act of "narrating" to the lower-categorized act of "singing," suggested by someone good at the latter but not at the former, nor to switch from "masculinization" to "feminization." Rather, however gentle, quiet, and tacit, hers is an ambitious statement, by a maestro capable of performing in the male-centric mainstream, that doing the "men's" job well is simply not good enough.

Takemato Koshikô

Excerpt from Interview with Maki Isaka (2019)[9]

Gidayû music is certainly a dynamic narrating art created for men, but there are also some parts in it, usually at a climax, that are to be sung up melodiously, just like arias of opera, you see. It's said that it can be done naturally through women's bodies, not so much artificially or forcefully, so it's comfortable to listen to, so it is said. One of the strong suits of females' *gidayû* lies in such, no doubt.

Please see the Works Cited for further information on the sources used in this essay.

Notes

1 Japanese names are given in the Japanese order: surname first, followed by the given name. In subsequent references for *gidayû* musicians, this essay uses their first names.
2 The 1629 proclamation prohibited "female kabuki players and the like" from performing. Subsequent bans specifically targeted female *gidayû* players.
3 Michel Foucault's influential study, *Discipline and Punish* (1977), examines the carceral state historically and its ongoing influence on society at large.
4 For a discussion of this phenomenon focusing on new "actresses," see Ayako Kano, *Acting Like a Woman in Modern Japan: Theater, Gender, and Nationalism* (New York, NY: Palgrave, 2001). For a discussion of how female actors in *kabuki* (another all-male theatre closely related to *bunraku*) were obliterated in relation to this phenomenon, see Maki Isaka, *Onnagata: A Labyrinth of Gendering in Kabuki Theater* (Seattle, WA and London: University of Washington Press, 2016). An analysis of female *gidayû* musicians surviving the very same ordeal that ended up expunging their *kabuki* sisters necessitates a longer essay than is possible here.
5 Simplifying to the extreme, it might be dubbed a conquest of "femmes fatale" by "honorary men," a phenomenon of great moment that deserves a full-scale analysis.
6 Takemoto Koshikô states, "some parts [of *gidayû*] are to be *sung* up melodiously, just like arias of opera [. . . which] can be done [more] naturally through women's bodies [than through men's bodies] [. . .]. One of the strong suits of females' *gidayû* lies in such" (emphasis Maki Isaka).

7 A full analysis of both "melodious singing-voice" and "naturally" lies outside the scope of this essay.

8 This perception is not unique to male *gidayû* performers and critics but is shared by successful female performers as well. Female *gidayû* chanter Toyotake Danshi (1891–1989) applauds Toyotake Roshô (1874–1930) for her beautiful voice, emphasizing that we "won't have such a beautiful voice like hers after her, never," but nevertheless criticizes her performance *because of* that: "So her *jôruri* [i.e., *gidayû*] was something that anybody feels like listening to again, but she wasn't skillful at all. She can't get skilled cause her voice was way too good. The life of *jôruri* is in lines, isn't it. But if your voice is too good, you'd end up *singing*, so your lines won't get improved. My voice is just average, nothing more, so I've made every effort to practice lines" (Hayashi Yoshiki, *Onna Gidayû Ichidai: Toyotake Danshi Jôruri Jinsei*. Kobe: Kôbe Shinbun Shuppan Sentâ, 1988. 179; translation and emphasis Maki Isaka).

9 Translated from Japanese by Maki Isaka.

Suggestions for Further Reading

Coaldrake, A. Kimi. *Women's Gidayû and the Japanese Theatre Tradition*. London: Routledge, 1997.

Gabrovska, Galia Todorova. "Onna Mono: 'Female Presence' on the Stage of the All-Male Traditional Japanese Theatre." *Asian Theatre Journal* 32.2 (Fall 2015): 387–415.

Mizuno, Yûko. *Edo Tôkyô Musume Gidayû no Rekishi*. Tokyo: Hôsei Daigaku Shuppankyoku, 2003.

89 ÉMILIE MONNET (b.1979)

Lindsay Lachance

Introduction

Dreams, rivers, beavers and birch trees are the images that come to mind when I think of Émilie Monnet's *Okinum* (2020). Many Indigenous theatre artists across Turtle Island, and particularly in what is now known as occupied Canada, use their theatre and performance practices to exercise their culturally specific intellectual traditions, (re)learn Indigenous languages, activate political or legal systems and build dramaturgies based on material cultures like weavings, birch bark biting, traditional tattoos and other systems. This signals how Indigenous theatre practitioners are articulating and embodying theoretical understandings of life, culture, storytelling and community that are constructed differently than Western theories and worldviews. Within the field of critical Indigenous studies, there are growing numbers of Indigenous scholars, artists and activists who work within resistance and resurgence frameworks. Resistance and resurgence frameworks both stem from a deep love of the land, proudness of our ancestors and respect for our nations.

Through an Indigenous lens, we can understand and appreciate Émilie Monnet's (b.1979) play *Okinum* as a work of resurgence theory. For Michi Saagiig Nishnaabeg scholar, writer and artist Leanne Betasamosake Simpson, kwe, meaning woman in Anishinaabemowin[1], is understood as resurgent method. In her chapter "Kwe as Resurgent Method," in *As We Have Always Done: Indigenous Freedom Through Radical Resistance,* Simpson explains how "as political orders, [Indigenous] bodies, minds, emotions, and spirits produce theory and knowledge on a daily basis without conforming to the conventions of the academy" (31). Dreams, rivers, beavers and birch trees become the theoretical map for Monnet to question her identity, memory and ancestral history through an interdisciplinary theatre and immersive performance experience. Amik (the beaver) came to Anishinaabe artist Émilie Monnet in her dream. A giant amik visited Monnet three times while she was fighting cancer, speaking to her in Anishinaabemowin and carrying medicine in its paw. This led Monnet to refuse Western medical cancer treatment, and she began her work with Elders, the language and the land.

Monnet exemplifies resurgence practices in her real life and her artistic practice. Her personal healing journey was devoted to learning her language, spending time at the Ottawa River, learning about amik's medicines and reconciling the intergenerational trauma carried in her own body. Therefore, both formally and in terms of its content, *Okinum* resists and refuses traditional notions of Western (male) dramaturgy. Kwe as resurgent method, in this context, means that kwe is also a theorist. For

DOI: 10.4324/9781003006923-90

Simpson, Indigenous women's bodies and life are a part of our research, and we can use this knowledge to critique and analyze.

Émilie Monnet is an actor, playwright, producer and the founder of Onishka Productions based out of Montreal, Quebec, Canada. In 2019, Onishka Productions partnered with O'Kaadenigan Wiingashk Collective to present Indigenous Contemporary Scene Scotland, a month-long program of performing arts and creative conversations featuring Indigenous artists from across Canada, presented during the Edinburgh Fringe Festival and also at the Edinburgh International Festival and the Edinburgh International Book Festival (cross-festival programming). Monnet's work as an Anishinaabe/French artist creates bridges between Indigenous and non-indigenous audiences who are mutually interested in challenging and transforming the world we live in. Monnet's work is essential in bringing Francophone and Anglophone Indigenous artistic communities together not only in Quebec, Canada but also across the globe.

Okinum, which means dam, is a beautiful piece written in French, English and Anishinaabemowin that follows Monnet's healing journey. It is accented with a soundscape of her homelands, phrases from her language teacher and the echoes of amik chewing on some bark. Monnet uses her piece to demonstrate theatre's expansive abilities to involve characters, stage presences and Indigenous structures that refuse the well-made play model. In the excerpts included here, Anishinaabe kwe theory and worldview transport us between various temporal realities: the dream world, the animal plain, histories of settler colonialisms and back to real time. Braided through *Okinum* is kwe as theory, kwe as art and kwe as survival.

A dam is a great metaphor for how Western dramatic theory and criticism does not consider Indigenous worldviews and ways of being in its pedagogy and methodology. A dam that is blocking water flow, or causing build-up, may cause more harm than good. Instead, *Okinum* is a dam that centres and celebrates Indigenous experiences, intelligences and practices. The theoretical landscape – our rivers and trees, and the animals who make this land their home – help Indigenous theatre artists build culturally specific dramaturgies and vessels to carry our stories. With works like Émilie Monnet's *Okinum*, we see how embodied knowledge, lived experiences, land-based work and language revitalization influence both the structure and the content of a piece, building a theory of its own.

Émilie Monnet

Excerpts from Okinum *(2020)*

SCENE 2: Small Game

In my bed,
spread out in the shape of a star,
I listen
to my heart
Beating fast
too fast since I left my dream
and landed here
awake.

I have an appointment at the hospital this morning.

Pause. We shift into dream world.

I dreamt I was on the trap line.
I dreamt of Wabush, caught in a snare.
I see Wabush struggle
trying to break free from the metallic fangs grasping at their neck.
I watch
without moving
mesmerized by rabbit's instinct to survive.

I look at Wabush
right in the eye
Holding on to this moment
so fleeting
when life spills out
when fur becomes still.
I'm transfixed.
Right here
Right in front of me
I watch Wabush die.

I admire their fight
Fur is white
as snow
Wabush finally surrenders.
Body stops shaking
Heart stops beating.

Without a cry
or a plea
Wabush offers their life
In the crisp silence of winter.

I start to undress Wabush
remove their fur.
The flesh is pink
Warm
Naked.
I watch the blood
drip onto the snow
Nothing's more beautiful than this red spill
this blood-offering
now soaking into the white.

The woman stands up.

We hear a voice in Anishnaabemowin saying the following. The woman repeats some of the words.

Pakidadenagewin panema kida togon kijdja madiziwin.
Kek oshka madiziwin ki abidan.[2]

Pause.

My heart beats faster
It means I'm alive.
Right?

And since I found the lump,
since I've entered this dance
with ultrasounds
mammograms
biopsies
scans
needles under my skin
life

MY life
pulses,
A dam about to break.

I have an appointment at the hospital this morning.

I feel like Wabush:
Dépecée, exposée[3]
Dépecée, exposée
Dépecée, Exposed, raw
Raw, vulnérable,
Skinned, vulnerable, dépecée
À vif, à vif, à vif[4]

The rumbling starts again and beaver sounds intensify. We tip into Beaver world.

SCENE 3: First Beaver Dream

Pre-recorded words in Anishnaabemowin interweave with live text, enveloping the audience in the sounds of language. Sounds of water. There is a river nearby.
We shift into Dream world again.

A beaver
Giant
Fur shiny

She recognizes Amik the beaver

Amik
Taller than me.
Eyes lock.
Amik
Walks towards me
Stands in front of me
Looks familiar.

Amik
Grabs my hand.
Puts something into my hand.
A pouch.

Amik says:

Pre-recorded voice in Anishnaabemowin comes in.

Owe ni mashkikim.
Kin oo aji.
Mino abijiton.[5]

Now we hear a pre-recorded conversation between the woman and Véronique, her Anishnaabemowin teacher. The woman asks her teacher what the words spoken by the beaver in her dream meant. The teacher translates the words into English and corrects the woman's pronunciation.

Véronique: Owe ni mashkikim
Émilie: Owe ni mashkikim
Véronique: Owe ni mashkikim. This is my medicine
Émilie: Then he said, Kin oo aji (pronounced incorrectly)
Véronique: Kin oo aji Kin oo aji
Émilie: Kin oo aji (repeating)
Véronique: Hmum, This means it's yours now
Émilie: wow
Véronique: because he gives it to you
Émilie: and then he said, Mino abijiton (pronounced incorrectly) something like that
Véronique: Mino abijiton
Émilie: abijiton
Véronique: Mino abijiton. It means use it well. Abijiton means use it.
    Mino, it means carefully or well more even for the better.
    So, this is what it means mino abijiton
Émilie: Mino abijiton.
Véronique: abijiton
Émilie: abijiton.

End of recording

SCENE 4: A Dam in the Throat

We hear the National Geographic jingle. The woman steps down from the platform and speaks directly to the audience. Black and white documentary-style video footage of beavers in action.

In July 1990, the same summer as the Oka/Kanehsatake resistance, an enormous beaver dam was photographed by a NASA satellite. Nobody knew of its existence. Not until Google Earth…

The dam is right in the middle of Wood Buffalo National Park in Northern Alberta. It measures 850 meters which is quite exceptional. Beaver dams rarely measure more than 10 meters.

Many generations of beaver worked on the construction of the dam and, to this day, the dam still continues to grow.

Where beavers build dams, new bodies of water appear, like deep stagnant ponds. These ponds also allow for new bacteria to develop in the water, breaking down pollutants caused by the overuse of chemical fertilizers.

It's remarkable how beavers restore life and how they repopulate their territories, after being hunted continuously, for hundreds of years.

Beavers are the only species along with humans able to leave a trace on Earth that is visible from outer space.

> An imprint left on Earth
> A dam for protection
> But only visible from the stars

The woman crawls back onto the platform, as if pulled in by what she sees projected in it. We hear a pre-recorded conversation between her and Veronique:

Émilie: What does it mean « okinum »?
Véronique: Is a dam, a beaver dam
Émilie: beaver dam
Véronique: Beaver dam, «amik» is the beaver, «okinum» is the damn
Émilie: and what's the root?
Véronique: Etymologically, it's «okin » meaning bones,
> *because the trees, they look like bones gathered together.*
> *So «okinum», it's like the corpses of trees or their skeletons that have been gathered together*
> *by the beaver. put together. « okinum »*
Émilie: « okinum »

Pause

The woman repeats the word Okinum. The 'O' transforms into a sound throat, as if she tries to unblock her throat.

Véronique: Menjesh Chapeney
Émilie: Menjesh Chapeney?
Véronique: Menjesh Chapeney, Menjesh Chapeney
Émilie: And what does it mean?

Véronique: « cancer ».
Émilie: But what does it mean exactly?
Véronique: « Menjesh », the insects that give you disease;
*   « Chapeney», means lack of health: what the Menjesh have done to you.*
Émilie: So it is like insects eating you inside?
Véronique: The insects are like eating all your wellness.

SCENE 8: Beaver's Teeth

The National Geographic jingle starts. In a lecture style delivery, the woman removes the rest of the beaver pelts, stacking them in a pile.

From the 17th to the 19th century, beaver hats were one of the most important features in a man's wardrobe in Europe. At the time, it was a common belief that wearing a beaver hat would make you smarter. And a deaf person could even recover their hearing.

In Europe, beavers were almost extinct by the end of the 17 hundreds. North America became a major supply source to sustain fashion in Europe, and it's around that time that the Hudson's Bay Company was created to export as many beaver pelts as possible. Overhunted, beavers here almost vanished completely by the end of the 18 hundreds.

The beaver pelts were a form of currency in the development of the colonial economy, which enabled Canada to come into existence. It explains why the beaver became the official symbol of Canadian sovereignty in 1975 and why it was chosen to be on the nickel back in 1937. But in 2011, Senator Nicole Eaton proposed a new law to replace the beaver on the coin with a polar bear. The Senator considered the beaver to be a 'has been', and no longer reflected Canadian values.

'The beaver is a rat, a big rat. Every winter, they destroy the docks at our cottages'. The Senator's proposal was rejected and the beaver continues to be the iconic symbol of this country.

> Amik needs to work all the time
> because their teeth never stop growing.
> If Amik stops working
> The teeth will pierce their throat.

She chokes.

Beaver sounds transform into the sounds of birch-bark biting, a traditional art form practiced by Indigenous women across Turtle Island.

SCENE 9: The Art of Making Marks on Bark

The image of a birch bark flower is projected on the platform.

> Mani is in a forest of birch trees
> She cuts through the bark with her knife
>
> A drop falls.
> Then another one.

It's the first water of the year.
It's Spring.

Mani hangs a birch bark basket on the tree's skin
collecting every precious drop.
There's an image on the basket.

We hear the pre-recorded word mazinibaakajige repeated several times. On the video screens the image of Thérèse Telesh Bégin from Mashteuiatsh appears. She is biting at the birch bark.

Mazinibaakajige
Making marks on the bark Mazinibaakajige
The art of making images on the birch bark with your teeth.

We hear the pre-recorded voice of Telesh, in French, sharing knowledge about the art of birch bark biting:

Telesh: «*It takes a lot of concentration to make images. What you imagine is what you will get. When I start folding, I start thinking about what I can do, what I will draw with my teeth. Most of the drawings I make, I do them in the bush, when I'm at peace, when I'm alone. That's what I've learnt.*
When Spring arrives, after Winter, that's when we feel a lot of energy and I always get excited because I know the bark will be beautiful.
The sap will go up and the bark will detach itself easily from the tree.
And at the same time the bark will be softer which will help to make the designs.
At this point I say to people around me: don't ask me any more questions because I'm going to my forest. I'm going on a journey into the forest when I make the drawings....
And by the way, it's in the way the bark is folded that you get the symmetry in the drawing... Of course when you start to unfold, you have to be very careful because the bark is very thin.
When you look at it in the light, it will look like lace. It's exactly that.
Why do I love doing this? Because of so many generations of women before me who practiced this art form, I don't want it to disappear. They're traditions, womens' traditions. I'm proud to be able to share my art. I don't want it to disappear. That's why I love to share it.»

End of the recording.

The woman rips long strips of the bark, lets go, and watches the bark curl back on itself. The platform is transformed into a beautiful birch bark tapestry.

Mani
More and more I find it hard to resist your call. It sounds like the song of an old beaver

SCENE 11: The Flood

Pre-recorded conversation between the woman and Véronique.

Véronique: «*Nowé anowé*»: *I want to speak.*
Émilie: *Will I be able to speak it one day?*

Véronique: Speak up: «Nowé anowé». Don't say: «Will I speak it one day?»
Émilie: «Nowé anowé»
Véronique: Nowé anowé: I want to speak it.
Émilie: Speak up. Loud and clear: «Nowé anowé».

End of the recording.

> Some secrets gnaw at you
> until you get sick
> My stories are too sad to be told
> elle m'a dit[6]
> too sad
> Infinite sadness under layers and layers of secrets
> I have secrets inside of me I will never tell...
> *Chut*
> A knot on the bark
> A lump in my throat
> Insects gnawing and biting
> to the point of
> *Chut!*

[Here and below, a pre-recorded Voice in Anishnaabemowin comes in.]

> *Voice: Ahhhh Nten*

> Some stories give power
> when they're told
> Stories can heal
> Put pieces together
> Decipher
> layer after layer after layer
> Go back in time
> Lorsqu'Amik était mon parent[7]
> Amik is my kin
>   *Voice: Micha Amik Aki*

> Les castors géants ont réellement existé[8]
> Their stories continue to be told
> Ronge, ronge[9]
> Gnaw
> Bite into it.
>   *Voice: Ndeto Mitigok Odabimimawa Okegendanawa.[10]*

> Keep going
> Continue
> Don't give up
> Ne pas abandonner[11]
> C'est une priorité.[12]
>   *Voice: Paneme he.*

An elder told me
they recognize me but they don't understand what I'm saying
It's too hard
   Voice: Panama mojik.

Apprendre[13]
réapprendre[14]
Don't give up
Keep learning new words
Mojik
Mashkwizewin
Widjegabowitojin
Obedi okegendan
Mishkikiwos mitikgok.
Mani only spoke Anishnabemowin
   Voice: N'mushumis.

N'mushumis
Papi
the last one to
Speak it
When I pray to Mani she doesn't understand me
So what's the use of praying?
   Voice: N'djumen.[15]

Quand est-ce que le cordon est complètement coupé?[16]
When do we stop being Anishnaabe?
   Voice: Anishnaabewin ki tebenamigon[17]

I have to keep going
Continue
Never give up
   Voice: Panima oshamesh ijitigemwin

PANIMA OSHAMESH IJITIGEWIN
My mantra to give courage
Même si...[18]
PANIMA OSHAMESH IJITIGEWIN
Garder le cap[19]
Not a clear path
   Voice: Kawin pegadedaken[20]

Au fond de mes entrailles,[21]
Buzzing sounds in my ears
   Voice: Showapishken

In my ears
HER voice
   Voice: Nidjikag[22]

Help me, Mani help me
Même si je ne comprends pas,[23]
In my palm
Un cadeau.[24]
Mishkikiwin.
    Voice: Mashkikiwog mitikgok[25]

Don't give up
M'engager jusqu'au bout.[26]
    Voice: Mashkikiwog mitikgok

Panima oshamesh ijitigewin
Spend time with elders
Prepare the teas
Follow the instructions,
Activate the medecine with a good mind
    Voice: Sogodewin[27]

Basta
ça suffit[28]
c'est fini[29]
The blue heron above me
Same color as my hospital gown
    Voice: Odji madiziwin[30]

I need courage
to change
dig
rip
bring back
heal further back than me
Générations de femmes qui s'effacent[31]
My burden
My gift
    Voice: Kawin Segeziken[32]

MENDJESH CHAPENEY NIGODJIKWA,
C'est ma décision[33]
MY decision
    Voice: Kawin Segeziken

Wake up the bear
As big as Amik in my dream,
MICHA AMIK MAKWA ADIZIN
It's MY decision,
    Voice: Makwenden Makwadizen[34]

Sogodewin
Shoapishken

Sogwenden
Odji madiziwin
Makwenden makwadizen
Become the bear.
She roars.

SCENE 12: Inside the Lodge

The woman sings. The beams of light shining down on the platform resemble tipi poles.

It's summer
It's hot
inside the lodge

Clothes stick to the skin
Outside
sky is pitch black
Inside
Colours
Dancing in the flames
Cascading onto drum
Transforming into song

This is my thank you ceremony:
The black spots that kept growing with each of my ultrasounds have
disappeared.

Memory of Amik is in my bones
Make good use of it
The bones of trees form dams
Make good sense of it
It will be ok
Mino Abijiton

The woman sings again, this time in Anishnaabemowin. Her song brings the beavers in, they are swimming around her. She sits amongst the beavers.

Kitci Meegwetch Kokom Mani
egi ijinjawotc Amik kidja wejibamok mii e aji e pedjimiwooga
Ni moshomisimik koki kija
Ka kanidanan tabi ke ijaik kishpen kendanmik tebi e odjibawik.

A video projection of the woman wrapped in a big piece of tent canvas appears while she's singing. She climbs on top of a beaver lodge

SCENE 13: Beaver Lodge

The woman stands up and leaves the platform.

The images on the copper screens change to close-ups of hands building a sweat lodge.

Pre-recorded conversation between Émilie and Véronique comes in:

Émilie: A beaver lodge makes me think of a belly. A big belly. Or a sweat lodge.
Véronique: Yes it does seem like a sweat lodge. Well there are similarities because the beaver lodge
is made of trees, medicinal trees, because that's what the beaver uses. They're medicinal
trees. The scent in there must be very ha...[she exhales] It must be very nice and secure
with the scent of the beaver.
Émilie: Yes. Dark and warm and secure.
Véronique: Yes. And the beavers live in there as a big family. They must be feeling well, healthy...
Healthy in the big belly (laughs)
Émilie: Yes in the big belly.
Véronique: In the big beaver lodge (laughs).

Beaver sounds intensify. Lights go off.

There should be no applause at the end. People are invited to stay in the space and share tea.
The space, theatrical until now, morphs back into installation mode like at the beginning of the
performance.

Please see the Works Cited for further information on the sources used in this essay.

Notes

1   The Anishinaabe language.
2   Life is a constant birth. Sacrifice brings new life. One life is given up for another to
begin.
3   Cut up/carved; exposed.
4   Alive.
5   This is my medicine. This medicine is yours now. Make good use of it.
6   She told me.
7   When Amik was my parent.
8   The giant beavers really existed.
9   Gnaw.
10   Listen to trees, roots remember it all.
11   Don't give up.
12   It's a priority.
13   To learn.
14   To relearn.
15   My little one.
16   When is the cord completely cut?
17   Your umbilical cord connects you to being Anishnaabe.
18   Even if.
19   Keep focus.
20   Don't give up on your path.
21   At the depth of my soul.
22   My palm.
23   Even if I don't understand.
24   A gift.
25   Trees carry the medicine.
26   Commit to the end.
27   Courage.
28   That's enough.
29   It's finished.

30 Courage for life.
31 Generations of women who fade away.
32 Don't be afraid.
33 It's my decision.
34 Remember the power of the bear.

Suggestions for Further Reading

Mojica, Monique. "In Plain Sight: Inscripted Earth and Invisible Realities." *New Canadian Realisms*. Eds. Roberta Barker and Kim Solga. Toronto: Playwrights Canada Press, 2012. 218–242.

Mojica, Monique. "Stories from the Body: Blood Memory and Organic Texts." *Native American Performance and Representation*. Ed. S.E. Wilmer. Tucson, AZ: University of Arizona Press, 2011. 97–109.

Nolan, Yvette. *Medicine Shows: Indigenous Performance Culture*. Toronto: Playwrights Canada Press, 2015.

Simpson, Leanne Betasamosake. *Dancing on Our Turtle's Back*. Winnipeg: Arbeiter Ring Publishing, 2011.

Works Cited

"12x12: Gabriela Sanchez" https://www.leeway.org/events/12x12_gabriela_sanchez/#.XwIcXShKiM8. Accessed 5 Jul. 2020.

"About: History and Awards." Playwrights Horizons. https://www.playwrightshorizons.org/about/who-we-are/history-and-awards/. Accessed 3 Feb. 2022.

"Action for Women in Theatre: A Study on Employment Discrimination Against Women Playwrights and Directors in Non-Profit Theatre (1969–1975)." https://www.google.com/url?esrc=s&q=&rct=j&sa=U&url=https://witonline.org/2017/03/18/on-the-gender-parity-movement-jenny-lyn-bader/&ved=2ahUKEwjf1NLq5P32AhVYTDABHTteAL4QFnoECAEQA-g&usg=AOvVaw0hElHnn2ll4UM8GY6x3mQB. Accessed 12 Jan. 2022.

Adam, Julie. "The Implicated Audience: Judith Thompson's Anti-Naturalism in *The Crackwalker, White Biting Dog, I Am Yours,* and *Lion in the Streets.*" *Judith Thompson. Critical Perspectives in Canadian Theatre in English.* Vol. 3 Ed. Ric Knowles. Toronto: Playwrights Canada, 2005. 41–46.

Adebayo, Mojisola. "Everything You Know About Queerness You Learnt from Blackness: The Afri-Quia Theatre of Black Dykes, Crips and Kids." *Queer Dramaturgies: International Perspectives on Where Performance Leads Queer.* Eds. Alyson Campbell and Stephen Farrier. London: Palgrave Macmillan, 2016. 131–149.

_____. *Moj of the Antartic: An African Odyssey. Mojisola Adebayo: Plays One.* Ottawa: Oberon Books, 2011.

_____. *Mojisola Adebayo: Plays One.* Ottawa: Oberon Books, 2011.

_____. *Mojisola Adebayo: Plays Two.* Ottawa: Oberon Books, 2020.

_____. *Muhammed Ali and Me. Mojisola Adebayo: Plays One.* Ottawa: Oberon Books, 2011. 65–149.

_____. "Revolutionary Beauty Out of Homophobic Hate: A Reflection on the Performance I Stand Corrected." *Applied Theatre: Aesthetics.* Ed. Gareth White. London: Bloomsbury, 2015. 123–155.

Adebayo, Mojisola and Caoimhe McAvinchey. "Mojisola Adebayo: Interview and Introduction by Caoimhe McAvinchey." *Performance and Community: Commentary and Case Studies.* Ed. Caoimhe McAvinchey. London: Bloomsbury, 2014. 63–73.

Adebayo, Mojisola and Lynette Goddard. "Mojisola Adebayo in conversation with Lynette Goddard." *Hidden Gems.* Ed. Deirdre Osborne. Ottawa: Oberon Books, 2008. 142–148.

Adebayo, Mojisola and Patrick O'Kane. "Mojisola Adebayo." *Actors' Voices: The People Behind the Performances.* Ed. Patrick O'Kane. Ottawa and London: Oberon Books, 2012. 63–87.

Adebayo, Mojisola, Valerie Mason-John, and Deirdre Osborne. "'No Straight Answers': Writing in the Margins, Finding Lost Heroes." *New Theatre Quarterly.* 25.1 (2009): 6–21.

Agate, James. *London Times.* 4 Apr. 1925.

Aldrich, Richard. "This Week in the Worlds Of Music And Opera: Revival Of Gluck's 'Orfeo' At The Metropolitan Opera House." *The New York Times.* 19 Dec. 1909.

Allana, Amal. "Introduction." *The Act of Becoming: Actors Talk.* New Delhi: National School of Drama and Niyogi Books, 2013. xvii–xxiii.

Allen, Robert Clyde. *Horrible Prettiness: Burlesque and American Culture.* Chapel Hill, NC: The University of North Carolina Press, 1991.

Alt-Africa Review. (2019). "Talking to Winsome Pinnock Ahead of Passages: A Windrush Celebration at Royal Court" at https://alt-africa.com/2019/03/10/talking-to-winsome-pinnock-ahead-of-passages-a-windrush-celebration-at-royal-court/. Accessed 17 Mar. 2020.

"Amelia Ann Everard Chesson." *Athenaeum.* 1902: 145.

"American Revolutions." *Oregon Shakespeare Festival.* https://www.osfashland.org/artistic/American-revolutions.aspx. Accessed 26 Oct. 2020.

"American Theatre Again." *The New Yorker.* 12 May 2017. www.newyorker.com/books/page-turner/with-her-eerily-indecent-paula-vogel-unsettles-american-theatre-again?source=searchgoogledspaide&gclid=CjwKCAjw26H3BRB2EiwAy32zhWLMd-m3Kd0gohwdZe97W9nggFY3dMAwH9Y16fShG9yOkg6ej5GFOhoC7KwQAvDBwE. Accessed 1 June 2020.

"Amusements: Theatrical. Mr. Mathews in 'Not Such A Fool As He Looks,' At Fifth-Avenue Theatre. 'Jack Sheppard' At The Olympic." *The New York Times.* 16 May 1871.

Anderson, Misty G. *Female Playwrights and Eighteenth-Century Comedy: Negotiating Marriage on the London Stage.* Houndsmill, Basingstoke: Palgrave, 2002.

Andrews, Jennifer. "A Conversation with Diane Glancy." *American Indian Quarterly.* 26.4 (2002): 645–658.

Angeletti, Gioia. *Nation, Community, Self: Female Voices in Scottish Theatre from the Seventies to the Present.* Milano: Edizioni Mimesis; series Mimesis International, 2018.

Anzaldua, Gloria. *Borderlands/La Frontera: The New Mestiza.* 2nd ed. Iowa City, IA: Aunt Lute Books, 1999.

Archer, William. "A Pre-Shakespearean Playwright." Rev. of *A Father's Tragedy, William Rufus, Loyalty or Love* by Michael Field. *Pall Mall Budget.* 33 (1885): 28.

Arliss, George. "Introduction." *On the Stage.* By Frances Anne Kemble. New York, NY: Dramatic Museum of Columbia University, 1926.

Armstrong, Ann Elizabeth, Kelli Lyon Johnson, and William A. Wortman, eds. *Performing Worlds into Being: Native American Women's Theater.* Oxford, OH: Miami University Press, 2009.

Asleson, Robyn. *The Notorious Muse: The Actress in British Art and Culture, 1776–1812.* New Haven, CT: Yale University Press, 2003.

Ashwell, Lena. "Beauty in Strange Places." *The Stage.* London: Geoffrey Bles, 1929. 9–34.

Astin, M., *Mary Russell Mitford: Her Circle and her Books.* London: N. Douglas, 1930.

Aston, Elaine. "Agitating for Change: Theatre a Feminist 'Network of Resistance'." *Theatre Research International.* 41.1 (2016): 5–20.

_____. *Caryl Churchill.* 3rd ed. Oxford: Oxford University Press, 2018.

_____. "Feeling the Loss of Feminism: Sarah Kane's *Blasted* and an Experiential Genealogy of Contemporary Women's Playwriting." *Theatre Journal.* 62.4 (2010): 575–591.

_____. *Feminist Theatre Practice: A Handbook.* New York, NY and London: Routledge, 2005. www.theatresonline.com › theatres › loughborough-theatres

_____. *Feminist Views on the English Stage: Women Playwrights, 1990-2000.* Cambridge: Cambridge University Press, 2003.

_____. *A Good Night Out for the Girls: Popular Feminisms in Contemporary Theatre and Performance.* London: Palgrave Macmillan, 2013.

_____. *An Introduction to Feminism and Theatre.* London: Routledge. 1995.

_____. *Restaging Feminisms.* London: Palgrave Macmillan, 2020.

_____. *Sarah Bernhardt: A French Actress on the English Stage.* Oxford and Providence RI: Berg, 1989.

Aston, Elaine and Sue-Ellen Case, eds. *Staging International Feminisms.* London: Palgrave Macmillan, 2007.

Aston, Elaine and Elin Diamond, eds. *The Cambridge Companion to Caryl Churchill*. Cambridge: Cambridge University Press, 2009.

Aston, Elaine, ed. *Feminist Theatre Voices: A Collective Oral History: Six Feminist Theatre Groups in Interview*. Leicestershire: Loughborough Theatre Texts, 1997. www.theatresonline.com 'theatres' loughborough-theatres. Accessed 15 Jan. 2022.

Aston, Elaine and Geraldine Harris. *Performance Practice and Process: Contemporary [Women] Practitioners*. London: Palgrave Macmillan, 2007.

Aston, Elaine and George Savona. *Theatre as a Sign System: A Semiotics of Text and Performance*. Cambridge: Cambridge University Press, 2013.

Aston, Elaine and Janelle Reineldt, eds. *The Cambridge Companion to Modern British Women Playwrights*. Cambridge: Cambridge University Press, 2000.

Atkinson, Brooks. "No Theatre Openings Prove That Spring Is Here." *The New York Times*, 2 May 1937. X1.

_____. "Theatre: Seamy Side; 'Single Men at a Party' Opens Off-Broadway." *The New York Times*. 22 Apr. 1959. 30.

Atkinson, Clarissa W. *Mystic and Pilgrim: The Book and the World of Margery Kempe*. Ithaca, NY: Cornell University Press, 1983.

Augustine of Hippo. Sermon 280, "On the birth of the martyrs Perpetua and Felicitas." Ed. J.P. Migne. Paris: Patrologia Latina, 1841. Vol. 38, col. 1281–1284.

Babb, Lawrence. "The Cave of Spleen." *The Review of English Studies*. 12.46 (1936): 165–176.

Baillie, Joanna. *Dramatic and Poetical Works*. London: Longman, Brown, Green, and Longmans, 1851.

_____. "To the Reader." *A Series of Plays in Which It Is Attempted to Delineate the Stronger Passions of the Mind, Each Passion Being the Subject of a Tragedy and Comedy*. London: T. Cadell and W. Davies, 1798. Dramatic and Poetical Works, 228–235.

Baillie, Matthew. *Lectures and Observations on Medicine*. London: Richard Taylor, 1825.

Bain, Audrey. "Loose Canons: Identifying Women's Tradition in Playwriting." *Scottish Theatre Since the Seventies*. Eds. Randall Stevenson and Gavin Wallace, Edinburgh University Press, 1996. 138–145.

Baker, George Pierce. *Dramatic Technique*. Boston, MA: Houghton Mifflin Co., 1919.

Balme, Christopher. "Playbills and theatrical public sphere." *Representing the Past: Essays in Performance Historiography*. Eds. Charlotte Canning and Thomas Postlewait. Iowa City, IA: University of Iowa Press, 2010. 37–62.

Barish, Jonas. *The Antitheatrical Prejudice*. Berkeley, CA: University of California Press, 1981.

Barlow, Judith E. "Introduction." *Women Writers of the Provincetown Players*. Ed. Judith Barlow. Albany, NY: State University of New York Press, 2009. 1–23.

Barnes, Djuna. *The Antiphon*. Los Angeles: Green Integer, 2000.

_____. *The Dove. At the Roots of the Stars: The Short Plays*. Los Angeles: Sun & Moon Press, 2005. 147–161.

_____. "When the Puppets Come to Town." *New York Morning Telegraph Sunday Magazine*. 8 July 1917.

Barnett, Claudia. "Judith Thompson's Ghosts: The Revenants that Haunt the Plays." *Judith Thompson: Critical Perspectives in Canadian Theatre in English*. Vol. 3. Ed. Ric Knowles. Toronto: Playwrights Canada Press, 2009. 92–98.

Baudrillard, Jean. *De la seduction*. Paris: Editions Galilée, 1979.

Bay-Cheng, Sarah. *Mama Dada: Gertrude Stein's Avant-Garde Theater*. New York, NY and London: Routledge, 2004.

Beckett, Samuel. "Dante...Bruno...Vico...Joyce." *Disjecta*. Ed. Ruby Cohn. London: John Calder, 1983. 19–33.

Behn, Aphra. *The Feign'd Curtezans; or, A Night's Intrigue. The Works of Aphra Behn*. Vol. 2. Ed. Montague Summers. London: William Heinemann, 1915. 301–412.

Bell, John. *American Puppet Modernism: Essays on the Material World in Performance*. London: Palgrave Macmillan, 2008.

Bennett, Susan. "Who Speaks? Representations of Native Women in Some Canadian Plays." *Canadian Journal of Drama and Theatre*. 1.2 (1991): 13–25.

Bentley, Eric, ed. *Thirty Years of Treason: Excerpts from Hearings before the House Committee on Un-American Activities, 1938-1968*. New York, NY: Viking Press, 1971.

Ben-Zvi, Linda. "'A Different Kind of the Same Thing': The Early One-Act Plays of Susan Glaspell and J.M. Synge." *Eugene O'Neill Review*. 39.1 (2018): 33–47.

_____. "Silent Partners: The 'Trifling' Nature of Language in the Theatre of Susan Glaspell and Samuel Beckett." *On Glaspell's* Trifles *and "A Jury of her Peers": Centennial Essays, Interviews and Adaptations*. Eds. Martha C. Carpentier and Emeline Jouve. Jefferson, NC: McFarland & Company, Inc., 2015. 45–61.

_____. *Susan Glaspell: Her Life and Times*. Oxford: Oxford University Press, 2005.

Bergman, Mary Bernardine, trans. "Hrotsvit of Gandersheim: The Establishment of Gandersheim." *Medieval Hagiography: An Anthology*. Ed. Thomas Head. New York, NY: Routledge, 2001. 237–254.

Bernhardt, John W. *Itinerant Kingship and Royal Monasteries in Early Medieval Germany, c. 936-1075*. Cambridge: Cambridge University Press, 1993.

Berrian, Brenda and Micere Githae Mugo. "Interview with Micere Githae-Mugo. [Department of Literature, University of Nairobi, 4 Juy 1979]." *World Literature in English*. 21.3 (1982): 521–531.

Berschin, Walter. "Hrotsvit and her Works." *A Companion to Hrotsvit of Gandersheim: Contextual and Interpretive Approaches*. Eds. Phyllis R. Brown and Stephen L. Wailes. Leiden and Boston: Brill, 2012. 23–34.

Berschin, Walter, ed. *Hrotsvit: Opera Omnia*. Leipzig: Teubner, 2001.

Beshero-Bondar, Elisa E. "Mitford, Mary Russell, Drama." *The Encyclopedia of Romantic Literature*. Gen. Ed. Frederick Burwick. Chichester and Hoboken, NJ: Wiley-Blackwell, 2012. 857–864.

Best, Tony. "Barbara Ann Teer and the Liberators." *New York Amsterdam News*, 12 Nov. 1975, D10.

Bhabha, Homi K. *The Location of Culture*. New York, NY and London: Routledge, 1998.

Bhattacharji, Santha. "Sutton, Katherine (d. 1376)." *The Oxford Dictionary of National Biography*. Oxford: Oxford University Press, 2004. Online ed., by subscription. Accessed 11 March 2022.

Biers, Katherine. "Stages of Thought: Emerson, Materlinck, Glaspell." *Modern Drama*. 56.4 (2013): 457–477.

Billington, Michael. "Elizabeth MacLennan Obituary." *The Guardian*, 29 June 2015, www.theguardian.com/stage/2015/jun/29/elizabeth-maclennan. Accessed 1 Jan. 2020.

"Biographical Character of the Late Mrs. Cowley." *Gentlemen's Magazine*. 79.1 (1809): 377.

A Biographical Dictionary of Actors, Actresses, Musicians, Dancers, Managers, and Other Personnel in London, 1660-1800. Eds. Philip H. Highfill, Kalman A. Burnim, and Edward A. Langhams. 16 vols. Carbondale, IL: University of Illinois Press, 1973–1993.

The Biographical Dictionary of Scottish Women. Eds. Elizabeth Ewan, Sue Innes, Sian Reynolds. Coordinating editor Rose Pipes. Edinburgh: Edinburgh University Press, 2006, p. 365.

"BIPOC Demands for White American Theatre." *We See You*. Weseeyouwat.com. Accessed 12 Oct. 2020.

Bishop, John George. *Strolls in the Brighton Extra-Mural Cemetery*. London: Fleet, 1867.

Bjorkman, Edwin. *The Freeman*. 11 Aug. 1920.

Black, Cheryl. *Women of the Provincetown*. Tuscaloosa, AL: University of Alabama Press, 2002.

Blank, Antje. "Introduction." *Eighteenth-Century Women Playwrights*. Ed. Derek Hughes. 6 vols. London: Pickering & Chatto, 2001.

Blau, Herbert. *The Audience*. Baltimore, MD: Johns Hopkins University Press, 1990.

_____. "Universals of Performance: Or, Amortizing Play." *SubStance*. 37–38 (1982): 140–161.

Blundell, Graeme. *Australian Theatre: Backstage with Graeme Blundell*. Melbourne: Oxford University Press, 1997.

Boaden, James. *Memoirs of Mrs. Inchbald: Including Her Familiar Correspondence with the Most Distinguished Persons of Her Time*. 2 vols. London: Richard Bentley, 1833.

Boal, Augusto. *Theatre of the Oppressed*. Trans. Charles A. and Maria-Odilia Leal McBride. London: Pluto, 1979.

Bodarwé, Katrinette. "Hrotsvit and her Avatars." *A Companion to Hrotsvit of Gandersheim: Contextual and Interpretive Approaches*. Eds. P.R. Brown and S.L. Wailes. Leiden and Boston: Brill, 2012. 329–362.

Bolton, Betsy. *Women, Nationalism and the Romantic Stage: Theatre and Politics in Britain, 1780-1800*. Cambridge: Cambridge University Press, 2001.

Bornstein, Kate. *A Queer and Pleasant Danger: A Memoir*. Boston, MA: Beacon Press, 2012.

_____. *Gender Outlaw: On Men, Women, and the Rest of Us*. New York, NY: Knopf Doubleday Publishing Group, 2016

_____. "Theater, and the Future of the Body." *Women & Performance*. 14.2 (2005): 15–17.

Borsa, Paolo and Christian de Vento. "Italian Tragedy, 1820-1827." *Rassegna europea di letteratura italiana*. 44 (2014): 59–88.

Bowerbank, Sylvia and Sara Mendelson, eds. *Paper Bodies: A Margaret Cavendish Reader*. Peterborough and Ontario: Broadview Press, 2000.

Boyce Davies, Carol. *Black Women: Writing and Identity*. New York, NY and London: Routledge, 1994.

Brandt, George W. "Introduction." *Modern Theories of the Drama*. Ed. George W. Brandt. Oxford: Oxford University Press, 1999. xiii–xx.

Brecht, Bertolt. "The Popular and Realistic." *Brecht on Theatre*. Ed. John Willett. New York, NY: Hill and Wang, 1964. 107–115.

Bremmer, Jan N. and Marco Formisano, eds. *Perpetua's Passions: Multidisciplinary Approaches to the Passio Perpetuae et Felicitatis*. Oxford: Oxford University Press, 2012.

Broe, Mary Lynn, ed. *Silence and Power: A Reevaluation of Djuna Barnes*. Carbondale and Edwardsville, IL: Southern University Press, 1991.

Brooks, Ann. *Women, Politics and the Public Sphere*, Chicago, IL: The University of Chicago Press, 2019.

Brooks, Helen. *Actresses, Gender, and the Eighteenth-Century Stage: Playing Women*. London: Palgrave Macmillan, 2015.

Brown, Ian. *Scottish Theatre: Diversity, Language, Continuity*. Amsterdam and New York, NY: Rodopi, 2013.

Brown, Mark. "RSC Chooses Female Directors for All Plays in Summer 2018 Season." *The Guardian*, Guardian News and Media, 12 Sept. 2017, www.theguardian.com/stage/2017/sep/12/royal-shakespeare-company-chooses-all-women-directors-summer-2018-season.

Brown, Phyllis R. and Stephen L. Wailes, eds. *A Companion to Hrotsvit of Gandersheim (fl. 960): Contextual and Interpretive Approaches*. Leiden and Boston, MA: Brill, 2013.

Bryan, Patricia and Thomas Wolf. *Midnight Assassin*. Chapel Hill, NC: Algonquin Books of Chapel Hill, 2005.

Bryant-Jackson, Paul K. and Lois More Overbeck, eds. *Intersecting Boundaries: The Theatre of Adrienne Kennedy*. Minneapolis, MN: University of Minnesota Press, 1992.

Buck, Gertrude. *The Social Criticism of Literature*. New Haven, CT: Yale University Press, 1916.

Bukenya, Austin L. and Pio Zirumu. "Oracy as a Skill and as a Tool for African Development." *The Arts and Civilization of Black and African Peoples*. Vol. 4: *Black Civilization and African Languages*. Ed. Joseph Okpaku. Miami, FL: Third Press International, 1986. 89–106.

Burney, Frances. *The Complete Plays of Frances Burney*. Ed. Peter Sabor. London: Pickering & Chatto, 1995.

_____. *Diary and Letters of Madame D'Arblay*, Volume III – 1788–1796. Ed. Charlotte Barrett. London: Bickers and Son, 1890.

_____. *The Early Journals and Letters of Fanny Burney*, Volume II – 1774–1777. Ed. Lars E. Troide. Oxford: Clarendon Press, 1990a.

_____. *The Early Journals and Letters of Fanny Burney*, Volume III – The Streatham Years, Part I: 1778–1779. Eds. Lars E. Troide and Stewart J. Cooke. Oxford: Clarendon Press, 1990b.

_____. *The Early Journals and Letters of Fanny Burney*, Volume IV. Eds. Lars E. Troide and Stewart J. Cooke. Oxford: Clarendon Press, 1990c.

_____. *The Journals and Letters of Fanny Burney (Madame d'Arblay)*. Ed. Joyce Hemlow et al. 12 vols. Oxford: Clarendon Press, 1972–1984.

_____. *The Streatham Years, Part II: 1780-1781*. Ed. Betty Rizzo. Oxford: Clarendon Press, 2005.

Burroughs, Catherine, *Closet Stages: Joanna Baillie and the Theater Theory of British Romantic Women Writers*, Philadelphia, PA: University of Pennsylvania Press, 1997.

_____. *Women in British Romantic Theatre: Drama, Performance and Society, 1790-1840*. Cambridge: Cambridge University Press, 2000.

Butler, Judith. *Gender Trouble: Feminism and the Subversion of Identity*. New York, NY and London: Routledge, 1990.

Burwick, Frederick. "Joanna Baillie, Matthew Baillie, and the Pathology of the Passions." *Joanna Baillie, Romantic Dramatist: Critical Essays*. Ed. Thomas C. Crochunis. New York, NY and London: Routledge, 2004. 48–68.

Cabral, Amilcar. "National Liberation and Culture." *Return to the Source: Selected Speeches of Amilcar Cabral*. New York, NY: Monthly Review Press, 1974. 39–56.

Campagna, Vanessa. "Gesturing toward Queer Utopia: The Children's World of Paula Vogel's *And Baby Makes Seven*." *Journal of Dramatic Theory and Criticism*. 32.1 (2017): 107–126. www.doi.org/10.1353/dtc.2017.0024. Accessed 15 June 2020.

Campbell, Thomas. *Life of Mrs. Siddons*. 2 vols. London: Wilson, 1834.

Caplan, Harry, ed. and trans. *[Cicero]: Ad C. Herennium de ratione dicendi*. Cambridge, MA: Harvard University Press, 1989.

Carlile, Susan. *Charlotte Lennox: An Independent Mind*. Toronto: University of Toronto Press, 2018.

Carlson, Marvin. *The Haunted Stage: The Theatre as Memory Machine*. Ann Arbor, MI: University of Michigan Press, 2001.

Carmody, Broane. "Dorothy Hewett's Daughters Say Grown Men Preyed on them as Children." *Sydney Morning Herald*. June 2018.

Case, Sue-Ellen. "The Affective Performance of State Love." *Performance, Feminism and Affect in Neoliberal Times*. Eds. Elin Diamond, Denise Varney, and Candice Amich. London: Palgrave Macmillin, 2017. 15–23.

_____. "Classic Drag: The Greek Creation of Female Parts." Special Issue: *Staging Gender*. Ed. Timothy Murray. *Theatre Journal*. 37.3 (1985): 317–327.

_____. *The Divided Home/Land: Contemporary German Women's Plays*. Ann Arbor, MI: University of Michigan Press, 1992.

_____. *The Domain-Matrix: Performing Lesbian at the End of Print Culture*. Bloomington, IN: Indiana University Press, 1996.

_____. *Feminism and Theatre*. London: Methuen, 1988.

_____. *Feminist and Queer Performance: Critical Strategies*. London: Palgrave Macmillan, 2009.

_____. "From Split Subject to Split Britches." *Feminine Focus: The New Women Playwrights*. Ed. Enoch Brater. Oxford: Oxford University Press, 1989. 126–146.

_____. "Miss Piggy the Seer in the Land of Trump's Blind: Elfriede Jelinek's On the Royal Road: The Burgher King." *Critical Perspectives on Contemporary Plays by Women: The Early Twenty-First Century*. Eds. Penny Farfan and Lesley Ferris. Ann Arbor, MI: University of Michigan Press, 2021. 249–256.

_____. *Performing Feminisms Feminist Critical Theory and Theatre*. Baltimore, MD: Johns Hopkins University Press, 1990.

_____. *Performing Science and the Virtual*. New York, NY and London: Routledge, 2007.

_____. *Split Britches: Lesbian Practice/Feminist Performance.* New York, NY and London: Routledge, 1996.

_____. "Towards a Butch-Femme Aesthetic." *Discourse.* Special Issue: *BODY//MASQUERADE.* 11.1 (1988–1989): 55–73.

_____. "Tracking the Vampire." *Differences.* 3.2 (1991): 1–20.

Castagno, Paul. *New Playwriting Strategies: A Language-Based Approach to Playwriting.* New York, NY and London: Routledge, 2001.

Catalogue of Five Hundred Celebrated Authors of Great Britain Now Living; the Whole Arranged in Alphabetical Order; and Including a Complete List of Their Publications, with Occasional Strictures, and Anecdotes of Their Lives. Ed. Thomas Gisborne Marshall. London: Printed for R. Faulder, New-Bond Street, 1788. iv–v.

Catalogue of John Larpent's Plays, San Marino, CA: Huntington Library. Processed by Dougald MacMillan in 1939; supplementary encoding and revision by Diann Benti in January 2018. San Marino, CA: Huntington Library, 1939.

Catanese, Brandi Wilkins. *The Problem of the Color [blind]: Racial Transgression and the Politics of Black Performance.* Ann Arbor, MI: University of Michigan Press, 2011.

Cattel, Tracy. "Transmitting the Thinking: The Nineteenth-Century Stage Manager and the Adaptation of Text for Performance." *Nineteenth-Century Theatre and Film.* 42.1 (2015): 39–49.

Cavendish, Margaret. "An Oration concerning Playes, and Players." *Orations of Divers Sorts Accommodated to Divers Places Written by the Lady Marchioness of Newcastle.* London: s.n., 1662. Early English Books Online Text Creation Partnership, 2004. Online ed., by subscription. Accessed 18 Sept. 2019.

_____. *CCXI Sociable Letters Written by the Thrice Noble, Illustrious, and Excellent Princess, the Lady Marchioness of Newcastle.* London: William Wilson, 1664. *Early English Books Online Text Creation Partnership,* 2004. Online ed., by subscription. Accessed 18 Sept. 2019.

_____. *The Description of a New World, Called the Blazing World Written by the Thrice Noble, Illustrious, and Excellent Princess, the Duchess of Newcastle.* London: A. Maxwell, 1666. *Early English Books Online Text Creation Partnership,* 2004. Online ed., by subscription. Accessed 3 Nov. 2019.

Cavendish, Margaret and William Cavendish. *Plays written by the thrice noble, illustrious and excellent princess, the Lady Marchioness of Newcastle.* London: A. Warren, John Martyn, James Allestry, and Tho. Dicas, 1662. *Early English Books Online Text Creation Partnership,* 2004. Online ed., by subscription. Accessed 18 Sept. 2019.

Cerasano, S.P. and Marion Wynne-Davies, eds. *Renaissance Drama by Women: Texts and Documents.* London: Routledge, 1996.

Chambers, Jane. "The Arrogant Playwright as Humble Actor." *Gay Theatre Alliance Newsletter.* 3.2 (April 1981): 1–3.

_____. *Last Summer at Bluefish Cove.* New York, NY: JH Press, 1982.

Chesson, Amelia. Diaries. John Rylands Library. REAS/10 Amelia Chesson's diary (1858), REAS/11 Frederick Chesson (1854–1870).

_____. "The Handel Festival. Second Day's Performance." *Morning Star* (London), 18 June 1857.

Childress, Alice. "The Black Experience: Why Talk About That?" *Negro Digest.* 16 (1967): 17–21.

_____. "Black Writers' Views on Literary Lions and Values." *Negro Digest.* 17 (1968): 36; 85–87.

_____. "But I Do My Thing." Published in the Series "Can Black and White Artists Still Work Together?" *The New York Times.* 2 Feb. 1969: D9.

_____. "A Candle in a Gale Wind." (orig. pub. 1953). *Black Women Writers (1950-1980): A Critical Evaluation.* Ed. Mari Evans. New York, NY: Doubleday, 1984. 112–116.

_____. "For A Negro Theatre." *Masses and Mainstream.* 4 (Feb. 1951): 61–64. Reprinted as "For a Strong Negro People's Theatre." *The Daily Worker.* (16 Feb. 1951): 11.

_____. "The Negro Woman in American Literature." *Freedomways* 6 (Winter 1966): 14–19. Reprinted as "A Woman Playwright Speaks Her Mind." *Anthology of the American Negro in the Theatre: A Critical Approach.* Ed. Lindsay Patterson. New York, NY: Publishers Co., 1968. 75–79.

Chinoy, Helen Krich. "Art versus Business." *The Drama Review.* 24.2 (1980): 3–10.

Cima, Gay Gibson. "Elizabeth Robins: The Genesis of an Independent Manageress." *Theatre Survey.* 22.2 (1980): 145–163.

_____. "Ibsen and the Critical Actor." *Performing Women: Female Characters, Male Playwrights, and the Modern Stage.* Ithaca, NY and London: Cornell University Press, 1993. 20–59.

Cixous, Hélène. "Aller a la mer." Trans. Barbara Kerslake. *Modern Drama.* 27.4 (1984): 546–548.

_____. "The Laugh of the Medusa." *Signs.* 1.4 (1976): 875–893.

_____. "Theatre Surprised by Puppets." *Politics, Ethics, and Performance: Helene Cixous and the Theatre du Soleil.* Ed. and trans. Lara Stevens. Melbourne: re.press, 2016. 64–74.

Cixous, Hélène and Frederic-Yves Jeannet. *Recontre terrestre.* Paris: Galilee, 2005.

Clarke, Mary Cowden. *The Girlhood of Shakespeare's Heroines.* London: W.H. Smith & Son, 1852.

Clinton, Catherine. *Fanny Kemble's Civil Wars: America's Most Unlikely Abolitionist.* Oxford: Oxford University Press, 2000.

Cloud, Christine. "A Long Line of Vendidas." *Loving in the War Years: lo que nunca pasó por.* 26.1 (2010): 84–97.

Cochrane, Kira. "The Fourth Wave of Feminism: Meet the Rebel Women." *Guardian.* 10 December 2013. http://www.theguardian.com/world/2013/dec/10/fourth-wave-feminism-rebel-women. Accessed 22 May 2015.

Cockin, Katharine. *Edith Craig (1869-1947): Dramatic Lives.* London: Cassell, 1998.

_____. *Edith Craig and the Theatres of Art.* London: Bloomsbury Methuen Drama, 2017.

_____. *Women and Theatre in the Age of Suffrage: The Pioneer Players 1911-25.* Basingstoke: Palgrave, 2001.

Cohn, Ruby. "A Fornes Calendar." *Conducting a Life: Reflections on the Theatre of Maria Irene Fornes.* Eds. Maria M. Delgado and Caridad Svich. Hanover, NH: Smith and Kraus Publishers, 1999. 7–13.

Collins, Charles. "Cornelia Otis Skinner is Entire Cast in 'Edna His Wife'; Opening Tomorrow." *Chicago Tribune.* 16 Jan. 1938. *Proquest Historical Papers.* www.proquest.com. Accessed 9 Feb. 2022.

Collins, H. "On Theatre: An Interview with Hélène Cixous." *Selected Plays of Hélène Cixous.* Ed. Eric Prenowitz. London and New York, NY: Routledge, 2004. 1–24.

Colón, Christine. *Joanna Baillie and the Art of Moral Influence.* New York, NY: Peter Lang, 2009.

Congdon, Constance. "How to Talk to a Playwright." *Dramaturgy in American Theater: A Source Book.* Eds. Susan Jonas, Geoffrey S. Proehl, and Michael Lupu. Fort Worth, TX: Harcourt Brace College Publishers, 1997. 180, 187.

Constable, Neil. "Statement regarding the Globe's future Artistic Direction." *Shakespeare's Globe Blog,* 25 Oct. 2016, https://www.shakespearesglobe.com/discover/blogs-and-features/.

Constantine-Simms, Delroy, ed. *Homosexuality in Black Communities.* New York, NY: Alyson Books, 2011.

Conway, Colleen, M. *Sex and Slaughter in the Tent of Jael: A Cultural History of a Biblical Story.* Oxford Scholarship Online, 2016. https://oxford.universitypressscholarship.com/view/10.1093/acprof:oso/9780190626877.001.0001/acprof-9780190626877. Accessed 3 Mar. 2022.

Copeland, Rita. *Rhetoric, Hermeneutics, and Translation in the Middle Ages.* Cambridge: Cambridge University Press, 1999.

Cotsell, Michael. *The Theater of Trauma: American Modernist Drama and the Psychological Struggle for the American Mind, 1900-1930.* New York, NY: Peter Lang, 2005.

Coture, Selena. "Siddons's Ghost: Celebrity and Gender in Sheridan's *Pizarro*." *Theatre Journal.* 65 (2013):183–196.

Coulthard, Glen and Leanne Betasamosake Simpson, "Grounded Normativity/Place-Based Solidarity." *American Quarterly.* 68.2 (2016): 249–255.

"The Count 2.0." The Dramatists Guild, 2018. https://www.dramatistsguild.com/advocacy/the-count. Accessed 4 Apr. 2022.

Cowley, Hannah Parkhouse. "Advertisement." *A Day in Turkey or, the Russian Slaves. A comedy, as Acted at the Theatre Royal, in Covent Garden.* London: G.G.J. and J. Robinson, 1792.

_____. "Address." *A School for Greybeards, or The Mourning Bride.* London: G.G.J. and J. Robinson, 1787.

_____. *Albina, Countess Raimond, a Tragedy.* London: J. Dodsley, R. Faulder, L. Davis, and others, 1779.

_____. *A Day in Turkey, or The Russian Slaves, A Comedy, as Acted at the Theatre Royal, in Covent Garden.* London: G.G.J. and J. Robinson, 1792.

_____. *The Plays of Hannah Cowley.* Ed. and intro. Frederick Link. 2 vols. London and New York, NY: Garland, 1979. Reprt. From 1776–1795 eds.

_____. "Preface." *The Town Before You. A comedy, as acted at the Theatre Royal, in Covent Garden.* London: G. Woodfall, for T.N. Longman, 1795.

_____. "Prologue." *Who's the Dupe? The Plays of Hannah Cowley.* Vols 1; 5–6. Ed. Frederick M. Link. New York, NY: Garland Publishers, 1979.

_____. *The Runaway.* London, printed for the author and sold by Mr. Dodsley, Mr. Becket and Mr. Cadell, Mr. Langman and Carnan and Newbery, 1776.

_____. *A School for Greybeards or the Mourning Bride.* London: G.G.J. and J. Robinson, 1786.

_____. *Who's the Dupe? A Farce: As It Is Acted at the Theatre Royal in Drury-Lane.* London: J. Dodsley, 1779.

Cox, Jeffrey N., "Baillie, Siddons, Larpent: Gender, Power, and Politics in the Theatre of Romanticism. *Women in British Romantic Theatre Drama, Performance, And Society, 1790-1840.* Ed. Catherine Burroughs. Cambridge: Cambridge University Press, 2009. 23–47.

_____. "Staging Baillie." *Joanna Baillie, Romantic Dramatist: Critical Essays.* Ed. Thomas C. Crochunis. New York, NY and London: Routledge, 2004. 146–167.

Craig, Edith. "Producing a Play." *Munsey's Magazine.* June 1907. 311–314.

Craig, Edward Gordon. *The Art of the Theatre.* Edinburgh: T.N. Foulis. 1905.

Crow, Brian and Michael Etherton. "Popular Drama and Popular Analysis in Africa." *Tradition for Development: Indigenous Structures and Folk Media in Non-formal Education.* Eds. Ross Kidd and Nat J. Colletta. Bonn and Eschborn: German Foundation for International Development, 1980. 57–94.

Cummings, Scott T. *Maria Irene Fornes.* London: Routledge. 2013.

_____. "Naomi (French) Wallace." *Twentieth-Century American Dramatists: Third Series.* Ed. Christopher J. Wheatley. Farmington, MI: Gale, 2002. *Dictionary of Literary Biography* Vol. 249. *Gale Literature Resource Center.* Online ed., by subscription. Accessed 17 Aug. 2020.

Cusk, Rachel. "The Other Self." *The New York Times,* 10 Oct. 2014. BR9.

Dace, Tish. "For Whom the Bell Tolled." *The New York Native.* 24 Oct.–6 Nov. 1983. 47.

Daniels, Ron. "Naomi is inside My Head." *The Theatre of Naomi Wallace: Embodied Dialogues.* Eds. Scott T. Cummings and Erica Stevens Abbitt. London: Palgrave Macmillan, 2013. 195–201.

D'Aponte, Mimi Gisolfi, ed. *Seventh Generation: An Anthology of Native American Plays.* New York, NY: Theatre Communications Group, 1999.

Darby, Barbara. "Feminism, Tragedy, and Frances Burney's *Edwy and Elgiva.*" *Journal of Dramatic Theory and Criticism.* 11.2 (1997): 3–24.

_____. *Frances Burney, Dramatis: Gender, Performance, and the Late Eighteenth-Century Stage.* Lexington, KY: University of Kentucky Press, 1997.

Darby, Jaye T., Courtney Elkin Mohler, and Christy Stanlake, eds. *A Critical Companion to Native American and First Nations Theatre and Performance: Indigenous Spaces.* London: Methuen, 2020.

Dasi, Binodini. *Amar katha* (My Story). 1912. Eds. Soumitra Chattopadhyay and Nirmalya Acharya. Kolkata: Kathashilpa, 1964. [Excerpts trans. Suddhaseel Sen.]

_____. *My Story and My Life as an Actress.* Trans. and ed. Rimli Bhattacharya. New Delhi: Kali for Women, 1998.

"Davenport, E(dward) L(oomis) (1815–1877)." *The Cambridge Guide to Theatre.* Ed. Martin Banham. 2nd ed. Cambridge: Cambridge University Press, 2000.

David, Christopher. "Matthew Lewis's *The Monk* and James Boaden's *Aurelio* and *Miranda*— From Text to Stage." *Theatre Notebook.* 65.3 (2011): 152–189.

Davis, Tracy C. "Theatre Critics in Late-Victorian and Edwardian Periodicals: A Supplementary List." *Victorian Periodicals Review.* 17.4 (1984): 158–164.

Däwes, Birgit. *Native North American Theater in a Global Age: Sites of Identity Construction and Transdifference.* Heidelberg: Universitätsverlag, Winter, 2007.

Day, Carolyn and Amelia Rauser. "Thomas Laurence's Consumptive Chic: Reinterpreting Lady Manners's Hectic Flush in 1794." *Eighteenth-Century Studies.* 49. 4 (2016): 455–474.

De Almeida, Hermione. "Burney, Frances." *The Encyclopedia of Romantic Literature.* Ed. Frederick Burwick. Chichester: Blackwell, 2012. 183–189.

DeFrantz, Thomas F. and Anita Gonzalez, eds. *Black Performance Theory.* Durham, NC: Duke University Press, 2014.

de Kooning, Elaine. "Hans Hofmann Paints a Picture." *Art News* [February 1950] 19 November 2012: https://www.artnews.com/art-news/news/hans-hofmann-paints-a-picture-2125/.

Dean, Jodi. *The Communist Horizon.* London: Verso, 2012.

Delgado, Maria M. and Caridad Svich. "Maria Irene Fornes Discusses Forty Years in the Theatre with Maria M. Delgado." *Conducting a Life: Reflections on the Theatre of Maria Irene Fornes.* Eds. Maria M. Delgado and Caridad Svich. Lyme, NH: Smith and Kraus, 1999. 248–276.

Demastes, William. *Staging Consciousness: Theater and the Materialization of the Mind.* Ann Arbor, MI: University of Michigan Press, 2002.

Dewey, John. "My Pedagogic Creed." *School Journal.* 54 (Jan. 1897): 77–80.

Dharwadker, Aparna Bhargava, ed. *A Poetics of Modernity: Indian Theatre Theory, 1850 to the Present.* New Delhi: Oxford University Press, 2019.

Diamond, Elin. "Brechtian Theory/Feminist Theory: Toward a Gestic Feminist Criticism." *TDR.* 32.1 (1988): 82–94. *JSTOR,* www.jstor.org/stable/1145871. Accessed 6 Jan. 2020.

———. *Unmaking Mimesis: Essays on Feminism and Theatre.* New York, NY and London: Routledge, 1997.

DiCenzo, Maria. *The Politics of Alternative Theatre in Britain: The Case of 72:84 (Scotland).* Cambridge: Cambridge University Press, 1996.

Dictionary of National Biography. Volume LIX. Ed Sidney Lee. Wakeman-Watkins, London: Smith Elder & CO., 1899. 97–98. https://archive.org/details/dictionaryofnati59stepuoft/page/74/mode/2up/search/wallace. Accessed 1 June 2023.

Dinshaw, Carolyn. "Margery Kempe." *The Cambridge Companion to Medieval Women's Writing.* Ed. Carolyn Dinshaw and David Wallace. Cambridge: Cambridge University Press, 2003. 222–239.

Dodds, Lara. *The Literary Invention of Margaret Cavendish.* Pittsburgh, PA: Duquesne University Press, 2013.

Dolan, Jill. *The Feminist Spectator as Critic.* Ann Arbor, MI: University of Michigan Press, 1991.

———. *The Feminist Spectator in Action: Feminist Criticism for the Stage and Screen.* London: Palgrave Macmillan, 2013.

———. "Gender Impersonation Onstage: Destroying or Maintaining the Mirror of Gender Roles." *Women and Performance.* 2 (1985): 1–19.

———. *Geographies of Learning: Theory and Practice, Activism and Performance.* Middletown, CT: Wesleyan University Press, 2001.

———. "Preface." *Memories of the Revolution: The First Ten Years of the WOW Café Theater.* Eds. Holly Hughes, Carmelita Tropicana, and Jill Dolan. Ann Arbor, MI: University of Michigan Press, 2015, pp. vii–xiv.

———. *Presence and Desire: Essays on Gender, Sexuality, Performance.* Ann Arbor, MI: University of Michigan Press, 1994.

———. *Utopia in Performance: Finding Hope at the Theater.* Ann Arbor, MI: University of Michigan Press, 2005.

Donkin, Ellen. *Getting into the Act: Women Playwrights in London, 1776-1829.* London: Routledge, 1994.

Doody, Margaret Anne. "Shakespeare's Novels: Charlotte Lennox Illustrated." *Studies in the Novel.* 19 (1987): 296–310.

"Dr. Barbara Ann Teer's National Black Theatre." *Lortel Archives: Internet Off-Broadway Database.* 2020. http://iobdb.com/CreditableEntity/48077. Accessed 10 Jan. 2020.

Dronke, Peter, ed. *Nine Medieval Latin Plays.* Cambridge: Cambridge University Press, 1994.

Dugan, Olga. "Telling the Truth: Alice Childress as Theorist and Playwright." *The Journal of Negro History.* 18.1 (1996): 123–136. *JSTOR.* Accessed 18 May 2018.

Duras, Marguerite. "General Remarks." *India Song.* Trans. Barbara Bray. New York, NY: Grove Press, 1988, pp. 5–6.

Edwards, Brent Hayes. *The Practice of Diaspora: Literature, Translation, and the Rise of Black Internationalism.* Cambridge, MA: Harvard University Press, 2003.

Ekine, Sokari and Hakima Abbas, eds. *Queer African Reader.* Nairobi, Dakar and Oxford: Pambazuka Press, 2013.

Elfenbein, Andrew. *Romantic Genius: The Prehistory of a Homosexual Role.* New York, NY: Columbia University Press, 1999.

Ellison, Ralph. "Indivisible Man." *The Collected Essays of Ralph Ellison.* New York, NY: Random House, 1995. 357–400.

The Elizabeth Robins Web. Project Director: Joanne Gates. https://www.jsu.edu/robinsweb/. Accessed 1 Mar. 2022.

Engel, Laura. "Mommy Diva: The Divided Loyalties of Sarah Siddons" *Stage Mothers: Women, Work, and the Theater, 1660-1830.* Eds. Laura Engel and Elaine McGirr. Lewisburg, PA.: Bucknell University Press, 2015. 217–232

_____. *Women, Performance and the Material of Memory: The Archival Tourist.* New York, NY and London: Palgrave Macmillan, 2019.

Engel, Laura and Elaine McGirr, eds. *Stage Mothers: Women, Work, and the Theater, 1660-1830.* Lewisburg, PA: Bucknell University Press, 2015.

The English Chronicle; or Universal Evening Post. 10 April 1788.

"entertain, v." *OED Online,* Oxford University Press, Sept. 2020. www.oed.com/view/Entry/62849. Accessed 26 Oct. 2020.

Epprecht, Marc. *Sexuality and Social Justice in Africa: Rethinking Homphobia and Forging Resistance.* London: Zed Books, 2013.

Escott, Angela. *"The Celebrated Hannah Cowley": Experiments in Dramatic Genre, 1776-1794.* Vermont and London: Pickering and Chatto, 2012.

Esslin, Martin. *The Theatre of the Absurd.* London: Penguin Press, 1968.

Evans, Bertrand. *Gothic Drama from Walpole to Shelley.* Berkeley, CA: University of California Press, 1947.

Faison, Nabii. Personal Interview with the author. 13 Jul. 2010.

Fanon, Frantz. *Black Skin, White Masks.* London: Pluto Press, 1986.

_____. *The Wretched of the Earth.* Trans. Charles Lam Markmann. New York, NY: Grove Press, 1967.

Farfan, Penny. "From *Hedda Gabler* to *Votes for Women:* Elizabeth Robins's Early Feminist Critique of Ibsen." *Theatre Journal.* 48.1 (1996): 59–78.

_____. "Monstrous History: Judith Thompson's *Sled.*" *Judith Thompson. Critical Perspectives in Canadian Theatre in English.* Vol. 3. Ed. Ric Knowles. Toronto: Playwrights Canada Press, 2005. 99–105.

Feinberg, Leslie. *Stone Butch Blues: A Novel.* Atlanta, GA: Firebrand Books, 1993.

Field, Michael. *Callirhoë. Fair Rosamund.* London: George Bell & Sons, 1884.

_____. *Canute the Great. The Cup of Water.* London: George Bell & Sons, 1887.

_____. *The Father's Tragedy. William Rufus. Loyalty or Love.* London: George Bell & Sons, 1885.

_____. *The Tragic Mary.* London: G. Bell, 1890.

Finberg, Melinda C. "Introduction." *Eighteenth-Century Women Dramatists*. Ed. Melinda Finberg. Oxford: Oxford University Press, 2001. ix–xlvii.

Finch, Anne. *The Anne Finch Wellesley Manuscript Poems: A Critical Edition*. Eds. Barbara McGovern and Charles H. Hinnant. Athens, GA: University of Georgia Press, 1988

———. *The Poems of Anne Countess of Winchilsea: From the Original Edition of 1713 and From Unpublished Manuscripts*. Ed. Myra Reynolds. Chicago, IL: The University of Chicago Press, 1903.

Fisk, May Isabel. "The Art of Giving a Monologue." *Monologues and Duologues*. New York, NY: Samuel French, 1914.

Fitzgerald, Christina M. and John T. Sebastian, eds. *The Broadview Anthology of Medieval Drama*. Peterborough and Ontario: Broadview Press, 2015.

Fitzmaurice, James. "Shakespeare, Cavendish, and Reading Aloud in Seventeenth-Century England." *Cavendish and Shakespeare: Interconnections*. Eds. Katherine Romack and James Fitzmaurice. Aldershot, Hampshire: Ashgate, 2006. 29–46.

Flanagan, Hallie. *Arena*. New York, NY: Duell, Sloan and Pearce, 1940.

———. *Dynamo*. New York, NY: Duell, Sloan and Pearce, 1943.

———. *Shifting Scenes*. New York, NY: Coward-McCann, Inc., 1928.

Flower of the Jacobins: Containing Biographical Sketches of the Characters at Present at the Head of Affairs in France. Eds. D.J. Owen and H.D. Symonds. 3rd ed. 1793. https://babel.hathitrust.org/cgi/pt?id=njp.3210103757325 8&view=1up&seq=11. Accessed 1 June 2023.

Foley, Helene P. *Reimagining Greek Tragedy on the American Stage*. Berkeley, CA: University of California Press, 2012.

The Folger Collective on Early Women Critics, eds. *Women Critics, 1660-1820*. Bloomington, IN: Indiana University Press, 1995.

Fornés, María Irene. "Creative Danger." *American Theatre*. 1 September 1985: 15–16.

———. "'I Write These Messages That Come.' From an interview conducted and edited by Robb Creese." *The Drama Review*. 21.4 (Dec. 1977): 25–40.

———. "Maria Irene Fornes." *In Their Own Words: Contemporary American Playwrights*. Ed. David Savan. New York, NY: Theatre Communication Group, 1988, 51–69.

———. "Maria Irene Fornes." The 'Woman' Playwrights Issue. *PAJ*, 7.3 (1983): 90–91.

———. "Maria Irene Fornes Discusses Forty Years in the Theatre with Maria M. Delgado." *Conducting a Life: Reflections on the Theatre of Maria Irene Fornes*. Eds. Maria M. Delgado and Caridad Svich. Lyme, NH: Smith and Kraus, Inc., 1999. 248–276.

———. "Playwright's Preface." *Playwrights for Tomorrow: Volume 2*. Ed. Arthur H. Ballet. Minneapolis, MN: University of Minnesota Press, 1966: 9–10.

———. *The Summer in Gossensass. What of the Night? Selected Plays*. New York, NY: PAJ Publications, 2008. 47–95.

Forsgren, La Donna L. "'Set Your Blackness Free': Barbara Ann Teer's Arts and Activism During the Black Arts Movement." *Frontiers*. 36.1 (2015): 136–159.

Forster, Antonia. "Thomas Holcroft and Reviewing Traditions." *Re-Viewing Thomas Holcroft, 1745-1809: Essays on His Life and Work*. Eds. Miriam L. Wallace and A.A. Markley. 2012. London and New York, NY: Routledge, 2016. 167–180.

Franc, Miriam A. *Ibsen in England*. Boston, MA: Four Seas, 1919.

Fraser, Nancy. "Feminism, Capitalism and the Cunning of History." *New Left Review*. 56 (March-April 2009): 97–117.

Freire, Paulo. *Pedagogy of the Opressed*. Trans. Myra Bergman Ramos. London and New York, NY: Continuum, 2000.

Freud, Sigmund. "The 'Uncanny'" (1919). *The Complete Psychological Works*, Volume XVII. Trans. Alix Strachey. London: Hogarth Press, 1955. 217–256.

Friedl, Bettina, Ed. *On to Victory: Propaganda Plays of the Woman Suffrage Movement*. Boston, MA: Northeastern University Press, 1987.

Friedman, Muriel Sanderow. "The Theatrical Career of John O'Keeffe." 1974. PhD dissertation, Loyola University of Chicago.

"Friends of the Jenin Freedom Theatre." *Thefreedomtheatre.org.* https://www.thefreedomtheatre. org/friends-supporters/new-york/. Accessed 26 Oct. 2020.

Fuchs, Elinor. "Adrienne Kennedy and the First Avant-Garde." *Intersecting Boundaries: The Theatre of Adrienne Kennedy.* Eds. Paul K. Bryant-Jackson and Lois More Overbeck. Minneapolis, MN: University of Minnesota Press, 1992. 76–84.

_____. *The Death of Character: Perspectives on Theater After Modernism.* Bloomington, IN and Indianapolis, IN: Indiana University Press, 1996.

Führkötter, Adelgundis with Angela Carlevarlis, eds. *Hildegardis Scivias.* Corpus Christianorum Continuatio Medievalis 43A. Turnholt: Brepols, 1978.

Gale, Maggie B. "Going Solo: An Historical Perspective on the Actress and the Monologue." *The Cambridge Companion to the Actress.* Eds. Maggie B. Gale and John Stokes. Cambridge: Cambridge University Press, 2007. 291–313.

García-Romero, Anne. *The Fornes Frame: Contemporary Latina Playwrights and the Legacy of Maria Irene Fornes.* Tucson, AZ: The University of Arizona Press, 2016.

_____. "Fugue, Hip-Hop and Soap Opera: Transcultural Connections and Theatrical Experimentation in Twenty-First Century US Latina Playwriting." *Latin American Theatre Review* 53.1 (Fall 2019): 87–102.

Gardner, Lyn. "Winsome Pinnock: 'I used to think we needed change – now we need a revolution'." *The Guardian,* 23 May 2018 at https://www.theguardian.com/stage/2018/ may/23/winsome-pinnock-leave-taking-bush-theatre. Accessed 17 Mar. 2020.

Garrett, Martin. "Mitford, Mary Russell." *Oxford Dictionary of National Biography.* Online ed., by subscription. Accessed 29 Jan. 2022.

Garwood, Rebecca. "Sophia Lee (1750-1824) and Harriet Lee (1757-1821)." Chawton House Library. https://chawtonhouse.org/wp-content/uploads/2012/06/Sophia-Lee-and-Harriet-Lee.pdf. Accessed 14 Feb. 2022.

Gates, Joanne E. "Elizabeth Robins and the 1891 Production of *Hedda Gabler.*" *Modern Drama.* 2844 (1985): 611–619.

_____. *Elizabeth Robins 1862-1952: Actress, Novelist, Feminist.* Tuscaloosa, AL and London: University of Alabama Press, 1994.

_____. "Henry James's Dictation Letter to Elizabeth Robins: 'The Suffragette Movement Hot from the Oven'." *Henry James Review.* 31.3 (2010): 254–263.

_____. "Introduction to *Votes for Women* by Elizabeth Robins." *Modern Drama by Women 1880s – 1930s.* Ed. Katherine E. Kelly. London and New York, NY: Routledge, 1996. 108–111.

_____. "Stitches in a Critical Time: The Diaries of Elizabeth Robins, American Feminist in England, 1907-1924." *A/B: Auto/Biography.* 4.2 (1988): 130–139.

_____. "The Theatrical Politics of Elizabeth Robins and Bernard Shaw." *Shaw.* 14 (1994): 43–55.

Gay, Penny. *Jane Austen and the Theatre.* Cambridge: Cambridge University Press, 2002.

Gayle, Jr. Addison. *The Black Aesthetic.* Garden City, NY: Doubleday & Company, Inc., 1971.

Geiogamah, Hanay, and Jaye T. Darby, eds. *Stories of Our Way: An Anthology of American Indian Plays.* Los Angeles, CA: UCLA American Indian Studies Center, 1999.

Genest, John. *Some Account of the English Stage from the Restoration in 1660 to 1830.* Bath: H.E. Carrington, 1832.

Gentile, John Samuel. *Cast of One: One-Person Shows from the Chautauqua Platform to the Broadway Stage.* Champaign, IL: University of Illinois Press, 1989.

Gevirtz, Karen Bloom. "Ladies Reading and Writing: Eighteenth-Century Women Writers and the Gendering of Critical Discourse." *Modern Language Studies.* 33 (2003): 60–72.

_____. "Peer Reviewed: Elizabeth Inchbald's Shakespeare Criticism." *Shakespeare and the Culture of Romanticism.* Ed. Joseph M. Ortiz. Burlington, VT: Ashgate, 2013. 31–49.

Gilbert, Sandra M. and Susan Gubar. *The Madwoman in The Attic.* New Haven, CT: Yale University Press. 1984.

Gillespie, Benjamin. "Detonating Desire: Mining the Unexplored Potential of Aging in Split Britiches' Unexploded Ordanances (UXO)." *Performance Research*. 24.3. Special Issue "On Aging and Beyond." (2019): 89–98.

Gilman, Charlotte Perkins. "Dame Nature Interviewed on the Woman Question as It Looks to Her." *Kate Field's Washington*. 1890. Ed. Maurine Beasley. Washington, D.C.: Records of the Columbia Historical Society, Washington, 138–140.

_____. "The Quarrel." "The Ceaseless Struggle of Sex: A Dramatic View." *Kate Field's Washington*. 1890. Ed. Maurine Beasley. Washington, D.C.: Records of the Columbia Historical Society, Washington, D.C. 49 (1973/1974): 392–404.

_____. *Women & Economics: A Study of the Economic Relation Between Men and Women as a Factor in Social Evolution*. Boston, MA: Small, Maynard & Company, 1898.

Gilroy, Paul. *The Black Atlantic: Modernity and Double Consciousness*. Cambridge, MA: Harvard University Press, 1993.

_____. "'…to be real': The Dissident Forms of Black Expressive Culture." *Let's Get It On: The Politics of Black Performance*. Ed. Catherine Ugwu. Winnipeg: At Bay Press, 1995. 12–33.

Glancy, Diane. "Author's Statement on *Pushing the Bear*." *Performing Worlds into Being: Native American Women's Theatre*. Eds. Ann Elizabeth Armstrong, Kelli Lyon Johnson, and William A. Wortman. Oxford, OH: Miami University Press, 2009. 126.

_____. *Claiming Breath*. Lincoln, NE: University of Nebraska Press, 1992.

_____. "Further (Farther): Creating Dialogue to Talk about Native American Plays." *American Gypsy: Six Native American Plays*. Norman, OK: University of Oklahoma Press, 2002. 200–204.

_____. "Native Dramatic Theory in a Bird House." *Twenty-First Century Perspectives on Indigenous Studies: Native North America in (Trans)Motion*. Eds. Birgit Däwes, Karsten Fitz, and Sabine N. Meyer. New York, NY: Routledge, 2015. 31–41.

_____. *Salvage. The Native American New Play Festival: A Four Year Celebration*. Ed. Sarah d'Angelo and Regina McManigell Grijalva. South Gate, CA: No Passport Press, 2016. 106–162.

Glaspell, Susan. *The Complete Plays*. Eds. Linda Ben-Zvi and J. Ellen Gainor. Jefferson, NC: McFarland & Company, Inc., 2010.

_____. "A Jury of Her Peers." *Her America: "A Jury of Her Peers" and Other Stories*. Eds. Patricia L. Bryan and Martha C. Carpentier. Iowa City, IA: University of Iowa Press, 2010. 81–102.

_____. *The Road to the Temple*. Ed. and with a new Introduction and Bibliography by Linda Ben-Zvi. Jefferson, NC: McFarland & Company, 2005.

_____. ["Speech on the Federal Theatre Project"]. The Henry W. and Albert A. Berg Collection of English and American Literature, The New York Public Library, Astor, Lenox and Tilden Foundations.

_____. *Trifles. The Complete Plays*. Eds. Linda Ben-Zvi and J. Ellen Gainor. Jefferson, NC: McFarland & Company, Inc., 2010. 24–34.

_____. *The Verge. The Complete Plays*. Eds. Linda Ben-Zvi and J. Ellen Gainor. Jefferson, NC: McFarland & Company, Inc., 2010. 227–267.

Goddard, Lynette. *Staging Black Feminisms: Identity, Politics, Performance*. London: Palgrave Macmillan, 2007.

Goldberg, Isaac. *The Drama of Transition*. Cincinnati, OH: Stewart Kidd Co.,1922.

Goldring, Douglas. *Regency Portrait Painter: The Life of Sir Thomas Lawrence*. London: Macdonald, 1951.

Goode, C.T., *To the Crystal Palace*. Bracknell: Forge Books, 1984.

Goodman, Elizabeth. "'Divina': A Report from Turin." *New Theatre Quarterly*. 7.25 (1991): 97–99.

Grace, Sherrill. "Going North on Judith Thompson's *Sled*." The Masks of Judith Thompson. Ed. Ric Knowles. Ontario: Playwrights Canada Press. 2009. 59–73.

Green-Rogers, Martine Kei et al. "Continuing the Conversation: Responses to Gabriela Serena Sanchez and Quiara Alegria Hudes." *Theatre Topics*. 29.1 (2019): E 15–21.

Gregory, Lady Augusta. "The Felons of Our Land." *Cornhill Magazine*. 8.47 (May 1900). 622–634.

_____. *Selected Writings.* Eds. Lucy McDiarmid and Maureen Waters. London: Penguin, 1995.

Greig, David. "Emma Rice's Exit from Shakespeare's Globe Feels a Bit Brexity." Accessed 26 Oct. 2016, https://www.newstatesman.com/culture/music-theatre/2016/10/emma-rices-exit-shakespeares-globe-feels-bit-brexity.

Green-Rogers, Martine Kei et al. "Continuing the Conversation: Responses to Gabriela Serena Sanchez and Quiara Alegría Hudes." *Theatre Topics.* 29.1 (Mar. 2019): E 15–21.

Grijp, Louis Peter. "De zingende Hadewijch: Op zoek naar de melodieën van haar Strofische Gedichten." *Een zoet akkord: Middeleeuwse lyriek in de Lage Landen,* Ed. Frank Willaert. Amsterdam: Prometheus, 1992. 72–92.

Grimm, Jacob. *Lateinische Gedichte des 10. und 11. Jahrhunderts.* Göttingen: Dieterichsche Buchhandlung, 1898.

Guide to the Elizabeth Robins Papers. New York, NY: Fales Library Special Collections. New York University Libraries. http://dlib.nyu.edu/findingaids/html/fales/mss_002/. Accessed 20 April 2023.

Gunderson, Lauren. "Survival of the Storied: Why Science Needs Art and Art Needs Science." Lauren Gunderson, 2015.

"Handel Festival." *Illustrated London News.* 13 June 1857, p. 572.

Hanna, Gillian, ed. *Monstrous Regiment: A Collective Celebration.* London: Nick Hern, 1991.

Harris, Aleshea. "The Lighthouse." "Adrienne Kennedy: A Liberating Beacon." *American Theatre,* "A Tribute to Adrienne Kennedy" Special Issue, 4 Sept. 2019. americantheatre.org/2019/09/04/adrienne-kennedy-a-liberating-beacon/. Accessed 4 Mar. 2020.

Hart, Lynda, ed. *Making a Spectacle: Feminist Essays on Contemporary Women's Theatre.* Ann Arbor, MI: University of Michigan Press, 1989.

Harvie, Jen. "Constructing Fictions of an Essential Reality, or 'This Pickshur is Niiiice:' Judith Thompson's *Lion in the Streets.*" *The Masks of Judith Thompson.* Ed. Ric Knowles. Ontario: Playwrights Canada Press, 2009. 47–58.

Harvie, Jen and Lois Weaver, eds. *The Only Way Home is Through the Show: The Performance Work of Lois Weaver.* London and Bristol: Live Art Development Agency and Intellect, 2015.

Hauser, Thomas. *Muhammad Ali: His Life and Times.* London: Pan Books, 2007.

Hay, Samuel A. *African American Theatre: An Historical and Critical Analysis.* Cambridge: Cambridge University Press, 1994.

Hayashi, Yoshiko. *Onna Gidayu Ichidai: Toyotake Danshi Joruru Jinsei.* Kobe: Kobe Shinbun Shuppan Senta, 1988.

Heath, Mary T. "A Crisis in the Life of the Actress: Ibsen in England." Phd Diss. University of Massachussetts-Amherst, 1986.

Heddon, Deirdre. *Autobiography and Performance.* New York, NY: Palgrave Macmillan, 2008.

Heller, Adele and Lois Rudnick. "Introduction." *1915: The Cultural Moment.* Eds. Adele Heller and Lois Rudnick. Newark, NJ: Rutgers University Press, 1991. 1–13.

Hemans, Felicia. "Italian Literature: No. II The Alcestis of Alfieri." *Edinburgh Magazine and Literary Miscellany.* 7 (Dec. 1820): 512–516.

_____. "Italian Literature: No. III Il Conte di Carmagnola, a Tragedy by Alessandro Manzoni." *Edinburgh Magazine and Literary Miscellany.* 8 (Feb. 1821): 122–132.

_____. "Patriotic Effusions of the Italian Poets." *Edinburgh Magazine and Literary Miscellany.* 8 (June 1821): 513–515.

Hewett, Dorothy. *The Chapel Perilous.* Sydney: Currency Press, 1972. Revised ed. 1977.

_____. "Why Does Sally Bow?" *The Chapel Perilous.* Sydney: Currency Press, 1972. Revised ed. 1977.

_____. *Wild Card.* Ringwood, Australia: McPhee Gribble for Penguin Books, 1990.

Hewitt, Martin. *The Dawn of the Cheap Press in Victorian Britain: The End of the 'Taxes on Knowledge', 1849–1869.* London: Bloomsbury, 2014.

Higa, Jade. "Charlotte Charke's Gun: Queering Material Culture and Gender Performance." *ABO: Interactive Journal for Women in the Arts, 1640-1830.* 7.1 (2017). Online ed., by subscription. Accessed 1 June 2023.

Highfill, Philip H. et al. *A Biographical Dictionary of Actors, Actresses, Musicians, Dancers, Managers & Other Stage Personnel in London, 1660-1800.* 3 vols. Carbondale, IL: Southern Illinois Press, 1975.

hooks, bell. "Critical Reflections: Adrienne Kennedy, the Writer, the Work." *Intersecting Boundaries: The Theatre of Adrienne Kennedy.* Eds. Paul K. Bryant-Jackson and Lois Overbeck. Minneapolis, MN: University of Minnesota Press, 1992. 179–185.

_____. *Feminism is for Everybody: Passionate Politics.* Cambridge, MA: South End Press, 2000.

_____. *Salvation: Black People and Love.* London: The Women's Press, 2001.

Hotten, John Camden. *The Slang Dictionary: Etymological, Historical, and Anecdotal.* London: Chatto and Windus, 1874.

Houston, Velina Hasu. "Introduction." *But Still, Like Air, I Will Rise: New Asian American Plays.* Ed. Velina Hasu Houston. Philadelphia, PA: Temple University Press, 1997.

_____. "Introduction." *The Politics of Life: Four Plays by Asian American Women.* Ed. Velina Hasu Houston. Philadelphia, PA: Temple University Press, 1993.

_____. "*matchabook.*" https://matchabook.wordpress.com/about/. Accessed 24 Jan. 2022.

Hudes, Quiara Alegría, "Artistic Statement." *Contemporary Plays by Women of Color.* 2nd edition. Ed. Roberta Uno. New York, NY and London: Routledge, 2018. 77–79.

_____. "Drama as Literature." *The Dramatist.* Jan./Feb. 2014: 10.

Huston-Findley, Shirley A. and Rebecca Howard, eds. *Footpaths and Bridges: Voices from the Native American Women Playwrights Archive.* Ann Arbor, MI: University of Michigan Press, 2008.

"In a Letter to a Lady." *The Lady's Magazine.* 30 (1799): 580.

Inchbald, Elizabeth. "Remarks on *King Lear.*" *The British Theatre; Or, A Collection of Plays, Which Are Acted at the Theatres Royal, Drury Lane, Covent Garden, and Haymarket.* Volume IV. London: Longman, Hurst, Rees & Orme, 1808.

Irigaray, Luce. *This Sex Which Is Not One.* Trans. Catherine Porter with Carolyn Burke. Ithaca, NY: Cornell University Press, 1985.

Isaka, Maki. *Onnagata: A Layrinth of Gendering in Kabuki Theater.* Seattle, WA and London: University of Washington Press, 2016.

Jameson, Anna Murphy. *Shakespeare's Heroines: Characteristics of Women: Moral, Poetical, and Historical* (1832). Ed. Cheri L. Larsen Hoeckley. Peterborough and Ontario: Broadview Press, 2005.

Janaczewska, Noelle. *Playing Awkward: A Response to The Chapel Perilous.* Sydney: Currency Press, 2014.

Jelinek, Elfriede. *Burgtheater.* Vienna: Frischfleisch & Löwenmaul, 1987.

_____. *Charges (the supplicants).* Trans. Gitta Honegger. London: Seagull Books, 2016.

_____. "Es ist Sprechen und aus!" 2013. https://www.elfriedejelinek.com/. Accessed 8 Feb. 2021.

_____. "Ich möchte seicht sein." *Theater: Jahrbuch der Zeitschrift Theater Heute.* Berlin: Friedrich-Berlin-Verlag, 1983: 102.

_____. *Meaning Immaterial. Body Useless. Theaterschrift.* 11 (1997): 23–31.

_____. *On the Royal Road: The Burgher King.* Trans. Gitta Honegger. London: Seagull Books, 2020.

_____. *Schwarzwasser. Zwei Theaterstücke.* Hamburg: Rowohlt Verlag, 2020.

_____. *Sports Play.* Trans. Penny Black. London: Oberon Books, 2012.

_____. *zum Theater.* 39 texts on theatre. http://elfriedejelinek.com/ Accessed 8 Feb. 2021.

Jellicoe, Ann. *3 Jelliplays.* London: Faber & Faber, 1975.

_____. "Ann Jellicoe Interviewed by Harriet Devine." *The Legacy of the English Stage Company.* Lyme Regis: British Library, 2008.

_____. *Community Plays: How to Put Them On.* London: Methuen, 1987.

_____. *The Giveaway: A Comedy.* London: Faber & Faber, 1970.

_____. *The Knack and The Sport of My Mad Mother: Two Plays.* New York, NY: Dell, 1964.

_____. *The Reckoning.* Lyme Regis: Unpublished, 1978. "Ann Jellicoe Collection." London: London V&A Theatre and Performance Collections.

_____. *The Rising Generation*. London: Unpublished. 1967. "Ann Jellicoe Collection." London: London V&A Theatre and Performance Collections.

_____. *Shelley, or The Idealist*. London: Faber & Faber, 1966.

_____. *Some Unconscious Influences in the Theatre*. Cambridge: Cambridge University Press, 1967.

_____. *The Western Women*. Lyme Regis: Unpublished, 1984. "Ann Jellicoe Collection." London: London V&A Theatre and Performance Collections.

John, Angela V. *Elizabeth Robins: Staging a Life 1862-1952*. London and New York, NY: Routledge, 1995.

Johnson, E. Patrick. "'Quare' Studies, or (Almost) Everything I Know about Queer Studies I Learned from My Grandmother." Black Queer Studies: A Critical Anthology. Eds. E. Patrick Johnson and Mae G. Henderson. Durham, NC: Duke University Press, 2005. 124–57.

Johnson, E. Patrick and Mae G. Henderson, eds. *Black Queer Studies: A Critical Anthology*. Durham, NC: Duke University Press, 2005.

_____. "Introduction: Queering Black Studies/'Quaring' Queer Studies." *Black Queer Studies: A Critical Anthology*. Eds. E. Patrick Johnson, and Mae G. Henderson. Durham, NC: Duke University Press, 2005. 1–17.

Johnson, Samuel. *The Life of Dryden*. Transcribed Jack Lynch. http:/jacklynch.net/Texts/dryden.html. Accessed 21 Feb. 2020.

Jones, Jennifer. "In Defense of Woman: Sophie Treadwell's *Machinal*." *Modern Drama*: 37.3 (1994): 485–496.

Jones, LeRoi. "The Revolutionary Theatre," *Liberator*. 5 Jul. 1965, 4–5.

Jones, Robert Edmond. "Art in the Theatre." *The Dramatic Imagination*. Seattle, WA: Theatre Arts Books, 1969. 23–42.

Jordan, Julia. *The Count 2.0*. New York, NY: The Dramatist Guild, 2018.

Kabira, Wanijuki Mukabi. *The Oral Artist*. Nairobi: Heineman, 1983.

Kamlongera, Christopher. *Theatre for Development in Africa with Case Studies from Malawi and Zambia*. Oxford: Foundation for International Development, 1989.

Kano, Ayako. *Acting Like a Woman in Modern Japan: Theater, Gender, and Nationalism*. New York, NY: Palgrave, 2001.

K-D 265 and 1st ed. (Larpent Plays, LA 1104, q.v.): Minor differences; printed in three acts. Catalogue of John Larpent's Plays. San Marino, CA: Huntington Library. Processed by Dougald MacMillan in 1939; supplementary encoding and revision by Diann Benti in Jan. 2018.

Keats, John. Letter to George and Tom Keats, 21-27 December 1817. *John Keats: Selected Letters*. Ed. Robert Gittings, Oxford: Oxford University Press, 2002. 40–42.

Kellaway, Kate. "Emma Rice: 'I Don't Know How I Got to Be so Controversial'." *The Guardian*, Guardian News and Media, 1 Jul. 2018, https://www.theguardian.com/stage/2018/jul/01/emma-rice-controversial-shakespeares-globe-wise-children.

Kelly, Henry Ansgar. *Ideas and Forms of Tragedy from Aristotle to the Middle Ages*. Cambridge: Cambridge University Press, 1993.

Kemble, Frances Anne, *Journal of a Residence on a Georgia Plantation*, 1838–39. Ed. John A. Scott. Athens, GA: University of Georgia Press, 1984.

_____. "On the Stage." *Notes Upon Some of Shakespeare's Plays: Macbeth, Henry VIII, The Tempest, Romeo* and *Juliet*. London: Richard Bentley and Son, 1882. 3–17.

Kenlon, Tabitha. https://wwp.northeastern.edu/context/#kenlon.performances.xml. Accessed 2 Jan. 2022.

Kennedy, Adrienne. "Adrienne Kennedy by Suzan Lori Parks." *The Bomb*. Vol. 54. (1 Jan. 1996). bombmagazine.org/articles/adrienne-kennedy/. Accessed 15 Nov. 2019.

_____. *People Who Led to My Plays*. New York, NY: Alfred A. Knopf, 1987.

Kent, Christopher. "Periodical Critics of Drama, Music, & Art, 1830-1914: A Preliminary List." *Victorian Periodicals Review*. 13.1/2 (1980): 31–55.

Kershaw, Baz. "(Patricia) Ann Jellicoe." *British and Irish Dramatists Since World War II. Second Series.* Ed. John Bull. *Dictionary of Literary Biography.* Vol. 233. Detroit, MI: Gale, 2001. *Gale Literature Resource Center.* Online ed., by subscription. Accessed 30 April 2023.

_____. *The Politics of Performance: Radical Theatre as Cultural Intervention.* London: Routledge, 1992.

Keymer, Thomas. "Shakespeare in the Novel." *Shakespeare in the Eighteenth Century.* Eds. Fiona Ritchie and Peter Sabor. Cambridge: Cambridge University Press, 2012. 118–140.

Keyssar, Helene. *Feminist Theatre.* Houndsmills: Macmillan Publishers Ltd., 1984.

Keyssar, Helene, ed. *Feminist Theatre and Theory.* New York, NY: St. Martin's Press, 1996.

Khalidi, Ismail. "Being the 'Other': Naomi Wallace and The Middle East." *The Theatre of Naomi Wallace: Embodied Dialogues.* Eds. Scott T. Cummings and Erica Stevens Abbitt, 2013. 211–213. Kindle edition.

Kidd, Ross and Martin Byram. "De-Mystifying Pseudo-Freirian Non-Formal Education: A Case Description and Analysis of Laedza Batanani." *Canadian Journal of Development Studies/ Revue canadiennes d'études du développement.* 3.2 (1982): 271–289.

Kidd, Ross and Nat J. Colletta, eds. *Tradition for Development: Indigenous Structures and Folk Media in Non-Formal Education.* Toronto: German Foundation for International Education and International Council for Adult Education, 1980.

Kimmerer, Robin Wall. *Braiding Sweetgrass: Indigenous Wisdom, Scientific Knowledge and the Teaching of Plants.* Minneapolis, MN: Milkweed Editions, 2013.

Kiper, Florence. "Some American Plays from the Feminist Viewpoint." *The Forum.* 51 (1914): 921–931.

Kirkwood, Lucy. *NSFW.* London: Nick Hern Books Ltd., 2012.

Kleist, Heinrich von. "On the Marionette Theatre." Trans. Thomas G. Neumiller. *TDR: The Drama Review* 16:3 (September 1972): 22–26.

Knapp, Oswald, G. *An Artist's Love Story.* London: George Allen, 1905.

Knowles, Ric, ed. *Judith Thompson: Critical Perspectives in Canadian Theatre in English.* Vol 3. Ontario: Playwrights Canada Press, 2005.

_____. "Judith Thompson in Criticism." *The Masks of Judith Thompson.* Ed. Ric Knowles. Ontario: Playwrights Canada Press, 2009. vii–xiv.

_____. *The Masks of Judith Thompson.* Ed. Ric Knowles. Ontario: Playwrights Canada Press, 2009.

Kodicek, Catherine. "Fittings, food and thanks – my costume resolutions for directors". *The Stage,* 11th January 2018. https://www.thestage.co.uk/opinion/catherine-kodicek-fittings-food-and-thanks--my-costume-resolutions-for-directors. Accessed 1 Dec. 2019.

_____. "Gendered job titles have to go for the sake of equality". *The Stage.* 29th May 2018. https://www.thestage.co.uk/opinion/catherine-kodicek-gendered-job-titles-have-to-go-for-the-sake-of-equality. Accessed 1 Dec. 2019.

_____. "Let's have a grown-up conversation about how we pay costume supervisors". *The Stage.* 29th January 2019. www.thestage.co.uk/opinion/2019/costume-designer-catherine-kodicek-lets-grown-conversation-pay-people-fees/. Accessed 1 Dec. 2019.

_____. "Stop tipping your dresser – it's time to pay costume professionals properly". *The Stage.* 21st August 2018. www.thestage.co.uk/opinion/2018/stop-tipping-dresser-time-pay-costume-professionals-properly/. Accessed 1 Dec. 2019.

_____. "Stop treating costume professionals as second-class workers." *The Stage.* 7 Nov. 2017. www.thestage.co.uk/opinion/2017/catherine-kodicek-stop-treating-costume-professionals-as-second-class-workers/. Accessed 7 Nov. 2017

Kois, Dan. "Is America's Favorite Playwright Too Much for New York?" *Slate,* 6 Oct. 2019. https://slate.com/culture/2019/10/lauren-gunderson-profile-most-popular-playwright-marie-curie.html. Accessed 20 Oct. 2019.

Kolawole, H. "Look Who's Taking the Stage." *The Guardian,* 26 July 2003. https://www.theguardian.com/stage/2003/jul/26/whoswhoinbritishtheatre.features. Accessed 17 Mar. 2020.

Kucich, Greg, "Reviewing Women in British Romantic Theatre." *Women in British Romantic Theatre: Drama, Performance, and Society, 1790-1840.* Ed. Catherine Burroughs. Cambridge: Cambridge University Press, 2000. 48–76.

Kushner, Tony. "Introduction." *Tales of the Lost Formicans and Other Plays.* Constance Congdon and New York, NY: Theatre Communications Group, 1994. ix–xii.

_____. "One of the Greats." *Conducting a Life: Reflections on the Theatre of Maria Irene Fornes.* Eds. Maria M. Delgado and Carida Svich. Lyme, NH: Smith and Kraus Publishers, 1999.

LA 1093 The Whim. Comedy, 2 acts. Eglantine, Lady Wallace. Application Sept. 7, 1795, Thomas Shaw, Margate. Not produced. (License refused.) MS: endorsed, by Larpent, Prohibited from being acted. Comp. 2d ed., Margate, 1795.

Lafler, Joanne. *The Celebrated Mrs. Oldfield: The Life and Art of an Augustan Actress.* Carbondale, IL: Southern Illinois University Press, 1989.

Lahr, John. "Surreal Life: The Plays of Sarah Ruhle." *The New Yorker.* www.newyorker.com/magazine/2008/03/17/surreal-life. Accessed 17 Mar. 2008.

Leavitt, Dinah L. "Megan Terry." *Women in American Theatre: Careers, Images, Movements: An Illustrated Anthology and Sourcebook.* Eds. Helen Krich Chinoy and Linda Walsh Jenkins. New York, NY: Crown Publishers, Inc., 1981. 285–292.

Lee, Esther Kim. *A History of Asian American Theatre.* Cambridge: Cambridge University Press, 2006.

Lehmann, Hans-Thies. *Postdramatic Theatre.* London and New York, NY: Routledge, 2006.

Levin, Laura. "Environmental Affinities: Naturalism and the Porous Body." *The Masks of Judith Thompson.* Ed. Ric Knowles. Ontario: Playwrights Canada Press, 2009. 123–135.

Lewis, Earl. "To Turn as on a Pivot: Writing African Americans into a History of Overlapping Diasporas." *American Historical Review.* 100.3 (1995): 765–787.

The Life of Dick Turpin. Devonport: S.&J. Keys. c.1840-1845.

Littlewood, Joan. Letter to Ewan MacColl. n.d. Joan Littlewood Correspondence. Ewan MacColl & Peggy Seeger Archives. Ruskin College, Oxford.

_____. *Political Science Notebook.* n.d. The Michael Barker Collection of Joan Littlewood. Harry Ransom Center, University of Texas, Austin. Series I, Joan Littlewood 1937-1975. Subseries A, Notebooks, Box 1, Folder 6.

_____. "The Theatre and Communism by Joan Littlewood: Some ideas inspired by a recent visit to Czechoslovakia." n.d. The Michael Barker Collection of Joan Littlewood. Harry Ransom Center, University of Texas, Austin. Series I, Joan Littlewood 1937-1975. Subseries A, Notebooks, Box 1, Folder 3.

Lobban-Viravong, Heather. "The Theatricals of Self-Sentiment in *A Narrative of the Life of Ms. Charlotte Charke.*" *Auto/Biography Studies.* 24.2 (Winter 2009): 194–209.

Lochhead, Liz. *Dracula.* London: Nick Hern Books, 2009.

_____. *Blood and Ice.* London: Nick Hern Books, 2009.

_____. *Mary Queen of Scots Got Her Head Chopped Off.* London: Nick Hern Books, 2009.

_____. "In The Cutting Room." *Dreaming Frankenstein and Collected Poems.* Edinburgh: Polygon Books, 1984.

Lock, Charles. "Maurice Browne and the Chicago Little Theatre." *Modern Drama.* 31.1. (Spring 1988):106–116.

Logan, Olive. *Apropos of Women and Theatres with a Paper or Two on Parisian Topics.* New York, NY: Carleton Publishing, 1869.

Londré, Felicia. "Megan Terry." *Speaking On Stage: Interviews with Contemporary American Playwrights.* Eds. Philip C. Kolin and Colby H. Kullman. Tuscaloosa, AL: University of Alabama Press, 1996. 138–149.

The London Stage, 1660-1800: Part 5, 1776-1800: A Calendar of Plays Entertainments & Afterpieces Together with Casts, Box-receipts and Contemporary Comment. Ed. and Intro. by Charles Beecher Hogan. 3 vols. Carbondale, IL: Southern Illinois Press, 1968.

The London Stage Database, 1660-1830: Eighteenth-Century Drama: Censorship, Society, and the Stage. Adam Matthew Digital. https//:www.eighteenthcenturydrama.amdigital.co.uk. Accessed 10 Mar. 2022.

López, Tiffany Ana. "Performing Aztlán: The Female Body as Cultural Critique in the *Teatro* of Cherríe Moraga." *Performing America: Cultural Nationalism in American Theater*. Eds. Jeffrey D. Mason and J. Ellen Gainor. Ann Arbor, MI: University of Michigan Press, 1999. 160–177.

Lorde, Audre. "Age, Race, Class and Sex: Women Redefining Difference (1986)." *Literary Theory: An Anthology*. Eds. Julie Rivkin and Michael Ryan. London: Blackwell, 1998. 630–636.

———. *Zami: A New Spelling of My Name: A Biomythography*. Trumansburg, NY: Crossing Press, 1982.

Lovvan-Viravong, Heather. "The Theatrics of Self-Sentiment in *A Narrative Life of Mrs. Charlotte Charke*." *a/b: Auto/Biography Studies*. 24 (2009). https//doi.org/10.1080/08989575.2009.10815208.

Ma, Shen-mei. "The Necessity and Impossibility of Being Mixed-Race in Asian American Literature." *Reconstructing Hybridity: Post-Colonial Studies in Transition*. Eds. Jopi Nyman and Joel Kuortti. Leiden: Brill Rodopi, 2007. 163–190.

MacColl, Ewan. *Journeyman: The Autobiography of Ewan MacColl*. London, Sidgwick & Jackson Ltd., 1990.

Macheski, Cecelia. *Remarks for the British Theatre (1806-1809), by Elizabeth Inchbald*. Delmar, NY: Scholars' Facsimiles and Reprints, 1990.

Macgowan, Kenneth. *New York Globe*. 15 November 1921.

Mackay, James. "Introduction: Red State Poet." *The Salt Companion to Diane Glancy*. Ed. James Mackay. Cambridge: Salt, 2010. 1–14.

Mackay, James, ed. *The Salt Companion to Diane Glancy*. Cambridge: Salt, 2010.

MacLennan, Elizabeth. *The Moon Belongs to Everyone: Making Theatre with 7:84*. London: Methuen, 1990.

Maeterlinck, Maurice. "The Tragical in Daily Life [Le Tragique quotidien]." *European Theories of the Drama*. 1918. Rev. Ed. Henry Popkin. New York, NY: Crown Publishers Inc., 1972. 393–394.

Malina, Judith. *Living Theatre Records*. New Haven, CT: Beinecke Rare Book & Manuscript Library, Yale University.

Mansbridge, Joanna. *Paula Vogel*. Ann Arbor, MI: University of Michigan, 2014.

Manzoni, Alessandro, *The Count of Carmagnola* and *Adelchis*. Introduced and trans. Federica Brunori Deigan. Baltimore, MD and London: The Johns Hopkins University Press, 2004.

Manzor, Lilliana. "From Minimalism to Performative Excess; The Two Tropicanas." *Latinas on Stage: Practice and Theory*. Eds. Alicia Arrizón and Lilliana Manzor. Berkeley, CA: Third Woman Press, 2000.

Marcus, Jane. *Art and Anger: Reading Like a Woman*. Columbus, OH: Ohio State University Press, 1988.

———. "The Divine Rage to Be Didactic: Introduction to Elizabeth Robins' *The Convert*." *The Convert*. Old Westbury, CT: The Feminist Press, 1980.

Marra, Kim. *Strange Duets: Impresarios and Actresses in the American Theatre, 1865-1914*. Iowa City, IA: University of Iowa Press, 2006. 73–141.

Marsden, Jean. "Charlotte Charke and the Cibbers: Private Life as Public Spectacle." *Introducing Charlotte Charke: Actress, Author, Enigma*. Ed. Philip E. Baruth. Champaign, IL: University of Illinois Press, 1998. 65–82.

———. "Sex, Politics, and She-Tragedy: Reconfiguring Lady Jane Grey." *Studies in English Literature, 1500-1900*. 42 (2002; 2006): 501–522.

Martin, John, Mojisola Adebayo, and Manisha Mehta. *The Theatre for Development Handbook*. London: Pan Intercultural Arts, 2010.

Maufort, Mark. *Labyrinth of Hybridities: Avatars of O'Neillian Realism in Multi-ethnic American Drama (1972-2003)*. New York, NY: Peter Lang, 2010.

Mbiti, John S. *African Religions and Philosophy*. Portsmouth, NH: Heinemann, 1969.

McCallum, John. *Belonging*. Sydney: Currency Press, 2009.

McCauley, Mary Carole. "50 monologues expose 'My America' at Center Stage." *The Baltimore Sun*. 21 Sept. 2012. https://www.baltimoresun.com/entertainment/arts/bs-ae-my-america-intro-20120921-story.html. Accessed 22 Oct. 2020.

McEvoy, William. "'Leaving a Space for the Non-Theorisable:' Self and Other in Hélène Cixous's Writing for Theatre." *The European Legacy*. 14.1 (2009): 19–30.

McGlennen, Molly. "Diane Glancy's Creative/Critical Politics." *The Salt Companion to Diane Glancy*. Ed. James Mackay. Cambridge: Salt, 2010. 59–74.

McGurty, Eileen Maura. "From NIMBY to Civil Rights: The Origins of the Environmental Justice Movement." *Environmental History*. 2.3 (1997): 301–323. www.jstor.org/stable/3985352. Accessed 4 Nov. 2020.

McMillan, Dorothy Porter. "Liz Lochhead and the Ungentle Art of Clyping." *Liz Lochhead's Voices*. Eds. Robert Crawford and Anne Varty. Edinburgh: Edinburgh University Press, 1993. 17–37.

McMillin, Linda A. "The Audiences of Hrotsvit." *A Companion to Hrotsvit of Gandersheim*. Eds. P.R. Brown and S.L. Wailes. Boston, MA: Leiden, 2012. 311–327.

McPherson, Heather. *Art and Celebrity in the Age of Reynolds and Siddons*. State College, PA: Penn State University Press, 2017.

McRobbie, Angela. *The Aftermath of Feminism: Gender, Culture and Social Change*. London: Sage, 2009.

McRuer, Robert. *Crip Theory: Cultural Signs of Queerness and Disability*. New York, NY: New York University Press, 2006.

Mda, Zakes. *When People Play People*. Johannesburg: Oxford University Press, 1993.

Meek, Heather. "Elitist Anti-Circumcision Discourse as Mutilating and Anti-Feminist." *Case Western Review*. 47.2 (1997): 461–480.

_____. "Medical Discourse, Women's Writing, and the 'Perplexing Form' of Eighteenth-Century Hysteria." *Early Modern Women: An Interdisciplinary Journal*. 11.1 (2016): 177–186.

_____. "Of Wandering Wombs and Wrongs of Women: Evolving Conceptions of Hysteria in the Age of Reason." *English Studies in Canada*. 35.2–3. (Sept. 2009): 105–28.

Mellor, Anne K. "'Am I not a Woman, and a Sister?': Slavery, Romanticism, and Gender." *Romanticism, Race and Imperial Culture, 1780-1834*. Eds. Alan Richardson and Sonia Hofkosh. Bloomington, IN: Indiana University Press, 1996. 311–329.

Melville, Joy. *Ellen and Edy: A Biography of Ellen Terry and Her Daughter, Edith Craig, 1847-1947*. London: Pandora, 1987.

Metwaly, Ati. "A Year of Revolutionary Theatre." *Al-Ahram*. 29 Dec. 2011-4 Jan. 2012.

Mĩcere Gĩthae. Mũgo. *African Orature and Human Rights*. Roma, Lesotho: Institute of Southern African Studies, National University of Lesotho, 1991.

_____. "The Battle of the Mind." *Ufahamu: A Journal of African Studies*. 13.2–3 (1984): 239–248.

_____. *Daughter of My People, Sing!* Nairobi: East African Literature Bureau, 1976.

_____. "Elitist Anti-Circumcision Discourse as Mutilating and Anti-Feminist." *Case Western Reserve Law Review*. 47.2 (1997): 461–480.

_____. *The Long Illness of Ex-Chief Kiti*. Nairobi: East African Literature Bureau, 1976.

_____. *My Mother's Poem and Other Songs*. Nairobi: East African Educational Publishers, 1994.

_____. "Popular Paradigms and Conceptions." *Writing and Speaking from the Heart of My Mind*. Trenton, NJ: Africa World Press, 2012. 87–104.

_____. "Popular Paradigms and Conceptions: Orature-Based Community Theater." *Out of One, Many Africas: Reconstructing the Study and Meaning of Africa*. Eds. William G. Martin and Michael O. West. Champaign, IL: University of Illinois Press, 1999. 197–212.

_____. "Towards a Definition of African Orature Aesthetics." *Third World Book Review*. 2.3 (1987): 40–41.

_____. *Visions of Africa: The Fiction of Chinua Achebe, Margaret Laurence, Elspeth Huxley, and Ngũgĩ wa Thiong'o*. Kenya: Kenya Literature Bureau, 1978.

_____. "The Woman Artist in Africa Today: A Critical Commentary," *Africa Development/ Afrique et Développement*. 19.1 (1994): 49–69.

_____. *Writing and Speaking from the Heart of My Mind: Selected Essays and Speeches*. Trenton, NJ: Africa World, 2012.

Mĩcere Gĩthae, Mugo and Adeola James. "Mĩcere Gĩthae Mugo [Interview at University of Zimbabwe, Harare 12 July 1986]." *In Their Own Voices: African Women Writers Talk.* Ed. Adeola James. London: James Currey, 1990. 92–101.

Mĩcere Gĩthae, Mũgo and Jane Wilkinson. "Micere Githae Mugo [interview in London, 6 July 1985]." *Talking with African Writers: Interviews by Jane Wilkinson.* Eds. Jane Wilkinson and James Currey. Oxford: Oxford University Press, 1992. 111–120.

Miller, Henry D. *Theorizing Black Theatre: Art Versus Protest in Critical Writings, 1899-1965.* Jefferson, NC: MacFarland, 2011.

Milling, Jane. "'A Gotham Election': Women and Performance Politics." *Restoration and Eighteenth-Century Theatre Research.* 21.2 (2006): 74–89.

Milman, Henry Hart. "Il Conte di Carmagnola; tragedia di Alessandro Manzoni, Milano, 1820. Ricciarda; tragedia di Ugo Foscolo, Londra, 1820. Francesca da Rimini; tragedia di Silvio Pellico, Milano, 1818." *Quarterly Review.* 24 (1820): 72–102.

"Miss Edith Craig." *Vote.* 12 March 1910. 233.

Mitford, Mary Russell, *The Dramatic Works*, 2 vols. London: Hurst and Blackett, 1854.

Mlama, Penina Muhando. *Culture and Development: The Popular Theatre Approach in Africa.* Uppsala: Nordiska Africainstitutet, 1991.

Moon, Krystyn. *Yellowface: Creating the Chinese in American Popular Music and Performance, 1850s-1920s.* New Brunswick, NJ: Rutgers University Press, 2004.

Moraga, Cherríe. "Art in América con Acento." *The Last Generation.* Boston, MA: South End Press, 1993.

_____. "Can You Keep a Secret?" *New Connections 99: New Plays for Young People.* Eds. Nick Drake et al. London: Faber and Faber, 1999. 93–137.

_____. "An Irrevocable Promise: Staging the Story Chicana." *A Xicana Codex of Changing Consciousness.* Durham, NC: Duke University Press, 2011. 34–46.

_____. "A Long Line of Vendidas." *Loving in the War Years: lo que nunca pasó por sus labios.* Boston, MA: South End Press, 1983. 90–142.

_____. "A Xicana Lexicon." *A Xicana Codex of Changing Consciousness.* Durham, NC: Duke University Press, 2011. xxi–xxii.

Morpurgo, Michael. "They Must Have Known Emma Rice Was Never Going to Treat Shakespeare as Holy Writ." *The Guardian,* Guardian News and Media, 27 Oct. 2016, https://www.theguardian.com/books/2016/oct/27/michael-morpurgo-globe-emma-rice-never-treat-shakespeare-holy-writ. Accessed 15 January 2022.

Morrison, Kevin A., "Mitford, Mary Russell, Prose" in *The Encyclopedia of Romantic Literature.* General Editor. Frederick Burwick. Chichester: Wiley-Blackwell, 2012. 865–871. Accessed 20 January 2022.

Morrison, Richard. "Richard Morrison: The Globe Has Been a Success Story - and Emma Rice Is Wrecking It." *Times2|The Times,* 30 Sept. 2016. https://www.thetimes.co.uk/article/richard-morrison-the-globe-has-been-a-success-story-and-emma-rice-is-wrecking-it-xrrgxz3ml. Accessed 1 June 2023.

Moses, Caro. "Winsome Pinnock: One Under," 6 Dec. 2019. thisweeklondon.com/article/winsome-pinnock-one-under/. Accessed 17 March 2022.

Mouffe, Chantal. *Agonistics: Thinking the World Politically.* London: Verso, 2013.

Muholi, Zanele. *Faces and Phases.* Munich, Berlin, London and New York, NY: Presetel, 2010.

Mulligan, Jim. "Something to Be Reclaimed." jimmulligan.co.uk. https://www.jimmulligan.co.uk/interview/winsome-pinnock-can-you-keep-a-secret. Accessed 17 Mar. 2020.

Muñoz, José Esteban. "Feeling Brown, Feeling Down: Latina Affect, The Performativity of Race, and the Depressive Position." *The Routledge Queer Studies Reader.* Eds. Donald E. Hall, Annamarie Jagose, Andrea Bebell, and Susan Potter. London: Routledge, 2013. 412–421.

Murphy, Vincent. *Page to Stage: The Craft of Adaptation.* Ann Arbor, MI: University of Michigan Press, 2013.

Myers, Victoria. "An Interview with Paula Vogel." *The Interval.* 18 Apr. 2017. https://www. theintervalny.com/interviews/2017/04/an-interview-with-paula-vogel/. Accessed 30 Apr. 2020.

———. "An Interview with Quiara Alegría Hudes." *The Interval.* 17 May 2016. https://www. theintervalny.com/interviews/2016/05/an-interview-with-quiara-alegria-hudes/. Accessed 5 Jul. 2020.

Myers, Victoria. "Joanna Baillie's Theatre of Cruelty." *Joanna Baillie, Romantic Dramatist: Critical Essays.* Ed. Thomas C. Crochunis. New York, NY and London: Routledge, 2004. 87–107.

"Nance Oldfield: The Tragedy Queen: A Comic Drama in One Act." *Manuscript.* n.d. Women's Theatre Collection, University of Bristol.

Neal, Larry. "The Black Arts Movement." *The Drama Review: TDR.* 12.4 (Summer 1968): 28–39.

Newey, Katherine, "Women and History on the Romantic Stage: More, Yearsley, Burney, and Mitford." *Women in British Romantic Theatre: Drama, Performance, and Society, 1790–1840.* Ed. Catherine Burroughs. Cambridge: Cambridge University Press, 2000. 79–100.

Newman, Barbara. *Sister of Wisdom: St. Hildegard's Theology of the Feminine.* Berkeley, CA: University of California Press, 1987.

Ngũgĩ wa Thiong'o. *Decolonising the Mind: The Politics of Language in African Literature.* London: James Currey, 1986.

———. "The Oral Native and the Writing Master: Orature, Orality, and Cyborality." *Globalectics: Theory and the Politics of Knowing.* New York, NY: Columbia University Press, 2012. 63–85.

———."Oral Power and Europhone Glory: Orature, Literature, and Stolen Legacies." *Penpoints, Gunpoints, and Dreams: Towards a Critical Theory of the Arts and the State in Africa.* Oxford: Clarendon, 1998. 103–128.

Ngũgĩ wa Thiong'o and Mĩcere Gĩthae Mũgo. *The Trial of Dedan Kimathi.* Portsmouth, NH: Heinemann, 1977.

———. "Oral Power and Europhone Glory: Orature, Literature, and Stolen Legacies." Penpoints, Gunpoints, and Dreams: Towards a Critical Theory of the Arts and the State of Africa. Oxford: Clarendon Press, 1998. 103–128.

———. "The Oral Native and the Writing Master: Orature, Orality, and Cyborality." *Globalectics: Theory and the Politics of Knowing.* New York, NY: Columbia University Press, 2012.

Nobel Media. "The Nobel Prize in Literature, 2004." https://www.nobelprize.org/prizes/ literature/2004/summary/. Accessed 8 Feb. 2021.

Nothof, Anne. "Judith Thompson." *Canadian Theatre Encyclopedia.* www.canadiantheatre.com/ dict.pls?term=Thompson%@C%20Judith. Accessed 3 Jan. 2020.

Nunn, Robert C. "Spatial Metaphor in the Plays of Judith Thompson." *The Masks of Judith Thompson.* Ed. Ric Knowles. Ontario: Playwrights Canada Press, 2009. 20–40.

Nussbaum, Felicity. *Rival Queens: Actresses, Performance, and the Eighteenth-Century British Theater.* Philadelphia, PA: University of Pennsylvania Press, 2011.

Nyong'o, Tavia. "'Rip it Up': Excess and Ecstasy in Little Richard's Sound." *Black Performance Theory.* Eds. Thomas F. DeFrantz and Anita Gonzalez. Durham, NC: Duke University Press, 2014. 169–183.

O'Connor, John S. "*Spirochete* and the War on Syphilis." *The Drama Review: TDR.* 21.1 (1977): 91–98.

O'Connor, John and Lorraine Brown. *Free, Adult, Uncensored: The Living History of the Federal Theatre Project.* New York, NY: New Republic Books, 1978.

Odom, Glenn. *World Theories of Theatre.* London: Routledge, 2017.

Ogden, Dunbar H. *The Staging of Drama in the Medieval Church.* Newark, DE: University of Delaware Press, 2003.

O' Gorman, Frank. *The Long Eighteenth Century: British Political and Social History 1688-1832.* London: Hodder Arnold, 2005.

Okagbue, Osita and Kene Igweonu "Introduction." *Performative Inter-Actions in African Theatre 1: Diaspora Representations and the Interweaving of Cultures.* Newcastle: Cambridge Scholars Publishing, 2014. 1–16.

O'Keeffe, Adelaide. *The Broken Sword, or, A Soldier's Honour: A Tale of the Allied Armies of 1757*. London: Groombridge, 1854.

———. *Dudley*. 3 vols. London: Longman, 1819.

———. *Llewellin: A Tale*. 3 vols. London: Cawthorn, 1798–1799.

———. "Memoir." *O'Keeffe's Legacy to his Daughter, Being the Poetic Works of the Late John O'Keeffe, Esq., the Dramatic Author*. Ed. Adelaide O'Keeffe. London, 1834. Xi–xxxviii.

———. *Patriarchal Times; or, The Land of Canaan: A Figurative History*. London: Rivington, 1811.

———. *A Trip to the Coast. Or Poems Descriptive of Various Interesting Objects on the Sea-Shore*. London: Darton, 1819.

———. *Zenobia, Queen of Palmyra; A Narrative, Founded on History*. 2 vols. London: Rivington, 1814.

O'Keeffe, Adelaide et al. *Original Poems for Infant Minds*. 2 vols. London: Darton, 1804-1805.

O'Keeffe, Lynda. Personal correspondence. 12 Dec. 2018.

O'Neill, Michael. "'Anxious Cares': From Pope's Spleen to Coleridge's Dejection." *Studies in the Literary Imagination*. 44.1 (2011): 99–118. Online ed., by subscription. Accessed 1 June 2023.

"Operatic Developments." *New York Daily Times*. 6 Mar. 1855.

O'Quinn, Daniel, "Hannah Cowley's *A Day in Turkey* and the Political Efficacy of Charles James Fox." *European Romantic Review*. 14 (2003). 17–30.

Osborne, Dierdre, ed. *The Cambridge Companion to British Black and Asian Literature (1945-2010)*. Cambridge: Cambridge University Press, 2016.

Osborne, Elizabeth A. *Staging the People: Community and Identity in the Federal Theatre Project*. New York, NY: Palgrave Macmillan, 2011.

"Our Stories: Power Street Theatre Company" https://www.cultureworksphila.org/stories/power-street-theatre-company. Accessed 5 Jul. 2020.

Our Private Wire. "Au Revoir Miss Ellen Terry: Off to America To-day: The First Lady Stage Manager of a Tour." *Yorkshire Evening Post*. 12 Jan. 1907: 5.

Ozieblo, Barbara. *Susan Glaspell: A Critical Biography*. Chapel Hill, NC: The University of North Carolina Press, 2000.

Ozieblo, Barbara and Jerry, Dickey. *Susan Glaspell and Sophie Treadwell*. New York, NY and London: Routledge, 2008.

Palmer, Jennifer and Dorothy Hewett, eds. *Contemporary Australian Playwrights*. Adelaide: Adelaide University Union Press, 1979.

"Parisian Dramas: The Story of Mademoiselle Cora Pearl." *New York Times*, 5 Jan. 1873.

Parks, Suzan-Lori. "From Elements of Style." *The America Play and Other Works*. New York, NY: Theatre Communications Group, 1994. Online ed., by subscription. Accessed 11 Jan. 2020.

Patton, Cindy and Beningo, Sanchez-Eppler, eds. *Queer Diasporas*. Durham, NC and London: Duke University Press, 2000.

Payne, Tony. "Is Neoliberalism at Last Unravelling in Britain?" SPERI.comment: The Political Economy Blog. 5 November 2014. http://speri.dept.shef.ac.uk/2014/11/05/neoliberalism-unravelling-britain/. Accessed 22 May 2015.

Pearce, Michael. *Black British Drama: A Transnational Story*. London and New York, NY: Routledge, 2017.

Pelligrini, Ann. *Performance Anxieties: Staging Psychoanalysis, Staging Race*. New York, NY: Routledge, 1997.

Pepys, Samuel. *The Diary of Samuel Pepys*. Eds. Robert Latham and William Matthews. 11 vols. Berkeley, CA and Los Angeles, CA: University of California Press, 1970–1983.

Peters, Margot. *Bernard Shaw and the Actresses*. New York, NY: Doubleday, 1980.

Phelan, Peggy. "Lessons in Blindness from Samuel Beckett." *PMLA*. 119.5 (Oct. 2004): 1279–1288.

———. *Live Art in LA: Performance in Southern California, 1970-1983*. New York, NY: Routledge, 2012.

———. *Unmarked: The Politics of Performance*. London: Routledge, 1993.

Phelan, Peggy and Helena Ricket, eds. *Art and Feminism*. New York, NY: Phaidon, 2001.

Phelan, Peggy and Jill Lane, eds. *Ends of Performance*. New York, NY: New York University Press, 1998.

Pietropoli, Cecilia. "The Story of the Foscaris, a Drama for Two Playwrights: Mary Mitford and Lord Byron." *The Languages of Performance in British Romanticism*. Bern: Peter Lang, 2008, 115–126.

Piggott, J.R. *Palace of the People: The Crystal Palace at Sydenham 1854-1936*. Madison, WI: University of Wisconsin Press, 2004.

"Pinocchio Dies in New York as Federal Theatre Drops Curtain." *Life*. 7.3 (July 17, 1939). 20.

Pinnock, Winsome. *Can You Keep a Secret? New Connections 99: New Plays for Young People*. Eds. Nick Drake et al. London: Faber and Faber, 1999. 93–137.

_____. *A Hero's Welcome. Six Plays by Black and Asian Women Writers*. Ed. Kadija George. London: Aurora Metro Publications, 1993. 21–55.

_____. *Leave Taking. First Run: New Plays by New Writers*. Ed. Kate Harwood. London: Nick Hern Books, 1989. 139–189.

_____. *Mules*. London: Faber and Faber, 1996.

_____. *One Under*. London: Faber and Faber, 2005.

_____. *The Principles of Cartography. Black Lives, Black Words*. Ed. Reginald Edmund. London: Oberon Books, 2017. 136–142.

_____. *A Rock in Water. Black Plays 2*. Ed. Yvonne Brewster. London: Methuen, 1989.

_____. *Rockets and Blue Light*. London: Nick Hern Books, 2020.

_____. *Taken. Charged: Six Plays*. Clean Break Theatre Company Edition. London: Nick Hern Books, 2010. 57–80.

_____. *Talking in Tongues. The Methuen Drama Book of Plays by Black British Writers*. Ed. Lynette Goddard. London: Methuen, 2011. 119–200.

_____. *Tituba. Women Centre Stage: Eight Short Plays By and About Women*. Ed. Sue Parrish. London: Nick Hern Books, 2018. 57–72.

Pinter, Harold. "Writing for the Theatre." *Harold Pinter: Complete Works*, Vol. 1. New York, NY: Grove Press, 1976. 9–16.

Pollack-Pelzner, Daniel. "With Her Eerily Timely 'Indecent,' Paula Vogel Unsettles American Theatre Again." *The New Yorker*. 12 May 2017. www.newyorker.com/books/page-turner/with-her-eerily-timely-indecent-paula-vogel-unsettles-american-theatre-again?source=search_google_dsa_paid&gclid=CjwKCAjw26H3BRB2EiwAy32zhWLMdm3Kd0gohwdZe97W9nggFY3dMAwH9Yl6efShG9yOkg6ej5GFOhoC7KwQAvD_BwE. Accessed 1 June 2020.

_____. "You've Probably Never Heard of America's Most Popular Playwright." *The New Yorker* 16 Oct. 2017, https://www.newyorker.com/books/page-turner/youve-probably-never-heard-of-americas-most-popular-playwright. Accessed 20 Dec. 2019.

Poore, Benjamin. "Liz Lochhead and The Gothic." *The Edinburgh Companion to Liz Lochhead*. Ed. Anne Varty. Edinburgh: Edinburgh University Press, 2013. 86–104.

Pope, Alexander. *Poetry and Prose of Alexander Pope*. Ed. Aubrey Williams. New York, NY: Houghton Mifflin, 1969.

Potts, Kathleen. "Quiara Alegría Hudes: Water by the Spoonful." *Guernica*, July 2, 2012. https://www.guernicamag.com/water-by-the-spoonful/. Accessed 5 Jul. 2020.

Powell, J. Kerry. "Oscar Wilde, Elizabeth Robins and the Theatre of the Future." *Modern Drama*. 37.1 (1994): 220–237.

_____. *Women and Victorian Theatre*. Cambridge: Cambridge: University Press, 1997.

Power Street Theatre Company. https://www.powerstreettheatre.com/. Accessed 5 Jul. 2020.

Prenowitz, Eric. "On Theatre: An Interview with Hélène Cixous." *Selected Plays of Hélène Cixous*. Ed. Eric Prenowitz. London and New York, NY: Routledge, 2004. 1–24.

Puar, Jasbir K. *Terrorist Assemblages: Homonationalism in Queer Times*. Durham, NC: Duke University Press, 2017.

Pursell, Madeline. "Freedom Theater's 'The Siege' Arrives at Skirball." *Washington Square News*, 17 Oct. 2017. https://nyunews.com/2017/10/17/freedom-theatres-the-siege-arrives-at-skirball/. Accessed 26 Oct. 2020.

Putzel, Stephen "Virginia Woolf and the Theatre." *Edinburgh Companion to Virginia Woolf and the Arts*. Ed. Maggie Humm. Edinburgh: Edinburgh University Press, 2010.

Radic, Leonard. *Contemporary Australian Drama*. Blackheath: Brandl and Schlesinger, 2006.

Rancière, Jacque. *The Emancipated Spectator*. 2009. Trans. Gregory Elliott. London: Verso, 2011.

Ranger, Paul, '*Terror and Pity Reign in Every Breast': Gothic Drama in the London Patent Theatres, 1750-1820*. London: Society for Theatre Research, 1991.

Rankin, Peter. *Joan Littlewood: Dreams and Realities. The Official Biography*. London: Oberon Books, 2015.

Read, Robyn. "Who is the Stranger?: The Role of the Monstrous in Judith Thompson's *Capture Me*." *The Masks of Judith Thompson*. Ed. Ric Knowles. Ontario: Playwrights Canada Press, 2009. 111–122.

Rebellato, Dan. *1956 and All That: The Making of Modern British Drama*. London: Routledge, 1999.

Reed, Josephine. "Interview with Spiderwoman Theater's Muriel Miguel." National Endowment for the Arts. https://www.arts.gov/stories/podcast/muriel-miguel#transcript. 2017. Accessed 19 Jan. 2022.

Reinelt, Janelle. "Generational Shifts." *Theatre Research International*. 35.3 (2010): 288–290.

_____. "Performance at the Crossroads of Citizenship." *The Grammar of Politics and Performance*. Eds. Shirin M. Rai and Janelle Reinelt. Abingdon, Oxon: Routledge, 2015. 34–50.

Rice, Emma. Feast "Wise Children." *Wise Children*. https://www.wisechildren.co.uk/. Accessed 26 Aug. 2019.

_____. "A Letter from Artistic Director, Emma Rice." *Shakespeare's Globe Blog*. 19 April 2017.

Richards, Sandra. *The Rise of the English Actress*. New York, NY: St. Martin's Press, 1993.

Richardson, Alan. "A Neural Theatre: Joanna Baillie's 'Plays on the Passions.'" *Joanna Baillie, Romantic Dramatist: Critical Essays*. Ed. Thomas C. Crochunis. New York, NY, and London: Routledge, 2004. 130–145.

Ridinger Smorul, Kate. "Of Marionettes, Boxers, and Suffragettes: Djuna Barnes's Performative Journalism." *Journal of Modern Literature*. 39.1 (2015): 55–71.

Ritchie, Fiona. *Women and Shakespeare in the Eighteenth Century*. Cambridge: Cambridge University Press, 2014.

Roach, Joseph. *Cities of the Dead: Circum-Atlantic Performance*. New York, NY: Columbia University Press, 1996.

_____. *The Player's Passion: Studies in the Art of Acting*. Ann Arbor, MI: The University of Michigan Press, 1993.

_____. "'Pretty Ghost, a Duet': On Dying While You Still Look Good." *Theatre and Ghosts: Materiality, Performance and Modernity*. Eds. Mary Luckhurst and Emilie Morin. London and New York, NY: Palgrave Macmillan, 2014. 128–140.

Roach, Stephanie. "Chronology." *The Cambridge Companion to American Women Playwrights*. Ed. Brenda Murphy. Cambridge: Cambridge University Press, 1999, xix–xxxviii.

Robbins, Phyllis. *Maude Adams: An Intimate Portrait*. New York, NY: G.P. Putnam's Sons, 1956.

_____. "Remembrances of Miss Maude Adams: Scrapbooks Compiled by Phyllis Robbins." Volumes I-IV. 1898-1953. Maude Adams Collection, Harvard Theatre Collection. Cambridge, MA.

_____. *The Young Maude Adams*. Francestown, NH: M. Jones, 1959.

Roberts, Philip. *The Royal Court Theatre and the Modern Stage*. Cambridge: Cambridge University Press, 1999.

Roberts, R. Ellis. *Manchester Guardian*. 17 Jul. 1925.

Roberts, Vera Mowry. "Olive Logan and 'The Leg Business.'" *The Journal of American Drama and Theatre.* 2.1 (1990): 5–10.

Robins, Elizabeth. *The Convert.* New York, NY: Macmillan, 1907.

_____. "Henrik Ibsen." *Time and Tide.* 9. 11. (16 Mar. 1928): 242.

_____. "Henrik Ibsen: The Drama of Ideas." *Times.* (17 Mar. 1928): 13–14.

_____. *Ibsen and the Actress.* London: Hogarth Press, 1928.

_____. *Votes for Women.* London: Mills and Boon, 1909.

Robinson, Marc. *The Other American Drama.* Baltimore, MD: The John Hopkins University Press, 1994.

Rohe, Alice. "The Story of Susan Glaspell." *Morning Telegraph.* 18 Dec. 1921, 2:4.

Romero, Elaine. *Barrio Hollywood.* New York, NY: Samuel French, 2008.

_____. "Personal Interview." 19 Oct. 2020.

_____. *The Fat-Free Chicana and the Snow Cap Queen. Puro Teatro: A Latina Anthology.* Eds. Alberto Sandoval-Sánchez and Nancy Saporta Sternbach. Tucson, AZ: University of Arizona Press, 2000. 89–144.

_____. "The Power of Space." *Theatre and Cartographies of Power: Repositioning the Latina/o Americas.* Eds. Jimmy A. Noriega and Analola Santana. Carbondale, IL: Southern Illinois Press, 2018. 164–169.

_____. *Walking Home. The Chicano/Latino Literary Prize: An Anthology of Prize-Winning Fiction, Poetry, and Drama.* Ed. Stephanie Fetta. Houston, TX: Arte Público Press, 2008. 229–234.

Rourke, Constance. *American Humor: A Study of the National Character.* New York, NY: Harcourt, Brace, 1931.

Rousseau, George. "Depression's Forgotten Genealogy: Notes Towards a History of Depression." *History of Psychiatry.* 11.41 (2000): 71–106.

Royce, Graydon. "Welcome to the new Jungle: Sarah Rasmussen takes over the Minneapolis Theater." *StarTribune,* 11 Feb. 2016, www.startribune.com/welcome-to-the-new-jungle-sarah-rasmussen-takes-overthe-minneapolis-theater/368488341/. Accessed 4 Mar. 2023.

Ruhl, Sarah. *100 Essays I Don't Have Time to Write: On Umbrellas and Sword Fights, Parades and Dogs, Fire Alarms, Children, and Theater.* New York, NY: Farrar, Straus and Giroux, 2014.

_____. *The Oldest Boy.* New York, NY: Theatre Communications Group, 2016.

_____. "When Woolf Saw Chekhov, Something of an Introduction." *Chekhov's Three Sisters and Woolf's Orlando: Two Renderings for the Stage.* New York, NY: Theatre Communications Group, 2013. x–xii.

Russell, Tilden. *Dance Theory: Source Readings from Two Millennia of Western Dance.* New York, NY: Oxford University Press, 2020.

Rutter, Carol. *Clamorous Voices: Shakespeare's Women Today.* London and New York, NY: Routledge, 1989.

Ruwe, Donelle. "Dramatic Monologues and the Novel-in-Verse: Adelaide O'Keeffe and the Creation of Theatrical Children's Poetry in the Long Eighteenth Century." *The Lion and the Unicorn.* 33.2 (2009): 219–234.

_____. "Mediocrity: Mechanical Keyboards and Music for Girls." *Literary Cultures and Eighteenth-Century Childhoods.* Ed. Andrew O'Malley. London: Palgrave Macmillan, 2018. 163–188.

_____. "*Zenobia, Queen of Palmyra*: Adelaide O'Keeffe, the Jewish Conversion Novel, and the Limits of Rational Education." *Eighteenth-Century Life.* 36.1 (2012): 30–53.

Saglia, Diego. "'Freedom Alone Is Wanting': British Views of Contemporary Italian Drama, 1820-1830." *British Romanticism and Italian Literature: Translating, Reviewing, Rewriting.* Eds. Laura Bandiera and Diego Saglia. Amsterdam and New York, NY: Rodopi, 2005. 237–254.

_____. "'Womanhood summoned unto conflicts' in the historical tragedies of Felicia Hemans and Mary Russell Mitford." *La Questione Romantica.* 14 (2003): 95–109.

Samuel, Raphael, et al., eds. *Theatres of the Left, 1880 – 1935: Workers' Theatres Movements in Britain and America.* London: Routledge and Keagan Paul, 1985.

Sanchez, Gabriela Serena and Quiara Alegría Hudes, "Pausing and Breathing: Two Sisters Deliver the ATHE 2018 Conference Keynote Address." *Theatre Topics*. 29.1 (Mar. 2019): E-1–13.

Sanchez, Maria C. and Linda Schlossberg, eds. *Passing: Identity and Interpretation in Sexuality, Race, and Religion*. New York, NY: New York University Press, 2001.

Sanjinés, Javier C. "Indianizing the Q'ara: Mestizaje Turned Upside Down." *Mestizaje Upside-Down: Aesthetic Politics in Modern Bolivia*. Pittsburgh, PA: University of Pittsburgh Press, 2004. 149–189.

Savile, Alice. "Black Lives, Black Words' at the Bush Theatre: Why This, Why Now?" *Time Out*, 22 Mar. 2017 at https://www.timeout.com/london/theatre/black-lives-black-words-at-the-bush-theatre-why-this-why-now. Accessed 17 Mar. 2020.

Savran, David. "Loose Screws: An Introduction." Paula Vogel, *The Baltimore Waltz and Other Plays*. New York, NY: Theatre Communications Group, 1996. ix–xv.

_____. "Maria Irene Fornes." *In Their Own Words: Contemporary American Playwrights*. Ed. David Savan. New York, NY: Theatre Communication Group, 1988, 51–69.

Schlueter, Jennifer. "'A theatrical race': American Identity and Popular Performance in the Writings of Constance M. Rourke." *Theatre Journal*. 60.4 (2008): 529–543.

Schmatz, Ferdinand and Jamie Owen Daniel. "Viennese Actionism and the Vienna Group: The Austrian Avant-Garde after 1945." *Discourse*. 14.2 (1992): 59–73.

Schmidman, Jo Ann, Sora Kimberlain and Megan Terry, eds. *Right Brain Vacation Photos: New Plays and Production Photographs 1972-1998*. Omaha, NE: Omaha Magic Theatre Foundation and Megan Terry, 1992.

Scott, John A. "Introduction." *Journal of a Residence on a Georgia Plantation in 1838-1839*. Ed. John A. Scott. Athens, GA: University of Georgia Press, 1984. ix–lxi.

Sedgwick, Eve Kosofsky. *Tendencies*. London: Routledge, 1994.

_____. *Touching Feeling: Affect, Pedagogy, Performativity*. Durham, NC: Duke University Press, 2003.

Segarra, Marta, ed. *The Portable Cixous*. New York, NY: Columbia University Press, 2010.

Selaiha, Nehad. "A Year of Revolutionary Theatre" *al-Ahram*. 29 December 2011–4 January 2012.

_____. "Art and Politics." *The Egyptian Theatre: New Directions*. Cairo: GEBO, 2003. 435–46.

_____. "Women Playwrights in Egypt." *Plays and Playwrights*. Cairo: GEBO, 2003. 443–46.

Shakespeare, William. *A Midsummer Night's Dream*. *The Riverside Shakespeare*. 2nd ed. Ed. G. Blakemore Evans. Boston and New York, NY: Houghton Mifflin Company, 1997. 256–283.

Shaver, Anne, ed. *The Convent of Pleasure and Other Plays*. Ed. Margaret Cavendish. Baltimore, MD: Johns Hopkins University Press, 1999.

Shaw, Bernard. *Our Theatres in the Nineties*. 3 vols. London: Constable and Company, 1932.

Shepard, Alan and Mary Lamb. "The Memory Palace in Paula Vogel's Plays." *Southern Women Playwrights: New Essays and Criticism*. Eds. Robert L. McDonald and Linda Rohrer Paige. Tuscaloosa, AL: University of Alabama Press, 2002. 198–217.

Shevelow, Kathryn. *Charlotte: Being a True Account of an Actress's Flamboyant Adventures in Eighteenth-Century London's Wild and Wicked Theatrical World*. London: Picador, 2005.

Shimakawa, Karen. "Swallowing the Tempest: Asian American Women on Stage." *Theatre Journal*. 47.3 (1995): 367–380.

Siddons, Sarah Kemble. *The Reminiscences of Sarah Kemble Siddons, 1773-1785*. Ed. William Van Lennep. Cambridge, MA: Harvard University Library, 1942.

Silver, Brenda R. "'Anon' and 'The Reader': Virginia Woolf's Last Essays." *Twentieth Century Literature*. 25.3/4 (1979): 356–441.

Simkin, Stevie. *Cultural Constructions of the Femme Fatale: From Pandora's Box to Amanda Knox*. London: Palgrave Macmillan, 2014.

Simpson, Leanne Betasamosake. *As We Have Always Done: Indigenous Freedom Through Radical Resistance*. Minneapolis, MN: University of Minnesota Press, 2017.

Singh, Dalbir. "Staging the Post-Colonial Monster in Judith Thompson's *Capture Me*." *The Masks of Judith Thompson*. Ed. Ric Knowles. Ontario: Playwrights Canada Press, 2009. 106–110.

Skinner, Cornelia Otis. "Monologue To Theatre: An Exponent of a Solo Art Discusses Its Rise from the Ranks of the Amateurs." *The New York Times*, 27 Dec. 1931, sec. Arts & Leisure. *Proquest Historical Newspapers*.

Smith, David. "Lauren Gunderson: The Most Popular Playwright in America Today." *The Guardian*, 4 Jan. 2018, https://www.theguardian.com/stage/2018/jan/04/lauren-gunderson-america-most-popular-playwright-interview. Accessed 15 Dec. 2019.

Smith, Elton E. *Charles Reade*. Boston: Twayne, 1976.

Smith, Hannah. "Susanna Centlivre, 'Our *Church*'s Safety' and 'Whig Feminism'." *Religion and Women in Britain, c. 1660-1760*. Eds. Sarah Apetrei and Hannah Smith. Farnham: Ashgate, 2014. 145–162.

Smith, Zadie. "Fascinated to Presume: In Defense of Fiction." *The New York Review of Books*. 51.16 (2019): 4–11.

Sobecki, Sebastian. "'The writyng of this tretys': Margery Kempe's Son and the Authorship of Her Book." *Studies in the Age of Chaucer*. 37 (2015): 257–83.

Sofer, Andrew. *The Stage Life of Props*. Ann Arbor, MI: University of Michigan Press, 2003.

Solga, Kim. "Building an Ethical Architecture: Judith Thompson's *Habitat* and the Shape of Radical Humanism." *The Masks of Judith Thompson*. Ed. Ric Knowles. Ontario: Playwrights Canada Press, 2009. 136–148.

Solomon, Alisa. "Forword." Adrienne Kennedy, *The Alexander Plays*. Minneapolis, MN: University of Minnesota Press, 1992. ix–xvii.

Sontag, Susan. "Notes on Camp." *Partisan Review*. 31.4 (Fall 1964), 515–530

_____. "Preface." Maria Irene Fornes, *Plays*. New York, NY: PAJ Publications, 1986. 7–10.

Spaliviero, Antonia, ed. *Divina: Vicende di vita e di teatro*. Tirrenia Stampatori, 1992.

Split Britches. "Public Address Systems." http://www.split-britches.com/public-address-systems. Accessed 8 Jan. 2022.

Staley, Lynn. *Margery Kempe's Dissenting Fictions*. University Park, PA: Pennsylvania State University Press, 1994.

Stanlake, Christy. *Native American Drama: A Critical Perspective*. Cambridge: Cambridge University Press, 2009.

Stanton, Elizabeth Cady, Susan B. Anthony, and Matilda Joslyn Gage. *History of Woman Suffrage*. Vol. 2. Rochester, N.Y.: Charles Mann Printing Co., 1881.

Stanton, Judith Phillips, "'This New–Found Path Attempting': Women Dramatists in England, 1660–1800." *Curtain Calls: British and American Women and the Theater, 1660 – 1820*. Eds. Mary Anne Schofield and Cecilia Macheski. Athens, OH: Ohio University Press, 1991. 325–354.

Staves, Susan. *A Literary History of Women's Writing in Britain, 1660-1789*. Cambridge: Cambridge University Press, 2010.

Stein, Gertrude. *Lectures in America*. New York, NY: Random House, 1935.

Steinmetz, Katy. "The Transgender Tipping Point." *Time Magazine*. 29 May 2014. https://time.com. Accessed 4 Mar. 2023.

St John, Christopher, ed. *Ellen Terry and Bernard Shaw: A Correspondence*. New York: G. P. Putnam's Sons, 1931.

_____. "The First Actress." 1911. Lord Chamberlain's Manuscripts 14, British Library.

_____. "Miss Ellen Terry's American Tour." *Morning Post*. 11 Jan. 1907. 8.

Stockton, Kathryn Bond. *Beautiful Bottom, Beautiful Shame: Where "Black" Meets "Queer."* Durham, NC and London: Duke University Press, 2006.

Stokes, James. "Women and Mimesis in Medieval and Renaissance Somerset (and Beyond)." *Comparative Drama*. 27 (1993): 176–196.

Stowell, Sheila. *A Stage of Their Own: Feminist Playwrights of the Suffrage Era*. Ann Arbor, MI: University of Michigan Press, 1992.

Straub, Kristina. *Sexual Suspects: Eighteenth-Century Players and Sexual Ideology.* Princeton, NJ: Princeton UP, 1992.

Straznicky, Marta. *Privacy, Playreading, and Women's Closet Drama, 1550-1700.* Cambridge: Cambridge University Press, 2009.

Sutton Williams, Natasha. "Playwright Winsome Pinnock on Identity, Otherness and the Artistic Benefits of Ageing." 26 Sept. 2019. Diabilityarts.online. https://disabilityarts.online/magazine/opinion/playwright-winsome-pinnock-on-identity-otherness-and-the-artistic-benefits-of-ageing/. Accessed 16 Mar. 2020.

Takemoto, Koshikô. Personal interview. 24 Aug. 2019.

TallBear, Kim. "Caretaking Relations, Not American Dreaming." *Kalfou.* 6.1 (2019): 24–41.

Tamale, Sylvia, ed. *African Sexualities: A Reader.* Nairobi: Pambazuka Press, 2011.

Taylor, Ann and Jane, et al. *Original Poems for Infant Minds.* 2 vols. London: Darton, 1804-05.

Taylor, George. *The French Revolution and the London Stage.* Cambridge: Cambridge University Press, 2000.

Teer, Barbara Ann. "We Can Be What We Were Born to Be." *The New York Times,* 7 Jul. 1968. D1.

Templeton, Joan. *Shaw's Ibsen: A Re-Appraisal.* London: Palgrave Macmillan, 2018.

Terry, Megan. *Ex-Miss Copper Queen on a Set of Pills.* New York, NY: Samuel French, 1966.

_____. *Molly Bailey's Traveling Family Circus featuring Scenes from the Life of Mother Jones.* Music by Joann Metcalf. New York, NY: Broadway Publishing Co., 1983.

_____. *Right Brain Vacation Photos.* Eds. Megan Terry, Jo Ann Schmidmann and Sora Kimberlain. Omaha, NB: OMT Press, 1992.

Thain, Marion. *Michael Field: Poetry, Aestheticism and the Fin-de-Siècle.* Cambridge: Cambridge University Press, 2007.

Thomas, Lundeana. "Barbara Ann Teer: From Holistic Training to Liberating Minds." *Black Theatre: Ritual Performance in the African Diaspora.* Eds. Paul Carter Harrison and Victor Leo Walker II. Toronto: Playwrights Canada Press, 1981.

Thomas, Sue. "Elizabeth Robins (1862-1952): A Bibliography." *Victorian Fiction Research Guide.* Queensland: University of Australia, 1994. https://victorianfictionresearchguides.org/elizabeth-robins/. Accessed 1 Mar. 2020.

Thompson, Ann and Sasha Roberts. *Women Reading Shakespeare, 1660-1900: An Anthology of Criticism.* Manchester: University of Manchester Press, 1997.

Thompson, Jessie. "Winsome Pinnock: 'I'd go to the theatre with my sister - we'd be the only black people in the audience'." *Evening Standard,* 25 May 2018. https://www.standard.co.uk/go/london/theatre/winsome-pinnock-id-go-to-thetheatre-with-my-sister-wed-be-the-only-black-people-in-the-audiencea3848521.html. Accessed 13 Mar. 2020.

Thompson, Judith. *Body and Soul.* Toronto: Playwrights Canada Press, 2011.

_____. *Capture Me.* Toronto: Playwrights Canada Press, 2006.

_____ *The Crackwalker.* Toronto: Playwrights Canada Press, 2016.

_____. *Habitat.* Toronto: Playwrights Canada Press, 2002.

_____. *Hedda Gabler and Sirens: Elektra in Bosnia.* Toronto: Playwrights Canada Press, 2017. 107–112.

_____. "Inciting a Riot: Digging Down Into a Play." *Writing Creative Writing: Essays from the Field.* Eds. Rishma Dunlop, Daniel Scott Tysdal, and Priscila Uppal. London: Dundurn, 2018. 210–220.

_____. *Lion in the Streets.* Toronto: Playwrights Canada Press, 1992.

_____. *The Other Side of the Dark: Four Plays.* Toronto: Playwrights Canada Press, 1997.

_____. *Palace of the End.* Toronto: Playwrights Canada Press, 2007.

_____. *Perfect Pie.* Toronto: Playwrights Canada Press, 2000.

_____. "The Return." *Luminous Ink: Writers on Writing in Canada.* Eds. Dionne Brand, Rabindranath Maharaj, and Tessa McWatt. Toronto: Cormorant Books, 2018.

_____. *Sled.* Toronto: Playwrights Canada Press, 1997.

_____. *Such Creatures.* Toronto: Playwrights Canada Press, 2011.

_____. "That Stinking Hot Summer." *Theatre Journal.* 62.4 (2010): 505–510.

_____. *The Thrill.* Toronto: Playwrights Canada Press, 2015.

_____. *Watching Glory Die.* Toronto: Playwrights Canada Press, 2017.

_____. *White Biting Dog, and Other Plays.* Toronto: Playwrights Canada Press, 2014.

Todd, Janet, *The Sign of Angellica: Women, Writing and Fiction, 1660-1800.* London and Bloomington, IN: Indiana University Press, 1996. 311–329

Toles, George. "'Cause You're the Only One I Want:' The Anatomy of Love in the Plays of Judith Thompson." *The Masks of Judith Thompson.* Ed. Ric Knowles. Ontario: Playwrights Canada Press, 2009. 1–19.

Tolhurst, J. B. L., ed. *The Ordinale and Customary of the Benedictine Nuns of Barking Abbey.* Henry Bradshaw Society 65. 2 vols. London: Harrison and Sons, 1927.

Tran, Diep. "The Top 20 Most-Produced Playwrights of the 2019-20 Season." *American Theatre.* Sept 2019. https://www.americantheatre.org/2019/09/18/the-top-20-most-produced-playwrights-of-the-2019-20-season/. Accessed 1 Oct. 2019.

Treadwell, Sophie. "Writing a Play." 1925. Manuscript. University of Arizona Libraries Special Collections.

"Troubles of the Opera Singers–their Salaries and Profits.: SUPREME COURT–SPECIAL TERM." *New York Daily Times.* 3 Sept. 1857.

Trueman, Matt. "Katie Mitchell: 'I Was Uncomfortable Coming Back to Work in the UK'." *The Stage.* 26 Feb. 2016. www.thestage.co.uk/features/katie-mitchell-i-was-uncomfortable-coming-back-to-work-in-the-uk. Accessed 10 Mar. 2022.

_____. "Matt Trueman talks to Winsome Pinnock and Amit Sharma about the Reworking of *One Under*". https://graeae.org/matt-trueman-talks-to-winsome-pinnock-and-amit-sharma-about-the-reworking-of-one-under/. Accessed 3 Mar. 2020.

Turney, Eleanor. "Women in Theatre: Beyond the Glass Ceiling and the Ghetto." *Guardian*, 6 Mar. 2012. https://www.theguardian.com/culture-professionals-network/culture-professionals-blog/2012/mar/06/female-theatre-companies-agent-160. Accessed 16 Jan. 2022.

Ukaegbu, Victor. "Grey Silhouettes: Black Queer Theatre on the Post-war British Stage." *Alternatives within the Mainstream 2: Queer Theatres in Post-War Britain.* Ed. Dimple Godiwala. Newcastle: Cambridge Scholars Publishing, 2007. 322–338.

Usui, Masami, and Miles Xian Liu. "Velina Hasu Houston." *Asian American Playwrights: A Bio-bibliographical Critical Sourcebook.* Ed. Miles Xian Liu. Westport, CT: Greenwood Press, 2002. 103–120.

Van Acker, L., ed. *Hildegardis Bingensis Epistolarium.* Corpus Christianorum: Continuatio Mediaevalis 91A. Antwerp and Brussels: Turnholt: Brepols, 1991.

van Beek, Cornelius Iohannes Maria Ioseph, ed. *Passio Sanctarum Perpetuae et Felicitatis.* Gelderland: Nijmegen, 1936.

Vekeman, H.W.J., ed. and trans. (modern Dutch). *Het Visioenenboek van Hadewijch, Uitgegeven naat handschrift 941 van de Bibliotheek der Rijksuniversiteit te Gent.* Nijmegen: Dekker and Van de Vegt, 1980.

Venn Creative. "Emma Rice--Directing Tristan & Yseult." *Kneehigh Cookbook.* 27 Oct. 2015. https://thisiskneehigh.co.uk/. Accessed 22 Mar. 2022.

"Vestvali in Court: SUPREME COURT CHAMBERS. Before Judge Barnard." *The New York Times*, 2 Aug. 1865.

Vogel, Paula. "Bake-Offs: A History." www.paulavogelplaywright.com/bakeoff. Accessed 1 June 2020.

Wailes, Stephen L. "Hrotsvit's Plays." *A Companion to Hrotsvit of Gandersheim: Contextual and Interpretive Approaches.* Eds. Phyllis R. Brown and Stephen L. Wailes. Boston: Leiden, 2012. 121–46.

Wailes, Stephen L., and Phyllis R. Brown. "Hrotsvit and her World." *A Companion to Hrotsvit of Gandersheim: Contextual and Interpretive Approaches.* Eds. Phyllis R. Brown and Stephen L. Wailes. Boston: Leiden, 2012. 3–22.

Walcott, Rinaldo. "Somewhere Out There: The New Black Queer Theory." *Blackness and Sexualities*. Eds. Michelle M. Wright and Antje Schuhmann. Munster: Lit Verlag, 2007. 29–40.

_____. "Outside in Black Studies: Reading from a Queer Place in the Diaspora." *Black Queer Studies: A Critical Anthology*. Eds. E. Patrick Johnson and Mae G. Henderson. Durham, NC: Duke University Press, 2005. 90–105.

Walker, Craig Stewart. "Judith Thompson: Psychomachia." *The Buried Astrolabe: Canadian Dramatic Imagination and Western Tradition*. Montreal: McGill-Queen's University Press, 2001. 74–91.

Wallace, Lady Eglantine. *The Conduct of the King of Prussia and General Dumourier Investigated by Lady Wallace*. London: J. Debrett, 1793.

_____. *The Whim, a comedy in three acts, by Lady Wallace. With an Address to the Public, upon the arbitrary and unjust Aspersion of the Licenser against its Political Sentiments*. Margate: W. Epps, 1795.

Wallace, Michele. *Black Macho and the Myth of the Super-woman*. New York, NY: Verso, 1979.

Wallace, Naomi. "Let the Right One In: Resistance, Hospitality, and New Writing for the American Stage." *American Theatre* 30.1 (January 2013). https://www.americantheatre. org/2013/01/01/let-the-right-one-in/. Accessed 3 Mar. 2023.

_____. "On Writing as Transgression: Teachers of young playwrights need to turn them into dangerous citizens." *American Theatre*. 25.1 (January 2008): 98–102. Online ed., by subscription. Accessed 20 Oct. 2020.

_____. Personal communication. 8 Aug. 2020.

_____. "Radical Vision and Form: A Conversation with Naomi Wallace." Interview with Joel Murray. *Americantheatre.org*. November 10, 2015. Accessed 8 Oct. 2020.

Wallace, Naomi and Ismail Khalidi. "Shattering the Spectacle of Trump: toward a theatre of holistic dissent." *American Theatre*. 34.9 (November 2017): 38–42. Online ed., by subscription. Accessed 10 Oct. 2020.

Wallace, Naomi and Claire MacDonald. "Intimate Histories." *PAJ: A Journal of Performance and Art*. 28.3 (Sept. 2006): 93–102.

Walter, Harriet. *Actors on Shakespeare: Macbeth*. London: Faber and Faber, 2002.

_____. *Brutus and Other Heroines: Playing Shakespeare's Roles for Women*. London: Nick Hern Books, 2016.

_____. *Facing It: Reflections on Images of Older Women*. London: Facing it Publications, 2011.

_____. "The Heroine, the Harpy and the Human Being." *New Theatre Quarterly*, 9.34 (1993): 110–120.

_____. *Other People's Shoes: Thoughts on Acting*. London: Nick Hern Books, 2003.

Wandor, Michelene. *Post-War British Drama: Looking Back in Gender*. London: Routledge, 2001.

Warner, Marina. "Memories of the Martyrs: Reflections from a Catholic Girlhood." *Perpetua's Passions: Multidisciplinary Approaches to the Passio Perpetuae et Felicitatis*. Eds. Jan N. Bremmer and Marco Formisano. Oxford: Oxford University Press, 2012. 354–356.

Washington, Mary Helen. *The Other Blacklist: The African American Literary and Cultural Left of the 1950s*. New York, NY: Columbia University Press, 2014.

Wearing, J.P. *The London Stage, 1890-1899: A Calendar of Plays and Players*. Lanham, MD: Scarecrow Press, 1976.

Weaver, Lois and Hannah Maxwell. "Care Café: A Chronology and a Protocol." *The Scottish Journal of Performance*. 5.1 (2018): 87–98.

Weber, Bruce. "Maria Irene Fornes, Writer of Spare, Poetic Plays, Dies at 88." *The New York Times*. 31 Oct. 2018: Sec. B14.

"Wellesley to See Styles in Acting By Dorothy Sands," *The Christian Science Monitor*, 13 Jan. 1933, *Proquest Historical Newspapers*.

Wetzsteon, Ross. "Irene Fornes: The Elements of Style." *The Theater of Maria Irene Fornes*. Ed. Marc Robinson. New York, NY: PAJ Books, 1999: 25–38.

"We See You, White American Theater." *We See You. weseeyouwat.com/statement*. Accessed 12 Oct. 2020.

Wiener, Oswald, and David Britt. "Remarks on Some Tendencies of the 'Vienna Group'". *October.* 97 (Summer 2001): 121–130.

Wilson, Katharina. *The Ethics of Authorial Stance: Hrotsvit and her Poetics.* Leiden: Brill, 1988.

Williams, Gweno. "Chapter 7: 'Why May Not a Lady Write a Good Play?'" *Readings in Renaissance Women's Drama: Criticism, History, and Performance, 1594-1998.* Eds. S.P. Cerasano and Marion Wynne-Davies. New York, NY and London: Routledge, 1998. 95–107.

Winchilsea, Anne Kingsmill Finch. *The Anne Finch Wellesley Manuscript Poems: A Critical Edition.* Eds. Barbara McGovern and Charles H. Hinnant. Athens, GA: University of Georgia Press, 1998.

Witham, Barry. *The Federal Theatre Project: A Case Study.* Cambridge: Cambridge University Press, 2003.

Wollstonecraft, Mary. *A Vindication of the Rights of Woman: With Strictures on Political and Moral Subjects.* London: J. Johnson, 1792.

Wong, Helen Jean. "Playing the Palace Theatre: A Chinese American's Recollections of Vaudeville." *Chinese America, History and Perspectives.* 3 (1989): 111–116.

Woolf, Virginia. *Between the Acts.* New York, NY: Houghton Mifflin Harcourt, 2008.

_____. *The Diary of Virginia Woolf, Vol 3.* New York, NY: Houghton Mifflin Harcourt, 1980.

_____. "Ellen Terry." *Collected Essays.* Vol. 4. London: The Hogarth Press, 1925. 67–72.

_____. *Freshwater: a comedy.* New York, NY: Houghton Mifflin Harcourt, 1976.

_____. *Mrs Dalloway.* New York, NY: Houghton Mifflin Harcourt, 2005.

_____. "Notes on an Elizabethan Play." *The Essays Of Virginia Woolf.* Vol. 4. Ed. Andrew McNeillie. New York, NY: Harcourt Brace, 1994. 62–70.

_____. *Orlando: Biography.* New York, NY: Houghton Mifflin Harcourt, 2006.

_____. "Professions for Women." 1931. *Selected Essays.* Ed. David Bradshaw. Oxford: Oxford University Press, 2008. 140–145.

_____. *A Room of One's Own.* New York, NY: Houghton Mifflin Harcourt, 2005.

_____. *Three Guineas.* New York, NY: Houghton Mifflin Harcourt, 2014.

_____. *To The Lighthouse.* New York, NY: Houghton Mifflin Harcourt, 2005.

_____ "Twelfth Night at the Old Vic." *The Death of the Moth and Other Essays.* New York, NY: Houghton Mifflin Harcourt, 1947.

_____. *The Waves.* New York, NY: Houghton Mifflin Harcourt, 2006.

Worrall, David. *Theatric Revolution: Drama, Censorship and Romantic Period Subcultures 1773–1832.* Oxford: Oxford University Press, 2006.

Wren, Celia. "The Golden Ruhl." *American Theatre.* 22.8 (2005): 30–32.

Yarbro-Bejarano, Yvonne. *The Wounded Heart: Writing on Cherríe Moraga.* Austin, TX: University of Texas Press, 2001.

Yardley, Anne Bagnell. *Performing Piety: Musical Culture in Medieval English Nunneries.* New York, NY: Palgrave Macmillan, 2006.

Young, Karl. *The Drama of the Medieval Church.* 2 vols. Oxford: Clarendon Press, 1933.

_____. *Samuel Johnson on Shakespeare: One Aspect.* Madison, WI: University of Wisconsin Press, 1923.

Yung, Judy. *Unbound Voices: A Documentary History of Chinese Women in San Francisco.* Berkeley, CA: University of California Press, 1999.

Zampelli, Michael, S.J. "The Necessity of Hrotsvit: Evangelizing Theatre." *A Companion to Hrotsvit.* Eds. Phyllis R. Brown and Stephen L. Wailes. Leiden: Brill, 2012. 47–200.

Zeydel, Edwin. "Were Hrotsvitha's Dramas Performed during Her Lifetime?" *Speculum* 20 (1945): 443–456.

Zwagerman, Sean. "The Scholarly Transgressions of Constance Rourke." *Transgressive Humor of American Women Writers.* Ed. Sabrina Fuchs Abrams. New York, NY: Springer International Publishing, 2018. 59–79.

Index

Note: Page references with "n" denote endnotes.

Printed in the United States
by Baker & Taylor Publisher Services